GOD'S EMPOWERING PRESENCE

GOD'S EMPOWERING PRESENCE

THE HOLY SPIRIT

IN THE LETTERS

OF PAUL

GORDON D. FEE

HENDRICKSON PUBLISHERS

Library of Congress Cataloging-in-Publication Data

Fee, Gordon D.
    God's empowering presence: the Holy Spirit in the letters of Paul /
Gordon D. Fee
        p.   cm.
    Includes bibliographical references and index.
    ISBN 0–943575–94–X
    1. Holy Spirit—Biblical teaching.   2. Bible.   N.T.   Epistles of
Paul—Criticism, interpretation, etc.   I. Title
BS2655.H67F44   1994
231'.3'09015—dc20   93-41933
                                                                          CIP

Material from "Pauline Literature" in the *Dictionary of Pentecostal and
Charismatic Movements*, Stanley M. Burgess and Gary B. McGee, eds.,
Patrick H. Alexander, assoc. ed., © 1988 Stanley M. Burgess, Gary B.
McGee, and Patrick H. Alexander, was used with the permission of
Zondervan Publishing House.

Portions of chapter 4, "1 Corinthians," were adapted from Gordon D. Fee,
The First Epistle to the Corinthians, in the New International Commentary
series, © 1987 by Wm B. Eerdmans Publishing Company, and is used with
the gracious permission of the publisher.

for
Carl and Betsy
Michael and Rosemary
Peter and Donna
Paul and Gail
and
Maudine
with gratitude for providing a context
for the birthing of this book;
may God's Empowering Presence
be your portion

TABLE OF CONTENTS

Part II—Synthesis

ABBREVIATIONS

AB	Anchor Bible
ACNT	Augsburg Commentary on the New Testament
ACQ	*American Church Quarterly*
AGJU	Arbeiten zur Geschichte des antiken Judentums und des Urchristentums
AnBib	Analecta biblica
ASV	American Standard Version
ATR	*Anglican Theological Review*
AusBR	*Australian Biblical Review*
AUSSDS	Andrews University Seminary Studies Dissertation Series
BAGD	W. Bauer, W. F. Arndt, F. W. Gingrich, and F. W. Danker, *Greek-English Lexicon of the New Testament and Other Early Christian Literature*
BAR	*Biblical Archaeology Review*
BBC	Broadman Bible Commentary
BDF	F. Blass, A. Debrunner, and R. W. Funk, *A Greek Grammar of the New Testament and Other Early Christian Literature*
BETL	Bibliotheca Ephemeridum Theologicarum Lovaniensium
BETS	*Bulletin of the Evangelical Theological Society* (see also *JETS*)
Bib	*Biblica*
BJS	Brown Judaic Studies
BNTC	Black's New Testament Commentaries
BSac	*Bibliotheca Sacra*
BT	*The Bible Translator*
BZ	*Biblische Zeitschrift*
BZNW	Beihefte zur ZNW
CBC	Cambridge Bible Commentary
CBQ	*Catholic Biblical Quarterly*
CBSC	The Cambridge Bible for Schools and Colleges
CGTC	Cambridge Greek Testament Commentaries
CGTSC	Cambridge Greek Testament for Schools and Colleges
CJT	*Canadian Journal of Theology*
CNT	Commentaire du Nouveau Testament
CQR	*Church Quarterly Review*

CTM	*Concordia Theological Monthly*
DPL	G. F. Hawthorne, et al. (eds.), *Dictionary of Paul and His Letters*
EB	*Etudes Bibliques*
EBC	Expositor's Bible Commentary
EDNT	Exegetical Dictionary of the New Testament
EGT	Expositor's Greek Testament
EKKNT	Evangelisch-Katholischer Kommentar zum Neuen Testament
ET	English Translation
ETL	*Ephemerides theologicae Lovanienses*
EvQ	*Evangelical Quarterly*
EvT	Evangelische Theologie
Exp	*Expositor*
ExpT	*Expository Times*
GNB	Good News Bible
GTJ	*Grace Theological Journal*
Herm	Hermeneia
HNT	Handbuch zum Neuen Testament
HNTC	Harper's New Testament Commentaries
HTKNT	Herders theologischer Kommentar zum Neuen Testament
HTR	*Harvard Theological Review*
IB	Interpreter's Bible
IBS	*Irish Biblical Studies*
ICC	International Critical Commentary
IKZ	*Internationale Kirchliche Zeitschrift*
Int	*Interpretation*
JB	Jerusalem Bible
JBL	*Journal of Biblical Literature*
JBR	*Journal of Bible and Religion*
JETS	*Journal of the Evangelical Theological Society*
JJS	*Journal of Jewish Studies*
JSNT	*Journal for the Study of the New Testament*
JSNTSup	Journal for the Study of the New Testament Supplement Series
JSOT	*Journal for the Study of the Old Testament*
JTS	*Journal of Theological Studies*
KJV	King James Version
Knox	R. Knox, *The Holy Bible: A Translation from the Latin Vulgate in the Light of the Hebrew and Greek Originals*
Louw and Nida	J. P. Louw and E. A. Nida, *Greek-English Lexicon of the New Testament: Based on Semantic Domains*
LSJ	H. G. Liddell, R. Scott, and H. S. Jones, *A Greek-English Lexicon*
LTP	*Laval théologique et philosophique*
LWC	Living Word Commentary
LXX	Septuagint
MajT	Majority Text (= the Byzantine texttype)
MeyerK	H. A. W. Meyer, *Kritisch-exegetischer Kommentar über das Neue Testament*
MHT	J. H. Moulton, W. F. Howard, and N. Turner, *Grammar of New Testament Greek*

MM	J. H. Moulton and G. Milligan, *The Vocabulary of the Greek Testament*
MNTC	Moffatt New Testament Commentary
Moffatt	J. Moffatt, *The New Testament: A New Translation*
MS(S)	Manuscript(s)
MT	Masoretic Text
NA^{26}	E. Nestle, K. Aland, *Novum Testamentum Graece* (26th ed.)
NAB	New American Bible
NASB	New American Standard Bible
NCB	New Century Bible
NCBC	New Century Bible Commentary
NClarB	New Clarendon Bible
NEB	New English Bible
Neot	*Neotestamentica*
NIBC	New International Biblical Commentary
NICNT	New International Commentary on the New Testament
NIDNTT	Colin Brown (ed.), *The New International Dictionary of New Testament Theology*
NIGTC	New International Greek Testament Commentary
NIV	New International Version
NJB	New Jerusalem Bible
NouvRT	*Nouvelle Revue Theologique*
NovT	*Novum Testamentum*
NovTSup	Novum Testamentum, Supplements
NRSV	New Revised Standard Version
NT	New Testament
NTD	Das Neue Testament Deutsch
NTM	New Testament Message
NTS	*New Testament Studies*
OL	Old Latin
OT	Old Testament
OTP	J. H. Charlesworth (ed.), *The Old Testament Pseudepigrapha*
PE	Pastoral Epistles
PNTC	Pelican New Testament Commentaries
RB	*Revue Biblique*
REB	Revised English Bible
ResQ	*Restoration Quarterly*
RevExp	*Review and Expositor*
RevistB	*Revista biblica*
Robertson, Grammar	A. T. Robertson, *A Grammar of the Greek New Testament in the Light of Historical Research*
RSR	*Recherches de science religieuse*
RSV	Revised Standard Version
RThR	*Reformed Theological Review*
RV	Revised Version
SBLDS	Society of Biblical Literature Dissertation Series
SBT	Studies in Biblical Theology
SD	Studies and Documents
SE	*Studia Evangelica*

SEÅ	*Svensk Exegetisk Årsbok*
SecCent	*Second Century*
SH	W. Sanday and A. C. Headlam, *Romans*, ICC
SJT	*Scottish Journal of Theology*
SJTOP	Scottish Journal of Theology Occasional Papers
SNTSMS	Society for New Testament Studies Monograph Series
StBibT	*Studia Biblica et Theologica*
SWJT	*Southwestern Journal of Theology*
TBC	Torch Bible Commentary
TCNT	Twentieth Century New Testament
TDNT	G. Kittel and G. Friedrich (eds.) *Theological Dictionary of the New Testament*
Textual Commentary	B. M. Metzger, *A Textual Commentary on the Greek New Testament*
Th	*Theology*
THKNT	Theologischer Handkommentar zum Neuen Testament
TLZ	*Theologische Literaturzeitung*
TNTC	Tyndale New Testament Commentaries
TR	Textus Receptus
TRev	*Theologische Revue*
TrinJ	*Trinity Journal*
TS	*Theological Studies*
TynB	*Tyndale Bulletin*
TZ	*Theologische Zeitschrift*
UBS[4]	United Bible Societies Greek New Testament (4th ed.)
VoxEv	*Vox Evangelica*
VoxR	*Vox Reformata*
WBC	Word Biblical Commentary
WEC	Wycliffe Exegetical Commentary
WMANT	Wissenschaftliche Monographien zum Alten und Neuen Testament
WPC	Westminster Pelican Commentaries
WTJ	*Westminster Theological Journal*
WUNT	Wissenschaftliche Untersuchungen zum Neuen Testament
ZAW	*Zeitschrift für die alttestamentliche Wissenschaft*
ZNW	*Zeitschrift für die neutestamentliche Wissenschaft*
ZTK	*Zeitschrift für Theologie und Kirche*

PREFACE

The occasion and raison d'être of this book are found in chapter 1, especially its relationship to the article on the Spirit in the Pauline letters that appeared in the *Dictionary of Pentecostal and Charismatic Movements*. The twofold burden of the present study emerged from having spent long years studying and living with the apostle Paul in his letters. First, by and large the crucial role of the Spirit in Paul's life and thought—as the dynamic, experiential reality of Christian life—is often either overlooked or given mere lip service. This oversight has sometimes been "corrected" at the popular level by a variety of emphases in various sectors of the church—e.g., some mystics, the holiness movement, the deeper life movement, the Pentecostal movement—but in many instances these lack any sound exegetical base (experience tends to precede exegesis in most cases) or betray inadequate theological reflection. My burden here, therefore, is to demonstrate what I perceive to be the crucial role of the Spirit in Pauline experience and theology, but to do so as the result of exegetical labor.

Second, I am equally convinced that the Spirit in Paul's experience and theology was always thought of in terms of the personal presence of God. The Spirit is God's way of being present, powerfully present, in our lives and communities as we await the consummation of the kingdom of God. Precisely because he understood the Spirit as God's personal presence, Paul also understood the Spirit always in terms of an empowering presence; whatever else, for Paul the Spirit was an *experienced* reality. This is not something that I so much set out to prove, as it is a conviction that has grown up over many years and that I trust the exegesis presented in the book adequately demonstrates.

Just a few words about other presuppositions. Since the original article dealt with the Pauline literature, all thirteen of the canonical epistles attributed to Paul are brought into the picture. But in this case, this also reflects my own convictions that the major ten are in fact from Paul himself (including the three most often suspected: 2 Thessalonians,

Colossians, Ephesians), and that the Pastoral Epistles are Pauline, how-ever one finally decides as to the actual writer of the letters (on these matters cf. the discussions in Luke Timothy Johnson, *The Writings of the New Testament: An Interpretation* [Fortress, 1986]). As I argued in my commentary on these letters (NIBC 13; Hendrickson, 1988), I think the case for Pauline "authorship" still resolves more of the problems than otherwise. And in any case, contrary to the opinion of many, the Spirit language of these letters appears to be quite in keeping with what one finds in Paul elsewhere.

On the matter of their chronological order, with the exception of Galatians, I follow the generally accepted historical sequencing (see, e.g., the major Introductions). But I am also convinced that an earlier gener-ation of scholars had the better of it in the dating of Galatians, which almost certainly is not the earliest of the letters. Its relationship to Romans is so close, and their relationship to one another so unlike the others, that I find it difficult to imagine a gap of seven years or so between the writing of two such ad hoc documents; the difficulty is further heightened if, in the meantime, Paul had written the two Thessalonian and Corinthian letters. How does one explain the absence of the Galatian themes and language in these letters, only to have them reappear seven years later, and in the same general sequence of argument, in Romans? In any case this is the assumed chronological order in which both the discussion of texts takes place and all biblical references are given.

Several words about procedure, which in effect are also something of an apology. First, when I began, I had no idea that the book would evolve into something so big. The net result is that it has been over two years in the writing; in the meantime I have learned far more than I could have imagined. Careful work on text after text has led me to change my mind at several places, unexpectedly in many cases. But all of this also means that there may still be some rough spots between some of the earlier exegetical chapters and the later ones (which were not written in their present order). I have tried to remove as many of these as I could in a final reading, but some inconsistencies may still remain.

Second, during its evolution I had to struggle repeatedly with my target audience. It will not take long for one to recognize that I am basically trying to speak to two groups: pastors, students, and other church leaders; and the academic community. Whereas the former are my first concern, it was not possible to write this particular book without trying at the same time to speak to the academy. Whether I have suc-ceeded in bridging this gap remains for the readers to decide. Those more directly connected with the church may find it much too technical and cumbersome to be useful; the academy may find it too elementary—or homiletical?—at other points. In any case, I am aware of both the pitfalls and my own shortcomings in trying to reach two audiences.

Third, I determined early on in writing the exegetical chapters that I would do so as though from scratch—with my Greek NT and various tools, but without consulting the secondary literature. This means that when I finally came to the secondary literature, much of what I had discovered ("anew" for myself, as it were) had already been said by some, or many, before me—as well it should have been. But the question of "indebtedness" was thus ever present, because I also learned much from the literature as I made my way through it, letter by letter. I have tried to reflect these distinctions in the notes, but as all who do this kind of work know, one cannot always be sure when an idea is one's own and when the seed was dropped by someone else, sometimes years earlier.

In any case, my debt to the many who have previously written on this subject, including those with whom I have disagreed, will be obvious to all who are well read in these matters; much of this indebtedness is reflected in the footnotes. At the same time, since this volume covers such a wide range of biblical material, I am sure to be embarrassed by items that I have failed to note. I hope such authors will be generous in their forgiveness.

Fourth, as anyone who has worked closely with Paul knows, as well as anyone who is up to speed on the literature, one of the most vexing questions in this discipline has to do with "Paul and the law." I do not pretend that I have mastered either Paul or the secondary literature on this question. But I do need here to offer an explanation about usage. Because of what I perceive to be a play on the word νόμος ("law") in Rom 7:20–8:2, I have chosen to capitalize "Law" whenever I refer to what Paul in expanded form calls "the works of the Law." Thus, I perceive the word to refer primarily not to the OT nor even to the Pentateuch, but to the "laws" connected with the covenant on Sinai and recorded in the Pentateuch. That is, for Paul "the Law" refers primarily to the *legislation* of the Sinaitic covenant, which by the time of Paul carried both religious significance (having to do with one's relationship with God) and sociological significance (having to do with the Law as the special privilege of Judaism, that marked Israel off from the Gentiles). I have often interchanged this use of "the Law" with the word "Torah," well understanding that what Paul would have meant by the word "law" may not necessarily reflect the common understanding of Torah, and especially how this latter word functions in some quarters of the Jewish community today. I may be faulted for this, but at least this explanation of usage seemed necessary.

Fifth, because of my conviction that for Paul the Spirit is to be understood in personal terms, as the way God is currently present among the people of God, I frequently find it necessary to use personal pronouns to refer to the deity. In view of our lack of pronouns for God, I follow the historic practice of using the masculine pronouns; but I do not for a minute think that God is male (or female). God is God, and includes in himself all that is essential to our being male and female, while at the same time transcending such distinctions. I do not wish to offend those whose sensibilities are alert to the problem of using masculine pronouns for God; but neither can I bring myself to eliminate the intensive pronoun from our talk about God nor to use such monstrosities as "God Godself."

Sixth, the translations that appear in the Analysis are my own; in most cases they tend to be quite literal for the sake of exegetical comment. Thus they reflect the Greek text more than my exegetical conclusions. When passages containing the word πνεῦμα or χαρίσματα are judged not to refer to the Holy Spirit, smaller type is used.

Thanks are due to the following:

To Gary McGee and Stan Burgess, editors of the Dictionary in which some of the material in Part II originally appeared, for their patience and persistence that I should write that article, and for allowing me extra time far beyond the original deadline.

To Zondervan Publishing House for permission to lift some paragraphs (sometimes unchanged) from that article.

To Eerdmans Publishing Company for permission to use so much material from my 1 Corinthians commentary in this present volume.

To several friends who read some of the chapters and saved me from some errors—and varying degrees of embarrassment: Paul Barnett, David Chotka, Phil Towner, Archie Hui, J. I. Packer, Walt Hansen, my wife Maudine, and especially Rikk Watts, who interacted vigorously with several of the early exegetical chapters.

To the Board of Governors at Regent College for their generous sabbatical policy, which allowed Maudine and me to move out to Galiano Island for the fall of 1992 to bring the book to its completion.

To my teaching assistant, Rick Beaton, who assembled the table of abbreviations and the bibliography, and who compiled the Scripture and subject indexes.

And finally to Steve Hendrickson, David Townsley, and Patrick Alexander of Hendrickson Publishers, for their invitation to publish the present volume—and for carrying through with it after it grew so large!—and especially to the latter for his editing skills that have made it a better book.

Regent College
Advent 1992

1

INTRODUCTION

For good or ill, and despite appearances, this is a book on Pauline *theology*. Not the whole of that theology, nor even its chief element, but an aspect of the *experienced faith* of Paul and his churches that stood much closer to the center of things for him—and for them—than seems to be true for us. For Paul the Spirit, as an experienced and living reality, was the absolutely crucial matter for Christian life, from beginning to end. That, at least, is the contention of this book.[1] For the contemporary church it seems much less so, both in the academy, in its understanding of Pauline theology,[2] and in the actual life of the church. I do not mean that the Holy Spirit is not present; he is indeed, or we are not of Christ at all. Nonetheless, despite the affirmations in our creeds and hymns and the lip service paid to the Spirit in our occasional conversations, the Spirit is largely marginalized in our actual life together as a community of faith. At least that seems to be true of my own experience of the church; it also

---

[1]Cf. C. Pinnock, "The Concept of Spirit in the Epistles of Paul" (unpubl. Ph.D. dissertation; Manchester, 1963) 2: "His entire theology without the supporting pinion of the Spirit would crumble into ruins"; and S. Neill and N. T. Wright, *The Interpretation of the New Testament 1861–1986* (Oxford: University Press, 1988) 203: "Paul's doctrine of the Spirit is far more central and characteristic than his doctrine of justification by faith."

[2]This is evidenced in any number of ways, including the lack of a comprehensive study of Pauline pneumatology such as this book offers. Note, e.g., how little space is given to the Spirit in the otherwise quite helpful little book on *Pauline Christianity* by John Ziesler (Oxford: University, 1983; about 2 pages out of 144!); cf. the magisterial *Paul: An Outline of His Theology* by Herman Ridderbos (Grand Rapids: Eerdmans, 1975), where the Spirit fares only a little better proportionately (e.g., there are five times as many pages devoted to "sin" as to the Spirit). See also the two papers (by J. D. G. Dunn and B. Roberts Gaventa) on the theology of Galatians in the Pauline Theology Seminar at the Society of Biblical Literature in which neither, as presented at the seminar, mentioned the Spirit even once (see *The Society of Biblical Literature 1988 Seminar Papers* [ed. D. J. Lull; Atlanta: Scholars, 1988] 1–16, 17–28). And this in papers in which the question of "identity markers" was clearly recognized.

seems to be reflected in the thousands of ways individual believers have longed for a greater sense of God's presence in their lives.

A "THEOLOGY" OF THE SPIRIT?

For some a book on the Spirit as "theology" is the kiss of death; and in many ways I am in that camp. But we lack a better word; and in the final analysis, the health of the contemporary church necessitates that its *theology* of the Spirit and its *experience* of the Spirit correspond more closely. Ordinarily "theology" has to do with reflective understanding of things divine. That is scarcely what we find in Paul regarding the Holy Spirit, any more than we find him "reflecting" on the significance of the Lord's Table or on the relationships within the Godhead which he pre-supposes and which tantalizingly "pop out" here and there.

Yet theology is what Paul is doing all the time. But it is seldom the reflective theology of the academy, dealing with how the various matters we believe about God and God's ways can be put into some kind of coherent whole. Rather, it is what has been called "task theology," the theologizing that takes place in the marketplace, where belief and the experience of God run head-on into the thought systems, religions, and everyday life of people in the Greco-Roman world at the beginning of the second half of the first century CE. Such "task theology" is the more complex because it takes place in an extremely heterogeneous environ-ment. In part, therefore, the issues raised for Paul have to do with what the God of the Jews (the one and only God) was doing in history through Christ and the Spirit, for him within a primarily Gentile context.

Into this kind of setting Paul came preaching, experiencing, rethink-ing, and re-articulating old and new truths, as he wrestled with what it meant for Jew and Gentile together to be the one people of God at the turning of the ages ushered in by Christ's resurrection and the gift of the Spirit. In the process he was constantly "doing theology," grappling with how the gospel works—and works out—in this new context that was so radically different from that in which it first appeared in history.

Our present concern is with what Paul says about the Spirit, since it is through what he says that we basically have entrée into his under-standing. But our theological concern lies deeper than merely collating all the passages and running them through some kind of theological grid, for in the case of the Spirit we are dealing with the essential matter of early Christian experience. Here was how the early church came to appropriate the salvation that Christ had brought; and here was how believers came to understand their own existence as essentially eschato-logical, with the Spirit as both the evidence that God's great future for the people of God had already made its way into the present and the guarantee that God would conclude what he had begun in Christ. Thus the Spirit is absolutely presuppositional to their entire experience and understanding of their present life in Christ; and as often happens with such presuppositional matters, one rarely looks at them reflectively. They are simply part of the "stuff" of ongoing life; and what one says about such matters is often off-handed, matter-of-fact, and without considered articulation. As a result, trying to write a "theology of the Spirit" in Paul can be a somewhat tenuous affair. In any case, we must try to wrestle not only with what Paul says explicitly, but with some of the experiential undercurrents that are reflected in some of the things he articulates.

At the same time, since the Spirit is only part of the larger picture of Pauline theology, two other matters of Paul's theologizing must always be kept before us as we theologically think through his experience and understanding as these are reflected in his letters.

First, there is the issue of continuity and discontinuity between the old covenant and the new, between God's word to Israel, articulated by prophet and poet, and God's new word through Christ Jesus, articulated by apostles and others. What carries over as theological presupposition? Wherein does continuity lie? And how is the new related to the old? Does it supersede, as a truly *new* covenant? Does it fulfill, and in so doing carry with it much of what was there before?

Second, and related, is the issue which Christiaan Beker[3] has taught us to consider, of coherence and contingency, of the (basically) "unchanging core" in Paul's theological understanding and the contingent rearticulation of that "core" as it impacts, and is impacted by, contingencies and conflicts in the Pauline churches. Do we try to do theology by finding and articulating what is "coherent" in Pauline theology? Or do we do our theologizing by looking at the disparate elements that come to us in somewhat random fashion in his highly "contingent" letters? Or do we assume that there is coherence, and then work at articulating how the "coherent" and "contingent" interface in the Pauline letters?

So what do we mean by offering a book on the theology of the Spirit as that emerges in the letters of Paul? Let me begin with three basic convictions about the matters just articulated.

First, I am convinced that the only worthwhile theology is that which is translated into life; and here is where this book has theological concern at its very heart. Paul's "understanding" of the Spirit—language that will recur throughout this book, as I understand Paul's understanding—is ultimately a matter of what Jeremias in another context called *gelebte Glaube*, "lived-out faith." Thus in Paul we find moments of theological reflection; but mostly we find occasional words that give us all kinds of insight into his understanding of the role/experience of the Spirit in the new age that has *come present* with Christ and the Spirit. My concern is with our coming

---

[3]See *Paul the Apostle: The Triumph of God in Life and Thought* (Philadelphia: Fortress, 1980) 11–36.

to terms both with the *experienced realities* themselves and with Paul's understanding of them, as much as we can do that fairly and with integrity.

Furthermore, since I believe that these texts are at the same time God's word, which function as Scripture for the church, I understand my task as theologian to be both descriptive and normative. That is, the first task is the exegetical one, to *describe* as carefully as possible, Paul's own understanding of life in the Spirit; but I am convinced that such description, if properly and carefully done, should lead to obedience, to our own coming to terms with the role of the Spirit in the ongoing life of the church. The interplay between the descriptive task and the normative carries on throughout the book. I am convinced that those who take Scripture seriously as God's word to themselves and to the church need especially to come to terms with the implications of Paul's experience and understanding of the Spirit for our own day.

Second, I am convinced that in order to understand Paul aright we must take both continuity and discontinuity with equal seriousness. Paul not only stands in the direct line with the people of God in the Old Testament, but despite his deep convictions about the radical implications of the coming of Christ and the Spirit, he regularly reaffirms that continuity. He includes a primarily Gentile church in the events of the Exodus: "all *our* forefathers were baptized into Moses in the cloud and in the sea" (1 Cor 10:1–2). To Gentiles who were in danger of succumbing to circumcision he not only appeals to Abraham and the promises of the old covenant, but he asks frankly, "Tell me, you who wish to be under the Law, do you not hear the Law?" and then expounds the "true meaning" of Sarah and Hagar, Isaac and Ishmael, in light of Christ and the Spirit (Gal 4:21–31). Paul never speaks of a "new Israel" or "new people of God"; his language is "God's Israel" (Gal 6:16), an *Israel* composed of Jew and Gentile alike as one people of God. But just as clearly, the people of God have now been *newly* constituted. Christ is the "goal of the Law" (Rom 10:4), and the Spirit is "the promised Holy Spirit" (Gal 3:14). Christ's death and resurrection have brought an end to Torah observance; the Spirit has replaced Torah as God's way of "fulfilling" Torah.

Thus any "theologizing" of Paul must continually wrestle with the relationship of the old and the new, of the nature of the continuity and discontinuity. The Christian Bible, composed of *both* testaments, two discrete collections of documents held together in a common volume, is an expression of that continuity and discontinuity. I do not pretend to address this issue directly in this volume; but the very nature of the texts and their "theology" forces us to deal with that question again and again.

Third, I am also convinced—despite frequent demurrers to the contrary—that there is a substantial amount of "coherence" in Paul's understanding of Christ and the Spirit, much of which is presuppositional for him, based on his sense of continuity with the old; but much of which is to be found in what he simply calls "the gospel." It seems to me to be an inadequate reading of Paul which does not recognize that for him there was *content* to the gospel—content held in common with all other early Christians. The "contingencies" in Paul, as I understand them, have to do with his working through the implications of that common content for the Gentile mission, to which he devoted the last two decades of his life.

Thus this book attempts to analyze and synthesize what Paul says about the Spirit, both as person and as experienced reality within the life of the believer and the believing community. It will be clear to those who read further that I believe the Spirit to lie near the center of things for Paul, as part of the fundamental core of his understanding of the gospel. The reason for that in part stems from the eschatological framework of his Jewish roots, with its eager awaiting of the Spirit as part of the realization of the messianic age. Essential to Paul's becoming a follower of Christ was his conviction that this hope had already been realized by the advent of the Spirit in the present; hence the significance of the Spirit for both continuity and discontinuity in Paul's understanding of the gospel, as well as the reason for Paul's seeing the Spirit as a fundamental component of reality.

This book is theological in another sense as well, in the sense of theology proper. For when we deal with Paul's understanding of the Spirit, even though the emphasis will ultimately be where Paul's tends to be—in soteriology—nonetheless we are dealing with the basic presupposition to everything: the reality (I started to write "doctrine") of God.

In the course of working through the pertinent texts I became profoundly aware of how crucial God is to the whole of Paul's urgencies; and how much his understanding of God has been affected by OT realities— God as creator and redeemer, full of love and grace—and that these realities have been fleshed out in our human history through the work of Christ; and finally how all of this continues in the present through the ongoing work of the Holy Spirit. It is not that I did not know, or believe, this before. But the close work on these texts has had a profound impact on my own life as a Christian believer, both in my thinking and (especially) in my praying. And it is this personal dimension, my own encounter with God the Holy Spirit, that led to the title and therefore the urgencies of this book.

GOD'S EMPOWERING PRESENCE

Each word of this title expresses one of my urgencies, because I became convinced they were Paul's own urgencies, either articulated as such or inherent to his understanding of the gospel. Thus: the Holy Spirit as *person*, the person of God himself; the Holy Spirit as God's personal *presence*; and the Holy Spirit as God's *empowering* presence.

The Holy Spirit as Person. For most of us our understanding of the Spirit falls considerably short of personhood. We have a certain immediate empathy with the student who once told a colleague of mine: "God the Father makes perfectly good sense to me; and God the Son I can quite understand; but the Holy Spirit is a gray, oblong blur."

This was illustrated vividly for me on Pentecost Sunday during the final writing of this book. It was during the children's time in the small island church where Maudine and I spent our sabbatical. Our good friend MaryRuth Wilkinson was trying to illustrate the reality of "Spirit" by blowing on a piece of paper and letting it "fly" away. The Spirit is like that, she was saying to the children; it is like the "wind," very real in its effects, even though invisible to us. At which point a six-year old boy blurted out, "But I want the wind to be un-invisible!" I whispered to Maudine: "Of course; what a profound theological moment!" How often we all feel this way about God as Spirit, as Holy Spirit. "I want the Holy Spirit to be un-invisible!" And because he is not, we tend to think of him in nonpersonal terms. At which point our images take over; we think of the Spirit as wind, fire, water, oil—impersonal images all—and refer to the Spirit as "it." No wonder many regard the Spirit as a gray, oblong blur.

It is otherwise with God and Christ. Even though we start with the primary biblical understanding of God, that he cannot be imaged by what is created, we nonetheless have had much less difficulty in identifying with God, because in the Old Testament the images and anthropomorphisms at least let us catch a glimpse of true personality. And with the coming of Christ, all of that has been given a moment of historical focus. Our understanding of God is forever marked by the fact that he has been "fleshed out" at one point in our human history. Even if God seems distant, transcendent, "from eternity to eternity," we are not in the dark about God and his character. As Paul put it, the glory of God has been imaged for us in the one true human who bears the divine image, Christ himself; and by beholding his "face" we see the glory of the eternal God (2 Cor 3:18; 4:4, 6).

The burden of this book is that we must recognize the same to be true about the Spirit, not simply theoretically, but really and experientially. The Spirit is not lightly called the Spirit of Jesus Christ. Christ has put a human face on the Spirit as well. If we are truly to understand Paul, and to capture the crucial role of the Spirit in his theology, we must begin with his thoroughly Trinitarian presuppositions. Not only has the coming of Christ changed everything for Paul, so too has the coming of the Spirit. In dealing with the Spirit, we are dealing with none other than the *personal presence of God* himself.

The Holy Spirit as God's Presence. Absolutely central to Paul's theology of the Spirit is that the Spirit is the fulfillment of the promises found in Jeremiah and Ezekiel: that God himself would breathe on us and we would live; that he would write his law in our hearts; and especially that he would give his Spirit "unto us," so that we are indwelt by him. What is crucial for Paul is that we are thus indwelt by the eternal God. The gathered church and the individual believer are the new locus of God's own presence with his people; and the Spirit is the way God is now present.

One of the key images, therefore, that Paul associates with the indwelling Spirit is that of "temple," part of the significance of which is that it functions for Paul for the corporate, gathered community as well as for the individual believer. With this imagery in particular Paul picks up the Old Testament motif of God's "presence" with the people of God. This theme is one of the keys to the structure of the book of Exodus, where Israel comes to the holy mount, the place of God's "dwelling," the place where they are forbidden to go on the threat of death. Only Moses is allowed into God's presence. But God plans to "move" from the mount and dwell among his people by means of a "tabernacle." So after the giving of the Book of the Covenant (chs. 20–24), Moses receives the precise instructions for constructing the tabernacle (chs. 25–31). But this is followed by the debacle in the desert (ch. 32), followed by God's announcing that "my presence will *not* go with you"; an angel will go instead (ch. 33). Moses recognizes the inadequacy of this solution and intercedes: "If your Presence does not go with us, do not send us up from here. How will anyone know that you are pleased with me and with your people unless you go with us? What else will distinguish me and your people from all the other people on the face of the earth?" (33:15–16 NIV). God's Presence with Israel is what distinguishes them, not the Law or other "identity markers." This in turn is followed by the further revelation of God's character (34:4–7) and the actual construction of the tabernacle (chs. 35–39), all of which concludes with the descent of God's glory which "filled the tabernacle" (40:35). With that, they journey to the place which "the Lord your God will choose as a dwelling for his name" (Deut 12:11 and passim). At a later point in time the motif of the divine presence, as outlined here, was actually equated with "the Holy Spirit of the Lord" (Isa 63:9–14).

In a canonical reading of the Old Testament the Deuteronomy promise is finally fulfilled in the construction of Solomon's temple, where the same glory as in Exodus 40 descended and "filled his temple" (1 Kgs 8:11). But Israel's failure caused it to forfeit God's presence. This is the tragedy. The temple in Jerusalem, the place where God has chosen to dwell, is finally destroyed; and the people are not only carried away captive, but the captives and those who remained were no longer a people distinguished by the presence of the living God in their midst—although it is promised again in Ezekiel's grand vision (40–48). The second temple itself evinces mixed feelings among the people. In light of Solomon's temple and the promised future temple of Ezekiel, Haggai complains, "Who of you is left who saw this house in its former glory? How does it look to you now? Does it not seem to you like nothing?" (2:3).

It is this complex of ideas and images that Paul picks up in 1 Cor 3:16–17 and 6:19. His introductory, "do you not know that . . . " followed by "you are *the* temple of God [in Corinth]," strongly suggests that this is the rich history that Paul here has in mind. The church, corporately and individually, is the place of God's own personal presence, by the Spirit. This is what marks God's new people off from "all the other people on the face of the earth." Hence Paul's consternation with the Corinthians' present behavior which has the effect of banishing the Spirit, the living presence of God that makes them his temple.

This is the context of continuity in which we should read scores of Spirit texts in the apostle. This is how we know God's love for us in Christ (Rom 5:5); this is what makes us certain that we are God's very children (Gal 4:6; Rom 8:15–16); this is why holiness is not optional (1 Thes 4:7–8), why we must not grieve the Holy Spirit of God (Eph 4:30), why Timothy must not flag in the context of external pressures (2 Tim 1:6–7)—because we are indwelt by God himself. The Spirit is the fulfillment of God's promise to dwell in and among his people; the Spirit is God *present* among us.

The Holy Spirit as God's Empowering Presence. In keeping with Paul's Old Testament roots, the presence of God by the Spirit also meant for Paul the powerful and *empowering* presence of God. We are not left on our own as far as our relationship with God is concerned; neither are we left on our own to "slug it out in the trenches," as it were, with regard to the Christian life. Life in the present is empowered by the God who dwells among us and in us. As the personal presence of God, the Spirit is not merely some "force" or "influence." The living God is a God of power; and by the Spirit the power of the living God is present with and for us.

But in Paul, power is not to be thought of merely in terms of the miraculous, the extraordinary. Rather, because of his basic eschatological framework (see ch. 12) Paul understood the Spirit's power in the broadest possible way. On the one hand, the future had broken in so powerfully that signs and wonders and miracles are simply matter-of-fact (1 Cor 12:8–11; Gal 3:5); on the other hand, the Spirit also empowers for endurance in the midst of adversity (Col 1:11; 2 Cor 12:9–10)—and for everything else as we endure, awaiting the final glory, of which the Spirit is the guarantee.

Person, Presence, power: these three realities are what the Holy Spirit meant for the apostle Paul. Because this was so, he "theologizes" about Christian life in a way that makes him neither triumphalist nor defeatist, but realist. To recapture the Pauline experience and understanding is the key to our finding our way into the "radical middle," where we expect neither too much nor too little. Here we will know life and vitality, attractive life and vitality, in our personal lives and in the community of faith. Here we will constantly have the veil removed so that we might behold God's own glory in the face of Christ, so that we are constantly being renewed into his likeness. Here we will regularly expect, and see, both the working of miracles and the fellowship of his sufferings, without sensing frustration in either direction. If we do not have the Spirit, Paul says, we do not belong to God at all; my concern is that in our having his Spirit, we not settle for a watered down understanding that gives more glory to Western rationalism and spiritual anemia than to the living God.

In the final analysis I am perhaps trying to do far more than I can hope to deliver. On the one hand, I want to speak to the academy, to urge that Paul's theology without a greater sense of Pauline pneumatology is to sell short Paul's own understanding of the gospel. On the other hand, I want to speak to all who belong to Christ, to call us to a greater awareness—an experienced awareness if you will, more along Pauline lines—of the Spirit in our lives and in the life of the church. Whether both of these can happen in a single volume remains to be seen. But to these ends, at least, I have written.

ABOUT THE BOOK ITSELF

I obviously did not need a book of almost a thousand pages to make the preceding points. The length of the book came about in the interest of thoroughness and because of my conviction that careful exegesis of all the texts should precede an attempt to theologize on any of them. The net result is that I have looked carefully at every text that even remotely whispered of the Spirit's presence; indeed, I am sure that reviewers will accuse me of finding the Spirit under every rock. To be sure, after going over all these texts with some care, I am convinced the Spirit really is there under most of these rocks—and probably under a good many more as well. But perhaps a few further words are in order as to the occasion and purpose of the present study.

This book offers the exegetical basis for, and a considerable elaboration of, my contribution entitled "Pauline Literature" (with emphasis on the Holy Spirit) in the *Dictionary of Pentecostal and Charismatic Movements*.[4] While working on that article, I became aware of a singular lacuna in this area. There are books devoted to the Spirit in the New Testament,[5] that include Pauline sections; and there are books on Pauline or New Testament theology, that include sections on Paul's pneumatology. But in English only an obscure work by R. B. Hoyle,[6] now

---

[4]Grand Rapids: Zondervan, 1988, 665–83.

[5]See, e.g., H. B. Swete, *The Holy Spirit in the New Testament* (London: Macmillan, 1909; repr. Grand Rapids: Baker); E. F. Scott, *The Spirit in the New Testament* (London: Hodder and Stoughton, 1923); F. Büchsel, *Der Geist Gottes im Neuen Testament* (Gütersloh: Bertelsmann, 1926); S. Horton, *What the Bible Says about the Holy Spirit* (Springfield, Mo.: Gospel Publishing, 1976); D. Ewert, *The Holy Spirit in the New Testament* (Harrisburg: Herald, 1983); M. Green, *I Believe in the Holy Spirit* (2d ed.; Grand Rapids: Eerdmans, 1985).

[6]*The Holy Spirit in St. Paul* (London: Hodder and Stoughton, 1928).

considerably out of date, deals exclusively with the subject of the Spirit
in Paul's letters and theology.[7] With this book I hope to fill that lacuna.[8]

As with my commentary on 1 Corinthians,[9] it seemed fitting that one
such book at least be written by a New Testament scholar who is also a
Pentecostal both by confession and by experience. In his watershed
exegetical study of "The Baptism in the Holy Spirit," J. D. G. Dunn
observed that for traditional Pentecostalism, which bases its theology
primarily on Acts, "Paul need not have written anything. Indeed Paul
seems to be more of an embarrassment than an asset."[10] Conversely, it
might be observed that most non-Pentecostals, of both the sacramental
and nonsacramental variety, find Paul to be most convenient to their
theologies, while Acts is determined to be decidedly nontheological.
Therefore, in evaluating the role of the Spirit in the life of the believer
(especially on the matter of "conversion-initiation," to borrow Dunn's
term), both groups tend to find a canon within the canon.

The same holds true for their respective emphases on the ongoing
life in the Spirit. But here there is a "canon within the *Pauline* canon."
Pentecostals, on the one hand, at times could be rightly accused of
neglecting most of Paul for 1 Corinthians 12 to 14. Here they find biblical
justification for the ongoing exercise of the spiritual gifts in their midst,
especially the more extraordinary gifts. Non-Pentecostals, on the other
hand, tend to regard 1 Corinthians as an embarrassment, both to Paul
and to the later church (or else they use it as a negative paradigm). Their
"canon within the canon" is Galatians 5 and Romans 7–8; for them the
key to Pauline Spirit language resides in ethical life (the fruit of the
Spirit). I find both forms of truncated canon less than satisfactory, hence
part of the reason for this study.

The concern of the present book is mirrored in part in its format.
Historically, there are two ways of going about this task. The first is to
arrange all of the material in a logical, thematic fashion and to exegete
the texts as they appear in that logical scheme.[11] Although this might be

---

[7]But see the unpublished dissertations by Pinnock, "Concept," and by W. C.
Wright, Jr., "The Use of Pneuma in the Pauline Corpus with Special Attention to the
Relationship between Pneuma and the Risen Christ" (Fuller Theological Seminary,
1977). The closest thing to what I have tried to do here, but still on a slightly different
tack, is K. Stalder, *Das Werk des Geistes in der Heiligung bei Paulus* (Zürich: Evz-Verlag,
1962). On the French side see M.-A. Chevallier, *Esprit de Dieu, Paroles d'Hommes*
(Neuchâtel: Delachaux and Niestlé, 1966).

[8]I have made no attempt to trace the history of scholarship on the subject; brief
overviews may be found in the unpublished dissertation by Lemmer (see bibliog. on
ch. 9) and R. P. Menzies, *The Development of Early Christian Pneumatology, with special
reference to Luke–Acts* (JSNTSup 54; Sheffield: JSOT, 1991) 18–46.

[9]In the NICNT.

[10]*Baptism in the Holy Spirit* (SBT 2/15; London: SCM, 1970) 103.

[11]As in my dictionary article; cf. Ewert, et al.

useful, it has the distinct disadvantage of requiring an index to locate a discussion of the texts themselves, and if the exegetical discussion is lengthy, as at times it must be, then the flow of the presentation tends to get lost in the exegetical detail. Not only so, but all too often the exegetical discussions are *not* lengthy, and one is often left wondering how the conclusions were reached. The second approach is to analyze all the texts in their canonical order and simply let them speak for themselves, as much as that is exegetically possible. H. B. Swete followed this approach; but this leaves the reader with simply a presentation of textual data with scarcely any significant conclusions as to how the pieces fit together in Paul's thinking.

This book combines these two approaches. Part I (Analysis) offers a systematic, detailed exegesis of the relevant passages in their assumed chronological order. But this is not a full-scale commentary. As with all proper exegesis, the first concern has to do with what the text meant in its original historical-literary context. But in each case the emphasis is especially on the significance of the Spirit-language or phenomena in these texts. Part II (Synthesis) offers a theological and practical elaboration of the aforementioned article, now radically rewritten, and with the opportunity to refer directly to the exegetical bases of the conclusions as they are argued in Part I. Hence another reason for the book: The New Testament scholar in me experienced no little frustration in offering conclusions, demanded by the dictionary format, without being able adequately to justify—or explain—their exegetical basis.

The reader should consider Part I as the exegetical basis for Part II; at all times the conclusions in Part II are what (the terribly long) Part I is aiming at. I have no illusions that anyone will read the book through in its entirety. Hopefully, however, the reader will want to read in and around Part I, since the texts themselves form the basis for everything, and there is occasional theologizing going on there as well.

FINDING THE ELUSIVE "CENTER"

Before turning to the texts, one further introductory word about Pauline theology is necessary. There has been a long debate in scholarship as to what constitutes the "heart" of Pauline theology.[12] The traditional view, fostered by the Reformers and perpetuated by generations of Protestants, is that "justification by faith" is the key to Paul's theology. This view emphasizes Christ's historical act of redemption and its appropriation by the believer through faith. The inadequacy of such a view should be apparent to anyone carefully reading Paul's letters. Not only

---

[12]For a helpful overview of this debate, especially in its more recent expressions, see J. Plevnik, "The Center of Pauline Theology," *CBQ* 61 (1989) 461–78.

does it focus on one metaphor of salvation to the exclusion of others, but such a focus fails to throw the net broadly enough to capture all of Paul's theological concerns.

In response to this, others have sought this center in Paul's "mystical experience of being *in Christ*."[13] This view shifts the focus from Christ's historical work and its appropriation by the believer to the believer's (especially Paul's) ongoing experience of Christ. While in some ways this serves as a corrective to the traditional view, most contemporary Pauline scholars have recognized the inadequacy of both of these somewhat limiting approaches.

It is my conviction that the reason the center is so "elusive" is that Paul's theology covers too much ground for one to simplify it into a single phrase. It would seem far better for us to isolate the essential elements of his theology that lie at the very heart of matters for Paul and around which all other concerns cluster.[14] In such a view, at least four items must be included:

- The *church* as an eschatological community, which comprises the new covenant people of God;

- The *eschatological framework* of God's people's existence and thinking;

- Their being constituted by God's eschatological *salvation* effected through the *death and resurrection of Christ*;

- Their focus on *Jesus* as Messiah, Lord, and Son of God.

To put this another way:

- The *foundation*: A gracious and merciful God, who is full of love toward all.

- The *framework*: Eschatological existence as already but not yet.

- The *focus*: Jesus, the Son of God, who as God's suffering servant Messiah effected eschatological salvation for humanity through his death and resurrection, and who is now the exalted Lord and coming King.

- The *fruit*: The church as an eschatological community, who, constituted by Christ's death and the gift of the Spirit, and thus restored into God's likeness, form God's new covenant people.

---

[13]See esp. A. Deissmann, *Die neutestamentliche Formel "in Christo Jesu"* (Marburg: N. G. Elwert, 1892). For English readers see Deissmann's *St. Paul: A Study in Social and Religious History* (trans. L. R. M. Strachan; London: Hodder and Stoughton, 1912 [Ger. original 1911]); and A. Schweitzer, *The Mysticism of Paul the Apostle* (London: A & C Black, 1931).

[14]Cf. Plevnik, "Center," 477–78; but without mention of the Spirit!

Summary. Through the death and resurrection of his Son Jesus, our Lord, a gracious and loving God has effected eschatological salvation for his new covenant people, the church, who now, as they await Christ's coming, live the life of the future by the power of the Spirit.

If this is a correct assessment of things Pauline (and the rest of the New Testament, for that matter), then one might distill all of this still further. On the one hand, it seems impossible to understand Paul without beginning with *eschatology* as the essential framework of all his theological reflection; on the other hand, *salvation in Christ* is the essential concern within that framework. Salvation is "eschatological" in the sense that final salvation, which still awaits the believer, is already a present reality through Christ and the Spirit. It is "in Christ" in the sense that what originated in God was effected historically by the death and resurrection of Christ, and is appropriated experientially by God's people through the work of the Holy Spirit—who is also the key to Christian life "between the times," until the final consummation at Christ's *parousia*. All of this to say, then, that any understanding of Paul that does not recognize the crucial role of the Spirit in his theology quite misses Paul's own concerns and emphases.

Thus in the theological chapters in Part II, we will devote separate chapters to the Spirit's role in Paul's eschatology, his theology proper, his soteriology, and his ecclesiology—the theological words for his understanding of history and time, God, salvation, and church. And all the time, we will keep an eye open toward the issues of continuity and discontinuity, since it is not possible to understand the Spirit in Pauline theology without recognizing that for Paul the coming of the Spirit was God's fulfillment of the promised new covenant.

Finally, the aim of all of this is not simply informational. I would be less than honest if I did not admit to trying to persuade. But persuasion in this case is not a matter of being "right" or "wrong." My ultimate concern, for myself and for the contemporary church, is to persuade that we would do well to return to our biblical roots on this matter, if the church is going to count for anything at all in the new millennium that lies just around the corner.

2

PRELIMINARY OBSERVATIONS ON USAGE

In the Analysis that follows (Part I), an attempt has been made to examine carefully all the possible texts in the Pauline corpus in which the Spirit is mentioned directly or indirectly or in which Spirit activity seems to be in view. The clue to the relevance of most of these texts lies in the language itself; however, there is just enough flexibility in language to make precision difficult to come by at times—especially with the key words πνεῦμα (spirit), πνευματικός (spiritual), and χάρισμα (gracious gift). Not only is Paul's usage itself at times ambiguous, but scholars disagree on some fundamental points. For that reason it seemed worthwhile to isolate the basic issues and to suggest some solutions in an introductory chapter, so that these matters would not need to be repeated continually in the subsequent exegesis—although the latter should reinforce the observations made here.

THE USE OF πνεῦμα IN PAUL[1]

The word πνεῦμα occurs 145 times in the thirteen Pauline letters; the vast majority of these unambiguously refer to the Holy Spirit, although the full name occurs but 17 (or 16) times.[2] Paul also uses the term "the Spirit of God"/"His Spirit" 16 times;[3] and "Spirit of Christ" or its equiva-

---

[1] *Bibliography:* F. J. **Badcock**, " 'The Spirit' and Spirit in the New Testament," *ExpT* 45 (1933–34) 218–22; K. H. **Easley,** "The Pauline Use of *Pneumati* as a Reference to the Spirit of God," *JETS* 27 (1984) 299–313; D. P. **Francis,** "The Holy Spirit: A Statistical Inquiry," *ExpT* 96 (1985) 136–37; N. **Turner,** *Grammatical Insights into the New Testament* (Edinburgh: T. & T. Clark, 1965) 17–22.

[2] 1 Thes 1:5; 1:6; 4:8; 1 Cor 6:19; 12:3; 2 Cor 6:6 (although this is debated; see the discussion in ch. 5); 13:13[14]; Rom 5:5; 9:1; 14:17; 15:13; 15:16; Eph 1:13; 4:30; Titus 3:5; 2 Tim 1:14. "Holy" has been added to the text by various MSS in two other instances (1 Cor 2:13 [MajT]; Rom 15:19 [considered original by Westcott and Hort]).

[3] 1 Thes 4:8 ("his Holy Spirit"); 1 Cor 2:11; 2:14; 3:16; 6:11; 7:40; 12:3; 2 Cor 3:3; 3:17 (perhaps = "the Spirit of the Lord"; see exegesis in ch. 5); Rom 8:9; 8:11; 8:14; 15:19; Eph 3:16; 4:30 ("the Holy Spirit of God"); Phil 3:3.

lent 3 times.[4] The word refers to Satan once (Eph 2:2), and at least once in the plural it denotes demons (1 Tim 4:1).[5] In one instance (2 Thes 2:8, q.v.) Paul also echoes an OT usage, when he alludes to the "breath" from the Lord's mouth by which the Lawless One will be slain. Paul also uses πνεῦμα to refer to the basic interior component of the human personality,[6] although there has been some debate here.[7] The difficulties in usage occur in three areas.

THE HOLY SPIRIT OR A HOLY SPIRIT

Because of some flexibility in Paul's use of the definite article with the noun πνεῦμα, some have suggested that when Paul does *not* use the definite article, he means something closer to "a spirit," intending a sort of divine influence or "a spirit from God," but something less than personality, and probably not the Holy Spirit. Such a view occasionally surfaces in the commentaries;[8] it was taken up by Nigel Turner and offered as a "grammatical insight."[9] Turner begins his discussion with the assertion that "if the New Testament writers took 'spirit' into their vocabulary for an *unclean* demon, equally probably they had a demon in mind when they referred to *holy* spirit."[10] He then proceeds to argue for a distinction between "a spirit and the Spirit" on the basis of the presence or absence of the definite article with πνεῦμα. Although Turner primarily discusses Luke–Acts, what he says about Luke applies equally to Paul. For the most part contextual exegesis in itself reveals the inadequacy of this perspective;[11] but some factors of usage, not observed by Turner, seem to indicate that he has given us no "grammatical insight" into this matter at all.

---

[4]Gal 4:6 ("the Spirit of his Son"); Rom 8:9 ("the Spirit of Christ"); Phil 1:19 ("the Spirit of Jesus Christ").

[5]For this possibility regarding the term "the discerning of spirits" in 1 Cor 12:10, see the discussion in ch. 4.

[6]The following have been judged to be exclusively so in the exegesis of this book: 1 Thes 5:23; 1 Cor 2:11; 5:5; 7:34; 14:14; 16:18; 2 Cor 2:13; 7:13; Gal 6:18; Rom 1:9; 8:16; Phlm 25; Phil 4:23; 2 Tim 4:22.

[7]See the discussion of 1 Thes 5:23 below.

[8]E.g., Plummer, *2 Corinthians*, 297: "Sometimes we are not sure whether . . . when [Paul] is speaking of the Divine Spirit, how far he regards the Spirit as personal. . . . This is especially the case in the expression ἐν πνεύματι"; cf. Parry, *1 Corinthians*, 176, 177; Best, *1 and 2 Thessalonians*, 75 (who cites Turner); Robinson, *Ephesians*, 38–39; Patzia, *Ephesians*, 164–65.

[9]See n. 1 above.

[10]*Grammatical Insights*, 18.

[11]This is particularly true of those several places where the Spirit is under discussion and Paul fluctuates between an articular and an anarthrous usage. For example, in 1 Cor 6:9–20; Gal 5:16–25; Rom 8:1–17, the usage goes back and forth, sometimes in the shortest possible span.

Some years ago I had reason to take interest in the use/non-use of the article with proper names, especially with "Jesus," in the Gospel of John.[12] That study arose out of a concern to discover Johannine "style"; in the course of things it became obvious that well-known peculiarities of Johannine usage of the article were primarily related to stylistic features, including case and word order. The application of a similar method to Paul's use/non-use of the article with πνεῦμα is equally revealing. The following data tell their own story. [For those without Greek the following technical analysis can be skipped; I give it in full here for the sake of the scholarly community. The conclusions at the end of this section are what bear significance.]

1. πνεῦμα *in the Nominative.* The word πνεῦμα occurs 17 times in the nominative, clearly referring to the Holy Spirit.[13] In 15 of these it is articular:

Rom 8:10   τὸ δὲ πνεῦμα ζωὴ διὰ δικαιοσύνην

Rom 8:11   εἰ δὲ τὸ πνεῦμα τοῦ ἐγείραντος τὸν Ἰησοῦν . . . οἰκεῖ ἐν ὑμῖν

Rom 8:16   αὐτὸ τὸ πνεῦμα συμμαρτυρεῖ

Rom 8:26   ὡσαύτως δὲ καὶ τὸ πνεῦμα συναντιλαμβάνεται τῇ ἀσθενείᾳ ἡμῶν

Rom 8:26   αὐτὸ τὸ πνεῦμα ὑπερεντυγχάνει στεναγμοῖς ἀλαλήτοις

1 Cor 2:10   τὸ γὰρ πνεῦμα πάντα ἐραυνᾷ

1 Cor 2:11   οὐδεὶς ἔγνωκεν εἰ μὴ τὸ πνεῦμα τοῦ θεοῦ

1 Cor 3:16   τὸ πνεῦμα τοῦ θεοῦ οἰκεῖ ἐν ὑμῖν

1 Cor 12:4   διαιρέσεις δὲ χαρισμάτων εἰσίν, τὸ δὲ αὐτὸ πνεῦμα

1 Cor 12:11   πάντα δὲ ταῦτα ἐνεργεῖ τὸ ἓν καὶ τὸ αὐτὸ πνεῦμα

2 Cor 3:6   τὸ δὲ πνεῦμα ζῳοποιεῖ

2 Cor 3:17   ὁ δὲ κύριος τὸ πνεῦμα ἐστιν

2 Cor 3:17   οὗ δὲ τὸ πνεῦμα κυρίου, ἐλευθερία

Gal 5:17   τὸ δὲ πνεῦμα [ἐπιθυμεῖ] κατὰ τῆς σαρκός

1 Tim 4:1   τὸ δὲ πνεῦμα ῥητῶς λέγει

The two anarthrous instances are among those which most clearly refer to the Holy Spirit:

Rom 8:9   εἴπερ πνεῦμα θεοῦ οἰκεῖ ἐν ὑμῖν

Eph 4:4   ἓν σῶμα καὶ ἓν πνεῦμα, καθὼς καὶ ἐκλήθητε ἐν μιᾷ ἐλπίδι

---

[12]See "The Use of the Definite Article with Personal Names in the Gospel of John," *NTS* 17 (1970/71) 168–83.

[13]The usage in 1 Cor 15:45 does not easily fit any category (it is a predicate nominative; does not refer to the Holy Spirit; exists because of the LXX text which Paul is "interpreting"). See the discussion in ch. 4.

In both cases the non-use of the article can be explained on other grounds: in Eph 4:4 the modifier "one" functions the same way as the definite (= defining) article ("There is the one body [the church] even as there is the one Spirit [who created the one body]"); in Rom 8:9 the context itself, with at least 6 articular uses surrounding this one (and its companion in the accusative πνεῦμα Χριστοῦ), makes it certain that this can refer only to the Holy Spirit as the Spirit of God. The non-use of the article is stylistic, related to a usage with the genitive noted below.

These statistics suggest that Paul regularly employs the article when the Spirit is the subject of a clause; this holds true whether πνεῦμα is qualified or not. In the two instances where he does not use the article, the qualifiers and the contexts make it plain that the Holy Spirit is in view.

On four occasions πνεῦμα functions as the subject of a clause where the human spirit is in view, and these are all articular:

1 Cor 2:11   εἰ μὴ τὸ πνεῦμα τοῦ ἀνθρώπου τὸ ἐν αὐτῷ

1 Cor 5:5   ἵνα τὸ πνεῦμα σωθῇ

1 Cor 14:14   τὸ πνεῦμά μου προσεύχεται

2 Cor 7:13   ἀναπέπαυται τὸ πνεῦμα αὐτοῦ

2. πνεῦμα *in the Genitive*. Apart from usage in prepositional phrases controlled by the genitive case (see 3. below), πνεῦμα occurs 30 times in the genitive, 28 of which refer to the Holy Spirit.[14] Of these, 18 are articular:

Rom 8:2   ὁ γὰρ νόμος τοῦ πνεύματος τῆς ζωῆς

Rom 8:5   τὰ τοῦ πνεύματος

Rom 8:6   τὸ δὲ φρόνημα τοῦ πνεύματος ζωὴ καὶ εἰρήνη

Rom 8:23   τὴν ἀπαρχὴν τοῦ πνεύματος ἔχοντες

Rom 8:27   οἶδεν τί τὸ φρόνημα τοῦ πνεύματος

Rom 15:30   διὰ τῆς ἀγάπης τοῦ πνεύματος

1 Cor 2:14   οὐ δέχεται τὰ τοῦ πνεύματος τοῦ θεοῦ

1 Cor 6:19   ναὸς τοῦ ἐν ὑμῖν ἁγίου πνεύματός ἐστιν

1 Cor 12:7   ἡ φανέρωσις τοῦ πνεύματος

2 Cor 1:22   δοὺς τὸν ἀρραβῶνα τοῦ πνεύματος

2 Cor 3:8   ἡ διακονία τοῦ πνεύματος ἔσται ἐν δόξῃ

2 Cor 5:5   ὁ δοὺς ἡμῖν τὸν ἀρραβῶνα τοῦ πνεύματος

2 Cor 13:13   καὶ ἡ κοινωνία τοῦ ἁγίου πνεύματος

---

[14]One of the other two (2 Cor 7:1) has been argued in ch. 5 as referring primarily to the Spirit, but in an indirect way. The other (1 Cor 5:4) occurs in a genitive absolute; it is one of the instances noted in the next section where some kind of interrelationship between Paul's own spirit and the Holy Spirit is in view.

Gal 3:14	ἵνα τὴν ἐπαγγελίαν τοῦ πνεύματος λάβωμεν
Gal 5:22	ὁ δὲ καρπὸς τοῦ πνεύματός ἐστιν
Eph 4:3	σπουδάζοντες τηρεῖν τὴν ἑνότητα τοῦ πνεύματος
Eph 6:17	δέξασθε καὶ τὴν μάχαιραν τοῦ πνεύματος, ὅ ἐστιν ῥῆμα θεοῦ
Phil 1:19	καὶ [τῆς] ἐπιχορηγίας τοῦ πνεύματος Ἰησοῦ Χριστοῦ

and 10[11?] are anarthrous:

Rom 7:6	ἐν καινότητι πνεύματος
Rom 15:13	εἰς τὸ περισσεύειν ὑμᾶς . . . ἐν δυνάμει πνεύματος ἁγίου
Rom 15:19	ἐν δυνάμει πνεύματος θεοῦ
1 Cor 2:4	ἐν ἀποδείξει πνεύματος καὶ δυνάμεως
1 Cor 2:13	ἀλλ᾽ ἐν διδακτοῖς πνεύματος
2 Cor 3:6	καινῆς διαθήκης, οὐ γράμματος ἀλλὰ πνεύματος
[?]2 Cor 7:1	ἀπὸ παντὸς μολυσμοῦ σαρκὸς καὶ πνεύματος
Phil 2:1	εἴ τις κοινωνία πνεύματος
1 Th 1:6	μετὰ χαρᾶς πνεύματος ἁγίου
2 Th 2:13	ἐν ἁγιασμῷ πνεύματος καὶ πίστει ἀληθείας
Tit 3:5	ἔσωσεν ἡμᾶς διὰ . . . ἀνακαινώσεως πνεύματος ἁγίου

Two observations are needed. First, the numbers themselves weigh heavily in favor of an articular usage with the genitive. Second, those instances that are not articular are in every case to be explained by another phenomenon of usage. For the most part, Paul's habit when using the genitive is either to make both the modified word and its genitive articular or to make both words anarthrous.[15] When the controlling word is anarthrous, it is either a matter of taste (apparently) or a matter of following the conventions of the language (nonarticular with abstract substantives, etc.). But the presence of the article with the Spirit is always controlled by whether the noun it modifies is articular or not, not by a distinction between "a spirit" and "the Spirit." Thus in 2 Cor 13:13[14] Paul speaks of ἡ κοινωνία τοῦ ἁγίου πνεύματος (the fellowship of the Holy Spirit), while in Phil 2:1 he asks εἴ τις κοινωνία πνεύματος (if any fellowship of Spirit?). There can be little question that he has the same experience of the Holy Spirit in mind in both cases. In Philippians the modifier

[15]This makes the usage in 2 Cor 3:17 (τὸ πνεῦμα κυρίου) especially unusual, the solution to which is that Paul is here picking up the anarthrous use of κύριος from the "citation" of the LXX in the preceding verse (v. 16). See the discussion in ch. 5. The other apparent exception (1 Cor 6:19) is probably not so, but is another reflection of the accuracy of E. C. Colwell's observation, sometimes called "Colwell's rule," that when a definite predicate noun precedes its verb it is almost always anarthrous.

τις causes the κοινωνία to be anarthrous; hence πνεύματος is also anarthrous. All of this is confirmed by passages like Rom 15:19, ἐν δυνάμει πνεύματος θεοῦ (by *the* power of *the* Spirit of *the* [one and only] God), where this phenomenon occurs with both genitive nouns. This also explains one of the anarthrous instances in the nominative (Rom 8:9), where πνεῦμα θεοῦ means "*the* Spirit of *the* [one and only] God." The lack of the article appears to be a matter of style, pure and simple, for in 1 Cor 2:11 and 3:16 Paul has τὸ πνεῦμα τοῦ θεοῦ. There simply can be no difference in meaning or emphasis. One may as well argue that Paul, in not using the article with θεός in this case, means "a spirit of a god," as to argue that he means "a spirit" in similar constructions with πνεῦμα.

3. πνεῦμα *with the Genitive (in prepositional phrases)*. A similar phenomenon appears when πνεῦμα occurs with certain prepositions taking the genitive case. There are 13 such, 9 of which refer to the Holy Spirit (6 of them articular):[16]

Rom 5:5	διὰ πνεύματος ἁγίου τοῦ δοθέντος ἡμῖν
Rom 8:11	ζῳοποιήσει . . . διὰ τοῦ ἐνοικοῦντος αὐτοῦ πνεύματος ἐν ὑμῖν
1 Cor 2:10	διὰ τοῦ πνεύματος
1 Cor 12:8	ᾧ μὲν γὰρ διὰ τοῦ πνεύματος δίδοται
Gal 5:17	ἡ γὰρ σὰρξ ἐπιθυμεῖ κατὰ τοῦ πνεύματος
Gal 6:8	ἐκ τοῦ πνεύματος θερίσει ζωὴν αἰώνιον
Eph 3:16	ἵνα δῷ ὑμῖν . . . δυνάμει κραταιωθῆναι διὰ τοῦ πνεύματος αὐτοῦ
2 Thes 2:2	μήτε διὰ πνεύματος μήτε διὰ λόγου
2 Tim 1:14	φύλαξον διὰ πνεύματος ἁγίου τοῦ ἐνοικοῦντες ἐν ἡμῖν

and 4 to the human spirit (all articular).

Gal 6:18	μετὰ τοῦ πνεύματος ὑμῶν
Phil 4:23	μετὰ τοῦ πνεύματος ὑμῶν
Phlm 25	μετὰ τοῦ πνεύματος ὑμῶν
2 Tim 4:22	μετὰ τοῦ πνεύματός σου

Of the 3 anarthrous instances which refer to the Holy Spirit,[17] two (Rom 5:5; 2 Tim 1:14) are qualified by the addition of "Holy" and a substantival participle, thus making them references to the Holy Spirit; the other (2 Thes 2:2) is an indirect reference (= through a prophetic utterance

---

[16]Left out of this discussion is the occurrence in 2 Cor 3:18, καθάπερ ἀπὸ κυρίου πνεύματος, which has been judged to be an appositive.

[17]Assuming my exegesis of 2 Thes 2:2 in ch. 3 to be correct.

that comes from the Spirit). Again, articular usage prevails, and anarthrous usage has other explanation.

4. πνεῦμα *in the Accusative*. Although one would ordinarily discuss the dative case next, that is where most of the difficulties have been seen to lie; and since the usage in the accusative (direct object) and with prepositions is very much like that in the genitive, it is appropriate to offer these data next.

(a) Arthrous, referring to the Holy Spirit

1 Cor 2:12	ἀλλὰ [ἐλάβομεν] τὸ πνεῦμα . . . τοῦ θεοῦ
2 Cor 4:13	ἔχοντες δὲ τὸ αὐτὸ πνεῦμα τῆς πίστεως
Gal 3:2	ἐξ ἔργων νόμου τὸ πνεῦμα ἐλάβετε
Gal 3:5	ὁ οὖν ἐπιχορηγῶν ὑμῖν τὸ πνεῦμα
Gal 4:6	ἐξαπέστειλεν ὁ θεὸς τὸ πνεῦμα τοῦ υἱοῦ αὐτοῦ
Eph 4:30	μὴ λυπεῖτε τὸ πνεῦμα τὸ ἅγιον τοῦ θεοῦ, ἐν ᾧ ἐσφραγίσθητε
1 Thes 4:8	τὸν καὶ διδόντα τὸ πνεῦμα αὐτοῦ τὸ ἅγιον
1 Thes 5:19	τὸ πνεῦμα μὴ σβέννυτε

(b) Arthrous, referring to the human spirit

1 Cor 16:18	ἀνέπαυσαν γὰρ τὸ ἐμὸν πνεῦμα καὶ τὸ ὑμῶν
1 Thes 5:23	ὁλόκληρον ὑμῶν τὸ πνεῦμα . . . τηρηθείη

(c) Anarthrous, referring to the Holy Spirit

Rom 8:9	εἰ δέ τις πνεῦμα Χριστοῦ οὐκ ἔχει
1 Cor 7:40	κἀγὼ πνεῦμα θεοῦ ἔχειν
1 Cor 12:13	πάντες ἓν πνεῦμα ἐποτίσθημεν
2 Cor 11:4	εἰ μὲν γὰρ . . . πνεῦμα ἕτερον λαμβάνετε

(d) Anarthrous, referring to "a spirit of":

Rom 8:15	οὐ γὰρ ἐλάβετε πνεῦμα δουλείας πάλιν
Rom 8:15	ἀλλὰ ἐλάβετε πνεῦμα υἱοθεσίας
Rom 11:8	ἔδωκεν αὐτοῖς ὁ θεὸς πνεῦμα κατανύξεως [LXX]
Eph 1:17	δώῃ ὑμῖν πνεῦμα σοφίας καὶ ἀποκαλύψεως
2 Tim 1:7	οὐ γὰρ ἔδωκεν ἡμῖν ὁ θεὸς πνεῦμα δειλίας ἀλλὰ δυνάμεως

(e) Arthrous with prepositions (all referring to the Holy Spirit):

1 Cor 12:8	κατὰ τὸ αὐτὸ πνεῦμα
Gal 6:8	ὁ δὲ σπείρων εἰς τὸ πνεῦμα

(f) Anarthrous with prepositions (all referring to the Spirit):

Rom 1:4	κατὰ πνεῦμα ἁγιωσύνης
Rom 8:4	ἀλλὰ κατὰ πνεῦμα

Rom 8:5   οἱ δὲ κατὰ πνεῦμα

Gal 4:29   ἐδίωκεν τὸν κατὰ πνεῦμα

These data reflect phenomena similar to usage with the genitive. Two observations are in order: (1) Good explanations are forthcoming for every anarthrous usage. Either there is a qualifying modifier (as with the genitive above),[18] some form of fixed, or formulaic, usage (as for example with κατὰ πνεῦμα), or some other contextual—or stylistic[19]—reason. (2) When referring to the human spirit, as with usage in the genitive, Paul always uses the article. The "spirit of" usage will be noted below.

5. πνεῦμα *with the Dative.* Most of the difficulties in Pauline usage have emerged here, especially with the formula ἐν πνεύματι and πνεύματι.[20] What is of particular interest is that most of the data noted in the other three cases are now reversed. Thus, there are 37 occurrences where the Holy Spirit is either directly or indirectly in view; 32 are anarthrous and 5 arthrous:

Rom 2:29   ἐν πνεύματι οὐ γράμματι

Rom 8:9   ὑμεῖς δὲ οὐκ ἐστὲ ἐν σαρκὶ ἀλλὰ ἐν πνεύματι

Rom 8:13   εἰ δὲ πνεύματι τὰς πράξεις τοῦ σώματος θανατοῦτε

Rom 8:14   ὅσοι γὰρ πνεύματι θεοῦ ἄγονται

Rom 9:1   συμμαρτυρούσης μοι τῆς συνειδήσεώς μου ἐν πνεύματι ἁγίῳ

Rom 14:17   δικαιοσύνη καὶ εἰρήνη καὶ χαρὰ ἐν πνεύματι ἁγίῳ

Rom 15:16   ἡγιασμένη ἐν πνεύματι ἁγίῳ

1 Cor 4:21   ἔλθω . . . ἢ ἐν ἀγάπῃ πνεύματί τε πραΰτητος

1 Cor 12:3   οὐδεὶς ἐν πνεύματι θεοῦ λαλῶν

1 Cor 12:3   οὐδεὶς δύναται εἰπεῖν . . . εἰ μὴ ἐν πνεύματι ἁγίῳ

1 Cor 12:13 ἐν ἑνὶ πνεύματι ἡμεῖς πάντες . . . ἐβαπτίσθημεν

1 Cor 14:2   πνεύματι δὲ λαλεῖ

1 Cor 14:16 εὐλογῇς ἐν πνεύματι

2 Cor 3:3   ἐγγεγραμμένη οὐ μέλανι ἀλλὰ πνεύματι θεοῦ ζῶντος

2 Cor 6:6   [συνιστάντες ἑαυτοὺς] . . . ἐν πνεύματι ἁγίῳ

---

[18]The items in (c), for example, are simply further examples of phenomena noted above with the genitive.

[19]This term may seem bothersome at this point, but it is a descriptive, not definitive, term. That is, this is a stylistic phenomenon of Pauline usage which may be so described, even if as yet there is no explanation for it.

[20]There is no substantive difference in this formula with or without the ἐν, except that the simple πνεύματι seems usually to be instrumental—although even in some of these cases one could make a case for locative of "sphere." The use with ἐν, because more numerous, covers a broad range of usage (means, manner, sphere, association). On this usage see Easley, "Pauline Use."

Gal 3:3	ἐναρξάμενοι πνεύματι νῦν σαρκὶ ἐπιτελεῖσθε;
Gal 5:5	ἡμεῖς γὰρ πνεύματι ἐκ πίστεως ἐλπίδα δικαιοσύνης ἀπεκδεχόμεθα
Gal 5:16	πνεύματι περιπατεῖτε
Gal 5:18	εἰ δὲ πνεύματι ἄγεσθε
Gal 5:25	εἰ ζῶμεν πνεύματι
Gal 5:25	πνεύματι καὶ στοιχῶμεν
Gal 6:1	καταρτίζετε τὸν τοιοῦτον ἐν πνεύματι πραΰτητος
Eph 2:18	ἐν ἑνὶ πνεύματι πρὸς τὸν πατέρα
Eph 2:22	συνοικοδομεῖσθε εἰς κατοικητήριον τοῦ θεοῦ ἐν πνεύματι
Eph 3:5	ὡς νῦν ἀπεκαλύφθη τοῖς ἁγίοις . . . προφήταις ἐν πνεύματι
Eph 5:18	ἀλλὰ πληροῦσθε ἐν πνεύματι
Eph 6:18	προσευχόμενοι ἐν παντὶ καιρῷ ἐν πνεύματι
Phil 1:27	στήκετε ἐν ἑνὶ πνεύματι, μιᾷ ψυχῇ συναθλοῦντες
Phil 3:3	οἱ πνεύματι θεοῦ λατρεύοντες
Col 1:8	ὁ καὶ δηλώσας ἡμῖν τὴν ὑμῶν ἀγάπην ἐν πνεύματι
1 Thes 1:5	ἐγενήθη . . . καὶ ἐν δυνάμει καὶ ἐν πνεύματι ἁγίῳ
1 Tim 3:16	ἐδικαιώθη ἐν πνεύματι

1 Cor 6:11	καὶ ἐν τῷ πνεύματι τοῦ θεοῦ
1 Cor 12:9	ἐν τῷ αὐτῷ πνεύματι
1 Cor 12:9	ἐν τῷ ἑνὶ πνεύματι
2 Cor 12:18	οὐ τῷ αὐτῷ πνεύματι περιεπατήσαμεν
Eph 1:13	ἐν ᾧ . . . ἐσφραγίσθητε τῷ πνεύματι τῆς ἐπαγγελίας τῷ ἁγίῳ

When the primary referent is to the human spirit (9 instances), however, usage continues to be articular only:

Rom 1:9	ἐν τῷ πνεύματί μου
Rom 8:16	τῷ πνεύματι ἡμῶν ὅτι ἐσμὲν τέκνα θεοῦ
1 Cor 5:3	παρὼν δὲ τῷ πνεύματι
1 Cor 7:34	καὶ τῷ σώματι καὶ τῷ πνεύματι
1 Cor 14:15	προσεύξομαι τῷ πνεύματι[21]
1 Cor 14:15	ψαλῶ τῷ πνεύματι
2 Cor 2:13	οὐκ ἔσχηκα ἄνεσιν τῷ πνεύματί μου

---

[21]On these two instances in v. 15, see the discussion in ch. 4. The primary referent is almost certainly to his own "spirit," which is aided by the Holy Spirit.

[?]Eph 4:23   ἀνανεοῦσθαι δὲ τῷ πνεύματι τοῦ νοὸς ὑμῶν
Col 2:5   ἀλλὰ τῷ πνεύματι σὺν ὑμῖν εἰμι

Several observations are in order about this usage: (1) Paul's preferences in this case are manifest; with the formula πνεύματι/ἐν πνεύματι there is a decided preference for what appears to be something of a conventional or stereotypical anarthrous usage. The five instances with the article are easily explained: 1 Cor 6:11 appears in a balanced prepositional phrase where the use of the article is determined by the article with "in/by the name of our Lord Jesus Christ."[22] The two in 1 Cor 12:9 are in a context where it is being argued that the "one and the same Spirit" is responsible for the diversity of gifts; the context calls for this repetition. So also in 2 Cor 12:18, where the emphasis on "the same" Spirit determines the usage. In Eph 1:13 the article came about because of an almost solemn emphasis; note that the same usage appears in the accusative in Eph 4:30.

(2) Over one-third of the anarthrous instances occur in the three major discussions of the role of the Spirit in Christian life in 1 Corinthians 12–14, Galatians 5, and Romans 8. Since in each case they are surrounded by other references to the Spirit, mostly articular, it is simply not possible that Paul in these contexts means other than the Holy Spirit when using this formula as well.

(3) Likewise in most of the other occurrences, the context demands that Paul can only intend "by [the Holy] Spirit," not "by a spirit." Thus, e.g., both the qualifier "Holy" and the fact that the Spirit elsewhere in Paul is so closely linked with power demand that "by the Holy Spirit" is what Paul intends in 1 Thes 1:5. Similarly in 2 Cor 3:3, where both the qualifier, "of the living God," and the succeeding argument which contrasts the ministries of the two covenants in terms of the Spirit and the letter mean that πνεύματι θεοῦ ζῶντος can refer only to the Holy Spirit, as the Spirit of the living God. One can show the same for the majority of items in this list.

(4) That we are here dealing with a kind of stereotyped usage,[23] similar to κατὰ πνεῦμα and κατὰ σάρκα, is finally made certain by the fact that the same phenomenon occurs with other words as well, when used with the dative in this way. This is especially true of σάρξ (flesh), the natural opposite of πνεῦμα, as well as such pairs as "law" and "grace." In the nominative and accusative these words are almost always articular; whereas in the dative (instrumental) they are nearly always anar-

---

[22]So also Easley, "Pauline Use," 311.

[23]So clearly stereotypical is this formula that Bultmann considered it "a formula of ecstasy" (2 Corinthians, 97). That in itself does not seem to be an adequate view, since many of these have nothing to do with ecstasy as such. If one speaks in tongues πνεύματι (1 Cor 14:2; in/by the Spirit), so does one walk and behave πνεύματι (Gal 5:16, 25). But such a suggestion is the clear recognition of a formulaic expression.

throus. That Paul can put πνεύματι/ἐν πνεύματι side by side with σαρκί/ἐν σαρκί, where the latter can mean only "in/by *the* flesh," is the clear evidence that Paul also—and always—by this formula means "in/by *the* Spirit."

Conclusions. On the one hand, this analysis should help to put an end to speculation about the presence or absence of the article as determining whether Paul meant to refer to the Holy Spirit or not. The evidence confirms that Paul knows no such thing as "a spirit" or "a holy spirit" when using πνεῦμα to refer to divine activity. He only and always means the Spirit of the living God, the Holy Spirit himself.[24] All of this is further corroborated by a passage like 2 Cor 13:13[14], where the Holy Spirit appears in triadic formula alongside, and distinct from, Christ and the Father. If one begins with such a text as thoroughly presuppositional to Paul's understanding, as one should, and then notes how often this triadic formula is presupposed in the many soteriological texts that mention the separate activities of the triune God, it is a cause for wonder that another view of Paul's usage took root at all.

Not only so, but this evidence weighs entirely against those translations and commentators who would understand passages such as 2 Thes 2:13; 1 Cor 14:2; 2 Cor 6:6; Eph 2:18; 5:18; or 6:18 as referring to the human spirit. As the exegesis of these texts shows, in each instance πνεῦμα can refer only to the Holy Spirit. The evidence on usage given here substantiates fully that exegesis.

It also needs to be noted—and this will spill over into the next section—that not a single anarthrous πνεῦμα occurs in the corpus when Paul unambiguously refers to the human spirit. All of this, then, may serve as a clue to the very difficult usage in Rom 12:11, where one cannot be sure by means of context whether τῷ πνεύματι ζέοντες means be zealous "in spirit" or "by the Spirit." Here the articular usage would seem to tilt the evidence in favor of the former, although this may be a case where both are intended (on this see below).

HOLY SPIRIT OR HUMAN SPIRIT

Although for the most part, as we have noted above, Paul's usage can be determined with a high degree of confidence, there are two types of πνεῦμα language in Paul where clarity is difficult to achieve, primarily

---

[24]This evidence seems also to render quite inadequate, as far as Paul is concerned, the study by Francis ("Holy Spirit"), who tries (rather unsuccessfully) to distinguish between instances where emphasis is on person (articular) and power (anarthrous). But the fact that πνεῦμα with the nominative is always articular and with the dative rarely so already loads the deck toward his conclusions; when "reception" and "giving" language is presupposed to refer to "power" not "person," one can be sure that Pauline usage is going to be missed by too much.

because in both cases Pauline usage seems to be a bit fluid. One of these is the three instances in 1 Corinthians 12–14 of the plural πνεύματα; the other has to do with several texts where Paul speaks of "my spirit," but it is clear in context that the Holy Spirit is very much in view as well. The probable solution to these passages lies in Paul's apparent conviction that the believer's spirit is the place where, by means of God's own Spirit, the human and the divine interface in the believer's life.

The resolution of these ambiguities is first of all to be found in the three plurals in 1 Corinthians 12–14: "the discerning of spirits" (12:10), "since you are zealots for spirits" (14:12), and "the spirits of the prophets are subject to the prophets" (14:32). The key lies with the context of 14:32, where "the πνεύματα of the prophets" almost certainly refers to "the prophetic Spirit" by which each of them speaks through his or her own spirit;[25] thus the prophetic utterance, inspired by the divine Spirit, is subject to the speaker and must be "discerned" by others in the community. It is argued in chapter 4 that this usage might best be translated by the inelegant "S/spirits of the prophets," as a way of trying to capture the apparent interfacing lying behind these plurals.

This usage in turn is the clue to the following passages:

1 Cor 5:3   παρὼν δὲ τῷ πνεύματι

1 Cor 5:4   συναχθέντων ὑμῶν καὶ τοῦ ἐμοῦ πνεύματος

1 Cor 6:17   ὁ δὲ κολλώμενος τῷ κυρίῳ ἕν πνεῦμά ἐστιν

1 Cor 14:14   τὸ πνεῦμά μου προσεύχεται

1 Cor 14:15   προσεύξομαι τῷ πνεύματι

1 Cor 14:15   ψαλῶ τῷ πνεύματι

Col 2:5   ἀλλὰ τῷ πνεύματι σὺν ὑμῖν εἰμι

Although these represent three different kinds of texts and language, the resolution of each is probably similar. In every instance one might best render πνεῦμα as "S/spirit," since this almost certainly approximates what Paul's somewhat flexible language intends. Thus in 1 Cor 14:14–15 Paul's ultimate point of reference is to the Spirit of God, who prays through my praying. Thus he means "my S/spirit prays/sings" in the sense that his own spirit is worshipping, but this transpires by the direct influence of the indwelling Spirit of God. Similarly, the whole argument of 1 Cor 6:12–20 suggests that v. 17 means something like, "he/she who

---

[25]See Fee, 1 Corinthians, 696; cf. the discussion in ch. 4 below. That Paul himself believed in a plurality of "good spirits" is emphatically denied by 12:4, 8–11: "the same Spirit, the one Spirit, the one and the same Spirit." Whether this also combats a concept of plurality of spirits on the part of the Corinthians is moot. The curious affirmation in 14:12, that they are "zealots of spirits," at least allows as much; but Paul's own use of this language in 14:32, where it cannot mean that, suggests something closer to what is here proposed.

is joined to the Lord becomes one spirit/Spirit with him." The same holds true for the difficult language of 1 Cor 5:3–5, where Paul speaks of being present in their gatherings "in S/spirit." In light of this usage—and of the difficulties involved—perhaps this is also how one should finally understand Rom 12:11 ("be fervent in S/spirit").

In any event, this kind of pedantic rendering of Paul's Greek would seem to get at the sense of these various texts, which indicate that for Paul "spirit" and "Spirit" are understood as closely related in the actual expression of Spirit manifestations.

"THE SPIRIT OF" OR "A SPIRIT OF"

Eleven times in his extant letters Paul uses πνεῦμα with a genitive modifier referring to some quality or attitude.[26] One cannot immediately be sure in these instances whether Paul intends something more strictly attitudinal or whether he is in fact referring to the Spirit who brings about the qualities mentioned in the genitive (e.g., 1 Cor 4:21, "a spirit of gentleness" [= a gentle spirit] or "the Spirit of gentleness" [= gentleness that the Spirit brings]). Both background and context suggest that Paul primarily has the Holy Spirit in mind in this usage, although in some cases there is just enough ambiguity to leave the matter open.

The usage itself is a Semitism, which Paul apparently adopted from his own reading of the Bible. In the OT conception,[27] humans did not so much possess a "spirit" as something innate to their humanity, as the very fact that they lived (and therefore "breathed") meant that they had been given the πνεῦμα of life (= the breath/spirit of life). Such a view of being human meant that many of the activities or dispositions of such "living beings" were expressed in terms of their having, or having been given, "a spirit of . . . "[28] This did not mean that they had received an individual entity or "substance" called "a spirit of . . . ," but that those in whom God had breathed the πνεῦμα of life, and who evidenced certain qualities or dispositions, also thereby had been given "a spirit" of such. At times this is nothing more than a periphrasis for the activity or attitude itself; at other times, and especially so when such language comes to be associated with God's own πνεῦμα that has been given to

---

[26]1 Cor 2:12 (τοῦ κόσμου, "of the world"); 4:21 (πραΰτητος, "of gentleness"; cf. Gal 6:1); 2 Cor 4:13 (τῆς πίστεως, "of faith"); Rom 1:4 (ἁγιωσύνης, "of holiness"); Rom 8:15 (δουλείας, "of slavery"); 8:15 (υἱοθεσίας, "of adoption"); Rom 11:8 [LXX] (κατανύξεως, "of stupor"); Eph 1:17 (σοφίας καὶ ἀποκαλύψεως, "of wisdom and revelation"); Eph 4:23 (τοῦ νοὸς ὑμῶν, "of your minds"); 2 Tim 1:7 (δειλίας . . . δυνάμεως καὶ ἀγάπης καὶ σωφρονισμοῦ, "of cowardice . . . of power, love, sound-mindedness").

[27]For helpful overviews of OT usage of רוּחַ (rûaḥ; LXX πνεῦμα) see F. Baumgärtel, TDNT 6.359–68; and E. Kamlah, NIDNTT 3.689–93.

[28]See, e.g., Num 5:14, 30 ("a spirit of jealousy"); Deut 34:9 ("a spirit of understanding"); Isa 61:3 ("a spirit of despair").

certain people for their divinely appointed task, "a spirit of . . . " comes very close to meaning "the Spirit who" so empowered them with such a disposition.[29]

In the eleven occurrences of this phrase in Paul, the usage seems to run the gamut. At one end are those instances which seem to be a periphrasis for an attitude or disposition, pure and simple. This is especially true of his citing of the LXX in Rom 11:8[30] ("a spirit of stupor" = "stupor"); cf. "a spirit of gentleness" in 1 Cor 4:21. On the other hand, the majority of such occurrences lean toward expressing something about the presence of the Spirit in the believer's life. For example, in Gal 6:1, where Paul refers to restoring a fallen person ἐν πνεύματι πραΰτητος, repeating the phrase from 1 Cor 4:21, the context seems to demand a secondary reference to the Spirit. That is, it still refers to the believer's attitude, but as that is now a fruit of the Spirit. The entire argument to this point (from Gal 5:16) has to do with life in the Spirit, one of whose fruit is πραΰτης ("gentleness"; 5:23). In 6:1, therefore, Paul is referring back to this fruit of the Spirit as the manner or means whereby the transgressor is restored.

A similar usage occurs in Rom 8:15, but now in one of Paul's standard "not . . . but" contrasts (cf. 1 Cor 2:12; 2 Tim 1:7). English translations tend to render the negative part "a spirit of" and then become ambiguous with the positive part (sometimes "but the Spirit"; sometimes "but a spirit"). Here Paul's usage is unmistakable. In each case he intends to refer to their reception of the Holy Spirit, which did not come from the "world" or bring "slavery" or "cowardice"; rather, the Spirit comes from God (1 Cor 2:12) and brings "adoption" (Rom 8:15) and "power, love, and sound-mindedness" (2 Tim 1:7). To put all of that another way, had Paul not set up his concern by the emphatic negative clause, no one would ever have imagined that Paul was referring to anything but the Holy Spirit in speaking of the "Spirit of adoption," "the Spirit of God," and "the Spirit of power, love, and sound-mindedness." These rather clear and unmistakable uses should cause us to lean in that way in the others as well—although not all will be so persuaded in some cases.

Ultimately, these latter can be resolved only contextually. Paul surely intends the Holy Spirit by "the Spirit of life" (= the Spirit who brings life) in Rom 8:2; so also Rom 1:4 (the Spirit characterized by holiness), 2 Cor 4:13 (the Spirit who brings faith), and Eph 1:17 (the Spirit who gives wisdom and revelation). The usage in Gal 6:1 may be the clue to the identical phrase in 1 Cor 4:21, although in the latter the primary emphasis falls more likely on Paul's own attitude. But even here, where the

---

[29]See esp. Exod 31:3 and 35:31 (of Bezalel, where it is actually qualified with the adjective "divine") and Isa 11:2 (of the Messiah).

[30]On this "merged" citation see the discussion in ch. 7.

accent lies on the quality expressed in the genitive, Paul speaks of a πνεῦμα of gentleness, not so much to refer to "a spirit of" that quality, but to point to the Spirit as its source.

It is altogether likely, therefore, that even in what may appear to be more impersonal uses of πνεῦμα, Paul enlists this word because the characteristic or quality to which he refers is either a characteristic of the Spirit himself, or the result of the Spirit's activity in the life of the believer.

THE MEANING OF THE ADJECTIVE πνευματικός[31]

This is an almost exclusively Pauline word in the NT, occurring 24 of 26 times in his letters, 15 times in 1 Corinthians alone.[32] It appears in various ways:

(a) As a substantive.

(i) In the masculine (referring to people):

1 Cor 2:15   ὁ δὲ πνευματικὸς ἀνακρίνει πάντα

Gal 6:1   ὑμεῖς οἱ πνευματικοὶ καταρτίζετε τὸν τοιοῦτον

(ii) In the neuter (plural):

Rom 15:27   εἰ γὰρ τοῖς πνευματικοῖς αὐτῶν ἐκοινώνησαν τὰ ἔθνη

1 Cor 2:13   διδακτοῖς πνεύματος, πνευματικὰ πνευματικοῖς συγκρίνοντες

1 Cor 9:11   εἰ ἡμεῖς ὑμῖν τὰ πνευματικὰ ἐσπείραμεν

1 Cor 12:1   περὶ δὲ τῶν πνευματικῶν

1 Cor 14:1   ζηλοῦτε δὲ τὰ πνευματικά

(iii) In the neuter plural (referring to demonic spirits):

Eph 6:12   πρὸς τὰ πνευματικὰ τῆς πονηρίας ἐν τοῖς ἐπουρανίοις

(b) As an adjective.

(i) Referring to people:

1 Cor 3:1   οὐκ ἠδυνήθην λαλῆσαι ὑμῖν ὡς πνευματικοῖς

---

[31]On this word in the NT see the "Additional Note" by E. G. Selwyn, *The First Epistle of St. Peter* (London: Macmillan, 1946) 281–84. This is a helpful piece, although I tend to go in some slightly different directions. See also the brief, but helpful, overview by E. Schweizer, *TDNT* 6.436–37.

[32]The adverb πνευματικῶς occurs once only in the NT, in 1 Cor 2:14, where, contra Selwyn (*1 Peter*, 283) it clearly refers to the Spirit (= discerned by the Spirit). See ch. 4 below.

1 Cor 14:37   εἴ τις δοκεῖ προφήτης εἶναι ἢ πνευματικός

(ii) Modifying impersonal nouns:

Rom 1:11   ἵνα τι μεταδῶ χάρισμα ὑμῖν πνευματικόν

Rom 7:14   ὁ νόμος πνευματικός ἐστιν

1 Cor 2:13   διδακτοῖς πνεύματος, πνευματικοῖς πνευματικὰ
              συγκρίνοντες

1 Cor 10:3   πάντες τὸ αὐτὸ πνευματικὸν βρῶμα ἔφαγον

1 Cor 10:4   καὶ πάντες τὸ αὐτὸ πνευματικὸν ἔπιον πόμα

1 Cor 10:4   ἔπινον γὰρ ἐκ πνευματικῆς ἀκολουθούσης πέτρας

1 Cor 15:44   ἐγείρεται σῶμα πνευματικόν

1 Cor 15:44   ἔστιν σῶμα ψυχικόν, ἔστιν καὶ πνευματικόν

1 Cor 15:46   ἀλλ' οὐ πρῶτον τὸ πνευματικόν ἀλλὰ τὸ ψυχικόν

1 Cor 15:46   ἔπειτα τὸ πνευματικόν

Eph 1:3   ὁ εὐλογήσας ἡμᾶς ἐν πάσῃ εὐλογίᾳ πνευματικῇ

Eph 5:19   ἐν ψαλμοῖς καὶ ὕμνοις καὶ ᾠδαῖς πνευματικαῖς

Col 1:9   ἐν πάσῃ σοφίᾳ καὶ συνέσει πνευματικῇ

Col 3:16   ψαλμοῖς ὕμνοις ᾠδαῖς πνευματικαῖς

This is another of the words in the NT that bears a strong Pauline stamp. It does not occur in the LXX. In classical and Hellenistic Greek it had to do primarily with wind or air; thus it is found only rarely in Hellenistic texts as an adjective pertaining to the human πνεῦμα.[33]

Unfortunately, its meaning in Paul tends to be obscured by one of the rare impoverishments of the English language, in that our translations of this word are limited almost exclusively to the small case "spiritual." The net result is one of those "slippery" words that tends to mean whatever its user wants it to mean (and who often could not define it, if required to do so). But such users seldom stray close to Pauline usage, where the word functions primarily as an adjective for the Spirit, referring to *that which belongs to, or pertains to, the Spirit.* Several considerations converge to make this certain.

The basic meaning of the adjective. The word itself belongs to a class of adjectives ending in -ικος, formed from their corresponding nouns and bearing the meaning, "belonging to, or pertaining to,"[34] the corresponding noun. Thus, in the same way that κυριακός in 1 Cor 11:20 is an

---

[33]The closest thing to it is an obscure passage in Philo (*Her.* 242); a bit later than Paul, Plutarch appears to use it to refer to the nonmaterial side of human existence, but even this passage is disputed.

[34]See W. F. Howard, MHT 2.377–79; cf. Selwyn, *1 Peter,* 282, who translates these adjectives, "concerned with."

adjective referring to "the Lord" (hence "the Table pertaining to the Lord" or "the Lord's Table"), and σαρκικός is an adjective for "flesh," meaning that which belongs to, or pertains to, the flesh, so πνευματικός is an adjective for πνεῦμα, meaning that which belongs to, or pertains to, "spirit." Since the word πνεῦμα primarily refers to the Holy Spirit in Paul, one might expect the corresponding adjective to function similarly. Indeed, in the case of the adjective, there is no certain instance in all of Paul's uses, where he refers to the "spiritual" (= inner or noncorporeal) nature of people, as over against their "physical" or "earthly."

The Pauline usage (in the masculine singular/plural). The word emerges for the first time in 1 Corinthians, and in a manner suggesting strongly that the usage stems from his difficulties with this community. Whatever else, here is where he and they are at odds—on what it means to be "spiritual," having to do in particular with what it means to be people of the Spirit. Thus, when Paul uses πνευματικός in its several polemical contexts in this letter (2:6–3:1; 12:1–14:40; 15:44–46), it refers almost exclusively to God's people as πνευματικοί, or to various activities and realities as belonging especially to the sphere of the Spirit.

The argument in 2:6–3:4 is especially pertinent in this regard, since it has such a high incidence of this word (5 including the adverb in v. 14). With biting irony for those who regard themselves as πνευματικοί (Spirit-people), Paul argues that in their by-passing the cross for "wisdom" (1:18–31), they have taken their place with the world, who in its wisdom "crucified the Lord of glory"! With that he sets out the starkest possible contrast between believers and nonbelievers, those who have gone the way of God's wisdom and those who have not. The key to all of this is the Spirit, whom believers—including the Corinthians—have received. That the "foolishness of the cross" is God's wisdom has been revealed by the Spirit (v. 10), for only the Spirit of God knows the mind of God and has revealed it to us (v. 11). In receiving the Spirit, we did not receive that which makes us think like the world, but the Spirit of God himself, by whose presence in our lives we understand what God has graciously done in our behalf (v. 12). Therefore what things we speak (about Christ crucified; cf. v. 2) are not in keeping with human wisdom but are taught us by the Spirit (v. 13), which means that we explain πνευματικά ("spiritual things"; i.e., the things freely given us by the Spirit of God, v. 12) πνευματικοῖς ("by spiritual means"; i.e., by means of the words taught by the Spirit).[35]

In contrast to us, who by the Spirit understand what God has been about in the cross, Paul continues in v. 14, there is the *psychikos* person (the person who is merely human, without the Spirit of God). Such a person does not receive the things of the Spirit of God—indeed cannot

---

[35]On the meaning of this complex verse, see the commentary in ch. 4.

know them—precisely because such matters are discerned only by "spiritual" means (that is, by means of the Spirit). The one who is spiritual (the Spirit person), on the other hand, discerns all things (v. 15), precisely because by the Spirit believers have received the mind of Christ (v. 16).

Then, with full irony, in 3:1–4 Paul presses his advantage. Even though they regard themselves as—and in reality are—Spirit people, their thinking and behavior is that of non-Spirit people, so he has had to treat them accordingly, as mere babies. As long as quarreling and strife continue among them, Paul asks, are they not acting like mere human beings, that is, precisely like people who do not have the Spirit? The point of Paul's argument, of course, is "Stop it." My point is that for Paul the Spirit alone distinguishes believer from nonbeliever. God's people have the Spirit, and are by that very fact "spiritual" (= Spirit people), while others are not, nor can they be "spiritual" in any meaningful (for Paul) sense of that word, precisely because they lack the one criterion for "spiritual" life, the Spirit of the living God.[36]

This same emphasis on πνευματικός as pertaining to the people and/ or activities of the Spirit is likewise in view in such passages as 1 Cor 12:1; 14:1, 37; Gal 6:1; Rom 1:11; Col 1:9; 3:16; and Eph 5:19. Thus, for example, in Gal 6:1, in the context of walking/living/being led by the Spirit, οἱ πνευματικοί (you who are spiritual! [NIV]) can refer only to those who are so walking/living/being led by the Spirit. Indeed even its negative usage in Eph 6:12 confirms this understanding, where in the neuter plural it refers to "the spirit powers of evil." Just as there is only one Holy Spirit, so there are many "spirits" of the evil spirit (Eph 2:2), who are at work in the world to tear down and destroy (cf. the plural "spirits" in 1 Tim 4:1).

In the neuter plural. These are the more difficult instances, where material support is "physical" in contrast to the benefits of the gospel that are "spiritual," and in several instances where the adjective modifies an impersonal noun. But even here, as the exegesis of these passages will show, it is arguable that the ultimate referent is the Spirit. Material support, for example, which is designated as "fleshly," has to do with the material needs of this earthly life; but Paul's having "sown spiritual things" among them does not mean "religious" or the like, but rather refers to the gospel, in which the Spirit plays such a key role. Thus in

---

[36]Cf. Schweizer, *TDNT* 6.436–37. In light of all of this, and especially since the word is used to refer to people as such in so few instances (1 Cor 2:15; 3:1; 14:37; Gal 6:1), one wonders whether Betz can be right in asserting that "in antiquity, this name was an almost technical self-designation of people who regarded themselves as having more or less reached the final goal of 'salvation' already here on earth" ("In Defense of the Spirit: Paul's Letter to the Galatians as a Document of Early Christian Apologetics," in *Aspects of Religious Propaganda in Judaism and Early Christianity* [ed. E. Schüssler Fiorenza; Notre Dame, 1976] 99–114 [106]). I would agree that this was the Corinthian attitude, but where is the evidence for this outside 1 Corinthians itself?

passages like 1 Cor 9:11 and Rom 15:27 τὰ πνευματικά most likely refers
to the "things of the Spirit." Perhaps the most ambiguous usage in this
regard is in Eph 1:3 ("God has blessed you with all spiritual blessings in
heavenly places in Christ Jesus"). Because of the occurrence of "heavenly
places," some argue that this means "heavenly" blessings, in contrast to
those of earth. More likely, however, especially in light of Paul's usage
in the rest of this letter and of vv. 13–14 with which this benediction
concludes, Paul is referring to the benefits that the Spirit bestows through
the work of Christ that is elaborated in vv. 4–12. So also the "spiritual
songs" in Col 3:16 and Eph 5:19 refer to songs that are inspired of the
Spirit which people sing in the gathered community. And in 1 Cor 15:44–
46, it is not a nonmaterial body that awaits us, but a "heavenly, supernatural one," adapted to the final life of the Spirit in the eschaton.

Conclusion. All of this is to say that the small case "spiritual" probably
should be eliminated from our vocabulary, when it comes to this word
in the Pauline corpus. All the more so, when one thinks of the Greek
overtones underlying most contemporary uses of this word, where "spiritual" tends to mean either "religious," "nonmaterial" (a meaning absolutely foreign to Paul), something close to "mystical," or, even worse,
"the interior life of the believer." In fact, there is not a single instance in
Paul where this word refers to the human "spirit" and has to do with
"spiritual life," as this word is most often understood in modern English.
For Paul it is an adjective that primarily refers to the Spirit of God, even
when the contrasts are to "earthly" bodies and "material support."

THE TERM χάρισμα IN PAUL[37]

As with the adjective πνευματικός, the word χάρισμα is an almost
exclusively Pauline word in the NT, occurring 16 of 17 instances in his
letters.[38] Indeed, it occurs more often in Paul than in all other known
instances in Greek antiquity, up to and including the first Christian
century.

Because of its association with the Spirit in 1 Corinthians 12, it is
commonly translated "spiritual gift." But again, as with πνευματικός, this

---

[37] *Bibliography:* H. **Conzelmann**, *TDNT* 9.402–6; **Dunn**, *Jesus*, 205–9; G. D. **Fee**,
DPL, 339–47; K. S. **Hemphill**, *Spiritual Gifts: Empowering the New Testament Church*
(Nashville: Broadman, 1988); J. **Koenig**, *Charismata: God's Gifts for God's People*
(Philadelphia: Westminster, 1978); S. **Schatzmann**, *A Pauline Theology of Charismata*
(Peabody, Mass.: Hendrickson, 1987).

[38] The only other NT usage is 1 Pet 4:10. It occurs with some regularity in the
apostolic fathers and in later Christian writings, but under the influence of NT usage.
In Paul the word occurs 6 times each in 1 Corinthians and Romans, and once each
in 2 Corinthians, 1 Timothy, and 2 Timothy.

tends to mislead. On its own the word has little or nothing to do with the Spirit; it picks up Spirit overtones only by context or by explicit qualifiers.

In this case the noun has been formed from χάρις (grace), as a way of concretely expressing the abstract noun. Χάρις issues in a χάρισμα; and that is what it means in its every instance in Paul—a concrete expression of grace, thus a "gracious bestowment." In nearly half of its uses, therefore, χάρισμα lacks any reference at all to the Spirit, but simply designates a variety of ways God's grace is evidenced in the midst of, or in the lives of, his people. It includes such diverse "gifts" as eternal life (Rom 6:23; cf. 5:15, 16), the many special privileges granted to Israel (Rom 11:29, referring to 9:4–5), celibacy and marriage (1 Cor 7:7), and deliverance from a deadly peril (2 Cor 1:10).

On the other hand, the word frequently relates to special manifestations or activities of the Spirit, indicating "gracious gifts" of the Spirit, which is why it has come to be thought of as a Spirit activity as such. That its basic relationship is to "grace," while at the same time pointing toward the "gifting" that comes from the Spirit, surfaces in two texts. First, in 1 Cor 1:4–7 God expresses his grace concretely in the rich number of χαρίσματα (charismata) he bestows upon this community; it is in this way, especially as the word is picked up in chapter 12, that χαρίσματα comes to be understood as "gifts of the Spirit." Second, in Rom 1:11 Paul specifically associates these ideas by qualifying the noun χάρισμα with the adjective πνευματικόν. Thus Paul hopes that in coming to Rome he might be an instrument through whom the Spirit will further benefit the Roman believers, by means of a "Spiritual gift."

This in turn serves as the basis for the special usage in 1 Corinthians 12 (vv. 4, 9, 28, 30, 31). In three of these (vv. 9, 28, 30) Paul employs the phrase "χαρίσματα of healings." Here he probably refers not to some "gift" that enables people to heal others, but to the various concrete expressions of the Spirit's power bringing physical healing to members of the community; hence "gifts of healings." But in v. 4, at the head of this discussion, this word is associated with the Spirit in a way that seems intended to include what in v. 7 Paul styles "manifestations of the Spirit." Thus there can be little question that the "manifestations" listed in vv. 8–10 are to be understood as χαρίσματα, gracious bestowments of the Spirit in the gathered community for the sake of building up the people of God.

More difficult is the recurrence of this word in the imperative at the end of this discussion in 12:31, in which he urges them "eagerly to desire the greater χαρίσματα." For several reasons noted in the exegesis of this passage (see pp. 195–97 below), this imperative almost certainly does not refer to the preceding potpourri of people, ministries, and Spirit manifestations that "God has placed in the church" (v. 28). Rather, the imperative begins the argument on intelligibility and order in chapter 14, which is interrupted so as to place all of these things in the context of love.

When *resuming* this imperative in 14:1, Paul replaces χαρίσματα with τὰ πνευματικά (the things of the Spirit), which have to do, as in 12:4–11, with Spirit manifestations in the community gathered for worship. It is doubtful, therefore, whether Paul intends to describe such people as apostles[39] and teachers, or such ministries as helpful deeds and acts of guidance, as χαρίσματα. At least in its only specific appearances in this argument the term seems to be limited to Spirit manifestations in the community, and thus probably means something like, "concrete expressions of grace manifested through the Spirit's empowering."

This leads in turn to the more difficult usage in Rom 12:6, where Paul speaks of "having χαρίσματα that differ, in keeping with the χάρις given to us." Here again is the distinct joining of χαρίσματα with "grace" itself, as concrete expressions of the latter. The problem is that in context Paul does not so much as mention or allude to the Spirit. But this is true of almost all of Romans 12–14. That the Spirit is assumed to lie behind all of this behavior can be inferred from the relationship of this material to ch. 8.[40] Not only so, but the first χάρισμα mentioned in this list is prophecy, which in Paul is understood to be a Spirit gifting par excellence.

Nonetheless, despite such obvious associations with the Spirit that come from the larger context of Romans and 1 Corinthians, it is not at all plain that Paul intended everything that he calls χαρίσματα in 12:6b–8 to be understood as special gifts *of the Spirit*, at least in the same way that he expressly equates this term with the Spirit's manifestations in 1 Corinthians 12. The list in vv. 6b–8 is so heterogeneous and covers such a broad range of behavior, it seems far more likely that for Paul the emphasis lies on the "grace of God" here being worked out among them in concrete ways, rather than on the empowering of the Spirit for such behavior or on "Spirit gifting" as such. Thus the list includes items such as prophecy, teaching, and exhorting/encouraging, which in 1 Corinthians 12 come under the purview of Spirit χαρίσματα, as well as various forms of serving others within the believing community (service, contributing to the needs of others, giving aid, and showing mercy), which are never elsewhere in Paul attributed directly to the Spirit as *his* gifts. These latter items move away from the idea of "gifts" per se, at least in terms of Spirit manifestations, to proper ethical behavior, in which the fruit of love finds concrete expression in their midst. That these are indeed the outworking of the Spirit in Pauline theology need not be doubted. What

---

[39]It is popular to refer to apostleship as "the greatest charisma of all"; it is doubtful, however, whether Paul actually considered his apostleship a gift *of the Spirit*. His apostleship in particular is related to God's will and Christ's commissioning; he himself never calls it a Spirit-gifting as such.

[40]Especially significant in this regard is the similar relationship of the paraenesis in Galatians 5–6 with the argument of that letter, which in this case is expressly designated as Spirit-empowered behavior.

is doubtful is that our translation "gifts *of the Spirit*" is an adequate understanding of Pauline usage. While both enumerations are called χαρίσματα, only that in 1 Cor 12:8–10 is tied specifically by Paul himself to the activities of the Spirit in the community.

In any case, the items listed in Romans 12 will not be pursued in this study, any more than will other listings of "graces" such as in Col 3:12—except in the exegesis of the Romans passage itself and under the larger rubric of the various ways that love, the primary fruit of the Spirit, concretely manifests itself.

Finally, the two uses in 1 Tim 4:14 and 2 Tim 1:6 should be noted, because in these instances the χάρισμα is singular, is said to be "in Timothy," and occurs in contexts referring to Timothy's ministry as such. Thus in its first instance it probably concerns his "giftedness" for ministry, which came to him through prophetic utterances. In 2 Tim 1:6, however, the χάρισμα seems more likely to point to the Spirit himself, although that in turn probably is a metonymy for Timothy's Spirit-given ministry that came to him "through prophetic utterances."

All of this to say, then, that when χάρισμα is specifically related to the activity of the Spirit, it seems to indicate some concrete ways in which the Spirit manifests himself in the believing community, granting them "gracious bestowments" to meet their various needs and thus to build them up as the eschatological people of God; whereas χάρισμα as such is a much broader term and is probably incorrectly translated "spiritual gift" or "gift of the Spirit."

THE SPIRIT AND THE LANGUAGE OF POWER

In contrast to the common understanding of contemporary believers, first-century believers understood—and assumed—the Spirit to be manifested in power. So much is this so that the terms "Spirit" and "power" at times are used interchangeably.[41] Luke, for example, interchanges the two words in the balanced lines of Semitic poetry in Luke 1:35; and since Jesus' whole public ministry is to be understood in terms of the Spirit's activity (3:22; 4:1, 14), there can be little question that in 5:17 Luke meant the "power *of the Spirit*" was present with Jesus to heal.[42]

So also with Paul. Not only does he specifically use such terminology as "the power of the Spirit" (Rom 15:13, 19), but he also regularly joins the two terms in such a way that the presence of the Spirit means the presence of power (1 Thes 1:5; 1 Cor 2:4; Gal 3:5; Rom 1:4; Eph 3:16; 2 Tim

---

[41]See, e.g., the discussion in J. D. G. Dunn, *Romans 9–11* (WBC 38B; Dallas: Word, 1988) 851.

[42]So James B. Shelton, *Mighty in Word and Deed: The Role of the Holy Spirit in Luke–Acts* (Peabody, Mass.: Hendrickson, 1991) 75–76; contra Menzies, *Development,* 124–25.

1:7). Several of these references occur in the context of Paul's own ministry (1 Thes 1:5; 1 Cor 2:4; Rom 15:19), but others refer to the powerful working of the Spirit in the lives of believers. One may thus assume not only that Paul's other references to the Spirit always imply the presence of power, but also that many of his references to power imply the presence of the Spirit (e.g., 2 Thes 1:11; 1 Cor 4:20; 5:4; 2 Cor 4:7; 6:7; 12:9, 12; 13:4; Col 1:11, 29; Eph 1:19, 21; 3:7, 20; 2 Tim 1:8).

Such texts as these, therefore, will also be analyzed in detail, to see to what degree this association can be seen in Paul's understanding of the Spirit. What becomes abundantly clear is that "power" includes a broad range of "meaning" for Paul. Thus the relationship between the Spirit, power, and weakness and suffering must also be explored, as it will be in chapter 12.

PART 1

ANALYSIS

3

THE THESSALONIAN CORRESPONDENCE

Commentaries:[1] E. **Best** (BNTC, 1972); F. F. **Bruce** (WBC, 1982); John **Calvin** (1540[1]; ET 1960); E. **von Dobschütz** (1909[7]); C. J. **Ellicott** (1861); G. G. **Findlay** (CGT, 1925); J. E. **Frame** (ICC, 1912); W. **Hendriksen** (1955); D. E. **Hiebert** (1971); D. H. **Juel** (1985); J. B. **Lightfoot** (1895 [= *Notes on the Epistles of St Paul*]); I. H. **Marshall** (NCBC, 1983); C. **Masson** (CNT, 1957); G. **Milligan** (1908); J. **Moffatt** (EGT, 1910); A. L. **Moore** (NCB, 1969); L. **Morris** (NICNT, 1959); W. **Neil** (MNTC, 1950); A. **Plummer** (1 Thes, 1918; 2 Thes, 1918); B. **Rigaux** (ET, 1956); R. L. **Thomas** (EBC, 1978); W. **Trilling** (EKKNT, 2 Thes, 1980); C. A. **Wanamaker** (NIGTC, 1990); R. A. **Ward** (1973); D. E. H. **Whiteley** (NClarB, 1969).

Other significant works are referred to by the following short titles:

Collins, *Studies* (= Raymond F. Collins, *Studies on the First Letter to the Thessalonians* [BETL 66; Leuven: University, 1984]); **Giblin**, *Threat* (= Charles H. Giblin, *The Threat to Faith: An Exegetical and Theological Re-examination of 2 Thessalonians 2* [AnBib 31; Rome: Pontifical Biblical Institute, 1967]); **Hughes**, *Rhetoric* (= Frank Witt Hughes, *Early Christian Rhetoric and 2 Thessalonians* [JSNTSup 30; Sheffield: Academic Press, 1989]); **Jewett**, *Correspondence* (= Robert Jewett, *The Thessalonian Correspondence: Pauline Rhetoric and Millenarian Piety* [Philadelphia: Fortress, 1986]); **Jewett**, *Terms* (= Robert Jewett, *Paul's Anthropological Terms: A Study of their Use in Conflict Settings* [AGJU 10; Leiden: Brill, 1971]); **O'Brien**, *Thanksgivings* (= Peter T. O'Brien, *Introductory Thanksgivings in the Letters of Paul* [NovTSup 49; Leiden: Brill, 1977]).

In these earliest of the extant Pauline letters, the Holy Spirit is mentioned by name or alluded to six times (1 Thes 1:5, 6; 4:8; 5:19; 2 Thes

---

[1]The following commentaries are referred to in this chapter only by the author's last name.

2:2, 13),[2] chiefly in contexts that refer either to the Thessalonians' origins or to their life as believers. Two items are significant about these references. First, apart from the possibly corrective passage in 1 Thes 5:19–22, most of them are quite incidental, in the sense that Paul is not trying to say something about the Spirit as such. Rather, he refers in passing to the Christian life of these very recent converts, and in a matter-of-fact way he describes that life in terms of the Spirit.

Second, although not numerous, the various texts touch on most of the issues in Pauline pneumatology. Thus in 1 Thes 1:5 he reminds them of his Spirit-empowered ministry among them. In both 1 Thes 1:6 and 2 Thes 2:13 he recalls for them their own experience of conversion, and in both cases he mentions the central role of the Spirit. In 1 Thes 4:8, as well as 2 Thes 2:13, the emphasis is on the Spirit as the one who fits them for ethical life. The final two passages (1 Thes 5:19–22 and 2 Thes 2:2) reflect the community at worship. The former insists on the testing of prophetic utterances, without eliminating them altogether; the latter illustrates in a practical way the need for such testing.

1 THESSALONIANS

1 THESSALONIANS 1:4–6[3]

[4]*knowing, brothers and sisters beloved by God, your election,* [5]*how that*[4] *our gospel came to you not in word alone, but also with power, namely,*[5] *with the*

---

[2]Although see the discussion below on 1 Thes 5:23 and 2 Thes 1:11.

[3]As noted in the Preface, the "translations" in each case do not reflect the exegesis that follows, but are attempts to render the Greek as literally as possible, so as to make comment on the text easier.

[4]Rather than "causal," as in most translations and commentaries (cf. O'Brien, *Thanksgivings*, 151n49; Wanamaker 78), the ὅτι that begins this clause is probably epexegetic and offers an elaboration-explanation as to how the Thessalonians can be sure that God's love for them has resulted in their election. For this usage in Paul (οἶδα, followed by an object, followed by an epexegetic ὅτι), see esp. 2:1; cf. 1 Cor 16:15; Rom 13:11.

[5]This translation is based on the textual choice which omits the ἐν before πληροφορίᾳ with א B 33 lat. This is the best candidate for being the original text, since one can offer no reasonable explanation for its omission by scribes (esp. in light of its certain presence before the two preceding nouns, "power" and "Holy Spirit"), whereas that very fact easily explains why subsequent scribes would have added an ἐν before πληροφορίᾳ as well—to make all three nouns coordinate (so also Rigaux 374). What this means, therefore, is that we are not here dealing with a "triad" (Collins, *Studies*, 192n95, Thomas 244), but with epexegesis, where the second (compound) phrase further qualifies the first (cf. Moffatt 24).

Holy Spirit and[6] *full conviction, just as you know what manner of men we were toward*[7] *you for your sakes;* [6]*and you became imitators of us and of the Lord, having received the message amid great affliction, accompanied by the joy of*[8] *the Holy Spirit.*

These two sentences (vv. 3–5, 6) contain the earliest reference to Christian conversion in the NT. Significantly, they occur in Paul's thanksgiving at the opening of the letter.[9] The emphases reflect the historical setting. Although full precision is not possible, two items that recur in 1 Thessalonians 1–3 enable us to make some educated guesses as to the nature of that setting. On the one hand, Paul more than once refers to their suffering in the face of opposition (1:6–7; 2:13–16; 3:2–4); on the other hand, he also offers a considerable defense both of his ministry while among them (2:1–12) and of his actions since leaving (2:17–3:5). These are undoubtedly related themes; i.e., the persecution the Thessalonian believers are undergoing from their former pagan associations (2:15) is in some way related to their becoming the converts of an itinerant Jewish propagator of a new (non-Greek) religion,[10] in which

---

[6]For the textual choice in this case, see the preceding note.

[7]The textual choice between ὑμῖν (ℵ A C P 048 33 81 104 326* 945 1739 1881 pc) and ἐν ὑμῖν (B D F G Maj sy) is not an easy one. The change could have been purely accidental: an additional ἐν or its omission resulting from dittography or haplography (from the preceding ἐγενήθημεν). On the one hand, from the perspective of intrinsic probability (in this case, author's style), one could argue for its presence in the Pauline original, since the use of two prepositional phrases in this manner (ἐν ὑμῖν δι' ὑμᾶς) is quite in keeping with Paul's style (cf. 3:7; 4:14). On the other hand, on the grounds of transcriptional probability—assuming the change was not accidental—ὑμῖν is most likely the original, since scribes would tend to add prepositions, unless a reason could be found for their having omitted it, which is not forthcoming in this case. Since this reading also has the better external support (it is clear that B abandons its relatives in this case), it should probably be preferred as the original. Although the overall sense of the sentence comes out at about the same place, the text without ἐν emphasizes Paul's (and Timothy's/Silas's) relationship *toward,* or *before* (so Frame), the Thessalonians; whereas ἐν ὑμῖν emphasizes their conduct while *among* them. The argument of 2:1–12, which emphasizes Paul's *relationship with the Thessalonians* while present among them, also favors the former reading.

[8]Codex B and some Vulgate MSS add a καί between "joy" and "Holy Spirit," resulting in: "accompanied by joy and the Holy Spirit." This is in all likelihood secondary.

[9]This is one of three instances where the work of the Spirit is mentioned as part of a thanksgiving (see 1 Cor 1:4–9 and Col 1:8–9).

[10]This view is rejected by G. Lyons, *Pauline Autobiography: Toward a New Understanding* (SBLDS 73; Atlanta: Scholars Press, 1985) 177–201, in an argument that I find not wholly convincing. Part of his reason for rejection is the failure of scholarship to establish a polemical context for the letter, which assumes some opposition to Paul in the church community. On this matter I quite agree; but the opposition, I would argue, is not against Paul—and therefore within the Christian community—but is pagan opposition to the Thessalonians (as 2:14–16 suggests), and Paul's role in their conversion is very likely a part of that opposition.

part of the charge originally laid against them had to do with the legitimacy of such religion and the honor of Caesar (see Acts 17:7).[11] Paul's own concern is over whether they are standing firm in their new-found faith, despite his hurried leave-taking[12]—and probably before they were as firmly planted in the faith as he would have desired.[13]

Hence in the thanksgiving, as often in his letters, Paul anticipates some of the issues that he will later address, by reminding them that he is constantly praying for them, and that in his prayer he thanks God for them and their faithfulness to Christ (vv. 2–3). In the process (v. 4) he offers divine love and election as the foundation of their faith that prompts his thanksgiving. This is probably intended also to be a theological undergirding of their faith, to lead to yet further faithfulness, which is precisely where v. 5 fits in. The evidence[14] of their election is to be found in their conversion itself. What is significant in this reminder is the experiential, evidential nature of what is to be recalled. Their election itself is a *positional* reality;[15] but their own appropriation of that reality came about through a combination of experiential factors: Paul's powerful, Spirit-inspired preaching of the gospel, resulting in their joyful experience of conversion, all orchestrated by the Holy Spirit.

Paul's concern seems obvious. He grounds their experienced faith in God's prior love and election (v. 4); but since he is appealing to their own conversion as a means of encouragement in the midst of present suffering,[16] the reminder is twofold: of the nature of *Paul's proclamation* of the gospel, that it was accompanied by the Holy Spirit's power (v. 5); and of their own *experience* of receiving the gospel (the word), that it

---

[11]That the situation in Thessalonica may well be related to the charge against Paul in Acts 17:7 has been suggested by E. A. Judge, "The Decrees of Caesar at Thessalonica," *RTR* 30 (1971) 1–7; cf. K. P. Donfried, "The Cults of Thessalonica and the Thessalonian Correspondence," *NTS* 31 (1985) 342–52; Wanamaker 113–14.

[12]This assumes that the picture in Acts 17:1–10 is a generally accurate one. Paul's obvious anxiety over their welfare, which had led to repeated attempts to return (2:18), to Timothy's being sent in his place (3:1–2), and finally to his great relief in finding out that they were persevering in their faith (3:6–8), join to give credence to the account in Acts. It also seems to be corroborated by the need to defend his ministry among them (2:1–12; anticipated in the present passage [vv. 5–6, 9]), since the (probably Greek) persecutors of these new believers most likely knew of his sudden departure in the dead of night—from their point of view to "protect his own skin."

[13]See esp. 2:17–3:10, where his concern over their faith(fulness) is the basic reason for his trying over and again to return (2:18) and his sending Timothy instead (3:1–2). Note also his genuine relief that they are indeed standing fast in their faith (3:8), yet his awareness that there are "deficiencies" (3:10).

[14]See n. 4. Wanamaker 78 agrees, but sees the evidence as beginning in v. 6.

[15]That is, their salvation as an objective reality based on their "position" in Christ.

[16]This seems to be the ultimate reason for this recall, even though it is expressed in terms of his (and Silas's and Timothy's) recollection of their conversion when giving thanks in prayer.

was accompanied by an untrammeled joy produced by the Holy Spirit—despite the sufferings they also came to experience (v. 6).[17]

5 If the point of this clause in its present context seems clear enough, what is less so is Paul's intention in this first mention of the Spirit in his letters. At issue is the precise referent in the twin phrases "in/with power" and "in/with the Holy Spirit and deep conviction."[18] Does this refer to Paul's actual preaching of the gospel,[19] to "signs and wonders" that accompanied that preaching (as in the similar passage in Rom 15:19),[20] or, as is almost certainly true of the similar passage in 1 Cor 2:4–5 (q.v.), to the Thessalonians' actual conversion?[21] Or perhaps do two or all three of these somehow coalesce in this sentence?

Most likely the answer lies with this last suggestion, so that at least the two realities of Paul's Spirit-empowered preaching and their Spirit-experienced conversion are both in view, the latter being the consequence of the former (or in this case, they represent the two sides of one reality). Nonetheless, even though in context (especially vv. 2–4 and 6–10) the overall emphasis is on their becoming and being Christian believers, the *primary* emphasis in v. 5 seems to be on Paul's Spirit-empowered preaching of the gospel that brought about their conversion. This seems certain from the contrasting phrase, "not only in word," as well as from the concluding clause, "even as you know what manner of men we were toward you for your own sakes." The latter in particular focuses on Paul's and his co-workers' preaching and behavior—and surely anticipates 2:1–12.

The phrase "not only in word," it should be noted, is not an attempt to play the Spirit off against the Word.[22] Paul accomplishes two objectives with this contrast: First, he is setting up the argument in 2:1–12, that his preaching and their response are quite unrelated to the kind of "word" one finds among the religious and philosophical charlatans. As they well know, and as he will argue in 2:1–12, his manner of life among them as proclaimer

---

[17]This appeal to the *experience* of conversion, evidenced by the work of the Spirit, is not dissimilar to that found in Gal 3:1–5.

[18]On these as "twin phrases" and not a "triad," see n. 5 above.

[19]As most commentaries.

[20]As, e.g., Giblin, *Threat*, 45: "Paul's teaching was given in the power of the Spirit in that it was attended with miracles (1 Thes 1,5 . . .)." Cf. Marshall 53–54; Wanamaker 79; W. Grundmann, *TDNT* 2.311.

[21]As, e.g., Whiteley 36: "The *power* associated with the *gospel* was . . . the power to work the 'miracle' of causing the heathen to believe."

[22]On this point Kemmler's critique of much of the exegesis of this text is well taken. But his own solution, which sees the "but with" phrases as "additional testimonies" to the effectiveness of Paul's "word," seems to miss Paul's concern and argument by too much (see D. W. Kemmler, *Faith and Human Reason: A Study of Paul's Method of Preaching as Illustrated by 1–2 Thessalonians and Acts 17,2–4* [NovTSup 40; Leiden: Brill, 1975] 149–68).

of the gospel contrasted starkly with such purveyors of empty words, who used "flattery as a mask for greed" (2:5). Paul's "word" was accompanied by the power of the Holy Spirit and carried deep conviction.

Second, Paul wants to remind them, as he will the Corinthians in yet another context (1 Cor 2:1–5), that the message of the gospel is truth accompanied by experienced reality. It did indeed come "in word," meaning in the form of proclaimed truth, as a message from God himself (see 2:4 and 13). But for this appeal the proof is in the eating. Thus it was not "in word *alone*." God verified its truthfulness by a display of his power through the ministry of the Holy Spirit.

What this means, then, is that the twin phrases, "but in power" and "with the Holy Spirit and deep conviction," refer primarily to Paul's preaching, but not so much to the *manner*[23] (or style) of the preaching, as to its Spirit-empowered *effectiveness*. This seems to be the best way to make sense of what might at first look like a mere compounding of words. Contrary to some,[24] the appeal can scarcely be to Paul's *own sense* that his ministry was accompanied by power. The sentence insists that his gospel "came *to you*"[25] in a certain manner. Thus the initial phrase on the positive side is not "with the Holy Spirit and power,"[26] but simply "in power," precisely because for Paul that is the proper contrast to coming merely "with speech" (cf. 1 Cor 2:1–5; 4:19). But lest "power" not be fully understood, Paul immediately qualifies by adding, "that is, with the Holy Spirit and deep/full conviction." Thus, the Holy Spirit is being designated as the source of the power in his preaching the gospel, the evidence of which was the full conviction that accompanied his preaching and resulted in their conversion.

To be sure, the meaning of the latter expression ("full conviction") is not all that certain. Rigaux (377), for example, argues that the noun πληροφορία[27] should carry its ordinary meaning of "fullness" and thus refer to the great results of the work of the Spirit. Some[28] would see it as

---

[23]Contra Frame 81, among others.

[24]For example, O'Brien, *Thanksgivings*, 132, who argues that "ἐν δυνάμει does not so much refer to the outward signs of the presence of the Holy Spirit, as to the sense the preachers had that their message was striking home." That seems to miss Paul's own emphasis, which throughout is on the Thessalonians' recollection of their conversion, including their remembering Paul's preaching as Spirit-empowered—and thus effectual *in their behalf.*

[25]Gk. ἐγενήθη εἰς ὑμᾶς. The idiom basically means "to come to someone."

[26]As for example in 1 Cor 2:4 ("with the demonstration of the Spirit and power") and Rom 15:19 ("with the power of the Spirit").

[27]A noun that does not appear in classical Greek authors. In fact, apart from PGiess. 87 (see MM), it is used only by Christian authors. It derives from the verb πληροφορέω and means either "fullness" or "full assurance, certainty."

[28]For example, Masson, Moore, Bruce, Findlay, and Dunn (*Jesus*, 226, 417n138; for his earlier position see *Baptism*, 105).

referring to what happened to the Thessalonians in their hearing and receiving the gospel; others,[29] to the assurance and confidence with which the missionaries presented the message. Most likely, as with the former phrase, it refers in a way both to Paul's preaching and to their response to it. His preaching was accompanied by the power of the Holy Spirit so as to carry great conviction, which finally was evidenced by their conversion.

Whether this language also presupposes accompanying "signs and wonders" is less certain. Very likely it does that as well. That is, even though the primary referent in the phrase "with power, that is, with the Holy Spirit and full conviction" is to Paul's Spirit-empowered proclamation of Christ, such passages as 2 Cor 12:12 and (especially) Rom 15:18–19 indicate that his Spirit-empowered word was regularly accompanied by Spirit-empowered miracles as well. Not only so, but the evidence from Gal 3:1–5 shows that his converts' own experience of the Spirit was also accompanied by experiential phenomena to which Paul can appeal as evidence of their having become the children of God by faith. Thus, even though the first referent in the present language is almost certainly to Paul's Spirit-anointed preaching of Christ, the presence of the "power of the Spirit" most likely implies these other accompanying phenomena as well. And in any case, the Thessalonians undoubtedly experienced such phenomena, so that the reminder of Paul's preaching and their conversion as accompanied by the "power of the Spirit" would have brought to mind this whole complex of empowering phenomena.

In sum, this sentence points primarily to Paul's Spirit-empowered preaching that led directly to the Thessalonians' own reception of the Spirit in conversion, which is what Paul will go on to remind them in v. 6. What is finally significant, of course, is that in both cases—his preaching and their conversion—the Spirit is the key; and there was an evidential expression to the work of the Spirit, that Paul refers to as power, to which he can appeal so as to make his point stick.

6 This sentence has extremely close ties to the preceding. Indeed, even though most English translations follow the Greek editors and put a full stop at the end of v. 5, it seems more likely that the καί (and) with which the present clause begins is to be understood as a coordinating conjunction.[30] This would probably be seen more clearly had Paul not included the somewhat parenthetical καθώς (just as) clause at the end of

---

[29]This is the majority view, held inter alia by Ellicott, Lightfoot, Frame, Moffatt, Whiteley, Hendriksen, Best, Morris, Hiebert, O'Brien, Marshall, and Dunn (*Baptism*, 105).

[30]Parataxis (beginning sentences with καί [and] in the Semitic fashion) is unusual for Paul; in most cases it can be shown to be intentionally linking sentences that are coordinate in some way.

our v. 5. Thus the full sentence probably has the following structure (abbreviated in order to see its essential parts):

Knowing your election,

> *that* our gospel came (ἐγενήθη) to you . . . with power,

> (just as you know how we were toward you),

> *and* you became (ἐγενήθητε) imitators of us . . .

Thus, even though the thanksgiving is getting away from him somewhat,[31] this clause still forms part of the thanksgiving and elaborates the two concerns of vv. 4–5: the reality of their own election and its relationship to Paul's ministry. It begins with the latter but concludes, and thus emphasizes, the former. Paul has just said: "You know how *we* were toward you for your sakes"; now he adds: "indeed *you yourselves*[32] became imitators of us—and of the Lord." The content of their "imitation" is then spelled out in terms of their having received the word[33] in the midst of great affliction, but accompanied by the joy of the Holy Spirit.[34]

It should be noted that the concept of becoming "imitators" means far more than this for Paul.[35] His present concern, however, is with their maintaining faith in the midst of suffering. Hence he reminds them that in this matter—suffering as believers—they have his own example (cf. 2:1–2, 15; 3:7), not to mention that of the Lord.

What strikes one here is what he recalls for them as the evidence of their genuine conversion: their experience of *joy*, resulting from the Holy Spirit's invasion of their lives. The little phrase, "with the joy of the Holy Spirit," probably tells us much about both the paganism from which they had come and the life of the Spirit into which they had entered. On the

---

[31]So much so, that in 2:13 he *resumes* the thanksgiving ("and for this reason *also* we give thanks"), which by 2:12 had totally gotten away from him; what he thanks God for once more is in fact their reception of his preaching as the very word of God.

[32]Cf. Rigaux 380, "vous de votre coté."

[33]Gk. λόγος, i.e., the message of the gospel.

[34]The genitive in this case is most likely to be understood as an ablative of source. The joy has come *from* the Spirit whom they had received. Jewett (*Correspondence*, 100), as partial support for his historical reconstruction, asserts that this joy is thus "from a supernatural force manifesting itself in an ecstatic manner." Perhaps so, but this text neither says nor implies as much, and the exhortation to "rejoice always" in 5:16 suggests that they need to be reminded to keep alive in worship what they had experienced in conversion.

[35]Indeed, his calling on his converts to "imitate" him as he "imitated" Christ is almost certainly the key to the ethical instructions given in his churches, where they have no "book" to follow. 1 Cor 11:1 provides the starting point: Paul considered himself a follower of the example and teaching of Christ; his following Christ then served as "model" for his churches, who in turn, as v. 7 in our present passage makes clear, became "models" for one another. On this matter, see Fee, *1 Corinthians*, 187–88, 490 (on 4:16 and 11:1), and the bibliography noted therein.

one hand, life as a pagan may have had its moments of happiness, as it does for humanity in general, but by and large it was for them a life of heaviness and toil, arid in religion and empty in personal fulfillment— especially for the slaves and poor freedmen who would have made up the majority of the typical early Christian congregation (cf. 1 Cor 1:26).[36] But in coming to Christ and thus receiving the Holy Spirit, they had been filled with such an untrammeled joy, which was such an experienced reality for them, that even in the midst of genuine hardships related to their having become believers, this is the one characteristic of their life in the Spirit that Paul recalls for them as evidence of their conversion. This suggests in the strongest possible way that for Paul joy is one of the certain hallmarks of genuine spirituality (Spirit-uality?).

Thus we find here that remarkable collocation of joy and suffering found throughout the NT.[37] The early church understood suffering to be part of its lot, and believers were not to be surprised by it (1 Thes 3:2–3); yet because they had experienced their new life as the indwelling of the Spirit, they also lived with great joy. In the midst of present suffering, their experience of the eschatological Spirit had given them a foretaste of the life to come.[38] Precisely because of the Spirit's presence in this way, Paul will later in this letter describe the "will of God" in the form of three imperatives, the first of which is, "Rejoice always" (5:16–18).

Although he does not express it elsewhere in quite this way, Paul will regularly pick up on the theme of joy in his letters, and in Gal 5:22 will place this quality of life in the Spirit as second in the list of the Spirit's "fruit."

In sum, without overly pressing the point, in many ways this first appearance of the Spirit in the corpus resounds with theological overtones, either explicit or implicit, that lie at the heart of Paul's understanding of the Spirit.

1. Although for Paul salvation has to do with the death and resurrection of Christ (cf. 5:9–10 below), the actualization or appropriation of that saving work in the lives of believers results from the effective working of the Spirit. Thus, for him there is no coming to Christ that does not have the experience of the Spirit as its primary element.

2. In keeping with that point, and even though it is not explicit, here also is the first instance of what is thoroughgoing in Paul—salvation as the activity of the triune God. Here in a presuppositional way one

---

[36]Despite E. A. Judge et al. to the contrary; on this matter see the discussion in Fee, *1 Corinthians*, 80–82.

[37]Cf., e.g., 2 Cor 8:2; Rom 5:3–5; Acts 5:41; James 1:2; 1 Pet 1:6.

[38]As Rom 14:17 demonstrates, believers in Christ have indeed become subjects of a new kingdom, whose consummation they eagerly await, but whose present manifestation is joy in the Holy Spirit. Therefore Wanamaker (82) is probably right that this experience of joy is in part related to their confidence in their imminent salvation by the return of Christ, to which Paul explicitly refers in vv. 9–10.

encounters Paul's "soteriological" (economic) Trinitarianism—and always in this fashion, although the language will vary greatly. Salvation is first of all predicated on, and thus initiated by, God's love; it was effected historically by Christ, a point that is more by implication in this passage than explicit (in the language "election," "gospel," and "imitators of Christ"). The Holy Spirit is the one who effects salvation experientially, effectively appropriating the benefits of Christ's saving work to their lives. This passage, then, is the beginning of many such Trinitarian soteriological texts in Paul.[39]

3. It needs also to be pointed out that this earliest mention of the Spirit in the Pauline letters posits the closest kind of relationship between the Spirit and power.[40] In this case, the Spirit stands in apposition to "coming to you with power." This matter-of-fact way of speaking of the Spirit as the evidence of God's power at work in their midst is therefore presuppositional in Paul, and this usage sets the stage for our understanding of the Spirit as power and of Paul's use of "power" language as frequently an indirect reference to the Spirit.[41]

4. Finally, and related to what was just said, these two sentences manifest the basic "tension" (for us) in Paul's understanding of life in the Spirit. On the one hand, the Spirit's presence means power, in this case effective and evidentially expressed and experienced power. On the other hand, the joy of the Spirit takes place in the context of present weaknesses and suffering. Paul never resolves such tension, precisely because for him it was not tension. Rather, this broad understanding of the Spirit and his activity in the life of the believer is predicated on his "already-but-not-yet" eschatological perspective; power and weakness co-exist precisely because we live "between the times." For Paul, therefore, the Spirit's power and the Spirit's joy in suffering are not "either/or" but "both/and." Again, this is a thoroughgoing perspective throughout the corpus.

---

[39]See esp. the semi-creedal soteriological passages, such as 2 Thes 2:13–14; 1 Cor 6:11; 2 Cor 1:21–22; 13:13[14]; Gal 4:4–7; Rom 5:1–5; 8:3–4; 8:15–17; Eph 1:13–14; 4:4–6; Titus 3:5–7. But see also many other such texts, soteriological or otherwise: 1 Cor 1:4–7; 2:4–5; 6:19–20; 12:4–6; 2 Cor 3:16–18; Gal 3:1–5; Rom 8:9–11; 15:16; 15:18–19; 15:30; Col 3:16; Eph 1:3; 1:17–20; 2:17–18; 2:19–22; 3:16–19; 5:18–19; Phil 1:19–20; 3:3.

[40]Cf. in this regard Hendriksen 51.

[41]I do not mean by this that they are in some way coterminous, but only that for Paul they have the closest kind of overlapping relationship. I would have no special quarrel with Best's way of putting it (75): "In the N.T. the Spirit is much more than a Spirit of power; he is also the Spirit of love and goodness. . . . Thus Paul is not writing tautologically when he conjoins power and Spirit, for the latter is much the wider term." Nonetheless, that seems to narrow the concept of "power" far too much. Surely the love and goodness that the Spirit effects in the lives of believers are but another form of the Spirit's empowering.

1 THESSALONIANS 2:15[42]

. . . who killed both the Lord Jesus and the prophets[43] and persecuted and drove us out,[44] and do not please God and are in opposition to all people.

This is the first occurrence of the word προφήτης (prophet) in the Pauline corpus; and in this case it almost certainly refers to the OT prophets. To be sure, had we only this sentence in the NT, one could well argue, as some have done,[45] that Paul is here referring to Christian prophets. Especially so, since τοὺς προφήτας (the prophets) is the compound object of "killed"[46] and *follows* "the Lord Jesus,"[47] which in turn is followed by Jewish persecution of Paul. That might suggest a natural chronological sequence of Christian persecution (Jesus, some early Christian prophets, Paul).[48]

Nonetheless, Paul seems far more likely to be picking up the common Jewish[49]—and later Christian—motif of the "killing of the prophets," to which Jesus also refers in Matt 23:30–31, 34, 37 (cf. 5:12; Acts 7:52). Paul's concern seems not to be simply with the fact of the Jewish persecution of Jesus and his followers, but that such persecution is quite in keeping with their history of "killing the

---

[42]A considerable literature has emerged in the past decade both pro and con over the authenticity of vv. 14–16. For a helpful overview see Jewett, *Correspondence*, 36–42.

[43]This reflects the reading (τοὺς προφήτας) of all the early witnesses—Greek, Latin, and Coptic—and is almost certainly the original. The later Byzantine tradition has made the sense "clear"—from their perspective—by adding ἰδίους (= "their own prophets"), i.e., the Jews killed Jesus, just as they had a history of doing to their own prophets.

[44]This is an attempt to get at the force of the compound ἐκδιωξάντων (cf. Lightfoot 33). BAGD translate "persecute severely," but they also note that in the LXX it means to "drive away," which seems to be the general sense here, since Paul is reflecting on his treatment by the "Jews" (= Judeans).

[45]See Findlay 54; cf. Kirsopp Lake, *The Earlier Epistles of St. Paul* (2d ed.; London: Rivingtons, 1914) 87n2.

[46]As difficult in some ways as this sentence is, that τοὺς προφήτας functions as the second member of the compound object of "killed" seems to be demanded by the structure of Paul's sentence: the placement of καί before τὸν κύριον makes little sense otherwise. Hence, "who killed *both* the Lord Jesus *and* the prophets, and who . . . " Cf. Rigaux 447, whose grammatical point is slightly different, namely, that a construction in which an added subject or object found at the end of the clause or phrase is common in Paul (cf. καὶ τοῦ κυρίου in 1:6; καὶ ὁ θεός in 2:10). Otherwise Findlay, Milligan, Thomas; but their arguments chiefly express concern over Paul's chronology ("to avoid the slight anticlimax," Milligan 30) or a desire to highlight apostolic suffering by placing them in the same category as those of the OT prophets. Cf. Goodspeed's translation: "who killed the Lord Jesus and persecuted the prophets and us."

[47]Probably because Paul shared the view of the early church, reflected in Jesus' parable of the "wicked tenants," that the killing of Jesus was the climax of the "killing of the prophets," hence he is here listed in first position.

[48]This is precisely the point Findlay argues; but for the most part this runs aground on the grammar (see n. 46).

[49]See, e.g., H.-J. Schoeps, "Die jüdischen Prophetenmorde," in *Aus frühchristlicher Zeit* (Tübingen: Mohr, 1950) 126–43.

prophets,"[50] which outburst here has probably been triggered by the memory of his own fellow-countrymen's complicity in his being persecuted while in Thessalonica. In any case, in context this seems to be what Paul intended, rather than Christian "prophets." Especially so, since there is no other NT evidence that the earliest Christian martyrs in Jerusalem were considered "prophets."[51]

1 THESSALONIANS 4:8

For that very reason the person who rejects [this instruction][52] does not reject a man but rejects the God who also[53] gives[54] his Holy Spirit unto you.[55]

As the earlier references to the Spirit in this letter recall their conversion experience, so now in the context of paraenesis (ethical instruction/exhortation), Paul reminds them of God's call to Christian life (v. 7)

---

[50]This, of course, is not so much anti-Judaic, as is so often alleged, as it is in keeping with Paul's—and other early Christians'—view that Christ and his followers are the true succession of the OT people of God, and that those responsible for his crucifixion and for subsequent persecution of his followers are in the succession of those who repeatedly rejected God and his covenant, as illustrated by their rejection of the prophets (hence the "killing" motif) who had been sent to them.

[51]One might also note that apart from Eph 2:20; 3:5; and 4:11 Paul does not refer to "*the* prophets" as a discrete group of people within the Christian community. Rather, in 1 Corinthians 12 and 14 "prophets" as a noun refers primarily to those within the community who prophesy, i.e., the emphasis lies on the *function* of prophesying, not on persons called prophets.

[52]There is no object to the verb "rejects," but the context demands something like this, rather than a rejection of Paul himself.

[53]The presence (א D* F G Maj lat Clement) or absence (A B I 33 1739* b pc) of this καί is not easy to resolve; but in the final analysis, it seems more likely that scribes omitted it as unnecessary than that it was added (precisely because it is difficult to imagine *why* they would have done so); cf. the similar expression in 2:12, where no such "addition" exists in the textual evidence. The presence of this καί would be especially telling against those various commentators who think the emphasis here is on the substantival idea of "God the giver," rather than on the verbal, "the one who gives." See the discussion below.

[54]Gk. διδόντα (א* B D F G I 365 2464 pc); later witnesses (A Ψ Byz sy co) changed it to the aorist δόντα, on the pattern of Paul's usage elsewhere (Rom 5:5; 2 Cor 1:22; 5:5; cf. Gal 3:2: 4:6; Rom 8:15). Rigaux (514) adopts it on the pattern of the preceding aorist ἐκάλεσεν, but as Frame (156) had pointed out many years earlier, this is but another reason for later scribes to make the change. As to whether the present tense is significant, see the discussion below.

[55]The ἡμᾶς (us) found in A 6 365 1739 1881 a f m t pc is probably a secondary conformation to the ἡμᾶς found in v. 7. An earlier generation of Catholic scholars adopted this reading and used it as support for the apostolic succession, i.e., to reject Paul's teaching is the same as to reject God, who gave his Spirit to Paul in order to teach authoritatively. But even if ἡμᾶς were the original reading, it would mean "us Christians collectively" (Frame), as elsewhere in Paul where in semi-creedal formulations he changes from the second person plural to the all-inclusive first person plural (e.g., Gal 4:6).

and of the gift of the Spirit (v. 8) as his final court of appeal for them to abstain from sexual immorality.

This is the first of two matters where their "faith" is "deficient" (3:10),[56] about which he has just prayed that they might be "blameless" at the coming of the Lord (3:12–13), and about which he had formerly instructed them (4:1–2). The commendation that they are indeed "walking so as to please God," coupled with the exhortation that they "do so all the more" (v. 1), suggests that the majority are indeed living the Christian ethic, but apparently not all are. So in vv. 3–8 Paul again addresses the matter of sexual immorality.

The emphasis in this passage is twofold: positively, Paul calls them to "holiness" (ἁγιασμός); negatively, and specifically, he commands those persisting in sexual immorality to desist, precisely because sexual immorality is incompatible with the "holiness" to which God has called them (v. 7). Hence, rejecting Paul's instruction on this matter means to reject God himself, who is holy, and who gives his *Holy* Spirit to them, so that they, too, might be holy. The net result is that indulgence in sexual sin is a rejection of the Holy Spirit, God's own personal presence in and among them.

This argument has several crucial implications as to Paul's understanding of the Spirit. First, the full designation "Holy Spirit" is not simply the Spirit's name—although that is also true. But just as "our Lord Jesus Christ" is both name and reality,[57] so also the Spirit, who in the OT is most frequently designated "the Spirit of God," is in the NT designated the "Holy Spirit," both as name and reality—the Spirit is none other than the Spirit of God, himself "holy."[58] As the *Holy* Spirit he is thus to be distinguished from all other "spirits." In the final analysis, therefore, we are here dealing with the character of God, and with Paul's understanding of the Christian ethic as the Spirit's reproducing that character in his people. Thus in a context where God's will is defined in terms of the Thessalonians' living in *holiness* (v. 3), so that they "gain mastery over their own vessels"[59] in *holiness* (v. 4), because God has

---

[56]The other is with the "unruly-idle," whose failure to work with their own hands is a failure of love. This is addressed first in 4:9–12, and again in 5:14 and 2 Thes 3:6–15.

[57]Jesus of Nazareth is Lord (= the LXX designation for God himself) and Messiah (= the fulfillment of Jewish eschatological hopes).

[58]This is made emphatic in this case by the word order, τὸ πνεῦμα αὐτοῦ τὸ ἅγιον (the Spirit of Him, the holy), where not only is there emphasis on the fact that God gives them *his* Spirit, but that that Spirit is also designated *holy*.

[59]This literal translation is an attempt to keep what I am convinced is a euphemism for the male sexual organ (cf. the use of the Hebrew כְּלִי in 1 Sam 21:5); this was first suggested by J. Whitton ("A Neglected Meaning for σκεῦος in 1 Thessalonians 4:4," *NTS* 28 [1982] 142–43, and apparently favored by Bruce 83). Many think that this is a metaphor for "wife" (the most significant argument for which is by

called them not to uncleanness but to live in *holiness* (v. 7), it is hardly surprising that the source of such "holiness" is the "Holy" Spirit whom God gives to them.[60]

Second, in this first mention in the Pauline corpus of the actual "gift of the Spirit," he designates the Spirit as being given εἰς ὑμᾶς (into you). This somewhat unusual usage is reminiscent of LXX Ezek 37:6 and 14 (καὶ δώσω τὸ πνεῦμά μου εἰς ὑμᾶς, "I will give my Spirit into you"), which probably means something like, "I will *put* my Spirit in you."[61] This usage reflects a Pauline understanding of the gift of the Spirit as the fulfillment of OT promises that God's own Spirit will come to indwell his people, "and you shall live" (Ezek 37:14; cf. 11:19). In later letters Paul will make this same point by referring to the Spirit as "given (or sent) into your hearts" (2 Cor 1:22; Gal 4:6; cf. the emphatic statement in 1 Cor 6:19, "the temple of the in you Holy Spirit").[62]

Third, despite some debate here, the use of the present participle, "who also gives," almost certainly stresses the ongoing work of the Spirit in their lives. Although their previous conversion by the Spirit is the obvious presupposition of this usage, had Paul intended to refer to their conversion as such (as in 1:5–6),[63] he would have used the simple aorist, as in v. 7 and as he does elsewhere with regard to the Spirit (see n. 54 above).[64] This is very similar to the use of the present tense with "calls"

C. Maurer, in *TDNT* 7.358–67; but see also R. F. Collins, "This is the Will of God: Your Sanctification [1 Thess 4:3]," *LTP* 39 [1983] 27–53; and O. L. Yarbrough, *Not Like the Gentiles: Marriage Rules in the Letters of Paul* [SBLDS 80; Atlanta: Scholars, 1985]; cf. the rebuttal by M. McGehee, "A Rejoinder to Two Recent Studies Dealing with 1 Thess 4:4," *CBQ* 51 [1989] 82–89); nonetheless, such a view has two telling strikes against it. First, one has yet to explain why Paul should use such an unusual metaphor for "wife," if that's what he intended. On the one hand, he is perfectly capable of saying "take a wife" if he so intends (cf. 1 Cor 7:27); on the other hand, there is nothing in all of Paul's letters that even remotely suggests that "to take a wife" would be such a delicate thing to say that he would feel compelled to resort to such an oblique metaphor. Second, the negative assertion "not in passionate lust like the Gentiles who do not know God" makes very little sense about "taking a wife." One can marry "in holiness and honor," to be sure, but it is difficult to see how one "takes a wife" *not* in passionate lust as the Gentiles; whereas both ideas make perfectly good sense as a euphemism for one's sexual organ (or "body," as others prefer).

[60]Although he also makes this point, Collins (*Studies*, 292) considers the addition of "Holy" to be Paul's way of making it "clear that it is to the Holy Spirit of Christian faith that the prophet [Ezekiel] was making reference."

[61]Cf. Frame 156, "the εἰς is for dative or for ἐν; 'give to be in,' 'put in.' "

[62]We note in passing that this is the first expression of the "Presence" motif in the corpus.

[63]As Hiebert 176, e.g., explicitly says.

[64]Apparently to avoid the implication of the present participle, some suggest that the emphasis is substantival, "God the Giver of the Holy Spirit" (e.g., Moffatt 35; Findlay 90; Hiebert 176; Dunn, *Baptism*, 106, at least as referring to conversion). The expressed concern here is to avoid the concept of "continuous or successive impar-

in 2:12 and 5:24, and especially to the use of the present tense with the "granting" or "supplying" of the Spirit in Gal 3:5 (cf. Phil 1:19). All of this is to say that Paul's concern here is not with their conversion, but with their present experience of God's *Holy* Spirit, given to them by God precisely so that they might walk in holiness. Thus the Spirit is understood as the constant divine companion, by whose power one lives out holiness, i.e., a truly Christian ethic.

Fourth, both the nature of this argument (which brings in the presence of the Spirit in their lives as the clincher) and the emphasis on the "presentness" and "indwelling" nature of the Spirit as gift point to *effectual power* in the struggle against sin. This does not mean that the Spirit guarantees perfection—hardly so—but it does mean that one is left without argument for helplessness. As Plummer asserts: "This [gifting of Spirit] transformed their whole life; and it put an end to the pagan plea that man has no power to resist impure desires" (63). For Paul the presence of the Spirit was not simply God's gift as *an option* against sin; nor would he have understood the Spirit as present but ineffectively so. To the contrary, the dynamic that makes Paul's argument against sexual impurity possible is the experienced reality of the Spirit.

Thus for Paul the Spirit is not only the key to becoming a believer, but is the power for truly Christian behavior, which is not a matter of regulations and observances, but of living in the Spirit so as to behave in keeping with the Spirit (cf. Gal 5:13–6:10).

1 THESSALONIANS 5:16–18

[16]*Always rejoice;* [17]*continually pray;* [18]*in everything give thanks; for this is the will of God in Christ Jesus for you.*

Although it is not immediately obvious that these imperatives are "Spirit texts," there are sound reasons for including them in this study. First, vv. 14 and 19–22 indicate that this final set of imperatives (that begin in v. 12) is basically to be understood within the context of the gathered community at worship, the context in which the letter itself would be read.[65]

Furthermore, as will be noted below, the set of imperatives that immediately follows (vv. 19–22) come as something of a surprise, in the sense that nothing in the letter itself or in the immediate context quite prepares us for what is there said. But one element of surprise, its place

---

tation" (Moffatt). But that is to avoid "second blessing theology" by an unnecessary expedient. Paul's concern is not on "successive gifts" of the Spirit, but on the present, ongoing work of the Spirit in their lives.

[65]Contra Thomas 290, e.g., who seems to reflect Western individualism more than Paul by entitling these verses, "Responsibilities to oneself."

in the immediate context, is alleviated somewhat if one recalls that for Paul the activities of rejoicing and prayer presuppose the activity of the Holy Spirit in the community. It is easy to imagine this first set of commands, which already assumed the Spirit as present in their midst, to have triggered those which follow.[66]

Finally, it should be noted that 1:6 has already prepared us for this understanding, where Paul recalls their experience of conversion as accompanied by both great affliction and the joy of the Holy Spirit.[67] The point is that Paul, in a thoroughgoing way, understood joy, prayer, and praise (thanksgiving) as the result and the evidence of the Spirit's presence. Thus in Gal 5:22, the second item on Paul's list of the "fruit" of the Spirit is joy, and in Rom 14:17 the joy of the Spirit is evidence of the presence of the kingdom of God. Similarly, 1 Cor 14:15, Rom 8:26–27, and Eph 6:18 all verify that for Paul prayer was especially an activity of the Spirit.

It should be noted here, however, that the emphasis on joy is not so much on the experience of joy, but the active expression of it. They are to "rejoice always," which Phil 4:4 bears out means not simply to express joy in general, but specifically to "rejoice *in the Lord.*"

For the role that this set of imperatives plays in the larger context of vv. 12–22, see the discussion of vv. 19–22 that follows. For now it must be noted that even though these may seem like a series of general exhortations, not dissimilar to Phil 4:4–6, for example, it would be an injustice to treat them solely on that basis. Whatever else we know from this letter, there can be no question that here is a church that is undergoing severe hardship because of its faith in Christ. God's will for such a community, both as individuals and as they gather for worship, is that they rejoice, pray, and give thanks in all circumstances—including especially those of their present lot.[68] Without a common understanding and experience of the eschatological Spirit, who has appropriated for them the work of Christ and guaranteed their future in Christ, these imperatives are merely pious platitudes that would weigh the soul with guilt and lead to illusion. But precisely because the joy is from the Holy Spirit, given by God (4:8) and experienced as God's own powerful presence (1:5–6), these imperatives are not only removed from the category of pious platitude, but also become the dynamic and living experience of

---

[66]So Ellicott 80. Cf. Findlay 128: "From *joy, prayer,* and *thanksgiving* it is a natural transition to *the Spirit* and *prophecy.*"

[67]Cf. Wanamaker 199–200, who also makes this point.

[68]The context and the structure strongly suggest that Paul intends the final clause ("for this is the will of God in Christ Jesus for you") to modify all three of the imperatives, not simply the giving of thanks in all circumstances. One should note further their christocentric nature. God's will in this regard, and for them (εἰς ὑμᾶς = purpose), has found its expression and location "in Christ Jesus." That is, God has expressed his will through Christ, and by putting them in Christ, God has purposed that they should fulfill his will in this way.

those who by that same Spirit are "in Christ." Life in Christ, and therefore life in the Spirit, is a life of joy, prayer, and praise—in any and all circumstances. And this is because Spirit people are truly living in the Spirit and have thus already tasted of the life to come; they already know the powerful presence of God in their lives.

Finally, Paul is as good as his word. See especially 3:9–10 and Phil 1:3–4, where he mentions joy and thanksgiving as inherent to his praying—and the latter in the context of a trying imprisonment.

1 THESSALONIANS 5:19–22

[19]*The Spirit do not quench;* [20]*prophecies do not despise;* [21]*But*[69] *test all things: hold fast to what is good,* [22]*keep away from every evil form.*[70]

This surprising series of imperatives is the earliest record in the NT of the basically charismatic[71] nature of the earliest Christian communi-

---

[69]The omission of this δέ in the TR (supported by ℵ* A 33 81 104 614 629 630 945 pm), along with the fact that each of these imperatives was assigned a verse number, has tended to destroy altogether the meaning of this series of imperatives—and to cause untold harm in separatist churches. The δέ in this case was in all likelihood omitted by scribes (in conformity to the whole series, all of which lack conjunctions), rather than added early and often by such a wide range of early witnesses (incl. B D G K P Ψ 181 326 436 1241 1739 pm it vg cop goth eth). Metzger (*Textual Commentary*, 633, following Lightfoot 84) suggests that the omission may have resulted from its being "absorbed by the following syllable," but it is hard to see how that could have happened in this case (since it is followed by the δοκ-, not the -τε, of δοκιμάζετε).

[70]The genitive πονηροῦ is ambiguous and may be either a substantive ("every form of evil"), as most understand it, or an adjective, as in my translation (cf. Lightfoot 86, Frame 208, Dunn, *Jesus*, 236). The reason for going against the majority here is based in part on Pauline usage and in part also on my conviction, argued below, that this clause refers singularly to the testing of prophetic utterances and is not some kind of generalized prohibition about abstaining from all appearance of evil. Pauline usage is not decisive, of course, but is suggestive. This order of πᾶς + noun + adjective occurs in Eph 1:3; 4:29; and esp. with the expression "every good work" in 2 Thes 2:17; 2 Cor 9:8; Col 1:10; 1 Tim 5:10; Titus 1:16; 3:1; 2 Tim 2:21; 3:17. Its opposite, "every evil work" (παντὸς ἔργου πονηροῦ), occurs in 2 Tim 4:18. On the other side, there is no instance where this order occurs and the adjective is to be understood as a substantive, which makes the absence of the article with πονηρός the more telling here (cf. 2 Thes 3:3).

[71]I use the word in this way with some misgivings, because there is a sense in which everything that is of the Spirit is "charismatic," not simply the more visible manifestations of phenomena such as prophecy, etc. Nonetheless, one of the current possibilities of meaning is this one—to refer to Christian communities (or people) who are open to, and experiencing, these kinds of Spirit activity. That the present passage presupposes this is self-evident, hence the use of the term "charismatic" in this sense to describe them—and the rest of the early church. On this matter, though somewhat overstated, see H. Gunkel, *The Influence of the Holy Spirit* (Philadelphia: Fortress, 1979 [Ger. original, 1888]) 30–42.

ties. They are surprising mostly because nothing else in the letter has prepared us for them, and because they seem to be so much more case-specific than the immediately previous, more general exhortations (in vv. 15, 16–18).[72] Not only so, but they are the only ones in the entire series of exhortations (from v. 12) which are expressed as prohibitions (vv. 19–20), and for which their positive counterparts in vv. 21–22 are qualifications. That leads us to make several contextual and structural observations before looking at each of the imperatives individually.

First, there is the issue of historical context. Because this instruction is so condensed and because related material in these two letters is so sparse, how are we to understand the specific historical setting of the concern here expressed?[73] The note about "Spirit" (probably in the form of prophecy) as a possible source of the misguided teaching in 2 Thes 2:2 (q.v.) opens the possibility that correction is more necessary than first meets the eye.

Part of the problem of historical context concerns the literary context of these imperatives, which has two facets: their place in the whole series of imperatives that begins in v. 12; and the role of the series (vv. 12–22) in the letter.[74] The problem is, how do these imperatives relate to the *formal* (structural) aspects of the letter, and how much do they *reflect the known situation* in Thessalonica (as reported to him by Timothy)?

Most likely the answer to both parts of the problem lies "somewhere in between." That is, in terms of form the whole has been set up by 5:11 ("therefore, exhort/encourage one another and build up one another, even as you are doing"). Thus, in the first instance these various imperatives spell out specifics in response to v. 11. Since v. 14 so clearly picks

---

[72]Morris 175–79, therefore, sees the whole of vv. 19–22 not as referring to prophetic utterances, but as general prohibitions, including one (v. 20) against despising prophecies. But this does not seem to take seriously enough either (1) the fact that the preceding three are a package of imperatives, (2) the structure of this particular series, or (3) the appearance and contrastive force of the δέ in v. 21, which is related specifically to prophecies.

[73]Some have made it the basis for all the troubles Paul addresses in Thessalonica. But that is probably to read too much into too little evidence. See esp. Jewett, *Correspondence*, 161–78. This book elaborates concerns previously spelled out in *Terms*. For a brief description of Jewett's view see below, n. 104.

[74]On the one hand, hortatory remarks such as these appear regularly as a part of the concluding materials in the Pauline letters (e.g., 1 Cor 16:13–18; 2 Cor 13:11; Rom 16:17–19; cf. Fee, *1 Corinthians*, 825–26), most often, as here, in the form of "staccato imperatives." Sometimes these imperatives pick up specific matters in the congregations; at other times they are simply general exhortations. On the other hand, in some of Paul's letters a section of paraenesis follows the so-called doctrinal section as a conclusion of the larger argument of the epistle, as, e.g., in Romans 12–15, Galatians 5–6, Colossians 3–4. In each case these can be shown to be integral to the argument of the letter, not simply "ethical instruction" following "right thinking on the Christian gospel."

up the majority of preceding concerns in the letter,[75] it is at least possible
that vv. 12–13 should also be read as specific to Thessalonica.[76]

On the other hand, since most of the content of vv. 12–13 and 15–18
occurs in similar or analogous form in Romans 12,[77] much of this material may be more generally intended; that is, this is the kind of paraenesis
that fits any Christian community and may only indirectly reflect specific
concerns in the Thessalonian church. Thus, the most likely answer to
the *formal* consideration is that it is basically general paraenesis, which
has been tailored in part to the situation in Thessalonica. If so, then the
lack of this kind of content elsewhere in the Pauline letters suggests that
this may be part of the "tailoring" to the situation in the local church,
rather than simply general exhortation.

Even so, the question still remains, what situation is Paul addressing?
Some structural observations are in order. As with the preceding set
(vv. 16–18), the five imperatives are intended to be read together. They
are given in two sets (vv. 19–20; 21–22): the first is a form of parallelism
in which the second member specifies the first; the second set, which is
in contrast to the first, specifies what they are to do instead, this time in
a set of three, the first giving the general rule, which the final two spell
out more specifically. Thus:

> The Spirit do not quench;
> Prophecies do not despise;
>
> > *but*
>
> Test all things:
>
> > Hold fast to the good;
> > Avoid every evil form.

The basic exegetical issue is whether the emphasis lies on the first
two imperatives (are some within the community less than delighted with
such phenomena in the assembly?), or on the final three (do the first two
set up the final three so that in correcting abuses they will not over-
correct?)—although it is altogether possible, of course, that since many of
his Gentile converts were already well acquainted with "ecstasy" from their

---

[75]As most commentators are quick to point out. The ἄτακτοι (idlers) refer back
to 4:9–12; the "faint hearted" to those who are suffering and concerned about the
recent death of members of the community; the "weak" to those in 4:3–8.

[76]Although it is unclear whether the issue was insubordination or simply a real
concern that leaders be recognized and appreciated.

[77]The concern over leaders (vv. 12–13a) corresponds in part to Rom 12:4–6; the
concern for "peace among yourselves" (v. 13b) to Rom 12:18; v. 15 recalls Rom 12:17;
and the exhortations to continual joy, prayer, and thanksgiving resemble Rom 12:12.
This is the evidence that causes Best 223 to consider them all not as case-specific but
as general, and thus the kind of thing that could be said to any and every church.
For a fuller list of comparisons with Romans 12, see Marshall 145–46.

pagan past,[78] Paul is simply trying to offer some guidelines for perfectly valid—and normal—"ecstasy" within their own gatherings for worship.[79]

It is common to argue that the problem in Thessalonica results from some disenchantment with these phenomena, in the form either of too much "ecstasy" (usually glossolalia, as in Corinth) or of misguided "ecstasy" (either by the "unruly-idle," who are using prophecy to justify their behavior or by some whose mistaken predictions about the Day of the Lord have brought prophecy into disrepute). This is arguably supported by the grammar of the prohibitions themselves.[80]

But it is just as possible, more likely in my view, that Paul is here offering something preventative—perhaps related to their former experience with "ecstasy" of a more uncontrolled sort. The evidence from 2 Thes 2:1–2, at least, might suggest that Timothy has already informed Paul of some tendencies in worship that needed "adjustment"—but not elimination. Thus, some months later (2 Thes 2:2), even though Paul apparently does not know the precise source of the misrepresentation of his teaching, he does know that "Spirit" (= a prophetic utterance) is one of the possibilities. That is probably why in the same letter (2:15; cf. 2:5) he urges them to stay close to what has already been taught them during his first (and founding) visit and in our present letter.

In any case, here is our earliest encounter with the life of the Spirit in an early Christian community, and instead of urging them to "fan into flame" or "earnestly seek" the Spirit and his manifestations among them, he urges them not to quench the Spirit in this regard, but by "not quenching" or "not despising" neither is he suggesting that anything goes in the name of the Spirit. They are to "test all things," holding fast the good and avoiding every evil form, but testing is not to lead to quenching the Spirit or his gifts.

19 Paul begins this series in the most general way,[81] "Do not quench the Spirit."[82] Were this not followed by v. 20, one could justifiably

---

[78]See Fee, 1 Corinthians, 574–82 (on 1 Cor 12:1–3).

[79]Cf. Wanamaker 201, who suggests that "Paul wished to encourage pneumatic activity as a sign of the eschatological times in which the Thessalonians found themselves." This passage seems to imply that the phenomena are more integral to early Christian initiation and experience than Wanamaker allows. Paul hardly needs to "encourage" what would have been *presuppositional* in the Pauline churches.

[80]μή with the present imperative often has the force of "stop doing something," implying the forbidden action is already taking place. This is argued, e.g., by Hiebert 243 and Moore 83; but see Bruce 125, who correctly notes that "like the positive imperatives in vv 16–18 and 21–22, [these negative imperatives] indicate what they must habitually do (or refrain from doing)."

[81]Gunkel (*Influence*, 30–31), who believes glossolalia to be "the Spirit's most striking and characteristic activity," therefore considers πνεῦμα in this sentence to be "set next to προφητεία as the capacity for speaking in tongues."

[82]Since τὸ πνεῦμα holds first place in the sentence, one might argue that the

understand this as a more general word that included both ethical life and charismatic manifestations. But the next clause and the structure of the whole suggest that Paul already has something more specific in mind here.

Although the metaphorical use of the verb "quench"[83] goes beyond the common literal sense of "putting out [a fire]," the frequent collocation of the Spirit with fire[84] is the probable reason for the metaphor here.[85] Nonetheless the emphasis lies not on the "fire" dimension of the metaphor, but on the stifling of the Spirit in their midst and, just as in 2 Thes 2:2, τὸ πνεῦμα most likely refers to "charismatic manifestations."[86] Despite the fact that the ministries of the Spirit can be abused in the Christian community, Paul's own deep appreciation for the central role of the Spirit in individual and corporate life will not allow for correcting abuse by commanding disuse.[87] Rather, the antidote for abuse is proper use. Hence he begins these exhortations with the general caution, "Do not put out the Spirit's 'fire.' "

20 This next imperative spells out the general caution of v. 19. "By not 'quenching' the Spirit," he goes on, "I mean in particular, 'Do not despise prophetic utterances.' " This is the earliest mention of προφητεία ("prophecy" or "prophetic utterance") in the NT. Although not a frequent term in the Pauline corpus, it occurs in the earliest and latest of the letters, as well as in 1 Corinthians and Romans.[88] The presupposition of the present passage as well as the argument of 1 Corinthians and the matter-

---

emphasis lies here; however, this word order seems less emphatic than merely formal, since in each case the verb is the last member of the sentence (as was also true in the preceding set of "staccato imperatives," vv. 16–18). More significantly, the definite article with πνεῦμα assures us that Paul is referring to *the* Spirit, that is, the Spirit of the living God, whom each of them had come to experience at conversion (1:5–6).

[83] Gk. σβέννυμι. MM offer a similar metaphorical usage from the first century ("you quenched the sunlight in us both").

[84] But in the Pauline corpus only here and 2 Tim 1:6–7 ("fan into flame the gift").

[85] On this see esp. W. C. van Unnik, " 'Den Geist löschet nicht aus' (1 Thessalonicher v 19)," *NovT* 10 (1968) 255–69.

[86] The language is from von Dobschütz 225 and is cited favorably by van Unnik (see preceding n.)—although his distinction between v. 19 as referring to oneself and v. 20 to others is perhaps too finely drawn.

[87] This can be seen most clearly in 1 Corinthians 12–14. Even after some rather strong words of correction about the Spirit's activity among them, Paul refuses to allow these correctives to become a form of "quenching the Spirit's fire." Thus he concludes the whole, by repeating the command that they "be zealous for prophecy, and not forbid speaking in tongues." The corrective is to be found in their doing so "decently and in order."

[88] Besides this passage see Rom 12:6; 1 Cor 12:10; 13:2, 8; 14:6, 22; 1 Tim 1:18; 4:14. The verb, which speaks of the activity itself, occurs 11 more times and includes the participation of women in 1 Cor 11:5.

of-fact mention of it in Rom 12:6 strongly suggest that this was a normal expression of the Spirit's activity in the early Christian communities.

For a discussion as to what "prophecy" entails, see below on 1 Cor 12:10 and the summary discussion in chapter 15. For now it should simply be noted that Paul is referring to some kind of spontaneous utterance within the community,[89] which is understood to be from the Holy Spirit, which is not absolute as revelation (since it must be tested), and which for them is to be understood as evidence that God is in their midst (see 1 Cor 14:24–25). Such utterances were probably a means of their hearing from God, perhaps in the form of his giving direction and encouragement to a persecuted community. Because such utterances are from the Holy Spirit, they must not be "despised"[90]; but also because such utterances come through merely human vessels, they must be tested, which is the point that he now moves on to make.

21a The adversative δέ (but) which begins this sentence sets the whole matter in perspective. Even though they must not quench the Spirit by showing contempt for prophetic utterances, neither must they simply accept every utterance of this kind as from the Spirit. They must "test[91] all things."[92] In all likelihood this is an earlier form of what in 1 Cor 12:10 and 14:29 Paul calls "discerning," or "weighing," the "spirits," meaning in the first instance the testing of prophecies. And this in turn is the early Christian version of "testing the prophets" found in Deut 18:21–22.

All of that seems easy enough; the difficulty for us at this distance is determining *how* such prophecies are to be tested: How does Paul understand such testing to take place, and by what criteria? For the most part we are standing on the outside looking in, since nowhere in Paul are criteria specifically offered. Nonetheless two passages give us some clues.

---

[89]Contra Collins, *Studies*, 62, who suggests that "the . . . notion of the charism does not, of itself, imply an extraordinary phenomenon." This does not seem to take the whole of the Pauline data quite seriously enough.

[90]Gk. ἐξουθενέω, which here, as often in the NT, implies to "reject with contempt" (BAGD; see Acts 4:11; Gal 4:14).

[91]Gk. δοκιμάζω, which here means to "put to the test," in the sense of "examine" as to its trustworthiness. Cf. Luke 14:19, where one excuses himself from the banquet so that he may go and "test/examine" a purchase of oxen.

[92]From a very early time this saying was related to an *agraphon* of Jesus, "Be approved money-changers." Cf. esp. the form in which it is cited by Clement: "Be ye approved money changers, who reject much, but retain the good." As Jeremias points out, this is probably how the logion itself was originally to be understood (J. Jeremias, *Unknown Sayings of Jesus* [London: SPCK, 1958] 89–93). But despite this Clementine form, which has some obvious linguistic overtones with Paul, there is no reason to believe that Paul either knew or used the saying; and in any case Paul's concern moves in a considerably different direction.

First, in the discussion of 2 Thes 2:2 below, it is suggested that 2 Thes 2:15 may help. In a context where some of them have been badly shaken by a misrepresentation of his teaching about the Day of the Lord, Paul exhorts them to "stand fast and to hold firm the *traditions that you were taught,* whether through *word* [= his original preaching of the gospel and the teaching that followed their coming to faith] or through *letter* [= in this case our 1 Thessalonians]." If this be so, then the first test is the apostolic proclamation/teaching of Christ. This is a test that has to do with the theological or doctrinal content of the utterance.

Second, in 1 Cor 14:3 Paul specifically says that the one who prophesies speaks edification, encouragement (or exhortation), and comfort. This is the test of purpose, as well as content, and has to do with its helpfulness to the believing community.[93]

The imperatives that follow offer help in yet another direction, but without specification: that somehow, presumably by the content, they should be able to discern the "good" from the "evil."

21b–22 Paul now concludes this brief set of imperatives about prophecies in their assembly by indicating what their twofold response to the testing should be. On the one hand, they are to "hold fast to what is good"; on the other hand, they are to "keep away from every evil form." The first of these is easy enough. According to Paul in a later passage (1 Cor 14:1–19), the reason for earnestly desiring prophecy in the community is that it "edifies" and is therefore an expression of love; in 14:20–25 it is also a sign for them that God is truly in their midst (because of its effect on unbelievers). This criterion, therefore, is but another way of saying what recurs frequently in the Pauline paraenesis, that the aim of all such activity is the "common good" (τὸ συμφέρον; 1 Cor 12:7), the building up of others.

The difficulty lies with the final clause (lit. "abstain[94] from every evil form"). Since this comes as the final imperative in the series that began in v. 12, and since the verb is used earlier (4:3) in a context of "avoiding evil" in the ethical sense, this clause can easily get separated from its context and become a form of general paraenesis for the Christian community. Just as they are to "abstain from sexual immo-

---

[93]Among the "criteria" passages, one might add 1 Cor 12:3, but as I have noted in my commentary (*1 Corinthians*, 581), "Paul's point in context is not to establish a means of 'testing the spirits,' but to remind them that 'inspired utterance' as such is not evidence of being 'led of the Spirit.' "

[94]Gk. ἀπέχεσθε. Cf. 4:3: ἀπέχεσθαι ὑμᾶς ἀπὸ τῆς πορνείας (that you abstain from sexual immorality); and 1 Tim 4:3 (where false teachers command "abstinence from foods, etc.").

rality," so now he commands finally that they "abstain from every form of evil."[95]

But despite some difficulties with the language,[96] Paul intends that they "avoid" or "keep distant from" every expression of "prophecy" that is not "good," but rather is an "evil kind." For the most part the difficulties with the language can be accounted for. The choice of the verb ἀπέχω (keep away) is to be explained by Paul's use of κατέχω (hold fast) in the preceding clause as its natural rhyming antonym. The use of ἀπέχω then further explains the differences in the way the objects are expressed.[97]

What is more difficult to explain is the choice of the noun εἶδος (form), rather than simply "what is evil," as in the preceding clause ("what is good"). The word εἶδος in this sense occurs only here in Paul, and means something close to "kind."[98] Thus, they are to "shun every kind that is evil." The best explanation here would seem to be an older one, that in Paul's view "good" is singular, whereas "evil" takes many forms. In any case, the context and the verbal plays between the two final clauses seem to demand that this final clause also refers to prophetic utterances.

It seems unlikely that Paul would actually allow that such "kind" are truly of the Spirit. What he is urging rather is the testing of all "inspired" utterances, so that the Thessalonian believers may distinguish "the good" (= those from the Spirit) from every kind that when tested is found wanting, and therefore not of the Spirit. While we cannot be certain as to how Paul would have understood the latter, in terms of either source or content, possibly he would look upon the misrepresentation of his own teaching about the Day of the Lord in 2 Thes 2:2 as "an evil kind" of utterance which they must shun.

It should perhaps be noted in conclusion that the first mention of prophecy in the NT includes the imperative that all such prophecies (and by implication all other such "Spirit utterances" in the community) are to be tested. The awe with which many contemporary charismatics hold prophecy and "prophets," which in effect causes them almost never to be "tested," stands in basic contradiction to this Pauline injunction.

---

[95]This possibility is often entertained by commentators (e.g., Moore and Hiebert).

[96]The choice of verbs seems especially perplexing to some, since Paul has an ample vocabulary to express "reject." Even more difficult is the adverb modifier, ἀπὸ παντὸς εἴδους πονηροῦ [see n. 70 above], which does not balance the simple object, "the good," in the preceding clause.

[97]In the middle, which is the only form of ἀπέχω that means "to avoid" or "keep distant from," it naturally takes the preposition ἀπό to complete its meaning.

[98]As BAGD; see, e.g., its use in Sir 23:16; 25:2; cf. Jos. Ant. 10.37, for a similar expression: πᾶν εἶδος πονηρίας (every form/kind of wickedness). One wonders whether lying behind this usage is a correlation of "sin" with "idolatry" in the Jewish mind?

1 Thessalonians 5:23–24

[23]*Now may the God of peace himself sanctify you wholly,*[99] *and may each of you in entirety*[100]—*spirit, soul and body—be preserved blamelessly at the coming of our Lord, Jesus Christ.* [24]*Faithful is the one who calls you, who also will do it.*

The reasons for including this benedictory prayer[101] in the present study are not self-evident from the text itself. Its inclusion stems from two quarters. First, because of its clear, and therefore almost certainly intentional, reminiscence of the language of 4:3–8,[102] H. B. Swete included it in his discussion of the Spirit in this letter.[103] In 4:7–8 Paul argues that God has called them to holiness and purposed to accomplish it in their lives by giving them his Holy Spirit. Paul here simply picks up this concern one final time in the form of a concluding prayer (cf. 3:13).

---

[99] Gk. ὁλοτελής (NT *hapax legomenon*), an adjective in the predicate position that here probably functions adverbially; it is a quantitative (or "collective"; Milligan 78, Rigaux 596) term for which BAGD offer "through and through" as a possible translation. Lightfoot 87 considers the predicate usage preferable: "as proleptic, . . . 'may he sanctify you so that ye be entire.' " Cf. Jewett (*Terms*, 176), who considers the adverbial use "indefensible" here, since Paul could have used the corresponding adverb ὁλοτελῶς. The adverbial understanding, however, which seems demanded by the emphasis and context, goes back as far as the Vulgate (*per omnia*). Moreover, it is not at all clear how "being entire" or "integral" (Jewett) makes much sense with the clearly ethical intent of ἁγιάσαι.

[100] Gk. ὁλόκληρον, according to BAGD, "a qualitative term," which they translate "complete, or sound." It is difficult to see much essential difference in meaning from ὁλοτελεῖς. The best solution seems to be that of Milligan and Rigaux (preceding note), who, on the basis of derivation, see ὁλοτελεῖς as collective and ὁλόκληρον as distributive (i.e., "completely" and "in every part"). For the present translation see the discussion that follows.

[101] This is my terminology; Paul is praying for them, but its form and placement at the end of the letter indicates that it serves as a benediction as well. Cf. R. Jewett, who styles it a "homiletic benediction" ("The Form and Function of the Homiletic Benediction," *ATR* 51 [1969] 18–34; *Terms*, 175–83). G. P. Wiles (*Paul's Intercessory Prayers* [SNTSMS 24; Cambridge University Press, 1974] 63–68) uses the language "wish–prayer" for this and all the prayers in the optative in the Pauline corpus. The literature on the passage, besides the commentaries, is considerable. For a review of much of the recent continental literature, in several of the European languages, see Collins, *Studies*, 68–89.

[102] Note, e.g., the following significant correspondences: (1) the preceding prayer in 3:11–13, which anticipates the argument of 4:1–8, includes a desire for them to be ἀμέμπτους (blameless) in "holiness" (ἁγιωσύνη) at the coming of Christ; (2) the noun ἁγιασμός occurs three times in 4:3–8, and nowhere else in the epistle; the corresponding verb ἁγιάζω occurs only here (in 5:23) in the letter; (3) in 4:7 God, who gives them the Holy Spirit, has "called" them to "holiness"; here the God who sanctifies them (v. 23) is the God who also "calls" them to such holiness (v. 24).

[103] See *The Holy Spirit in the New Testament*, 174–75. It is of some interest to note how few commentators in English over the past one hundred years have made this connection.

Second, in emphasizing the completeness of the sanctifying work that he desires for them, and that he prays and believes God will bring to pass in them, Paul uses the noun πνεῦμα to begin his listing of some components of the human person. Some have seen in this an oblique, or in some cases a rather direct, reference to the Holy Spirit, picking up τὸ πνεῦμα from v. 19.[104]

The relationship with 4:3–8 is a point well taken; however, there is little more to say here about the activity of the Spirit in the sanctifying process, since Paul merely *presupposes*, but does not explicitly press that concern here. The point to make, of course, is that 4:7–8 was an *exhortation* to holiness, with the clear admonition that to reject this Pauline imperative was to reject the God who called them to himself—called them thereby to the kind of holiness that reflects his own character—and who *gives* them his Holy Spirit precisely so as to enable a holy life. In the present case the same "admonition" comes by way of prayer, but it concludes with typical Pauline confidence that the character of God—his faithfulness—will prevail, and so the prayer will be answered.

But the second point, that the use of πνεῦμα in this passage refers either obliquely or directly to the Holy Spirit, will probably not hold up. It is not at all clear that Paul ever understood the Holy Spirit as taking the role of the human spirit, as Jewett argues. Moreover, the way the three terms are used together here, makes it especially difficult to imagine that the Thessalonians could have perceived the first term in this way. The emphasis after all lies on *their* being sanctified (not on the presence of the Spirit in their lives) and on the *entirety* of the human person that needs this sanctifying work of God (although "through his Spirit" would be implied).

On this most are agreed; the problems lie in the exact meaning of some of the details, which are brought about by three factors: (1) the unusual (for Paul) tripartite way of speaking of the human person, spirit/soul/body, and how he would have understood the first two of these terms; (2) the structure of the

---

[104]See, e.g., Frame 211–13, following von Dobschütz. This view, which has been generally rejected (e.g., Hendriksen 147) or disregarded, has been recently revived by Jewett (*Terms*, 175–83) as a significant part of his understanding of this letter and of Paul's usage of πνεῦμα in general. According to Jewett the occasion of 1 Thessalonians can best be explained in terms of a "radical millinarism," in which an ardent expectation of Christ's return combined with unbridled ecstasy to produce the various troubles in Thessalonica. The issue in 4:3–8 would then have been a "spiritual" separation of spirit and body, so that in "Spirit" one can do as one wills with the body, including illicit sexuality. That is because in their view they have been taken over by the divine Spirit. Hence, Paul urges that God's sanctifying activity excludes the notion that only "Spirit" will be redeemed (πνεῦμα = the apportioned Spirit, i.e., the Spirit of God that has been severally apportioned to individual believers and more or less assumes the role of the human πνεῦμα) and that it includes "the whole person—not just the pneumatic inner man" (181). But it is not at all clear that the problem in Thessalonica is with "opponents," rather than simply with a lack of understanding and growth on the part of Gentile converts fresh out of paganism. Jewett probably reads a bit too much into only a few snippets of material from these two letters, and in the case of this verse, takes the additional step of seeing Paul as taking over the language of his opponents and reforming it. This seems too much to ask of the prayer, since one can make good sense of it by taking it in a more straightforward way.

sentence itself and how we are to understand the second part; and (3) the meaning of the adjective ὁλόκληρον in the second part (which I translated "in entirety") and its relationship to the adverb ἀμέμπτους (blamelessly).

To take up the second and third matters—for herein lies the clue to the first—Paul's sentence in this case is especially complex, calling forth alternative translations and interpretations, especially of the second clause.[105] The solution to Paul's own intent resides first in the structure of the whole, and secondly in the emphatic juxtaposition of the two adjectives, ὁλοτελεῖς, καὶ ὁλόκληρον. First, the two parts appear to form a kind of synonymous parallelism:

Line 1 – May the God of peace sanctify you wholly;

Line 2 – and may in entirety your spirit, soul, and body be preserved blamelessly at the appearing of our Lord Jesus Christ.

Seen in this way the two lines together emphasize a concern over the thoroughgoing nature of the sanctification he desires for them.

If so, secondly, the two adjectives, although grammatically predicate, function in a kind of adverbial sense, and respectively also emphasize the thoroughgoing nature of their sanctification.[106] The distinctions between them would thus mean something like "totally" (with emphasis on wholeness) and "in every possible expression of your humanity." The final adverb, "blamelessly," then adds the ethical/moral dimension to this thoroughgoing work of the

---

[105] The two basic understandings may be found in the NRSV and NIV: "may your spirit and soul and body be kept sound and blameless" (NRSV); "may your whole spirit, soul and body be kept blameless" (NIV). P. A. van Stempvoort argued for a different structure altogether: "May the God of peace sanctify you completely and in all parts [understanding πνεῦμα to represent 'you' or 'human beings']. May soul as well as body be protected unblemished at the coming of our Lord Jesus Christ" ("Eine stylische Lösung einer alten Schwierigkeit in I. Thessalonicher v. 23," NTS 7 [1961] 262–65). But as far as I can discern he has found no followers. The καί between ὁλοτελεῖς and ὁλόκληρον seems far more likely a form of parataxis between two sentences than a simple conjunction between two parts of the first sentence.

[106] Many also see in the two lines a kind of chiasmus. In its barest form the sentence reads: ἁγιάσαι ὑμᾶς ὁλοτελεῖς . . . ὁλόκληρον ὑμῶν τὸ πνεῦμα . . . τηρηθείη. Thus there is an ABC CBA order to (A) the verb, (B) the "you" and "your spirit etc.," and (C) the predicate adjective modifier of "you" and "your spirit." Understood in this way, the sentence is most often read: "May the God of peace sanctify you wholly; and may your spirit, soul, body be preserved complete [or "sound"]."

But this seems to make very little sense of Paul's sentence, especially when one comes to the adverb "blamelessly," which is usually turned into another adjective, resulting in (as the RSV): "May your spirit and soul and body be kept sound and blameless at the coming of our Lord Jesus Christ." The problem here is that the first adjective (ὁλοτελεῖς) is treated as an adverb, but the second (ὁλόκληρον) as an adjective, while the one true adverb (ἀμέμπτως) in the sentence becomes a predicate adjective. Paul's concern does not seem to be for the "wholeness" or "soundness" of one's spirit, soul, and body at the parousia, but that the "whole" person (i.e., spirit, soul, and body, and any other part of one's being) would be blamelessly preserved at the coming.

Spirit. Just as in 3:13, Paul desires the final form of this activity to be expressed in their standing "blameless" before God at the coming of our Lord Jesus Christ.[107]

If this is the correct way of viewing the structure and emphases of the prayer, then it is highly unlikely that the term πνεῦμα in this sentence refers even obliquely to the Holy Spirit. Most of the discussion on the three anthropological terms has centered either in determining whether or not Paul intended some kind of distinction between the first two terms—and if so, what?—or in the related question as to whether Paul was a dichotomist or trichotomist. That discussion, however, while not insignificant, has missed Paul's concern altogether. His use of πνεῦμα may indeed have been occasioned by its proximity to v. 19; nonetheless, Paul's concern is singular: that they be sanctified completely.[108] In the context of this letter, and especially in light of the verse's ties to 4:3–8, the present emphasis lies with *his inclusion of the body*. Very much as in 1 Cor 6:12–20, although without the express language of the body as the Spirit's temple, Paul is concerned that this early, almost totally Gentile (cf. 1:9–10), congregation understand that salvation in Christ includes the sanctification of the body: it is now to be holy, and wholly for God's own purposes. Thus he wants them to stand blameless in holiness before God at the coming of Christ, and he insists (now in prayer) that such holiness be thoroughgoing in their lives, including the purity of the body.

What, then, shall we say of the first two terms? First, it is very likely, given the way Paul here expresses himself, that he might think of the human spirit and soul as distinct entities in some way. But how he might think of them as different is not at all clear from the rest of his letters. Since he tends to use such terms both broadly and somewhat interchangeably, one is hard pressed to come to final conclusions. Moreover, the emphasis on entirety suggests that he could easily have included "mind" without for a moment deviating from his concern. That is, whatever distinctions he may have understood are quite secondary to the greater concern of completeness.

Paul does not often refer to the human spirit.[109] Whatever else πνεῦμα may signify, it refers to the interior, nonmaterial component of the human personality (see esp. 1 Cor 2:11). Those who see this usage as denoting that part of human existence that serves as the place of intersection between the human and the divine by means of the Holy Spirit are most likely moving in the right direction.[110] In any case, the concern here is that the body as well as the human spirit be kept blameless until the coming of Christ.[111]

---

[107] Thus, even though not quite precise as to the meaning of ὁλόκληρον and its grammatically being a predicate adjective, the NIV seems to have Paul's *sense* right: "May God himself, the God of peace, sanctify you through and through. May your whole spirit, soul, and body be kept blameless at the coming of our Lord Jesus Christ."

[108] Cf. the usage in the similarly expressed love command in Mark 12:30 (par.), where "heart, soul, mind, and strength" function in the same way.

[109] There seem to be only 14 instances in which πνεῦμα refers exclusively to the human spirit; see ch. 2, n. 6.

[110] Despite Jewett to the contrary. Thus, e.g., Findlay 133: "for with man's spirit the Holy Spirit directly associates Himself (Rom. viii.16)."

[111] On yet another front Juel's point (250) is well taken: sanctification here is not to be understood as a gradual progress toward a goal, but as a living out of the

2 THESSALONIANS

One of the incongruities of NT scholarship is its rejection of this epistle as genuinely Pauline. The rejection in this case is based, not as elsewhere on the *differences* between this letter and the other Paulines, but rather on its high level of *similarity* to 1 Thessalonians. Paul here is too much like himself to be genuine(!)—although not far below the surface in every case of rejection is some dissatisfaction with its content, especially the themes of judgment frequently expressed in a more apocalyptic mode of language.[112]

But the reasons for including it among the genuine Pauline corpus far outweigh any considerations against it. The similarities are precisely what one might expect of a letter written shortly after the first one,[113] and dealing for the most part with several of the same issues. Moreover, it is nearly impossible to find a *reason* for pseudepigraphy in this case,[114] since so little seems to be gained by it. Furthermore, the exegesis of 2:1–2 and 15 offered below presents a simple and historically viable reason for the letter within the framework of the context of Paul and Thessalonica that emerges in the first letter.

The occasion, purpose, and content of the letter are easily outlined. Soon after the first letter had been received in Thessalonica, someone in the community had begun to interpret the Pauline message of the Day of the Lord as "having already come." For believers undergoing severe persecution this caused great anxiety—not only in regard to their continuing suffering but also in regard to the "justice of God." At the same time, such teaching also added fuel to the fire of the "unruly idle," who

---

gift that has already been bestowed by grace. "Discipleship is life between the times, for God has not yet finished what he began. But the life of faith is not a striving for more; it is living more fully in what has already been given, knowing that even efforts to live more appropriately as 'saints' (4:1–3) depend upon God who sanctifies."

[112] The letter is said to lack the "warmth" of the first one, to show occasional breaks with "genuine" Pauline thought, and to reflect a different eschatology. See these kinds of arguments esp. in Hughes, *Rhetoric*, 14, whose various objections stem from what appears to be faulty, or simply prejudicial, exegesis of the passages he notes as unlike Paul. For similar arguments, see Trilling, and the refutation in Marshall 34, who has noted, "it is very doubtful whether a set of weak arguments adds up to one powerful one."

[113] I find the arguments of Wanamaker 37–45 for reversing the order of the epistles to be particularly unconvincing, especially since one can make such good sense of our letter in light of the exegesis of 2:2 and 2:15 offered below.

[114] The absence of allusions to or linguistic similarities with the other Pauline letters leaves only two options: it was written very early, when only 1 Thessalonians was known, or it was written by someone later who had access only to 1 Thessalonians. Neither of these is attractive historically.

now had even greater cause not to work with their own hands, but to live off the largess of the well-to-do within the community.[115]

Thus Paul responds by taking up first their present suffering, since the Day of the Lord had not yet come. In the opening thanksgiving (1:3–10) he reassures them that at the parousia of Christ, God will deal justly with those responsible for their suffering; therefore he prays (11–12) for God to fulfill his work in them in the present in light of their certain glorious future. That in turn leads to the primary concern of the letter, to correct the misrepresentation of his own teaching about the Day of the Lord (2:1–12), which leads to further thanksgiving for their own life in Christ and prayer for their standing firm therein (13–17). After a further request for prayer and some words of encouragement (3:1–5), which look as if the letter is about to wrap up, he takes up once more the matter of the "unruly idle" from the first letter, urging them to change their behavior and advising "excommunication" if they do not (6–15).

The passages of interest for us lie in the opening prayer (1:11), in the statement as to the letter's occasion (2:1–2), in the apocalyptic description of the anti-Christ figure (2:9), and finally in the second thanksgiving (2:13–14).

2 THESSALONIANS 1:11

To this end we also pray for you always that our God may make you worthy of the call and by his power[116] bring to fulfillment every resolve for goodness[117] and every[118] work of faith.

---

[115] For a slightly different reading of the situation, which views the problem as more totally related to misguided ecstasy, see Jewett, *Correspondence*, 101; cf. Dunn, *Jesus*, 269–70.

[116] This prepositional phrase, ἐν δυνάμει (with power), actually appears at the end of the clause (after "work of faith"). One cannot be certain whether Paul intended it to go with both verbs ("make you worthy"/"bring to fulfillment") or simply with the latter one. The overall structure of the sentence suggests this translation is what Paul had in mind in adding this phrase at the end, but it would not be far off course to suppose that it covers the whole of God's activity.

[117] Contrary to most of my translations elsewhere, I have here abandoned "literalness" (= every good will of goodness) as not making good sense. Paul's Greek, πᾶσαν εὐδοκίαν ἀγαθωσύνης, is a typically ambiguous genitive, that can be either "subjective" (= every expression of good will flowing from goodness), in which case it most likely refers to God himself, or objective, as above (= every good resolve for goodness). In favor of the former is the fact that the following phrase is almost certainly "subjective" (= work resulting from faith). But overall the latter seems to make the most sense of Paul's concern in prayer. So also Ellicott, Lightfoot (who translates "every delight in well-doing"), Milligan, Frame, Bruce, Best, Marshall, et al.

[118] Although one cannot have absolute certainty, most likely Paul intended the πᾶσαν to modify both sets of nouns ("desire for goodness" and "work of faith").

As in 1 Thessalonians, Paul's opening thanksgiving (vv. 3–4) gets away from him a bit in vv. 5–10, as a further word of encouragement flowing out of what is said in the thanksgiving proper. There he focused on their love, faith, and patient endurance in hardship—the matters to be taken up in the letter in detail.[119] The mention of their "patient endurance in persecution and hardship (θλῖψις)" prompts a reaffirmation of God's own justice, including his judgment on those causing the θλῖψις, which concludes with the final note of Christ at his Parousia being "glorified" in his saints and "marveled at" by all who believe. This final word concludes with something of a parenthetical note to include the Thessalonians themselves as among the believing and marveling. It is "to this end also," i.e., their being included in the "glorification" of v. 10, that Paul prays for them and includes a report of the content of his prayer.

The prayer picks up the twin concerns of love and faith from v. 3, that God will (1) make them worthy of their calling (living *faith*fully till the end, vv. 4, 10), and (2) bring to fulfillment their every desire for goodness and work that flows out of their faith. At the end of this clause (v. 11), probably for emphasis,[120] he adds that God will accomplish these things in them ἐν δυνάμει (with power).[121] With this phrase Paul probably intends "by the power of his Holy Spirit."[122] There are several considerations that suggest as much.

First, that Paul is not thinking here of "power" as a more abstract expression of one of the attributes of God (that God is the all-powerful one)[123] seems certain since he has just referred to God in this way (v. 9, "the glory of his might"); there he used the more appropriate word (ἰσχύς).

Second, in the thanksgiving in 1 Thes 1:5 (q.v.), Paul has already referred to his preaching as coming to them ἐν δυνάμει, which is immediately qualified as referring to the Holy Spirit (καὶ . . . ἐν πνεύματι ἁγίῳ).

Finally, and more significantly, Paul elsewhere attributes these divinely wrought activities among God's people to the activity of the Spirit. Indeed, both ἀγαθωσύνη (goodness) and πίστις (= faith-full) are included, together and in this order, in Gal 5:22 as fruit of the Spirit.

---

[119] Faith (in the sense of faithful trust) and patient endurance are spoken to in 2:1–15, especially in light of the fact that the Lord's Parousia is *not* immediate; love—or its abuse in this case (cf. 1 Thes 4:9–12)—in 3:6–16.

[120] So also Rigaux 640.

[121] Without justification Hughes (*Rhetoric*, 55) translates this phrase with the preceding one, "every work of faith and power."

[122] So Whiteley (indirectly), Frame, and Bruce. Many would translate it adverbially "that he powerfully fulfill" (e.g., Lightfoot, Ellicott; most recently, Wanamaker), but this seems to miss Pauline usage elsewhere as well as its emphatic position here.

[123] Cf. Hiebert 297: "the characteristic power inherent in His nature."

Thus, even though because of the context Paul expresses it in terms of "power," one may be reasonably sure that the Spirit's power is in view.

Three features of this text are worthy of further note, having to do with some basic "tensions" in Pauline theology. First, a healthy tension between divine activity and human responsibility runs throughout Paul's letters. Our present text indicates that the Pauline emphasis lies with God's prior action.[124] Their being made worthy of God's call, as evidenced by their goodness and faithful work, is first of all something that God brings about in their lives, and he does so by the power of the Spirit. This does not remove the imperative in Paul—not by a long way. Elsewhere he will urge such activities on his believing communities, often without mentioning the prior activity of God. This text demonstrates that for Paul the presupposition behind all such imperatives is the work of the Spirit in the life of the believing community.

Second, even though this text has to do with the Parousia, the prayer itself is concerned with their life in the present as they await the Parousia. That is, even though he prays that they might be found this way at the End—having lived "worthy" of their calling (cf. 1 Thes 2:12), exemplified by their goodness and faith-producing work—his concern is that this will be their standing at the End inasmuch as God by his Spirit has already been effecting such in their lives in the present. Thus the prayer is typical of Paul's eschatological stance of "already/not yet," with regard to life in the present.

Third, even though one may be quite sure that behind the word "power" is the divine Spirit, nonetheless Paul does use δύναμις here, not πνεῦμα, because that is his present emphasis. He is truly grateful to God that they are patiently enduring their present persecution and suffering; but he also knows that what they need in order to continue is God's *power* at work in their lives. In contrast to so much of subsequent Christianity, in which ethical life is often taken much too lightly, Paul knows no genuine Christian life that is not also lived in such a way as to be worthy of this calling. But the church—and its individual members—are not left to "slug it out in the trenches" on their own. Rather God has committed himself to them to empower such a life through the indwelling Spirit.

Finally, v. 12 gives the reason for all of this, namely, that God himself will be glorified through those who walk in his ways and thus bear and share his glory. Once again the final emphasis rests upon the grace of God that brings any and all of this about.

---

[124]In this regard one should note further how the prayer report finally ends in v. 12: "that the name of the Lord Jesus might be glorified in you, and you in him, *according to the grace* of our God and the Lord Jesus Christ."

2 Thessalonians 2:1–2[125]

[1]*Now, brothers and sisters, we beg you concerning the coming of our*[126] *Lord Jesus Christ and our gathering unto him* [2]*that you not be too easily*[127] *shaken in mind nor disturbed, whether by Spirit or word or letter, as though by us, to the effect that the Day of the Lord*[128] *has come.*

This passage is at once the most crucial and most problematic in this letter. It is the most crucial because Paul now articulates for his and their sakes his understanding of what has been recently reported to him about the situation in Thessalonica; thus it serves as the primary occasion for the letter. Indeed the other concerns—their unjust suffering (ch. 1) and the continuing difficulty with the "unruly idle" (ch. 3)—are best understood as related to this one. Whatever some of them had come to believe about "the Day of the Lord" (see 1 Thes 5:1–11), it had resulted in their being shaken with regard to their present sufferings and had caused others to take a dim view toward "working with their own hands."

At the same time, however, this passage is also the most problematic, because, being as crucial as it is, what it finally means is far from certain. The difficulty is twofold: (1) *What* has been communicated to them? That is, what does it mean, "the Day of the Lord has come"? (2) *How* has this been communicated to them, and how is that communication related to Paul? It is at this latter point that this becomes one of the crucial "Spirit" texts in these letters.

The first matter—what they had come to believe—is not essential to our present concern. Nonetheless, since it is crucial to the whole letter and relevant to the interpretation of the first part of v. 2, a summary of conclusions is in order.

First, it seems nearly impossible not to see this as related to some kind of misunderstanding of 1 Thes 5:1–11, with its repeated mention of the Day of the Lord (vv. 2, 4) and subsequent play on the themes of "day" and "night."

---

[125] For a more complete presentation of the point of view argued for here, see G. D. Fee, "Pneuma and Eschatology in 2 Thessalonians 2.1–2—A Proposal about 'Testing the Prophets' and the Purpose of 2 Thessalonians," in *Telling the Mysteries* (forthcoming, Sheffield Academic Press).

[126] B J 33 and a few others (including sy[h] and some MSS of the Vulgate) omit the ἡμῶν. Were this more widely attested, most textual critics, including this one, would think that the other witnesses had added the pronoun (as in 1:2), since this is Paul's more usual form. But more likely here we have omission for stylistic reasons, in light of the ἡμῶν that follows a few words later.

[127] For this sense of ταχέως, see BAGD, who also offer Gal 1:6 and 1 Tim 5:22 as further examples. The emphasis is only partly on "haste." Rather it lies more on "quickly" in the sense of "too easily" taken in by new things.

[128] Against all earlier evidence in all forms (Greek, versions, Fathers), the MajT has substituted Χριστοῦ for κυρίου. This seems to be a later attempt to make sure that "Lord" equals "Christ" in this passage, which in fact it almost certainly does.

Second, in all probability the content of the misunderstanding has to do with someone's teaching that the Day of the Lord is already present, or perhaps more likely in light of the emphases in ch. 1, that it had already *begun* in some way. This alone seems to make sense of the argument that follows, in which Paul insists that, just as he had previously taught them, particular observable events must transpire *before* that Day comes. The Day not only will be *preceded* by certain events, but also the events surrounding the Day will simply be too visible for any of them to miss it when it does come.

Third, such erroneous teaching that the Day has already come in some way also helps to explain the emphases in chs. 1 and 3. In light of what Paul had said in the earlier letter, the increase—and unjust nature—of their sufferings gives them considerable reason for anxiety, if the Day has already appeared. Hence, Paul's assurance in chapter 1 both of their own (future) vindication and of the just judgment of their adversaries. But the same reality would also add fuel to the fire of the reasoning of the unruly-idle. Since the Day of the Lord has already arrived, and since they probably also took a dim view of work in any case,[129] why should they return to their former occupations?

The question for us, then, is *how* has this thoroughly misguided understanding arisen among them, and how is it related to anything Paul may have said or written? The problem is both *linguistic* (what does "Spirit" mean here, especially as the first member of an apparently equivalent triad that includes "word" and "letter"?) and *grammatical* (how is the final phrase "as though by [διά] us" related to the preceding triad, which also is "by [διά]" these possible means?). The resolution of these difficulties involves two points.

First, one must take more seriously than have most commentators that Paul is not at all sure as to the exact source of the misinformation. That is, he truly does not know whether it has come through Spirit, word, or letter. Furthermore, one must take equally seriously the explicit statements in 2:5 and 15 that Paul has indeed previously spoken to this question both when he was among them (= λόγος, "word") and in his earlier letter (= 1 Thessalonians). All of this becomes the more problematic when one considers on the basis of vv. 3–12 and 1 Thes 5:1–11 that Paul himself has been quite clear on this matter and that their present position is a far cry from what he has taught or written. Thus we are faced with a situation in which Paul knows (1) that his own teaching has been either ignored, misunderstood, or misrepresented (probably the

---

[129] On this matter see esp. R. Russell, "The Idle in 2 Thess 3.6–12: An Eschatological or a Social Problem?" *NTS* 34 (1988) 105–19; and David C. Aune, "Trouble in Thessalonica: An Exegetical Study of I Thess 4:9–12, 5:12–14 and II Thess 3:6–15 in Light of First Century Social Conditions," unpubl. Th.M. thesis (Vancouver, B.C.: Regent College, 1989).

latter), and (2) that even though he is not sure how this came about, he is considered to be the agent of what is currently being taught.

That leads us to the little phrase ὡς δι' ἡμῶν (as though through us), which in Paul's sentence follows hard on the heels of "whether by Spirit, whether by word, whether by letter."[130] Frequently this has been understood as referring to the final item only (= nor through a letter as though it had come from us).[131] This is usually supported by the signature in 3:17, that Paul in this case "signs" the letter in his own hand so that they will not mistake it for some forgery. Tempting as that reconstruction might be, it seems to run aground on what Paul actually says. (a) Such a position has great difficulty with 2:15, where Paul affirms that they are to hold fast to what came to them from him by way of "word" and "letter." (b) If this were his intent then one would expect ὡς ἀπ' ἡμῶν or παρ' ἡμῶν (as though *from* us). Indeed the repetition of the "through" in this phrase not only tends to spell the death knell to this traditional understanding,[132] but also probably offers the clue to what he did intend.

Because of the difficulty of the διά many have suggested that it goes with all three of the preceding words.[133] Although this has more going for it grammatically, the problem with this solution lies with understanding how "the Spirit" might have been understood as mediated "through us," since Paul has not recently been on the scene. Nor is it easy to see how this erroneous view about the Day could have been attributed to Paul on the basis of what we know he has said in 1 Thessalonians.

The resolution to this, therefore, would seem to lie in seeing the sentence as somewhat elliptical, although it is easy to see what probably happened. The enigmatic ὡς δι' ἡμῶν is best understood as referring not directly to the *form* by which the misinformation has been mediated to

---

[130] See the helpful discussion in Jewett, *Correspondence*, 181–86, who categorizes three approaches to this phrase: (1) to view the phrase as the work of a forger [which Jewett rightly sees breaks down in trying to interpret 2:15]; (2) to deny that the phrase has any implications of forgery; (3) to view 1 Thessalonians as the letter, but to understand it as being misrepresented in some way [the view argued for in this study].

[131] E.g., Moffatt, Moore, Bruce.

[132] This point of grammar is usually overlooked or ignored in the commentaries and translations (von Dobschütz 266 and Giblin, *Threat*, 149, are exceptions). But that will not do, since Paul elsewhere shows considerable precision in the use of these two prepositions. When he refers to the source of something he uses ἀπό (see, e.g., 1 Thes 3:6: "now that Timothy has come to us *from* you"); when he refers to a secondary agent, that through which something has been mediated, he uses διά. In this regard see esp. the well-known demurrer in Gal 1:1 that his apostleship is neither ἀπ' ἀνθρώπων nor δι' ἀνθρώπου (it neither has its source in humans nor has it been mediated through any human). We must conclude it is simply wrong to translate this phrase, "either *by* spirit or *by* word or *by* letter, as though *from* us" (NRSV; cf. NIV). Paul is not here referring to the *source* of the misinformation, but its unknown *mediation* to them.

[133] This is by far the more common option in the English commentaries.

them (i.e., Spirit, word, letter), but to the *content* of it (i.e., to the clause that follows). In this view, Paul is not saying that the letter did not come from him—it did indeed—but that *what they are now believing about the Day of the Lord did not come through him.*[134]

Thus the "logic" of the sentence goes something like this. Paul's difficulty is twofold: first, he is aware that the misinformation has ultimately been attributed to him; but second, he is not quite sure how it was communicated. He therefore begins with the latter item, the uncertain source, the first member of which is most likely the key to the whole. "Spirit" in this case in all likelihood refers to a "prophetic utterance."[135] By means of the "Spirit" someone could easily have represented himself/herself as speaking in Paul's behalf. But for Paul it would be equally possible that such a "prophecy" may have been given in the form of an authoritative interpretation of what he had previously taught or written (e.g., "the Spirit says that what Paul really meant was . . . "). In any case, having mentioned the uncertain source by the repeated "whether through . . . ," he now moves toward the misrepresented content. Using the same suppositional language, "as though through us," he anticipates the final clause in the sentence. Thus: "Do not be too easily shaken or disturbed," he urges them, "whether it comes through the Spirit, or through what I have previously taught or written, as though the teaching came through us to the effect that the Day of the Lord has already come."

This also helps explain the otherwise awkward ὡς ὅτι that introduces the final clause. Paul's intent is clear enough; here finally is the content of what has been said in their midst that is currently troubling them. But the sentence has begun to get out of hand grammatically. The ὅτι (that) introduces the content of what has been said among them; the preceding ὡς picks up the same sense of misrepresentation as in the preceding phrase, and thus ties the two together. Teaching of this sort cannot in any way be attributed to Paul.

Such a view, it should be noted, makes sense of several matters in these letters. As noted above on 1 Thes 5:19–22, Paul has already anticipated the need for this community to be a bit more perceptive about "Spirit" utterances. Furthermore, and most significantly, this explains

---

[134] This view has been suggested, inter alia, by Frame 247 ["he disclaims simply all responsibility for the statement: 'the day of the Lord is present' "]; cf. von Dobschütz 266–67, Dibelius 44, Findlay 165 ["*supposing that* it is through us,' viz. that the announcement of the arrival of 'the day' comes from the Lord through His Apostles and has their authority"]; Jewett, *Correspondence*, 184–86.

[135] Cf. the NIV, which actually translates πνεῦμα "by some prophecy." The view argued for here was anticipated by Giblin, *Threat*, 149–50, 243, although his solution took the form of the question of authority. As with his view of πνεῦμα in 1 Thes 5:19, Gunkel (*Influence*, 31) considers it to refer to glossolalia here. But how, one wonders, could such a miscommunication occur through a phenomenon that is not understood by either speaker or hearer?

why in 2 Thes 2:15 he refers again to διὰ λόγου and δι' ἐπιστολῆς (through word or through letter),[136] and urges them to hold fast to what they have *previously been taught by him*. He knows that his former teaching was not ambiguous; they must therefore hold fast to what has been "handed down" to them *directly* from him. What is conspicuously missing in this instance, of course, is the first member of the former triad, "through the Spirit"—because in this view that is what Paul himself most likely believed to be the ultimate source of his difficulty.[137]

Again, as before, such abuses of "prophetic utterances" are not in themselves directly condemned, probably in this case because he is not certain that this is the actual cause. On the other hand, if we have approximated Paul's intent in 2:2, then he is in 2:15 also offering a criterion for "testing the spirits": "the *traditions* you were taught, whether orally or by our letter." This sets the pattern for the church at a later time, which now of course has the "traditions" only in their written form.

2 Thessalonians 2:8

And then the Lawless One shall be revealed, whom the Lord Jesus shall slay with the breath of his mouth and shall abolish at the manifestation of his parousia,

In his description of Christ's ultimate defeat of the anti-Christ figure at his Parousia, Paul uses language reminiscent of Isa 11:4 ("He shall strike the earth with the rod of his mouth, and with the breath of his lips he shall kill the wicked"[138]). The word "breath" in both cases (the LXX and Paul) is πνεῦμα, which Giblin interprets as "the Spirit from the mouth of the Lord."[139]

But such a view runs aground at two points: (1) It does not take the metaphorical language seriously enough as metaphor. It is doubtful whether either Isaiah or Paul thought in terms of the Spirit of God in using this metaphor. (2) The use of the definite article with πνεύματι in this instance points away from reference to the Spirit, rather than toward it, as was noted in the discussion of

---

[136] In support of what has been argued above (n. 132) about Paul's use of διά, note that the δι' ἐπιστολῆς in 2:15 does *not* refer to the *source*, but the *means* whereby the "traditions" have been given to them.

[137] For a different view on the relationship between 1 Thes 5:19–22 and 2 Thes 2:2; 2:15, see Hughes, *Rhetoric*, 56–57, who interprets the author of 2 Thessalonians as denying the validity of "spirit," which is contrary to the genuine Paul in 1 Thes 5:19–20 ("a particularly jarring contrast" to the exhortation not to quench the Spirit—as though Paul had not written vv. 21–22 as well!). Cf. Giblin, *Threat*, 45, who also sees 2:15 as "factoring out" a "heavy reliance on charismatic utterances," but as a "modification," rather than a "follow up," of 1 Thes 5:19–22.

[138] On the probable meaning of this metaphor, as referring to the authoritative command of the king, see R. Watts, "The Meaning of *Alaw Yiqpesu Melakim Pihem* in Isaiah LII 15," *VT* 40 (1990) 327–35 (330–31).

[139] See *Threat*, 91–95; Milligan 103 attributes this view also to Athanasius (*ad. Serap.* 1.6).

this idiom in chapter 2. Hence it is extremely doubtful whether this text advances our understanding of the Spirit in Paul.

2 THESSALONIANS 2:9

whose parousia is in accordance with Satan's working with all power, with signs and wonders from falsehood.[140]

In this clause Paul goes on to describe the "parousia" of the anti-Christ figure, which immediately precedes that of Christ. His coming, Paul says, will be accompanied by the same phenomena that elsewhere (Rom 15:19; 2 Cor 12:12) are mentioned as accompanying (and in part authenticating) his own apostolic ministry. In the same way, the early church understood such phenomena—and used the same language to describe them—as authenticating the ministry and person of Jesus (Acts 2:22). According to Mark 13:22 (cf. Matt 24:24), Jesus himself predicted the rise of "false christs [plural]," who would perform great signs and wonders—probably the source of the traditional material reflected here.

Two matters are significant for our present purposes: First, in Rom 15:19 Paul specifically equates "the power of signs and wonders" with "the power of the Spirit of God." These are the "signs of an apostle" in the sense that such apostleship is derived from and dependent on the Spirit. Secondly, Paul indicates here that "signs and wonders" can accompany both truth and falsehood. By describing those of the Lawless One as stemming from falsehood, he does not mean that they are "counterfeit"[141] in the sense of not really occurring. To the contrary, miracles they are indeed; but they issue from falsehood and as such are intended to deceive, to lead people astray after Satan. Indeed, in Paul's view they are empowered by the "spirit" responsible for all falsehood, Satan himself (cf. Eph 2:2).

One wonders, therefore, whether this is not one of the reasons why in 2 Corinthians 10–13 Paul is so reluctant to bring forward his "signs and wonders" as authenticating his ministry. He does not thereby deny

---

[140]It is not absolutely certain how Paul intended the adjective πάσῃ (all) and the final genitive ψεύδους (of falsehood) to be understood. The NRSV takes the former to go only with "power" and the latter only with "wonders" ("all power, signs, lying wonders"); the NIV takes them both to go with all three words ("all kinds of counterfeit miracles, signs, and wonders"). Since πάσῃ is singular and modifies the singular δυνάμει, the NRSV probably has the better of it here; ψεύδους is more difficult, but since it *follows* τέρασιν, and therefore *can* include both nouns, and since the two words seem so clearly to go together and thus speak of a single reality, it seems likely that Paul intended it to cover both of the preceding nouns, not just the final one. Hence my translation.

[141] Since this is the only real meaning of "counterfeit," one wonders whether the NIV is not quite misleading to call them "counterfeit miracles, etc." See also RSV, which is even worse: "with pretended signs and wonders"—now corrected in NRSV.

them; but neither does he put much stock in them as marks of authentication. For him the evidence of apostleship lies ultimately not in the miraculous—in the sense of "signs and wonders," since Satan can also produce these—but in his own "imitation of Christ" in his sufferings and in the fruit of such imitation, the conversion of the Corinthians themselves.

In any case, in both instances, the true and the false, the "signs and wonders" are the work of "spirit," either the false spirit, as here, or the Holy Spirit, as in Paul's case.

2 THESSALONIANS 2:13

But we, on the other hand, are bound always to give thanks to God for you, brothers and sisters beloved by the Lord, that God chose you to be firstfruits[142] for salvation by means of the sanctifying work of the Spirit and your own belief in the truth.

This final Spirit text in the Thessalonian correspondence is also one of the more intriguing. As in 1 Thes 2:13, Paul offers a second thanksgiving for them—although in this case it is not a resumption but part of the conclusion to the present argument. In fact, the thanksgiving begins a series of materials (vv. 13–17), which seem clearly designed to conclude

---

[142]On the surface, this is one of the more difficult textual choices in 2 Thessalonians (between ἀπαρχήν, "firstfruits" [B F G P 33 81 326 1739 it^{c,dem,div,f,x,z} vg syr^h cop^{bo}] and ἀπ᾽ ἀρχῆς "from the beginning" [ℵ D K L Ψ 104 181 pler it^{ar,e,mon} sy^p cop^{sa}]). The external evidence is nearly evenly divided, both East and West. Nor is the change likely to have happened by pure accident (except in the sense noted below that a scribe looked at one thing but "saw" another). The commentaries tend to favor ἀπ᾽ ἀρχῆς (Best, Ellicott, Frame, Hendriksen, Hiebert, Marshall, Morris, Plummer, Thomas, Wanamaker; otherwise Weiss, Moffatt, Bruce), while the English translations are more divided ("from the beginning," KJV RSV NASB JB NEB NIV; "firstfruits," GNB NAB Moffatt Knox). Nonetheless, the weightier arguments both transcriptional and intrinsic point to ἀπαρχήν as the original text. Given both its lack of theological grist in comparison with "from the beginning," it is easily the *lectio difficilior*. That this same interchange (from ἀπαρχή to ἀπ᾽ ἀρχῆς) happens twice elsewhere in the NT (Rom 16:5 [P^{46} D* g m]; Rev 14:4 [ℵ 336 1918]) illustrates the ease with which scribes, who were actually looking at one thing, in fact "saw" another (in each case ἀπαρχή lay before them; they "saw," or anticipated Paul to have said, ἀπ᾽ ἀρχῆς). The primary argument usually raised against ἀπαρχήν is that the Thessalonians were not in fact the "firstfruits" of Macedonia; but this makes the rather unwarranted assumption that Paul would indeed have intended "of Macedonia" had he used this word (it is common to note that although Paul uses ἀπαρχή elsewhere [Rom 8:23; 11:16; 16:5; 1 Cor 15:20, 23; 16:15], only in Rom 11:16 does he use it without a qualifying genitive [most recently Wanamaker 266]). To the contrary, Paul almost certainly intended "the firstfruits of Thessalonica," wanting them to see themselves as the "firstfruits" of many more in Thessalonica who would come to know the Savior—despite (or as the result of?) the persecution that they are presently enduring. Added to this is the fact that when Paul elsewhere wishes to place something "in eternity," he never uses the phrase ἀπ᾽ ἀρχῆς or anything close to it (cf. 1 Cor 2:7; Col 1:26; Eph 1:4).

the argument that began in v. 1—in three ways: first, with a *thanksgiving* (13–14), which sets them off in sharp contrast to the unbelievers described in vv. 10–12; second, with an *exhortation* (15) to hold fast the traditions which they had been taught (harking back to vv. 3–5); and third, with a *wish-prayer* (16–17) that God and Christ encourage and firmly establish them, thus bringing closure to vv. 1–2. The concern in all of this lies with the exhortation to stand firm (v. 15) and is the result of the misrepresentation of Paul's teaching that is "shaking them up" (vv. 1–2).

Thus Paul's reasons for the thanksgiving seem plain. He has just described those who have been taken in by the Lawless One and who will thus be judged along with him. They are people who have rejected the truth (v. 10) and through deceit have come to believe the lie (v. 11), and thus take pleasure in unrighteousness (v. 12). In the light of their eventual demise, and thus by way of the strongest possible contrast, Paul says that he feels obliged to thank God for the Thessalonian believers, because they are loved by Christ and elected unto salvation, with eternal glory as their destiny. That leads him to yet another description/reminder of their own conversion. The emphasis falls on God's prior activity and, as with the exhortation and prayer that follow, is intended to fortify them both in the midst of their unjust suffering (ch. 1) and in their having been "shaken" by the misrepresentation of his teaching (2:1–2).

Our interest lies in the twofold prepositional phrase[143] that (apparently) describes the means by which God effected their salvation: the sanctifying work of the Spirit[144] and their own belief in the truth.

First, this is the first of several semi-creedal soteriological passages in which Paul refers to the saving event as the combined activity of the triune God.[145] Here the Father "elects," the Son "has loved" (in the cross), and the Spirit effects it in their lives by "sanctifying" them. Granted this is not Trinitarian in a later sense, but the later outworking is the direct result of such texts as these. Whatever else, the "three persons of the Godhead" are mentioned in distinctly separate ways, and each is active in the work of salvation.[146]

---

[143] Rather than "twin phrases," since one preposition controls both "the sanctifying work of the Spirit" and "belief in the truth."

[144] Findlay 189–90 and Moffatt 50 argue that by ἐν ἁγιασμῷ πνεύματος Paul intends "sanctification of (your) spirit" (Findlay). In its favor they argue (1) from the absence of the article with πνεύματος, and (2) that the second member of the phrase is an objective genitive, so this one should be as well. This is finally defeated on the grounds of Pauline usage (the absence of the article speaks in *favor* of the Spirit [see ch. 2]; Paul avoids speaking of salvation in terms of the human spirit [except for 1 Cor 5:5, q.v.]). For the Spirit as the agent of sanctification see 1 Cor 6:11 and Rom 15:16.

[145] See n. 39 above.

[146] Cf. Whiteley 104, who of this text says, "We have the close functional association of Father, Son, and Holy Spirit which provided the biblical material for the later doctrinal constructions."

Second, and closely related, although in such passages Paul usually refers to the work of Christ as effecting salvation, here such reference is to be found only in the preceding "loved by the Lord," and more obliquely in the language "belief in the truth." The reason for the present emphasis is simple; Paul wants to draw a contrast between the Thessalonian believers and the unbelievers in vv. 10–12. The latter are expressly said to have been deceived by the working of Satan, so that they *do not believe the truth* but rather *take pleasure in wickedness.* Thus, in the former passage he has underscored both the "working" of Satan and the twofold result of unbelief and unrighteousness. Now, by way of contrast, he emphasizes the "working" of the Spirit and its twofold result of holiness and faith.

Third, it is of more than passing interest that he should describe their *conversion* in terms of "sanctification," or "holiness." This seems designed to pick up the concern in 1 Thes 4:1–8 and 5:23 (q.v.). The call to Christ, and its effective appropriation by the Spirit, has inherent in it that they are to become God's holy people. Thus "sanctification" in Paul, as 1 Cor 1:30 and 6:11 also make plain, is not a second work of grace, nor does it refer primarily to something that takes place in the believer after conversion—although that, too, is surely expected. Rather, their conversion itself may be described in terms of "sanctification," both in its sense of their being now set apart for God's purposes and in its more ethical sense of their walking in God's ways, so as to reflect his character. As in 1 Thes 4:8, for Paul this is the work of the Holy Spirit in the life of the believer. This is not Paul's only metaphor for "salvation in Christ," nor is it even a predominant one; on the other hand, there is for him no genuine conversion that does not include the sanctifying work of the Spirit.

Fourth, as noted above on 1:11, there is a happy tension between the divine and human in Pauline theology, but as always the order (the work of the Spirit, followed by their belief in the truth) says it all in terms of Paul's own theological emphases. If that misses the "logic of chronology," it is fully in keeping with Paul's "logic of theology." Whether that also implies that faith, too, is the work of the Spirit seems to me to be moot.

CONCLUSION

As noted at the outset, even though there is no direct "teaching" on the Spirit in these letters, what we do find in the several passages is a rather full-orbed understanding, even if at times in the form of presuppositions, of the work of the Spirit as lying at the heart of Christian life, from beginning to end. The call to Christ through the apostolic preaching was made effective through the "power of the Spirit" in that preaching; their own experience of conversion was effected by the Spirit, whose coming into their lives was intended among other things to produce "holiness." They are to continue their life in Christ in terms of willing and doing good and of faithful work, but even that is effected by the Spirit (God's power at work in their lives). Not only so, but their new life in Christ is also manifest by their joy (and prayer and thanksgiving), which is the direct result of the Spirit's indwelling. And finally in their gatherings for worship the Spirit is both actively and visibly present in the form of prophetic utterances; but since such activity can also go astray, they must always make sure by "testing all things" that what is spoken as a prophecy is indeed from the Spirit of God.

If Paul does not stress much of this himself, the very fact that the Spirit lies so close to the surface in his conversations with these early—and new—believers says much in terms of the presuppositions of Paul's understanding of Christian faith and life.

4

FIRST CORINTHIANS

Commentaries:[1] P. E.-B. **Allo** (Ebib, 1934); C. K. **Barrett** (HNTC, 1968); F. F. **Bruce** (NCB; 1971); J. **Calvin** (ET, 1960); H. **Conzelmann** (Hermeneia, 1975); C. T. **Craig** (IB, 1953); E. **Fascher** (THNT, 1984³); G. D. **Fee** (NICNT, 1987); G. G. **Findlay** (EGT, 1900); F. **Godet** (ET, 1886); H. L. **Goudge** (WC, 1903); F. W. **Grosheide** (NICNT, 1953); J. **Héring** (ET, 1962); C. **Hodge** (1857); C. **Holladay** (LWC, 1979); R. **Kugelman** (JBC, 1968); R. C. H. **Lenski** (1937); J. J. **Lias** (CBSC, 1896); H. **Lietzmann** (ed. W. G. Kümmel, HNT, 1949); J. B. **Lightfoot** (1895); J. F. **MacArthur** (1984); W. H. **Mare** (EBC, 1976); J. **Moffatt** (MNTC, 1938); L. **Morris** (TNTC, 1958); J. **Murphy-O'Connor** (NTM, 1979); W. F. **Orr** and J. A. **Walther** (AB, 1976); R. St J. **Parry** (CGTSC, 1926²); D. **Prior** (1985); A. **Robertson** and A. **Plummer** (ICC, 1914²); J. **Ruef** (WPC, 1971); A. **Schlatter** (1962); C. **Senft** (1979); M. E. **Thrall** (CBC, 1965); J. **Weiss** (MKNT, 1910⁹); H. D. **Wendland** (NTD, 1968).

Other significant works are referred to by the following short titles:

Aune, *Prophecy* (= David E. Aune, *Prophecy in Early Christianity and the Ancient Mediterranean World* [Grand Rapids: Eerdmans, 1983]); **Cranfield,** *Romans* (= C. E. B. Cranfield, *The Epistle to the Romans* [2 vols.; ICC; Edinburgh: T & T Clark, 1975, 1979]); **Ellis,** *Prophecy* (= E. Earle Ellis, *Prophecy and Hermeneutic in Early Christianity: New Testament Essays* [Grand Rapids: Eerdmans, 1978]); **Grudem,** *Gift* (= Wayne A. Grudem, *The Gift of Prophecy in 1 Corinthians* [Washington: University Press of America, 1982]); **Hurd,** *Origin* (= John C. Hurd, *The Origin of 1 Corinthians* [2d ed.; Macon, Ga.: Mercer University, 1983]); **Martin,** *Spirit* (= Ralph P. Martin, *The Spirit and the Congregation: Studies in 1 Corinthians 12–15* [Grand Rapids: Eerdmans, 1984]); **Murphy-O'Connor,** *Corinth* (= J. Murphy-O'Connor, *St. Paul's Corinth* [GNS 6; Wilmington, Del.: Michael Gla-

---

[1]The following commentaries are referred to in this chapter only by the author's last name.

zier, 1983]); **O'Brien,** *Thanksgivings* (= Peter T. O'Brien, *Introductory Thanksgivings in the Letters of Paul* [Leiden: Brill, 1977]); **Zuntz,** *Text* (= Gunther Zuntz, *The Text of the Epistles* [London: British Academy, 1953]).

Although the basic emphases on the Spirit are already to be found in 1 and 2 Thessalonians, the greatest amount of Spirit language in Paul appears in the four great letters of the third missionary tour (1 and 2 Corinthians, Galatians, Romans).[2] Our present letter is especially crucial in this regard, since much of what Paul says about the Spirit is purposely corrective to some misunderstandings on the part of the Corinthians. That leads him at some point or another to touch on almost every aspect of the Spirit and Christian life that one finds in the corpus, from the person of the Spirit, to the Spirit as the essential matter of Christian existence, to the Spirit in the community and in its worship.

The language itself tells the story. In this letter there are at least 27 (probably 31) references to the Holy Spirit; 15 of 24 occurrences of the adjective πνευματικός (*pneumatikos*, Spirit-ual); the only occurrence of the adverb "spiritually" (2:14, where Paul clearly intends "by means of the Spirit"); all 20 of the (direct) references to glossolalia (speaking in tongues); all 11 of the occurrences of the verb "to prophesy"; 6 of 11 occurrences of the noun "prophecy"; and 6 of 14 instances of "prophet." Furthermore, chs. 12–14, although basically intended as corrective, include the fullest discussion of the "manifestations" of the Spirit in the community, commonly called "Spiritual gifts."

Since so much Spirit material appears in this letter, and since so much of it is directly related to the situation in Corinth, a brief overview of that situation seems necessary.[3] Our letter is the third in a series of exchanges between Paul and this community (see 5:9 and 7:1), each of which I take to be in direct response to the preceding one.[4] In his first letter Paul had forbidden certain practices (5:9); their letter to him (7:1), rather than seeking his counsel on matters over which they are divided internally (the common view), more likely takes exception to the prohibitions in his first letter. In response, our 1 Corinthians aims at convincing them he is right and they are wrong on these issues, now based on some additional inside information about the community reported to him by Chloe's people (1:10–12).

This suggests, in turn, that although some strife exists within the community, the greater conflict is between the community, led by a few,

---

[2] Plus Ephesians, which I take to be Pauline and from the next period of letters (see on ch. 9).

[3] What follows, of course, is my perception of it; for a more detailed discussion and defense, see the Introduction to Fee, 4–15.

[4] Although this is the most natural view of an exchange of letters, it is one of the idiosyncrasies of NT scholarship that hardly anyone holds this view—all of which is predicated on the prejudgment of reading the letter in the light of 1:10–12.

and Paul himself. He and they are at odds on almost every issue; and their conflicting understandings of the Spirit and his activity seem to lie at the heart of things. Whatever else, they consider themselves to be πνευματικοί (Spirit people);[5] because of Paul's bodily weaknesses and non"wisdom," nonrhetorical presentation of the gospel they are less than sure about him. At issue throughout the letter, therefore, in most of its various parts, is a basic conflict over what it means to be people of the Spirit.

Their view apparently has a touch of overrealized, or more properly, overspiritualized, eschatology. That is, because of their understanding of glossolalia as angelic speech (the dialect of heaven),[6] they consider themselves already to have arrived at the ultimate spiritual existence, except to slough off the body in death. They are already experiencing the existence of the future, a kind of ultimate spirituality which puts them *above* the present world. Thus some of them are denying sex within marriage, or marriage itself, while others are indulging themselves in various ways, including sexually. The "spiritual" nature of baptism and the sacraments helps to protect them while they continue to visit the pagan temples for sacred meals with their friends. The customary (apparently) head-covering is being discarded as evidence that "male" and "female" are no longer meaningful designations for those who are as the angels.

Thus, all the while they are prating about being πνευματικοί, they are also indulging in theological and behavioral fancies that have removed them far from the real life in the Spirit, where one lives out the future in the present even in weakness, not in triumphalist terms, but in terms of the ethical life of those "who have been sanctified in the name of Christ and by the power of the Spirit" (6:11).

Thus for Paul, too, the Spirit is the key to everything. But in contrast to them, being πνευτματικός means to live empowered by the Spirit in contradiction to the (merely human) wisdom they are now advocating; it means to understand the cross as God's power at work in the world (1:18–25; 2:6–16). Their internal strife is evidence that, even though they are Spirit people because they are Christ's, they are acting like anything but; in fact they are acting like "fleshly" people, like mere human beings, who know nothing of the Spirit of God (3:1–4; cf. 2:14). Indeed, by the Spirit, they form God's temple in Corinth (3:16), but their strife in the name of wisdom is destroying God's temple, putting them in danger of

---

[5]This seems certain not only by the various arguments in the letter (esp. 2:6–3:1; 12:1; 14:37; 15:45–49), but also by two additional phenomena: (1) The high incidence of this adjective in the letter, most often in polemical contexts. (2) The argument in ch. 14, which comes to a climax with the challenge in v. 37, "If anyone thinks that he or she is a prophet or πνευματικός (a Spirit person), let that person take note of what I write that it is the command of the Lord." This is the nub of the conflict: his opponents think they are; they are less sure about Paul.

[6]For this view see the discussion of 13:1 below.

his wrath (3:17). Moreover, what the Spirit has formed in Corinth is Christ's body (12:12–26), which means that their singular and unhealthy interest in tongues in the gathered community is also destroying the body by eliminating its necessary diversity.

Thus, everywhere one looks in this letter there are corrective—and sometimes presuppositional—words about true life in the Spirit, both to the individual and to the community. Their conversion was the result of Paul's preaching, which was accompanied by the Spirit's power (2:4–5); and the Spirit is still at work in Paul as he writes to them (7:40; 14:37). Indeed as this letter is being read to them, Paul himself is to be understood as present by the Spirit (5:3–4). The washing, sanctifying, and justifying act of God in their lives was also effected by the Spirit (6:11); and by the Spirit they acknowledge Jesus as Lord (12:3). The Spirit thus marks off God's people from those who do not know him (2:14) and reveals to them that the weakness represented by the cross is truly God's wisdom and power at work in the world (2:10–13). The Spirit who appropriates salvation is also the Spirit who sanctifies the body of the believer and thus separates him or her unto holy living (6:19–20). And above all else the Spirit is the key to their life together as God's people, a people fashioned by the Spirit into one body (12:13), indwelt by the Spirit as his one temple, his alternative to Corinth (3:16–17). Their gatherings, therefore, should be full of the Spirit, but precisely so that believers might be built up (14:1–19, 26–33) and outsiders might be exposed before God and fall on their faces before him in repentance (14:24–25).

The Corinthians are quite right about the importance of the Spirit as the key to Christian life; but they are wrong as to what that life looks like and how such people live and behave in the present world. Thus, Paul's second letter to them, our 1 Corinthians, is full of Spirit concerns, and therefore full of what truly Christian life is all about.[7]

1 CORINTHIANS 1:4–7

[4]*I thank my God always for you because of the grace of God given you in Christ Jesus,* [5]*that in every way you have been enriched in him, in all*[8] *speech and all knowledge,* [6]*even as our witness to Christ*[9] *was confirmed among you,* [7]*so that*

---

[7]Two passages in particular (2:6–16; 12:1–14:40) are of such length and significance that I have treated them much more like a commentary. Hence much of that material will bear considerable likeness to my commentary, with the generous permission of Eerdmans Publishing Co.

[8]With abstract nouns, as here, πᾶς usually has the sense of "every kind of." See BAGD 1aβ. Cf. Barrett 36–37 and O'Brien, *Thanksgivings*, 117.

[9]Several MSS, incl. B* F G 81 1175, read θεοῦ (God), instead of "Christ," probably as an assimilation to the wording of 2:1.

you are lacking no gracious gift as you eagerly await the revelation of our Lord Jesus Christ.

As with 1 Thessalonians, the first mention of Spirit activity in 1 Corinthians is found in the thanksgiving period; similarly it specifically reflects the issues that will be raised in the letter. What is most remarkable about this thanksgiving is the apostle's ability to thank God for the very things in the church that, because of abuse, are also causing him grief.[10]

Paul thanks God first of all for the community of believers itself, because as possessively as he will speak about them in the two preserved letters, they are nonetheless God's own possession, not his.[11] That about them for which he is specifically grateful is that "in every way you have been enriched in Christ Jesus, in every kind of speech (λόγος, *logos*) and knowledge (γνῶσις, *gnōsis*)." Indeed, he goes on, the net result of God's enriching you through our preaching Christ among you, is that "you are lacking in no gracious gift (χάρισμα, *charisma*), as you await the coming of Christ." One will quickly recognize that λόγος, γνῶσις, and χάρισμα are not only related items (see 12:8–9), but also register high among the difficulties Paul faced in this church.

Nonetheless, Paul simply refuses to domesticate the faith by eliminating what could prove troublesome; the problem after all lay not in the Corinthians' giftedness, but in their attitude toward such gifts.[12] Precisely because the gifts come from God, Paul is bound to give thanks for them, since as chs. 12 and 14 demonstrate these are *good* things that have gone sour.[13] In his thanksgiving, therefore, Paul accomplishes two objectives: he gives genuine thanks to God both for the Corinthians themselves and for God's having "gifted" them, but at the same time he redirects their focus.

The redirection of their focus in this case will set the tone for the rest of the letter. Four matters are especially noteworthy:[14] (1) its christocentric

---

[10]So much so, that some have suggested that the thanksgiving is ironical (see, e.g., Craig 18, Allo 4). But this view misses too much, including vital features in Paul's theology and spirituality.

[11]On the significance of this reality for Pauline spirituality, see G. D. Fee, "Some Reflections on Pauline Spirituality," in *Alive to God: Studies in Spirituality presented to James Houston* (ed. J. I. Packer and Loren Wilkinson; Downers Grove: InterVarsity, 1992) 96–107.

[12]Cf. the observation of O'Brien, *Thanksgivings*, 114: "The Corinthians had forgotten that what they had received were 'gifts' (note the biting words of 4:7, 'What have you that you did not receive? If then you received it, why do you boast as if it were not a gift?'), sovereignly distributed by the Holy Spirit (12:4–11, esp. v. 11) and that their purpose was 'for the common good' (12:7), or that the church might be edified (14:5)."

[13]Cf. Lightfoot 148: "St Paul here gives thanks for their use: he afterward condemns their abuse."

[14]The significance of these matters for this letter should not be underestimated by their mere notation here; for further detail see Fee, 36–46.

focus;[15] (2) everything is the result of God's own gracious activity to-ward/among them;[16] (3) Paul's role in their being so gifted;[17] and (4) the gifts belong to the present, to the time of awaiting the final consummation.[18]

As to the "giftedness" itself, several matters need to be noted:

1. The first occurrence of the word χάρισμα in the Pauline corpus (v. 7) is especially instructive, since it demonstrates that the first empha-sis in the word is on its root χάρις ("grace"), not on either the Spirit or the gifting per se.[19] Thus, even though Paul has concrete expressions of "grace" in view (in this case "speech" and "knowledge"), and even though in ch. 12 these concrete expressions are understood as the direct result of Spirit activity, there seems to be no real justification for the translation "spiritual gift" for this word. Rather, they are "gracious endowments" (where the emphasis lies on the grace involved in their being so gifted), which at times, as in this letter, are seen also as the gracious activity of the Spirit in their midst.

Thus the specific basis of Paul's thanksgiving is "because of the *grace of God* given you in Christ Jesus" (v. 4). Although this is commonly viewed as a thanksgiving for grace understood as the gracious out-pouring of God's mercy in Christ toward the undeserving, here χάρις probably points to the concrete expressions of God's gracious activity in his people, namely, λόγος (speech) and γνῶσις (knowledge), which in v. 7 are referred to as χαρίσματα.[20] The relationship of these "gifts" to the

---

[15]Grace was given them *in Christ Jesus* (v. 4), *in whom* they were enriched with these gifts (v. 5), just as Paul's own testimony *to Christ* was confirmed among them (v. 6) as they await *the revelation of Jesus Christ* (v. 7). Moreover, the God who will also keep them blameless until *the day of our Lord Jesus Christ* (v. 8) is the same faithful God who has called them into fellowship with his Son, *our Lord Jesus Christ* (v. 9).

[16]This note is struck in two ways: the mention of χάρις in v. 4 as that for which he specifically gives thanks; and the so-called divine passives, which imply God as the subject of all the verbs in the thanksgiving. Thus, God "gave you grace" (v. 4), "enriched you" (v. 5), "confirmed our testimony among you" (v. 6), "will also confirm you blameless at the end" (v. 8), and "called you" (v. 9).

[17]This seems to be the only viable explanation for the awkward intrusion of v. 6 into the sentence. Unlike many interpreters (e.g., O'Brien, *Thanksgivings*, 120) and English translations (NIV, NEB), I take the καθώς in v. 6 to carry its ordinary comparative sense ("just as," "even as"). Paul is thus suggesting that their gifts, for which he is genuinely thankful, are the *evidence* that "our testimony about Christ was confirmed in you." If we take seriously that the implied subject of the passive verb is "God," then the clause says that God himself confirmed Paul's witness to Christ among them by gifting them with Spirit endowments. As throughout the thanksgiving, the emphasis in this clause is on Christ; nonetheless, Paul at the same time alludes to his own ministry among them, since in this community these two stand or fall together.

[18]On this see especially the argument in 13:8–13. With others I see this emphasis as an attempt at the beginning to redirect their "overspiritualized eschatology."

[19]See the discussion in ch. 2 above (pp. 32–35); cf. Dunn, *Jesus*, 205–7.

[20]Cf. Rom 12:6, where believers are given differing χαρίσματα, according to the χάρις given to them.

Spirit, therefore, is not through the word χάρισμα but through the specific connection made by Paul in ch. 12.

2. As to the "gifts" themselves, even though he notes their abundance ("in every way" v. 5; "lacking no χάρισμα" v. 7), Paul specifies only "with all λόγος and all γνῶσις." Ordinarily, these would not be the only—or ordinary—things for which one were to give thanks among a group of new Christians.[21] They are selected here because, as chs. 1–4, 8–10, and 12–14 make clear, they were both noticeably evident in this community and also highly prized among them. Paul's emphasis, of course, differs considerably from theirs. They stressed the gifts per se; he the gracious activity of *God*. Because *God* gives them and because they express *God's* grace, there can be no grounds for boasting on their part. Indeed, he will argue in 8:1–2, without the corresponding fruit of the Spirit, love, which builds up, γνῶσις only puffs up. Paul's dilemma is to convince the Corinthians to share his view about these benefits, since they arrogantly boast over the very things that as gifts may only be gratefully received (cf. 4:7).

A considerable discussion has arisen around the specific "graces" intended by the words λόγος and γνῶσις;[22] but the context of the letter itself supplies all the help one needs. Since both terms occur most often in 1 Corinthians in polemical contexts,[23] they are probably first of all

---

[21]In fact it is often noted that Paul does not in their case mention such qualities as love, faith, or hope (as e.g., in 1 Thessalonians, Philippians, or Colossians). This is true, of course, but it does not necessarily imply that they lack these; after all, in a nearly parallel passage in 2 Cor 8:7, the two items mentioned here are again included, along with faith, earnestness, and love.

[22]Lightfoot 147, followed by O'Brien, *Thanksgivings*, 118, lists four possibilities: (1) that λόγος refers to the lower, γνῶσις to the higher knowledge (which they rightly dismiss as impossible); (2) that λόγος refers to tongues, γνῶσις to prophecy (which is also to be dismissed as too narrow a view); (3) that λόγος refers to the gospel which came to them, and γνῶσις to their hearty acceptance of it (which is discredited by the whole context of 1 Corinthians); and (4) the position they prefer, that λόγος refers to the outward expression, γνῶσις to the inward conviction and apprehension of the gospel. But this latter also seems to ignore the point in the context of 1 Corinthians. Other options have been offered: Zuntz (*Text*, 101), suggests that one refers to "rational" the other to "ecstatic" gifts, which again seems to ignore the actual data of 1 Corinthians. K. Grayston suggests, even less convincingly, that λόγος refers to those who were insisting on following the remembered words of Jesus in a legalistic way (they had traded one form of law for another), while γνῶσις refers to those who had "an awareness of the cosmic relationships between God the Father, the Lord Jesus Christ, and the Christian," so that they were, through Christ, absolved from "the conventional rules" ("Not With a Rod," *ExpT* 88 [1976] 13–16).

[23]Cf. 1:17 "with σοφίᾳ λόγου [wisdom characterized by clever speech, or reason]"; 2:1–5 "with pretensions of λόγος [clever speech?] or wisdom"; 4:17–20, the kingdom of God does not consist of λόγος but of power. So also with γνῶσις, which occurs especially in their argument with Paul in chs. 8–10 as the basis for their actions over against his prohibitions. "We all have γνῶσις," they have argued in their letter, apparently as the predicate for attending idol feasts (see Fee, 357–63).

Corinthian terms, which Paul will play back to them in positive and negative ways.

Thus the term λόγος here probably means something akin to "every kind of utterance," including "Spirit utterances," and would refer especially to the various speech gifts noted in chs. 12–14 (knowledge, wisdom, tongues, prophecy, etc.)—even though as those chapters indicate, the Corinthians' interest in "speech" is more singular. But in chs. 1–4, the term refers in a pejorative sense to what is merely human in contrast to the λόγος of the cross (1:17–18; cf. 2:1–4). Not every form of "word" is necessarily a "gracious endowment"; some speech to which they are attracted is merely human and stands in contrast to truly Spirit-inspired λόγος. So also with γνῶσις. As a χάρισμα in chs. 12–14 it refers to the gift of special knowledge, probably related to prophetic revelation (12:8; 13:2; 14:6). Yet in 8:1–13 it serves as their basis for Christian conduct, and as such comes under severe criticism from Paul. Thus, as with λόγος, not all γνῶσις is truly of the Spirit.

Paul therefore appears to be picking up on two terms in their spiritual vocabulary about which they are perhaps a bit too *self*-confident. In the places where they boast in such things as "utterance" or "knowledge," Paul argues that they are acting in merely *human* ways and are not "in Spirit" at all. Nonetheless, these same items appear as legitimate gifts of the Spirit that belong to the present age (12:8–11; 13:8–12), and set in proper perspective they will edify the church (14:6). Because they are gracious endowments of the Spirit (v. 7), given by God in Christ Jesus, Paul can be genuinely grateful for them.

3. The language "in every way" in v. 5 and "lacking in no χάρισμα" in v. 7[24] presents us with some ambiguities, especially regarding the scene in Corinth. On the one hand, this language suggests an abundant and diverse supply of such gifting. On the other hand, the nature of the argument in chs. 12 and 14 suggests that with regard to "speech" gifting, they were more narrowly focused on the gift of tongues alone.

---

[24]It is not certain what is intended by "you do not lack any χάρισμα." The verb "lack" ordinarily takes a genitive for its object and in that case would mean that they potentially have at their disposal all the gifts of God. But here the verb is modified by a prepositional phrase ("in no χάρισμα") and therefore could mean that they do not come short, either in comparison with others or in normal expectations of Christians who have the Spirit, in any of the gifts that they do possess. Most likely the syntax is influenced by v. 5 ("enriched in every way") and merely repeats negatively what was already affirmed positively in v. 5. They have been enriched in every way, so that none of the gracious endowments of the Spirit is lacking in their midst. This also means that the word χάρισμα, which could be seen to refer more broadly to the gracious gift of redemption (as some do; e.g., Calvin 22; O'Brien, *Thanksgivings*, 124), is to be understood as in v. 5 to refer more specifically to those special endowments of the Holy Spirit mentioned in chs. 12–14 (cf. Rom 12:6).

The resolution to this matter probably lies with the twofold reality that the Spirit did richly and diversely manifest himself in their midst, but that the Corinthians took special interest in the one form of "speech" that was for them evidence of their having attained heavenly status (see on 13:1), which also was evidenced by their special gifting in "wisdom" and "insight" (knowledge).

4. Finally, by adding the eschatological note at the end of the sentence (vv. 7–8), Paul also apparently attempts to set their present giftedness into the proper eschatological perspective of "already/not yet."[25] Thanksgiving for present gifts simply is not the final—nor the only—word. Gifts are ever to be realized in the context of "eagerly awaiting the revelation of our Lord Jesus Christ."[26]

Even though Paul's theological perspective is thoroughly eschatological, a comparison of this thanksgiving with that in 1 Thes 1:2–5 indicates that an eschatological note is not a necessary element in his thanksgivings (in fact it occurs only in Philippians and Colossians in the later letters).[27] Why, then, this additional note about the coming of Christ? It may of course mean nothing more than that this concern is ever present with the apostle, since salvation for Paul was primarily an eschatological reality, begun with Christ's coming, to be consummated by his soon return. But it is also probable in this instance that that ever present concern is heightened by the Corinthians' own apparently overrealized eschatological understanding of their existence, which for them was related in particular to their experience of the "spiritual gift" of tongues (see on 13:1). Paul's gratitude for their giftedness, therefore, includes a reminder that they still *await* the final glory, since it seems to be the case that some among them do not actually have such eager expectation (see on 4:8 and 15:12).

Nonetheless, even though Paul is concerned to remind the church that they have not yet arrived, at the same time in v. 8 he reassures them that by God's own action they will indeed make it in the end. Consequently, by means of thanksgiving, Paul redirects their confidence from themselves and their own giftedness towards God, from whom and unto whom are all things.

---

[25]For this essential framework to Paul's theology, see the Introduction to Fee 16–17.

[26]Indeed, there is perhaps a correlation in the contemporary church between its general loss of such "graces" and its lack of eager expectation of the final consummation.

[27]Thus O'Brien, *Thanksgivings*, 124, does not seem quite precise to speak of "the customary eschatological climax of the introductory thanksgivings." This perspective is the result of analyzing the thanksgiving periods *formally* without giving chronology its due. An "eschatological climax" is missing in 1 Thessalonians, Romans, and Philemon.

Therefore, even though the Spirit is not mentioned specifically in this opening thanksgiving, the language reflects the actual situation in Corinth and anticipates not only some abuses in the community but also the discussion of Spirit phenomena which concludes the letter.[28]

1 CORINTHIANS 2:4–5

[4]*My message and my preaching were not with the persuasion of wisdom,*[29] *but with a demonstration of the Spirit's power,*[30] [5]*so that your faith might not rest on human wisdom, but on God's power.*

This first mention of the Spirit in the letter comes at the conclusion of an argument with the Corinthians (from 1:17) in which he has brought his full arsenal to bear on the problem of their present fascination with "wisdom." It is thus full of irony, inasmuch as both wisdom and Spirit are Corinthian claims, almost certainly to be understood in conjunction with one another; i.e., the gift of Spirit is in their view the source of their "wisdom." But Paul has another view of wisdom and Spirit, and both are integral to the message of the gospel,

---

[28]This assumes, e.g., with Martin (*Spirit*), that the issue in ch. 15 forms an integral part of the argument of chs. 12–14, having served for them as a kind of theological basis for their perception of Spirit phenomena.

[29]Later MSS, on the analogy of v. 13, add ἀνθρωπίνης (human), which is patently secondary. But after that, there is considerable difficulty in deciding the original text. The text of (ℵ*) B D 33 181 1175 1506 1739 1881 pc reads πειθοῖς σοφίας λόγοις (cf. NA[26], Lietzmann, Barrett, Conzelmann; NIV, "wise and persuasive words"). The difficulty with this reading is the word πειθοῖς, apparently the dative of πειθός, a term that is otherwise unknown in all of Greek literature (see the discussion of πειθός and πειθώ in BAGD). Paul, or course, is capable of creating such a word, and the early Greek Fathers do not have any difficulties with it. The problem, however, is complicated by the reading of P[46] F G, πειθοῖς σοφίας. Zuntz (*Text*, 23–24) has (cogently) argued that this reading alone explains how the various corruptions arose. The σ at the end of πειθοῖς is a simple corruption of doubling the initial σ of σοφίας. The λόγοις was then added, also on the analogy of v. 13, to make sense of what had now become an adjective. With some reluctance this is the position adopted here, for two reasons: (1) this reading is unquestionably the *lectio difficilior* and more easily explains how the others came about than vice versa. It is extremely difficult to account for the "omission" of λόγοις on any grounds; and in this case it would need to have happened twice, once each in the ancestors of P[46] and F G; (2) the absence of the word πειθός in the entire Greek rhetorical tradition is difficult to explain had there ever been such a word; whereas the regular adjective, πιθάνος is common. On the other hand, the noun πειθώ is plentiful in this tradition. Given that Paul is here reflecting so much of the language of this tradition, a Pauline creation seems less likely than a scribal corruption. Thus the translation offered here.

[30]The Greek literally reads "the Spirit and power." For this translation see the discussion below.

with its central focus on God's foolishness and weakness manifest in the crucified One.

Paul has argued (1:18–2:5) that the message of the cross which brought them to faith and the Corinthians' very existence as believers contradict their present stance. This paragraph serves as a final illustration to demonstrate the point of 1:18–25,[31] this time in terms of Paul's effective ministry among them despite his weaknesses and failure to rely on the kind of speech (λόγος) that they are enamored with. Thus, not only the *means* (the cross; 1:18–25) and the *people* (the church in Corinth; 1:26–31), but also the *preacher* (Paul; 2:1–5) declare that God is in the process of overturning the world's systems.[32] At the same time, however, the entire paragraph exhibits a strong apologetic overtone, and this is where the Spirit language emerges. Despite Paul's weaknesses which they seem to deplore, his own ministry as truly of the Spirit has been justified before them by its results.

The paragraph has two parts (vv. 1–2, 3–5).[33] The first two verses, which pick up the language of 1:17 and 23, remind the Corinthians of the *content* of Paul's preaching and emphasize that he intentionally preached a crucified Messiah, God's weakness. Verses 3–4 then remind them of the *form* of his preaching, which bears the same character as the message itself—"weakness." Nonetheless, as in 1:22–25, in this "weakness" the power of God is at work, now expressed in terms of the Spirit. A final purpose clause in v. 5 gives the reason for all this, that their faith might be of God and in God alone and not in human wisdom (cf. 1:31).

But Paul does not glory in his weaknesses for their own sake or simply to contrast himself to the sophists. Rather it is to remind the Corinthians, as they should well remember, that the real power lies not in λόγος and σοφία, but in the work of the Spirit, evidenced by their own existence. Although his preaching lacked—indeed he deliberately avoided the very thing that now fascinates them—"the persuasion of wisdom," it did not thereby lack "persuasion." After all, they themselves came to faith through it. What it lacked was the kind of persuasion they *now* delight in, where the power lay in the person and his delivery. Paul's

---

[31]The paragraph is replete with themes from 1:17–25: v. 1, "not in word or wisdom" (cf. 1:17); v. 2, "Jesus Christ and him crucified" (1:23); v. 3, I came "in weakness" (1:25); v. 4, my preaching was not in "persuasion of wisdom" (1:17), but in "demonstration of power" (1:23–5); v. 5, that your faith might not rest "on [human] wisdom, but on God's power" (1:25).

[32]Cf. Conzelmann 53: "Just as the attitude of the community must accord with the word of the cross, so also must the form of the preaching and the bearing of the preacher." Conzelmann makes more sense of the argument as a whole than do those who see this paragraph as somewhat independent from 1:18–31 (e.g., Barrett, Mare, Murphy-O'Connor). Cf. the discussion in L. Hartmann, "Some Remarks on 1 Cor. 2:1–5," *SEÅ* 34 (1974) 109–20.

[33]Both begin with the somewhat unusual (for Paul) κἀγώ, "and I."

preaching had no such power; rather, it had the real thing, the power of the Spirit, at work despite (through?) Paul's weaknesses, and producing the desired results, their faith in the living God. In keeping with the message itself (cf. 1:23–25), his preaching exhibited "the weakness of God" that is stronger than human strength (1:25).

Thus, Paul describes his preaching in rhetorical terms, as accompanied by "a demonstration[34] of the Spirit's power." What is less certain is what specifically he intends by this description. The Greek literally reads, "of the Spirit and power,"[35] which some see as referring to two realities, "spiritual gifts and miracles."[36] But for Paul the terms "Spirit" and "power" are at times nearly interchangeable;[37] to speak of the Spirit is also to speak of power. The combination here, therefore, is close to a hendiadys (the use of two words to express the same reality: "the Spirit, that is, Power"), hence "the Spirit's power" (cf. NIV).

But to what powerful demonstration of the Spirit does this refer? The answer is not at all certain; in this case it is complicated by the argument in context, on the one hand, and the related passages in 1 Thes 1:5 and Rom 15:18–19, on the other. It is possible, for example, and is often argued for or simply assumed, that in keeping with Rom 15:19 this refers to the "signs and wonders" of 2 Cor 12:12. But that would seem to play directly into the Corinthians' hands, to build up the very issue he is trying to demolish (cf. 2 Cor 12:1–10). More likely, therefore, especially in the context of personal "weakness" and in keeping with 1 Thes 1:5–6, it refers to their actual conversion, with its coincident gift of the Spirit, probably evidenced by Spirit manifestations, especially tongues. The evidence lies not in external "proofs" which Paul will muster against mere wisdom and rhetoric. Rather the evidence lies with the Corinthians themselves and their own experience of the Spirit as they responded to the message of the gospel.[38]

---

[34]Gk. ἀποδείξει (a NT hapax legomenon), a word suggesting more than simply "manifestation," but something akin to "evidence" or "proof." In Greek rhetoric it was a technical term for a compelling conclusion drawn from the premises. Cf. Quintilian 5.10.7 ("an ἀπόδειξις is clear proof" [Loeb, 2.205]) and Cicero, *Acad.* 2:8 ("Therefore this is the definition of logical proof, in Greek ἀπόδειξις: 'a process of reasoning that leads from things perceived to something not previously perceived' " [Loeb, 19.501]). Paul thus turns the word on its head, arguing that the "proof" lies not in compelling rhetoric, but in the accompanying *visible* ἀπόδειξις of the Spirit's power. Cf. Hartmann, "Remarks," 116–117; Dunn, *Jesus,* 226–27.

[35]The genitives are at least objective (= evidence that the Spirit is present in power); Barrett 65 suggests that they are subjective as well (= the manifested Spirit and power bring proof and conviction), although this seems less likely.

[36]Recently, Ellis, *Prophecy,* 64–65.

[37]See below on 5:4; cf. inter alia the discussion of 1 Thes 1:5; 2 Thes 1:11; Rom 15:13, 19 and *supra,* pp. 35–36.

[38]Cf. W. C. Robinson, Jr., "Word and Power," in *Soli Deo Gloria: Essays for W. C. Robinson* (ed. J. M. Richards; Richmond, 1968) 68–82. However, Robinson is too intent on emphasizing their conversion to the exclusion of their own experience of the gifts

Hence the power of Paul's "nonrhetoric": He is almost certainly turning the tables on them. They are moving toward a form of triumphalism, with great emphasis on the Spirit and power and a concomitant rejection of all forms of present weakness, and are thus opposed to Paul. He, too, is for Spirit and power, but as that which evidences itself through weakness, as God did in the cross—and in Paul's preaching which brought them to faith and the experience of the Spirit!

This is probably the crucial point of difference between Paul and the "arrogant" who have opposed him (4:18). For them "Spirit" meant the gift of tongues; it meant to have arrived in the "excellence of wisdom" (v. 1; cf. 4:8, 10), to have entered into a new existence that raised them above merely earthly existence, quite unrelated to genuine ethical behavior. For Paul, on the other hand, "Spirit" *included* inspired utterances—as long as they edified—but for him the emphasis lay on the Spirit's *power*, power to transform lives (as here), to reveal God's secret wisdom (2:6–16), to minister in weakness (4:9–13), and to effect holiness in the believing community (5:3–5). In other words, the purpose of the Spirit's coming was not to transport one above the present age, but to empower one to live within it.

Therefore, with the concluding purpose clause of v. 5 the argument that began in 1:18 comes full circle. The message of the cross, which is folly to the "wise," is the saving power of God to the believing. The goal of all the divine activity, both in the cross and in choosing them, and now in Paul's preaching which brought the cross and them together, has been to disarm the wise and powerful so that those who believe must trust God alone and completely. Thus v. 5 concludes the paragraph: "so that your faith might not rest on human wisdom, but on God's power." In another context this might suggest that faith rests on evidences; but that would scarcely apply here. The power of God throughout this passage has the cross as its paradigm. The true alternative to wisdom humanly conceived is not "signs," but the gospel, which the Spirit brings to bear on people's lives in powerful ways.

1 CORINTHIANS 2:6–3:2

6We do, however, speak wisdom among "grown-ups,"[39] *but not the wisdom of this age or of the rulers of this age, who are being brought to nothing. 7Rather we speak God's formerly hidden wisdom, kept in secret, which God destined for our glory before the ages, 8which none of the rulers of this age understood;*

---

of the Spirit. That concern probably reflects a later time in the church where the coming of the Spirit is less visibly manifested than seems to have been the case in the NT. It is hard to imagine the Corinthians' being able to make the distinction. For them to hear the words "the Spirit and power" would automatically have recalled the visible evidences of the Spirit's presence.

[39]For this translation, as a play on terms with "infants" in 3:1, see Fee, 102–3.

for if they had understood, they would not have crucified the Lord of glory, [9]*but just as it is written:*

> *"What things no eye has seen,*
> *and no ear has heard,*
> *and no mind has conceived,*
> *what God has prepared for those who love him";*

[10]*for*[40] *to us God has revealed it by the*[41] *Spirit. For the Spirit searches all things, even the depths of God.* [11]*For who among humans knows a person's thoughts except the spirit*[42] *of the person that resides within? In the same way also no one knows the thoughts of God except the Spirit of God.* [12]*Now the Spirit we received was not of the world but the Spirit who is from God, so that we may understand the things that God has freely given us.* [13]*What things also we speak are not with words taught us by human wisdom but with words taught by the Spirit,*[43] *explaining the things of the Spirit by the Spirit's means.* [14]*But the ordinary human does not receive the things that come from the Spirit of God,*[44] *but considers them foolishness and cannot understand them, because they are discerned*[45] *by means of the Spirit.* [15]*But Spirit people discern all things,*[46] *but are not themselves subject to anybody else's discernment:*

---

[40]Contrary to the NA²⁶–UBS⁴ (δέ, following ℵ A C D F G Maj latt sy; cf. NIV), the γάρ of P⁴⁶ B 6 88 181 326 365 1739 1877 2127 2492 m sa bo^mss Clement is to be preferred on all counts. Not only (1) does it have the better external attestation, but (2) it is easily the *lectio difficilior* (a copyist would scarcely have deliberately created a text with three γάρ's in a row, whereas the substitution of a δέ for a γάρ would have been natural and could have been deliberate or accidental); (3) it fits Pauline style (cf. esp. Rom 15:3–4); and (4) it makes better sense of the argument (see below). See G. D. Fee, "Textual-Exegetical Observations on 1 Corinthians 1:2, 2:1, and 2:10," in *Scribes and Scripture: New Testament Essays in Honor of J. Harold Greenlee* (ed. D. A. Black; Winona Lake: Eisenbrauns, 1992) 1–15.

[41]The text without αὐτοῦ is supported by P⁴⁶ ℵ* A B C 630 1739 1881 pc cop. The "his" of the MajT, incl. D F G latt, is undoubtedly what the definite article intends in this case (hence the translation in the NIV).

[42]A few Western MSS (F G a b Pel) omit the words τοῦ ἀνθρώπου, resulting in a text that translates, "except the spirit (Spirit?) that resides within."

[43]The MajT, with no early Greek or versional support, adds "Holy" to "Spirit."

[44]On the basis of the citations from several Fathers, Zuntz (*Text*, 221–23) argues that τοῦ θεοῦ is an interpolation (cf. the {C} rating in the UBS³). Unlike its predecessor, UBS⁴ does not even acknowledge a variant reading exists. This illustrates a highly questionable use of patristic evidence to support a "shorter text" (cf. G. D. Fee, "The Text of John in *The Jerusalem Bible*: A Critique of the Use of Patristic Citations in New Testament Textual Criticism," *JBL* 90 [1971] 170–72). Not one of the patristic citations is more than probable; none is certain. Internal considerations support the full description, which is carefully balanced with what is said about the believer in v. 12.

[45]Gk. ἀνακρίνεται; on the difficulty of rendering this verb in its three occurrences in this passage, see below on v. 14.

[46]The majority of MSS replace the τά of τὰ πάντα with a μέν, thus conforming the τὰ πάντα to v. 10 and placing the emphasis on the second clause. See the discussion in Metzger, *Textual Commentary*, 547, and Zuntz, *Text*, 109–10 and 198.

> [16]"For who has known the mind of the Lord;
>   who shall instruct him?"

But we have the mind of Christ.[47] [3:1]And I, brothers and sisters, was not able to speak to you as to Spirit people, but as to those still in the flesh, as to mere infants in Christ. [2]I gave you milk, not solid food; for you were not able to take the latter. Indeed, not yet even now are you able.

This passage is at once one of the most significant and most abused of the Spirit passages in the Pauline corpus. Its significance will be noted as we proceed; the abuse is basically the result of not recognizing—or not caring—how it fits into Paul's argument. Thus, even though Spirit language does not appear until v. 10, the whole passage needs careful contextual analysis before looking at the Spirit material in detail.

The problem that Paul addresses in 1:10–4:21 is several-fold. Its most obvious dimension is some internal strife and division that is taking place in the name of their former (itinerant) teachers. But it is clear from Paul's argument that this is only symptomatic of two deeper issues: some of the division seems to be the direct result of an anti-Pauline sentiment that has arisen among them (hence the reason for the concluding argument in ch. 4); and all of this is being carried on in the name of σοφία (wisdom), which in this case seems to carry its semi-technical philosophical sense. The net result, and for Paul the more serious issue, is a desperately flawed understanding of the gospel and, with that, of the church and ministry. In effect, their present fascination with wisdom and rhetoric, with their concurrent rejection of Paul's apostleship, has issued in a rejection of the message of the cross (milk?) for something more akin to the Greek wisdom tradition (solid food?).

To this point, in a series of three paragraphs, Paul has shown how their existence as believers radically contradicts their present stance regarding "wisdom." The message of the cross which brought them to faith, although the ultimate expression of God's power and wisdom, is sheer madness from the point of view of "wisdom" (1:18–25); moreover, their own existence—the fact that God chose *them* for salvation, not the world's "beautiful people"—stands in contradiction to "wisdom" (1:26–31), as does Paul's preaching, discussed above, which brought them to faith (2:1–5).

Therefore, till now Paul has been rather hard on "wisdom"—because he is arguing against a Corinthian attitude toward it that has undermined his authority and questioned the nature of the gospel. But not all is pejorative. He also asserted that God acted by means of his own wisdom (1:21) and that he made Christ to become "wisdom" for us; but in so doing

---

[47]A few MSS (B D* F G 81 it) replace χριστοῦ with κυρίου, thus assimilating Paul to the citation of Isa 40:13.

Paul transformed "wisdom" from a philosophical, rhetorical term, into a historical, soteriological one (1:24, 30). Taking up the language of v. 4 ("not in the persuasion of wisdom, but with a demonstration of the Spirit's power"), he now makes a turn in the argument in order to reassert that the gospel he preaches is actually the wisdom of God. And this is where the crucial Spirit material surfaces. The gospel can never be perceived as divine wisdom by those who are pursuing σοφία; it is recognized as such only by those who have the Spirit, since it comes only by the Spirit's revelation.

As with much of 1:18–2:5 the argument of the paragraph is full of bite. The Corinthians, enamored by wisdom and thinking of themselves as πνευματικοί (spiritual = Spirit people) are less than enchanted by Paul's message, which they apparently regard as mere "milk." With fine irony Paul demolishes their misperceptions and false boastings. The gospel of the crucified Messiah is wisdom all right, he affirms, but not of the kind they are now pursuing. True wisdom is indeed for the πνευματικοί, to whom the Spirit has revealed what God has really accomplished in Christ. Because they do have the Spirit, and thus the mind of Christ, they should have seen the cross for what it is—God's wisdom— and thereby have been able to make true judgments. By pursuing σοφία they are acting just like those without the Spirit, who are likewise pursuing wisdom but see the cross as foolishness. The net result—and the irony—is that they are "spiritual," yet "unspiritual"; they are pursuing "wisdom," yet missing the very wisdom of God.

The argument, which is in four parts, can easily be traced:

(1) Vv. 6–10a set forth the nature of God's wisdom in terms of the basic contrast between those for whom it was destined and those who cannot perceive it. God's wisdom, predestined by him to bring *us* to glory, was therefore held "in mystery," hidden from the present age and its leaders. (2) Vv. 10b–13 explain how we are let in on the secret, and why the others are left out. We have received the Spirit, who knows the mind of God and has revealed to us what God is up to. (3) Vv. 14–16 conclude by reaffirming all this in terms of "natural" and "spiritual" people. The people of this age, who are pursuing mere "wisdom" and so consider the cross "foolishness," do not have the Spirit; therefore, they cannot understand true wisdom (v. 14) or make valid judgments (v. 15), an activity that is properly available only to those who have the Spirit. The paragraph concludes with a citation from Isa 40:13, which offers biblical support for peoples' inability to comprehend, a situation that is now reversed for those who have the Spirit and therefore the "mind of Christ." (4) 3:1–4 then apply all of this to their present situation, with devastating irony. Even though they are Spirit people, he could not address them as such because both their thinking and behavior are contrary to the Spirit. But neither can he refer to them as merely "natural," since they do have the Spirit; so the contrast is changed to Spirit and flesh. His ultimate

point, of course, is "Stop it"; but he makes that point in grand fashion. Their behavior is the giveaway, the sure evidence, that even though they do have the Spirit, they are acting like "mere human beings"!

Unfortunately, despite what appears to be a simple—and explicable—turn in the argument, this paragraph has suffered much in the church, both at the hands of scholars and in popular preaching and Bible reading. The reasons for this have to do partly with the *language* (e.g., wisdom, mystery, hidden, rulers of this age, deep things of God, spiritual/natural people, the mind of Christ) and partly with the several *contrasts* set up. As a result the paragraph has been variously viewed as an example of Paul's playing the Corinthians' game after all—that he really does argue that there is a "deeper wisdom" for those who are truly spiritual, and thereby establishes two classes within the church, one "spiritual" and "mature," the other "natural" (or "worldly") and "immature" (or "babes").[48] But such a view runs counter not only to the argument as a whole (not to mention this paragraph), but to the whole of Pauline theology. Indeed, such an argument would effectively destroy the very point of everything said in 1:18–2:5.[49] Paul is not here rebuilding what he has just torn down. He is retooling their understanding of the

---

[48]This has taken several forms. Traditionally (e.g., Goudge 16), Paul is seen to be arguing that despite what he has said in 2:1–5, he nevertheless does have "deep truth to reveal," which "requires a developed spiritual character for its appreciation." Those continuing to take some form of this approach see Paul as addressing a special group ("the mature" or "the spiritual"), the differences having to do with how the special group is perceived. See, e.g., Conzelmann 57: "The section is dominated by a pneumatic enthusiasm, a distinction between two classes. The pneumatics here do not comprise all Christians, but only a superior class"; cf. R. Bultmann, *Faith and Understanding* (ET: New York: Harper, 1969) 70–72, and U. Wilckens, *Weisheit und Torheit* (Tübingen: Mohr, 1959) 52–96. R. Scroggs argues convincingly against Wilckens's basic position (that Paul is here adopting the position of his Gnostic opponents and thus betrays his own theology), but continues to promote the idea that Paul "must have had an esoteric wisdom teaching entirely separate from his kerygma" ("Paul: ΣΟΦΟΣ and ΠΝΕΥΜΑΤΙΚΟΣ," *NTS* 14 [1967–68] 35). Ellis (*Prophecy*, 25–26), on the other hand, sees Paul as addressing only the πνευματικοί, who are defined as those who with Paul possess spiritual gifts. The position argued for here essentially agrees with R. W. Funk ("Word and Word in 1 Corinthians 2:6–16," in *Language, Hermeneutic, and Word of God* [New York: Harper, 1966] 275–305); cf. B. E. Gärtner, "The Pauline and Johannine Idea of 'To Know God' Against the Hellenistic Background," *NTS* 14 (1967–68) 215–21; and J. Francis, " 'As Babes in Christ'—Some Proposals regarding 1 Corinthians 3.1–3," *JSNT* 7 (1980) 41–60.

[49]This is admitted by both Wilckens and Conzelmann (see previous n.), both of whom see Paul as using the ideas and language of his opponents or of a prior "schema," which he fails adequately to integrate, thus creating tension or paradox. The logic of this position is finally taken by M. Widmann ("1 Kor 2:6–16: Ein Einspruch gegen Paulus," *ZNW* 70 [1979] 44–53), who argues that the passage is a gloss introduced by Paul's Corinthian opponents as a reply to Paul. See the response by Murphy-O'Connor, "Interpolations in 1 Corinthians," *CBQ* 48 (1986) 81–84.

Spirit and Spirit-uality, in order that they might perceive the truth of what he has been arguing to this point.

While it is true that much of the *language* of this paragraph is not common to Paul, the explanation of this phenomenon is, as before, to be found in his using *their* language but filling it with his own content and thus refuting them.[50] The theology, however, is his own, and it differs radically from theirs. For Paul—as for them—the Spirit is the key to everything. For him the Spirit is an eschatological reality, marking the turning of the ages. This becomes crucial for understanding the several *contrasts* in the passage. On the one hand, those who are still of *this* age, who have not received the Spirit, do not understand the wisdom of God in Christ crucified. But their wisdom is under divine judgment and already on its way out. Those who have the Spirit, on the other hand, have "the mind of Christ" and thus understand God's activity, revealed to them by the Spirit. This is why Paul comes down so hard on his Corinthian friends. They do have the Spirit; they are part of the coming age that God is now ushering in. But their present conduct and stance toward wisdom are precisely those of this age/world, which is passing away. Paul's contrast, therefore, is between Christian and nonChristian, between those who have and those who do not have the Spirit. His concern throughout is to get the Corinthians to understand who they are—in terms of the cross—and to stop acting as non-Spirit people. At the same time, as with 2:1–5, there is an unmistakable note of personal apologetic lying just below the surface, if not in fact right out in the open.

The net result for our present purposes is a considerable amount of instruction, both intentional and incidental, about the Spirit and Christian faith. The Spirit, who is above all "the Spirit of God," is also therefore "from God." Through the analogy of the human spirit, the Spirit is understood as the interior expression of God's own being; yet the Spirit is clearly distinct from the Father. In terms of his relationship to us, the Spirit is first of all the *revealer* (vv. 10–11), the one who, to use John's language, "takes the things of Christ and makes them known to us." He is therefore also the *instructor* in the ways of God and Christ (vv. 12–13). At the same time the Spirit is also the crucial—and only—differentiator between those who are Christ's and those who are not (vv. 14–16), and therefore, as in 1 Thessalonians, he is the source and power of distinctively Christian living (implied, 3:1–4). All of this is best understood by a careful analysis of the passage, verse by verse, with an eye to the Spirit material in particular.

---

[50]Cf. Funk, "Word," 300n107: "Paul has simply turned their language, and thus their expectations, inside out in the interest of bringing them face to face with the word of the cross." One must exercise due caution here—not every new term must come from them loaded with foreign nuances—but in the present case this seems to make the most sense of the data.

10a Although the main point of this sentence is clear enough, its relationship to what has preceded, especially to v. 9, is less so. On the analogy of Rom 15:3–4, the citation in v. 9 is best understood as the conclusion to vv. 6–8 and as a transition to the rest of the argument. Thus it first offers scriptural support for vv. 6–8: what God was doing in Christ simply could not be conceived by merely human minds. But the final line, "what God has prepared for those who love him," prepares the way for the main concern of the entire passage, namely, that God's wisdom can be known only by God's people because they alone have the Spirit. Thus, the explanatory "for" picks up line 4 in the citation. The others could not understand the things that "God has prepared *for those who love him*, for *to us* God has revealed[51] (them)[52] by the Spirit." The contrast, therefore, despite the emphatic position of "to us,"[53] lies not so much between "us" and "them" as between the *reason* they could not, but we can, understand the things that God has prepared for his people. That is, as vv. 10b–13 make clear, the emphasis lies on the *means* of revelation, the Spirit, not on the recipients themselves, although the latter of course are always in view and will be picked up again in vv. 14–16. Thus this sentence asserts the revelatory role played by the Spirit; what follows will explain the assertion.

10b–11 With a second explanatory "for," Paul proceeds to explain how the formerly hidden wisdom of God (the gospel of a crucified Messiah) has been revealed to us by the Spirit. The basis of the argument will be the Greek philosophic principle of "like is known only by like,"[54] that is, humans do not on their own possess the quality that would make it possible to know God or God's wisdom. Only "like is known by like"; only God can know God. Therefore, the Spirit of God becomes the link between God and humanity, the "quality" from God himself who makes the knowing possible. This is a felicitous bit of reasoning, for two reasons: (1) This is what Paul really believes about human ability to know the

---

[51]Gk. ἀπεκάλυψεν, the verb that became the technical one for the "divine revelation of certain supernatural secrets" (BAGD); see, e.g., Ps 98:2 (LXX 97:2). This becomes a particularly developed idea in Jewish and Christian "apocalyptic," e.g., Dan 2:22 (cf. vv. 19 and 28 Theod.). For Paul this is the ordinary verb for supernatural revelation of any kind.

[52]There is no object to the verb ἀπεκάλυψεν in Paul's sentence. Probably, as Godet 147 observes, that is because the emphasis lies on the *fact* of revelation here, not on what is revealed. The context makes it certain that something very much like "his wisdom" is what is in view.

[53]The emphatic position of ἡμῖν is not so much to contrast "us" with those who cannot perceive God's ways, but to place "us" in immediate juxtaposition with "those who love him." Thus: "For to us, namely those who love him, God has revealed what is otherwise hidden."

[54]On this question see esp. Gärtner, "Idea" (see n. 48).

ways of God that are otherwise "past finding out"; the natural person on his or her own cannot know God by reason or intuition, as Paul affirms in v. 14. (2) This is the linkage he needs in his argument with the Corinthians. Their experience of the Spirit, accompanied by ecstasy, had led them to a triumphalist, over-realized, and anti-physical spirituality. In contrast Paul is about to present the Spirit as the key to *the proper understanding of the gospel itself*, both his preaching of it (v. 13) and their experience of it as grace (v. 12); in this context, as always, the gospel is God's salvation through the crucified One.

The Spirit is thus first of all linked with God: "The Spirit searches all things, even the depths of God." The language "depths of God" is part of the reason for an "elitist" interpretation of this passage. But that is to miss both the argument and Pauline theology. Elsewhere Paul speaks of the "depth of the riches of the wisdom and knowledge of God" (Rom 11:33), reflecting his sense of the profound greatness of God, which is part of his Jewish heritage, both OT and apocalyptic.[55] The idea of the Spirit's "searching" all things, including the depths of God, is thus best understood in light of Paul's own explanation by way of analogy in v. 11.[56] The "depths of God," therefore, have to do not with "deeper truths" available only to "insiders," but with the formerly hidden wisdom of God now revealed as such through the Spirit—salvation through a crucified Messiah.

Perhaps this sentence, too, contains a tinge of irony. They considered Paul's preaching as "milk"; to the contrary, he implies, redemption through the cross comes from the profound depths of God's own wisdom, which his Spirit, given to those who love him, has searched out and revealed to us.

In v. 11, with yet another explanatory "for,"[57] Paul offers the supporting analogy for the fact that the Spirit knows the things of God and makes the further point that he *alone* knows them. Here in particular the principle of "like is known by like" is spelled out in detail, in this case of course influenced by the OT motif that no one has ever seen God. The analogy itself is a simple one, and insists that just as the only person who knows what goes on inside one's own mind is oneself, so only God knows

---

[55]See, e.g., a passage like Dan 2:20–23. Although there is no mention of the Spirit as the agent of revelation, the linguistic parallels with v. 22 ("God reveals deep and hidden things") are of such nature that one scarcely needs to search Greek or Gnostic sources for this terminology.

[56]What lies behind such an idea can be illustrated from Rom 8:27, where God is called the One who searches people's hearts (an epithet with deep OT roots: e.g., 1 Sam 16:7; Ps 139:1, 2, 23). In this passage the fact that God searches the hearts of others functions as the presupposition that he must a fortiori also know the unspoken desires of his own Spirit. On this see Cranfield, *Romans*, 1.424.

[57]Gk. γάρ. This piling up of γάρ's is a typical feature of Pauline style. Cf. 1:17, 18, 19, 21; 3:3, 4; 9:15, 16, 17; and many others.

the things of God.[58] Paul makes that point by use of the language πνεῦμα, because first of all he is talking about the Holy Spirit, and secondly because it is for him a common word for the interior expression of the human person.[59]

In fairness to Paul's own argument, of course, his concern is with neither anthropology nor pneumatology as such. It is analogy, pure and simple, having to do not with the constituents of personality, but with our common experience of personal reality. At the human level, I alone know what I am thinking, and no one else, unless I choose to reveal it in the form of words. So also only God knows what God is about. His Spirit, therefore, who knows his mind, becomes the link to our knowing him also, because as v. 12 goes on to affirm: "we have received the Spirit *of God.*"

The net result, however, is that we do learn much about Paul's understanding of the Spirit. Here is the certain evidence that the Spirit is at once both fully God, as a constituent part of the divine reality, and distinct from the Father. On the one hand, the closest kind of intimate, interior relationship exists between the Father and the Spirit, so close that the only proper analogy for it is that of the human spirit, as the interior expression of personality. As with Christ in the creed, the Spirit is God very God. To put that in experiential terms, in our reception of the Spirit, we are on intimate terms with none other than God himself, personally and powerfully present, as the one who in this case reveals God's ways to us. But at the same time the Spirit is not identical with the Father. The Spirit, as a distinct personality, alone knows—and reveals to us—God's thoughts, God's ways. In the same way Paul will assert in Rom 8:27 that the Father has the same intimate knowledge of the Spirit. Distinct, they nonetheless function as one. To be sure, one must be careful not to read too much later Christian theology back into Paul's language here. Nonetheless, passages like this one, and 12:4–6, serve as the "stuff" out of which the later full Trinitarian formulations are legitimately mined.[60]

12 With this sentence and the next we come to the central issue in the paragraph.[61] The argument began with the assertion that Paul does

---

[58]The one difference in the two parts of the sentence is with the verb "to know" (οἶδεν/ἔγνωκεν). The older commentators suggested that the differences have to do with the capacity for "knowing" itself (e.g., Lightfoot 179, Robertson-Plummer 44); more likely ἔγνωκεν is chosen in the second instance because it constitutes a truer perfect and suggests the sense of "no one has ever known" (cf. Barrett 74).

[59]Despite Jewett's arguments to the contrary (see the discussion of 1 Thes 5:23, esp. n. 104). The phrase "the person's spirit within him," it should be noted, is almost identical to the LXX of Zech 12:1: πνεῦμα ἀνθρώπου ἐν αὐτῷ.

[60]On this question see D. W. Martin, " 'Spirit' in the Second Chapter of First Corinthians," *CBQ* 5 (1943) 181–95.

[61]The δέ that joins the sentence to what precedes is "consecutive" or "re-

indeed speak wisdom among the "grown-ups" of God's people. That
wisdom, which is not esoteric knowledge of deeper truths about God but
simply his own plan for saving his people, is contrasted to that of the
leaders of the present age, who cannot know God's wisdom because it is
his "secret, hidden" wisdom, destined for, and finally revealed to, those
who love him. That revelation has been given by the Spirit, who alone
knows the inner secrets of God, and whom, as this verse now affirms,
"we[62] have received." Since "like is known by like," the Spirit of God
becomes the link on the human side for our knowing the ways of God.

As in vv. 6–9 Paul makes that point by way of antithesis to those of
the present age.[63] He thus reminds the Corinthians that they belong to
a different world order, a different age, and therefore must not do as they
are now doing—pursue or think in terms of merely human σοφία. In
receiving the Spirit,[64] it was not "the spirit of the world" that "we have
received." By this Paul is not suggesting that there is a "spirit" of the
world comparable to the Holy Spirit; neither is he referring to demonic
"spirits."[65] He is rather saying something about the Holy Spirit. The
Spirit whom we have received is not "of this world"; he neither comes
from this world nor belongs to this world. Rather he is "the Spirit who

---

sumptive." Thus our translation "now," resuming the point of v. 10a, after the mild
digression of vv. 10b–11.

[62]As throughout the passage, the interpretation of the "we" is crucial to one's
understanding of the sense of the whole. Those who see this as polemical (in the sense
of the Corinthians vis-à-vis Paul) suggest that he is here arguing with them that he,
too, has the Spirit and not they alone (e.g., Conzelmann 66–67). But it is Paul's regular
habit to revert to "us" when his argument moves toward soteriological realities he
shares with his readers (see, e.g., 1 Thes 1:9–10; 4:13–18; 5:5[!]; Gal 3:13; 4:5–6; Rom
8:4; and throughout his letters). Thus his first point of reference is always the
Corinthians; but since he has a share in these same divine realities ("what God has
freely given us" echoes "our glory" in v. 7 and "to us, who love him" in vv. 9 and
10) he reverts to the first person plural.

The usage in vv. 7–10, plus the connection of this verse with v. 10 by means of
the resumptive δέ (see preceding note), and the fact that in Paul the language "receive
the Spirit" elsewhere refers only to believers in general (see n. 64) seem also to deny
the force of the assertion by W. C. Kaiser that "Paul is not talking about the Spirit
that animates believers, but about the Holy Spirit's operation in delivering the
Scripture to the apostle" (see "A Neglected Text in Bibliology Discussions: I Corinthians 2:6–16," *WTJ* 43 [1981] 301–19 [315]). Kaiser's concern is indeed picked up
in v. 13, although the language "delivering the Scripture to the apostle" seems to be
a considerable distance from Paul's own concern and intent.

[63]Note the interchangeability of αἰών ([this] "age," vv. 6, 8) and κόσμος ([this]
"world"). Cf. 1:20.

[64]This is the first occurrence in Paul's letters of this ordinary NT language for
the gift of the Spirit; cf. Acts 2:38; 10:47; 19:2; 2 Cor 11:4; Gal 3:2, 14; Rom 8:15. In
Paul it refers primarily to Christian conversion.

[65]This was suggested, e.g., by Ellis, *Prophecy*, 29–30, on the assumption that it
is related to "the rulers of this age" in vv. 6 and 8, whom he incorrectly understands
to be demonic powers. Cf. Barrett 75.

is from God."[66] The implication, of course, is that since the Holy Spirit whom they have received is not of this world, they should desist thinking like this world.

The final clause of the sentence picks up the point of vv. 6 and 10 and thereby gives the reason, in *this* context, for our having received the Spirit, namely, "that we may understand[67] what God has freely given us." This latter phrase in particular echoes the motif of v. 9, "what things God has prepared for those who love him," and gives us the one glimpse into the *content* of the wisdom that God has revealed to his people by his Spirit. The verb (χαρίζομαι) may deliberately allude to the "grace" (χάρις) of God, or the "gift" (χάρισμα) of salvation (as Rom 6:23);[68] its neuter plural form ("what things have been freely bestowed") reflects the neuter plurals of v. 9. This language seems determinative: in talking about God's wisdom in this passage, Paul is referring to salvation through the crucified One (as in 1:23–24; 2:2), which God's people "understand" precisely because they have received the Spirit.

13 Having argued that their common gift of the (revelatory) Spirit is what enables the Corinthians and him to understand God's wisdom, Paul returns to his own preaching of that wisdom, first mentioned in vv. 6 and 7, and he links it to the same reception of the Spirit. This sentence, therefore, not only continues the argument at hand,[69] but also recalls the preceding paragraph (2:1–5) with its underlying apologetic motif. "What we preached to you was God's wisdom, all right," he asserted (vv. 6–7), despite what they may think. Now he returns to that assertion by way of the explanation of vv. 10–12. Just as we have all received the Spirit so as to understand the gift of salvation, so also the message I[70] preach is given "in words taught by the Spirit."[71] The Spirit is therefore also our divine instructor.

---

[66]This seems clearly to be the sense of the contrast in this sentence, but such a translation misses the exact repetition of the designation from v. 11. Thus: " . . . except *the Spirit of God*; and we have . . . received *the Spirit of God*."

[67]Gk. εἰδῶμεν, picking up the verbs from v. 11.

[68]Conzelmann 67 candidly acknowledges as much, but is so enamored with Hellenistic parallels in the paragraph that he immediately qualifies it by saying that "χάρις, too, can assume the tenor of the mysteries and denote the power within the pneumatic, thus becoming synonymous with πνεῦμα. It will therefore be necessary to look for further indications." But why should one do so when both the argument itself and the terminology are so thoroughly Pauline?

[69]Gk. ἃ καὶ λαλοῦμεν, lit. "what things *also* we speak." The "what things," of course, refers to "the things God has freely given us." λαλοῦμεν repeats the verb from vv. 6 and 7 and therefore seems clearly resumptive.

[70]Since λαλοῦμεν repeats the verb of vv. 6 and 7, it is also likely that the "we" here picks up the editorial "we" of those sentences. Hence "I."

[71]The noun πνεύματος lacks the definite article, thus indicating that the presence or absence of the article with πνεῦμα does not determine whether Paul intends *the* Spirit in any given instance. See the discussion in ch. 2

The Spirit is thus the key to everything—Paul's preaching (vv. 4–5, 13), their conversion (vv. 4–5, 12), and especially their understanding of the content of his preaching to be the true wisdom of God (vv. 6–13). As throughout the paragraph—and the entire argument from 1:17—what he says positively about his own ministry is placed in antithesis to what is merely human: "not in words (λόγοις) taught by human wisdom (σοφία)."[72] The ties to 2:1–5 are obvious. "Words" of course does not mean simply language itself, but the meaning, or message, contained in the words as they give expression to the gospel.

What is less obvious is the further explanation of this teaching. Here for the first time in the corpus we meet the adjective πνευματικός (*pneumatikos* = Spirit-ual), which, as noted in ch. 2, is a possessive adjective referring primarily to the Holy Spirit. This is made the more certain by the remarkable collocation of Spirit words in Paul's sentence, beginning with the final word in v. 12, πνεύματος πνευματικοῖς πνευματικά (by the Spirit, with the Spirit's [words], the things of the Spirit). But this combination, along with the participle συγκρίνοντες, also poses considerable difficulties for interpretation. Did Paul intend "expressing spiritual truths in spiritual words" (NIV), or "interpreting spiritual truths to spiritual people" (NIV[mg]), or "comparing spiritual things with spiritual" (KJV, RSV[mg])?[73] The problems are two: (1) finding a proper meaning for the verb συγκρίνοντες, and (2) determining whether πνευματικοῖς refers to the just mentioned "words taught by the Spirit" or whether it means "Spirit people" and anticipates the antitheses of vv. 14–15.[74]

On this second matter the possibility that it anticipates what follows has in its favor the immediate contrast of the "non-spiritual person" in v. 14. In this context that reading of the text could make a lot of sense. Nonetheless, the grammar, and especially the immediate juxtaposition of the adjective with the noun "Spirit" in v. 12, would seem to favor the view that Paul is explaining further what he has just said.[75] "We speak words

---

[72]Orr-Walther 158 suggest the alternative possibility of "learned words of human wisdom," but they make too much of the subtle shades of meaning. Héring 20, on the unfounded assertion that the common translation would only be possible if διδακτός were a noun, adopts a conjectural omission of λόγοις and translates: "amongst people instructed in human philosophy." But such conjectures are unnecessary, especially since the "subjective" or "agency" use of the genitive with this adjective is found also in John 6:45, which Héring overlooks.

[73]The KJV translated "comparing spiritual things with spiritual," giving rise to the popular use of this text to support the analogy of Scripture, i.e., comparing one text with another so as to derive its meaning from within Scripture itself. That is a useful hermeneutical principle, based on the belief of the common inspiration by the Spirit of all Scripture, but it is quite beside Paul's present point.

[74]It is possible, though less probable, that it is neuter and simply means something like "spiritual means" or "spiritual things" in general.

[75]The participial construction, modifying λαλοῦμεν, also argues for the closest possible tie to what has already been said, not a loose addition anticipating what

taught by the Spirit," he has just asserted, "which means," he now adds, "that we [explain] spiritual things (i.e., the things of the Spirit, probably referring to the 'things freely given us by God,' v. 12) by means of, or with, the words (in the sense just noted in v. 12) taught us by the Spirit."

As to the meaning of the verb, only Paul uses it elsewhere in the NT, in 2 Cor 10:12 (twice), where it plainly means "compare," a meaning that does not seem appropriate here. Some have argued that it should carry its classical sense of "combining";[76] however, Paul's septuagintal background argues in favor of "explaining" or "interpreting." Most likely, therefore, he intended something like, "explaining the things of the Spirit (as described in v. 12) by means of the words taught by the Spirit," that is, "in language appropriate to the message, not with human wisdom."[77]

Thus here is no "deeper life" theology, nor does this clause deal with "the analogy of Scripture." Paul's concern is with the central role of the revelatory Spirit both in his preaching and in the Corinthians' hearing and understanding the gospel. He reinforces that by adding this explanatory clause to what he meant by "words taught by the Spirit."

14 Until now Paul has sketched God's wisdom, its "what" (formerly hidden, destined for our glory) and its "how" (revelation by the Spirit), always with an eye toward its opposite—the "wisdom of this world," currently so attractive to the Corinthians. Now (in vv. 14–16), in light of what has been said about the work of the Spirit *in us*, Paul sets forth the negative side of the antithesis: what it is like *for them*—those who do not have the Spirit, yet with whom the Corinthians are currently aligning themselves. At the same time, therefore, he is setting them up for the polemic of 3:1–4.

The people of this age, those who in their merely human wisdom miss out on God's wisdom, are designated ψυχικοί ("the natural man/woman," NASB et al.) in contrast to those with the Spirit (the πνευματικοί, v. 15). Although there has been considerable debate over this term, the ensuing description demonstrates that, whatever else, it refers to those who do not have the Spirit, therefore, the merely human. But why this usage, since Paul elsewhere prefers some form of σάρξ (flesh) when contrasting

---

follows. Furthermore, one would expect the definite article with πνευματικοῖς if "those who have the Spirit" were intended.

[76]Most recently by Kaiser, "Bibliology," 318, and MacArthur 63; cf. Lightfoot 180–81 and Goodspeed (translation). Kaiser does so on the basis of the not totally relevant assertion, borrowed from Godet, that "the meaning of 'interpreting' for this verb is foreign in the NT and Classical Greek." But neither is there any NT usage meaning "combine"(!), and the comparison with classical Greek is particularly irrelevant since the word was regularly used with the meaning of "interpreting" or "explaining" in the LXX (e.g., Gen 40:8, 16, 22; 41:12, 13, 15; Num 15:34; Dan 5:7), but never in the "classical" sense.

[77]Holladay 47.

with πνεῦμα (Spirit), as he does in the polemical paragraph that immediately follows? Some have argued that it is a Corinthian term that Paul is adopting and turning against them.[78] More likely the term originated in Paul's own Jewish background, where the Greek noun ψυχή had been used to translate the Hebrew nepeš, which often simply denotes humanity in its natural, physical existence.[79] This at least is Paul's present point. With this term he is designating outsiders, people who have never been believers. They are people who know only the "wisdom of this age" (v. 6). Thus, Paul never uses the term to refer to believers. When he does address the Corinthians, who are acting just like these people without the Spirit, he calls them σαρκίνοι (3:1), which possesses a different nuance altogether.

Paul describes the ψυχικοί in three ways, each in terms of their [= the ψυχικοί] non-relationship to the Spirit. First, they do "not accept the things that come from the Spirit of God." This description conspicuously contrasts with the "we [who] have received . . . the Spirit of God" of v. 12. The verb in this case is the ordinary one for "receiving" or "accepting" another person. This implies not that ψυχικοί people are simply incapable of understanding the things of the Spirit, but that, because of their being "merely human," they reject the things of the Spirit.

Second, the reason for their "not accepting/rejecting" is that the things of the Spirit "are foolishness to them." Because they lack the Spirit, in the sense of v. 12, their view of everything is from the bottom up, twisted and distorted. Paul, of course, is continuing the argument of 1:18–2:5, that Christ crucified, which they see as folly, is God's wisdom over against human folly, which they deem wisdom. Response to the cross reveals people for who they are; to see it as foolishness means to stand over against God and his ways—and to stand under his judgment as one without his Spirit and therefore apart from "what he has freely given us."

Third, again in antithesis to v. 12, the "natural man/woman cannot understand" the things that the one who has received the Spirit can. Here the emphasis falls on their inability. Again, "like is known by like" (see v. 11); without the Spirit they lack the one essential "quality" necessary for them to know God and his ways—"because they are spiritually

---

[78]This is the view of Wilckens, Weisheit, 89–91, who sees it as a Gnostic term being taken over by Paul; cf. B. Pearson, The Pneumatikos-Psychikos Terminology in 1 Corinthians: A Study in the Theology of the Corinthian Opponents of Paul and Its Relation to Gnosticism, SBLDS 12 (Missoula, Mont.: SBL, 1973) 38–39; R. A. Horsley, "Pneumatikos vs. Psychikos: Distinctions of Spiritual Status among the Corinthians," HTR 69 (1976) 269–88; and J. A. Davis, Wisdom and Spirit: An Investigation of 1 Corinthians 1:18–3:20 Against the Background of Jewish Sapiential Traditions in the Greco-Roman Period (Lanham, Md.: University Press of America, 1984) 117–25, who see it as evidence of Philonic influences. The problem with this is to discover how the Corinthians might have been using it, unless they were describing Paul in this manner.

[79]See the discussion of these terms in TDNT 9.608–63 (E. Schweizer), and NIDNTT 3.676–86 (G. Harder).

discerned." This last phrase demonstrates the fluidity of Paul's use of language. The word "spiritual" is now an adverb;[80] the context makes it certain that Paul intends "by means of the Spirit," not "by some intuitive process." For Paul, "to be spiritual" and "to discern spiritually" simply means to have the Spirit, who so endows and enables.[81]

The verb translated "discern"[82] is crucial. The fact that it occurs only in this letter in the Pauline corpus (ten times), and that in every case but one (14:24) it appears in a polemical or ironical context, suggests that it is a Corinthian word that Paul enlists against them. Finding a proper meaning for it is the difficulty. Technically it can mean to "examine" in a judicial sense, and clearly has that meaning in the two instances where Paul charges them with "judging" him (4:3–4; 9:3).[83] Here there seems to be a play on the word; many think it is also ironical, anticipating the usage in 4:3–4. Probably it means something very close to "discern" in the sense of being able to make appropriate "judgments" about what God is doing in the world; and the person "without the Spirit" obviously cannot do that. As such it is immediately picked up in v. 15 as the one proper activity of the true Spirit person.

This sentence in particular, along with Gal 3:2–5, demonstrates that in Pauline theology, the Spirit is the sine qua non, the absolutely essential, crucial matter, in becoming a part of the people of God. The Spirit—alone—distinguishes believer from nonbeliever. This is why the latter "are perishing" and consider the cross foolishness; this is why they do not understand the ways of God in Christ. The Spirit differentiates between what is of Christ and what is not.

15–16 With these sentences the argument of the present paragraph, as well as the argument of the whole section that began in 1:17, concludes. At the same time they lead into the strong polemical application of all this to the Corinthians and their quarreling (3:1–4). The four parts form something of an AB-B'A' pattern of argument:

A The Spirit person "judges" all things;

  B But he/she in turn is "judged" by no one.

  B' For who has known the mind of the Lord; who shall instruct him?

A' But we have the mind of Christ.

---

[80]Gk. πνευματικῶς; cf. Rev 11:8, a word that is found in later Christian literature, but is unknown outside the Christian tradition.

[81]See further the discussion in ch. 2.

[82]Gk. ἀνακρίνω; cf. v. 15[2x]; 4:3[2x], 4; 9:3; 10:25, 27; 14:24.

[83]The emphasis lies on the process of examining, rather than the verdict itself, implied in the root verb κρίνω.

The first line stands in sharp contrast[84] to the final word about the ψυχικός person in v. 14. That person is totally unable to understand the things of the Spirit, because such things are "examined/discerned" by means of the Spirit, whom the ψυχικός does not have. But the πνευ-ματικός, the person with the Spirit,[85] is not at such a disadvantage. This person can "make judgments about all things." Such a statement must not be wrested from its context. Since it is the Spirit who "searches all things, even the depths of God" (v. 10), the one having the Spirit can therefore discern God's ways. Not necessarily *all things*, of course, but all things that pertain to the work of salvation, matters formerly hidden in God, but now revealed through the Spirit. Thus, nothing new is being said here; the point of vv. 10–14 is being reiterated in a new way.

The second line, which contrasts with the first, reverses the order of things in light of what has just been said in v. 14. But here there seems to be a play on the word ἀνακρίνω (discern/examine). The person lacking the Spirit cannot discern what God is doing (v. 14); the one with the Spirit is able to because of the Spirit (line A); therefore, the one without the Spirit cannot "examine," or "make judgments" on, the person with the Spirit (line B). In its first instance this simply means that the person who belongs to this age is not in the position to judge as "foolish" the person who belongs to the age to come. Those whose lives are invaded by the Spirit of God can discern "all things," including those without the Spirit; but the inverse is not possible.[86]

But one wonders whether there is not in these words also a subtle moving of the argument toward the next paragraph, and even more so toward the conclusion in 4:1–5. The Corinthians regard themselves as "spiritual," and as such they are also "examining" the Apostle. Paul allows that the truly "spiritual" person, the one who understands what God has done in Christ crucified, discerns, "examines" all things. Thus he himself will be able to make the necessary judgments about them that follow. Indeed the whole of this letter will be the spelling out of the principle detailed in line A. But also because he has so understood "the mind of Christ," he disallows their judging him. To the contrary, by their actions they have proved themselves—and not Paul—to be less than truly "spiritual"; indeed they are "fleshly," acting like mere humans who do not have the Spirit. Thus as a "spiritual person" he himself is "not

---

[84]Set off in the Greek text by an adversative δέ.

[85]Such a meaning for πνευματικός seems demanded by the context. To suggest, as does Grudem, *Gift*, 158, that it means "spiritually mature" misses Paul's argument.

[86]Here is another sentence which, taken out of its context, has suffered much in the church. There are always some who consider themselves full of the Spirit in such a way as to be beyond discipline or the counsel of others. Such a reading of the text is an unfortunate travesty, since these people are usually among those most needing such discipline.

subject to anybody else's judgment." As he will insist in 4:3–4, he is not subject to any merely human court because he belongs to the Lord, who alone will judge him, as well as all others.

The third line (B′) gives scriptural support for the assertion of the second (B). But it does so in this case without an introductory formula (e.g., "it is written"). Rather, he reworks Isa 40:13[87] in such a way that it serves as a rhetorical question, demanding the answer, "No one."[88] "For," he asks rhetorically in light of line B, "who has known the mind of the Lord that he may instruct him?" Again, in the context of the argument this probably has a double punch. On the one hand, it simply asks rhetorically of the ψυχικοί how they can expect to know true wisdom and thereby pass judgment on the one who has the Spirit, when they do not have the mind of the Lord. "Who is the person who wants to match wits with God?" he asks. But surely this, too, is directed now at his Corinthian friends. "Who among his detractors, now enamored with human wisdom and passing judgment on Paul, is so capable of knowing the mind of the Lord that he or she can bypass the wisdom of God itself as it is revealed in the cross?" Indeed, whoever would pursue wisdom so as to avoid the word of the cross fares no better than one who would have the ultimate folly of thinking he or she could instruct the Lord.

The final line (A′) corresponds to the first assertion in v. 15, but now in direct response to the rhetorical question of v. 16a. "But," in contrast to those who lack the Spirit and thereby do *not* know the mind of the Lord, "*we* have the mind of Christ."[89] By "mind" he probably means Christ's own understanding of his saving significance, as revealed to us by the Spirit. In fact in the Greek Bible that Paul cites, the word "mind" translates the Hebrew *rûaḥ*, which ordinarily means "spirit" (Isa 40:13).

Thus the argument is brought full circle. He began by insisting that his message is in fact an expression of wisdom—God's own wisdom,

---

[87]He has left out the middle line of three ("who has become his advisor?"), since it would fail to serve his present purpose. According to Robertson (*Grammar*, 724), the ὅς that introduces the second line of the quote "denotes a consecutive idea, 'so as to.' " It should be noted in passing that with this citation Paul is reflecting the very point of Isaiah 40–48, where Israel's "second-guessing" of God is the whole issue.

[88]Cf. Wilckens, *Weisheit*, 95. This line is often interpreted otherwise, namely, as in support of line A, implying that the question from Isaiah is open-ended at this point, to be answered by the next line. That is, "The spiritual person judges all things, . . . for who has known the mind of Christ? The answer? We have." But that puts too much stress on the grammar (the δέ of the final line is better understood as an adversative, especially in light of the emphatic "*we*" and the change to "mind *of Christ*") and does not fit the argument as well.

[89]The substitution of "Christ" for the "Lord" of the Isaiah passage probably has no significance for the present argument, but it does indicate something of Paul's own Christology! For him Christ is Lord; therefore when the OT speaks of the Lord, he sees in such language references to Christ himself. See also in this regard the interchange of the "Spirit of God" and the "Spirit of Christ" in Rom 8:9.

revealed as such by the Spirit. He at least—in contrast to the merely ψυχικός person, the mere human being without the Spirit—understands the mind of Christ. As those who possess the Spirit the Corinthians also potentially possess that same mind. However, as he will now turn to point out, their behavior betrays them. They do, but they don't. The concern from here on will be to force them to acknowledge the folly of their "wisdom," which is expressing itself in quarrels, and thereby is destroying the very church for whom Christ died.

3:1 Paul now applies the argument of 2:6–16 specifically to the Corinthian situation: "We who have received the Spirit do indeed have the mind of Christ and understand the wisdom of the folly of God. And I, for my part, brothers and sisters, was not able to address[90] you as πνευματικοί (Spirit people)." Two concerns now drive the Apostle: their "spirituality" and their divisions. For Paul these are mutually exclusive. The problem is that the Corinthians *think* of themselves as the one—"spiritual"—while *in fact* they are the other—"divided." Thus Paul does two things, which flow directly out of 2:6–16 and lead directly into 3:5–17.

First, picking up the theme of being "spiritual" from what has just preceded, he makes a frontal attack and pronounces them as not Spiritual at all! Indeed, they are just the opposite; they are "fleshly"—still thinking like mere human beings, who do not have the Spirit. With this charge Paul has exposed himself to centuries of misunderstanding. But his concern is singular: not to suggest classes of Christians or grades of spirituality, but to get them to stop *thinking* like the people of this present age.[91]

Secondly, and more importantly in their circumstance, he also wants them to stop *behaving* like the people of the present age. In the argument, therefore, their quarrels become Exhibit A of the charge in vv. 1 and 2.[92]

---

[90]Gk. λαλῆσαι, the infinitive of the same verb used about his preaching in 2:6, 7, and 13.

[91]This seems by far the best answer to the question of whether Paul himself distinguishes between believers within the congregation, an idea that almost all commentators, including those who believe he does, recognize as inherently problematic—given the current problem of divisiveness within the congregation and Paul's theology as it is seen elsewhere. Cf. Funk, "Word," 299: "Does Paul nevertheless make a distinction within the congregation? Indeed he does! The question is what kind of distinction and on what basis?" After giving a theological basis for what Funk refers to as a "dialectical" tension, he says of this passage: "Thus it may be said that Christians both have (insofar as they walk according to the spirit) and do not have (insofar as they fall short of the norm) the spirit." But to suggest *two* meanings for πνευματικός (e.g., P. J. du Plessis, ΤΕΛΕΙΟΣ: *The Idea of Perfection in the New Testament* (Kampen, 1959), 183–85, and Mare 204) misses Paul's point. What Mare suggests as necessitating a different meaning here from 2:14–15 can better be subsumed under the ironical usage argued for here, without the difficulties of the other view.

[92]He then proceeds to address this question directly for three paragraphs, but interestingly not in terms of quarreling per se but in terms of their misunderstanding

Their behavior is that of "mere humans." Is it not true then that they are not truly "spiritual," but "fleshly"?

Paul, of course, does not mean to say they do not have the Spirit. They do; and that's the problem, because they are thinking and behaving otherwise. The argument has considerable bite, therefore, since his ultimate message is: "Stop it! People of the Spirit simply must stop behaving the way you are."

But by saying that he "could not address (them) as spiritual," he seems to be allowing that there are "unspiritual" Christians—which is both true and not true. On the one hand, it is *not* true in the sense that the Spirit is the crucial factor as to whether one is or is not a believer; one cannot be a Christian and be devoid of Spirit.[93] On the other hand, the Corinthians are involved in a lot of unchristian behavior; and in that sense they are "unspiritual," not because they lack the Spirit but because they are thinking and living *just like* those who do lack the Spirit. But these theological niceties that so often concern us are quite beside Paul's purpose. He is "after them," as it were; and he uses their language, now based on his own content that has just been given, to shame them into reality (despite the demurrer of 4:14).

Not only could he not address them as "spiritual," but they were in fact quite the opposite—"fleshly."[94] For those whose spirituality had denigrated present physical existence to the point of denying a future bodily resurrection (15:12), this word can only be biting irony. The word used here, σαρκίνοι, emphasizes especially their humanness and the physical side of their existence as over against the nonphysical.[95] The change to σαρκικοί in v. 3 only strengthens the blow.[96] They were not only "of the flesh" when Paul first was among them, but even now their behavior is "fleshly," a word with decidedly ethical overtones of living from the perspective of the present age, therefore out of one's sinfulness. Furthermore, σαρκίνος is *not* a synonym for ψυχικός in 2:14. The change

---

of the nature and role of leadership in the church (3:5–15), which in turn reflects their misunderstanding of the nature of the church itself (3:16–17). See below on 3:16–17.

[93]This is quite the point of 2:14 above; cf. Rom 8:9; Gal 3:2–3; Titus 3:5–7.

[94]Gk. σαρκίνος (fleshly = composed of flesh). In v. 3 Paul shifts to σαρκικός (fleshly = having the characteristics of flesh; associated with flesh). Paul keeps this distinction in his use of σαρκίνος in 2 Cor 3:3 ("but on tablets of human hearts" [NIV], i.e., on hearts composed of flesh) and σαρκικός in 2 Cor 1:12 ("worldly wisdom," i.e., wisdom based on the point of view of the sinful nature). The later witnesses, not surprisingly, read σαρκικοῖς here against the σαρκινοῖς of P[46] ℵ A B C* D* 6 33 945 1175 1739 pc.

[95]This stands against the commonly held view that these words mean basically the same thing. If so, then one wonders why Paul himself uses two words. If the difference is somewhat subtle, it is nonetheless by Paul's own choice and needs to be taken seriously. See, e.g., Robertson-Plummer 52 and Moulton (MHT 2.378).

[96]This is the first instance in Paul's extant letters with the contrast between "flesh" and "Spirit." See further, 2 Cor 1:17 and 22; 5:16–17; Gal 5:13–25; Rom 7:5–8:17.

is deliberate. The latter word had just been used to describe the person totally devoid of Spirit, who could not even understand Paul's present argument, because it would be folly to him/her. Because the Corinthians *had* received the Spirit, he could not call them ψυχικοί—even if they were acting that way. So the shift to σάρκινοι fits him in every way. He avoids accusing them of not having Spirit altogether, but at the same time he forces them to have to face up to their true condition.

This section of 1 Corinthians has endured a most unfortunate history of application in the church. Paul's own purpose has been almost totally lost in favor of an interpretation that is nearly 180 degrees the opposite of his. Almost every form of spiritual elitism, "deeper life" movement, and "second blessing" doctrine has appealed to this text. To receive the Spirit according to their special expression paves the way for people to know "deeper truths" about God and to view the rest as "carnal."[97]

Paul's concern needs to be resurrected throughout the church. The gift of the Spirit does not lead to special status among believers; rather, it leads to special status vis-à-vis the world. But it should do so always in terms of the centrality of the message of our crucified/risen Savior. The Spirit should identify God's people in such a way that their values and world-view are radically different from the wisdom of this age. Believers do know what God is about in Christ; they do live out the life of the future in the present age that is passing away; they are marked by the cross forever. As such they are the people of the Spirit, who stand in bold contrast to those who are merely human and do not understand the scandal of the cross. Being Spirit people does not lead to elitism; it leads to a deeper understanding of God's profound mystery—redemption through a crucified Messiah.

1 CORINTHIANS 3:16–17

[16]*Do you not know that you yourselves are God's temple and that God's Spirit dwells in you?* [17]*If anyone destroys God's temple, God will destroy*[98] *that person; for God's temple is holy, and you are that temple.*

---

[97]One special brand of this elitism surfaces among some who have pushed the possibilities of "faith" to the extreme and regularly make a "special revelation" from the Spirit their final court of appeal. Other "lesser" brothers and sisters are simply living below their full privileges in Christ. Indeed, some advocates of this form of spirituality bid fair to repeat the Corinthian error in its totality. What is painful about so much of this is not simply the improper use of this passage, but that so often there is an accompanying toning down of the message of the cross. The result is that one is hard-pressed to hear the content of "God's wisdom" ever expounded as the paradigm for truly Christian living.

[98]"Influenced by the preceding word, several witnesses, chiefly Western, read the present tense φθείρει (D[gr] G[gr] L P 81 [pc]) instead of φθερεῖ " (Metzger, *Textual Commentary,* 549).

This is the first of three instances in Paul's letters[99] where he uses temple imagery to refer to the church as a corporate reality, in which the Spirit plays the leading role.[100] As such it is also one of the most important passages in the corpus for uncovering his understanding of the nature and significance of the local community of faith as a people of the Spirit. Since it comes to us in the context of correction and warning, we must begin by placing it in the present argument.

For Paul the problem of strife and division in the name of σοφία (merely worldly wisdom) with former teachers as points of reference is but symptomatic of two much deeper issues in the Corinthian assembly— a radical misunderstanding of the gospel, with a consequent failure to understand church and ministry. Having dealt with the former in 1:18– 3:4, he now turns to the latter.

With v. 5 Paul set out to correct their false view of church leadership by redirecting their focus from the teachers to God, who owns all, and whose alone they are (vv. 5–9). At the same time he must also correct their impaired understanding of the nature of the church, which is where our short paragraph fits in. In v. 9 he concluded the first analogy by asserting that the church is *God's* field, with the emphasis on God as owner and producer. Paul then changes imagery; the church is also God's building. With this image he will first warn those who are currently constructing the building, that they must do so with utmost care, making sure that the superstructure is built with material compatible with the foundation—Christ crucified (vv. 10–11). Their current fascination with σοφία adds up to building with wood, hay, and stubble, which will not endure the eschatological test.

With our paragraph the argument turns slightly, as Paul carries the imagery of vv. 9b–15 a step further by specifying the *kind* of building that he and the others have been erecting—God's *temple* in Corinth. Two issues concern him: He attempts, first, by the imagery itself, to help the Corinthians to see the nature and significance of their being God's people in Corinth; and, second, by picking up the motif of judgment from vv. 13–15, he sternly warns those who are in process of destroying the church by their wisdom and divisions. Thus he presents us with a remarkable metaphor to describe the nature of the local church and offers the strongest warning in the NT against those who would take the local church lightly.

He turns to rhetoric: "Do you not know[101] who you are?" he asks them. It is clear from their current behavior that they do not know, or

---

[99]See also 2 Cor 6:16 and Eph 2:20–22.

[100] Cf. the other two primary images for church in Paul, body and family, in which the Spirit also plays the leading role (see 1 Cor 12:13 and Eph 4:4 for Spirit and body; Gal 4:6 and Rom 8:15–16 for Spirit and family).

[101] Gk. οὐκ οἴδατε ὅτι. The fact that he uses this device ten times in this letter (3:16; 5:6; 6:2, 3, 9, 15, 16, 19; 9:13, 24), chiefly in contexts where he is exercised, and

at least have not seriously considered the implications of who they are as God's people in Corinth.

The church as God's temple is pregnant imagery—for both the Jewish Paul and the Gentile Corinthians. Paul's word (ναός) refers to the actual sanctuary, the place of a deity's dwelling, in contrast to ἱερόν, which designates the temple precincts as well as the sanctuary.[102] In its first instance, therefore, the imagery picks up the motif of God's presence with his people, which begins in the book of Exodus and runs throughout the OT.[103] God's presence, eventually understood as referring to the Spirit of the Lord,[104] was responsible for leading Israel through the desert and into "their rest." God's presence, Moses argues with God himself, is the crucial matter for Israel's existence (Exod 33:15–16). Not Torah, not circumcision, not Sabbath keeping, but God's presence, first in the tabernacle and later in the temple in Jerusalem, alone distinguishes God's people from all other peoples on the earth. For Paul, therefore, the temple imagery first of all echoes this OT motif: God is now present among his people in Corinth by his Spirit.

This imagery very likely also had eschatological overtones for Paul.[105] Such an understanding would flow from two sources: Jewish eschatological hopes as reflected in a variety of sources,[106] and a tradition that goes back to Jesus himself, that he would rebuild the temple "in three days."[107] The present experience of the church as the place where

---

that it occurs only one other time in his letters (Rom 6:16), probably says much about his feelings toward the Corinthians and their behavior. Some have suggested that Paul's question implies that he had previously given them this image. See, e.g., Weiss 84 and B. Gärtner, *The Temple and the Community in Qumran and the New Testament* (SNTSMS 1; Cambridge: University Press, 1965) 57. But that is to put too much weight on what seems rather to be a rhetorical device in this letter. Given their own emphasis on wisdom and knowledge, however, in this case it may be more than simply a rhetorical device, moving closer to irony or sarcasm: "Can it be that you who boast in γνῶσις do not know that?"

[102] See O. Michel in *TDNT* 4.880–90. The distinction between the two words does not necessarily hold in all the Greek of the NT period, but the usage in the LXX, where the distinction is common, seems to have influenced Paul here.

[103] Indeed, as noted in ch. 1 (pp. 6–8), this motif is arguably the key to the structure of Exodus.

[104] See Isa 63:9–14 (NRSV): "It was no messenger or angel but his presence that saved them. . . . But they rebelled and grieved his holy spirit; . . . Like cattle that go down into the valley, the Spirit of the Lord gave them rest. Thus you led your people, to make for yourself a glorious name." See the further discussion on Eph 4:30 below.

[105] This suggestion has been frequently made, and it is probably correct, given the Qumran eschatological parallels (see Gärtner, *Temple*) and Paul's overall eschatological frame of reference; but nothing in Paul's usage itself demands such an understanding. See, among others, Weiss, Barrett, Bruce, Conzelmann, Senft.

[106] E.g., Isa 28:16 (cf. 1 Cor 3:10); Ezekiel 40–48; *Jub.* 1:17; 1 Enoch 91:13; 4QFlor.

[107] As represented in the charges of the false witnesses in Mark 14:58. The "falseness" has not to do with the statement, but with what would have been meant

the eschatological Spirit dwells would thus be the restored temple of Ezekiel's vision (chs. 40–48), where God promised "to live among them forever" (43:9) and out of which flowed the river of fresh water that restored the land (47:1–12).

Paul's unique contribution lies with his remarkable, but understandable, transfer of images: the believing community themselves are God's temple in Corinth. In the OT the Israelites are never called God's temple as such, although they are God's people among whom God chose to "dwell" by tabernacling in their midst.[108] The Corinthians' experience of the eschatological Spirit, as indwelling the believer and present in the gathered community, is the key to this transfer of images. The Spirit was how Isaiah 63 understood God to be present among his ancient people and how Paul now understands God to be present among his newly constituted eschatological people.

This imagery would also have been easily understood by the Corinthians from their own religious background as well. As practicing pagans[109] most of them would have frequented the many pagan temples and shrines (ναοί) in their city.[110] Indeed some of them were arguing for the right to do so still.[111] But now Paul calls their attention to the fact that the living God has only one temple in pagan Corinth, and they are it.[112] They became so in that "God's Spirit dwells in you." Most likely Paul meant by this not that the Spirit dwelt in each of them, true as that would be for him (cf. 6:19), but that the Spirit of God "dwells in your midst." That is, Paul is here reflecting on the church as the corporate place of God's dwelling, who when gathered in Jesus' name, through the Spirit experienced the presence and power of the Lord Jesus in their midst (5:4–5). Again, as in 2:10–13 (cf. 2:4–5), the Spirit is the crucial reality for life in the coming age, now present. The presence of the Spirit and that *alone* marks them off as God's new people, his temple, in Corinth.

It is difficult to overemphasize the significance of this text for Paul's understanding of the church—as primarily a people of the Spirit. This is

---

by it. The same tradition is reflected in John 2:19–21, and probably among the Hellenists in Acts (whence arose Paul), who rejected the temple in Jerusalem as "made with hands" (Acts 6:13; 7:48–50).

[108] Cf., e.g., Ps 114:2: "Judah became his sanctuary," plus the rich imagery of God's dwelling in their midst in the desert.

[109] As is made clear from 6:9–11; 8:7, 10; 12:2.

[110] According to the later account of Pausanius, 26 in all.

[111] At least in my view; see the discussion of chs. 8–10 in Fee, *1 Corinthians*.

[112] Although one perhaps should not make too much of it, Paul's word order, ναὸς θεοῦ ἐστε, is probably emphatic and an illustration of "Colwell's rule" (that predicate nouns that precede the verb are usually definite, even if they do not have the definite article). If so, then Paul is saying, "Do you not know that you are *the* temple of God in Corinth?"

true not only when they are thought of as a corporate reality, a kind of new race[113] in the local setting where they are placed, but also when they are thought of as a gathered community, worshipping the living God and thereby ministering to one another. Although the former is probably in view here, the latter follows close behind, since it is in their corporate gatherings that much of their corporate life is expressed.

In any case, as God's temple in Corinth, they are intended to be his alternative to Corinth, to both its religions and vices. In contrast to the "gods many and lords many" of pagan religion with their multiplied temples and shrines, there was now a temple of the living God in Corinth—and they did not so much as have a building; *they* were the building. And in contrast to the sexual immorality, greed, enmity, and broken relationships that marked Corinthian society, they were the people of the living God, where God by his Spirit had effected purity, compassion, forgiveness, and love. What made them God's alternative, his temple in Corinth, was *his own presence* in and among them. By his Spirit the living God had made his abode in Corinth itself!

This is precisely the reason given that concludes the dire threat in v. 17: "for God's temple is 'holy,'[114] and you are that temple."[115] The language "holy" maintains the imagery of temple, a place set apart for God and not to be desecrated in any way. As imagery, such language no longer refers to ritual holiness, but to "holy" in the moral-ethical sense. Thus the statement, although an indicative, in keeping with the imagery itself, becomes a functional imperative by the addition of "and that temple you are." God is holy; his temple is therefore also holy, set apart for his purposes; and as his temple, his people are by implication also to be holy. As this letter reveals, this is not one of their strong suits. So the threat, which is real, is at the same time turned into an invitation for them to become what in fact they are by the grace of God, "God's *holy* temple in Corinth."[116]

---

[113] This is language taken from Eph 2:11–22, where Jew and Gentile together as God's new people form a new ἄνθρωπος, a new humanity out of the two former "races."

[114] Gk. ἅγιος (holy, sacred), the same word that is used in the NT as part of the Spirit's "Christian" name.

[115] This translation reflects what is most likely the correct understanding of a very difficult Greek construction, οἵτινές ἐστε ὑμεῖς. The plural compound relative pronoun, οἵτινες, does not have a proper antecedent and can refer to either "temple" or "holy." The reason for the plural is to be explained as an attraction to the following ὑμεῖς. The antecedent is most likely "temple," which rounds off the sentence by referring again to v. 16. To emphasize that "holy" is what they in fact are seems to ask too much of the context.

[116] Cf. E. Käsemann, "Sätze Heiligen Rechts im Neuen Testament," *NTS* 1 (1954–55) 248–60; ET, *New Testament Questions of Today* (Philadelphia: Fortress, 1969) 66–81, esp. 68.

But the Corinthian believers, by their worldly wisdom, boasting, and divisions, were blowing it. Since their unity as a people was created by the Spirit,[117] their disunity in the form of strife and division had the effect of banishing the Spirit and thus of dismantling God's temple, the only alternative God had in their city. Hence, following the rhetoric that calls attention to who they are, Paul solemnly warns those who were thus wreaking havoc in the church: "If anyone destroys[118] God's temple, God will destroy that person."[119] One can scarcely circumvent the awful nature of the warning. God obviously takes the local church far more seriously than did the Corinthians—and most contemporary Christians. The church is the apple of his eye; his holy people set apart by his Spirit for his holy purposes in Corinth. Those who are responsible for dismantling the church[120] may therefore expect judgment in kind; it is difficult to escape the sense of eternal judgment in this case, given its close proximity to vv. 13–15.[121] Although it takes the form of casuistic law, this is a strongly prophetic word in the apostle[122] that needs to be heard accordingly.[123]

---

[117] See esp. on 12:12–13 below.

[118] As in vv. 12–13, this is almost certainly a present particular supposition: "If anyone is destroying . . . "

[119] As Käsemann ("Sentences," 66–68) has pointed out, this has all the earmarks of a "sentence of holy law," in which the *lex talionis* and chiasm combine to express the fearful judgment of God on the last Day (note esp. the near word play brought about by the juxtaposition of the two verbs: φθείρει/φθερεῖ ("If anyone the temple of God destroys, destroy this person will God"). But see the critique by Aune, *Prophecy*, 167, 237.

[120] According to BAGD, the imagery is that of "the destruction of a house."

[121] On this question Robertson-Plummer 67 are worth quoting: "But . . . φθερεῖ here . . . must [not] be pressed to mean annihilation (see on v. 5). Nor, on the other hand, must it be watered down to mean mere physical punishment (cf. xi.30). The exact meaning is nowhere revealed in Scripture; but terrible ruin and eternal loss of some kind seems to be meant." Cf. BAGD and G. Harder, *TDNT* 9.93–106.

[122] Cf. Käsemann, "Sentences," 68; and C. J. Roetzel, "The Judgment Form in Paul's Letters," *JBL* 88 (1969) 305.

[123] Some interpreters are dismayed that Paul can now speak of a person within the community as "being destroyed," especially after the provision of escape was given in v. 15. It is commonly suggested that Paul is dealing with two different groups of people in the two passages (so, e.g., Godet, MacArthur, and Barrett [to a lesser extent]). But neither rhetoric nor prophetic threat—not to mention Paul—is so logical. This threat takes the warning of vv. 10–15 to its next step. The whole is addressed to the church. If a distinction is to be made between the "anyone" of this passage and of vv. 10–15, it would be that the focus is more specific in this case upon those few who seem to be the prime movers of the present quarreling.

The theological question as to whether a true "believer" could be destroyed by God lies beyond Paul's concern. In any case, one must be careful not to let the "logic" of one's system (as in the case of MacArthur 86, for example) prejudge the plain meaning of Paul's words. That these people were members of the Corinthian community seems beyond reasonable doubt; that Paul is also serving up a genuine

As with 2:6–16, this passage has endured a long history of unfortunate interpretation in the church. Because the imagery of the temple is reapplied in 6:19–20 (q.v.) to the individual Corinthian who was going to the prostitutes, many have read that usage back into this passage as though it were a word of warning to individual believers as to how they treat their bodies or how they live out their Christian lives. Both the context and the grammar disallow such interpretations, even by "extended application," which are all the more unfortunate because this is one of the few texts in the NT where we are exposed to an understanding of the nature of the local church (God's temple indwelt by his Spirit) and where the warning of v. 17 shows how important the local church is to God.

The church desperately needs to recapture this vision of what it is by grace, and therefore also what God intends it to be. In most Protestant circles one tends to take the local parish altogether too lightly. Seldom does one sense that it is, or can be, experienced as a community that is so powerfully indwelt by the Spirit that it functions as a genuine alternative to the pagan world in which it is found. It is perhaps not too strong to suggest that the recapturing of this vision of its being powerfully indwelt by the Spirit and serving as a genuine alternative ("holy" in the most holistic sense) to the world is the church's single greatest need.

1 CORINTHIANS 4:18–21

[18]*Some of you have become puffed up, as if I were not coming to you.* [19]*But I will come to you very soon, if the Lord is willing, and then I will find out not only the word of those who are puffed up, but their power.* [20]*For the kingdom of God is not with word but with power.* [21]*What do you prefer? Shall I come to you with a whip, or in love and with the S/spirit of gentleness?*

The argument that began in 1:10 concluded at 4:13; but Paul did not. The most delicate issue still remained: in light of all that has been said, how can he reestablish his authority over them without destroying the very thing he has been arguing so strongly for—the servant nature of church leadership, including his own? He does this in v. 14 with a change of metaphors, from servant and household (4:1–5) to father and children, where he appeals to their loyalty. Our passage, which appears at the end

---

threat of eternal punishment seems also the plain sense of the text. The theological resolution of such tension will lie either with the concept of the visible church being composed of more than the real church, destined by God for glory, or with the supposition that some, who by all appearances do belong to the community of faith, have, for reasons beyond our understanding, opted out and are once again pursuing a path leading to destruction. The net result is the same in either case. Paul does not consider any of the Corinthian "bent ones" to be there—yet; and the warning is intended to keep it from happening.

of this appeal, includes two passing references to the Spirit that call for some comment.

The first of these is the "word" (λόγος)/"power" (δύναμις) contrast in vv. 19–20, which recalls the language about his ministry among them in 2:1–5, but now with powerful irony. Those who are puffed up against Paul[124] are so partly because he lacks significant λόγος ("word, speech," see 2:1–5; cf. 1:17). But in contrast to the λόγος characterized by wisdom that they demand of him, he has already reminded them of his real λόγος (preaching), which was not "with persuasion of wisdom" but was accompanied by the δύναμις of God, i.e., by the powerful work of the Spirit (2:4–5). Now he threatens the arrogant. When he returns, will they merely have λόγος, or will they in their "wisdom" also be able to demonstrate the δύναμις of God? They claim to have the Spirit; will they evidence what for Paul is the crucial matter, the powerful, dynamic presence of the Spirit among them to save and to sanctify (cf. 5:1–5)? He apparently has little fear of the outcome of such a confrontation.

Some have expressed concern that Paul appears to be undoing what he has been arguing earlier, especially in 1:18–2:5 and 3:5–4:13, about the servant nature of his gospel and his ministry. But that is a false fear, and misses the point of this text. The gospel of Christ crucified with all of its apparent weakness is nonetheless the power of God unto salvation for those who believe. Paul, therefore, is challenging the arrogant not on their grounds, but on his own. They lacked the true power of the Spirit, which gives people birth to new life in Christ (v. 15), which can change people's lives—can "take the poor lost sinner, lift him from the miry clay and set him free," as the gospel song has it.

That this is the nature of the challenge he sets before the "puffed up" is confirmed by the explanatory word of v. 20: "For the kingdom of God is not a matter of λόγος but of δύναμις." The real action is not where they are currently trying to place it, in merely human wisdom that "boasts" in men. What Paul is concerned about is "the kingdom of God." This is one of the rare occurrences in Paul[125] of a term that dominates the

---

[124] Cf. the use of this same verb in v. 6, where they are "puffed up" for the one (Apollos) against the other (Paul). See Fee 166–70. It is noteworthy that at the end of this long argument, carried on against the entire community indiscriminately, Paul zeros in on the instigators of the trouble. These are the people who have disdained both Paul's authority and his theology. They were probably in view in several references throughout the argument (2:15; 3:12–15, 17, 18; 4:3, 6–7). The problem, of course, is that they have had considerable influence on the entire community. To the degree that the community has tolerated (or adopted) so much unchristian behavior as the result of this sub-Christian theology, they too are at fault. Hence the letter is addressed to the church; but continually, as here, it evidences tension between the "some" and the whole.

[125] Cf. 6:9–10; 15:24, 50; 2 Thes 1:5; Gal 5:21; Rom 14:17; Col 1:13; 4:11; Eph 5:5; 2 Tim 4:18.

ministry and teaching of Jesus. But its casual appearance here indicates that it was a regular part of his own understanding of the gospel. In most instances in Paul the term refers to the consummation of the kingdom at the coming of Christ (cf. e.g., 6:9–10; 15:50); but this passage, along with Rom 14:17, makes it certain that for him the kingdom was "now" as well as "not yet." The kingdom that has already been inaugurated by the resurrection of Jesus and the coming of the Spirit is characterized by the *power* of the Spirit.

Here is the place of ultimate demarcation between their view of spirituality and Paul's. They were living in the Spirit as though the future had dawned in its fullness,[126] hence they were above the weaknesses that characterized Paul's life and ministry. Paul, on the other hand, lived in the kinds of weaknesses that characterized his Lord, but through those weaknesses the power and grace of God were at work in the world bringing people into God's kingdom (cf. Col 1:13) and assuring them of that same kingdom as their inheritance (6:9–10). This same point will be made even more strongly, and with explicit Spirit language, in Rom 14:17.

The second occurrence of Spirit language in this passage (in v. 21) is more problematic. Being reminded by what he has just said about the opposition of "some" to him, he concludes with the threat of discipline— which the church is in no danger of exercising among themselves, as what immediately follows attests![127]

If they will allow this letter and Timothy's coming to serve as the proper inducement to correcting their behavior, he may come the way a father would prefer, not with a *rod*,[128] but "in love and in the Spirit of gentleness." Love, of course, the first-mentioned fruit of the Spirit (Gal 5:22), must control all Christian conduct. One should not make too much of the fact that it seems to be set in contrast to his coming with a rod of discipline. Paul is simply continuing the father-child metaphor;[129] his

---

[126] See esp. 4:8: They had already entered their "reign."

[127] It is arguable that this final threat is directed especially against the "arrogant" of vv. 18–20. But that would miss the function of this sentence as a lead-in to the argument that follows, especially to 5:1–13 and 6:1–11. What is remarkable about both of those passages is that the heavy guns are aimed in each case at the community itself, not at the wrong-doers. That seems to be the sure evidence of the pervasive influence of the "some who are arrogant" in their midst (v. 18). It probably also indicates that Paul's own apostleship, and his capacity to speak prophetically among them, comprises a key point of tension between him and the Corinthians, both the ringleaders and the community as a whole that has been influenced by them.

[128] The imagery is the "rod of correction," found throughout the OT (Exod 21:20; 2 Sam 7:14; Prov 10:13; 22:15; Isa 10:24; Lam 3:1). Cf. also Plato, *Leg.* 3.700c; Plut. *Mor.* 268D, 693F.

[129] Craig 59 suggests that this is "the schoolmaster's whip," apparently following the argument of C. Schneider, *TDNT* 6.966–70 (cf. Lightfoot 201). But this is an unfortunate breaking of the imagery, as well as lexically unsound, as D. Daube has

contrasts relate to the *manner* of his coming, not the motive, which would express love in either case. This is confirmed by the next phrase, where the problem in interpretation lies, "the πνεῦμα of gentleness."

Ordinarily, as in most English translations, this would seem to be a case where πνεῦμα means something close to "attitude," thus reflecting the picture given in the list of apostolic hardships in vv. 11–13. But "gentleness" is also one of the fruits of the Spirit in Gal 5:22–23; moreover, this exact phrase recurs in Gal 6:1 (q.v.), where it refers to "the Spirit's gentleness." Consequently, even though the emphasis here lies on "attitude," the very expression implies the presence of the Spirit who produces such an attitude in Paul.[130]

The word "gentleness" echoes the teaching of Jesus, who described himself as "gentle in heart" (Matt 11:29; cf. 2 Cor 10:1) and who pronounced God's congratulatory blessing on those who are likewise (Matt 5:5).[131] Thus, even though the phrase in one sense is simply a further expression of the metaphor, it is so as a reflection of our Lord himself, whose earthly life of "gentleness" was lived out in the power of the Spirit. The Spirit of Christ is therefore understood as reproducing "the spirit of Christ," in whose "spirit of gentleness" Paul desires to come to them. As such it again starkly contrasts with the arrogance of the Corinthian troublemakers. Not only so, but it also makes certain that "power" in vv. 19–20 is not misunderstood in authoritarian terms, but rather reflects the understanding suggested above.

1 Corinthians 5:3–5

³*And I for my part,*[132] *although*[133] *absent in body, nonetheless being present in S/spirit, have already, as present, passed judgment*⁴ *in the name of our Lord Jesus,*[134] *on the one who did this. When you and my S/spirit are assembled,*

---

shown. See "Paul a Hellenistic Schoolmaster?" in *Studies in Rationalism, Judaism and Universalism in Memory of Leon Roth* (ed. R. Loewe; London, 1966) 67–71.

[130] Cf. Findlay 806, "the thought of [the Spirit] is latent in every reference to the 'spirit' of a Christian [person]"; cf. H. D. Betz, *Galatians* (Hermeneia; Philadelphia: Fortress, 1979) 297n.48, who says of the identical phrase in Gal. 6:1 that "it refers both to the divine and to the human spirit."

[131] For a thorough discussion of this term both for Jesus and for the Christian ethic in general, see R. Guelich, *The Sermon on the Mount* (Waco: Word, 1982) 79–83. See the further discussion on Gal 5:22–23.

[132] This is an attempt to give the proper nuance to Paul's ἐγὼ μὲν γάρ. The μέν has no coordinate δέ, but contrasts the ἐγὼ of this sentence with the καὶ ὑμεῖς of the preceding one.

[133] The concessive force of the participle ἀπών is made certain in the Western text, followed by the MajT, by the addition of ὡς.

[134] The MSS are divided between: (1) "the Lord Jesus" [A Ψ 2495 pc]; (2) "the Lord Jesus Christ" [ℵ a]; (3) "our Lord Jesus" [B D* 1175 1739 pc b d]; and (4) "our Lord Jesus Christ" [P⁴⁶ F G Maj]. This is further complicated by the similar corruptions at

along with the power of our Lord Jesus,[135] *⁵hand this man over to Satan for the destruction of the flesh, so that his spirit might be saved on the day of the Lord.*[136]

In one of the more difficult passages in the Pauline corpus, there are two occurrences of πνεῦμα (vv. 3–4[2x] and 5), which are not only part of the present difficulty, but also problematic with regard to the concerns of this study.

The historical situation is easy enough: a believer is living in an incestuous relationship with his step-mother.[137] Paul's answer is also easy enough: no less than four times in vv. 2–13 he tells the community to put the incestuous man outside their fellowship. How a believer came to such a lifestyle and how the church could be puffed up about it (in spite of it?) are more difficult, but need not detain us here. The real difficulty, highlighted by the awkwardness of the literal translation given above, lies in our understanding what Paul envisioned should take place within the Corinthian community as his letter was being read, and in response to it. And here is where the πνεῦμα language appears.

Two matters seem firm. First, in v. 2 Paul remonstrates with the Corinthians, telling them what they ought to have done—they should have removed the incestuous man from their midst and mourned his (and their?) sinfulness. Second, our sentence—all of vv. 3–5—tells them what he has done by way of contrast, and therefore what they are to do when his letter is read among them.

---

the end of the verse (see next n.). The addition of Χριστός is probably also related to the syntactical problem of finding which verb form the prepositional phrase modifies (see discussion). Contra Zuntz (*Text*, 235), the Χριστός most likely is an addition, probably by a scribe who interpreted the passage the way Zuntz and I do (cf. RSV): to heighten the solemn words of judgment ("I have pronounced judgment in the name of our Lord Jesus Christ"). An "omission," on the other hand, could only have happened by accident. A judgment on the word ἡμῶν is more difficult, although the MS evidence seems to support its presence. It fits well with "the Lord Jesus" here, and could easily have been omitted with the addition of "Christ." On the other hand, it could have been added on the analogy of the next phrase.

[135] Cf. previous note. A similar set of variants occurs: (1) "our Lord Jesus" [א A B D* sa]; (2) "the Lord Jesus" [P⁴⁶ P Ψ 629 2495 pc]; (3) "the Lord" [630 1739]; and (4) "our Lord Jesus Christ" [F G Maj]. In this case variants (1) or (2) are to be preferred to the others (Zuntz, *Text*, 235, leans toward the reading of 1739, but its reading can easily be explained as an accidental omission due to homoeoteleuton). Of these two, the inclusion of ἡμῶν is preferred on exegetical grounds.

[136] The MSS variously add Ἰησοῦ (א Ψ Maj), Ἰησοῦ Χριστοῦ (D pc), and ἡμῶν Ἰησοῦ Χριστοῦ (A F G P 33 104 365 1881 pc). The translated text is that of P⁴⁶ B 630 1739 pc Tert Epiph. Although this may look like more of the same (see two previous notes), it is not so. Here the use of "the day of the Lord" in Paul is the decisive factor (cf. 1 Thes 5:2; 2 Thes 2:2); the very variety of the additions indicates that the shorter reading is the original.

[137] For a detailed presentation of the problem within its cultural milieu, see Fee 196–201.

There are three especially problematic exegetical matters that affect one's view of vv. 3–5: (1) the sense of Paul's "although absent in body, but present τῷ πνεύματι" (which is referred to twice more: "as present," and "when you and my τοῦ πνεύματος are assembled"); (2) the placement of the two prepositional phrases, as to what they modify: "in the name of our Lord Jesus"[138] and "with the power of our Lord Jesus"; and (3) what exactly Paul expected to happen to the man himself, especially the meaning of the contrasts: "for the destruction of his σάρξ (flesh)" and "in order that τὸ πνεῦμα (his spirit) might be saved."

None of these is easily solved. In many ways the second is the more crucial for the overall sense of the sentence; but since it affects our present concerns the least, I simply sketch the conclusions to what is more carefully argued in my commentary (206–8). Several grammatical and syntactical considerations point to a resolution which understands the first phrase to modify the main verb in the sentence (i.e., "I have already pronounced judgment in the name of the Lord Jesus on the one who has perpetrated this deed") and the second to modify the genitive absolute, "when you and my πνεῦμα are assembled with the power of the Lord Jesus."[139] Thus my translation.

But what does Paul intend with this (for us) obscure πνεῦμα language? In the first instance, about his own πνεῦμα being present in their gathering, several considerations have led to the somewhat abstruse translation, "S/spirit," suggesting that Paul considers himself actually to be present among them by the Spirit when his letter is read in their midst.[140] First, the emphatic "and I for my part,"[141] stands in contrast to "and *you* are puffed up." By these words he asserts his own authority in their midst. To their collective shame, the Corinthians are "puffed up" and have done nothing, not even mourned the man's sin. Paul, however, has taken decisive action. But the action cannot be his alone. It must be

---

[138] This is the more difficult one; it has been variously understood to go (1) with the main verb, as I have translated it (cf. RSV); (2) with the genitive absolute, "when you and my S/spirit are assembled in the name of the Lord Jesus" (cf. NIV; although its translation of the genitive absolute itself is without warrant); or (3) with the verb form it immediately follows, "the one who did this thing in the name of the Lord Jesus" (cf. Murphy-O'Connor).

[139] This placement of the prepositional phrase seems to be beyond any reasonable dispute, since the grammar demands it. The two genitives "you" and "my πνεῦμα" can only function as the compound subject of the participle συναχθέντων (gathered together), and the σύν of the prepositional phrase seems obviously intended to modify the verb with its corresponding σύν-compound (thus, συναχθέντων σύν . . .).

[140] Cf. Col 2:5. The language is not exact, but close. Here Paul contrasts τῷ σώματι (in the body) with τῷ πνεύματι (in the spirit); in Colossians the first member is τῇ σαρκί (in the flesh), which in this instance means the same thing.

[141] See n. 132 above.

carried out in the context of the gathered assembly, where both he and
the power of Christ are present by the Spirit.

Second, in saying he is not "physically present" but is there "in
πνεῦμα," Paul almost certainly does *not* intend something similar to our
use of this idiom, "you are in my thoughts."[142] It is extremely doubtful
that Paul, or any first-century person for that matter, would have used
this contrast for such an idea; in any case, Paul uses plain speech when
this is what he intends, as the many prayer reports in his letters evidence.
It is, after all, quite different for him to say that he thanks God "at every
remembrance" of someone, and to say that he considers himself actually
to be present with them ἐν τῷ πνεύματι ("in his spirit" or "in the Spirit").

Third, even if not altogether clear to us, that Paul understood himself
actually to be present "in spirit/Spirit" in the gathered community[143] is
confirmed by the phrase ὡς παρών (as present). Although usually translated "*just as if I were* present," what is said in verse v. 4 shows that he
intends, "as actually present."[144] That is, he is not allowing that because
he is not physically present, he is not truly present and therefore he must
act *as though* he were. Rather, he emphasizes that he is indeed present
in Spirit, and that is *why* he can act as he does.

Fourth, the phrase "and my spirit" in v. 4, with its emphatic use of
"my"[145] and the fact that it serves with "you" as the compound subject
of the verb "when assembled," is what finally makes this certain. Paul
does not say, as the NIV and others, "when you are assembled and I am
with you in spirit." He says, "when you and my spirit are assembled."

What finally he understood this to mean is more difficult to pin down,
but it is undoubtedly related to his understanding of life in the Spirit. The
person in Christ has "received the Spirit of God" (2:12–13), has "become
one πνεῦμα with the Lord" (6:17), so that he/she is a "temple of the Holy
Spirit, whom [referring to the Spirit] one has from God" (6:19). Related

---

[142]Cf. Barrett 123: "Paul is using the word in a 'quite popular sense' (Weiss), that
is, psychologically rather than theologically. . . . Paul refers to his thoughts, and his
concern for the Corinthian church." Of v. 4 he says further: "He will make his
contribution, as the Corinthians reflect on what they remember of his convictions,
character, and ways, and on what they know of his mind in the present matter"
(124). This seems to miss the dynamic character of their gathering in the power of
the Spirit.

[143]Cf. Wiles, *Prayers*, 145–46.

[144]Cf. Findlay 808, who is one of the few commentators to catch the significance
of this insertion: "ὡς παρών means 'as being present,' not 'as though present'—which
rendering virtually surrenders the previous ἀπὼν . . . παρὼν δέ"; and Murphy-
O'Connor ("1 Corinthians, V,3–5," *RB* 84 [1977] 244n20): "There is no justification
for translating *hos paron* by 'as if present'. . . . Hence, 'as one who is present.' "

[145]Gk. ἐμοῦ, the possessive adjective serving as possessive pronoun in the
emphatic position. This is seldom noted by commentators, but it must not be
overlooked. Elsewhere with this idiom Paul uses the simple, unemphatic μου (14:14;
2 Cor 2:13; Rom 1:9).

to this kind of "receiving/having/being joined to the Spirit" language, Paul further speaks of "my spirit" in ways that seem ambiguous. Sometimes he simply means his own person with no reference to the Spirit of God (e.g., 16:18; 2 Cor 2:13); but in 1 Cor 14:14–15 ("my spirit prays") he means that his own spirit prays as the Holy Spirit gives the utterance. In this case we might then translate, "my S/spirit prays." Something very much like that seems to be intended here. Thus, in saying, "when you and my S/spirit are assembled together, along with the power of the Lord Jesus," Paul does not mean that in some vague way they are to think about him as though he were actually among them, even though he really is not.[146] Rather, when the Corinthians are assembled, the Spirit is understood to be present among them (see on 3:16); and for Paul that means that he, too, is present among them by that same Spirit.[147] If all of that is not easy for us to grasp; we must nonetheless not try to make Paul think or talk like us. This letter, of course, communicates his prophetic word to them on this matter; he probably therefore thinks of the reading of the letter in the gathered assembly as the tangible way in which the Spirit communicates his prophetic-apostolic ministry in their midst (cf. 2 Cor 10:10–11).

His actual presence by the Spirit probably harks back to the "arrogance" of those who say he is not returning (4:18). "To the contrary," Paul says, "I am present among you in Spirit, whereby I speak the prophetic word of judgment in your midst."[148] Thus he has "already passed judgment on the one who did this," namely, that this man is to be handed over to Satan (v. 5). But the action is not to be Paul's alone; nor is it to be understood as some sort of ecclesiastical tribunal.[149] Rather it is to be a community action, carried out in the context of the Spirit, where "you and my S/spirit are assembled together, along with the power of the Lord Jesus."

---

[146] The NIV seems especially to fall into this trap. By eliminating all reference to the Spirit, it takes the whole to say, "physically" = actually present, and "spiritually" = but not really. Thus they translate the first clause, "I am with you in spirit," meaning "I am not really present because I am not there physically." The next clause then makes this "not really" clearer by the translation, "just as if I were present," implying "but I am not because I am only with you in spirit" (v. 4). But this misses Paul by a wide margin, and is an especially unfortunate rendering of καὶ τοῦ ἐμοῦ πνεύματος, which functions in Paul's sentence as the compound subject, along with ὑμῶν, of the verb συναχθέντων (when you and my S/spirit are assembled).

[147] Cf. E. Schweizer, *TDNT* 6.434–35; for a somewhat different view see Jewett, *Terms*, 184–97, 451–53.

[148] For the probability that we are dealing with a prophetic judgment, as in 3:17, see Käsemann, "Sentences," 70–71.

[149] This is an especially popular position in the nonexegetical literature, although it can be found at times elsewhere. See, e.g., Roetzel, "Judgment," 113–24, who simply assumes juridical procedures are in view and discusses the passage accordingly.

Moreover, similar to the usage in 2:4–5 and 4:19–20, the term
"power" in a context like this is almost certainly a further reference to
the Spirit, who is dynamically present among them when they are assembled together. In such a context Paul's word of prophetic judgment
is to be heard and acted upon. The whole community must carry out the
action, because the "leaven" has affected them as a community; and as
a community of the Spirit (3:16) they must act in accordance with the
Spirit's direction that has now been given them through Paul.

That leads, then, to the equally difficult set of contrasts in v. 5, as to
what Paul expected to happen to the man as a result of their corporate
action. As before, this passage is filled with notorious difficulties; also as
before, my own resolutions are briefly outlined here, for which the full
argumentation can be found in the commentary.

Most of the ink has been spilt in this case on the infinitive phrase,
"to hand him over to Satan," and on its modifying prepositional phrase,
"for the destruction of his flesh." The first matter is more easily resolved
and seems to mean something like "to turn him back out into Satan's
sphere." In contrast to the gathered community of believers, where the
Spirit, as the power of the Lord Jesus, is to be visibly manifest in edifying
gifts and loving concern for one another, this man is to be put back out
into the world, where Satan and his "principalities and powers" still hold
sway over people's lives to destroy them.

As to the second matter, most interpreters consider the prepositional
phrase to express purpose. But since there is one clear purpose clause in
the sentence, "that his πνεῦμα might be saved on the day of the Lord
Jesus," it is more likely that the prepositional phrase expresses anticipated
result.[150] Thus, the "destruction of his flesh" is the *anticipated result* of the
man's being put back out into Satan's domain, while the *express purpose* of
the action is his redemption.[151] Given the context of "salvation," therefore, the "flesh" in this case most likely refers to the man's sinfulness.[152]

What this means, then, is that we have a typically Pauline contrast
between "flesh" and "spirit," although not necessarily typically expressed. What Paul was desiring by the man's being put outside the
believing community was the destruction of what was "carnal" in him,
so that he might be "saved" eschatologically.[153] In this case, "flesh" and

---

[150] For which, see BAGD 4e. Paul is not adverse to doubling purpose clauses, but
he does so by twin clauses, not by this preposition and a final clause. See, e.g., ἵνα . . .
ὅπως (1:28–29; 2 Thes 1:11–12; 2 Cor 8:14); εἰς τὸ . . . ἵνα (Rom 7:4; 15:16); ἵνα . . . ἵνα
(1 Cor 4:6; 7:5). The only expression similar to this is in Rom 6:4, but the εἰς τόν does
not express purpose.

[151] This point is unfortunately missed in most of the literature (cf. NIV).

[152] For this argument, and especially for the many weaknesses in the notion that
Paul expects either physical suffering or death, see Fee 210–12.

[153] Apart from Tertullian (*pudic.* 13–15), who knew his view was contrary to
common opinion, this was the standard view in the early church, being found

"spirit" each "designates the whole person as viewed from different angles. 'Spirit' means the whole person as oriented towards God. 'Flesh' means the whole person as oriented away from God."[154] The "destruction" of one's "flesh" would thus belong to the same kind of imagery as in "crucifying" it (Gal 5:24; cf. Rom 7:5–6); the salvation of "his spirit" is therefore a basically anthropological expression, very much as in 2 Cor 7:13: "his spirit was refreshed," meaning "he" was refreshed. So also here, Paul simply means that "he" will be saved; he expresses it in this more unusual way because of the preceding language "flesh."

The intent of this action, therefore, is the man's salvation. He is not being "turned over to Satan for destruction," an idea that is quite foreign both to Paul and the rest of the NT, but is being excluded from the Christian community with its life in the Spirit. The inevitable consequence is that he is back out in Satan's domain, where it is hoped by Paul that his "flesh" might be destroyed, which in turn will result in his salvation on the day of the Lord. By this latter term Paul does not intend that he must wait until the final Day to be saved. Rather this is one of Paul's ordinary ways of expressing salvation. Salvation is primarily an eschatological reality, experienced in the present to be sure, but to be realized fully at the day of the Lord.

It should be noted finally, in support of our conclusions in ch. 2, that in both of these cases, where the primary referent is the human spirit in contrast to "body" and "flesh," Paul uses the definite article with πνεῦμα, which he tends to do in the vast majority of instances where the human spirit is in view.

1 Corinthians 6:11

And that is what some of you were. But you were washed, you were sanctified, you were justified in the name of our Lord Jesus[155] and by the Spirit of our God.

This highly significant sentence concludes Paul's revulsion that two members of this believing community were adjudicating a legal matter before the local magistrates in Corinth, while the church stood by and did nothing. After shaming the church for its failure to act as God's

---

explicitly in Origen, Chrysostom, and Theodore of Mopsuestia.

[154] Murphy-O'Connor 42.

[155] As often happens with the Lord's name in the Pauline corpus, there is a range of textual options here. Some have added "our" (B P 33 1739 lat syr bo al), which is probably an assimilation to the following phrase ("our God"); the more difficult choice is between "Jesus" (A Ψ Maj) and "Jesus Christ" (P46 ℵ D* pc). An omission could have happened due to homoeoteleuton or because the shorter form is more common with this formula ("in the name of"); more likely "Christ" was added through liturgical influence.

eschatological community in Corinth (vv. 1–6), he asks the offended man why he could not have behaved a bit more like his Lord and "suffer wrong" (v. 7a). Beginning with v. 7b he directs his concern toward the one who did the defrauding in the first place. With the severest of warnings (vv. 9–10), he reminds the whole community that people who live in this way, namely, those outside of Christ, will not inherit the eschatological kingdom. His point, of course, is that some within the believing community are behaving just like those who will not inherit the kingdom. They must change their behavior or come under the same threat of judgment.

But Paul simply cannot bring himself to conclude on the note of warning,[156] especially since it might leave the impression that the Corinthians were actually still among "the wicked." Thus he ends by reaffirming: "And these things[157] are what some of you *were*."

Our interest lies in the rest of the sentence, which offers the soteriological basis for this premise: "But you were washed,[158] but you were sanctified, but you were justified in the name of the Lord Jesus and by the Spirit of our God." As such it is also one of the more important theological words in the epistle. Paul's concern is singular: "Your own conversion, effected by God through the work of Christ and the Spirit, is what has removed you from being among the wicked, who will not inherit the kingdom." An inherent imperative is implied: "Therefore, live out this new life in Christ and stop being like the wicked."

This is the second of such soteriological moments in Paul,[159] in which Paul refers to peoples' conversion in latent Trinitarian language, in which God the Father saves,[160] through the work of Christ, effected experientially by the Spirit. In this case, however, that pattern is less

---

[156] Note how often in this letter Paul concludes on a positive note after such an argument or warning: e.g., 3:22–23; 4:14–17 (as a conclusion to all of 1:18–4:21); 5:7; 6:20; 10:13; 11:32.

[157] Gk. ταῦτα, referring to the whole list. The neuter is striking; one would expect τοιοῦτοι. The neuter functions in a more dramatic way to express horror or contempt (= these abominations).

[158] Gk. ἀπελούσασθε (only here and Acts 22:16 in NT). Some make a considerable point that the verb is middle and offer such forced translations as "you had yourselves washed," making further theological significance that this is a voluntary act on the part of one who is being baptized (e.g., G. R. Beasley-Murray, *Baptism in the New Testament* [Grand Rapids: Eerdmans, 1962] 163; R. Y. K. Fung, "Justification by Faith in 1 & 2 Corinthians," in *Pauline Studies: Essays Presented to Professor F. F. Bruce on his 70th Birthday* [ed. D. A. Hagner and M. J. Harris; Grand Rapids: Eerdmans, 1980] 250; Robertson-Plummer 119). But much of that discussion will not "wash," since the verb occurs almost altogether in the middle. This is a middle that functions like a passive. Cf. Dunn, *Baptism*, 123 and most English translations.

[159] See on 2 Thes 2:13 and the note there.

[160] Although the text does not actually so specify, this is inherent in the "divine passives." See the discussion below.

explicit, and more needs to be said about how Paul views the various relationships expressed in this pregnant sentence.

The *structure* of the sentence holds the key. It begins with three verbs, each introduced with the strong adversative "but," adding force to the "once you were, but now you are not" emphasis of the sentence. As in 1:30, the three verbs are primarily metaphors of salvation, each expressing a special facet of their conversion in light of the preceding sentences: they had been "washed" from the filth of their former lifestyles expressed in the preceding list; they had been "sanctified," set apart by God for holy, godly living that starkly contrasts with their former wickedness; they had been justified, who were formerly "unjust,"[161] so that now right with God they may inherit the kingdom that before they could not. Each of the verbs is thus chosen for contextual, not dogmatic, reasons; and their sequence is theologically irrelevant.[162] "Washing" comes first because that most naturally follows the "filth" of the vice catalogue. Finally, since the three verbs refer essentially to the same reality, and since each of them is in the "divine passive" with "God" as the implied subject, the two prepositional phrases are best understood as modifying all three verbs.[163] God has effected the salvation expressed by these rich metaphors "in the name of the Lord Jesus Christ and by his Spirit."

If the two prepositional phrases modify the three verbs, then they probably carry the same grammatical freight, in this case instrumental (cf. GNB, NEB). The reference to "the name" of Christ, as in 1:10 and 5:4 (cf. 2 Thes 3:6), thus refers to the authority of Christ on behalf of the believer, especially in terms of his saving work; and the reference to the Spirit reflects Paul's understanding of the Spirit as the means whereby God in the present age effects the work of Christ in the believer's life. Together, then, the two prepositional phrases refer to what God has done *for* his people *through Christ*, which he has effected *in* them by *the Spirit*. This also means that one should not press the relationship of the Spirit

---

[161] It is difficult to resist seeing in this verb (δικαιόω) something of a word play on the adjective ἄδικοι in vv. 1 and 9 and on its cognate verb ἀδικέω in vv. 7–8. This, after all, is the main thrust of the entire section (6:1–11).

[162] Some are anxious about the ordering of these verbs, as if Paul were thereby making some kind of theological statement that does not seem to fit our own dogmatic categories. This is true even of C. A. A. Scott's attempt to read the verbs in reverse order (i.e., behind each action lay the former one; see *Christianity according to St. Paul* [Cambridge: University Press, 1927] 120).

[163] The repetition of the ἀλλά before each verb also argues for this (cf. Fung, "Justification," 251). Contra Scott, (previous n.). Cf. the less than convincing presentation by K. Bailey ("Paul's Theological Foundation for Human Sexuality: 1 Cor. 6:9–20 in the Light of Rhetorical Criticism," *ThRev* 3 [1980] 28–29), who argues that the sentence has step parallelism, with each verb corresponding in sequence to the persons of the Trinity mentioned in the prepositional phrases (washed = Christ; sanctified = Spirit; justified = God). This destroys Paul's own parallelism found in the two nicely balanced prepositional phrases.

to the three metaphors expressed by the three verbs. In each case, Christ's death was the place in history where such saving activity took place; they were saved in these various aspects "by the name of our Lord Jesus Christ." But because they were all experientially appropriated at conversion, which is essentially the work of the Spirit, they were also saved in these various aspects "by the Spirit of our God."

Since all these verbs function as metaphors for various aspects of salvation, they all refer primarily to the work of Christ in our behalf. Nonetheless, they also occur elsewhere in Paul as activities of the Spirit, in contexts where the focus is on the experienced reality. Thus "washed" occurs as the activity of the Spirit in Titus 3:5; "justified," in the form of its cognate noun "righteousness/justification," occurs as the work of the Spirit in 2 Cor 3:8–9 and Gal 5:5; for obvious reasons "sanctified" occurs more often as a Spirit activity (1 Thes 4:7–8; 2 Thes 2:13; Rom 15:16) than it does in connection with Christ.[164]

Once more, as in 5:6–8, Paul urges the Corinthians to become what they are; and he predicates that imperative on the prior work of Christ. In this case, however, the imperative is only implied. The emphasis on the work of Christ falls less on the objective reality of his sacrifice and more on their own experience of that reality by means of the Spirit. They are to *be* and *behave* differently from the wicked, because God in his mercy has already removed the stains of their past sins, has already begun the work of ethical transformation, and has already given them forgiveness and right standing with himself. This is precisely why Paul adds "and by the Spirit of our God" to the work of Christ. The concern is not simply with positional realities, but effected realities. The Spirit not only brought these realities to bear on their lives at conversion but, in Pauline theology, the Spirit also effectively empowers them for life in the present. This seems the more certain in light of the qualifier, "of our God," which Paul tends to add whenever ethical life is at stake. As always in Paul, such a qualifier indicates the closest relationship between the Spirit and the Father and implies that the presence of the Spirit in the lives of believers is none other than the presence of God himself.

Many interpreters also detect in this sentence close ties between the Spirit and water baptism, understanding "you were washed" not to be (only) a metaphor for cleansing from sin, but to refer to the waters of baptism.[165] But Paul does not say, "you were baptized," which he was perfectly capable of doing if baptism were his concern. This verb (ἀπολούομαι) is not used elsewhere in the NT to denote baptism.[166]

---

[164] See 1 Cor 1:2; Eph 5:26, where it is Christ's activity.

[165] See, e.g., the discussion in Beasley-Murray, *Baptism*, 162–67; for the contrary view, see Dunn, *Baptism*, 120–23.

[166] It is linked with baptism in a metaphorical way in Acts 22:16; despite suggestions to the contrary (e.g., H. M. Ervin, *Conversion-Initiation and the Baptism in*

Besides appealing to the connotation in the verb "washing" itself, the argument most frequently used in favor of a reference to baptism is the association with the first prepositional phrase, "in the name of our Lord Jesus Christ."[167] But this is to read Paul through the eyes of Luke. Two matters of usage suggest otherwise: (1) This proposed use of ἐν (in) with "baptism" does not correspond to Paul's usage elsewhere. In the NT ἐν with "baptize" refers always to the element into which one has been baptized;[168] with the combination "baptize" and "name," Paul uses the preposition εἰς (into): one is "baptized *into* the name" (cf. 1:13–15)[169] or "into Christ" (Gal 3:28).[170] (2) The two prepositions and three verbs all go together; and there is no parallel in Paul's usage that one is "baptized in the name of Christ and in the Spirit of our God," or that one is sanctified or justified at baptism.

This is not to say that the verb for Paul may not have carried with it an indirect allusion to baptism; rather Paul is not here concerned with the Christian initiatory rite, but with the spiritual transformation made possible through Christ and effected by the Spirit. The three metaphors emphasize the aspects of Christian conversion found in the theological terms "regeneration, sanctification, and justification";[171] and for Paul these are the work of the Spirit in the believer's life, not the result of baptism.[172]

It needs only be noted once more how crucial the role of the Spirit is to Paul's view of salvation in Christ. It is not that the Spirit saves; that

---

the Holy Spirit [Peabody, Mass.: Hendrickson, 1984] 93), it is *not* the actual verb for baptism itself.

[167] See, e.g., Ervin, *Conversion-Initiation*, 94. Ervin's comments, because they are directed so specifically against Dunn's *Baptism*, have several questionable moments.

[168] For Paul, see 1 Cor 10:2 and 12:13.

[169] This is standard usage in the NT, except for Acts 2:38, which has ἐπί; this would suggest, therefore, that the ἐν τῷ ὀνόματι Ἰησοῦ Χριστοῦ in Acts 10:48 goes *not* with βαπτισθῆναι, but as elsewhere in the NT, with the verb "command," which makes far more sense of this passage in any case.

[170] It should perhaps also be pointed out that the collocation of "the name of Jesus" with baptism does not occur in Paul. In the name of Jesus one "commands" (2 Thes 3:6), "appeals" (1 Cor 1:10), "judges" (5:3–4), "does all things" (Col 3:17), "gives thanks" (Eph 5:20), and "is washed, sanctified, justified" (here); but nowhere is one "baptized" ἐν τῷ ὀνόματι of Jesus.

[171] For these latter two words see Fee 86–87 on 1:30; for "sanctify" see also on 1:2, and for "justify" see on 4:4. Some have argued that the verb "justify" here does not have the full theological significance that obtains in Galatians and Romans (e.g., R. Bultmann, *Theology of the New Testament* [2 vols.; trans. K. Grobel; New York: Scribners, 1951–55] 1.136); but there are no valid lexical or contextual grounds for so arguing. See the discussion in Fung, "Justification," 250–51; cf. Conzelmann 107.

[172] For a similar view see Dunn, *Baptism*, 120–23; cf. Barrett 141, who allows that "baptism is in mind," but that "it is the inward meaning rather than the outward circumstances of the rite that is important to Paul." For the view that it refers to baptism see, Beasley-Murray, *Baptism*, 162–67, and most of the other literature on baptism, as well as most commentaries.

is the work of the Father through the Son. But the Spirit appropriates God's salvation in the life of the believer in such a way that new life and behavior are the expected result; and without the latter, the effective work of the Spirit in the believer's life, there has been no true salvation—in any meaningful sense for Paul.

1 CORINTHIANS 6:14

And God both raised the Lord and will raise us through his power.

The reason for including this sentence in this study is the final phrase, that God has raised Christ, and will also raise us, "through his power." Ordinarily the use of the word "power" in a passage like this might lead one to think that the Spirit were lurking just beneath the surface.[173] However, nothing inherent either in this text or in Pauline usage elsewhere suggests that Jesus was raised by the power of the Spirit.[174] The closest thing to it is Eph 1:19–20, when interpreted in light of 3:16. The "power" at work in believers, which is almost certainly a reference to the Spirit, is the same "power" that raised Christ from the dead. Nevertheless, the emphasis even there is on the power of God at work in believers, not on the presence of the Spirit as such.

All told, it seems unlikely that Paul is here trying to say something about the Spirit. The addition, "through his power," actually throws the sentence out of balance with the previous sentence in v. 13b, with which it is otherwise intentionally in parallel.[175] The phrase may have been added not because of the mention of Christ, but because of the mention of the resurrection of believers, which lies still in the future. The sentence, therefore, anticipates the more detailed argument in ch. 15, where some are denying a future resurrection of believers (15:12). As in that argument, our resurrection is predicated on the resurrection of Christ: "God both raised the Lord, and he will raise us." This affirmation sharply opposes the Corinthian view of spirituality, which looked for a "spiritual" salvation that would finally be divested of the body. But God by his power will in fact raise us "bodily" at the future resurrection of believers; whether that, too, is an activity of the Spirit is a moot point and cannot be demonstrated with finality one way or the other.

1 CORINTHIANS 6:17

But the one who has been joined to the Lord is one S/spirit.

---

[173] As e.g., in 2 Thes 1:11; Col 1:11; Eph 3:16, 20. See the discussion in ch. 2.

[174] Although some would see this connection in Rom 1:3–4; 8:11; and 1 Tim 3:16. See esp. the discussion on Rom 8:11, and in ch. 12, pp. 808–11.

[175] Except, of course, for the repetition of the verb, since in this case one action has already taken place, while the other is still future, whereas in v. 13b both actions are still future: "God will destroy both the one [the stomach] and the other [food]."

This kind of sentence discloses that Paul is often more interested in his rhetoric and the balanced parallelism of his sentences than he is with their linguistic precision. Consequently, the *reason* for this sentence, and the way it is expressed, is far easier to determine than the exact sense that Paul intended—although that, too, can be determined with a fairly high degree of certainty.

The *form* of the sentence has been determined by v. 16, "the one who has been joined to a prostitute is one body." The verb "joined" was chosen because of its sexual connotations; the "one body" (rather than the "one flesh" of Gen 2:24, which Paul goes on to cite) was chosen because of the argumentation to this point, all of which has to do with the Corinthians' obviously negative view toward the physical body.[176]

They have argued that since food is for the stomach and the stomach for food, and since neither will go on into eternity, so also regarding the body and sex (v. 13). But Paul reformulates their slogan by insisting that "the body is *not* for *porneia*, but for the Lord," as is evidenced by the resurrection (v. 14). In vv. 15–17 Paul sets out to explain his reformulation by applying it directly to their going to the prostitutes. The argument is in two parts, both introduced by the formula, "Do you not know that?" Verse 15 asserts, on the basis of v. 14, that the bodies of believers are "members" of the "body" of the Lord and therefore cannot be joined to a prostitute, to become "members" of her body. Verses 16–17 further explain v. 15, asserting on the basis of Gen 2:24 that in sexual intercourse two bodies become one, which is how a man becomes a "member" of her body. To have sexual intercourse with a prostitute involves an illicit sexual joining of one's body to that of another (literally). It is not the sexual union itself that is incompatible with union with Christ; it is such a union *with a prostitute*. This constitutes bodily union with a person who is not a member of Christ, whose own body therefore is not destined for resurrection.

And that is what sets up the unusual parallel in v. 17, where "Lord" is substituted for "prostitute" and πνεῦμα for "body." Paul's concern is easy to see, even if stated in complex fashion. The illicit union is now being contrasted to the believer's union with Christ. In light of vv. 19–20, Paul's primary referent is to the work of the Holy Spirit, whereby through the "one Spirit" the believer's "spirit" has been joined indissolubly with Christ.[177] Thus, by the Spirit the believer is united to the Lord and thereby has become one S/spirit[178] with him. This does not mean that

---

[176] On this matter see the discussion in Fee 250–57.

[177] Cf. Dunn, *Baptism*, 123–24. For a considerable argument against those who see this usage as contrasting "spirit" with "body," with the latter being a lesser union, see R. H. Gundry, *SOMA in Biblical Theology with emphasis on Pauline Anthropology* (SNTSMS 29; Cambridge: University Press, 1976) 65–69. Such an idea is so foreign to the context, one wonders how any could have convinced themselves of its validity.

[178] On this proposed translation, see on 5:3–5; cf. esp. 14:14–15.

Paul is now abandoning the concern over the body; vv. 18–20 indicate that he is not. Since the language has been dictated by its parallel, and since the union it contrasts was constituted through sexual intercourse, he could scarcely describe it in terms of becoming "one body" with the Lord. Even though the concern is still with the believer's physical body, which belongs to the Lord on the basis of his resurrection, the union in this case is of a different kind; the way to express that union is in terms of the Spirit.

Thus Paul's point is singular: to demonstrate that the physical union of a believer with a prostitute is not an option, because the believer's body already belongs to the Lord, through whose resurrection one's body has become a "member" of Christ by his Spirit.

Because the language has been dictated by the argument, one needs to use special caution as to how the Spirit language is understood. It is especially doubtful whether this says anything significant about Christology, as though Paul considered the risen Christ and the Spirit to be one. Such a proposal misses the argumentation by too much. Moreover, it is equally doubtful whether it says anything about one's "mystical" union with Christ through the Spirit. If such theology is to be found in Paul, this sentence does not support it. What the text does affirm is what is plainly said in scores of other places, namely, that the Spirit is responsible for our being "in Christ." And here that is most likely understood as having happened at conversion. Anything beyond that presses Paul's language far beyond his own intent and away from his own theology.

1 Corinthians 6:19–20

[19]*Or do you not know that your body*[179] *is the temple of the Holy Spirit within you, whom you have from God, and that you are not your own?* [20]*For you were purchased at a price; therefore, glorify God in your body.*[180]

---

[179] Gk. τὸ σῶμα ὑμῶν; for this use of the Semitic "distributive singular," see the discussion on Gal 6:18. Some later MSS (A L Ψ 33 81 pm), apparently uncomfortable with this usage, turn "body" into the plural ("your bodies").

[180] One of the manifestly theological textual corruptions to this letter is the addition of the words καὶ ἐν τῷ πνεύματι ὑμῶν, ἅτινά ἐστιν τοῦ θεοῦ (and with your spirits, which are God's), read by the MajT, with no supporting evidence earlier than the seventh century. The addition may have been the result of early Christian liturgy, as Lightfoot 218 suggests. Unfortunately, it also became Scripture to generations of Christians and had the net result of deflecting Paul's point toward the position of the Corinthian pneumatics. Not that the addition is untrue; rather, it completely misses the concern of the present argument, which stands over against the Corinthian view that the body counts for nothing and therefore it matters not what one does with it. To the contrary, Paul argues throughout, the body is included in the redemptive work of God and therefore may not be involved in sexual immorality.

With these words Paul concludes the argument of 6:12–20, offering theological justification and explanation for the prohibition of v. 18.[181] At the same time the content of the question in v. 19 reinforces and elaborates the theology of the body expressed in vv. 13–17. Using two images (temple and purchase of slaves = the Spirit and the cross) Paul reasserts that the body even in its present existence belongs to God. Thus the body is included in the full redemptive work of Christ—crucifixion, resurrection, and the present work of the Spirit. All of which leads to the final inferential imperative: they must therefore glorify God in their bodies, which in this context means no sexual immorality.

The Spirit language of this passage is full of theological bite. Their understanding of Spirit had led to disdain for the body; they belong to another world, the heavenly one, where there will finally be no body. So in their view, since "all things are lawful" in any case (v. 12), the body has very little to do with anything—least of all with life in the Spirit.

As throughout, Paul embraces another view, the view from above. The Spirit, he insists—and this must have come as an extraordinary idea to them—has everything to do with the body. Not only is the body destined for resurrection—indeed he will argue in 15:44–49 that the resurrection body is nothing less than πνευματικόν!—but it is even now the habitation of the Spirit, the Spirit's very temple. "Or do you not know," he asks—and they obviously did not—"that your body is the temple of the Holy Spirit, who is in you, whom you have received from God, and that you are not your own?"

The final clause, "and that you are not your own," probably forms part of the question,[182] the two parts complementing each other. The body is the present habitation of God's Spirit, which implies that one belongs to the God whose Spirit dwells within. At the same time, the second part results in a shift of metaphors, so that God's proper ownership of the body is affirmed in terms of their being "bought at a price." The accent, therefore, falls especially on the body as "for the Lord" (see v. 13) in the sense of being God's rightful possession, which is evidenced both through the indwelling Spirit and redemptive work of Christ. Here is yet another of the semi-creedal soteriological passages, in which God's salvation is seen as the work of the triune God.[183] None of these passages is the same, but all of them have in common that God saves through Christ by the Spirit.

In referring to the body as the temple of the Spirit, of course, Paul adopted the imagery that first of all belongs to the church as a whole (cf.

---

[181] That they must flee sexual immorality because it is sin; in this case sin of a special kind, since it is the one sin that is deliberately against one's own body.

[182] This is not demanded by the Greek text, but makes far better sense of it. See Findlay 821; Barrett 151; cf. NRSV, NASB (contra NIV, NEB).

[183] See 1 Thes 1:5–6 and the list in n. 39; cf. 6:11 above.

3:16; 2 Cor 6:16; Eph 2:21–22) and applied it to the individual believer.[184] The use of the possessives reflects something of the difference. In 3:16 the church through the Spirit is *God's* temple in Corinth, in contrast to all the pagan temples and shrines. Through the phenomenon of the indwelling Spirit, Paul now images the body as the *Spirit's* temple, underscoring that it is the "place" of the Spirit's dwelling in the individual believers' lives. In the same way that the temple in Jerusalem "housed" the presence of the living God, so the body of the believer "houses" the presence of the living God by his Spirit. This is imagery pure and simple, affirming the significance of the body for the present; it is not intended to be a statement of Christian anthropology, as though the body were the mere external casing of the spirit or Spirit. But what *is* significant is that the believer is the present *locus* of God's own *presence*. The God who tabernacled among his people, whose same glory filled Solomon's temple, now tabernacles among his eschatological people by his Spirit (3:16). But more than that; for Paul the gift of the Spirit is also the fulfillment of the new covenant promises made through Jeremiah and Ezekiel.[185] Hence God not only dwells *among* his people, but is himself present, by his Spirit, *within* his people, sanctifying their present earthly existence and stamping it with his own eternity.

Thus, the Spirit's indwelling is the *presupposition of the imagery*, reinforced here by the two modifiers, "who is in you"[186] and "whom you have from God." What Paul seems to be doing is taking over their own theological starting point, namely, that they are "spiritual" because they have the Spirit, and redirecting it to include the sanctity of the body. The reality of the indwelling Spirit is now turned against them. They thought the presence of the Spirit negated the body's value; Paul argues the exact opposite: The presence of the Spirit in their bodily existence is God's affirmation of the body.

Thus, a variety of Spirit motifs that have already been found in earlier texts are sketched once more, in both intentional and less intentional ways. (1) Salvation is an activity of the triune God; the role of the Spirit in this case is not so much for the appropriation of Christ's work, as for life in the present. (2) The Spirit has been sent forth from God and is "received"[187] by individual believers. (3) As such the Spirit indwells the

---

[184] Otherwise R. Kempthorne, "Incest and the Body of Christ: A Study of I Corinthians VI.12–20," *NTS* 14 (1967–68) 568–74 (cf. K. Romaniuk, "Exégèse du Nouveau Testament et ponctuation," *NovT* 23 [1981] 199–205), who considers the passage, especially from v. 15, to be dealing with the church as the body of Christ. See the refutation in Gundry, *SOMA*, 76. On the imagery itself, see 3:16.

[185] See on 1 Thes 4:8 and 2 Cor 3:6.

[186] Gk. ἐν ὑμῖν; in contrast to 3:16 this is distributive, referring to the Spirit in the life of each of them. Paul's phrase actually reads "the in you Holy Spirit" (cf. 1 Tim 4:14).

[187] Paul's clause reads, "which you have from God"; the emphasis, however, is

believer, as God's own sanctifying presence. (4) The Spirit is here given his full name, which often happens when holiness is part of the concern. (5) Sanctification includes the body, which through Christ's resurrection has been made his own possession and is thereby destined for resurrection. To be Spirit-ual, therefore, does not mean to deny the physical side of our human life; neither, of course, does it mean to indulge it. The presence of the Spirit means that God himself, who created us with bodies in the first place, has taken keen interest in our whole life, including the life of the body. The creation of the body was pronounced *good* in the beginning; it has now been purchased by Christ and is sanctified by the presence of God himself through his Holy Spirit. We must therefore "sanctify" it as well ("therefore glorify God in your bodies"), by living the life of the Spirit, a life of holiness.

The message of this text needs to be sounded repeatedly in the face of every encroachment of Hellenistic dualism that would negate the body in favor of the soul. God made us whole people; and in Christ he has redeemed us wholly. According to the Christian view there is no dichotomy between body and spirit that either indulges the body because it is irrelevant or punishes it so as to purify the spirit. This pagan view of physical existence creeps into Christian theology in any number of subtle ways, including the penchant on the part of some to "save souls" while caring little for people's material needs. Not the immortality of the soul, but the resurrection of the body, is the Christian creed, based on NT revelation. That creed does not lead to crass materialism; rather it affirms a holistic view of redemption, which is predicated in part on the doctrine of creation—both the physical and spiritual orders are good because God created them—and in part on the doctrine of redemption, including the consummation—the whole fallen order, including the body, has been redeemed in Christ and awaits its final redemption. The unmistakable evidence of this is the presence of the Spirit, which does not move us toward a false, Hellenistic "spirituality," but toward the biblical view noted here.

1 CORINTHIANS 7:7

But every person has his or her own gracious gift from God, one[188] of one kind, and one of another.

---

not on possession but on God as the source. Thus the "received" of the NIV is a legitimate translation.

[188] For the o μεν . . . o δε of ℵ* A B C D F G P 6 33 81 630 1739 1881 2464 pc, P46 and the MajT have ὃς μέν . . . ὃς δέ (favored by Zuntz, *Text*, 52, on the grounds that it is an Atticism, which scribes would not likely have rejected). The original is almost certainly o μεν . . . o δε; but the question of accenting remains. The critical editions (NA26) favor the article: ὁ μέν . . . ὁ δέ, thus highlighting the person(s) with the

This second occurrence of χάρισμα (gracious endowment) in this letter, and thus in the Pauline corpus (see on 1:7), functions along with the usage in 2 Cor 1:11 and Rom 6:23 as evidence that the concept of "Spiritual gift" is ancillary to this word at best, not inherent to it. For Paul the emphasis in this word is always primarily on God's grace, of which the "gift" is the concrete expression. That is especially so in this case.

The Corinthians apparently have used Paul's own celibacy as part of their argument for asserting that "it is good for a man not to touch a woman [= engage in sexual relations]" (v. 1b). But for Paul there is a difference between his celibacy and mere singleness. His celibacy was not singleness by choice, predicated as some of theirs was on the questionable grounds that marriage is sin, but by χάρισμα—it was his as giftedness resulting from God's grace. Celibacy, therefore, was an expression of giftedness that had freed him from the need for sexual fulfillment, thus making it possible for him to live without marriage. But lest he be understood to make celibacy a higher calling, he immediately qualifies, "one χάρισμα of one kind, another χάρισμα of another kind." Thus, if celibacy is χάρισμα, so is marriage.

Even though Paul obviously prefers his own status, and "wishes that others were as he is," he also recognizes that the Corinthian pneumatics' attitude toward singleness was predicated on a false spirituality that tended toward making celibacy a requirement. Lest their "slogan" in v. 1b become the "rule," he reminds them that *everything* is χάρισμα, and that "giftedness" differs from one person to the next. Celibacy is for the celibate, who are so by gracious endowment. By their very nature as concrete expressions of grace that differ from one person to another, χαρίσματα cannot be reduced to principle or made into requirements.

All of this suggests rather strongly that Paul, who uses the word χάρισμα in 16 of its 17 occurrences in the NT, would never have imagined that the word means "Spiritual gift," as though all χαρίσματα were Spirit manifestations of some kind.

1 Corinthians 7:34

Both the unmarried woman and the virgin are concerned about the things of the Lord, that they might be holy in both[189] body and spirit.

χάρισμα(τα), just as in the textual variation. However, since this would be a unique usage in the NT, which otherwise always has the relative pronoun with the indefinite "the one–the other," it is far more likely that such is the case here. Thus Paul would have intended ὃ μέν . . . ὃ δέ, referring to the χάρισμα itself ("one χάρισμα of one kind . . . another χάρισμα of another kind").

[189] A number of early and diverse witnesses do not have this first καί (P46 A D P 33 1175 2495 a t), a reading Zuntz (*Text*, 199) prefers on stylistic grounds. Conzelmann (131n5) suggests that the text of P46 et al. means "in the body and the Spirit," but that is both unnecessary and almost impossible.

Although this is not an especially easy text to interpret in its context,[190] the meaning of the final phrase, ἐν τῷ πνεύματι (in spirit) seems certain in this case to be a purely anthropological usage. The exegetical difficulty has to do with what it might mean and why it was added in this way in the larger context. The options are two. If the verb μεριμνᾷ is negative (as the cognate adjective, "without anxiety," in v. 32 might suggest), then Paul is reflecting the Corinthians' point of view: those who are avoiding sexual relations for ascetic reasons are being anxious about how they might please the Lord with their bodies as well as with their spirits. If the verb is positive (as in my translation, but without conviction), then this usage reflects a perspective very close to that of 1 Thes 5:23 (q.v.), where the two words together ("both body and spirit") mean "entirely," that is, "holy in every possible way." See the similar usage in 2 Cor 7:1.

1 Corinthians 7:40

But she is the more blessed if she remains unmarried, according to my opinion. And[191] I think that I also have the Spirit of God.[192]

Paul's final word in ch. 7 is also his only mention of the Spirit in the long twin sections in which he deals with matters from their letter related to marriage and singleness. Apart from divorce (vv. 10–11), he is dealing with matters not inherently ethical and therefore on which there is no "word from the Lord" in the Christian ethical tradition (v. 12). Thus Paul has had to speak for himself, as it were, even though he considers his opinion as quite trustworthy (see vv. 6, 12, 25, 40a). This final word should therefore come as no surprise: He believes that "he also has the Spirit of God," thus enabling him to speak to these issues.

But given the nature of the argument throughout, one is not quite sure how the Corinthians were to take the little word, "I also."[193] Is this simply an additional note to follow the mention of his opinion?[194] That is, even though he has given this final advice as his opinion, he none-theless also has the Spirit to help him, so that his opinion is not simply given willy-nilly?[195] Or does this final clause serve also as a final word over against them: if they think they have the Spirit, and have therefore

---

[190] See the discussion in Fee 345–46.

[191] For this δέ B 6 33 104 365 630 1739 1881 2495 pc t substitute an explanatory γάρ. See the discussion in Zuntz, *Text*, 204.

[192] P15 and 33 substitute "Christ" for God, thus conforming it to 2:16.

[193] It appears in the contracted form κἀγώ, which, when it stands first in its clause means "and I." But when it occurs after its verb, or after a conjunction like καθώς, it means "I also."

[194] As most commentators and English translations, e.g., the GNB, which con-strues the two items as one sentence: "That is my opinion, and I think that I too have God's Spirit."

[195] Note the similar immediate qualification of his "opinion" in v. 25.

argued as they have in their letter,[196] he *too* has the Spirit, even when he is giving forth his opinion on these matters.

In light of the similar qualification in v. 25, and since what Paul says here is something on which they and he would tend to be agree, it is more likely that the former is intended, although it may also be a subtle word against those who were not so sure that he in fact did possess the Spirit.

In either case, the net result is the same. Paul considers his instruction to have its ultimate source in the Spirit—who is once more called "the Spirit of God." This designates the Spirit as not simply from God, but as the way God himself is present in the apostle's ministry. But in this case the Spirit as "ultimate source" of his teaching does not mean in the sense of "revelation," as in 2:12–13, where he is referring to the gospel. Rather, it is in the sense that as he is one who lives in and by the Spirit and whom God regards as trustworthy (v. 25), the Spirit serves as the ultimate ground even for Paul's opinions on matters where there is no revelation. Thus "having the Spirit," even for an apostle, does not guarantee every word to be a word of revelation, nor does it allow even Paul to use the Spirit on such matters as a whip for his authority. The Spirit in this case is not the guarantor of Paul's words, but of Paul's life, which makes these words more than simply one man's personal opinion.

1 CORINTHIANS 9:11

If we have sown for you the things of the Spirit, is it such a great thing that we shall reap of your fleshly things?

In one of the strangest arguments on record, and with some of the most vigorous rhetoric to be found in his letters, Paul argues in 9:1–14 for his apostolic "rights" to material support from the Corinthian church. The strangeness of the argument rests with the fact that he cares not a whit for their support; indeed he has regularly refused it. Why, then, such vigor for something that he intends in vv. 15–18 to go on to offer his reasons for having refused? The answer stems almost certainly, as 2 Cor 11:7–12 and 12:13 later make plain, from their viewing his refusal of patronage as grounds for calling his apostleship into question.[197] So

---

[196] Their whole argument apparently was predicated on their false Spirit-uality that has so denigrated the body, that some had even argued that "marriage is sin" (vv. 28, 36). Although the present argument carries less passion than elsewhere in this letter, it seems nonetheless clear that they have hardly written to Paul asking for his opinion on these matters; the nature of the argumentation will scarcely allow such a view. Rather, as elsewhere, he and they are at odds on this matter. For this reconstruction, see Fee 267–70.

[197] After all, the entire section begins on this note: "Am I not free? Am I not an apostle? . . . If I am not an apostle to others, surely I am one to you!" Their syllogism

with one rhetorical question pouring forth over another, he first insists on his full apostolic rights to their patronage, before he goes on to explain why he has felt constrained in their case not to accept it.

Our text lies toward the end of the first round of this argument. Its point is as straightforward as anything in the section. As the one responsible for having preached Christ among them so that, as vv. 1–2 emphatically point out, they came to faith through his ministry, they in reciprocity owe him their material support. This is not only the way things are in the "natural" order (vv. 7–10), but is also the way of Israel (v. 13) and the way of Christ (v. 14).

But he says this in our passage by way of metaphor, keeping alive by application the sowing and reaping imagery from the OT that he has just used in vv. 9–10. The two adjectives are what hold our interest. On the one hand, his preaching of the gospel is described as "sowing τὰ πνευματικά," which in this case must refer to the "things of the Spirit"—not "spiritual" in the sense of religious or sacred as over against merely earthly, secular, or temporal. This is yet another ironic moment in the letter. They who think of themselves—because they truly are—people of the Spirit, must not forget who sowed among them the things of the Spirit that made it possible for them to be so. Here is another instance where the adjective "spiritual" must be understood as referring primarily to the Holy Spirit. It therefore means "Spiritual."[198]

On the other hand, and typically, the contrast to the things of the Spirit is τὰ σαρκικά (the things of the flesh). As the context makes plain in this case, this word enjoys a great deal of flexibility in Pauline usage, since here it can refer only to material support. Therefore, there is nothing pejorative in its present usage.[199] It is simply the natural contrast with Spirit, where the one refers to the preaching of the gospel and the other to material benefits in return. On this usage see also Rom 15:27.

1 CORINTHIANS 10:3–4

[3]*And they all ate the same*[200] *spiritual food* [4]*and all drank the same spiritual drink; for they drank from the spiritual rock that accompanied them, and that rock was Christ.*

---

seems to be: Major premise: Apostles accept patronage (in light of Apollos). Minor premise: Paul did not accept patronage. Conclusion: therefore, Paul is no apostle, or at least it is questionable.

[198] See the discussion in ch. 2.

[199] Any more than in the same contrast in Rom 1:3–4, where Jesus is born of the seed of David, "according to the flesh," meaning by natural descent.

[200] p46 and A, plus a few others in each case, omit the αὐτό here and in v. 4. Most likely the omission is the result of homoeoteleuton (TOAYTO).

Although Spirit concerns lie just below the surface throughout much of the argumentation of this long section of the letter (8:1–11:1),[201] these sentences contain the only other explicit mention of the Spirit, again in the adjective form πνευματικός, and in a way that is not at all easy to interpret.

The nature and form of Paul's argumentation suggest that the reason for the wording lies in Corinth itself. The best solution to the whole section is to see the issue as having to do not with the eating of market-place food, for which Paul cares almost nothing at all,[202] but with their insisting on the right to continue to eat such food in the pagan temples.[203] Therefore, "unpacking" the present argument (10:1–22), and especially the unusual analogies from the Exodus in vv. 1–5, depends upon appreciating their understanding of baptism and the Lord's Supper as affording a kind of Spiritual security for them when they attend the pagan feasts.

Not so, Paul argues vigorously, beginning with analogies from Israel itself. The Israelites had their own form of "baptism" (vv. 1–2) and "Lord's Supper" (vv. 3–4); yet they were not only *not* secured by such, but in fact the great majority of them were scattered all over the desert. It is in the mention of their form of "Lord's Supper" that Paul designates Israel's food and drink in terms of the Spirit. In so doing he also let loose in the church a long history of a "spiritual" understanding of our Supper that not only misses the Spirit, but is considerably removed from the apostle himself.

In the same way as the Red Sea was Israel's form of being "baptized into Moses," so Paul describes Israel's experience of the miraculous bread (Exod 16:4–30) and miraculous drinking of water from the rock (Exod 17:1–7; Num 20:2–13)[204] as a form of "spiritual eating,"[205] unquestion-

---

[201] Especially in the language on which their whole argument is predicated, "we all have γνῶσις." On γνῶσις as evidence of the Spirit, see the discussion on 1:4–7, which will suffice for this section of the letter as well.

[202] As 10:23–11:1 makes especially clear; so, too, with 9:19–23, where he appears to be defending his own stance with regard to such food when eaten in homes.

[203] As 8:10 specifically suggests; and as the whole of 10:1–22 is specifically directed toward. Their γνῶσις, which comes from the Spirit, has not simply "helped" them with regard to the food itself—on this he and they are quite in agreement (cf. Rom 14:17)—but has led them to argue that monotheism means the idols do not exist (8:4); and that since food is an irrelevancy (8:8), then surely not only *what* we eat but *where* we eat it must be a matter of indifference to God.

[204] It should be noted that these are not the only references to these events in the OT, but they are the primary historical ones; and in Exod 16–17 the miraculous feeding and drinking immediately follow one another. Although the two events are mentioned separately in subsequent traditions (e.g., Deut 8:3, where the bread is already being interpreted "spiritually"), more often they appear together (e.g., Deut 8:15–16; Neh 9:15, 20; Ps 78:15–31; 105:40). Cf. John's Gospel, where the eschatological "bread from heaven" is the theme of ch. 6, followed by the eschatological water in 7:37–39.

[205] Goppelt (*TDNT* 6.146), following Dibelius, Weiss, and Käsemann, argues on the basis of the Corinthian fondness for this word and the usage in Did. 10:3 that this was already a term current in Corinth for the eucharistic elements. If so, it cannot

ably viewing it as a type/analogy of the Lord's Supper:[206] "They all ate the same[207] spiritual food; and they all drank the same spiritual drink."

But what does he intend in calling their food and drink "spiritual"?[208] That question is perhaps best answered by asking what other word he might have used to accomplish two ends simultaneously: (1) to refer to that food and drink which for Israel were supernaturally given and thus divinely sustained them in the desert; and (2) at the same time to suggest the analogy or type of the Lord's Supper, including the special food and drink of Christians to be distinguished from ordinary meals. That, in any case, is his concern and the reason for this choice of words. At the same time, the christological interpretation of the rock that follows[209] should alert us to the possibility that πνευματικόν here also carries its proper adjectival sense of "belonging to, or pertaining to the Spirit," or perhaps in this case, "deriving from the Spirit," emphasizing its divine origins. But "belonging" or "pertaining" to the Spirit in what way? That is the more difficult question, because the analogy suggests that whatever he meant about Israel's experience of supernatural provision, he means as well to apply to the Christian Eucharist.

It seems extremely doubtful that Paul was trying to say something about the sacramental character of the food, or that in some way it *conveyed* the Spirit.[210]

---

be demonstrated convincingly. For example, the usage in the Didache could be dependent on this passage, rather than reflecting widespread common usage in the early church. One simply cannot know.

[206] Contra Dunn, *Baptism*, 125, whose anti-sacramental stance causes him in this instance to reject any analogical/typological reference to the Eucharist here. Not only does the language nearly demand a eucharistic typology, but in the prohibition of the next paragraph (vv. 14–22) Paul begins with his understanding of the Eucharist as the reason why the Corinthians *cannot* go to the pagan meals.

[207] Calvin 204, followed by T. C. A. Edwards, *A Commentary on the First Epistle to the Corinthians* (3d ed., London: A. C. Armstrong, 1897) 245 and A. T. Hanson, *Jesus Christ in the Old Testament* (London, 1965) 19, argues that "same" here means "the same which we Christians eat." But that is quite beyond Paul's concern, which is to emphasize that *all* enjoyed the same privileges, including those whose bodies were scattered about the desert; cf. Héring 86, Barrett 221–22. Cf. v. 17; *all* eat the *one* bread.

[208] For a full discussion and critique of the various options, see W. L. Willis, *Idol Meat at Corinth: The Pauline Argument in 1 Corinthians 8 and 10* (SBLDS 68; Chico, Calif.: Scholars Press, 1985) 130–42, and R. M. Davidson, *Typology in Scripture: A Study of hermeneutical* τύπος *structures* [AUSSDS 2; Berrien Springs, Mich.: Andrews University Press, 1981] 225–31, 245–47.

[209] On the meaning of this sentence see the discussion in Fee 447–49.

[210] As e.g., E. Käsemann, "The Pauline Doctrine of the Lord's Supper," in *Essays on New Testament Themes* (ET; SBT 41; London: SCM, 1960) 108–35, who is characteristically bold: "βρῶμα and πόμα πνευματικόν undoubtedly mean 'food and drink which convey πνεῦμα,'" followed by Jewett, *Terms*, 38–39. But this is to place the emphasis on the sacraments in a way that Paul does not; his concern is with the Corinthians' idolatry, not their false sacramentalism. Moreover, the adjective is

Not only are such ideas foreign to Paul—and this use of an otherwise obscure adjective hardly argues to the contrary—but such a view puts the emphasis in the wrong place. More likely, as with the christological word that follows, Paul is concerned to establish that what Israel experienced in the desert truly is analogous to the Corinthians' own life in Christ. In their own way the Israelites not only experienced Christ in prefigurement, but they likewise had their own prefigurement of the Spirit.

If such is the case, then that does say something about how Paul understood the food of the Lord's Table as the place where the Spirit regularly applies the benefits of the cross, as represented in the food, to the life of the believer. Paul's understanding of the Table, therefore, falls not on the side of a kind of sacramentalism, where the food is regarded as conveying grace in some way, but, on the side of the Spirit as present at the Table, freshly appropriating the benefits of Christ to the believers' lives. Thus, the food of the Table is the Spirit's food in the sense that the Spirit, as the real presence, once more appropriates the provision of the cross to the one who eats by faith, in celebration with others.

This might seem to put a bit more stress on the Spirit as present at the Table than the text itself allows; but one simply must take seriously not only the basic meaning of the word πνευματικόν in Paul as primarily having reference to the Spirit but also the especially high incidence of this word in a letter to a church that apparently held this word, or the ideas inherent in the word, in such high regard. The Spirit does indeed have a role at the Table; but it is a role quite similar to that in conversion. The saving benefits come from Christ. They are realized anew at the Table, experientially and by faith, through the effective work of the Spirit as we eat together "in remembrance of the Lord."

1 CORINTHIANS 11:4–5

⁴Every man praying or prophesying, having down the head shames his head; ⁵but every woman praying or prophesying, uncovered as to the head, shames her[211] head.

---

properly a possessive and means something closer to "belonging to πνεῦμα," not "conveying Spirit."

At the same time it also exceeds the evidence, and probably misses Paul's intent, to suggest as Davidson does (*Typology*, 246), that "the apostle seems to intimate that ancient Israel also partook of sacramental gifts which conveyed the Spirit" (cf. 247: "Both are sacraments, charged with πνεῦμα, and salvific"). In this case Davidson's prior interest in typology, not simply as prefiguring but in some way as being *devoir-être* (must needs be), surpasses Paul's concerns in the text.

[211] In place of the (clearly original) αὐτῆς (her) of the rest, B D² 6 629 945 and a few others read ἑαυτῆς (her own). The context, and especially the way the argument is set up in v. 3 by designating certain relationships with the metaphor "head," demands that the shame is not on her own (literal) head, but on her metaphorical head (in this case "the man," probably "husband").

It is hardly possible here to resolve the exegetical difficulties of this extremely problematic passage; therefore, as before, I note some conclusions. The problem lay squarely on the head; in this case on the women's heads literally. We can only guess what they were doing (probably doffing a customary head covering) and why (probably because they considered themselves already as the angels, where sexual distinctions no longer mattered—and especially so in Christian worship where all spoke in tongues, the language of angels, as evidence of their having attained to this degree of heavenly existence).

In any case, Paul feels strongly enough about what they were doing to speak to it, which he does by starting in v. 3 with a theological construct about certain special relationships as one being "head" of another.[212] If men were to appear in worship as women (that is, with something hanging from their heads) they would thus bring shame to Christ; likewise if women appear as men (discarding the customary head covering) they bring shame on their husbands (presumably).

Our interest in the passage is singular: to note that quite in passing, in referring to both men and women in the worshipping assembly, he describes their activity in terms of "praying and prophesying." Several things should be noted about this first mention of the phenomenon of prophesying[213] in this letter.

1. That Paul is referring to the church gathered for worship cannot be doubted.[214] But Paul has no interest in describing Christian worship. The casual way in which he mentions the two activities of worship, praying and prophesying, is therefore instructive, precisely because it is so presuppositional for Paul. How else might one describe worship, Paul would be wont to ask. These two activities, therefore, probably represent the two basic kinds that would happen in Christian worship. Together they designate the two foci of worship—God and the believing community. Thus prayer (and song and tongues [according to 14:2 and 15], etc.) is directed Godward; and prophesying represents the many forms of

---

[212] Much ink has been spilt on the meaning of this metaphor. Despite demurrers (see esp. P. Cotterell and M. Turner, *Linguistics and Biblical Interpretation* [Downers Grove, Ill.: InterVarsity, 1989] 141–45) the early Greek Fathers probably had it right in seeing the metaphor as anatomical, where the head was the source—responsible for the life of—the body. For this discussion see Fee 501–5.

[213] On the meaning of prophesying itself, see the discussion of this term in 12:8 and in ch. 15, pp. 890–92.

[214] Although some have done so from time to time (e.g., P. Bachmann, *Der erste Brief des Paulus an die Korinther* [3d ed.; Kommentar zum Neuen Testament; Leipzig: A. Deichert, 1921]); but this is to create every imaginable exegetical difficulty. One may pray privately, but not so with prophecy! Ellis, *Prophecy*, 27, would limit the activity to "the prayer sessions of the pneumatics," but there is no such self-limiting suggestion either within the text or the letter.

speech—in this letter, Spirit-inspired speech—which are directed toward the people of God for their edification (14:26), or to outsiders to disclose the secrets of their hearts (14:24–25).

2. The fact that "prophesying" is the form of Spirit-inspired speech singled out for the sake of the community is also probably instructive. It seems clear from 1 Thes 5:19–20, and even more so from the argument in ch. 14 of this letter, that prophecy regularly occurred in the Pauline churches; from Paul's point of view it was the preferred expression of worship that was directed toward the people of God for their edification.

3. In terms of participation, both men and women apparently shared equally in the praying and prophesying. This is quite in keeping with 14:23, where again somewhat in passing Paul says that "all may prophesy." The problem in this case, therefore, is not with the *fact* that women prayed and prophesied in the assembly, but that they were doing so attired in the same fashion as men, which Paul considers to be an expression of shame. That women fully participated in the worship of the Pauline churches, including the more preferred expression of Spirit-inspired speech, prophecy, moves considerably beyond the norm of Paul's Jewish background and seems to be quite in keeping with the rest of the NT evidence, as little as it is.

1 CORINTHIANS 12:1–14:40[215]

This is the single largest block of Spirit material in the Pauline corpus; it is also one that has received an enormous amount of scholarly and popular attention, especially since the advent of the charismatic renewal in the 1960s. Because there is so much Spirit material, spanning such a lengthy argument, the present section of this chapter proceeds more along the lines of a commentary, so that all the pertinent issues, as well as much of the scholarly debate, might have ample hearing.[216]

---

[215] *Bibliography:* A. **Bittlinger,** *Gifts and Graces: A Commentary on 1 Corinthians 12–14* (ET; Grand Rapids: Eerdmans, 1967); D. A. **Carson,** *Showing the Spirit: An Exposition of 1 Corinthians 12–14* (Grand Rapids: Baker, 1987); **Dunn,** *Jesus*; **Ellis,** *Prophecy*; **Grudem,** *Gift*; J. W. **MacGorman,** *The Gifts of the Spirit: An Exposition of I Corinthians 12–14* (Nashville: Broadman, 1974); **Martin,** *Spirit*; C. H. **Talbert,** "Paul's Understanding of the Holy Spirit: The Evidence of 1 Corinthians 12–14," in *Perspectives on the New Testament: Essays in Honor of Frank Stagg* (ed. C. H. Talbert; Macon, Ga.: Mercer University Press, 1985) 95–108.

[216] Cf. 2:6–16; Gal 5:13–6:1; Rom 8:1–17. Much of this section follows my commentary very closely, with two exceptions: (1) there has been some rewriting so as to focus especially on the issue of the Spirit in Pauline theology, and therefore (2) some paragraphs have been omitted altogether, or are briefly outlined, inasmuch as they do not deal directly with the concern of this study.

In this instance in particular, one must begin with a provisional understanding of the situation in Corinth that they have addressed (presumably) in their letter, or in any case, that has called forth this lengthy response.

Since 8:1 Paul has been dealing with matters related to worship. In 8:1–10:22, he forbade Christian participation in pagan worship. That is followed by three issues involving their own gatherings for worship. Our section is the third of these. It also appears to be the most important from Paul's point of view, because here in particular the differences between him and them come to a head, especially over what it means to be πνευματικοί (Spirit people). That seems also to be the reason for the close relationship between these chapters and the final issue—the future bodily resurrection of believers (ch. 15). Together these four chapters bring the letter, with all of its preceding arguments, to its fitting climax. Being "spiritual" in the present means to edify the community in worship (chs. 12–14), because the perfect has not yet come (13:8–13). When it does come it will include a bodily resurrection, albeit in a "spiritual body" (ch. 15).

Most likely the present issue was raised in their letter;[217] nonetheless,[218] both the length[219] and the nature of Paul's response allow for a fairly straightforward reconstruction of the problem.[220] What is more difficult is to determine what they might have said in their letter that called for this response. On the basis of ch. 12 alone,[221] one might conclude that they were asking questions about Spirit manifestations;[222]

---

[217] This is a nearly universal conviction, based on the recurrence of the περὶ δέ (now about) formula in 12:1. See the discussion in Hurd, *Origin*, 186–95.

[218] When a problem is *reported* to him, Paul feels compelled to tell them what he knows (cf. 1:11–12; 5:1; 6:1; 11:17–22); thus we, too, have a better idea of what was going on. When responding to their letter, unless he quotes from it (7:1; 8:1, 4), he picks up right at that point, so we are not always informed of the precise nature of the problem.

[219] In NA[26] it covers 159 lines of Greek text; chs. 1:10–4:21 cover 161 lines; chs. 8–10 cover 143.

[220] Although a glance at the various reconstructions discussed by Hurd, *Origin*, 186–87, 190–91, should make one duly cautious as to what seems "straightforward." Robertson-Plummer's view (257) that the phenomena here dealt with "were to a large extent abnormal and transitory," not being "part of the regular development of the Christian church," probably says more about them and their notion of what should be "regular" than it does about either Paul or the primitive church.

[221] Cf. W. J. Bartling, "The Congregation of Christ—A Charismatic Body. An Exegetical Study of 1 Corinthians 12," *CTM* 40 (1969) 67: "If we had only ch. 12, we would probably never have surmised that the focus of Paul's practical concern throughout chs. 12, 13, and 14 of First Corinthians is the tongues phenomenon."

[222] This is the most common view, repeated in a modified form most recently by Martin, *Spirit*, 7–8. This frequently assumes that there was division among the Corinthians themselves on this matter. See, e.g., J. M. P. Sweet, "A Sign for Unbelievers: Paul's Attitude to Glossolalia," *NTS* 13 (1967) 240–57, among many

but ch. 14 indicates that, as throughout the letter, Paul's answer is intended to be *corrective*, not instructional or informational. Thus, even if they presented themselves to Paul in the form of a question (or questions), his response takes *exception* to their viewpoint,[223] not simply informs them in areas where they lack understanding.

The problem is an *abuse* of the gift of tongues.[224] This is revealed first of all by the structure of the argument. It begins with a more general word (ch. 12), followed by a theological interlude (ch. 13), and concludes with a specific response to the matter in hand (ch. 14). Since the whole argument aims at the specific correctives in ch. 14, it is appropriate to begin our analysis there. This argument is in two parts: (1) In vv. 1–25, with a running contrast between tongues (unintelligible inspired speech) and prophecy (representing intelligible inspired speech), Paul argues for *the absolute need for intelligibility* in the assembly. This is so both for the sake of fellow believers (vv. 1–19), since only what is intelligible can build them up, and for unbelievers (vv. 20–25), since only what is intelligible can lead to their conversion. (2) In vv. 26–40, he offers some specific guidelines for *the absolute need for order* in the assembly.

Two related concerns emerge from this argument. First, as in 11:2–16 and 17–34, the problem is one of corporate worship. This is specifically indicated by the language "in church" and "when you assemble together" (vv. 18–19, 23, 26); it is implied throughout.[225] Second, the correctives are *all* aimed at the abuse of tongues in the assembly, which seems to be both singular in its emphasis and disorderly in its expression (cf. 14:12, 23, 33, 40). Since this is unquestionably the focus of ch. 14,[226] it is reasonable therefore to assume the argument in chs. 12 and 13 leads to these correctives. Thus, after setting forth the basic criterion for distinguishing what belongs to the Spirit and what does not (vv. 1–3), in 12:4–30 Paul emphasizes the need for *diversity* of gifts and manifestations

---

others. But this is read into the text from ch. 13; little or nothing in the argument itself hints of such. There is a tendency among other scholars to see 12:1–3, and the problem of "testing the spirits," as the basic thrust of their letter. See the discussion in Hurd, *Origin*, 186–87.

[223] See on 14:6, 18–19, 23, 33, and esp. 36–38.

[224] Variously called "kinds of tongues" (12:10, 28), "to speak in/with tongues" (14:2, 4, 5, 6, 13, 18, 23, 27, 39), or simply "tongues" or a "tongue" (13:8; 14:22, 26).

[225] In vv. 1–5 by the intelligibility/edification motif; in vv. 6–12 by analogies that require hearers; in vv. 13–17 by the inability of others to respond by saying the Amen to what is said in tongues; in vv. 26–31 by the orderly sequencing of utterances.

[226] Although see D. L. Baker, "The Interpretation of 1 Corinthians 12–14," *EvQ* 46 (1974) 224–34, who thinks the key lies with the Corinthians' use of τὰ πνευματικά, by which they meant "spiritual gifts," and of which only two were of interest to them (prophecy and tongues). Paul's point in ch. 14 in this view is simply to answer *their* inquiries about these gifts and to give some guidelines for the use of each. But that does not adequately come to terms with the argument, especially the insistence on intelligibility over against tongues in the assembly.

in the unity of the one Spirit.[227] That is the clear concern of vv. 4–11, as well as the major note struck in the analogy of the body in vv. 12–26 and in the concluding reiteration in vv. 27–30. This emphasis is best understood vis-à-vis their singular enthusiasm for tongues.

It should be noted at this point that only tongues is included in every list of "gifts" in these three chapters.[228] Its place at the *conclusion* of each list in ch. 12, but at the beginning in 13:1 and 14:6, suggests that the problem lies here. It is listed last *not* because it is "least," but because it is the problem. He always includes it, but at the end, after the greater concern for diversity has been heard.[229]

This view of the problem also makes sense of the argument of ch. 13. Their passion for tongues in the assembly indicated further their failure to love one another (cf. 8:2–3). Love, however, is set out not in *contrast* to tongues, but as the necessary ingredient for the expression of all spiritual gifts.[230] The reason for the gifts is the edification of the church, which is precisely what love aims at, but uninterpreted tongues does not.[231] Thus he concludes this argument, and therewith begins the final one, by saying (14:1): "Aim at love, which will have as its concomitant that you be zealous for Spirit manifestations, especially the intelligible ones, so that the church may be edified."

All of this seems clear enough. Less clear are the *reasons* for this attitude on the part of the Corinthians and *what* it was they communicated to Paul. Although this point is more speculative, what transpires here between Paul and the Corinthians may actually be the key to much

---

[227] It is common to read this section as emphasizing the Corinthian need for unity. One has been set up for reading it this way both by the problem of quarreling in chs. 1–4 and 11:17–34 and by Paul's previous use of the body imagery in 10:17 to make that very point, not to mention the fact that vv. 20 and 25 do suggest as much. But a careful reading of the whole indicates that *diversity* is Paul's concern, not unity, which is the presupposition of the argument. See on 12:12–14.

[228] See 12:8–10, 28, 29–30; 13:1–3, 8; 14:6, 26.

[229] See G. D. Fee, "Tongues—Least of the Gifts? Some Exegetical Observations on 1 Corinthians 12–14," *Pneuma* 2 (1980) 3–14. It is of some interest that in a community that lacked genuine unity, there should be concern for uniformity in Spirit manifestation. Unity and uniformity are not the same thing, not even close.

[230] So also Talbert ("Understanding," 100): "Chapter 13, then, focuses on love as the motivation for applying the gifts"; Carson, *Showing*, 56–57; and most recent interpreters. J. Smit ("The Genre of 1 Corinthians in the Light of Classical Rhetoric," *NovT* 33 [1991] 193–216), has recently argued to the contrary that the chapter "is entirely antithetical in character" (212n36). But for all its learning, this article seems to be an attempt to use rhetorical criticism to circumvent the plain sense of Paul's own statements and theology. Since both "gifts" and "fruit" come from one and the same Spirit, and since Paul urges both—both here and elsewhere—by means of imperative, one seems hard pressed to see love in antithesis of Spirit manifestations.

[231] It should be noted, however, that this "discussion" on love that puts gifts into their proper framework also reflects the larger concerns of the letter, in which their form of spirituality is not marked by proper Christian ethical behavior.

of the rest of the letter. First, there is not a single suggestion in Paul's response that they were themselves divided on this issue[232] or that they were politely asking his advice. More likely, the crucial issue is their decided position over against him as to what it means to be πνευματικός (spiritual).[233] Their view apparently not only denied the material/physical side of Christian existence (hence the reason why ch. 15 follows hard on the heels of this section),[234] but also contained an element of "spiritualized (or over-realized) eschatology."

The key probably lies with 13:1, where tongues is referred to as the "tongues of angels." The Corinthians seem to have considered themselves to be already as the angels, thus truly "spiritual," needing neither sex in the present (7:1–7) nor a body in the future (15:1–58). Speaking angelic dialects by the Spirit was evidence enough for them of their participation in the new spirituality, hence their singular enthusiasm for this gift.[235]

But Paul viewed life in the Spirit differently. His view not so much removed one from present existence, but enabled one to live in the present simultaneously in weakness and power (see, e.g., 2:1–5; 4:9–13). Life in the present is conditioned by the life of the future that has already begun with Christ's death and resurrection (cf. 4:1–5; 7:29–31); but that life has only begun, it is not yet consummated. Thus in the present they must live in loving, responsible relationships with one another in the body of Christ. Their times of public worship must be for the edification of one another, not for heightened individualistic spirituality, which in their case had become a false spirituality.

---

[232] This is the standard view; see n. 222 above. Implied, or indeed more often stated, is the idea that the glossolalists (enthusiasts) were after the more "showy gifts" over against others (sometimes viewed as those who preferred prophecy). This is so commonly held that a full bibliography would be tedious. See, e.g., Sweet, "Sign," 241; Martin, *Spirit*, 20 and passim. But not a single sentence in these chapters indicates such an attitude on the part of the Corinthians.

[233] This may be further reflected in his sudden shift to the first person singular at key points in the argument (13:1; 14:6, 14–15, 18, 37), intimating that they may have disapproved of him precisely because of his failure to "come to them speaking in tongues" (14:6). Otherwise, Grudem, *Gift*, 157–62, but his arguments seem to miss the overall nature of the conflict between this church and its apostle; moreover, his contention that πνευματικός basically means "spiritually mature" does not hold up exegetically.

[234] See further on 2:6–16; 6:12–20; 7:1–7, 25–40.

[235] Although it is not possible from this response to reconstruct what they might have said in their letter, there is much to be said for Hurd's view (*Origin*, 226–28) that this is not the first interchange between them and Paul on this matter—although Hurd's own solution is not fully satisfactory. He follows the many who have argued that the major point of contention is over the "testing" of "spirits." Since Paul's answer reflects little concern over this matter as such, it seems more likely that it had to do with the value and significance of tongues for spiritual life in the assembly.

In so doing Paul does not "damn tongues with faint praise."[236] Rather, he is concerned to put that gift into a broader context, where it functions privately as much as one pleases, but in the community only in the context of edification, which requires intelligibility. Hence in the assembly it must always be accompanied by interpretation; it must be in orderly sequence; and in any case prophecy is preferable.

1 CORINTHIANS 12:1–3

¹Now about the things of the Spirit, brothers and sisters, I do not want you to be ignorant. ²You know that when[237] you were pagans, you were carried away, as you were continually being led about[238] to mute idols. ³Therefore I make known to you that no one speaking[239] by the Spirit of God says, "Jesus is cursed," and no one can say, "Jesus is Lord," except by the Holy Spirit.

At first reading this opening paragraph seems quite unrelated to the topic at hand; nonetheless, Paul intends to set the stage for much that follows. Despite some notorious exegetical difficulties in vv. 2 and 3, one thing seems certain: His initial concern is to contrast their former experience as idolaters with their present experience as Christians, who speak "by the Spirit of God." The structure of the argument verifies this. He begins by telling them "I do not want you to be ignorant" (v. 1). He

---

[236] This is frequently suggested, because Paul so clearly tries to put tongues in its proper place. But nothing in the argument indicates that he is trying to eliminate it. If so, then one must allow that he argues out of both sides of his mouth. Among those who take this position see esp. D. Walker, *The Gift of Tongues* (Edinburgh, 1908) 72; H. Chadwick, " 'All Things to All Men' (I Cor. IX.22)," *NTS* 1 (1954–55) 268–69; Hurd, *Origin*, 188–90; D. W. B. Robinson, "Charismata versus Pneumatika: Paul's Method of Discussion," *RefThRev* 31 (1972) 49–55; and A. C. Thiselton, "The Interpretation of Tongues: A New Suggestion in Light of Greek Usage in Philo and Josephus," *JTS* 30 (1979) 15–36. But see R. Banks and G. Moon, "Speaking in Tongues: A Survey of the New Testament Evidence," *Churchman* 80 (1966) 285, who correctly observe: "He makes it clear, however, that the correct treatment for abuse is not disuse, but proper use," an attitude, they go on to point out, that is "grounded in the belief that the Spirit is the source of the gift"! So also T. W. Harpur, "The Gift of Tongues and Interpretation," *CJT* 12 (1966) 164–71, esp. 165. Cf. W. Richardson, "Liturgical Order and Glossolalia in 1 Corinthians 14:26c–33a," *NTS* 32 (1986) 144–53, esp. 145–46.

[237] The combination ὅτι ὅτε, which makes Paul's sentence ungrammatical, has resulted in the omission of one or the other in a variety of witnesses. One of the more intriguing solutions to the grammar is the textual one offered by Westcott-Hort, that ὅτε was probably originally ποτε (= "that at one time you were pagans, carried away to dumb idols, however you were being led"). Nonetheless, the simplest solution is the one adopted here, namely, to insert an additional "you were" before the participle ἀπαγόμενοι.

[238] This is an attempt to give the proper iterative force to ὡς ἄν.

[239] The Western tradition omits the λαλῶν, probably seeing it as redundant, which in this case it is not; rather, it anticipates the discussion of "speaking" in tongues by the Spirit.

follows this by reminding them of something about which they are *not* ignorant, namely, what it was like to be pagans (v. 2; led about to mute idols). In light of that experience, therefore, he now makes known to them (v. 3) the proper criterion for what is genuinely the work of the Spirit of God.

What is less certain is (1) the meaning of the genitive plural of πνευματικός that introduces the matter at hand (whether "spiritual gifts" or "spiritual people"); (2) the significance of the reference to their former idolatry (whether it refers simply to idolatry as such or to "ecstatic"[240] experiences, which Paul considered to be inspired by demonic spirits; cf. 10:20–21); and (3) how to understand the words of contrast in v. 3, "Jesus is cursed."

When all of that has been sorted out, and especially in light of their zeal for tongues, it seems most likely that Paul's concern at the outset is singular: To insist that it is not "inspired utterance" in itself that marks what is truly Spiritual, but the intelligible content of that utterance, content that is ultimately tested by the basic Christian confession of the lordship of Jesus Christ.

1 The new topic is marked both by the repeated "now about" and the vocative, "brothers and sisters."[241] The difficulty lies with the content, τῶν πνευματικῶν, which may be either masculine (= Spirit people) or neuter (usually understood to mean "Spiritual gifts"). On the one hand, what favors the former[242] is the usage in 2:15, 3:1, and especially 14:37, where Paul says rhetorically, "If anyone thinks he or she is πνευματικός." It would also fit well with the problem in Corinth as we have reconstructed it above, where the conflict with Paul is not simply over Spirit manifestations, but over the significance of tongues for "spiritual" life. On the other hand, the use of the neuter plural in 14:1 in the imperative to be "zealous for τὰ πνευματικά," where it refers at least to prophecy and tongues, plus the overall argument that deals primarily

---

[240]One of the real difficulties in discussing these matters is the looseness with which many of us use terminology, the term "ecstasy" being a primary case in point. Technically, this should refer to experiential activity in which the person is "beside himself or herself," i.e., either out of control or out of touch with the present surroundings (e.g., a trance of some kind). Cf. T. Callan, "Prophecy and Ecstasy in Greco–Roman Religion and 1 Corinthians," *NovT* 27 (1985) 125–40. But very often it is used as a synonym of "enthusiasm" to denote any number of kinds of spiritually inspired activity or speech. In this study I shall use "inspired utterance" or "inspiration" for the latter kinds of spiritual activity and "ecstasy" in its more technical sense.

[241]Although Paul's vocative is the standard "brothers," 11:2–16 shows that women prophesied. Since they were obviously present in the worship for the reading of the letter, contemporary usage demands the translation, "brothers and sisters."

[242]See inter alia, Weiss 294, Bruce 116, Hurd, *Origin*, 194.

with Spirit manifestations in the church, not with individual spirituality, has caused most commentators to opt for "Spiritual gifts."[243]

This debate, however, has probably narrowed the options too rigidly. The word is probably neuter, as in 9:11 and 14:1. As noted in ch. 2, for Paul the primary focus of this adjective is on the Spirit. Paul's immediate—and overall—concern has to do with what comes from "the Spirit of God" (v. 3). Moreover, elsewhere in ch. 12 he uses χαρίσματα for the specific manifestations of the Spirit's activity. Therefore, even though at points the two words are nearly interchangeable (as 12:31a and 14:1 would imply), the emphasis in each case reflects the root word. When the emphasis is on the manifestations, the "gifts" as such, Paul speaks of χαρίσματα; when the emphasis is on the Spirit, he speaks of πνευματικά.[244] Hence our translation, "the things of the Spirit," which would refer primarily to manifestations/gifts from the perspective of the *Spirit's* endowment; at the same time, the expression also points toward those who are so endowed.

In saying, "I do not want you to be ignorant" (cf. 10:1), Paul does not intend to give new information, but an additional slant or a corrective to their understanding of "the things of the Spirit."

2 Paul begins his correction of their "ignorance" by reminding them of something from their pagan past[245] of which they were well aware. Our primary exegetical difficulty is to determine the *reason* for this sentence in the argument. There are basically two options: (1) Some have argued for a minimal view, that Paul intends only to contrast their former life as idolaters with their new life as Christians (that is, pagans are led to idols; Christians are led by the Spirit).[246] A modification of this

---

[243]For more complete arguments in favor of this meaning, see Grudem, *Gift*, 157–62, and Martin, *Spirit*, 8. Robinson, "Charismata," has argued that πνευματικά is a Corinthian word by which they have narrowed the gifts basically to "tongues and other ecstatic utterances"; cf. Baker, "Interpretation." But this does not correspond with Pauline usage elsewhere.

[244]For another view see Martin, *Spirit*, 8, who follows J. Goldingay (*The Church and the Gifts of the Spirit* [Bramcote, 1972]), and Koenig, *Charismata*, in seeing πνευματικά as the broader term while χαρίσματα refer more specifically to πνευματικά to be practiced in the context of the assembly at worship.

[245]This sentence offers the clearest evidence in the letter of the predominantly Gentile character of the church in Corinth (cf. 6:9–11 and 8:1–10:22). The attempt by J. D. M. Derrett, "Cursing Jesus (I Cor. XII. 3): The Jews as Religious 'Persecutors,'" *NTS* 21 (1974–75) 553, to circumvent this so as to give the problem a basically Jewish life-setting is less than convincing. Cf. the earlier, even less convincing, suggestion in this regard by J. M. Ford, "The First Epistle to the Corinthians or the First Epistle to the Hebrews," *CBQ* 38 (1966) 410.

[246]As in 1 Thes 1:9; Gal 4:8–9. See, e.g., M. Barth, "A Chapter on the Church—The Body of Christ. Interpretation of I Corinthians 12," *Int* 12 (1958) 131, who says, "A short introduction (vss. 2 and 3) reminds the readers that a miraculous operation

position sees Paul as contrasting their former experience with idols either (a) as a way to remind them of their "sheer lack of experience with true 'inspired' speech" (thus implying that they have no basis from which to make judgments about speech inspired of the Spirit),[247] or (b) to contrast Christian prophets and their Spirit-inspired utterances with the Corinthians' former experience with totally mute idols.[248] While this view, in one of its several forms, is possible, the difficulty with finding an adequate reason for making such a point in this introductory paragraph has caused most scholars to look elsewhere for an answer.

(2) Others see Paul's larger concern to be the setting forth of a pagan example against which they are to understand both "inspired utterances" and the significance of "tongues." If so, then it seems probable that what is in view is their former experience of "ecstasy" or "inspired utterances" as pagans. Although neither verb on its own necessarily implies this, the unusual compounding of the verbs,[249] with emphasis on the Corinthians' being acted upon by others (implied in the two passives), leads in this direction.

In keeping with his Jewish heritage,[250] Paul scorns the idols as mute because they cannot hear and answer prayer; nor can they speak—in contrast to the Spirit of God who can. But he has also argued earlier that the mute idols represent demons (10:20–21)—who can and do speak through their devotees. Most likely, therefore, he is reminding them of what they well know, that in some of the cults "inspired utterances" were part of the worship, despite the "mute idols."[251] If so, then his concern

---

of the Holy Spirit has freed them from service to dumb idols and makes them confess distinctly that 'Jesus is Lord' "; cf. K. Maly, "1 Kor 12,1–3, eine Regel zur Unterscheidung der Geister?" BZ 10 (1966) 82–95.

[247] Grudem, Gift, 162–65; his argument is formulated so as to demonstrate the nonecstatic character of prophecy. He (rightly) makes a considerable point that the sentence must stand in contrast with v. 3, but he fails to show how this minimal view sustains Paul's concern either in these three verses or in the larger argument of chs. 12–14, which after all is trying to place "tongues" into proper perspective, not give teaching on the nature of prophecy.

[248] See Maly, "Regel"; and Derrett, "Cursing," 552–53.

[249] The combination ἤγεσθε ἀπαγόμενοι, which is strange at best, seems emphatic, a point generally overlooked by those who take the minimalistic position. Grudem, Gift, 162–64, tries to minimize this by looking at each verb separately; but that will not do, since it is the combination that is so striking. On this question see Parry, 175; Maly, "Regel"; and Jouette M. Bassler, "1 Cor 12:3—Curse and Confession in Context," JBL 101 (1982) 416–17.

[250] Cf. e.g., Hab 2:18–19; Ps 115:5; 3 Macc 4:16.

[251] For a thorough discussion of this phenomenon in pagan antiquity, see Aune, Prophecy, 23–79. It is unlikely that Paul is also thinking of the frenzied ecstasy and mania of some of the cults (Bacchus, Dionysus, Cybele, etc.), since nothing in the text moves in that direction. Paul's concern is not with mania as such, but with pressing the point that "inspired utterances" in themselves are no guarantee that one is speaking by the Spirit.

is to establish early on, as v. 3 corroborates, that it is not "inspired speech" as such that is evidence of the Spirit. They had already known that phenomenon as pagans. Rather, what counts is the *intelligible and Christian content* of such utterances.

3 With an emphatic "therefore,"[252] Paul concludes this opening word. The verb "I make known to you" recalls the "I do not want you to be ignorant" of v. 1, but now by way of what was said in v. 2. "Therefore," he says, "since I do not want you to be ignorant about the things of the Spirit, and since you have already known about inspired utterances as pagans, I make known to you what follows." But what follows turns out to be another of the more difficult passages in the letter. In two nearly balanced clauses Paul indicates what one who is speaking by the Spirit *cannot* say, and contrariwise that only by the Spirit can one utter the primary Christian confession. The difficulty lies primarily with the first clause, "No one who is speaking by the Spirit of God[253] says, 'Jesus is cursed.' " But it also has to do with the relationship of all this to the argument that follows. However one finally answers the first matter, which is probably "past finding out," that answer must explain two issues: (a) how it functions in relationship to v. 2, and (b) how it relates to the larger issue of their inordinate enthusiasm for the gift of tongues.

The problem is especially perplexing—in two ways: First, it is difficult to imagine either that anyone actually cursed Jesus in the gathered Christian assembly, or that, if he or she did, Paul would take it so casually as to speak to it only here and in this totally noncombative way. Second, how is it possible that Paul would have to "make known to them" that no one speaking in the Spirit would say such a thing as "Jesus is/be[254] cursed"? Of the many and varied solutions offered, two have the least number of difficulties.[255]

---

[252] Gk. διό (cf. 14:13); the conjunction emerges as a predominant one in 2 Cor.

[253] Parry 176, 177, following Hort, makes a point of the anarthrous use of πνεύματι as though it implied an "intermediate sense" in which each manifestation is the work of "a holy spirit." But that misses Pauline usage altogether. Verse 9 alone indicates that such is not true ("by the same Spirit"; "by the one Spirit"). On this usage see ch. 2.

[254] It is not easy to determine whether an imperative ("Jesus be cursed") or an indicative ("Jesus is cursed") is intended. Most often an imprecation (imperative) is assumed; but it is likewise generally assumed (for good reason) that the following confession is indicative. Cf. W. C. van Unnik, "Jesus: Anathema or Kyrios (I Cor. 12:3)," in *Christ and Spirit in the New Testament* (ed. B. Lindars, S. Smalley; Cambridge: University Press, 1973) 115–16, who objects to making this an imperative.

[255] Most scholars continue to hold to some explanation that assumes that someone actually said such a thing in the Christian assembly. For an overview, see Fee 580–81. The multiplicity of solutions as to how that might have been possible only demonstrates how difficult any such solution might be. In the first place, how could a *believer* under any circumstances in the Christian assembly say such a thing,

(1) An increasingly popular option is that no one in the Christian assembly actually said such a thing; rather, this is a hypothetical alternative, framed in light of v. 2, to the real issue, that "inspired utterances" or true Spirit-possession will be recognized by the criterion of the primitive confession, "Jesus is Lord" (cf. Rom 10:9).[256] The problem with this option is the equal difficulty of imagining the Jewish-Christian Paul to have created such a blasphemous alternative had it never actually been said.[257] Moreover, the clause "Jesus is/be cursed" possesses all the earmarks of an actual curse formula.

(2) The alternative view is that this is exactly the kind of outcry that may have occurred in the pagan settings that Paul is alluding to in v. 2, by those who are "inspired" by demonic spirits. This is an attractive option, since it would help us better to understand the reason for v. 2. Furthermore, it would be precisely the kind of contrast between their pagan past and Christian present that would help them to see the difference between "spirits" and *the* Spirit, between any type of "inspired utterance" and that which is truly of the Spirit of God. Hence it is not tongues per se that is evidence of the Spirit's activity, but the intelligible, Jesus-exalting content of such activity. The difficulty with this option lies in the language *anathema*,[258] which seems to reflect a Jewish usage not frequently found among Greeks.[259]

---

and how is it that he or she would need such instruction? Moreover, if this were actually happening in the Corinthian assembly, one is hard pressed to explain both how this introduces the rest of the argument and why Paul does not challenge such blasphemy with his usual vigor.

[256] Among others, see Hurd, *Origin*, 193; Conzelmann 204; Bruce 118; Pearson, *Terminology*, 47–50; Bassler, "1 Cor 12:3"; J. W. MacGorman, "Glossolalic Error and Its Correction: 1 Corinthians 12–14," *RevExp* 80 (1983) 392; Aune, *Prophecy*, 257.

[257] But see Pearson, *Terminology*, 48–50, who insists (correctly, one would think) that "it is impossible for *any* kind of Christian to curse Jesus, no matter how erroneous his views or how loose his behavior" (48) and concludes that "Paul's argument is a shocking one, and was undoubtedly intended to be such" (50). Bassler, "1 Cor 12:3," 147, has argued that it serves as an *analogy* by way of v. 2 to their "experience in pagan cults when the δαίμων exercised total control over their actions. Thus they should recognize that the Christian likewise does not make the confession of faith by his own will, but shows thereby the controlling presence of the Holy Spirit." In this she is following Weiss 296 and Conzelmann 206.

[258] Cf. 16:22. This word in Greek ordinarily refers to a votive offering set up in a temple (cf. Luke 21:5); but it was picked up by the LXX translators to translate ḥerem, which more often refers to what is devoted not for consecration but for cursing. Thus it often means "that which is under the *ban*," or "the accursed thing" (cf. Deut 7:26; 13:17; Josh 6:18; etc.), referring to "something delivered up to divine wrath, dedicated to destruction and brought under a curse" (J. Behm, *TDNT* 1.354). This usage is known in the Greek world only from a single inscription from the first or second century CE, in a table of curses (see A. Deissmann, *Light from the Ancient East*, 95–96). For Paul's use of the term see esp. van Unnik, "Jesus," 116–21.

[259] However, it is possible that the language is Paul's, while the curse itself could

In the final analysis it is difficult to choose between these options, since neither is without problems, although I tend to lean toward the latter. But in either case, Paul's point is not to establish a means of "testing the spirits," but to remind them that "inspired utterance" as such is not evidence of being "led of the Spirit."

Paul's insistence that "no one can say, 'Jesus is Lord,'" except by the Holy Spirit," has also troubled later readers, since anyone could seemingly say these words at will. But that misses the radical nature of this confession for the earliest Christians. The use of "Lord" in such a context meant absolute allegiance to Jesus as one's deity and set believers apart from both Jews, for whom such a confession was blasphemy,[260] and pagans, especially those in the cults, where the deities were called "lords."[261] Thus this became the earliest Christian confession,[262] tied in particular to Jesus' having been raised from the dead and therefore having become the exalted One.[263] Paul's point, of course, is that just as formerly they had been "led about and carried away" to mute idols, so now one who is indwelt by the Spirit of the living God is led to the ultimate Christian confession: "Jesus (the crucified One) is (by his resurrection) Lord (of all the universe)." As in 2:10–13, only one who has the Spirit can truly make such a confession, because only the Spirit can reveal its reality.

Because of its less than clear relationship to the rest of chs. 12–14, especially for those whose chief interest in this section is in learning about spiritual gifts, this paragraph is generally quickly passed over. But if our interpretation is correct, then it continues to stand as a particularly pertinent word for the church, in which many of these spiritual phenomena are recurring. The presence of the Spirit in power and gifts makes it easy for God's people to consider the power and gifts as the real evidence of Spirit's presence. Not so for Paul. The ultimate criterion of the Spirit's activity is

---

have been part of a pagan setting. Although there is no evidence for such *oracular* imprecations from pagan antiquity (at least none is noted in Aune, *Prophecy*), nonetheless since curses of all kinds abound, there is no good reason to doubt that they could have occurred in the "inspired utterances" of pagan religion. Cf. e.g., Lucian, *Alex.* 38, where Alexander begins with a "cursing" of Christians. For Christian examples, see Gal 1:8–9; Rev 22:18–19. Those who think the curse to be hypothetical also generally assume it would have been spoken in some setting outside the Christian community, not within (cf. Aune, *Prophecy*, 257).

[260] Cf. Acts 7:54–60.

[261] See Fee 371–76 on 8:5–6. Eventually, of course, it would set them in opposition to the cult of the emperor as well, which came about precisely because of the absolute nature of this confession for Christians.

[262] Cf. Rom 10:9–10; Phil 2:6–11; and Acts 2:36. See the discussions in W. Neufeld, *The Earliest Christian Confessions* (Grand Rapids: Eerdmans, 1967) 42–68, and W. Kramer, *Christ, Lord, Son of God* (ET; SBT 50; London: SCM, 1966) 65–107.

[263] See esp. the motif of humiliation-exaltation and the tie to the resurrection in the passages noted in the preceding note.

the exaltation of Jesus as Lord. Whatever takes away from that, even if they be legitimate expressions of the Spirit, begins to move away from Christ to a more pagan fascination with spiritual activity as an end in itself.

1 CORINTHIANS 12:4–11

[Since much of the interpretation of this section revolves around the twin emphases in the opening sentence ("diversities" but "the same Spirit"), the translation is this case is given by means of a structural display of the whole, in a very literal translation, with these emphases highlighted (the emphasis on "diversity" is CAPITALIZED; the emphasis on "the same Spirit" *italicized*)]:

[4]DIVERSITIES of gifts   there are, but *the same Spirit*;
[5]DIVERSITIES of services   there are, but *the same Lord*;
[6]DIVERSITIES of workings   there are, but *the same God*,[264]
                  who works ALL THINGS
                  IN ALL PEOPLE.

[7]TO EACH is given the manifestation *of the Spirit*
          for the common good.

    for
[8]TO ONE   is given   a message of wisdom,   *through the Spirit*;
TO ANOTHER   a message of knowledge, *by the same Spirit*;
[9]TO ANOTHER[265]   faith,   *by the same Spirit*;
TO ANOTHER   gifts of healings,   *by the one[266] Spirit*;
[10]TO ANOTHER   workings of miracles;[267]

---

[264]B 1739 and the MajT add ἐστιν (at different places), a clearly secondary addition (cf. Zuntz, *Text*, 187).

[265]This enumeration follows standard Hellenistic patterns (ᾧ μὲν, followed by ἄλλῳ δὲ, . . . μὲν ἄλλῳ δέ), except for two idiosyncrasies: (1) The third and eighth items (faith and kinds of tongues) are enumerated by the synonym ἑτέρῳ. This stylistic variation is not unknown (cf. Matt 16:14; Heb 11:35–36), but in these cases it is a simple twofold enumeration ἄλλος δὲ . . . ἕτερος δέ. (2) Although there is some textual variation in each case, what is most likely Paul's original text also lacks the ordinary δέ in the two instances where he has ἑτέρῳ. This may simply be variety for variety's sake; but it is also arguable that this most unusual expression of variety has some purpose to it. Very likely this is Paul's own clue—subtle though it might be and therefore not terribly significant—as to how the list is to be "grouped." See the discussion below; cf. Findlay 888–89, Conzelmann 209. (For a different view of the textual question, see Zuntz, *Text*, 106.)

[266]The majority of witnesses (ℵ D F G 0201 Maj) conform this ἑνί to the preceding twice-repeated αὐτῷ (A B 33 81 104 630 1175 1739 1881 2464 pc lat); P[46] omits altogether. See Metzger, *Textual Commentary*, 563.

[267]P[46] reads ἐνεργήματα δυνάμεως, the genitive understood as descriptive (= powerful workings; cf. the Western tradition, ἐνεργεία δυνάμεως = miraculous power). The latter is preferred by Zuntz, *Text*, 100, who argues that the plural δυνάμεων of the majority has been conformed to the preceding ἰαμάτων. More likely P[46] and the Westerns reflect an attempt to "improve" a difficult plural that seemed tautologous.

TO ANOTHER	prophecy;
TO ANOTHER	discernments[268] of spirits;
TO ANOTHER[269]	kinds of tongues;
TO ANOTHER	interpretation of tongues;

[11]ALL THESE THINGS works *the one and the same Spirit*,
    DISTRIBUTING to EACH ONE,
      even as he wills.

Paul began his argument with the Corinthians by placing the phenomenon of "inspired utterances" into the broader context of the Spirit's role in their confession of Jesus as Lord.[270] Now he zeroes in on the specific problem in Corinth by emphasizing the need for a wide variety of the one Spirit's manifestations within the church. The argument is in three parts vv. 4–11, 12–26, 27–31a, each stressing the need and value of diversity within unity.

Paul's point seems clear: Diversity, not uniformity, is the essential matter for a healthy church. At the same time he urges that all of this is God's doing and part of his divine purposes, a point he repeats throughout (vv. 6, 7, 11, 18, 24, 28). The one God who is himself characterized by diversity within unity has decreed the same for his church. Very likely this emphatic theological framework forms part of the corrective: Perhaps their emphasis on spirituality, manifested by tongues, had become an end in itself, so that they were focusing more on these events than on God. In any case, the opening paragraph (vv. 1–3) put the work of the Spirit into a proper christological perspective; this section puts it into a proper theological one. Diversity within unity belongs to the character of God. Although there is but one Spirit, one Lord, and one God, a great variety of gifts and ministries characterizes each of the divine Persons (vv. 4–6). Such diversity in God manifests itself, Paul argues further, by God's distributing to the many of them different manifestations of the Spirit for the common good. Paul then offers several of these as illustrations (vv. 7–11).[271] In the final analysis, everything, absolutely every-

---

[268] The original here (supported by P^{46} ℵ A B Maj sy^h bo) is plural, not found in any known English translation. The English tradition reflects the move toward the singular found in C D F G P 0201 33 1175 pc latt $sy^{p\ sa}$.

[269] See n. 265 above.

[270] Martin, *Spirit*, 10–11, observes that v. 3 puts them into the orbit of the *gift* of the Spirit, whereby they confess Jesus as Lord and become one of his; now he will move on to talk about the *gifts* of the Spirit for the building up of the life of the community. The gift is one; the gifts are many.

[271] As we will note, he goes on in vv. 12–26 to reinforce all this by means of a common political-philosophical analogy—the "body" politic now viewed as the "body" of Christ, focusing on their *common* experience of the Spirit in conversion as the key to unity (v. 13), but illustrating from the analogy itself the need for diversity if there is to be a true body and not simply a monstrosity. By its very nature the analogy shifts focus momentarily (vv. 20–25) from the gifts per se to the diversity of

thing—gifts, persons, church—owes its origin to the one God who works all things in all of his people (v. 6).

Contemporary interest in this paragraph, however, has tended to focus not on Paul's argument, but on the list of "gifts" in vv. 8–10; in this regard, therefore, one must underline at the outset that Paul's argument is entirely ad hoc, reflecting the Corinthian situation.[272] His own concern is *not* with instruction about "spiritual gifts" as such, their number and kinds. Indeed, the list of nine items in vv. 8–10 is neither carefully worked out nor exhaustive; it is merely *representative* of the diversity of the Spirit's manifestations.[273] Paul offers a *considerable* list so that they will stop being singular in their own emphasis.

All of this suggests not only that do we not have here a systematic discussion of "spiritual gifts," but also that there is some doubt as to whether the apostle himself had precise and identifiably different "gifts" in mind when he wrote these words. He himself would probably not recognize the schematizing that some later interpreters have brought to these texts.

---

people who make up the community. Finally, all of this is replayed once more by means of yet another list (given twice, though not precisely) that combines both gifts and persons (vv. 27–31a). The emphatic point once again is that "not all" are the same, nor are all "gifted" in the same way.

[272] Note esp. that the list begins with language (λόγος, σοφία, γνῶσις) which reflects the opening thanksgiving (1:5–7), where he thanked God that they had been enriched in all λόγος and γνῶσις, lacking no χάρισμα. Speech, wisdom, and knowledge, of course, are part of the *problem* in this church (see Fee 63–66, 365–67, on 1:17 and 8:1); it is hardly accidental that they now head Paul's list—in the same way that it is hardly accidental that tongues comes at the end.

[273] This is demonstrated in two ways: (1) The fact that Paul has six other lists in this argument (12:28, 29–30; 13:1–3, 8; 14:6, 26), each of which is also ad hoc (simply spun off at the moment for the purpose of the argument) and no two of which (even 12:28 and 29–30!) are exactly alike either in language, number, or character. (2) There is considerable flexibility in Paul's use of language on these matters, both here and in the rest of the NT. For example, (a) in v. 4 he speaks of the Spirit's χαρίσματα, which in v. 7 are called "manifestations," while χαρίσματα appears again in v. 9 (and vv. 28, 30) narrowly confined to "healings," only to reappear in v. 31 to refer to the broader categories; (b) in v. 6 the activities of God are called ἐνεργήματα (workings) which he ("works"), yet ἐνεργήματα occurs again in v. 10 as one of the *Spirit's* "manifestations," and in v. 11 the Spirit is said to ἐνεργεῖ all these things; (c) the "workings of miracles" is simply "miracles" in vv. 28–29; (d) one finds the λόγος of "knowledge" in v. 8, "knowing all mysteries and all knowledge" in 13:2, and simply "knowledge" in 13:8 and 14:6; (e) "prophecy" is a "manifestation" in v. 10; prophets themselves are mentioned in vv. 28–29 (cf. 14:29 and 37); but it is not at all clear that "prophecy" is the private province only of some who are called "prophets" (cf. "teachers" and "teaching" in 12:28 and 14:6, 26); (f) in v. 5 the activities associated with the Lord are called διακονίαι, a word that appears again as a χάρισμα in Rom 12:6–7, but in a context where the Spirit (though perhaps assumed on the basis of Rom 8) is not mentioned at all. It is fair to say at this point that far greater confidence is often expressed on some of these matters in both the scholarly and popular literature than the evidence itself warrants.

4–6 These opening sentences seem intended to give the theological context within which all that follows is to be understood. Each begins with the word "different kinds of,"[274] showing where Paul's accent lies; and each is followed by a noun that characterizes the activity of one Person of the Trinity.[275] The repetition of "same" with each divine Person underscores that the *one* Spirit/Lord/God each manifests himself in a wide variety of gifts and ministries. Thus the unity of God does not imply uniformity in gifts; rather, the one and the same God is responsible for the variety itself.

Given the flexibility of language noted above (see n. 273), one should probably not overanalyze the different words used to describe the individual activities of the divine Persons:[276] "gifts,"[277] "ministries" or "services,"[278] "workings."[279] They are simply three different ways of looking at what in v. 7 Paul calls "manifestations" of the Spirit.[280] This is supported by the fact that (1) both "gifts" and "workings" occur again in the list (associated with "healings" and "miracles" respectively) and that (2) both "God" and "the one and the same Spirit" are respectively the subject of the same verb ("works") in vv. 6 and 11. In addition, the word χάρισμα is probably too narrow to embrace the great variety of things mentioned in this argument. Apostles and prophets (v. 28), for example, would better be described as "ministries," whereas "prophecy" is a

---

[274] Gk. διαιρέσεις. Because of the appearance of the cognate verb διαιρέω in v. 11, where it means "apportion" or "distribute," BAGD suggest the meaning "allotments" for these three occurrences of the noun; cf. Barrett 283 and most commentators. But the meaning "difference" or "variety" is also well established; the context rules in favor of the latter here. Cf. Parry 177, who would combine the ideas: "there are varieties of gifts assigned." Martin, *Spirit*, 12–13, makes the intriguing suggestion that διαιρέσεις might be a word play on the αἱρέσεις of 11:19.

[275] I recognize this language is anachronistic for Paul, but as will be noted below, this kind of construction is part of the "stuff" out of which the later articulations and language arise. As Barth has rightly said, "Trinity is the Christian name for God."

[276] But see Bittlinger, *Gifts*, 20–21, who sees χάρισμα as reflecting the source of the gifts (the divine χάρις), the διακονίαι as reflecting the way in which they become real in practice, and the ἐνεργήματα as indicating their results (definite effects); cf. Findlay 887 and Dunn, *Jesus*, 411n51.

[277] For this word see the discussion on 1:4–7 above. In this chapter (at least in vv. 4 and 31), contra Grosheide 283, it probably refers to the more concretely visible manifestations of the Spirit's activity, such as those listed in vv. 8–10.

[278] Gk. διακονίαι, the emphasis being on "service." Paul regularly calls his own ministry in the gospel a διακονία (e.g., 2 Cor 3:7–9; 4:1) and himself and his co-workers διάκονοι of the gospel (see Fee 130–31 on 3:5). But so, too, is the collection for the poor saints in Jerusalem a διακονία unto them (2 Cor 8:4; 9:1, 12–13). See further 16:15 and 2 Tim 4:11.

[279] Gk. ἐνεργήματα, found only here and in v. 10 in the NT. The emphasis seems to be on the "effects" produced by work, not simply on activity in and of itself (contra BAGD); cf. Findlay 887.

[280] Cf. Bruce 118: "*Gifts, service* and *working* are not distinct categories."

χάρισμα. But such distinctions belong to our interests, not Paul's, for
whom the emphasis is simply on their variety and divine origin.

At the same time, however, the three nouns do reflect what for
Paul would be a primary aspect of the three divine Persons. Thus, even
though elsewhere the word χάρισμα is not ordinarily associated with the
Spirit,[281] the central concern of the present argument (chs. 12–14) is with
the Spirit and his "gifts." Hence it is appropriate that the argument begin
with this association.[282] Likewise, the correlation of "kinds of service"
(or "ministries") with "the same Lord" is especially appropriate, since this
word group is used everywhere in the NT to describe the "servant"
ministry of both Christ and his "ministers." The triad climaxes with the
sentence about God the Father.[283] The noun in this case is somewhat
rare; but its cognate verb, which appears in the qualifying clause, usually
connotes "effectual" working. Something is accomplished by the effort
put forth. Thus it is probably not so much individual "gifts" or "manifestations" that Paul has in mind with this noun, but the fact that *all things*
done in the church are ultimately effected by the powerful working of
God. This is further suggested by the final qualifying clause, "who works
(or effects) all of them[284] (meaning the χαρίσματα and διακονίαι as well)
in all people."[285] With this final clause Paul redirects the focus from the
statements about God to the diverse ways ("all of them") and the many
different people ("in all people") God uses to minister in his church. Paul
will now spell this out in detail in vv. 7–11.

The Trinitarian implications in this set of sentences, the earliest of
such texts in the NT, are striking.[286] As Barrett notes, "The Trinitarian
formula is the more impressive because it seems to be artless and unconscious" (284). It is not actually a Trinitarian construct per se; i.e., Paul's
interest is not in the unity of the *Persons* of the Godhead: the relationships

---

[281] Most often it is associated with God; see, e.g., 1 Cor 1:5–7; 7:7; Rom 6:23; 11:29;
2 Tim 1:6. But see Rom 1:11, where the adjective πνευματικόν modifies the noun
χάρισμα.

[282] Thus it is quite irrelevant to suggest as some do (e.g., Lietzmann 61) that the
sentences represent an ascending order of rank.

[283] Although Paul does not call God "Father" here, he regularly does so; see esp.
8:6 and the salutations ("God our Father and our Lord Jesus Christ"). Yet see 2 Cor
13:13[14].

[284] Gk. τὰ πάντα; this combination in Paul generally means "the whole of
everything," depending on the context. Sometimes it refers to the whole created order
(as in 8:6; 15:27–28), but other times, as here, it refers in a more limited way to the
subject at hand (cf. e.g., 2:15; 11:12; 12:19). Martin, *Spirit*, 5, prefers to take it
adverbially, "in every way."

[285] Gk. ἐν πᾶσιν, which could mean "in every case" (TCNT), but the context seems
to require "in all people" in this instance.

[286] In Paul cf. 2 Cor 13:13[14] and Eph 4:4–6. But note also the several texts noted
in 1 Thes 1:5–6 in which the working of the triune God in salvation is either directly
or indirectly stated.

are not spoken to at all, nor does he say that the Father, Son, and Spirit are one. Nonetheless, passages like this are the "stuff" from which the later theological constructs are correctly derived. Paul's use of language is somewhat fluid. On the one hand, in these sentences, as elsewhere in this letter (e.g., 3:22–23; 11:3; 15:23–28), the unity of God dominates his thinking in such a way that the Son and Spirit are subsumed under that unity, and their own activities are seen as functionally subordinate (e.g., God gives gifts "through the Spirit," vv. 8–9). On the other hand, there can be little question that he thinks of Christ and the Spirit in terms of their full deity. (For Christ see, for example, Fee 34–35, 373–76 on 1:3 and 8:6, plus the title "Lord" in the immediately preceding verse. For the Spirit the interchange of subjects in vv. 6 and 11 is the strongest kind of evidence.) The combination of texts like this one plus the full attributions of divine activities and attributes to the Son and Spirit become Paul's contribution to the later formulations.

7 Having grounded his appeal for diversity in the triune God, Paul proceeds to articulate how that diversity is worked out in the life of the church. This sentence states his thesis, which is then illustrated by the examples in vv. 8–10 and concluded in v. 11 by a restatement of the concern of this sentence, but with a slightly different accent.

This thesis sentence is simply stated; Paul's emphasis is to be found in holding together its three leading ideas. First, "each one," standing in the emphatic first position as it does, becomes his way of stressing diversity; indeed this is how that diversity will be emphasized throughout the rest of the paragraph.[287] Contrary to so much of the popular literature, Paul does not intend by this to stress that every last person in the community has his or her own gift.[288] That may or may not be true, depending on how broadly or narrowly one defines the word χάρισμα. But that is simply not Paul's concern. This pronoun is the distributive (stressing the individualized instances) of the immediately preceding collective ("in all people"), which emphasizes the many who make up the community as a whole.

Second, what "each one" is given in this case is not a χάρισμα, but a "manifestation of the Spirit." One should not make too much of this change of words, as if the following items would be wrongly called "gifts" because they are now called "manifestations."[289] Most likely, the change

---

[287] It is spelled out in particular in the unusual ninefold repetition in vv. 8–10 of "to one, to another," etc.

[288] When Paul wants to make that point he usually says εἷς ἕκαστος (every single one). See Fee 540–43 on 11:21. Grosheide 284 makes the opposite error: "Paul's words 'to each one is given' must mean: to everyone who has special gifts of the Spirit is given." Hardly.

[289] Esp. so, since in 1:5 he has already designated as χαρίσματα two words found on the following list, "speech" (λόγος) and "knowledge" (γνῶσις).

reflects Paul's own emphasis throughout these chapters, which is on the Spirit himself, not on the "gifts." Thus each "gift" is a "manifestation," a disclosure of the *Spirit's* activity in their midst.[290] These first two items together, therefore, are Paul's way of repeating the theme of diversity from vv. 4–6. His urgency, as vv. 8–10 show, is not that each person is "gifted," but that the Spirit is manifested in a variety of ways. Paul's way of saying that is, "to each one is given the manifestation of the Spirit."

Third, probably to give a proper balance to "each one," he concludes with the reason for this great diversity: "for the common good." By so doing he anticipates the concern of chs. 13 and 14, that in community the Spirit manifests himself for the building up of the entire community, not primarily for the benefit of the individual believer.[291]

8–10 To illustrate[292] the thesis of v. 7 Paul offers a sizable list of ways the Spirit is manifested in the Christian assembly. Because this is the first of several such enumerations in the Pauline corpus,[293] considerable interest has been generated over this passage in terms of the nature and meaning of the various gifts.[294] But as noted above, that lies outside Paul's interest, which is simply to illustrate the *diversity* of the Spirit's activities/manifestations in the church.[295]

---

[290]This is so whether the genitive is subjective or objective. In favor of an objective genitive is the verb δίδοται, which has "God" as its implied subject. Thus God gives to each, that is to the community at large, different gifts by which the Spirit is visibly evident in their midst. In favor of a subjective genitive is v. 11, where the Spirit himself is the one who distributes to each as he wills. The former seems the more likely, since the concern is not with the gifts, but with the manifestation of the Spirit through the gifts. Cf. Dunn, *Jesus*, 212: "It is difficult to exclude either sense."

[291] That is not to say that the building up of the individual believer is no concern of Paul's. To the contrary (see on 14:4). But the concern throughout this entire argument is with the effect of gifts in building up the community.

[292]Note esp. the γάρ; cf. BAGD 1d, "the general is confirmed by the specific."

[293]Besides the others in these chapters (cf. n. 228 above), see Rom 12:6–8 (apparently a later reflection on some items from this chapter) and Eph 4:11.

[294]As one might expect, the popular literature on this passage is immense, esp. among Pentecostal and charismatic groups. Two items from this material are worth noting. The first is by the prominent British Pentecostal, Donald Gee, *Concerning Spiritual Gifts* (Springfield, Mo.: Gospel Publishing House, n.d. [in an appendix dated Nov. 4, 1947, the author indicates that the present printed edition had appeared ten years earlier]). Although untrained in the "school" sense, Gee showed remarkable exegetical skills; this book is worthwhile both for its own insights and for understanding traditional Pentecostalism. The second is by George Mallone et al., *Those Controversial Gifts* (Downers Grove: InterVarsity, 1983), a collection of seven essays by four pastors within the more traditional evangelical framework who have experienced in their churches the renewal of some of the more visible gifts in this list.

[295]Paul is capable of simply listing gifts; but he does not do so here. In each case there is the prior "to one," "to another," etc. That is part of his emphasis.

Attempts to classify the several items are numerous and varied.[296] It has been suggested that they reflect a descending order of value.[297] Others have rearranged the items conceptually.[298] A popular grouping is (1) gifts of instruction (wisdom and knowledge); (2) gifts of supernatural power (faith, healings, miracles); and (3) gifts of inspired utterance (prophecy, discerning prophecies, tongues, interpretation of tongues).[299] It will be noted that the seventh item (discernments of spirits) is the one that tends to give trouble to most of these arrangements. If grouping is legitimate at all, it is most likely to be found in some clues Paul himself has given, by starting the third and eighth items (faith and tongues) with a different word for "another."[300] If so, then the first two are chosen for specific ad hoc purposes; "wisdom" and "knowledge" held high court in Corinth. He then adds a random list of five items that have as their common denominator a supernatural endowment of some kind, and he concludes with the "problem child" and its companion, tongues and interpretation.

What distinguishes this listing is the concretely visible nature of these items, especially of the last seven. These, after all, are not only "gifts," they are above all *manifestations* of the Spirit's presence in their midst,[301] chosen because they are, like tongues itself, extraordinary phenomena. It would scarcely do for Paul at this point to attempt to broaden their perspective by listing less visible gifts. That will come in time (especially through the analogy of the body and in the lists in vv. 28–30); but for now the emphasis is on the supernatural. Indeed, the truly remarkable feature about this list is the attribution to "each one"

---

[296] One wonders, for example, what motivated our present verse divisions, which were created in the sixteenth century in the Greek text. Although there are a large number of unfortunate choices, by and large they make enough sense that one cannot believe they were done willy-nilly. In this case the clue lies in the first instance in the similarity in content of the first two (hence v. 8); the second break was probably motivated by the presence of the phrase "by the same Spirit," which the second two share in common with the first two (hence v. 9). What remained was a list of five gifts with no qualifier (thus v. 10).

[297] E.g., Bruce 119.

[298] E.g., MacGorman, *Gifts*, 35, who arranges them in categories of (1) intelligible utterance (wisdom, knowledge, prophecy); (2) power (faith, healings, miracles); (3) spiritual discernment; and (4) ecstatic utterance (tongues, interpretation). Cf. the "traditional Pentecostal" view expressed by W. R. Jones, "The Nine Gifts of the Holy Spirit," in *Pentecostal Doctrine* (ed. P. S. Brewster, 1976) 47–61, who has the divisions: (1) illumination (wisdom, knowledge, discernment); (2) action (faith, miracles, healings); (3) communication (prophecy, tongues, interpretation).

[299] E.g., W. Baird, *The Corinthian Church—A Biblical Approach to Urban Culture* (New York: Abingdon, 1964) 139; Martin, *Spirit*, 12.

[300] See n. 265 above.

[301] Note that the emphasis on "the same/one Spirit" carries through the first four items; Paul surely intends that it should carry through to the end.

of a whole gamut of supernatural activities—in the same matter-of-fact way that contemporary clergy might list positions on an organizational chart![302] How, then, are the individual items to be understood?

(1) *The message (λόγος) of wisdom (σοφία).* This language harks back to the problem addressed in 1:17–2:16, where in the name of wisdom the Corinthians were rejecting both Paul and his gospel. Indeed, in contrast to their own criterion for "spiritual" excellence, Paul says he deliberately rejected coming to them either in "σοφία characterized by λόγος" (rhetoric; 1:17), or "with excellence of λόγος or σοφία" (2:1, 5). With a bold stroke of inspiration Paul now does two things: (a) He uses one of their own terms[303] to begin his list of "manifestations" in the assembly that demonstrate the great diversity inherent in the one Spirit's activities; and (b) he reshapes that term in light of the work of the Spirit so as to give it a significantly different content from their own.[304]

The phrase means either "a message/utterance full of wisdom" or "an utterance characterized by wisdom."[305] In either case its content should be understood in light of Paul's own argument in 2:6–16. There the "message of wisdom," revealed by the Spirit, is not some special understanding of the "deeper things" or "mysteries" of God.[306] Rather, it is the recognition that the message of Christ crucified is God's true wisdom.[307] This recognition comes only to those who have received the

---

[302] One is reminded of the words of J. B. Phillips, penned in the introduction to his translation of the book of Acts (*The Young Church in Action* [New York: Macmillan, 1949] p. vii): "Yet we cannot help feeling disturbed as well as moved, for this surely is the Church as it was meant to be. . . . If they were uncomplicated and naive by modern standards, we have ruefully to admit that they were open on the God-ward side in a way that is almost unknown today."

[303] The probability that both σοφία and γνῶσις were Corinthian terms taken over by Paul only increases our difficulty in determining the specific nature of these two gifts in Paul's own thinking. Cf. the discussion in Dunn, *Jesus*, 217–21.

[304] As Martin, *Spirit*, 13, says of these first two items: "He now rescues both terms from the Corinthian pneumatics and gives them a fresh stamp."

[305] The interpretation in the Living Bible, "the ability to give wise advice," has little or nothing to do either with the context of the letter or with the Greek word σοφία.

[306] In Pentecostal and charismatic circles this "gift" is often understood to be that special word of insight given by the Spirit when the community is going through a time of difficulty or decision. See, e.g., Bittlinger, *Gifts*, 28, who thus defines this gift: "In a difficult or dangerous situation a word of wisdom may be given which resolves the difficulty or silences the opponent." One need not doubt that the Holy Spirit speaks so to today's church, but it is unlikely that Paul had this in mind by this "gift." If he were to "label" such a phenomenon, it would probably be ἀποκάλυψις (revelation); cf. 14:6. The same is true of the so-called word of knowledge that has become such a frequent occurrence in these communities.

[307] Cf. Gee, *Gifts*, 20–26, who affirms that this is the primary meaning for Paul, although he adds the possibility noted in the preceding note on the basis of Jesus' word to his disciples in Luke 21:15.

Spirit. For only the Spirit, Paul says, whom we *have* received, understands the mind of God and reveals what he accomplished in Christ (2:10–13). Thus the "utterance of wisdom" that comes "through the Spirit" probably refers to an utterance that proclaims Christ crucified into this highly "wisdom"-conscious community. That this particular "gift" does not appear again in any further list or discussion further supports this interpretation; that is, that this is a largely ad hoc construct.

(2) *The message (λόγος) of knowledge (γνῶσις).*[308] As with the first item, this is first of all Paul's way of rescuing this gift of the Spirit[309] from their own fascination with "knowledge" and its concurrent pride (see Fee 365–69, 378–81 on 8:1–3, 7). In this case, however, Paul's own understanding of the gift as a "manifestation" of the Spirit is more difficult to determine, since "knowledge" as gift recurs in the ensuing discussion in three significant texts (13:2, 8–12; and 14:6), which also have some ambiguities. Some have suggested that Paul here has in mind a supernatural endowment of knowledge, factual information that could not otherwise have been known without the Spirit's aid,[310] such as frequently occurs in the prophetic tradition and is assumed to be true in the pagan prophetic oracles. But since here knowledge is a descriptive genitive with the word λόγος, others see it as referring to something more akin to inspired teaching,[311] perhaps related to receiving Christian insight into the meaning of Scripture.[312]

Since "knowledge" has also been taken over from the Corinthians and is so closely tied to the preceding "utterance of wisdom," the two should probably be understood as parallel in some way. Most likely, therefore, it is a "Spirit utterance" of some revelatory kind.[313] This is suggested by its place between "revelation" and "prophecy" in 14:6 and by the fact that along with prophecy and tongues, it will cease at the Eschaton (13:8). How the *content* of such an utterance makes it

---

[308] See on 1:5, where these two words individually are singled out as illustrations of the Corinthians' giftedness.

[309] Conzelmann 209 distinguishes between διὰ τοῦ πνεύματος and κατὰ τὸ αὐτὸ πνεῦμα as the Spirit's being both the source and the norm; but he allows that the distinction cannot be taken strictly. BAGD give evidence κατά may mean "by way of."

[310] Peter's "knowledge" of Ananias' and Sapphira's misdeed in Acts 5:1–11 is often looked upon as this gift in action. That may well be (although "revelation" would be as fitting a label); but Luke himself does not so indicate. In fact the word "know" or "knowledge" does not occur in the narrative.

[311] Somewhat surprisingly, this is the position argued for at some length by Gee, *Gifts*, 27–34 and 110–19, who insists that the list does not require this gift to be a supernatural manifestation.

[312] Cf. Bittlinger, *Gifts*, 30, who says it "consists of the old message spoken in the new situation in such a way that it still remains the old message." This may be so, but it lacks an exegetical basis.

[313] Cf. Dunn, *Jesus*, 218, who suggests that the "utterance" in 8:4, "an idol is nothing in the world," may be a Corinthian "λόγος of knowledge."

γνῶσις as distinguished from "wisdom" or "revelation," is perhaps forever lost to us.[314]

(3) *Faith*.[315] With this word Paul moves on to include several more clearly supernatural manifestations of the Spirit.[316] While Paul probably considered the "faith" that leads to salvation to be the work of the Spirit in the believer's life,[317] what is in mind here is the special gift of supernatural faith that can "move mountains," mentioned again in 13:2. It probably refers to a supernatural conviction that God will reveal his power or mercy in a special way in a specific instance.[318] Although it is listed separately, as given "to another," there is a sense in which this and the following two items belong together—and indeed, they would at times seem not quite possible to differentiate. Faith that "moved a mountain" could also rightly be called the working of a miracle.

(4) *Gifts of healings*.[319] What this refers to needs little comment. Jesus, Paul, and the rest of the early church lived in regular expectation that God would heal people's physical bodies. This expectation was based in part on the OT promises that in the messianic age God would "heal" his people.[320] According to Acts, such healings accompanied Paul's own ministry; they are probably also referred to by Paul himself in "the signs of an apostle" in 2 Cor 12:12 (cf. Rom 15:19).[321] What is of interest in this case is the language "gifts of healings," which recurs in the two lists in vv. 28 and 30. Probably this language reflects two things: (a) the use of χάρισμα

---

[314] In any case, as Dunn (*Jesus*, 221) has rightly argued, "for Paul wisdom and knowledge as such are not thought of as charismata; only the actual utterance that reveals wisdom or knowledge to others is a charisma."

[315] On the question of the relationship of this gift to "the measure of faith" in Rom 12:3, see Dunn, *Jesus*, 211–12; cf. the discussion of Rom 12:3 below, pp. 604–11. Cf. also Gal 5:22, where "faith" (= faithfulness) is listed as a "fruit" of the Spirit.

[316] The difference between αὐτῷ and ἑνί in the two prepositional phrases in this verse is purely rhetorical; cf. v. 11, where the two are joined.

[317] See the discussion of 2 Cor 4:13 below; cf. the discussion in ch. 14, pp. 853–60.

[318] Both Gee, *Gifts*, 36, and Bittlinger, *Gifts*, 32–33, suggest the story of Elijah at Carmel (1 Kings 18) as an OT example of such a gift in operation.

[319] Gk. χαρίσματα ἰαμάτων; both are plural, as are also "workings of miracles," "discernments of spirits," and "kinds of tongues."

[320] Cf., e.g., Matthew's use in 8:17 of Isa 53:4 to refer to Jesus' ministry of healing the sick. The Isaiah passage itself is ambiguous; it is clearly a metaphor for salvation, but in the prophetic tradition such salvation also included the healing of the people's wounds incurred in their judgment. Thus in the NT Isa 53:4 is understood both as a metaphor for salvation (1 Pet 2:24) and as a promise for physical healing (Matt 8:17).

[321] In a "scientific age" it is common to reject the possibility of God's healing the sick. Unfortunately, this is also true of many contemporary Christians, whose theology has made a severe disjunction between the "then" and "now" of God's working. This seems to be a seriously flawed understanding of the kingdom, which according to the NT was inaugurated by Christ in the power of the Spirit, who continues the work of the kingdom until the consummation. Indeed, this seems to be a thoroughgoing denial of the NT view of the Spirit.

itself in this case suggests that the "manifestation" is given not to the person who is healed, but to the person God uses for the healing of another;[322] (b) the plural χαρίσματα probably suggests not a permanent "gift," as it were, but that each occurrence is a "gift" in its own right.[323] So also with the plurals in the next item.

(5) *Workings of miracles.*[324] Although gifts of healings would probably also be considered by Paul as the "workings of miracles," this manifestation most likely covers all other kinds of supernatural activities beyond the healing of the sick. The word translated "miracles" is the ordinary one for "power," and as was pointed out in ch. 2, it is especially associated in Jewish antiquity with the Spirit of God. The present context suggests that it covers a broad range of supernatural events that ordinary parlance would call miraculous.[325] In the duplicated list of vv. 28–30, the word appears by itself in the plural. That "miracles" were common stock in the Pauline churches is further evidenced by the argumentation in Gal 3:5 (q.v.).

(6) *Prophecy.*[326] With this word Paul returns to verbal manifestations. In light of the running contrast in ch. 14 between this gift and tongues, he is probably also consciously moving toward the conclusion of this list with its mention of tongues. Also because of that running contrast, we have a fairly good idea as to how Paul understood this phenomenon. Several things need to be noted: (a) Although prophecy was an especially widespread phenomenon in the religions of antiquity,[327] Paul's understanding—as well as that of the other NT writers—was thoroughly conditioned by his own history in Judaism. The prophet was one who under inspiration of the Spirit spoke to God's people (e.g., Mic 3:8). The "inspired utterance" came by revelation and announced judgment (usually) or salvation. Although the prophets often performed symbolic acts, which they then interpreted, the mainstream of prophetic activity, at least as it came to canonized, had very little to do with

---

[322] Otherwise Dunn, *Jesus*, 211.

[323] Cf. the similar suggestion by Bittlinger, *Gifts*, 37: "Every healing is a special gift. In this way the spiritually gifted individual stands always in new dependence upon the divine Giver."

[324] Gk. ἐνεργήματα δυνάμεων; see Fee 94–97 on 2:4–5. Cf. 2 Cor 12:12, where Paul claims the "signs of an apostle" were "effected" (κατειργάσθη) among them in the form of "signs (σημεῖα), wonders (τέρατα), and miracles (δυνάμεις)."

[325] Weiss 301 and Héring 126 see it as especially referring to exorcisms. It would certainly include but not be limited to these. See Dunn, *Jesus*, 210.

[326] Because of the more universal nature of this phenomenon in antiquity, it has received considerable attention among scholars. The more significant studies for understanding prophecy in Paul are: H. Krämer, R. Rentdorff, R. Meyer, G. Friedrich, *TDNT* 6.781–861; D. Hill, *New Testament Prophecy* (Atlanta: John Knox, 1979); Grudem, *Gift*; and Aune, *Prophecy*. Aune includes a considerable review of both the *TDNT* article and Hill. For a helpful overview see C. M. Robeck, *DPL*, 755–62.

[327] See Aune, *Prophecy*, 23–88.

"ecstasy," especially "frenzy" or "mania."[328] For the most part the prophets were understood only too well! Often the word spoken had a futuristic
element, so in that sense they also came to be seen as "predictors"; but
that was only one element, and not necessarily the crucial one.

(b) With the outpouring of the Spirit at the end of the age, the early
Christians understood the prophecy of Joel 2:28–30 to have been fulfilled,
so that "prophecy" not only became a renewed phenomenon, but was
also potentially available to all, since all now possessed the Spirit in
fullness (cf. Acts 2:17–18). This especially fits what we learn in the
Pauline letters. It appears to have been a widespread phenomenon (cf.
1 Thes 5:19–22; 2 Thes 2:2: Rom 12:6).

(c) The evidence in ch. 14 indicates that it consisted of spontaneous,
Spirit-inspired, intelligible messages, orally delivered in the gathered
assembly, intended for the edification or encouragement of the people.[329]
Those who prophesied were clearly understood to be "in control" (see
14:29–33).

(d) Although some people are called "prophets," probably because
they were frequent speakers of "prophecies,"[330] in ch. 14 the implication
is that it is a gift widely available—at least potentially—to all.[331]

(e) Although the prophetic tradition of the OT probably lay behind
Pauline understanding, at no point does he understand the prophet to
be speaking anything other than an ad hoc word. This is evidenced by
the fact that for Paul it must be "weighed" or "tested." Thus, there is
never any sense that a prophetic word was to be raised to the level of
"inspired text."

(f) There is no Pauline evidence for the phenomenon known in
contemporary circles as "personal prophecy," whereby someone prophesies over another as to very personal matters in their lives. Where such
might appear to be the case (e.g., 1 Tim 1:18; 4:14), there is community
affirmation (testing?) by way of the laying on of hands by the elders.

---

[328] However one is to understand the "ecstasy" of Saul and the others in 1 Sam
19:19–24, e.g., it scarcely belongs to the canonical understanding, and the latter is
what influenced Christ and the early Christians. By "canonical understanding," I
mean the influence of the "canon" of OT Scripture on the Judaism of Paul's day. Since
the Saul phenomena were also in the OT text, one might argue that this, too, is
canonical. Our evidence from Paul, however, seems to move in quite a different
direction. First, whenever he refers to OT prophecy or prophets, he invariably refers
to the stream of prophetism that was recognized as authentic, either within the
preserved data of the OT or by the canonizing process (1 Thes 2:15; Rom 1:2; 3:21;
11:3; 16:26). Second, he so utterly rejects any form of Spirit-inspiration that borders
on "ecstasy" (1 Cor 14:23–25, 32).

[329] Thus it is *not* the delivery of a previously prepared sermon.

[330] Although this may also have become a term for some who emerged as
"charismatic leaders" within the communities; cf. e.g., Acts 13:1 and Eph. 2:20.

[331] See on 11:4–5; 14:1–5, 23–24, 29–31. This does not mean that all do (cf. 12:29),
but that it is not limited strictly to "prophets," as is so often suggested in the literature.

Otherwise prophecy seems to be a strictly community affair, for the sake of the community's corporate life.

(7) *Discernments of spirits.* This is language over which there has been considerable debate, and little agreement, among scholars. The question is, to what does it refer? To the phenomenon associated with "testing the spirits, to see whether they be of God" (1 John 4:1), meaning the ability to discern what is truly of the Spirit of God and what comes from other spirits?[332] Or to the phenomenon noted in 14:29, "and let the others weigh carefully [i.e., discern or judge rightly] what is said," in which the cognate verb of this noun appears?[333]

Most likely, given Paul's own use of language in ch. 14, it refers to both, but particularly to the phenomenon of "discerning, differentiating, or properly judging" prophecies in 14:29.[334] There are several reasons for taking this position: (a) Both 1 Thes 5:20–21 and 1 Cor 14:29, the two places where Paul mentions the functioning of prophecy in the church, call for a "testing" or "discerning" of prophetic utterances. It therefore seems likely, given that the noun used in this passage is the cognate of the verb in 14:29, that the same is true here, since it immediately follows "prophecy." (b) That seems all the more likely in this case, since these two are followed immediately by "tongues" and "interpretation." This same pattern of tongues plus interpretation and prophecy plus discernment is found again in the instructions on order in 14:26–29. (c) The real difficulty lies with the word "spirits." The probable key to understanding lies not in 1 John 4:1,[335] but with Paul's own usage in 14:12, 14, and especially 32, where he tends to use the term in a much more flexible way than most of us are comfortable with. The Spirit who speaks through the prophets is also speaking through "the spirit" of the prophet; when Paul is praying in the Spirit, he speaks of "my spirit" praying (cf. on 5:3–4). The Corinthian zeal for "spirits" in 14:12, therefore, is zeal for

---

[332] E.g., as Paul in Acts 16:16–18. This position is taken, inter alia, by Bittlinger, *Gifts*, 45; Grudem, *Gift*, 58–60 and 263–88; and most Pentecostal interpreters.

[333] See, e.g., Findlay 888–89, Moffatt 182, Holladay 161; Hill, *Prophecy*, 133; and Martin, *Spirit*, 14. A unique view is offered by G. Dautzenberg, "Zum religionsgeschichtlichen Hintergrund der διακρίσεις πνευμάτων (I Kor. 12.10)," *BZ* 15 (1971) 93–104 (cf. his *Urchristliche Prophetie* [Stuttgart: Calwer, 1975] 122–48), who argues that it means "interpreting the utterances of the prophets." Grudem, *Gift*, 263–88, has thoroughly refuted Dautzenberg, but is less than convincing in arguing that the term does not have to do with "discerning" prophecies.

[334] Similarly Barrett 286; Dunn, *Jesus*, 233.

[335] Where among those who have "charisms" (2:27) they are told to "test the spirits to see whether they are of God." But one must not make the prior assumption that what is going on in 1 John is a well-known phenomenon, by which this present passage is to be understood. Very likely that passage is to be understood in light of these chapters in Paul.

manifestations of the Spirit (especially tongues) as he quickens their spirits to pray.

Thus in this present listing, it seems most likely that Paul is referring to the same phenomenon as in 14:29, but is using the language of "spirits" to refer to the prophetic utterances that need to be "differentiated" by the others in the community who also have the Spirit and can so discern what is truly of the Spirit.

(8) *Different kinds of tongues*. This is obviously the "controversial gift," both then and now.[336] If our interpretation of ch. 14 is correct,[337] then their singular preference for this manifestation is what lies behind this entire argument. Thus, after listing several equally visible and extraordinary manifestations of the Spirit, Paul includes their favorite as well,[338] along with its companion "interpretation." As with prophecy, enough is said in chs. 13–14 to give us a fairly good idea as to how Paul understood it. The following seems certain: (a) It is Spirit-inspired utterance; that is

---

[336] The literature here is immense, especially since the outbreak of this, or a similar, phenomenon in the traditional churches in the late 1950s. Before 1960 there were basically two studies in the scholarly journals devoted solely to tongues: C. Clemens, "The 'Speaking with Tongues' of the Early Christians," *ExpT* 10 (1898–99) 344–52; and I. J. Martin, "Glossolalia in the Apostolic Church," *JBL* 63 (1944) 123–30. See also the monograph by G. B. Cutten, *Speaking with Tongues* (New Haven: Yale University, 1927).

Since 1960 nearly every major journal has had at least one article. The following is a highly selective representation of these (Eng. titles only, in chronological order): R. H. Fuller, "Tongues in the New Testament," *ACQ* 3 (1963) 162–68; F. W. Beare, "Speaking with Tongues," *JBL* 83 (1964) 229–46; W. G. MacDonald, "Glossolalia in the New Testament," *BETS* 7 (1964) 59–68; S. D. Currie, " 'Speaking in Tongues.' Early Evidence Outside the New Testament Bearing on 'Glossais Lalein,' " *Int* 19 (1965) 174–94; Banks–Moon, "Tongues"; R. H. Gundry, " 'Ecstatic Utterance' (N.E.B.)?" *JTS* 17 (1966) 299–307; Harpur, "Tongues"; E. L. Kendall, "Speaking with Tongues," *CQR* 168 (1967) 11–19; Sweet, "Sign"; J. M. Ford, "Toward a Theology of 'Speaking in Tongues,' " *TS* 32 (1971) 3–29; B. L. Smith, "Tongues in the New Testament," *Churchman* 87 (1973) 183–88; S. Tugwell, "The Gift of Tongues in the New Testament," *ExpT* 84 (1973) 137–40; R. A. Harrisville, "Speaking in Tongues—Proof of Transcendence?" *Dialog* 13 (1974) 11–18; D. M. Smith, "Glossolalia and Other Spiritual Gifts in a New Testament Perspective," *Int* 28 (1974) 307–20; E. Best, "The Interpretation of Tongues," *SJT* 28 (1975) 45–62; R. A. Harrisville, "Speaking in Tongues: A Lexicographical Study," *CBQ* 38 (1976) 35–48; V. S. Poythress, "The Nature of Corinthian Glossolalia: Possible Options," *WTJ* 40 (1977) 130–35; T. L. Wilkinson, "Tongues and Prophecy in Acts and 1st Corinthians," *VoxR* 31 (1978) 1–20. See also the unpubl. dissertation by N. I. J. Engelsen, "Glossolalia and Other Forms of Inspired Speech According to 1 Corinthians 12–14" (Yale, 1970).

For further bibliography, including a helpful bibliographical essay, see W. E. Mills, *Glossolalia: A Bibliography* (New York: Edwin Mellen Press, 1985); for a convenient overview see C. M. Robeck, *DPL*, 939–43.

[337] See the introduction to this section.

[338] But it is prejudicial to say, as Conzelmann 209, e.g., "Paul indicates his criticism by the very order of the enumeration." This does not seem to take seriously enough Paul's own spirituality, as indicated in 14:15–19.

made explicit both in vv. 7 and 11 and in 14:2. (b) The regulations for its use in 14:27–28 show that the speaker is not in "ecstasy" or "out of control."[339] Quite the opposite; the speakers must speak in turn, and they must remain silent if there is no one to interpret. (c) It is essentially unintelligible speech both to the speaker (14:14) and to others (14:16).[340] (d) It is speech directed basically toward God (14:2, 14–15, 28);[341] one may assume, therefore, that what is "interpreted" is not speech directed toward others, but the "mysteries" spoken to God.

What is less certain is whether Paul also understood the phenomenon to be an actual language. In favor of such a view is (a) the term itself, (b) the need for "interpretation, and (c) the evidence from Acts 2:5–11.[342] In the final analysis, however, this question seems irrelevant. Paul's whole argument is predicated on the phenomenon's unintelligibility to both speaker and hearer; he certainly does not envisage someone's being present who would be able to understand it because it was also an earthly language. Moreover, his use of earthly languages as an *analogy* in 14:10–12 implies that it is not a known earthly language, since a thing itself is not usually identical with that to which it is analogous. Most likely, therefore, the key to Paul's—and their—understanding lies in the term "the language of angels" in 13:1 (q.v.).[343] On its usefulness or lack thereof to the community and the individual, see on 14:1–5 and 13–19.

(9) *The interpretation of tongues.* This is the obvious companion to "tongues," precisely because of the unintelligibility of the latter. Although this term could mean something close to "translation," it can also mean "to put into words";[344] in this context it probably means to articulate for the benefit of the community what the tongues-speaker has said. The evidence from 14:5, 13, and 27–28 indicates (a) that this, too, is a "Spirit-inspired" gift of utterance and (b) that it may be given either to the tongues-speaker or to another.

---

[339] Contra Gunkel, *Influence*, 31; Callan, "Prophecy," and many others. Callan would distinguish between prophecy and tongues in terms of prophecy's being nonecstatic while tongues was "accompanied by trance" (137). But he uses the idea of trance in a loose way and seems to miss the point of the evidence in 14:27–28.

[340] Bruce 119, taking his clue from Acts 2, suggests that this includes languages "intelligible to some hearers." But there is nothing in 1 Cor. 12–14 to suggest that Paul thought of it in these terms.

[341] Cf. Bittlinger, *Gifts*, 48–51, who discusses this gift under the heading, "praying in the Spirit."

[342] See esp. Gundry, "Utterance," who is followed by Ford, "Theology"; cf. also Wilkinson, "Tongues." Dunn, *Jesus*, 244, concludes: "It is evident then that Paul thinks of glossolalia as language. But can we go on from that to conclude that he equates glossolalia with 'human language foreign to the speaker' (Gundry)? I think not"; cf. Richardson, "Order," 148.

[343] Cf. Barrett 299–300; Conzelmann 209; Dunn, *Jesus*, 244.

[344] See esp. the discussion by Thiselton, "Interpretation," 15–36.

11 After the long list of manifestations illustrating the thesis of v. 7, Paul closes this section of the argument by summing up what has been said thus far. The language "the one and the same Spirit" echoes both vv. 4–6 and 8–9, again emphasizing that the diversity is the product of the one God, who by his Spirit "works" (same verb that was used with "God" in v. 6) "all these," referring to the preceding list of manifestations.[345] The participial phrase, "distributing to each person,"[346] picks up the noun translated "different kinds of" in vv. 4–6, emphasizing in this case both the variety and the active work of the Spirit in apportioning to the many these manifestations. Only the final clause is new: "just as he determines."[347] In this context it might best be translated, "just as he sees fit (or pleases)." The emphasis is less on the Spirit's deliberation in action than on his sovereignty in distributing the gifts or perhaps in manifesting himself. Thus the gifts, even though they are "given" to "each person," ultimately express the Spirit's sovereign action in the life of the believer and the community as a whole.[348] This is the Pauline version of "the wind/Spirit blows where it/he wills" (John 3:8).

Thus, from beginning to end the single emphasis of the paragraph is the great diversity of gifts that the one God distributes/manifests through his one Spirit for the sake of the community. The reason for such emphasis is not immediately evident from what is said here, but before Paul finishes, the Corinthians should have no doubt about Paul's concern, and the *corrective* nature of this present argument.

Apart from the traditional Pentecostal movement, the church showed very little interest in this paragraph until the outbreak of some of these phenomena both in Roman Catholic and in traditional Protestant circles in the late 1950s. The result has been a considerable body of literature, both scholarly and popular, on the gifts enumerated in vv. 8–10. Most of this literature assumes that such gifts were available to Christians during all ages of the church. Although some have taken a dim view of the phenomena, most have been moderately cautious, suggesting openness to what the Spirit might do, but usually also offering correctives or guidelines. However, there has also been a spate of literature whose sole urgency has been to justify the limiting of these gifts to the first-century church. It is fair to say of this literature that its authors have found what they were looking for and have thereby continued to reject such manifestations in the church. It can also be fairly said that such rejection is

---

[345] Robertson-Plummer 268 note that the πάντα is very emphatic.

[346] Gk. ἰδίᾳ ἑκάστῳ; the addition of ἰδίᾳ emphasizes the individual nature of the Spirit's dealings with each; cf. Barrett, "individually to each one"; Conzelmann, "to each in particular."

[347] Gk. βούλεται, by the Koine period roughly synonymous with θέλω.

[348] Cf. Conzelmann 209, "This denies the pneumatic any power of his own."

not exegetically based, but results in every case from a prior hermeneutical and theological commitment.[349]

Perhaps the greater tragedy for the church is that it lost touch with the Spirit of God in its ongoing life, and as a result it often settled for what is only ordinary. Equally grievous is the urgency of some to justify such shortsightedness. The hope, of course, lies with v. 11, that the one and the same Spirit will do as he pleases, despite the boxes provided for him by those on both sides of this issue.

1 CORINTHIANS 12:12–14

[12]*For just as the body is one and has many parts, and all the parts of the body[350] though many form one body, so it is with Christ.* [13]*For indeed we all were baptized in one Spirit unto one body—whether Jews or Greeks, slave or free—and we were all given one Spirit[351] to drink.* [14]*For indeed the body is not one part but many.*

In order to press the point made in the previous paragraph, the need for diversity within unity, Paul adopts a common analogy from antiquity and directs it toward the Corinthian situation. In so doing, as often happens with such rich metaphors, he also makes further points about attitudes that need correcting in Corinth. Since effective analogies by their very nature are open to independent application, and since this one is so well known in the church, one must be especially careful to read the text with Paul's concerns in view.

The argument consists of three parts (vv. 12–14, 15–20, 21–26).[352] This first paragraph sets out the basic presupposition of the imagery (the body is one) and its urgency (but has many members). This is followed by a twofold elaboration of the metaphor, the first part stressing diversity (vv. 15–20), the second unity (vv. 21–26). Since Spirit language and

---

[349]I do not mean this to be unkind; by "exegetical," I mean that the questions and answers arise from the text itself. When one asks of the text, "When will these phenomena cease?" one has already asked a nonexegetical question, in the sense that it does not arise from the text itself. This is true even of a book like R. Gaffin's *Perspectives on Pentecost* (Phillipsburg, N.J.: Presbyterian and Reformed, 1979), whose exegetical skills are obvious, but who has nonetheless set up the questions and goes after the results in terms of his prior questions quite apart from Paul's own interests. See my critique of Gaffin and this kind of hermeneutics in *Gospel and Spirit: Issues in New Testament Hermeneutics* (Peabody, Mass.: Hendrickson, 1991) 76–77.

[350]The MajT, following several Western witnesses (D b Ambrosiaster), add τοῦ ἑνός, thus: "all the parts of the *one* body."

[351]A few late MSS (630 1881 2495 pc sy^h) read πόμα for πνεῦμα, thus making this a reference to the Lord's Supper: "We were all given one drink to drink."

[352]NA^{26}, followed by NIV and others, breaks the paragraphs as vv. 12–13, 14–20, 21–26. But this misses the structures of Paul's Greek. See below.

concerns occur only in vv. 12–14, the application of the metaphor in vv.
15–26 will be noted more in passing.

Paul's primary concern with this imagery is not that the body is one
even though it has many members,[353] thus arguing for their need for unity
despite their diversity. Rather, his concern is expressed in v. 14, that *even
though the body is one*, it does not consist of one member, but of many,
thus arguing for their need for diversity, since they are in fact one
body.[354] The structure of the argument in vv. 12–14 bears this out. The
opening sentence somewhat redundantly strikes both notes with equal
force:

For just as	the body is one,	A
and	has many members,	B
and	all the members, though many,	B'
	are one body,	A'
So also is	Christ.	

Thus the first clause (AB) strikes the note of diversity; the second (B'A')
the note of unity.

The two following sentences (vv. 13 and 14) begin with the identical,
but unusual, "for indeed,"[355] suggesting that in turn they will elaborate
(or explain) what has just been said. Thus v. 13 takes up the presuppositional statement (the body is one) and explains *how* the many of
them became one body: They were all immersed in and made to drink
the same reality—the Spirit. Verse 14 then picks up the second theme,
but rephrases it so as to highlight the real urgency of the analogy: The
one body is not one member, but many.

The key to both their unity and diversity is their common lavish
experience of the Spirit, as v. 13 says with powerful metaphors. Although
this is the only mention of the Spirit in the entire section (vv. 12–26), this
presuppositional statement seems intended to control the Corinthians'
understanding of the whole. And how different from what they understood—and what is so often the experience of later Christians. They and
Paul were agreed at one point—the lavish experience of Spirit is the key
to their life in Christ; they were disagreed over the reason for such
lavishness. The Corinthians understood it basically in terms of the gift of

---

[353] The NIV reflects this traditional understanding, but the Greek simply does not
support it.

[354] Cf. Conzelmann 212, commenting on v. 14: "Now the accent again lies (as in
vv 4–11) upon the notion of differentiation." This stands over against both the NIV
and a large number of interpreters, who, despite the structure and all the signals to
the contrary, see the passage as emphasizing unity. See most recently, Talbert,
"Understanding," 98–99.

[355] Gk. καὶ γάρ; this combination of particles also appears elsewhere in 1 Corinthians as an emphatic explanation of a prior assertion. See 5:7; 11:9; 14:8; cf. 1 Thes
3:4; 2 Thes 3:10; 2 Cor 5:2–4; Rom 11:1; 15:3; 16:2.

tongues, which they took as testimony that they had entered into a kind of heavenly existence in the present. Paul understood it as the basis for unity, but not uniformity, and therewith as the guarantor of rich diversity in terms of the Spirit's manifestations in their midst.

Our present interest lies primarily with what is said about the Spirit in v. 13; but a few contextual words are necessary also about vv. 12 and 14, lest we isolate v. 13 from its present argument, as so often happens in the literature on this verse.

12 The "for" with which this sentence begins indicates that what follows is intended to offer further explanation of the point made in vv. 4–11. The explanation returns to the imagery of the church as the "body of Christ," first used in 10:17 and picked up again in 11:29.[356] The imagery itself was common in the ancient world,[357] and was therefore probably well known to the Corinthians. It suits Paul's present concern perfectly.[358]

In its first instance (10:17) Paul insists that the many are one body, a point made on the basis of the many of them eating of the one loaf at the Lord's Table. That note is struck again here, but now as the presup-

---

[356] On these two significant texts and their importance to the present argument, see Fee 468–70 and 563–64. On the possible "sources" or "origin" of this analogy in Paul, see E. Best, *One Body in Christ* (London: SPCK, 1955) 83–95, although the very commonplaceness of the imagery renders some of that discussion irrelevant. Less likely still is the suggestion that the "source" was the temple of Asclepius with its many clay replicas of "dismembered" parts of the body. See A. E. Hill, "The Temple of Asclepius: An Alternative Source for Paul's Body Theology?" *JBL* 99 (1980) 437–39; and G. G. Garnier, "The Temple of Asklepius at Corinth and Paul's Theology," *Buried History* 18 (1982) 52–58.

[357] In none of the other known usages is the same *point* made as in Paul. Thus the fable of Menenius Agrippa (ca. 494 BCE) recorded in Livy, *Hist.* 2.32 (the parts are upset with the stomach and choose not to feed it, resulting in their common emaciation), stresses the *interdependence* of the many on one another (in his case the need for the plebeians not to be seditious). Josephus (*War* 4.406) uses the analogy in a negative way to describe the spread of sedition; his usage is comparable to 12:26 ("if one part suffers, all parts suffer together"), but his concern is radically different from Paul's. So also with the Stoic philosophers, whose concern is that any one part is ultimately subservient to the whole, which is the greater. Cf. Marc. Aur. Ant. 2.1; 7.13; Epict. 2.10.3–4; Seneca, *Ep.* 95.52, whose language comes the closest to Paul's: "All that you behold, that which comprises both god and man, is one—we are the parts of one great body." He is also concerned that the parts are mutually interdependent.

[358] For Paul it is metaphor, pure and simple, whose interest is not the nature of the church per se, but the need for it to experience its proper diversity in unity. This makes most of the *theological* discussion, which moves in the other direction, to be "by the way" in terms of Paul's concerns. Cf. B. Daines, "Paul's Use of the Analogy of the Body of Christ—With Special Reference to 1 Corinthians 12," *EvQ* 50 (1978) 71–78; and G. L. O. R. Yorke, *The Church as the Body of Christ in the Pauline Corpus: A Re-examination* (Lanham, Md.: University Press of America, 1991).

position; this is not what Paul will argue *for*, but argue *from*. In this passage the emphasis shifts to the many who make up the one body. Nonetheless, in this opening sentence both points are made: The body is one, yet the body has many parts. In saying that it is one, his concern is for its essential unity. But that does not mean uniformity. That was the Corinthian error, to think that uniformity was a value, or that it represented true spirituality. Paul's concern is for their unity; but for him there is no such thing as true unity without diversity. Hence the need to strike that note so strongly.[359]

13 This verse and the next pick up the two parts of v. 12 by way of explanation/elaboration. The present sentence further explains the presupposition, "the body is one." In keeping with the preceding argument, as well as with the section as a whole, the explanation is given in terms of the Spirit. But in this case one suspects that this is not simply an ad hoc theological construct, but rather is inserted precisely because it reflects the heart of Pauline theology.[360] What makes them one is their common experience of the Spirit, the very Spirit responsible for, and manifested in, the great diversity just argued for in vv. 4–11. For Paul the reception of the Spirit is the *sine qua non* of Christian life. The Spirit is what essentially distinguishes believer from nonbeliever (2:10–14); the Spirit is what especially marks the beginning of Christian life (Gal 3:2–3); the Spirit above all is what makes a person a child of God (Rom 8:14–17). Thus it is natural for him to refer to their unity in the body in terms of the Spirit.

What needs to be pointed out, however, is that, despite the considerable literature on this text suggesting otherwise, Paul's present concern is *not* to delineate *how an individual becomes a believer*, but to explain *how the many of them, diverse as they are, are in fact one body*.[361] The answer: The Spirit, whom all alike have received.

To make that point Paul refers to their common reception of the Spirit, presumably at the beginning of their Christian experience, by means of parallel sentences:

---

[359] In saying "so it is with Christ," Paul is probably using metonymy, where "Christ" means the church, as a shortened form for the "body of Christ." The evidence for this is v. 27: "Now you are the body of Christ, and each one of you is a part of it," followed by v. 28, "And in the church God has appointed . . . "

[360] Cf. Dunn, *Jesus*, 199–202. So also E. Käsemann, "The Theological Problem Presented by the Motif of the Body of Christ," in *Perspectives on Paul* (ET; London: SCM, 1971) 104, who, however, sees the "heart" to be the sacramental aspect rather than the Spirit.

[361] Missing this concern is what mars Beasley-Murray's—and so many others'—discussion of this text (*Baptism*, 167–71); cf. in the same vein, Ervin (*Conversion-Initiation*, 98–102), whose urgency to respond to Dunn causes him to discuss this text without ever asking the basic exegetical question as to its meaning in context.

> "We[362] all were baptized in the one Spirit,"
> 　and
> "We all were caused to drink one Spirit."

The first clause is further qualified by the prepositional phrase, "unto/into[363] one body," which in turn is modified by the parenthetical addition, "whether Jews or Greeks, slave or free."

But there is considerable difference of opinion as to what experience(s) this language refers. Because of the verb "baptize," it is often assumed[364] that Paul is referring to the sacrament of water baptism,[365] and it is then often argued further that this text supports the close tie of the reception of the Spirit with baptism itself.[366] But that assumes far more than is actually said. While it is true that early on this verb became the technical term for the Christian initiatory rite, one may not thereby assume that *Paul* intended its technical sense here. In fact he does not say "we were all *baptized*," which on its own would almost certainly imply "with water," but specifically says, "we were all *baptized in one Spirit*."[367] Moreover, it is *not* baptism but the *one* Spirit, repeated in both clauses, that in Paul's present argument is the basis for unity (cf. vv. 4–11). In any case, one is hard pressed in Paul's letters to find an equation between baptism and the reception of the Spirit.[368] Both are assumed to be at the beginning of Christian experience, to be sure, but there is no specific tie of the two in such a way that the Spirit is received at baptism.[369] This

---

[362] For this use of "we" in the middle of an argument where Paul begins to identify with the Corinthians, esp. in their common experience of life in Christ, see 2:7; 5:7–8; 6:3; 8:8; 10:16; 11:31; cf. 2 Cor 1:21–22; 3:18; 5:18; Gal 3:13–14; 4:5, 6, et al.

[363] Gk. εἰς, which can be local, indicating that into which all were baptized, or it can denote the goal of the action, indicating the purpose or goal of the baptismal action (= so as to become one body). The argument in context favors the latter.

[364] This is the stance of most commentaries, which for the most part do not even raise the question.

[365] See the argument for this position in Beasley-Murray, *Baptism*, 167–71, whose "considerations" that seem to "demand" this view are not convincing. In Paul's argument it is not *baptism* that makes them one, but the *one Spirit*.

[366] Even Beasley-Murray (appropriately) backs off here: "There is nothing automatic about this association of baptism and the Spirit" (*Baptism*, 170).

[367] For the Corinthians, of course, the point of reference for the metaphor would be their own baptism (immersion) in water. But that is not the same as suggesting either that Paul intended the rite here or that they would have thought him to be referring to it.

[368] See the assertion by R. Schnackenburg, *Baptism in the Thought of St. Paul* (ET; Oxford: Blackwell, 1964) 83: "That baptism and the reception of the Spirit are associated is not to be doubted, according to I Cor. vi. 11; xii. 13." But that is precisely what is to be doubted in both cases (see above on 6:11). The argument thus becomes circular. See also the discussion of 2 Cor 1:21–22; Eph 1:13–14; and Titus 3:6.

[369] On this matter see the full discussion in ch. 14 below, pp. 853–64.

text supports such a view *only* on the unsupported grounds that Paul himself makes that assumption.

But the greater difficulty for this view lies with the second clause, "and we were all given one Spirit to drink." Some have argued that this clause points to a *second* experience of some kind,[370] but the lack of such usage elsewhere in Christian literature militates against it. Rather, as indicated above, this is most likely a piece of Semitic parallelism, where both clauses argue essentially the same point.[371] It is the clearly *metaphorical* sense[372] of this parallel clause which, along with the modifier "in the Spirit," argues most strongly for a metaphorical, rather than literal, meaning for "baptism" in the first clause.[373]

If so, then to what do the two clauses refer? For what Christian experience do they serve as metaphors? Some have argued for "Spirit baptism," by which they mean a separate and distinguishable experience from conversion.[374] But this has against it both Pauline usage (he does not elsewhere use this term or clearly refer to such a second experi-

---

[370] Some (including Calvin, Luther, Käsemann, Conzelmann; for a more complete list see Schnackenburg, *Baptism*, 84) have suggested the Lord's Supper, a view that has nothing in its favor except the verb "to drink," and has everything against it (nowhere is such a metaphor used for the Table; there is not a hint that anyone in the early church ever thought of drinking the cup as an imbibing of the Spirit). A traditional Pentecostal view sees the two clauses as referring to conversion and Spirit baptism (see, e.g., R. E. Cottle, "All Were Baptized," *JETS* 17 [1974] 75–80, defending a view put forth by R. Riggs, *The Spirit Himself* [Springfield, Mo.: Gospel Publishing House, 1949]; cf. more recently, Ervin, *Conversion-Initiation*, 101–2). The traditional Roman Catholic view is that it refers to confirmation (see Schnackenburg, 84; cf. J. Hanimann, " 'Nous avons été abreuvés d'un seul Esprit.' Note sur 1 Co 12, 13b," *NouvRT* 94 [1972] 400–405). These views seem to reflect vested interests that lie beyond the concern of Paul's argument.

[371] This is a common device in Paul; cf. e.g., vv. 15–16, 17, 21, 22–23 below; cf. 10:23.

[372] Cf. the usage in the Gospel of John, where "water" is used as a symbol for the Spirit (4:10, 14; 7:37–39). An attractive option that has been gaining adherents suggests that the metaphor reflects the idea of "watering" (cf. 3:6–7), esp. referring to OT motifs of the "pouring out" on the land of the eschatological Spirit, as in Isa 32:15; 44:3. Thus, "we were all saturated with the one Spirit." See the considerable argument in its favor by Schnackenburg, *Baptism*, 84–86, and Dunn, *Baptism*, 130–31; cf. Wendland 97; Beasley–Murray, *Baptism*, 170; Cottle, "All," 79; G. J. Cuming, "ἐποτίσθησαν (I Corinthians 12. 13)," *NTS* 27 (1981) 283–85; Martin, *Spirit*, 24; Carson, *Showing*, 46. The most crippling blow to this position is the accusative ἓν πνεῦμα; the LXX of Isa 29:10 has the dative, which one would certainly expect here had Paul intended πνεῦμα to be instrumental. See further, E. R. Rogers, " Ἐποτίσθησαν Again," *NTS* 29 (1983) 139–42.

[373] There is, after all, no experience called "drinking the Spirit"! Among others who adopt the present view, see Wendland 97; Dunn, *Baptism*, 127–31; Talbert, "Understanding," 98–99.

[374] Most recently, H. Hunter, *Spirit-Baptism: A Pentecostal Alternative* (Lanham, Md.: University Press of America, 1983) 39–42.

ence[375]) and the emphasis in this context, which is not on a special experience in the Spirit beyond conversion, but on their *common* reception of the Spirit.

Most likely, therefore, Paul is referring to their common experience of conversion, and he does so in terms of its most crucial element, the receiving of the Spirit. Such expressive metaphors (immersion in the Spirit and drinking to the fill of the Spirit), it needs to be added, imply a much greater experiential and visibly manifest reception of the Spirit than many have tended to experience in subsequent church history (see on 2:4–5). Paul may appeal to their common experience of Spirit as the presupposition for the unity of the body precisely because, as in Gal 3:2–5, the Spirit was a dynamically experienced reality, which had happened to all.

If this is the correct understanding of these two clauses, and the full context seems to argue for such, then the prepositional phrase "in the Spirit" is most likely locative,[376] expressing the "element" in which they have all been immersed, just as the Spirit is also that which they have all been given to drink. Such usage is also in keeping with the rest of the NT. Nowhere else does this dative with "baptize" imply agency (i.e., that the Spirit does the baptizing),[377] but always refers to the element "in which" one is baptized.[378]

In this sentence the *goal* of their common "immersion" in the one Spirit is "into/unto one body," which of course is the point in context, picking up the concern of v. 12. The precise nuance of this preposition is not certain. It is often given a *local* sense, suggesting that all are baptized

---

[375] Which does not mean that he did not know of such. *Pace* Hunter (*Spirit-Baptism*, 30–63), whose texts are all exegeted on the prior assumption that such *may* have been the case, there is no clear statement in Paul that speaks to such a question.

[376] It is possible, as the NIV, to see it as instrumental, esp. in light of v. 9; cf. e.g., Moffatt 186; O. Cullmann, *Baptism in the New Testament* (ET; London: SCM, 1950) 30; Schnackenburg, *Baptism*, 27–29; and argued for vigorously by Ervin, *Conversion-Initiation*, 99. But usage elsewhere in the NT, plus the present argument in context, suggests otherwise.

[377] The usage in 6:11 that is often appealed to is not parallel. See the discussion above.

[378] This is always true of "water" (Matt 3:11; Mark 1:8; Luke 3:16; John 1:26, 31, 33; Acts 1:5; 11:16; cf. Matt 3:6; John 3:23;); it is likewise true in the other instances of "Spirit baptism," which are always set in contrast to water baptism (Matt 3:11; Mark 1:8; Luke 3:16; John 1:33; Acts 1:5; 11:16). See esp. Paul's own usage in 10:2. Cf. Dunn, *Baptism*, 127–28. Both Hunter (*Spirit-Baptism*, 41) and Ervin (*Conversion-Initiation*, 99) argue that Paul may go his own way on this matter of usage. While that is possible, it does not make it necessary, as both seem to imply. The Pauline usage in v. 9 is not quite as significant as they wish to make it, since the crucial issue is *usage with the passive of* βαπτίζω, not with the verb δίδωμι (in other words Paul's usage in 10:2 is more significant in this regard than in v. 9, since local context is quite irrelevant for this kind of grammatical nuance).

"into" the same reality, namely, the body of Christ, the implication being that there is a prior entity called the body of Christ, which one becomes part of by being immersed in the Spirit.[379] But with verbs of motion like "baptize" this preposition most often has the sense of "movement toward so as to be in."[380] In the present case the idea of "goal" seems more prominent. That is, the purpose of our common experience of the Spirit is that we be formed into one body. Hence, "we all were immersed in the one[381] Spirit, so as to become one body." This phrase, of course, expresses the reason for this sentence in the first place. How did the many of them all become one body? By their common, lavish experience of one and the same Spirit.

To emphasize that the many ("we all") have become one through the Spirit, Paul adds parenthetically, "whether Jews or Greeks, slave or free." As in 7:17–24, these terms express the two basic distinctions that separated people in that culture—race/religion and social status.[382] In Christ these old distinctions have been obliterated, not in the sense that one is no longer Jew or Greek, etc., but in the sense of their having *significance*. And, of course, having significance is what gives them value as distinctives. So in effect their common experience of the Spirit had eliminated the significance of the old distinctions, hence they had become one body.

14 With another "for indeed"[383] Paul elaborates the second motif of v. 12 and the real concern behind this analogy: that even though they are one body, made so by their common experience of the Spirit (v. 13), the body itself, though one, is not one "part," but "many." Though echoing the theme from v. 12, this is not simply reiteration. In v. 12 it is stated matter-of-factly: "The *body* is *one*; the *one body* has *many* members." Here Paul mixes the two themes with a negative contrast: "The *one body* is *not* one member; *rather*, it is composed of *many* constituent parts." This negative way of reiterating v. 12 is surely the point of the whole; otherwise why say it at all, especially in this sentence which intends to elaborate v. 12?

---

[379] See, e.g., Schnackenburg, *Baptism*, 26. One need not doubt the general truth of such a statement. The question is whether Paul intended it here, since his question is not, "How do people become believers?" but "How do the many believers become one body?"

[380] Dunn, *Baptism*, 128.

[381] Note the repetition of this qualifier from vv. 4–11 (esp vv. 9 and 11). The basis of their unity is still the unity of God himself, expressed here in terms of the "one Spirit."

[382] In 7:17–24 the same four groups are mentioned in the same order. Cf. Gal 3:28, where Paul adds the final distinction between people, "male and female." For a different expression of this kind of list, see Col 3:11.

[383] See n. 355 above.

From here Paul proceeds to develop the imagery of the "body" (referring always to the church) in two slightly different directions (vv. 15–20, 21–26), which will in fact apply both parts of the figure (many members, one body) to their situation; but the primary concern, as this verse indicates, is with the "many parts."

In sum (regarding the Spirit in this passage): 1. Along with 2:10–16 and elsewhere (e.g., Gal 3:2–5), this passage makes it clear that for Paul the Spirit is the *sine qua non*, the one absolutely crucial element of entrance into life in Christ. The common experience of the Spirit in all of God's people lies behind this argument as its basic presupposition. Thus, even though this is not a "conversion" text per se, Paul's point stands or falls on the fact that he is referring to their common reception of the Spirit at their conversion.

2. The metaphors in v. 13 imply that their common experience of the Spirit was a lavish and experienced reality, very much as in Gal 3:2–5. On this matter Paul and the Corinthians have the same starting point, not as argumentation, but as common experience. It seems difficult to get around the further implication that the experience of the Spirit was therefore accompanied by visible, evidential phenomena.

3. The Spirit is understood by Paul to be responsible for making "one body" of the many people who become "members" of the new people of God. While the emphasis is not on the unity of the body as such, the implication of v. 13 is that the Spirit is indeed responsible for their unity.

1 CORINTHIANS 12:15–26

[24b]*But God composed the body by having given greater honor to the parts that lacked it* [25]*in order that there might be no division in the body but that the parts might show the same concern for one another;* [26]*and if one member suffers, all the members suffer together; if one member is honored, all the members rejoice together.*

Although neither of the paragraphs (vv. 15–20, 21–26) in this extended application of the body metaphor mentions the Spirit as such, we need at least to wrestle with their place in the argument, since for many they hold the keys to understanding the whole. At issue is the intent of the second analogy, with its language of *apparently* "weaker"/"less honorable" members, who are "indispensable"/receive "the greater honor." To whom is Paul referring, and who within the community considers them so? And how, then, do vv. 24b–26 fit in as Paul's concluding response to this matter? In order to speak to these questions, a brief overview seems necessary.

The two paragraphs elaborate the imagery of the body by illustrating both concerns of vv. 12–14, *diversity* in *unity*. Verses 15–20 continue the thought of diversity in v. 14, "the body is not one member but many," but conclude by once more stressing unity (v. 20), which is then taken up in the second illustration (vv. 21–26).[384] The structure of both illustrations is similar. In each case Paul begins with a personification of some of the parts of the body. These parts are disallowed to say things either about themselves (vv. 15–16) or about others (v. 21), which express absurdities, as far as the body is concerned. The absurdity is pressed in the first instance with rhetorical questions (v. 17) and in the second with observations about how certain parts of the body are treated (vv. 22–24a). Paul then "applies" these pictures to the body itself (vv. 18–20; 24b–26); in each case Paul obviously intends the application to fit the situation in Corinth as well: *they* are the "body" being spoken about. The ultimate exegetical concern is to determine how the Corinthians were expected to understand these applied pictures, and thus to determine the place of this section in the total argument.

In the first analogy, Paul's rhetorical questions in vv. 17 and 19 argue that all members are necessary if there is to be a body and not a monstrosity. Verses 18 and 20 respond to this rhetoric by indicating the true nature of the body as it was divinely ordained: one body with many parts. In context, therefore, this first application illustrates the concern of v. 14, "the body is not *one* member, but *many*." Even though v. 18 embraces the people involved, the focus seems still to be on their need to experience a *variety of Spirit manifestations* within the gathered community. That is (probably), their gatherings should not be given to speaking in tongues exclusively (= the body is not *one* member), but should also include other Spirit workings such as those enumerated in vv. 8–10 (the body is *many* members).

In the second analogy, the focus shifts toward the people themselves and the *attitude of some toward others within the community*. This illustrates the point of v. 13, "all immersed in the one Spirit so as to form one body, whether Jew or Greek, slave or free." The need for diverse Spirit manifestations thus recedes momentarily in favor of an emphasis on showing special concern for the "apparently weak and insignificant," so as to eliminate "division" in the body. At issue, therefore, are (1) how, or whether, this is also related to their enthusiasm for tongues, and (2) how, or whether, either of these (attitudes toward one another and enthusiasm for tongues) is related to previous expressions of (apparent) "division" within the community (especially 1:10–3:23; 8:1–13; and 11:17–34). This latter issue is especially complex, inasmuch as: (a) the "division" in 1:10–3:23 does not emerge along ideological lines, but focuses on

---

[384]These elaborations become analogies in their own right and are capable of independent application (as often happens to them). However, even though in Paul's hands analogies are often less than precise—the analogy seems to make one point while Paul's own application makes another (cf. 2 Tim 2:20–21)—nonetheless we must go with Paul's own application, not with the imagery as such.

loyalty to former teachers in the name of wisdom; (b) the tension in 8:1–13[385] generates from some who operate on the basis of "knowledge" and who are thus causing considerable distress for others lacking such "knowledge"; (c) the "division" in 11:17–34 is along sociological lines, where the "haves" are abusing the "have-nots" at the Lord's Table. It should also be noted that the two prior occurrences of the imagery of the church as Christ's body, with emphasis on unity and mutual concern, appear in these latter two instances (10:17 and 11:29). The question is, how does all of this relate?

On the one hand, on the basis of the context, it seems likely that both of the present applications have glossolalists in view. First, they are being encouraged to see the ministry of the Spirit on a much broader scale than has been their wont (vv. 15–20); second, they are being admonished not to take an elitist view of tongues, which allows them to disdain others and thus to divide the community (vv. 21–26). At the same time, the "admonition" in the second application has so many similarities with the attitude of those with "knowledge" in ch. 8 (including Paul's calling on them to function on the basis of love), that it is a very small step for us to see some kind of identification between the two. That they might also have been enthusiastic about tongues because of its allegedly "showy" nature, which is often suggested as well, seems moot. Nothing in the text suggests as much; it has rather been inferred from the analogy, with its mention of more honorable, less honorable, etc. But the inference is neither necessary nor supported by the rest of the argument.

On the other hand, there are also some inherent difficulties with this view: (1) Nothing else in the present argument seems specifically directed toward internal strife over the issue of tongues-speaking. Indeed, when Paul finally speaks directly to the issue of tongues in 14:1–40, there is not a hint of what is said here, either in terms of the attitudes of the glossolalists toward their "gift" or of any "division" among the Corinthians on this matter. This is particularly telling in the final "so then" of 14:39, which merely reiterates the instruction of vv. 1–33, but now in terms of their "not forbidding tongues" in light of what he has argued. If an elitist attitude toward tongues, *which also created division among them*, were the bottom-line issue, one wonders how Paul avoided saying a final word about it at the end. In fact, the only specific conflict that emerges in ch. 14 is between the glossolalists and Paul, which vv. 36–37 confirm; it seems to lie just below the surface in vv. 6, 13–15, and 18–19 as well. (2) The final applications of the analogy that Paul makes in vv. 25b–26 ("showing mutual care" and "suffering with those who suf-

---

[385] Which is never referred to as "division" or "quarrelling," nor does Paul suggest or imply that the Corinthians themselves are "divided" on this matter. Some are abusing others, pure and simple.

fer") do not seem to fit well with division based on Spirit manifestations. That is, the "division" to which Paul refers is specifically related to the attitude of some toward others based on *their status within the community* as "weak" and "insignificant"; and the call is to mutual care—obviously from "the top down"—so that their mutual interdependence as a body expresses itself in "suffering together with one another" and "rejoicing together."

That leads then to a modification of the common view, which tries to keep its strengths but to do so in light of these difficulties. Rather than using this second application to deal exclusively with glossolalia, Paul more likely is now addressing the larger question of "divisions" within this community—of any and all kinds. This is not to exclude application to glossolalists; but it is to suggest, in light of how Paul concludes in vv. 25–26, that this application throws the net more broadly and includes all forms of such strife, including the attitudes of the rich toward the poor (masters toward slaves? since the one body now includes "slave and free"?). Since they are one body in Christ, formed by their common experience of the Spirit, there can be *no* "looking down" on others (those with weak consciences regarding temple meals; the poor who miss out on the Lord's Supper as it is currently "celebrated"; and those who might not have the same exalted view of glossolalia as do others). It is as though Paul were saying at v. 21, "And by the way, while we are on this matter of one body with many parts, let's not miss the broader implications; not only may none of you disdain others on any issue for any reason, but you are so interdependent that as one body you must instead show mutual care for one another, and that includes suffering with the suffering and rejoicing with those who receive honor."

The advantages of this view are that it does not remove it from its immediate context, but neither does it try to identify the glossolalists too closely with any of the former issues in the letter (although I personally lean toward an identification with the issue in chs. 8–10). Moreover, it keeps us from having to read into ch. 14 what is not there—strife within the community over tongues; and it makes sense of the real conflict which does emerge—between the church and its apostle, not suggesting that all are so inclined to be against Paul, but that those who are currently influential among them have moved in that direction.

Finally, in terms of the present context, two matters are of significance for Paul's argument: (1) The urgency over "showing mutual concern" for people within the community is in keeping with Paul's concern over diversity "for the common good" (v. 7), on the one hand, and for intelligibility for the sake of edification (14:3, 5, etc.), on the other. The Spirit does not divide; the Spirit promotes the welfare and edification of others, because the *one* Spirit is common to *all* and has made the many into one body. (2) The slight shift in focus in the second application, from the Spirit manifestations of the various members to the various members, leads Paul to a conclusion (vv. 27–30) in which people and gifts will merge in a common list, intended once more to score the point from the beginning—the whole, though one body is not one thing, in terms of either positions, people, or giftedness.

1 CORINTHIANS 12:27–31

²⁷Now you are the body of Christ, and members each for his/her part; ²⁸and whom God has placed in the church are first apostles, second prophets, third teachers, then miracles, then gifts of healings, helpful deeds, acts of guidance, kinds of tongues. ²⁹Are all apostles? Are all prophets? Are all teachers? Are all miracles? ³⁰Do all have gifts of healing? Do all speak in tongues? Do all interpret? ³¹But eagerly desire the greater³⁸⁶ gifts. And now³⁸⁷ I will show you the most excellent way.

This paragraph concludes the argument that began in v. 4 by tying together its two parts (vv. 4–11 and 12–26) and thus returning to the original emphasis. In v. 27 the preceding imagery of the body (vv. 12–26) is now applied specifically to the church in Corinth, again focusing on the many who make it up. In vv. 28–30, now by way of v. 27, Paul returns once more to the concern of vv. 4–11, the need for diversity, not uniformity, in gifts and ministries.

He argues this view by means of another ad hoc list, which this time includes persons and their ministries as well as some of the χαρίσματα/Spirit-manifestations from vv. 8–10. As before, at issue is neither *instruction* about gifts and ministries, nor *ranking* them. Rather, the preceding illustrations implied that the body has both different kinds of parts and differences within the same kind. The former focused on gifts (vv. 15–20), the latter on the persons (vv. 21–26). Now he simply combines them all, beginning with "persons" and ending again with "tongues."

---

³⁸⁶ The Westerns and MajT substituted the misleading κρει(ττ)ονα (better) for Paul's original μείζονα (greater), read by P⁴⁶ ℵ A B C 6 33 81 104 326 630 1175 1739 1881 pc co. See Zuntz, *Text*, 135, who is worth quoting: "The 'non-Alexandrian' reading makes Paul end on a truism: if there are any charismata 'better' than others, of course they ought to be sought; it moreover credits him with a use of the word κρεῖσσον for which there is no parallel in his writings. . . . The essence of Paul's exhortation is that some spiritual gifts are 'greater' than others (cf. xiv.5) because they benefit the wider community. Even so, he opposes outright the notion that any one is superior or inferior to another." On the other side see A. Harnack, "The Apostle Paul's Hymn of Love (1 Cor. XIII.) and its Religious-Historical Significance," *Exp* 8:3 (1912) 385–408, 481–503 [387–88], which appeared originally in *Sitzungsberichte der Preussischen Akademie der Wissenschaften* (Berlin, 1911) 132–63.

³⁸⁷ The difficulty with this ἔτι is demonstrated by the reading of P⁴⁶ (and perhaps D* F G), εἴ τι (= "If there is anything beyond, I point out the way to you"). But this reading is almost certainly a corruption. Cf. the discussion in Zuntz, *Text*, 90–91, who is tantalized by it, but admits the difficulties.

But he has not lost sight of his goal, which comes out forcefully in the rhetoric of vv. 29–30: "Are all one thing?" "Do all have the same gifts?" "Of course not," is the intended reply. This is simply v. 19 now being applied directly to the situation of the church. Diversity within unity is Paul's concern; and diversity *includes* tongues, but will not allow tongues to be *exclusive*.

Thus, even though the Spirit is not mentioned as such, the whole continues to deal with Spirit phenomena in the church.

27 This sentence, which ties all the preceding pieces together, spells out what the Corinthians must have known right along, that the foregoing analogies were all about them. In v. 12 Paul asserted that the body, with its diversity in unity, is like Christ. Now he says plainly, "you[388] are Christ's body,"[389] meaning that collectively in their common relationship to Christ through the Spirit they are his one body (vv. 12–13). At the same time individually they make up its many parts (v. 14). As the next verses make plain, this means that individually they are members with a variety of "assigned" parts. As before, the emphasis lies on the many who give the one body its necessary diversity.

28 With this sentence Paul gives substance to the preceding application, that individually they are parts of the one body of Christ. Now he reiterates two points from the preceding argument: First, he reasserts that God is responsible for the diversity that makes up the one body (cf. vv. 4–6, 11, 18, 24b).[390] The sentence begins on this emphatic, somewhat ungrammatical,[391] note: "and[392] whom[393] God has placed in the church

---

[388] The pronoun takes the emphatic first position.

[389] There is no definite article in the Greek text. Paul is not trying to say something about their relationship to other churches, but about their relationship to Christ and to one another. Thus, he does not mean *the* body, as if they were the whole, nor does he mean *a* body, as if they were one among many (true as that might otherwise be). Rather he means something like, "Your relationship to Christ (vv. 12–13) is that of being his body." The genitive "of Christ" is thus possessive. Cf. Parry 185. So intent is Mare 266 to make this passage refer to the church universal that he limits his discussion to this anarthrous usage and quite disregards the emphatic ὑμεῖς δέ!

[390] The correspondence with v. 18 is especially noteworthy. As in that verse the emphasis here is on God's responsibility for the diversity, for "arranging" the many parts in the body as he wished.

[391] Although Paul's intent seems clear enough, the grammar breaks down some, making a literal translation difficult at best.

[392] Gk. καί, probably coordinate here, develops not "the thought of the church as an organic structure" (Barrett 293), but that of the many kinds of parts that make up the one body.

[393] Gk. οὓς μέν, which expects a coordinate οὓς δέ ("some of one kind, . . . others of another"; see on 7:7). Instead Paul abandons this construction for an ordinal enumeration, which creates something of an *anacolouthon*.

[are]." Since this sentence is coordinate with v. 27, with its emphatic "you are," meaning the church in Corinth, there can be little question that by the phrase "in the church" Paul primarily intends the local assembly in Corinth.[394] In his earlier letters, whenever he means something like our term "church universal," he always uses the plural, "in the churches."

Second, Paul illustrates that diversity by means of another enumeration (cf. vv. 8–10) possessing several remarkable features: (1) He begins by listing *persons* (apostles, prophets, teachers), whom he ranks in the order of first, second, third. (2) With the fourth and fifth items ("miracles" and "gifts of healings") he reverts to two manifestations from the list in vv. 8–10. These are both prefaced with the word "then," as though he intended the ranking scheme to continue. (3) The sixth and seventh items ("helpful deeds" and "acts of guidance"), which are *deeds of service*, merit note in three ways: (a) they are the only two not mentioned again in the rhetoric of vv. 29–30; (b) they are not mentioned again in the NT; (c) they do not appear to be of the same kind, i.e., supernatural endowments, as those on either side (miracles, healings, tongues).

Thus, whether Paul intended so or not, this list includes personal ministries, χαρίσματα, and deeds of service, concluding with tongues. These represent a whole range of "ministries" in the church and were probably chosen for that reason. What one is to make of this mix is not certain. At best we can say that the first three emphasize the persons who have these ministries, while the final five emphasize the ministry itself.[395] The NIV has tried to overcome these differences by making the whole list personal: "miracles" becomes "workers of miracles," and "helps," "those who help others." This may be justifiable in light of vv. 29–30, where the nature of those questions demands a more personal expression.[396] But in truth Paul lists gifts and deeds, not persons. That

---

[394] Cf. Dunn, *Jesus*, 262–63. But its use in this kind of context seems also to prepare the way for its broader use in the Prison Epistles to refer to the church universal—especially so, since the first item "God has placed in the church" are "apostles" (plural). Cf. Martin, *Spirit*, 31, who says this in reverse, that "what Paul had in view was the universal church of which the Corinthian Christians formed a local outgrowth." His entire exegesis, as with most interpreters, is then predicated on the more universal nature of the ministries at the head of this list. On the other side see R. Banks, *Paul's Idea of Community* (Grand Rapids: Eerdmans, 1980) 35–37, who would limit the term strictly to the local community.

[395] It is common to assert, as e.g., Parry 187 that "a marked line is drawn . . . between the permanent functions already enumerated and the occasional manifestations of spiritual power." Whether some functions were permanent or occasional may or may not be true, but the text itself does not make that claim. It is an assertion only, no matter how often it is repeated.

[396] See on vv. 29–30, where Paul seems to sense the difficulty himself. He tries to keep to the "gifts" as such, but the question, "Are all miracles?" makes such little sense (in Greek or in any other language) that he makes the final three personal by

probably suggests that the first three items therefore are not to be thought of as "offices," held by certain "persons" in the local church, but rather refer to "ministries" as they find expression in various persons; likewise the following "gifts" are not expressed in the church apart from persons, but are first of all gracious endowments, given by the Spirit to various persons in the church for its mutual upbuilding.

That leads to the further question, Did Paul intend *all* of these to be "ranked" as to their role or significance in the church? The answer seems to be *No*. He certainly ranked the first three. One might argue also for the rest on the basis of the "then . . . then" that preface the next two. But that poses problems, since (1) he drops the enumeration with the sixth item, (2) the fourth and fifth items are in reverse order from their earlier listing, and (3) there seems to be no special significance as to whether miracles precedes healings, or vice versa, or whether these precede or follow helpful deeds and acts of guidance. The gift of tongues, as noted earlier, is listed last not because it is least but because it is the problem. As before, Paul includes it because it is a proper part of the necessary diversity; but it is included at the end so that the emphasis on diversity will be heard first.

Why, then, does Paul rank the first three? That is more difficult to answer; but it is almost certainly related to his own conviction as to the role these three ministries play in the church. It is not so much that one is more important than the other, or that this is necessarily their order of authority;[397] rather, one has *precedence* over the other in the founding and building up of the local assembly.[398] In light of 14:37 and the probability that those who have taken the lead against Paul are considered "prophets," one is tempted to see here a subordinating of such people to the apostle, who is giving them "the Lord's command" over against their "prophets." It is perhaps noteworthy that none of these "ranked persons" is *addressed* as such in this letter, which suggests further that we are not dealing with recognized "offices" in the Corinthian assembly.

---

adding a verb. The fact that he begins by simply listing a gift suggests that the emphasis is still on the gift, rather than on the persons who express that gift.

[397] Although that would certainly be true of "apostles." But the question of "authority structures" is not asked here and in terms of the argument is altogether irrelevant. It is of some note that those most interested in this question have relegated the first two ministries to the first century only (although some, without textual warrant, would make "prophet" equal "preacher"), so that the third, teacher, now assumes the first position (see, e.g., MacArthur 322–24). One wonders whether a teacher first designed this hermeneutics!

[398] Cf. Grudem, *Gift*, 56–57, although his term is not "precedence" but "usefulness in building up the church." There is nothing in the text to support the oft-repeated suggestion that these three are itinerant ministries, while the rest would be local. See Martin, *Spirit*, 32–33. On this debate in German scholarship see Conzelmann 215.

As to the individual items:

(1) *First, apostles.* It is no surprise that Paul lists "apostles" first. The surprise is that they are on this list at all, and that he lists them in the plural. The meaning of the term "apostle" is not as certain as usage in the church suggests.[399] Paul had already used it in his earliest letter (1 Thes 2:7[6]) as a designation for himself and his co-workers. Its several occurrences in our letter[400] demonstrate that it had already become a fixed term in the Pauline churches to designate a particular group of authoritative people. It obviously includes the Twelve, but also goes considerably beyond them (15:5–7; Rom 16:7).

Our problem with the term stems from two realities: First, this is often an area of conflict between Paul and his churches; and one is not sure whether the churches understand apostleship in the same sense of authoritative self-designation as the apostle himself. Second, even in Paul it is still a considerably flexible term, referring both to *function* and *position*, in at least some semi-official sense. Thus, on the one hand, he used it to describe some who are "sent" by Christ to preach the gospel (cf. 1:17) or by the churches in some official capacity in their behalf (2 Cor 8:23; Phil 2:25). On the other hand, those who were "sent" by Christ, especially those who founded churches as a result of their evangelizing, came to be known as *apostles*, a designation that had inherent in it a sense of "position" as well (especially for those who were directly associated with Christ in his earthly ministry; cf. 15:5–7). Paul's understanding of his own apostleship is predicated on two realities: his having seen the risen Lord and his having founded churches.[401]

Thus in Paul the functional and positional usages nearly coalesce. The problem is to determine the sense it carries in this instance. Since the term "in the church" refers primarily to Corinth, and since "apostleship" is a bone of contention between him and them,[402] this could

---

[399] The literature here is enormous. Among other items see K. H. Rengstorf, *TDNT* 1.407–45; ch. 2 in H. von Campenhausen, *Ecclesiastical Authority and Spiritual Power in the Church of the First Three Centuries* (ET; Stanford: University Press, 1969; 1st Ger. ed. 1953) 12–29; R. Schnackenburg, "Apostles Before and After Paul's Time," in *Apostolic History and the Gospel* (ed. W. W. Gasque, R. P. Martin; Grand Rapids: Eerdmans, 1970) 287–303; and J. A. Kirk, "Apostleship since Rengstorf: Towards a Synthesis," *NTS* 21 (1974–75) 249–64. For an overview of the literature on its origins, see F. H. Agnew, "The Origin of the NT Apostle-Concept: A Review of Research," *JBL* 105 (1986) 75–96.

[400] 1:1; 4:9; 9:1, 2, 5; 12:28, 29; 15:7, 9[2x]; cf. 2 Cor 1:1; 8:23; 11:5, 13; 12:11, 12.

[401] See esp. how these function in the argument in 9:1–2, and how the "founding of churches" functions in the argument of 2 Cor 10–13, where the "super-apostles," whom Paul obviously considers not genuine, are partly so because they work in his field rather than found churches themselves.

[402] Based in part on their apparent triumphalism, stemming from his and their conflicting views of what it meant to be πνευματικός; cf. the introduction to this chapter. In the current context his failure to come to them "speaking in tongues"

assert—indeed, probably did to some degree—his own authority among them. Nonetheless, in keeping with the other members on this list, "apostle" is probably primarily "functional" here, perhaps anticipating the concern for the "building up" of the body that he has already hinted at in v. 7 and will stress in ch. 14.[403] Most likely with this word he is reflecting on his own ministry in this church;[404] the plural is in deference to others who have had the same ministry in other churches (cf. 9:5; 15:7–11).[405]

In any case, there is no other evidence of any kind that Paul thought of a local church as having some among it called "apostles," who were responsible for its affairs. Moreover, and of special interest for our purposes, there is no place in Paul where there is a direct connection between the Spirit and apostleship.[406] His apostleship is received "from Christ" (Rom 1:4–5) and "by the will of God" (1 Cor 1:1); it is never suggested to be a "charism" of the Holy Spirit, as though the Spirit gifted some people for this "office."

(2) *Second, prophets.* On this term see on vv. 8–10. The question is whether Paul is here thinking of a specific group of people known as "prophets" vis-à-vis "apostles" and other members of the community, or whether this is a purely functional term for him, referring to any and all who would exercise the gift of prophecy. The answer is probably yes and no. As noted on v. 10, the evidence of ch. 14 suggests that all Spirit people were potentially "prophets," in the sense that they could prophesy. But this list, as well as the similar kind of language in Eph 2:20 and 4:11, suggests that for Paul, as for Luke, there were some who, because they regularly functioned in this way, were known as "prophets." The term here is probably a designation for the latter, although the emphasis would still be on their *function* to build up the community.

(3) *Third, teachers.* This is the first mention of this ministry in the extant Pauline letters. All attempts to define it from the Pauline perspective are less than convincing, since the evidence is so meager.[407] As with

---

probably accounts in part for their dim view of his apostleship. See below on 14:6, 13–15, 18–19.

[403]Cf. the list in Eph 4:11, which also begins with apostles and includes prophets and teachers, whose reason for being "given" to the church is "the equipping of the saints for the work of the ministry" and the "building up of the body of Christ."

[404]Note esp. on 9:1–2 that the "authority" of an "apostle" from Paul's perspective was *not* over the church universal, but over the churches he founded. On this point see Dunn, *Jesus,* 274.

[405]Dunn, *Jesus,* 275, on the basis of 9:6, would limit the term here to Paul and Barnabas.

[406]In Eph 3:5, the mystery of the gospel is revealed to the apostles and prophets by the Spirit; but that is a different thing from being designated or "anointed" for this ministry by the Spirit.

[407]See, e.g., Dunn, *Jesus,* 282–84, who sees their primary functions as "passing on and interpreting the traditions." This is attractive, and may be correct, but it lies beyond our ability to demonstrate from the evidence alone.

prophecy, the noun "teaching" will appear again as a gift (14:6, 26; q.v.), without concern for the person of the teacher. Probably the same relationship sustains between teaching (as an inspired utterance) and the teacher, as between prophecy and the prophet. There were some who regularly gave a "teaching" in the communities, who thus came to be known as teachers. But again, as ch. 14 indicates, the concern is with their *function*, not their office.[408]

(4, 5) *Then, miracles; then, gifts of healings.* On these gifts see on vv. 8–10. It is of interest that these two appear in their reverse order from vv. 9–10, thus suggesting the irrelevancy of rank from here on. As noted above, the emphasis is not on the people who have these gifts, but simply on the presence of the gifts themselves in the community.

(6) *Helpful deeds.* This word occurs only here in the NT, although it is known in the LXX, where it functions as a verbal noun meaning to help, assist, or aid someone.[409] Perhaps it is similar to the final three items in the list of χαρίσματα in Rom 12:8 (giving, caring for others, doing acts of mercy).[410] In any case it implies that some minister to the physical and spiritual needs of others in the community.

(7) *Acts of guidance.*[411] Although the cognate personal noun of this word occurs in Acts 27:11 and Rev 18:17, meaning "steersman" or "pilot," this noun occurs three times in the LXX,[412] where it carries the verbal idea of giving "guidance" to someone. Most contemporary translations prefer the word "administration"; but in contemporary English that word conjures up the idea of "administrative skills," which is probably a far cry from what Paul had in mind—although it is likely that it refers to giving wise counsel to the community as a whole, not simply to other individuals.[413]

(8) *Different kinds of tongues.* On this gift see on v. 10. As noted above, it is no surprise that it is listed last; what is unusual is that it stands by

---

[408]Since the emphasis seems to be on the function of these first three terms, it is very likely that in terms of persons there was some overlap. That is, the apostle Paul, e.g., is among those in Antioch known as "prophets and teachers" (Acts 13:1); and 14:37 seems to imply that Paul considered himself also among the "prophets." The terms probably finally came to be attached to certain people on the basis of their most common function in the church.

[409]Usually of divine aid, or in the papyri of help sought from a king. But it is purely gratuitous, on the basis of this usage, to argue as Parry 187 does that "it has therefore the definite suggestion of assistance given by governing authorities."

[410]An observation made also by Dunn, *Jesus,* 252; the oft-repeated suggestion that these would be the duties of the "deacons" speaks to the concerns of a later time. Cf. the list of "good deeds" attributed to the "genuine widow" in 1 Tim 5:10.

[411]Gk. κυβερνήσεις; also a NT *hapax legomenon.* Equally gratuitous to the linking of "helps" with "deacons" (see preceding n.) is that of linking this word with "bishops."

[412]Prov 1:5; 11:14; 24:6.

[413]Cf. Dunn, *Jesus,* 252, who translates, "giving counsel."

itself at the end of this list as a gift of utterance. It surely seems out of place after the preceding four items. This increases the probability that our interpretation is correct, that it is not at the bottom of a descending list, but is finally included in a truly heterogeneous listing of gifts and ministries in the church. Thus he concludes, "and this includes tongues as well."

29–30 Paul now ends the argument of this chapter with a crescendo of rhetorical questions. His concern throughout has been the need for diversity, which of course must function in unity. With these questions that is made plain. "Are all one thing? Do all function with the same ministry?" The implied answer is, "of course not." Paul's point, then, is: "Correct; so why don't you apply this to yourselves and your singular zeal for the gift of tongues?" Tongues are fine, he will go on to affirm, provided they are interpreted. But not all should be speaking in tongues when they assemble for worship. That makes all become the same thing, which is like a body with only one part.

The list repeats the items from v. 28,[414] with the omission of "helpful deeds and acts of guidance," and the addition of the "interpretation of tongues" at the end. Nothing should be made of these differences, since the rhetoric indicates Paul's interest. The addition of the verbs "have" and "speak" with "gifts of healing" and "tongues"[415] is simply a way of avoiding the awkwardness that began with the fourth question, "Are all miracles?"[416] The next three questions make it certain that he intended, "Do all work miracles?"

The tension that some feel between this rhetoric and the question as to whether anyone is therefore excluded from any of these gifts is again related to our own concerns for precision. The "wish" in 14:5 that all speak in tongues (apparently privately is intended) and the imperative of 14:1, "eagerly desire spiritual gifts, especially that you may prophesy," plus the statement in 14:31 that "all may prophesy," suggest that such gifts are potentially available to all. But that is *not* Paul's point or concern here. His rhetoric does not mean, "*May* all do this?" to which the answer would probably be "of course"; but "*Are* all, *Do* all?" to which the answer is "of course not." That is, the questions are not theological or theoretical in nature, but practical and experiential. *All* may prophesy, Paul later tells them; but in actual reality all do not prophesy, he here reminds

---

[414]Making it clear that this is the point of that list, not the number or rank of ministries.

[415]Cf. also the use of the verb instead of the noun for "interpretation."

[416]Cf. Barrett 296, "Paul's sentence breaks down." Yes and no. As noted above, it is atrocious Greek, as it is English. But it keeps the emphasis on the gifts, not on persons as such.

them. The singular concern of this argument has led to this rhetoric, which concludes in a resounding fashion as a plea for diversity.

31 After the argument of vv. 4–30 and especially after the rhetoric of vv. 29–30, the imperative with which this verse begins, "but eagerly desire[417] the greater gifts," is a puzzle. It is not so for many, of course, since it is common to read v. 28 as intended to *rank* the various ministries and gifts, so that Paul might place tongues as the last and least of the gifts.[418] This imperative is then read as urging them to seek the gifts at the top of the list, as opposed to those at the bottom, which the argument in ch. 14 is seen to support (prophecy as the "greater" and tongues as the "least"). The difficulties with this view, however, are too numerous to make it viable: (1) Paul's own emphasis throughout the argument falls consistently on the need for diversity, not on ranking some gifts as "greater" than others. (2) This is confirmed by the rhetoric of vv. 29–30, which quite disregards any concern for rank, and has only to do with variety. (3) By the same reasoning that puts tongues as the least, "apostles" should be the "greater" gift, yet all are agreed that this is the one gift that none of them may properly "eagerly desire." (4) Although prophecy is used as the primary example of intelligibility in ch. 14, its place in the two lists in ch. 12 is ambiguous—sixth on the first one, second on the other. (5) The lack of concern for ranking is manifest by Paul's failure to include five of the nine items from the first list in the second one, and of the four he does include, the first three are in reverse order. (6) Such a view seems to run full in the face of the concern in the second application of the body imagery (vv. 21–26), where Paul stressed their mutual interdependence with no one as "superior" to others.

Thus, common as it is, this view must finally be rejected as contradictory both to the spirit and the intent of the preceding argument. But if so, then what does one do with this imperative, which likewise seems contradictory to what has preceded? Three alternatives have been offered.

(1) Some have suggested that this is a citation from the Corinthian letter, as though Paul were saying, "But 'earnestly desire the greater gifts,' you say; well, I will show you a way far superior to that."[419] This

---

[417] Gk. ζηλοῦτε (cf. 14:1, 39, and ζηλῶται in 14:12), which may very well have the full force of the present tense, "keep on eagerly desiring." With its adj. ζῆλος (see Fee 126–27 on 3:3) it can be used either in a positive sense (as here; cf. 2 Cor. 11:2) or negative ("have rivalry, be jealous," as in 13:4).

[418] On this as a misunderstanding of Paul's use of μείζονα, see the quote from Zuntz in n. 386 above.

[419] See, e.g., Baker, "Interpretation," 226–27; following M.-A. Chevallier, *Esprit*, 158–63.

is supported not only by the fact that in previous places Paul seems to cite their letter[420] but by the language of 14:12 as well: "Since you *are* zealots for 'spirits.' " The difficulty with this option is the lack of signals in the argument that indicate either that Paul is quoting them or that what follows is a qualification of the kind found, for example, in 6:13–14; 7:2; or 8:2–3.

(2) It is possible to read the verb as an indicative (cf. NIV[mg]).[421] Thus Paul, after arguing for diversity against their overenthusiasm for tongues as the premier evidence of being "spiritual," has remonstrated, "But you are seeking the so-called greater gifts. Rather I will show you a 'more excellent way.' " He then urges the pursuit of love, and in *that* context that they eagerly desire not "greater gifts," but simply "spiritual gifts."[422] And when one does both—pursues love and desires spiritual gifts—he or she will seek for an intelligible gift such as prophecy (or others listed in 14:6), for only what is intelligible will edify the community. This is supported further, as with the prior option, by Paul's statement to this effect in 14:12. What basically stands against this option[423] is the appearance of the same verb form in 14:1 and 39, where it can only be an imperative and not an indicative.[424]

(3) Despite some attractive features to this second option, the preferable alternative is that the verb is an imperative, as in 14:1, but that it is not intended to be in contrast to 12:4–30, or to the prior enumerations of gifts. Rather, the preceding argument has concluded with the rhetoric of vv. 29–30. With this imperative Paul is about to launch his next argument, namely, 14:1–25 and the need for intelligibility in the community; and in the community *all* the intelligible gifts are "greater" than tongues, because they can edify while tongues without interpretation

---

[420]See, e.g., 6:12, 13; 7:1, 25; 8:1, 4.

[421]For this argument see G. Iber, "Zum Verständnis von I Cor. 12:31," *ZNW* 54 (1963) 43–52. Cf. Bittlinger, *Gifts*, 73–75, who also adopts this alternative. Martin, *Spirit*, 34–35, combines these first two options, following Chevallier in making a considerable distinction between τὰ χαρίσματα in this v. and τὰ πνευματικά in 14:1. See next n.

[422]However, Chevallier, Baker, and Martin (see nn. 243 and 419) make a considerable point that πνευματικά in 14:1 is a deliberate change of words on Paul's part, reflecting the heart of the controversy between him and them. The difficulty with this view is that it makes χαρίσματα the Corinthian word which Paul then tries to put into a new context with the use of πνευματικά. But that seems to run counter to the rest of the evidence of this letter that πνευματικός was a Corinthian word vis-à-vis Paul.

[423]One would also expect the emphatic pronoun ὑμεῖς δέ (but as for you), if this were Paul's intent.

[424]But as Iber points out, when it does reappear as an imperative in 14:1, it lacks what he views as the pejorative qualifier "greater." Thus Paul is saying, "You are seeking the *greater* gifts; you should be simply seeking spiritual gifts in the context of love."

cannot.[425] But before he gets to that, Paul interrupts himself to give the proper framework in which the "greater gifts" are to function—love. In this view 14:1 is resumptive. "Pursue love," he commands, "and in that context *eagerly desire* the things of the Spirit, especially those gifts that are intelligible and will thus edify the community."

If this is the correct view of this passage, then the words, "and now I will show you the most excellent way," serve to interrupt the argument in order to put the entire discussion into a different framework altogether. It is often suggested that Paul is setting out love as the greatest of all the gifts, and therefore the "greater gift" that all should pursue. But this is not quite precise. Not only does Paul not call love a gift, either here or elsewhere, but this clause stands in *contrast* to the immediately preceding imperative, not as its proper complement. What Paul is about to embark on is a description of what he calls "a *way*[426] that is beyond comparison."[427] The way they are currently going is basically destructive to the church as a community; the way they are being called to is one that seeks the good of others before oneself. It is the way of edifying the church (14:1–5), of seeking the common good (12:7). In that context one will still earnestly desire the things of the Spirit (14:1), but precisely so that others will be edified. Thus it is not "love versus gifts" that Paul has in mind, but "love as the only context for gifts"; for without the former, the latter have no usefulness at all—but then neither does much of anything else in the Christian life.

1 CORINTHIANS 13:1–3

[1]*If I speak in the tongues of men and of angels, but do not have love, I am only a resounding gong or a clanging cymbal.* [2]*If I have prophecy and know all mysteries and all knowledge, and if I have all faith so as to move mountains, but do not have love, I am nothing.* [3]*If I parcel out all my property for food and if I deliver over my body so that I may boast,*[428] *but do not have love, I gain nothing.*

---

[425] See esp. on 14:5, where prophecy is specifically called μεῖζον for this very reason.

[426] Cf. the brief excursus on the concept of ὁδός in Conzelmann 216; see also C. Spicq, *Agapè dans le Nouveau Testament* (3 vols.; EB; Paris: Gabalda, 1958–59) 2.64–66 (ET [but without the copious notes], *Agape in the New Testament* [trans. M. A. McNamara and M. H. Richter; St. Louis: B. Herder, 1963] 2.143). (In further notes page nos. refer to the French original, with English translation in parentheses.)

[427] See BAGD under κατά, II.5bβ.

[428] The textual choice in this instance is one of the truly difficult ones in the NT. There are three readings:
  (1) καυχήσωμαι P46 ℵ A B 6 33 69 1739 cop Origen Jerome
  (2) καυθήσωμαι K Ψ 614 1881 Maj Chrysostom Cyril Theodoret
  (3) καυθήσομαι C D F G L 81 104 630 1985 latt arm

Both the imperative in 12:31a and the resumptive nature of the imperatives in 14:1, not to mention the lyrical nature of the vv. 1–8,[429] indicate
that ch. 13 is something of an interlude in Paul's argument. But as with
all such moments,[430] it is fully relevant to the context, and without it
the succeeding argument would lose much of its force. In a series of three
paragraphs, Paul sets out to put their zeal for tongues within a broader
ethical context that will ultimately disallow uninterpreted tongues in the
assembly. That context is love for others over against self-interest,[431]
which in ch. 14 will be specified in terms of "building up" the church.

At the same time, however, much of the language suggests that Paul
is also picking up on some of the differences between himself and them
that have emerged throughout the letter.[432] Thus the structure of the
argument, lyrical as it is, also reflects his continuing argument with
them. At issue have been opposing views of Spirituality. They speak in
tongues, to be sure, which Paul will not question as a legitimate activity
of the Spirit. But at the same time they tolerate, or endorse, illicit sexuality, greed, and idolatry (5:9–10; illustrated in 5:1–5; 6:12–20; 6:1–11;
8:1–10:22). They have a spirituality which has religious trappings (asceticism, knowledge, tongues) but has abandoned genuinely Christian ethics, with its supremacy of love. For Paul, in contrast, Spirituality meant

---

Although Zuntz, *Text*, 35–37, favors #2, few others do, since it is a grammatical
monstrosity (future subjunctive; otherwise unknown in the Koine period, but occurring in the Byzantine). The choice then is between a basically Western reading (#3,
"that I may burn") or Egyptian (#1, "that I may boast"), with the Western reading
finally having prevailed. Given the generally excellent quality of the Egyptian
tradition, the external evidence favors #1. So, too, does transcriptional probability: It
is difficult to imagine that in a time when martyrdom by burning was common a
copyist seeing καυθήσομαι would change it to καυχήσωμαι, either accidentally or
deliberately, especially since the basic difficulty that anyone has ever had with reading
#1 is to find an adequate sense for it. But these matters are ultimately indecisive in
themselves; the question must finally be determined on the basis of intrinsic
probability. On this see the discussion below. For arguments in favor of #1 see Metzger,
Textual Commentary, 563–64. For arguments favoring #3 see J. K. Elliott, "In Favour
of καυθήσομαι at I Corinthians 13:3," *ZNW* 62 (1971) 297–98, and R. Kieffer, " 'Afin
que je sois brûlé' ou bien 'Afin que j'en orgueil'? (1 Cor. xiii. 3)," *NTS* 22 (1975) 95–97
(cf. Barrett 302–3 and Conzelmann 217n1).

[429] For a discussion of a whole variety of issues about this chapter (its alleged
poetic nature, its "origins," etc.), which are of little moment for the concerns of this
study, see the introduction to ch. 13 in Fee 625–28—except to note that whatever
else, this is not a "hymn about love." There is nothing hymnic about it at all; and its
poetic nature scarcely goes beyond vv. 1–3. Exalted prose, yes; but hymn, hardly.

[430] Cf. the "B" section in the various A-B-A arguments in this letter: 2:6–16;
7:29–35; 9:1–27.

[431] But not over against tongues as such. Since tongues is an activity of the Spirit
(14:2), that would pit the Spirit against the Spirit; and Paul would have none of that.

[432] Cf. M. Miguens, "1 Cor. 13:8–13 Reconsidered," *CBQ* 37 (1975) 80, who also
makes the point that it has ties to the letter as a whole, as well as to the immediate
context of chs. 12–14.

first of all to be full of the Spirit, the *Holy* Spirit, which therefore meant to behave as those "sanctified in Christ Jesus, called to be his holy people" (1:2), of which the ultimate expression always is to "walk in love." Thus, even though these opening sentences reflect the immediate context, Paul's concern is not simply with their overenthusiasm about tongues, but with the larger issue of the letter, where their view of spirituality has caused them to miss rather widely both the gospel and its ethics.

He begins in this first paragraph by setting out several Spirit activities as not benefiting the person doing them if that person's life is not also characterized by the primary fruit of the Spirit, love.[433] That is followed in vv. 4–7 by a description of love especially adapted to the Corinthian situation[434] and their differences with Paul.[435] This in turn leads to a contrast of love with selected χαρίσματα, including tongues, in terms of the absolute, eternal nature of the one and the relative, temporal nature of the other, placed within the context of their "already/not yet" eschatological existence (vv. 8–13). This does not make χαρίσματα less valuable for life in the present as one awaits the consummation, but it posits against their "overrealized" spirituality that these things have a relative life span (for the "already" only), while love is both for now and forever. Thus vv. 1–3 urge the absolute *necessity* of love; vv. 4–6 describe the *character* of love; and vv. 8–13 illustrate the *permanence* of love—all to the one end that they eagerly desire "the things of the Spirit" (14:1) for the sake of the common good (12:7).

Thus Paul begins his description of "the way that is beyond comparison" with a series of three conditional sentences,[436] whose powerful

---

[433]Because of the lyrical nature of this section, it is easy to think of love as an abstract quality. That is precisely to miss Paul's concern. Love is primary for him because it has already been given concrete expression in the coming of Jesus Christ to die for the sins of the world (cf. Gal 2:20; Rom 5:6–8; 8:31–32; Eph 5:1–2). Love is not an idea for Paul, not even a "motivating factor" for behavior. It *is* behavior. To love is to act; anything short of action is not love at all.

[434]See, e.g., Robertson-Plummer 285–86 ("Most of the features selected as characteristic of [love] are just those in which the Corinthians had proved defective"); and Spicq, *Agapè*, 77n3 (150n123): "[These characteristics] are neither exhaustive nor arbitrary, but were chosen with reference to the virtues most neglected by the Corinthians." Cf. the less than adequate reconstruction by I. J. Martin, "I Corinthians 13 Interpreted by its Context," *JBR* 18 (1950) 101–5, who imagines Paul to be opposing glossolalists, but who lacks a single *linguistic* tie to the context.

[435]See Fee 635–42 on vv. 4–7 for this point of view. Because there is no mention of the Spirit in this paragraph, it will be passed over in the current study.

[436]Each is a present general (if ever the one condition prevails, so also does the other). Each is carefully structured in three parts: (a) a protasis (in the second and third instances a double protasis), (b) an adversative clause, "but have not love," and (c) an apodosis. The balance is maintained by having a longer apodosis in v. 1, where the protasis is shorter, and the briefest possible apodosis in vv. 2 and 3, where the protasis is elaborated. The whole is a work of art, with marvelous cadences and dramatic effect.

cadences, and order of appearance, should have had a sobering affect on the Corinthians—and on all subsequent Spirit people. He begins with tongues, because that is where the problem lay; and for that reason it also receives individual treatment. He then expands it to include a variety of the χαρίσματα from ch. 12, which he himself had argued for so vigorously as part of the need for diversity. Finally he includes examples of self-sacrificial deeds. In each case the conditional clause presupposes that both he and they are agreed that the activity has value. Thus it is not the activity that is at stake without love, but the person. These are good things; what is not good is religious performance, gifts on display by one who is not otherwise acting as described in vv. 4–7. It is not, these things *or* love, or even these things motivated *by* love, but these things by a person whose whole life is otherwise also given to love. If not, that person's life before God adds up to zero.

1 This opening sentence is the reason for the entire argument: "If I speak in the tongues of men and of angels." One may be quite sure that the Corinthians believed they were; indeed, this best accounts for the sudden shift to the first person singular (cf. 14:14–15).[437] On its own this could mean nothing more than "speak eloquently," as some have argued and as it is popularly understood. But since it is not on its own, but follows directly out of 12:28–30 and anticipates 14:1–25, most likely this is either Paul's or their understanding (or both) of "speaking in tongues." "Tongues of men" would then refer to human speech,[438] inspired of the Spirit but unknown to the speaker; "tongues of angels" would reflect an understanding that the tongues-speaker was communicating in the dialect(s) of heaven.

That the Corinthians at least, and probably Paul, thought of tongues as the language(s) of the angels seems highly likely—for two reasons: (1) There is some evidence from Jewish sources that the angels were believed to have their own heavenly language (or dialect) and that by means of the "Spirit" one could speak this dialect. Thus in the *Testament of Job* 48–50 Job's three daughters are given "charismatic sashes,"[439] which when put on allowed Hemera, for example, to speak "ecstatically in the

---

[437] That is, Paul uses himself as the hypothetical person precisely because many of the Corinthians were like this in reality. Bringing them into the argument in this more indirect way is its own form of powerful argumentation. At the same time, as in 14:6, this use of the first person could reflect an undercurrent of their disapproval of him for *not* being known to speak in tongues, hence of his not being truly πνευματικός; cf. on 2:15.

[438] See on 12:10. Martin, *Spirit*, 43, along with many others, sees the two genitives as suggesting "eloquence and ecstatic speech," with eloquence reflecting the Corinthian interest found in chs. 1–2. That is certainly possible, but it seems more likely, given the context, that Paul is simply describing "tongues" in two different forms.

[439] The language is that of R. P. Spittler, "The Testament of Job," in *OTP* 1.865. For a discussion of the other possible reflections of this phenomenon see 866 n. "f."

angelic dialect, sending up a hymn to God with the hymnic style of the angels. And as she spoke ecstatically, she allowed 'The Spirit' to be inscribed on her garment."[440] Such an understanding of heavenly speech may also lie behind the language of 1 Cor 14:2 ("speak mysteries by the Spirit"). (2) One can make a good deal of sense of the Corinthian view of "spirituality" if they believed themselves already to have entered into some expression of angelic existence. This would explain their rejection of sexual life and sexual roles (cf. 7:1–7; 11:2–16) and would also partly explain their denial of a future bodily existence (15:12, 35). It might also lie behind their special interest in "wisdom" and "knowledge." For them the evidence of having "arrived" at such a "spiritual" state would be their speaking the "tongues of angels." Hence the high value placed on this gift.

But Paul's concern lay elsewhere. Their "spirituality" showed evidence of all kinds of behavioral flaws. Their "knowledge" led to pride and the "destruction of a brother for whom Christ died" (8:2, 11). Their "wisdom" had led to quarrels and rivalry (1:10; 3:4). Their "tongues" were neither edifying the community nor allowing pagans to respond to the prophetic word (14:1–25). In short, theirs was a spirituality that lacked the primary evidence of the Spirit: behavior that could be described as "having love."

In saying "but not have love"[441] Paul does not mean to suggest that love is a possession of some kind. The language has been formed by the elevated style of the prose. To "have love" means to "act lovingly," just as to "have prophecy" in v. 2 means "to speak with the prophetic gift."[442] And to act lovingly means, as in the case of Christ, actively to seek the benefit of someone else. For Paul it is a word whose primary definition is found in God's activity in behalf of his enemies (Rom 5:6–8), which was visibly manifested in the life and death of Christ. To "have love," therefore, means to be toward others the way God in Christ has been toward us. Thus, in the Pauline paraenesis, for those who "walk in the Spirit" the primary ethical imperative is "love one another," which is found at the heart of every section of ethical instruction,[443] of which the other exhortations are but the explication.

---

[440]T. Job 48:3 (Spittler's trans.).

[441]Gk. ἀγάπη, rare but not unknown in Greek literature. The LXX often used this word to speak of God's love, and probably became the source of its use among the early Christians. The latter probably used ἀγάπη to designate a love differing esp. from ἔρος (desiring love) and also from φιλία (natural sympathy or mutual affection). See the discussion by W. Günther and H.-G. Link, NIDNTT 2.538–47; and by G. Quell and E. Stauffer, TDNT 1.221–54. See also the important monographs by J. Moffatt, Love in the New Testament (New York: Macmillan, 1930); A. Nygren, Agape and Eros (ET; London, 1932, 1939); and esp. Spicq, Agapè (1959).

[442]Otherwise Ellis, Prophecy, 52n29, who argues that it "here includes the perception of mysteries."

[443]See 1 Thes 4:9; Gal 5:13, 22; Rom 12:9; 13:8; Col 3:14; Eph 5:2.

The final coup in this sentence is the language "resounding gong" and "clanging cymbal." Although it is not certain as to what the former designates,[444] at least it is a metaphor for empty, hollow sound.[445] The latter in fact was an "instrument" expressly associated with the pagan cults.[446] Perhaps, then, this is an allusion to 12:2 and their former associations with such cults.[447] To speak in tongues as they were doing, thinking themselves to be "spiritual" but with no concern for the building up the community, is not merely to speak unintelligible words; it makes one become like the empty, hollow noises of pagan worship.

2 In this second sentence Paul widens the perspective to include three of the χαρίσματα from 12:8–10, a list which in that argument came from Paul himself as his way of expanding their horizons as to the work of the Spirit. Thus he includes *prophecy*, the gift he regularly considers to be of primary significance for the community;[448] *knowledge*, which was another of the Corinthian favorites (cf. 1:5; 8:1); and *faith*, which by its qualifier, "that can move mountains," means the gift of special faith for mighty works (see on 12:9).[449] In order to make this point as emphatic as possible, Paul thrice repeats, *all* mysteries, *all* knowledge, *all* faith. If one person could embrace a whole range of χαρίσματα and the full measure of any one of them, but at the same time fail to be full of love, such a person is in fact *nothing* in the sight of God.[450]

---

[444]Gk. χαλκὸς ἠχῶν (= lit. "echoing bronze"). Of the two items, this is the more puzzling, since there is no known evidence for its use as an "instrument." Recently it has been suggested that it reflects the bronze "amplification" systems of the stone amphitheaters. See W. Harris, "Echoing Bronze," *Journal of the Acoustical Society of America* 70 (1981) 1184–85; idem, " 'Sounding Brass' and Hellenistic Technology," *BAR* 8 (1982) 38–41; cf. Murphy-O'Connor, *Corinth*, 76–77; and W. W. Klein, "Noisy Gong or Acoustic Vase? A Note on I Corinthians 13.1," *NTS* 32 (1986) 286–89.

[445]Cf. K. L. Schmidt, *TDNT* 3.1037–39, and Spicq (*Agapè*, 69–70 [146]), who suggest that it may reflect a commonplace scoffing at the empty sophist or rhetorician (cf. the introduction to 1:10–4:21 in Fee).

[446]In particular with the cult of Cybele, where also some of the more bizarre forms of "ecstasy" occurred. See the evidence in E. Peterson, *TDNT* 1.227–28; and K. L. Schmidt, *TDNT* 3.1037–39; cf. J. Quasten, *Musik und Gesang in den Kulten der heidnischen Antike und christlichen Frühzeit* (Münster, 1930).

[447]Cf. H. Riesenfeld, "Note supplémentaire sur I Cor. XIII," *Coniectanea Neotestamentica* 10 (1946) 50–53.

[448]See on 1 Thes 5:19–20; 1 Cor 11:4–5; 14:1–25.

[449]This qualifier is another certain evidence of Paul's acquaintance with the teaching of Jesus, reflecting a saying found variously in Mark 11:23 and Matt 17:20 (cf. Luke 17:6). On this question see Fee on 4:16; 7:10, 25; and 9:14.

[450]This latter idea is not in the text per se, but is surely what Paul means by "nothing" in this sentence and "profit nothing" in the next. Cf. Spicq, *Agapè*, 71 (147).

But what did Paul intend by the second item, "know[451] all mysteries and all knowledge"? These terms appear together as a regular feature of Jewish apocalyptic,[452] especially with regard to the unfolding of God's final eschatological drama. Paul now uses this language to refer to God's present revelation of his ways, especially in the form of special revelations by means of the eschatological Spirit whom Christians have received (cf. 14:6).[453] This is most likely how we are also to understand both the "utterance of knowledge" in 12:8 and the "knowledge" that accompanies tongues and prophecy in vv. 8–13 that follow.

Given the longer protasis, Paul concludes with a shorter apodosis, "I am nothing." That eloquently speaks for itself. As before, expression of χαρίσματα is no sure sign of the Spirit; Christian love is.

3 Enlarging his perspective yet further, this time quite beyond χαρίσματα as that word would be understood under any standard definition, Paul next offers examples of great personal sacrifice.[454] Inasmuch as these are not uniquely Spirit activities, or at least are not so defined by Paul, we will skip a detailed analysis here.[455] What *is* important is the inclusion of these two examples at all, which makes it clear that love is not here being set out in contrast to gifts; rather, Paul is arguing for the absolute supremacy and necessity of love if one is to be Christian in any sense. Paul will continue to "give his body so that he might boast"; he will especially urge the Corinthians to desire prophetic utterances; and he will encourage tongues in their life of personal prayer. But these things must be brought forth in lives that above all "have put on love"; for without love one misses the point of being Christian in the first place. And even though Paul does not in this letter or in this argument associate love with the Spirit, it is absolutely clear from other contexts that he sees love as the primary work of the Spirit in the life of the believer. This is made especially plain in the argument in Gal 5:13–23 (q.v.).

---

[451] The vb. εἰδῶ controls both nouns, "all mysteries" and "all knowledge." Here it must mean "understand"; hence the NIV's "fathom."

[452] See, e.g., Dan 2:19–23, 28 where in the LXX the repeated language includes σοφία, γνῶσις, μυστήρια and ἀνακαλύπτω; cf. also the recurring "he showed me all the mysteries of . . . " in 1 Enoch (41:1; 52:2; 61:5; 63:3; 68:5; 71:4).

[453] Friedrich, TDNT 6.853–54, asserts, but without textual support: "Γνῶσις is one of the 'rational gifts of the Spirit.' It is attained speculatively, by thinking about the mysteries of the faith. . . . In contrast, prophecy rests on inspiration. Knowledge is given to it by sudden revelation. The prophetic thought or image strikes the prophet from without." This is hard to square with Paul's own language in 12:7–11 and 14:1–6.

[454] Spicq, *Agapè*, 71 (147), suggests a connection with the ἀντίλημψις in 12:28; this is doubtful, since the emphasis here is not on helping others as such.

[455] Which may be found in Fee 633–35.

1 CORINTHIANS 13:8–13[456]

⁸Love never fails.[457] *But where there are prophecies, they will be pass away; where there are tongues, they will cease; where there is knowledge,*[458] *it will pass away. ⁹For we know in part and we prophesy in part, ¹⁰but when what is complete comes, what*[459] *is in part passes away. ¹¹When I was a child, I talked like a child,*[460] *I thought like a child, I reasoned like a child. When*[461] *I became a man, I put away the things of childhood. ¹²For we as yet in a figurative way of speaking look through a looking-glass; then we shall see face to face. As yet I know in part; then I shall know fully, even as I am fully known. ¹³And now these three remain: faith, hope, and love. But the greatest of these is love.*

Paul began this little interlude on love with a set of contrasts in which he insisted that χαρίσματα and good works benefit the speaker or doer not at all if he or she does not also have Christian love. Now, following the lyrical description of ἀγάπη (love) in vv. 4–7, he closes this argument with another set of contrasts: Love is the "way that is beyond comparison" because, in contrast to the χαρίσματα, which function within the framework of our present eschatological existence only, ἀγάπη characterizes our existence both now and forever. Accordingly, love is superior, not because what exists only for now (χαρίσματα) is lesser, but because what is both for now and forever (ἀγάπη) must dictate *how* the χαρίσματα function in the life of the church.

The greater urgency of this argument, however, is with the "*only-for-the-present*" nature of the gifts, not with the permanence of love— although that is always lingering near the surface. Love is scarcely mentioned (vv. 8a, 13 only); the fact that the gifts will pass away forms the heart of the whole argument (vv. 8b–12). The clue to this emphasis

---

[456]Even though vv. 4–7 are absolutely crucial to Paul's argument, especially since so many of the words about love have their opposites in Corinthian behavior, we have skipped this paragraph because it has no Spirit language or direct Spirit concerns as such.

[457]The Westerns and MajT read the compound ἐκπίπτει; P⁴⁶ ℵ* A B C 048 243 33 1739 pc read πίπτει. The latter is almost certainly original, despite Harnack, "Hymn," 481n2.

[458]A few MSS (ℵ A F G 33 365 pc a) make this plural, conforming it to the preceding plurals and thus making it clear that it refers to the "utterances of knowledge" in 12:8.

[459]The MajT, with no early support, adds τότε, probably under the influence of v. 12. But it misses the point of the later τότε altogether, which is not a logical "then" but a contrast between the present "now" and the eschatological "then."

[460]For the argument for the word order of P⁴⁶ and the MajT ("as a child I talked, etc.") as the original, see Zuntz, *Text*, 128–29, who is almost certainly correct. As he notes, Paul's emphasis lies not on the verbs, but on the repeated ὡς νήπιος.

[461]The MajT, with some Western support, adds a δέ, which is spurious by all counts. See Zuntz, *Text*, 189n8.

lies with the Corinthians' understanding of tongues as evidence of their spirituality. The problem is with an "overspiritualized" eschatology, as if tongues, the language of the angels, meant that they were already partakers of the ultimate state of spiritual existence.[462] Hence the underlying polemical tone of this passage. This does not condemn the gifts; it puts them into eschatological perspective. In 1:7 Paul had already stated his own perspective: "You do not lack any χάρισμα as you eagerly wait for our Lord Jesus Christ to be revealed." Now he urges over and again that gifts do *not* belong to the future, but only to the present. On this they are deluded: The irony is that the gifts, their evidence of their future existence, will pass away (v. 8a); they are "in part" (v. 9); they are as childhood in comparison with adulthood (v. 11); they are like looking into a mirror in comparison with seeing someone in person (v. 12).

One must not mistakenly equate this emphasis with a devaluation of Spirit manifestations.[463] The fact is that we are still in the present, where gifts are one of the ways the Spirit builds up the community; but love must prevail as the *reason* for all such manifestations. Therefore, Paul will go on in ch. 14 not only to correct an imbalance with regard to the gifts, but to urge their proper use. Pursue love (14:1), he says, because that alone is forever (13:8, 13); but love also means that in the present you should eagerly desire manifestations of the Spirit that build up the community (14:1–5).

8 This paragraph begins with the famous line, "Love never fails,"[464] but it is not immediately clear what Paul intends. On the one hand, it could conclude v. 7 and mean something like "love is never defeated, is never brought to the ground; it persists even when rebuffed." On the other hand, several items indicate that it serves as the beginning of the present paragraph[465] and is intended to be set in contrast both to the verb "remain" in v. 13 and the verbs "pass away" and "cease" in v. 8. If so, then it would mean something like "never comes to an end, becomes invalid." Perhaps the very ambiguity of such figurative language allows for both nuances. There is a sense in which love is never brought down; it reflects God's character, after all, and cannot fluctuate from what it is. Yet that same reality also gives it eternal character, so that it "remains"

---

[462]The close proximity of the argument in ch. 15 is especially relevant here.

[463]That the Spirit is the source of the gifts and that Paul himself holds prophecy in such high regard make this an impossible position. See also n. 236 on 12:1–14:40.

[464]Gk. πίπτει, which lit. means "to fall," is used figuratively to refer to "falling" into guilt, sin, or apostasy (cf. 10:8, 12) or to "become invalid, deprived of its force" (Luke 16:17). See the discussion by W. Michaelis, *TDNT* 6.164–66.

[465]Esp. (1) the repetition of the subject ἡ ἀγάπη, which suggests in the strongest way that it is no longer part of the preceding series; (2) the δέ and repeated εἴτε before the three gifts indicate that these are intended to be in contrast to this sentence; and (3) the verb πίπτει contrasts with the μένει with which the paragraph concludes.

even after all other things have come to their proper end. In any case, the latter idea is what is now in focus.

Despite the majestic description of love that has just preceded, Paul has not lost sight of his overall argument. Thus he sets forth three χαρίσματα,[466] which by way of contrast to the nonfailing character of love, are destined "to come to an end." If there is any significance to this choice of gifts, it lies with the fact that the first, "prophecies," is his preference for the edification of the community, while the other two are Corinthian favorites. In both cases, and therefore in all cases, these are manifestations of the Spirit for the church's present eschatological exist-ence, in which God's new people live "between the times"—between the inauguration of the End through the death and resurrection of Jesus with the subsequent outpouring of the Spirit and the final consummation when God will be "all in all" (see 15:20–28). Thus the basic verb chosen to describe the temporal, transitory nature of the χαρίσματα is typically an eschatological one, used elsewhere in the letter to refer to the "passing away" of what belongs merely to the present age.[467] This choice of verbs, which recurs in v. 10, already indicates that the contrasts in the passage have to do with eschatology, not with maturity of some kind.

It needs only to be noted further that "knowledge" in this passage does not mean ordinary human knowing or learning, but refers rather to that special manifestation of the Spirit, the "utterance of knowledge" (12:8), which understands revealed "mysteries" (13:2).[468] It has especially to do with "knowing" the ways of God in the present age.[469] This is made certain by vv. 9 and 12b, where this form of "knowledge" is referred to as "in part," in contrast with a "face to face" knowing at the Eschaton that is "complete," i.e., which is of the same character as God's knowl-edge of us.

---

[466] All three appear in the original list in 12:8–10; they also reappear in the current argument in 13:1–2.

[467] Gk. καταργέω (cf. 1:28; 2:6; 6:13; 15:24–26; 2 Thes 2:8), used here with both "prophecy" and "knowledge." Some (e.g., MacArthur 359; cf. S. D. Toussaint, "First Corinthians Thirteen and the Tongues Question," *BSac* 120 [1963] 311–16) have argued that the change of verbs (including the change of voice) with tongues (παύσονται) has independent significance, as though this meant that tongues might cease before prophecy and knowledge. But the change of verbs is probably rhetorical; to make it otherwise is to elevate to significance something Paul himself shows no interest in. Just as one can scarcely distinguish between "cease" and "pass away" in English, when used in the same context, neither can one distinguish between καταργέω and παύω in this context (although the NIV's choice of "be stilled" for tongues is felicitous). The middle voice came along with the change of verbs.

[468] Cf. N. Johansson, "I Cor. xiii and I Cor. xiv," *NTS* 10 (1964) 389, and Miguens, "Reconsidered," 82, although they differ considerably as to the *content* of such γνῶσις. This usage probably prevails in 2 Cor 8:7 and 11:6 as well (q.v.).

[469] Cf. 2 Cor 11:6, where Paul's gift of knowledge is probably to be understood in terms of the "knowledge of God" in 10:5.

9–10 Paul now sets out to explain[470] what he has asserted in v. 8. He does so with the language "in part" to describe the "for now only" nature of the gifts[471] (repeating the verb "pass away" from v. 8 to indicate what happens to them) and "the perfect/complete"[472] to describe the time when what is "in part" will come to an end. The use of the substantive, "the perfect/complete," which sometimes can mean "mature," plus the ambiguity of the first analogy (childhood and adulthood), has led some to think that the contrast is between "immaturity" and "maturity."[473] But that is unlikely, since Paul's contrasts have to do with the partial nature of the gifts, not with the immaturity of believers them-

---

[470]Note the return of the explanatory γάρ, last seen in 12:12–14 (cf. its frequency in chs. 1–11), evidence that Paul is returning to his argumentative style, which will predominate throughout ch. 14.

[471]The choice of prophecy and knowledge from the preceding verse does not "mean" anything. Partly this is due to style, partly to the fact that "tongues" does not lend itself easily to the way these sentences are expressed. "We speak in tongues in part" is not particularly meaningful; but tongues, as well as all the other χαρίσματα in 12:8–10, are to be understood as included in the argument. Otherwise Miguens, "Reconsidered," 90, and Martin, *Spirit*, 53–54, who suggest that "knowledge" is the Corinthians' prized gift that is basically being taken to task here. The argument of ch. 14 (esp. v. 6) refutes this.

[472]Gk. τὸ τέλειον; cf. 2:7. This is the adjective of the verb τελειόω. Both mean to "bring to an end, to complete" something, although they also carry the further sense of "making" or "being perfect." That is, the completing of something is the perfecting of it. God may thus be described as τέλειος (Matt 5:48), which can only mean "perfect." Its present meaning is determined by its being the final goal of what is ἐκ μέρους, "partial." Thus the root sense of "having attained the end or purpose" (BAGD), hence "complete," seems to be the nuance here.

[473]This has taken several forms, depending on how one understands τὸ τέλειον. (1) Some see it as referring to love itself. In this view the Corinthians' desire for gifts reflects their immaturity; when they have come to the fullness of love they will put away such childish desires (e.g., Findlay 900; Bruce 128; Johansson, "I Cor. xiii," 389–90; Miguens, "Reconsidered," 87–97; Holladay 174). (2) Others see "the perfect" as referring to the full revelation given in the NT itself, which when it would come to completion would do away with the "partial" forms of charismatic revelation. Given its classical exposition by B. B. Warfield, this view has been taken over in a variety of ways by contemporary Reformed and dispensationalist theologies. This is hermeneutically suspect, since Paul himself could not have articulated it. (3) Still others see it as referring to the maturing of the body, the church, which is sometimes also seen to have happened with the rise of the more regular clergy (Eph 4:11–13 is appealed to) or the coming of Jews and Gentiles into the one body (see, e.g., J. R. McRay, "*To Teleion* in I Corinthians 13:10," *RestQ* 14 [1971] 168–83; and R. L. Thomas, " 'Tongues . . . Will Cease,' " *JETS* 17 [1974] 81–89). This view has almost nothing to commend it except the analogy of v. 11, which is a misguided emphasis at best.

It is perhaps an indictment on Western Christianity that we should consider to be "mature" our rather totally cerebral and domesticated—but bland—brand of faith, with the concomitant absence of the Spirit in terms of his supernatural gifts! The Spirit, not Western rationalism, marks the turning of the ages, after all; and to deny the Spirit's manifestations is to deny our present existence as eschatological, as belonging to the beginning of the time of the End.

selves.[474] Furthermore, that approach gives the analogy, which is ambiguous at best, precedence over the argument as a whole and the explicit statement of v. 12b, where Paul repeats verbatim[475] the first clause of v. 9, "we know[476] in part," in a context that can only be eschatological. Convoluted as the argument may appear, Paul's distinctions are between "now" and "then," between what is incomplete (though perfectly appropriate to the church's present existence) and what is complete, when its final destiny in Christ has been reached and "we see face to face" and "know as we are known."[477]

That means that the phrase "in part" refers to what is not complete, or at least not complete in itself. The phrase by itself does not carry the connotation of "temporary" or "relative"; that comes from the context and the language "now . . . then" in v. 12. But the implication is there. It is "partial" because it belongs only to this age, which is but the beginning, not the completion, of the End. These gifts have to do with the edification of the church as it "eagerly awaits our Lord Jesus Christ to be revealed" (1:7). The nature of the eschatological language in v. 12 further implies that the term "the complete" concerns the Eschaton itself, not some form of "perfection" in the present age.[478] It is not so much that the End is "the perfect," language which does not make tolerably good sense; rather, it is what happens at the End, when *the goal* has been reached. At the coming of Christ the final purpose of God's saving work in Christ will have been reached; at that point those gifts now necessary for the building up of the church in the present age will disappear, because "the complete" will have come. To cite Barth's marvelous imagery: "*Because* the *sun* rises all lights are extinguished."[479]

11 Echoing the themes of "in part" and "the complete" plus the verb "pass away"[480] from v. 10, Paul expresses the intent of vv. 9–10 by way

---

[474]Even though Paul says, "*we* know in part," the emphasis is not on the immaturity of the Corinthians, but on the relative nature of the gifts. This is demonstrated (1) by the γάρ that ties it to v. 8, where it is said of these gifts that *they* will pass away, not that the Corinthians need to grow up, and (2) by the clause, "we prophesy in part," which makes sense only as having to do with the prophecies, not with the prophets.

[475]With the exception of the change from the plural to the singular.

[476]No significance can be attached to the use of the verb instead of the noun. The usage in 8:1–2 indicates that the verb here means "to have knowledge," which in this context means to have the gift of knowledge.

[477]Cf. Grudem, *Gift*, 148–49, esp. the discussion of ἐκ μέρους in n. 59.

[478]Cf. the discussion in Grudem, *Gift*, 210–19, which also includes a refutation of the views in n. 473.

[479]*The Resurrection of the Dead* (ET; London, 1933) 86.

[480]But now in the active. This is the only occurrence in the letter where it is not necessarily eschatological. It was chosen here because of its use in the preceding sentences, and means "do away with," or in keeping with the imagery "set aside."

of analogy. The analogy is commonplace.[481] The adult does not continue to "talk" or "think" or "reason" like a child.[482] Because of the use of the verb "talk," which elsewhere in this section is used with tongues, and because of the contrast in 14:20 between thinking like children and adults, it is common to see this analogy as referring to speaking in tongues.[483] Tongues is the "childish"[484] behavior that the Corinthians are now being urged to set aside in favor of love. But such a view runs contrary to the argument itself, both here and in 12:4–11 and 14:1–40.[485]

Paul's point in context has to do not with "childishness" and "growing up," but with the difference between the present and the future. He is illustrating that there will come a time when the gifts will pass away.[486] The analogy, therefore, says that behavior from one period in one's life is not appropriate to the other; the one is "done away with" when the other comes. So shall it be at the Eschaton. The behavior of the child is in fact appropriate to childhood. The gifts,[487] by analogy, are appropriate to the present life of the church, especially so since from Paul's point of view they are the active work of the Spirit in the church's corporate life. On the other hand, the gifts are equally inappropriate to the church's final existence because then, as he will go on to argue in v. 12, "I shall know fully, even as I am fully known." Hence the implicit contrast with love, which will never come to an end. Love does not eliminate the gifts in the present; rather, it is absolutely essential to Christian life both now and forever. The gifts, however, are not forever; they are to help build up the body—but *only* in the present, when such edification is needed.

12 Paul now moves to another analogy, to which he appends an immediate application. With their repeated "as yet, but then" language, these sentences further sharpen the contrast between the Corinthians' present existence and that of the future. The fact that they are tied to v. 11 by an explanatory "for" further indicates, that the previous analogy

---

[481] See Conzelmann 226n84.

[482] Gk. νήπιος, which ordinarily, as here, refers to a very young child.

[483] But as Conzelmann 226n85 notes, that breaks down with the use of the past tense and the first person singular. After all, Paul speaks in tongues more than all of them (14:18).

[484] Cf. the NIV, "childish ways"; "childish" is much more pejorative in English than Paul's analogy suggests.

[485] Although the "childishness" is seen in their eagerness for tongues, the net result is that spiritual gifts, which for Paul are "manifestations of the Spirit," are disparaged.

[486] Cf. Parry 195: "It is an illustration merely: no ref. to the metaphorical use of νήπιος and τέλειος."

[487] Not simply tongues, which is not taken up as such in the argument after v. 8. Tongues at this point is but one among all the Spirit-inspired gifts (note the special emphasis on the Spirit's role in 12:7–11) which are part of the present life of the church.

has basically to do with two modes of existence, not with "growing up" and putting away childish behavior.

The first sentence, "For as yet[488] we look through[489] a looking-glass ἐν αἰνίγματι,[490] but then[491] face to face"[492] is particularly relevant to their setting, since Corinth was famous as the producer of some of the finest bronze mirrors in antiquity.[493] That suggests that the puzzling phrase ἐν αἰνίγματι is probably not as pejorative as most translations imply.[494] More likely the accent is not on the *quality* of seeing that one experiences in looking into a mirror—that would surely have been an affront to them—but to the *indirect nature* of looking into a mirror[495] as opposed to seeing someone face to face.[496] The analogy, of course, breaks

---

[488]Gk. ἄρτι, an adverb that in classical Greek meant "just now" (cf. Matt 9:18), but in Hellenistic Greek it took on the further connotation of "now in general," referring especially to "the present time." This is the predominant usage in the NT, and it can mean nothing else when set in contrast with τότε, as here.

[489]This is a bit stilted. Because of the peculiar nature of the reflection in a mirror, the Greeks thought of one as looking "through" the "glass," in contrast to our looking "in" or "into" it.

[490]This Greek word, which appears only here in the NT, literally means "in a riddle, or figurative way." Very likely this echoes Num 12:8 (LXX), where God spoke with Moses directly ("mouth to mouth"), not as to the prophets, to whom he spoke through visions or dreams (v. 6), "in figures," implying that they received "pictures" of the truth that were not as clear as the direct words to Moses. The problem is whether it means "indistinctly" (thus, "obscurely, dimly," etc.) or "indirectly" (thus "in riddle" as over against "direct speech"), referring to the form rather than the content. The majority of interpreters have taken the former position, but cf. the critique by S. E. Bassett, "I Cor. 13:12, βλέπομεν γὰρ ἄρτι δι᾿ ἐσόπτρου ἐν αἰνίγματι," *JBL* 47 (1928) 232–36; and esp. N. Hugedé, *La métaphore du miroir dans les Epitres de Saint Paul aux Corinthiens* (Neuchâtel, 1957) [Eng. synopsis by F. W. Danker, "The Mirror Metaphor in 1 Cor. 13:12 and 2 Cor. 3:18," *CTM* 31 (1960) 428–29].

[491]The coming of Christ is implied.

[492]A biblical idiom for direct personal communication. See Gen 32:30; cf. Num 12:8, "speak 'mouth to mouth.' "

[493]See, e.g., *Corinth: A Brief History of the City and a Guide to the Excavations*, published by the American School of Classical Studies in Athens, 1972, p. 5. It is thus surely not by accident that only in the Corinthian correspondence does this analogy occur in the Pauline letters (cf. 2 Cor. 3:18); cf. in a similar way the relevance of the analogy in 9:24–27.

[494]As e.g., by "darkly" (KJV), "we are baffled" (Montgomery), "only blurred" (Norlie), "dimly" (TCNT). In fact the idea that their mirrors were of poor quality and therefore one did not get a true image is a purely modern misconception. See Hugedé, *Métaphore*, 97–100.

[495]Cf. among others, Bassett, "I Cor. 13.12"; Barth, *Resurrection*, 85; Hugedé, *Métaphore*, 145–50; Danker, "Mirror," 429; Conzelmann 228.

[496]This imagery has elicited considerable discussion, with a whole range of suggestions. Most of these are quite unrelated to the context and especially to the *point* of the analogy, which is made plain in the second half of the verse. The most probable of these options is that of G. Kittel, *TDNT* 1.178–80, who argues that "through a mirror in riddles," refers to "seeing in the Spirit," meaning to "see prophetically."

down a bit, since one sees one's own face in a mirror, and Paul's point
is that in our present existence one "sees" God (presumably),[497] or understands the "mysteries," only indirectly. It is not a *distorted* image that we
have in Christ through the Spirit; but it is as yet *indirect*, not complete.
To put all this in another way, but keeping the imagery, "Our present
'vision' of God, as great as it is, is as nothing when compared to the real
thing that is yet to be; it is like the difference in seeing a reflected image
in a mirror as over against seeing a person face to face." In our own
culture the comparable metaphor would be the difference between a
photograph and seeing someone in person. As good as a picture is, it is
simply not the real thing.

With the second set of sentences in this verse, Paul brings into focus
all that has been argued since v. 8. Picking up the words of contrast from
v. 12a ("at the present time, then") but the *content* of v. 9, he concludes,
"Now I[498] know in part, but then I shall know fully[499] even as I also am
fully known." By this Paul intends to differentiate between the "knowing" that is available through the gift of the Spirit and the final eschatological knowing that is complete. What is not quite clear is the exact
nuance of the final clause that expresses the nature of that final knowing,
"even as[500] I also am fully known." It is often suggested that the passive,
"as I am fully known," "contains the idea of electing grace."[501] Attractive as that is theologically, most likely it simply refers to God's way of
knowing. God's knowledge of us is immediate—full and direct, "face to
face,"[502] as it were. At the Eschaton, Paul seems to be saying, we too
shall know in this way, with no more need for the kinds of mediation
that the mirror illustrates or that "prophecy" or the "utterance of knowledge" exemplify in reality.

13 This sentence, which is related to v. 8 through its use of the verb
"remain," is at once both the best known and most difficult text in the
paragraph. There can be little question that it is intended to bring the
point of the present paragraph to a conclusion, probably the whole chapter as well. But how? There are five interrelated problems: (1) Whether
the words "and now" carry a temporal or logical force; (2) in conjunction

---

See the critique of the other suggestions in Hugedé, *Métaphore*, 37–95.

[497] Otherwise Miguens, "Reconsidered," 87.

[498] For this sudden switch to the singular see on v. 1.

[499] The verb in this final clause is the compound, ἐπιγινώσκω, which probably is
intended to carry its precise nuance, "to know exactly, completely, or through and
through" (BAGD).

[500] Gk. καθώς; Spicq, *Agapè*, 102 (166), notes that Paul uses this word 25 times,
always with the connotation "exactly as," i.e., "it makes an exact comparison."

[501] The language is Conzelmann's (228), but the suggestion occurs throughout
the literature (cf. e.g., Martin, *Spirit*, 54).

[502] Cf. Gen 32:30.

with that, whether "remain" has to do with the present or the future; (3) the sudden appearance of "faith and hope" in an argument that heretofore has had to do not with these virtues but with love and spiritual gifts; (4) how love is "greater than" these other two; and (5) how, then, this sentence concludes the paragraph.

Despite the long debate over the temporal or logical force of the combination, "and now,"[503] it is difficult under any circumstances to divest the adverb "now" of all temporal sense. That is, even if its basic thrust is logical (= but as it is),[504] it carries the force "as it is in the present state of things." This seems to be all the more so here, given the present tense of the verb "remain," and the fact that these three opening words conjoin directly to the preceding eschatological words. Thus, however we finally translate them, these opening words seem to imply some kind of *present* situation over against what is yet to be, when "I shall know fully, even as I am fully known."

The real issue, then, has to do with the sudden appearance of "faith and hope" with love, and in what sense these three "abide." First, there is solid evidence to suggest that this was a familiar triad in early Christian preaching, and therefore that it would have been well known to the Corinthians.[505] Together these words embrace the whole of Christian existence, as believers live out the life of the Spirit in the present age, awaiting the consummation. They have "faith" toward God, that is, they trust him to forgive and accept them through Christ. Even though now they see him not (or see, as it were, "a reflection in a mirror"), they trust in his goodness and mercies. They also have "hope" for the future, which has been guaranteed for them through Christ. Through his resurrection and the gift of the Spirit, they have become a thoroughly future-oriented people; the present age is on its way out, therefore they live in the present "as if not" (cf. 7:29–31), not conditioned by the present with its hardships or suffering. They are on their way "home," destined for an existence in the presence of God that is "face to face." And through the same Spirit they have "love" for one another, as they live this life of faith and hope

---

[503] Gk. νυνὶ δέ; see 12:18 and 15:20; cf. 2 Cor 8:11, 22; Rom 3:21; 6:22; 7:6, 17; 15:23, 25; Phlm 9, 11; Col 1:22; 3:8.

[504] The debate is carried on, of course, by those who want to interpret the sentence eschatologically, that is, that faith, hope, and love all remain forever, even into eternity. This view demands a logical force to the νυνὶ δέ, since a strictly temporal sense eliminates it as a possibility. But it must be noted that adopting a "logical" sense to the νυνὶ δέ does not demand an eschatological view, it merely makes it possible.

[505] In Paul see 1 Thes 1:3; 5:8; Gal 5:5–6; Rom 5:1–5; Col 1:4–5; Eph 4:2–5 (cf. Titus 2:2). Beyond Paul see Heb 6:10–12; 10:22–24; 1 Pet 1:3–8. Beyond the NT see Barn. 1:4; 11:8; Polycarp, *Phil.* 3:2–3. Cf. the discussion in A. M. Hunter, *Paul and his Predecessors* (2d ed.; London: SCM, 1961) 33–35, who has argued convincingly that the formula antedates Paul, and suggests that the words τὰ τρία ταῦτα might be translated, "the well-known three."

in the context of a community of brothers and sisters of similar faith and hope. In the present life of the church "these three remain (or continue): faith, hope, and love."[506]

But why this triad in the present context where the contrast has been between gifts and love? The answer lies beyond our immediate reach, since it is probably related to his former association with this church, where he had spent eighteen months preaching and teaching. Both the evidence of his letters and the express language of this sentence suggest that he is here reminding them of something they know very well. Thus in pointing them to the way that is better by far, he concludes by reminding them of the "well-known three," with which they are especially well acquainted. Just as love is "greater" than the gifts because it belongs to eternity, being the essential character of God and therefore belonging to the present as well as the future, so too its place among the well-known three. Along with the gifts, these three "remain" as long as present life endures. But in the immediate context the greatest of these is love, both because the emphasis lies here, with the ethical dimension of life in Christ, and because it precedes them on into the final glory. Love will still remain when faith and hope have been realized; hence "the greatest[507] of these is love." If this understanding moves in the right direction, then by concluding with the "well-known three," Paul puts the "only for now" emphasis on the χαρίσματα into its broader perspective.

With this sentence Paul is basically drawing the present argument to a close. The concern has been over the "only for now" aspect of the gifts, which stands in contrast to love. The gifts are "in part"; they belong to the "now," which will be brought to an end with the "then" that is to be. Love, on the other hand, is not so. It never fails; it will never come to an end. Along with its companions, faith and hope, it abides in the

---

[506] Those who interpret the passage as eschatological would not disagree with most of this; the question is whether by "remain" Paul meant "forever." The obvious difficulty with the eschatological view—that all who adopt it struggle with in some way—is how Paul could envision "faith" and "hope" to continue into eternity, especially since in 2 Cor 5:7 he contrasts faith with the final glory in the words "for we walk by faith and not by sight," and in Rom 8:24 says that "hope that is seen is not hope." Despite a variety of suggestions as to how these two virtues could still be a part of our eternal existence, I find the idea especially incompatible with Rom 8:24. "Hope" is not a meaningful concept once it has been realized. Among those who argue for an eschatological sense for μένει, see Parry 196–98; Robertson-Plummer 300; Barrett 308–10; M.-F. Lacan, "Les Trois qui demeurent (*I Cor.* xiii, 13)," *RSR* 46 (1958) 321–43; F. Neirynck, "De Grote Drie. Bij een nieuwe vertaling van I Cor. XIII 13," *ETL* 39 (1963) 595–615.

[507] Gk. μείζων, as in 12:31a and 14:5; here it is probably taking the place of the superlative, as it often does in Hellenistic Greek. Otherwise, R. P. Martin, "A Suggested Exegesis of 1 Corinthians 13:13," *ExpT* 82 (1971) 119–20, who gives it its true comparative force, suggesting it should be translated, "but greater than these [three] is [the] love [of God]."

present. But it is greater, at least as the point of this argument, because it abides into eternity.

1 CORINTHIANS 14:1–25

With this section and the next (vv. 26–40) Paul at last offers specific correctives to the Corinthians' apparently unbridled use of tongues in the assembly. He began by setting forth the broader theological framework in which these correctives are to be understood. In ch. 12 he argued for diversity, tongues being only one among many manifestations of the Spirit, who gives gifts to each as he wills for "the common good" (vv. 7–11). In ch. 13, reflecting on the theme of "the common good," he insisted that none of them, himself included, counts for anything, no matter how "spiritual" they are, if they do not likewise manifest love. Now he puts these together, by insisting that in the gathered assembly the single goal of their zeal for the Spirit should be love (v. 1). Love, as in 8:1, is expressed in the language of "building up" the church (vv. 3–5, 12, 17, 26).[508] This latter theme is developed in two ways: by insisting on *intelligibility* in the gathered assembly and by giving guidelines for *order*.

This first section (vv. 1–25) takes up the issue of intelligibility.[509] The argument is in two parts: Verses 1–19 argue for intelligibility for the sake of fellow believers—that they might be edified; vv. 20–25 make the same point for the sake of unbelievers—that they might hear the word of the Lord and be converted. Paul argues his case in two ways: (1) In vv. 1–5 and 20–25 he urges that they seek prophecy vis-à-vis tongues, because, being understandable, it can both edify and lead to conversion. However, both the list of gifts in v. 6 and the argument of vv. 6–19 indicate that the real issue is not tongues and prophecy per se, but the building up of the community, and that can only be effected by understandable utterances, primarily prophecy.

(2) In vv. 6–19 Paul directly addresses the issue of tongues, as to its unintelligibility and therefore inability to edify the community. After a series of analogies illustrating the basic lack of benefit from what is unintelligible (vv. 7–11), he applies this point to their situation (vv. 12–13), arguing that prayer and praise must be intelligible if the community is to be edified (vv. 14–17). This section begins (v. 6) and ends (vv. 18–19) on personal notes that suggest that Paul is also offering an apologetic for his not comporting with their standard for spirituality. For him to come to them speaking in tongues would not benefit them; thus, even though

---

[508] Contra Conzelmann 233, whose view that ch. 13 is an editorial intrusion allows him to say of this opening: "A unified line of thought can be discovered only with difficulty."

[509] So also Carson, *Showing*, 102: "The context specifies that the issue is *intelligibility*."

he speaks in tongues more than them all, *in church* he will do only what edifies, i.e., only what is intelligible.

1 CORINTHIANS 14:1–5

¹*Pursue love and eagerly desire the things of the Spirit, especially that you might prophesy.* ²*For the one speaking in a tongue does not speak to people but to God. Indeed,*[510] *no one understands*[511] *the speaker; but by the Spirit he or she speaks mysteries.* ³*But the one prophesying speaks edification, encouragement, and comfort to people.* ⁴*The one speaking in a tongue edifies oneself, but the one prophesying edifies the church.* ⁵*I would like all of you to speak in tongues, but I would rather that you prophesy. The one prophesying is greater than one speaking in tongues, unless he or she interprets, so that the church may be edified.*

This opening paragraph sets out the basic contrasts and the central themes of what follows. The concern is edification (vv. 3–5), the issue intelligibility. Tongues is not understandable (v. 2), hence it cannot edify the church (v. 4). Prophecy is addressed to people precisely for their edification (v. 3), and in that sense it is thus the greater gift.

Although there can be little question that Paul prefers prophecy to tongues in the gathered assembly, v. 5 indicates that the real issue is not tongues per se, but *uninterpreted tongues* (cf. v. 13), since an interpreted tongue can also edify. That means, therefore, as vv. 2–3 imply, that the real issue is with intelligibility in the assembly. Furthermore, it is also clear from vv. 2–5 that Paul is not "damning tongues with faint praise." In both cases the contrasts are not between tongues and prophecy as to their inherent value, but as to the direction of their edification. The edification of the individual believer is not undesirable; it simply is not the point of gathered worship.

1 These opening imperatives reflect a single purpose: to serve as transition from the preceding argument(s) to the issue at hand, namely, their abuse of tongues in the gathered assembly. Thus in chiastic order[512] Paul says "follow the way of love," namely ch. 13, and in that context "eagerly desire the things of the Spirit," resuming the argument from 12:31a that was interrupted by the exhortation to love. In the earlier

---

[510] Gk. γάρ, almost certainly inferential in this case.

[511] Gk. ἀκούει; although this usage does not occur often in the NT, it is otherwise well-attested. It combines the two ideas of "hearing with the understanding."

[512] Thus: (12:31)   Be zealous for τὰ χαρίσματα   A
               Yet I point out the superior way   B
      (13)   Description/exhortation about love   C
      (14:1)   Pursue love   B′
               Be zealous for τὰ πνευματικά   A′

exhortation (12:31a) he had said "eagerly desire the *greater* χαρίσματα"; now he indicates (v. 5) that by the greater gifts he means those that edify the community. His choice to represent those greater gifts is, "especially that you may prophesy."[513] A further word about each of these.

The command to "follow[514] the way of love" puts into imperative form what was implied throughout the preceding argument. The "love" that they are to pursue, of course, is that described in 13:4–7, since without it the Spirit person amounts to zero (vv. 1–3); furthermore (vv. 8–13), love is the great imperishable, which alone—not the χαρίσματα (nor faith and hope)—will abide into eternity.

The imperative "eagerly desire the things of the Spirit,"[515] although it resumes the argument from 12:31, is nonetheless not a precise repetition. The verb remains the same, but the object is no longer "the greater χαρίσματα," but τὰ πνευματικά, which probably means something like "utterances inspired by the Spirit" (see on 12:1). Some have argued for more significant differences between these two words;[516] probably it is a matter of emphasis. At the end of ch. 12, where he had been speaking specifically of the *gifts* themselves as gracious endowments, he told them, "eagerly desire the greater χαρίσματα." Now in a context where the emphasis will be on the activity of the Spirit in the community at worship, he says, "eagerly desire the things of the Spirit." But this interchange also illustrates that in a context of Spirit utterances within the community there is also a degree of overlap in usage. From one

---

[513] It should be noted that the imperatives are directed to all, not to a select group of "prophets." One may assume, therefore, that even though in reality not all will be "prophets" (12:29), nonetheless prophesying is as available to all as are the command to pursue love and the wish that *all* may speak in tongues (v. 5); cf. Barrett 315. Otherwise Ellis, *Prophecy*, 24–27, who argues that only "pneumatics" are in view in ch. 14.

[514] Gk. διώκετε, lit. "pursue, strive for, seek after, aspire to" (BAGD). The word most often means to pursue in a negative sense, thus "persecute." But in Paul it is a favorite metaphor for spiritual effort (cf. 1 Thes 5:15; Rom 9:30–31; 12:13; 14:19; Phil 3:12; 1 Tim 6:11; 2 Tim 2:22). The present imperative implies continuous action, "keep on pursuing love."

[515] Martin, *Spirit*, 65–66, following Chevallier and Baker (see on 12:31), argues that these words are best understood as a quote from the Corinthian letter. Although this option has some attractive features, it has several strikes against it: (1) The form of the verb is imperative; it is not easy to imagine why the Corinthians would have spoken to Paul in this manner, especially in a setting where they are basically over against him. (2) To make this approach work Martin suggests that the following ἵνα is imperatival; but that will not do, since it is grammatically dependent on the ζηλοῦτε, which means further that both verbs must be part of *Paul's* exhortation. That is, one could well understand how he could quote them and then qualify their position with an imperative—but not with a ἵνα-clause that is grammatically dependent on the quote itself. (3) That the ἵνα-clause is not imperatival is further suggested by the exact repetition of the μᾶλλον δὲ ἵνα προφητεύητε in v. 5, where it cannot be so.

[516] See the discussion on 12:1.

perspective prophecy is therefore a χάρισμα, a *gracious gift* from the Spirit; from another perspective it is a Spirit utterance, a manifestation of the Spirit's presence within the community.

What must be emphasized is that this imperative is now to be understood singularly in light of the exhortation to love that has preceded it. If the two imperatives are not kept together, the point of the entire succeeding argument is missed. Thus he immediately qualifies the imperative with a clause that literally says, "but rather[517] that[518] you prophesy."[519] In the following sentences Paul gives the reasons for this qualification.

2–4 Paul now explains[520] why they should especially seek to prophesy. In light of v. 1, which does *not* mention tongues, that the first sentence should be about tongues rather than prophecy should catch our attention. That is, even though he has said that they should especially seek to prophesy, his explanation comes in the form of a contrast of prophecy with tongues, whose aim is to point out, first, the focus of each form of speech and therefore, second, who is edified thereby. The argument is best seen in light of its structure. With two balanced pairs (vv. 2–3) Paul first contrasts tongues and prophecy with respect to who is addressed (in bold) and their basic purpose (in italics); the second pair (v. 4) then interprets the first pair in terms of who is being edified:

> *For*
> (a) The one speaking in a tongue   speaks *not*   **to people,**
>   *but*   <u>**to God**</u>.
>   Indeed, no one understands him/her;
>   he/she   speaks *mysteries* by the Spirit.
>   *On the other hand,*[521]

---

[517] Gk. μᾶλλον δέ, which could be intensive, "especially." More likely, in light of the exact repetition in v. 5, Paul intends it to be slightly adversative, introducing "an expr[ession] or thought that supplements and thereby corrects what has preceded" (BAGD). The "correction" in the present case is toward specifying with greater exactness the point of the preceding imperative.

[518] Gk. ἵνα, which in this case is probably epexegetic, functioning like a ὅτι. Thus, "Be eagerly desiring the things of the Spirit, but rather *namely that* you prophesy." That is as awkward in Greek as it is in English, but the point seems clear enough.

[519] On the gift of prophecy, see on 12:10. Throughout the argument, both for prophecy and tongues, the *verbs* "prophesy" and "speak in tongues" predominate over the corresponding nouns. The verb "prophesy" appears in vv. 1, 3, 4, 5[2x], 24, 31, 39; the noun "prophecy" in vv. 6 and 22, and "prophet" in vv. 29, 32[2x], 37. The combination "speak in tongues" occurs in vv. 2, 4, 5[2x], 6, 13, 18, 23, 27, 39; the noun "tongue(s)" in vv. 14, 19, 22, 26.

[520] Note the explanatory γάρ.

[521] Gk. δέ; even though there is no μή in the previous clause, the two sets are so plainly set up in contrast that such a translation makes that point clearer.

(b) The one prophesying	speaks	to people,
	edification,	
	encouragement,	
	comfort.	
(a) The one speaking in a tongue	edifies him/herself;	
on the other hand,		
(b) the one prophesying	edifies the church.	

Paul's emphasis—and concern—is unmistakable, the edification of the church. The one activity, tongues, edifies the speaker, but not the church, because it is addressed to God and no one understands him or her; indeed we learn in vv. 14–15 that not even the speaker understands what is being said. The other activity, prophecy, edifies the church because it is addressed to people and speaks "edification, encouragement, and comfort" to them.

Although trying to cool their ardor for congregational tongues-speaking, he does not disparage the gift itself; rather he seeks to put it in its rightful place. Positively, he says three things about speaking in a tongue.[522] These are best understood in light of the further discussion on prayer and praise in vv. 13–17: (1) Such a person is "speaking to[523] God," that is, he or she is communing with God by the Spirit. Although it is quite common in Pentecostal groups to refer to a "message in tongues," there seems to be no evidence in Paul for such terminology. The tongues-speaker is addressing not fellow believers, but God (cf. vv. 13–14, 28). This means that Paul understands the phenomenon basically to be prayer and praise.[524]

(2) The content of such utterances is "mysteries" spoken "by the Spirit."[525] It is possible that "mysteries" means something similar to its usage in 13:2; more likely it carries here the sense of that which lies outside the understanding, both for the speaker and the hearer. After all, "mysteries" in 13:2 refers to the ways of God that are being revealed by the Spirit to his people; such "mysteries" would scarcely need to be spoken back to God.[526]

---

[522] On the nature of the gift, see on 12:10.

[523] Grosheide 317 understands this to be a dative of advantage, but the standard usage with the verb "to speak" makes this especially difficult to sustain.

[524] Cf. Dunn, *Jesus*, 245.

[525] Not "with his spirit" as the NIV; cf. Godet 266, Héring 146, Parry 200, Morris 191. That is not precise even for vv. 14–15 (q.v.). On the absence of the article with Spirit in the dative see ch. 2. Chapter 12 verses 7–11 show that tongues is the manifestation of the Spirit of God through the human speaker. It does not seem remotely possible that in this context Paul would suddenly refer to speaking "with one's own spirit," rather than by the Holy Spirit. Cf. Holladay 175.

[526] Although it is a moot point as to whether Rom 8:26 reflects glossolalia, as I argue, the main thrust of that passage echoes what is said here.

(3) Such speech by the Spirit is further described in v. 4 as edifying to the speaker. This has sometimes been called "self-edification" and therefore viewed pejoratively.[527] But Paul intended no such thing. The edifying of oneself is not self-centeredness, but the personal edifying of the individual believer that comes through private prayer and praise. It is hard to imagine the circumstances in which Paul would think this a bad thing in itself, especially in light of his own experience of "speaking in tongues more than all of them" (v. 18). But "private prayer" is not the reason for public worship. Although one may wonder how "mysteries" that are not understood even by the speaker can edify, the answer lies in vv. 14–15. Contrary to the opinion of many, spiritual edification can take place in ways other than through the cortex of the brain.[528] Paul believed in an immediate communing with God by means of the S/spirit[529] that sometimes bypassed the mind; and in vv. 14–15 he argues that for his own edification he will have both. But *in church* he will have only what can also communicate to other believers through their minds (vv. 16–19).

But despite these favorable words about tongues, Paul's concern is not with private devotion, but with public worship. Therefore, he urges by implication that they *not* speak in tongues in worship (unless it be interpreted, vv. 5, 13, 27), but rather that they seek to prophesy (or in light of v. 6 bring forth any form of intelligible utterance). The reason for prophecy is that it speaks "edification, exhortation, and comfort" to the rest of the people.[530] These three words[531] set forth some parameters of the divine intent of prophecy for the sake of believers and indicate that in Paul's view the primary focus of a prophetic utterance is not the future, but the present situations of the people of God. For the sake of an unbeliever, prophecy functions in a considerably different way (vv. 24–25).

---

[527] See, e.g., O. Michel, *TDNT* 5.141: "It is thus wrong for the man who speaks in tongues to edify himself"; cf. R. G. Gromacki, *Called to Be Saints: An Exposition of 1 Corinthians* (Grand Rapids, 1977) 168. MacArthur 372, whose biases intrude on his interpretation, considers it sarcastic here. See the critique of this position in Carson, *Showing*, 102n89.

[528] See Bittlinger, *Gifts*, 100–106, for a discussion of the gift of tongues in terms of its psychological benefits; but such discussions lie quite beyond what one can say exegetically.

[529] On this way of translating the concept of the divine Spirit speaking through the human spirit, see on v. 14 below (cf. 5:3–5).

[530] There is some ambiguity as to whether the edifying of others is to be viewed in terms of edifying the other individuals who are present, or whether it refers to the community corporately. Verse 3 implies the former; v. 4 the latter. Probably they run together in the apostle's mind. The edification of the whole at the same time includes the edification of the various parts.

[531] They function grammatically as the compound *direct object* of the verb λαλεῖ, hence the translation. Some see the second two as defining the first (e.g., Wendland 109; Conzelmann 234–34; Ellis, *Prophecy*, 132n13). Otherwise, Findlay 902 (explicitly) and most commentators implicitly.

The first word, "edification,"[532] controls the thought of the entire chapter. In 8:1 Paul had said, "love builds up"; now the sequence runs, "Pursue love, and in that framework seek the things of the Spirit, especially prophecy, because prophecy builds up." Thus the reason for the preceding chapter:[533] Since love builds up, in their zeal for Spirit utterances they are to seek prophecy because it is intelligible and thus builds up the body. The second word[534] is more ambiguous, meaning alternatively "encouragement,"[535] "comfort,"[536] or "exhortation (appeal)."[537] It is joined in this instance by its companion "comfort."[538] The question is whether these two words are, as in other instances, near synonyms meaning to encourage or comfort, or whether they embrace the broader categories of exhorting and comforting.[539] In either case, the aim of prophecy is the growth of the church corporately, which also involves the growth of its individual members.

5 This verse summarizes the point of vv. 1–4 by making explicit Paul's preference for prophecy over tongues in the assembly. As in vv. 2–4, he begins with tongues: "I would like you all to speak in tongues." This sentence is often viewed as "merely conciliatory," especially in light of 12:28–30 where he asserts that all do not speak in tongues.[540] But that is not quite correct. Paul has already indicated that tongues have value for the individual, meaning in private, personal prayer (cf. vv. 14–15 and 18–19). Now he says of that dimension of spiritual life that he could wish all experienced the edification that came from such a gift of the Spirit.

---

[532] Gk. οἰκοδομή, which occurs 4 times in this chapter (vv. 3, 5, 12, 26), the verb 3 times (v. 4[2x], 26). Neither form of the word occurs in the preceding two sections of the argument. For this word in 1 Corinthians, see also 3:10; 8:10; and 10:23.

[533] Conzelmann 233, in his desire to isolate ch. 13 from the present context, makes the curious comment: "The criterion is no longer ἀγάπη, 'love,' but οἰκοδομή, 'edification, upbuilding.' "

[534] Gk. παράκλησις; cf. esp. the combination of verbs in v. 31: "you can all *prophesy* in turn so that all may learn and all παρακαλῶνται." Note also the collocation of the two nouns, παράκλησις and παραμυθία, probably as near synonyms, in Phil 2:1.

[535] So translated here by NIV, RSV, GNB, NAB, JB, Moffatt, Montgomery, Beck. For this usage in Paul see, e.g., Rom 15:4–5.

[536] See the many examples in 2 Cor 1:3–7.

[537] So translated here by KJV and NASB. For this usage in Paul see 1 Thes 2:3; 2 Cor 8:17, and the cognate verb frequently.

[538] Gk. παραμυθία; cf. Phil 2:1 and the combination of cognate verbs in 1 Thes 2:12.

[539] Cf. e.g., Findlay 902, who sees παράκλησις as addressing duty, παραμυθία sorrow or fear; Dunn, *Jesus*, 229–30, implies that the two words *together* suggest both exhortation and encouragement/comfort. See also Hill, *Prophecy*, 122–32, who tries, not totally successfully, to build a case from these words that the basic function of prophecy in Paul was "pastoral teaching."

[540] See, e.g., H. W. House, "Tongues and the Mystery Religions of Corinth," *BSac* 140 (1983) 135–50.

But that of course is not his present point; thus he quickly qualifies that "wish" by repeating the language of v. 1: "but rather that you prophesy."

After such a summary one would expect in this letter that it might be followed by an explanatory "for" and a reason. In this case, however, he concludes with the proposition, "Greater is the one who prophesies than the one who speaks in tongues." With these words two matters from the preceding argument are brought into focus. First, this defines the meaning of "greater gift" in the exhortation in 12:31; second, the *reason* prophecy is greater is related to the edification of the community, as the preceding argument makes certain. Thus it is not inherently greater, since all gifts come from the Spirit and are beneficial. It is greater precisely because it is intelligible and therefore can edify.

This last point is ensured by the final qualifying clause added to speaking in tongues: "unless he or she interprets,[541] so that the church may be edified." The problem is not with tongues per se but tongues without interpretation—which from the context seems very likely what the Corinthians were doing. The interpretation of the tongues-speech brings it within the framework of intelligibility, which in turn means that it too can edify the community. This does not imply that such a tongue is to be understood as directed toward the community, but that what the person has been speaking to God has now been made intelligible, so that others may benefit from the Spirit's utterance.[542] Thus, even though from Paul's perspective prophecy is clearly preferable, it seems equally clear that the real urgency is not with tongues and prophecy, but with intelligible utterances in the gathered assembly so that all may be edified.

1 CORINTHIANS 14:6–19

⁶But as it is, brothers and sisters, if I come to you speaking in tongues, how shall I benefit you, unless I speak to you by means of revelation, or by means of knowledge, by means of prophecy or[543] teaching? ⁷Even in the case of lifeless

---

[541] This is not in conflict with 12:30 or 14:28, as some imply, since the former verse says that not *all* are or do the same thing, not that anyone may do *only* one thing; and the latter text allows for interpretation to come from others than the tongues-speaker. According to 12:10, this too is a gift of the Spirit; therefore, it is potentially available to anyone, including the tongues-speaker (cf. v. 13, where the tongues-speaker is encouraged to pray for this gift, so that his tongue might edify).

[542] Dunn, *Jesus*, 247–48, wants to raise the question, that if this is the case, why then tongues at all, implying that "Paul is trying to rationalize a form of charismatic worship in Corinth with which he is not altogether happy." Paul himself certainly does not suggest as much.

[543] Each of these nouns appears with an ἐν (= in the form of, by means of). The ἐν is missing with διδαχῇ in P⁴⁶ ℵ* D* F G 0243 630 1739 1881 pc, which then would tie it more closely with prophecy (as in this translation). This is not an easy textual choice. On the one hand, it is difficult to account for its omission by scribes, either accidentally or intentionally; on the other hand, it is equally difficult to account for

things giving sound, whether flute or harp, if they make no clear distinction in their tones, how will anyone know what the flute or harp is playing? ⁸For indeed, if the trumpet does not sound a clear call, who will get ready for battle? ⁹So also you, if you do not speak an easily recognizable word with your tongue, how will what is being said be known? For you will be speaking into the air. ¹⁰Undoubtedly there are all sorts of languages in the world, and none⁵⁴⁴ is without meaning. ¹¹If then I do not understand the meaning of what is said, I shall be a barbarian to the speaker, and the one speaking a barbarian from my perspective.⁵⁴⁵ ¹²So also you, since you are zealots for spirits,⁵⁴⁶ strive that you may abound unto the building up of the church. ¹³Therefore let the one speaking in a tongue pray to interpret. ¹⁴If⁵⁴⁷ I pray in a tongue, my S/spirit prays, but my mind is unfruitful. ¹⁵What then? I will pray with my S/spirit, and I will also pray with my mind; I will sing with my S/spirit, and I will also sing with my mind. ¹⁶Otherwise if you are blessing⁵⁴⁸ God by the Spirit how can the one filling the place of the unlearned say "Amen" to your thanksgiving, since such a person does not know what you are saying? ¹⁷You, to be sure, are giving thanks well enough, but the other person is not being edified. ¹⁸I thank God⁵⁴⁹ I speak in tongues more than all of you. ¹⁹But in church I would rather speak five words with my mind, so as to instruct others, than ten thousand words in a tongue.

This long paragraph⁵⁵⁰ elaborates Paul's the concern over the unintelligible, and therefore nonedifying, character of uninterpreted tongues

---

Paul's having omitted it in this instance when the rest of the list is so carefully balanced. On the whole it seems more likely that Paul himself omitted it, but it is unlikely that he "meant" anything by it. See the discussion in Barrett 312 and 317.

⁵⁴⁴For the sake of smoothness, the MajT has added an αὐτῶν (cf. NIV).

⁵⁴⁵P⁴⁶ D F G 0243 6 81 365 1175 1739 1881 al b vg bo read ἐμοί. As Zuntz notes (*Text*, 104), this is most likely a harmonization to the preceding τῷ λαλοῦντι. The original (ℵ A B Ψ Maj lat sy bo) reads ἐν ἐμοί (= from my perspective); cf. Barrett 312.

⁵⁴⁶Paul wrote πνευμάτων (spirits); the change to πνευματικῶν was actually made by P 1175 pc a r syᵖ co. See the discussion below.

⁵⁴⁷Despite the support of P⁴⁶ B F G 0243 1739 1881 pc b sa, the γάρ (included with brackets in NA²⁶; cf. NIV) is by all counts not original. Its omission would be almost impossible to account for, either accidentally or deliberately—even more so independently across two early traditions (Egyptian and Western). One can easily account for the addition, given both the frequency of this conjunction in this letter and the apparent awkwardness of the asyndeton. Cf. Zuntz, *Text*, 194, who adds the note that both here and in v. 18, where Paul suddenly brings in his own person, the text is asyndetic.

⁵⁴⁸P⁴⁶ F G 048 and the MajT read the aorist εὐλογήσῃς here, almost certainly in error. The aorist, which is the more common nonindicative "tense" in Greek (cf. vv. 6, 7, 8, 9), is the one toward which change most often occurs. As in v. 14, this sentence is most likely a present general condition.

⁵⁴⁹A ὅτι is supplied in the Latin tradition (F G lat) for the same reason the NIV has in English. The lack of a conjunction tends to heighten the significance of the second sentence. See Robertson-Plummer 413.

⁵⁵⁰Most translations consider vv. 6–12 and 13–19 to be separate paragraphs; but

in the assembly. The opening rhetorical question (v. 6) sets the agenda: Hearers benefit not at all by what is not understandable. This is followed by a series of examples from musical instruments, including trumpet calls for battle (vv. 7–8) and foreign languages (vv. 9–11), each of which is applied to the Corinthians with a similar, "so it is with you" (vv. 9 and 12). The second application concludes on the same note with which the paragraph began—the edification of the church, which should rule their zeal for Spirit utterances. That leads to further application, this time specifically with regard to their public worship. After urging the one who speaks in tongues to pray for the gift of interpretation (v. 13), he argues in vv. 14–15, on the basis of his own experience, that since praying in the Spirit means that the understanding is unfruitful, he will do both— pray in the Spirit and with the mind—adding that he will do the same in praise (in this case, singing). As vv. 16–17 demonstrate, this latter item is his basic concern, praising God with the mind (= intelligibly) for the sake of others, who cannot otherwise say the corporate "Amen" to what is said. Verses 18–19 conclude on another personal, and probably apologetic, note (cf. v. 6), putting the whole into perspective: For the sake of others, only what is intelligible in church; thus no uninterpreted tongues.

Thus the entire section deals with speaking in tongues; prophecy is not mentioned after v. 6, although perhaps it is alluded to at the end (v. 19).[551] Tongues becomes intelligible through interpretation, as already suggested in v. 5. Here in particular it is evident that for Paul "tongues" is an expression of prayer and praise, not a word directed primarily toward the community. As far as the one speaking is concerned, everything said about tongues is quite positive; nonetheless, as before, the purpose of the whole is to check the unbridled use of uninterpreted tongues in the assembly.

At the same time, one perceives an undercurrent of apologetic between Paul and the Corinthians. If our reconstruction is correct, that not only are they high on tongues as evidencing true spirituality, but at the same time negative toward Paul for his shortcomings in this matter, then the form of v. 6 is especially relevant: "If I *come to you* speaking in tongues, how shall I benefit you?" This motif seems to carry through v. 19. Paul has not lost his primary focus of putting their gift into proper perspective, especially as the community gathers for worship. At the same time, he takes the opportunity to put his own practice into perspec-

---

since it is difficult to decide whether v. 13 goes with vv. 6–12 or 14–19, and since vv. 6 and 18–19 form an *inclusio* in terms of what Paul might do among them, there is no valid reason to break this argument into separate paragraphs.

[551] Dunn, *Jesus*, 228, suggests that "praying with the mind" in v. 15 is to be equated with prophecy. This is doubtful. It may have the same effect—intelligibility— but all of vv. 14–17 deal with God-directed utterances; and prophecy, whatever else, is not a God-directed word.

tive for them. Even though he speaks in tongues more than all of them (v. 18), and determines to pray and sing both in the Spirit and with his mind (v. 15), he likewise refuses to "come to them" as they might prefer, speaking in tongues, because that will not benefit *them* at all.

6 This opening sentence functions as a transition: It carries forward the argument of vv. 1–5; at the same time it sets the stylistic pattern for the first set of analogies ("If . . . how shall . . . ?"[552]), which argue vigorously against unintelligibility (= tongues), since it has no usefulness for its hearers.

Even though the sentence is probably designed to present a hypothetical setting for the argument,[553] both the combination, "but as it is,"[554] and the language, "if I come to you,"[555] support[556] the suggestion that this is more than merely hypothetical; probably it also indicates the way things are between them and him, implying his rejection of their criterion for being πνευματικός. Paul in effect refuses to "come to [them] speaking in tongues." The reason for this echoes the motif of edification from vv. 3–5. By following their criterion he would not "profit them."[557]

The alternative is for him to come speaking some form of intelligible utterance, which he illustrates with yet another list of Spirit phenomena, in this case, Spirit utterances. This list is both illuminating and intriguing.[558] On the one hand, the appearance of prophecy in the third position intimates, as has been argued regarding vv. 1–5, that the real issue is not tongues and prophecy as such, but tongues and intelligibility, for which prophecy serves as the representative gift. On the other hand, as with the other lists in this argument,[559] this one is also especially ad

---

[552] Cf. vv. 6, 7, 8, 9, each of which basically follows the same form: an ἐάν clause, followed by an interrogative particle (τί, πῶς, τίς), followed by a future indicative.

[553] Cf. Conzelmann 235, who sees it as rhetorical, in diatribe style.

[554] Gk. νῦν δέ, which in this case, in contrast to the clearly temporal usage in 5:11 and 7:14, seems to function in a logical sense, as in 12:20 (cf. the νυνὶ δέ in 12:18; 13:13; and 15:20). Even so the sense of time is never quite missing from this use of the adverb. Hence the translation, "but (δέ) as it is (νῦν)."

[555] Cf. 2:1; 4:18–19, 21; 16:2, 5. Apart from 2:1 each of these refers to his anticipated next visit. The choice of this language for the hypothetical setting is striking.

[556] Perhaps this is true of the vocative as well, since this sudden very personal address does not otherwise seem to fit with an appeal whose main content will be a series of analogies.

[557] Gk. ὠφελέω (cf. 13:3); cf. the concern in 12:7 for "the common good."

[558] Some (e.g., Calvin 438, Robertson-Plummer 308; Ruef 148, Grudem, *Gift*, 138–39, with qualification) see an "artful" arrangement, in which there are two pairs, the latter two expressing the "administration" of the former two. But given Paul's usage throughout this argument, this is a discovery that would most likely come as a surprise to him. On the basis of 13:2 ἀποκάλυψις corresponds more with γνῶσις than with prophecy. In any case the list is too ad hoc for such schemes.

[559] Cf. 12:8–10, 28, 29–30; 13:1–2, 8; 14:26.

hoc. Paul wants to specify various kinds of Spirit-inspired utterances that have intelligibility as their common denominator. Thus he includes two items from previous lists, "knowledge" and "prophecy" (see 12:8–10; 13:2, 8). The other two call for additional comment.

The word "revelation" is used in a variety of ways by Paul,[560] but only in the present argument to suggest some kind of utterance given by the Spirit for the benefit of the gathered community.[561] What its content might be and how it would differ from "knowledge" or "prophecy" is not at all clear. For example, along with "teaching" it appears in the final list in v. 26, a list which includes neither "prophecy" nor "knowledge." Yet in the subsequent discussion of the ordering of utterances (vv. 27–33), Paul takes up tongues and prophecy, not "revelation," although its cognate verb does appear in the discussion of prophecy in v. 30. This latter passage in particular suggests that there is a general lack of precision in Paul with regard to these various items.[562] Perhaps in the final list (v. 26) this word covers both prophecy and knowledge as the more inclusive term. In any case, it implies the disclosure of divine "mysteries," either about the nature of the gospel (cf. 2:10) or perhaps about things otherwise hidden to the "natural person."[563]

Equally intriguing is the appearance of "teaching,"[564] which corresponds to "the teacher" in 12:28 as prophecy does to the prophet. Probably this has to do with a Spirit-inspired utterance that took the form of instruction,[565] rather than with the more common usage that implies formal teaching of some kind. Again, how this differs in terms of content from the other items on this list is a matter of speculation, since the data are so meager. See the discussion on 12:28.

---

[560] Gk. ἀποκάλυψις (cf. v. 26) sometimes refers to visible disclosures associated with the return of Christ (1:7; 2 Thes 1:7; Rom 2:5; 8:19). In other places it refers to the "revelation" of the gospel given to Paul by Christ (Gal 1:12) or of God's will in his life (Gal 2:2). The latter may be associated with the kind of Spirit utterance referred to in this passage. On the other hand, there are the "revelations" of the Lord given to Paul in the visionary experiences of 2 Cor 12:1, 7, which he was not allowed to share with others. For this word in Paul see M. Bockmuehl, *Revelation and Mystery in Ancient Judaism and Pauline Christianity* (WUNT 2/36; Tübingen: Mohr-Siebeck, 1990).

[561] Those who equate Gal 2:1–10 with the famine visit recorded in Acts 11:27–29 see the reference in Gal 2:2 to his going up to Jerusalem "by revelation" as related to the prophecy of Agabus in Acts. But see the discussion of this text in ch. 6 below.

[562] Cf. Barrett, 317: "All these activities . . . shade too finely into one another for rigid distinctions."

[563] Cf. the discussion in Dunn, *Jesus*, 230.

[564] Gk. διδαχή; referring to the utterance itself, not to "doctrine" (KJV).

[565] This is supported by three pieces of evidence: (1) Its appearance here in a list of items that are otherwise unquestionably to be understood as Spirit-inspired χαρίσματα; (2) the fact that the whole section has to do with πνευματικά (v. 1) and the Corinthians' zeal for "spirits" (v. 12); and (3) its appearance in v. 26 in a similar context of inspired utterances. Cf. Dunn, *Jesus*, 236–37.

Despite our lack of certainty about the exact nature and content of these forms of utterance, however, their common denominator is their intelligibility, and to that question Paul now turns in the form of analogies.

7–11 Paul illustrates his point from three analogies—musical instruments, a battle call, and foreign languages—which in themselves seem self-evident. Tongues, Paul is arguing in the first two instances, is like the harpist running fingers over all the strings, making musical sounds but not playing a pleasing melody,[566] or like a bugler who blows the bugle without sounding the battle cry. In both cases sounds come from the instrument, but they make no sense; hence they do not benefit the listener. So it is with tongues.

The third analogy, the phenomenon of different languages, which would have been commonplace in a cosmopolitan center like Corinth, is the one most closely related to the immediate problem. The analogy is not that the tongues-speaker is also speaking a foreign language, as some have suggested,[567] but that the hearer cannot understand the one speaking in tongues any more than he or she can the one who speaks a foreign language. Indeed this is the certain evidence that Paul does not understand Spirit-inspired speaking in a tongue to be speaking an actual earthly language. The analogy, of course, emphasizes the perspective of the hearer. It is not that the different languages do not have meaning to their speakers; rather they do not have meaning to the hearers.

Again, the application to their setting and "speaking in tongues" is obvious. Just as the hearer of one speaking in a foreign language cannot understand what is said, so the other worshipers in the community cannot understand what is spoken "in tongues." Thus it is of no value to them.

12 This second application begins exactly as in v. 9: "So it is with you." But in this instance instead of applying the obvious point of the preceding analogy, Paul ties all this together by picking up two motifs from vv. 1–5. First, "since you are zealots[568] for spirits."[569] As many have seen, this clause probably holds the key to much. Whatever else it means, it explicitly indicates that zeal for what is at issue in these chapters is a

---

[566] In modern culture the appropriate analogy would be the cacophony of the symphony orchestra tuning instruments and warming up just before the conductor raises the baton.

[567] E.g., Gundry, "Utterance?" 306. The point of the analogy is that "tongues" functions *like* this. Cf. Dunn, *Jesus*, 244: "That which is not self-evident (the uselessness of unintelligible glossolalia in the assembly) is illuminated by that which is self-evident (the uselessness of unintelligible foreign language in the assembly)." See also the discussion on 12:10.

[568] Gk. ζηλωταί, the cognate noun of the verb ζηλόω (eagerly desire) in v. 1.

[569] For this usage, cf. the discussion on 5:3–4.

Corinthian trademark. This has caused some, therefore, to read the two imperatives in 12:31 and 14:1 as quotations from the Corinthian letter. But that is an unnecessary expedient. Paul was not commanding them in those cases to do what they were already doing. Rather, just as in this verse, he was urging them to direct that zeal toward Spirit phenomena that edify (14:5).

The more difficult concept is their zeal for "spirits." On the basis of 14:1, this is almost universally understood to refer to their alleged zeal for "spiritual gifts" in general.[570] But that is unlikely, in terms both of this choice of words and of the historical context as a whole. More likely this refers especially to their desire for one particular manifestation of the Spirit, the gift of tongues, which was for them the certain evidence of their being πνευματικός (a person of the Spirit).[571] The plural "spirits" does not mean that "the one and the same Spirit" of 12:7–11 is now to be understood as a multiplicity of spirits.[572] Rather, this is Paul's way of speaking about the Spirit's manifesting himself through their individual "spirits." The clue lies in the usage in v. 32, where the "spirits of the prophets" refers to the Holy Spirit's speaking prophetic utterances through the one who is prophesying. Likewise in vv. 14–15, Paul will pray with "my spirit," meaning "by means of the Holy Spirit through my spirit." Hence they have great zeal for their spirits, through speaking in tongues, to be the mouthpiece for the Spirit.

Paul desires to capitalize on their zeal, or more accurately, as before, to redirect their zeal. Thus the second motif from vv. 1–5, and the purpose of everything: "Strive to abound[573] in the building up of the church." This was the explicit concern in vv. 1–5; it has been the implicit concern in the several analogies of this paragraph. Utterances that are not understood, even if they come from the Spirit, are of no benefit, i.e., edification, to the hearer. Thus, since they have such zeal for the manifestation of the Spirit, they should direct that zeal in corporate worship away from being "foreigners" to one another toward the edification of one another in Christ.

13 The strong inferential "therefore,"[574] indicates a close relationship between this sentence and v. 12. It functions to conclude vv. 6–12 by applying the principle of "building up the church" to their zeal for

---

[570] So e.g., KJV, NASB, NIV, GNB, NAB.

[571] Cf. Dunn, *Jesus*, 234, who interprets it to mean "eager to experience inspiration, . . . particularly the inspired utterance of glossolalia." Ellis, *Prophecy*, 31, suggests it implies "an interest in the powers that lie behind and attend those manifestations," but that seems both unnecessary and unlikely.

[572] As suggested by Weiss 326–27, who quite misses Paul's point and the larger context.

[573] Gk. ἵνα περισσεύητε, where a ἵνα-clause functions as an infinitive of purpose.

[574] Gk. διό (cf. 12:3).

tongues.[575] Its content, therefore, comes as something of a surprise. In light of the total argument thus far, one might have expected, "For this reason let the one who speaks in tongues seek rather to prophesy." But prophecy is not Paul's first concern, intelligibility is; thus he moves toward that concern by urging, "let the one speaking in a tongue pray to interpret."[576] The point is that of v. 5;[577] The interpretation of the tongue makes it an intelligible utterance;[578] therefore it can satisfy the concern of v. 12, the edification of the church. As before, the Corinthians' practice of uninterpreted tongues is what is being challenged, not tongues as such. This is further confirmed by vv. 27–28, which again disallow uninterpreted tongues, but otherwise *regulate* the expression of the gift *when there is interpretation*.

14 With this sentence Paul begins the specific application of the argument against unintelligibility in vv. 7–13. He does so, as he will again in v. 18, by referring to his own experience of speaking in tongues.[579] But the *point* of this sentence is less than certain. Probably he is using his own experience to highlight a basic principle, which will be elaborated in v. 15 and then applied to their assembly in vv. 16–17.

This seems to make the best sense of what is otherwise a very difficult sentence in the middle of this argument.[580] Paul is not contending that

---

[575] This observation, plus the asyndeton in v. 14 (see n. 547 above), suggests that the sub-paragraphs should probably be vv. 6–13, 14–17, and 18–19.

[576] Some earlier interpreters suggested a different meaning for this sentence, viewing "prayer" as the "praying in a tongue" in v. 14 and the ἵνα clause as telic (purpose). Thus, "Let him that has the gift of tongues pray with tongues, but let him do so with the purpose of interpreting his utterance afterwards" (Edwards 365; cf. Godet 277–78, Beet 245). But this breaks down both grammatically and contextually. On the matter of the tongues-speaker also interpreting, see n. 541 on v. 5.

[577] This verse seems to function in relationship to vv. 6–12 as v. 5b did to vv. 1–5.

[578] But not necessarily having "the effect of converting it into prophecy, or teaching," as Barrett 319 suggests.

[579] As suggested on v. 6, this probably also carries an undercurrent of apologetic. He does indeed speak in tongues—more than all of them (v. 18)—despite what they may think.

[580] Made the more so by the addition of the explanatory "for" found in the majority of witnesses (and the NIV); see n. 547 above. This is seldom noted by interpreters; nevertheless, the contextual difficulties are considerable if the γάρ is original and the intent is that the tongues-speaker should pray for the gift of interpretation for the benefit of his or her own understanding, a view espoused by, inter alia, Calvin 292, Grosheide 325–26, Morris 194, Ruef 150, Mare 273. Not only does this contradict vv. 2, 4, and 15, but it places a premium on the mind as the only means whereby one may be edified personally, which also contradicts the intent of vv. 2 and 4. Furthermore, it is out of keeping with the whole context, which has the edification of the church in view.

One way out of this difficulty has been to make ἄκαρπος "active" in meaning, thus "my mind produces no results for anyone" (Williams; cf. Goodspeed, Moffatt, the tongues-speaker should also interpret for the benefit of his or her own understanding. That would be a considerable "rock" in the middle of this argument for the edification of others through intelligibility. It would also contradict what is said in vv. 2 and 4 and intimated in v. 15, that the one who speaks in tongues is edified by his or her communion with God through the Spirit, without the need of perceptual understanding. Paul's point is a simple one, and one which they themselves should fully recognize: When I pray in tongues[581] I pray in the Spirit, but it does not benefit my mind—the implication being, as he will go on to argue in vv. 16–17, that neither does it benefit the minds of others.

As suggested before,[582] in the present context the difficult wording, "my πνεῦμα prays," seems to mean something like "my S/spirit prays." On the one hand, both the possessive "my" and the contrast with "my mind" indicate that he is here referring to his own "spirit" at prayer. On the other hand, there can be little question, on the basis of the combined evidence of 12:7–11 and 14:2 and 16, that Paul understood speaking in tongues to be an activity of the Spirit in one's life; it is prayer and praise directed toward God in the language of Spirit-inspiration. The most viable solution to this ambiguity is that by the language "my spirit prays" Paul means his own spirit is praying as the Holy Spirit gives the utterance.[583] Hence, "my S/spirit prays."

As v. 15 makes certain, Paul does not mean that praying in the Spirit is undesirable because it does not benefit his understanding; rather, this states the simple realities of things. What he *does* go on to say is that he will do *two* things, one apparently for his own sake, the other for the sake of others.

15 Paul now elaborates the principle set forth in v. 14, with an eye toward turning it into application in vv. 16–17. In light of the simple reality stated in v. 14, he asks rhetorically, "what then?"[584] His answer is that he will do both. On the one hand, "I will pray with my S/spirit"[585]

Conzelmann). Although that moves the concern in the right direction, it seems unlikely that the intended contrast (Gk. δέ) between "my spirit" and "my mind" is that between "what benefits me and what benefits others."

[581] The conditional sentence is a present general; hence, whenever I am praying in a tongue, this is the consequence.

[582] See on v. 12 above; cf. the discussion on 5:3–4; 12:10; and 14:32.

[583] Cf. the language of Acts 2:4: "They began to speak in other tongues, as the Spirit gave them utterance" (RSV). This is not far removed from, but seems to be a preferable way of stating, the alternative favored by Barrett 320 and others that "my *spirit* is the spiritual gift entrusted to me."

[584] Gk. τί οὖν ἐστιν; (cf. 14:26); cf. also the simple τί οὖν of Rom 3:9; 6:15; 11:7, which is the more classical form. The idiom means, "what then is the upshot of what has just been said?"

[585] Gk. τῷ πνεύματι. If the analysis offered above (ch. 2, pp. 24–26) is correct, then

meaning, as vv. 14 and 19 show, "I will pray[586] in tongues." Although this is obviously not Paul's immediate concern, it joins with v. 18 in suggesting that such was his regular practice and that he was edified thereby, even if perceptual understanding did not enter into such praying.[587] On the other hand, and the combination "but also"[588] indicates the emphasis lies here, "I will *also* pray with my understanding,"[589] meaning "I will also pray and praise in Greek for the sake of others."

Although it is not explicitly stated, this contrast between praying and singing with my S/spirit and my mind ultimately aims at relegating the former to the setting of private praying, while only the latter is to be exercised in the assembly. This is implied in vv. 16–17, where he allows that the tongues-speaker is praising God all right, but to no one else's benefit. In v. 19 this distinction is made explicitly.

To "praying" Paul adds "singing with the S/spirit" and "with the understanding." Singing was a common part of worship in Judaism and was carried over as an integral part of early Christian worship as well, as v. 26 and Col 3:16//Eph 5:19 illustrate.[590] The evidence from Colossians and Ephesians suggests that some of the singing was corporate; the language of these passages[591] further indicates that besides being addressed as praise to God, such hymns also served as vehicles of instruction in the gathered community. Furthermore, both passages, as well as this one, indicate that some of the singing might best be called "a kind of charismatic hymnody,"[592] in which spontaneous hymns of praise were offered to God in the congregation, although some may have been known beforehand. The present passage, as well as v. 26, indicates that some of

---

this arthrous usage does not refer directly to the Holy Spirit, but to "my spirit" in v. 14. The usage in v. 16, on the other hand, is anarthrous and probably refers more directly to the Spirit.

[586] This future must be understood as volitional, not temporal, expressing determination.

[587] This in itself speaks against an understanding of v. 14 that sees Paul as encouraging the tongues-speaker to pray for the gift of interpretation so that his or her mind might also benefit from what is said. Obviously for Paul the latter is not always necessary.

[588] Gk. δὲ καί; cf. 15:15.

[589] Gk. νοῦς, as in v. 14; although the word means "mind," Paul's concern is with the "understanding" involved, not the "location," as it were. E. Käsemann, *Perspectives on Paul* (trans. M. Kohl; Philadelphia: Fortress, 1971) 131, also seems quite wrong to suggest that this means "without his will." Incomprehensible and unwilling are not in the same category of reality.

[590] See, e.g., G. Delling, *TDNT* 9.489–503; K. H. Bartels, *NIDNTT* 3.668–75 (who, however, misses the point of this text); R. P. Martin, *Worship in the New Testament* (2d ed.; Grand Rapids: Eerdmans, 1974) 39–52; Dunn, *Jesus*, 238–39.

[591] "Speaking to one another" (Eph 5:19) and "teaching and admonishing one another" (Col 3:16). See esp. the discussion on Col 3:16 below (ch. 8).

[592] The language is Dunn's (*Jesus*, 238).

this kind of singing was "solo." This text also adds a further dimension to our understanding of "speaking in tongues." Not only did one *pray* in this way, but one also *praised* God in song in this way. Hence the verbs in vv. 16–17 that pick up this theme are "bless" and "give thanks."

16 Paul now moves from his own determination to praise in both ways—in tongues to be sure, but *also* with his understanding—to their need to do especially the latter in the assembly: "Otherwise,[593] if you[594] are praising[595] God[596] by the Spirit, [meaning here, praising God in tongues in the assembly], how can another say 'Amen' to your thanksgiving,[597] since they will not know what you are saying?" Saying the (customary)[598] "Amen"[599] assumes a corporate worship setting, where this word, also taken over from the Jewish synagogue, indicated wholehearted response to and endorsement of the words of another.[600] Paul's point, the same one he has been making throughout, is unmistakable: Praising God (or praying) in tongues, even though it is by the Spirit, does not build up anyone else in the assembly (v. 17), since what is said is unintelligible.

---

[593] Gk. ἐπεί, which ordinarily is causal ("since"; cf. v. 12). For the usage here cf. 5:10 and 7:14, where it functions in a similar way.

[594] This "you" is singular; for this sudden shift to the second singular in applicational or paraenetic sections see Fee 158–60, 315–18, 330–32 on 4:1; 7:21 and 27. Probably Paul is here supposing an interlocutor, who is understood to be taking the opposite position of his own (cf. Rom 8:2).

[595] The sentence, as with v. 14, is a present general condition: "Whenever you praise God in this way, you may expect these results." The verb εὐλογέω is most frequently used in the LXX to translate the Heb. *barak*, "bless." Thus this instance is often considered to refer to specific kinds of prayers, such as the blessings in the Jewish synagogue. But that will not work since it is the verb for "praising" in tongues. Most likely it covers in a more general way both activities mentioned in v. 15.

[596] This word is not in the Greek text, but is obviously implied.

[597] Gk. εὐχαριστία; the cognate verb appears in v. 17. Thus the two verbs, εὐλογέω and εὐχαριστέω, are nearly interchangeable here, as in 10:16 and 11:24.

[598] This is implied by the use of the article τό before ἀμήν. The continuation of the practice in the early church is noted by Justin, *Apol.* 65: "When he has finished the prayers and the thanksgiving, the whole congregation present assents, saying, 'Amen.'"

[599] A borrowed word from the Hebrew, meaning "that which is sure and valid." In the NT it most often appears at the conclusion of doxologies to God or Christ. See Gal 1:5; Rom 1:25; 9:5; 11:36; 16:27; Phil 4:20; Eph 3:21; 1 Tim 1:17; 6:16; 2 Tim 4:18; Heb 13:21; 1 Pet 4:11; 5:11; Jude 25. Cf. the magnificent scene in Revelation 5, where at the conclusion of the hymns of praise to God and to the Lamb, the four living creatures say, "Amen" (v. 14). On the use of this word in early Christian worship, see H. Schlier, *TDNT* 1.336–38; and Martin, *Worship*, 36–37.

[600] See Dunn, *Jesus*, 282, who emphasizes the importance of the corporate sense of the worship, in which all joined together, both in the "ministry" of the gifts and in the response to what God was saying. The "Amen" would function as the affirmation following the "testing" of the utterances.

Paul's description of the person who cannot say the "Amen," however, is puzzling: "the one who fills the place of the ἰδιώτης." The problem is twofold: (1) whether the expression "fills the place of"[601] is to be taken literally or figuratively; and (2) what ἰδιώτης means here. The problem is complicated by two factors: (a) Although the word ordinarily means "nonexpert," hence "an ordinary person" in contrast to one who is skilled, there is also evidence that it was a technical term in religious life for nonmembers who still participated in the pagan sacrifices.[602] (b) In the present context this same person in v. 17 is referred to as not being "built up," which in Paul has to do with believers, yet the word ἰδιώτης reappears in v. 23 in close connection with unbelievers.

Those who presuppose that the word refers to the same person here and in v. 23 most often[603] consider the ἰδιώτης to be a person who stands somewhere between nonbelievers and "full-fledged Christians."[604] Often he or she is also viewed as having a special place reserved for them in the Christian assembly (thus, literally "fill the place" of the "inquirer"). But considerable difficulties attend these viewpoints. First, even though such language was used at a later time in the church for catechumens, it is probably anachronistic to assume that there were already "non-baptized converts" who had special "places" reserved for them in the early house churches. Second, the larger context seems to be against it. The concern until now has been the edification of *the church*. In v. 17 this ἰδιώτης is referred to as "the other person" who "is not edified" by hearing praise in tongues. Elsewhere in this argument such language refers to a believer. Moreover, Paul says this person is unable to say the customary "Amen" *to your thanksgiving*, which implies the whole-hearted endorsement by one who regularly affirms the praise of the living God.

The (preferable) alternative is to take the verb in a figurative sense of "one who finds him/herself in the place or role of an ἰδιώτης," with the latter word being used in its nontechnical sense to refer to such a person's inability to comprehend the tongues-speaker. This does not mean, as is often suggested, that such people do not themselves have "spiritual gifts," so that they are also being "put down" by the one speaking in tongues.[605] Rather, it refers to any and all in the community

---

[601] Gk. ὁ ἀναπληρῶν τὸν τόπον. The verb ordinarily means to "fill up," or "fill a gap, replace."

[602] See the evidence in BAGD; cf. H. Schlier, *TDNT* 3.215–17.

[603] A few consider the person to be an "outsider" (RSV) in both cases.

[604] "As a kind of proselytes or catechumens" (BAGD). This has been the traditional stance of German scholarship in general. Cf. Schlier (n. 602); see also Morris 195–96; Martin, *Spirit*, 71; "inquirer" (NIVmg).

[605] Despite the frequency of this suggestion (among others, Goudge 127, Robertson-Plummer 313, Lenski 594, Grosheide 327, Héring 151), it has almost nothing to commend it. The issue is not between those who do and do not have this gift, but between intelligibility and this gift in the assembly. Even other tongues-speakers will

who become ἰδιῶται to the tongues-speaker—perhaps in the further sense of being "untrained" (cf. Acts 4:13) in the "language" being spoken—precisely because they do not understand what is being said.[606] The reason for the singular is that it corresponds to the second person singular of the person being addressed. Thus, rather than speak to all in the second plural, Paul strengthens his case with the singular, with the person addressed representing those speaking in tongues in the community, and the "person taking the place of the unlearned" representing all the rest in the community who at any time must listen to the uninterpreted tongues without understanding. This, after all, is Paul's concern throughout the argument, and it is further supported by his own follow-up explanation in v. 17.

17 This sentence, which is joined to v. 16 with an explanatory "for," spells out why that situation is unacceptable. The contrasts are emphatic. Still keeping to the singulars, he says: "*You*, to be sure,[607] are giving thanks[608] well enough,[609] but *the other person* is not being edified." The "you" and the "other person" are the two mentioned in v. 16, the one praising God in tongues, and the one who takes the place of the "unlearned" because he or she does not understand. As in vv. 1–5 and 6–13 intelligibility and edification are tied together. In the assembly the latter cannot happen without the former. "To be sure, you are giving thanks." But that is not adequate in the assembly. What is needed in giving thanks is *intelligibility*, so that others may benefit as well.

18 Paul concludes the argument on yet another personal note, which in itself is not surprising, since both the larger section (beginning with v. 6) and the more immediate sub-paragraph (beginning with v. 14) both begin on such a note.[610] What is surprising is its *content*: "I thank

---

be ἰδιῶται in the sense that Paul is using the word, since neither will they be able to understand what is being said by the others.

[606]Cf. Godet 282: "Paul thus designates all the members of the Church, because in this situation they play the part of unintelligent hearers in relation to the glossolalete." See also Barrett 321; Carson, *Showing*, 104–5.

[607]Gk. μέν, followed in this case by the stronger ἀλλ' (= to be sure . . . but).

[608]Gk. εὐχαριστεῖς. On the basis of vv. 15 and 16 this is a straightforward statement of fact: "You are giving thanks well enough." Cf. Barrett 321, who is one of the few English translators to catch this: "You indeed are giving thanks well enough." The subjunctive rendering of the NIV is unwarranted—and prejudicial: "you may be giving thanks well enough."

[609]There is no cause to make the καλῶς ironical here, as Robertson-Plummer 314 suggest. That fails to take v. 15 as well as the language of "praise" and "thanksgiving" to God associated with this gift seriously.

[610]As with v. 14, this one is also asyndetic; the argument concludes on the same abrupt note with which it began.

God I speak in tongues more than[611] all of you." Indeed, one wonders who is the more greatly surprised, the Corinthians or the contemporary reader.

It has been common to treat the earlier personal references as rhetorical and therefore hypothetical; this one, however, indicates that those references do indeed reflect Paul's own spirituality. Along with vv. 14–15 and 2 Cor 12:1–10, this assertion lets us in on aspects of Paul's personal piety for which we otherwise would have been quite unprepared.[612] Apparently his life of personal devotion was regularly given to praying, singing, and praising in tongues. Granted that this is probably somewhat hyperbolic;[613] it thereby only makes the reality the more emphatic. The fact that he can say it at all, and say it as a matter for which he can thank God, and say it without fear of contradiction to some who are quite taken by this gift, must be taken seriously.

If our suggestion has been correct, that there is an undercurrent of apologetic in these references, where Paul is both defending his own status with regard to their criterion—the gift of tongues—but also rejecting their use of it, then these sentences are intended to fall as something of a bombshell in Corinth. Despite what they may think, he can assert— with thanksgiving to God![614]—"I speak in tongues more than all of you." His concern throughout has been with uninterpreted tongues in the assembly, because they cannot edify the church. With this sentence he outmaneuvers the Corinthians altogether. He herewith affirms their gift in the strongest of terms; but he does so in order to reorder their thinking about what was going on in the assembly.

Thus this sentence corresponds to the first clause in v. 17. "When praising in tongues, you are thanking God well enough. Indeed, I do this more than all of you. But what goes on in church is another story altogether." Hence v. 19 will be his own personal response to v. 18, which in turn corresponds to the second clause of v. 17—the edification of others in the assembly.

---

[611] Gk. μᾶλλον, used with the genitive of comparison, rather than the customary ἤ. One cannot tell whether the intent is primarily qualitative (Bruce 132, "a richer endowment") or quantitative (with greater frequency). Although it is not necessary to decide, it is probably the latter.

[612] These passing references in the Corinthian correspondence should give us reason to pause whenever we think we know about as much about the apostle as can be known. More likely the extant correspondence is but the tip of the iceberg.

[613] After all, one may legitimately ask how he knew, to which the answer would be that he didn't.

[614] This asseveration is probably something of a mild oath, a way of calling on God to witness to the absolute truthfulness of what follows (cf. his use of "I tell the truth, I am not lying" in Gal 1:20; Rom 9:1; 1 Tim 2:7; cf. also 2 Cor 1:23; 11:10). At the same time, it also says something about his own attitude toward this gift.

19 Having set them up with the surprising words of v. 18, he now drops the other shoe. When it comes to tongues as such, he has just asserted, I surpass all of you. But so what? The crucial question is not whether one speaks in tongues or not, but *what is appropriate in the assembly*. Heretofore one may only have suspected that Paul was making distinctions between private devotion and public worship; this sentence makes it explicit.

The contrasts, which return in part to the language of v. 15, are stark. In church[615] "five words with my mind" are to be preferred to "ten thousand[616] words in a tongue."[617] Only the language for edification has changed: "to instruct[618] others."[619] This language suggests that "the intelligible words" in this sentence are moving away from the prayer and singing (praising) of vv. 15–16, including the interpretation of such praise, back toward the other intelligible gifts mentioned in v. 6.

Thus the section has come full circle. If Paul came[620] to them as they wished, speaking in tongues, it would not benefit them. He must speak in intelligible ways. Now he affirms that he does indeed speak in tongues—more than all of them—but in church, so that others might be instructed, he would rather speak just five words that could be understood than countless words in a tongue. The obvious implication is that they should wish to do the same.

1 Corinthians 14:20–25[621]

[20]*Brothers and sisters, stop being children in your thinking, on the contrary, be infants regarding evil, but in your thinking be grown-ups.* [21]*In the Law it is written:*

---

[615] There is no article in the Greek. "In church" is to be preferred to the "in the church" of the NIV and others as the more appropriate English idiom for the actual gathering together of God's people; in contemporary English the addition of the article tends to move the idiom toward the concept of the *place* of gathering, which is totally foreign to its sense here.

[616] Gk. μυρίους (cf. 4:15), the adjective for "ten thousand," the largest word for numbers available in Greek. As an adjective it means "countless, innumerable, tens of thousands."

[617] This use of the singular γλώσσῃ, following immediately on the plural γλώσσαις in v. 18, is the certain indication that there is no real significance to the singular or plural. It scarcely now means "a foreign language"; probably it implies "in any given instance of speaking in tongues."

[618] Gk. κατηχέω (cf. Gal 6:6; Rom 2:18); not the ordinary word for "teach"; rather it has to do with "informing" or "instructing" another in religious matters.

[619] Paul now shifts back to the plural from the singulars of vv. 16–17.

[620] Or perhaps "had come." This may refer to their present judgment of him, as they reflect back on his presence with them in light of their "new" criteria.

[621] *Bibliography:* W. A. **Grudem**, "1 Corinthians 14.20–25: Prophecy and Tongues as Signs of God's Attitudes," *WTJ* 41 (1979) 381–96 (repr. in *Gift*, 185–210);

"With other[622] tongues and through the lips of others[623]
I will speak to this people,
but even then they will not obey me," says the Lord.

[22]*So then, tongues are for a sign, not for believers but for unbelievers; prophecy,*
however, is not for unbelievers but for believers. [23]*Therefore, if the whole*
church comes together at the same place and everyone speaks in tongues, and
some who are uninstructed or unbelievers come in, will they not say that you
are mad? [24]*But if an unbeliever or uninstructed person comes in while every-*
body is prophesying, such people will be convicted by all, are called to account
by all, [25]*and[624] the secrets of their hearts will be laid bare, and thus falling on*
their faces they will worship God, exclaiming, "God is truly among you!"

Paul is still challenging the Corinthians' use of uninterpreted
tongues in the assembly. Not only are they incapable of edifying the
church, but, he now goes on to explain, they have disastrous effects on
unbelievers as well. Despite some notorious difficulties involving v. 22,
the *structure* of the present argument makes it plain that the single issue
being taken up is the effect of tongues on unbelievers:[625]

[20]Exhortation:	Redirect your thinking (about the function of tongues)			
[21]OT text:	Tongues do not lead people to obedience			
[22]Application:	So then —			
Assertion 1–	Tongues	a sign	not for believers	A
			but for unbelievers	B
Assertion 2–	Prophecy	[a sign]	not for unbelievers	B
			but for believers	A
[23]Illustration 1–	Effect of tongues (1)		on unbelievers	(B)
[24-25]Illustration 2–	Effect of prophecy (2)		on unbelievers	(B)

B. C. **Johanson**, "Tongues, a Sign for Unbelievers?: A Structural and Exegetical Study
of I Corinthians xiv. 20–25," *NTS* 25 (1979) 180–203; P. **Roberts**, "A Sign—Christian
or Pagan?" *ExpT* 90 (1979) 199–203; O. P. **Robertson**, "Tongues: Sign of Covenantal
Curse and Blessing," *WTJ* 38 (1975) 45–53; R. **Schnackenburg**, "Christian Adulthood
According to the Apostle Paul," *CBQ* 25 (1963) 365; **Sweet**, "Sign."

[622]NIV, "through men of strange tongues." Apparently this is in the interest of
OT parallelism; but it is not what Paul said—or intended. His emphasis is not on *"men
of* strange tongues," but on the phenomenon of "other tongues."

[623]In place of ἑτέρων (א A B Ψ 0201 0243 6 33 81 104 326 1739 2464 pc), P[46] D[s]
F G Maj lat co have ἑτέροις, making it modify "lips" and thus equivalent to
ἑτερογλώσσοις (other tongues and other lips). As Zuntz (*Text*, 174n4) points out, this
is less suited to Paul's argument, which implies by ἑτέρων "that 'others' (i.e., the
believers) will vainly speak in tongues to the nonbelievers."

[624]The MajT, against all the early evidence, adds a premature καὶ οὕτως to the
argument (see the next clause).

[625]Cf. the structural analysis in Johanson, "Tongues," 186–90.

Although one is led to expect something else from the two assertions, Paul's basic concern is easily discernible, from the flow of thought and from the fact that both illustrations deal only with unbelievers. As in the preceding section it has to do with the effect of unintelligibility in the corporate setting. Uninterpreted tongues *do not edify believers*, he has just argued (6–19); *neither do they benefit unbelievers* who may visit their assembly, he now argues. Indeed, the effect would be quite the opposite. As the illustration in v. 23 shows, instead of leading to conviction of sin and thus to repentance, the use of tongues in the assembly turns out to fulfill the word of Isa 28:11–12 (cited in v. 21), that "even then [by speaking in tongues] they will not obey me." But that is not the final word. As with believers, however, prophecy will have the opposite effect; it will lead to their conversion.

Thus even though in v. 22 Paul speaks of the effect of both tongues and prophecy on *believers*, he has already dealt with that, so in this paragraph he speaks *only* to how each affects *unbelievers*.[626] Although this analysis does not resolve all the difficulties with the language of v. 22, it does indicate the direction in which the resolution must lie.

20 Another turn in the argument is marked by the vocative ἀδελφοί (cf. v. 6) and by the rather abrupt appearance of the exhortation to stop being children[627] in their thinking.[628] Some have seen this as related to 13:10–11 and have thus argued that Paul considered speaking in tongues itself as childish behavior to be outgrown,[629] yet both the preceding argument—especially vv. 15 and 18—and the structure of this sentence suggest otherwise.[630] With the familiar A-B-A pattern of argument, Paul uses this imagery to appeal in two directions: that they cease being like children *in their thinking*; and that they be as innocent as babies *in their behavior*. In Paul's sentence this is the basic contrast, brought out in

---

[626] Cf. Johanson, "Tongues," 187: "The main concern of *vv.* 21–25 has to do with the relation of tongues to unbelievers in contrast to the relation of prophecy also to unbelievers." In an otherwise helpful study, Roberts, "Sign," makes a crucial leap of logic so that the concern turns out to be with the Corinthians themselves rather than with the ineffectiveness of unintelligibility in the community.

[627] Gk. παιδία, the only occurrence of this word in Paul; in 3:1–2 he uses νήπιος (cf. 13:11), the verb form of which appears in the next clause.

[628] Gk. φρεσίν (only here in the NT), referring to understanding or discernment. Cf. the similar appeal to their thinking sensibly that begins the final prohibition against idolatry in 10:15. Although this exhortation begins the paragraph, it undoubtedly is intended also to apply to all that has been said since v. 1. Some (e.g., Findlay 908; Martin, *Spirit*, 72) break the paragraph after v. 20.

[629] As recently as Martin, *Spirit*, 71.

[630] Cf. Schnackenburg, "Adulthood," 365: "Not that glossolaly itself is childish behavior, but rather it is childish to have an unreasonable preference for this gift of the Spirit."

the first two clauses, while the third balances the first as its opposite. Thus (literally):

Do not	be children	in your thinking;[631]		A
but[632]	be infants[633]	in evil;		B
rather (δέ)		in your thinking	be adults.	A

Similar to the usage of this same imagery in 3:1–2, there is probably a degree of irony intended.[634] Their childishness consists of *thinking* improperly about tongues, that it serves as evidence of their new transcendent spirituality and thus marks off the spiritual quality of their gatherings,[635] while they actually evidence all kinds of ethical/behavioral aberrations.

In the context of the OT passage Paul invokes, the prophet Isaiah prefaces the cited words with this rhetorical question: "To whom is he explaining this message? To children weaned from their milk?" In Isaiah this was probably spoken to the prophet by his mockers. It seems likely that Paul has this context in mind; for him the Corinthians are in danger of playing the role of those "children" who rejected the word of the Lord. Thus this exhortation gets them to reconsider their own evaluation of tongues and at the same time to prepare the way for the final argument against unintelligibility in the community.

21 Paul begins the redirecting of their thinking by adapting a passage from Isa 28:11–12, which he introduces as a citation from "the

---

[631] In each case this is a dative of reference.

[632] Gk. ἀλλά, which with the preceding μή indicates that *Paul's* contrasts lie here. Otherwise Johanson, "Tongues," 186, who sees the second clause as parenthetical.

[633] Gk. νηπιάζετε; probably no significance is to be attached to the differences between παιδία and νήπιος, especially since in 13:11 Paul refers to thinking like a νήπιος (infant). The fluidity of Paul's images is reflected in his positive use of the "infant" metaphor here, which was negative in 3:1–2 and neutral in 13:11. Here it implies the need for innocence with regard to evil.

[634] Because of the abrupt nature of the transition from v. 19 to v. 20, R. M. Grant suggested that Paul is taking up another topic from Corinth, i.e., their justification for their "childish behavior" as having "the sanction of the Lord's command," as found in Mark 10:15 and parallels ("Like Children," *HTR* 39 [1946] 71–73). The possibility that Paul is taking on their own point of view here seems viable, but more likely in the form of irony than in direct refutation of an alleged use of a Jesus word.

[635] See the introductions to chs. 12–14 and to 14:1–25, as well as the discussion on 13:1. As can be seen, it fits again with the overall argument of the letter. Johanson, "Tongues," and Sweet, "Sign," presuppose that this paragraph, as well as the whole of chs. 12–14, is dealing with internecine strife between glossolalists and prophets. This view fails at a number of significant points; this presupposition, which in both cases is integral to their respective analysis of the paragraph, mitigates what are otherwise some helpful insights.

Law."[636] The citation itself is not precise;[637] it seems to have been chosen
for two interrelated reasons: the occurrence of the language "other
tongues"[638] and the fact that in the OT context this "speaking in tongues"
by foreigners served as judgment against those who would not hear
straight talk (from the prophet). To underscore his concerns Paul adapts
the Isaiah passage in four ways. (1) He inverts the order of "stammering
lips" and "other tongues" to put his interest, "other tongues," in first
position. (2) He changes "stammering lips" to "the lips of others"; the
"others" now being the Corinthian believers, whose speaking in tongues
would have a deleterious effect on unbelievers. (3) In keeping with the
MT, but against the LXX, Paul alters "the Lord will speak" to "I will speak"
and concludes with the formula, "says the Lord," probably to increase
its impact on the Corinthians.[639] (4) Most significantly, he skips a considerable section in the Isaiah passage, picking up at the end of v. 12,
where he modifies "and they would not hear (ἀκούω)," referring to the
intelligible words of the Lord, to "and even so [referring now to the 'other
tongues'] they *will not obey* (εἰσακούω) me." In Paul's context this refers
to the outsiders of v. 23, who on hearing the Corinthians' speaking in
tongues would declare them mad. For Paul such a reaction by unbelievers would thus "fulfill" this "word of the Lord"; tongues will not lead
them to obedience. To the contrary, unintelligibility leads to their judgment—in a time of grace when they need to hear a clear word about Christ.

22 With the strong inferential conjunction, "so then,"[640] Paul de-
duces two antithetical assertions from the Isaiah passage just quoted.[641]
But what he says has become a notorious crux. The problem is twofold:

---

[636] On the use of this formula in Paul, see Fee 406–9 on 9:9. Citing from the
prophets as "in the Law" reflects Paul's Jewish heritage (cf. Rom 3:19; John 10:34).
Cf. W. Gutbrod, *TDNT* 4.1036–78.

[637] Paul follows neither the LXX nor the MT, although he is closer to the latter.
Since there are some correspondences between this citation and the later (ca. 100
years) translation of Aquila (in the combined form ἑτερόγλωσσος, and in the inversion
of "tongues" and "lips," including the form χείλεσιν ἑτέρων), it is possible that Paul
and Aquila both depended on an earlier form of Greek text no longer available. See
the argument in Harrisville, "Study," 42–45.

[638] Gk. ἐν ἑτερογλώσσοις; only here in the NT. The LXX has διὰ γλώσσας ἑτέρας
(cf. Acts 2:4: ἑτέραις γλώσσαις).

[639] On this usage, see Ellis, *Prophecy*, 182–87. He advances the (highly speculative)
hypothesis that this formula may indicate the utterances of Christian prophets.

[640] Gk. ὥστε; in 1 Corinthians, see 3:7, 21; 4:5; 5:8; 7:38; 10:12; 11:27, 33; 14:39;
15:58. For this usage see C. F. D. Moule, *An Idiom Book of New Testament Greek* (2d
ed.; Cambridge: University Press, 1963) 144. Johanson, "Tongues," 189, considers it
consecutive, but his own discussion implies otherwise.

[641] Martin, *Spirit*, 72, would resolve the difficulties by viewing v. 22 as a midrash
on v. 21, without its pointing forward to vv. 23–25. But this seems to break down in
light of the structural analysis presented above.

(1) the meaning of "sign," including whether he intended it to be repeated for the second assertion, and if so, what it also meant there; and (2) how to square what is said here with the illustrations that follow,[642] especially the second assertion with the second illustration.[643] As noted above, the solution to this lies chiefly in the recognition that Paul's point in the paragraph is made in vv. 23–25 and especially in the way v. 23 "fulfills" the Isaiah passage. This means that, contrary to many interpretations, this text (v. 22) needs to be understood in light of what follows, not the other way around.

The first assertion flows directly out of the quote: "Tongues are for a sign[644] not for[645] believers but for unbelievers." Although it cannot be finally proven, the flow of the argument from v. 20, including the strong "so then" of this sentence, suggests that Paul is setting up this antithesis with the Corinthians' own point of view in mind.[646] That is, "In contrast to what you think, this word of the Lord from Isaiah indicates that tongues are *not* meant as a sign for believers. They are not, as you make them, the divine evidence of being πνευματικός or of the presence of God in your assembly. To the contrary, in the public gathering, uninterpreted tongues function as a sign for *un*believers." The question for us is, what kind of sign? In light of v. 21, for which this is the inferential deduction,

---

[642]Johanson, "Tongues," 190–91, has made the helpful distinction that the assertions express the relation of tongues and prophecy to the two groups in terms of *function*, whereas the OT citation and the illustrations do so in terms of *effect*.

[643]This is so severe that J. B. Phillips, without textual warrant, opted for radical surgery and transposed "believer" and "unbeliever" in his translation. He noted: "This is the sole instance of the translator's departing from the accepted text. He felt bound to conclude, from the sense of the next three verses, that we have here either a slip of the pen on the part of Paul, or, more probably, a copyist's error" (346). Cf. Parry 205, who prefers to see v. 22 as a gloss.

[644]Gk. εἰς σημεῖον; the NIV translates "are a sign," a rendering also favored by Grudem, *Gift*, 192–93, esp. n. 23. The supporting evidence in its favor, however, is basically Semitic—even the passages in Paul that are mustered as evidence are all citations of the LXX (e.g., 1 Cor 6:16; 15:45). More likely the preposition carries its more ordinary telic force (= tongues are meant as a sign), as Moule 70; Johanson, "Tongues," 190n5; cf. 1 Cor 4:3—although the meaning is not greatly affected.

[645]Dative of advantage/disadvantage.

[646]This has also been suggested, but with differing agenda in mind, by Sweet, "Sign," 241; Johanson, "Tongues," 193–94; and Roberts, "Sign," 201. Johanson sees the *whole* of v. 22, including the internal antitheses in each assertion, as the point of view of the Corinthian glossalalists, which Paul is reproducing in the form of rhetorical questions. Thus σημεῖον is positive (because it expresses their outlook); Paul's response is found in the illustrations of vv. 23–25, which stand in opposition to the glossalalists, in favor of those who prefer prophecy. Although this has some attractive features, it finally breaks down both grammatically (Paul's use of ὥστε in 1 Corinthians—the alleged analogous usage in Gal 4:16 is not similar) and contextually (there is otherwise not a hint in this chapter that Paul is responding to an in-house division over this matter—not to mention that in chs. 1–4 where there is internal division Paul refuses to take sides).

"sign" in this first sentence can function only in a negative way. That is, it is a "sign" that functions to the disadvantage of unbelievers, not to their advantage.

Paul is using the word in a way that is quite in keeping with his Judaic background, where "sign" functions as an expression of God's attitude;[647] something "signifies" to Israel either God's disapproval[648] or pleasure.[649] In this case, his disapproval is in view; but not in the sense that God *intends* unbelievers during this time of grace to receive his judgment. To the contrary, tongues *function* that way as the result of their *effect* on the unbeliever, as the illustration in v. 23 will clarify. Because tongues are unintelligible, unbelievers receive no revelation from God; they cannot thereby be brought to faith. Thus by regarding the work of the Spirit—tongues—as madness, they are destined for divine judgment—just as in the OT passage Paul has quoted. This, of course, is not the divine intent for such people; hence, Paul's urgency is for the Corinthians to cease thinking like children, to stop the public use of tongues, since it only drives the unbeliever away rather than leading him or her to faith.

With a balancing antithetical clause Paul adds that "prophecy, however," also functions as a sign,[650] but "not for unbelievers, but for believers." With this sentence he resumes the contrast between tongues and prophecy that was last expressed in vv. 1–6 (although it is alluded to in v. 19 in anticipation of this argument). This is also the clause where all the difficulties have arisen, because in the illustration that corresponds to this assertion (vv. 24–25) he does not so much as mention believers, but indicates only how prophecy affects unbelievers. Further, he does so in a way that makes one think that it is really a sign for *them*, that is, to *their* advantage.

The solution again lies first of all in the nature of the conflict between Paul and the Corinthians. Contrary to their preference for tongues, he is asserting that it is prophecy, with its intelligibility and revelatory character, that functions as the sign of God's approval, of God's presence in their midst.[651] The evidence of this is to be found in the very way that it affects unbelievers. By the revelatory word of prophecy unbelievers are

---

[647]For the argument in favor of this viewpoint see Dunn, *Jesus*, 230–32, and Grudem, *Gift*, 194–202 (apparently independently of Dunn, given the nature of the addendum to n. 25, p. 196).

[648]See, e.g., Num 26:10 (those who died in Korah's rebellion became a sign); cf. Deut 28:46. See further, Grudem, *Gift*, 195.

[649]E.g., Gen 9:12 (the rainbow); Exod 12:13 (the blood on the doorpost).

[650]This is not specifically said in the Greek text; but the sentence is most likely an ellipsis, since the verb εἰσιν is omitted as well. This means that the two sets of antitheses are to be understood as in perfect balance. Cf. Grudem, *Gift*, 193–94.

[651]Barrett 324 sees prophecy as a sign of "judgment" on the believers, since they prefer tongues to the very kind of intelligibility that can lead to salvation.

convicted of their sins, and falling on their faces before God they will exclaim that "God is really among you!" That exclamation as response to prophecy is a "sign" for believers, the indication of God's favor resting upon them.[652]

Thus, tongues and prophecy *function* as "signs" in two different ways, precisely in accord with the *effect* each will have on unbelievers who happen into the Christian assembly.

23 With this sentence and the next Paul proceeds[653] to illustrate the two assertions of v. 22 in terms of the effect of each on unbelievers. Both sentences take the same form: a present general condition in which the protasis expresses the hypothetical situation of the gathered church into which unbelievers enter and the apodosis expresses their response—first to tongues, then to prophecy. Although hypothetical, and probably overstated, the protases must nonetheless be taken seriously as real possibilities; otherwise the argument is to no avail. Thus these illustrations offer several insights into an early Christian gathering for worship.

(1) The language for their assembling together is nearly identical to that in 11:20: "the whole church comes together at the same place." Along with the salutation[654] and the evidence from Rom 16:23[655] this implies that all the believers from all the house churches met together in some way.[656] Given the limitations of size in even the most commodious of well-to-do homes,[657] does this imply that the church was smaller than we might tend to think? Or is it possible that one of the houses was considerably larger than archaeology has uncovered in Corinth to this point? We simply do not know.

(2) Both this text and v. 26, as well as 11:4–5, where women are praying and prophesying in the assembly, indicate that at least one expression of their worship was "charismatic" in the twofold sense that

---

[652] Cf. such OT passages as Isa 29:10; Mic 3:6; Lam 2:9, for indications that the absence of prophecy is a sign of judgment or of the loss of God's favor.

[653] The illustrations are joined to v. 22 by means of an inferential οὖν. As with the two assertions, the two illustrations are connected with an adversative δέ (on the other hand).

[654] See 1:2; the letter is written to *the* church in Corinth.

[655] Writing from Corinth, Paul sends greetings from "Gaius, host to me and to *the whole church*."

[656] Cf. Banks, *Paul's Idea*, 38, who argues that the use of ὅλη (whole) here implies a more regular meeting of smaller groups. Parry 207 allows that it could refer to "the whole of any particular congregation," but that seems doubtful in light of all the evidence.

[657] See Murphy-O'Connor, *Corinth*, 153–61; present archaeological evidence indicates that the largest house in Corinth could have accommodated only 30 to 50 guests.

there was general participation by all the members, including the women, and that there was considerable expression of the more spontaneous gifts of utterance.

Two matters should be noted in regard to the language "and all speak in tongues." (a) Even though this is probably overstated, one can hardly escape the implication that *all* of the believers could potentially do so. This means that Paul's point in 12:29–30, as we noted there, was to discourage "all" from doing so; he did not mean that only a few could be so gifted (cf. v. 5). The same is true of prophecy. (b) Again, even though it is overstatement, this is probably a generally realistic description of the current scene in Corinth. Not that all were necessarily speaking in tongues at the same time; nonetheless, the guidelines in vv. 27–33 imply that many were doing so on a regular basis.[658] If so, then not only did the unintelligibility lead to the exclamation of "madness," but so also would the general chaos of so much individualized worship with no concern for the general edification of the body as a whole.

(3) These gatherings of the "whole church" were also accessible to unbelievers. The term "unbeliever" (ἄπιστος) is the same as in v. 22, making it certain that these verses illustrate those assertions. Added to "unbeliever" in both instances is the word ἰδιώτης from v. 16. The close ties of this word with "unbeliever" and the nature of their response to tongues and prophecy indicate that such people are not believers. It is also doubtful for the same reasons that it is a technical term for an "inquirer," who stands in some kind of halfway position. As before, it carries the nontechnical sense of anyone who is "unlearned," in this case "untutored" with regard to the Christian faith.[659] Indeed, it is possible that Paul did not intend to designate a second kind of person at all;[660] rather, he simply begins his description of unbelievers in general with this word. Thus, the visiting "unbeliever" is also "untutored" in the faith. Paul may very well have in mind an unbelieving spouse accompanying the believer to his or her place of worship. Such a person is both outside of Christ and as yet uninstructed in Christ.

---

[658] So also Barrett 324. Robertson-Plummer 317 object on the basis of v. 24, that since πάντες cannot mean "all simultaneously" there, it also cannot here. But that has Paul's argument in reverse. Verse 24 receives its *form* from v. 23; it is not necessary to think that Paul would have envisioned "all prophesying" to put them in disarray, which apparently he did of their speaking in tongues.

[659] Cf. Findlay 910: "unacquainted with Christianity." Since the term in both cases is nontechnical, there can be no objection to its referring to believers in v. 16, who are "unacquainted" with the meaning of the "tongue" and therefore cannot say the "Amen," and to unbelievers here, who are quite "untutored" with regard to the Christian faith and would see their corporate tongues-speaking as "madness."

[660] So Barrett 324, who joins the two words into one by translating "unbelieving outsiders." Cf. Conzelmann 243.

(4) The response of the unbeliever to the community's collective speaking in tongues is to equate the Christian gathering with the mania that attended some of the mystery cults.[661] "Madness,"[662] they will say. For Paul such a response is totally unworthy of the gospel of Christ. Hence tongues fulfills the prophetic word of Isaiah, that with "other tongues" God will speak to "this people," yet even so they will not obey. This is Paul's final word about uninterpreted tongues in the assembly; with it he is once more urging them to stop such activity. Not only do tongues alone not edify the congregation; neither are they the "evidence" the Corinthians think them to be. To the contrary this response would be the sure evidence that they have quite missed what it means to be God's "Spirit people" in the eschatological age that has dawned with Christ.

24–25 Once more prophecy is set forth as the alternative to the unintelligibility of uninterpreted tongues. In this case it is viewed as leading directly to the conversion of the visiting unbeliever. This passage in particular implies that prophesying is *potentially available* to all believers, since all are Spirit people.[663] That is, Paul does not say, "If the prophets all prophesy," but, "If *all* prophesy . . . the unbeliever will be convicted by *all* [not all the prophets] . . . and he or she will be judged by *all*." The nature of this argumentation excludes the option that this gift was limited to a group of authoritative people who were known in the community as "the prophets." Again, as with tongues, it does not mean that Paul expects everyone to prophesy; it does imply the extensive involvement of the whole community in the worship, especially in the Spirit manifestations of inspired utterance.

In contrast to the negative response in v. 23, Paul offers a considerable description of the unbeliever's response to such prophesying. One cannot tell from what is said whether these prophecies would be similar to those in v. 3 that edified believers, or whether some of the prophecies would be more specifically directed toward the unbeliever as such— more likely the latter. In either case, quite in keeping with the OT view of prophecy, Paul understands the inspired word to penetrate deeply into the moral consciousness of the hearers. There are several dimensions to this.

---

[661] See Fee 498n23 and 509n75, on 11:2–6.

[662] Gk. μαίνεσθε; cf. John 10:20; Acts 26:24, 25. The cognate noun is μανία, which occurs in various texts reflecting the ecstasies of the mysteries. E.g., Pausanius 2.7.5: "These women they say are sacred to Dionysus and maddened by his inspiration"; cf. Herodotus 4.79.

[663] This kind of language expresses the prophetic ideal that in the coming age of the Spirit all of God's people will be "prophets" (cf. Joel 2:28–30 and esp. the citation on the Day of Pentecost in Acts 2:17–18).

First, the unbeliever is "convicted[664] by all, is called to account[665] by all." These two verbs together imply the deep probing work of the Holy Spirit in people's lives, whereby they have their sins exposed and thus are called to account before the living God. Lying behind the word "convicted" is the OT view that one is exposed before the living God through the prophetic word; inherent in such "exposure" is the call to repentance,[666] the summons to have one's exposed sins forgiven by a merciful God.

The second word appeared previously in this letter to describe the Corinthians' "examination" of Paul and his apostleship (4:3–4; 9:3); it was also used in 2:14–15 to describe the proper sphere of activity for the "spiritual person," where it means something like "discern." Perhaps there is an intended deflection by the use of this word here. Instead of "examining" Paul on their grounds of spirituality, they should seek to prophesy in the assembly so that the proper "examining" might take place, namely, that of the Spirit in the heart of the unbeliever, bringing him or her to a place of repentance.

The result of this convicting process begins as an internal work in the sinner: "the secrets of his or her heart will be laid bare."[667] The emphasis here is on the revelatory aspect of the prophetic utterance.[668] The story of the Fall suggests that one of its first effects on humanity is the great sense of need to hide from the living God; it is the folly of our sinfulness that allows us to think we can. Thus, one of the sure signs of the presence of God in the believing community is this deep work of the Spirit, whereby through prophetic revelation the curtains are pulled back and the secrets of the heart laid bare.[669] No wonder the Corinthians preferred tongues; it not only gave them a sense of being more truly "spiritual," but it was safer!

All of this suggests that some expressions of prophecy, besides being directed toward believers for *their* edification (v. 3), are also directed toward the unbelieving to expose them before God so as to be called to

---

[664]Gk. ἐλέγχεται; in Paul cf. Eph 5:11, 13; 1 Tim 5:20; Titus 1:9, 13; 2:15; 2 Tim 4:2. Cf. also John 16:8–11. For a discussion of biblical usage see F. Büchsel, *TDNT* 2.473–76.

[665]Gk. ἀνακρίνω; only in 1 Corinthians (10x) in Paul. See the discussion on 2:15.

[666]Büchsel, *TDNT* 2.474: It means "to show someone his sin and to summon him to repentance." Hence the NIV, "he will be convinced by all that he is a sinner."

[667]Cf. 4:5, where nearly identical language describes the eschatological judgment of God. Now he uses it to refer to the judgment that takes place in the present through the Spirit.

[668]The Greek for "laid bare" is φανερός; the adjective of the verb "to reveal," which according to 2:10–12 is one of the activities of the Spirit.

[669]It is a biblical axiom that sin is first of all a matter of the heart. Therefore, conversion also includes not only the forgiveness of one's sins, but the regenerating work of the Spirit in the heart, from whence are the issues of life.

him. Here is another evidence that the "Spirit" knows all things—not only the "depths of God" (2:11) and the deep groanings of the believer's heart (Rom 8:26), but also the deep recesses of the hearts of those who do not believe. He exposes only that he might also convict and thereby effectively apply the grace of God that has effected salvation through Christ. Thus the Spirit plays the leading role from beginning to end in terms of the *experience* of grace.

The final result of such exposure before God is conversion, which is what Paul's language unmistakably intends. The language is thoroughly steeped in the OT. First, "they will thus fall on their faces[670] and worship God." This is biblical language for obeisance and worship. That Paul intends this to mean conversion is confirmed in the final exclamation, which is a conscious reflection of Isa 45:14 (cf. Zech 8:23): God, speaking through the prophet, says that the Egyptians will come over to you and "will worship" before you and say, "surely God is with you." Paul simply changes the singular "with you," referring to Israel, into a plural, "among you," referring to the gathered community.[671] This final confession of the unbeliever is thus the "sign" that prophecy is for "believers"; it is evidence of God's favor resting on his people.

With these powerful words Paul concludes his argument with the Corinthians against both the use of uninterpreted tongues in the assembly and the thinking that lay behind it. In the gathered community he insists that only what is intelligible is permissible—because what is intelligible, especially prophecy, edifies God's people and leads to the conversion of others. But this is only part of the problem. Their use of tongues was apparently also disorderly; so to that question he now turns before he concludes the argument by directly confronting them over his right to order them and over who in fact is truly πνευματικός.

Along with the great need for local communities to be edified, the reason set forth in this paragraph ought to be sufficient to lead the church to pray for the renewal of the prophetic Spirit in its ongoing life. It is not simply the presence of prophecy that signifies God's presence among his gathered people, but the powerful revealing work of the Spirit that convicts of sin and leads to repentance. Perhaps in our domestication of the Spirit we have also settled for a "safer" expression of worship, one in which very few are ever led to exclaim that "surely God is among you." When one has seen that actually take place, then it leads to prayer

---

[670] Gk. πέσων ἐπὶ πρόσωπον; in the LXX see, e.g., Gen 17:3, 17; Lev 9:24; Num 16:22; Ezek 11:13; and many others. In the NT see Matt 17:6; 26:39 (of Jesus in Gethsemane); Luke 5:12; 17:16; Rev 7:11; 11:16.

[671] The thoroughly biblical language used throughout vv. 24–25 to describe the effect of prophecy on the unbeliever is further evidence that this phenomenon in Paul is to be understood in light of his Jewish heritage rather than similar phenomena in Hellenism.

that v. 1 might be the church's ongoing portion: Love, Spirit manifestations, especially prophecy.

1 CORINTHIANS 14:26–33

[26]*What then, brothers and sisters? When you come together, each one*[672] *has
a hymn, has a teaching, has a revelation, has a tongue, has an interpretation.
Let all things happen for edification.* [27]*Whether anyone speaks in a tongue, let
there be two or at the most three, one at a time, and let one interpret.* [28]*But
if ever there is no interpreter, let the speaker be silent in church and let him
or her speak by himself and to God.*

[29]*And let two or three prophets speak, and let the others discern.* [30]*And if
a revelation comes to another who is seated, let the first be silent.* [31]*For you
can all prophesy one by one so that all may learn and all be encouraged.* [32]*And
the spirits*[673] *of the prophets are subject to the prophets.* [33]*For God is not a
God of disorder but of peace, as in all the congregations of the saints.*

If this material were in a nonpolemical letter, it would look very
much like instruction on the regulation of Spirit utterances. Its appearance here, however, indicates that, even though instructional, it is primarily correctional, especially in light of the argument that has preceded
and the rhetoric that follows (vv. 36–38).

The basic problem Paul has with the Corinthians' singular zeal for
the gift of tongues has now been addressed (vv. 1–25); because speaking
in tongues is unintelligible, it neither edifies the saints nor converts the
sinner. But that is not the only concern. What was hinted at in v. 23 is
implied more strongly in vv. 27–28. Apparently there was a degree of
disorderliness to their speaking in tongues as well. Although the evidence
is not conclusive, the present argument suggests that more than one of
them was used to speaking forth at the same time. Thus there appears
also to have been a high degree of individualized worship in their corporate gatherings. Paul, however, does not press this latter theme here, so
one must be duly cautious. His antidote is to offer guidelines for regulation, which taken together suggest orderliness, self-control, and concern
for others.

The opening paragraph of this section thus concludes the argument
of the chapter. He begins with a descriptive exhortation (v. 26): Each one
has something to contribute, and everything must be done to edify. This

---

[672]The Westerns and MajT have the understandable, but secondary, addition of
ὑμῶν. It is missing in P[46] ℵ* A B 0201 33 81 630 1175 1739 1881 pc, an "omission" that
can scarcely be accounted for, if ὑμῶν were original.

[673]A few MSS (D F G Ψ* 1241ˢ pc a b syᵖ) try to alleviate the difficulty of this
plural by making it singular—although in some cases this could be the result of an
accidental dropping of a τα.

is followed by guidelines, first for tongues and interpretation (vv. 27–28) and then for prophecy and discernment (vv. 29–31). The concluding word on prophecies (vv. 32–33) probably functions as a concluding word for the whole section. Christian inspiration is not out of control, for God himself is not like that; and this holds for all the congregations of the saints.

The two regulatory sections are quite similar in structure and content: He begins with a word about the number of speakers (two or three at the most); they must speak "one at a time"; tongues must be interpreted and prophecy "discerned"; under certain conditions silence is enjoined; and each concludes with words similar to the instruction in vv. 2–4 (without interpretation the tongues-speaker must speak privately to God; if properly regulated prophecies will bring instruction and encouragement).

What is said about tongues is precisely in keeping with what he has argued throughout; it affords further evidence that he has not been after tongues as such, but after tongues *without* interpretation in the assembly. Here he regulates the use of tongues *with* interpretation.

26 The combination of the formula, "what then [is the upshot of all this]?"[674] with the vocative, "brothers and sisters," signals another shift in the argument, but in this case one that seems intended to tie together several loose ends. The verb "when you come together," spoken now in the second person plural (as in 11:18, 20, 33–34), picks up the argument from vv. 23–25.[675] The first sentence, which describes what should be happening[676] at their gatherings, echoes the concerns of ch. 12, that *each one* has opportunity to participate in the corporate ministry of the body. The second sentence, the exhortation that all of the various expressions of ministry described in the first sentence be for edification,[677] echoes the basic concern of ch. 14—as well as of ch. 13. Accordingly, these concluding guidelines bring both sections of the preceding argument into focus.

As with all the former lists in these chapters, this final one is also ad hoc; it is intended neither to give the "order" of service[678] nor to be exhaustive of what "each one has" to offer by way of ministry. Given that neither prayer nor prophecy and "discernment" is listed (cf. 11:4–5), yet in the following sentences the latter two are "regulated," this list seems capable of yielding to an et cetera at the end. Each of these items has

---

[674] See n. 584 on v. 15.

[675] See on v. 23. This repetition of the verb in terms of what *should* be happening further supports the suggestion made there that v. 23 gives a generally realistic picture of what was actually going on.

[676] Some of this was perhaps already happening; but the rest of the context, including ch. 12, suggests that this is a corrective and not merely descriptive word. Martin, *Spirit*, 78, offers that the repeated "has" may be a form of reproof; however, nothing in the text itself mildly hints at disapproval here.

[677] The preposition πρός with οἰκοδομήν indicates the purpose of all these things.

[678] So also Conzelmann 244; cf. Robertson-Plummer 320; otherwise, Findlay 912.

appeared in the previous discussion; most likely they represent various *types* of verbal manifestations of the Spirit that should occur in their assembly. Since the latter three are Spirit-inspired utterances, and are therefore spontaneous, it is likely that the first two are to be understood in that way as well,[679] although that is not certain.

For a discussion of the "hymn" see on v. 15; this word probably covers for "prayer" as well, although the interpreted tongue could also fit that category. For "teaching" and "revelation" see on v. 6. As suggested there, the latter is perhaps a cover word for all other forms of intelligible inspired speech, including the "prophecies" of vv. 29–32, especially since the verb "revealed" occurs in the context of prophecy and discernment in v. 30. For "tongue" and "interpretation" see on 12:10. On the "charismatic" nature of this worship, see on v. 23. What is striking in this entire discussion is the absence of any mention of leadership or of anyone responsible for seeing that these guidelines were followed. This, of course, is true of the whole letter, and of most of the Pauline corpus, so too much must not be made of it. But there does seem to be a sense in which the Holy Spirit is understood to give basic leadership to the worship of the gathered body.[680] What is mandatory is that everything aim at edification.

27 Having commanded that "all things [i.e., the various ministries in the preceding list] be done for edification [of the church, being implied]" Paul shows how this may be accomplished for tongues and prophecy, the two gifts that have been at the forefront of the preceding discussion. He begins with the problem child, tongues.[681] Three guidelines are given.

First, "two or at the most three." One cannot be sure whether this means "at any one service" or "before there is an interpretation." In favor of the former is the phrase "at the most," plus the overall concern of the chapter that tongues not dominate the assembly; therefore in this guideline he would be suggesting that such manifestations be limited in any

---

[679] See the discussion on vv. 6 and 15.

[680] But see Parry 209, who says of vv. 27–28 that "these are rules for the chairman"!

[681] The sentence begins with an εἴτε, implying that he intended to "regulate" several items: "whether it be a tongue, do it thus; whether it be prophecy, etc." However, the first one apparently ended up longer that the εἴτε anticipated, especially with the qualifying sentence about interpretation in v. 28. Hence the discussion of prophecy skips the εἴτε and picks up with the guideline about two or three in succession.

It should also be noted that the sentence is a simple condition; as Richardson, "Order," 148, notes, "It is not a question of contingency, but an introduction to directives; not a matter of whether, but when."

given gathering. In favor of the latter is the similar recommendation for prophecies in vv. 29–31, which on the basis of vv. 24 and 31 is intended to limit the number of speakers in sequence, not the number of prophecies at any given service. On the whole, this is not easy to decide, but probably the word "at the most," which is missing in the guidelines for prophecies, tips the balance in favor of the former.[682]

Second, "and one at a time."[683] Two observations are in order. (a) There seems to be no good reason for such a word unless it is intended to be corrective. As in v. 23, the implication is that the Corinthians were doing otherwise. Not only did they have a singular passion for this gift, but apparently they had allowed it to dominate their gatherings in a way that reflected pagan ecstasy far more than the gospel of Christ. (b) This guideline clearly removes tongues from all forms of pagan ecstasy, as far as Paul's understanding is concerned. The admonition in v. 32 is probably intended as much for this gift as for prophecy. Whatever else, Christian inspiration, including both tongues and prophecy, is not "out of control." The Spirit does not "possess" nor "overpower" the speaker, but is subject to the prophet or tongues-speaker, in the sense that what the Spirit has to say will be said in an orderly and intelligible way. It is indeed the Spirit who speaks, but he speaks through the controlled instrumentality of the believer's own mind and tongue. In this regard it is no different from the inspired utterances of the OT prophets, which were spoken at the appropriate times and settings.

Third, "and let one interpret." This repeats what has already been said in vv. 6 and 13, except that in those two passages it is assumed that the tongues-speaker will also receive the interpretation. Here and in 12:10 and 28–30 it is assumed that the interpretation will be given to someone else.[684] What cannot be decided is whether "one" is to interpret after each utterance in tongues[685] or whether both of the first guidelines are intended to limit the number of expressions in tongues before there is an interpretation. Probably the latter, but there is no way to determine. This guideline receives further qualification in the next verse.

28 This qualification underscores what has been said throughout vv. 1–25. First, "if there is no interpreter,[686] let the speaker be silent in

---

[682] The factor of "amount of available time" that is often brought into this discussion is altogether too modern—and Western—to be relevant. Anyone who has sat through several hours of worship in Romania, West Africa, or Latin America will recognize such language as a Western phenomenon.

[683] Gk. ἀνὰ μέρους; for this idiom see BAGD, under ἀνά 2. Parry 209 suggests "share and share alike," which sounds too modern and lacks support.

[684] Although εἷς in this case could refer to one of two or three tongues-speakers.

[685] So Bittlinger, *Gifts*, 119; Martin, *Spirit*, 78.

[686] Gk. διερμηνευτής, the *nominal subject* for the verb διερμηνεύω that appears in v. 27 (cf. 12:30), which in turn refers to the activity described by the noun ἑρμηνεία

the assembly." This puts into the form of a regulation what was said in different ways in vv. 5, 6–13, and 14–19. It also accounts for the conclusion in v. 13 of the discussion in vv. 6–12 that urges the tongues-speaker to pray that he or she might also interpret. If they have not themselves experienced the gift of interpretation, and if there no one present who is known to have this gift, then they are to remain silent.

But as before Paul does not forbid the gift itself. Repeating the ideas of vv. 2 and 4, he admonishes that the tongues-speaker "speak by himself/herself and to God." Speaking "by himself"[687] (= privately) stands in contrast to "in the assembly" in v. 28, meaning he or she should pray "to God" in this way in private.

Apart from the final admonition in v. 39, this is the final word about tongues in this argument. Paul has been consistent throughout. It is the language of prayer and praise, directed toward God, but because it is unintelligible and therefore cannot edify, it should remain in the setting of personal prayer and devotion. Only when someone known to be gifted with interpretation is present may it be exercised in the assembly.

29 Paul next offers similar guidelines for prophetic utterances.[688] Because of the similarities with what was said about tongues, some have suggested that there were difficulties with this gift in Corinth as well. More likely, however, he advances these guidelines because this is the gift he has been arguing for throughout vis-à-vis tongues; since he has just "regulated" their gift, he goes on to do the same for the one he has been pressing for in its place. Hence the similarities.

He begins with the same ordering as in v. 27: "Let two or three prophets speak."[689] This does not mean that in any given gathering there must be a limit of only two or three prophecies. Even though that is commonly suggested, it lies quite beyond Paul's concern[690] and makes little sense at all of v. 24 ("when you come together and *all* prophesy"), nor of the concern in v. 31 that *all* have opportunity to participate. Rather it means that there should not be more than three at a time before "the others discern [what is said, is implied]." This latter item is the verb for

---

γλωσσῶν (the interpretation of tongues) in 12:10. As with "tongues" all of this is functional language. There was no group in Corinth known as "the interpreters of tongues"; the language of 14:5, plus the exhortation of v. 13, tells against such a possibility. See the discussion in v. 29 for how this affects our understanding of the word "prophet" in that passage.

[687] Gk. ἑαυτῷ; cf. BDF §188(2): dative of advantage.

[688] Grosheide 337, in a discussion lacking exegetical basis, argues that the "regulating" of prophecy in itself has the effect of putting it below preaching!

[689] The verb is λαλέω, the same used throughout in conjunction with tongues. This usage tells heavily against those who have regarded this verb as a somewhat technical term for tongues, indicating its less-than-articulate nature.

[690] See above on v. 27.

"discernments of spirits" in 12:10 (q.v.). As noted there, this is probably to be understood as a form of "testing the spirits," but not so much in the sense of whether "the prophet" is speaking by a foreign spirit, but whether the prophecy itself truly conforms to the Spirit of God,[691] who is also indwelling the other believers. Other than in 12:3, no criterion is here given as to what goes into the "discerning"[692] process.[693] Nor is there any suggestion as to how it proceeds. At best one can argue that prophecies did not have independent authority in the church, but must always be the province of the corporate body, who in the Spirit were to determine the sense or perhaps viability of what had been said.

Some have argued, on the basis of 12:28, that "prophets" refer to the special group of authoritative persons in the community who have been given this gift.[694] "The others"[695] in this case means "the other prophets,"[696] so that the whole text is intended to regulate the activities of the prophets, vis-à-vis regulating "prophecies" per se. But nearly everything else in the argument stands over against such a view. (a) The argument from v. 1 has been in the second plural, addressing the entire community. To all of them he urged that they "eagerly desire spiritual gifts, especially that you prophesy," without a hint that this gift is limited to the "prophets." (b) So with the rest of the argument; e.g., in v. 12 he exhorts, "since you are zealous for Spirit manifestations [referring to their collective enthusiasm for tongues], seek to excel in the building up of the church [meaning especially the gift of prophecy]." (c) The evidence in v. 24, even though hypothetical, is especially telling. As with v. 23, Paul implies a situation that could conceivably occur, namely, that "all prophesy," so that the unbeliever is convicted by *all* and judged by *all*. (d) So also in v. 31, he urges orderliness "because you may *all* prophecy in turn so that *all* may learn and *all* be encouraged/exhorted." It is gratuitous to suggest that the first "all" means "all the prophets," while the next two refer to the whole community.[697]

---

[691] Cf. Bittlinger's happy phrase: "The Spirit recognizes the Spirit" (*Gifts*, 121).

[692] Cf. Grudem, *Gift*, 58–60, who translates "evaluating." He also separates this activity from that of 12:10 beyond what seems warranted—or necessary.

[693] But see the useful discussion in Dunn, *Spirit*, 293–97.

[694] This has become an increasingly popular view. See inter alia, Ellis, *Prophecy*, 139n48; Hill, *Prophecy*, 120–21.

[695] Gk. οἱ ἄλλοι; cf. on 12:8 and 10. This word basically means "others different from the subject." Whereas it could mean "the rest," had Paul intended that idea the more correct term would have been οἱ λοίποι (cf. 9:5, οἱ λοίποι ἀπόστολοι). To put that in another way, the use of οἱ λοίποι would almost certainly have meant "the rest of the same class," i.e., prophets. Paul's word could mean that, but ordinarily it does not, referring simply to "someone else," or in the plural, "the others that make up the larger group." Cf. Barrett 328; Grudem, *Gift*, 60–62.

[696] Cf. Grosheide 338; Lenski 611; Friedrich, *TDNT* 6.855–56; H. Greeven, "Propheten, Lehrer, Vorsteher bei Paulus. Zur Frage der 'Ämter' im Urchristentum," *ZNW* 44 (1952–53) 6; Hill, *Prophecy*, 133. See the refutation in Grudem, *Gift*, 60–62.

[697] The lack of the definite article with προφῆται seems to clinch this argument.

This does not mean, of course, that all *will* or *do* prophesy. It is simply to note that Paul's concern here is not with a group of prophets, but with the *functioning* of prophecy in the assembly. The noun "prophets," therefore, is to be understood as functional language, similar to the use of "interpreter" in v. 28. It means, as in v. 3, "the one who is prophesying." Since he has an available noun in this case, which he does not with "the one who speaks in a tongue,"[698] the structure of the sentence called for its use here without implying that he is now speaking about a special group of *persons*.

30–31 These two sentences offer a further guideline for prophetic utterances, so that everything will be "done in a fitting and orderly way" (v. 40). The requirement seems to be aimed at those who might tend to dominate the meeting, although that is not certain. In any case, Paul presupposes that while one is speaking, "a revelation[699] [may come] to one who is seated."[700] The use of the verb "reveal" in this context suggests that for Paul this was the essential character of what was spoken in a prophecy. See on vv. 6, 24–25, and 26. When this happens then "let the first speaker," meaning the one already speaking, "be silent." The grounds for such a regulation will be given in v. 32; neither the tongues-speaker nor the prophet is out of control.

The "for" that begins v. 31 may be either explanatory, offering an explanation for what has just been said, or causal, giving its reason. In either case, he now offers a justification for the preceding regulation: "you can all prophesy one by one." As noted above, (1) "all" does not mean that everyone has this gift; the implication is that it is potentially available to everyone; and (2) this language makes almost no sense at all if Paul is referring to what should take place over several different meetings; the concern throughout, beginning with the verb "when you assemble" in v. 26, is with what takes place in a given gathering.

The appeal is to both self-control and deference. It is difficult to imagine two people prophesying simultaneously. But since they apparently were doing so with tongues, this at least anticipates their also doing so with prophecy—as well perhaps as keeping it in the category of "controlled" speech in contrast to pagan varieties.

The sentence begins with this word, but simply with "prophets," not *the* "prophets," implying on the basis of the structure of v. 27: "If some speak as prophets . . . "

[698] As in English, thus we are forced to such infelicities as "glossolalist" or "tongues-speaker."

[699] Gk. ἀποκαλύφθῃ; lit. "it is revealed (to another)." This is the verb for the noun ἀποκάλυψις in vv. 6 and 26.

[700] The clear implication is that the one prophesying stands while doing so; probably this would be true of the other manifestations as well. Cf. the Jewish rabbi who taught sitting down.

The reason for such orderliness is given in a final purpose clause. Paul is emphatic: "*All* may prophesy, so that *all* may be instructed and *all* may be encouraged/exhorted." As in ch. 12, and again in v. 26 with which this paragraph began, this reflects a concern for edification in which everyone contributes. Since the whole of the divine revelation is not given to just one or a few—or in simply one kind of manifestation—the concern is that all, including those who speak prophetically, should learn from[701] and be encouraged or exhorted by[702] what the Spirit has given to others. The result of such orderliness, therefore, is that the opening exhortation is fulfilled, that "everything be done for the edification of the church" (v. 26).

32 With this crucial sentence Paul offers his justification for the preceding regulations of the activities of both speaking in tongues and prophesying. Along with its theological basis given in the next verse, these two sentences also bring this section to its fitting conclusion. With these words Paul lifts Christian "inspired speech" out of the category of "ecstasy" as such and offers it as a radically different thing from the mania of the pagan cults. There is no seizure here, no loss of control; the speaker is neither frenzied nor a babbler.[703] If tongues are not intelligible, they are nonetheless inspired utterance and completely under the control of the speaker. So too with prophecy.

As noted earlier,[704] the phrase "spirits of the prophets" means "the prophetic Spirit" by which each of them speaks through his or her own spirit.[705] His point is that the utterances are subject to the speakers in terms of timing; the content is understood to be the product of the Divine Spirit who inspires such utterances. Thus Paul justifies their speaking one at a time, being silent with regard to tongues when no interpreter is present, and ceasing for the sake of another when a prophetic revelation is given to someone else. All of this is possible because "the S/spirits of the prophets are subject to the prophets."

33 To conclude Paul adds a significant theological justification for the foregoing guidelines. Everything has to do with the character of God and what God has already established to be true of his divine activity in

---

[701] Gk. μανθάνω (cf. 1 Tim 2:11); it means to *receive* instruction (= to learn) as over against giving it (= to teach).

[702] Gk. παρακαλέω; see on v. 3.

[703] For descriptions of the Hellenistic view of prophecy involving "ecstasy," see Plato, *Phaed.* 243e–245c; Philo *Spec.* 4.49; *Her.* 4.265. See esp. the discussion in Aune, *Prophecy,* 19–22, 33–34.

[704] See on v. 12; cf. 5:3–4 and 12:10 on "discernments of spirits."

[705] Ellis, *Prophecy,* 36–42, makes the unlikely suggestion that "spirits" here refers to "angelic spirits." See the refutation in Grudem, *Gift,* 120–22 (see 120–36 for a discussion of other views as well).

the rest of the churches. First, "for God is not a God of disorder[706] but of peace." This sentence, along with the final appeal in v. 40, corroborates the suggestion made on v. 23 that the Corinthian assembly had become unruly in its expression of tongues. Now Paul is arguing that the basis of all these instructions is ultimately theological. It has to do with the character of God, probably vis-à-vis the deities of the cults, where frenzy and disorder characterized their worship. The theological point is crucial: the character of one's deity is reflected in the character of one's worship.[707] They must therefore cease worship that reflects the pagan deities more than the God whom they have come to know through the Lord Jesus Christ (cf. 12:2–3). God is neither characterized by disorder nor causes it in the assembly.

This, of course, has further implications as to the Spirit. Since the Spirit is none other than the Spirit of the living God—whose character is *shalom*—then the Spirit cannot be responsible for that which contradicts God's own character. If the Spirit continually reminds us of the creative and unpredictable dimensions of God's character, so also the Spirit as God's presence in our midst should lead into that kind of worship that is fully in keeping with God.

The interesting opposite of "disorder," however, is not quietness or propriety, or even "order," but "peace." Minimally this refers to the sense of harmony that will maintain in a Christian assembly when everyone is truly in the Spirit and when the aim of everything is the edification of the whole (v. 26).[708] It is tempting, as in 7:15, to see a reflection of Paul's Jewish background in this usage, where God's people are called to live, in this case worship, "for the sake of peace," that is, in such a way as to win the favor of others.

Second, what is true of God in terms of Christian worship is so "in all the congregations of the saints."[709] Because of the awkwardness in speaking of God in this way, a number of scholars and translations prefer to take this final phrase with vv. 34–35. But there are a number of reasons for taking it as the concluding word to these instructions on "order." (a) As noted in the Excursus, substantial evidence indicates that vv. 34–35 are not authentic and therefore that Paul could not have intended it

---

[706]Gk. ἀκαταστασίας; cf. esp. 2 Cor 12:20, where it occurs in the list of sins that Paul fears may yet be going on in Corinth. There it may mean something closer to "disturbances," as it seems to in the list of his apostolic hardships in 6:5 of that same letter. See also James 3:16 where it stands in contrast to peace among other virtues.

[707]This probably says something regarding somber Christian worship as well, since joy is the order of the early church, indicating that God is a God of joy, who delights in the worship of his people as they delight in him.

[708]On the Spirit as responsible for "peace" in the community, see Gal 5:22; Rom 14:17; and Eph 4:3.

[709]This is the only occurrence of this combination in the NT, but that is not surprising in light of 1:2.

to go with what he did not write. In any case, the very early textual evidence in the Western church indicates that this phrase was not considered to be part of vv. 34–35.[710] (b) The two rhetorical questions in v. 36, both of which begin with "or," make the best sense when understood as referring directly to this statement. That is, "All the churches of the saints are intended to be orderly as we have just described, *or* did the word of God originate with you?" This seems to be the proper understanding of the rhetoric in v. 36, even if vv. 34–35 were authentic. (c) To take this phrase with v. 34 creates an even clumsier sentence: "As in all the churches of the saints women should remain silent in the churches." That is a redundancy that is nearly intolerable.[711] (d) This is now the fourth appeal of this kind in the letter (see 4:17; 7:17; 11:16); in each of the other instances this appeal concludes its sentence, and in two cases (4:17; 11:16) it functions as an addendum just as it does here. (e) Finally, and most importantly, this concern that they be like the other churches is more fitting at the conclusion of the major concern of this argument, just as in chs. 1–4 and 11:2–16, rather than with something that if authentic is an aside at best.

Thus, this final appeal continues the theological word with which the sentence began.[712] God is not only like this, but he has so commanded that his character be appropriately displayed in worship in all the churches. This particular appeal, which in this letter began in the opening words of salutation (see 1:2), tells the Corinthians that their view of tongues and spirituality that has allowed this kind of disorderly conduct is out of keeping with what God is doing elsewhere through the gospel. They are marching to their own drum; Paul is urging them not only to conform to the character of God, but also to get in step with the rest of God's church.

By and large the history of the church indicates that in worship we do not trust the diversity in the body. Edification must always be the rule, and that carries with it orderliness so that all may learn and all be encouraged. But it is no great credit to the historical church that in opting for "order" it also opted for a silencing of the ministry of the many. That, it would seem, is at least the minimal point of the paragraph.

---

[710] Cf. Chrysostom, *Hom. 36 and 37 on 1 Cor.*, who breaks these two homilies between vv. 33 and 34 and understands 33b to belong to 33a. The idea that v. 33b goes with v. 34 seems to be a modern phenomenon altogether.

[711] So much so that the NIV, e.g., tries to alleviate it with a different translation for the two clauses. Some suggest the second phrase means, "in every congregational meeting in Corinth"; but that runs counter to Pauline usage. See Fee 706.

[712] Grosheide 341 objects that the words of the first clause in v. 33 "refuse to take any further qualification." But that is an assertion unsupported either theologically or grammatically in Paul.

But perhaps the most important word in this paragraph is the final one. Some Pentecostal and charismatic assemblies would do well to heed these directives; confusion and disorder are simply not in keeping with the character of God. At the same time, v. 26 makes it clear that the "peace" and "order" in v. 33 does not necessarily mean somber ritual, as though God were really something of a "stuffed shirt." If our understanding of God's character is revealed in our worship, then it must be admitted by most that God is not often thought of in terms of allowing spontaneity or of joy.

1 CORINTHIANS 14:36–40[713]

[36]*Or did the word of God originate with you? Or are you the only people it has reached?* [37]*If anyone thinks he or she is a prophet or a Spirit person, let such a person acknowledge that what I am writing to you is the Lord's command.*[714] [38]*If he or she ignores this, they themselves will be ignored.*[715] [39]*Therefore, my*[716] *brothers and sisters, eagerly desire to prophesy, and do not forbid speaking in tongues.* [40]*But let all things be done in a fitting and orderly way.*[717]

Paul's long response to the Corinthians' enthusiasm for tongues is now finished. At the heart of the matter is what it means to be πνευ-ματικός (a Spirit person); and on this issue Paul and they are deeply divided. They think it has to do with speaking in tongues, the language of the angels, the sure evidence that they are already living the pneu-matic existence of the future. For this reason they have great zeal for this

---

[713] For some comments on vv. 34–35, which I take to be spurious, but which others see as regulating tongues or the discerning of prophecies in some way, see the Excursus at the end of this chapter.

[714] The singular ἐντολή is read by P[46] (א) B 048 0243 33 1241[s] 1739* pc vg[ms]. Various attempts were made to ameliorate this difficult reading (following the plural ἅ). Some witnesses (D* F G b Ambrosiaster) omit the word altogether; the majority change it to a plural. Otherwise Zuntz, *Text*, 139–40 (cf. Barrett 314, Bruce 136, Murphy-O'Connor 133), who thinks the Western text best explains how the others came about; but in this case one has considerable difficulty explaining how a scribe would have created the singular ἐντολή as a "clarifying addition." See Metzger, *Textual Commentary*, 566.

[715] The early MSS cross "party lines" between ἀγνοεῖται (א* A*vid D [F G] 048 0243 b 33 1739 pc b bo [favored by NIV[text] and Metzger, *Textual Commentary*, 566]) and ἀγνοείτω (P[46] א[2] A[c] B D[2] Ψ Maj sy; NIV[mg] and Zuntz, *Text*, 107–8). The former is easily the "more difficult" reading—from any perspective—as even Zuntz, who thinks it is too difficult, acknowledges. See the discussion below.

[716] Although the μου is missing in many witnesses (P[46] B[2] D* F G 0243 Maj lat), Zuntz, *Text*, 179, has noted that in every case in this letter when the pronoun occurs, some MSS omit it; whereas the opposite does not occur.

[717] For a discussion of the various readings that make up this final clause, but with differing results, see Zuntz, *Text*, 29–31, and Metzger, *Textual Commentary*, 566–67. Zuntz makes an unconvincing attempt to derive "meaning" from what he considers to be the original form.

gift (cf. v. 12), including an insistence on its practice in the gathered assembly. Apparently in their letter they have not only defended this practice, but by the same criterion have called Paul into question for his lack of "spirituality." Hence the undercurrent of apologetic for his own speaking in tongues in vv. 6, 15, and 18, but in private, not as they would have Paul "come to them."

Paul's response to all this has been twofold. First, they are to broaden their perspective to recognize that being Spirit people by its very nature means a great variety of manifestations, gifts, and ministries in the church (ch. 12). Second, the whole point of the *gathered* people of God is *edification*, the true expression of love for the saints. Whatever they do in the assembly must be both intelligible and orderly so that the whole community might be edified; thus it must reflect the character of God, which is how it is (or is to be) in all the churches of the saints (v. 33).

Paul is now about to wrap all this up, which he does in vv. 39–40 with a final summation of the argument, by reaffirming the priority of prophecy, without forbidding tongues (vv. 1–25), yet insisting that all must be done in a fitting and orderly way (vv. 26–33). But before that, the mention of how things are in "all the churches of the saints" spins off into a moment of ad hominem rhetoric, in which he not only dresses them down for "marching to their own drum" (v. 36), but also confronts them directly on the matter of who is truly πνευματικός, they or he (v. 37). He concludes with a prophetic word against any who reject the corrections given in this response (v. 38). All of this is reminiscent of the final parting shot in 4:18–21 and the defense in 9:1–23.

36 These two questions are a direct confrontation with the Corinthians over their attitude toward Paul on some issue,[718] in which he tries to give them perspective by reminding them of their own place in the history of "the word of God" (i.e., the gospel of Christ).[719] "Did the message of Christ originate with you?" he asks with sarcasm. "Are you the fountainhead from which all Christian truth derives that you can act so in this matter?" "Are you the only ones to whom it has come," he asks further, "so that you can carry on in your own individualistic way, as if there were no other believers in the world?" This is biting rhetoric, which flows directly out of the (probably) immediately preceding clause (v. 33), "as in all the churches of the saints." Who do they think they are

---

[718] Both in style and content these questions are so thoroughly Pauline and fit the context so well that one is puzzled by Conzelmann's including them as part of the interpolation of vv. 34–35—all the more so since there is no textual warrant.

[719] Cf. the usage in 1 Thes 2:13; 2 Cor 2:17; 4:2; Col 1:25 (in Rom 9:6 it refers to God's former "word" spoken in Scripture); cf. "the word of the Lord" in 1 Thes 1:8; 2 Thes 3:1. In each case this means "God's message" or "the message that comes from God."

anyway, is the implication; has God given them a special word that allows them to reject Paul's instructions, on the one hand, and be so out of touch with the other churches, on the other?

But to what does this rhetoric refer? Probably not to vv. 34–35,[720] which are most likely unauthentic; in any case, one can make far better sense of the argument to see this as referring to the larger matter at hand, namely, to their and his disagreements over the nature of being πνευματικός and the place of tongues in the assembly. Both questions begin with the conjunction "or," implying that the first question flows directly out of the immediately preceding sentence.[721] This conjunction in fact goes very poorly with v. 35,[722] but makes excellent sense following v. 33: "For God is not a God of disorder but of peace, as in all the churches of the saints; or did the word of God originate from you? Or are you the only people it reached?" They are dead wrong on this matter; this rhetoric, therefore, is not only trying to get them to see that they are out of step with the other churches, but also leads directly to the two conditional sentences that follow.

37 This is now the third instance in this letter where Paul attacks their own position head-on with this formula, "if anyone thinks he or she is" (see on 3:18 and 8:2). Each occurs in one of the three major sections of the letter (1–4; 8–10; 12–14); and the argument in each case indicates that Paul by this formula is zeroing in on the Corinthians' perspective as to their own spirituality. They do indeed think of themselves as "the wise" (3:18) and as "having knowledge" (8:2), probably in both cases because they also think of themselves as being πνευματικοί (see on 2:15 and 3:1).

In this case, however, it is probably not the Corinthians as a whole whom he is taking on, although they are certainly in view as well; more likely, as in 4:18 and 9:3, he is speaking directly to those who have been leading the church into its anti-Pauline sentiments. These people consider themselves to be "prophets" and "Spirit people." These two words are probably to be understood as closely linked. In contrast to the functional use of "prophet" in the immediately preceding argument, the word "prophet" here reverts back to the usage in 12:28, where it refers to those who had a "ranked" position of ministry in the local assembly. Crucial is the addition, "or πνευματικός" (= a person of the Spirit). As argued throughout, this is the central issue. There seems to be no other good

---

[720] This is the traditional view, as though the Corinthians were allowing women to speak in the assembly against Paul's own instructions and the custom of the churches elsewhere.

[721] As elsewhere in this letter; see, e.g., 6:2, 9, 16, 19; 9:6.

[722] So much so that the KJV and others (RSV, Montgomery, TCNT) resorted to translating it "What!" for which there is not a shred of linguistic evidence.

reason for Paul to have spoken to them in this way, unless they did indeed consider themselves to be πνευματικοί, the primary evidence of which was the gift of tongues. They were sure of themselves, that they were Spirit people; they were less sure of the apostle.

But in 12:28 Paul had already anticipated what he says now. God has placed in the church *first* apostles, *second* prophets. He is not denying that those who oppose him are prophets or that the Corinthians as a whole are πνευματικοί. He seems to be arguing that he is first of all an apostle, who is therefore also a prophet, and who thus is "writing to you the Lord's command."[723] The emphasis in Paul's word order is on "the Lord" (referring to Christ) as the source of what he has been writing. The word "command" therefore is best understood as a collective singular referring to all that he has written on this present matter, especially the need for intelligibility and order in their assembly so that all may be edified.[724] Since both he and they have the Spirit, the true "person of the Spirit" will thus "acknowledge"[725] that what Paul writes is from the Lord.

38 With the authority of the same Lord from whom he received the "command," Paul pronounces sentence on those who do not recognize the Spirit in what he writes: "If anyone [i.e., the one who thinks he is a Spirit person] ignores[726] this, he himself will be ignored."

Paul's point is clear; the precise meaning of the repeated verb is slightly less so. He seems to be making a double play on words. The verb "to ignore" (ἀγνοεῖ) is here the antonym of "acknowledge" (ἐπιγινώσκω) in v. 37. Thus, a Spirit person should "recognize" what Paul writes as "from the Lord"; if anyone "fails to acknowledge" it as such, that person will in turn not be "recognized/acknowledged." Although it is possible that Paul meant the subject of this last clause to be himself or the church (= not recognized to be a prophet or πνευματικός), more likely "God" is intended.[727] That is, failure to recognize the Spirit in Paul's letter, will

---

[723] Gk. κυρίου ἐστὶν ἐντολή; BAGD are probably incorrect to list this usage under the category of "the precepts of Jesus." Paul is almost certainly referring to the instructions of the preceding argument. But see the discussion by C. H. Dodd, ""Ἔννομος Χριστοῦ," in *Studia Paulina in honorem Johannis de Zwaan Septuagenarii* (ed. J. N. Sevenster, W. C. van Unnik; Haarlem: 1953) 96–110 [142n3]. On the textual question see n. 714 above.

[724] It is easy to forget that Paul's letters were not read in the quietness of one's own home, but in the assembly as it gathered for worship. Therefore, it had the effect of his speaking prophetically into their midst, even though he was not present "in body." See the discussion on 5:3.

[725] Gk. ἐπιγινωσκέτω (cf. 13:12); here it means "recognize to be so," hence "acknowledge."

[726] Gk. ἀγνοεῖ; cf. 10:1; 12:1.

[727] Cf. Käsemann, "Sentences," 68–69; so also Conzelmann 246; cf. Barrett 334.

lead to that person's failure to be "recognized" by God (cf. 8:2–3). Hence it is a prophetic sentence of judgment on those who fail to heed this letter.[728]

One can hardly escape Paul's own sense of authority in the Spirit in these words. He does not deny the Spirit to those who oppose him in Corinth. But the Spirit recognizes the Spirit; and the true nature of their own Spirituality will be found in their recognizing Paul's letter as the Lord's command, given through the Spirit, and in their thereby being recognized by the Lord whose apostle he is.

39–40 Since the rhetorical confrontation in vv. 36–38 is something of an aside—although in Paul never irrelevant!—he closes the preceding argument with a three-part summation. It is signaled by the strong inferential conjunction "so then," common to this letter,[729] and yet another vocative. After the rhetoric of the preceding verses, in this case he adds the personal possessive, "*my* brothers and sisters."

The first clause repeats the imperative with which Paul began in v. 1: "eagerly desire to prophesy." The second speaks to their favorite: "and do not forbid speaking in tongues." As in the argument itself, he is not forbidding tongues, nor will he allow anyone else to take the preceding correction as prohibition. Tongues are permissible in the assembly accompanied by interpretation and may be experienced as much as one wishes in private. These two clauses together thus summarize vv. 1–25.

The third clause (v. 40) summarizes the point of vv. 26–33: "Let all things be done in a fitting and orderly way." The word "fitting"[730] argues again for propriety in the assembly (cf. 11:13); the word "orderly" echoes its opposite, "disorder," from v. 33, and along with that verse strongly implies that the assembly in Corinth was in disarray. The implication of the argument throughout has been that speaking in tongues is the guilty party. With these words, therefore, the argument is brought to its fitting conclusion.

But the letter itself is not finished. Behind their view of spirituality is not simply a false view of Spirit manifestations, but a false theology of "spiritual" existence. Since their view of "spirituality" had also brought them to deny a future resurrection of the body, it is fitting that this matter be taken up next. The result is the grand climax of the entire letter, at least in terms of its argument.

---

[728] This also makes better sense of the sentence than does the variant reading (see n. 715), which makes the play on words in the second clause go in a different direction: If the hearer fails to recognize Paul's word as the Lord's command, let him/her continue in ignorance. In a more circuitous way that, too, is a form of judgment; but the indicative is to be preferred.

[729] See on v. 22 and the note there.

[730] Gk. εὐσχημόνως; cf. 1 Thes 4:12; Rom 13:13. Cf. the use of εὐσχημοσύνη in 12:23, which moves into the area of propriety.

1 CORINTHIANS 15:42–46

⁴²*So also the resurrection of the dead. It is sown in a perishable state; it is raised in an imperishable state.* ⁴³*It is sown in humiliation; it is raised in glory. It is sown in weakness; it is raised in power.* ⁴⁴*It is sown a natural body; it is raised a "spiritual" body. If there is a natural body, there is also a "spiritual" body.* ⁴⁵*So also it is written: "The first man, Adam, became a living being"; the last Adam, a life-giving spirit.* ⁴⁶*But the "spiritual" did not come first, but the natural, then the "spiritual."*

In order to navigate one's way through the complex use of πνεῦμα/πνευματικός language in this passage, several essential contextual matters must be kept in mind. (1) The primary issue being addressed in all of ch. 15 is that "some of them" deny the resurrection of believers (v. 12), to which Paul first responds in vv. 1–11 (they already believe in the resurrection of Christ) and vv. 12–34 (Christ's resurrection makes that of believers both necessary and inevitable). So significant is this question that Paul has already spoken of the resurrection of Christ as God's way of giving our mortal bodies eternal significance (6:14). (2) The basic reason for this denial appears in the argument of vv. 35–58: As already πνευματικοί (through the Spirit they have arrived at true "spiritual" existence, which denied any significance to the body) they are distressed (offended?) by the concept of the body rising from the dead. The issue for them, therefore, is primarily over the question, "*how* will the dead be raised, i.e., with what kind of *body* will they come forth?" (v. 35). (3) Paul's argument in this section is basically to demonstrate from a series of different analogies that the raised body will have both continuity and discontinuity with the present body. It will have continuity in that it is the *present body* that is raised; it will have discontinuity in that it will be "transformed" and thereby fitted for the life of the future, the life of heaven.

Our passage comes at the crucial point in this second part of Paul's argument (vv. 35–58). In vv. 42–44 he sets out to apply the various analogies that have just preceded (vv. 36–41), which in vv. 45–49 he validates by means of Scripture in the form of a (functional) christological interpretation of a key passage found in Gen 2:7. The use of πνευματικος is crucial for both the application (v. 44) and the christological interpretation of Gen 2:7 (vv. 45–46). What is absolutely crucial to this whole argument, and to Paul's use of Spirit language, are the twin realities that Christ's resurrection is the ground for the (necessary and inevitable) resurrection of believers who have died (vv. 12–28) and for the kind of body that believers will assume at the resurrection, which in Phil 3:21 Paul calls "the body of his glory" (i.e., the form of body that Christ has assumed in his glorified state).

44 With pairs of striking contrasts, Paul has already (vv. 42–43) described the nature of the body that is laid in the grave (perishable, humiliation, in weakness) and that which is raised (imperishable, glorified, with power). On this final contrast he will pause briefly to elaborate: It is sown a ψυχικόν body; it is raised a πνευματικόν body.

It is hard to imagine the shock these words must have registered when first read aloud to the church in Corinth. A "spiritual body" is an oxymoron in any language; it would surely offend those whose view of the material world is such that "spirituality" at least minimally has to do with being done with the physical body. Almost certainly their worldview becomes part of the reason that Paul chooses what appears to us as such strange language. That it is probably partly in response to their view of things will also help us to comprehend what Paul understood this combination to mean.

First, this is the fourth in a rhetorical compounding of contrasts. The first three concern the "nature" or "form" of the former and later bodies, not their *substance*. Consequently, it is highly unlikely that Paul intends πνευματικόν to describe what the resurrected body "consists of." The same holds true of the description ψυχικόν for the present body. It does not consist of "soul" or "spirit" in either case.

Second, the clue to the meaning of πνευματικόν lies first of all with the similar contrast between it and ψυχικός in 2:14–15. There, the ψυχικός person is one who does not have the Spirit and is therefore merely "natural"—i.e., living in the present as any other human being who has not yet been invaded by the Spirit of the living God and therefore stamped with eternity. Likewise the πνευματικός person is a Spirit person, one who is Christ's by virtue of having received the Spirit. In this new context, one might expect similar contrasts. This view is strengthened by the choice of Gen 2:7 (LXX) as the supporting evidence for this assertion.

The present body is ψυχικός, "natural," in the sense that it is fitted for life in the present age. Belonging to the present, it is thereby subject to decay, humiliation, and weakness. The new body will be πνευματικόν, "spiritual," in the sense that it belongs to the final world, the world of the Spirit, of which the Spirit also presently serves as God's down payment or firstfruits in the life of the believer. Thus, in keeping with the possessive form of the adjective, the "spiritual body" is a body that belongs to the Spirit in its final "glorified, imperishable" expression.

Nonetheless, finding an adequate English translation for this idea presents a difficulty. Perhaps in the final analysis, the best we can do is to translate ψυχικόν "natural" and πνευματικόν "supernatural," not in the sense of "miraculous," but in the sense of that which belongs to the world of Spirit that lies beyond this present "natural" existence.

In any case, having described the "now" and "then" expressions of the body as sown "natural" and raised "supernatural," Paul asserts further that "if there is a ψυχικόν body [and there is], then there is also a πνευματικόν body." Our present body is *not* the final one; but neither will there be a kind of pneumatic existence that is without the body. Nevertheless, these two expressions of bodily existence do not exist simultaneously. The whole argument has to do with the *future, bodily* resurrection of believers; thus the "supernatural" body lies in the future.

45 Since the final assertion in v. 44—that the existence of one means the existence of the other—is not particularly self-evident, Paul feels compelled to vindicate it, which he now assays to do by Scripture and on the basis of Christ's resurrection. But in so doing he uses πνεῦμα language in two further statements that, from our distance, are equally knotty: (a) that in his resurrection Christ became a life-giving πνεῦμα; and (b) that the πνευματικόν does not come first, but the ψυχικόν, then the πνευματικόν.

First, two contextual words: (1) The concern in Paul's statement, "the last Adam, a life-giving πνεῦμα," is *not* christological, at least in any ontological sense;[731] rather, it is a purely soteriological concern, having to do with the effects of Christ's resurrection on ours. In the argument it demonstrates from Scripture the reality of v. 44, that just as there is a ψυχικόν body, there is also a πνευματικόν body. As we have suggested, this must have come as something of a shock to the Corinthian pneumatics. (2) The Adam-Christ analogy *presupposes* its prior use in vv. 21–22 and therefore deals with the *effects of the resurrection of Christ*, now in terms of the resurrection body. To miss these two points can lead one astray in terms of what is actually said.

In vv. 21–22 Paul had argued that "in Adam all die, but in Christ all will be made alive." He now returns to that analogy by way of Scripture to support his contention in v. 44, that believers will be raised with a "spiritual body," that is, a "supernatural" body acquired through resurrection and adapted to the life of the Spirit in the coming age. He begins by citing the LXX of Gen 2:7 in a kind of midrash pesher (= a quotation that is at once citation and interpretation; cf. 14:21):[732]

---

[731] A considerable amount of scholarly energy has been expended on vv. 45 and 47 in terms of their christological implications. But these are quite beside Paul's point, which, as in vv. 21–22, has to do with *Christ's resurrection* being the ground of ours. The *language* has been dictated by the argument itself, especially the use of Gen 2:7. See n. 739 below, and the discussion in ch. 13.

[732] Cf. E. E. Ellis, *Paul's Use of the Old Testament* (Edinburgh: Oliver and Boyd, 1957) 141–43; it is doubtful, however, whether Paul is here citing a midrash that had already taken hold in Christian circles (95–97). Paul is perfectly capable of such pesher. J. D. G. Dunn argues that the whole sentence "stands under the οὕτως γέγραπται— including verse 45b, as the absence of δέ indicates" ("I Corinthians 15.45—last Adam, life-giving Spirit," in *Christ and Spirit in the New Testament: Studies in Honour of Charles Francis Digby Moule* [ed. B. Lindars, S. Smalley; Cambridge, 1973] 127–41 [130]). Yes and no. This is true of the pesher as such, but Paul hardly intends the second clause

ἐγένετο   ὁ πρῶτος ἄνθρωπος   Ἀδὰμ εἰς ψυχὴν ζῶσαν
           ὁ ἔσχατος   Ἀδὰμ εἰς πνεῦμα ζῳοποιοῦν

Several observations about this citation-turned-interpretation are needed: (1) Paul's modifications of the LXX in the first line—the additions of the adjective "first" and of the name "Adam"—are specifically designed to lead to the second line, where his real concern lies. (2) The two words that describe Adam and Christ respectively are the cognate nouns for the adjectives ψυχικόν and πνευματικόν in v. 44. This in fact is the *only reason* both for the citation and for the language used to describe Christ. This clear linguistic connection implies that the original bearers of the two kinds of bodies mentioned in v. 44 are Adam and Christ.[733] That is, the two "Adam's" serve as evidence that even as there is a ψυχικόν body (as the first Adam demonstrates; Gen 2:7), so also Christ, the second Adam, by his resurrection is evidence that there must be a πνευματικόν body.[734] (3) Not only so, but Paul's *reason* for saying that Christ became "a life-giving πνεῦμα" is that the LXX had said of Adam that he became "a living ψυχή." That is, the *language of the citation* called for the *parallel language about Christ*. (4) Even though the content of the second line is neither present nor inferred in the Genesis text, it nonetheless reflects the language of the prior clause in the LXX, "and he *breathed* into his face the *breath of life* (πνοὴν ζωῆς)"; now in speaking about Christ, Paul makes a play on this language. The one who will "breathe" new life into these mortal bodies—with life-giving πνεῦμα (as in Ezek 37:14) and thus make them immortal—is none other than the Risen Christ. (5) The language "life-giving" repeats the verb used of Christ in the previous Adam-Christ analogy in v. 22, indicating decisively, it would seem, that the interest here, as before, is in Christ's resurrection as the ground of ours ("in Christ all will be made alive"). Thus the argument as a whole, as well as the immediate context, suggests that even though Christ has now assumed his exalted position in a σῶμα πνευματικόν and is thus a "life-giving πνεῦμα," his function in this role will take place at the resurrection of believers, when he "makes alive" their mortal bodies so that they too assume a σῶμα πνευματικόν like his.

Despite some subtleties at work here, one may, from these observations, draw the following conclusions about Paul's intent. First, the *reason* for the citation lies with Paul's desire to demonstrate the reality of the resurrection body on the basis of the prior Adam-Christ analogy. The LXX's use of ψύχη to describe Adam gives Paul a biblical basis for the distinctions

---

to be understood as Scripture—even in a targumic way—in the same sense that the first line is.

[733] As Dunn also notes ("I Corinthians 15.45," 130).

[734] Cf. Max Turner, "The Significance of Spirit Endowment for Paul," *VoxEvang* 9 (1975) 56–69 [62].

he wants to make between the two kinds of *sōma*, and at the same time it allows him to connect that with what he had already said in vv. 21–22.

Second, as the further explanation in vv. 47–48 shows, the overriding urgency in this passage is to show in an analogical way that the two kinds of bodies "sown" and "raised" in v. 44 are already represented in the two archetypal "Adams." On the one hand, the first Adam, who became a "living ψύχη," was thereby given a ψυχικόν body at creation, a body subject to decay and death. This Adam, who brought death into the world (vv. 21–22), became the representative man of all who bear his ψυχικόν likeness. The last Adam, on the other hand, whose "spiritual (glorified) body" was given at his resurrection, not only became the representative Man[735] for all who will bear his πνευματικός likeness, but he is himself the source of both the πνευματικός life[736] as well as the πνευματικός body.[737]

Therefore, third, the shift from "living" with regard to Adam (he is merely life-receiving) to "life-giving" seems to have a double entendre with regard to Christ. In his resurrection whereby he assumed his "supernatural body," he also became the giver of life to all who will ever follow.[738] Paul's point seems to be that one can assume full πνευματικός existence only as Christ did, by resurrection, which includes a πνευματικόν body. His way of saying this was to keep the parallelism with "Adam" intact, by using the noun πνεῦμα to correspond with the noun ψυχή, used for Adam in the LXX.

The concern of line 2, therefore, is not christological, as though Christ and the Spirit were somehow now interchangeable terms for Paul.[739] Indeed, he does not intend to say that Christ became *the*

---

[735] Hence the reason he is called the "last Adam," meaning not just the final representative, but the "eschatological" Adam—and "Adam," not "man," because he is representative, not simply a model or pattern.

[736] Cf. Dunn, "I Corinthians 15.45," 132; however, his emphasis on the verb ζῳοποιέω as referring primarily to the present misses its clear tie to v. 22, where it is used of the resurrection.

[737] A. T. Lincoln (*Paradise Now and Not Yet: Studies in the Role of the Heavenly Dimension in Paul's Thought with Special Reference to his Eschatology* [SNTSMS 43; Cambridge: University Press, 1981] 43) suggests that by this collocation of Adam and Christ on the basis of Gen 2:7 Paul implies that at creation a different kind of body was already in view. Thus, "the Corinthians should not view the idea of a bodily form appropriate to spiritual existence as something so novel and unimaginable, for in fact this has always been God's purpose."

[738] Cf. Lincoln, *Paradise*, 43–44: "The last Adam however has a new quality of life, for as πνεῦμα ζῳοποιοῦν he is no longer merely alive and susceptible to death but rather has now become creatively life-giving."

[739] It is sometimes suggested, on the basis of this text and 2 Cor 3:17, that Paul "does not draw any hard and fast line between the Spirit and Christ" (Ruef 173). But that reflects an inadequate understanding of Paul's Christology, not to mention of 2 Cor 3:17, which is not saying something about Christ at all. See the discussion in

life-giving Spirit, but a life-giving spirit. Christ is not *the* Spirit; rather, in a play on the Genesis text, Paul says that Christ through his resurrection assumed his new existence in the spiritual realm, the realm of course that for the believer is the ultimate sphere of the Spirit. Thus, just as the first man came to have "natural" (ψυχικός) life through creation, so Christ entered into the "supernatural" (πνευματικός) realm through resurrection. And just as through Adam we have borne the body of the one existence, so too through Christ we shall bear the body of the new existence.

Part of Paul's point in all of this seems to be to deny, on the basis of Christ's resurrection, that they are completed pneumatics now. They, too, must await the resurrection (or transformation, v. 52) before their "spirituality" is complete, since as with Christ it *must* include a somatic expression. This is the point he will pick up with the second use of this text and the Adam-Christ analogy in vv. 47–49; but before that he takes another swipe at their misguided, over-spiritualized eschatology, which leads us to the final instance of Spirit language in this passage.

46 Since v. 47 follows so naturally out of v. 45, the present verse is a truly puzzling text in the argument, both as to what "spiritual" and "natural" here refer (Christ and Adam, or the two kinds of bodies) and why it is said at all, especially with the adversative "but" (ἀλλά) and the "not/but" contrast that emphatically declares the "spiritual" to come second. Of several suggestions the best solution lies in the preceding citation of Gen 2:7 and is to be regarded as over against the Corinthians. On the one hand, in asserting that the last Adam became "a life-giving spirit," Paul alluded to the prior act of God in breathing life into the *first* Adam. Now Paul corrects any misimpressions that allusion may have created. The "last Adam" refers to the *eschatological* reality of Christ's resurrection and of his subsequently giving life to his own at their resurrection. Accordingly, the πνευματικόν comes *after* the ψυχικόν, in terms both of Adam and Christ and of the two forms of somatic existence people will bear. The debate over Adam/Christ or the two bodies, therefore, is probably too narrowly conceived. The words most likely refer to the two orders of existence connoted by this language, of which Adam and Christ are the representatives and the two bodies the concrete expressions.[740]

---

ch. 5. Although he has correctly rejected the improper use of 2 Cor 3:17, Dunn ("I Corinthians 15.45") has unfortunately perpetuated this kind of "Spirit Christology" for the present text. See my critique "Christology and Pneumatology in Romans 8:9–11—and Elsewhere: Some Reflections on Paul as a Trinitarian," in the I. H. Marshall Festschrift, *Jesus of Nazareth: Lord and Christ* (ed. J. B. Green and M. Turner; Grand Rapids: Eerdmans, 1994) 312–31, and the discussion in ch. 13 below.

[740]Cf. Lincoln, *Paradise*, 44: "What started out as a comparison between two forms of bodily existence moved to a comparison between the two representatives of those forms and now proceeds to include the two world-orders which the first and last Adam exemplify."

At the same time, however, the emphatic "not/but" suggests that he is asserting this order of things over against the Corinthians. This does not mean, as some have suggested, that the Corinthians were asserting some kind of Philonic[741] or Gnostic[742] understanding of the priority of the spiritual to the physical. After all, in neither of those systems is there a concern for the chronology of one to the other. The order set out in v. 23 insists that each comes in its own order, Christ first, then those who are his. Against the Corinthians, who assumed themselves already to have entered into the totality of pneumatic existence while they were still in their ψυχικός body, Paul insists that the latter comes *first*, i.e., that they must reckon with the physical side of their present life in the Spirit. "Then," meaning at the Eschaton, comes the πνευματικός; and they must reckon with the reality that since the ψυχικός comes first and has a body, so too the πνευματικός that comes after will also have a body, a transformed body appropriate to eschatological spiritual life.[743]

Finally, the net result of this passage as to Paul's view of the Spirit is that the Spirit is the key to both expressions of bodily existence. According to 6:19–20 the body is the temple of the Spirit, belonging to him because of Christ's purchase and his own coming to indwell the believer. Therefore, everything that is done in the body should reflect the holiness of the Holy Spirit. Now we are told that the new body is also related to him, so much so that it is actually referred to in terms of πνευματικός, belonging to the Spirit. Thus the Spirit is the down payment, not only of our final inheritance, but also of our final bodily existence. If that is too somatic for those whose deepest roots are in the basically dualistic Western philosophical tradition, it is not so for Paul. The body belongs to the present and to the future, although its future expres-

---

[741] Among those who view this as a response to Philonic views, see Allo 427–28; Héring 178; Barrett 374–75; W. D. Davies, *Paul and Rabbinic Judaism: Some Rabbinic Elements in Pauline Theology* (rev. ed.; New York: Harper & Row, 1967) 51–52; Pearson, *Terminology*, 17–23; Horsley, "Pneumatikos." This view has been (rightly) rejected by R. Scroggs, *The Last Adam: A Study in Pauline Anthropology* (Oxford: Blackwell, 1966) 115–22; A. J. M. Wedderburn, "Philo's 'Heavenly Man,' " *NovT* 15 (1973) 301–26; and Lincoln, *Paradise*, 44.

[742] Cf. W. Schmithals, *Gnosticism in Corinth: An Investigation of the Letters to the Corinthians* (trans. J. E. Steely; Nashville: Abingdon, 1971) 169–70; Jewett, *Terms*, 352–56; E. Brandenburger, *Adam und Christus* (WMANT 7; Neukirchen, 1962). See the critique, esp. of Brandenburger, in S. Kim, *The Origin of Paul's Gospel* (2d ed., rev.; WUNT; Tübingen: J. C. B. Mohr [Paul Siebeck], 1984) 162–93, based in part on the unpubl. dissertation of A. J. M. Wedderburn, "Adam and Christ" (Cambridge, 1970).

[743] Cf. Wedderburn, "Heavenly Man," 302, and Lincoln, *Paradise*, 45. In Wedderburn's words: "Taken in this way the verse becomes a polemic against an unrealistic spiritualizing of this present life, a blending of heaven and earth that does away with the earthiness of the latter; the Corinthians erred in holding to a *one-stage soteriology*, rather than in reversing the order of a two-stage one" (italics mine).

sion will be adapted for the life of the future, which can finally be described only in terms of the Spirit: it will be πνευματικός, a body for the Spirit.

1 CORINTHIANS 16:18

For they refreshed my spirit—and yours.

For this usage in Paul, and for arguments against R. Jewett, who thinks this passage reflects "the apportioned divine Spirit," see the comments on the similar expression in 2 Cor 2:13; cf. 1 Thes 5:23; Gal 6:18.

CONCLUSIONS

It is not my purpose here to draw out this long chapter by further rehearsing or even summarizing all that has been said. Rather, I wish to comment on the reason for its length and relate that to Pauline pneumatology in general.

The obvious reason for so much more Spirit talk in this letter than in any of the others, and especially talk about Spirit manifestations in the community, is that something had gone astray in Corinth. This seems to be the case, whether one accepts my reconstruction as to what needs "fixing" or adopts another. This factor has caused some to see the Pauline emphases here as having little to do with the "ordinary" Paul and much to do with an early "charismatic" congregation, whose emphasis on "spiritual gifts" had led them astray. The implication is that since this kind of thing does not come up front and center in other letters, we would do well to relegate it to the periphery as well—or better, basically be done with it altogether.[744]

But as the full data of this letter, not to mention the rest of the letters, make plain, that is scarcely a valid view of the apostle. One may as well argue that, because the Lord's Table is mentioned only in 1 Corinthians, and here only because it needed "fixing," therefore, Paul himself does not hold much stock in the Table—and in trying to "fix" it was merely trying to get them to put it aside altogether. All the more so, since not once does he ever mention it either in passing or as something to which he can appeal either theologically or as a basis for correct behavior.

In the case of Spirit manifestations, however, we are not dealing with only one church and its wrong-headedness (wrong-Spiritedness?). Indeed, the cumulative evidence, which comes from 1 and 2 Thessalonians,

---

[744]All of this, of course, stems from a fundamental failure to take the thoroughly ad hoc nature of all the letters seriously enough.

Romans, Galatians, and 1 and 2 Timothy, seems incontrovertible: that the Pauline churches were thoroughly charismatic in the full sense of that term.

What this letter makes plain, and in this regard it simply picks up where 1 and 2 Thessalonians left off, is that Paul cannot think of Christian life without the Spirit. If that will become even more clear in Galatians and Romans, it is fully in evidence here. Apart from the corrections of chs. 12–14, which may also lie behind several other mentions of the Spirit (e.g., 2:4–5, 10–16, 15:44–46), there is much that is said not simply because the Corinthians had got it wrong regarding life in the Spirit, but because for Paul the Spirit is the key to Christian life under any circumstances.

Thus we meet in this letter the most wide-ranging references to the Spirit and his activity, both in individual and corporate life, that we find in Paul's letters. The Spirit leads one to Christ (by revealing one's sins and drawing to Christ; 14:24–25), accompanies the preaching of Christ, so that it might be seen for the wisdom that it is (2:12–13); thus the Spirit makes the preaching of Christ effective (2:4–5) and effectively appropriates the "washing, justifying, sanctifying" work of Christ in such an empowering way that it changes one's life and lifestyle (6:11). As the indwelling Spirit, he also sanctifies the body in the present (6:19–20) and characterizes it in terms of the life of the future (15:44–46). Much of this either repeats or adds further insights to what we have already seen in 1 and 2 Thessalonians.

But because the problem in Corinth is a corporate one, the largest amount of Spirit material relates to their life as a believing and worshiping community. And here there is much that we learn in every way—too much to recount here, except to note how rich and diversified Paul's understanding is. The Spirit is the essential ingredient for their life together—indeed, they became a body by their common, lavish experience of the Spirit (12:13); and the Spirit among them is alone what distinguishes them from all other communities in Corinth (3:16–17). Furthermore, the Spirit manifests himself in their gathered worship precisely for their common good (12:7), so that they may be built up together as the people of God (14:3, 6, 26), and so that others will be brought into that people (14:24–25).

Finally, although this is not Paul's point, their very errors in understanding permit us to catch a glimpse of what otherwise would be unknown, namely, Paul's own interior life in the Spirit. We know from all the letters that he was a man of prayer, joy, and thanksgiving; what we learn here is that his "spirituality" included a continual life of praying and singing in the Spirit—in this case, with glossolalia. But we also learn from this letter what will become even more pronounced in 2 Corinthians, namely, his reluctance to make this part of his life a matter of public record or a means of validation. Perhaps here, more than at any other juncture, he tends to part company with so many in the modern charismatic and Pentecostal movements. He simply could not imagine such private matters having a kind of prominence so as to make them count for anything in terms of sharing them with others or of validating his own life in the Spirit.

The reason for all of this is also obvious from this letter, although because of the nature of this study, it did not receive that much attention in this chapter. Specifically, Paul was a man of the Spirit precisely so that he could all the more be a man in Christ. Jesus Christ crucified and risen is where everything finally focuses for Paul. Any Spirit talk that does not also lead to that focus totally misses the apostle and his concerns. It is unfortunately one of the dangers of Spirit manifestations that they occur in mere mortals such as ourselves, who in our fallenness sometimes think the action lies there; whereas for Paul the action lies only and always with Christ. This is what makes the next letter—and especially the Spirit material in it—so crucial for our full picture. The Spirit manifests himself in and through Paul's weaknesses so that Christ and his power alone can be seen.

EXCURSUS: ON THE TEXT OF 1 CORINTHIANS 14:34–35

In my commentary I argued that these verses were neither original to this letter nor authentic to Paul. Since several reviewers took exception to this position, usually quite cavalierly, dismissing it without acknowledging the difficulties. I subsequently wrote up the textual evidence for presentation to the academy, at the NT Text Criticism Section of the 1990 annual meeting of the Society of Biblical Literature.[1] Since the issue for me is primarily a textual one, I present much of that paper here, with the exception of the final section, which is elaborated in the interest of addressing two interpretations of the passage that see it as referring directly to some form of Spirit utterance on the part of women in the gathered community in Corinth.

Three questions need to be addressed in some detail, and in this order: (1) the nature and significance of the Western evidence, which has this passage at the end of ch. 14; (2) the application of Bengel's first principle[2] to the question of transcriptional probability; and (3) the question of intrinsic probability, including the difficulties that have to be faced by all who think of the verses as authentic.

---

[1]November 17–20 in New Orleans; after this paper was written a more complete reply to the presentation in the commentary has been offered by D. A. Carson (" 'Silent in the Churches': On the Role of Women in 1 Corinthians 14:33b–36," in *Recovering Biblical Manhood and Womanhood: A Response to Evangelical Feminism* (ed. J. Piper and W. A. Grudem; Wheaton: Crossway, 1991) 140–53. I have expanded the notes in this excursus to respond further to Carson, although he basically attempts to speak against a few of my concerns, but offers no new resolution to the textual issue; and unfortunately, he does not speak to some of the textual issues as they are expanded in this present study.

[2]Which in my own language goes, "That reading which best explains how all the others came about is to be preferred as the original." No one who takes textual criticism seriously denies that this is indeed the "first principle." Disagreements arise in this case—and others—as to which reading best explains the others.

THE WESTERN EVIDENCE

The Western witnesses to 1 Corinthians have a text which translates as follows (beginning with v. 33, translating Claromontanus):

> For God is not a God of confusion, but of peace, as in all the churches of the saints. Or did the word of God originate with you, or are you the only ones to whom it came? If anyone thinks he is a prophet or a Spirit person, let him recognize that what I write to you is of the Lord. If anyone does not recognize this, he is not recognized. So then, brothers, be zealous to prophesy and do not forbid glossolalia; but let all things happen decently and in order. Let your women keep silence in the churches; for it is not permitted for them to speak, but let them be in submission, even as the Law says. If in fact they want to learn anything, let them ask their own husbands at home, for it is a shameful thing for a woman to speak in the assembly.

Admittedly, the evidence for this reading does not appear to be great, being limited to:

1. The three bilingual Western MSS:

    Claromontanus (D/d; 5th c.)

    Auginesis (F/f; 9th c.)

    Boernerianus (G/g; 9th c.)

2. The first hand of codex 88 (12th c.; a "Western" cursive)

3. Two other Old Latin MSS:

    Sangermanensis (e/76; 9th c.)

    Armachanus (ar/61; 9th c. [although this MS also omits vv. 36–39, so that its text reads vv. 33, 40, 34–35, in this order])

4. Two Latin Fathers:

    Ambrosiaster (4th c.)

    Sedulius Scotus (9th c.)

While this does not appear to be a significant array of witnesses, three matters about this evidence need to be underscored, which in turn leads us to the problem of transcriptional probability and Bengel's rule.

First, it is common to belittle this evidence either as "chiefly Western" (and therefore untrustworthy), late,[3] or quantitatively small. But such belittling in this case fails to catch its significance, for this collection of

---

[3]See, e.g., Ben Witherington III, *Women in the Earliest Churches* (SNTSMS 59; Cambridge University Press, 1988) 91: "The witnesses . . . are generally late and chiefly Western."

witnesses represents not simply a few Western MSS which happen to read the text in this way, but in fact the *whole* of the known non-Vulgate, and therefore pre-Vulgate, evidence for the Western text.[4] While it is true that the MSS are somewhat late, it has been demonstrated beyond reasonable doubt that the heart of this evidence, the three bilinguals D F G, in fact represent a form of text nearly identical to that of Hippolytus of Rome.[5] Therefore they can be said to bear witness to a form of the Western text known in Italy as early as the late second century. Consequently, to argue that the evidence is untrustworthy because it is late, is to reveal a lack of understanding of the nature of this evidence. What this means, then, is that one simply may not say of this evidence, "several Western MSS read these vss. at the end of chapter 14," or "a few manuscripts which elsewhere tend to edit the text."[6] For here we are dealing neither with a few Latin MSS per se, nor with MSS that elsewhere tend to edit. We are dealing with the entire surviving evidence for the shape of the text in the West before 385 CE.

Second, it should be noted that I, and others who take this position, have not argued that the Western tradition preserves the *original* order of Paul's argument. At this point in our argument, the question of "original text" is irrelevant. What I am urging first of all is that no one dismiss this evidence out of hand because it is thought to be secondary in character or not original at this point. Both of these may be readily admitted, but have no bearing in this case. What counts is the fact that this evidence is early and the only text known in the West before Jerome.

Third, the point, of course, is that the Western text is equally as early as the standard text. In fact, one can be sure of it: had Jerome not translated his Vulgate in Jerusalem, the Western reading would have been the only one known in the entire Latin tradition and would therefore have been taken far more seriously by scholarship. To put this another way, the two known readings were not vying with one another as original at any given point of geography in the first four Christian centuries. To the contrary, had one been a Christian anywhere in the West up to 400 CE, the Western text is the *only* way one would have

---

[4]The other OL MSS listed in our apparatuses as supporting the standard text are Vulgatized MSS, which reflect the evidence of Jerome, not the pre-Vulgate OL.

[5]See G. D. Fee, "The Majority Text and the Original Text of the New Testament," *BT* 31 (1980) 113–14; C. D. Osburn, "The Text of the Pauline Epistles in Hippolytus of Rome," *SecCent* 2 (1982) 97–124.

[6]J. B. Hurley, *Man and Woman in Biblical Perspective* (Grand Rapids: Zondervan, 1981) 185. Hurley's rejection of the textual evidence, in which he castigates those who think differently from himself as either "not having done their homework" or as "allowing their prejudices to sway their judgments," is itself a prejudicial approach to textual criticism. Unfortunately, Hurley himself does not work through the *textual* issues at all.

known Paul's argument; and so likewise in the East, the text we know best through an accident of history is the only one known on the Greek side of the Empire.

The point of my argument is simple: Since one cannot dismiss the Western evidence as that of so many lesser MSS (since it is the only reading known in the entire pre-Vulgate Western tradition), and since it is therefore as early as the reading that came to predominate in the East, both readings must theoretically be given equal weight as external evidence for Paul's original text. That leads me then to the second question, that of transcriptional probability.

THE TRANSCRIPTIONAL PROBABILITY

Given the early nature of the evidence for both readings, it was the question of transcriptional probability that finally convinced me that neither of these readings represents Paul's original text. Here is where Bengel's first principle, as always, must prevail in textual decisions: That form of the text is more likely the original which best explains the emergence of all the others. In this case there are two options: (a) Either some form of *transposition* had occurred (either the standard text or the Western text is original and some very early scribe in the East or West deliberately rearranged Paul's argument), or (b) the evidence points to a marginal gloss that was subsequently *interpolated* into the text at two different places. Of these two options, the latter is easily the one that best fits Bengel's first principle, for the following reasons:

(1) In terms of Paul's argument, one can make an equally good case for these sentences' appearing in either position. That is, neither of them *inherently* commands our allegiance as the original because it makes the best sense of Paul's argument; likewise neither of them commands our allegiance because the other is "smoother" or "more difficult." On the one hand, if these sentences originally belonged as vv. 34–35, one can show that the operative word is the third person imperative of σιγάω (σιγάτω vv. 28, 30; σιγάτωσαν, v. 34). Just as there is a time for glossolalists and prophets to be silent, so there is a time (always and absolutely) for women to be silent. On the other hand, if these sentences stood originally as vv. 41–42, then they come as a concluding afterthought to a carefully argued section on intelligibility and order in the assembly with regard to tongues and prophecy.

Likewise, if they can be shown to "fit" reasonably well in either place, they can both be shown equally as well *not* to fit well in either place. On the one hand, as vv. 34–35 they interrupt a tight argument between Paul and the Corinthians over the character and quality of what it means to be πνευματικός. Into this argument these two verses stick out like a rock, not to mention that the context has altogether to do with the exercise of χαρίσματα by *them all*, not with kinds or classes of people as such.

On the other hand, as vv. 41–42 they are exactly as described, an afterthought; and so much so, one wonders why Paul should have cared to contradict himself so thoroughly on the matter of women speaking in the assembly without some hint as to why.

Because one can make an equally good case *for or against either reading* most comments on the reason for the change become irrelevant. If, for example, the reason given is an attempt "to find a more appropriate location in the context for Paul's directive concerning women," as Metzger states,[7] then it must be admitted that this could go either way. Neither of the two extant ways of reading Paul's argument is persuasively "more apparent" than the other.

But it is also precisely because one can make an equally good case both for and against either reading that interpolation is the more viable option. That is, one can scarcely find a viable reason for such a total disruption of Paul's argument, if either of the early texts were original; by the same token, one can give perfectly good reasons for the double interpolation, since the argument can be made to work quite well when this material is in either location.

(2) To argue that either the Western text or the standard text is a transposition of the other is to use the word "transposition" in a way that is otherwise unknown in NT textual criticism. Transposition ordinarily refers to changing the position of items that are either (a) contiguous, as in letters, words, phrases, or sentences, or (b) in the case of words, sometimes noncontiguous, but still within their own phrases or sentences. To call the present textual phenomenon a transposition, therefore, is to press the meaning of that word quite beyond its ordinary sense.

If original to either location, what will have happened in this case is not a simple transposition of adjoining sentences, but a *radical rewriting of Paul's argument*. The problem here is not whether such could or could not have been done, but that such a total disruption of an author's argument on the part of a scribe has no precedent in the entire NT textual tradition.[8]

The complete lack of precedent for such a "transposition," on the one hand, with the concomitant existence of such precedent for a double interpolation, on the other, is what favors the theory of interpolation, rather than a theory of radical rewriting, as best explaining the textual data. That is, since this is a question of history as such, historical probability lies with an explanation predicated on *known* phenomena, not on one that is otherwise a historical solecism.

(3) Even more difficult is to imagine the historical circumstances of the scribe who would have disrupted an author's argument in this

---

[7] *Textual Commentary*, 565.

[8] Unless, of course, one is prepared to argue, despite all the evidence against it, that John 7:52–8:12 is original there and has been "transposed" to its various other settings in the tradition.

fashion. While it is true that not all scribes were careful workmen and that the Western text often shows signs of scribes who took considerable liberties with the text, this change reflects neither carelessness nor ordinary liberty.

Whatever else, scribes were chiefly copyists, trying to reproduce a second—readable and useful—copy of a written document. In this case, however, the "scribe" who "transposed" Paul's argument in this fashion can only have done so by deliberately rewriting the entire argument; it could not have happened by accident. It is arguable, of course, that the scribe left out a considerable portion and then reinserted it at a convenient place. But that is a merely *possible* solution without an ounce of historical probability. We are talking about dropping several lines of text (seven in P[46]), which could hardly be accounted for as a copying error per se.

On the other hand, because one can make sense of either text as they appear in the manuscript tradition, one can scarcely make a sound *historical* case for someone's having deliberately rearranged the text.[9] It is not that scribes did not, or could not, think. But in light of how many of Paul's arguments have been left untouched (think only of 1 Cor 14:22–25), no valid *historical* reason for such a radical alteration of this argument can be posited. The scribe, after all, is *copying* a text. If his mind is *not* at work, there is no possibility of his making this major change; if his mind *is* in his work, there is equally no accounting for his choosing to place these words at another location in the argument. If vv. 34–35 were original, one should note, there are two major strikes against such a radical rewriting of the text:

First, the scribe would be copying a text without a break between letters, words, and sentences. What we must imagine is someone who was copying a line that would have read something like this:

ΤΩΝΑΓΙΩΝΑΙΓΥΝΑΙΚΕΣΕΝΤΑΙΣ

who would then have paused after the ΑΓΙΩΝ, left out the next four sentences, holding them in abeyance, then picked up his copying again with the H in the middle of a line that would have looked something like this:

---

[9]Grudem (*Gift*, 241) tries to make a case for this, but it does not seem to have been thought through carefully in terms of historical probability. He states: "In fact, some early scribes *thought* that vss. 34–35 were *out of place* and *transposed* them to follow vs. 40" (emphases mine; an argument repeated by Carson, "Silent," 142–43, but with no further explanation as either to *why* or *how* an early scribe could have been imagined to do such a thing). Grudem adds that this "point[s] to an early uneasiness about these verses which extends to the present day." That is easily asserted, but in fact there is no precedent for this in the entire NT textual tradition. (That scribes [plural] would have done such a thing is well-nigh impossible [it may have happened once, but twice independently exceeds the bounds of historical probability]).

ΕΝΕΚΚΛΕΣΙΑΗΑΦΥΜΩΝΟΛΟΓΟΣ

only to reinsert the omitted four sentences a bit later in the middle of yet
another line that would have looked something like this:

ΤΑΧΙΝΓΙΝΕΣΘΩΓΝΩΡΙΖΩΔΕΥΜΙΝ

I would not argue that such could not have been done; after all, all things
are possible. But I would argue that not all possible things are equally
probable historically. And the improbability of such a rewriting of a text
is high indeed, not to mention without historical precedent.

But secondly, why *should he do so?* Since there are scores of places in
Paul where one could reasonably have rearranged the argument, and
yet this was *not* done in the scribal tradition, under what historical rubric
will one wish to argue for someone's having done so in this one instance?
Especially so, when one can make sense of either text in its present
arrangement. In fact the oft-repeated argument, "to find a more appropriate location in the text," simply will not wash.

The strength of this argument can be seen by putting the question
of "transposition" in reverse, and ask, as I did one time, since the Western
text is equally as early as the standard text, then why not assume for the
moment that it represents the original; how then would one explain its
having been moved from its location at the end of this section forward
to its setting in the Eastern tradition? The answer given was, "But no one
would have done such a thing." Precisely![10]

Copyists are copyists; and even when they try to assist an author
by additions, grammatical improvements, or local transpositions, they
nonetheless remain copyists. There is no precedent for their becoming
redactors of this particular kind, at least not in the Pauline corpus.

(4) Finally, now to bring parts I and II together, if the Western text
of Paul shows *some* of the characteristics of that text in the Gospels and
Acts (in the sense of its being an independent witness and reflecting a
somewhat undisciplined copying tradition), it fails on the whole to do so
either so consistently or so radically in the Pauline corpus. One would
be hard pressed ever to write a meaningful volume on the "theological
tendencies" of the Western text of the Pauline letters. It simply does not
exist in that way in the apostle.

All of this evidence together argues especially strongly, despite the
lack of direct manuscript evidence, for interpolation as the best solution
to the textual problem. Those who wish to maintain the authenticity of

---

[10]And if one were to argue (with Carson, "Silent," 143–44) that the Eastern text
is the *lectio difficilior* (with which I would tend to agree, but with very little conviction),
the obvious reply is that a less likely historical solecism hardly makes it any less a
historical solecism.

these verses must at least offer an *adequate* answer as to how the Western arrangement came into existence, if Paul wrote them originally as our vv. 34–35. Failure to offer an answer, and it must have historical credibility to be adequate, must also be seen as evidence in favor of interpolation.[11]

THE INTERNAL EVIDENCE

It is usually assumed, and sometimes baldly asserted, that the real reason for arguing for the inauthenticity of these verses "depends on the conviction that they seriously conflict with 11.5 and other passages in Paul."[12] That they do indeed, but the problem of resolving the textual evidence itself poses the greater problem in my case.[13]

Nonetheless, once one sees on textual grounds the unlikelihood of Paul's having written these words—and at this point in his argument—all kinds of matters of intrinsic probability are more easily answered. Besides the issue of contradiction just noted, there is the structural argument presented above in the discussion of vv. 26–33 and 36–40. The rhetorical "Or did the word of God originate with you?" follows perfectly from "as in all the churches of the saints," whereas one has to perform some exegetical gymnastics to get the "or" with which v. 36 begins to fit meaningfully as a response to v. 35. The "What!" of the KJV, RSV, and others, has no known linguistic evidence from Greek antiquity—all the more so in light of Paul's use of this double "or" to begin rhetorical questions in this letter.

There are also several linguistic irregularities in these two verses, any one of which is possible, but which together form a considerable package in four brief sentences. They include (a) the use of the plural "in the churches," which occurs nowhere else in Paul; (b) the appeal to the law—in an absolute sense, without quoting or referring to a specific passage—which is unknown in Paul; (c) the appeal to shame in v. 35 as a general cultural matter (which is quite unlike the appeal to "shaming" one's spouse in 11:5).

---

[11] While one may well agree with Carson ("Silent," 142) that "adequacy is in part in the eye of the beholder," at least one should offer a historical answer that matches what we know elsewhere to be true of the scribal tradition. That has not been forthcoming in this case, nor does an appeal to the way this tradition handles the Gospel and Acts fit well here, since the same kind of handling of the text is demonstrably *not* so in the Pauline corpus.

[12] Grudem, *Gift*, 241.

[13] One might easily turn this argument about and say that the failure to the take the Western textual evidence seriously is based on a prior commitment to authenticity. In most cases I would be loathe so to argue; but I would point out that such argumentation can easily cut both ways.

But there are two contextual matters that are especially difficult. The first is the fact that these two verses so thoroughly intrude into the argument. The entire argument from 14:1 to 40 deals with tongues and prophecy as manifestations of the Spirit within the community; only in v. 29 are people mentioned ("prophets"), and as noted in the preceding exegesis, this is much less likely referring to people per se than to the functioning of prophecy within the assembly. The present verses, on the other hand, do not so much as mention gifts, ministries, or the Spirit; they deal with people as such, women in this case, and absolutely deny them the privilege of speaking in the assembly.

Second, most attempts to give meaning to these verses in terms of the context of tongues and prophecy spend most of their time trying to get around the plain sense of the text, which requires women to be silent in all the churches, and without qualification. That is, the command is absolute, with no modifier or qualifier: "The women must be silent in the churches"; "it is not permitted them to speak"; "if they wish to learn let them ask their husbands at home"; "it is shameful for a woman to speak in the assembly." Thus, these sentences not only do not fit the context of the present argument in terms of content, but they contradict the emphasis on the participation of "all" throughout the chapter.

Of those who have tried to make sense of the passage as in some way dealing with the argument of the section, two are noteworthy. On the basis of the verb "speaking," which is used throughout the argument when tongues is mentioned, some have tried to limit the silence to tongues, the implication being that the "eschatological women" are themselves basically responsible for the problem.[14] But that faces insuperable difficulties: (a) Paul uses the same verb for "speaking" prophetic utterances; (b) whenever the verb refers to "tongues," the latter word invariably modifies the verb; (c) v. 35 implies the asking of questions for the sake of learning, not the alleged thrusting on the congregation of their own Spirit utterances; (d) and the prohibition takes a more absolute form than this view allows.

Still others have tried to make it, some four sentences later, to be Paul's own qualifier on "the discerning of prophecies" in v. 29b;[15] but it is hard to imagine how, without some internal clue or some kind of qualifier, the Corinthians, in hearing this letter read in their assembly, could have picked out *only the second part of v. 29b as being qualified*, in light of all that has preceded and especially in light of the absolute way silence is enjoined.

---

[14]See, e.g., Martin, *Spirit*, 85–88.

[15]A view that appears to have been advanced first by Thrall 102. See the more complete presentation in Grudem, *Gift*, 239–55; cf. Hurley, *Man and Woman*, 185–94; Carson, *Showing*, 129–31 (repeated in "Silent," 151–53).

Both Grudem (241) and Martin (84) have argued that if one can make good sense of the text in its context (in its position in the East), then that should be reason enough to accept the words as authentic. Even if one were to allow that argument, which I find especially difficult in light of the textual evidence, my problems still remain. Having gone over both of their arguments with great care, I find them especially unsuccessful in dealing with what the text actually says (absolute prohibition, which both deny, despite the clear evidence of the text itself) or in giving it a reasonable sense in the argument in context. One needs internal clues of some kind to make their answers stick; and there are none. The only internal clue, "that they ask their husbands at home if they wish to learn," is made to mean something other than what it plainly says in both cases; and in neither case do they adequately explain why *this* is the only clue given, why not something about "tongues" or "discerning" or "judging" or something, if that is what Paul was talking about.

On the whole, therefore, the case against these verses is so strong, and finding a viable solution to their meaning so difficult, that it seems best to view them as an interpolation. If so, then one must assume that the words were first written as a gloss in the margin by someone who, perhaps in light of 1 Tim 2:9–15, felt the need to qualify Paul's instructions even further. Since the phenomenon of glosses making their way into the biblical text is so well-documented elsewhere in the NT (e.g., John 5:3b–4; 1 John 5:7), there is no good historical reason to reject the possibility here. That these words occur in all extant witnesses[16] only means that the double interpolation had taken place before the time of our present textual tradition, and could easily have happened before the turn of the first century.

Thus, this passage is almost certainly not by Paul, nor does it belong to this argument. That means, of course, that it offers no help in our search for the place of the Spirit in the Pauline experience of Christ and in his theology.

---

[16]This is admittedly the strongest argument for authenticity, as Carson ("Silent") most recently emphasizes. But see now P. B. Payne, "Fuldensis, Sigla for Variants on Vaticanus, and 1 Cor 14.34–35," *NTS* (forthcoming), who has argued convincingly that the early Vulgate MS, Fuldensis, bears witness to a text *without* these verses.

5

SECOND CORINTHIANS

Commentaries:[1] P. **Barnett** (BST, 1988); C. K. **Barrett** (HNTC, 1973);
G. R. **Beasley-Murray** (BBC, 1971); J. H. **Bernard** (EGT, 1897); F. F.
Bruce (NCB, 1971); R. **Bultmann** (1976; ET 1985); J. **Calvin** (ET, 1964);
D. A. **Carson** (1987 [10–13 only]); J.-F. **Collange** (1972 [2:14–7:4 only]);
F. W. **Danker** (ACNT, 1989); V. P. **Furnish** (AB, 1984); R. P. C. **Hanson**
(TBC, 1954); M. J. **Harris** (EBC, 1976); J. **Héring** (ET, 1967); C. **Hodge**
(1891); P. E. **Hughes** (NICNT, 1962); C. **Kruse** (TNTC, 1987); H. **Lietz-
mann** (ed. W. G. Kümmel; HNT, 1949); R. P. **Martin** (WBC, 1986); H. A. W.
Meyer (1879); A. **Plummer** (ICC, 1915); R. H. **Strachan** (MNTC, 1935);
C. H. **Talbert** (1989); R. V. G. **Tasker** (TNTC, 1958); M. E. **Thrall** (CBC,
1965); H. D. **Wendland** (NTD, 1968); H. **Windisch** (MeyerK, 1924).

Other significant works are referred to by the following short titles:

Belleville, *Reflections* (= Linda Belleville, *Reflections of Glory: Paul's Polemical Use of Moses-Doxa Tradition in 2 Corinthians 3.1–18* [JSNTSup 52;
Sheffield; JSOT, 1991]); **Martin,** "Spirit" (= Ralph P. Martin, "The Spirit
in 2 Corinthians in Light of the 'Fellowship of the Holy Spirit' in 2 Corin-
thians 13:14," in *Eschatology and the New Testament: Essays in Honor of
George Raymond Beasley-Murray* [ed. W. H. Gloer; Peabody, Mass.: Hendrick-
son, 1988] 113–28); **Sumney,** *Opponents* (= Jerry L. Sumney, *Identifying Paul's
Opponents: The Question of Method in 2 Corinthians* [JSNTSup 40; Sheffield;
JSOT, 1990]); **Young-Ford,** *Meaning* (= Frances Young and David F. Ford,
Meaning and Truth in 2 Corinthians [Grand Rapid: Eerdmans, 1987]).

In turning to this letter from 1 Corinthians, one has the sense of entering
a new world. Almost none of the issues raised in the earlier letter seem
to appear here, except the concern over the collection,[2] which has now

---

[1]The following commentaries are referred to in this chapter only by the author's
last name.
[2]See chs. 8–9 of this letter; cf. 1 Cor 16:1–11.

taken a considerably new turn. On further reflection, however, this sense of newness turns out to be but a surface reading of the two letters. What holds them together in fact is not so much the specific issues addressed in each, but the overriding tension one finds in both over Paul's apostleship, and thus over his authority and that of his gospel.[3] And it is precisely at this point where the ministry of the Spirit looms large in the letter,[4] despite the much smaller number of specific references than in 1 Corinthians.[5]

Part of the problem in dealing with these texts, however, relates to a factor that emerges scarcely if at all in 1 Corinthians. The problems between Paul and this church that had surfaced at the writing 1 Corinthians seem largely to have been at the instigation of a few within the community.[6] The letter, therefore, is addressed to the entire community, always in the second person plural,[7] and with scarcely a hint that there are outsiders who might make up part of the problem. The only possible hint of external influence occurs in 9:12, "if others share in your material benefits, should not we do so the more?" In the context of 1 Corinthians, especially since there is no other hint of outsiders being currently among them, the "others" in this text most likely refers to Apollos and Cephas, when they were among them (cf. 9:4–6).

But in both letters that form 2 Corinthians (chs. 1–9, 10–13) all of this has changed. Outsiders first emerge in 2:14–4:6, where Paul refers to

---

[3]For a helpful discussion in this regard, see Young-Ford, *Meaning*, 44–52.

[4]It is therefore with considerable insight into the heart of things that Karl Prümm entitled his theological study of this letter *Diakonia Pneumatos* (διακονία πνεύματος, from 3:6, 8), Rome: Herder, 1960.

[5]Because the letter is so intensely personal, and so intensely ad hoc, it has more than its share of difficulties in terms of overall design and purpose. Included in these difficulties is the question of its integrity (whether our present letter was one letter or a compilation of two or more). Resolving this issue in this case does not affect the overall exegesis of the various passages. For my own position on this question see "ΧΑΡΙΣ in II Corinthians i.15: Apostolic Parousia and Paul-Corinth Chronology," *NTS* 24 (1977–78) 533–38, which is similar to that of Barrett and Furnish—that chs. 1–9 are a single letter sent from Macedonia by way of Titus and two other brothers (8:16–24), basically to have them pick up the collection, but at the same time to explain his more recent relations with them in light of Titus' report that things between them are much better than he had previously hoped. But at issue in all of this is his own form of apostolic lifestyle, and with it his apostolic authority. Chapters 10–13 form a fifth letter to Corinth written very shortly after chs. 1–9, when Titus had apparently beat a hasty retreat to Macedonia because earlier problems had not only resurfaced but worsened. This letter (our 2 Cor 10–13), written in anticipation of his own soon-to-be-realized third visit, is also primarily about his apostleship; consequently, it continues the discussion of chs. 1–9 in a more vigorous way, making the two letters easily form one in overall design, if not in actual time of writing.

[6]Note, e.g., "each of you says" (1:12), "some [of you, is implied] are puffed up as though I were not coming to you" (4:18), "how can some among you say" (15:12).

[7]Except for a few instances where he reverts to the second person singular, so as to make his point even more telling.

some opponents (apparently) as "peddlers of the word" (2:17), who "need letters of commendation" (3:1), and in contrast to whom Paul "does not use deception or distort the word of God" (4:2). It is in this context that the largest single block of Spirit material occurs in the letter (3:3–18), as Paul contrasts his own ministry and its effectiveness in Corinth with that of his opponents: his is of Spirit, theirs of "letter." When this conflict fully emerges in chs. 10–13, Paul accuses these outsiders of preaching "another Jesus" and the Corinthians of having thus received "another Spirit." These passages suggest that even though the ground has shifted a bit, in that the opponents are probably Jewish Christians who are pressing for some form of "Jewishness" as part of their understanding of Christ and the Spirit,[8] they probably have found some common cause with the Corinthians in their understanding of apostleship and its relationship to the Spirit. Hence they have struck the chord of triumphalism once again, with its emphasis on visible and powerful demonstrations of Spirit life; so Paul must wrestle with this issue once more, this time along the lines of the "new thought" that has made its way among them.

As a result there are two passages in particular, 2:14–4:6 and 12:1–12, that require a rather thorough examination, both for their meaning in context and for our grasping Paul's understanding of life in the Spirit. Both of them come out of strongly polemical contexts,[9] but what emerges is a view of the Spirit that is quite in keeping with what we have seen thus far—although some of the language changes rather dramatically. Here in particular, the eschatological dimension of the coming of the Spirit stands out; for all the continuity Paul experiences with his Jewish past, the Spirit especially is the key to the element of discontinuity. In the gospel of Christ, we are dealing with "newness of Spirit";[10] where the Spirit of the Lord is, there is "freedom," especially toward God, but also from the letter that kills. The death and resurrection of Christ and the gift of the eschatological Spirit (the down payment on the future, 1:22;

---

[8]This is an area of considerable difficulty, and therefore of considerable discussion. For a helpful overview of the debate, and for a "minimalistic" approach to its resolution, see Sumney, *Opponents*. The problems in identification are large, having to do with the limited amount of material from this letter, found basically in polemical contexts, and with whether or not the alleged opponents are related to those in other letters as well. I am impressed with the specific Jewishness that Paul singles out in 11:22, combined with the argumentation of ch. 3, but I doubt whether we may thereby "define" their theological perspective with any confidence. To describe what they were presenting as an expression of "Jewishness" is intended not to be pejorative, but simply to find a word that covers this side of the difficulty, a difficulty exacerbated by the fact that the word "law" does not appear in this letter.

[9]This is debated with regard to 2:14–4:6; see the discussion in Belleville, *Reflections*, 143–48.

[10]This language comes from Rom 7:6; that it also describes the basic thrust of the argument in ch. 3 can hardly be doubted.

5:5) mark the end of the old order, even if it is still very much with us. But as in 1 Corinthians, the evidence of Spirit activity in Paul's new life—and by implication therefore in theirs—is not ecstasy as such or an abundance of revelations from the Spirit. Paul indeed had these, but what counts is the Spirit's making it possible for him to live by the grace of Christ, even in his bodily weaknesses (12:1–12).

At the same time, as with the earlier letters, there is also a considerable number of "incidental" mentions of the Spirit, which, as before, tend to cover the broad range of concerns. Thus, as in the earlier letters, the mention of Christian origins for any group of believers invariably involves Paul in Spirit talk, this time (1:21–22) with a rich supply of metaphors (anointing, seal, down payment). It is the Spirit who brings faith (4:13), and Paul and Titus both walk by the same Spirit (12:18). Although not mentioned directly, the Spirit is again the key to their being God's temple; it is by God's Spirit that God dwells among them, thus calling them to holiness (6:16–7:1). And here, too, in the form of a benedictory prayer, we find one of the clearest, unequivocal references to the Spirit as one of the three Persons of the Godhead (13:13[14]), each of whom is designated by that special ministry indicative of each.

One other related phenomenon of this letter needs to be noted, and that is the high incidence of the language "flesh" as a pejorative term,[11] and always in polemical contexts. Because of its usage in Galatians and Romans we are used to thinking of the "flesh/Spirit" contrast as central to Paul's thinking. In fact that direct contrast occurs rarely in Paul's letters. Its earliest appearance is in 1 Cor 3:1–4. In a context where the Corinthians considered themselves πνευματικοί (= Spiritual; people of the Spirit), Paul says that they are actually acting like people who operate on the basis of "flesh" more than of Spirit. In the present letter they seem to have turned that argument around on Paul and variously accuse him of being "fleshly," precisely because he does not share their current triumphalist presuppositions. Even though these various passages do not appear in direct contrast to the Spirit in this letter, we need to note them in passing, because this usage will have some bearing on Paul's later usage of this contrast in Galatians and Romans.

Thus even in this intensely personal, intensely emotional, letter, one cannot escape the central role the Spirit plays in Paul's understanding of the gospel and of the Christian life.

2 CORINTHIANS 1:11

[10] . . . *And he will yet rescue* [11]*as you also help by joining in prayer for us, so that from many people thanksgiving may be offered through many on our behalf for the gracious gift given us.*

---

[11]1:12, 17; 5:16[2x]; 10:2, 3[2x], 4. See the further discussion of this in ch. 12.

This terribly complex sentence which concludes the opening "blessing" of this letter is included in this study because of the occurrence of the word χάρισμα (translated "gracious gift"). Frequently in Paul χάρισμα is associated with the Spirit. But as already noted on 1 Cor 1:7 (cf. 7:7), the concept of "spiritual gift" is ancillary to the word χάρισμα, not inherent to it. As a rule of thumb, some contextual reason must usually be present in order for us to understand this word as referring to the activity of the Spirit; χάρισμα refers rather to some concrete expression of grace received.[12] In this case the χάρισμα is most likely to be understood as the gracious activity of God on Paul's behalf in rescuing him from a deadly peril, from which at one point he did not expect to recover.

What is unusual about this present usage is its apparent reference to a specific event in Paul's life. In 1 Cor 7:7, for example, it referred to that kind of "giftedness" that enabled one to live as a true celibate—or within marriage ("one of one kind, one of another"). Or in Rom 6:23 the χάρισμα is the gift of salvation itself, given through Christ. But here it refers apparently to his recovery from some debilitation, sickness or otherwise, that had caused him to despair of life itself. Thus, finally, the χάρισμα is the gift of life itself, given specifically through his recovery from his θλῖψις ("distress," "affliction").

This usage in particular should alert the reader of Paul not to be too hasty to refer to Spirit manifestations as χαρίσματα in such a way as thereby to truncate the much broader semantic field in which this word operates.

2 CORINTHIANS 1:12

For our boasting is this, the witness of our conscience, that in the holiness and sincerity of God, and not by fleshly wisdom but by the grace of God, have we conducted ourselves in the world, and especially toward you.

It is striking that Paul should begin the body of the letter on this decidedly apologetic note. Why he should do so is to be explained in part by the deteriorating relationship between him and them that was already manifesting itself when he wrote 1 Corinthians. In the meantime, matters had obviously worsened. Despite Titus' basically good report that some past difficulties had been healed, it is clear from the way this letter begins that Paul still feels compelled to explain, and thus to defend, his own relationship with them, and in so doing once more to defend his apostleship before them.

Thus, these opening words take the form of a denial and an affirmation. The denial is that he has ever conducted himself toward them on the basis of "fleshly wisdom." Although not mentioned directly, a contrast between such an outlook and the life of the Spirit lies close to the surface. For reasons to be spelled out throughout this letter, he chooses in this instance to contrast "fleshly wisdom" with "the grace of God." Our present interest lies with the fact that this is now the second instance

---

[12]On this matter see especially the discussion in ch. 2, pp. 32–35.

in the corpus that a pejorative view of "the flesh" emerges. The first occurrence was in 1 Cor 3:1–4, where it arose specifically as a way of his contrasting what they claimed to be (Spirit people)—and by grace were indeed—with what their present stance toward "wisdom" implied, namely, that their outlook and behavior were anything but that of the Spirit; rather, they were acting like people who lived on the basis of "the flesh." (For the meaning of this term, when used in this pejorative way, see the discussion of 5:16–17 below.)

2 CORINTHIANS 1:21–22

[21]*Now the one who establishes us, along with you,*[13] *unto Christ, and has anointed us, is God,* [22]*who indeed*[14] *sealed us and gave us the down payment of the Holy Spirit in our hearts.*

With these remarkable words Paul concludes the first part of his argument that began in v. 12 and carries through to 7:16.[15] What is remarkable is not so much the words themselves, but that they should conclude this particular argument. At issue is Paul's *integrity*, as it relates to his relationship with the Corinthian community. Although Titus' return had indicated that there had been a measure of reconciliation between them and Paul (7:5–16), Titus probably also had to report that there was some lingering bad feeling. Some of this undoubtedly stems from an earlier time and is reflected in 1 Corinthians.

In any case, Paul feels a decided urgency to explain his recent relationships with them, and especially his recent change of itinerary—for a second time.[16] But at stake still more than his own integrity is his apostleship. That has been called into question by some of them for a considerable time, as 1 Cor 4:1–21 and 9:1–23 make plain. His change of announced plans to return to Corinth after traveling to Macedonia,

---

[13]A few scattered witnesses (C 104 630 pc sy[h]) have the two pronouns, "us" and "you," in reverse order. This appears to be a simple and characteristic scribal error; the sense of Paul's argument demands the order of the standard text.

[14]As will be noted in the exegesis below, this καί is most likely explicative (ascensive), not connective or something "in addition to." That is, the God who "anointed us" thereby also "sealed us" by "having given us the down payment of the Holy Spirit."

[15]This of course recognizes that 2:14–7:4 forms a considerable—though understandable—break in this argument, and in fact is also the longest single block of material in this letter.

[16]The evidence from 1 Cor 16:5–7 and 2 Cor 1:15–17 and 1:23–2:4 indicates that the visit mentioned in 2 Cor 1:15–16, 23–24 does *not* correspond to that proposed in 1 Cor 16:5–7 (thus one change in plans); further, he has obviously not followed through on the second plan mentioned in 2 Cor 1:15–16. It is this latter change of plans that he is hereby explaining to them. See Fee, "XAPIΣ"; but see also the response in Furnish 142–45, who reconstructs the proposed visits differently.

returning to Ephesus instead, has apparently fueled the fires of his detractors, now supported by some outside opposition.[17] Paul can be no
apostle of the truth that is in Christ, since he so obviously says both *yes*
and *no* out of the same side of his mouth.

Therefore, precisely because his apostleship is at stake, Paul feels compelled not simply to explain himself, but also to establish his integrity—
ultimately on theological grounds. Thus the strange and, to us, apparently
convoluted nature of the present argument. He begins by giving the reason
for the first change of plans (vv. 15–16),[18] insisting that that plan had
not been made with levity nor did changing it mean duplicity on his part
(v. 17). "Are my plans made like a mere worldling,"[19] he asks rhetorically,
"full of duplicity, meaning both 'yes' and 'no' at the same time?" The
form of the rhetoric carries its own intended response, "of course not."

But that is not sufficient for Paul, so he launches into a singular
theological vindication of his integrity in which he is intent to tie his
"words" (about itineraries, etc.) to his "word" (his preaching of the
gospel), and thus to God's own faithfulness as revealed in Christ his Son
and in the gift of the Spirit. This is bold stuff, based on the absolute
conviction expressed in 1:1 that his apostleship is predicated altogether
on God's will. Thus, despite appearances, the logic of the argument in its
various parts can be easily traced out:

(a) The first statement following the rhetorical denial of his duplicity
is the boldest of all (v. 18a, "God is faithful"). Paul's integrity is predicated
first of all on God's faithfulness, or trustworthiness.

(b) God's faithfulness is what guarantees Paul's "word" to them
(v. 18b). An obvious word play is in progress here: in its first sense this
guaranteed "word" is that of vv. 15–17; but that is only part of the play.
The real "word" that validates all other "words" is his preaching of
Christ, which is the true "word" that is "to them" (v. 18) and was
preached "among them" (v. 19).

(c) The clear evidence that Paul's "word" is trustworthy is to be
found in the faithful God's Son, whom Paul (and his companions)

---

[17] These people, who are mentioned only in chs. 1–9 (e.g., 2:14–4:6) but who have
bid fair to take over in chs. 10–13, seem to have seized on these doubts about Paul's
authority as basic to their proclamation of "another Jesus" (11:4).

[18] In v. 15; in order that "they might have double opportunity for grace"; that is,
the privilege of helping him on to Macedonia and of being the "sending church" for
the mission to Jerusalem. For this interpretation of δευτέραν χάριν, see Fee, "ΧΑΡΙΣ."

[19] Gk. κατὰ σάρκα (lit. "according to the flesh"). Cf. 1:12, the accusation in 10:2,
and especially the argument in 5:16 that he does not view anyone from this
perspective, hence neither should they. Thus, this is a distinctively pejorative term
that frequently stands in contrast to Spirit, as it seems to do here (v. 22; cf. 1 Cor 2:1),
and that has to do with living from the perspective of the present age and its values.
See on "worldly" wisdom in 1 Cor 2:6–16, and, especially for this contrast, Gal
5:16–6:8.

preached so effectively in Corinth. The "for" that begins v. 19 is explanatory, or evidential. Thus, "for the Son of God, Jesus Christ, whom we preached, is himself God's yes," not only to his own promises, but by implication also to Paul's "word."

(d) Indeed, he will explain further (v. 20a), in apparent anticipation of chapter 3 (and 11?), all of God's promises to Israel have found their divine *yes* in Christ. There is nothing more to be had.

(e) Not only so, he adds (v. 20b), but in our corporate worship it is "through Christ" that we (both Paul and the Corinthians) affirm God's trustworthy word, found in Christ and preached by us, by saying the "Amen" to God, unto his eternal glory.

(f) Finally, he concludes (vv. 21–22), the same trustworthy God, whose Son is his *yes* to his promises, is the one who confirms us; and not only us, but you as well. This confirmation is the outflow of his having already "anointed" us, that is, his having "sealed" us by giving us the Holy Spirit as God's down payment on our sure future.

It should be noted, finally, that this is one of the most God-centered, God-focused paragraphs in the Pauline corpus. As such it is a clear reflection of Paul's essential theology, and is even more telling because it is such an "off-the-cuff," nonreflective moment. Paul's integrity—and their own existence in Christ that is so integrally tied up with that integrity[20]—ultimately rests in the *character* of God (his trustworthiness, whose promises have all been realized in Christ) and in the *saving activity* of God, which is but an outflow of his character. Thus, as always in Paul, God's own character stands as both the ground and the initiative of his saving activity, which was effected historically by his Son and appropriated in the lives of believers by his Spirit, who is also the present guarantor of the final eschatological glory. What is true of the paragraph as a whole, it should be further noted, is also played out in particular in the final sentence (vv. 21–22), where the God who presently "confirms" in Christ is the one who previously had anointed ("christed") believers by giving them the Holy Spirit.

Thus, the primary role of the Spirit in this argument is to confirm Paul's integrity—and ministry.[21] But the inclusion of the Corinthians at the end indicates that the Spirit, whom they equally have experienced, should certify Paul's own trustworthiness to them.

21–22 Here is a Pauline sentence that requires some structural and grammatical analysis before one looks at the details, since structure and grammar determine so much as to its meaning. First, the whole is a single

---

[20]A point that is often made in the two extant letters to this congregation. See, e.g., 1 Cor 4:14–17; 9:1–2; and in our present letter especially 3:1–3 and 13:1–10.

[21]Cf. Martin, "Spirit," 168: " . . . this confession of faith . . . is also an *apologia* for apostolic service."

nominal[22] sentence, whose basic word order I have tried to keep in the translation. The sentence begins with two substantival participles ("he who confirms" and "who anointed"), followed by the predicate noun "God," which in turn is followed by two further substantival participles ("who sealed" and "who gave"). This structure and word order suggest that the "is" most likely should be understood as coming before the θεός, not after it. Thus, "the one who . . . *is* God," not "the God who . . . *is* the one who also . . . "

A structural display of the sentence, therefore, looks like this:

```
The one    who        confirms us
                           along with you
                               unto Christ
                           and
           who         anointed us is God
           who indeed  sealed us
                           and
                       gave us the down payment
                               of the Spirit
                                   in our hearts
```

Second, such an unusual sentence, with "God" as its central moment, should be taken seriously as reflecting present concerns. The emphasis seems to lie first of all on Paul's being presently "confirmed" by God (and by extension therefore all of them); at the same time the whole emphasizes the absolutely central and crucial role taken by God.

Third, the fact that the first participle is present tense, while all the others are aorist, can hardly be accidental. Thus, the present tense of βεβαιῶν ("confirms") brings the current argument about Paul's integrity to its fitting conclusion; but his immediate inclusion of the Corinthians ("us along with you") in Christ not only reaffirms the absolute interconnectedness between his ministry and their existence as believers, but also launches him into a moment of reflection on their mutual present "confirmation" as predicated on the past event of their reception of the Spirit, presumably at conversion. Thus, the one who "confirms" is the very God who previously "anointed us."

Fourth, apart from the second phrase in v. 21 ("and anointed us") the whole is dominated by a commercial metaphor ("confirms" = guarantees; "seals" = ownership and guarantee; and "down payment" = the guarantee of the future). The "odd phrase out" ("anointed") is almost certainly the result of yet one more word play. In Paul's sentence it immediately follows the mention of Christ (thus, εἰς χριστὸν καὶ χρίσας

---

[22]That is, a sentence without a verb. In such sentences a form of "to be" is understood.

ἡμᾶς); but since his concern is with the "confirmation" metaphor, which in Paul's thinking is ultimately the role of the Spirit in Christian life, he immediately follows the subject "God" by elaborating on the metaphor "anoints" in terms of the Spirit, using two further "confirmation" metaphors in so doing. What this means structurally, therefore, is that the final two participial phrases that make up v. 22 are elaborations of the "anointing" metaphor of v. 21; this in turn means that the καί which follows the ὁ ("he who") in v. 22 is probably to be understood neither as conjunctive (= "and") nor as "additional" (= "also"), but as ascensive (= "who indeed," i.e., "who in having anointed thereby also sealed"). Finally, since the last two metaphors ("seal" and "down payment") refer to one and the same reality, the gift of the Spirit, the καί that joins them should also be understood as epexegetical, wherein the second gives content to, or further elaborates, the first. Thus, "God indeed is the one who sealed us, by having given us the down payment of the Holy Spirit."[23]

The net result is a sentence that in elaborated translation goes something like this: "Now the one who confirms us (in our integrity) and you therefore along with us unto Christ, and who anointed us ('christed us' = made us Christ's people), is God, who thereby also sealed us, by having given us the down payment of the Holy Spirit in our hearts." What this means, then, is that the present sentence is affirming the presence of the Spirit as the crucial ingredient not only in their own existence as believers but at the same time of his own ministry among them as an apostle—an argument that anticipates both the nature and the content of the argument of chapter 3 that follows.

If that is what the sentence as a whole means, then what of its various parts, especially its metaphors?

Anointed. This is the only occurrence of this metaphor in the Pauline corpus, which at first blush is striking, given its OT linkage to the Spirit and the rich possibilities of the metaphor.[24] The reason for this singular usage in Paul lies close at hand. As noted above, the metaphor in this case is probably the result of a play on words: in putting us into *Christ*, God *christed* us, which means something like "made us Christ's people." If we take seriously that Luke–Acts springs from the same milieu as Paul's, and therefore probably reflects the Jesus tradition as found in the Pauline churches,[25] Luke's own restriction of this terminology to refer to Christ's having been anointed by God with the Holy Spirit probably gives us the clue for NT usage.[26] "Anointing" came to be associated especially

---

[23]Cf. Martin, "Spirit," 119.

[24]All the more, when one considers how often this metaphor functioned in the later church in talking about the work of the Spirit, beginning with 1 John (2:20, 27).

[25]For a discussion of this perspective, as it relates to the words of institution in 1 Cor 11:23–25, see Fee, *1 Corinthians*, 546–47.

[26]Cf. Dunn, *Baptism*, 133, who puts it in slightly different form.

with Jesus and the gift of the Spirit whereby he was appointed/affirmed for his role as Messiah (= Christ). He therefore was the "Anointed One" in a unique sense, so that in time the title became part of the name by which he was known in the early church ("Jesus the Christ" came to be simply "Jesus Christ"). That usage probably also accounts for the general reluctance to apply this imagery to believers.

Hence what Paul does here is unique to the NT. His first point of reference is almost certainly to his and the Corinthians' relationship to Christ. By joining them to the Anointed One, God has thereby anointed them as well.[27] But such terminology was profuse with the OT traditions of the anointing of kings and priests and, especially in Isaiah, of the anointing of the Messiah with the Spirit. This latter usage is what Paul picks up on here, as he proceeds in v. 22 to elaborate on this "anointing," this relationship with Christ, in terms of the Spirit.

But Paul does not further press the metaphor, nor should we. Even though the metaphor has primarily to do with one's relationship to Christ, inherent in it is Christ's own anointing by the Holy Spirit; thus when Paul goes on to elaborate, he returns to the commercial imagery of the first verb ("confirms") in the form of two further metaphors, which he explicitly interprets as the gift of the Spirit in his and their hearts.

Sealed. With this imagery Paul returns to the commercial metaphor begun with the verb "confirms"[28] and applies the whole directly to the work of the Spirit in the believer's life. The imagery derives from a wide variety of transactions in the Greco-Roman world, most often in the form of a stamped imprint in wax bearing the "seal" of the owner or sender. Primarily such a seal denoted ownership and authenticity; this thereby guaranteed the protection of the owner.[29] Paul uses it metaphorically seven times in all, with several different nuances.[30] In this case, as in Eph

---

[27]Some (e.g., Meyer 159, Plummer 39, Strachan 59), following Chrysostom, have argued that with this metaphor Paul is referring to his "anointing" to the office of apostle, thus excluding the Corinthians from the ἡμᾶς. But in light of v. 22 and Paul's use elsewhere of the metaphors in that verse, this view has almost nothing to commend it. Cf. Bultmann 42: "The ἡμᾶς cannot refer to Paul alone. Rather the σὺν ὑμῖν dominates the entire statement." So most commentators; J. J. Kijne leans this way, but waffles ("We, Us and Our in I and II Corinthians," *NovT* 8 [1966] 176–77).

[28]Which here is probably a metaphor for the selling of property.

[29]See BAGD 2b; MM 617–18; and the discussions in *TDNT* 7.939–43 (Fitzer) and *NIDNTT* 3.497 (Schippers).

[30]The verb occurs here and in Rom 15:28; Eph 1:13; 4:30; the noun in 1 Cor 9:2; Rom 4:11; and 2 Tim 2:19. The usage in Rom 15:28 is unique and apparently refers to the "sealing" of a bag of produce to guarantee that it was ready for market; thus the gift for the church in Jerusalem is "handed over under seal as it were" (Fitzer, *TDNT* 7.948). In Rom 4:11 circumcision functions as God's "seal," ratifying Abraham's righteousness by faith before he was circumcised. In 1 Cor 9:2 the emphasis is primarily on authentication; the Corinthians themselves are God's seal, authenticating Paul's apostleship.

1:13 and 4:30, it metaphorically refers to the Spirit as the "seal" of God's ownership and therefore the guarantee of the believer's final inheritance.

As the usage in Eph 1:13 and 4:30 ensures, the "seal" is the Spirit himself, by whom God has marked believers and claimed them for his own. Thus the Spirit is the proof of Paul's apostleship, not simply because he was a Spirit person himself, but because the Spirit bore fruit through him in the form of those in the Corinthian church, who through his ministry were themselves sealed by the Spirit as God's own possession, both for now and forever. This point will be pursued with some vigor in 3:1–18. The eschatological guarantee in the metaphor is expressly stated in Eph 4:30 ("with whom you were sealed *for the day of redemption*"). If the structural analysis suggested above is correct, then the same is true in this case. God has sealed us "by having given us the *down payment* [on the inheritance], namely, the Spirit himself."

Down payment.[31] This metaphor occurs three times in the NT, all in Paul (here; 5:5; Eph 1:14) and all with reference to the Holy Spirit. Although there is no contemporary evidence for its metaphorical usage, ἀρραβών is amply attested in the Greek commercial papyri as a technical term for the first installment (hence "down payment") of a total amount due, either from sales or services.[32] As such, it both establishes the contractual obligation and guarantees its fulfillment.[33] As Eph 1:14 makes certain, the genitive "of the Spirit" here and in 5:5 is to be understood as in apposition to "down payment." Thus the Spirit himself *is* the down payment, God's down payment in our lives that guarantees our certain future. Not only so, this metaphor also (especially) suggests that what is given is part of the whole. For Paul the gift of the Spirit is the first part of the redemption of the whole person, the beginning of the process that will end when believers assume their "spiritual" bodies (= enter into a mode of existence determined solely by the Spirit; see 1 Cor 15:44).

That leads us finally to several further notes about the Spirit in this text:

1. This is the fourth in a series of semi-creedal soteriological texts in Paul that are full of Trinitarian implications.[34] In this case, as always,

---

[31]Gk. ἀρραβών, apparently a Semitic loanword, probably by way of Phoenician merchants.

[32]See esp. MM 79; for its metaphorical meaning in Paul see, most recently, A. J. Kerr, "ΆΡΡΑΒΩΝ," *JTS* 39 (1988) 92–97.

[33]Kerr, "ΆΡΡΑΒΩΝ," 95, points out that in its common usage as a contract for services, the reception of the ἀρραβών also places the one who receives it, who will perform the services, under obligation to perform. But for all the usefulness of that dimension of the metaphor, it does not seem to be the direction of Paul's emphasis, which is on God's part in giving it, not on ours in receiving.

[34]See above on 2 Thes 2:13 and 1 Cor 6:11 (cf. n. 39 on 1 Thes 1:4–6). This point is noted by several commentators; see Plummer 41–42, Hughes 39, Héring 12, et al., who accept it with varying degrees of enthusiasm in terms of Paul's own theology.

the saving event is the result of God the Father's own activity, which he has effected in the Son, his *yes* to all of his earlier promises made to Israel; the effective working out of this salvation in the life of the believer and the believing community is again the work of the Spirit, who both applies the work of Christ and serves as God's own resident guarantee that it will be finally fully realized.

2. The metaphors in this text also demonstrate in striking ways that the Spirit for Paul is principally an eschatological reality. The presence of the Spirit as God's seal and down payment is the unmistakable evidence of salvation as "already but not yet." The future is already in evidence through the "down payment," the present guarantee; but he is present only as "down payment"; the final inheritance, which he guarantees, is yet to be realized.[35]

3. This is yet another text that makes a point of the Spirit as "indwelling" the believer. God has given us the Spirit "in our hearts." We have already seen this emphasis in 1 Thes 4:8 and 1 Cor 6:19; it will recur often (e.g., Gal 4:6; Rom 8:9–26). The Spirit is none other than God himself resident in our present human life, the life which we now live by "faith in the Son of God."

4. Even though by the time we come to this sentence at the end of the section we are somewhat removed from the rhetoric that started it in v. 17, it is nonetheless worthy of note that the gift of the Spirit that confirms Paul's ministry among them is the sure evidence that he did not make his plans κατὰ σάρκα.[36] This is now the second,[37] somewhat indirect, occurrence of this contrast in the corpus. Nothing more can be made of it here; but this linkage probably stands behind the strong language in 5:16–17 (q.v.); and of course it becomes a predominant motif in the next two letters (Galatians and Romans).

5. And all of this, in this context, is to emphasize that God, through the gospel of his Son and through their common gift of the indwelling Spirit, has authenticated Paul's ministry, so that even his failure to follow through regarding his itinerary does not negate his integrity or throw doubt on his apostleship. The significance of all of this will be elaborated in 2:14–4:6.

6. There seem to be no grounds in the text, therefore, for viewing this passage as also referring to water baptism.[38] In fact, not one of its several

---

[35]For a similar discussion of these metaphors, see Judith M. Gundry Volf, *Paul and Perseverance: Staying in and Falling Away* (WUNT 2/37; Tübingen: Mohr, 1990) 27–33, whose concern lies with the theme of perseverance inherent in the metaphors and Spirit language.

[36]So also Harris 325.

[37]See Fee, *1 Corinthians*, 121–28 on 1 Cor 3:1.

[38]This linkage has a considerable history; it has been argued vigorously by Erich Dinkler, "Die Taufterminologie in 2 Kor. i21f," in *Neotestamentica et Patristica* [Fest-

metaphors is ever used in the NT, either individually or together, to refer to or allude to Christian baptism; moreover, in this text and others Paul designates the Spirit, not baptism, as God's "seal" of ownership. The linkage itself is circuitous: one begins with mid-to-late-second century evidence for the imagery of "seal" as referring directly to baptism,[39] then presupposes the (questionable)[40] assumption that Paul understood believers to receive the Spirit at baptism, then finally assumes the metaphors (especially "anointing" and "seal") to have baptism *inherently* in them.[41]

But to make this work, this final assumption needs full demonstration in the form of clear evidence that *Paul himself* either directly, or in some allusive way, linked these metaphors with baptism so that the latter is to be understood as *inherently within the metaphor itself*. Such demonstration seems particularly difficult to come by, since Paul not only designates the Spirit by these metaphors, but also makes a point by means of these metaphors that is quite foreign to any point he makes when referring to Christian baptism.[42] Here is a place where one may

---

schrift Oscar Cullmann] (NovTSup 6; ed. W. C. van Unnik; Leiden: Brill, 1962) 173–91; and Beasley-Murray, *Baptism*, 171–77. It is adopted, inter alia, by W. Grundmann in *TDNT* (on χρίω) [vis-à-vis Fitzer (on σφράγις)], and Schippers in *NIDNTT*; cf. Bernard 45, Plummer 41, Strachan 60, Lietzmann 103, Bultmann 42, Furnish (hesitantly) 148–49. Barrett 80–81, who considers Dinkler to have "exaggerated" the evidence [indeed, is there any evidence from Paul at all?], would see implicit "the whole complex of their entry into the Christian life—conversion, faith, baptism, the reception of the Spirit" (quoted with approval by Martin 29). But this seems to be asking a bit too much of the metaphors in an effort to please all sides.

[39] Especially in 2 Clement and the Shepherd of Hermas. See the references in BAGD, σφράγις 2b. Bultmann 42 considered these as more significant than Ephesians in determining Paul's intent!

[40] On this matter see the discussions of 1 Cor 6:11; 12:13; and Titus 3:6.

[41] For this line of reasoning, see Beasley-Murray, *Baptism*, 171–77. The "jumps" in the reasoning are especially pronounced when he affirms (correctly) that "the Spirit *is* the anointing and the seal" (175), but then through reference to 1 Cor 6:11 and 12:13 asserts that the "seal of the Spirit" is "'*the baptism of the Spirit' in association with the laying of the Name of Jesus on a believer in the rite of baptism*" (174, emphasis his). This seems to be assertion and conjecture, pure and simple; nothing said in this text or in the other Pauline texts validates it. The assertion rests on the prior assumption that Paul linked the gift of the Spirit with baptism in water and that therefore any metaphorical reference to the reception of the Spirit must also carry inherently within it a reference to water baptism. That seems to ask a great deal of the evidence. It should be noted that Dinkler also argues on the basis of the "Amen" in v. 20 that this is a "liturgical" text and therefore that vv. 21–22 reflect liturgy. Even if this could be demonstrated, it tends to confuse "liturgies," where presumably the "liturgy of the Word" to which one would respond with the Amen would be considerably different from a "liturgy of baptism." But all of this is conjecture.

[42] That is, when Paul directly refers to the significance of Christian baptism, he never makes the point of ownership or authenticity or eschatological guarantee, which is the point of these metaphors. In Paul's theology these are all activities of the Spirit.

conclude rather decisively that baptism is strictly read into the passage from without, and in this case from a later time; nothing that Paul explicitly says here justifies such a linkage.[43]

2 CORINTHIANS 2:13

my spirit had no rest because I did not find my brother Titus there.

R. Jewett[44] posits this as another case in Paul where πνεῦμα refers to what he terms "the apportioned divine spirit" that is given to Christians when through faith in Christ they enter the eschatological age. But Jewett's position overlooks other evidence from Paul. Of interest in this case is Paul's use of σάρξ in the nearly identical parallel, when this argument resumes in 7:5 ("our flesh had no rest"). In both cases these are anthropological terms, which function as something of a periphrasis for "I." In each case the emphasis lies on a different aspect of Paul's lack of rest. In the present text the problem is with anxiety pure and simple; the anthropological term that fits that concern is "spirit." In the next instance the emphasis shifts to his being "afflicted in every way," beginning with external disputes, hence he had no rest in his "flesh." If one may not be certain as to how precisely Paul viewed the human spirit, there can be little question that here πνεῦμα refers to the interior dimension of the human person.[45]

2 CORINTHIANS 3:1–18[46]

Although specifically mentioned only six times (vv. 3, 6, 8, 17[2x], 18), the Spirit dominates Paul's thinking and argumentation in this

---

[43]Cf. Dunn, *Baptism*, 131, "water-baptism . . . does not enter the thought at all"; and Héring 12. Those who do not even raise the question may be assumed to think so as well (Calvin, Meyer, Hodge, Hanson, Tasker, Harris, Barnett). Hughes 43–45 allows the possibility, but thinks otherwise.

[44]*Terms*, 192–94.

[45]See further the discussion on 1 Thes 5:23; 1 Cor 2:11; and Gal 6:18.

[46]*Bibliography:* W. **Baird**, "Letters of Recommendation. A Study of II Cor. 3:1–3," *JBL* 80 (1961) 166–72; **Belleville**, *Reflections*; C. **Blomberg**, "The Structure of 2 Corinthians 1–7," *Criswell Theological Review* 4 (1989) 3–20; J. D. G. **Dunn**, "2 Corinthians III.17—'The Lord is the Spirit,' " *JTS* 21 (1970) 309–20; J. A. **Fitzmyer**, "Glory Reflected on the Face of Christ (2 Cor. 3:7–4:6) and a Palestinian Jewish Motif," *TS* 42 (1981) 630–44; D. E. **Garland**, "The Sufficiency of Paul, Minister of the New Covenant," *Criswell Theological Review* 4 (1989) 21–37; P. **Grech**, "2 Corinthians 3,17 and the Pauline Doctrine of Conversion to the Holy Spirit," *CBQ* 17 (1955) 420–37; D. **Greenwood**, "The Lord is the Spirit: Some Considerations of 2 Cor 3:17," *CBQ* 34 (1972) 467–72; S. J. **Hafemann**, "The Comfort and Power of the Gospel: The Argument of 2 Corinthians 1–3," *RevExp* 86 (1989) 325–44; S. J. **Hafemann**, *Suffering and the Ministry in the Spirit: Paul's Defense of his Ministry in 2 Corinthians 2:14–3:3* (Grand Rapids; Eerdmans, 1990; a slightly abridged ed. of the author's Ph.D. diss. which

passage.[47] Indeed, as full of difficulty as some of its statements are, this is one of the most significant Spirit passages in the Pauline corpus. Here for the first time in his extant letters the old and new (covenants and ministry) are set out in sharp contrast—as of letter and Spirit, death and life, condemnation and righteousness, the "glory" of the new being in part the confidence, freedom, and reality that the Spirit brings, and in part the sure inheritance of God's final glory.[48] But before looking at the Spirit texts in particular, one needs to have a sense of the whole, so as to see the predominant role the Spirit plays throughout.[49]

Verses 1–18 form the middle section of an argument that begins in 2:14 and extends to 4:6, which is the first part of a long "digression" (2:14–7:4),[50] in which four concerns are woven together into a continu-

appeared first in WUNT 2/19; Tübingen: Mohr, 1986); A. T. **Hanson**, "The Midrash of II Corinthians 3: A Reconsideration," *JSNT* 9 (1980) 2–28; A. T. **Hanson**, *Studies in Paul's Technique and Theology* (Grand Rapids: Eerdmans, 1974) 139–42; I. **Hermann**, *Kyrios und Pneuma: Studien zur Christologie der paulinischen Hauptbriefe* (Munich: Kösel-Verlag, 1961); C. J. A. **Hickling**, "The Sequence of Thought in II Corinthians, Chapter Three," *NTS* 21 (1975) 380–95; M. D. **Hooker**, " 'Beyond the Things that are Written': St Paul's Use of Scripture," *NTS* 27 (1981) 295–309; E. **Käsemann**, "The Spirit and the Letter," in *Perspectives on Paul* (London: SCM, 1969) 138–66; J. **Lambrecht**, "Transformation in 2 Cor. 3,18," *Bib* 64 (1983) 243–54; C. F. D. **Moule**, "2 Cor. 3:18b, καθάπερ ἀπὸ κυρίου πνεύματος," in *Neues Testament und Geschichte* (Festshrift O. Cullmann; ed. H. Baltensweiler, B. Reicke; Tübingen, Mohr, 1972) 233–37; J. **Murphy-O'Connor,** "PNEUMATIKOI and Judaizers in 2 Cor. 2:14–4:6," *AusBR* 34 (1986) 42–58; T. E. **Provence**, " 'Who is Sufficient for These Things?' An Exegesis of 2 Corinthians ii 15–iii 18," *NovT* 24 (1982) 54–81; D. A. **Renwick**, *Paul, the Temple, and the Presence of God* (BJS 224; Atlanta: Scholars, 1991); E. **Richard**, "Polemics, Old Testament and Theology—A Study of II Cor. III,1–IV,6," *RB* 88 (1981) 340–67; C. Kern **Stockhausen**, *Moses' Veil and the Glory of the New Covenant* (AB 116; Rome: Biblical Institute, 1989); **Sumney**, *Opponents*; W. C. **van Unnik**, " 'With Unveiled Face,' An Exegesis of 2 Corinthians iii 12–18," *NovT* 6 (1963) 153–69; N. T. **Wright**, "Reflected Glory: 2 Corinthians 3:18," in *The Glory of Christ in the New Testament: Studies in Christology in Memory of George Bradford Caird* (ed. L. D. Hurst, N. T. Wright; Oxford: Clarendon, 1987) 139–50.

[47]Since this is so clear, and is verified in every possible way both from this text and from Paul's usage elsewhere, one reads with some astonishment in Hughes, 96–102, 115–17, that πνεῦμα language in this argument refers not to the Holy Spirit, but to something "inward" in contrast to the letter of the law.

[48]This point is not expressed as such here, but is quite evident in 1:22 and 5:5. As we will note below, it seems inherent to the contrast in v. 11 that the new covenant "remains" (cf. v. 18, "from glory to glory").

[49]What is presented here is basically the result of my own work on the text, although it is hardly possible in this case not to have been influenced in part by the work of so many who have written on the passage. I intend to resist in this case an interaction with this literature on the passage as a whole, and limit interaction to those passages where the Spirit is mentioned specifically.

[50]Indeed, this is one of the classic "digressions" in ancient literature. This statement, of course, assumes several things: (1) that chs. 1–9 are to be understood as a single letter, not a later compilation by someone else (on the unlikelihood of such

ous thread: (1) a defense of Paul's apostleship, and thereby his gospel, which (2) though characterized by suffering and weakness, is nonetheless full of the Spirit and therefore of glory, as is evidenced (3) by the Corinthian believers themselves and by their own experience of the Spirit; therefore (4) they should not succumb to the wiles of some outsiders, who, despite letters of commendation, are nonetheless "peddlers of the word of truth." The concern is primarily with a defense of his apostleship, not so much the *fact* of it, as its *character*. He seems especially concerned throughout to demonstrate that his apostolic "style" is quite in keeping with the message—marked by the cross, but effective in its results.[51] That at least seems to be the point of the beginning (2:14–17) and end (4:1–6) of this section of the argument.

Thus in 2:14–16a, through the powerful imagery of the Roman triumphal procession Paul glories once more in his "weaknesses"[52]—although that word does not yet occur. Even though he is constantly being led to death, as it were in the arena, his life and ministry are nonetheless an aroma leading to life or death. In v. 16b, he then asks the leading question, "Who is sufficient for these things (i.e., for such ministry)?" which he answers (positively)[53] in this first instance by contrasting himself to the "peddlers" (v. 17). As over against them, Paul speaks as one who lives in the presence of God.[54]

Since the implication that Paul is "sufficient" for such ministry may sound like so much self-commendation, he turns to rhetoric in 3:1–3 to assert otherwise. In contrast to the others who apparently had made a point of their having "references," Paul needs no outside commendation at all, least of all in the form of letters (v. 1). The mention of "letters of

---

"scissors-and-paste" compilation, see G. D. Fee, "II Corinthians vi.14–vii.1 and Food Offered to Idols," *NTS* 23 [1976–77] 140–61 [142–43]); (2) that this is therefore a kind of "digression," as 2:13 and 7:5 reveal, although I would doubt that it is digressive in the ordinary sense of that word, having had in this case a great deal of thought and intent to it (hence the quotation marks); and (3) that Paul's letters were in fact a form of "literature," since they were intended to be read in the gathering of God's people and therefore had an intentionally public aspect to them from the beginning.

[51]Cf. 1 Cor 2:1–5; 4:1–17; Gal 6:12–17.

[52]For a full and convincing discussion that this imagery refers to Paul's place at the end of the procession as one destined to die in the arena, see Hafemann, *Suffering*, 7–39; cf. Fee, *1 Corinthians*, 174–75, on the similar imagery in 1 Cor 4:9.

[53]For the debate (and therefore bibliography) over whether Paul expected a negative or positive answer to his question, see the helpful discussion in Hafemann, *Suffering*, 90–98, who concludes (convincingly) for the positive. Indeed, not only the γάρ in v. 17 seems to demand such, but so also does the entire argument in ch. 3.

[54]Cf. Renwick, *Paul*, 61–74, for an argument in favor of this understanding of v. 17. This study came in hand many months after this chapter had been written, hence I have not interacted with it except by way of a note or two. Although I am not convinced by much of the exegesis in this study, the author has (correctly) highlighted this very important motif in the argument of this passage.

commendation" in turn spins off a whole series of images, all of which are designed to defend his own apostleship, especially as evidenced by the Corinthians' reception of the Spirit. Thus, Paul argues once more that they are the living proof of the effectiveness, and therefore of the integrity and veracity, of his apostleship.[55] As above in 1:21–22, the key to this argument is the Spirit, evidenced in the first instance by the Corinthians' own reception of the Spirit.

That in turn leads him back to his own ministry in vv. 4–6, and to the question begun in 2:16b, "Who is sufficient for such ministry?" As elsewhere and always, Paul's confidence rests on the threefold work of the triune God. His ministry is "from God" (v. 5) and "before God" (v. 4), and has come to Paul "through Christ" (v. 4). It is the ministry of the new covenant, characterized by the Spirit, the giver of life (v. 6). In making this point, Paul presents his ministry in contrast to the old covenant, which is characterized as merely "letter," which kills (i.e., deals in death).

And here begin some contrasts that are carried through the rest of vv. 7–18, which in turn create a number of exegetical difficulties. Not the least of these is how much, if any, of this contrast, both in v. 6 and in the explication that follows, has to do with the opponents, and how much simply flows out of Paul's argumentation and digressions.[56] On this matter, I tend toward a middling position: On the one hand, in light of the decided emphasis in chs. 10–12 on the Jewishness of these opponents, it seems likely that the contrast between himself and Moses, in terms of the glory of the former and present covenants, is in some way in response to the opponents. On the other hand, I have less confidence than some that we can thereby recreate either the theology or the origins of the opponents on the basis of what is said here. There is simply too much that is allusive and therefore elusive.

In any case, vv. 7–18 are primarily a defense, by way of explication, of what is said in v. 6. Paul's concern remains the same: his apostleship, despite its weaknesses, is a ministry of the new, life-giving covenant of Spirit, their existence serving as the primary evidence—apparently now over against those who would add "Jewishness" to the pure gospel of Christ.

Paul begins (vv. 7–11) with a contrast between the respective δια-κονίαι ("ministries") of the two covenants, with "glory" appearing as the dominant motif. To our surprise, Paul's point is that *both* ministries came with glory. The problem, it turns out, was not with Moses, but with those who heard (hear) Moses. They did not perceive that the former covenant

---

[55]For this point in 1 Corinthians see especially the rhetoric in 9:1–2. His apostleship and their existence are so interwoven that to deny the one (his apostleship) is to endanger the other (their existence).

[56]See nn. 5 and 50 above.

was coming to an end for the very reason that that covenant was merely "letter" and did not have "Spirit." But crucial to his argument is that the former ministry, and therefore former covenant, had *glory*. On this predicate Paul uses a series of *a fortiori* arguments to make the point that even though the former came with "glory," it was a glory that could not be seen by the original recipients and that was in any case intended to fade away (i.e., be replaced by one with greater glory). But if such a ministry—of "letter," dealing in death and therefore leading to condemnation—had "glory," how much more does Paul's ministry—of Spirit, that is life-giving and effects righteousness—come with "glory." His point, of course, is that despite appearances, because of the Spirit his ministry is full of "glory," glory that is both for now and forever; this glory surpasses by far the former glory. That glory was "fading" glory; the glory of the new continues, because it is of the Spirit.

It only remains, then, for Paul to demonstrate the *nature* of the glory resident in his ministry through the Spirit. But to do this (vv. 17–18), Paul takes the long route through Exod 34:28–35, to which he had alluded in vv. 7–11. In an argument that is no longer transparent, Paul appears to draw several threads together as well as to weave in a few new ones. One of the keys to this paragraph (vv. 12–18) is the inclusion of the Corinthians in the "we" of v. 18 ("we all"), and perhaps therefore already anticipated in the "we" of v. 12. Thus there is once more a slight shift from his ministry as such (picked up again in 4:1) to the effect of his ministry on those who hear, the Corinthians in particular—set out in stark contrast to what currently takes place in the synagogue.

Thus he begins in v. 12 by asserting that because we have such a hope—that the life-giving ministry of the new covenant is accompanied by a glory that "remains" and therefore is forever—"we" use great boldness/freedom.[57] While this first mention of "freedom" and "boldness" refers to his ministry, it anticipates that of vv. 17–18, where the Corinthians are included. His way of getting there is by means of those who first heard (vv. 13–14a), and those who now read (vv. 14b–15), the older

---

[57]Gk. παρρησία, one of the more difficult words in the Pauline letters. Its basic meaning is "outspokenness" or "plainness of speech" that "conceals nothing and passes over nothing" (BAGD); but it soon crossed over to mean "openness to the public," hence "publicly," and eventually took on the nuance of "bold speech," "confidence/boldness," of the kind that only the privileged would have before those in authority. The meaning here is most likely intentionally ambiguous, that is, in its first instance it probably carries the nuance of "boldness" (= "confidence" with regard to his ministry); but what follows picks up the theme of "openness," playing on the theme of the veil, thus anticipating the "freedom" in the Spirit of v. 17. This freedom is finally expressed in terms of "unveiled face" before God, the ultimate—and original—sense of παρρησία. Such nuanced meanings make translation especially difficult. For a more complete discussion of the options and the debate, see Belleville, *Reflections*, 194–98.

covenant—in contrast to the Corinthians,[58] who with Paul stand before God by means of the Spirit with unveiled faces (vv. 16–18).

The link in all of this—from Israel to contemporary Judaism to the Corinthians—is the "veil," which in the original Exodus account covered Moses' face,[59] but which now is seen in a metaphorical way to cover the "minds/hearts" of Paul's fellow-countrymen whenever they hear "Moses" read in the synagogue, which "veil" cannot be removed except by Christ.[60] But, he goes on in v. 16, whenever anyone turns to the Lord (as Moses in Exod 34:34), the veil is removed, which in vv. 17–18 is interpreted as the function of the Spirit. Thus the Spirit brings "freedom," the kind of freedom that allows God's new covenant people to be, as Moses was, in God's very presence and there to behold the *glory* of God, Christ himself, as though looking at him in a mirror. The result of this new unveiling by the Spirit, by which God's people have now entered God's presence with freedom, is that they themselves are being transformed by the same Spirit into God's own likeness in an ever-increasing measure.

Thus, despite the considerable contrasts involved and the running commentary on the contrasted glory between the old and the new, the argument from beginning to end has to do with the activity of the Spirit, both in Paul's own ministry and in the Corinthians' lives as the result of that ministry. Set in contrast as it is (apparently) to some emphases on things Jewish by his opponents, the rhetoric of the climax of the argument simply soars. With extraordinary language, both in its flexibility and in its vivid imagery and bold declarations, Paul asserts that the Spirit has to do with "freedom," not only from the letter and death of the old but also toward God, so much so that by the Spirit God's newly constituted people are brought into God's presence so as to "behold" him and thus to be continually transformed into his own likeness. As with Moses,

---

[58]This seems to be so even if one thinks, as Belleville, *Reflections*, 245–46, that vv. 14b–15 are to be linked with 4:2–4 as response to an accusation as to why Paul's own ministry has seemed to be so ineffective among his own people. Paul's point throughout remains singular: for the Corinthians now to pick up the Law is to retrogress—in this case, to be like the very people who still have veils over their hearts because they lack the freedom of the Spirit.

[59]One of the especially difficult exegetical decisions in this passage concerns the intent of the purpose clause in this sentence, "so that the children of Israel [the original recipients of the covenant] could not gaze at the τέλος (goal? end?) of that which was fading away, but their hearts were hardened." For a full and helpful discussion, see Belleville, *Reflections*, 199–225.

[60]This seems to be the case, despite the precision called for by Hanson, *Studies*, 139–41, who observes, probably correctly, that the verb καταργεῖται (v. 14) must first of all apply to the old covenant, since strictly speaking that is the only thing that can be "abolished." Nonetheless, the use of the imagery throughout is just fluid enough that when we come to vv. 17–18 it is the "veil" that has been removed, not just the old covenant, since the latter remains, but with a veil over it for those who continue to read it without the veil removed.

but unlike former and present Israel, the veil is removed when one turns
to the Lord, that is, when we come into God's very Presence, made
available to us by the Spirit of God. With these words we are brought
face to face with a kind of Spirit-empowering that one could only have
guessed at in earlier passages, and one far below which, if the truth were
told, most of God's people tend to live.

But Paul's argument is not over. In 4:1–6[61] he returns to the themes
with which he began in 2:14–16, by applying the argument of 3:1–18
directly to his own present situation. Picking up the theme of "veil," with
all of its ramifications, he insists that his ministry has no "hiddenness"
to it at all (v. 2), but rather is an open manifestation of the truth. If there
is "hiddenness," he adds, it comes from Satan's blinding the minds of
unbelievers (vv. 3–4). Paul's Spirit-filled ministry is full of glory, the glory
that is now expressed in terms of Christ (v. 4), who reveals the knowledge
of God. The Spirit is not mentioned explicitly in this final application;
nonetheless, since the paragraph flows directly out of 3:17–18, and in
light of Paul's usage elsewhere, one may assume that the Spirit, as the
source of the believer's "knowledge of God's glory in the face of Jesus Christ"
(v. 6), lies behind all of the "revelation" and "enlightening" language.

Having examined the larger argument, we can now analyze the
Spirit texts in some detail.

2 CORINTHIANS 3:3

*. . . since you are being manifested that you are Christ's epistle, served by us,
inscribed not with ink but by the Spirit of the living God, not on stone tablets
but on the fleshly tablets of the heart.*

Although this clause abounds with a variety of imagery, this first
specific mention of the Spirit in the argument is in some ways the easiest
of all to understand. Paul has argued vigorously in vv. 1 and 2 that, first
(v. 1), he needs no letters of commendation, because, second (v. 2), the
Corinthians themselves serve as such for him. Now he clarifies and
explains how all of this came about.

Paul has just called the Corinthian believers "our epistle"; what he
meant by this, in keeping with the imagery, is that they function as his
letter of commendation in the same way that literal letters function for
others. Three further points are thus made: First, since letters of commendation come from someone else and are carried by the one commended,[62] he needs to clarify that though the Corinthians are "written

---

[61]This is one of the more unfortunate chapter breaks in the NT. The close tie to
what has preceded, as application to his own situation, begins with the "therefore,
having *this ministry*," and continues throughout. See the discussion below on 4:1–6.

[62]Along with the overwhelming external support, this phenomenon is what
makes it seem certain that Paul really did intend in v. 2 to say "written on *our* hearts,"

on *his* heart" (and thus carried about by him), they are actually *Christ's* epistle. Accordingly, they have their origin in Christ and belong to him.

Second, Paul's role in their becoming Christ's letter was that they were διακονηθεῖσα ὑφ' ἡμῶν (lit. "served by us"). Whatever Paul intended in terms of the imagery,[63] the choice of this verb is deliberate, since it sets in motion the whole of the rest of the argument, which has to do with his διακονία ("service/ministry").[64]

Third, two sets of contrasts are added regarding the means and nature of this letter of commendation; and here is where the Spirit language begins, which launches the rest of the argument. In contrast to the literal letters carried by his opponents, the Corinthians, as letter, were not "written" with ink, but by the Spirit. This, of course, is for Paul the key to everything; in light of the argumentation of 1 Corinthians, this also has to be a telling point in the present argument. To make that point and the contrast even more telling, he describes the Spirit as the Spirit *of the living God.*Usually this very Jewish description of God occurs when Paul is making a point over against paganism.[65] Here it seems to be an emphasis over against mere "stony tablets" and anticipates the contrast with the "letter" of the old covenant that issued in death (v. 6).

In some ways the second set of contrasts ("tablets of stone/of fleshly hearts") comes as a surprise, at least in the sense that "letter" imagery hardly leads to it. But in typical fashion, Paul's imagery is fluid, as one image leads to another that leads to yet another.[66] Thus, even though the new imagery jars us a bit, for Paul everything has been moving toward this final set of contrasts. The mention of the Spirit of the living God evokes a contrast between Law and Spirit by means of the language of Exod 34:1 (the decalogue was written on πλάκας λιθίνας, tablets of stone) and Ezek 11:19 and 36:26 (in giving them his Spirit God will implant in his people [in place of hearts of λιθίνας] a καρδίαν σαρκίνην [fleshly heart]).[67] The language itself should have made this plain; the argument that follows confirms it.

---

even though it seems a bit awkward to us. After all, he is the one who must carry about such a letter, if the imagery is going to mean anything at all.

[63]There is some discussion in the literature as to whether Paul intended "written by us" or "delivered by us," the resolution of which is neither critical to the argument nor relevant to our discussion.

[64]See vv. 7, 8, 9[2x], 4:1.

[65]See on 6:16 below; cf. 1 Thes 1:9.

[66]Belleville, *Reflections*, 146–49, rejects this view of things, arguing that "the theme of ministerial credibility and the issue of appropriate credentials" is the linkage. That may indeed hold things together, but it does not necessarily mean that my way of describing it is thereby denied. Paul knows where he is going; the shifting from image to image helps him get there.

[67]For the influence of the language of Ezek 36:26–27 on Paul's Spirit language see also 1 Thes 4:8.

In this first instance, it must finally be noted, the emphasis is on the Spirit at work in the lives of the Corinthians. They are those who have had the Spirit of the living God "engraved" on their hearts; thus, Gentiles though they are, the Corinthians are the recipients of and in some ways the fulfillment of the promised covenant of Spirit[68] that Paul will now go on to describe in the language of Jer 31:31 as the "new covenant."

2 CORINTHIANS 3:6

[5] . . . But our sufficiency is from God, [6]who made us sufficient as ministers of the new covenant, not of letter, but of the Spirit, for the letter kills, but the Spirit gives life.

This clause serves both as a conclusion to the argument to this point (from 2:14, by way of 3:1–3) and as a transition to the next section, in which Paul will contrast the two covenants in terms of their function, results, and relationship to the Spirit. The language of "sufficiency" picks up the question from 2:16a; the present argument makes it clear that Paul intended a positive response to his question. He only needs to explain, as he does in this paragraph, that his confidence in ministry is anything but self-confidence; rather, it is predicated on God's enabling and empowering.

What is new is the language "new covenant,"[69] which, in keeping with v. 3, is specified as the "covenant of Spirit," in which "the Spirit gives life." This concept of a "new covenant" as a "covenant of Spirit" comes from a combination of ideas from Ezek 36:26–27 and Jer 31:31–34 (LXX 38:31–34). Through Jeremiah God had promised to make a new covenant with his people, because they had broken the former covenant; through Ezekiel God had promised to replace his people's hearts of stone with "fleshly hearts," interpreted as "putting my Spirit in you." Furthermore, the related oracle that follows (Ezek 37:1–14) pictures the Spirit as breathing "life" into God's people and concludes with the promise, "I will put my Spirit in you and you will live" (v. 14).

In light of this kind of intertextuality,[70] one can scarcely miss the eschatological implications of Paul's understanding of the Spirit—as fulfillment of God's promised gift of Spirit at the end of the ages, which according to 1 Cor 10:11 he understands already to have come. Thus the

---

[68]A point Paul will make specifically in Gal 3:14.

[69]Although the "new covenant" is probably already in view in 1:20: "as many as are the promises of God, they find their Yes in Christ." Cf. the emphasis in 5:14–17 on the passing of the old (order) and the coming of the new, and the citation of Isa 49:8 (LXX) in 6:2, emphasizing that God's eschatological salvation is now and that Paul is the minister of such. I owe these last insights to Paul Barnett.

[70]On this term and its meaning in Paul see below on the discussion of Phil 1:19.

Spirit is the key to both continuity and discontinuity with the OT people of God. The continuity lies with God and his promises, especially the promise of a new covenant of "Spirit" with his people; the discontinuity lies with the Spirit's coming so as to fulfill the promise and thus usher in a new day, which includes the Gentiles, since they, too, have received the same Spirit by faith (see esp. Gal 3:6–14).

Our difficulty in this passage lies with the language Paul uses of the former covenant, that it is a "covenant of letter" and that "the letter kills."[71] Such language about the Law occurs later in Rom 2:29 and 7:6. The path to understanding this usage lies in two directions.

First, this initial instance of Paul's referring to the Law as mere "letter" is evoked by the context. The "letters of commendation" used by his opponents to credit themselves and discredit Paul are from his point of view mere "letters on papyrus" and in reality amount to nothing. His ministry—of the new covenant of Spirit—led to their conversion, so that the Ezekiel and Jeremiah promises had been fulfilled in them. Since those who have come to introduce a "new Jesus," leading to a "new Spirit," seem keen on things Jewish, they were probably introducing the old covenant as a means to righteousness (not ethical, but covenantal). Thus Paul accuses those whose letters are written merely on papyrus with ink of also coming with the old covenant which, first engraved on stone tablets, is now figuratively also a matter of mere "letter," precisely because it was neither then nor now accompanied by the one crucial factor that made it workable, the Spirit of the living God. That is, the essential contrast between letter and Spirit is neither "external" versus "internal,"[72] nor "letter" as representing human striving after righteousness based on Law versus the gift of Spirit;[73] rather, it is between the Law as

---

[71]On this question, and especially on the meaning of the contrast between "letter" and "Spirit," see: E. Kamlah, "Buchstabe und Geist. Die Bedeutung dieser Antithese für die alttestamentliche Exegese des Apostels Paulus," *EvT* 14 (1954) 276–82; Käsemann, "Spirit," 138–66; P. Richardson, "Letter and Spirit: A Foundation for Hermeneutics," *EvQ* 45 (1973) 208–18; B. Schneider, "The Meaning of St. Paul's Antithesis 'The Letter and the Spirit,' " *CBQ* 15 (1953) 163–207; S. Westerholm, " 'Letter' and 'Spirit': The Foundation of Pauline Ethics," *NTS* 30 (1984) 229–48.

[72]In its baldest form see the arguments by Hughes 96–102, a view that has almost nothing to commend it. Another such view that goes back to Origen and is found repeatedly in the popular literature and sermons is the distinction between the "plain" or "surface" meaning of a text and the "spiritual" meaning. It thus becomes a kind of Pauline "hermeneutical principle." This is to use Paul's words for a thoroughly non-Pauline idea. Others consider "letter" to refer to "external rites," while "Spirit" refers to internal reality.

[73]For this view, see especially Käsemann, "Spirit" (cf. Barrett, Furnish). But see the refutation in Westerholm, " 'Letter.' " Westerholm's view that "letter" refers to the OT in its written form as made up of concrete demands has much to commend it—although this view is easier to support on the basis of the two passages in Romans than on this one. Whether this is the precise referent or not, it moves in the right

demand for obedience but unaccompanied by the empowering of the
Spirit and the coming of the Spirit who makes Law in the former sense
obsolete, since what the Law requires is now written on the heart.[74]

Thus it is not the Law itself that is "letter"; the Law is holy and
good and even πνευματικός (Rom 7:12, 14). But the Law as specific
demands requiring obedience is merely letter; and its time is past
because it was incapable of bringing life and righteousness—of the
real kind. Thus, to introduce the old covenant in whatever specific form
it may take to people who already live by the Spirit is retrogression—
because the promised Spirit of the new covenant has come, and he
"writes the Law on the heart" so that God's people will be moved to obey
him (Ezek 36:27).

But second, and even worse, such introduction of the former covenant leads only to death—precisely because in this case it is not accompanied by the Spirit, who alone gives life. How the Law leads to death is
not elaborated here. But the casual, almost cryptic, way in which Paul
in 1 Cor 15:56 introduces the Law as ultimately leading to death through
sin, suggests in the strongest possible way that Paul has formerly spoken
about these matters, so that the Corinthians can fill in the gaps themselves. For us these gaps must be filled in from Galatians 3 and Romans
7, where Paul explicates in the context of Jew-Gentile relationships to God
through the one Spirit that the Law failed because (1) even though
"Spiritual," it was not accompanied by the Spirit in the lives of those who
received it, and (2) this good thing therefore led to death due to the sin
resident in human "flesh," which the Law aroused. It is in this sense that
"the letter kills," because it can arouse sin but is powerless to overcome
it; the Torah lacks the one essential ingredient for life,[75] the Spirit. In
many ways Rom 8:2 serves as Paul's own commentary on this passage:
"For the 'law' of the Spirit who endows life has in Christ Jesus set you
free from the 'law' of sin and death."

Thus to depict the Spirit as the "giver of life" is especially significant.
As suggested above, the first reason for it lies with Ezekiel's prophecy.
God's intent was to "put my Spirit in you, and you shall live." That
eschatological promise has now been fulfilled. However, this is also a
primary designation for God himself; he is the living God, who is both
the author and giver of life.[76] Now it is "the Spirit of the living God" who
is designated as "the giver of life."

---

direction. In any case, all of these latter scholars also recognize and emphasize the
thoroughly eschatological dimension to the contrast.

[74]For a similar eschatological emphasis regarding this contrast see Bruce 190–91.

[75]Cf. Gal 3:21: "if a law had been given that was able to give life."

[76]Cf. 1 Cor 15:45, where Christ is also designated "a life-giving spirit," regarding
our future bodily resurrection.

The "life" here referred to is almost certainly "eternal life," that is, the life of God that belongs to eternity that is made available to his people now through the Spirit. This is the χάρισμα of God through Christ (Rom 6:23), in whom we have been raised "to newness of life" (Rom 6:4) through "the newness of the Spirit" (Rom 7:6). Thus it becomes a key word throughout Romans to describe what it means to be God's people, and especially in Romans 8, where the Spirit is again described as "the Spirit of life" (= the Spirit who gives life). Therefore, to call the Spirit the "life-giver" is to designate him in terms of personhood and deity.

2 CORINTHIANS 3:8

How much more shall not the ministry of Spirit be with glory?

This sentence, which occurs in the first of the three *a fortiori* arguments[77] that make up this paragraph (vv. 7–11), flows directly out of the final word in v. 6 ("the letter kills; the Spirit gives life"). Together the three "if the one . . . how much more the other" sentences function in three ways in the argument. First, they continue the contrasts between the two covenants, picking up first the contrast between "death" and "[the life-giving] Spirit," then adding the further contrasts that the one leads to condemnation, the other to righteousness, and that the one is "fading away" while the other "remains" ("forever" being implied).

Second, although the contrasts are between the two covenants themselves, the emphasis continues to lie on the "ministry" of each, not so much intending (apparently) a contrast between Paul and Moses personally, as between the ministry that necessarily accompanied the old and that which now accompanies the new. Paul's ministry is obviously in view in the latter.

Third, very much in keeping with the basic concern of the argument in Rom 7:7–25, this paragraph insists that the older covenant, even though it dealt in condemnation and death and was destined to fade away, nonetheless had its own form of "glory." This becomes the equivalent in this letter of saying that the Law is holy, good, and Spiritual in Rom 7:12, 14. The point Paul wants to make in both instances seems clear. Even though from his present perspective in Christ the old covenant leads to condemnation and death, it was nonetheless God's thing and therefore was accompanied with glory. The problem lay not in the Law itself, but in the fact that it was powerless to lead to life, since it was not accompanied by the gift of Spirit.

Hence, as already noted in v. 6, Paul's contrast between Spirit and letter continues to be basically eschatological. Because the former cove-

---

[77]In this case we have clear examples of arguing *a minori ad maius,* "from the lesser to the greater." This is why it is so important for Paul's case that the former covenant had its own form of "glory." If so, then "how much more the new covenant."

nant lacked Spirit and therefore led to condemnation and death, it was destined to be replaced by a new one; God himself had so promised through the prophets. With the coming of Christ and the Spirit, the new covenant has now come, making the old obsolete. It is this eschatological dimension of Spirit and Law that makes it so difficult for Paul to deal with those who want to maintain in the present age what was destined to come to an end once the Spirit had been given. "We have been there," is Paul's point, "and it didn't work; it was a covenant that dealt in death precisely because it lacked the Spirit. So now that the Spirit has come, who gives life apart from the Law, why should anyone want to return to, or introduce Gentiles to, the older covenant which the covenant of Spirit has replaced?"[78]

Our present sentence, therefore, simply picks up the language of v. 6 and moves it forward. In v. 3 Paul had used the verb διακονέω ("to serve, minister") to describe his role in the Corinthian community's becoming "Christ's epistle." The cognate noun διακονία pervades the present paragraph. Thus, the "letter" that "kills," described again in terms of "engraved on stones," is now referred to as "the ministry of death." That is, even though Moses' ministry was accompanied with glory, the net result of his "ministry," because he served Israel with the Law, was that it led to death. If such ministry, Paul now argues, was accompanied with glory, how much more shall the "ministry of Spirit" be accompanied with glory? In context, therefore, the "ministry of Spirit" means his ministry in Corinth that brought to them the life-giving Spirit.

That same sense prevails in the second set of contrasts as well; the one led to condemnation, the other to righteousness, or justification. To be sure, neither Paul nor the Spirit brought about the justification that leads to life; that was accomplished by Christ. But Paul's Spirit-endowed, Spirit-empowering ministry of the gospel, which has God's justifying of sinners at its heart, has in turn been effected in the lives of the believers in Corinth by the Spirit. Thus the "ministry of the Spirit" is also "the ministry of justification," that is, the ministry that has brought the experience of justification to them through the Spirit.[79]

As noted above, this paragraph basically affirms that the former covenant did have glory; therefore the new covenant must have even greater glory. At this juncture the argument is merely asserted, by way of *a minori ad maius*, as obvious; Paul will next describe the nature and content of that glory, which is also where Spirit language next appears.

---

[78]Thus in every place in the Pauline churches (as known through his letters) where someone has tried to introduce the old covenant, Paul opposes it in terms of their present life in the Spirit. See further Gal 3:1–4:7; Phil 3:3 (cf. Rom 7:5–6; 8:1–17).

[79]For a similar relationship of justification/righteousness to the Spirit, see on 1 Cor 6:11 and Gal 5:5.

2 CORINTHIANS 3:16–18

¹⁶But whenever he turns to the Lord, the veil is removed. ¹⁷Now "the Lord" is the Spirit; and where the Spirit of the Lord, freedom.[80] *¹⁸Now all*[81] *of us, with unveiled faces, beholding the glory of the Lord as in a mirror, are being transformed into the same likeness from glory to glory, just as from the Lord, the Spirit.*

With these sentences, difficult as parts of them may seem to us, the conclusion to Paul's argument that began in v. 4 takes wings; it also turns out to be one of the more significant Spirit passages in his letters. Fortunately, the difficulties for the most part can be resolved, and in any case they do not impede our basic understanding of Paul's point. Two matters are crucial: First, Paul is tying up several loose ends to an argument that assumes the opponents of 3:1 as the backdrop; thus many of the clues lie in what has preceded. Second, vv. 17–18 function specifically as Paul's interpretation of Exod 34:34 as "cited" in v. 16, in terms of the ministry of the Spirit vis-à-vis that of the older covenant, where a veil still exists, keeping those who rely on it from entering God's presence and beholding the glory of God.

In vv. 7–11 Paul had argued that if the former "ministry" of the old covenant that dealt in condemnation and death came with glory, how much more will glory attend the new "ministry" of the Spirit that deals with righteousness and life. Then in the immediately preceding sentences (vv. 12–15) Paul used the story of Moses and his "veiled" glory from Exod 34:28–35 to establish (1) the temporary nature of the old covenant and (2) that the veil now represents the hardened hearts of those who still adhere to the old even though the new has come. The possibility for removing this "veil," which is Paul's obvious concern, was accomplished, as we should expect, in the work of Christ (v. 14).

Thus several previous themes are tied together in the conclusion in vv. 17–18: the Spirit as the evidence of the new covenant; for those who have the Spirit the veil is now removed; such "unveiling" therefore means "freedom" (cf. v. 12: "boldness, freedom"); the "freedom" that comes with the removal of the veil means that people now have access to God's presence so as to behold the "glory" which the veil kept them from seeing; the "glory" turns out now to be that of the Lord himself. In beholding this glory God's people are thereby "transformed into the same likeness, from glory to glory." Thus, in the final analysis, the Spirit of the

---

[80]The Western MSS, followed by the later MajT, add an ἐκεῖ ("there") before "freedom." This appears to be a "translational" variant which arose in Latin for the very reason one senses the need for it in my literal translation. It is surely what Paul intended, even if not expressed.

[81]A few witnesses omit this πάντες (P⁴⁶ vg^mss Spec), but in so doing blunt Paul's argument, which now intentionally includes the Corinthians as the recipients of the "ministry of Spirit."

living God not only gives us the life of God, but serves for us as God's presence and enables us to behold God's glory so that we are being transformed into his likeness. That is "glory" indeed!

16 This sentence serves as the transition from the argument of vv. 12–15 to the conclusion in vv. 17–18. It is tied to v. 15 by its common beginning: ἡνίκα ἄν . . . ἡνίκα δὲ ἐάν ("whenever Moses . . . ; but whenever he . . . ").[82] This obvious tie creates our first difficulty in understanding the present verse. The grammar demands that the unexpressed subject of the verb is "he" (= Moses). But it is equally clear from the context that the subject has been intentionally unexpressed, because in the end it means "he" (= "anyone");[83] thus, "when *anyone* turns to the Lord." The interpretation in v. 17 seems to make that certain.

Thus in "citing" Exod 34:34 in this intertextual way,[84] Paul makes a few crucial changes to the text of the LXX[85] that allow him to interpret it as he intends in vv. 17–18, by way of analogy. (1) As already noted, the subject "Moses" is deliberately omitted; (2) the verb εἰσεπορεύετο ("used to go into") is altered to ἐπιστρέψῃ ("turn to"), which in Pauline/Lukan circles had become a quasi-technical term for "conversion";[86] (3) having omitted "Moses," Paul also therefore omitted the purpose clause, "to talk to him [God]"; and (4) most significantly, in altering the word order of the final clause, Paul also changed the verb from an imperfect middle ("he [Moses] used to remove") to a present passive, so that, in line with v. 14c, Paul's version reads, "the veil is being removed" (by the work of Christ, being the obvious implication).

Thus by these several changes Paul is setting out what happens to a person who has "turned to the Lord."[87] But in light of what has already

---

[82]Since this conjunction occurs nowhere else in Paul, and in fact in v. 16 is borrowed from the LXX, it seems certain that Paul therefore already had this citation in mind when he began v. 15.

[83]In context the subject should not be overly generalized; in the first instance it would refer to anyone from v. 15b, those who have a veil over their hearts at the reading of the old covenant. It is doubtful whether Paul specifically intends himself as an example of such, as Belleville contends (*Reflections*, 249–50). Paul's own role in the argument is never fully lost sight of, but this verse stands some distance from v. 12, where Paul was last mentioned; it is difficult to imagine how the Corinthians might have caught on that Paul had intended himself to be the subject.

[84]For this technique of "citation" in literature of all kinds, see on Phil 1:19.

[85]ἡνίκα δ' ἄν εἰσεπορεύετο Μωυσῆς ἔναντι κυρίου λαλεῖν αὐτῷ, περιῃρεῖτο τὸ κάλυμμα.

[86]*Pace* Renwick, *Paul*, 151–54. For Paul see 1 Thes 1:9; for Luke see Acts 3:19; 9:35; 11:21; 14:15; 15:19; 26:20; 28:27. Cf. 1 Pet 2:25; James 5:20. Otherwise Belleville, *Reflections*, 252–53, who sees it in terms of LXX usage, referring to the Jews themselves as "turning" to God (from their idols, etc.).

[87]There is considerable debate as to whom "the Lord" refers in this sentence, whether Christ or Yahweh (see Belleville, *Reflections*, 254–55). In light of Paul's interpretation in v. 17a, this debate seems nearly irrelevant. In the sense that he is

been said about Christ in v. 14, one is not quite prepared for the interpretation that follows—which only shows how thoroughly this whole
passage is dealing primarily with the work of the Spirit, rather than of
Christ. And all of that, because the Spirit is the key (1) to Paul's ministry
and to the Corinthians' conversion—vis-à-vis his opponents, who, as
mere peddlers of the word relying on "letters" and Law, are bringing to
the Corinthians what he will later call another Jesus and another Spirit
(11:4)—and (2) to his and their experience of God's presence, which is
what vv. 17–18 pick up more specifically.

17 That this verse is intended to be an interpretation of the newly
transformed "citation" of Exod 34:34 in v. 16[88] is made certain by the
introductory formula, ὁ δὲ κύριος. A formula such as this, in which a
word from a previously "cited" biblical text is now re-introduced with δέ,
occurs three times in Paul (cf. 1 Cor 10:4; Gal 4:25). It also occurs
regularly throughout Jewish literature as a formula for interpreting
words from a text that has just been cited.[89] The usage in Gal 4:25 is
instructive, since it is nearly identical to this one, and there it is even
more clearly a literary device for picking up a word from a previous
sentence and elaborating on its meaning. Paul had already told us he
was interpreting the Sarah and Hagar stories as analogies (v. 24a). Thus,
"these are two covenants, one from Mount Sinai, begotten for slavery,
which is Hagar. Now 'Hagar' stands for Mount Sinai in Arabia." So here.
"Whenever anyone turns to the Lord [so as to be converted], the veil is
removed. Now 'the Lord' stands for the Spirit."[90]

Once this literary device has been observed, much of the debate over
Paul's language in this text tends to become irrelevant. By "the Lord,"
Paul does not intend either God or Christ; he intends the Spirit.[91] That

---

"citing" the LXX, the reference would seem to be Yahweh; but his concern is to
"contextualize" the text, so he argues that in fact it refers to the Spirit.

[88]This passage is a famous crux in Paul. Having missed Paul's exegetical method,
many have despaired of making sense of it; Schmithals has even argued that it is a
Gnostic interpolation (*Gnosticism*, 315–25). For discussion and bibliography, see
Belleville, *Reflections*, 256–57.

[89]See the helpful list in Belleville, *Reflections*, 263–66.

[90]For an earlier version of this argument, see G. D. Fee, "Hermeneutics and
Common Sense: An Exploratory Essay on the Hermeneutics of the Epistle," in
Inerrancy and Common Sense (ed. R. R. Nicole, J. R. Michaels; Grand Rapids, Baker,
1980; repr. as ch. 1 in *Gospel and Spirit: Issues in New Testament Hermeneutics* [Peabody,
Mass.: Hendrickson, 1991] 18–19). Cf. inter alia, Barrett 122; Dunn, "2 Corinthians
iii.17," 309–20; Furnish 212; Belleville, *Reflections*, 263–67.

[91]This is, after all, a pneumatological passage, not a christological one. Paul is
not trying to identify Christ with the Spirit; neither is he suggesting that the Spirit is
in some way to be equated with the risen Christ. This is an interpretative device, pure
and simple, in which he keeps alive his argument that his ministry is that of "the
new covenant of Spirit." Here he is about to explain the ultimate implications of that

is, he is interpreting the text of Exodus in light of the present argument. The Lord in that text, he is saying, is now to be understood (not literally, but in an analogical way) as referring to the Spirit—not because this is the proper identification of the Lord in the Exodus text, but because in this argument that is the proper way to understand what happens to those who, as Moses, now "turn to the Lord." The Spirit, who applies the work of Christ to the life of the believer, is the key to the eschatological experience of God's presence. With the veil removed from the hardened heart, God's people enter into freedom.

That this captures Paul's intent is confirmed by the clause that follows, where the Spirit is designated "the Spirit of the Lord." Three things seem to be going on here. First, by designating him now as "the Spirit of the Lord," Paul seems intent to remove any potential misunderstandings of the previous clause. He therefore circumvents an absolute identification of the Spirit with Yahweh (probably) or with Christ. Thus: "in interpreting 'the Lord' in the Exodus passage as referring to the Spirit, I do not mean that the Spirit is Lord; rather, the Spirit is, as always, the Spirit *of the Lord*."

Although it is not certain, and tends to go against Paul's ordinary usage, most likely the "Lord" in this case refers to Yahweh.[92] The reasons for this are several: (1) Paul is citing the LXX in v. 16, where the original reference is certain. Moreover, it is the habit of the LXX translators to avoid the article when using κύριος for Yahweh, a habit which remains invariable in all of Paul's OT citations as well. (2) The passage in fact is not christological, but pneumatological, and Paul far more often refers to the Spirit as "the Spirit of God" (cf. v. 6) than as "the Spirit of Christ."[93] (3) The use of τὸ πνεῦμα κυρίου is unique to the entire Pauline corpus; otherwise he either has the article with both nouns or has it with neither. This use of the article with πνεῦμα, followed by an anarthrous κυρίου, is best explained as Paul's picking up the reference to Yahweh in v. 16.[94] (4) Finally, and for me decisively, in v. 18 the "glory of the Lord," which believers behold, seems to refer to Christ; that is, Christ himself is the glory of the Lord Yahweh, which is quite the point made in 4:6.

ministry. Missing Paul's method here has led several to argue that Paul here identifies the Spirit with Christ (esp. I. Hermann, *Kyrios und Pneuma*, who bases his entire case on his misreading of this text; cf. also N. Q. Hamilton, *The Holy Spirit and Eschatology in Paul* [London: Oliver and Boyd, 1957] 4–8). See the critique in ch. 13 below.

[92]This is debated, of course, and much of the debate rests on how one understands v. 17a. Those who think "Lord" throughout refers to Yahweh include Bernard 58; Collange 103–4; Dunn, "2 Corinthians iii.17," 317; Moule, "2 Cor. 3.18b," 235; Harris 339; Furnish, 213; Martin 30; Belleville, *Reflections*, 255. The majority think it refers to Christ (Meyer, Hodge, Plummer, Strachan, Tasker, Wendland, Bruce, Barrett, Bultmann, Danker).

[93]See ch. 2, pp. 14–19.

[94]This is a more precise way of making the point that is found in more general terms in Harris 339 and Belleville, *Reflections*, 255.

Second, although Paul himself does not here press the point, this usage presupposes the Spirit as the fulfillment of the Presence of God motif in a thoroughgoing way. The Lord to whom Moses turned is the one whose "Presence" tabernacled in the midst of his people Israel. By removing the "veil" of the old covenant, Christ has ushered in the new covenant. The "Lord" to whom God's newly constituted people turn, whose "Presence" is now in their hearts, is none other than the life-giving Spirit of the living God. With the passing of the old covenant and with the removal of our sins, as Paul will argue in 5:20–21, we now know the Presence of God in an eternal way; as we are indwelt by the living God himself, in the person of God's Spirit.

Third, Paul's point in the present argument is to interpret both his preceding sentence and the argument of vv. 12–16 in light of the effective ministry of the Spirit. Just as his ministry of the Spirit has given him "boldness" or "confidence" before God; so now in turning to the Lord, understood as God's presence by the Spirit, the believer enters into freedom. Thus the two parts of v. 17 together interpret the two sides of v. 16: When one "turns to the Lord" (now "the Lord" stands for the Spirit, who is the key to ministry in the new covenant), "the veil is removed" (through the Spirit of the Lord who thus brings one into freedom).[95]

The meaning of "freedom" here has been much debated and, at the popular level, much abused. In context, it refers primarily to the freedom from "the veil" as that has been interpreted in v. 15, as lying yet over the hearts of those in the synagogue at the hearing of the old covenant. Precisely because they do not have the Spirit, they cannot behold God's glory that shines in Christ (v. 18). In this argument that further involves freedom from the covenant of letter that leads to condemnation and death.[96] After all, this is what the analogy of the veil is all about. All other kinds of freedom, which evolve from this first kind, are at best ancillary (e.g., freedom from sin), at worst distortions (e.g., freedom from ritualism[97]), at least as far as this text is concerned. To put all of this in another way, the emphasis in context is less on "freedom *from*" and more on "freedom *for*." What the Spirit has done for us in appropriating the

---

[95]I am indebted to Belleville, *Reflections*, 257, for this insight.

[96]Which is why the preaching of "another Jesus" to those who have the Spirit is such an anathema to Paul. Those who are still there, in the old covenant, are as those with veils over their hearts, who know nothing of the freedom that the Spirit has brought. So why bring that in among those who live in the new covenant of the Spirit?

[97]Some have objected to this on the grounds that the old covenant, with its requirements of religious duties and rites, was "letter" precisely because it was full of ritual without substance. But Paul does not object to rites or ritual. He objects to the imposition of the old covenant on Gentiles as an "identity marker," as though these expressions of the old covenant guaranteed that Gentiles were true members of the people of God. See further the introduction to Galatians in the next chapter.

work of Christ to our lives ("removing the veil") is to give us freedom,
boldness if you will, to enter into God's presence and behold his glory
"with uncovered faces"; freedom to be transformed into his likeness from
one degree of glory to yet another. This is the glorious freedom of the
children of God, made available through the Spirit, which will be explicated in the final sentence that wraps it all up.

18 With this sentence we reach the heights.[98] No wonder Paul
considers his opponents as mere peddlers of the word. They would lead
God's Spirit people back into bondage, back under the now obsolete
covenant that led to condemnation and dealt in death. Even though that
covenant had glory, he allowed, it was nothing at all in comparison with
the glory of the new. Not only has the old passed away (cf. 5:17) and the
new come to abide forever (v. 11), but, he has argued, "what [once] had
glory [now] has no glory at all in comparison with the surpassing glory
[of the new]" (v. 10). This concluding sentence (v. 18) now spells out "the
surpassing glory" of the "covenant of Spirit."

We have already noted that Paul here deliberately returns to the
beginning of his argument and includes the Corinthians in the experience of glory that the Spirit provides.[99] We need now to note that this
factor will have considerable bearing on how one understands v. 18 as a
whole—whether the basic contrast is between Paul (with others) and
Moses in v. 13, or between the Corinthians (with Paul) and those in
vv. 14–15. This matter is further complicated by the verb κατοπτριζόμενοι,
which ordinarily means "to look at in a mirror," but which may also
mean "to reflect as in a mirror."

In the first option the contrast is primarily between Moses, who had
to *veil* his face so that the glory could not be seen by others and who
therefore was not allowed to "reflect" the glory of his face, and Paul (and
others), whose faces are *unveiled* precisely so that through the Spirit they

---

[98]In more subdued fashion, Furnish 238 notes that this verse is "distinguished
formally by its almost confessional style."

[99]Not all think this; the majority take it to refer to all Christian believers, and in
a secondary sense it does. Cf. Furnish 238, who recognizes that it first of all refers to
Paul and the Corinthians, but who also suggests that "we all" means "all Christians"
(213). What appears to me as the Achilles' heel in Belleville's interpretation (see next
notes) is her limiting this phrase to Paul and to "all true gospel ministers without
exception" (276). This seems to miss Paul's own usage and tendencies by too much.
The best explanation for the "we all" lies close at hand, in 1:21–22, where Paul
concludes a similar defense of his apostolic integrity by including his readers in the
benefits of the Spirit's activity. Cf. this same kind of inclusion of the Corinthians in
the "with you" in 4:14 and "we all" in 5:10. This kind of inclusion more often goes
the other way, where in second person plural contexts, Paul will suddenly shift to
the first person plural when he speaks of the benefits of salvation (see, e.g., 1 Cor 1:18,
30; 5:7; 6:14, and throughout).

might *reflect* the glory of the Lord.[100] Here the emphasis lies still with the contrasts between *ministries,* both of which have glory; but the glory of the latter so far surpasses the former that there is no real comparison, because God's own glory has come through the latter—despite the weaknesses of the form in which it came.

In the second option the contrast is between the *recipients* of the two ministries and has to do with the *effect* of each ministry on them. The former have "veils over their hearts" (v. 15), which only Christ can remove. The latter, who have "turned to (the Spirit of) the Lord," have had the veil removed so as to experience God's presence with freedom. Further, they also experience freedom from the old and for the new as they *behold* the glory of God in the face of Jesus Christ and are therefore transformed into that same likeness with ever-increasing glory.

On the one hand, in favor of the former option are several factors: (1) The most obvious is the return to the use of "veil" with the "face," which earlier had to do with Moses, not the people. (2) It is possible that v. 18 is a further reflection on Exodus 34, in this case v. 35, "the Israelites *saw* that Moses' *face* had been *glorified.*" Thus, by way of contrast, Paul's face is unveiled so that people may see the glory of the Lord by the Spirit.[101] (3) This sentence also recalls the theme of "glory" from vv. 7–11, where the contrast was singularly between the two ministries, that of Moses and the old with that of Paul and the new. (4) This, in turn, is in keeping with the chief concern of the argument throughout, beginning with 2:14, namely, a defense of Paul's ministry, especially in contrast to the "peddlers" of 2:17. Finally (5), as in 1:21–22 and 3:1–3, his "ministry of Spirit" is what has brought the "glory of the Lord" to the Corinthians. Even if one goes with the next option, as I do, one must take seriously that what is said here is still ultimately in defense of Paul's ministry, which he makes plain in the verses that immediately follow (4:1–6).

On the other hand, there are also several factors that favor the latter option, which I find more convincing in terms of the total argument: (1) The inclusion of the Corinthians seems deliberate by the emphatic "we all" at the beginning of the sentence. (2) More significantly, the flow of the argument, beginning with v. 14b, has intentionally moved from Moses to contemporary Jews, who have "veiled hearts" because they continue in the old covenant which still has the veil over it. The contrasts

---

[100] See especially Belleville, *Reflections,* 273–96, whose case in part rests on what she perceives to be a continuation of the interpretation of Exodus 34 (now v. 35).

[101] Belleville, *Reflections,* tends to rest her case on this, which in her argument moves from a possibility to a certainty, so that Paul is "dependent" on Exodus 34 (p. 284). That seems to be something of an overstatement for the rather allusive nature of the linguistic ties between this verse and Exod 34:35. Under any circumstances the ties are not in the same category as in vv. 16–17 and those verses' relation to Exod 34:34.

in vv. 15 and 16 are deliberate; and they clearly focus on the *recipients* of the two ministries, as does v. 17, which interprets v. 16 in terms of the receiving of the Spirit. (3) In 4:1–6, Paul seems to be *returning* to the theme of his ministry, which in vv. 3–4 specifically refers to those who have *not* received his ministry of Spirit. That is, it focuses on his ministry in terms of its recipients (in this case, nonrecipients). (4) The imagery of v. 18 finally seems to make more sense in terms of their (Paul's and the Corinthians') shared experience of the glory—they are both being transformed into Christ's likeness from glory to glory—than in terms of emphasis on Paul's ministry as such over against the peddlers. Finally (5), as we will note momentarily, this also seems to explain better the mirror imagery, which ordinarily has to do with "looking into" a mirror, not with the mirror's reflecting an image.

If that is the case, then the shift of the imagery of veil back to the face, in this instance the faces of both Paul and the Corinthians, should not surprise us. Although "unveiled face" surely recalls the veiled face of Moses in v. 13, that "veil" has already moved from Moses' face to the old covenant to the hearts of those who cannot see the glory because of the "veil" over the covenant. Since the "freedom" of the Spirit has removed the veil over the heart, the imagery now shifts once more to the "face" of those who have experienced this freedom. Especially so, in light of the final use of this imagery in 4:3–4, where the "veil" is applied in terms of "the blinding of the minds" of those who do not believe, so that they do not *see the light of the gospel, which reveals the glory of Christ, who is the "likeness" of God.*

But the question still remains as to the basic thrust of the mirror imagery inherent in κατοπτριζόμενοι,[102] whether it means to "look at something in a mirror," hence "contemplate," or "to reflect as a mirror." That is, it is not immediately clear who is doing the seeing, whether *we all* are beholding God's glory and are thus being transformed into the same image, or whether with unveiled faces, as Moses of old, we are reflecting God's glory so that it might be seen by others.

Despite some obviously attractive features to the latter understanding, there finally are four matters that favor the former: (1) Mirror imagery occurs only twice in Paul's letters, here and in 1 Cor 13:12. This usage is a clear case of Paul's "contextualizing," since Corinth was famous throughout Greco-Roman antiquity for the superior quality of its bronze mirrors.[103] In its former usage the imagery was that of "beholding [God]" in the present in a way that is analogous to looking into ("through" is the Greek idiom) a mirror. The analogy is not "indistinctly"

---

[102] It occurs only here in early Christian literature; not surprisingly, neither is it found in the LXX.

[103] See, e.g., *Corinth: A Brief History of the City and a Guide to the Excavations,* published by the American Schools of Classical Studies in Athens, 1972, p. 5.

or "in a distorted way," but *indirectly* as over against our eschatologically seeing him "face to face."[104] The imagery, therefore, is something quite positive, and it worked for Paul precisely because it allowed him to postulate a real "seeing," yet one that in the present age falls short of actually seeing the Lord "face to face" as it were. Given the clear sense of this earlier usage, therefore, one would seem to need especially compelling reasons to abandon it for another sense in the present passage.

(2) This in fact is the primary meaning of the verb. Although some evidence can be mustered for the meaning "reflect,"[105] the verb normally means "to look into a mirror."

(3) Not only so, but even in the present passage the thrust of the imagery concerns our "beholding," rather than our "reflecting." This makes far better sense of the main verb and its modifiers, "*we are being transformed* into the same likeness, from glory to glory," than otherwise.[106] That is, *our* being transformed is better understood as taking place in us as we "behold the glory as in a mirror,"[107] rather than as we continually reflect the glory with unveiled faces.

(4) Paul's application of the imagery in 4:3–6 seems decisive. Once again, now in terms of those who have not believed his gospel through his ministry, he picks up the three themes of veiling, glory, and likeness. In this case, the veiling is clearly over the hearts of those who do not believe so that they might *not* see what those who believe the gospel *do* see, namely, the *glory* of God himself in the *face* of Jesus Christ, who is the *likeness* of God. That is because they do not have the Spirit, who has made all of this experiential to those who have "turned to the Lord."

We should note, finally, that this further application in 4:3–6 also seems to be the clue for resolving most of the remaining difficulties in the text. The Lord, whose glory we now behold by the Spirit, is none other than God. Through the gospel, Paul says in v. 4, we see the glory of Christ. This phrasing might make one think that "the Lord" in the phrase "glory of the Lord" in our text also therefore refers to Christ. But he further says that Christ is the "likeness" of God (v. 4), and in v. 6 repeats all of this by declaring that God has shined into our hearts[108] so that through that "light" we might see his glory, which is located "in the face of Jesus Christ."[109]

---

[104] On this see the discussion in Fee, *1 Corinthians*, 647–48.

[105] See Belleville, *Reflections*, 279–81, for what appears to be the best possible case.

[106] Belleville, *Reflections*, 281, acknowledges that this presents a real difficulty for many regarding her point of view; her response, and especially the texts mustered to support her view, suggest that the depth of this problem is not adequately recognized.

[107] See especially, Lambrecht, "Transformation," 249–54.

[108] This seems deliberately to recall, by way of contrast, those whose "minds are blinded" (v. 4a) because they have a "veil over their hearts" when the old covenant is read (3:15).

[109] But see Lambrecht, "Transformation," 245–46, who would put the emphasis on v. 4, and make the "Lord" here refer to Christ.

This passage (4:3–6) seems also to resolve the question of "the same image/ likeness."[110] The use of "image" comes from the metaphor of looking into a mirror; an "image" is what is seen. Some have suggested that this means that Paul and the Corinthians together share the same likeness as they exist together in Christ;[111] however, since Paul has already indicated that what is actually seen, as though we were beholding an image in a mirror, is "the glory of the Lord," this is the "same" image into which we are being transformed—that of God as his glory is seen in the face of Christ.[112] Paul employs similar language in Rom 8:29 to express the goal of the entire redemptive process ("that we be conformed [συμμόρφους] to the image [εἰκών] of his Son"), which suggests that the Adam-Christ analogy is deeply woven into Pauline theology. As Adam was created in God's εἰκών ("image/likeness"), but rolled that image in the dust, so the second Adam truly bears that likeness with all of its resplendent glory. And we, too, now bear that likeness as we are "in Christ," or in the words of this passage, as "we are transformed into the same likeness from glory to glory," precisely because the goal is that we be finally "conformed into the likeness of his Son."

Thus the phrase "from glory to glory"[113] most likely goes back to the motif of v. 11, that the glory of the old was destined to become obsolete, whereas the glory of the new not only would not fade away but would remain forever. In context therefore this phrase emphasizes the non-fading reality and ever-increasing dimension of the glory that is now ours through the ministry of the Spirit—as we continually behold Christ and are being constantly renewed into his likeness.

That leads us finally to the little coda with which both this sentence and the entire argument conclude, "just as from the Lord, the Spirit."[114] In many ways this is the most difficult expression of all. Is it true finally

---

[110] Gk. εἰκών. This is the word used in the LXX for the creation of humans in God's "image." Thus, in his incarnation Christ perfectly bears the εἰκὼν τοῦ θεοῦ. This is the image, or likeness, that we, through Christ, are now able to bear once again. Cf. Rom 8:29.

[111] See, e.g., van Unnik, "Unveiled Face," 167; Dunn, "2 Corinthians iii.7," 320; Wright, "Reflected Glory," 148–50; and Belleville, *Reflections*, 290, who thinks of it, however, in terms of "true ministers of the gospel."

[112] Cf. Lambrecht, "Transformation," 244–45. Thus, the objection that there is no proper antecedent for "same" does not seem to hold up. The "same" image is that which they behold "in the mirror," namely, that of the Lord whose glory they behold.

[113] Gk. ἀπὸ δόξης εἰς δόξαν. When Paul uses this kind of phrase to stress source and goal ("from the one so as to become the other") he uses ἐκ . . . εἰς (see 2:16; Rom 1:17).

[114] Gk. ἀπὸ κυρίου πνεύματος. This phrase could just possibly mean "from the Spirit of the Lord" (cf. v. 17, τὸ πνεῦμα κυρίου). But if that is what Paul intended, this change of word order is especially curious, all the more so with an anarthrous usage in which both nouns are ambiguously in the same case. In most such cases word order should prevail.

that Paul is identifying Christ with the Spirit? Not likely. The best solution of several is the contextual one. The point of the entire argument has been the role of the Spirit in Paul's ministry and thus in the lives of the Corinthians, which validates that ministry as one that has come with glory. This little phrase simply reinforces that point, but it does so in this case by taking us back to v. 17, to the original word of the "interpretation" of v. 16, "the 'Lord' stands for the Spirit." In the meantime Paul has explained the glory of the covenant of Spirit in terms of our relationship to Christ, in whom we behold God's own glory, and into whose likeness we are constantly being transformed. To bring this particular reality back into the realm of the ministry of the Spirit, he concludes by way of the emphasis with which he began, "just as from the Lord, the Spirit." As in v. 17, he is identifying neither Christ nor Yahweh with the Spirit. This a literary moment, pure and simple, in which all that has preceded is neatly rounded off. We already know from v. 17b that the Spirit in any case is the "Spirit of the Lord." The Spirit, we are now reminded, is the key to our experience of the presence of God.

Thus Paul's present argument (from v. 1) has come full circle. He will go on to apply it directly to his own ministry, especially vis-à-vis his opponents and in terms of those who do not believe. But for now his point has been made. He needs no letters of commendation as do the peddlers, because he is a minister of the new covenant, the covenant of Spirit that gives life. In contrast to them, who are dealing in condemnation and death because of their attachment to the old covenant, Paul's ministry belongs to the time of the fulfilled promise, in which the Spirit is now available to all. The coming of the Spirit has brought the old to an end and has appropriated the work of Christ, through whom the effects of the Fall have been radically reversed. Indeed, through Christ and by the Spirit we are being transformed so as to bear the likeness for which we were intended at the beginning. In the freedom the Spirit provides, we have seen the glory of God himself—as it is made evident to us in the face of our Lord Jesus Christ—and we have come to experience that glory, and will do so in an ever-increasing way until we come to the final glory. One takes the Spirit lightly in Pauline theology and Christian experience only at great risk, for herein lies the "glory," that by the Spirit we not only come to know God, but come to live in his Presence in such a way as constantly to be renewed into God's image.

To theologize this passage in such a way as to remove its experiential dimension in Pauline spirituality is to divest it of its "real life" setting, both in Paul and in Corinth. Whatever else, Paul was a passionate lover of God; his heart panted after God as the deer for the water brook. For him the Law with its "covenantal righteousness" had failed at this very point. The experience of the Spirit had done what the old covenant could not do, it had brought him into God's own Presence and empowered him to bear the divine likeness—to do what the Law required because in

freedom he had been, and was being, transformed into God's own likeness, i.e., to live in such a way as to reflect God's character. Any talk of
the Spirit as experienced reality that falls short of this misses the primary
role of the Spirit in Pauline theology and the argumentation of Galatians
5–6 and Romans 8–15.

We need to note, finally, that this is the next in the series of many
texts[115] in which Paul's Trinitarian presuppositions are plainly visible.
Indeed, the Trinitarian implications are thoroughgoing, rather than confused, as Ingo Hermann has suggested. The "high Christology" of the
passage can scarcely be missed; to behold Christ is to see the glory of the
Lord, because Christ is the "image/likeness of God." So with the "high
pneumatology." The Spirit is none other than the Spirit of the living God,
who by his working in our lives not only frees us from former tyrannies
but transforms us into God's own likeness. Through our experience of
the Spirit we have entered into God's presence with unveiled faces. As
everywhere in Paul, the one God has effected our salvation as Father,
Son, and Spirit. Thus the redemptive work of Christ (v. 14), which has
God's keeping covenant with his people as its predicate (v. 11), is realized
in our lives through the "inscribing" work of the life-giving Spirit; not
only so, but the aim of that redemptive work, our being re-created into
God's likeness, likewise flows from the redemption that is in Christ and
is effected in our lives as the Spirit "removes the veil" and transforms us
into the likeness of the Father as that is seen in the Son.

2 Corinthians 4:1–6

[1]*Therefore, having this ministry even as we have received mercy, we do not
lose heart;* [2]*rather, we have renounced the hidden things of shame, neither
walking in craftiness nor falsifying the word of God, but by manifestation of
the truth commending ourselves before God to every person's conscience.* [3]*If
indeed our gospel is hidden, it is hidden to those who are perishing,* [4]*among
whom the god of this age has blinded the minds of the unbelieving so that they
might not see the light of the gospel which reveals the glory of Christ, who is
God's image.* [5]*For we do not proclaim ourselves, but Jesus Christ as Lord, and
ourselves as your slaves for Jesus' sake,* [6]*because it is the God who said, "Out
of darkness light will shine forth," who has shone forth in our hearts in order
to give the light of the knowledge of the glory of God in the face of Christ.*

Although there is no direct reference to the Spirit here, this paragraph is so closely tied to the preceding argument that a few items need
to be noted as to the implied work of the Spirit that lies just below the
surface. Indeed, this is the kind of passage which offers clear evidence

---

[115] See above on 1:21–22; cf. n. 39 on 1 Thes 1:4–6.

that Paul does not always need to mention the Spirit by name in order for us to recognize his implied presence in an argument.

The reference to "this ministry," with which the paragraph begins, is the linkage with what has preceded, recalling 3:6 and 8 in particular, where Paul's ministry was described in terms of the new covenant of the Spirit. The rest of chapter 3 gives content to this ministry of the Spirit, as one of freedom in God's presence and with a glory that so outstrips the former glory as to render it no glory at all. It is this ministry of the Spirit to which Paul is now referring once more. Because he has this ministry of Spirit, which brings freedom and glory to others, he can do what the others cannot: commend himself *before God* to everyone's conscience. Thus in v. 2, Paul's ministry is now said to come as "the manifestation/revelation of the truth." The relationship of the Spirit to such manifestation is expressly stated in 1 Cor 2:12–13.

The same holds in vv. 4 and 6, as we have already noted above. Those who do not believe are said to be "blinded" (thus "veiled") by the god of this age, so that they cannot see what the Spirit, by removing the veil, makes possible for God's people, namely (literally), "to see the light of the gospel of the glory of Christ, who is the image/likeness of God." In its own way this repeats, and therefore interprets, v. 18. It is repeated again in v. 6, but now with the living God as the subject and "in our hearts" as the object. In contrast to the god of this world who blinds people, the living God has "shone" in our hearts, so as to "enlighten" us with the knowledge of his glory, as that is seen in the face of Jesus Christ. Again, the Spirit lies close at hand in the language of "shining"[116] and "enlightening."

All of this suggests, then, that as elsewhere in Paul "the god of this age" is to be understood as in contrast to the Spirit of the living God. The evil spirit "veils" the hearts of those who do not believe; the Holy Spirit removes the veil so that we can see the glory that is found in Christ.

2 CORINTHIANS 4:7

But we have this treasure in earthenware vessels, so that the surpassing splendor of the power might be God's and not from ourselves.

As in vv. 1–6, the Spirit is not expressly mentioned in this sentence; nonetheless, both the context and the mention of "power" in v. 7, plus the reflections on "life" and "death" in vv. 10–12, keep the whole firmly within the context of Paul's ministry of Spirit, which first found expression in 3:3. Indeed, with this passage the argument that began in 2:14 is being brought back full circle—from the theme of his "weakness" and integrity in 2:14–17, through the "glory" of his ministry despite the weaknesses, a glory that is the work of the Spirit, back to the theme of

---

[116] Cf. Young-Ford, *Meaning*, 257.

weakness. The argument shifts back from the ministry, which was full of glory, to the minister, who in his personal presence and style is anything but—a theme that will now receive theological reflection.

Two things are at work here: First, this is the second in a series of arguments in this letter in which Paul sets forth his own weaknesses in their starkest form,[117] so that he might emphasize that the "glory" of his ministry comes only from the Spirit and has nothing to do with himself. In this case the contrast takes the form of Paul's being a "clay vessel" but his ministry as being of "all-surpassing splendor of power," which is from God.

Second, although the imagery, and therefore much of the language, has changed, this is nearly a repeat of what he had already argued with them in 1 Cor 2:1–5. There, in a context of personal weakness (v. 3), he had refused to come to them with wisdom and rhetoric, but came instead in the demonstration of the Spirit's power (v. 4), so that their faith might finally rest in the "power of God" (v. 5). Now, he has this treasure (the gospel of vv. 4 and 6) in "an earthen vessel," an especially powerful imagery of his own personal weaknesses and physical frailty, which is what the argument that follows will spell out in detail. Nonetheless, in keeping with the argument of 3:1–18, despite the frailty of his person, his ministry was accompanied by the Spirit, with God's "surpassing splendor of power." As before, power has to do with the effectiveness of his ministry, with the Corinthians as Exhibit A, not with miracles and wonders as such, which for the Corinthians and the insurgents had apparently become a kind of end in itself leading to improper boasting.

All of this to observe, then, that once more lying close to the surface in Paul's use of "power" language is the implicit ministry of the Holy Spirit in his life.

2 CORINTHIANS 4:10–12

[10]*always carrying about the death of Jesus in the body in order that the life of Jesus might also be manifested in our body.* [11]*For we who live are always being handed over to death for Jesus' sake, in order that the life of Jesus might also be manifested in our mortal flesh,* [12]*with the result that death is at work in us, but life in you.*

As this argument unfolds, Paul again does not mention the Spirit as such, but the language he uses is full of recollections of the preceding argument in chapter 3. In this case he picks up the language of "life," which in 3:6 is singled out as the ministry of the Spirit. Here the "life" is qualified in particular as "the life of Jesus," which is undoubtedly related to Jesus' resurrection.[118] Such life is "manifested" in Paul, even in the

---

[117] The first appears in 2:14–16a; see also 6:3–13; 11:21–12:10; 13:3–4, 9–10.

[118] Some have argued that "the life of Jesus" refers here to Jesus' earthly life: e.g.,

midst of his constantly being handed over to death, so that it might also be made available to the Corinthians. Thus, the "life" is that of the Risen Lord; it is made available to the Corinthians through the power of the Spirit, who is at work in the ministry of Paul and who finally gives life in the sense of Ezek 37:1–14, as eschatological fulfillment, so that "these dry bones shall live."

2 CORINTHIANS 4:13

But having the same Spirit of faith that is in keeping with what is written, "I believed, therefore I spoke," we also believe, and therefore we also speak.

Although many understand πνεῦμα here to refer to a "disposition of faith,"[119] several factors suggest that Paul intends to refer to the Holy Spirit:[120] (1) The most significant factor is the place of this new paragraph in the present argument. The tie with what has preceded is marked by the repetition of the verb, "having," which since 3:4 has occurred at every significant shift in the argument, but as a continuation of the argument.[121] Thus this passage must be seen as a continuation of what has been in process since 2:14. In this regard it is difficult to imagine that the word πνεῦμα should now occur in some lesser sense as "attitude" or "disposition," since the Spirit has been the crucial matter right along. (2) Had Paul intended "the same faith as the Psalmist," he could easily have said that; but that in fact is not what he says. Paul's concern is twofold: that he and the Psalmist share the same faith, because they share the same Spirit who engendered such faith. (3) Part of the argument in ch. 3 contrasted the old covenant and the new, the former being a matter of letter, the latter a matter of Spirit, which makes the former obsolete. But Paul would never understand the OT, or the Law as such, thereby to go by the way. To the contrary, the OT is God's story, the story of his creating a people for his name, a story which now includes Paul and the Corinthians—and ourselves. The OT, therefore, is not obsolete; it

---

Meyer 497; J. Murphy-O'Connor, *The Theology of the Second Letter to the Corinthians* (Cambridge: Cambridge University Press, 1991) 46–47; J. A. Crafton, *The Agency of the Apostle* (JSNTMS 51; Sheffield: JSOT Press, 1991) 91. But this fails on all counts: the larger context of this passage, beginning in v. 14, makes a considerable point of the "already/not yet" of Christ's resurrection in Paul's present life—despite Paul's present weaknesses (described as "death at work" in him) Jesus' resurrection brings about "life" now (for them and him) and guarantees his (and their) future resurrection; moreover, if Jesus' earthly life were in view, the proper term for that is βίος, not ζωή.

[119] That is, "a believing frame of mind"; see inter alia, Bernard 63; Plummer 133; Hughes 147; Strachan 96; and probably those who translate with a lower case *s* and make no comment at all (e.g., Martin).

[120] So also Meyer 241, Hodge 97, Bultmann 121, Barrett 142, Furnish 258.

[121] See 3:4, "we have"; 3:12, "having therefore"; 4:1, "having therefore"; 4:7, "we have"; 4:13, "but having."

is Scripture,[122] inspired of the Holy Spirit, all of which pointed to the present fulfillment of the promised new covenant of Spirit. By this sudden appeal to the OT, Paul in effect brings the Spirit and the faith of the OT writer into the arena of the new covenant, since faith ultimately comes from the Spirit. Finally, (4) as Wendland put it, "Spirit and faith belong together."[123] For Paul it is the Spirit who not only gives life but also engenders the faith that causes one to receive the Spirit and thus enter into life. Thus this seems clearly to be a Spirit passage in Paul, which spells out the life of faith as the gift of the Spirit.

2 Corinthians 4:16

Therefore, we do not shrink back; but if our outer person is decaying, our inner person is being renewed day by day.

The verb ἀνακαινοῦται ("is being renewed"), which does not appear often in Paul, does occur in Titus 3:5 as a noun, and as the work of the Spirit. Thus, even though the Spirit again is not mentioned, this sentence is very much in keeping with vv. 10–12 above, where the body, full of the frailty of a clay vessel, is constantly being handed over to death. But the "inner person," who has been given life by the Spirit, is also constantly being renewed by that same Spirit. On this usage see also on Col 3:10 and Rom 12:2.

2 Corinthians 5:5

Now the one who has fashioned[124] us for this very thing is God, who gave us the down payment of the Spirit.

This reference to the Spirit as God's down payment, which repeats the language of 1:22, occurs in one of the thorniest passages in the Pauline corpus.[125] For the purposes of this study, it is not necessary to

---

[122] On the distinction between the old covenant and the OT, which is too often blurred in biblical scholarship, see especially Hanson, *Studies*, 136–39.

[123] "Geist und Glaube gehören zusammen" (190); cf. Héring, 34: "these two gifts of grace [Spirit and faith] are inseparable."

[124] Gk. κατεργασάμενος, which has been altered to the present tense by the Western MSS, presumably on the pattern of 4:17. It is not easy to find an appropriate English word with which to render this verb. Most translations opt for "prepare," but that contains connotations in English that miss the concept of "working, creating, accomplishing," which is basic to this verb. Here I have followed the NAB, which seems best to have captured the nuance in this context.

[125] *Bibliography:* R. **Berry,** "Death and Life in Christ," *SJT* 14 (1961) 60–76; F. F. **Bruce,** "Paul on Immortality," *SJT* 24 (1971) 457–72; R. **Cassidy,** "Paul's Attitude to Death in II Corinthians 5:1–10," *EQ* 43 (1971) 210–17; L. **Cranford,** "A New Look at 2 Corinthians 5:1–10," *SWJT* 19 (1971) 95–100; E. E. **Ellis,** "II Corinthians V.1–10 in Pauline Eschatology," *NTS* 6 (1959–60) 211–24; J. **Gillman,** "A Thematic Comparison: 1 Cor 15:50–57 and 2 Cor 5:1–5," *JBL* 107 (1988) 439–54; K. **Hanhart,** "Paul's Hope

resolve all of the issues involved, including its difficult details, nor to interact with the several positions on the passage that have emerged in the literature; but a few words as to how I perceive the point of the passage and its place in context are necessary in order to explicate my understanding of the role of the Spirit in the argument.

Two things seem to be going on: First, in the argument to this point, beginning with 4:7, Paul has been reflecting on the twin processes that are at work in the present. On the one hand, he is constantly being handed over to death; on the other hand, life is also at work in him, both through him for others (v. 12) and in his own inner person that is constantly being renewed by the Spirit (v. 16). This paragraph (5:1–10), which stands as something of a digression to the argument, spells out the outcome of these two processes, now in terms of the body in particular. In its present form the body is wasting away; but that is not the final word. In vv. 13–14 he had struck the note of resurrection as the final outcome of the process of the death that is at work in the mortal body. Thus, as he had already argued in 1 Cor 15:44–49, there awaits a supernatural (Spiritual) body which will replace the former at resurrection and/or transformation.

Second, since Paul has recently already spoken to this issue in 1 Corinthians 15, rather than to think that Paul here has changed his mind or is offering additional information, it is far more likely that he is covering the same ground one more time. Here is a place where he and they have been at odds; thus, lest they seize his apparent denigration of present bodily existence as supporting their own viewpoint, he now reemphasizes from 1 Corinthians 15 that there awaits a heavenly expression of the present body.

The structure of the argument seems plain enough. He begins with an assertion (v. 1), which is then elaborated with two clauses beginning with καὶ γάρ ("for indeed"; vv. 2 and 4).[126] The difficulties lie with the imagery, which is typically fluid, one image calling for another, so that neither of them can be pressed as images per se. Thus he shifts back and forth from "house" to "clothing," with the "dwelling" often functioning as the "clothing."

---

in the Face of Death," *JBL* 88 (1969) 445–57; M. J. **Harris,** "2 Corinthians 5:1–10: Watershed in Paul's Eschatology?" *TynB* 22 (1971) 33–57; R. F. **Hettlinger,** "2 Corinthians 5:1–10," *SJT* 10 (1957) 174–94; W. **Lillie,** "An Approach to II Corinthians 5:1–10," *SJT* 30 (1977) 59–70; **Lincoln,** *Paradise,* 55–71; J. **Osei-Bonsu,** "Does 2 Cor. 5:1–10 Teach the Reception of the Resurrection Body at the Moment of Death?" *JSNT* 28 (1986) 81–101; A. C. **Perriman,** "Paul and Parousia: 1 Corinthians 15:50–57 and 2 Corinthians 5:1–5," *NTS* 35 (1989) 512–21; G. **Wagner,** "The Tabernacle and Life 'in Christ': Exegesis of 2 Corinthians 5:1–10," *IBS* 3 (1981) 145–65; J. **Yates,** "Immediate or Intermediate? The State of the Believer Upon Death," *Churchman* 101 (1987) 310–22.

[126] Cf. the similar structure in 1 Cor 12:12–14 and 2 Cor 13:3–4.

Verse 1, therefore, asserts, as an explanation of vv. 17–18, that the "eternal weight of glory" that awaits in the resurrection (vv. 13–15) far outstrips the present affliction. "For," he says, "when the time comes[127] for our earthly 'tent-dwelling' to be 'dismantled,'[128] we have another dwelling, an eternal one in the heavens." With new imagery this says precisely what Paul has already said in 1 Cor 15:44–55.

The two "for indeed" sentences elaborate by going back to the argument of 4:7–18, that in our present bodily existence we "groan"[129] to be delivered and finally to "put on" the new "dwelling." In the first instance this takes the form of longing to be "overclothed" with the new, which is not an explanation of Pauline anthropology, as some suggest, but a repetition of 1 Cor 15:50–55 and the possibility of the living being transformed without going through death. All of this is repeated once more in v. 4. The concern is not with "nakedness" per se, and thus with some intermediate state, but with a longing for the future to be realized this side of death. We do not want to die, he seems to be saying, but to experience the transformation of the living in which "what is mortal is actually 'swallowed up' by life itself."

And here is where our sentence fits in. Whether we die or are transformed, God has fashioned us for this future bodily existence, in which the present mortal body is swallowed up by life. The clearest evidence for this is the gift of the Spirit, which functions for us as God's down payment that we shall indeed inherit the very thing God has fashioned us for, namely, a new form of bodily existence in a πνευματικὸν σῶμα ("Spiritual body"; 1 Cor 15:44) or σῶμα τῆς δόξης (a "body of glory"; Phil 3:21).

Two things need to be emphasized about this second appearance of "down payment" imagery in the letter: First, as we have already noted on 1:22, this is a case where the Spirit serves as the evidence for Paul of our essentially eschatological existence. We are destined for a glorious future, which is guaranteed precisely because the down payment of that future, the Spirit himself, is already our present possession. In giving us his Spirit, God has guaranteed our future. Thus, we live in the present, "already" but "not yet."

Second, as in 1 Cor 6:19–20 and 1 Cor 15:44–45, the Spirit is also the affirmation of our present bodily existence. We may "groan" a bit in it;

---

[127] This is to press Paul's ἐάν as expressing a present general condition, which in this case looks to the time in the future when it will actually happen.

[128] There is an obvious play on words here; our οἰκία τοῦ σκήνους ("dwelling in the form of a tent") will eventually καταλύθη ("be taken down").

[129] Furnish 295–99 suggests that the use of στενάζομεν is probably related to the similar usage in Rom 8:26, where the believer "sighs" in the Spirit, awaiting the final glory. This may very well be the case, especially in light of v. 5, where the Spirit is the "down payment" on the future resurrection of the body (cf. Rom 8:23). But one cannot be sure.

but it is not to be despised. As down payment, the Spirit in our present earthly existence also serves, as this passage makes abundantly clear, to verify that this mortal body is going to be "overclothed" with another body, which in 1 Cor 15:44 Paul called a "Spiritual" body and here images as a "heavenly dwelling, eternal, not made with hands."

It is impossible to know how the Corinthians responded to 1 Cor 15:35–58. Very likely, they did so with less than enthusiasm. For them the Spirit meant present ecstasy, life above and beyond mere bodily weaknesses, and thus evidence of being finally released from bodily existence altogether; for Paul the Spirit meant present empowering for life in the midst of bodily weaknesses in a body obviously in process of decay. But now he is reaffirming his position from 1 Cor 15:35–58, that the presence of the Spirit also means that these "decaying bodies" have also been stamped with eternity; they are destined for resurrection and thus transformation into the likeness of Christ's now glorified body. God himself, Paul here argues, "has fashioned us for this"; and the Spirit, whom the Corinthians have come to understand in a triumphalistic way, is rather the guarantee, the down payment, from God that these bodies are also destined for a "Spiritual" (= glorified) future.

2 CORINTHIANS 5:13

For if I am "beside myself" it is toward God; if I am in my "sound mind" it is for your sakes.

This is another of the difficult sentences in this letter. The problem here is threefold: finding an adequate meaning for its details; finding an adequate reason for it in the present argument; and determining whether being "beside himself" has reference to Spirit "ecstasy," as many think. All of this is complicated by whether this is basically affirmation on Paul's part, or whether he is picking up the language of the Corinthians and turning it against them.

The only one of these issues that can be resolved with any degree of satisfaction is the contextual one, and in this case only in the sense of describing its role in the argument, not of resolving what it actually means.[130] In v. 11 Paul returns to the defense of apostleship that began in 2:14 and was carried on in a variety of ways through 4:18. Following the "digression" indicating the outcome of the twofold process of death and life currently at work in his physical existence (5:1–10), but now flowing directly out of v. 10, Paul states that two things are true about

---

[130] Cf. Harris 351, "Whatever the background to this difficult verse, its general import seems clear. Paul disowns self-interest as a motive for any of his actions; all is for God's glory." For the same general sense as to its place in the argument, see Martin 126; Sumney, *Opponents*, 144.

his apostolic ministry. On the one hand, in light of the sure future judgment he tries without apology to "persuade people"; on the other hand, as to his own person and ministry, he is God's servant first and always, and therefore an open book before God—although he adds that he hopes he is equally manifest before their consciences as well. But in saying that, he goes on (v. 12), even though he does not intend to be commending himself, he does want them to have legitimate grounds for boasting in their founding apostle, and this in light of those who have come among them boasting in "externals" and not in what takes place in the heart.[131] With its connecting γάρ ("for"), our verse further explains two of the preceding themes: (1) that what he does is with a view either toward God or toward them, and therefore (2) there is not a moment of self-interest in whatever he does.

The problem lies with the distinctions "beside himself"[132] or "sound-minded"[133] as to what precisely is intended in the first item. The fact that this verb occurs only here in Paul, and in a context where he is defending himself, strengthens the possibility that the language comes from Corinth.[134] But even so, it is not clear whether Paul is giving it back to them ironically, that is, whether he is playing their note to a different tune, or whether he is making his own affirmation about his spirituality and ministry.[135]

Two options commend themselves. First, it could be that by "beside himself" Paul does not refer specifically to Spirit manifestations of some kind, but rather speaks directly to some slanderous accusations such as those brought against Jesus in Mark 3:31–35.[136] Thus, if they think he is beside himself in some way, so be it; what he is, he is ultimately before God, just as he has already said in v. 11. In this case, Paul would be making a positive assertion about his ministry. Indeed, he would be saying, I am "crazy like Jesus," in the sense that I am completely given up to God for the sake of others. This is the point made about Jesus in the Gospel story (Mark 3:31–35); it could well be the way we are to understand what follows in vv. 14–15. Love demands that I be a man for others in the same way as our Lord. In context, and in light of the

---

[131] This seems to hark back to 3:1–6, where these opponents have come with letters of commendation, and also with the mere "letter" of the old covenant, as over against the real epistle, the Spirit in the heart.

[132] Gk. ἐξέστημεν; found only here in the Pauline corpus. Elsewhere in the NT it ordinarily means "to be amazed"; however, it is used in Mark 3:21 as an accusation against Jesus that he is "out of his mind."

[133] Gk. σωφρονοῦμεν; cf. Rom 12:3. Its cognate noun occurs in 2 Tim 1:7 (q.v.), as a work of the Spirit in Paul and Timothy.

[134] This is so argued, correctly I would judge, by Belleville, *Reflections*, 123–24.

[135] For this distinction see Sumney, *Opponents*, 144–45.

[136] In some form or other this is the view of Calvin 73–74, Hodge 131–32, Plummer 172, Strachan 106, Tasker 84, Hughes 191, Héring 41, Bruce 207, Danker 78.

uncertainties, this view has much to commend it. In this case, it lies quite beyond the interests of this study, in that Spirit activity is not necessarily alluded to.

Second, Paul may mean something close to "ecstasy" in its proper sense, as referring to Spirit experiences that are out of the ordinary, "out of the body" as it were.[137] What favors this view is the fact that it immediately follows the mention of the self-commendation of his opponents, who boast in externals. One of their boasts, as 12:1–6 shows, is in "visions and revelations," which are there described as being experiences "out of the body."[138] There is some evidence that the verb ἐξίστημι may be used for such religious experiences.[139] Not only so, Paul himself makes the disclaimer about tongues in 1 Cor 14:2 that such experiences are "before God" and are not for the sake of others. If this is the general intent of Paul's statement, then he is arguing as elsewhere that rather than using them as "for others," in this case as "external" verification of his apostleship, they are for him strictly for his own building up before God.

In the final analysis it is difficult to choose between these options, mainly because the language itself is imprecise and because in either case so much guesswork is involved. On the whole, however, the explanatory γάρ which connects it with the immediately preceding judgment against the intruders, that they boast in "externals" not in matters of heart, suggests that the latter alternative is the better fit in context. His point would be that with regard to the "externals" about which they boast, these are strictly between me and God. What goes on between me and you is sober talk, for your sakes. And with that he will launch into one of the crucial moments of "sober talk" for their sakes in the letter.

If this be the case, we need only note that nothing is added to our understanding of Paul and the Spirit that is not explicitly said elsewhere. Special experiences of the Spirit are deeply personal and have to do with

---

[137] In which case it may be either accusation, which is less likely, or affirmation about themselves, which Paul is now saying is true in his own case as well; but he refocuses the direction and significance of such experiences. In the form that it is found in most recent commentaries, this view goes back to E. Käsemann, "Die Legitimität des Apostels: Eine Untersuchung zu 2 Korinther 10–13," ZNW 51 (1942) 33–71. It is the view of Bultmann 149, who asserts: "In antithesis to σωφρονεῖν, ἐξίστασθαι can only mean a 'being-outside-oneself' in pneumatic ecstasy"; cf. Wendland 201, Collange 250, Barrett 166, Furnish 308, 324–25, Martin 127.

[138] Bernard 70 sees this connection but takes it exactly in reverse, namely, that Paul did boast of such visions, which were then turned against him by his opponents (cf. Barnett 106 about tongues). But this does not capture adequately the nature of the rhetoric in 12:1–10, where it seems clear that Paul ordinarily does *not* boast in such things and did so in this case strictly because they "forced him" to it (12:11).

[139] See esp. the evidence given by Furnish 308, where similar contrasts are made between sane speech and otherwise; the difficulty with this evidence, of course, is that the verb for "madness" itself, μαίνω, not ἐξίστημι, occurs in these texts. Nonetheless, the contrasts are indeed much in the same mode as this one.

people's own relationship with God; they do not serve as verification or as grounds for boasting about that relationship, nor as grounds for authentication of ministry—a point that will be made with marvelous rhetoric in 12:1–10.

2 CORINTHIANS 5:16–17

[16]*So then, from now on we regard no one from the perspective of the flesh;*[140] *if indeed we considered Christ from this perspective, but now we know him [in this way] no longer.* [17]*So then, if anyone is in Christ, a new creation; the old things have passed away; behold the new have come.*

In his appeal to the Corinthians in vv. 11–13, that he is an open book before God, and hopefully before them as well, Paul also contrasted himself with his opponents in terms of their boasting in "externals," matters that for Paul are strictly between him and God. In terms of his relationship with the Corinthians he is committed to "sober-minded" straight talk. With that he launches into a moment of "sober-mindedness," which has as its singular aim the retelling of the essential story of the gospel so that he can apply it to their judgments about him, judgments that have nothing at all to do with Christ and the Spirit and have everything to do with the present age that has itself been judged and condemned by Christ and therefore is on its way out.

Thus, in vv. 14–15 Paul repeats the essential gospel story, that Christ died for all and was raised so as to give life to all. But his point in this case is a theological/eschatological one that he will apply in verses 16–17 to their (wrong) way of viewing him and his apostolic ministry. "If our basic story is the right one," he declares—and love for them compels him to say these things—"then we must own up to the fact that Christ's death for all people means that everyone has come under God's sentence of death; and that means further that the only people who currently live are those brought to life by Christ to live for him and his purposes." He will now apply that in terms of (1) its eschatological consequences, that a new order has come that changes everything, and (2) how that affects our perspective on people and ministry. In effect, this passage becomes the 2 Corinthians counterpart to the argument of 1 Cor 1:18–2:16. Christ's death and resurrection mark the turning of the ages, so much so that nothing, absolutely nothing, is any longer the same. For those who are in Christ, the old has gone, the new has come.

In making this point, even though he does not directly use Spirit language, Paul characterizes the present age, which continues but which

---

[140]Gk. κατὰ σάρκα, "according to the flesh"; the use of "knowing" and "seeing" verbs here calls for this translation (= "from the point of view of life lived in the old age, which is according to the flesh").

has come to an end for those who have been raised to new life in Christ, as κατὰ σάρκα (lit. "according to the flesh," = "from the perspective of the old age that is passé in Christ").[141] We know from a variety of passages that Paul's natural contrast to life κατὰ σάρκα is life κατὰ πνεῦμα, life that has undergone death and resurrection and is now lived from the perspective of, and in the power of, the Spirit. Thus, "from now on" (from the time of the death and resurrection in v. 14 and the subsequent gift of the Spirit), one can no longer regard anyone (their view of him is implied), least of all Christ, "from the perspective of the flesh." The reason is that we are among those who in Christ have experienced death and resurrection and therefore live now "from the perspective of the Spirit." In this case both Paul's language and argument simply demand this implicit contrast between "flesh" and Spirit.

Furthermore, this statement in v. 16 is followed in v. 17 with the language of the "new" and "old," in this instance the new and old orders; the old order has gone, the new "creation" has come in its place—not just in the life of the individual, but in the total sense of what God is doing in the world through Christ and the Spirit. The new creation itself has come; the old order is on its way out. This, of course, is the language used in chapter 3 to describe the two covenants, which reflect God's specific activities toward his people in these two orders. The old covenant is now obsolete because the new covenant, the covenant of Spirit, has come.

These two verses, therefore, belong together as the result (v. 16) and further explanation (v. 17) of vv. 14–15; as such it would be hard to overemphasize their significance for Paul's basic understanding of the cosmic, eschatological significance of the Christ and the Spirit—and of Christian life therefore as basically eschatological, lived by the power of the Spirit and over against the old order ("flesh") that is passing away. The problem Paul has had with this community of believers is that in rejecting him and his gospel of the crucified One they are giving up the very thing the Spirit has brought them to—and has revealed to them— and in its place have adopted the perspective of the world, a world that has been condemned in the death and resurrection of Christ. Thus one of the ironies of the present situation and of Paul's relationship with this

---

[141] This interpretation, therefore, takes a decided stance on the issue of whether κατὰ σάρκα modifies "Christ" or the verb "to know." Not only does Paul's word order (twice) clearly point to κατὰ σάρκα as a way of knowing, but there is no explicit evidence in this letter that there is a christological dispute between Paul and his opponents (see below on 11:4). Not only so, but the view adopted here is quite in keeping with Paul's use of this phrase in all of its other theological instances. For an especially helpful overview of this debate, see J. Louis Martyn, "Epistemology at the Turn of the Ages: 2 Corinthians 5:16," in *Christian History and Interpretation* (Festschrift John Knox; ed. W. R. Farmer, C. F. D. Moule, R. R. Niebuhr; Cambridge: Cambridge University Press, 1967) 269–87; for a more complete defense of the position taken here, see Furnish 312, 330–32.

church: having the Spirit and experiencing "ecstasy" in the form of tongues, they see themselves as "Spiritual" and consider Paul to be using "fleshly wisdom" (1:12) and "walking according to the flesh" (10:2–4). But in fact, as evidenced by their attitude toward him and his weaknesses, which have the cross as their paradigm, it is the Corinthians, not Paul, who view things from the perspective of the flesh.

The death and resurrection of Christ—Paul's current emphasis flowing out of vv. 12–13—plus the gift of the Spirit—Paul's emphasis in chapter 3—have changed everything. The former order of things is described in terms of "flesh," that basically self-centered, creature-oriented point of view, which has caused the Corinthians to regard Paul as he had formerly regarded Christ, as "weak" and therefore not of God. Thus "the flesh" perceives life from the old age point of view, where value and significance lie in power, influence, wealth, and wisdom (cf. 1 Cor 1:26–31)—and apostles are validated by persuasive rhetoric, miracles, and visions.[142] But in Christ, all of that has passed away; behold, the new has come, the time of the Spirit, in which there has been a total, radical restructuring of value and significance. The paradigm, Paul has argued regularly with this church, is the cross; the power lies not in externals, but in the Spirit, who indwells the believer and by grace is renewing the "inner person" (4:16), transforming us into God's own likeness, which has had its ultimate portrayal in Christ through his cross.

God's people, therefore, live "between the times," between the time of the passing of the old, and the dawning of the new; these two ages are described eschatologically by Paul as κατὰ σάρκα and κατὰ πνεῦμα, as lived out in keeping with sin and self or in keeping with and empowered by the Spirit of the living God. Thus, even though the Spirit is only implicit, this passage serves as the theological basis lying behind all such flesh and Spirit contrasts in the Apostle. They are primarily eschatological realities and take on existential and ethical dimensions as they reflect what is essential to life in either of the two orders. This will become crucial for our understanding of these contrasts in Galatians 5–6 and Romans 7–8.

2 CORINTHIANS 6:6–7

[6] . . . by purity, by knowledge, by longsuffering, by kindness, by the Holy Spirit, by genuine love, [7]by the word of truth, by the power of God.

---

[142]This, of course, finally presents Paul with some problems, because he *has* experienced visions of surpassing splendor (12:1–6), and signs and wonders through the power of the Spirit have always accompanied his ministry (12:12; cf. Rom 15:18–20). What he rejects is that these things in themselves *validate* his apostleship. For him that validation comes in his being conformed to the image of Christ and therefore in his sharing in Christ's "death" and "life." This is the heart of the argument of ch. 4, and it will be repeated in 12:7–10. Cf. 1 Cor 4:6–13.

At first glance, this is one of the more problematic occurrences of Spirit language in the Pauline letters. So much so that the NRSV translates the phrase ἐν πνεύματι ἁγίῳ ("by the Holy Spirit") as "holiness of spirit."[143] But that is to miss Paul's usage by too much. The reason for such translation is easy enough to discover; the mention of the Holy Spirit in this enumeration stands like a rock in the middle of items that otherwise seem more experiential or attitudinal. But a careful analysis of this list in context indicates that Paul is referring to the Holy Spirit, his gifts and empowering, as one of the ways that he is now commending himself in every way as a servant of God.

First, a twofold contextual note. (1) Verses 4b–10 form the second of the so-called hardship catalogues, which occur several times in these two letters.[144] What is remarkable about this list, not found in the others, is that right in the middle of them (vv. 6–7a), he describes Christian graces and the empowering of the Holy Spirit.[145] Thus, even though these are followed by further "hardships," this is not simply a "hardship cata- logue," and the ἐν παντί ("in every way") of v. 4 must be taken with much more seriousness than it often is. Not only do his "hardships," as expressions of his "weaknesses," serve to "commend" his ministry, but so also do the gifts and empowering of the Spirit. As elsewhere in these two letters, these are to be understood as empowering in the midst of weakness, not as his detractors would have it, to overcome or extricate him from such.

(2) That this list is given to "commend" his διακονία ("ministry") should not come as a surprise. In terms of letters of commendation and (apparently) self-commendation on the part of his opponents, who seem to pride themselves in their "powers" and "revelations" (see 11:1–12:12), Paul simply refuses to enter into their game. He needs no such letters; his commendation comes from God and is found in God's power working through his weaknesses (4:7) to bring others into existence (3:1–3). On the one hand, he refuses to "commend himself," when thought of in their terms (3:1; 5:12), yet when put into his own perspective of weakness and Spirit-empowering, he is quite ready to commend himself (4:2; 6:3–4). Thus the role of the Spirit in this catalogue. Weakness/hardship and Spirit-empowering go together in Paul's thinking.

---

[143] Cf. Plummer 196, who so argues probably because he misses the form and structure of this catalogue. So also Barrett 186–87, who considers πνεῦμα to refer to the human spirit, thus "a holy spirit."

[144] See 1 Cor 4:11–13; 2 Cor 4:7–12; 11:23–33. For a helpful analysis of this phenomenon and its possible background in the Greek philosophical tradition, see John T. Fitzgerald, *Cracks in an Earthen Vessel: An Examination of the Catalogues of Hardships in the Corinthian Correspondence* (SBLDS 99; Atlanta: Scholars, 1988).

[145] Fitzgerald, *Cracks*, 195, suggests that this is a catalogue of "virtues," which "serves to indicate the manner and means by which Paul deals with his hardships and persecutors."

As to the list itself, distinct groupings seem so evident that it is nearly impossible for the list to be merely random. That is, even though it is an ad hoc list, apparently spun off in the course of the argument as in all such cases, it is not randomly spun off. He begins with a series of hardships, set forth in three groups of three, under the general rubric "with great endurance." The first triad includes three synonyms for hardships as such; the second expresses hardships endured from others; the third contains hardships related to his itinerant ministry.[146]

> in much endurance:
>
>> in afflictions
>> in hardships
>> in calamities
>>
>> in beatings
>> in imprisonments
>> in violence
>>
>> in labors
>> in sleepless nights
>> in fastings

These are followed by the list of "graces" and "empowerings" that interest us, again with the Greek preposition "in," this time in two sets of four:

>> in purity
>> in knowledge
>> in longsuffering
>> in kindness
>>
>> in the Holy Spirit
>> in genuine love
>> in the word of truth
>> in the power of God

This structural analysis[147] reveals that, as always in Paul, ἐν πνεύματι ἁγίῳ refers to the Holy Spirit. But more can be said. Of the four words comprising the first set, three are elsewhere specifically related to the

---

[146] All of these are in the form of the Greek prepositional phrase, ἐν with the dative. They express either locative, "in these kinds of hardships," or manner, "with these kinds of hardships"—or perhaps a kind of intermediate combination of the two: "we commend ourselves and our ministry in the following ways, through the following means."

[147] Hughes 226–27 suggests that the arrangement is by sound, not sense. That is, it is the "sound" of the words, their poetic lilt, that is responsible for their order. I do not deny the presence of sound; but the list also makes especially good sense.

activity of the Holy Spirit: "knowledge" is one of the Spirit giftings in 1 Cor 1:7 and 14:6 (cf. 12:8), which Paul will lay claim to again in 11:6 and will allow in 8:7 that the Corinthians are also abundantly supplied with; "longsuffering" and "kindness" are listed fourth and fifth in the listing of the fruit of the Spirit in Gal 5:22 and appear in 1 Cor 13:4 in their verb form as the two primary attributes of God's love. The first term appears in 2 Cor 11:3 in combination with "sincere concern"[148] as the virtues in the character of Christ to which Paul appeals. Is Paul by these words intending to suggest, as in the argument about the cross in 1 Cor 1:18–31, that the character of God shines through the weaknesses themselves?

In any case, the close relationship of the Spirit to these Christian graces is what probably prompts Paul to list the Holy Spirit as the first member of the final tetrad.[149] What follows the Holy Spirit are two items, "genuine love" and "message of truth," which are specifically noted elsewhere as the outworking of the Holy Spirit in Paul's life.[150] These two correspond to the previous tetrad as the umbrella terms for patience and kindness, on the one hand, and knowledge, on the other. That is, according to 1 Cor 13:4 love manifests itself in longsuffering and kindness; and the message of truth comes in some instances as a "message of knowledge," all of which are effected by the powerful working of the Holy Spirit. Hence the final item sums up the work of the Spirit in terms of "the power of God." In effect the Holy Spirit serves as a kind of *inclusio* for the final four, thus placing all of these virtues, graces, and empowerings as the work of the Spirit's power in Paul's life.

What is striking in all of this is the inclusion of the powerful working of the Holy Spirit in the midst of a list that fully affirms weakness, in the form of hardship and apparent defeat (see vv. 9b–10), as a part of his apostolic ministry. This theme receives a thoroughgoing workout in this letter and is brought to its climax in 12:6–10 and 13:1–10. As noted before, the Spirit for Paul leads not to triumphalism, but to triumph in Christ (= death in the arena, as it were), even in the midst of those things that others reject or avoid as signs of weakness and powerlessness. For Paul the power lies elsewhere, not in deliverance from hardships, but in the powerful working of the Spirit that enables and empowers him for ministry even in the midst of such adversity.

---

[148] This seems to be the original text; see Metzger, *Textual Commentary*, 583–84, for the difficulty and the discussion.

[149] Which in each case is now a two-word item: Holy Spirit, genuine love, word of truth, power of God.

[150] For love as the fruit of the Spirit, see Gal 5:22; Rom 5:5; 15:30; Col 1:8; for the "message of the truth" as an activity that requires the Holy Spirit to make it effective, see 1 Thes 1:5; Rom 15:18–19.

2 CORINTHIANS 6:16–7:1[151]

[16]*And what concord does the temple of God have with idols? For we are the temple of the living God,*[152] *just as God said: "I shall dwell among them and walk in their midst, and I shall be their God and they shall be my people" [Lev 26:11–12];* [17]*therefore "Come out from among them and be separated, says the Lord; and touch not the unclean thing, and I shall accept you" [Isa 52:11],* [18]*and "I shall become a father for you and you shall become my sons and daughters, says the Lord almighty" [2 Sam 7:14].* [7:1]*Therefore, since we have these promises, beloved, let us cleanse ourselves from every pollution of the flesh and spirit, perfecting holiness in the fear of God.*

For many this may well be one of the more surprising inclusions of texts in this volume. But despite the enormous difficulties this passage poses for us contextually,[153] and despite the current tendency by many to view it as a non-Pauline interpolation, in fact the whole is thoroughly Pauline and filled with implied Spirit language—until the actual mention of πνεῦμα in 7:1. It is not my concern here to resolve the overall problem

---

[151] *Bibliography:* H. D. **Betz**, "2 Cor. 6:14–7:1: An Anti-Pauline Fragment?" *JBL* 92 (1973) 88–108; N. A. **Dahl**, "A Fragment in its Context: 2 Corinthians 6:14–7:1," in *Studies in Paul* (Minneapolis: Augsburg, 1972) 62–69; J. D. M. **Derrett**, "2 Cor. 6:14ff. a Midrash on Dt. 22:10," *Bib* 59 (1978) 231–50; G. D. **Fee**, "II Corinthians vi.14–vii.1 and Food Offered to Idols," *NTS* 23 (1976–77) 140–61; J. A. **Fitzmyer**, "Qumran and the Interpolated Paragraph in 2 Cor 6:14–7:1," in *Essays on the Semitic Background of the New Testament* (London: Chapman, 1971) 205–17; J. **Gnilka**, "2 Cor 6:14–7:1 in Light of the Qumran Texts and the Testaments of the Twelve Patriarchs," in *Paul and Qumran* (ed. J. Murphy-O'Connor; London: Chapman, 1968) 48–68; J. **Gunther**, *St. Paul's Opponents and Their Background* (NovTSup 35; Leiden: Brill, 1973) 308–13; J. **Lambrecht**, "The fragment 2 Cor. vi.16–vii.1. A plea for its authenticity," in *Miscellanea Neotestamentica* II (ed. T. Baarda, A. F. J. Klijn, W. C. van Unnik; Leiden: Brill, 1978) 143–61; J. **Moffatt**, "2 Corinthians vi.14–vii.1," *ExpT* 20 (1908–09) 429–30; D. **Rengsberger**, "2 Corinthians 6:14–7:1—A Fresh Examination," *StBibT* 8 (1978) 25–49; M. E. **Thrall**, "The Problem of II Cor. vi.14–vii.1 in some Recent Discussions," *NTS* 24 (1977–78) 132–48.

[152] A variety of textual variations arose in the manuscript tradition to alleviate the sudden shift from the second plural (in v. 14 and implied in the five rhetorical questions) to the first person plural of this clause. That shift makes the reading ἡμεῖς . . . ἐσμεν (found in B D* L P 6 33 81 326 365 1175 1881 2464 pc co; cf. ℵ 0243 1739 pc) the more difficult and therefore the one that best explains the others. The shift from the singular "temple" to the plural in ℵ* 0243 1739 pc is equally secondary, individualizing what in Paul refers to the community as a whole.

[153] As I have argued in "Food," 142–43, in terms of context nothing is to be gained by making it an interpolation. First, there are simply no analogies for such in the copying tradition; second, the problem of context still remains. By making it an interpolation we try to make Paul a tidier writer than he is, as we know from all kinds of data from his letters; to explain why an "interpolator" would have written it into his text at this point, in the process of editing the letter by copying it, is even more difficult.

of content and context; rather, I am interested in this as yet one more passage in this letter in which the Spirit may be assumed to be intrinsic to Paul's thinking even if not specifically mentioned, and therefore useful for our understanding of the Spirit in Paul's theology. The following matters are significant in this regard:

1. The whole passage (from v. 14) is filled with sacral language, with many ties to 1 Cor 10:14–22,[154] especially in the rhetorical questions that ask about the "fellowship" and "participation" of believers with nonbelievers. As vv. 16–18 show, the issue has to do with idolatry, which is precisely the concern of 1 Cor 10:14–22. The absolute incompatibility of believers with idolatry is the point of the rhetoric in vv. 14–16a; our passage (16b), which begins with an explanatory γάρ ("for"), gives the theological and scriptural reasons for such incompatibility.

2. The basic reason for this incompatibility lies with who the church is, as the people of God. To make this point Paul returns to the imagery of 1 Cor 3:16, where the Corinthians are called God's temple inasmuch as the Spirit indwells/dwells among them. Here again the church is "the temple of the living God" because God dwells in its midst. The reason for not explicitly mentioning the Spirit is to be found in the several OT passages which Paul cites, which make the same point as in 1 Cor 3:16, but without mention of the Spirit.

3. Despite a long history in the church of interpreting this passage as threat or warning, 7:1 indicates that Paul understood the citations chiefly as promises.[155] The promises are twofold: (a) By God's dwelling and walking in their midst, they will become/be known as God's *people* (this is the primary language for the OT people of God); (b) by their rejecting idolatrous associations they will also become/be known as his *children*. What is significant for our purposes is that elsewhere in Paul both images— temple and family—are the direct results of the presence of the Spirit.[156]

Thus, to bring items 2 and 3 together, if Paul does not use explicit Spirit language, it is because he is using OT sacral language, but language that is full of new covenant promises, that God would dwell among, walk with, be a father to his people. This is exactly the role of the Spirit in Paul's theology. Thus, by God's Spirit the church becomes "the temple of the living God,"[157] by his Spirit, God "dwells among them," and by his

---

[154] On this matter see Fee, "Food."

[155] Cf. 1:20; this language appears once again to reflect the new covenant. On this whole question, and on the thematic tie of these "promises" to the context of reconciliation and covenant in 2 Corinthians, see G. K. Beale, "The Old Testament Background of Reconciliation in 2 Corinthians 5–7 and its Bearing on the Literary Problem of 2 Corinthians 6.14–7.1," *NTS* 35 (1989) 550–81.

[156] For temple see 1 Cor 3:16; 6:19; Eph 2:21–22; for family see esp. Gal 4:6 and Rom 8:14–17.

[157] On the language "living God," see on 3:6, where the Spirit is specifically designated in this way, as "the Spirit of the living God." The reason for its occurrence

Spirit, God "has become a father for you." Since this letter is written in some close conjunction to our 1 Corinthians, it is well-nigh impossible for the Corinthians not to have caught all of this in terms of the Spirit—especially in a basically oral culture that thrives on images as a way of understanding and remembering.

4. In the concluding call for cleansing and "perfecting" holiness, which in 1 Thes 4:7–8 are also noted as the activity of the Spirit, one is not surprised that the language includes both "flesh" and "spirit." It is possible that this is simply a way of saying "completely," as in 1 Cor 7:34. However, that contrast in Paul is usually made with the terms "body" and "spirit," not "flesh" and "spirit." In light of the context, and especially in light of 5:16–17, "flesh" here probably has nothing to do with the body, but everything to do with living as people who are still oriented to the old age that is passing away. After all, idolatry is one of the unmistakable sins of the flesh in this sense (Gal 5:20), not in the physical sense that demands some form of asceticism. Since the old has gone, including walking in the "flesh" and therefore making judgments about idolatry from the perspective of fallenness, and the new has come, they are to "cleanse themselves from every kind of pollution that has to do with flesh."

This suggests that πνεῦμα, therefore, is not simply an anthropological term, indicating the "inward" vis-à-vis the "outward" with regard to our human existence, but is that "inner reality" of our humanity that is open to spirits or the Spirit. Since in Pauline understanding, idolatry in particular is the worship of demons (1 Cor 10:20–22), it should not surprise us that here he concerns himself with cleansing from the "pollution of spirit." Not only must the "flesh" be gone, but also the "spirit" must be the place of the Spirit's habitation (1 Cor 6:17), not a place where one is open to "spirits."

All of this to say, then, that as elsewhere in Paul's letters, the Spirit is the way God indwells his people and walks among them. He is the experienced expression of the divine presence who also creates and guarantees membership in God's family. Therefore, God's people must walk in his ways, by the Spirit's perfecting holiness in the fear of the Lord.

2 CORINTHIANS 7:13

In addition to our own encouragement, we rejoiced all the more greatly over Titus' joy, because his spirit had been refreshed by all of you.

in this context is obvious; over against all forms of idolatry, with their lifeless and mute idols, stands the living God.

For the use of "spirit" in this passage, which is undoubtedly an anthropological term referring to the interior dimension of one's person,[158] see the discussion on 1 Cor 16:18, where the same language occurs.

2 CORINTHIANS 8:7

But just as you abound in every way, in faith and word and knowledge and all earnestness and in the love that has come from us and abides in you,[159] that you may also abound in this grace.

In a context in which Paul is appealing to the Corinthians to get on with, or perhaps get back to, their promised contribution to the collection for the poor in Jerusalem, part of that appeal is to the abundant expression of other "graces" bestowed on them as a community of believers. Apart from "earnestness," a word especially prominent in chs. 7–8 of this letter, this list is composed of items that occur elsewhere in 1 and 2 Corinthians as ministries of the Spirit. Two matters are of interest in this regard:

First, as in 1 Cor 1:4–5 and 7, that these items are here designated by the word χάρις ("grace") indicates that when they are also elsewhere called χαρίσματα ("gracious bestowments"), the emphasis on these "gifts" is on the "grace" that Christ has brought to them and that is manifested thereby. As noted in chapter 2, this is the primary sense of the word *charisma*, so that it is probably not quite precise to refer to them as *Spiritual* gifts, even though the Corinthians abound in such "graces" because of the Spirit.

Second, the combination of "word" and "knowledge" mirrors 1 Cor 1:5, where Paul gives thanks for evidence of these "graces" as God's work among them. Their being listed again in this off-handed way indicates most strongly that he does not intend to demean these expressions of their giftedness. Although they need to be brought under the banner of the cross, they are not thereby to be eliminated. Indeed, Paul twice appeals to his own gift of "knowledge" in this letter as evidence that God is at work in his ministry (6:6; 11:6).

Again, as so often in this letter, even though the Spirit is not mentioned by name, he would nonetheless be understood by the Corinthians to be the source of these "graces" in their lives, in terms of their being manifestations of God's presence.

---

[158] *Pace* Jewett, *Terms*, 192–94.

[159] An exceptionally difficult textual choice lies behind this translation. Is Paul referring to their love for him (ὑμῶν ἐν ἡμῖν; ℵ C D F G Ψ Maj lat sy[h]) or his love for them, or perhaps as I have tried to render it, love that has initially come from him but is now to be found in them (ἡμῶν ἐν ὑμῖν; P[46] B 0243 6 104 630 1175 1739 1881 pc r sy[p] co Ambrosiaster)? As Metzger acknowledges (*Textual Commentary*, 581), the latter is plainly the more difficult reading; it is probably also the original.

2 CORINTHIANS 10–13

In our view these chapters represent yet a fifth letter from Paul to Corinth, but written so soon after the fourth (chs. 1–9) and taking up very specifically the crucial issue from the former—Paul's apostleship vis-à-vis the insurgents—that it was natural for them to be joined together and distributed as one.

The whole of these chapters is given over to Paul's frontal attack against these opponents in which he attempts simultaneously to recapture the minds and hearts of the Corinthians by bringing them again into obedience to Christ and to vanquish the opposition. In so doing he once again sets out in its starkest form the differences between his perspective and theirs about Christ and apostleship; thus we are led once more to the cross as the paradigm and to the apostle as one in whom Christ's power is evidenced through weakness.

He begins with an appeal for obedience (10:1–6), including a defense of his authority (vv. 7–11) and some biting remarks over the issue of "jurisdiction"—the opponents are working his turf, and that goes against "the rules" of proper boasting in Christ (vv. 12–18). That is followed by his "fool's speech," which includes a long introduction (11:1–21a), the speech itself (11:21b–12:10), and a conclusion (12:11–13).[160] All of this is followed by final appeals (and threats) in light of his imminent third visit (12:14–13:10).

Although there are few references to the Spirit as such in this letter, they do occur at crucial moments in the argument: in 11:4 in his description of what has happened in Corinth as the result of the intruders' activities; and in the "fool's speech" (12:1–10 and 12) in his rejection of their false criteria for apostleship (and therefore authentic Christian life). The Spirit is also mentioned in passing in the appeal regarding his and Titus' conduct among them (12:18) and in the concluding benediction (13:13[14]).

2 CORINTHIANS 10:2–4

²I beg of you that when I come present I need not be bold with the confidence I reckon to dare to have toward those who reckon us as walking according to

---

[160] This language apparently stems from Windisch; H. D. Betz (*Der Apostel Paulus und die sokratische Tradition* [Tübingen: Mohr, 1972]) has offered helpful insight into the form of this material by comparing it with Socrates' "apology" to his students vis-à-vis the sophists. But as with many such studies, the content becomes subservient to the form. Cf. A. T. Lincoln's more cautious approach: "It is unlikely . . . that Paul is consciously following the Socratic 'apology' as such . . . and more likely that he is making effective use of elements from this tradition with which he is acquainted from their employment in popular culture and conventions" (" 'Paul the Visionary': The Setting and Significance of the Rapture to Paradise in II Corinthians XII. 1–10," *NTS* 25 [1979] 206).

the flesh. ³For even though we walk in the flesh, we do not carry on warfare according to the flesh; ⁴for the weapons of our warfare are not fleshly but powerful before God, . . .

In his opening salvo, Paul makes a frontal attack against the opposition; and in so doing, lets all kinds of things fall into place for us, in terms of our grasping what has transpired between him and them since the writing of 1 Corinthians. In that letter he accused them of being "fleshly" (3:1–4), which was revealed both by their attitude toward the cross and himself in their new-found "wisdom" and by the strife which this new perception of Christ and the gospel engendered among them. This is now the fifth mention of the "flesh" in this pejorative way in our present 2 Corinthians.[161] What we suspected from 1:12 and 17, turns out to be so. They have turned his language against him: He is the one "walking according to the flesh," not they. One cannot be sure from this how they would have understood this term, whether it meant "walking in the weakness of the flesh (i.e., with bodily weakness), and therefore not in the power of the Spirit," or whether they understood it in Pauline eschatological terms, having to do with perceiving things from the perspective of the present age that has been condemned by Christ on the cross and is in process of passing away. In either case, their criteria of being "Spiritual" and therefore of apostleship condemned Paul as living "in keeping with the flesh."

So one more time, just as in 5:14–17, he takes up this language and turns it around. With a word play on the term "flesh," he acknowledges that he does indeed "walk *in* the flesh." But for Paul this is not pejorative; it merely reflects his OT roots, where "flesh" described human creatureliness over against God, not in terms of sinfulness, but in terms of weakness and vulnerability.[162] Paul, as well as all others, are "in the flesh," in the sense that in this "between the times" existence we still live in the weaknesses and limitations of "our mortal flesh," through which, nonetheless, the life of Christ is fully manifested (4:11). But what we do not do, Paul insists, is "walk in keeping with the flesh," flesh now thought of in terms of human fallenness over against God in its self-centered, basically anti-God frame of reference. Nor do we carry on our warfare by means of "weapons" that reflect such a perspective. To the contrary, since we walk by the Spirit our "weapons" are "powerful with reference to God."

Here, then, is another implicit contrast between flesh and Spirit in Paul. What is clear is that one can be "*in* the flesh" and "*in* the Spirit" at the same time; indeed, as long as one is still "of the earth" it cannot be otherwise for the believer. But as we will see in Galatians and Romans,

---

[161] See above on 1:12; 5:16–17; 7:1.
[162] See, e.g., Ps 78[77 LXX]:39; Isa 40:6–8; cf. A. C. Thiselton, *NIDNTT* 1.678–82; cf. the discussion in ch. 12 below.

one cannot be *"according to* the flesh" and *"according to* the Spirit" at the same time.[163] At one level we must live in two worlds; but at the essential level of our new eschatological existence ushered in through Christ and the Spirit, we live in only one of these worlds. Through Christ we have died to the one (5:14–17; Gal 5:24; Rom 7:4–6); by the Spirit we live in the other. Therefore, our thinking and our behavior must be in conformity to the Spirit. And here is where Paul and they are at odds, as to what life in the Spirit and life in the flesh looked like. Apparently in their new-found wisdom they had confused "being in the flesh" with "living according to the flesh." Paul's concern throughout the rest of this argument is to disabuse them of such confusion.

2 CORINTHIANS 11:4

For indeed if the one who comes preaches another Jesus whom we did not preach, or you receive a different Spirit whom you did not receive, or a different gospel which you did not accept, you put up with it well enough.

With this most unusual way of expressing himself, Paul isolates the heart of the difficulty between himself and the insurgents.[164] Here is the sure reason that even though these "super apostles" consider themselves "servants of Christ" (v. 23), they are from Paul's perspective "servants of Satan, who are masquerading as servants of δικαιοσύνη" ("righteousness"; v. 15). Despite the rhetoric of 11:21–12:18, at issue for Paul is not his apostleship alone, and especially it is not a matter of rival claimants to Corinthian affections. At issue, as always, is the gospel itself. Paul's jealousy is that of God (v. 2)—to present the Corinthians as a "pure virgin" to her betrothed (= the church to Christ at his Parousia). But as Eve was deceived, so too they are being led astray; their virginity is in grave danger of being sullied. Our verse indicates that the problem is with a false gospel, or false understanding of the one gospel, which the opponents are perpetrating.[165]

---

[163] Dunn's denial (by assertion) of these distinctions mars his study of "flesh and Spirit" ("Jesus—Flesh and Spirit: An Exposition of Romans I. 3–4," *JTS* 24 (1973) 40–68 [49]). This blurring of what Paul makes distinct unfortunately serves as the basis of much that seems wrong with Dunn's view of this contrast as to the ethical side of Christian life. By denying these distinctions Dunn assumes, as Paul's Corinthian opponents, that being "in the flesh" means to be "according to the flesh," so that anyone in the flesh is always driven by the desires of the flesh. That is hardly Paul's point of view (see on Gal 5:16, 24; Rom 7:4–6; 8:5–8, 9–11, 12–13); see further the discussion in ch. 12.

[164] But not in the way suggested by Käsemann ("Legitimität") and those who have followed his lead (e.g., D. Georgi, *The Opponents of Paul in Second Corinthians* (ET; Philadelphia: Fortress, 1986); Martin), that it serves as "a key for the understanding of the opponents who appeared on the scene at Corinth and for the interpretation of ch. 10–13" (Käsemann, 38; Martin's trans.).

[165] Cf. the language of Gal 1:6–9, where the agitators there are also accused of

Speculations as to the content of this false gospel are endless, but that will help us none here.[166] They and he both know the content;[167] Paul's immediate concern is with the *fact* of it, not its content. These outsiders, in coming onto Paul's turf and currying the favor of his Corinthian friends (10:7–18), are in fact ultimately leading them away from the gospel of Christ to something that from his perspective is no gospel at all.[168]

What we receive in this passage, despite the unusual—and therefore striking—use of language ("*another* Jesus, *a different* Spirit, *a different* gospel), are the essential matters for Paul with regard to the gospel and its reception.[169] That is, he is not trying to define his opponents' gospel in some way; his concern in this sentence is with what is happening to the Corinthians.[170] From Paul's perspective their following these outsiders ultimately means to abandon "salvation in Christ" for something else. Paul puts that in its starkest form, and he does so with the absolutely essential elements of his gospel, Christ and the Spirit. That is most likely the reason for the apparently unusual order, in which the gospel is mentioned last—so as to clarify the first two items as the essential matters with regard to the gospel. Thus it is not that the opponents were actually preaching a different Jesus as such, as though the issue were

---

preaching a "different gospel." Calvin 141–42 seems to miss the concern here in suggesting that "another Jesus" does not refer to a false gospel but to one that is from a ministry other than his own.

[166] The basic presupposition of many studies (e.g., Käsemann, Georgi, Martin) that here we have clues to the *content* of their teaching is what has led to this speculation. Thus Bultmann and others find "Gnostic pneumatics"; Barrett and others find Judaizers; Georgi, Martin, and others a "divine man" Christology. In all of these, this text plays a key role—despite the fact that there is no suggestion in the text itself or in the argument that follows that "another Jesus" actually describes the *content* of the false preaching. The language in vv. 13–15 (servants of δικαιοσύνη) and vv. 22–23 (are they Hebrews, etc.) seems most strongly to favor Barrett et al. If so, as I think, then all the more this suggests that the issue is *not* Christology, but soteriology, and all of these items together refer to what is ultimately happening to the gospel, not to their understanding of the person of Christ or the Spirit.

[167] Which in light of v. 22 and 3:6–18 most likely had some form of "Jewishness" to it; that Christology itself is involved is highly unlikely. See n. 8 above and the discussion on 3:6. Cf. Carson 88, that this is "the best guess" in light of the evidence.

[168] Cf. Furnish 500 for a similar assessment as to what can here be gleaned about the content of the opponents' preaching.

[169] Cf. Hanson 79: "Notice St. Paul's three-word summary of Christianity—Jesus, Spirit, Gospel."

[170] This seems supported by the awkwardness of the syntax. Flowing directly out of vv. 2–3, it begins with a contrast between the opponents' preaching and his own. But since the emphasis is on what is happening to the Corinthians, rather than on what is being preached by others, Paul shifts to the awkward, "or *you receive* another Spirit whom *you did not receive*; or another gospel which *you did not accept*." This emphasis on the Spirit as something "received" by the Corinthians is what makes the use of this term as a component of the false teaching a dubious exercise at best.

Christology;[171] rather, by their introducing the old covenant (as we may assume from 3:1–18), the net result is "another Jesus" from the one Paul preached, which in turn results in their "receiving another Spirit" precisely because the Spirit whom they received through Paul's preaching of Christ had freed them from any possible commitments to the now obsolete older covenant (3:17–18).

For Paul, authentic Christian life is the combined result of Jesus, who is "preached," and the Spirit, who is "received." This combination alone makes up the genuine reception of the gospel. As elsewhere in Paul, preaching "Jesus" refers to the proclamation of the saving event itself and all that Christ provided for us through his death. The "Spirit" refers to the actual appropriation, the actualization of the saving event.

Others have suggested that πνεῦμα here refers to something attitudinal or to some aspect of Christian lifestyle;[172] but that will hardly do in this argument. Against it is (1) that the mention of Spirit comes between Jesus and gospel; in such a context it is difficult to imagine that it will bear some meaning unrelated to the other two; and (2) that the verb "received," which Paul uses elsewhere for the reception of the Holy Spirit,[173] hardly goes well with any other understanding of the word πνεῦμα. How does one "receive" some aspect of Christian lifestyle or attitude? But the contextual questions seem decisive. In the context of this letter and of this church, the Spirit is absolutely crucial to the argument. Whatever else, the Corinthians were into Spirit. What jars Paul is that Spirit people have now let themselves be turned aside to that which has nothing at all to do with the Spirit.[174]

All of this, then, to say that Paul does not think of them as actually receiving another "spirit,"[175] that is a demonic spirit, or the "spirit of the world," or a "bad attitude." After all, just as there is not actually a Jesus other than the one Lord Jesus Christ, so there is only one Spirit, the Holy

---

[171] *Pace* Georgi and others; cf. Martin 336, "the issue is basically a christological one." That is bold indeed, considering that Christology neither is pursued in this argument, nor emerges as such throughout 2 Corinthians.

[172] See, e.g., Plummer 297, Hughes 378, Carson 87–88, Martin 336. Both Martin's reason for going this way (otherwise it assumes that "we would have to suppose that they had a heterodox . . . Trinitarian teaching") and his attempt to make sense of "spirit" (as "the effects of Christian living seen in outward deportment") highlight the difficulties with this position—and the basic error in presupposing that content is what is involved.

[173] See Rom 8:15; 1 Cor 2:12; Gal 3:2.

[174] This, of course, is precisely the argument of 3:1–18 and Gal 3:1–5.

[175] In this regard cf. the discussion in ch. 2 on "a spirit of . . . ," especially in the three texts which are set up by the negative contrasts, "not a spirit of, but the Spirit," in which he almost certainly does not intend in the first part to suggest that there is "another spirit" that people receive (1 Cor 2:12; Rom 8:13; 2 Tim 1:7). Rather, he intends, "in receiving the Spirit of God, you did not receive this negative characteristic."

Spirit. Thus, their current understanding of the gospel and their current behavior and attitudes toward him prove that the opponents are not preaching the pure gospel of Christ; and the direction the Corinthians are currently going is not in keeping with the Spirit whom they have in fact already received. Hence, it is "another Spirit," just as the form of the "gospel" they are now giving credence to proclaims "another Jesus."[176]

If this is the correct understanding of this passage, and it seems to make the best sense of the argument in context, then we have yet another instance where the actualization of the gospel in the lives of believers is thought of in terms of Christ and the Spirit. The Spirit is not at the center; Christ is, now and always. But without the Spirit there has been no receiving of Christ, no realization of the benefits of Christ in the life of the believer and the community. Hence the inclusion of the Spirit with Jesus in this crucial passage that speaks of the net effect of the work of the outsiders in their midst.

2 Corinthians 11:6

But if indeed I am untrained in speech—but not in knowledge—but in every way having been manifest in all things for your sakes.

This thoroughly ungrammatical sentence brings the present paragraph (vv. 1–6) to conclusion and at the same time serves as transition to what follows. Here Paul is explaining how it is that he is not one whit inferior to their "super apostles." In so doing he picks up several themes from this letter and from 1 Corinthians and replays them for the sake of his readers. Lying behind all of this is the activity of the Holy Spirit.

The two words set in contrast, "speech" (λόγος) and "knowledge" (γνῶσις) first appeared together in the thanksgiving in 1 Cor 1:5, as *charismata*. As noted in that discussion, these are two of their favorites and are understood by them, as well as by Paul, as manifestations of the Spirit. But it is also obvious that they do not think of Paul as gifted with the first one, "speech," as 10:10 (his λόγος is contemptible) confirms. In 1 Cor 2:1–5 Paul argued that the evidence for the presence of the Spirit in his ministry was in his λόγος, not understood in their terms (rhetoric, fine speech, etc.), but in his own (as the Spirit-empowered preaching of Christ that brought about their conversion). Here he is yielding once more to their use of the term.[177]

But he will not yield on the matter of "knowledge." Their understanding of "knowledge" is decidedly perverse; it leads to their being

---

[176] In Gal 1:6–7 Paul makes a similar charge, but there qualifies himself, "not that there is really another gospel." There is no good reason to think that he intends anything else here. He does not so qualify it here because the rhetoric carries its own power and meaning—which they would have well understood.

[177] In this case in particular he refers to himself as ἰδιώτης τῷ λόγῳ (= "nonprofessional"); cf. 1 Cor 14:16, 23.

puffed up, rather than loving (1 Cor 8:1–13). Paul's understanding of "knowledge" has to do with the gospel, in which the "knowledge" of God (2 Cor 10:5) is manifested through Christ by the Spirit (4:4–6). He allows that they do indeed have γνῶσις (8:7), but so does he (6:6); now he turns on them with regard to their following those who preach another gospel. Their "knowledge," to the degree that it minimizes or deflects from a proper understanding of the cross, is defective. Paul's "knowledge," which comes by the Spirit, is manifest for all to see, since it has to do with the gospel itself, as that has been given us in Christ Jesus. Thus, as in 1 Cor 1:5 and 2 Cor 8:7, the Holy Spirit hovers just beneath the language of this apologia, as the source of Paul's "knowledge," for which he will now contend with vigorous rhetoric.

2 CORINTHIANS 12:1–10[178]

[1]*It is necessary*[179] *to go on boasting.*[180] *There is no advantage to it; but I shall go on to visions and revelations of the Lord.* [2]*I know a man in Christ fourteen years ago (whether in body I do not know or whether outside the body I do not know; God knows), such a one having been caught up to the third heaven.* [3]*And I know such a man (whether in body, or whether apart from*[181] *the body I do not*

---

[178] *Bibliography:* H. D. **Betz**, "Eine Christus-Aretologie bei Paulus (2 Kor 12.7–10)," *ZTK* 66 (1969) 288–305; H. **Binder**, "Die angebliche Krankheit des Paulus," *TZ* 17 (1961) 319–33; D. A. **Black**, *Paul, Apostle of Weakness: Astheneia and Its Cognates in the Pauline Literature* (New York: Peter Lang, 1984) 138–59; J. W. **Bowker**, " 'Merkabah' Visions and the Visions of Paul," *JJS* 16 (1976) 157–73; J. **Cambier**, "Le critère paulinien de l'apostolat en 2 Cor 12, 6s." *Bib* 43 (1962) 481–518; A. T. **Lincoln**, *Paradise*, 71–86; **Lincoln**, " 'Paul the Visionary,' " 204–20; T. Y. **Mullins**, "Paul's Thorn in the Flesh," *JBL* 76 (1957) 299–303; P. **Nisbet**, "The Thorn in the Flesh," *ExpT* 80 (1969–70) 126; G. G. **O'Collins**, "Power Made Perfect in Weakness: 2 Cor 12:9–10," *CBQ* 33 (1971) 528–37; D. M. **Park**, "Paul's ΣΚΟΛΟΨ ΤΗ ΣΑΡΚΙ: Thorn or Stake?" *NovT* 22 (1980) 179–83; R. M. **Price**, "Punished in Paradise (An Exegetical Theory on 2 Corinthians 12:1–10)," *JSNT* 7 (1980) 33–40; H. **Saake**, "Paulus als Ekstatiker, Pneumatologische Beobachtungen zu 2 Kor. xii 1–10," *NovT* 15 (1973) 153–60; N. G. **Smith**, "The Thorn that Stayed. An Exposition of 2 Cor 12:7–9," *Int* 13 (1959) 409–16; R. P. **Spittler**, "The Limits of Ecstasy: An Exegesis of 2 Corinthians 12:1–10," in *Current Issues in Biblical and Patristic Interpretation* (Festschrift M. D. Tenney; ed. G. F. Hawthorne; Grand Rapids: Eerdmans, 1975) 259–66; J. D. **Tabor**, *Things Unutterable: Paul's Ascent to Paradise in its Greco-Roman, Judaic, and Early Christian Contexts* (Lanham, Md.: University Press of America, 1986); J. **Zmijewski**, "Kontextbezug und Deutung von 2 Kor 12, 7a: Stilistische und Strukturale Erwägungen zur Lösung eines alten Problems," *BZ* 21 (1977) 265–77.

[179] There is some considerable confusion in the text at the beginning of this sentence; the translation is that of P[46] B F G H L P 0243 1739 pm, adopted by UBS[4].

[180] Gk. καυχᾶσθαι (present middle infinitive). Although I tend to avoid this more pedantic approach to the Greek present, the context seems to demand that in this case the continuous present is in view. Cf. Martin 388, 394.

[181] The change from ἐκτός in v. 2 to this χωρίς (read only by P[46] B D*) is probably purely stylistic; despite the preponderance of evidence for a repeated ἐκτός here, it is

know; God knows), ⁴that he was caught up to Paradise and heard unutterable utterances, which are not permitted for a person to speak about. ⁵I shall boast about such a man, but about myself I shall not boast except in my[182] *weaknesses.*

⁶*For if ever I should wish [so] to boast, I shall not be a fool, for I speak the truth; but I forbear, lest anyone consider me beyond what he or she sees in me or hears anything*[183] *from me* ⁷*especially by reason of the extraordinary quality of the revelations.*[184] *Therefore, in order that I might not be exalted, there was given to me a thorn in the flesh, a messenger of Satan, in order that I might not be exalted.*[185] ⁸*About this matter three times I besought the Lord that it might be removed from me;* ⁹*and he said to me, "My grace is sufficient for you, for power*[186] *reaches perfection in weakness." Therefore I will the more gladly boast in my weaknesses, in order that the power of Christ may dwell in me.* ¹⁰*Therefore I delight in weaknesses, in mistreatments, in hardships, in persecutions and*[187] *difficulties, which are for the sake of Christ; for whenever I am weak, then I am powerful.*

Although not explicitly mentioned in this remarkable passage, the Spirit lies behind both the phenomenon and its narration ("whether in or out of the body" Paul does not know), as well as Paul's actually describing the phenomenon in terms of ἀποκαλύψεις ("revelations") in vv. 1 and 7 and in the final purpose clause, "that the power of Christ might dwell in me" (v. 9). To recognize that is easy;[188] the difficulty lies

---

nearly impossible to account for a change to χωρίς across two textual traditions had ἐκτός been original.

[182] I am here translating the ταῖς; the addition of μου, which probably originated in the West under the influence of the Latin, simply adds the possessive pronoun which the context otherwise makes clear is intended in the article.

[183] The very awkwardness of this τι, found in P⁴⁶ D* Ψ 0243 Maj f syʰ, argues for its being the original text.

[184] This translation assumes the punctuation of UBS⁴ to be correct in seeing this phrase as part of the preceding sentence rather than the beginning of v. 7—over against the great majority of English translations, including Barrett 313 (but see now the NRSV). The *primary* reason for this view is that elsewhere in Paul, and the entire NT as well, the conjunction διό always stands in first position in its clause. For more complete arguments in favor of this view see Zmijewski, "Kontextbezug," and the summary of his arguments in Furnish 528. As early as P⁴⁶ (followed by D Ψ Maj) this difficulty was alleviated by the omission of διό, which of course is the strongest argument in favor of its being original.

[185] For obvious reasons, the rhetorically powerful repetition of this clause was omitted in a large group of witnesses (ℵ* A D F G 33 629* pc lat).

[186] The addition of μου ("my"; in ℵ² A D² Ψ 0243 Maj), though understandable, is secondary on all counts. It undoubtedly comes from "the power of Christ" in the next sentence; whether it is what Paul intended is moot.

[187] This is the (almost certainly correct) text of P⁴⁶ ℵ* B 104 326 1175 pc, which was understandably changed to ἐν in the majority to conform to the rest of the list.

[188] Cf. Lincoln, *Paradise*, 85–86, who entitles the final section of his discussion, "The heavenly vision as a manifestation of the Spirit." Cf. E. Käsemann, "The Cry

in our trying to gain some measure of insight into the phenomenon itself and Paul's understanding of it.[189]

As often in such passages, one can have a fairly high degree of confidence as to Paul's overall point in the narrative and to the flow of the argument. Having purposely turned the insurgents' boast in their accomplishments on its head by "boasting" in his still greater "accomplishments" for Christ in the form of every manner of weakness, he now turns to their (apparent) boast in Spiritual experiences, especially those of a truly extraordinary kind. Thus, in continuing his boast, he continues on their grounds in terms of what he perceives as false criteria for apostolic legitimacy (namely, an "abundance of revelatory experiences"), in order that he may conclude this "fool's speech" by emphasizing the *real* criterion (namely, the powerful work of the Spirit in his ministry, especially in the presence of his weaknesses, so that all glory may go to Christ). The one who boasts, he repeated in 10:17,[190] must boast in the Lord and in what he accomplishes, since not the one who commends himself on criteria such as these, but only the one "whom the Lord commends"—on radically different grounds—is genuinely approved (v. 18).

The unfolding of the narrative shows that Paul is not denigrating experiences such as the one he describes; what he finds uncomfortable is talking about them at all—because for him they are personal and private—and especially therefore making them some kind of criterion for authentic apostleship. For him revelatory experiences per se have nothing at all to do with his apostleship; they have to do only with his own personal relationship with God (5:13). So much is this so, that apart from the Corinthians' own false criterion for Spirituality (in 1 Corinthians 12–14) and for apostleship (in this passage), we would know nothing about Paul's own inner life of the Spirit (speaking in tongues and an abundance of revelations). Our tendencies tend to be two: to disregard as insignificant such expressions of life in the Spirit because Paul puts such little stock in them in terms of their public consumption; or, in trying to counter such a mistaken reading of Paul's personal Spirituality, to do the very thing he would not—to make too much of them. The *via media* in this matter lies in paying close heed to the present narration, which seems to have a twofold aim: in vv. 1–5 to invalidate the criterion

---

for Liberty in the Worship of the Church," in *Perspectives on Paul* (London: SCM, 1971) 130.

[189] As one might well expect of such a cryptic passage, a considerable literature has sprung up over it, with a great deal of speculation. For our purposes matters such as Paul's cosmology ("the third heaven") or the meaning of the term "paradise" will not detain us, since to resolve those (if indeed, they can be resolved) is quite unrelated to our concerns.

[190] See the citation of the same Jeremiah passage in 1 Cor 1:31, in a context much like this one, except for the absence of outsiders, who are here stirring up the pot.

without denying the substance, precisely as in 1 Cor 14:14–18; and in
vv. 6–10 to shift the criterion from ecstasy to Christ himself, who as the
crucified one is God's power at work in the world (13:3–4; cf. 1 Cor 1:18–2:5).

The argument, therefore, can be easily traced. In vv. 1b–4 Paul goes
on to "visions and revelations"; but he obviously has real difficulty
here—probably not only because of the private nature of such experiences but also because he really does have difficulty moving over onto
their turf. Thus he narrates a single experience—a "revelation" with no
revelatory word—in the third person, as a way of distancing himself from
what he is presently about.

Verses 5–6, which serve as transition from the narrative of vv. 2–4
to his own reasons for disowning such criteria in vv. 7–10, are the key
to much. On the one hand, Paul says "about such a man I will boast";
and in so doing he would not be a fool, for what has been narrated is in
fact true. But about *himself* he will not boast, except in his weaknesses.
The reasons for this are given in v. 6. He will spare them such narratives
about himself so that *no one will regard him, because of the abundance of
such revelations, beyond what they can see or hear for themselves.* That is, if
he tells them of such experiences, they might think more highly of him
as the result of his having had such revelations than their value warrants, and especially that they might think more highly of him—and for
the wrong reasons(!)—than what they themselves see or hear of him.
Under any circumstances, such revelations are simply not verifiable; so
Paul will "boast" only of what is before their very eyes, which, as in 1 Cor
2:3–5, is the twofold reality of personal weakness on the part of Paul
himself but of undoubted power in terms of what Christ is accomplishing
through him. And that is the point of vv. 7b–10. On the one hand, lest
Paul also think too highly of himself, God gave him his infamous "thorn
in the flesh," whatever that may have been; and when he sought its
removal, on the third time around the Lord finally gave him a "revelatory
word"[191] he could share with others, namely, that all is of grace, and
grace is enough, since Christ's power is best seen in the presence of
weakness (as in 1 Cor 1:18–25). All of this is then explained in vv. 9b–10
as the ultimate reason for Paul's engaging in this "fool's speech" in the first
place, since the weaknesses that he boasted in are not a matter of personal
boast but a matter of boasting in Christ, whose power can best be seen
as Christ's own when he works mightily through Paul's weaknesses.

A few further words are in order on some of the verses in terms of
what we might here learn about Paul's understanding of the Spirit.

1 The language Paul uses to describe the category of experience he
is about to narrate is "visions and revelations of the Lord." This is the

---

[191] Cf. Lincoln, "Paul the Visionary," 204–5: "We must also assume that the
saying of the Risen Christ recorded in v. 9 was given to Paul by revelation."

only occurrence of the word "visions" in Paul's letters; it is not possible to determine solely from the phrasing whether Christ is the object of the vision or the one from whom visions about other realities came.[192] The word "revelation" occurs elsewhere in Paul as a specific activity of the Spirit, usually having to do with something that God is saying to his people or to Paul individually.[193] The obviously extraordinary character of the experience described here, however, suggests that "revelation" in this case is but a synonym for "vision." This means finally that we cannot really tell what is to be understood by "revelation" here in terms of content, especially since Paul not only refuses to describe that content, but also cannot tell about any of the things he heard. Thus whatever he saw or heard is totally outside the possibility of our ever knowing—deliberately so.

2–4 For any number of reasons, one best understands what is narrated here as referring to a single experience,[194] which suggests that whatever it finally means in terms of Paul's own cosmology, the third heaven and Paradise are terms that refer to the same reality—almost certainly in this case what Paul would understand to be the ultimate heaven, the very presence of God. What is of interest for our purposes is the language "caught up"[195] and the parenthetical phrase in v. 2, repeated in v. 3, that the experience was of such nature that even Paul was never able to ascertain whether he was there "in body" or "out of the body." Most likely with this language Paul is trying to emphasize its transcendent reality.[196] For him the experience itself was so real that he could never tell whether he was actually "transported"[197] there in his present bodily form[198] or whether he was there "in Spirit" in some way

---

[192] Lincoln, "Paul the Visionary," 205, has argued, probably correctly, that "since the majority of the visions mentioned in the letters and in Acts involved seeing Christ and receiving a revelation from him we may well assume that the same holds in this case." Cf. Hughes 428n97; Barrett 307; Dunn, *Jesus*, 414n88. One might note that in Gal 1:16 (ἀποκαλύψαι τὸν υἱὸν αὐτοῦ), the "Son" is clearly the object of the revelation.

[193] In this regard see on 1 Cor 14:6, 26; and Gal 2:2.

[194] Basically because the two are held together by such balanced clauses and because the first is dated, not to mention that the vision happened to him as to one "in Christ." So the vast majority of interpreters.

[195] Gk. ἁρπάγεντα, ἡρπάγη; cf. 1 Thes 4:17, where it is said of the living at the Parousia of Christ that they "will be caught up" to meet the Lord in the air.

[196] Jewett, *Terms*, 278; Lincoln, "Paul the Visionary," 215; and others suggest that it might also be carefully designed in light of the opposition. This seems altogether possible, but how it might be so is much more speculative.

[197] This seems to be the meaning of "caught up"; contra Tabor, *Things Unutterable*, whose *religionsgeschichtlich* interests in this phenomenon lead him to several unlikely conclusions about the passage, including such language as "making preparations" for the journey and "ascent into Paradise," as though Paul prepared himself for this heavenly journey. Paul's language belongs to a different world.

[198] Similar to the narrative about Philip in Acts 8.

in an experience so real, that even though visionary, he could, as it were, touch the furniture and smell the smells.[199] That is, the experience of ecstasy was not a matter of his "having died and gone to heaven,"[200] but of its being such a vividly real moment in God's presence that he could never quite discern whether the Spirit literally "took him there" or merely let him into the heavenly realm by way of the vision itself. In either case, the Spirit is certainly to be understood as the "means of transport," whether truly there in body or otherwise.

6–7a In v. 6a Paul asserts that he could legitimately boast in such experiences and not be a fool, since he would be speaking sober truth. Now he gives the first reason for refusing to do so. It might make others think more highly of him, and therefore from his perspective less highly—or less correctly—of his Lord, than he is willing to allow. The final phrase in this sentence gives the reasons why some might do so, by reason of "the extraordinary quality of the revelations." In returning to the word "revelations" to describe this category of experience, two points are made from before: First, there has been more than one such moment in Paul's life in the Spirit; there have been several revelations, as the plural noun and the whole phrase demand.[201] Second, they have been such extraordinary moments that Paul can only describe them as ὑπερβολή, far surpassing what is merely ordinary.[202]

Again, even though Paul plays down the significance of such moments in terms of their usefulness for authenticating him before others, the argument of the whole verse reveals that they were indeed significant moments in Paul's personal pilgrimage[203]—so much so that, he will now go on to explain, God had to counterbalance them in his life lest he think too highly of himself. Again, he cannot bring himself to deny the substance; but both for himself and for others he insists that such moments be put into perspective in terms of their usefulness for ministry.

What is striking is how often in the later church Paul's point is missed by those in ministry. Those who have had such experiences can hardly be other than deeply affected by them; but unfortunately such experiences also have an aura of fascination. At times one may feel that his or her ministry is not taken quite seriously enough by others and be

---

[199] As in the narrative of Peter's "vision" in Acts 11.

[200] This is sometimes suggested in the literature. But in 1 Cor 15:35–58 and 2 Cor 5:1–10 Paul vehemently argues against heaven as being a "bodiless" existence. He could hardly be bringing in such a dualistic understanding through this back door.

[201] This is true even if he does not frequently mention them (as e.g., Gal 2:2, q.v.). As with the "signs and wonders" in v. 12, Luke narrates several of these that Paul never mentions (Acts 9:12; 16:9; 18:9–11; 22:17–22; 23:11).

[202] This term could refer to quantity rather than quality. Dunn's suggestion (*Jesus*, 215) that this may be an exaggeration would seem to contravene Paul's point.

[203] So also Lincoln, "Paul the Visionary," 205.

tempted to narrate such experiences as though to imply that God has thereby given one significance—and that others should as well. Paul obviously thinks otherwise.

7b–8 That brings us to something that is not related to the Spirit in Paul's life, but that must be discussed in this study because there are so many in the contemporary church whose view of life in the Spirit does not allow that Paul actually carried about in his body some form of physical infirmity.[204] But the argument seems to demand exactly such a view of Paul's "thorn in the flesh," rather than its being some spiritual attack or literal enemy who was trying to bring him down in some way.[205] The only circumstance that favors this latter view is that the thorn is further described in very personal terms, as "an angel/messenger of Satan." Three matters argue that "flesh" refers to his physical body.

First, the language "in the flesh" and "buffet" point strongly to a physical infirmity of some kind. On the one hand, there is no evidence in Paul that, when speaking of his present life as a believer, he ever used the term "in the flesh" to refer to anything other than "in the present form of bodily existence."[206] For him to be "buffeted in his flesh" as if it meant his sinful nature makes little or no sense.[207] "Flesh" in that sense is always pejorative in Paul; further it does not describe his present life in Christ; nor would it be something to be "buffeted" by Satan himself. Paul considered his—and our—"flesh" to have been to be crucified with Christ (Gal 5:24; Rom 7:6), so that his present life in Christ was life in the Spirit, not "in the flesh," as Gal 5:16–25 and Rom 8:1–30 make abundantly clear. Furthermore, this language closely resembles that of Gal 4:13–15, where Paul describes his reason for coming to Galatia in the first place as the direct result of "some weakness/illness in his flesh." This use of "flesh" to describe present bodily existence in terms of its weakness and being subject to decay is precisely in keeping with his OT background, where "flesh" often appears to describe one's creatureliness.

Second, the context suggests that whatever the infirmity was, it occurred not on three different occasions, but rather it was regularly with him, and three different occasions he specifically asked the Lord for relief.[208] On the third entreaty he was told that it would not be removed,

---

[204] I have almost no interest in what that might have been, since that lies totally in the area of speculation, which as in vv. 2–4 does not really help exegetically. The list in BAGD proves the uselessness of such speculation. In Paul himself the only passage that might help, and I am quite open to this possibility, is the apparent reference to an eye ailment in Gal 4:13–15.

[205] For a sane and balanced overview of the various options, pro and con, see Furnish 547–50.

[206] See above on 2:13 regarding 7:5, for example; cf. 10:2–3.

[207] Despite Calvin and others.

[208] So also Bruce 249.

precisely so that Christ might be glorified through it. An argument along these lines makes little sense when thought of in terms other than of the physical body. Not only so, but the larger context of glorying in his weaknesses, the vast majority of which are related to his life "in the flesh," also leads us in this direction.

Third, it seems likely in light of the larger context that an "unhealed" σκόλοψ is one of the very items seized on by his detractors as evidence that he was not a "super-apostle" of the same kind as the interlopers. That is, rather than to think of this as some kind of personal, private matter between him and his Lord, more likely Paul's "thorn" was a well-known matter in Corinth; and it stood so contrary to their own triumphalist view of life in the Spirit that it was regularly thrown up against him and his Spirituality. An actual physical difficulty of some kind, which was evident to all, would make far more sense of the reason for mentioning it all in this particular context.

Finally, even though we have no way of knowing what the infirmity was, Paul continued to be plagued by a physical problem, even after seeking relief from God. What needs to be emphasized is that for Paul the infirmity was not incompatible with life in the Spirit; indeed, to the contrary, in itself it had little or nothing to do with life in the Spirit, except as a means whereby Christ would gain the more glory to himself by being powerfully at work in Paul's life despite all such forms of weakness. And that is the point Paul will go on to make in the concluding word in vv. 9–10.

9–10 What interests us in these final words is their dominant theological theme of power in weakness, which upon further reflection one should note to be a recurring theme throughout 1 and 2 Corinthians, perhaps *the* recurring theme in the latter. As is clear from 1 Cor 1:18–25 and 2:3–5, when thought of in terms of God's activity in behalf of God's people and our salvation, power is what Christ was about; but when thought of in terms of ministry, power is what the Spirit is about. These two themes conjoin here. Power is designated as "the power of Christ" that "dwells in him," because it is Christ who had spoken to Paul (v. 9a) and whose gospel is in focus, as 13:3–4 finally make clear. The power dwelling in Paul is the power of the gospel at work in the world for the sake of others.

But whenever Paul thinks of that power in terms of its actual effectiveness through his ministry, resulting in the conversion of those who hear his preaching of the gospel, then the power is spoken of in terms of the Spirit. As elsewhere in Paul, his language can fluctuate between God, Christ, and Spirit, depending on the emphasis of a given passage, which also says much about how Paul viewed Christ and the Spirit in terms of deity and inter-relationship.

In any case, Paul's point is now made. His weaknesses do not render him less than a fully Spiritual man; indeed, he can delight in them precisely because the manifestation of Christ's power in his life despite such hindrances means that the ultimate focus is where it belongs—on Christ himself, not on the messenger. This, too, I submit, is a work of the Spirit in Paul's life.

2 Corinthians 12:12

The[209] signs of an apostle were performed among you with all endurance, by means both[210] of signs and wonders and of deeds of power.

In many ways this is one of the most surprising sentences in this letter, not to mention in the present argument. After the long "fool's speech" in which Paul has deliberately focused on his hardships and weaknesses, including his nonheroic escape through the wall of Damascus to avoid capture (11:31–33) and his total downplaying of visions and revelations, one is not quite prepared for this sentence. Does Paul have some afterthoughts? Has the emphasis on his weaknesses been such that the Corinthians might forget that there were miracles as well? The answer to the contextual question must finally be resolved by observing the nature of the argument that began in the preceding verse, which serves as transition from the long "fool's speech" to his final response to false charges and direct appeal to their return to him and his gospel.

Thus in v. 11 three points are made: he has played the role of the fool; they have forced him to it; they should have been on the other side, commending him against these intruders. The key to the present text lies with the second matter, that they "forced him" to play the role of the fool. How so? In two ways: first, because they have set the criteria (falsely, to be sure), and he has felt compelled to play their game; this he does by stepping into the role of the "fool," who in Greek plays spoke the truth the author might otherwise be in some trouble for speaking, but could get away with in the mouth of the fool. Second, because they should have been on his side but were not, he felt compelled to play the game on their terms to show them how foolish those terms really are.

---

[209]This sentence begins with a μέν, which has been left untranslated (so also Furnish 553), since there is no corresponding δέ. Although the μέν might have concessive force in such cases, it is more likely that this is an instance similar to 1 Cor 11:19, where Paul very likely intended to offer an "on the other hand," but changed direction slightly when he came to the end of the present sentence.

[210]This is an awkward attempt to catch the force of Paul's Greek, σημείοις τε καὶ τέρασιν καὶ δυνάμεσιν, which suggests that the "signs and wonders" go together as a unit, followed by "the mighty deeds." The later MS tradition, including the MajT and the TR, has rewritten σημείοις τε to ἐν σημείοις, thus balancing the three nouns and making them clearly instrumental.

Now he gives them the straight reasons why they should have commended him, because in fact he was "in no way inferior to their super apostles" (12:11).[211] This point has been made right along. He was equal to them in pedigree (11:22); he was their superior in terms of serving Christ (11:23–29); and he was at least their equal in terms of ecstatic experiences (12:1–5). It is in this vein that he finally reminds them that "the signs of an apostle were [also] done among them," if they will but pause to remember. In the parallel in Rom 15:18–19, Paul specifically attributes such miracles to the "power of the Holy Spirit." Here the Spirit is not mentioned, but is implied in the passive verb, "were performed among you." Paul did no miracle; but the Spirit accompanied his preaching of Christ with miracles of all kinds.

What is remarkable, and the same is true of the parallel in Romans 15, is that this is said so matter-of-factly. He is not trying to "prove" anything, even about his apostleship. Rather, he is simply reminding them that what they seem keen on was, after all, also a part of his own ministry, as they well know. Thus, even here these do not prove his apostleship; they simply occurred as a matter of course,[212] and therefore prove nothing.

But some details are less clear. First, what is one to make of the phrase, "the signs of the apostle," which occurs only here in the NT?[213] Does this phrase suggest that miracles are some kind of special province of apostleship, a sort of special evidence for it, or does it merely assume an expectation with regard to the miraculous on the part of apostles that would be more a matter of course? On the whole the latter is much to be preferred, especially in light of 1 Cor 12:10 and 28–29, where the working of miracles and healing of the sick are ministries of people within the congregation, quite unrelated to apostleship. On the one hand, for Paul himself, as Rom 15:18–20 seems to imply, such miracles were

---

[211] Even here he cannot quite bring himself to such comparisons, so he adds "even though I am nothing." That means, of course, that so are the super apostles!

[212] In this regard see especially Jacob Jervell, "The Signs of an Apostle: Paul's Miracles," in *The Unknown Paul: Essays on Luke–Acts and Early Christian History* (Minneapolis: Augsburg, 1984) 77–95, who emphasizes that in both Pauline and Lukan theology "word" and "power" go together. Neither could have imagined the proclamation of the gospel without its being accompanied by the miraculous— precisely because both were essentially Spirit events. Martin 436 seems to miss both Jervell and Paul here by some margin, especially in light of Rom 15:18–19, by arguing against Jervell that "Paul does not consider the miraculous as the main criterion by which to judge apostleship." Jervell does not say they do; but to suggest, as Martin seems to, that they are nearly irrelevant misses the Pauline evidence, not to mention the rest of the NT.

[213] It is purely gratuitous to assert, as do e.g., Käsemann, "Legitimität," 35; Bultmann 231; Rengstorf, *TDNT* 7.259, that this is a stereotyped and widespread formula that Paul is picking up. It may just as easily have been Pauline coinage based on the present argument. Cf. Jervell, "Signs," 171n35.

simply a matter of course. The fact that his ministry in its entirety was in the power of the Spirit also meant that it would be accompanied by the miraculous. But it is extremely doubtful whether by this phrase he also thought of such miracles as the special province of apostleship. On the other hand, precisely because he would have so understood them—as a matter of course—he would probably *also* expect such "signs" to accompany all whose ministry might be termed "apostle."[214]

Second, as to the specifics of "both signs and wonders and deeds of power," one can only speculate, which does not serve many purposes exegetically. The combination "signs and wonders" stems from the OT, having become an almost technical term for God's mighty deeds rendered at the Exodus;[215] the term "deeds of power" occurs regularly throughout the NT for miracles of many kinds. Whatever else, therefore, Paul can be referring only to what in ordinary parlance are termed *miracles*; no other view fits the evidence.[216] But two further points can be made. (1) In 1 Cor 12:9–10 and 28–30, Paul seems to distinguish between "gifts of healings" and "workings of miracles" (here translated "deeds of power"). There we guessed that the distinction is between the healing of the body and all other types of miraculous manifestations. (2) That is precisely the range of "signs, wonders, and deeds of power" that one finds in the large variety of narratives in Acts.[217] All of which suggests, then, that Paul is using this language to cover the broad range of miracles that attended his ministry through the power of the Holy Spirit.

What is quite evident is that he sees no tension at all between the Spirit's activity in his ministry in this way and his own personal weaknesses about which he has been boasting. Just as Jesus performed no miracle in his own behalf, but always in behalf of others, so the "signs of an apostle" here probably refer to that large number of ways that the Spirit worked powerfully through him, not for his own benefit, but for that of others. In this case, he clearly is referring to miracles that

---

[214] For the ambiguity of the term "apostle" in Paul's letters, see on 1 Cor 12:28 in ch. 4.

[215] See Exod 7:3, 9; 11:9–10; Deut 4:34; 6:22; 7:19; 11:3; 26:8; 29:3; 34:11; Neh 9:10; Ps 78:43; 135:9; Jer 32:20–21; Wis 10:16. Eventually the combination came to refer to any and all mighty deeds of God (cf. Dan 4:2–3; 6:27; Wis 8:8).

[216] It goes quite beyond all the linguistic evidence to suggest (as e.g., Strachan 34, Hughes 456) that it would refer primarily to their conversion. It is not that conversion was not "miraculous," but that it would never have occurred to someone in the first century to use these terms for it. Jervell, "Signs," 91, rightly scores such a view. Furthermore, this quite misses the OT background to this language.

[217] Given the matter-of-fact way that Paul speaks of such events as realities in his ministry, it is a cause of some wonder that so many scholars consider the narratives in Acts to border on fiction. In fact, they are precisely the kinds of things that one would expect to lie behind this language in Paul.

occurred in Corinth; they were "accomplished[218] *among you.*"[219] That, of course, is what Paul finds so perplexing in their attitude toward him.[220]

Third, perhaps that is how we are to understand the rather puzzling prepositional phrase, "with all endurance," a word that occurs elsewhere in Paul usually in the context of hardship or difficulty, or at least of patiently enduring the present as one awaits the final glory. Indeed, in Rom 5:3 he says that "affliction *accomplishes* endurance." Its role in this sentence, therefore, is something of a puzzle.[221] The phrase almost certainly modifies the verb "accomplished"; it immediately follows the phrase "among you." Does he add this note because the Corinthians could not keep "signs and wonders" and "endurance in affliction" in tension? In any case, the evidence is thoroughgoing that Paul could. This was part of his understanding of the Kingdom as already and not yet. Both miracles, evidence of the "already," and "endurance," evidence of the "not yet," were held together in his understanding precisely through the presence of the Spirit, whom earlier in this letter he has designated as God's "down payment" of the future. As already present, he has touched our human life with some measure of the future, hence "both signs and wonders and deeds of power"; but as only the down payment of the future, these "signs" take place in the context of "every kind of endurance."

2 CORINTHIANS 12:18

I urged Titus to go, and sent the brother with him. Surely Titus did not defraud you, did he? Did we not walk in the same Spirit? In the same footsteps?

Although I have translated πνεῦμα as referring to the Holy Spirit, that is not the common view;[222] it will need substantiation. The context itself is easy enough. Here Paul is responding to a final charge, to the effect that even though they grant that he himself did not "burden them" (= accept patronage), he was crafty enough to get their money by send-

---

[218] Gk. κατειργάσθη, the same verb that occurs in 5:5 (q.v.) and in Rom 5:3 noted below.

[219] Despite the fact that Luke records no such miracles in Corinth, this language from Paul himself is the certain evidence for such; "accomplished ἐν ὑμῖν" can scarcely bear another meaning.

[220] Jervell's answer to this ("Signs," 94) is to be found in the fact of Paul's own ailment noted in 12:7: "He is an ailing miracle worker, an ailing miraculous healer, and the miracle worker cannot remove this ailment (2 Cor. 12:7ff.)."

[221] It is hard to imagine, as some think (Calvin, Hughes), that this is one of the "signs of an apostle." It is likewise not probable that he intended "all possible steadfastness in fully exhibiting the signs of an apostle" (Meyer 484). Héring 95 would similarly get around it by translating "with perfect constancy."

[222] But see Meyer 489, who without argument asserts that it refers to the Holy Spirit. Cf. RV, NASB[mg] ("by the same Spirit"). Hodge 294 allows either.

ing Titus and the brother to pick up the collection for Jerusalem. It is moot whether such a charge was actually leveled against him, or whether he is merely heading it off. On the one hand, v. 16 has all the earmarks of an actual charge, to which Paul responds with considerable rhetoric. On the other hand, since the collection has been so long in their purview (see 1 Cor 16:1–4 and 2 Cor 8–9), it is arguable that he is merely heading off such a charge; i.e., in his frustration with them over their misreading of him and his motives on so many fronts, he finally concludes by deflecting the issue of the collection, lest they accuse him of bad faith here as well.

In any case, he can now point to Titus' conduct among them as something so exemplary that they must come to terms with the fact that fraud relating to the collection is simply out of the question. The rhetoric begins by reasserting the closest possible tie between Titus and himself ("I urged him to go, and sent the brother along as well"). Knowing that they cannot fault Titus' conduct he asks rhetorically, "Surely Titus did not defraud you, did he?" The μήτι ("surely") presupposes that the only possible answer is No.

Having established the tie between himself and Titus, and Titus' own faultless conduct, he asks further, "Did we not walk in/with τῷ αὐτῷ πνεύματι?" The question is, what is the referent of this final phrase? Is Paul reminding them that when he was with them he conducted himself as a Spirit person, just as more recently Titus had done, and therefore that fraud in unthinkable? Or is the phrase more anthropological here, referring simply to an attitude or upright manner in which both of them had walked?[223]

In light of the final phrase ("in the same footsteps"), which seems to give further meaning to "in the same spirit," it is arguable that Paul meant little more than "spirit" = attitude.[224] Nonetheless, in light of Paul's usage elsewhere, and in light of the overall context of Paul's relationship with this church, it seems far more likely the primary referent is the Holy Spirit, even if, as in other places, the Spirit is to be understood in the closest possible relationship to the human spirit.

First, "walking" is Paul's most common metaphor for Christian deportment and behavior, occurring 17 times in his letters either as an imperative or as a description of such behavior.[225] Furthermore, from the way Paul uses it in Gal 5:16, it is arguable that "walking in/by the Spirit" is the basic form of Paul's ethical imperative. For Christian life, therefore,

---

[223] E.g., GNB, "act from the very same motives."

[224] So Plummer 365, who sees the two phrases together as referring to "harmony . . . both in mind and conduct"; cf. Tasker 184, Hughes 467n155, Barrett 326, Furnish 560, Martin 449. One may assume that the many commentators who do not speak to it at all probably also go this way, since the translations have "spirit."

[225] On this usage see especially the discussion on Gal 5:16.

"walking" is a matter of living in the Spirit so as to follow in the ways of the Lord. It is fair to conjecture that had Paul not written the second phrase, the majority of scholars, on linguistic and theological grounds, would understand this as referring to the Holy Spirit. The question, then, is whether "in the same footsteps" is intended to be in apposition to ἐν αὐτῷ πνεύματι, as further explanation.

In light of Pauline usage, both of Spirit language and of metaphors, the second clause is most likely not intended to be an explanation of "the same spirit," thought of in terms of similar dispositions, but rather is the natural development of the *metaphor* for "walking" used in the first clause. Indeed, this phrase is probably where the imagery was heading in the first place; as a metaphor for human conduct, one "walks in the same footsteps" as someone else. But instead, since "walking" is also Paul's primary metaphor for Christian behavior, and because the life of the Spirit has been such a festering issue between him and this community, his first instincts are to speak in terms of the basic form such behavior takes: he and Titus both "walked in the Spirit"—the "same" Spirit, because there is only one. Having scored that point, he adds, referring now to the observable evidence of such walking in the Spirit, that Titus thus "walked in the same footsteps."

Finally, there is no analogy in Paul for the use of πνεῦμα, modified by "the same," to refer to some kind of general attitude or deportment.[226] But Paul does use this very phrase in 1 Cor 12:9, along with "by the one Spirit," to emphasize the unity of the Holy Spirit—that there is indeed only the one Spirit responsible for all the diverse manifestations in the Corinthians' midst. As in Phil 1:27 (q.v.), that is probably the emphasis here. Paul's conduct in their midst was just like that of Titus; they are both walking in the way of, and by the power of, the one and the same Spirit, who is also at work in the lives of the Corinthian believers.

In light of this evidence, it seems most probable that Paul is once again referring to the Spirit as the key to Christian conduct. On the meaning of "walking in the Spirit" itself, see on Gal 5:16–6:10.

2 CORINTHIANS 13:3–4

[3] *. . . since you seek proof that the one speaking in me is Christ, who is not weak toward you but powerful among you;* [4]*for indeed he was crucified in weakness, but he lives by the power of God. For indeed, we are weak in him, but we shall live with him by the power of God unto you.*

This difficult text is included in this study for two reasons: first, some have seen the Spirit to lie behind the mention of Christ's being raised by

---

[226]Unless, of course, one wishes to see this usage in 4:13; but the case for such usage there is even weaker than here.

the power of God (cf. 1 Cor 6:14); second, this is the final appearance in the letter of the motif of "weakness" and "power," a motif that has considerable bearing on Paul's understanding of life in the Spirit.

The first issue may be addressed and dismissed in brief. Throughout the corpus Paul invariably attributes Christ's resurrection to God, sometimes through the agency of God's power.[227] But even though "power" and "Spirit" are sometimes nearly interchangeable in Paul, they are not in fact coterminous.[228] As in 1 Cor 6:14, there is nothing in the context to make one think that Paul was using "power" here as a periphrasis for the Spirit. Indeed, it is quite the opposite. The reason for "power" language is the direct result of the contrast with "weakness." Christ's death and resurrection represent the ultimate divine paradigm of these two terms. What is going on in this text, therefore, is not a hidden reference to the Spirit, but a mixture of word play, irony, and reality, related to the preceding argument and to Paul's long-term difficulties with this congregation. And that leads us to the second matter, since the difficulties in the text are related to the play on words, all of which must be understood within Paul's basic "already but not yet" eschatological framework.

Since 12:14 Paul has been making his final appeal—and warning—stemming from the Corinthians' misguided theology and their current attitude toward him, on the one hand, and the fact that he is soon to visit them, on the other. He fears he will not find them as he ought (12:20), that he may have to reverse his former gentleness while among them and use harsher methods (13:2; cf. 10:1–6). With this sentence he offers them his willingness to submit to their demand for "proof" of his apostleship (= that Christ speaks through him). But what he will not back down on are the criteria as to what constitutes "proof." Their criteria are all lined up on the "power" side of things, as they perceive "power": visions, revelations, miracles, wisdom—but no "weakness." Their acquiescence to "another Jesus" and their receiving "another Spirit" (11:4) result from their continuing to circumvent the weakness of the cross, where God's true power lies. In eschatological terms, they are long on the "already" but short on patient endurance in the "not yet" (see on 12:12 above).

Thus the reality and the irony. In v. 3 Paul accedes to what he has himself argued right along (cf. 1 Cor 2:4–5), that Christ has been among them with power; Christ is not weak toward them. After all, their own conversion came about through a powerful working of the Holy Spirit in their midst. But that is also now the irony, because Christ's power toward

---

[227] See 1 Thes 1:10; 1 Cor 6:14; 15:15; 2 Cor 4:14; Gal 1:1; Rom 4:24; 6:4; 8:11; 10:9; Col 2:12; Eph 1:20; plus the texts where Christ's resurrection is expressed in the "divine passive" (1 Thes 4:14; 1 Cor 15:12, 20; 2 Cor 5:15; Rom 4:25; 6:9; 7:4; 8:34).

[228] See esp. on 12:10 above.

them was predicated first of all on the fact of his crucifixion; and his crucifixion was predicated on weakness,[229] a weakness without which they would not now know his power toward them. The power, of course, is predicated on his resurrection from the dead. These are the twin realities of the gospel, neither of which is Paul willing to lose. And it is on the strength of these twin realities that he will come among them for his third visit: weak in Christ, but living by the power of God, and all of this with reference to them.

The problem, of course, is that in his "already" but "not yet" exist-ence, Paul can—he insists, must—maintain these two realities simulta-neously. Just as Christ was crucified in weakness, and that message itself is the power of God, so too Paul lives his present apostleship as a disciple of him who suffered for our sakes. Thus, Paul's bodily presence and his life of apostleship are full of the weaknesses that find their paradigm in the cross. But he lives in these weaknesses by the power of God, exhibited in the resurrection of Christ and now realized by the indwelling Spirit (cf. Rom 8:10–11). The weaknesses neither negate his apostleship nor betray the gospel. To the contrary, they function first of all to model the gospel with its message of a crucified Messiah and secondly to put Paul in a place where he lacks control, and thus where the power of God can be truly manifest because it will be evident that the power lies not with the apostle himself, but with the God who raised Christ from the dead (12:9–10).

But that is precisely where the Corinthians have their difficulty. They, too, know that Christ's crucifixion was predicated on weakness and that his resurrection was predicated on "the power of God." And they prefer it this way: crucifixion, as a past event and the basis of our new life in Christ, giving way to the present empowering evidenced in the resurrection. But Paul will have none of that. Our present existence is both already and not yet; it includes living in present weakness so that God's glory might be seen most truly, but the enabling source for living in such weakness is the power of God exhibited in the resurrection of Christ—and now available through the eschatological Spirit.

Thus the irony. Christ has been with them in precisely these two ways, and that occurred through Paul's own preaching. When Christ came to them through Paul's preaching, he came as the crucified One, crucified in weakness and raised in power—for their sakes. Though the message centered in the cross, God's power in weakness, the result was that Christ was not weak among them, but powerful. But now they want only the power, and they will pay heed only to apostles who come with displays of power. The irony rests in the word play: For Paul "power" meant "the power of the Spirit" who brought about their conversion

---

[229] Hence the reason for the prepositional phrase, ἐξ ἀσθενείας, which in this case most likely means "from a basis of ἀσθενείας."

based on the proclamation of the ultimate divine folly and weakness, a crucified Messiah (1 Cor 2:4–5); for the Corinthians it meant Christ now "powerfully" among them in the form of Spirit manifestations, visions, and revelations (2 Cor 5:13 q.v.). Paul refuses to come with the latter, but is about to come with displays of "power" of a different kind in which he will "not spare" those who reject the truth of the gospel by their fascination with power without the cross.

Thus, even though the Spirit is not mentioned, since the context demands language related to Christ's death and resurrection, the theological content of such a passage fits perfectly with what Paul says elsewhere about the Spirit as present in power, but empowering in the midst of weakness, not circumventing weakness with displays of power for the sake of "proof" that the Spirit is indeed present among them.

2 CORINTHIANS 13:13[14]

The grace of our Lord Jesus Christ and the love of God and the fellowship of the Holy Spirit be with you all.

This remarkable grace-benediction is the only one of its kind in the extant Pauline corpus. In keeping with first-century conventions, Paul concludes all of his letters with a grace-benediction, usually with the simple "the grace of our Lord Jesus Christ be with you," as in the first part of this one. But this one has two remarkable features: first, the fact that it is elaborated at all; and second, the Trinitarian form in which the elaboration is expressed. It is arguable that in ways that may not immediately meet the eye this is a singularly significant conclusion to all of the theological and behavioral concerns of this letter.

Although we cannot at this distance suppose to penetrate the mind of Paul as to his reasons for this elaboration, it seems more likely than not to have directly resulted from matters in this letter. That is, even though Paul may be simply reflecting a liturgical formulation already used in his churches, more likely these words originated at this point and were expressed in light of what is going on in Corinth and what has been said in this letter—especially so, since nothing like this appears anywhere else in his letters, particularly in letters after this one. Ad hoc elaboration alone accounts for the unusual order of Lord (Christ), God, and Spirit. What appears to have happened is that Paul began with his ordinary benediction and then elaborated in the now "logical" order of God and Spirit. That the three expressions reflect the Pauline understanding of the soteriological functions of the Trinity seems to clinch the matter.[230]

---

[230] In the case of Christ and God at least, these are the most characteristic words in Paul's vocabulary to express the essence of their being and activity; the Spirit is associated with "fellowship" in Phil 2:1.

In many ways this benediction is the most profound theological moment in the Pauline corpus. On the one hand, it encapsulates Paul's basic soteriology, expressed more explicitly in other passages (e.g., Gal 4:4–6; Rom 5:1–11), where God in love determined to save his people and thereby took the initiative to bring it about (Rom 5:18–21). The "grace of our Lord Jesus Christ" in turn concretely expressed that love; through suffering and death in behalf of his loved ones he effected salvation for them at one point in our human history (5:14–15). The "fellowship of the Holy Spirit"[231] conveys the ongoing appropriation of that love and grace in the life of the believing community (3:6–18).

On the other hand, it also serves as our entrée into Paul's theology proper, that is, into his understanding of God, which has been so radically affected by the twin realities of the death and resurrection of Christ and the gift of the eschatological Spirit. As Barth put it with extraordinary insight, "Trinity is the Christian name for God." Here we begin to glimpse Paul's understanding of that reality, namely, that to be Christian one must finally understand God in a Trinitarian way. Paul's understanding begins with the OT (in part by way of the LXX), which is always presuppositional for him. God's relationship with his people is principally predicated on his love for them (Deut 7:7–8); what characterizes that love preeminently is his חֶסֶד (ḥesed; covenant love), usually translated ἔλεος ("mercy") in the LXX. What Paul has come to see is that God's love, which has manifested itself in compassion for his people, especially in his covenant loyalty with them, has found its singularly concrete historical expression in the death and resurrection of Christ. It is equally clear—if not always articulated with clarity—that Paul recognized that in Christ *God himself* had come "to reconcile the world unto himself" (5:19). But that is not all. Through the gift of his Holy Spirit, the Spirit of the living God, God has now arrived in the new creation as an abiding, empowering presence—so that what most characterizes the Holy Spirit is κοινωνία, which primarily means "participation in," or "fellowship with."[232] This is how the living God not only brings us into an intimate and abiding

---

[231] Cf. Phil 2:1 below, the only other place where this language occurs in the corpus.

[232] There has been some debate as to whether "of the Spirit" is an objective or subjective genitive. That is, are we in fellowship with the Spirit, or does he create the fellowship of the saints, as it were? Since the two prior clauses reflect something both of God's character and of his activity on behalf of his people in light of that character, it seems most likely that something similar is in view here. Since the word primarily means "participation in," the view presented here seems to capture the essence of the "direction" of the Spirit's activity and of the meaning of the word itself. This view goes back at least as far as Meyer, 514. It received its recent impetus from H. Seesemann, *Der Begriff* KOINΩNIA *im Neuen Testament* (BZNW 14; Giessen: Töpelmann, 1933); cf. Windisch 428; Lietzmann 162; Bultmann 251; Barrett 344; Furnish 584; Martin 505; Dunn, *Jesus*, 261.

relationship with himself, as the God of all grace, but also causes us to participate in all the benefits of that grace and salvation, indwelling us in the present by his own presence, guaranteeing our final eschatological glory.[233]

Granted that Paul did not wrestle with the ontological questions which such statements beg to have addressed. Nor does he here *assert* the deity of Christ and the Spirit. But what he does is to *equate the activity of the three divine Persons* (to use the language of a later time) *in concert and in one prayer*, with the clause about God the Father standing in second place. This suggests that Paul was truly Trinitarian in any meaningful sense of that term—that the one God is Father, Son, and Spirit, and that in dealing with Christ and the Spirit one is dealing with God every bit as much as one is with God the Father.

It is not difficult to see why such a profound moment of theology—in the form of *prayer* for the Corinthians—should be the single most appropriate way to conclude this letter. What Paul wishes for them is all of this, and nothing less. He has brought them this gospel of God's love and Christ's grace; in turning to God they have received the Holy Spirit, who has removed the veil from their hearts (regarding the old covenant of stone and letter) and from their faces (so that they might be in fellowship with God himself, beholding his glory in the face of Christ and being transformed into that glory). For them to abandon Paul and his apostolic ministry, Paul recognizes in a most discerning way, is to abandon Christ and the Spirit, and thus the very love of God. For them to continue in their sinful ways (meals in the idol-temples and sexual immorality; 6:14–7:1; 12:19–21) and for them to take up with their "super apostles" and be brought under "externals" (whether in the form of Jewish casuistry/requirements or of the validation of spirituality by ecstasy) is to turn from true righteousness to condemnation, from life to death. It means to go after "another Jesus," who is no Lord Jesus Christ at all; and it means to "receive another spirit," who is not the Spirit whom they have received, who has brought them into this participation/fellowship (11:4).

As Ralph Martin put it, with considerable insight:

> Paul invokes the Holy Spirit with one master concern. He is seeking to establish the Holy Spirit as *the authentic sign of the new age, already begun but not yet realized in its fullness,* and he is building his case on *the readers' participation in the Spirit as the hallmark of their share in both the new world of God's righteousness and the Pauline apostolate that represents it.*[234]

It needs to be noted, finally, how thoroughly and unmistakably Trinitarian this prayer is. That Paul would include the Holy Spirit as an

---

[233] On this view of things, especially the absolutely necessary Trinitarian understanding of God and salvation, see below on Rom 5:5.

[234] Martin, "Spirit," 127 (emphasis his).

equal member of this triadic formula, and that he would pray to the Spirit in their behalf, says as much about his understanding of the Spirit both as person and as deity as any direct statement of this kind ever could. If there is no explication as to how a thoroughgoing monotheist can speak of Christ and the Spirit in this way, that does not lessen the impact of Paul's language. It is for the later church to try to understand the ontological implications, how God is three in one; its reason for doing so at all comes about precisely because the church is forced to come to terms with Paul's understanding of God's character and activity in our behalf expressed in this kind of prayer.[235]

CONCLUSION

As with 1 Corinthians, one cannot escape the central role the Spirit plays in Paul's thinking and Christian experience. If there is not such a full accounting of the Spirit's person and activity in this letter, what does emerge is in some ways even stronger evidence. It was suggested in the preceding chapter that much of our hearing about the Spirit in 1 Corinthians came about as a direct result of the Corinthians' emphases on what it means to be Spirit people. But that seems to be less so in this letter. If the Spirit as evidence that the future had made its way into the present is presuppositional in 1 Corinthians, here it is in fact argued for, probably because of the nature of some outside opposition. As Spirit people, they are here brought face to face with the theological and experiential consequences.

What is given here for the first time—that the Spirit, as an eschatological reality, and as fulfillment of the promised new covenant, renders the old covenant obsolete—will get its impassioned hearing in the next letter (Galatians), and its less impassioned but perhaps more complete hearing in the next (Romans). The presence of the Spirit in the life of the believer and the church means that all other boundary markers, all other identity symbols, must go. To receive the Spirit means to experience God's very presence, and to do so in freedom; the Spirit leads one to behold God's glory, so that one is actually transformed into the likeness of Christ, the ultimate image of God.

As before, therefore, the Spirit means empowering, but empowering of the kind already seen in 1 Corinthians, where by his Spirit God effectively reconciles people to himself and transforms them into the image of

---

[235] For a helpful discussion of the Trinitarian implications of this and other such texts in 1 Corinthians, see especially Young-Ford, *Meaning*, 255–60; cf. the further discussion in ch. 13.

his Son, and all of that despite the apostle's own weaknesses, so that they might see the glory of God in Christ, not the "clay vessel" of the apostle.

Along the way, of course, much more is said, since the Spirit is so crucial to the actual living out of the gospel. But for the most part, nothing new is said that we have not met in the earlier three letters. What this letter provides is the powerful articulation, with new and vivid images, of the role of the Spirit in the eschatological scheme of redemption, and therefore in the life of those who follow Christ—all to the glory of God.

6

Galatians

Commentaries:[1] D. C. **Arichea** and E. A. **Nida** (1976); H. D. **Betz** (Hermeneia, 1979); J. **Bligh** (1969); J. M. **Boice** (EBC, 1976); F. F. **Bruce** (NIGTC, 1982); E. D. **Burton** (ICC, 1921); J. **Calvin** (ET, 1965); R. A. **Cole** (TNTC, 1965); G. S. **Duncan** (MNTC, 1934); G. **Ebeling** (1981); C. R. **Erdman** (1930); R. Y. K. **Fung** (NIC, 1988); D. **Guthrie** (NCB, 1974); W. **Hendriksen** (1968); M.-E. **Lagrange** (EB, 1925); H. **Lietzmann** (HNT, 1910); J. B. **Lightfoot** (1865); R. N. **Longenecker** (WBC, 1991); J. **MacArthur** (1987); H. A. W. **Meyer** (MeyerK, 1870); F. **Mussner** (HTKNT, 1974); C. **Osiek** (NTM, 1980); W. M. **Ramsay** (1900); H. **Ridderbos** (NIC, 1953); J. **Rohde** (THKNT, 1988); H. **Schlier** (MeyerK, [13]1965); J. R. W. **Stott** (1968).

Other significant studies, cited by author's last name and short title:

Barclay, *Obeying* (= John M. G. Barclay, *Obeying the Truth: A Study of Paul's Ethics in Galatians* [Edinburgh: T & T Clark, 1988]); **Barrett,** *Freedom* (= C. K. Barrett, *Freedom and Obligation: A study of the Epistle to the Galatians* [London: SPCK, 1985]); **Betz,** "Defense" (= Hans Dieter Betz, "In Defense of the Spirit: Paul's Letter to the Galatians as a Document of Early Christian Apologetics," in *Aspects of Religious Propaganda in Judaism and Early Christianity* [ed. E. Schüssler Fiorenza; Notre Dame, 1976] 99–114); **Bruce,** "Spirit" (= F. F. Bruce, "The Spirit in the Letter to the Galatians," in *Essays on Apostolic Themes: Studies in honor of Howard M. Ervin* [ed. P. Elbert; Peabody, Mass.: Hendrickson Publishers, 1985] 36–48); **Cosgrove,** *Cross* (= Charles H. Cosgrove, *The Cross and the Spirit: A Study in the Argument and Theology of Galatians* [Macon, Ga.: Mercer, 1988]); **Hansen,** *Abraham* (= G. W. Hansen, *Abraham in Galatians: Epistolary and Rhetorical Contexts* [JSNTSup 29; Sheffield, JSOT, 1989]); **Hays,** *Faith* (= Richard B. Hays, *The Faith of Jesus Christ: An Investigation of the Narrative Substructure of Galatians 3:1–4:11* [SBLDS 56; Chico, Calif.: Scholars Press, 1983]); **Ladd,** "Holy Spirit"

---

[1]The following commentaries are referred to in this chapter only by the author's last name.

(= George E. Ladd, "The Holy Spirit in Galatians," in *Current Issues in Biblical and Patristic Interpretation* [FS M. C. Tenney; ed. G. F. Hawthorne; Grand Rapids: Eerdmans, 1975] 211–16); **Lull,** *Spirit* (= David John Lull, *The Spirit in Galatia: Paul's Interpretation of* Pneuma *as Divine Power* [SBLDS 49; Chico, Calif.: Scholars Press, 1980]); **Ropes,** *Problem* (=James Hardy Ropes, *The Singular Problem of the Epistle to the Galatians* [London: Oxford University Press, 1929]); **Williams,** "Justification" (= Sam K. Williams, "Justification and the Spirit in Galatians," *JSNT* 29 [1987] 91–100.)

Since the time of the Reformers, Galatians has been perceived primarily as the place where Paul contests most vigorously for his central doctrine of justification by faith, that is, that people are saved by faith in Christ not by works of the Law. While there is a profound sense in which this is a central concern for Paul, more likely at stake in this letter is the inclusion of Gentiles as full and equal members of the people of God. At issue is whether Gentiles who have believed in Christ must also accept the "identity markers" of Jewishness[2] in order to be genuine "children of Abraham," and thereby receive the promises of God's covenant with Abraham as expressed in Gen 12:3 and 18:18.[3] At the same time, because of the emphasis by the Reformers on the language of "justification" and "by faith," there has been a tendency to neglect the equally important matter of the life in the Spirit, which is the central focus of so much of the argument in this letter.[4]

There is in fact a much greater explication of the Spirit in the life of the *believer* in Galatians than in the earlier letters—because the issues are different. In 1 Corinthians the life of the community was at stake; here, it is the essential nature of Christian existence as such, both as to how one is related to God and how life in Christ is lived out. Thus the argument is not basically along *positional* lines, that one has right standing with God ("is

---

[2]Especially circumcision (3:3; 5:2–3, 11–12; 6:12), observance of the Jewish calendar (4:10–11), and probably food laws, given their significance as "identity markers" in the Diaspora and the way Paul weaves them into the argument in the crucial narrative of 2:11–14. This does not necessarily exclude the theological view of the Law—Torah as a means of right standing with God. In this letter the two ways of understanding the Law coalesce; but the predominant issue is not "works-righteousness" (= doing Torah to gain favor with God), but sociological (= doing Torah as necessary to belong to the people of God). The former flows naturally out of the latter.

[3]This is what one might call the "new look" on Galatians, which may be traced back as far as K. Stendahl's "The Apostle Paul and the Introspective Conscience of the West," in *Paul Among Jews and Gentiles and Other Essays* (Philadelphia: Fortress, 1976) 78–96 [repr. from *HTR* 56 (1963)]; cf. inter alia, T. D. Gordon, "The Problem at Galatia," *Int* 41 (1987) 32–43; Barclay, *Obeying,* 36–74; J. D. G. Dunn, "The Theology of Galatians; The Issue of Covenantal Nomism," in *Jesus, Paul and the Law* (Philadelphia: Westminster, 1990) 242–64.

[4]This emphasis is at last receiving its due hearing. See especially Lull, *Spirit;* Cosgrove, *Cross;* Betz, "Defense"; Bruce, "Spirit"; Williams, "Justification." See also the emphasis in Betz' commentary.

justified") by faith alone; rather, it is especially along *experiential* lines, that by faith one has received the Spirit, and that the Spirit and Torah observance (= "works of law") are absolutely incompatible. The one means freedom, the other slavery. Indeed, the issue raised by the agitators[5] is not how one *enters* life in Christ (surely the agitators would have agreed that this was through the death and resurrection of Christ), but how such life is brought to completion (3:3)—especially for Gentile believers.[6] For the agitators, the gift of the Spirit apparently meant the need to be "completed" by adhering to Torah, especially by submitting to circumcision. After all, this was common Jewish expectation, derived from Jer 31:31–34 and Ezek 11:19–20; 36:26–27, that the gift of the eschatological Spirit would lead people to obey the Law.[7] For Paul, the gift of the Spirit, along with the death and resurrection of Christ, meant the *end* of the time of Torah. The old covenant had failed precisely because it was not accompanied by the Spirit. Thus the advent of Christ and the Spirit meant an end to the old covenant; the new covenant, ratified through the death of Christ, had been instituted through the gift of the Spirit, who thereby replaced Torah.

The Spirit, therefore, beginning at 3:2 and carrying through to 6:10, plays a leading role in the argument of this letter. The word πνεῦμα, referring to the Spirit, occurs sixteen (or seventeen) times;[8] and πνευματικοί, referring to Spirit people, once (6:1). Another text (2:2) also seems to reflect a Spirit phenomenon, while 2:20, though expressed in terms of Christ, most likely in Pauline theology also reflects the Spirit's activity in the believer. Even though many of these texts presuppose the believing community,[9] for the most part they are concerned with the essential character of life in Christ, which is begun at the individual level.

---

[5]This is Paul's own language about his opponents, found in 1:7 and 5:10. According to 6:12, these agitators were "compelling" Paul's Gentile converts to accept circumcision (cf. 2:3; 5:2–3). Since they are referred to in the third person, over against the Galatians themselves, one may assume they are also outsiders.

[6]To use the language of E. P. Sanders, but not his conclusions in this case, at stake are not *entrance* requirements but *maintenance* requirements (for full membership into God's covenant people one must become Abraham's true child by means of circumcision). Sanders understands the issue in Galatians as "entrance requirements." See *Paul, the Law, and the Jewish People* (Philadelphia: Fortress, 1983). Cf. the critique in Cosgrove, *Cross*, 11–13.

For a different view altogether, see Cosgrove, who considers the question Paul raises in 3:5 as the essential matter and thus understands the agitators to be promoting Torah as the proper means for "sustaining and promoting life in the Spirit" (86); see esp. 39–86. This view was anticipated in part by J. L. Martyn, "A Law-Observant Mission to Gentiles: The Background of Galatians," *SJT* 38 (1985) 307–24.

[7]See, e.g., Ezek 36:27: "And I will put my Spirit in you and move you to follow my decrees and be careful to keep my laws."

[8]3:2, 3, 5, 14; 4:6, 29; 5:5, 16, 17[2x], 18, 22, 25[2x]; 6:1 (probably), 8[2x].

[9]See, e.g., 3:5 and especially 5:13–6:10, where the interplay between an individual believer and the believing community is thoroughgoing. See below on this passage.

What emerges in this letter is the absolutely crucial role the Spirit plays in Paul's understanding of Christian existence. The key element of Christian conversion is the Spirit, dynamically experienced (3:2–5; 4:6), as the fulfillment of the promise to Abraham (3:14). Indeed, the Christian experience of the Spirit sets the believer off from all other existences, which are alternatively seen as "under Law" (5:18) or "carrying out the desire of the flesh" (5:16). The Galatians had previously lived the latter; some agitators had turned up to place them under the former. Paul will have none of it. The Spirit alone is the antidote to the "works of the flesh"; Law not only does not help, but rather leads to bondage. Only in (or by) the Spirit is one truly free, but free for righteousness, of the real kind. Thus the person who walks, lives, is led by the Spirit is not under Law; indeed, the Spirit produces the very fruit which the Law aimed at but could not produce. At the same time the one who walks, lives, is led by the Spirit will not do as the flesh desires.

But for Paul all is not automatic. One must sow to the Spirit (6:8) and be led by the Spirit (5:18); indeed, "if we live [= have been brought to life after the crucifixion of the flesh, v. 24] by the Spirit," we must therefore also "accordingly behave by the Spirit" (v. 25). Thus the Spirit not only stands at the beginning of Christian existence, but is the key ingredient to Paul's understanding of the whole of that existence. Accordingly, the final argument (5:13–6:10) becomes one of the most significant in the corpus for our understanding of Pauline ethics as Spirit-empowered Christ-likeness lived out in Christian community as loving servanthood.

Since the Spirit plays such a crucial role in the entire argument of the letter (from 3:1), an overview of the argument will help to highlight that role. As I perceive it, the "argument" of Galatians is basically in four parts, interspersed with application and appeal.[10] (1) *1:13–2:14*. After an opening exordium (1:6–12) in which a curse formula replaces the standard thanksgiving and prayer, Paul begins the *argument* in the form of three narratives (1:13–24; 2:1–10; 2:11–14), which are intended to defend both his apostleship (as from God, not of human origin) and thus his gospel (likewise as from God, not of human origin). In turn the three narratives make three points: (a) that Paul's gospel and apostleship are quite independent of Jerusalem; (b) that his gospel nonetheless was in agreement with Jerusalem; and (c) that Jerusalem (in the person of Peter), not he, broke faith with the agreement.

---

[10]On the question of *form*, and especially the question of the "rhetoric" of Galatians, see esp. Cosgrove, *Cross*, 23–38. His observation (26) that whatever else Galatians might be, it is a *letter*, is too easily forgotten by those enamored by first-century rhetoric. If in fact these categories are useful at all, then the persuasive nature of the overall argument, in which Paul is trying to convince them that he is right and the agitators are wrong, demands that it is deliberative, not apologetic.

(2) *2:15–4:20*. The third narrative (2:11–14) concludes with a "speech" to Peter that in fact evolves into a "speech" for the sake of the Galatians (2:15–21), and sets forth the basic theological propositions of the argument that follows. Three things matter: (a) that righteousness is "not by works of Torah"; (b) that righteousness is "by faith in Christ Jesus," who also brought an end to Torah observance; and (c) that the indwelling Christ (by his Spirit, is implied) is the effective agent for living out the new righteousness. This, then, is followed by the first theological argument (3:1–4:7), in which the experience of the Spirit and Scripture combine to support the first two propositions (that Christ has brought an end to Torah; therefore righteousness cannot be by "works of Torah" but by "faith in Christ Jesus").

This argument is concluded in 4:8–11 by specific application to their situation, which in turn calls forth an appeal to their continuing loyalty to Paul, given their original loyalty to him and his gospel when he was first among them (4:12–20).

(3) *4:21–5:12*. In 4:21–31 Paul returns to the scriptural argument of 3:6–4:7, in which, by picking up the themes of Abraham, slavery, and freedom, he demonstrates by analogy that Torah means slavery, and Christ and the Spirit mean freedom. Again the Spirit plays a key role: the "free son" of the "free woman" (who represents believers in Christ) is designated as "born according to the Spirit," over against Ishmael (current Judaism), the son of slavery, who was born "according to the flesh."

This in turn is followed by a twofold application and appeal, directed first *toward* the Galatians themselves that they face up to the consequences of a capitulation to Torah (5:1–6) and second *about* the agitators (5:7–12), who are blistered for what amounts to abandoning Christ.

(4) *5:13–6:10*. Paul concludes by taking up the third proposition from 2:15–21, namely, that the indwelling Spirit has replaced Torah, because the Spirit can do what Torah could not do, effect the righteousness that Torah demands. Whereas Torah was unable effectively to deal with the "passions and desires of the flesh," the Spirit does that very thing. But in this case, Paul is dealing with more than mere argument; he applies the argument to the specific issue of disharmony within their local assemblies.

The Spirit thus plays little role in part I of the argument, for obvious reasons, since it takes the form of narrative and functions to defend Paul's gospel and apostleship. But in parts 2, 3, and 4 the Spirit, alongside Christ, plays a major role. Indeed, the argument of Galatians simply does not work without the Spirit. The Spirit is an experienced reality providing evidence that righteousness is not by Torah (3:1–5, 14; 4:6) and is the effective agent for righteousness now that the time of Torah is past (5:13–6:10).

GALATIANS 2:2

Now I went up in keeping with a revelation and[11] I laid before them—privately to those of prominence—the gospel I preach among the Gentiles.

Although the Spirit is not mentioned in this passage, Paul clearly understands ἀποκάλυψις ("revelation") as a working of the Spirit,[12] sometimes in more general terms,[13] and sometimes, as here, in more ad hoc moments, closely allied with prophecy—if not in some cases the same thing.[14] Since Paul reminds the Galatians in 3:5 that the Spirit continues to do miraculous deeds among them, it seems likely that the Galatians also would have understood Paul's present language in this way.

Such indeed is the view of many commentators,[15] some of whom, however, suggest a correlation between this language and the prophecy of Agabus related in Acts 11:27–28.[16] But such a correlation would surely catch the apostle by surprise! As noted above (n. 11), the first clause in this sentence is not to be understood as something of a parenthesis; rather it serves as the basis for the second clause ("Now [δέ] I went up in keeping with a revelation and I laid before them . . . the gospel I preach

---

[11]Both the Greek text (UBS⁴ and NA²⁶) and several English translations (RSV, NASB) place a full (or major) stop after ἀποκάλυψιν; but that makes this clause appear too parenthetical (as Duncan 37 actually suggests). Far more likely Paul's structures are otherwise. The δέ of this verse resumes the narrative from v. 1 by elaborating specifically on the *reason* for "going up." Since sentences beginning with "and" are so rare in Paul, the next clause (καὶ ἀνεθέμην κτλ.) should be understood not as a new sentence, but as the complement to ἀνέβην δὲ κατὰ ἀποκάλυψιν. The first clause in v. 2 therefore serves as the *basis* and the second as the *reason* for "going up." Thus:

> ¹Then after 14 years
>   I went up again   to Jerusalem,
>   with Barnabas
>   taking along Titus also;
> ²Now (δέ) I went up
>   in keeping with a revelation,
> *and* (καί) I laid before them . . .

[12]This is not true of every usage, of course, as for example in 1:12, where the "revelation of Jesus Christ" refers to his conversion/commissioning, with Christ as the object of the revelation (as vv. 15–16 seem to confirm).

[13]As e.g., in 1 Cor 12:10–12 and Eph 3:5.

[14]Cf. the discussion in ch. 4 above, on 1 Cor 14:6, 26, and 30.

[15]See, e.g., Lightfoot, Burton, Erdman, Duncan, Mussner, Bruce, Fung, Longenecker. Many others (e.g., Lagrange, Schlier, Guthrie, Betz, Ebeling, Rohde) simply note the wide variety of options here (direct revelation, vision, prophetic utterance) and suggest no preference.

[16]This is embraced with varying degrees of enthusiasm by Duncan, Cole, Stott, Fung, Longenecker; cf. W. M. Ramsay, *St Paul, the Traveller and the Roman Citizen* (14th ed., 1920; repr. Grand Rapids: Baker, 1951) 57.

among the Gentiles"). Thus, Paul and Barnabas (and Titus) went up to Jerusalem specifically in response to the Spirit's direction, and for the purpose of dealing with the issue of Paul's law-free (= circumcision-free) gospel among the Gentiles.[17] For Paul's immediate purposes, of course, this little note makes it plain that the meeting was not at the behest of Jerusalem, but was undertaken freely in response to the guidance of the Spirit.

What cannot be determined by such a reference, of course, is whether the "revelation" came to Paul privately,[18] or in the context of the community at worship, such as in Acts 13:2. Given the presence of Barnabas and Titus and Paul's free appeal to such "revelation" as something that could be verified or tested, I would lean toward the latter.[19] If so, this is another one of those side notes in Paul that indicate the presence of the "charismatic" Spirit in the life of the early church. Rather than a form of "personal prophecy," giving specific direction to one person's life, such a prophetic utterance would have been understood as a community moment, which, properly tested, would have been acted upon as a community sending of the three brothers.[20]

GALATIANS 2:19b–20

[19] . . . *I am crucified with Christ;* [20]*and I no longer live, but Christ lives in me. So the life I now live in "the flesh," I live by faith in the Son of God,*[21] *who loved me and gave himself for me.*

---

[17] See now W. O. Walker, "Why Paul Went to Jerusalem: The Interpretation of Galatians 2:1–5," *CBQ* 54 (1992) 503–10.

[18] As the "revelation of Jesus Christ" referred to in 1:12 and 16 must surely have been, as also the "abundance of the revelations" in 2 Cor 12:7. While it is true that both parts of the argument in 1:10–2:14 are thus specifically related to a "revelation," there is no reason thereby to think that the word refers to the same kind of experience in each case.

[19] Contra Meyer 67; Bruce 108; Fung 86; Aune (*Prophecy*, 249, "a dream or vision experience"), and others, who take the revelation to be private, in which case it can scarcely be the result of a prophetic word, nor related to 1 Cor 14:26–33.

[20] Cf. Lightfoot 102, who suggests that the revelation "either prompted or confirmed the decision of the Church" (referring to the account in Acts 15:1–2). If indeed these are the same events, as I believe, then Paul surely intends the former. For a view similar to the one suggested here see Dunn (*Jesus*, 217), who also freely admits (p. 222) that it could have been of a different sort as well.

[21] The current debate over the phrase ἐκ πίστεως Χριστοῦ (whether it means "on the basis of faith in Christ" or "by the faith[fulness] of Christ"), found first in v. 16 and repeated here in the modified form ἐν πίστει τῇ τοῦ υἱοῦ τοῦ θεοῦ, is already large and is growing on a regular basis (for a bibliography to 1980 see Longenecker 87; cf. Hays, *Faith*; Morna D. Hooker, "ΠΙΣΤΙΣ ΧΡΙΣΤΟΥ," *NTS* 35 [1989] 321–42; and esp. the recent debate between Hays and Dunn in *Society of Biblical Literature 1991 Seminar Papers* [Atlanta: Scholars, 1991] 714–44). The resolution of this debate lies beyond the

Whether this text should be discussed in this book is moot. In any case is it not an easy text to grasp in its context. But in light of the theologically crucial passage in Rom 8:9–10, and especially in light of the argument of the rest of the present letter, Paul's "but Christ lives in me" most likely is a kind of shorthand for "Christ by his Spirit lives in me." This is not to suggest that for him the risen Lord and the Spirit are the same;[22] rather, since the Spirit is indeed the Spirit *of Christ*, Pauline usage depends on the emphasis in a given context. Here the emphasis is on Christ and his work; hence he speaks of the indwelling Christ,[23] rather than of the indwelling Spirit.[24]

One of the reasons for thinking so is that Paul usually thinks of believers as "in Christ," whereas "indwelling" is common language regarding the Spirit. Romans 8:9–10 (q.v.) offers the theological clue to this language: Believers are those who are not in the flesh but *in the Spirit*, inasmuch as *the Spirit of God dwells in them*. If they do not *have the Spirit of Christ*, they do not even belong to him (Christ). The final consequence of such argumentation is that *if Christ be in you*, then "the Spirit bestows life on account of [the] righteousness [given by Christ]." Here is the clear evidence that in Paul's view Christ indwells his people by his Spirit. Hence the similar point in Phil 1:19–20 (q.v.), that as a result of the Philippians' prayers Paul is given a fresh supply of *the Spirit of Jesus Christ*, and Christ himself will be magnified when Paul stands trial. Such an understanding lies behind the present usage as well.

Later, in his personal appeal in 4:19, Paul images himself as in the travail of labor over the Galatians until "Christ be formed in you," probably intending "until Christ's own likeness be formed in your lives." How that will happen is quite the point of the argument of 5:13–6:10,

---

scope of our study. Although there are places where I think it probably means "the faithfulness of Christ" (e.g., Rom 3:22), I am less convinced that it means that here. In v. 16, where the phrase appears for the first time, it seems to have been coined on the basis of the contrast with ἐξ ἔργων νόμου, which can only mean "on the basis of works of law." Despite the protest that to understand ἐκ πίστεως Χριστοῦ as "faith in Christ" is to overload this sentence, that will hardly stand in this case. After all, no less than three times in this clause Paul says "not by works of law." Since part of the response to this is that "we have believed in Christ Jesus," it seems more probable to me that Paul is loading the sentence with a threefold, "not by works of law," contrasted by the threefold, "but by faith in Christ Jesus." If that is the case in v. 16, then that same meaning probably prevails here—although I have no objection to the other possibility in this instance.

[22]As Betz 124, e.g., maintains; cf. Burton 127 who speaks a bit more cautiously. On this question see ch. 13.

[23]Although Paul does not do so often (for him the more common expression has to do with believers being "in Christ"); but see 2 Cor 13:5; Rom 8:9–10; Col 1:27; and Eph 3:17.

[24]Similarly Duncan 72; Bruce 144; cf. Ebeling 149–50.

namely, as they learn to "walk by/bear the fruit of/conform to the Spirit." Especially significant in that argument is the combination of language in 5:24–25, where *crucifixion* of the flesh and *life* by the Spirit are juxtaposed. Thus, even though Paul does not here mention the Spirit, the implications of Pauline usage elsewhere suggest that he means "Christ by his Spirit lives in me."[25]

The more difficult question is what the passage means in its context, and why the emphasis on the indwelling of Christ. The answer to that lies in the argument itself, which begins at v. 11, where Paul is recounting Peter's betrayal of their agreement on Gentile inclusion without the need to submit to Jewish identity markers. Paul's "speech" to Peter on that occasion becomes the springboard for his argument with the Galatians. Indeed, the "speech" evolves into argument,[26] in which the two principal matters of this letter merge: a defense of his apostleship and preaching of Christ, and a defense of his "law-free" gospel for Gentiles. The preceding sentence, "for if I[27] build again those very things I tore down, I put myself in the position of a transgressor," looks like a thinly veiled reference to Peter's action in Antioch, in light of the previous agreement narrated in vv. 1–10. Verse 19, therefore, offers by way of further personal testimony (cf. v. 16) the believer's present life in Christ vis-à-vis the Law.

---

[25]So also Meyer 125; Ridderbos 106; Dunn, *Baptism*, 107; Bruce 144; Cosgrove, *Cross*, 173, 193–94; Longenecker 93.

[26]Betz, followed by Longenecker, refers to this as the *propositio* of an "apologetic letter." Perhaps so, but one needs to raise two cautions: (1) Since there is no known example of such a thing as an "apologetic letter," one may be properly skeptical as to whether this is what Paul intended (see esp. the critiques by W. A. Meeks, *JBL* 100 [1981] 304–7; and Cosgrove, *Cross*, 24–27); (2) the use of rhetorical categories sometimes has the effect of obscuring what is going on in the letter (e.g., to call this section a "summary of 1:11–2:14" [Longenecker 80–81] seems to miss too much—after all, this section still takes the form of narrative, not propositional argumentation). The question is, in which direction is this material pointing, toward Antioch and Peter or toward the Galatians? Even though the situation in Antioch is never quite lost sight of, the primary focus seems now to be on the Galatians, by way of anticipating the argument that follows. To that degree, it functions in part as a *propositio* (contra Cosgrove, *Cross*, who too summarily cuts the link between 2:16 and the argument of 3:1–14). Cf. B. Byrne, *'Sons of God'—'Sons of Abraham'* (AnBib 83; Rome: Pontifical Biblical Institute, 1979) 143.

[27]Note the sudden return to the first person singular, which was last used in v. 14. The "speech" to Peter, which begins in the second singular (v. 14b), shifts to the first plural in v. 15, which then continues through v. 17. How much of this is still intended to be part of that former "speech" is moot, of course, because whatever Paul said on that occasion forms the content of what now needs to be said to the Galatians. That is, at some point in vv. 15–17, the "speech" to Peter becomes a "speech" to the Galatians. Nonetheless, it is arguable that the concerns of that original event, since they are so similar to what is now happening in Galatia, still lie close to the surface of the current argument—although I doubt whether Paul is any longer consciously focusing on the Antioch scene.

On the one hand, as far as Torah is concerned,[28] death has brought an end to that relationship altogether because of the believer's intimate relationship with Christ, whose death brought an end to the time of Torah—which is the point of the entire argument of the letter from 3:6. On the other hand, with reference to God himself, despite the demise of Torah, the believer now lives. Our passage (vv. 19b–20) sets out to explicate "how so."

Thus in v. 20 the new, post-crucifixion life is characterized not as one's own rightful possession, but as a gift—life from the Living One himself, the crucified and now risen Christ. In context, therefore, especially in light of the preceding phrase, "I am crucified with Christ," it is only natural that the risen Christ is the one who now lives in him, thus making life possible at all. The rest of the argument of the letter, especially 4:4–7, makes it plain that Paul understands such a life of "sonship" to be the result of Christ's redemptive work, *appropriated by the Spirit's indwelling*, both of whom were sent forth from the Father.

It should be noted, finally, how reminiscent of 2 Cor 5:14–17 this passage is. Christ's death has meant death for all, so that any present "life" is a gift from the Risen One. Thus it is not "I" who now live, since "I" have already experienced death through Christ's death. For the believer, however, it is not simply a matter of "all dying in Christ's death" (2 Cor 5:14), but especially of the believer's being intimately joined to Christ in his death, so that what Christ died to bring to an end has been brought to an end for the believer as well (in this case, the Law). So also with life. Since "I" died in Christ's death, the only life now available is that of the risen Christ; hence the only people who truly live in the present are believers, and they live by virtue of their further intimate relationship with Christ, who "lives in me"—by his Spirit. Thus "the life 'I' now live 'in the flesh' I live by virtue of Christ, whose love for me was expressed by his death on the cross in my behalf."

From now on believers live "between the times" in the "already" and "not yet" of eschatological salvation. Death has occurred already, as well as life. "I" no longer "live"; yet I continue to live "in the flesh," not meaning "in my sinfulness" but, as in 2 Cor 10:3, "in this present existence." This existence is "already" stamped with eternity through Christ's death and resurrection and the gift of the Spirit, but it is "not yet" in that it is still subject to the vicissitudes of the present age. But the presence of Christ by his Spirit means that life "in the flesh" is not life under Law (cf. 5:18), nor subject to the desire of "the flesh" (5:16)—humanity viewed not simply as "human" but as fundamentally opposed to God in its fallenness.

---

[28] I take both datives νόμῳ and θεῷ to be datives of reference. With reference to Torah the believer is dead; with reference to God the believer is alive. Cf. Rom 7:1–6.

The net result, therefore, is that by way of personal testimony this passage spells out the essential theological thesis of the letter. Christ, by his death "for us," has brought an end to Torah, opening up a way of life that is based on faith alone; but that life is not merely "positional" righteousness, it is the real thing predicated on Christ by his Spirit living out God's own life in us. The rest of the letter spells this out in detail.

GALATIANS 3:1–4:11

Thus far in the argument Paul has insisted, first, that his (law-free) gospel for the Gentiles came to him by direct revelation; consequently, both his apostleship and his understanding of the gospel are *quite independent of* Jerusalem.[29] He needed no "credentials" such as the agitators apparently had—and in which they probably prided themselves (1:10–23). Second, although independent of them, his understanding of the gospel was *not different from* those of "prominence" in Jerusalem (2:1–10); to the contrary, when he and Barnabas finally had occasion to lay "their gospel" before them, it was agreed that the understanding of the gospel as law-free for the Gentiles was held in common; only the spheres of labor would differ (2:1–10).[30] Hence, Paul uses Peter's betrayal of this agreement in an incident at Antioch (2:11–14) as the launching pad for his argument with the Galatians as to the nature of the gospel, especially since the "betrayal" was over the very kind of issue that is now being urged on the Galatians by the agitators who have come in among them—allegedly with Jerusalem's blessing.[31]

---

[29]His independence of Jerusalem, of course, is quite in keeping with the agitators' point of view (i.e., they called his apostleship into question in part because he *lacked* authorization from Jerusalem). Paul is thus turning this "deficit" into capital; what they saw as a defect, he saw as to his great advantage—his apostleship and gospel, unlike theirs, came not "from men" but directly from God.

[30]Lull, *Spirit*, 10, offers the insightful suggestion that lying behind this passage is the implication that from Paul's perspective it was not he but the Jewish-Christian agitators who were thus at odds with Jerusalem.

[31]That the agitators touted their point of view as having the blessing of Jerusalem is the best way to make sense of the way the argument in chs. 1–2 proceeds, and especially of the fact that Paul uses Peter's betrayal of the Jerusalem agreement to launch his argument with the Galatians. Cf. Lincoln, *Paradise*, 10. From Paul's perspective the agitators cannot have Jerusalem's blessing, since he himself has it; but Peter serves as a prior example of one who allowed pressure from "some from Jerusalem" to cause him to capitulate on matters of observance in which Gentiles' "living like Jews" was at stake. Hence Paul's reason for transforming the "speech" to Peter into his present argument with the Galatians.

As noted above, that argument focuses on three particulars, to be elaborated in the rest of the argument: "not by works of Law," "by faith in Christ Jesus," and "Christ (by his Spirit) lives in me."[32]

The argument is about to pick up these threads and to demonstrate from Scripture, especially from the combined evidence of Genesis and Deuteronomy, that the coming of Christ has meant the end of the observance of Law, and therefore, as with Abraham, that the gift of righteousness rests on faith—for Jew and Gentile alike. The crucial *experiential* evidence that both of these are true is the indwelling, empowering presence of the Spirit.[33]

The argument can be easily traced, even if some of its details are a bit obscure to a later reader. It begins with the rhetoric of vv. 1–5, where the three themes are woven together as Paul urges that their own experience of the Spirit plays the lie to their wavering over the issue of Gentile circumcision.[34] The Spirit is Exhibit A that relationship with God is predicated *not* on "works of Law" but on "faith in Christ Jesus." Verses 6–14 pick up these two themes and argue from Scripture, first (vv. 6–9), that righteousness comes to Jew and Gentile alike "by faith in Christ Jesus," and, second (vv. 10–14), that it cannot be "by works of Law," inasmuch as Christ's having become a curse for us not only ended the time of Law but also made it possible for the blessing of Abraham to come to the Gentiles, a promise that was fulfilled in their reception of the Spirit. This is followed in vv. 15–18 by yet another argument from Scripture—and from everyday life—that since a ratified will can neither be annulled nor be added to, and since the "promise" to inherit *preceded* the advent of Torah (and circumcision), therefore Torah could not annul the promise, which has been fulfilled by the gift of the Spirit.

Since all of this sounds anti-Torah, in vv. 19–22 Paul takes up the matter of Torah: given what he has just argued concerning the relationship of Torah to the promise, then *why Torah at all?* Indeed, *does not Torah stand over against the promise?* Paul's response to the first question is that Torah had a (necessary) *temporary* role—to "hem people in because of transgressions"—which in turn sets up the rest of the argument in

---

[32]Contra Cosgrove, *Cross*, 32–33, who with a kind of literary tour de force basically eliminates 2:15–21 from consideration as a key to this letter.

[33]Both Cosgrove (*Cross*, 39–61) and C. D. Stanley, " 'Under a Curse': A Fresh Reading of Galatians 3.10–14," *NTS* 36 (1990) 492–95, in slightly different ways, read the argument in 3:1–14 as having mainly to do with the Galatians' reception of the Spirit. That is, both their experience and Scripture conjoin to demonstrate that they received the Spirit by faith and not by adding Law. While my own sympathies should lie in this direction, my sense is that both authors minimize the element of "righteousness" in this argument, and especially of its connection with the theme of "righteousness by faith" that precedes this section (2:16, 21) and follows (3:21, 24).

[34]At this point Cosgrove, *Cross*, 38, is onto something significant by suggesting that here is the place for us to "join the conversation" of Galatians.

3:23–4:7. His response to the second question is typical, "God forbid!" As in 2 Corinthians 3, the problem is not with Torah; it simply was not designed to do what the Spirit alone can do.

With the final two paragraphs (3:23–29 and 4:1–7) Paul ties together the loose ends of the argument. The first deals with the role of Christ in freeing people from Torah observance. Picking up on the function of Law to "imprison" people (from vv. 19–22), but shifting the analogy, Paul argues that being under Law is in effect to be in slavery (vv. 23–24), but that the coming of Abraham's "true seed" (Christ [vv. 15–18]) has brought freedom from such slavery and has given "true sonship" to all who believe in him (cf. vv. 6–9 with 25–29). But even more (4:1–7), freedom from slavery and being Abraham's "children" means "sonship" of the highest order. God sent both his Son—to redeem from slavery and for adoption as children—and *the Spirit of his Son*, whose cry of "Abba" (Jesus' own word of "sonship") from the heart of the believer is the evidence of such "adoption." All of which is then concluded in 4:8–11 by an appeal for the Galatian believers to apply all of this to their own situation.

Two further observations about this argument are pertinent. First, the "declarative" imperative in 3:7 ("Know therefore that those who are by faith [not 'by Law' is implied], these are the children of Abraham") serves as a kind of thesis statement for the whole argument.[35] Hence the double conclusion: in 3:29 ("Now if you are Christ's, *you are therefore Abraham's seed, heirs* according to *promise*") and 4:7 ("So then [because of Christ's redemption and the Spirit's indwelling], you are no longer a slave [under Law] *but a child*, and if a child, then also *an heir* through God"). This suggests (1) that the question being addressed throughout is, "Who are *Abraham's true children*, thus *heirs* of the *promise*?" and (2) that the agitators themselves had argued, probably from Genesis 17, that the true children of Abraham (and by implication, children of God) are those who, as Abraham, seal their faith by circumcision. For Paul it was in the happy providence of God that in Genesis 15, *before* the covenant of circumcision, God had already both declared Abraham to be righteous by faith and included Gentiles in the promise made to Abraham. Thus both the *language* of Scripture and the *timing* of events are crucial for Paul's argument.

Second, one can scarcely miss the absolutely crucial role the Spirit plays in all of this.[36] In 3:1–5 their own experience of the Spirit had

---

[35]Contra Stanley ("Under," 492), who argues that this fails on the grounds that Paul does not press for this theme immediately. But as with Stanley's own position, much has to do with how much of the argument is presuppositional between Paul and the Galatians. I am more impressed by the fact that this is where the larger argument seems to be heading in 3:29.

[36]Although see Lightfoot, whose commentary is nearly void of references to the Spirit!

preceded the coming of Torah (in the form of the agitators' insistence on circumcision), thus absolutely destroying the agitators' arguments. Not only so, but the evidence of Scripture shows that both the declaration of righteousness and the promise of blessing for the Gentiles, which are predicated on faith, also precede Torah. What is crucial for Paul is his interpretation of the "fulfillment" of the "promised blessing" in terms of their experience of the Spirit (v. 14). This double *entendre* with regard to the "promise"—that the blessing of "sonship/inheritance" for Gentiles has been fulfilled by the gift of the Spirit—is probably also at work in varying degrees in the further references to the "promise" that follow (vv. 16, 17, 18, 21, 22, 29). The argument concludes (4:6) with a final appeal to the indwelling Spirit as the ultimate evidence of "sonship" and thus of being heirs—of Abraham, but now especially of God.

Thus, in terms of the saving event, Christ is always and singularly the focus of the argument: redemption, freedom, adoption, and therefore righteousness have come through him, through his death and resurrection. Paul, as one "crucified with Christ" (2:20), so exhibited Christ in their midst (3:1). By hanging on a tree Christ redeemed Jew and Gentile alike from Torah observance and made "sonship" possible (3:13; 4:5). But in terms of the evidence that life in Christ is by faith alone and quite apart from Torah, both at its beginnings and in its continuing expression, the Spirit plays the major role.[37] Their own experience of the Spirit, in conversion and in their corporate life, is thus pressed on them as proof positive that the time of Torah is over and that the time of God's fulfillment of his promise to Abraham, including the blessing of the Gentiles, has come. A close look at these texts further demonstrates that this is the Pauline perspective.

GALATIANS 3:1–5

[1]*O foolish Galatians, who has bewitched you,*[38] *before whose eyes Jesus Christ was exhibited*[39] *as crucified?* [2]*This only I wish to learn from you: On the basis*

---

[37]Cosgrove, *Cross*, sees the relationship between the Spirit and the cross somewhat differently—as Paul's way of bringing their (legitimate) experience(s) of the Spirit under the larger aegis of Christ's suffering, so as to keep them from going the way of triumphalism. A point well taken, but not pressed in the actual argument of Galatians.

[38]Apparently because of the suddenness of this turn in the argument, for which very little heretofore has prepared us, the later textual tradition supplied the words τῇ ἀληθείᾳ μὴ πείθεσθαι ("so that you do not obey the truth") from the similar sentence in 5:7. The phrase is missing in all the early and best evidence (ℵ A B D* F G 6 33* 81 630 1739 pc lat sy^p co).

[39]The Western textual tradition (D F G lat), followed by the later Majority text, modified the verb with an added ἐν ὑμῖν ("among you"), apparently to reinforce that the "exhibit" took place as he lived among them while preaching the gospel. Lightfoot

of works of law did you receive the Spirit, or on the basis of the hearing of faith? [3]*Are you so foolish? Having begun by the Spirit, do you now come to completion*[40] *by the flesh?* [4]*Did you experience so many things in vain? If indeed it is in vain.* [5]*Therefore, he who supplies you with the Spirit and performs miracles among you, is it*[41] *on the basis of works of law or on the basis of the hearing of faith?*

The six (or five)[42] rhetorical questions with which this argument begins start with the Galatians' experience of Paul's preaching of Christ (v. 1), then move to their *initial reception* of the Spirit as proof positive that their new life in Christ is predicated on faith, not on "works of Law" (v. 2). That in turn leads to the twofold question which is the urgency of the entire letter, that they cannot begin one way and come to completion another (v. 3), which leads to yet one more moment of pure rhetoric: Have they experienced so much (of the Spirit's activity among them, is implied) in vain (v. 4)? Which in turn leads to an appeal to their *present experience* of the Spirit and his miraculous activity in their midst, that this too is by faith and has nothing at all to do with Law (v. 5).[43]

Thus, before engaging them in a scriptural demonstration that Abraham himself—and therefore all his "genuine" children—received both the covenantal promise and the blessing of God (in this case God's gift of righteousness) by faith, he begins by reminding them of their experience of the Spirit, which they received—and continue to experience—by faith.

1 From theologizing by way of personal testimony in 2:15–21, Paul turns to appeal directly to the Galatians and to their experience of Christ and the Spirit. But the appeal is scarcely reasoned argumentation. Rather, he goes straight for the jugular—with the arresting vocative,

---

134 expresses doubt, asking "how did it get in, if not original?" To which the answer is, "But why was it removed, if original?" The sentence is a historical anachronism under any circumstances—since the Galatians' eyes did *not* see Jesus Christ, and the removal of this phrase hardly mitigates the anachronism.

[40]Gk. ἐπιτελεῖσθε. Lull, *Spirit*, 42; Fung 133–34; and Longenecker 103 prefer the sense of "coming to perfection," as though the issue were Torah-observance as a way of being "perfect." But both the context of the letter as a whole and the use of these same two verbs in Phil 1:6 to refer to the "start" and "finish" of Christian life tell against such a view.

[41]Paul's sentence breaks down grammatically, since it has no verb. The supplying of these two words gets at his apparent intent.

[42]In the NA[26] Greek text the two clauses in v. 3 are punctuated as one question. More likely, as in my translation (cf. NRSV), they are two questions, which belong together to make a single point. Cf. Hansen, *Abraham*, 109.

[43]Having missed the central role of the Spirit in all of this, Lightfoot 136 implies that vv. 3–4 are a bit of a digression, and that v. 5 simply returns to the question of v. 2. This general view of things is shared by others (e.g., Fung, Longenecker), who, however, do not miss the role of the Spirit as Lightfoot does.

"O foolish[44] Galatians," and the even more arresting imagery of their being deceived by "an evil eye,"[45] those before whose eyes[46] Christ had been put on public display[47] as the crucified One. In terms of content, this first question thus picks up the emphasis in the preceding passage about Paul's being "crucified with Christ."[48] Here he describes his own ministry among them as the public exhibition of the reality of the crucifixion, wherein Christ "loved (us) and gave himself for (us)" (2:20). If righteousness came by means of "works of Law," then it is not of grace and Christ's death was of no avail (v. 21). Thus the first question, whose obvious point is that to submit to circumcision is to reject Christ.

2 But the appeal in v. 1, theologically necessary as it is and having priority as it does, is not sufficient in this situation to secure their allegiance to his gospel. Free people though they are in Christ, they are nonetheless freely submitting to the bondage of Jewish identity markers—as though Christ had died for nothing (2:21). To get to the argument of what Christ has done vis-à-vis the Law (vv. 6–22), Paul must first appeal to their own experience of life in Christ—that it began, and continues, on the basis of faith alone, quite apart from "works of Law." And so he turns to further rhetoric, reminding them of the experienced nature of their entrance into Christian life—through the dynamic working of the Spirit.

In view of their "bewitchment" and readiness to capitulate to "works of Law" (in this case, circumcision and the observance of days), Paul wants to learn "this one thing only"[49] from them. And he can narrow everything to this alone, because he was there when in their response to his preaching of Christ crucified they had received the Spirit.[50] Thus he begins his argument not with an appeal to theology but with an appeal to the life of the Spirit, which he will use to demonstrate the truthfulness of his theology—and the wrongness of their predilections.

---

[44]Gk. ἀνόητοι, which emphasizes the lack of ordinary good sense (cf. v. 3); cf. Burton 143: "The word . . . suggests failure to use one's powers of perception rather than natural stupidity."

[45]Gk. βασκαίνω, used in secular Greek to refer to being "bewitched" by spirits. See the references in Betz 131n31.

[46]Gk. οἷς κατ᾽ ὀφθαλμοὺς. This is probably a continuation of the metaphor; cf. Lightfoot 134.

[47]Gk. προεγράφη. This is the common word for the posting of public notices.

[48]Cf. Hays, *Faith*, who describes this phenomenon, which recurs in Galatians, as Paul's "operating 'in the mode of recapitulation.' "

[49]The τοῦτο μόνον ("this alone") stands in the emphatic first position in the sentence. He knows he has them on this one; their experience of the Spirit absolutely belies their willingness to submit to circumcision.

[50]On this point, Lull, *Spirit*, 53–95, is quite right that their dynamic, experienced reception of the Spirit came in response to Christian proclamation, not at the time of baptism. Cf. 1 Thes 1:5; 1 Cor 6:11; 2 Cor 1:21–22.

Paul's concern, of course, as the structure of the question and the context make plain, is that their relationship with God is predicated entirely on their trust in Christ, not on their submission to "works of Law." "On the basis of works of Law the Spirit did you receive, or on the basis of the hearing of faith (= believing what you heard)?" For our purposes, two matters in particular are significant from this second question.

First, along with many other passages throughout the corpus, this appeal to the "reception of the Spirit" as the evidence of entry into Christian life[51] demonstrates the crucial role the Spirit plays not only in Christian conversion but also as the singular "identity mark" of those who belong to Christ. After all, at issue throughout is proper evidence of identity. What uniquely distinguishes God's people, marks them off as inheritors of the promises made to Abraham? The agitators are urging circumcision, probably on the basis of Gentile inclusion in the covenant with Abraham in Gen 12:3 and 17:4–7, 12.[52] Paul argues for the Spirit. As this argument demonstrates, for Paul *the Spirit alone* functions as the seal of divine ownership,[53] the unmistakable evidence that one has entered into the life of the new aeon. As such, even though Paul's expressed contrasts for his present purposes are between "faith" and "works of Law," the ultimate contrast in this argument is between life under Law (= slavery) and life in the Spirit (= adoption as children).[54] The Spirit alone distinguishes God's people in the new covenant.

Second, the entire argument runs aground if this appeal is not also to a reception of the Spirit that was dynamically experienced.[55] Even

---

[51]Hunter, *Spirit-Baptism*, 33, suggests that the data "seem too ambiguous to determine what experience [of the Spirit] is in view." But the "ambiguity" rests with his tendency to read the text apart from its argument in context; thus he altogether slights the contrasts of "having begun" and "coming to completion" in this verse in favor of a view that sees v. 5 as the point of everything and vv. 2 and 3 existing merely to "offer an explanation of when and how the Spirit reception of v. 5 is effected." This not only turns Paul's concern on its head, but misses the emphasis on both their past (v. 2) and present (vv. 4–5) experience(s) of the Spirit *before the coming of Torah* as the certain evidence that Torah observance has no place at all in Christian life.

[52]That they were urging the circumcision of these Gentile converts is without question (see 5:2–3, 12; 6:12); that they were doing so on the basis of the Abrahamic covenant is the best way to make sense of the argument of 3:6–14 and 26–29.

[53]In light of the later church's penchant to tie the reception of the Spirit with water baptism, one is wont to add here, "and not water baptism" (cf. Lull, *Spirit*, 53–95, and Dunn, *Baptism*, 108–9). In the present case the idea that water baptism might have been involved with the reception of the Spirit is so foreign to the text, one would not even mention it negatively were it not so commonly assumed by others in their discussion of this passage. See also the discussion on 2 Cor 1:21–22.

[54]As 4:1–7 makes plain and as 5:13–6:10 will further amplify.

[55]A point that is all too frequently missed in the commentaries (although see Ramsay 326–28; Burton 147; Erdman 61; Mussner 208; Betz 130, 132). For example, Dunn, *Baptism*, 107–9, misses this emphasis in his desire to discount Pentecostalism in this passage—a point he rectifies somewhat in *Jesus*, 202.

though Paul seldom mentions any of the visible evidences of the Spirit in such contexts as these,[56] here is the demonstration that the experience of the Spirit in the Pauline churches was very much as that described and understood by Luke—as visibly and experientially accompanied by phenomena that gave certain evidence of the presence of the Spirit of God. Not only is this the clear point of the rest of the argument in vv. 4–5, but such an understanding alone makes the present rhetoric possible at all.[57] Not only so, but such an experienced reality best accounts for the way Paul picks up the argument about life in the Spirit in 5:13–6:10. Many of the difficulties moderns have with that passage (q.v.)—and its promises—lie with the general lack of appreciation for the dynamically experienced nature of life in the Spirit in the early church.

3 With two further questions, full of sting, Paul ties together and applies the rhetoric of the first two questions to the scene in Galatia, thus demonstrating their own self-contradiction.[58] Indeed, here is the heart of the matter—which drives the argument of the entire letter: "So foolish are you (cf. v. 1)? Having begun[59] by the Spirit[60] (v. 2) now by the flesh do you finish?"[61] This is the question to which the entire argument of the letter is devoted as a response. Which in turn means that the question is not, "How does one gain right standing with God? How are people saved?" but, "Once given right standing with God, how is such a relationship sustained or maintained?" The real question, finally, is the role of Torah observance at all in Christian life. On this Paul is adamant. There is none. As he will argue in 5:13–15, the *whole* of Torah is fulfilled

---

[56]The exceptions are 2 Cor 12:12 and Rom 15:18–19, where in sober matter-of-fact statements Paul notes what God had accomplished through him to bring about the obedience of the Gentiles, "by the power of signs and wonders, by the power of the Holy Spirit." If there are not more such statements in Paul, it is only because visible evidences of the Spirit's presence were presuppositional for him and his churches; and he refused to appeal to them for the very reason that they might deflect from the essential message of the gospel of a crucified Messiah. Even so, these are references to extraordinary evidences of the Spirit that accompanied his ministry, which is not precisely the same thing to which he is appealing here, namely, to the Galatians' powerful experience of the Spirit in their lives.

[57]So, e.g., Burton 147; Longenecker 102. MacArthur 167 tends to deny the dynamic and visible dimension altogether; but, then, he shows very little appreciation for the force of Paul's rhetoric.

[58]As Betz 133 has pointed out.

[59]Gk. ἐναρξάμενοι; cf. the similar use of these two verbs in Phil 1:6 to refer to the beginning and eschatological conclusion of their life in Christ. See also n. 51 above.

[60]Gk. πνεύματι; on this usage see the discussion in ch. 2 on Pauline usage. Given the arthrous usage in v. 2, "the Spirit did you receive," this passage is a clear example that the anarthrous usage in this dative formula can only mean "by the Spirit."

[61]Part of the power of the rhetoric is the perfect chiasmus in which this is expressed: ἐναρξάμενοι (A) πνεύματι (B) νῦν (C) σαρκὶ (B′) ἐπιτελεῖσθε (A′); which I have tried to capture in the translation.

in the one command, "You shall love your neighbor as yourself," which command is now fulfilled as the fruit of the Spirit.

This question also demonstrates the correctness of the observation made above, that the ultimate contrast with which Paul deals in this letter is not between "faith" and "works of Law," but between life in the Spirit—lived out always by faith—and Torah observance. This is what makes 5:13–6:10 a crucial part of the *argument* of Galatians, not simply a collection of paraenesis added at the end, after the theological argument is in place. The ethical result of the life of the Spirit is part of the essential argument of the letter, since this is the burning question, "How do believers *live?*" And the answer given here is the surprising one, but fully in keeping with Paul's theology as it emerges elsewhere. Not by "works of Law," which he here describes as "coming to completion *by means of the flesh*"!

This is the second appearance in the corpus of a direct contrast between "flesh" and "Spirit."[62] In this instance an obvious word play is in process. The word σαρκί ("by flesh") first of all refers to the literal cutting of the flesh in circumcision.[63] But in Paul it is never that simple, since σάρξ is also used as his main description of life before and outside of Christ. To live σαρκί is to live according to the values and desires of life in the present aeon that stands in absolute contradiction to God and his ways.[64] Hence the ultimate contrasts in Paul are eschatological: life "according to the flesh," lived according to the present age that has been condemned through the cross and is passing away; or life "according to the Spirit," lived in keeping with the values and norms of the coming aeon inaugurated by Christ through his death and resurrection and empowered by the eschatological Spirit.[65] The surprising dimension to this response is Paul's willingness to equate coming to completion "in the flesh" with submission to "works of Law," a point that will be clarified later in chapter 5 and will be made again in Romans 7–8 and Phil 3:2–3 (q.v.). Since life before and outside Christ is described as "flesh," and since compliance with the identity markers of the people of God under the former covenant is to revert to life before Christ, to submit to "works of Law" is therefore to revert to life in "the flesh." Not only so, but for Paul

---

[62]See 1 Cor 3:1–2; cf. 2 Cor 1:12, 17; 5:14–17; and 10:2–3, where this theological contrast underlines Pauline σάρξ language.

[63]As the usage in 6:12–13 confirms; cf. Betz 124. Burton 148 limits it to this meaning altogether (despite 4:29 and 5:16–6:8); Fung 134 and Longenecker 103, however, limit it strictly to the later theological usage. Cf. the similar word play in Phil 3:3.

[64]Thus "flesh" in Paul does not first of all refer to one's own "sinful nature," nor does it refer primarily to "what is merely human" (as Barclay, *Obeying*, 206). While it sometimes can mean the latter, when the usage is pejorative, it refers to what is "human and over against God in deliberate fallenness."

[65]On this whole matter see esp. the discussion on 2 Cor 5:14–17 in ch. 5.

the issue is finally theological; to submit to circumcision is to put one's confidence before God in that which is merely an expression of "flesh." This becomes, therefore, *self*-confidence, rather than trust in Christ and him alone for a proper relationship with God.

Understandably Paul is frustrated with the situation in Galatia. To yield to Jewish identity markers is neither an innocent rapprochement of Jewish believers nor necessary for Gentile inclusion into the full privileges of the covenant with Abraham. This is *not* the way to become members of the people of God in the new aeon; rather, it is to "rebuild" what Christ has dismantled (2:18), to try "to come to completion by means of the flesh."

4 Still reflecting on the absurdity of it all, Paul again turns to rhetoric—this time with yet another ad hominem question (cf. v. 1): "Did you experience so many things in vain?" This question is designed to point out the implications if they follow on their present course; it is the precursor of what is said with a plain indicative in 5:4. To capitulate to "works of Law" is to revert to life in the flesh; and to do that is to have experienced life in the Spirit "in vain." It is to "cut themselves off from Christ," to "fall away from grace." In this first instance, of course, Paul is not suggesting that such has yet happened. The rhetoric expresses disbelief that people who had had "such remarkable experiences"[66] should even consider coming under Torah. To do so is tantamount to having experienced life in the Spirit "in vain." This is simply another way of reinforcing the previous question (v. 3).

The idea that people could have genuinely believed "in vain" has traditionally been a stone of theological stumbling. But the question needs to be kept within its Pauline context. He speaks earlier and later of the possibility of his having labored "in vain" (2:2; 4:11); and expresses similar concern over his converts in 1 Cor 15:2.[67] In the present case he is not ready to allow that such has really happened; thus his quick disclaimer: "If indeed it has been in vain." Whether or not such *might* happen is yet another question, to which Paul would certainly allow a yes.[68] But whenever he comes close to allowing as much about any of his converts, he readily offers the disclaimer that he does not really believe that they have taken such a drastic step. And in this case, Paul has already said something similar about Christ's death in 2:21, which he obviously cannot believe is true either really or hypothetically.

More significantly for our purposes is that Paul can again appeal to "such remarkable experiences" when referring to their initial entry into

---

[66]This is the translation in BAGD (under τοσοῦτος 2 a β).
[67]Cf. also Phil 2:16.
[68]Cf. Bligh 232–33.

life in Christ through the Spirit. This question, and that in v. 5, seem to confirm what was argued above as to the visible and experiential nature of such Spirit life.

But in this case not all scholars think so, since the verb that Paul uses for "experienced" elsewhere in his letters always means "to suffer."[69] Thus many English translations have followed the KJV: "Have ye suffered so many things in vain?"[70] However, Pauline usage, significant as this is in most circumstances, is in this case the *only* thing in favor of translating the verb "suffered." Against it are: (1) the clear sense of the context, in which the traditional meaning of the word makes eminently good sense; (2) that in contrast to most of Paul's other letters there is not the slightest hint in this one that the churches of Galatia were undergoing suffering, not to mention suffering τοσαῦτα (so many things); and (3) that the word order puts the τοσαῦτα in the emphatic first position, referring to what has just been said in vv. 2–3, not to "so many things in general."[71] That v. 5 picks up on this question by putting their past experiences in light of their current experience of the Spirit seems to be the clincher. Otherwise the question sits in the middle of an appeal to their experience of the Spirit, past and present, as something of a rock, with no specific reference to the immediate context.

5 If the Galatians' past experience of the Spirit is not enough to convince them that their relationship to God is based on faith alone, Paul will try one more time—this time appealing to their ongoing life in the Spirit as a community of worshipping believers.[72] This question is thus joined to the others, and especially to the disclaimer in v. 4b, by an inferential "therefore," whose sense the NRSV captures best by translating, "well then."[73] It follows, Paul seems to be arguing, that if indeed you

---

[69]Gk. πάσχω; see the discussion in BAGD. The word traditionally meant "to experience, or be treated," referring to everything that can befall a person, whether good or ill. Eventually it came to be used predominantly of unfortunate experiences, although references to good experience still obtained. If indeed, as the context demands, the present usage refers to the experience of the Spirit in vv. 2–3, then this is the only time in the NT it is used in this positive way.

[70]Thus the NIV: "Have you suffered so much for nothing?" Cf. NASB, Williams, Living Bible, Phillips; so also Calvin, Meyer, Lightfoot, Burton, Erdman, Duncan (contra Moffatt's translation), Bruce, Michaelis (*TDNT* 5.905), Cosgrove (*Cross*, 185; a change from his dissertation). Otherwise NRSV: "Did you experience so much for nothing?" Cf. RSV, NAB, NEB, JB, Weymouth, Moffatt, Lietzmann, Ridderbos, Schlier, Hendriksen, Bligh, Mussner, Betz, Fung, Cole, Longenecker, Lull (*Spirit*, 78n35), Hays (*Faith*, 197).

[71]A point made also by Ridderbos 115 and Mussner 209.

[72]But see Cosgrove, *Cross*, 2, who sees this question as the key to the problem in Galatia.

[73]This οὖν is often seen to be resumptive, going back to v. 2 (so Lightfoot, Burton, Schlier, Longenecker). But see Cosgrove, *Cross*, 46, and Betz 135.

began life in the Spirit, and in light of how much of the Spirit's presence you have experienced—all by faith quite apart from Torah—then so too with your present experience of the Spirit:[74] the rich supply of the Spirit in your midst, including the working of miracles, *therefore*, cannot be related to Torah; to the contrary, everything is based on faith in Christ. What follows, then, is yet another question that again has as its focal concern that life in Christ is based on faith, not on "works of Law." But again, as in v. 2, what lies behind the question presuppositionally is of considerable importance to his being able to make this appeal. Three matters are of significance.

First, Paul turns the appeal toward God, by reminding them that God is the one who continually and liberally "supplies[75] you with the Spirit."[76] Thus their attention is once more drawn to God, as the one ultimately responsible both for the gift of the Spirit and thus for the work of the Spirit in their midst. Moreover, as with the similar passages in 1 Thes 4:8 and Phil 1:19, the clear implication is that even though they have already received the Spirit, there is another sense in which God "supplies" the Spirit again and again.[77] However, in contrast to the other two passages, here the emphasis is on what happens in the community. Every "manifestation" of the Spirit among them "for their common good" (cf. 1 Cor 12:7) is to be understood as God's supply of the Spirit in their community life.

Second, the close tie between the two participles, "who supplies the Spirit and works miracles," suggests that these two ideas are to be held firmly together. That is, God is present among them by his Spirit, and the fresh supply of the Spirit finds expression in miraculous deeds of various kinds. Thus Paul is appealing once more to the visible and experiential nature of the Spirit *in their midst*[78] as the ongoing evidence

---

[74]A point missed, e.g., by Burton 151; Ridderbos 116; Longenecker 105, who correctly see that the charismatic Spirit is in view, but somehow miss the change to the present tense and therefore view v. 5 as a resumption ("summary," Longenecker) of vv. 2–4.

[75]Gk. ἐπιχορηγέω. See on Phil 1:19 for a discussion of this word and its meaning in these two passages. That τὸ πνεῦμα serves here as the expressed object of the "supply" and that the verb is inherently transitive, even when in the passive, combine to verify this meaning for the similar language in Philippians. Lightfoot 136 suggests that the compound form (ἐπι-) especially implies "liberally." Cosgrove, *Cross*, 48, offers "sustaining" as an alternative translation, but without lexical support.

[76]Contra J. K. Parratt, "Romans i.11 and Galatians iii.5—Pauline evidence for the Laying on of Hands?" *ExpT* 79 (1967–68) 151–52, whose prior interest in finding "laying on of hands" in Paul dictates his exegesis, which disregards the linguistic and contextual evidence. He suggests that τὸ πνεῦμα refers to any charismatically endowed individual.

[77]So also Cosgrove, *Cross*, 47–48; otherwise Stott 71, who regards both passages as referring to the Galatians' conversion, from the two perspectives of their reception and the divine impartation.

[78]So most commentators, against Lightfoot 136, who curiously opts for "in you."

that life in the Spirit,[79] predicated on faith in Christ Jesus, has no place at all for "works of Law."

Third, the thoroughly presuppositional nature of this final appeal serves as further evidence, along with 1 Corinthians 14 and 1 Thes 5:19–22 (cf. 2 Thes 2:2), of the genuinely "charismatic" nature of the Pauline churches.[80] The evidence from 1 and 2 Thessalonians (and elsewhere) indicates that prophecy was a regular and expected phenomenon in his churches; 1 Corinthians indicates that speaking in tongues was also a part of the broad experience of Spirit phenomena. This text shows that what Paul elsewhere calls "signs and wonders" was also a regular and expected expression of their life in the Spirit. What we cannot know from this distance, of course, is all that Paul would have understood by the phrase, "works miracles among you." But similar phrasing elsewhere in the corpus suggests a variety of supernatural phenomena, including healings.[81]

Those who tend to think otherwise about these texts do so much less on exegetical grounds than on existential ones.[82] Our own experience of the church tends to cause us to be either unfamiliar or quite uncomfortable with such phenomena. We would prefer to believe that the Pauline churches were more like ours and less like the Pauline and Lukan documents suggest they really were. But the evidence in this case seems incontrovertible: the Spirit lay near the center of Pauline theology precisely because the experience of the Spirit in the life of the believer and the church was such a central feature of their experience and existence as believers.

From this appeal to their individual and corporate *experience* of the Spirit, Paul will now turn to take on the *biblical interpretation* of the agitators, by demonstrating from Scripture that the true inheritors of the Abrahamic covenant—his genuine children—are those who, as Abraham, live by faith and in Christ have become heirs of the covenantal promise, which Paul will argue, is fulfilled by none other than the Spirit (vv. 6–14).

---

[79]Lightfoot, Hendriksen, and MacArthur entertain the option that "miracles" have to do with the "moral world" (Lightfoot); but that flies full in the face of the argument, not to mention the meaning of this word in Paul.

[80]A point also made by Lull, *Spirit*, 53–95, correctly so in terms of conclusions, but at times with questionable exegesis as far as details are concerned.

[81]See the discussion above on 1 Cor 12:9–10. With a great deal more confidence than I could muster, Lull, *Spirit*, 70, asserts that "δυνάμεις comprise a well-known class of ecstatic phenomena." His ability to include speech phenomena under this category comes from a questionable analysis of the list of "charismata" in 1 Cor 12:8–10, while at the same time neglecting Paul's other uses of this terminology.

[82]As, e.g., MacArthur 69, who suggests that "miracles" here really means "powers," of basically nonmiraculous kinds, or that otherwise it refers to *past* miracles, at the beginning of their life in Christ. Such comments have very little to do with Paul and very much to do with theological pre-judgments.

GALATIANS 3:13–14[83]

[13]*Christ purchased us from the curse of the law, having become a curse for us—since it is written: "Cursed is everyone hanged on a tree"—*[14]*in order that the blessing of Abraham might in Christ Jesus be for the Gentiles, in order that we might receive the promise of the Spirit by faith.*

The question in v. 5 brings an end to Paul's appeal to their experience of the Spirit as the first line of evidence that the Galatian believers' attraction to Jewish identity markers is sheer madness (they are "bewitched" v. 1). With that he turns in vv. 6–14 to offer scriptural proof that the life of faith, verified by life in the Spirit, excludes any possibility that it also includes adherence to Torah. Up to this point (beginning in 2:16) he has repeatedly made the two points, that "righteousness," evidenced by the Spirit, is "not by works of Law" but "by faith in Christ Jesus." In vv. 6–9 he has argued on the basis of Gen 15:6 (LXX) and 12:3 (but in the language of 18:18) that it is "by faith in Christ Jesus."[84] Two matters were of significance for Paul in those texts: (1) that Abraham himself was declared righteous on the basis of faith; and (2) that it is in Abraham that all the Gentiles were to be blessed. Thus the Gentiles are already included as Abraham's children on the basis of what Torah says

---

[83]*Bibliography*: J. P. **Braswell**, " 'The Blessing of Abraham' versus 'the Curse of the Law': Another Look at Gal 3:10–13," *WTJ* 53 (1991) 73–91; F. F. **Bruce**, "The Curse of the Law," in *Paul and Paulinism* (ed. M. D. Hooker and S. G. Wilson; London: SPCK, 1982) 27–36; **Cosgrove**, *Cross*, 52–61; T. L. **Donaldson**, " The 'Curse of the Law' and the Inclusion of the Gentiles: Galatians 3.13–14," *NTS* 32 (1986) 94–112; James D. G. **Dunn**, "Works of the Law and the Curse of the Law (Gal. 3.10–14)," *NTS* 31 (1985) 523–42 (repr. in *Jesus, Paul and the Law*, 215–41); David **Hill**, "Salvation Proclaimed: IV. Galatians 3:10–14," *ExpT* 93 (1982) 196–200; J. **Lambrecht**, "Vloek en zegen. Een studie van Galaten 3,10–14," *Collationes* 21 (1991) 133–57; Martin **Noth**, "For All Who Rely on Works of the Law are under a Curse," in *The Laws in the Pentateuch and Other Studies* (Edinburgh/London: Oliver & Boyd, 1966) 118–31; **Stanley**, "Under," 481–511; Sam K. **Williams**, "*Promise* in Galatians: A Reading of Paul's Reading of Scripture," *JBL* 107 (1988) 709–20; N. T. **Wright**, "Curse and Covenant: Galatians 3:10–14," in *The Climax of the Covenant* (Minneapolis: Fortress, 1991) 137–56.

[84]Most commentators suggest that the καθώς that begins v. 6 is either an example of a (rare) absolute use at the beginning of a sentence or an abbreviated form of "even as it stands written." More likely it is neither, but rather belongs to v. 5 as an explanatory example. To Paul's question, "by works of Law or by the hearing of faith?" the implied answer is: "by the hearing of faith, just as Abraham 'believed God and it was credited to him as righteousness.' " Cf. Williams, "Justification," 93, and esp. Stanley, "Under," 493, who therefore also (correctly) argues that vv. 1–14 should be viewed as a single argument, in which Scripture is seen to verify their experience—although I would differ with him as to the aim of the whole argument (the Spirit as evidence of something else, as I am arguing, or a focus on the Spirit himself, and how they received the Spirit, as Stanley argues [cf. Cosgrove]).

about Abraham and about the Gentiles' relationship to Abraham, in that they live by faith as he did.

Now, in vv. 10–14, Paul argues that righteousness is "not by works of Law."[85] This, too, is supported by Scripture, in three ways: (1) everyone who is "by works of Law" is under a curse, from which they need redemption; the curse turns out to be the obligation to live by Torah, including the whole of Torah;[86] (2) Scripture, on the other hand, says that the δίκαιος ("righteous") person *shall live by faith*; Torah is not of faith, since Scripture also says that those who do them ("the laws"; in this case by yielding to circumcision) will live *by them* (meaning by Torah, and thus not by faith);[87] and (3) that Christ himself delivered us from the curse of living "by works of Law," because "cursed [also] is everyone who hangs on a tree."

Our sentence brings this argument to conclusion, in two ways: (1) by joining the experience of the Spirit in vv. 2–5 with the argument in vv. 6–12; thus the blessing of Abraham, which included the Gentiles, is based on faith and faith alone, the evidence for which is the gift of the Spirit, who is the fulfillment of the promise made to Abraham; and (2) by arguing that this was the ultimate goal of Christ's having become a curse for us. This goal is expressed in the two purpose clauses of v. 14: (a) in order that in Christ the "blessing of Abraham" might be realized for the Gentiles, and (b) that "we" by faith in Christ Jesus might receive the promise made to Abraham, which has been fulfilled by the Spirit's presence.

Since much of this is not especially self-evident, either in the texts or in the argument as it unfolds, a few further words of explanation are needed, especially regarding how Paul understands "the blessing of Abraham" and how that relates to the "promise," mentioned here for the first time in the argument, but a central feature in what follows.

First, one must decide on the relationship of the two ἵνα ("in order that") clauses to one another. In its barest form, and with Paul's emphases, the sentence reads:

---

[85]One should not miss the close ties of this paragraph with v. 9. Not only are they joined by an explanatory γάρ, but by the sharp contrasts between οἱ ἐκ πίστεως and ὅσοι ἐξ ἔργων νόμου ("those based on faith/as many as are based on works of Law") and between the former as "blessed" and the latter as "cursed." Stott's division of the argument, therefore, into vv. 1–9 and 10–14 (the latter entitled, "The Alternative of Faith and Works") probably says more about Stott's theological interests than about the form of Paul's argumentation.

[86]Contrary to what is often assumed, Paul's does *not* make the point—at least not here—that the curse lies in the fact that one must therefore keep the whole Law, which is something one cannot actually do. Rather the curse lies in being under Torah at all, which means that one must thereby *live by Torah*, thus excluding the other (essential) option, to *live by faith*.

[87]On the understanding of v. 12, cf. S. Westerholm, *Israel's Law and the Church's Faith: Paul and his Recent Interpreters* (Grand Rapids: Eerdmans, 1988) 111–12.

Christ	freed	*us*	from	the curse of the Law	
	by having become	for *us*	a curse		

	in order that	unto the Gentiles	the blessing	might be
			of Abraham	in Christ Jesus

	in order that	the promise		*we* might receive
		of the Spirit		through faith

Several observations are in order: (1) In light of Paul's own interpretation in vv. 11–12 of his citation of Deut 27:26 in v. 10, the genitive "of the Law" is probably in apposition to "the curse." Thus: by becoming a curse for us, Christ has freed us from the curse, from Torah with its regulatory obligations.[88] Further substantiation for this is 4:5, where with the same verb[89] Paul specifically says that the Father sent his Son in order to "redeem those *under Torah.*" This, after all, is the point of everything.[90] In one sense the concern throughout—apart from 19–22—is that Torah observance itself is a curse, for Jew and Gentile alike, which Christ's death has brought to an end. Paul's concern is not with the punishment that failure to keep Torah has engendered. True as that might be, and popular as such a view is,[91] Paul simply does not speak to such a question; not only so, but that would deflect from his central concern throughout his argument that Christ has brought an end to Torah observance. And Torah observance is the curse that has to be removed—by Christ having become a curse for us.

(2) The sudden appearance of "us/we" is noteworthy. To this point it has all been "you (Gentile Galatians)." But when he turns to *apply* the biblical text, Paul becomes inclusive, "Christ freed *us.*" This may mean nothing more than what often happens in such soteriological moments in Paul, where a third person narrative or second person argument becomes confessional, hence first person plural, so as to include himself with his readers.[92] But in this case it probably means more than that,

---

[88]For a similar view see Cosgrove, *Cross*, 52–61; Stanley ("Under," 496–507) offers a slightly different view, which comes out at a similar place. He sees the "curse of the Law" to be the *potential* curse that Gentiles would come under were they forced now to "live by doing the Law" (v. 12)—which excludes living by faith (v. 11)—inasmuch as they would not be able to "do all that is demanded" (v. 10).

[89]Gk. ἐξαγοράω, "purchase so as to set free."

[90]This is not to suggest that in its present form this sentence does not refer to the atonement. The language of "redemption" and "having become a curse ὑπὲρ ἡμῶν [*for us*]" indicates otherwise. But Paul's intent is not so much to make a statement about the nature of the atonement as such (as though the curse were the "punishment" of law-breaking from which we have been redeemed), as to locate the atonement as the place where Jew and Gentile alike were redeemed from the curse of "doing Law," which meant they could now live "by faith."

[91]This traditional view is based on the citation in v. 10 itself, *not* on Paul's explication of it in vv. 11–12.

[92]See, e.g., 1 Thes 5:9; 1 Cor 1:18, 30; 5:7; 15:3, 57; Rom 5:1–5; 8:4, 15; and throughout the corpus.

having to do also with himself as representing Jews. Thus he moves in turn from "Christ freed *us*," to "in order that the blessing of Abraham might be *for the Gentiles*," and then back again to "in order that *we* through faith might receive the promise of the Spirit."[93] In any case, the "we" in this final sentence, as in 4:5–6, most likely means "we believers, Jew and Gentile alike."

(3) These two points together suggest that the two clauses are to be understood as parallel to each other in some way,[94] most likely as a kind of "constructive" synonymous parallelism; that is, they are parallel to one another, but in a way in which the second takes the first a step further.[95] How so, will need explanation:

(a) The first clause points back to v. 8, where Paul cited Gen 12:3 in the language of Gen 18:18 to the effect that God had previously announced the good news to Abraham that "*in you* all the Gentiles will be blessed."[96] He is now arguing that by Christ's having become a curse "for us," he freed us—Jew and Gentile alike—from the curse of being under the obligations of Torah, so that, by removing what stood in the way of faith, Christ has made it possible for Gentiles to enter into their rightful inheritance in the "blessing of Abraham."

(b) In light of the argument of vv. 6–7, the language "the blessing of Abraham" in its first instance surely refers to Abraham's having "been reckoned as righteous through faith."[97] But Paul's concern is not simply with what happened to Abraham, but with the implications of these passages for Abraham's offspring. His urgency is to demonstrate that the

---

[93]None of this is self-evident, of course, and there is considerable debate on this issue. See the discussion in Donaldson, "Curse," who takes a position similar to the one argued here. Wright, *Climax*, 154, makes the second "we" refer to "we Christian Jews," but he allows that the position taken here may be right.

[94]That is, the shift from "the Gentiles" to "us" in the second clause seems to exclude the other grammatical option that the second clause is dependent on the first. Despite Stanley and others to the contrary, "that *we* might receive the promise of the Spirit" makes little sense as dependent on *the Gentiles* as present recipients of the blessing of Abraham. So Meyer 157; Burton 176; Lagrange 73; Ridderbos 125; Guthrie 99; Schlier 140; Hendriksen 131; Mussner 234–35; Boice 460; Bruce 167; Fung 151; Longenecker 123; Sanders, *PLJP*, 22; Byrne, '*Sons*,' 156. Otherwise Lightfoot 140; Duncan 103 (qualified); Betz 152; Stanley, "Under," 494.

[95]Cf. Hendriksen 131: "They cover the same ground, the second explaining the first."

[96]Although Paul does not explicitly make a point of it, this future tense, with its inherent promise of fulfillment, is what has now come to pass through the cross and the Spirit.

[97]By his dismissal of 2:15–21 as having significance for the argument, Cosgrove, *Cross*, 50–51, denies that Paul intends this at all. While I tend to agree that Paul's point rests ultimately in the application *he* makes, not in the OT text per se, it is difficult to escape the implication Cosgrove makes (35–37), that arguments build internally in this letter, so that a second or third mention of a motif—especially in a carefully selected quote—is intended to be heard in light of the earlier occurrences.

true offspring of Abraham, by way of his one true seed Christ Jesus (vv. 15–18), are those who, as Abraham, are *also* reckoned as righteous by faith—as the thesis statement in v. 7 makes clear. What he now wants to demonstrate is that this "promised blessing" for the Gentiles has been fulfilled through Christ's death, which did away with "works of Torah" for both Jew and Gentile.

(c) That leads us finally to the second clause, in which Paul declares that "*we* have received the promise of the Spirit through faith," a clause that by its function in parallel to the first clause and by its language seems intended to tie their experience of the Spirit in vv. 1–5 to the "blessing of Abraham" in vv. 6–9.[98] But it is a blessing in which Jew and Gentile participate together, because Christ has removed the curse—the necessity of Torah observance. Since the "blessing of Abraham" came in the form of a "promise," that word, even though it does not occur in the Genesis narrative, becomes the way Paul speaks of the "blessing of Abraham" throughout the rest of the argument. Indeed, this shift of language becomes crucial to the argument, because Paul's concern is not simply with the fact that the "blessing" included the Gentiles, but that for Abraham "and his seed" (vv. 15–18) it came only as *promise*—to be fulfilled later *in his seed*. In the rest of the argument the primary reference point of this "promised blessing" is the concept of "inheritance," which for Paul finally refers to "being Abraham's *heirs*," thus his true children.

(d) For our purposes the more significant turn in the second clause is that in its first occurrence in this argument "the promise" is fulfilled in their having experienced the Spirit.[99] The genitive, "the promise of the Spirit," in this case is probably not appositional in the strict sense, meaning either "the promise, that is, the Spirit" or "the promised Holy Spirit."[100] Rather, the "promised inheritance"—which includes the Gentiles—is now interpreted in light of vv. 1–5 as having been *fulfilled* for "us" through the gift of the Spirit.[101] Thus, in keeping with what has been said in vv. 1–5 and what will be said in the argument that follows, Paul asserts that the Spirit is the way the promised blessing made to

---

[98]So also Burton 177; Erdman 65; Ridderbos 128; Stanley, "Under," 495. Even though I disagree with the latter over the main focus of the present argument, I am in full agreement with his conclusions: "The Galatians' experience of receiving the Spirit by faith is a sign that God's promise to bless the Gentiles through Abraham has now become a reality in their midst. . . . The presence of God's Spirit among the Gentiles (including those in Galatia) is definitive proof that they have now entered into the full 'blessing' promised by God to his people."

[99]Cf. Cosgrove, *Cross*, 50: "Paul identifies the promise (explicitly) and the blessing (by implication) with the gift of the Spirit (3:14)."

[100]As, e.g., Burton 176 and others. In any case, it does not refer to the Spirit as guarantor of the (still) *future* promise, as in the metaphors "down payment" and "firstfruits." Cf. Williams, "*Promise*," 711.

[101]Cf. Lagrange 74; Erdman 65; and esp. Byrne, '*Sons*,' 156–57.

Abraham has been realized in all of Abraham's true children, who are "by
faith in Christ Jesus." The "blessing of Abraham" is not simply "justification by faith."[102] Rather, it points toward the eschatological life now
available to Jews and Gentiles alike, effected through Christ's death, but
realized through the dynamic ministry of the Spirit—and all of this by faith.

(e) Nonetheless, even though "the promise" in this case joins their
experience of the Spirit to their inheriting the blessing of Abraham, such
language in Paul is probably also to be understood in terms of "the
promised Holy Spirit" of the prophetic tradition. That is, despite the fact
that Paul does not here make a point of it, it is difficult to escape the
conclusion that in Pauline theology when "promise" refers to the Spirit,
it also inherently includes the theme of the promised new covenant of
Jeremiah by way of Ezekiel, whose purposes are fulfilled by the coming
of the Spirit. On this matter see the discussion of 2 Cor 3:1–18.

The net result of all of this is an understanding of the text that may
be paraphrased: "By having become a curse for us, Christ freed us from
the curse of being under the obligations of Torah . . . , so that Gentiles
might now receive the promised blessing of Abraham—sonship through
righteousness by faith—and thus, at the same time, that we both, Jew
and Gentile alike, might through faith experience the fulfillment of the
promise in the person of the Holy Spirit."

Thus, as in vv. 1–5, the Spirit is the primary evidence,[103] derived from
their having come to faith in Christ, that the Galatians have already
become the people of God and do not need to come under the obligations
of Torah, which for Paul means to come under the curse of having to
live by Torah and thus to exclude living by faith. At the same time the
Spirit is presuppositionally understood in terms of eschatological fulfillment. Here is the substantiation that the time of Torah and "flesh" is
past, that the new aeon has dawned. The promise of inheritance has
already been realized in measure by the coming of the Spirit. Here is the
fulfillment of the promised blessing of Abraham that Gentiles will join
Jews as Abraham's heirs. Thus, even though the Spirit is mentioned but
once—at the end of the paragraph—he again plays the key role in the
argument from Scripture that Torah's day has come to an end, the full
implications of which will be spelled out in 5:13–6:10.

GALATIANS 3:15–18[104]

*[15]Brothers and sisters, I give an analogy from everyday life: once a person's
will has been ratified no one can either set it aside or annul it. [16]Now [by way*

---

[102] As Boice 460 and others would have it.

[103] In keeping with his perspective on vv. 1–5, Lightfoot makes no comment on
the Spirit at all in this passage.

[104] Since I do not intend to exegete this paragraph as such, but only to wrestle

of application], the promises were made [by God] to Abraham and to his seed. That is, the biblical text does not say, "and to his seeds," as though the promise were made to many; but, as it were, to one, that is, "and to your seed," which we must therefore understand to be Christ. [17]Now I will apply this further: Torah, which came some 430 years later, does not annul the will that was ratified by God, so as to render the promise null and void. [18]For if the inheritance were based on Torah, it is no longer based on the promise. But in fact God graciously gave it [the inheritance] to Abraham on the basis of his promise to him.

This text is included in this discussion not because the Spirit is referred to, even indirectly, but because of the recurrence of the "promise" motif, which in v. 14 had been interpreted in terms of believers' having received the gift of the Spirit. "Promise" is the operative word in this paragraph, in which Paul is offering further scriptural proof for his position that "righteousness is not by works of Law but by faith in Christ Jesus," as is evidenced by the fact that these Gentile converts have already received the gift of the promised eschatological Spirit.

On the basis of "an everyday analogy" and of the language of Gen 13:15, Paul makes two crucial points: first, that Christ as Abraham's one true offspring, is the one who singularly inherits the promises made to Abraham; second, that the coming of the Law some 430 years after the promise was made to Abraham cannot set aside that promise. In a slightly different way Paul is repeating his twofold theme from 2:16, "not by works of Law" but "by faith in Christ Jesus."

Our concern is with the meaning of "promise" in this argument, which in v. 18a is indicated as having to do with "the inheritance." Here, then, is the first occurrence of another crucial word in the argument, especially in the double conclusions of 3:29 and 4:7, where people freed from the slavery of Law through Christ are Abraham's true children, the true heirs of the promised inheritance. Paul's fluid use of metaphors causes the argument to become a bit fuzzy at the end, but the "inheritance" most likely has to do with becoming God's children in the new aeon through the work of Christ and the Spirit, and especially with the inclusion of Gentiles among God's children (cf. vv. 7–9).[105]

In the present text, therefore, the "promise" does not so much refer directly to the Spirit,[106] despite v. 14, but to the "inheritance." But as v. 14 and 4:4–7 indicate, the "inheritance" is to be understood as having

---

with the concept of the promise contained herein, I have chosen in this instance to offer an expanded, somewhat paraphrastic, "translation" so as to point out the direction in which the exegesis would go.

[105] Cf. 4:5–6 and 4:29, where being God's children in the present age is predicated directly on the presence and ministry of the Spirit.

[106] As Cosgrove, *Cross*, 61–65, and Williams, *"Promise,"* contend.

been realized through the coming of the Spirit.[107] The Spirit is for Paul the means by which all the concerns of the letter are held together: righteousness by faith, Gentile inclusion, the blessing of Abraham, the promise(s) of God, the inheritance. These all merge in the double conclusions of 3:26–29 and 4:4–7, in which Gentile participation in the inheritance as God's true children apart from Torah has been effected by Christ and realized through the gift of the Spirit.

Because this is so, the Spirit lingers very near the surface throughout the rest of the argument, even when not directly mentioned—especially in vv. 21–22 that follow.

GALATIANS 3:21–22

[21]*Does the Law, then, stand over against the promises of God? Not at all! For if a form of Law had been given that was able to give life, then indeed righteousness would have been based on Law.* [22]*But the Scripture has imprisoned everything under sin, in order that the promise, based on faith in Christ Jesus, might be given to those who believe.*

Although this is another text in which the Spirit is not specifically mentioned, both the language and the implied contrasts in this sentence indicate that the Spirit is not only hovering nearby in Paul's thinking, but actually lies behind the language "to give life" and "the promise." This is all the more so, if our understanding of v. 14 is correct, that the "promise" in that verse is being interpreted in terms of the Spirit as the way in which the promise made to Abraham has found its fulfillment.

In vv. 19–22 the argument takes a slight turn. The appeals to their experience of the Spirit (vv. 1–5) and to the evidence from Scripture that righteousness is "by faith in Christ Jesus" (vv. 6–9) and "not by works of Law" (vv. 10–14), and especially the immediately preceding argument (vv. 15–18),[108] have not been particularly positive toward Torah. This paragraph, therefore, responds to the question, "Why Torah at all, if what you have just argued is true"? In light of the argument to here, verse 21 is therefore a variation of that theme: "Does the Law then stand over against the promises of God?" To which Paul responds in the words that interest us: "If [an expression of] Torah had been given that was able to give life, then righteousness would indeed be predicated on Torah." But since it could not—precisely because it lacked Spirit, the one essential ingredient for life—that means that Torah played a different role altogether (v. 22); it functioned to keep people "hemmed in 'under sin,' "[109] awaiting the fulfillment of "the promise," which was to be given

---

[107] So also Burton 185.

[108] Which in effect suggested Torah to be something of an afterthought.

[109] In light of v. 19, "Torah was added because of the transgressions," this unusual

"to those who believe." Although it is not certain how the Galatians would have heard these words, there can be little question, in light of the context and the language, that Paul understood them vis-à-vis the gift of the Spirit.[110]

That, after all, is quite the point of his (recent) argument with the Corinthians in 2 Cor 3:1–11. The problem with Torah is that is was not accompanied by Spirit; therefore it became death-dealing, not life-giving. The *new* covenant, however, is a covenant of Spirit over against the covenant of mere letter (= Torah observance)—in fulfillment of the new covenant passages in Ezekiel 36 and 37, where the Spirit is specifically referred to as the one who "gives life." Such a view of things almost certainly stands behind the language of v. 21.[111]

This is further confirmed by v. 22, where the "promise" has now been "given to those who believe." While the first referent of "promise" may again be the inheritance, both 3:14 and 4:4–7 show that Jew and Gentile alike have entered into that inheritance through the *Spirit*.[112] Thus, even though Spirit language as such does not occur in this passage, both in Pauline theology in general and in this argument in particular the Spirit is the one who fulfills the promise by "giving life," which was Torah's failure. All of this will be taken up in even greater detail in 5:13–6:10, where the Spirit "fulfills" Torah by doing "what Torah could not do."

GALATIANS 4:4–7[113]

[4]*But when the fullness of time came, God sent forth his Son, born*[114] *of a woman, born under Law,* [5]*in order that he might redeem those under Law, in*

---

phrase probably means not that Torah "imprisoned" people so that they sinned, but that because people were under sin, Torah functioned to keep them imprisoned until the means of release from sin would come.

[110] Cf. Williams, "Justification," 96–97. This is surprisingly seldom noted by commentators, although the connections with the immediate context and with 2 Cor 3:5–6 would seem to be determinative. But see Ridderbos 141 and (especially) Betz 174; Burton 195, 197 allows as much, but not exclusively so. For a more thorough presentation of this point of view see Cosgrove, *Cross*, 65–69.

[111] Thus it is not quite precise to argue as do Burton 195, E. P. Sanders (*Paul and Palestinian Judaism* [Philadelphia: Fortress, 1977] 503), and Bruce 180, that "to give life" and "to justify" are nearly synonyms here. While they may finally come out at the same place theologically, Paul does *not* use δικαιόω, but ζῳοποιέω, a word he has recently tied to the work of the Spirit in a context *over against* the Law.

[112] Cf. Fung 165.

[113] *Bibliography:* A. **Duprez**, "Note sur le rôle de l'Esprit-Saint dans la filiation du chrétien, à propos de *Gal.* 4:6," *RSR*, 52 (1964) 421–31; **Hays**, *Faith*, 85–137; J. M. **Scott**, *Adoption as Sons of God* (WUNT 2.48; Tübingen: Mohr [Paul Siebeck], 1992); for bibliography on the *Abba*-cry, see n. 150 below.

[114] Gk. γενόμενος (in both clauses), which literally means, "having become." In light of the similar usage in Phil 2:7b–8, these participles express "narrative action" (to borrow Hays's terminology [*Faith*, 105]), not state of being (as Burton, 218–19).

order that we might receive adoption as sons;[115] *⁶and because you are sons,
God*[116] *sent forth the Spirit of his Son*[117] *into our*[118] *hearts, crying out "Abba,
Father." ⁷So then you*[119] *are no longer a slave but a son; and if a son, then an
heir through God.*

With these words Paul concludes the argument that began in 3:1. As
throughout, the work of Christ and the Spirit are presented together as
evidence that the time of Torah has passed, hence the Galatians "are
being bewitched" by those who would insist on their circumcision. Earlier, in vv. 13–14, Paul had declared that "Christ freed us from the curse
of the Law, so that we might receive the promise [made to Abraham and
now fulfilled by] the Spirit." That same combination is now elaborated
in this final conclusion to the argument.

One must say "final conclusion," because vv. 26–29 in their own way
serve as a kind of "first conclusion." In that paragraph, Paul had tied
together various strands from the preceding paragraphs by asserting

---

When one "has become" from a woman, one is "born." Hence the common
translation, which has the misfortune of causing the English reader to miss its exact
parallel in the semi-creedal passage in Phil 2:7b–8a.

[115] Unfortunately, here is a place where the use of the more inclusivist term
"children," which gets at Paul's overall point well enough, misses something in terms
of the word play between Christ as God's Son and believers as God's "sons." For that
reason, I have chosen to translate υἱοί "sons." As a way both to signal the word play
and to avoid unnecessary gender exclusive language, I have put quotation marks
around the word whenever this usage appears in the following discussion.

[116] The expressed subject of the sentence, ὁ θεός ("God"), has been omitted in B
1739 sa. On the one hand, given this attestation and the tendency on the part of
scribes to add subjects, this might very well be the original. On the other hand, it is
far more likely that Paul himself is responsible for the perfect symmetry of this
sentence in relationship to v. 4, and therefore that the subject was omitted in B, or
its nearest relative, which was then picked up in the other two very closely related
witnesses.

[117] Quite missing the Pauline parallel, P⁴⁶ and Marcion (probably independently)
omit the words τοῦ υἱοῦ ("Son"), which produces a text that reads (v. 4) "God sent
forth his Son"; (v. 6) "God sent forth his Spirit." If this were a deliberate omission (as
it most likely was—although it could have been produced by homoeoteleuton), then
it was either for theological reasons—to avoid confusion about the Spirit, that he is
the Spirit of God, not the Spirit of Christ—or for less theological reasons of trying to
"clean up" what they assumed to be an awkward way of stating Paul's point, namely,
that God sent both the Son and the Spirit. But the omission simply misses too much;
see the discussion below.

[118] This is yet another example of Paul's shifting to the inclusive first person
plural in soteriological passages (cf. 1:4; 3:14; and 5:5 in this letter alone). Some of
the versions (the Syrian and parts of the Bohairic) and the later Majority text "clean
up" Paul's sentence by changing ἡμῶν ("our") to ὑμῶν ("your"); but this is unquestionably secondary. The text is supported by all the early evidence across all traditions
(P⁴⁶ ℵ A B C D* F G P 104 1175 1739 1881 lat sa bo^pt Tertullian).

[119] Only here in this letter Paul switches to the second person singular, when
addressing the whole people, probably as a way of individualizing his point.

(v. 26): "For *you* are the '*sons*' of God through the *faith* that is in *Christ Jesus*." Which is where the argument from v. 6 had been heading right along. All having been baptized into Christ means that Jew and Gentile alike belong to Christ; and if so, then through Christ (Abraham's true offspring) you *Gentiles* are also "Abraham's offspring, heirs in keeping with the *promise*" (v. 29). But precisely because their becoming Abraham's—and thereby God's—children is in keeping with the "promise," and since the promise in v. 14 was asserted to have been fulfilled by their reception of the Spirit, the Spirit is the one (crucial) strand that has been left hanging. Thus 4:1–7 serves as Paul's "final conclusion." By moving the Spirit back into the foreground, Paul brings the argument full circle.[120] What began as an appeal to their experience of the Spirit as evidence that *everything* (righteousness, "sonship," inheritance) is by faith in Christ—who has done away with Torah observance—is now concluded by indicating one specific and significant way in which they have experienced the Spirit so as to demonstrate that reality.

The close ties of this passage to vv. 23–29 are confirmed by several features: both begin with the similar imagery of the Law serving as our "pedagogue"; both conclude on the singular note of our being "heirs," imagery that began in v. 18 but which has been sharpened considerably by the addition of the pedagogue imagery; and in both the key imagery is "sonship." What unites these various motifs is made explicit in 4:1, namely, that the one who is "son" in the family, and thus "heir," is in fact no better than a "slave" as long as he is under the pedagogue slave. What is new in this final elaboration are: (1) the explicit contrasts between being "slaves" and "sons," thus "slave" and "free"—the motifs that become operative in the rest of the argument (4:21–31; 5:1, 13); (2) the language "enslaved to the στοιχεῖα [elemental substances/spirits] of the universe," which in v. 9 are by implication equated with their wishing to come under Torah; and, of course, (3) the reentry of the Spirit, now as evidence of "sonship."

Given the two realities—that this paragraph ties up the loose ends from 3:1, and the subtle shift in language to "slaves/slavery" and "sons/freedom," which takes over from here—it is arguable that vv. 4–7 serve as a kind of theological fulcrum for both what has preceded and what will follow. It is scarcely accidental, therefore, that the theological basis of the argument of the whole letter comes in one of the more striking soteriological[121] passages in the corpus. Here at the heart of this letter we once again encounter the thoroughly Trinitarian basis of Pauline

---

[120] So also Wright, *Climax*, 154n57 (from his student, Sylvia Keesmat).

[121] The passage is often termed "christological" (e.g., Hays, *Faith*, 86ff.; Betz 205ff.). It is that, too, of course, since in Paul one cannot have soteriology without Christology. But the focus here, as v. 5 certifies, is not on the person of Christ, but on his work.

soteriology, expressed in this case in a kind of semi-creedal formula, which has all the earmarks of being either created for this moment or so thoroughly adapted that any earlier form it might have taken is nearly irrelevant.[122] As everywhere in Paul, evidenced most strikingly in the compact phrases of the benediction in 2 Cor 13:13[14], salvation is initiated by God, effected by Christ through his death on the cross, and appropriated by "participating in the Spirit" (cf. Rom 5:1–5).

Verses 4–7 thus present God's alternative to the Galatians' coming under Torah, here expressed (vv. 1 and 3) in terms of being "minors, not yet of age"[123] and thus "no better than slaves." As Spirit people the Galatians must not regress to Torah observance.[124] Christ's death has redeemed ("freed") people from such and brought them into "sonship," confirmed by the indwelling Spirit of the Son, who cries out from within the believer in the language of the Son himself. Thus the Son has effected "adoption as sons," establishing for believers a relationship with God much like his own, which in Rom 8:14–17 Paul will amplify as "joint-heirship." For Paul, therefore, it is unthinkable that God's free "sons," made so by Christ and the Spirit, should revert to the slavery of a former

---

[122] The Pauline touches are thoroughgoing: e.g., the double ἵνα-clause, which functions just as in 3:14 to express the twofold effect of redemption in Christ; the subtle shift from "those" in the first clause to "we" in the second, which is also reminiscent of 3:14; the language of "redemption" found above in 3:13; the fact that "redemption" is for "those under Law," which is the point of the whole argument. Cf. the listing in Hays, *Faith*, 87–88.

Most contemporary scholars, however, are more enamored with its allegedly poetic form and some *unusual* phrasing—not to mention some matters that seem extraneous to the present argument—and thus argue for its prior existence. See esp. E. Schweizer, "Zum religionsgeschichtlichen Hintergrund der 'Sendungsformel' Gal 4,4f., Rm 8,3f., Joh 3,16f., 1 Joh 4,9," *ZNW* 57 (1966) 199–210 (see further bibliography in Hays, *Faith*, 127n1; for commentators for whom this is a driving issue, see Betz and Longenecker). Although possible, this can be neither proven nor disproved. And Schweizer's finding a "double sending formula" in Wis 9:7–18 is less than compelling; indeed it is a misguided use of sources (see my critique in the Appendix). My point is simple: the passage comes to us only in this context, in thoroughly Pauline language, and as the conclusion to his present argument. Even if it had prior form, that discovery would tell us next to nothing about its *present meaning*, which is to be found only in its Pauline context. Much of Betz' and Longenecker's concern, therefore, seems quite beside that of Paul. If it does reflect a prior creed, the significance would lie in the fact that Paul can appeal to it as common ground between him and the Galatians.

[123] Gk. νήπιος, which in Paul usually refers to infants or small children, but here takes on its legal sense of being a "minor."

[124] Which, of course, has been the issue right along, and which will be applied in vv. 8–11. Although most of those who have written on this passage recognize this point, they nevertheless frequently carry on conversation about v. 6 as if this central concern were no longer in view—which in turn has created much of the (unnecessary) verbiage on the relationship between vv. 5 and 6 in terms of the individual's experience of personal salvation.

time, the very slavery that not only failed to create true "sons" but also failed to effect true righteousness.

The passage is in four parts: (1) a statement about time (v. 4a), referring to the time when Torah observance was brought to an end through the work of Christ and the Spirit; (2) a soteriological-christo-logical statement (vv. 4b–5) similar to that of 3:13–14, but now expressed in terms of "receiving adoption as sons"; (3) a pneumatological statement (v. 6) which offers evidence for such adoption in terms of the indwelling Spirit's use of *the* Son's language, *Abba*; and (4) a summarizing word (v. 7) that ties "no slave, but a son" to v. 29, in that a "son" is also an heir. Our interest lies with what is said about the Spirit in v. 6, but to get there a few observations are needed about vv. 4–5.

4–5 This sentence offers the christological-soteriological basis for Paul's singular interest throughout—that because they are in Christ, the Galatian Gentiles do not need to come "under Torah." The sentence begins with language that ties what is about to be said to the preceding analogy (vv. 1–2) and its application (v. 3). In contrast[125] to a former time when God's people were no better off than "a minor," still under the tutelage of a slave-pedagogue, God's time for them to reach their maturity has now arrived. As Paul has argued in a variety of ways throughout, God's time came with Christ, especially through his redemptive work on the cross.

In the rest of the sentence, three points are made about Christ and his saving activity. First, in language that seems deliberately chosen so as to bring the work of Christ and the Spirit into conjunction, Paul says that "God *sent forth* his Son." Despite a few voices to the contrary,[126] the linguistic evidence,[127] the parallel in v. 6 about *sending forth* the Spirit,

---

[125] The δέ with which the sentence begins is adversative.

[126] See esp. J. D. G. Dunn, *Christology in the Making* (Philadelphia: Westminster, 1980) 38–44, whose case builds on a series of (correct) observations that on its own such language neither argues for (which is certainly true) nor necessarily presupposes preexistence. Thus he points to messenger and commissioning formulae which use this word, including Jesus' use of it in his parable of the wicked tenants, etc. This is a case of "divide and conquer," which fails to take into account the cumulative effect of what is here said and neglects altogether the significance of the parallel language of the Spirit in v. 6. It is true that the concern for Paul is not in fact Jesus' origins, but the cumulative weight of the evidence and the way all of this is expressed *presupposes* preexistence. Cf. Walter Kasper, *Jesus the Christ* (New York: Paulist, 1976) 173, and most commentaries.

[127] While it is true, as Dunn, *Christology*, 39, points out, that the compound ἐξαπέστειλεν is found in the LXX without concern for "origins" in the "commissioning" of human servants, it is also true, as he acknowledges, that it is used for the sending forth of divine messengers, where their prior existence is presupposed. Given the parallel in v. 6, it is hard to imagine that the Galatians would have heard this only in terms of commissioning, on the basis of the circuitous parallels that Dunn alleges.

and the otherwise unnecessary clause "born of a woman," combine to indicate that this is an assertion of Christ's preexistence—that the Son, himself divine, was sent by the Father to effect redemption. As with 3:5, the emphasis is on the activity of God; what God has done is reason enough for the Galatians to cease to listen to those who would bring them "under Torah." But in this case, it is even more. What God has accomplished, he has done as the eternal Trinity. As always God the Father is the subject of the saving verbs; but his saving activity has been carried out through the redemptive activity of God the Son, who has inaugurated God's eschatological salvation, with its inclusion of Jew and Gentile alike as his children.

Second, the two middle members of the sentence ("born under Torah, in order to redeem those who are under Torah") reiterate the central thrust of the whole argument. The Galatians must not be circumcised— because that means to "come under Torah," and Christ came "under Torah" so that no others would need to. This is the "curse" from which all of God's people have been redeemed by Christ (3:13–14).

Third, with a marvelous turn of images in the final clause Paul draws all sorts of ideas together: "in order that we[128] might receive the υἱοθεσίαν (adoption as 'sons')." In its most immediate context this picks up the analogy of vv. 1–2 and refers to the time when the "son" enters "maturity." But far more is going on with this choice of words. Although υἱοθεσία does not appear in the LXX, we know from Rom 9:4 that Paul understands God's election of Israel in terms of "adoption as a son."[129] With this word, therefore, Paul wraps up the argument from 3:6. The promised blessing of inheritance, which included Gentiles, has been effected by Christ, through the same act of redemption that also set people forever free from Torah observance. Thus *Abraham's true "sons,"* including Gentiles who through Christ get in on the promised blessing, are none other than *God's "sons,"* having become so through the adoption that *God's own Son* made possible. It is this relationship—"sonship" with God, thus taking up the "sonship" of Israel through Abraham's true seed—that is the point of everything for Paul's argument. Through Christ

---

Here it can only mean "God sent *forth* his Son," the presupposition of which is prior existence with God from whom he was sent forth. What is striking in Dunn's presentation is that he scours the NT and other ancient literature for possible parallels that *may* (and therefore for him *do*) suggest nothing more than an Adam Christology, while he ignores the immediate parallel in v. 6, which surely offers the interpretive key (on p. 39 he does mention v. 6, but without noting its significance for this passage).

[128] Note the similar shift from Israel under Law ("those under Law") to "we"— both Jews and Gentiles who believe—in 3:13–14.

[129] Cf. Exod 4:22; Isa 1:2; Hos 11:1; Jer 31:9. On the whole question of the meaning of this word ("adoption as sons" not "sonship" per se) and its possible OT background (2 Sam 7:14), see Scott, *Adoption*, who has added the full weight of all available evidence to a conclusion reached by Lightfoot (168–89) over a century earlier.

Gentiles are not merely freed from their own form of slavery to beings that are not gods; they are also thereby freed from that form of slavery to which Jews had been enslaved, under which the agitators would now bring them. Through Christ believers[130] are not slaves; they are free children, "with all the rights and privileges that pertain thereto."

But just as in 3:13–14, and in keeping with how the argument began in 3:1–5, the assertion of their "adoption as 'sons' " does not bring the argument to conclusion. That is what Christ effected indeed; nothing can add to or take away from that. But for Paul—and for them, if they will but pay attention—the sure *evidence* of such adoption is the gift of the Spirit. To put that another way, for Paul the work of Christ is a historical and objective reality. At one point in human history, when God's appointed time had arrived, Christ entered human history (born of a woman) within the context of God's people (born under Law), so as to free people from Torah observance by giving them "adoption as 'sons.' " But this historical and objective reality becomes realized (a "subjective reality" in this sense only) by the work of the Spirit.[131] It is this twofold reality, both its historical objectivity and its experienced realization, that makes his argument work, since it is *their experienced life of the Spirit who actualizes the "sonship" Christ provided,* which serves for Paul as the certain evidence that he is right and the agitators are wrong. Hence Paul has yet one more word.

6 This final word further certifies that the issue of this letter is not "justification by faith," but Gentile inclusion as Abraham's—and therefore God's—true children and thus rightful heirs of the final inheritance. God has brought about such "sonship" through the redemptive work of Christ. Now Paul concludes the argument by bringing back into focus the Galatians'—and his and others'[132]—experience of the Spirit (from 3:1–5) and showing how that relates to what has just been said about Christ. In so doing, Paul makes several significant assertions, and reveals several presuppositions vital for our understanding the role of the Spirit

---

[130] With the shift to "we" (see n. 128 above) and the verb "might receive," the sentence now begins to move toward the believers' own experience of redemption, which is finally realized in the next sentence (v. 6).

[131] Betz 209–10 rightly objects to the use of such language in this passage, noting that it is the result of bringing into the discussion external, dogmatic categories and suggesting in effect that the language is all backwards in any case—i.e., for Paul the "objective" reality to which he appeals and which demonstrates the truth of v. 5 is their experience of the Spirit!

[132] A point too easily overlooked. The awkwardness we sense with Paul's language is the result of his (apparent) inability to exclude himself and others from the rich benefits of salvation in Christ. Thus he begins, as the argument demands and despite the "we" at the end of v. 5, with "*you* are 'sons,' " which is evidenced by the Spirit in *our* hearts.

in Paul's understanding of the gospel. In this regard it is significant to compare the parallel in Rom 8:15–17, where some of this is said in slightly different, and apparently more deliberate, ways—a comparison that may illumine the concerns peculiar to the present argument.

In terms of the argument, two matters are crucial. First, Paul deliberately conjoins the work of the Son and the Spirit—in two ways: (a) By means of the identical "sending formula." In a historically particular moment for the Galatians—and others—"God sent forth [ἐξαπέστειλεν ὁ θεὸς] *the Spirit of his Son*" (v. 6), exactly as previously "God sent forth [ἐξαπέστειλεν ὁ θεὸς] his Son" (v. 4) at the right historical moment so as to redeem. As noted above (n. 122), this symmetry is almost certainly from Paul himself, and is therefore quite deliberate, even though the locus of the sending is considerably different.[133]

(b) He also conjoins the work of Son and Spirit by his use of the (rare) designation, "the Spirit *of his Son*"—the same Son whom God had sent to redeem people. This precise language in fact occurs nowhere else, but it is quite in keeping with that of Rom 8:9 ("the Spirit of Christ") and Phil 1:19 ("the Spirit of Jesus Christ"). These three passages, besides saying something significant in terms of Christology (it is no small thing that the Spirit *of God* can so easily also be called the Spirit *of Christ*), also say something significant about the Spirit (that the indwelling Spirit, whom believers know as an experienced reality, is the way both the Father and the Son are present in the believer's life).

Second, what lies behind this designation is in fact the goal of everything in terms of holding the present argument together. In one sense, Paul could have made his overall point had he simply said, "God sent forth his Spirit."[134] But Paul's interest in not in the Spirit as such, a concern given plenty of airing in 3:1–14. His interest now is to make sure that the Galatians understand who the Spirit is: none other than the Spirit *of Christ*—the same Christ who "loved [them] and gave himself for [them]," who now by his Spirit indwells them. But Paul's point goes even further. For the Spirit is not called "the Spirit of Christ" in that direct way, but "the Spirit of [God's] Son." That is the linchpin. The same Son whose death effected redemption and secured "sonship" for them, now indwells them by his Spirit, "the Spirit *of the Son*," whom God sent forth as he had the Son himself. The ultimate evidence of this "sonship" is their use of the Son's own address to the Father in prayer: *Abba*. Thus the "sonship" motif, that goes back as far as 3:7, is brought to its ringing climax with this sentence.[135]

---

[133] Within the context of human history and among the Jews, in the case of Jesus; within the hearts of believers, in the case of the Spirit.

[134] As in P[46] and Marcion; see n. 117 above.

[135] Cf. Wright, *Climax*, 44.

In sum: Paul's concern right along has had to do with Gentile believers as true "sons" of Abraham. That came about through the redemptive work of Abraham's one "seed," Christ, who made it possible for all who trust in him to share in his inheritance as fellow "sons." But beyond that, such "sons of Abraham" are "sons of God," made so through Christ (v. 5). The evidence of such shared "sonship" is the presence of the Spirit of the Son, who by crying out "Abba" from within the believer, bears witness to the presence of the Son who made us "sons," since that is his own distinctive term of address to God his Father. Thus: "Because you have received 'sonship' through Christ's redemption, God's confirmation of that for you experientially stems from his also having sent forth the Spirit of his Son into your hearts, evidenced by the fact that the Spirit of the Son cries out to God in the Son's own word of intimacy, 'Abba, Father.' "

That these are Paul's concerns here is reinforced by a comparison with the companion passage from Romans 8. Four matters are noteworthy: (a) Even though the language "adoption as sons" recurs in Rom 8:15, when the application is picked up in vv. 16–17, Paul shifts from the term "sons" (υἱοί) to the broader term "children" (τέκνα); thus the word play on υἱός is unique to Galatians; (b) rather than "the Spirit *of his Son*," in Rom 8:14–15 the Spirit is designated "the Spirit of God," who is also "the Spirit of sonship" (= the Spirit who effects sonship); (c) rather than the Spirit crying out "Abba," in Rom 8:15 "*we cry out* by means of the Spirit" (which obviously for Paul means the same thing, but our passage ties the cry more directly to the Spirit *of the Son*); and (d) although "becoming heirs" is the net result in both passages, in the immediate passage the connection of being a "son" with being "an heir" is the main thrust, as v. 7 makes clear, whereas in Rom 8:17 the main thrust has become eschatological and focuses on our shared "heirship" with Christ.

It should be noted further that this interest in joining as closely as possible the historic work of Christ with the Galatians' experience of the Spirit is surely the cause of the somewhat awkward, and for us unusual, way by which these two sentences are joined: "*Because*[136] you are 'sons.' " At first blush, that looks for all the world as though Paul considers the experience of the Spirit (v. 6) as subsequent to conversion (v. 5) and the

---

[136] This, of course, reflects a choice of the meaning of ὅτι that is in keeping with standard usage. The suggestion (made inter alia by Lagrange 103–4; Lietzmann 27; Moule, *Idiom Book*, 147; Duprez, "Note," passim; J. Jeremias, *The Prayers of Jesus* [SBT 2/6; London: SCM, 1967] 65n74; Lull, *Spirit*, 106; cf. NEB, GNB) that ὅτι is declarative here is an attempt to offer a *grammatical* solution to what is perceived as a "logical" problem (or problem of consistency). For this kind of argumentation that makes much too much of "consistency" and "logic," see esp. the discussion in Lull. But the alleged "problem" can be resolved much more easily, as here, by noting the "salvation history" dimension to these two sentences.

latter as the cause of the former.[137] But since such an idea occurs nowhere else in Paul, and since the concerns that unite the two sentences are so obvious, Paul's reasons for this language probably lie elsewhere. Three matters are worthy of note:

First, for Paul there is almost certainly a cause and effect relationship between the work of Christ and the subsequent work of the Spirit. But the "subsequence" for him, and especially so in this passage, is not that of two works of grace within the believer's experience. Rather it is the subsequence of "salvation history." As suggested above, Paul's intent in v. 5 is *not* to recount the *individual believer's personal salvation history.* That is, v. 5 does not immediately speak to the question of the individual believer's own experience of conversion at all. Rather, Paul sets forth the work of Christ as an objective, historical, once-for-all reality. In that objective, historical work the Son procured "sonship" for all who believe in him, which Paul makes personal for him and them by the final purpose clause, "so that *we* might *receive* adoption as 'sons.' " Subsequent to that is the experience of the believer—any believer—whereby that "objective sonship" procured by Christ is realized by the Spirit's indwelling. Thus Paul did not intend to offer here—nor does he presuppose—some chronology of personal salvation history. Rather, the cause and effect relationship is that between "sonship" as Christ has provided it historically *on the cross*[138] and "sonship" as the Spirit has appropriated it experientially *in the life of the believer.*[139] After all, the two sending clauses put Christ in the world to procure redemption and place the Spirit in our hearts as evidence of actualized redemption.

Second, such an understanding is the way forward through our sense of awkwardness in Paul's sentence, in which the entry clause implies

---

[137] Which is indeed the position taken by such diverse writers as Schlier 197–98; Mussner 275; J. K. Parratt, "The Witness of the Holy Spirit: Calvin, the Puritans and St. Paul," *EvQ* 41 (1969) 165; L. S. Thornton, *Confirmation: Its Place in the Baptismal Mystery* (Westminster: Dacre Press, 1954) 11–12; Hunter, *Spirit-Baptism*, 35–36; and Ervin, *Conversion-Initiation*, 86–88. In every case vested interests appear to precede a concern for discovering Paul's interests in this passage.

[138] The unfortunate result of analyzing this passage in terms of its pre-Pauline meaning can be seen in Betz' argument (207n51) that this passage and 3:13 "cannot be harmonized"—as though what Paul had said in 3:13 can now be disregarded by the Galatians when they come to this moment in the letter. To the contrary, as Hays (*Faith,* 92–125) has shown convincingly, both passages assume the same narrative framework about Christ and the meaning of his death; moreover, this narrative framework would have been well known to the Galatians, as the appeal in 3:1 substantiates.

[139] Cf. Dunn, *Baptism*, 114, who uses the language "logical, not chronological" to arrive at this same point. There is a sense, of course, in which the believer's appropriation of "sonship" by the Spirit is chronologically after the procuring of it by Christ; but "chronology" in this discussion usually refers to that of the individual believer.

that the coming of the Spirit is the *result* of the prior work of Christ, whereas the content of the sentence itself indicates that the Spirit is the *evidence* of "sonship." Both are true, in the sense outlined above. The Spirit's presence evidences the "sonship" that Christ's redemption has brought about. In that sense, Christ is the "cause" and the Spirit the "effect" as far as "sonship" is concerned.[140]

Third, a comparison with Rom 8:14–17 reinforces this understanding. When the relationship between the work of Christ and the Spirit is no longer central as in Galatians, and the work of the Spirit is the only one in immediate purview, Paul returns to normal language in speaking about the Spirit. Hence, it is the Spirit who brings "adoption as sons" to God's people, and surely in that passage Paul is referring to Christian conversion. What is presupposed there is the preceding argument from 3:21 to 5:11 where the prior action of Christ was spelled out in detail. The Spirit does not procure such adoption; but in terms of the believer's *experience* of salvation, the Spirit is the "Spirit of adoption," that is, the Spirit actualizes adoption for the believer.

This very discussion, it should finally be noted, is the result of our coming to the text with the wrong questions in hand (e.g., "what relationship does Paul envisage the charismatic Spirit to have with conversion?"). Paul is not setting forth, by either affirmation or presupposition, anything about the relationship between the believer's experience of Christ's redemption and the Spirit's *Abba*-cry; Paul's concern, in the well-chosen language of Cosgrove, is that "the Spirit comes with sonship in Christ; it is in no way dependent on lawkeeping" (52). To make more of this text than that tends to miss Paul by too much.

At the same time, there are in v. 6 a few further, somewhat interrelated, items concerning the Spirit that call for our attention. First, here is yet another text that emphasizes the presence of the Spirit in terms of "indwelling" the believer, in this case with the language "into our hearts." On this matter see especially the discussion of 1 Thes 4:8; 1 Cor 6:19; 2 Cor 1:21–22; and Rom 5:5. This consistent motif in Paul, expressed in a number of ways and in a variety of contexts, indicates the primary locus of God's presence in the present age. At work here is Paul's basic understanding of the Spirit as an eschatological reality in terms of the new covenant. The Spirit, whom the Galatians "received" as fulfillment of the promise to Abraham, also fulfills the new covenant promises of Jeremiah and Ezekiel, that God will write his Law on human hearts by putting his Spirit within them. For the moment Paul is not concerned

---

[140]Perhaps one should also point out that the discussion on the tenses of the verbs "you are" and "God sent," as though that says something significant about the "chronology" of conversion, is almost totally irrelevant (see, e.g., Duprez, "Note," 428n17; Mussner 275). Paul's usage is dictated by the realities he is trying to affirm, not by their order of occurrence.

with the ethical implications of such indwelling.[141] Here the emphasis is solely on their Spirit-inspired *Abba*-cry as evidence of their new *relationship* with God.

Second, as with most such texts in Paul, even though the *Abba*-cry is very much the realized experience of individual believers, the cry itself is most likely to be heard in the gathered worship of the community.[142] How this took place cannot now be determined with precision. Some would see it more liturgically, perhaps as referring to the address to God that begins the Lord's Prayer.[143] But the language of "crying out" suggests something much more spontaneous.

The use of the verb "cry,"[144] with the Spirit as the subject, has led other scholars to see the *Abba*-cry as a form of "ecstasy."[145] Although "ecstasy" is one of those elastic terms that tends to mean whatever the user wants it to mean in a given moment, usually it refers to an experience in which "there is no involvement of the 'ego,' except as an 'onlooker.' "[146] Our problems may be semantic, but since the language of "ecstasy" so often carries such a connotation of the "Spirit's takeover," as it were, a less loaded term such as "charismatic prayer" or, better, "Spirit-inspired prayer" is much to be preferred.[147] Such "crying out" by the Spirit would scarcely presuppose wild and uncontrolled utterance, given Paul's argument for "order" in 1 Cor 14:26–33 as reflecting God's

---

[141] A concern that properly drives Mawhinney (n. 150), but also causes him to read a bit too much into the *Abba*-cry.

[142] As over against Obeng (n. 150), who would place it at baptism as a cry before the world that people have become God's children. Any connection with baptism is gratuitous, since Paul himself never makes such a connection; elsewhere in Paul the community at worship is the certain locus of such Spirit-inspired prayer (1 Cor 14 passim).

[143] E.g., Bligh 354; O. Cullmann, *The Christology of the New Testament* (London: SCM, 1959), 209; Mawhinney 185 (see n. 150).

[144] Gk. κράζον, a word that implies loud speech, but not necessarily inarticulate or ecstatic speech. See W. Grundmann, *TDNT* 3.898–903.

[145] See Dodd, *Romans*, 129; Schlier 198n2; Betz 210; Lull, *Spirit*, 66–69; Käsemann, *Romans*, 227. Dunn, *Jesus*, 240, allows the possibility, but thinks it "less likely." Far less likely still are those who would tend to deny Spirit-inspiration altogether (e.g., Stott 107 who in commenting on this passage refers to "the quiet inward witness of the Spirit when we pray"!). This is especially the case with those who would stress its origins in the church in the opening address of the Lord's Prayer (see n. 143 above).

[146] Lull, *Spirit*, 67; cf. Dodd (*Romans*, 129): "People under the stress of strong spiritual excitement or exaltation would break out into loud cries. . . . These cries, which seemed independent of the thought or will of the speaker, were regarded as utterances of the Spirit within him." This probably says more about Dodd than it does about the early church.

[147] Cf. Dunn's "charismatic consciousness," which he intentionally sets over against "ecstatic," and by which he means both "the consciousness of being moved upon by divine power" and "the conscious willingness to be so used, the awareness and acceptance of the words and actions as one's own" (*Jesus*, 241).

shalom. Nonetheless, we need to take seriously that believers "cried out" to God within the assembly, and did so with full awareness that the Spirit was moving them so to do, and that they were thus using Jesus' own word of intimate relationship with the Father.[148]

Third, more needs to be said about the language "Abba," since in some ways this is what carries the argument for Paul and since a considerable amount of literature has grown up around this word. The landmark study in this regard was that of Joachim Jeremias,[149] who among other things concluded (1) that this was the address of intimacy, originating with small children, in an Aramaic home, (2) that Jesus' use of this term to address God was unique to him in all of known Jewish literature, (3) that the prayer thus revealed the uniqueness of his own self-understanding as Son of the Father, and (4) that he invited his disciples to use this term as his extension of grace to them. As with all such "landmarks" in NT scholarship, some correctives and advances are eventually made.[150] But when the dust has finally settled, and even if one were to assume the minimalist position of James Barr,[151] for example, much of this still remains. Indeed, Paul's usage here as much as anything tends to verify the basic soundness of Jeremias' conclusions.

For our purposes, several matters are of significance:

1. This usage by Paul both here and in Romans—written to a church that Paul has never visited!—presupposes the widespread usage of this prayer language in the Gentile churches.[152] Furthermore, these two passages together and the argument of this one in particular serve as primary evidence for its significance both in the life of Jesus and in the

---

[148] The best analogy in the Pauline corpus probably appears in the confession "Jesus is Lord" in 1 Cor 12:3, which no one can make except by the Spirit. In both cases, it is not ecstasy that is in view, but the presence of the Spirit, to whom such basic prayer and confession is ultimately attributable—as certain evidence that one is truly Christ's.

[149] As chapter 1 in *Prayers of Jesus*, 11–65 [the German original appeared in 1966].

[150] Since Jeremias, see Dunn, *Jesus*, 21–26; Cranfield, *Romans*, 1.399–402; J. M. Oesterreicher, " 'Abba, Father!' On the Humanity of Jesus," in *The Lord's Prayer and Jewish Liturgy* (ed. J. J. Petuchowski and M. Brocke; New York: Seabury Press, 1978) 119–36; G. Vermes, *Jesus and the World of Judaism* (London: SCM, 1983) 39–43; J. Fitzmyer, "Abba and Jesus' Relation to God," in *A cause de l'Evangile: Mélanges offerts à Dom Jacques Dupont* (ed. R. Gantoy; Paris: Cerf, 1985) 16–38; J. Barr, " 'Abba' isn't 'Daddy,' " *JTS* 39 (1988) 28–47; idem, " 'Abba, Father' and the Familiarity of Jesus' Speech," *Theology* 91 (1988) 173–79; A. Mawhinney, "God as Father: Two Popular Theories Reconsidered," *JETS* 31 (1988) 181–89; E. A. Obeng, "Abba, Father: The Prayer of the Sons of God," *ExpT* 99 (1988) 363–66; Dunn, "Prayer," in *Dictionary of Jesus and the Gospels* (ed. J. B. Green, S. McKnight, I. H. Marshall; Downers Grove: InterVarsity, 1992), 617–25, esp. 618–19; L. W. Hurtado, "God," in ibid., 275–76.

[151] Barr, " 'Abba.' "

[152] This is evidenced all the more by Paul's switch to "our hearts" in this clause, which implies that for him this is the common experience of believers in all churches.

early church. Such widespread, presuppositional usage of this prayer language—in its *Aramaic original*—is most easily accounted for historically on the grounds that this was Jesus' own term and that he invited his disciples to use his language after him.[153] Indeed, in the case of the present argument, everything hinges on the fact that believers now, by the Spirit *of the Son*, are using *the language of the Son*. To deny the origin of such usage to Jesus, and through him to the early church, is to push historical skepticism to its outer limits.

2. The jury is still out on the precise meaning, and therefore significance, of the term *Abba*. Jeremias had made a considerable case for intimacy on the grounds of its assumed origins as the word of infant children; Vermes and Barr have called that into question by offering evidence that it was the language of adult children as well. They may well be right on the question of origins; but its use by adult children in an Aramaic home does not thereby make it a more adult word.[154] Most likely the word was in fact an expression of intimacy, used by children first as infants and later as adults, reflecting what is true in many such cultures where the terms of endearment for one's parents are used lifelong—a circumstance generally not true in English-speaking homes. That it was used by adult children as well as small children is irrelevant. What is relevant is that it was probably the language of intimacy and endearment. If "Daddy" is not an exact equivalent—and it is not—the basic thrust of the term, and the significance of Jesus' use of it in addressing God, nevertheless carries considerable theological weight. If the term cannot be demonstrated, as Jeremias supposed, to be unique to Jesus,[155] it can surely be argued to be *distinctively* his form of address; and for Jesus it is best understood as a term denoting his own sense of unique Sonship—by his addressing God consistently in the language of the home. That he should invite his disciples to use his word after him was thus an expression of grace on his part.

3. It is more difficult to determine the precise wording of the cry in the early Christian churches. Despite the addition ὁ πατήρ to the *Abba* of Jesus' prayer in Mark 14:36, it is difficult to imagine that Jesus would have added the Greek equivalent to his own Aramaic prayer. It is possible, of course, that Mark added the Greek translation for the sake of his

---

[153] Cf. Dunn, *Jesus*, 22–26; Obeng, "Abba," 364; Hurtado, "God," and many others.

[154] Barr (" 'Abba' ") seems to miss the point here. While he is correct that it did not *originate* with the babbling of children (after all, why these sounds and not others?), that these (*abba* and *imma*) are the first words that most children would stammer needs to be noted. They do so, because these are the first words children are "taught," as it were (as in, "Say *abba*"). And in no language that I know are the more formal words for parents the first words they are "taught" to speak. Thus "origins" as such is irrelevant, but not so with usage and significance.

[155] So Vermes, Barr, Mawhinney.

Gentile readers; but more likely he reflects the usage of the Gentile churches, where the Greek equivalent was added at a very early stage, first as a translational equivalent,[156] but later as the deeply fixed language of piety.[157] That is probably what Paul is bearing witness to here and in Rom 8:15. By the time of these letters, Christians would have been using the two terms together, very much as *"Abba* Father," spoken together, has become the similar language of English-speaking piety, on the basis of the KJV.

4. Both the meaning of the term and the fact that such a cry comes from the heart suggest that for Paul a form of intimacy with God is involved.[158] Here is the ultimate evidence that we are God's children, in that we address God with the same term of intimate relationship that Jesus himself used. We are not slaves, but children. The Spirit has taken us far beyond mere conformity to religious obligations. God himself, in the person of his Spirit, has come to indwell us; and he has sealed that relationship by giving to us the language of his Son, the language of personal relationship. For Paul—and for us—this is the ultimate expression of grace. No wonder Paul was so opposed to Torah observance. It invariably breaks this relationship of child to parent in favor of one that can only be expressed in terms of slavery—performance on the basis of duty and obligation, in which one "slaves" for God, rather than being recreated in God's likeness (cf. 4:19), resulting in loving servanthood to all others (5:13). Christ has effected such a relationship; the Spirit makes it work. Damn all attempts to destroy it by Torah observance, as though one were related to God on the basis of religious obligation—which is undoubtedly Paul's sentiment, if not his language!

A final observation. With this text and its companion in Romans 8, we now have the third of Paul's primary images for the church, that of family (cf. 2 Cor 6:18). As with the prior two images of temple and body,[159] the Spirit is the essential ingredient of the imagery. As members of God's family, through the work of the Son, by whom we have become heirs together of God's own glory, God is "Father" and we are "brothers and sisters." The Spirit of the Son whom God has sent into our hearts makes this imagery a living reality. Thus it is the Spirit's presence that creates God's new temple; it is through our common lavish experience of the Spirit that we are formed into one body; and now it is the Spirit within who gives evidence that we are members of God's family.

---

[156] Barr (" 'Abba,' " 40–42) makes far too much of its being translated as an apparent declarative (ὁ πατήρ) rather than a vocative (πατέρ); but cf. Luke 8:54. Lightfoot 170, considered this a Hebraism that he styled "emphatic vocative." For this usage in biblical Greek see BDF §147(3).

[157] Cf. Dunn, "Prayer," 619.

[158] So most who have written on the subject, contra Barr.

[159] See above on 1 Cor 3:16–17 and 12:12–14.

GALATIANS 4:29

But just as the one who had been born according to the flesh used to persecute the one born according to the Spirit, so it is now as well.

In some ways this is the most remarkable sentence in the current argument—Paul's famous "allegory" of Hagar/Ishmael and Sarah/Isaac. However, it is precisely this surprising sentence, with its designation of Isaac as the one "born according to the Spirit" and the reference to the Jews (including the Jewish Christian agitators) as persecuting those who are "of Spirit," that puts the purpose of the allegory into perspective. Early in his "allegory" (v. 23) Paul had already designated the slave woman's son as born "according to the flesh" and the free woman's son as born "through promise." Now he will apply all of that to the Galatians' situation, including the "compulsion" on the part of the agitators that they be circumcised.

The argument/allegory is in four parts: (1) v. 21 challenges those who are succumbing to the persuasions of the agitators to interpret the OT text correctly; (2) vv. 22–23 set forth the basic data of the OT story, but do so in such a way as to tie the story to the present argument;[160] (3) vv. 24–27 give Paul's "allegorical" interpretation of these data, with the emphasis on the meaning of the two *mothers*; (4) vv. 28–31 then apply the interpretation to the situation in Galatia, in terms of the two *sons*.

The key to much lies in the way Paul sets forth the data in vv. 22–23. As the concluding application (vv. 28–31) makes clear, the basic concern throughout is with the two sons, one (Isaac) representing those who are in Christ, the other (Ishmael) representing contemporary Judaism.[161] The one exists as a result of the promise (which in 3:14 has been interpreted in terms of the Spirit); the other exists "according to the flesh." But to get to that point Paul first argues that the two mothers represent two covenants, pointing to the covenant of Law on Sinai (the only one actually singled out) and to the new covenant effected through Christ and the Spirit. Even more crucial for the argument is the fact that the mother of Ishmael in the LXX was called ἡ παιδίσκη ("the slave woman"). This language prompts Paul to designate Sarah the "free woman." These designations in turn relate the passage to the conclusions reached in 4:1–7, where Christ has "redeemed" (= freed from the slavery of the Law), and the Spirit has effected the "sonship" (= freedom)

---

[160] First, by picking up several motifs from 3:6–29 (Abraham, the question of Abraham's "true children," who are "according to the promise," and thus "inherit the promise"), but doing so, secondly, through the themes of 4:1–7 (slavery and freedom) and 3:3 (Spirit and flesh).

[161] And, in a circuitous way, the Jewish Christian agitators as well, since by insisting on circumcision they are rejecting Christ. Cf. 2:21; 4:9; 5:2, 4, 7–12; 6:12–13.

that Christ has procured, so that we are no longer "slaves" but "sons" and therefore "heirs."

The work of Christ, Paul argues, has in effect reversed the roles of the two mothers. On the one hand, the one (Sarah), who was *in fact* mother of the Jews, was also the mother of *the child of promise*, and therefore must now be seen as the mother of those who through Christ have received the promise (the Spirit) and therefore are "Abraham's seed" (3:29). Thus the "free woman" gives birth to the "free son"—*and his seed*. She is the formerly "barren one" who now rejoices in the multitude of her free children (v. 27).

Hagar, on the other hand, was *in fact* the mother of non-Jews (thus Gentiles). But because she was "the slave woman," and because the Law leads to slavery and not freedom, she is now seen as the mother of those who are in such slavery; she is therefore the "mother" of those who not only received the "slavery" of the Law on Mount Sinai, but who also in Paul's day persist in the same slavery (= "the present Jerusalem").

The application of this interpretation, which is based on reading the OT narrative in light of the event of Christ and the Spirit, is made in a straightforward way in vv. 28–31. "You Galatians," Paul says, "are, as Isaac, the children of promise," picking up the concern of the argument in 3:6–4:7. In v. 31 he states the same conclusion in light of the immediate argument: "Therefore, brothers and sisters, we are not children of the slave woman, but of the free woman." But in getting to this final application, he makes two assertions in vv. 29 and 30 that tie the previous argument (from 3:1) together and likewise anticipate the final application in 5:1–12.

The first of these (v. 29) makes two points:[162] First, the child of promise, Isaac, was born κατὰ πνεῦμα (according to the Spirit), which in light of vv. 23 and 28 comes as something of a mild surprise, since one might have expected "through the promise";[163] second, the child born κατὰ σάρκα (according to the flesh) used to—and still does—persecute the child of promise, the one who is of the Spirit.[164] Thus, first, by this way of putting it Paul once more, as in 3:14, links the promise to the gift of the Spirit, which for him is the primary evidence that one is truly of

---

[162] The second, made in v. 30, lies beyond our concern. By quoting the text of Gen 21:10, Paul indicates that the OT itself anticipates the time of doing away with Torah observance by stating that the child of the "slave woman" will not inherit with the "free son." Not only so, but by implication Paul is calling for the Galatians to "drive out the agitators from their midst," since they "shall not inherit" along with those who are heirs of the "free woman." See in this regard, Lincoln, *Paradise*, 27–29, and Hansen, *Abraham*, 147–50.

[163] Cf. Burton 266; Schlier 226.

[164] For a useful overview of the considerable discussion of Paul's use of the Genesis narrative, and the possible sources for this view, see Bruce 223–24; cf. Longenecker 200–206.

Christ and therefore without need to come under Law. By this designation, therefore, he keeps before them the thread of the Spirit and his work, which began in 3:2 and has been woven in continually throughout. Second, at the same time, he anticipates the application in 5:1–12, as well as the final indictment in 6:12–13, in which he roundly scores the Jewish Christian agitators, who by their insistence on circumcision are playing the role of "persecutor"[165] in the present Galatian scene.[166]

For our interests, two further matters need to be noted. First, the designation of the two sons as born κατὰ σάρκα and κατὰ πνεῦμα—which picks up language from 3:3 (q.v.), and anticipates the contrast which will dominate the argument in 5:16–6:10 (cf. Rom 8:4–17). In this its first occurrence there is considerable fluidity to Paul's usage, although his ultimate point with the language is clear enough. The son born "according to the flesh," of course, refers to Ishmael and to the fact that Abraham and Sarah took matters into their own (merely human, and thus fallen) hands to produce an offspring for God;[167] but this son now represents all who would secure their present position with God on the basis of Torah, which came to an end through Christ and the Spirit. Thus those who insist on Gentile Torah observance in the form of circumcision are here designated as "according to the flesh" (cf. 3:3). They may have "begun by Spirit," but they insist on coming to completion by the flesh.

Likewise the son born "according to the Spirit" refers first to Isaac, but then to all who are currently Christ's and thus "of the Spirit." But did Paul really think Isaac himself was born κατὰ πνεῦμα, or is this merely rhetoric, the use of words in an analogical way that has little or no bearing on the original account? In this case the answer lies somewhere in between. It may, of course, be simply analogy and nothing more. The prior use of κατὰ σάρκα to refer to Ishmael's birth (v. 23) indicates that Paul is already loading these terms with theological significance. But, as

---

[165] It is possible, as Burton 266 allows and Cosgrove (*Cross*, 80–85) assumes, that Paul is alluding to something more violent on the part of the Jewish synagogue; but in context it seems far more likely to refer to what the agitators are doing by "forcing" the Galatians to be circumcised. So most commentators.

[166] These are the two final issues of the letter. In 5:1–12 he speaks directly to the Galatians about their danger of being "estranged from Christ" (v. 4); in 5:13–6:10 he takes up the issue of life in the Spirit as the true fulfillment of the Law.

[167] In light of the demonstrably pejorative nature of the contrast, this is surely Paul's intent (as Betz 249; MacArthur 124; Hansen, *Abraham*, 111), rather than merely to designate Ishmael as born "in the ordinary course of nature" (as most commentators; cf. NIV). Some at least allow for this alternative (Ridderbos, Hendriksen); while Guthrie 123 opts for "natural birth," but then comments as though it had theological significance after all ("Ishmael was the result of Abraham's reliance on human planning rather than reliance on God's promises"). Bruce 217 goes so far as to assert that "no moral censure is implied." In light of this contrast throughout Paul, and especially in light of the further explication of this term in v. 29, this seems to go a bit too far in an attempt to exonerate Abraham.

Rom 4:18–22 makes clear, Paul did indeed consider Isaac's birth to be
wholly supernatural, hence it is not surprising for him to speak of it here
as κατὰ πνεῦμα.[168] In any case, Paul's interests here lie less with the birth
of Isaac and more with the birth of God's present children; and the
language, "according to the Spirit," which picks up this theme from
3:1–5, 14 and 4:6, at the same time points forward to the behavioral
dimension of life in the Spirit that will be explicated in 5:13–6:10.[169]

Second, the designation in v. 24 of the two mothers as representing
"two covenants" is equally important for our purposes. To be sure, Paul
does not here press for the meaning of the second covenant, since his
chief interest is in maintaining a Torah-free existence for Gentile believers and thus to point out the "slavery" of the first covenant. However,
given the context and the present argument, it is arguable that Paul
understood the "second" covenant in the terms set forth in 2 Cor 3:1–18,
where he contrasts the older covenant of Torah (letter) with the "new
covenant of the Spirit." The older covenant given on Mt. Sinai led to
slavery, not to the freedom of "sonship." Whereas the new covenant,
effected by Christ and realized by the Spirit, is precisely what will lie
behind the final wrap-up of the argument of this letter in 5:13–6:10. The
"whole Torah" is fulfilled in the word about love of neighbor, which is
effected not by the Law but by the Spirit, who has replaced Torah and
made true "righteousness" possible. As in 2 Corinthians 3, the Spirit is
sufficient precisely at the point where Torah was not. Thus our sentence
anticipates the concluding argument of 5:13–6:10 that follows the final
appeal of 5:1–12.

GALATIANS 5:4b–6

[4] . . . you who are achieving righteousness[170] by Law have fallen from grace;
[5]for we by the Spirit, on the basis of faith, eagerly await the hope of righteous-

---

[168] See, e.g., Meyer 278; Burton 253; Lietzmann 30; Lagrange 131; Ridderbos 182;
Hendriksen 187; Mussner 319; Schlier 217–18; Betz 243; Boice 483.

[169] Cf. Lincoln, *Paradise*, 26; Longenecker 216–17. As elsewhere (see on 3:1–5, 14),
Lightfoot does not so much as comment on the presence of the Spirit in this passage.

[170] Gk. δικαιοῦσθε. This particular usage demonstrates most of the difficulties in
translating this word "justify." Not only does this English verb eliminate the element
of "righteousness" in the Greek root (from the Hebrew צדק), but it tends to focus on
what happens at the *beginning* of one's relationship with God. Thus English translations in a variety of ways get around the present usage by adding such modals as
"you who are *trying to be*, or who *would be*, justified," whereas no such modal either
exists or is implied. Paul's Greek refers to what they are in fact doing; some are "being
righteous by Law." Cf. Cosgrove, *Cross*, 150–51, who notes, therefore, that the usage
is probably ironic. Those who "are righteous by Law" are going to get the opposite
of what they expect.

ness; ⁶for in Christ Jesus neither circumcision nor uncircumcision means anything; what means something[171] *is faith expressing itself*[172] *through love.*

These words conclude the first part[173] of Paul's appeal to the Galatians in 5:1–12, who by their (near?) capitulation to circumcision risk losing their freedom in Christ. Indeed, they are in danger of losing Christ altogether, since this appeal spells out what has been indicated right along, that Christ and Torah observance are absolutely mutually incompatible. Verse 1, therefore, flows directly from the application of the allegory in 4:28–31. In fact in Paul's original letter the first words in v. 1 would have been directly connected to the final words of our v. 31 without a word or paragraph break.[174] Thus he urges them to stand fast in their freedom in Christ and not be brought again under the "yoke of slavery" (in this case the Law, as it is expressed especially in circumcision).

The paragraph is designed to force the Galatians to take seriously the consequences of yielding to circumcision, which include return to slavery (v. 1), obligation to "do" the whole Law (v. 3), and becoming estranged from Christ by falling away from grace (v. 4). By way of contrast, vv. 5–6 express the alternative to losing out on Christ (v. 5) and reassert the net result of the work of Christ (v. 6). Some have suggested that these latter two verses serve as a summary of 2:15–4:7;[175] while this is correct in one sense, what is new here—its eschatological and ethical thrusts—are what give significance to this passage. In both sentences the Spirit again plays the major role alongside Christ, in v. 5 explicitly and in v. 6 implicitly (by anticipating 5:13–26). Thus these words come as one more emphatic expression of life in Christ as life in the Spirit, to be spelled out in some detail at the conclusion of the letter in 5:13–6:10.

5 To reinforce his appeal to the Galatians who are in danger of submitting to circumcision, Paul once more joins the three concerns of righteousness (justification), faith (in Christ), and the Spirit, now within

---

[171] This is the clear intent of the contrast set out by the ἀλλά.

[172] Gk. ἐνεργουμένη, the same verb used of the Spirit's work in 1 Cor 12:11. The present translation is that suggested by BAGD.

[173] In the second part of the appeal (vv. 7–12) Paul turns his full arsenal against the agitators. They are hindering the Galatians from completing the Christian race by persuading them to leave the truth (v. 7), a persuasion that does not come from God (thus by implication from Satan, v. 8); they are the little leaven about to leaven the whole lump of dough (v. 9), who will have to bear their own judgment (v. 10); Paul finally wishes they would castrate themselves if they want to use the knife at all on the male sexual organ (v. 12).

[174] τῆς ἐλευθέρας τῇ ἐλευθερίᾳ = "of the free woman for freedom." This is in part responsible for the several textual variations in v. 1, as various scribes tried to show the connection between the two sentences.

[175] E.g., Arichea-Nida, Betz, Longenecker.

the theological framework of the "already" and "not yet" of salvation in Christ. Since we have already been justified by faith, as evidenced by the gift of the Spirit, we therefore by that same Spirit[176] and faith live in sure hope of the final outcome of our justification, to be realized with the return of Christ.

The sentence is joined to v. 4 by an explanatory γάρ ("for"), which functions to describe us[177] who belong to Christ, over against those who submit to circumcision—but now in terms of (final) consequences. Over against Torah observance, which results in "being estranged from Christ" and thus (by implication) missing out on the eschatological goal, there stands *faith*—in Christ, who has brought Torah observance to an end, by freeing us from the slavery of Torah—and *the Spirit*, who has replaced Torah by effecting, and thus fulfilling, the righteousness found in Torah. Although not explicit here, there is probably a latent contrast with "flesh," from v. 4.[178] Those who are "being righteous by Law" are thereby yielding to life κατὰ σάρκα ("according to the flesh"), as 3:3 and 4:29 make clear.

It was suggested above on 3:1–5 that even though expressed in terms of "faith" and "works of Law," the ultimate contrast there—and throughout—is between life under Law and life in the Spirit. The order of words in this sentence, set as they are in sharp contrast to v. 4, bears out that observation. "By the Spirit" stands in first position in the sentence because this is how "we" live—as we await the final and certain outcome of our "righteousness"—in sharp contrast to "you" who are now being "righteous" on the basis of Torah observance.[179] Paul then immediately adds, "on the basis of faith [in Christ, is intended]," because this is the predicate underlying present life in the Spirit.[180] Paul's interest is not in

---

[176] In keeping with his overall perspective on this letter, Lightfoot 204 suggests that the sense is blurred here between "the spiritual in man" and the "Divine Spirit." For earlier commentators who held this view, see Meyer 288; even Lagrange 137 entertains it (cf. Schlier, Guthrie), because it was the majority view of the Latin Fathers. Both Pauline usage in general (see ch. 2) and the context of this letter make it an impossible view.

[177] In keeping with Paul's form of argumentation throughout this letter, whenever he speaks of the nature or results of salvation in Christ, he tends to shift from the second or third person into the first person plural so as to include him and them—and all other believers—together. See v. 1 in this paragraph; cf. 3:13–14; 4:3–6. ἡμεῖς stands in the emphatic first position here to highlight the contrast with the "you" in v. 4 who are being righteous by Law.

[178] So Burton 278; Fung 227.

[179] A point also recognized by Ridderbos and Hendriksen. But see Guthrie 129 and Boice 488, who suggest the emphasis lies on faith here (although this word has not appeared since 3:26) and that "by faith" is the proper contrast to v. 4. Both the word order and the rest of the argument favor what is argued here.

[180] For this reason, Cosgrove, *Cross*, 152, suggests that ἐκ πίστεως (on the basis of faith) modifies "by the Spirit." Thus, "the Spirit, which is from faith." This gets at the same idea, but seems less likely in terms of Paul's grammar.

how people are "justified," but in how "justified people" live; and life under Torah and life in the Spirit are mutually incompatible, which is precisely what he will say even more explicitly in v. 18.

By that same Spirit and on the basis of faith in Christ alone, we eagerly await our hope of realizing the eschatological goal, which is here expressed as "the hope of δικαιοσύνη (righteousness/justification)." This ambiguous genitive can mean either "the righteousness for which we hope" (NIV) or "the hope that our justification by faith in Christ and the Spirit has secured." Although the former can easily be fitted into Pauline theology,[181] in context the latter is much to be preferred.[182] Our present justification/righteousness based on the work of Christ and the Spirit is what will be realized—provided we continue in faith and the Spirit and do not return to slavery, which promises no eschatological reward, only death. In this proviso sense, of course, the final "verdict" is future. But that is not Paul's emphasis, which is on "life in the Spirit" vis-à-vis life under Torah observance. The latter not only fails to provide righteousness now, but offers no hope for the future; life in the Spirit, however, includes living a life of genuine righteousness now ("faith expressing itself through the Spirit's fruit of love") and having absolute certainty about its final outcome.[183] We have begun by the Spirit (3:3), and by the Spirit we have entered into our present realization of the promise of "sonship" (3:14; 4:6); moreover, by the Spirit we live in eager anticipation of final realization of the promise—life with Christ forever. But such "life in the Spirit" is not passive; hence the concluding explanation in v. 6, that what counts is neither circumcision nor its opposite, but "faith expressing itself through love."

In its own way, and similar to such passages as 2 Cor 1:21–22 and Eph 1:13–14, this suggests that the eschatological Spirit is the guarantee of final eschatological salvation. Here it is their status as Spirit people and therefore "free children," vis-à-vis their being under Torah, that guarantees the Galatians' hope of the final realization of justification—as well as providing evidence of their present justification, as argued in 3:1–5.

6 With yet another explanatory γάρ, Paul offers a kind of final summation of the present appeal, with its intransigent contrasts of the consequences of life under Torah and life "in Christ." In so doing, he repeats from 1 Cor 7:19 a fundamental "canon" (rule) of his gospel (cf. 6:15): that

---

[181] This is the majority view; see Meyer, Burton, Duncan, Ridderbos, Hendriksen, Bligh, Guthrie, Mussner, Bruce, Betz, Fung, Longenecker, Cosgrove (*Cross*, 152). Otherwise, Lagrange and J. A. Ziesler, *the Meaning of Righteousness* (SNTMS 20; Cambridge: Cambridge University Press, 1972) 179.

[182] See the full discussion in Fung 224–27, 232–35.

[183] The word ἐλπίς ("hope") in Paul, after all, is a "content" word, expressing surety, not uncertainty; cf. Rom 15:13.

neither circumcision nor uncircumcision counts for anything. As ever, he is unyielding on the matter of the circumcision of Gentiles, because such would mean that Torah observance rather than the Spirit identifies God's new covenant people; but neither does he allow that "not being circumcised" in itself is any virtue. This is why he does not demand "uncircumcision" on the part of Jewish believers. The death of Christ has forever eliminated the possibility of attributing significance to either state. The only thing that counts for one who is "in Christ" is *faith* in Christ, which in this case may move very close to the sense that it has in 5:22 of "faithfulness."

At the same time, these words anticipate the argument of 5:13–6:10, where the content of this sentence is spelled out in considerable detail. Thus "faith" is not some form of "easy believism"; neither does the elimination of Torah observance thereby eliminate righteousness. Rather, faith "works"—expresses itself—in the ultimate form of the Christian ethic, love. Since love is specifically asserted in the next section to be the work of the Spirit, that accounts in part for the mention of the Spirit in v. 5. We live now by faith, in the power of the Spirit. That frees us from all forms of religious rules and regulations; but as Paul will go on to argue, the presence of the Spirit does not free us from Christian behavior; freedom (from Torah) is not license to indiscriminate behavior. Indeed, it is quite the opposite; truly Christian behavior is the work of the same Spirit who serves as experiential evidence that we are justified by faith in Christ and not "by works of law."

Thus these two sentences encapsulate the two major theological agendas of this letter, that righteousness in terms of right standing with God is predicated on the work of Christ alone, and that righteousness in terms of righteous behavior is a necessary corollary of faith in Christ Jesus. As we have noted throughout, and will observe again in the final section of the letter, the Spirit plays the key role alongside the effective work of Christ in appropriating both kinds of "righteousness" in the life of the believer and the believing community.

GALATIANS 5:13–6:10

In some ways we come now to the crux for understanding Galatians as a whole. Historically this passage[184] has been understood to reflect a major shift in the letter, from the argument proper to a section of paraenesis (exhortation).[185] Thus Galatians is read as if in three parts: Chapters 1–2 are understood as autobiographical and apologetic; chap-

---

[184] This is true whether the passage is begun here—as one should, since the imperatives begin here—or earlier (usually at v. 1).

[185] For an esp. helpful historical overview of how this section has been understood within Galatians, see Barclay, *Obeying*, 9–26.

ters 3–4 as "doctrinal"; and chapters 5–6 (or beginning here) as "practical application" or as a series of exhortations.[186]

One can make far more sense of the letter as a whole, however, by viewing this section as the final (necessary) stage of the argument.[187] That is, this is not merely a kind of "now that we have got that matter settled, here is how you are to live, given that you are not under Torah." Some of that does exist here, to be sure. Nonetheless, even though this section comes by way of an occasional imperative,[188] it is absolutely essential to the argument that began in 3:1. It functions, in fact, as Paul's response to his own question in 3:3: "Having *begun* by the Spirit, do you now *come to completion* by the flesh?"

Two matters appear to drive the whole: On the one hand stands Paul's deep conviction of the failure of Torah to effect righteousness, both as right standing with God and as behavior that conforms to the character of God.[189] The argument from 2:15 to 4:31 has basically dealt with the work of Christ as effecting righteousness in the first sense, *evidence* for which, of course, is the experienced reality of the Spirit. This passage

---

[186] Perpetuated most recently by Fung 243. Even less convincing is that reading of the letter that sees Paul as fighting on two fronts: with "Judaizers" in 1:6–5:12 and with "libertines" in 5:13–6:10 (Ropes, *Problem*, and W. Lütgert, *Gesetz und Geist: Eine Untersuchung zur Vorgeschichte des Galaterbriefes* [Gütersloh: Bertelsmann, 1919]); see the discussion in Barclay, *Obeying*, 14–15). That the concern is with "libertine tendencies" within Galatia is also held by R. Jewett ("The Agitators and the Galatian Congregation," *NTS* 17 [1970/71] 198–212) and Longenecker; Betz takes a slightly different view that the Galatians themselves were struggling against fleshly desires. A "libertarian" point of view in Galatians is read into the situation from a text like 5:16; but in fact the only *specifics* mentioned (vv. 15, 26; 6:1–5) betray not "libertine" tendencies but conflict within the community. To call community conflict "libertine" is to stretch the meaning of that word beyond recognizable limits. Part of the reason for this view is the difficulty some have in believing that "those who want to be under Torah" (4:21) would at the same time live so contrary to Torah as to need these correctives. But this misses too much, especially the fact that "works of Law" have to do with Torah *observance*, not with genuinely Christian ethics. That is, "works of Torah" have to do with being "religious"; this section has to do with being truly "righteous" once Torah is gone. Thus Barrett has created a problem of his own making, not Paul's, when he suggests that "Paul is not (apparently) making it easy for himself to pass over into the realm of ethics" (*Freedom*, 56).

[187] For a more complete presentation similar to that offered here, see Barclay, *Obeying*. Frank Matera ("The Culmination of Paul's Argument to the Galatians: Gal. 5:1–6:17," *JSNT* 32 [1988] 79–91) has also argued for this section as integral to the argument of the letter. Although there are some helpful insights in this essay (e.g., the role of circumcision at the end of the argument), Matera fails to do justice to 5:13–6:10, esp. by downplaying the role of v. 13 and by focusing on the passages that mention Torah (vv. 14, 18, 23) without really coming to terms with the role of the flesh/Spirit contrast.

[188] As we will note below, there are very few imperatives as such.

[189] In this letter, and in keeping with Pauline theology in general, such behavior is specified as "faith expressing itself in love." See on 5:6; cf. 2 Cor 3:18; Rom 8:28–30.

now picks up the second conviction, the failure of Torah to effect righteousness in terms of behavior.

On the other hand, in terms of the argument of Galatians proper, there is the objection that was—or would be—raised by his opposition: If you eliminate Torah observance altogether—as Paul indeed does—what happens to obedience? Since the whole point of Torah is to lead God's people to obedience, if you take that away, what is to keep them from doing "whatever they wish" (5:17)?[190]

Paul answers both issues in this passage. Having begun by the Spirit, one comes to completion by the Spirit. The key to ethical life, including everyday behavior in its every form, resides in the fundamental Pauline imperative: "Walk by/in the Spirit, and you will not fulfill the desire of the flesh." The Spirit is the empowering for life that is both over against the flesh (so that one may not do whatever one wishes, v. 17) and in conformity to the character of God (here as the "fruit of the Spirit").

Paul's essential point in the argument, therefore, is twofold. First, precisely because of the *inadequacy of Torah* to empower, he argues (a) that in any case the whole of Torah is fulfilled in the love command, (b) that such love is the fruit of the Spirit, and therefore (c) that one who is led of the Spirit is not under Torah—indeed there can be no Torah (except for "the law of Christ") for those who live by the Spirit and so manifest the Spirit's "fruitfulness" (v. 23b).

Second, in an argument that anticipates Romans 6 and 8, Paul here maintains that Christ and the Spirit are God's own response to *life in the flesh*. Those who "walk by the Spirit," he affirms, will not carry out the ἐπιθυμίαν ("desire") of the flesh, precisely because those who are Christ's have crucified the flesh with its ἐπιθυμίαις ("desires"; v. 24).

The key element in all of this, just as in the main theological argument of 3:1–4:7, is their experience of the Spirit. Life in the Spirit means that one is *no longer under Law* (5:18); but it does not mean that one is "lawless." To the contrary, the Spirit person evidences the fruit of the Spirit and thus "fulfills" the whole of Torah (5:14; cf. 5:3)—by "fulfilling" the "law of Christ" (6:2). Life in the Spirit also means life *over against the flesh*, for the Spirit stands in absolute opposition to life in the flesh. As a result one may not do whatever one wishes, as one could when living in the flesh and apart from Torah.

Thus for Paul both flesh and Torah belong to the old aeon, whose essential power has been crippled by Christ's death and resurrection, which marked the dawning of the new aeon, the time of the Spirit. Although the flesh is still about, and stands in mortal opposition to the

---

[190] Cf. Burton 290; Lincoln, *Paradise*, 26; Barclay, *Obeying*, 111. This seems to be the best response to the issue raised by some, "How can Paul proclaim freedom from the Law in Galatians 3–4 and then go on 'to lay down the law' in Galatians 5–6?" Cf. n. 186 above.

Spirit, Christ's death has brought about our death—to Torah (2:19) and to the flesh (5:24). Having been raised with Christ, we now live empowered by the Spirit *of Christ*, who has already defeated our lifelong foe. Thus, as believers walk by the Spirit (i.e., with the Spirit's empowering), they are subject neither to the flesh's bidding (5:16) nor to the Law's enslaving (5:18).

The argument itself—and it is argument, not just a series of imperatives—is easy enough to follow,[191] even if some of its details have long eluded interpreters. It comes essentially in four parts: (1) 5:13–15 serve as a kind of thesis statement for the whole, weaving together two previous threads from 5:1 and 6 (the call to *freedom* [from Torah] and *love* [faith's true "work"]). Love is the proper way freedom from Torah's "slavery" expresses itself—with a new form of "slavery," in behalf of one another. Indeed, the love command is how the whole of Torah is fulfilled. The new element in the argument, which along with the Spirit will dominate from here on, is "the flesh," which apparently has found "an occasion" in their midst in the form of "biting and devouring one another" (v. 15).[192] In light of v. 26 and some of the particulars in 6:1–10, one suspects that Paul knows more about their situation than the mere fact that they are in danger of capitulation to Torah observance.[193] His point, then, in this thesis statement is that freedom from Torah does not mean freedom for the flesh (to chew up one's neighbor) but means freedom for love (to become servants to one another).

(2) 5:16–26 then go on to detail how vv. 13–15 can work—by means of the Spirit. But now it is not simply a matter of the Spirit's replacing Torah (although that point recurs in vv. 18 and 23), but Paul also addresses that area of human fallenness that Torah was incapable of dealing with—the life of the flesh. In vv. 16–18 he promises (by way of imperative) not only that "walking in the Spirit" is God's effective response to "making provision for the flesh" (v. 13), but also that such a person who is "led of the Spirit" is "not under Torah" (v. 18)—because the Spirit accomplishes the love that "fulfills" Torah. In vv. 19–23 he contrasts these two kinds of existence: the one, life in the flesh, is intentionally placed on the Torah (i.e., the "before Christ") side of life by the designation "*works* of the flesh." Nor is it accidental, in light of v. 15, that eight of the fifteen behaviors and attitudes so designated are sins of

---

[191] The pattern is similar to what has preceded: argument (3:1–4:7), followed by application (4:8–11, 12–20); argument (4:21–27), followed by application (4:28–31; 5:1–6, 7–12). In the present case, the "argument" is found in 5:13–26, the "application" in 6:1–10.

[192] As Bruce 242 correctly notes: "Internecine strife is the only 'work of the flesh' against which Paul specifically warns the Galatians." Cf. Cosgrove, *Cross*, 157, and Barclay, *Obeying*, 152–53.

[193] On this matter see esp. Barclay, *Obeying*, 146–77.

discord in the Christian community. The other existence, life in the Spirit, is described in terms of the fruit that is eventually manifested by those who walk by the Spirit. Verses 24–26 then bring closure to this section of the argument by reintroducing the work of Christ (his crucifixion spells the end of flesh) and by tying that work (through the motif of "life" following crucifixion) to that of the Spirit. To "live" by the Spirit demands behavior in keeping with the Spirit, which means no fleshly works that effectively destroy others (v. 26).

(3) 6:1–6 pick up the final exhortation in v. 26, and by way of positive and negative contrasts urge a life in the Spirit that expresses "the law of Christ." Here is spelled out in very practical ways, addressed specifically to their situation, how "being slaves to one another through love" is worked out in the community of the Spirit. It means a proper estimation of oneself (vv. 3–4), over against "conceit" (v. 26); it means "bearing one another's burdens and thus fulfilling the law of Christ" (v. 2), over against "envy" and "provocation" (v. 26).

(4) 6:7–10 finally bring the whole full circle by the metaphor of sowing and reaping. Since what one sows one also reaps, the Galatians are urged not to "sow to the flesh" (as described above), but to "sow to the Spirit," in the form of "doing good" to one another (vv. 9–10), so that they might also "reap" the eternal life that life in the Spirit promises (v. 8). Thus, the final word is like the first one: no "occasion" for flesh, but loving one another by doing good to one and all, and the Spirit as the essential—and sufficient(!)—constituent for this to happen.

Before looking at the argument in some detail, especially focusing on the role of the Spirit in all of this,[194] two further observations are needed: First, as noted above, what is striking about the material is the general paucity of imperatives, especially in 5:13–26.[195] The whole is indeed framed by imperatives, and the argument is carried forward at crucial places by imperatives (e.g., 5:16; 5:25; 6:1, 7). But by and large the imperatives are regularly explained or elaborated by material that is consistently in the indicative. Whatever else, this material (especially 5:13–26) is not just a series of exhortations; it is argument by way of exhortation. Thus, both the nature and structure of this material suggest that the section functions as part of the argument of the letter.

---

[194] In the exegesis that follows, we will at least overview each paragraph. Detailed exegesis will be reserved for those passages that deal directly with the Spirit.

[195] For example, in vv. 13–26 there are only two second person plural imperatives ("become slaves of one another" in v. 13 and "walk by the Spirit" in v. 16). As vv. 25–26 move the argument back to application, Paul shifts to "hortatory" imperatives ("let us . . . "). The number of imperatives do indeed increase in the practical application section, 6:1–10 (3 second plural imperatives; 2 hortatory subjunctives; and 2 third singular imperatives).

Second, quite in contrast to how this material is read by the most of us—and is presented in many of the commentaries[196]—the concern from beginning to end is with Christian life in community, not with the interior life of the individual Christian. Apart from 5:17c, which is usually completely decontextualized and misread (see below), there is not a hint that Paul is here dealing with a "tension" between flesh and Spirit that rages within the human breast—in which the flesh most often appears as the stronger opponent.[197] To the contrary, the issue from the beginning (vv. 13–15) and throughout (vv. 19–21, 26; 6:1–4, 7–10) has to do with Spirit life within the believing community. The individual is not thereby brushed aside; after all, one both enters and lives within the Christian community at the individual level. But that is where the individual believer fits into the argument. Within the context of the church each one is to live out his or her freedom by becoming love slaves to one another (v. 13). The imperative "walk by the Spirit" does not emphasize "the introspective conscience of the Western mind,"[198] but rather calls for a life in the Spirit that does not "eat and devour" one another (v. 15) and which does not through conceit provoke and envy others (v. 26). The "fruit of the Spirit" engenders "love, joy, and peace" within the community, not primarily within the believer's own heart (v. 22). Such a Spirit person will be among those who restore an individual who "is overtaken in a fault" (6:1). And the final expression of "sowing in the Spirit" is "to do good to all people, especially those of the household of faith" (v. 10).

GALATIANS 5:13–15

[13]*For you were called to freedom, brothers and sisters; only do not [allow]*[199] *your freedom to become an occasion for the flesh, but through love*[200] *perform the duties of a slave*[201] *to one another.* [14]*For the entire law is fulfilled*[202] *in*

---

[196] Duncan is a happy exception, but even he does not take this seriously until v. 25.

[197] See the discussion on v. 17 below.

[198] Language based on Stendahl's essay by that name. Stendahl has shown, convincingly to my mind, that one rather thoroughly misreads Paul, and especially this text, if one begins with the assumption that Paul is basically concerned with the problem of sin and conscience.

[199] Paul's sentence lacks a verb at this point; the negative particle μή indicates that an imperative is implied, much like the one supplied. Cf. NIV, NRSV, "do not use."

[200] Instead of διὰ τῆς ἀγάπης, the Western tradition (D F G 104 sa it Ambrosiaster) reads τῇ ἀγάπῃ τοῦ πνεύματος ("in/by the love of the Spirit")—with exegetical insight, we will argue below.

[201] Gk. δουλεύετε, which has the literal, technical sense of this translation. It means neither "be enslaved" (since it is not passive) nor "serve" in the milder sense of the verb διακονέω. Rather it means precisely this, "to perform the duties of a slave (by serving, etc.)."

[202] The Western tradition, followed by the Majority text, reads πληροῦται in place

one sentence, namely, "You shall love your neighbor as yourself." [15]*But if you eat and devour one another, beware lest you be consumed by one another.*

As noted above, this paragraph functions as a kind of thesis statement for the rest of the argument-appeal of the letter. In v. 6 Paul had just asserted that observance or nonobservance of religious obligation, in the form of circumcision, counts for absolutely nothing—in terms either of one's relationship with God or of one's membership in the people of God. What counts, on the contrary, is "faith that expresses itself through love." That is now spelled out by specific application to their situation. Indeed, verse 15 suggests that the whole section (5:13–6:10) has been determined by Paul's knowledge of their local situation(s). Thus, by the very nature of the material, the section that ties up the remaining loose threads of the argument of the letter at the same time serves in a very practical way to bring truly Christian behavior back into these communities.

Several matters emerge—and converge—in this first paragraph: First, in v. 13 Paul deliberately sets out to bring together the two crucial items from vv. 1–6: "freedom" (from Torah), and "love" (as the way faith "works"). Freedom from the enslavement of Torah paradoxically means to take on a new form of "slavery"—that of loving servanthood to one another.[203]

Second, love of this kind is the way the whole of Torah (in terms of human relationships) is "fulfilled," which is why Paul is not anxious about Christ's having brought the time of Torah to an end. The aim of Torah, which Torah was helpless to bring off, was to create a loving community in which God's own character and purposes are fulfilled as God's people love one another the way he loves them. Since love is later expressed as a "fruit of the Spirit," one may thus see in v. 14 what will be spelled out clearly in vv. 18 and 23, namely, that the Spirit has "replaced" Torah by fulfilling the aim of Torah.[204] Thus "love of neighbor" as the "fulfillment of Torah" fully anticipates the role of the Spirit in the subsequent argument.[205]

---

of the (surely original) πεπλήρωται of P[46] א A B C 062 0254 33 81 104 326 1175 1241 1739 pc. D* F G a b Ambrosiaster also add ὑμῖν before "in one word," thus making clear that in their understanding of Paul the Scripture is being fulfilled as the Galatians love one another. But that is *not* Paul's point, as is noted in the discussion below.

[203]On the meaning of this verb see n. 201 above.

[204]Thus the perfect passive "has been fulfilled" does not mean that the love command "sums up" the whole of the Law, since there is no incontrovertible evidence for such a meaning for this word. Rather it means what the verb ordinarily denotes, that the whole point of Torah is fulfilled, completed, by the practice of this one command, which, of course, as vv. 16–26 make clear, is now to be carried out by believers through the empowering of the Spirit. On this word see esp. Barclay, *Obeying*, 135–42, and Stephen Westerholm, "On Fulfilling the Whole Law (Gal 5.14)," *SEÅ* 51–2 (1986/87) 229–37.

[205]A point often overlooked in the commentaries (e.g., Ridderbos, Guthrie, Boice, Fung).

Third, and the apparent driving concern of the entire argument, "freedom (from Torah)" does not mean "lawlessness," now expressed as "providing an opportunity[206] for the flesh." Even though hinted at before (3:3; 4:23, 29), this is now the new element in the argument, which will replace Torah observance as the dominant negative motif in this section. In the present paragraph, the "flesh" manifests itself in the form of community strife, in which believers "bite and devour" one another.[207] It is precisely at this point, the "life of the flesh," that Torah had demonstrated itself to be inadequate. Torah obviously "laid down the law" against such behavior; but by deflecting Torah toward "works of Law" in the form of Jewish identity markers, one could be "religious" without being "righteous." Christ brought an end to Torah observance in part for that very reason. The Spirit replaced Torah so that God's people, Jew and Gentile alike, would have a new "identity": the indwelling of the Spirit of the living God himself. At the same time the Spirit would be sufficient to accomplish what Torah could not: effectively stand in opposition to the flesh.

Thus, even though the Spirit is not directly mentioned in this foundational opening exhortation, the Western text of v. 14 ("by the love of the Spirit serve one another") has it right in terms of Paul's meaning, as will be made plain in the argument that follows.

GALATIANS 5:16–18[208]

[16]*But I say, walk by the Spirit and you will not carry out the desire of the flesh;* [17]*for the flesh has desires over against the Spirit, and the Spirit over against*

---

[206] Gk. ἀφορμή, which literally referred to the starting-point or base of operations for an expedition. In its metaphorical denotations, especially in Paul, it can pejoratively express a kind of "pretext" for some action (e.g., 2 Cor 5:12; 11:12; 1 Tim 5:14); but here, even though distinctly pejorative, the literal sense seems to be the point of its metaphorical usage. Freedom is not to be turned into a kind of "base of operations" for the flesh. Otherwise Betz 272.

[207] There is considerable difference of opinion as to the place of v. 15 (and therefore 26 and 6:1–3) in the argument. Lightfoot, e.g., suggests (209) that it is "a sort of parenthetic warning"; those who see the whole as a kind of general paraenesis tend to view it this way. Betz 277 sees it as belonging to a "typos" and therefore unrelated to any specific situation in Galatia (cf. Meyer, Mussner). Most, however, see it as at least reflecting something going on in Galatia (e.g., Calvin, Burton, Duncan, Schlier, Hendriksen, Boice, Bruce, Fung, Cole, Longenecker). But they seldom make what seems to be the obvious connection between vv. 13, 15, 16, and 19–21 as "works of the *flesh*" (Bruce is a singular exception).

[208] *Bibliography:* P. **Althaus**, " 'Das ihr nicht tut, was ihr wollt.' Zur Auslegung von Gal. 5,17," *TLZ* 76 (1951) 15–18; J. D. G. **Dunn**, "Romans 7:14–25 in the Theology of Paul," in *Essays on Apostolic Themes: Studies in Honor of Howard M. Ervin* (ed. P. Elbert; Peabody, Mass.: Hendrickson Publishers, 1985) 49–70 [= *ThZ* 31 (1975) 257–73]; R. **Lutjens**, " 'You Do Not Do What You Want': What Does Galatians 5:17

the flesh; for[209] *these stand in opposition to each other, so that you may not
do whatever you wish.* [18]*Now if you are led by the Spirit, you are not under Law.*

That this paragraph functions as Paul's response to the various
matters in vv. 13–15 is confirmed in a number of ways.[210] First, the
solemn asseveration with which it begins, "but I say," stands in direct
contrast to v. 15 with its warning that their kind of "works of the flesh"
leads eventually to their being "consumed" by one another. "But I say,"
in contrast to that, "walk by the Spirit and you will not fulfill the desire
of the flesh," that is, you will not eat and devour one another[211]—not to
mention, of course, not engage in any other such behavior. Second, in
v. 16 the antidote to the possibility that freedom from Torah might
provide "a base of operations for the flesh" (v. 13) resides in the primary
Pauline ethical imperative, "walk by the Spirit." By so doing, Paul now
promises, one will thereby "not carry out the desire of the flesh" (= "not
make provision for the flesh"). Third, the sudden, seemingly disjointed,
mention of Torah in v. 18 ("Now if you are being led by the Spirit, you
are not under Law") is accounted for at this point as a response to v. 14.
That is, the Spirit who empowers love thereby "fulfills" Torah, so that
the one led by the Spirit is "not under Law." Its mention in the argument
here suggests that Paul's concern is to put forth the Spirit as God's
response to *both* the flesh and Torah, because the latter could *not* counteract the desire of the flesh, but the Spirit can and does.

Thus the flow of thought is easily accounted for. Verse 16, which
offers Paul's basic imperative, responds to the problem of the flesh as it
emerges in vv. 13–15. Verse 17 in turn explains how the assertion in v. 16
is true.[212] The reason walking by the Spirit means that one will thereby
not carry out the desire of the flesh is that the Spirit and the flesh are
absolutely antithetical to each other, and thus the Spirit opposes the flesh
precisely so that one may not do whatever one wishes, even though
Torah is gone; rather, one will carry out the purposes of the Spirit that
oppose those of the flesh. Further, Paul goes on in v. 18, that means that
one thus led by the Spirit is likewise not under Torah, because by walking

---

Really Mean?" *Presbyterion* 16 (1990) 103–17; David **Wenham**, "The Christian Life: A
Life of Tension? A Consideration of the Nature of Christian Experience in Paul," in
Pauline Studies (ed. D. A. Hagner, M. J. Harris; Grand Rapids: Eerdmans, 1980) 80–94.

[209]For the γάρ of P[46] ℵ* B D* F G 33 lat, the later Majority text (A C Ψ 0122
Byz) has substituted a δέ, a reading that is in keeping with the mistaken theological-
existential reading of this text as having to do with some internal struggle within the
human heart between "flesh" and Spirit.

[210]Cf. Meyer 305; Boice 493–94.

[211]On the question of the connection between vv. 13, 15, and 16 see n. 207 above.

[212]As over against the majority (of those who recognize the γάρ at all), who see
v. 17 as "explaining" the implied assumption of "warfare" found in v. 16—which
could be possible, if in fact it fitted at all with Paul's clear point: the sufficiency of the
Spirit vis-à-vis life under Law and against the flesh.

in the Spirit one both "fulfills" Torah (v. 14) and lives over against the flesh, in the face of which Torah had stood helpless. At issue, therefore, is not some internal tension in the present life of the individual believer,[213] but the sufficiency of the Spirit for life without Torah—a sufficiency that enables them to live so as not to revert to their *former* life as pagans (= life in the flesh, as vv. 19–21 make clear).

16 This opening sentence offers the divine antidote to the life of the flesh. It comes by way of imperative, "walk by the Spirit," and concludes with the note of promise, in response to vv. 13 and 15, that therefore "you will not carry out the desire of the flesh." That much seems easy enough, but several matters call for closer attention.

1. Even though this imperative occurs only here in the Pauline corpus, both the argument in which it occurs and the rest of Pauline theology indicate that this is Paul's basic ethical imperative.[214] To be sure, the love command, which many see as the basic imperative, occurs far more often in his letters.[215] But both the present context and the form suggest that this imperative is the prior one. As to the present context: (a) This imperative explains how vv. 13–14 work; that is, by walking in the Spirit one thus fulfills the love command which in turn fulfills Torah; and (b) love appears as the first of the Spirit's fruit in the life of the believer and believing community. By the very nature of things, that which empowers love precedes the love command. Moreover, by designating the "virtue list" in vv. 22–23 as "fruit *of the Spirit*," Paul puts all other such lists and ethical imperatives into proper theological perspective.

As to form, the verb "to walk," derived from his Jewish heritage, is Paul's most common word to describe or urge ethical behavior.[216] "To walk" in the ways of God is what Jewish understanding of ethics is all about; hence this verb occurs 17 times in the corpus with this ethical

---

[213] See nn. 222, 223, and 233 below. It should pointed out here that those who take this view of vv. 16–17 all fail to show how it fits into the overall argument of the letter, which to this point has had to do singularly with Gentiles' not needing to come under (now passé) Torah observance. How, one wonders, does this sudden shift to Christian existence as primarily one of (basically unsuccessful) conflict fit into this argument at all? No wonder it has been so popular to see this section (5:13–6:10) as basically unconnected "practical" exhortation. Cf. Barclay, *Obeying*, 112, who further observes that "the [immediate] context rules this interpretation out," because it places v. 17 in such unabashed contradiction to v. 16 and thereby "wholly undermines Paul's purpose in this passage." Not only so, but in terms of "reader response criticism," which understands the letter to be an attempt to *persuade*, one wonders what could possibly be the point of such persuasion that in effect contravenes the very thing he was trying to persuade them of in v. 16.

[214] Cf. Betz 277: "The imperative πνεύματι περιπατεῖτε . . . sums up the Apostle's paraenesis, and therefore defines Paul's concept of the Christian life."

[215] See, e.g., 1 Thes 4:9; 1 Cor 13:1–7, 13; 16:14; Rom 13:8–10; Col 3:14; Eph 5:2.

[216] See esp. the discussion on 2 Cor 12:18; cf. *TDNT* 5.940–45.

intent. Thus the combination of the imperative "walk," joined by the dative "by the Spirit," puts the two basic matters together. Ethical life is still a matter of "walking in the ways of God," but for Paul this is empowered for God's new covenant people by God's empowering presence in the person of his Holy Spirit.

As usual with such imperatives, it comes in the present (iterative) tense and refers to "the long obedience in the same direction."[217] Paul is not talking about what one does from time to time, but about a way of life in general. Thus, we might correctly translate, "go on walking in the Spirit."[218]

2. Here in particular, as noted above in chapter 2, the anarthrous πνεύματι ("Spirit" without the definite article) is certain evidence that by this formula Paul only and always means the Spirit of the living God, the Holy Spirit. In the immediate context this is made certain not only by the whole argument, but also by the articular usage in v. 17, which in Greek grammar is anaphoric. That is, in its second mention in v. 17 "Spirit" means "*the* one and only well-known Holy Spirit about whom we have talked so much in this letter."[219]

3. Nevertheless, here as elsewhere, the precise nuance of the dative is difficult to establish. It may be either instrumental ("walk by means of, i.e., empowered by, the Spirit") or locative of sphere ("walk in the sphere of the Spirit"). Although in the final analysis, and especially in light of the usage in v. 18, this formula is probably instrumental, I would argue for more of an overlap in Pauline usage than for rigid grammatical categories. That is, even though one is to walk by means of the Spirit, one does so because one is also to walk in the sphere of the Spirit, that is, in the arena of the Spirit's present life and activity.[220]

4. Picking up the contrasts in 4:29 of the two sons who were born "according to the flesh" and "according to the Spirit," Paul now places the life of the Spirit no longer over against Torah observance (except for vv. 18 and 23), but over against "the desire of the flesh." As noted elsewhere,[221] the term "flesh," which is one of the more fluid words in Paul's vocabulary, generally describes not the individual's "sinful nature"[222] but one's life before and outside of Christ. That is, "flesh" and

---

[217] See the book by this title by my colleague, Eugene Peterson (Downers Grove: InterVarsity, 1980).

[218] As does N. Turner in MHT 3.75.

[219] Contra Lagrange 147, who appears to be alone among modern interpreters in taking πνεῦμα as referring to the human spirit.

[220] Cf. Betz 277–78; it "expresses the origin as well as the quality of that way of life."

[221] On this see the discussion on 3:3 and 4:29 above; cf. also 2 Cor 5:14–17.

[222] As is most often suggested by those who comment on this passage. Even less possible is the alternative suggested by BAGD, "satisfy one's physical desires." The listing of "works of the flesh" in vv. 19–21, most of which lie quite apart from one's physical desires, render such a view impossible.

"Spirit" are first of all eschatological realities, denoting the essential characteristic of the two ages, before and after Christ. "Flesh," which began as a term denoting one's humanity and creatureliness, has for Paul taken on all the connotations of our humanity in its essential fallenness. As noted on 3:3, to live "according to the flesh" is to live in keeping with the values and desires of life in the present age that stand in absolute contradiction to God and his ways. Hence the ultimate contrasts in Paul are eschatological: life "according to the flesh," lived according to the present age that has been condemned through the cross and is passing away, or life "according to the Spirit," lived in keeping with the values and norms of the coming age inaugurated by Christ through his death and resurrection and empowered by the eschatological Spirit.

That such a view lies behind this contrast seems certain both from the context, where life "in the flesh" is described in terms of a former way of life (vv. 19–21a), whose eschatological end is that "such people shall not inherit the kingdom of God," and from v. 24 where the believer who now lives by the Spirit is described as having "crucified the flesh with its passions and desires." That is, Christ and the Spirit mark the turning of the ages; and therefore "life in keeping with the flesh" and "life by the Spirit" are mutually incompatible options, just as "faith in Christ" and "works of Torah" have been argued in 2:15–5:6 to be mutually exclusive options. Earlier (in 2 Cor 10:2–3, q.v.) Paul had said that even though he still lives "in the flesh," meaning in a body conditioned by this present age that is passing away, he does not thereby carry on warfare "according to the flesh," meaning with the weapons or from the perspective of the age that is passing away. So here, Paul is not setting out to describe the tension of Spirit life in the "already," in which the "flesh" still holds sway. However Paul may feel about that issue—and our existential problem is that he never speaks to it at all in these terms[223]—here he is describing life before and after Christ and the Spirit. Even though we do

---

[223] Here I fully agree with Stendahl ("Paul"), who points this out with striking clarity. One of the glaring weaknesses of Dunn's argument ("Romans 7:14–25") is methodological. He begins with a decided point of view on a text over which there is great controversy, then brings in a noncontextual reading of Gal 5:17 as support, and concludes by applying it to all other "weakness" and "flesh" texts in Paul, which simply will not hold up under scrutiny (see esp. the critique in Wenham, "Christian Life"). What Dunn fails to address is the fact that in no clear and unambiguous text does Paul ever so much as hint at the "normal" Christian life (= basically tension-filled and defeated) that Dunn espouses for him (e.g., referring to Gal 5:17, "In consequence the believer finds himself torn in two by conflicting desires and impulses, and his experience as a man of Spirit in the flesh is one of continuing frustration," p. 63). To the contrary, as Stendahl puts it, Paul reflects a rather "robust conscience," and never elsewhere (Romans 7 aside) so much as mentions "indwelling sin" within the believer, nor does he ever call his readers to deal with such. If this were as important to Paul theologically as Dunn would have us believe, one would think such a theological concern would emerge at some point clearly and unambiguously.

indeed live in the "overlap of the ages," believers are essentially eschatological people whose lives are marked by and determined by the indwelling and empowering Spirit. Nor is this triumphalism for Paul, as
2 Cor 11–13 has made abundantly clear. But the "tension" of the "already" and the "not yet" is not between an ever present "sinful nature"
and the "indwelling Spirit," but between the suffering and weaknesses
that still mark our present existence and the resurrection life of the future
by which we live—and endure—in the present sufferings.

This view of things is also the best explanation for the singular, "the
desire[224] of the flesh." Paul is first thinking not about the several "works"
of the flesh he will soon describe, but, as he will go on to explain in v. 17,
about the basic *perspective* of life in the flesh. Such a perspective, for
which those of the Spirit are to make no provision whatsoever, radically
opposes God and his ways, here designated as opposition to the Spirit.

5. This understanding of the sentence in context also helps to resolve
the form of the second clause, "you will never carry out[225] the desire of
the flesh." It is grammatically possible[226] that the two clauses together
mean "live by the Spirit and *do not* gratify the desires of the flesh" (NRSV).
But not only does that run a bit roughshod over what Paul actually
says[227]—after all, he is perfectly capable of expressing himself by two
coordinate imperatives if he so desires—but it also tends to be a noncontextual reading of the text in light of a view of v. 17c that is informed
not by this context but by a certain reading of Rom 7:14–25.

On the contrary, this clause functions similarly to the apodosis of a
"future most certain" conditional clause. As one "goes on walking by the
Spirit," one will thereby not carry out the desire of the flesh. This is Paul's
response to the issue raised in v. 13, concerning how it is possible to live

---

[224]Gk. ἐπιθυμίαν. Part of our difficulty with this passage lies with this word, which
the KJV most often translated "lust." The word, especially in secular Greek, is
completely neutral, referring to "desire" or "longing." Even in moral contexts, the
"longing" can be for something good (cf. 1 Thes 2:17; Phil 1:23) or evil (as most often
in the NT). Paul's explanation in v. 17 indicates that even though the flesh lies on the
negative, evil side of things, ἐπιθυμία does not inherently carry evil connotations (note
esp. that this word never occurs in the Pauline vice lists, except in Col 3:5, where it
is specifically modified by the adjective "evil"). After all, the Spirit is said to do this
as well (v. 17b). Thus "desire" is evil in this case not because it is so in itself, but
precisely because it is "the desire *of the flesh*." Thus the word here refers not to "lust,"
but to the kind of desires that one has who lives from the perspective of the flesh. Cf.
the discussion in Burton 199–200.

[225]Gk. οὐ μὴ τελέσητε. The verb τελέω means to "carry out" or "accomplish." Its
basic root has to do with goal or purpose; the one walking by the Spirit does not
accomplish the goals of the flesh.

[226]Because the clause is joined to the imperative "walk by the Spirit" with an
"and," and because in the OT the divine imperatives often took the form of a future
negation ("thou shalt not").

[227]So also almost all modern interpreters.

in freedom so as not to make it a base-camp from which the flesh can operate. Accordingly, Paul's clause takes the form of promise, not imperative.[228] As 6:1 and other passages make plain enough, Paul does not hereby suggest that Spirit people never sin. His concern is to describe how vv. 13–15 are worked out in the lives of those who no longer live under Torah. They began Christian life by the Spirit; as they "walk" by that same Spirit, they will thereby not follow after their former way of life, lived from the perspective of the old age that is passing away.

6. That leads finally to the question that is often less exegetical than existential. "That is all fine and good," it is often said, "but *how* does one go about walking by the Spirit" so as not to live from the perspective of the flesh? The best answer to that question is still the exegetical one, not an existential or formulaic one. Paul, of course, is speaking from within a historical context in which the Spirit was the primary, experienced reality of Christian life, as 3:2–5 has made plain. This appeal to the Galatians, therefore, is just that, an appeal to "go on walking by the very same Spirit by which you came to faith and with whom God still richly supplies you, including by the working of miracles in your midst." That is, a powerful and experiential—supernatural, if you will—presuppositional base lies behind this imperative.

But it comes by way of imperative, not by way of a passive indicative (as in v. 18). Life in the Spirit is not passive submission to the Spirit to do a supernatural work in one's life; rather, it requires conscious effort, so that the indwelling Spirit may accomplish his ends in one's life. One is urged to "walk by the Spirit" or "live by the Spirit" by deliberately "conforming one's life to the Spirit" (v. 25). If such a person is also described as being "led by the Spirit," that does not mean passively; it means to rise up and follow the Spirit by walking in obedience to the Spirit's desire.

The difference between "them" and "us" many centuries later is almost certainly at the experiential level, wherein their dynamic experience of the Spirit both at the beginning of life in Christ and in their ongoing life in the church would have made this imperative seem much more "practical" and everyday. Since the Spirit is God's own empowering presence, Paul expected God's supernatural aid to enable them to live in keeping with God's character and purposes. After all, Paul's point in all of this must not be lost sight of: in a world in which Torah observance no longer obtains, *the Spirit is sufficient and adequate to accomplish God's purposes in and among his people.* Spirit people march to a different drummer, and the Spirit empowers them to live in such a way that their lives

---

[228] So also Burton 299: "οὐ μὴ τελέσητε is equivalent to an emphatic promissory future . . . expressing, not a command, but a strong assurance that if they walk by the Spirit they will not, in fact, fulfill the flesh-lust." To take it otherwise is to opt for a sense that "rarely occurs."

evidence that fact; their behavior is of a decidedly different character from that of their former way of life. Just as with the "works of Torah," the time for the "works of the flesh" belongs to the past. Spirit people, by walking in the Spirit by whom they began life in Christ, will thereby not walk in the ways of their pagan past.

17 The phrasing of this sentence—flesh and Spirit as in opposition to each other and the final clause, "so that you may not do whatever you wish"—is what has caused vv. 16–17 to be lifted from context and made to refer to individual Christian life in general. At the same time the present verse is often read as though the Galatians had a copy of Romans in hand.[229] But that will scarcely do. In order to hear Paul, let us first note the structure and function of the three clauses that make up the verse, helped along by a visual display of the structure:

> *For* (γάρ)
> the flesh has desires
>   over against the Spirit
>   *and* (δέ)
> the Spirit
>   over against the flesh
>   *for* (γάρ)
> these (two) realities are in opposition to each other
>   *so that* (ἵνα)
>   whatever   things   you wish,
>   these   things   you may not do

The initial "for" signals that Paul is about to *explain* some matters from v. 16 *by way of elaboration.*[230] The reason why walking by the Spirit excludes carrying out the desire of the flesh is that flesh and Spirit have "desires" that stand as polar opposites, which is stated by the first two clauses and reaffirmed by the second "for" clause. Paul's point has to do with the *incompatibility* of life in the Spirit with life in the flesh;[231] they

---

[229] Not only so, but the assumption is that they also would have understood Rom 7:14–25 in a way *that is quite foreign to Paul's point.* See the discussion of this passage in the next chapter.

[230] Cf. Burton 300: "The γάρ is confirmatory and the whole sentence a proof of the statement of v. 16." So Schlier 248. Understandably, most commentators make no mention of the γάρ. The crucial question, of course, has to do with how one understands v. 16. The majority view assumes Paul now to be explaining the latent conflict mentioned in v. 16, which then leads to all the contextual difficulties noted above (n. 212). What, then, is the point of *persuasion*, one wonders. In any case, Barclay (*Obeying*, 111n11) rightly observes, "There is certainly no indication that 5.17 should be read as a *contrast* to 5.16."

[231] Just as 3:1–5 argues for the *incompatibility* of the Spirit and Torah observance.

belong to different worlds, to different ways of life altogether. The implication is that to live in one means *not* to live in the other.[232] This is why
walking by the Spirit excludes carrying out the desire of the flesh; flesh
and Spirit, Paul says, are not only incompatible, they stand in unrelieved
opposition to one another. There is not a hint in any of this that "warfare" is going on in the human breast, which in effect leaves the believer
in a state of helplessness (one *cannot* do what one wishes).[233] These
sentences belong to Paul's overall theological framework within which
eschatological salvation is being worked out. The "sphere" of the flesh is
obviously still about, and by implication the believer could fall prey to
its perspective. In that sense there is always "tension" for the Spirit
person. But this is also where the Spirit comes in—as the intractable foe
of the flesh. The good news for Paul is not only that the Spirit has come,
who is thus opposed to the flesh, but that the Spirit is also *God's enabling
power over against the flesh*, which is why he can urge upon them the bold
imperative and promise of v. 16.

This in turn leads to the troubling ἵνα-clause with which all of this
concludes. Since Paul's concern is both with the sufficiency of the Spirit
over against the flesh and with the mutual incompatibility of the two—so
that the Galatians in their freedom need not and may not make provision
for the flesh—this final clause, by the nature of grammar and logic, must
also speak to these two realities of life in the Spirit. That in itself,
therefore, negates the common interpretation, which sees the flesh and
the Spirit at war within the human heart, leaving the believer basically
helpless. On the contrary, Paul's sentence not only does not say any such
thing—nor does he even hint of it[234]—but his language and the context
suggest something else entirely.

---

[232] Cf. Barclay, *Obeying*, 112: "Their walk in the Spirit will set them against the
flesh and thus define the moral choices they must make."

[233] This view dominates, despite the problems it poses contextually (see n. 213
above). The view takes two forms: (a) that one is helpless because of the presence of
the flesh, which takes its extreme form in Lightfoot 210, whose paraphrase does not
reflect a single word or idea from Paul ("Have you not evidence of these two opposing
principles in your own hearts? How otherwise do you not always obey the dictates
of your conscience?"); cf. Althaus, Ridderbos, Hendriksen, Ebeling, Boice, Dunn, Cole;
(b) that the conflict between the two thwarts the believer (Meyer, Burton, Erdman,
Schlier, Mussner, Guthrie, Stott, Betz, Bruce, MacArthur, Rohde, Longenecker).

[234] Paul's basic clause, ἵνα ταῦτα μὴ ποιῆτε ("so that you may not do these
things"), does not have the slightest suggestion of *inability* to do them. A translation
like the NEB ("you cannot do"; cf. KJV, Knox) is fundamentally wrong and expresses
not what Paul actually says, but what scholars have assumed him to be talking about,
despite the language and context to the contrary. The assertion that this is "parallel"
with Rom 7:18–20 is just that, an assertion. What seems to be parallel is the language
"will" and the idea that the one "willing" cannot do what he or she "wills." But the
differences are far greater than this bit of imprecise "similarity." (1) In Romans the
context is that of Paul's attempt, in light of what he has argued up through 7:6 (q.v.),

Paul's direct statement in v. 16 is that the Spirit is fully sufficient to enable one to live so as not to go along with "the flesh." In explaining how this is so, Paul points out that the Spirit stands in utter opposition to the life of the flesh, here personified so as to heighten the effect.[235] Now he offers the net result[236] of the Spirit's opposition to the flesh, namely, that "you may not do whatever things you wish," which would refer not to what the Spirit "wills" but to what *the person who is no longer under Law* may wish. This also explains why he concludes with v. 18, which is otherwise totally alien to the argument. Thus, the reason he can say with such confidence that those who walk by the Spirit will not carry out what the flesh desires is that the Spirit stands over against the flesh in such a way that believers[237] no longer have the privilege of doing whatever they wish; they must now do as the Spirit leads, otherwise they are indeed carrying out the desire of the flesh.[238]

In context this would seem to mean that "eating and devouring" one another is not an option for those who live by the Spirit. Such people are to walk by the Spirit, who stands in fundamental opposition to such a life. On the contrary, through love they are to perform the tasks of a slave for one another. The one activity, eating and devouring one another,

---

to exonerate the Law as "good, holy, and Spiritual"; there is no hint of that in the present passage, where the only mention of Torah (v. 18) presupposes the preceding argument that its time is over. (2) In Romans the struggle is between indwelling sin, resident in one's flesh, and one's acknowledgment of the goodness of the Law, a struggle neither mentioned nor presupposed here; neither is there any hint of "indwelling sin." (3) In Romans Paul emphasizes one's *inability* and *helplessness* to do the good thing the Law requires; again, there is no hint of such here, where the opposition is between the Spirit and the flesh, and the Spirit overcomes the desire of the flesh (v. 16). (4) In fact there is no mention of the Spirit in the Romans passage at all; it is always imported from the outside (Rom 8:1–8) where Paul is referring to two different kinds of existence in the present world, not to some kind of internal struggle within the believer. Cf. the similar assessment in R. H. Gundry, "The Moral Frustration of Paul before His Conversion: Sexual Lust in Romans 7.7–25," in *Pauline Studies* (ed. Hagner, et al.), 238–39.

[235] Cf. Burton 301: "a rhetorical personification of σάρξ."

[236] Here seems to be a rather clear instance of ἵνα functioning in a "consecutive" or "result" clause. It is difficult to see how it might be "telic" under any understanding. So Turner (MHT 3.104); BAGD II,2.

[237] One should note that the whole of this paragraph is addressing the Galatians as a community and is thus expressed in the second person plural.

[238] This way of looking at the text goes back to Chrysostom and is advocated by Duncan 166–69 and Jewett, *Terms*, 106–7. Cf. Barclay, *Obeying*, 112–19, whose solution is slightly different. He sees the final clause as reflecting the result of the warfare imagery: "As [the Galatians] walk in the Spirit, they are caught up into a warfare which determines their moral choices. The warfare imagery is invoked *not to indicate that the two sides are evenly balanced* [my emphasis] but to show the Galatians that they are already committed *to* some forms of activity (the Spirit) and *against* others (the flesh)." Cf. Fung 251. This may very well be the correct nuance; in any case it comes out at the same place as the one presented here.

Paul will go on to say in vv. 19–21, belongs to "the *works* of the flesh"—this is how making provision for the flesh "works" out in everyday life. The other activity, in love performing the tasks of a slave for one another, is what the Spirit "produces" in the lives of those who "walk by the Spirit." But before that, he has one further loose end to tie up.

18 The point of this sentence, both on its own and in the overall context of this letter, seems clear enough: the fact that Christ has brought an end to the time of Torah observance does not mean that one has now entered a time of unbridled license. To be "Law-less" does not mean to be lawless. God's own provision for such is the life of the Spirit, here described as "being led by the Spirit."

All of that seems easy enough. The more difficult question in this case is how this sentence fits the immediate context of vv. 16–17. How does the fact that the one led by the Spirit is not under Torah follow the preceding imperative about "walking in the Spirit" and especially the elaboration on the incompatibility of flesh and Spirit that concludes, "so that you may not do whatever things you wish"?[239] Since it does not obviously follow in the logical, sequential sense, more likely it follows in the larger contextual sense, and our question, therefore, should not so much be "how does this follow?" but "what triggered this sentence right at this point?" Two suggestions come to mind.

First, beginning with v. 16 Paul really does intend to elaborate how the life of the Spirit responds to the various matters in vv. 13–15. Up to now he has dealt only with how the Spirit responds to "the flesh"; equally important for Paul's argument in this letter is the point made in v. 14, that the love command fulfills the purposes of Torah, hence one no longer needs to be "observant." Thus, in a sentence that looks like a non sequitur, Paul in fact ties up all the loose ends that concern him most.

Second, even though the sentence seems abrupt to us, it was probably less so for Paul and the Galatians. What apparently "triggers" it is what he has just said about the sufficiency of the Spirit to combat the life of the flesh, and especially the final result that those who walk by the Spirit may not thereby do whatever they please. On the one hand, the language "do whatever you please" probably harks back to the elimination of Torah that has been urged throughout the letter. Doing away with Torah does not lead to doing as one pleases. On the other hand, he

---

[239] This is an especially difficult question for those who take the common view that vv. 16–17 refer to the individual believer's helplessness in the midst of struggle between the flesh and Spirit. Ridderbos 204, e.g., finds the connection only by importing all kinds of theology about Paul and the Law which are not here (and belong not to the argument of Galatians but to reading it through the eyes of the "introspective conscience of the West").

is now quick to add, neither does that mean that one comes back under Torah. Precisely the opposite; walking by the Spirit means to follow the leading of the Spirit, which means that Torah observance is totally irrelevant.

Although at the popular level "being led by the Spirit" is sometimes understood to refer to direct guidance by the Spirit, Paul's concern lies elsewhere. In context it functions as the other side of the coin to the imperative "walk by the Spirit" in v. 16. That is, believers who walk by the Spirit do so because they are following where the Spirit leads; and the Spirit leads in "the law of Christ," in ways that both reflect and pattern after Christ himself—whom Paul has earlier described as "the one who loved me and gave himself for me" (2:20). This is why Torah observance is totally irrelevant; for the one led by the Spirit in "the law of Christ" the *aim* of Torah has been fulfilled. Thus, even though the main concern in this section is with the sufficiency of the Spirit over against the flesh, it is equally important for Paul to underscore the Spirit's sufficiency in a context where Torah observance no longer obtains. "It is all right to be done with Torah," he says, "because the Spirit can handle the flesh; indeed, to be led by the Spirit eliminates the need to be under Law."

What is finally significant for the concern of this letter is that *Paul herewith places the flesh and the Law on the same side of things over against the Spirit.*[240] It seems unlikely that he necessarily intended any close relationship between flesh and Torah, apart from that already pointed to in 3:3 and 4:29. The framework for all of this is Paul's eschatology, in which he sees Christ and the Spirit as setting the future in motion in such a way that neither circumcision nor uncircumcision has relevance, since "the new creation" has come (6:15; cf. 2 Cor 5:17). For him the Spirit is the principal evidence of this new eschatological existence that "eagerly awaits" its consummation (Gal 5:5). This means that everything before Christ, which was fundamentally eliminated by his death and resurrection and the gift of the eschatological Spirit, belongs to the same "old age" sphere of existence. In that sense the Spirit stands over against both the flesh and the Law, in that he replaces the latter and stands in opposition to the former.[241] Although Paul does not say so here, the argument of Romans 6–8 demonstrates that Torah was helpless in face of the flesh, while the Spirit is not, and for that reason replaces Torah.

---

[240]Cf. Bruce 256: "For Paul . . . the law and the flesh belong to the same pre-Christian order." Cf. further Rom 7:4–6.

[241]For a similar perspective on this paragraph, see J. L. Martyn, "Apocalyptic Antinomies in Paul's Letter to the Galatians," *NTS* 31 (1985) 410–24, esp. 416.

GALATIANS 5:19–23[242]

[19]*Now the works of the flesh are evident, which include sexual immorality,[243] impurity, licentiousness, [20]idolatry, sorcery, hostilities, strife,[244] jealousy,[245] outbursts of rage, selfish ambitions, dissensions, factions, [21]envies, drunken orgies, revelries, and the like. What I am telling you now is just as I told you before, that those who practice such things as these will not inherit the kingdom of God.*

[22]*But the fruit of the Spirit is love, joy, peace, forbearance, kindness, goodness, faith[fulness], [23]gentleness, self-control;[246] against such things as these there is no Torah.*

These lists of fifteen vices and nine virtues, which stand in sharp contrast to one another, are so well known that it is difficult for the modern reader to keep them in context, to listen to them as if in a Galatian assembly and for the first time. Having just reminded the Galatians one more time in this letter, now in terms of the Spirit's ministry, that the time of Torah is past (v. 18), Paul now returns to the theme of mutual incompatibility between the Spirit and the flesh spelled out in v. 17. These lists thus elaborate with specifics why flesh and Spirit stand in such unrelieved opposition to each other. The one describes the world *in which they once lived* and in which their pagan neighbors still live. These are the "evident works" of those who live according to "the desire of the flesh" (v. 16), and vividly illustrate the kind of life that those who "walk by the Spirit" must no longer be party to. The second describes what people will look like who walk by following the leading of the Spirit. It is difficult to imagine two more utterly contradictory ways of life.

---

[242]*Bibliography:* W. **Barclay**, *Flesh and Spirit: An Examination of Galatians 5.19–23* (Nashville: Abingdon Press, 1962); S. F. **Winward**, *Fruit of the Spirit* (Grand Rapids: Eerdmans, 1981).

[243]The MajT, following the Western tradition, places μοιχεία ("adultery") at the head of the list; it is missing in ℵ* A B C P 33 81 1175 1739 1881 2464 pc a vg syᵖ co Clement Tertullian and can hardly be original. But neither is it easy to see how or why the addition came into existence, except on the pattern of Matt 15:19, where it precedes πορνεῖαι in that vice list—although it does not appear to be added to Paul's lists elsewhere (but see 1 Cor 6:9).

[244]The MajT, again following the Western tradition, put this in the plural, thus conforming it to the plurals that surround it.

[245]See the preceding note; the same prevails here.

[246]The Western text (D* F G it vgᶜˡ Irenˡᵃᵗ Cyprian Ambrosiaster) appends ἁγνεία ("purity") to this list, which probably reflects a felt need to respond to the former list, and especially the sexual sins with which it begins. This perhaps also reflects how early the view arose in the church that the "desire of the flesh" in v. 16 is understood to refer to the male struggle with sexuality.

Vice and virtue lists such as these occur elsewhere in the Greco-Roman world[247] and throughout the Pauline corpus;[248] many of the same vices and virtues recur in several of them, although no two lists are alike either in content, order, or kinds of items included. Two observations are noteworthy about the present lists: (1) What elsewhere Paul either describes as "wickedness"[249] or lists without categorical names, he now specifically relates to the "flesh" and the Spirit, as "works" and "fruit" respectively; (2) although all such lists are ad hoc, and therefore several factors probably go into their specific content or order, in this case, as in others, the lists seem clearly adapted to the situation in Galatia as that emerges in v. 15.[250]

The lists, therefore, are not intended to be either delimiting or exhaustive, as though by a careful word study of these 24 items we would have a complete handle on either the works of the flesh or the fruit of the Spirit. Rather, as Paul indicates in both cases—by his use of τὰ ὅμοια τούτοις ("such things as these") and κατὰ τῶν τοιούτων ("against such things")—he intends these lists to be merely representative. Furthermore, even though these lists describe unbelievers and believers as such, Paul also intends them to describe the "before" and "after" of the Galatians themselves.[251] These "works of the flesh," and others like them, are the very things that "those who belong to Christ Jesus have crucified" (v. 24) and therefore are no longer an option for those who "walk by the Spirit" (vv. 13, 16).

Moreover, the two lists have formal similarities. Each begins with a title, followed by the list itself, to which is appended a concluding word. In both cases our comments will follow this formal structure.

19–21 *The title.* As already noted, in this single instance, and obviously deliberately, Paul associates the various sins enumerated here with "the flesh." Given v. 18, and the whole argument of the letter, that he describes them as "the *works* of the flesh" is hardly coincidental.

---

[247] For a helpful overview see Longenecker 249–52.

[248] Vice lists occur in 1 Cor 5:11; 6:9–10; 2 Cor 12:20; Rom 1:29–31; 13:13; Col 3:5, 8; Eph 4:31; 5:3–5; 1 Tim 1:9–10; Titus 3:3; 2 Tim 3:2–4. Elsewhere in the NT see Mark 7:21–22 (//Matt 15:19); 1 Pet 4:3; Rev 9:21; 21:8; 22:15. Virtue lists are far less common, since in the Pauline corpus the items that make this list occur in the context of Pauline paraenesis; but see Col 3:12.

[249] E.g., 1 Cor 6:9–10 and Rom 1:29.

[250] Cf. Hendriksen 220. Lightfoot 210 saw them as fitting the temperament of a Celtic people; Ramsay 446, on the other hand, saw in them "the faults of the South Galatic cities." That is perhaps to press too hard to make one's theories work?

[251] As we will note below on vv. 24–26, and in keeping with other such listings. See esp. in this regard how the vice lists appear in 1 Cor 6:9–11 ("but such were some of you") and Col 3:5–8 ("in which things you also once walked, when you lived in such things; but now . . . ").

This is almost certainly a deliberate association with the repeated "by *works* of Torah,"[252] which occurs in the earlier part of this letter.[253] This is not to suggest that Paul saw similarity between these two kinds of "works." Rather, by means of word association, he is reminding the Galatians that *both categories of "work"* (religious observance and sins of the flesh) *belong to the past* for those who are in Christ and now walk by the Spirit.

In saying that such "works" are "evident," he does not necessarily mean that the items that follow are always visible, but for those who live by the Spirit it should be self-evident that such vices belong to the "flesh" and have nothing to do with eschatological existence in Christ, as that is lived out by the empowering Spirit. These express the "desire of the flesh" against which the Spirit stands in such unrelieved opposition—to which reality God's people should joyfully respond, "Praise God."

The list. First, some words about form and content:

(a) The fifteen items fall into four categories:[254] illicit sex (3—sexual immorality, impurity, licentiousness), illicit worship (2—idolatry, sorcery), breakdown in relationships (8—hostilities, strife, jealousy, outbursts of rage, selfish ambitions, dissensions, factions, envies), and excesses (2—drunken orgies, revelries).

(b) In terms of specific content, the closest thing to this list is Paul's most recent one in 2 Cor 12:20, in which four of the relational sins occur in this same order and with the same combination of singulars and plurals (strife, jealousy, outbursts of rage, selfish ambitions)—as well as the three sexual aberrations (these three only but in a different order: uncleanness, sexual immorality, licentiousness).

(c) In terms of order, sexual sins followed by idolatry occurs also in the earlier list in 1 Cor 6:9–10 (but not in 5:11); otherwise sexual sin occur first only in Col 3:5.[255] The specific grouping of four kinds of sins does not appear in this way in any other list.

(d) What is striking in this case are the missing items, especially covetousness or greed (which makes most of the other lists)[256] and the related sins of theft and robbery, as well as the various sins of the tongue

---

[252] Gk. τὰ ἔργα τῆς σαρκός/ἐξ ἔργων νόμου. Cf. Burton 313; Longenecker 252–53.

[253] It occurs six times altogether: 2:16 (3x); 3:2, 5, 11.

[254] A frequent observation; see, e.g., Lightfoot 210; Burton 304; Lagrange 149; Duncan 170; Hendriksen 218–19; et al. For reasons that are not at all clear, Betz 283, followed by Longenecker 254, thinks the opposite—that this list is "chaotic" and the next "orderly."

[255] Neither sexual sins nor idolatry occurs in the (much longer) list in Rom 1:29–31; however, in this instance such sins have received full press in the preceding argument (vv. 19–27), so that the list at the end is representative of all kinds of other evils.

[256] Cf. Schlier 254.

(which is the category with the largest number of words when all the lists are collated). This suggests that whatever else "eating and devouring one another" meant, it most likely did not include various forms of verbal abuse. Also missing are sins of violence (murder, etc.).

Second, as to matters of significance for our purposes:

(a) This is *not* a list of sins of the *flesh*, i.e., having to do with the physical body or bodily appetites. The only items that fit this category are the three sexual aberrations which appear first and the two excesses which appear at the end. The majority of the items, in fact, can scarcely be located in the human body, indicating that the suggested alternative ("satisfy one's physical desire") offered in Bauer's lexicon for "the desire of the flesh" in v. 16 (q.v.) cannot possibly be Paul's intent, but is rather a carryover into this lexicon of the view of later interpreters.

(b) Moreover, for the most part the various sins are not the kind associated with internal warfare within the human breast. For example, noticeably missing are such items as "lust" and "covetousness," matters over which the individual often struggles in the face of temptation. Rather, this list basically describes human *behavior*, which for the most part is very visible and identifiable, "works" done by people who live in keeping with their basic fallenness and that of the world around them.

(c) Most noticeably, the majority (8 of 15) are sins of discord, which describe motivations or actions that lead to or express breakdowns in social relationships. Since such sins often make the Pauline lists, one should perhaps not make too much of their appearance here; but in light of what Paul says negatively in 5:15 and 26 and positively in 6:2 and 10, one may be justified in seeing their large number as the adaptation of a common rhetorical device.[257]

But having said all of that, a list is still a list; and one that concludes, as this one does, with "such things" is to be taken seriously by believers of all generations and geography. God is against such "works"; Christ has died to deliver us from their grip (v. 24); and the Spirit has come to empower us not to cave in to their "desire."

The concluding word.[258] In contrast to the fruit of the Spirit, the vice list concludes on an eschatological note: "those who practice such things as these will not inherit the kingdom of God." Similar language occurs in relation to the vice lists elsewhere in Paul (1 Cor 6:9–10; Eph 5:5).

---

[257] Cf. Barclay, *Obeying*, 153.

[258] On the basis of the language "I told you before" and some alleged non-Pauline expressions, Betz 285, followed by Longenecker 258, discerns here another piece of traditional material that Paul has taken over but not fully assimilated (cf. on 4:4–6). Both his method and conclusions are suspect, since the alleged "non-Pauline" expressions do occur in Paul elsewhere. Both note 1 Cor 6:9–10 as a parallel, but refer to the language as non-Pauline because it is rare! The discovery of traditional material will need to be made of sterner stuff.

Two observations are in order. First, for Paul there is an eschatological consummation of the kingdom of God that has already come present through Christ and the Spirit.[259] The outcome for any individual is predicated on whether or not one is a Spirit person, having become so through faith in Christ Jesus. Thus for Paul, "inheriting" or "not inheriting" the kingdom, the final eschatological glory, is a matter of whether or not one is a believer. The "works of the flesh," therefore, do not describe the behavior of believers, but of unbelievers.[260] It is not that believers cannot or never indulge in these sins;[261] Paul's point is that "those who *practice*[262] such sins," those who live in this way, have no inheritance with God's people. His concern here, as in 1 Cor 6:9–11 and Eph 5:5, is to warn believers that they must therefore not live as others who are destined to experience the wrath of God (Col 3:6).

Second, even though Paul is speaking negatively about the destiny of the ungodly, the positive implication of inheriting the kingdom for those who belong to Christ and thus live in the Spirit should not be missed—especially since the question of "inheritance" played such a major role in the argument of 3:6–4:7 (cf. 4:30). As earlier, "inheritance" belongs to those who, by the Spirit, give evidence that they are God's rightful "heirs." Not much is made of this here, except by implication. But in the corresponding passage in Romans 8 this motif plays a central role in the argument. Because such an inheritance is here implied for those who live by the Spirit, Paul concludes the next list by taking it in another direction altogether, namely, to come back to the issue of the Spirit and Torah observance.

22–23 *The title.* By describing the list of virtues as "fruit of the Spirit," Paul intends once more to set the Spirit in sharp contrast to the flesh. At the same time he contrasts the vices as "works" and the virtues as "fruit."

Two observations: First, by calling them "the fruit of the Spirit," Paul does not intend something passive on the part of the believer. To be sure, the contrast between "works" and "fruit" is almost certainly intentional

---

[259] On the presentness of the kingdom for Paul see on Rom 14:17 and 1 Cor 4:20.

[260] A point too often missed in the commentaries, apparently because of the way they handle v. 17. See, e.g., Calvin, Meyer, Fung, Betz, Longenecker.

[261] After all, Paul's emphasis on his having warned them before and now again makes that point plain enough!

[262] Gk. οἱ πράσσοντες, which Longenecker 258 (following Betz) considers evidence for a non-Pauline traditional saying here (see n. 258 above), since elsewhere in this letter Paul talks about "doing" (ποιέω) the Law. But that is to miss too much. Paul's use of ποιέω with regard to the Law is more "traditional" than this very Pauline word, since ποιέω occurs in this letter as the result of his citation in 3:12 of Lev 18:5; whereas the choice of πράσσω reflects not a concern about "doing" these works of the flesh, but "practicing" them, that is, living in this way in a habitual manner.

and significant. "Works" puts emphasis on human endeavor, "fruit" on divine empowerment.[263] The emphasis in this argument is on the Spirit's effective replacement of Torah. Not only do people who walk by the Spirit not walk in the ways of the flesh just described, but also the Spirit effectively produces in them the very character of God. Thus, the activities and attitudes of those who are "led by the Spirit" are designated as the Spirit's *fruit;* they are the "product" of life in the Spirit. Paul's point, of course, is that when the Galatians properly use their freedom, by serving one another through love, they are empowered to do so by the Spirit, who produces such "fruit" in/among them. But they are not passive; they must walk, live, conform to the Spirit. After all, in almost every case these various "fruit" appear elsewhere in the form of imperatives![264]

Second, it is common to make more of the singular "fruit," in contrast to the plural "works," than the language will allow.[265] Paul himself probably had no such contrast in mind, nor does he think of the "works" as many and individual but the "fruit" as one cluster with several kinds on it. The fact is that καρπός can function in Greek as a collective singular, very much as the word "fruit" does in English. In both Greek and English one would refer to "the fruit in the bowl," whether "they" are all of one kind or of several.[266]

The list. At the popular level, partly on the analogy of the so-called gifts of the Spirit in 1 Cor 12:8–10 (q.v.), it is common to refer to this list as "the ninefold fruit of the Spirit,"[267] or something similar, implying that by these nine words Paul has something delimited and definitive in mind. But as with the former list, this one also is representative, not exhaustive. Not only does the language "such things" in v. 23 indicate as much, but, as with the former list, what is surprising are the "omissions" of items that Paul elsewhere includes in such lists or in his paraenesis.[268]

---

[263] It should be noted, however, that when "human endeavor" is Paul's emphasis for the Spirit side of things, "works" is also the word that Paul will use, as at the end of the present argument (6:10, "let us work what is good," which becomes the "good works" of Eph 2:10). Anyone who thinks that Paul is not keen on good works either has not read Paul carefully or has come to the subject with emotional resistance to this language, usually predicated on the theological agenda of the Reformation.

[264] Cf. MacArthur 164–65, who sees this as somewhat "paradoxical."

[265] Perpetuated among others by Burton (with reservations), Lagrange, Erdman, Hendriksen, Guthrie, Schlier, Ebeling, Betz, MacArthur, Fung, Winward (*Fruit*).

[266] I suppose, however, that those who make much of this distinction could appeal to the precedent Paul himself sets with the similar kind of noun "seed" in 3:16! But my guess is that Paul would nonetheless be quite surprised to learn that he "intended" something significant by the present usage.

[267] As e.g., Hoyle, *Holy Spirit,* 76.

[268] In this regard see esp. 2 Cor 8:7; Rom 12:9–21; Col 3:12–17; Eph 4:32–5:2; the only other real "list" of this kind occurs in Col 3:12, where three of the five items in that list appear here as well.

Missing, for example, are thankfulness, forgiveness, humility, gracious talk, and endurance.[269]

Moreover, in contrast to the former list, one has much more difficulty in grouping the nine items mentioned here.[270] That love has pride of place does indeed reflect the Pauline perspective, as we have already noted on v. 14. But despite repeated suggestions to the contrary, no grouping into categories commends itself, except that the middle three may rightly be seen as belonging together for the reasons noted below. But overall, one is led to conclude that the list is much more random, where one word, for reasons not fully apparent, calls for the next. In any case, the virtues chosen stand in marked contrast to many of the preceding "works of the flesh." What results, therefore—and this does become significant for Pauline theology—is a list of virtues covering a broad range of Christian life, both collectively and individually, and which thereby helps to broaden our perspective as to the breadth and all-encompassing nature of the activity of the Spirit in Paul's understanding.

Three further matters of significance about this list should be noted. First, all of these words, or their cognates, appear elsewhere in the Pauline corpus in an ethical or paraenetic context. Even more significantly, several of them are used with reference to the character of God, often in terms of his motivation toward, and relationship to, his people.[271]

Second, as already noted, the decided majority of these items have to do not with the internal life of the individual believer, but with the corporate life of the community.[272] That is, while it is true that individuals must love, work toward peace, express forbearance, kindness, and goodness, or be characterized by gentleness, nonetheless in Pauline

---

[269] Indeed, it is the ad hoc nature of this particular list with its close association with the Spirit that makes a book of this kind tenuous in some ways. The very fact that this list is representative and not exhaustive suggests that in some ways all such moments of Pauline "ethics" should be examined, since this text makes it clear that the Spirit is the empowering presupposition behind them all. At the same time, it is precisely by a careful analysis of this passage that one can make such a judgment at all with regard to Pauline ethics in general. See the discussion in ch. 15 below (pp. 876–83).

[270] This is commonly noted. Some (Lightfoot, Schlier, Stott, Boice, Betz) think they find a "triadic" pattern here, but there is nothing inherent in the items to suggest as much. The obvious difficulty with it is in finding a proper term for the first three, which tend to make them individual dispositions, rather than community expressions. That might work for joy, but scarcely for love and peace. Even further from Pauline reality is Hoyle's suggestion (Holy Spirit, 76) that the first three—including love!— "express the Christian's emotions and attitude toward God."

[271] This reality, plus the fact that the terms are so deeply embedded in Paul through his lifelong association with the OT and the Jesus traditions, renders Betz' comment (282) strange: "The individual concepts are not in any way specifically 'Christian,' but represent the conventional morality of the time."

[272] Noted also by Meyer 313.

paraenesis these virtues characterize God and motivate his conduct toward his own, and therefore must do the same within the believing
community. This is demonstrated below in 6:1 by Paul's use of "the
S/spirit of gentleness" as the motivation behind their restoration of a
brother or sister who has sinned. Thus, when Paul admonishes in 6:4
that they are to "test" or "examine" themselves, that is not a call to
introspection, Christian "navel-gazing" as it were, but for them to see
whether as individuals the fruit of the Spirit are at work in each of them
for the sake of the "common good." Again, as with the preceding vice
list, lying behind much of this is the situation of the Galatian churches
as we get some insight into that from 5:15 and 26.

Third, it is common to compare this list with that of the *charismata*
in 1 Cor 12:8–10, and usually in such a way that either the latter are
damned with faint praise or the former are seen as the higher working
of the Spirit.[273] This perspective would undoubtedly have eluded the
apostle, as though, by way of analogy, prayer were of greater importance
in his mind than the Lord's Table because he speaks so often of the former
but only twice of the latter, and primarily to correct an abuse. The
context of this passage is *ethics*, not worship. To be sure, ethics and
worship are to his thinking closely related matters, as the presence of
1 Corinthians 13 in the midst of 12 and 14 attests. But that does not mean
that one is of more importance than the other, or that the other is
ultimately of lesser worth than the one. Apples and oranges have always
been poor objects of comparison, not because it is merely a matter of
individual taste, but because they are of equal worth, although suited for
different purposes—and in fruit salad they mix quite well. So it is with
the "gifts" and the "fruit" of the Spirit. Only fruit are mentioned here,
because only fruit fit the argument in context.

A few words about each:[274]

(1) *Love.* That love should assume pride of place is no surprise. Paul
has already accorded it such a place in this argument (5:6, 13–14), a place
it always holds in his ethics.[275] The reason for this is that in Paul's
theology, resulting from his long life in the OT (by way of the LXX), this
word captures the essence of the character of God as that is seen in his
relationship to his people.[276] Thus in the Trinitarian benediction of 2 Cor

---

[273] E.g., Burton 313–14; Duncan 173; Hendriksen 223; Fung 272.

[274] For more complete descriptions one is directed to the helpful discussion in
Burton, 314–18, and Bruce, 251–55, and the various articles in *TDNT*, *NIDNTT*, and
EDNT; see also the discussion in Barclay, *Flesh*, and Winward, *Fruit*. My interest is
in the Pauline dimension of these words, especially their place in the present context.

[275] See, e.g., 1 Thes 3:12; 4:9–10; 1 Cor 13:1–13; 16:14; Rom 13:8–10; Col 3:14;
Eph 5:2.

[276] See the key texts in Deut 7:7–8 and 10:15, picked up in the prophets (Hos 3:1;
11:1; Isa 41:8; 43:4; 48:14; 60:10; 63:9). As with many similar words, this background
in the LXX, not its classical or Koine usage, tends to determine Pauline usage.

13:13[14], in which the primary characteristics of the divine Persons are expressed, Paul prays for the Corinthians to know "the love of God." God's love for his people is what has been poured out into their hearts by the Spirit (Rom 5:5). For Paul this love has been expressed most powerfully in God's sending his Son, and in the Son's death on the cross (Rom 5:6–8). God's love is full of "forbearance" and "kindness" (see below) toward his people, and it finally expresses itself fully in the self-sacrificial death of Christ on behalf of his enemies.

But for Paul this is no mere theory or abstract reality; the Spirit had poured this love into his heart. In the present letter he has already described the indwelling Christ as the one "who loved me and gave himself for me" (2:20). This is surely what he intends by the "law of Christ" in 6:2 (q.v.), which lies behind the imperative by which all of this began in v. 13 ("through love perform the duties of a slave for one another"). Such love is the direct result of being loved by the God whose love has been lavished on us in the Son, who likewise loved us and gave himself for us, and by whose indwelling presence we now live. In Pauline theology, therefore, love is the result of a personal encounter with the living God, who above everything else loves his people. Love, therefore, is the *fruit of the Spirit* precisely because *the Spirit who poured out God's love into our hearts* and who now lives in us is *the Spirit of the One who loved us and gave himself for us.*[277]

Love, therefore, is not something one can do or feel on one's own. Neither is it to be distorted into its current North American version of "good feelings" toward someone, so that love is turned on its head: instead of self-sacrificially giving oneself for others, it has become identified with what I do or feel for another for the sake of my own fulfillment. Love heads this list of virtues over against the "works of the flesh" because it stands as the stark opposite of the self-centeredness of most of the items on the former list. As the fruit of the Spirit, love spells the end to "hostilities, strife, jealousy, outbursts of rage, selfish ambitions, dissensions, factions, envies," and the like.[278] This can only be lived out in the context of other people, especially other believers. Thus it is Paul's antidote in vv. 13 and 14 to their internecine strife in v. 15.

(2) *Joy.*[279] On this matter see the comments on 1 Thes 1:6 and 5:16. Joy is one of the foremost characteristics of genuinely Christian, and

---

[277] Cf. Rom 15:30 (q.v.), where love is expressly described as "the love of the Spirit"; cf. Col 1:8.

[278] In this regard, cf. the list of negatives in 1 Cor 13:4–7 that describe what love is not.

[279] Beginning with this virtue, we tend to read this list as though it were first of all a description of personal piety. Thus we most often use it as a kind of checklist to see "how we are doing." I would not hereby argue against this reading; my concern is that in context Paul probably intended these primarily as virtues that should

therefore genuinely Spiritual, piety. What is remarkable is its appearance in this list of virtues that are mainly ethical in character. As with love and peace that stand on either side of it, Paul is probably not thinking so much of the personal, individual experience of joy—although as with this whole list that can scarcely be excluded—but of the joy that characterizes life together in Christ. Life in Christ, and therefore life by the Spirit, is a life of joy; such joy is to characterize the Christian community above all else (1 Thes 5:16). In this regard the two other texts (Rom 14:17; 15:13) where joy, peace, and the Holy Spirit stand in collocation may be instructive. There joy and peace occur together, first as resolution and secondly as prayer, in a section (14:1–15:13) that is written specifically as an appeal for Jewish and Gentile believers to "accept one another" (15:7), rather than to judge or look down on each other (14:1–4). A righteousness that includes joy and peace in the Holy Spirit will have little room for internecine strife (Gal 5:15) or disdain of others (5:26–6:5).

For Paul, as for the rest of the NT in general, the presence or absence of joy is quite unrelated to one's circumstances, as Paul's letter to the Philippians makes plain. It is related in its entirety to what God has done for us in Christ through the Spirit. The Pauline imperative, stemming from joy as the *fruit* of the Spirit, is not simply, "rejoice"—although it often comes in that basic form as well—but "rejoice *in the Lord*." This focus is the key to our understanding the joy of the Spirit. A community that is "rejoicing *in the Lord* always" is not a community easily given to "eating and devouring one another" (v. 15), in which people think much too highly of themselves (6:4).

God has brought us eschatological salvation. The future has already made its appearance in the present. God's people have already tasted the life that is to be. Already they have received full pardon, full forgiveness. By the Spirit they cry out *Abba* to the God who has loved them and given his Son for them. This is cause for joy, untrammeled, uninhibited joy, as "by the Spirit we eagerly await the hope of righteousness" (v. 5). The fruit of the Spirit is *joy*, joy in the Lord. What must begin at the individual level must also therefore characterize the believing community, among whom God still generously supplies the Holy Spirit.[280]

(3) *Peace.* As with love, peace for Paul is especially associated with God and his relationship to his people. And as with love and joy, peace for Paul is particularly a community matter. That is, Paul's first concern

---

characterize the life of the Christian *community*, as it lives out its corporate life with one another in the world.

[280] One wonders, does the general lack of joy that characterizes so much of contemporary North American Christianity suggest that the life of the Spirit has been generally downplayed in the interest of a more cerebral or performance-oriented brand of faith?

with "peace" is not "the well-arranged heart"[281]—although again, it is difficult to have "peace" in a community where God's people know little peace individually. But here peace occurs in a list of virtues deliberately juxtaposed to the "works of the flesh," eight of which describe the causes or results of human discord.[282]

First of all then, as with love, God is often described as "the God of peace,"[283] the God who dwells in total *shalom* (wholeness, well-being) and who gives such *shalom* to his people in their life together. What is striking is that in every instance this divine ascription occurs in contexts where there is strife or unrest close at hand. Thus the antidote to unruly *charismata* in the community is the theological note that God is a "God of peace" (1 Cor 14:33); or in a community where the unruly-idle live off the largess of others, Paul prays that the God of peace will give them peace at all times (2 Thes 3:16); or in a context where believers are warned against those who "cause divisions and put obstacles in your way," he assures them that the God of peace will bruise Satan under their feet shortly (Rom 16:20).

Not only so, but in Paul the mention of peace in his letters (apart from the standard salutation) usually occurs in community or relational settings.[284] Christ is "our peace" who has made Jew and Gentile one people, one body (Eph 2:14–17), who are urged to "keep the unity of the Spirit through the bond of peace" (4:3); similarly in the argument of Rom 14:1–15:13, Jew and Gentile together are urged to "make every effort to do what leads to peace" (14:19); or in the community paraenesis of Col 3:12–4:6, they are urged to "let the peace of Christ rule in your hearts, *since as members of one body you were called to peace.*" Given the present context, both 5:15 and the fact that these fruit of the Spirit sharply contrast the works of the flesh just described, it is difficult to imagine that such is not the first setting for this fruit of the Spirit as well—not the only one, to be sure, since lists by their nature can carry a kind of independent existence apart from their first context.

(4) *Forbearance.* It is common to translate this word (μακροθυμία) as "patience." To be sure, in some cases it carries that meaning. But in English, "patience" tends to be individualistic; i.e., one is "patient" about all kinds of nonpersonal matters pertaining to life in general (burnt toast, e.g.). But in Paul μακροθυμία and its corresponding verb are always used in contexts involving one's forbearance toward others.[285] As such it often

---

[281] As e.g., Burton 314–15; Hendriksen 224; MacArthur 167.

[282] Cf. Meyer 313–14.

[283] See 1 Thes 5:23; 2 Thes 3:16; 1 Cor 14:33; 2 Cor 13:11; Rom 15:33; 16:20; Phil 4:9.

[284] Cf. V. Hasler, *EDNT,* 1.396.

[285] The KJV translated it "longsuffering." It is still hard to improve on the KJV on 1 Cor 13:4, "Charity [love] suffereth long, and is kind."

occurs, as it does here, as the passive side of love, of which its companion "kindness" is the active side. For instance, Paul describes God's attitude toward human arrogance as one of forbearance and kindness (Rom 2:4); these are the first two words that describe (God's) love in 1 Cor 13:4, and thus they occur together in Col 3:12 as part of Christian dress when one "puts on Christ."

Thus "longsuffering" has to do with one's long forbearance toward those who oppose or distress one in some way.[286] Nowhere else does Paul attribute such forbearance to the direct working of the Spirit; but its appearance here shows that Spirit-empowering is not simply for joy and miracles, but for this much-needed quality of "putting up with" those who need long and patient love and kindness (cf. Col 1:11). This is the antidote to "outbursts of rage" (v. 20) or "provoking one another" (v. 26).

(5) *Kindness*. This word and the next one, which are close synonyms,[287] are strictly Pauline words in the NT.[288] The meanings of both words are difficult to pin down with precision, because they occur most often in lists like this or in contexts where the general sense is easy enough to ascertain, but where nuanced differences are not at all easy to capture. The clues come most often from associations with other words. As is the case with the "forbearance" with which it is frequently allied, the key to understanding "kindness" is to be found in the instances where it describes God's character or activity toward people. Thus it occurs as a verb in 1 Cor 13:4 to express the active side of love, for which longsuffering expresses its passive side. In such a context it surely refers to God's active goodness, lavished upon those whom he loves. God's kindness, therefore, is to be found in his thousandfold acts of mercy toward people like ourselves who deserve his wrath. This is especially borne out by its usage in Eph 2:7, where the lavish expression of God's grace is demonstrated in his "kindness" toward us in Christ.

In this list, of course, where it occurs again in conjunction with forbearance, it has to do with the active expression of kindness toward others. As such it fits the larger context as another opposite to the "works of the flesh," with their self-centered, basically hostile-toward-others way of life. The Spirit not only empowers one to endure the hostility or unkindness of another; he also enables one to show kindness to such and actively to pursue their good. If longsuffering means not to "chew someone's head off" (see 5:15), "kindness" means to find ways actively to

---

[286] So also Burton 315.

[287] Evidenced by the fact that the LXX translators could use either word to render the Hebrew טוֹב *tôb*, the basic OT word for "good" or "goodness."

[288] Χρηστότης ("kindness") occurs ten times (2 Cor 6:6; Gal 5:22; Rom 2:4; 3:12; 11:22 [3x]; Col 3:12; Eph 2:7; Titus 3:4); its verb once (1 Cor 13:4); ἀγαθωσύνη ("goodness") four times (2 Thes 1:11; Gal 5:22; Rom 15:14; Eph 5:9).

show mercy to them, to take a towel and wash basin in hand and wash their feet.

(6) *Goodness.* As noted above, this word is closely allied with "kindness." If there is a difference, "goodness" is the more all-embracing quality, describing one's character. Although it does not occur often in the LXX, the adjective ("good") from which it is formed is a favorite word to describe God's character in the OT. Goodness, therefore, is something that believers may be described as "full of" (Rom 15:14). When put into practice it takes the form of "doing good." Indeed, goodness does not exist apart from its active, concrete expression. Thus, this is the quality of Christian grace, produced in the life of the believer by the Spirit, that Paul picks up on at the end to conclude the present argument (6:9–10). Again, as with the preceding words, its appearance here presupposes the present context. Those who "sow to the Spirit" are those who "do good to all"; obviously this stands as yet another antonym to those "works of the flesh" which have found a measure of existence among the Galatians.

(7) *Faith[fulness].* The word here is πίστις, Paul's normal word for "faith," having to do with one's basic stance toward God of utter trust in his trustworthiness. But in the LXX it was the basic Greek word for translating the concept of God's faithfulness. This is the sense that Paul picks up in Rom 3:3, that the "unfaithfulness" of God's people does not call into question God's own πίστις ("faithfulness"). Thus, even though one would have no theological objection to "faith" as the meaning of the word even here—i.e., that one of the fruit of the Spirit is one's trust in God—it is more likely, given the other virtues, and especially those that immediately surround it, that Paul is referring to faithfulness, i.e., one's faithful living out one's trust in God over the long haul.

The more difficult question, given the context, is whether it also carries a nuance of faithfulness in relationship to others. Since there are no other NT examples of this usage, it seems unlikely, despite the context, that Paul had that in mind here. More likely the sense is that of faithful devotion to God, which in turn will express itself toward others by means of the various other fruit in this list. True "faith" for Paul always includes the element of "faithfulness"; and thus true "faith" for him in this sense, as a fruit of the Spirit, expresses itself in love (5:6).

(8) *Gentleness.* In earlier versions this word (πραΰτης) was translated "meekness." For Paul it derives its Christian meaning from its relationship with Christ. In the Jesus tradition as recorded in Matt 11:25–30, this is one of the two words used to describe the character of Christ, which he, as the only Son of the Father, revealed about the character of the Father to the "infants" as over against the wise and understanding. That Paul knew this tradition, or one like it, seems certain from his appeal to the "meekness and gentleness of Christ" in 2 Cor 10:1.

As a Christian grace, reflecting the character of Christ himself, it occurs eight times in Paul.[289] This is the one fruit, more than the others, for which one has difficulty in finding an adequate English word.[290] Whatever else, it carries the sense of humility (i.e., a proper estimation of oneself over against God) and considerateness toward others.[291] Thus it is to this fruit that Paul will appeal in 6:1, when he urges those who walk by the Spirit to restore a brother or sister overtaken in a fault. One needs to do so in the "S/spirit of gentleness" both because the life of the other person is at stake and because one thereby remembers one's own frailties and susceptibility to temptation. In this list it stands as the exact antonym to the "work of the flesh" called ἐριθεία ("selfish ambition"). It is this fruit of the Spirit which is at work in those who do not think too highly of themselves (6:3), but who "in humility consider others better than themselves" (Phil 2:3)—in the sense that they look after others' needs and concerns before their own.

(9) *Self-control*. This last word on this list is unique in several ways. It is the one word on the list that does not appear elsewhere in Scripture with reference to the character of God. Indeed, the noun occurs only here in the Pauline corpus, although the verb occurs in 1 Cor 7:9 with reference to sexual continence and in 1 Cor 9:25 with regard to the self-discipline of the athlete.[292] Furthermore, it is the one virtue in the list that is clearly aimed at the individual believer. This is not something one does in community; it is a general stance toward excesses of various kinds.

Therefore, in contrast to the rest of the list which take aim at those eight "works of the flesh" that have to do with relational breakdowns, this one takes aim at either—or both—the sexual indulgences that appear as the first three "works of the flesh" or/and the excesses with which that list concludes. This, too, is the effective working of the Spirit in the life of the believer.

But in terms of Pauline ethics, what one may not do is to turn "self-control" into abstinence. Passages such as 1 Cor 10:31–33, Rom 14:1–23, Col 2:16–23, and 1 Tim 4:1–5 demonstrate that Paul is death on anything that even smacks of abstinence for its own sake as a Christian virtue. Therefore, because of this fruit of the Spirit, one is free to abstain from any and everything for the sake of others; but one may never turn the freely giving up of food or drink or whatever into some kind of virtue

---

[289] 1 Cor 4:21; Gal 5:23; 6:1; Col 3:12; Eph 4:2; 1 Tim 6:11; 2 Tim 2:25; Tit 3:2.

[290] In an uncharacteristic fashion, and precisely for this reason, BAGD offer a broad range of meaning: "*gentleness, humility, courtesy, considerateness, meekness* in the older favorable sense."

[291] Although Burton 316 would limit it to the latter use only in Paul.

[292] The adjective also occurs in the list of virtues required of an overseer in Titus 1:8.

on its own. Paul calls such abstemiousness merely "human traditions" in Col 2:22, the "teachings of demons," in 1 Tim 4:1.

The concluding word. That Paul has not done what we so often do with this passage—namely, to lose sight of the argument in context—becomes readily apparent by the concluding clause. Significantly, he does not conclude as before with an eschatological word, in this case a word of promise, probably because such a promise is already inherent in the previous concluding word; that word, after all, spoke not about the "wrath of God coming upon those in the flesh," but about their "*not* inheriting the *kingdom.*" Implied in that is the opposite reality, that Spirit people *will* inherit the kingdom. But the lack of an eschatological word in the present case, one would guess, is also because Paul cannot bring himself to say that "those who exhibit these virtues will inherit the kingdom." That inheritance, after all, is predicated altogether on their being God's children through Christ and the Spirit, not on the kind of life they exhibit as his children. Paul will indeed finally speak to the believer's involvement in making that calling sure—in the final wrap-up of this argument in 6:7–10, where he both warns and exhorts them to "sow to the Spirit" with the eschatological goal in mind. But for now the concern is quite different.

Paul's present interest lies once more with the main point of the argument of the entire letter, that the work of Christ and the coming of the Spirit have eliminated Torah from the agenda of God's people. Hence he concludes, "against such things[293] as these there is no Law." Paul's point seems clear enough, although this is stated a bit awkwardly to our thinking. After all, the Law exists because people are evil, not because they are good; it exists "against" sin, not "against" virtue. He therefore almost certainly intends that "when these virtues are evident in one's life because of the presence of the Spirit, Torah is an irrelevancy."[294] There is no need of Torah to say, "you shall not kill," to people who by the Spirit are loving one another, nor to say, "don't covet," to those who are actively pursuing the good of others out of kindness. This does not mean, of course, that such *reminders* are irrelevant—Paul himself is long on such—but that the need for Torah to "hem in human conduct because of the transgressions" (3:19, 22) has come to end with the advent of the Spirit, God's way of fulfilling his promised new covenant. This is Torah being etched on the heart, so that God's people will obey him (Jer 31:33; Ezek 36:27). Here also is the clear evidence that for Paul the elimination of Torah does not mean the end of righteousness. On the contrary, the

---

[293] Thus, as with most interpreters, understanding this term to be neuter, as in v. 21, not masculine as the Greek Fathers (cf. Moffatt).

[294] Calvin 168 put it slightly differently: "When the Spirit reigns, the law has no longer any dominion." I'm not sure that "reign" is the issue as much as relevancy; cf. Duncan 175–76; Betz 289.

Spirit produces the real thing, the righteousness of God himself, as his children reflect his likeness in their lives together and in the world.

GALATIANS 5:24–26

[24]*Now those who belong to Christ Jesus*[295] *have crucified the flesh with its passions and desires.* [25]*If we live by the Spirit, to the Spirit let us also*[296] *conform [our behavior].*[297] [26]*Let us not be conceited, provoking one another, envying one another.*

With these sentences Paul brings the present argument full circle, first by drawing the work of Christ back into the picture (v. 24), now vis-à-vis the flesh rather than Torah, and then in v. 25 by restating the basic imperative from v. 16, concluding in v. 26 with the reasons for these admonitions from v. 15. These sentences, therefore, belong integrally to what has preceded, but at the same time lead directly into the specific application that follows in 6:1–6. The appeal in v. 25 to conform our behavior to the Spirit thus wraps up what has been said in vv. 16–24 about life in the Spirit over against the flesh—repeating with different imagery the imperative to walk by the Spirit, now in light of the description of Spirit life in vv. 22–23 and on the basis of our having received life through the Spirit.

24 This sentence comes as something of a surprise, following hard on the heels of vv. 19–23 as it does, and since nothing in the present

---

[295] "Christ Jesus" is read primarily by Egyptian witnesses (‏א‎ A B C P Ψ 0122* 33 104* 1175 1241^S 1739 [1881] pc co); the rest, including P[46] D F G latt syr MajT, read "those who are of Christ." Good arguments can be mounted for either reading. An "addition" such as this occurs frequently in the Pauline letters; yet the use of the definite article with Χριστός is rare in Paul, even more so with the combination Χριστὸς Ἰησοῦς. Did scribes see the idiosyncrasy and omit "Jesus"? Probably (so Lightfoot 213), but in the final analysis, the textual choice in this case is a matter of preference for the supporting witnesses. If τοῦ Χριστοῦ Ἰησοῦ is the original text, then one has the further question of deciding whether "the Christ" is titular here with "Jesus" in apposition (= the Christ, Jesus). Might this be a gentle reminder that the Jewish Messiah himself did away with both Torah observance and the works of the flesh?

[296] The καί is missing in P[46] (F) G a b d. While this is not crucial to the sense, it seems more likely that scribes omitted the word as unnecessary to the sense (or perhaps by homoeoteleuton) than that they added it. The omission results in a much tighter pair of clauses; but it probably also misses the Pauline nuance that if by the Spirit believers have been given life following the crucifixion of the flesh, then they "also" (καί) must conform their behavior in keeping with the Spirit by whom they live. See the discussion below.

[297] This unfortunately awkward "translation" reflects an attempt to keep both the structural chiasm and the sense of the verb στοιχῶμεν. On both of these matters see the discussion below.

argument has quite prepared us for its content. Nonetheless Paul's concern seems clear, and the flow of thought is relatively easy to pick up. Here he offers the theological basis for the imperative and promise in v. 16, that those who walk by the Spirit will not carry out the desire of the flesh, as that is spelled out in the dreadful picture in vv. 19–21. He does this by picking up the language of his own testimony in 2:19–20[298] as that must now be understood in light of the argument in 3:6–4:7. Those who have put their trust in Christ, Paul has already said, have also been crucified with Christ, so that current "life in the flesh" is not predicated on the perspective of the flesh. Through their association with Christ in his death, they have been crucified (2:20; 6:14). Now he puts that in the active, purposely recalling their union with Christ in his death, but now as a bold metaphor as to what they have thereby done to their past way of life: they have nailed the flesh, with its passions and desires,[299] to the cross.

Just as in the argument of 3:1–4:7, where Paul seemed intent to tie the life of the Spirit to the work of Christ, so now by these words he seems equally intent to link the life of the Spirit to the preceding argument in which Christ plays the leading role.[300] The reason seems obvious: In Pauline theology, everything that God has done in the new covenant to create a people for his name he has done through Christ. Here is the source of Paul's confidence that those who walk by the Spirit will not carry out the desire of the flesh. By his crucifixion Christ has pronounced the death sentence on *all* that is "flesh" (2 Cor 5:14) and thus has effected for the believer a dramatic and real death regarding the former way of life. The time of the old order is over; the new order has come: behold *all things* are new (2 Cor 5:17); the only thing that counts is the "new creation" (Gal 6:15).

Thus, just as through Christ's death one has died to the Law (2:17; cf. Rom 7:1–4), so also through Christ's death one has died to the flesh. Spirit people have experienced a more radical way of dealing with the flesh than merely subjecting it to Law (v. 23); in Christ Jesus they have

---

[298] This is not always recognized by commentators, but the language and conceptual ties are thoroughgoing (cf. Dunn, *Baptism*, 107; Hendriksen, Betz, Bruce). The difference lies with that to which one has died—to Torah in 2:19–20, to the flesh here (cf. Bruce 256).

[299] Gk. τοῖς παθήμασιν καὶ ταῖς ἐπιθυμίαις. The combination indicates that both terms are pejorative in this sentence, although the former is rarely so otherwise and the latter only in context. For πάθημα see esp. Rom 7:5, where it occurs in a similar context of the flesh as that to which one has died. This combination carries forward the near personification of the σάρξ from vv. 16–17, suggesting that life in the flesh is prompted more from passionate desire, controlled by base appetites, than by the mind that has been renewed in Christ. Cf. Rom 12:1–2. On the two words, see Burton 320–21.

[300] Cf. Betz 289.

crucified it. To live according to the flesh is therefore no more an option under the new covenant than is living under Law. Christ's death has brought an effective conclusion to the reign of both. This is not wishfulness on Paul's part, but a declaration of eschatological realities. Having been crucified with Christ, the believer now lives by faith in Christ, who by his own Spirit has taken up residence within (2:20). At the same time, this is not to be understood as some form of triumphalism, as the exhortation that follows in v. 25 makes clear. Rather, this is to be understood within Paul's eschatological framework. Here is the "already" of eschatological salvation; the death of the flesh—the former way of life—has "already" taken place through Christ's death and resurrection.[301] But at the same time vv. 25–26 bring one back to the reality that there remains a "not yet." The *possibility for obedience* regarding the exhortations in vv. 25–26 rests on the twin facts (1) that the "flesh," which belongs essentially to the old order, has been crucified in Christ Jesus, and (2) that present life this side of that crucifixion is empowered by the Spirit.

25 With yet another striking chiasm,[302] which places emphasis on the Spirit, Paul responds directly to v. 24, both by the language ("live" following "crucified")[303] and by once more designating the Spirit as the source of the new life[304] that is lived over against the (now "dead") flesh. He thus rounds off the argument with an exhortation that harks back to the opening imperative in v. 16, where he had urged that walking by the Spirit is God's antidote to life in the flesh. Now, he urges, since Christ's crucifixion has spelled death for the flesh, believers are to behave in keeping with the Spirit, by whom they live and whose fruit they are to evidence.[305] Just as v. 16 responded directly to their "fleshly" behavior

---

[301] As Paul puts it in Romans, believers therefore must "reckon" themselves as dead, as far as sin is concerned, but as living, with reference to God (6:11). The aorist in this sentence (ἐσταύρωσαν) probably refers first to Christ's own crucifixion, but secondly to its appropriation by believers when they believed in him (cf. Bruce 256).

[302] The Gk. text reads (cf. 3:3 and 5:4 above):

εἰ ζῶμεν	If we live
πνεύματι	by the Spirit
πνεύματι	to the Spirit
καὶ στοιχῶμεν.	also let us conform.

[303] Another point seldom noted by commentators. But see Calvin, Meyer, Schlier.

[304] See above on 3:21; cf. 2 Cor 3:6 (q.v.); cf. Barclay, *Obeying*, 155. The protasis, "live by the Spirit," therefore, is not equivalent to "walk by the Spirit" in v. 16. That equivalent is found in the apodosis. Cosgrove, *Cross*, 164, correctly recognizes the point, but goes the wrong way with it (see next note).

[305] The protasis ("If we live by the Spirit") functions as an indicative (= "since, then, we have come to life by the Spirit"). This is the other side of v. 24 and describes Christian realities in terms of the Spirit. Barrett (*Freedom*, 78), therefore, is bringing in totally extraneous matter to suggest that this is basically in response to charismatics who are into tongues but not into ethical life, a position seconded by Cosgrove (*Cross*, 164–67) by especially circuitous argumentation (that "living by the Spirit" =

described in v. 15, so Paul now follows this summary exhortation by indicating in v. 26 how the Spirit affects community life; as argued in v. 17, life in the Spirit stands in utter contradiction to the flesh in the form of conceit, provocation, and envy—activity reminiscent of v. 15.

But this is also the text which shows that triumphalism is not what vv. 16, 22–23, and 24 are all about. In conjunction with v. 24, here one catches a glimpse of the "already/not yet" of Pauline soteriology, in which the (necessary) imperative follows hard on the heels of the divine indicative. The preceding sentence has put it boldly—death to the flesh through Christ. The protasis of this sentence follows that up in terms of life empowered by the Spirit that issues from that death; the apodosis calls for action based on the protasis. The reality lies in the protasis, which expresses not supposition but presupposition; God's new covenant people do in fact live by the Spirit. But precisely because this is so, one must heed the exhortation of the apodosis. Thus: "given that we[306] [have died with Christ and have been raised by him so as to] live by the Spirit, then let us also conform our lives to behave[307] in keeping with the Spirit [as that has been spelled out in vv. 22–23]." The Spirit is thus the key to effecting the realities of v. 24 (death to the flesh) and vv. 22–23 (the fruit of the Spirit) in everyday life.

26 That this exhortation brings the argument full circle is evidenced in two ways. First, following the positive exhortation to behave in conformity to the Spirit, one might well have expected something positive expressed in terms of the fruit of the Spirit. But what we get in fact are negatives, how people who conform to the Spirit are *not* to behave. Thus the concern does not seem to be with life in the Spirit in general, but especially with certain forms of life in the flesh that Paul is hoping to counteract. Secondly, even though not expressed in the same language as v. 15, these are the kinds of attitudes ("empty conceit,"[308] "envy") and

---

"being led by the Spirit" and that the latter refers to those who think of Spirit life in terms of charismatic empowering). But this misses both the contextual tie to v. 14 and Pauline usage elsewhere. This exegesis, which is central to Cosgrove's enterprise, mars what is otherwise a very helpful study; unfortunately it also weakens his central hypothesis (see n. 6 above).

[306] Note the return to the "we" as Paul moves to include himself with them in this eschatological/soteriological reality. This in itself, not to mention the argument and the context, rules out Barrett's and Cosgrove's suggestion (preceding note).

[307] This awkward and somewhat redundant expression is an attempt to capture the sense of the verb στοιχῶμεν, which occurs again in 6:14 and in Phil 3:16. The word, which originally meant simply to "draw up into a line," came to have the figurative sense of "being in line with," "holding to," or "conforming to" someone or something. Duncan 178 suggests that the verb was chosen precisely because community "life" is in view.

[308] Gk. κενόδοξος; lit. "empty/vain glory." The adjective occurs only here in Paul, but cf. the use of the noun in Phil 2:3, in an apparently similar setting.

actions ("provocation"[309]) that lead to their "eating and devouring" one another.[310] There are also some significant linguistic and conceptual links between this passage (through 6:5) and Phil 2:1–4, where the context also reflects disharmony within the believing community. In Philippians the believers are urged on the basis of their "participation in the Spirit" and their "mutual love" to do nothing out of "empty conceit," but rather with "humility" to "look out for" the interests of others, considering others as having precedence over themselves. Here they are urged to live by the Spirit in such a way that they do not live in "empty conceit," provoking one another, but rather in love ("fulfilling the law of Christ") they are to bear each other's burdens (6:2), since the one who thinks too highly of himself is thoroughly deceived (v. 3). Thus "life in the Spirit" precludes "life in the flesh," expressed specifically in terms of conflict in community relationships.

These three verses serve both as a conclusion to the argument from vv. 15 and 16 and as a transition from the more general imperatives and description of life in the Spirit in 5:13–26 to the specific applications of all this to their situation in 6:1–6.[311] In all of this the Spirit, following the work of Christ, is the prime mover. The Spirit is God's effective response to the problem of the flesh, whose reign was brought to an end through Christ and whose effect in the believer is negated by the empowering of the Spirit. But what Christ and the Spirit have effected, the believer must actively participate in—by walking by, and behaving in keeping with, the Spirit.

GALATIANS 6:1–3

[1]*Brothers and sisters, if indeed[312] a person[313] is overtaken[314] by a certain transgression, you who are Spiritual restore such a one in the S/spirit of gentleness, considering yourselves lest you also be tempted.* [2]*Bear each other's*

---

[309] Gk. προκαλέω, a word that is not necessarily pejorative, meaning to "call forth, invite, summon." But it also carries the pejorative sense of "summoning" so as to "challenge" someone, hence "provoking" someone into a fight or contest of some sort. See LSJ.

[310] So Lightfoot 214; Boice 500; Bruce 257; Fung 276; Cole 222. For a different view see Burton 323.

[311] So also Longenecker 266.

[312] The combination ἐὰν καί probably means something closer to "if indeed" than "even if." The ἐάν introduces a present general condition (= if this condition ever prevails, then the other will, or should, as well). The καί intensifies it as to its probability. That is, "if such a thing were indeed to happen, as it very likely will." Cf. 1 Cor 7:8. See Burton 326 for a full discussion.

[313] Although clearly not authentic, the addition of ἐξ ὑμῶν by P Ψ 1175 pc captures Paul's sense. It is not simply any person (ἄνθρωπος) to whom Paul refers, but precisely anyone *among them*. The ἐξ ὑμῶν was probably added because of Paul's use of ἄνθρωπος rather than ἀδελφός.

[314] See n. 321 below.

burdens and thus you will fill to the full[315] *the law of Christ.* ³*For if any think themselves to be something when they are nothing, they deceive themselves.*

Paul begins his direct application of what has preceded to their corporate life with a series of imperatives which illustrate how Spirit people should behave in their everyday relationships. The context is that of the community. Believers are to care for one another, on the one hand, and thus "fill to the full the law of Christ" (vv. 1–2). They are thereby to have a proper estimation as to their own worth (v. 3), on the other hand, by taking proper stock of themselves (v. 4) so as to know how to "carry their own weight" (v. 5).

One is not surprised that Spirit language does not occur often in such contexts, since it is presupposed—which makes the descriptions in v. 1 all the more telling. What is surprising is that translators historically have been so reluctant to see Paul's use of πνεῦμα language in this passage as referring directly to the preceding argument.[316] Our interest is in the language and meaning of v. 1 in particular, where both πνεῦμα and πνευματικός occur; but we must also note the relationship of v. 2 to 5:14, since both passages have the Spirit as presuppositional to what is said or urged. But first, a word or two about context.

Because a sequential flow to these various imperatives and their elaborations is not immediately evident, it is common to look upon all of 6:1–10 as a series of "gnomic sentences," somewhat randomly strung together.[317] On the other hand, if one assumes that 5:15 and 26 actually refer to specific matters within the Galatian congregations, then most of the material can be shown to have an "inner logic."[318] On this view vv. 1–3 form something of a unit in response to vv. 25–26. "Let us behave in keeping with the Spirit," Paul has urged in v. 25, meaning, let us *not* be full of empty conceit and provocation. On the contrary, as Spirit people

---

[315] Gk. ἀναπληρώσετε, which means to "fill a gap, make complete," hence to "fulfill." But it seems to have been chosen deliberately to distinguish it from πληρόω in 5:14. The future indicative (cf. 5:16) is read by P⁴⁶ B F G 323 pc latt co Marcion Cyprian; the rest read the aorist imperative. The future is to be preferred on all counts; not only is it supported by the earliest evidence across two text-types, but it is also the reading which best explains how the other came about. A scribe with a set of imperatives in the same sentence would not deliberately (or even accidentally) have changed the second to a future indicative; whereas it is easy to account for his having done so with the future indicative in front of him. He simply "saw" what he was expecting and "copied" the text accordingly.

[316] Lightfoot 215, e.g., notes the connection in the first instance, but not the second.

[317] For an articulation of this view, see Betz 291–92 (cf. Schlier 269); for an overview and critique see Barclay, *Obeying*, 147–55; cf. Longenecker 269–71.

[318] Betz 291–92 allows as much, himself using the language "inner logic" (which he never elaborates). In any case, one must take seriously that the connectives in vv. 3–5 (γάρ, δέ, γάρ) are those of "argument," not of randomly strung together sayings.

you should, for example, restore a fallen brother or sister, remembering your own susceptibility to temptation. Indeed, you ought to bear any and all of one another's burdens and so fulfill the law of Christ. For those who think themselves to be something when in fact they are nothing (who are thus full of empty conceit and thereby provoke rather than restore and assist others) are merely deceiving themselves. At the same time, Paul goes on in vv. 4–5, each one should put his/her own work to the test, and then alone will there be grounds for "boasting." In that sense, each person must mind his or her own affairs, carry his or her own load, and thus not envy or challenge one another. In any case, the Galatians are now about to see how love, peace, gentleness, self-denial, and goodness, for example, work out in everyday life.[319]

If this is the "flow" of thought, even if it takes the form of "stream of consciousness," the two parts to the first paragraph (vv. 1–3, 4–5) are thus a double-sided response to the "empty conceit" and "provocation/ envy" of 5:26, while vv. 7–10 bring the whole section (from 5:13, but now especially in light of 6:1–5) to its proper conclusion.

1 Both the grammar[320] and the language of this verse indicate that Paul is not starting something new, but rather is applying to their own situation what he has just been arguing. Here is the kind of Spirit activity that is exactly the opposite of that described in 5:26. The example describes a believer in the most vulnerable kind of situation—overtaken[321] by a transgression[322] that is known by others. Paul's point is that rather than provoke one another, which stems from the flesh and encourages a response in kind, those who live by the Spirit should see to it that the fallen one is fully restored to his or her former condition.[323] This

---

[319] Cf. Barclay, *Obeying*, 146 (note his chapter title for this material, "The Practical Value of the Spirit").

[320] Elsewhere in Paul the combination ἐὰν καί (or εἰ καί) always carries on some matter from the preceding sentence. See 1 Cor 7:11, 21, 28; 2 Cor 4:16; 5:3, 16; 7:8, 12; 11:15; 12:11; Phil 2:17; 3:12.

[321] Gk. προλημφθῇ, the aorist passive of προλαμβάνω, which in the passive can mean either "to be detected" or "to be overtaken, surprised"; cf. Wis 17:16[17]. While the former may be possible (cf. NIV, NRSV, Williams, Phillips, Erdman 115–16; although see Burton 327, who thinks it not possible at all), the latter seems much more in keeping with the context and especially with the final word of warning; the others are also susceptible to temptation, not to "being caught" in sin. The NEB heightens the element of "surprise" by translating, "do something wrong . . . on a sudden impulse." Cf. Lightfoot 215, Meyer 320–21, Burton 327, Fung 284.

[322] Gk. παραπτώματι. In keeping with his Jewish background, when Paul refers to Gentiles who do not have the Law at all, they are "Gentile sinners"; but when he refers to a specific "sin" of some kind, he reverts to the word that has Torah as its background—a "transgression."

[323] Gk. καταρτίζετε, which means to "restore" in this sense. It is used by Mark (1:19) to refer to the "mending" of nets, that is, bringing them back into their former proper condition.

means, of course, that neither may they act as "normal human beings" (= people without the Spirit) do under such circumstances and either neglect or disgrace the fallen one.[324] Here is the touch of realism, both the fallenness of the one and the susceptibility to temptation of all others, that should keep one from ever reading what has preceded in a triumphalistic way.

The subject of the apodosis is the first phrase that concerns us, ὑμεῖς οἱ πνευματικοί ("you who are Spiritual" = "you who, in keeping with v. 25, live by, and in conformity to, the Spirit"). The context demands that here is another instance in which by the use of this adjective (turned substantive) Paul means "Spirit people." Indeed, to translate this phrase with the lower case, "those who are spiritual," not only undermines it in terms of meaning for a contemporary English speaker, but also leads to connotations that are precisely the opposite of Paul's intent. With this word he is not, as some would have it, addressing a special group within the community who are, or think they are, "spiritual,"[325] who must restore a fallen one because he or she is (presumably) not "spiritual." In such a case, Paul would surely have said "*those* who are spiritual." Rather, Paul is addressing the whole community ("*you* who are Spiritual"), just as he does with all the second person plurals that have just preceded.[326] His point is to remind them of who indeed they are in Christ—people of the Spirit, who walk by the Spirit and live in keeping with the Spirit, and thus do not carry out the desire of the flesh so as "to eat and devour one another." If a distinction is to be made at all, it would be between those who are in fact already living by the *imperatives* in vv. 16, 18, 22–23, and 25, as over against those who are responsible for the works of the flesh that are disrupting the life of the community. But Paul himself does not make even that distinction.

Paul's concern, therefore, by using this form of direct address, is to tie together everything that has just been said about the life of the Spirit vis-à-vis the flesh as it relates to the specific behavioral ills that have crept into this community. That this is his intent is ensured by the final

---

[324] Cf. Calvin 170: "Most [people] seize on the faults of brethren as an occasion of insulting them."

[325] Cf., e.g., Lietzmann 38; Schlier 270; Cole 224–25; Barrett, *Freedom*, 78–79. This position assumes, on the basis of a given understanding of 1 Corinthians, that the substantive οἱ πνευματικοί has become something of technical term for a group of enthusiasts or spiritual elite. The difficulty with such a position, of course, is that the substantive is a purely Pauline phenomenon in all of known Greek literature; and there are considerable reasons to doubt that it ever carried this alleged technical sense. See above, pp. 28–32. Although he may not intend to do so, by translating the phrase "Spiritual believers," MacArthur perpetuates the idea of elitism.

[326] That also means that the suggestion of some that this reflects irony also runs aground. Cf. Barclay, *Obeying*, 157, who (correctly) considers this the *indicative* on which the following *imperative* is predicated.

clause, "looking out for your own selves,[327] lest you also be tempted." To be a person of the Spirit does not make one an elitist or a "pneumatic" in the midst of others who are not so. As all the preceding imperatives imply, a Spirit person is not a perfect person, but one who by the Spirit's empowering lives in keeping with the life the Spirit produces (the fruit of the Spirit). But such people are also always susceptible to temptation— the more so if they think not! And it is exactly our common vulnerability that causes people of the Spirit to restore the fallen, rather than kick them while they are down, as many of us are so prone to do.

That this is the Pauline concern is further corroborated by his description of the means whereby Spirit people are to restore the vulnerable one. They are to do so ἐν πνεύματι πραΰτητος (by the S/spirit of gentleness; cf. 1 Cor 4:21). This is another of those phrases in Paul that is extremely difficult to put into English. On the one hand, as some commentators are quick to observe,[328] the "gentleness" here invoked describes those who are doing the restoring. Thus it is with an attitude of, from a stance of, gentleness. On the other hand, given the presence of Spirit language throughout and thus its appearance here in a context where πνεῦμα has always and only referred to the Holy Spirit, it is difficult to imagine that this connection would have been lost on the Galatians themselves.[329] Consequently, as elsewhere, I have opted for the inelegant "S/spirit" as a way of catching Paul's nuance. In any case, the context rules out altogether translating it "a gentle spirit." Πραΰτης is what is called for— humility toward oneself and considerateness regarding others—and that as the fruit of the Spirit, not some mere human disposition.

Nevertheless, it can scarcely be doubted that this is a deliberate recall of the fruit of the Spirit from 5:23. The "gentleness" is the kind that is manifested by those who are Spirit people, and it is so precisely because they are just that, people *of the Spirit*, who has produced this fruit in their lives.

The net result, therefore, is that the entire sentence is a direct application of the point of the argument (from 5:13) to a specific congregational matter. This is how "freedom from Torah" evidences itself. This is how

---

[327] For the grammatical purist, Paul's grammar breaks down a bit here, in that this participle is singular, while the verb it modifies is plural. But here is the plain evidence that even though this is a community concern, one is tempted and overtaken by sin individually. This is merely another form of his saying "you [plural] each," as e.g., in Phil 2:4, where the same verb appears, but in the plural—and with "each" in the plural as well!

[328] That is, πνεῦμα refers at least to the human spirit or to an attitude. Thus Lightfoot, Burton, Ridderbos.

[329] So Meyer 321–22; Duncan 180; Schlier 260, 270; Guthrie 142; Betz 297n48; Bruce 260; Fung 286. One is struck by how often this clear connection is overlooked in the commentaries, or paid mere lip service.

as servants they love one another and so fulfill Torah. And this is what it means to walk by the Spirit so as not to carry out the desire of the flesh.

2 Although the matter just spoken to is probably to be included under the rubric "bear one another's burdens," the lack of a nuancing connective (e.g., "so," "therefore," etc.) suggests that this is a somewhat independent exhortation, but one which the preceding imperative has brought to mind. The connection therefore probably lies with the vulnerability of the erring one. Not only must the Spirit-led Galatians care for such people, but they must go beyond that by "bearing one another's burdens," lifting the load of the weak and needy, as it were. Since such "burden bearing" is further described as "filling to the full the law of Christ," one can be sure that with this sentence the Galatians are being brought back in a practical way to 5:13–15, especially v. 14. This is how one through love performs the task of a slave for one and all.

Since this surely recalls that verse, and since as we have noted above the Spirit is the presupposition for the empowering of that kind of love, so too the context suggests this to be yet one more way that behavior in keeping with the Spirit expresses itself. All the more so, in light of the tie to "sowing to the Spirit" and "doing what is good unto all" which concludes all of this in vv. 8–9.

But what does "the law of Christ" mean? Is Paul now suggesting, despite what he has just said in 5:23, that life in the Spirit is actually some new form of Torah, requiring observance or obedience? Hardly. The clue to this usage lies in three directions. First, as we will note in chapter 15 on Pauline ethics, God's glory is their *purpose*, the Spirit is their *power*, love is the *principle*, and Christ is the *pattern*. As we have already observed on v. 22, Christ serves as the pattern for the principle, love itself. Thus, "the law of Christ" is first of all an appeal not to some new set of laws or even to some ethical standards that the gospel imposes on believers,[330] but to Christ himself, who in this letter has been deliberately described as the one "who gave himself for our sins" (1:4) and who "loved me and gave himself for me" (2:20).[331] Thus he has already served as the paradigm for the argument in 5:13–14. " 'Tis the way the Master trod, should not the servant tread it still?"

Second, the combination of language—"fulfill" and "law of Christ"—points back to 5:14, where similar language was used of love as "fulfilling" Torah.[332] But at the same time, the choice of different verbs is

---

[330] On this debate see esp. R. B. Hays, "Christology and Ethics in Galatians: The Law of Christ," *CBQ* 49 (1987) 268–90, and Barclay, *Obeying*, 126–31.

[331] Cf. Hays ("Christology," 275): "a formulation coined . . . by Paul to refer to [the] paradigmatic self-giving Jesus Christ."

[332] Thus Barclay, *Obeying*, 131–35, who argues that "the law" here refers to the

probably deliberate. In the one case Torah has been fulfilled so as no longer to obtain;[333] in this case "the law of Christ" is "fulfilled" in every case where in love believers bear each others' burdens. Thus the "fulfillment" in the first instance is almost certainly to be understood in light of its further "being filled to the full" by those who, empowered by the Spirit, so live as Christ himself did.

Third, this turn of phrase in itself is one more gentle reminder that life free from Torah and flesh, empowered by the Spirit, does not lead to "lawlessness." Rather it leads to patterning one's life after the ultimate expression of the Law, namely, Christ, who through his death and resurrection "bore the burdens" of one and all. Above all, Christ is the one "who loved us and gave himself for us." This is "the law of Christ" which Spirit people are called to reproduce.

In light of such a "law," it is easy to see how in v. 3 Paul brings them back to 5:26. Those who are conceited, thinking too highly of themselves, are both self-deceived and unable to fulfill the law of Christ. Such people, therefore, are *not* living in conformity to the Spirit.

GALATIANS 6:7–10

[7]*Do not be deceived; God is not mocked. For whatever a person sows, that is what one will also reap.* [8]*Because the person who sows unto his or her own flesh shall from the flesh reap corruption, but the person who sows unto the Spirit shall from the Spirit reap eternal life.* [9]*Let us not flag in doing what is good, because we shall reap in due season, if we do not give out.* [10]*Therefore, as we have[334] opportunity,[335] let us labor at what is good unto all people, but especially unto those of the household of faith.*

Despite occasional suggestions to the contrary, these words are best understood as Paul's bringing to conclusion the argument that began at 5:13. Several matters of structure and content not only suggest such a view, but also seem to verify the basic correctness of the perspective here presented regarding this whole section.

Law of Moses (esp. from 5:14) as that has been "redefined and fulfilled by Christ in love" (134).

[333] That is, its purpose still obtains and is thus "fulfilled"; but as discrete covenant stipulations for Israel, and by extension to all who would be God's people, it no longer obtains.

[334] This ἔχομεν is read as the subjunctive ἔχωμεν by ℵ B* 6 33 104 326 614 al. This is too difficult a reading to be original and can be explained as a simple, and meaningless, itacism.

[335] Something of a word play is going on here which is very difficult to carry over into English. In v. 9 Paul said that we will reap καιρῷ ἰδίῳ (in its "own time," meaning at the "due season" for the harvest); here he picks up on "time" and talks about our using the present καιρός ("opportunity") for doing the good encouraged in v. 9.

First, all four verses clearly hold together as a unit. The opening warning and citation of what appears to be a common proverb leads directly into the application of the proverb in v. 8 in terms of the argument to this point. This application in turn becomes the basis for the final exhortation and promise in v. 9, now in terms of "doing what is good." Finally, v. 10, picking up the motif of "doing good," brings both this paragraph and the argument from 5:13 to conclusion with a final application in the form of exhortation. This holds together too nicely to be either accidental or random.

Second, in his application of the harvest metaphor in v. 8 Paul reunites the twin motifs that have dominated the entire argument—life in the Spirit over against life in keeping with the flesh—and does so by way of warning and encouragement in light of the eschatological outcome of each kind of life. To "sow unto the Spirit" is but another way of pressing the imperatives, expressed and implied, that dominate vv. 16–26: "walk by the Spirit," "being led by the Spirit," bearing the "fruit of the Spirit," "conforming one's life to the Spirit."[336] The harvest of such "sowing" is eternal life. Likewise, to "sow to the flesh" reflects the various opposites: "eating and devouring one another," doing the "works of the flesh," being "conceited, provoking one another, envying one another," "thinking oneself to be something when in fact one is nothing." Such sowing, as Paul has already asserted in 5:21, reaps non-inheritance, now expressed in terms of "corruption."

Third, the obvious point of the whole is a combination of warning and exhortation based on the harvest metaphor, with its unmistakable eschatological orientation. That the penultimate word of this whole section should be one of warning is particularly noteworthy. Such warning, we have noted above, lay just below the surface at several points (especially 5:21), and on the surface in 5:15 in the language "beware lest you consume one another." Here is the final warning that they desist in such "works of the flesh," for such sowing reaps destruction. Why else such a warning, one wonders, if the whole section has not been tailored to the conflict setting within the Galatian communities.

Fourth, it is also noteworthy that the final word of the whole should be one of encouragement toward "working at what is good for all, especially for those of the household of faith." This is what everything has been about. Those who are Christ's, who live by the Spirit, are thus no longer under Torah; its day has gone. But Spirit people are not lawless; they live by "the law of Christ," meaning that in love they perform the duties of a slave for one another. The problem in Galatia has

---

[336] Some (e.g., Burton 342–43) have argued for the human spirit here, but everything stands against such an option: the context, Pauline usage, and especially the contrast between "one's *own* flesh" and "*the* Spirit" (a point understood as early as Jerome).

been that some believers appear to have been quite willing to come under Torah, to become observant so as to be identified as God's people. But Torah observance would have done them no good at the one crucial point of internecine conflict within the communities. Thus they were willing to close the front door to observable "sin" by becoming Torah observant; but such "coming under Law" became a matter of self-deception. It allowed them to paint the barn red, but leave the dung inside. Real righteousness, that which is expressed in the "law of Christ," means to live in love, serving one another rather than biting one another, bearing one another's burdens rather than provoking one another; it means to live by the power of the Spirit so as not to carry out the desire of the flesh, but rather to evidence the fruit of the Spirit. The final word is that they sow to the Spirit, by working for the good of all, and especially for the good of those within their own communities.

That surely is the point of the whole section and of this final warning and exhortation in particular. Just a few further comments regarding the Spirit material in vv. 8 and 9–10 are needed.

1. As just noted the language of "sowing" to the flesh/Spirit belongs to the metaphor by which all of this began in v. 7. What is "sown" is almost certainly to be understood in terms of all that preceded since 5:13.[337] The two prepositional phrases, to sow "into" the Spirit/flesh and to reap "from" the Spirit/flesh, which seem a bit strange to our ears, simply keep the metaphor alive. As in vv. 16–17 the flesh comes close to being personified, standing in perfect parallel with the Spirit as it does. In terms of the metaphor, these are the two kinds of "soil" *into* which one puts the seed, and *from* which one reaps the harvest. Our difficulty is basically one of translation, since for us the two kinds of "soil" are not of a kind into which one would "plant" anything; thus, we make the slight change "*unto* the flesh/Spirit."

But the point of the metaphor seems transparent. On the one hand, to live out of selfish ambition, to give way to outbursts of rage, to sow discord and provoke hostility, to give way to sexual indulgence or excesses like drunkenness—this is to "sow unto *one's own* flesh." This is to give way to behavior that is just like that of those who do not belong to Christ. And as Paul has already said of them in 5:21, such "sowing" will reap destruction, for the flesh stands in utter and unyielding contradiction to the ways of God. On the other hand, to perform the tasks of a

---

[337] In a rare moment of missing the context, Calvin 178 rejects this in favor of, "to look forward to the wants of present life, without any regard to a future life." Others suggest a closer tie to v. 6, and thus regard the "sowing" as supporting the teacher (Paul or others; e.g., Burton 339–40; Bligh 483–86; cf. L. W. Hurtado, "The Jerusalem Collection and the Book of Galatians," *JSNT* 5 [1979] 46–62). That could be attractive were it not for the great number of links between this passage and all that has preceded.

slave for one another, to restore the fallen, to bear the burdens of another, to have a proper estimation of one's own worth, to bear with those who are hostile or slow to come along—this is to "sow unto the Spirit." This is to walk by the Spirit, to conform one's behavior to the Spirit by whom one now lives on this side of the cross. The final result of such eschatological salvation is its consummation, eternal life.

2. The difference between this final call to life in the Spirit and previous ones is its distinct eschatological focus. The eschatological consummation of each kind of life has already been mentioned in 5:5 ("by the Spirit we await the hope of righteousness") and in 5:21 ("those who do the works of the flesh will not inherit the kingdom"). Now this motif is the direct and express concern. Paul's point is that the eschatological outcome is determined by whether one is living from the flesh or by the Spirit. In 5:21 the outcome of life in the flesh was expressed in terms of unbelievers, people who follow this way of life; at the same time, of course, it served as a warning to Spirit people who persist in such behavior. Here that same point is made as an unmistakable warning. Those who persist in living from the flesh have de facto opted out of life in the Spirit. Again, this has nothing to do with being "overtaken in a trespass"; rather, it has to do with not coming under "obedience to the truth," resisting life in the Spirit for the indulgence of one's own sinfulness. Paul surely intends such warnings to be taken seriously.

Warning, however, is never the final word for Paul. The outcome for God's people, who by definition are those who "sow unto the Spirit," is the final realization of the "hope of righteousness"—eternal life. But as before, Spirit life is not automatic; it involves the making of choices. One must *sow* to the Spirit, that is, one must walk in the sphere of the Spirit by the Spirit's empowering; having been given life by the Spirit, one must live in conformity to what the Spirit wills, as illustrated in the fruit of the Spirit. Such fruitfulness is neither automatic nor optional. Hence, as before, all of this comes by way of imperative. The Spirit is sufficient; Torah never was. But the believer must go in the direction the Spirit leads. And such "sowing" has the promise of full harvest.

3. Lying being the final clause, "shall from the Spirit reap eternal life," is Paul's view of the Spirit as the primary reality of our eschatological existence as already and not yet. The Spirit who gives life (5:25; 2 Cor 3:6) is the same Spirit by whom we await our final hope (5:5) and because of whose presence within/among us we shall also enter into the final consummation of that life. This usage, therefore, reflects the same reality as the metaphors "down payment," "seal," and "firstfruits." The Spirit is both the evidence of our having entered into life in the present and the ground and guarantee of our final, full realization of that life.

4. Finally, vv. 9–10 bring the whole argument to conclusion by focusing on one fruit of the Spirit—goodness. Here is the clear evidence that goodness is not an abstract noun; as a fruit of the Spirit, goodness

means to keep on doing good, continually, without flagging or growing weary at it (v. 9).[338] As one thus "sows to the Spirit," one will reap at the time of harvest, as already promised in v. 8. It further means to work at what is good, with others as the recipients of such "good work." Quite in keeping with the thrust of the entire section, the final word is "especially to those who are members of the household of the faith"—"the faith" that has come with Christ (3:25–26), which expresses itself in love and "faith-fulness" within the believing community. Here is the proof that "having begun by the Spirit, they are also finishing by the Spirit."

The body of the letter thus concludes on the same note with which the argument proper began in 3:1–5. As we noted there, the ultimate contrast in Galatians is not between "works" and "faith," but between life under Torah and life by the Spirit. Life under Torah means to come under the very curse from which Christ has set us free; moreover life under Torah does not lead to righteousness, either in terms of relationship with God or in terms of godly behavior. Only the Spirit, who appropriates the righteousness secured through Christ's death and resurrection, can bring life and effect righteousness of the real kind. So having begun by the Spirit, the Galatians are urged to finish by the Spirit. And this, not only because here alone is the way of life in Christ, but also because here alone is God's antidote to the life of the flesh. Christ's death provided both freedom from Torah observance and crucifixion to the former way of life; the Spirit appropriates this freedom in such a way that the believer neither lives under the slavery of Law nor makes provision for the indulgence of the flesh. But to "finish" by the Spirit means to walk in/by the Spirit; it means, in the final words of the argument, to sow to the Spirit by working what is good to all people, especially those of one's own family in Christ.

GALATIANS 6:18

The grace of our[339] *Lord Jesus Christ be with your spirit, brothers and sisters. Amen.*

This is the first in a group of four letters, whose grace-benediction appears with this unusual form (see Phil 4:23; Phlm 25; 2 Tim 4:22). Heretofore (including the elaborated grace in 2 Cor 13:13[14]) Paul has signed off with, "The grace of our Lord Jesus Christ be *with you*" (1 Thes; 1 Cor; cf. Rom [16:20]; Col) or "*with you all*" (2 Thes; 2 Cor). But here, for reasons that are past finding out, the "with you" becomes "with your spirit."

---

[338] So also Betz 309 and Barclay, *Obeying*, 166.

[339] The ἡμῶν is missing in some significant witnesses (א P 1241ˢ 1739 1881 2464 pc). This very well may be the original text, since it is easier to imagine the pronoun being added (on the basis of familiarity with a standard Pauline pattern) than that a grandparent of these witnesses carelessly omitted it.

Robert Jewett has made a considerable point out of the singular of πνεῦμα occurring with the plural pronoun, asserting that "since the word 'spirit' is in the singular, reference is clearly being made to the single divine spirit rather than to the various human spirits with which the members of the congregation could have been thought to have been born." He adds: "But one thing is certain: the tradition which shaped this formula did not distinguish between the divine spirit and the spirit which a man could possess."[340]

But this is not nearly as "clear" and "certain" as Jewett would have it. In fact, this use of the plural pronoun with a singular noun is but another reflection of Paul's (Semitic) preference for a distributive singular, wherein "something belonging to each person in a group of people is placed in the singular."[341] Therefore, Paul almost certainly does *not* intend by this usage to refer to "the single divine spirit," nor is he thinking of the Spirit as apportioned to each them and in effect taking the place of the human spirit, as Jewett maintains. Paul means "be with your spirits," which he here substitutes for the more common "with you" that appears elsewhere.[342] One looks in vain in this case for a reference to the Spirit of God.

But, of course, that does not help us understand why Paul would choose such usage in these four letters. And at this point scholarship has tended to draw blanks. There does not seem to be anything unique to the four letters in which this variation appears that would provide a clue. What perhaps needs to be noted is that the other three letters (Philippians, Philemon, 2 Timothy) are the most overtly affectionate in the Pauline corpus. But Galatians? Perhaps this usage and the unique addition of ἀδελφοί ("brothers [and sisters]") are a kind of final offer of affection in a letter that otherwise has bristled with distress.

CONCLUSIONS

Because of the major role the Spirit plays in the argument of this letter, both by his explicit statements and by the implications lying behind much of what he says, Paul here opens the windows to give a rather full-orbed picture of the life of the Spirit in his experience and understanding. Christian life, individually and corporately, begins, is carried on, and comes to eschatological conclusion by means of God's empowering presence, the Holy Spirit.

1. As in the earlier letters, the Spirit is the absolute *sine qua non* of becoming a believer in Christ. Here is the verification that one belongs to him; the Spirit has now replaced Torah as the new "identity marker"

---

[340] *Terms*, 184.

[341] N. Turner, MHT 3.23. For this usage in Paul see (with σῶμα) 1 Cor 6:19, 20; 2 Cor 4:10; Rom 6:12; 8:23; (with καρδία) 2 Cor 3:15; 6:11 [LXX]; Rom 1:21; Eph 1:18; 4:18; 5:19; 6:5; Phil 1:7.

[342] Cf. E. Schweizer, *TDNT* 6.435.

of God's people. At the time of their conversion, God marked them as his children by sending the Spirit into their hearts, who enabled them to cry out "*Abba*" to God—the personal language of Jesus, God's Son, and therefore the evidence of "sonship."

At the same time, it is equally transparent that the coming of the Spirit was a dynamic, experienced reality—so much so that Paul can appeal without fear of contradiction to their reception of the Spirit as the impeccable proof that righteousness is predicated on faith in Christ and has absolutely nothing to do with Torah observance. The Galatians' own experience of the Spirit preceded the coming of Torah in the form of the agitators; for Paul this is evidence enough that the time of Torah is over. Thus those who are led by the Spirit are not under Torah.

2. The heart of the argument, however, has less to do with Christian beginnings and more to do with "coming to completion," i.e., with the ongoing life of the believer and the believing community. Here again the Spirit as God's empowering presence is the key to everything. At the heart of things in this letter, related to the controversy that triggered it, is the question of righteousness apart from Torah. For Paul the life of the Spirit—being led by the Spirit so as to walk in the ways of the Lord— means the end of Torah observance. Those who live by the Spirit will thus bear the fruit of the Spirit, and for such a life Torah as obligation has no significance at all.

But Paul's primary concern is not with the individual believer, but with the life of the Spirit as it works its way out in the community of faith. Hence this letter provides ample expression of this dimension of Spirit life as well. Included in this larger arena of life together by the Spirit is both their ethical life—their relationships with one another as evidencing the presence of the Spirit—and their corporate life of worship, since he can appeal to the ongoing presence of the miraculous in their midst as reason also that righteousness is by the hearing of faith, not by Torah observance.

3. Absolutely presuppositional to the Pauline understanding is the Spirit as the main eschatological reality, the certain evidence that the future has begun and the guarantee of its consummation. Although this note is sounded less here than elsewhere, it is so foundational for Paul that it can scarcely stay silenced. Hence in 5:5, besides everything else, the Spirit supersedes Torah precisely because his presence guarantees our hope that Christ's righteousness has afforded. But even more so, as in 2 Corinthians 3, Paul understands the Spirit himself as the fulfillment of God's promise, in this case, including the promise made to Abraham that included his blessing of the Gentiles (3:13–14).

4. Finally, it is noteworthy that the Spirit as God's *personal* presence is also presuppositional throughout. By his Spirit, Christ lives within the believer; the Spirit leads his people into the fulfilling of the righteousness the Law called for but could not produce.

As everywhere else in the apostle, the Spirit is not the central matter; that place is taken by Christ alone. But for the ongoing life that Christ has afforded through his death and resurrection, the Spirit is the key to everything: conversion, ethics, community life, miracles, revelation, eschatology. Without the Spirit there simply is no genuinely Christian life.

7

ROMANS

Commentaries:[1] P. J. **Achtemeier** (Interp, 1985); C. K. **Barrett** (BNTC, 1957); K. **Barth** (1933); M. **Black** (NCB, 1973); F. F. **Bruce** (TNTC, 1985²); J. **Calvin** (ET, 1961); C. E. B. **Cranfield** (ICC, 1975); idem (1985); J. **Denney** (EGT, 1900); C. H. **Dodd** (MNTC, 1959); J. D. G. **Dunn** (WBC, 1988); F. **Godet** (ET 1883); R. **Haldane** (1839); E. F. **Harrison** (EBC, 1976); C. **Hodge** (1864); E. **Käsemann** (ET, 1980); F. J. **Leenhardt** (ET, 1957); R. C. H. **Lenski** (1945); H. P. **Liddon** (1899); H. **Lietzmann** (1933); J. B. **Lightfoot** (1895); H. A. W. **Meyer** (MeyerK, 1881); O. **Michel** (MeyerK, 1966⁴); D. J. **Moo** (WEC, 1991); L. **Morris** (1988); J. **Murray** (NIC, 1959, 1965); A. **Nygren** (1949); W. **Sanday** and W. **Headlam** (= SH, ICC, 1896); T. **Zahn** (1910); J. **Ziesler** (1989).

Except for 1 Corinthians, Paul's letter to the church in Rome contains the largest amount of Spirit material in the corpus. The Spirit is explicitly mentioned at least 31 (perhaps 33) times,[2] 20 of which occur in chapter 8. The adjective πνευματικός (Spiritual) also occurs 3 times, χάρισμα (gracious gift) 6 times (twice referring to Spirit activity), and prophecy as a *charisma* once.

Because of the high incidence of Spirit language in chapter 8, the Spirit's crucial role in the argument of this letter has long been recognized. But also because of chapter 8, that role has most often been seen in terms of the sanctification of the believer, where the Spirit serves as the proper "successor" to Christ, whose justifying work is the primary concern of the letter. But there are good reasons for seeing this traditional interpretation as too facile, for Romans as a whole as well as for Paul's understanding of the Spirit's role in Christian life. How one under-

---

[1]The following commentaries are referred to in this chapter only by the author's last name.

[2]1:4, 9 (indirectly); 2:29; 5:5; 7:6; 8:2, 4, 5[2x], 6, 9[3x], 10, 11[2x] 13, 14, 15[2x], 16[2x], 23, 26[2x], 27, 9:1; 12:11[?]; 14:17; 15:13, 16, 19, 30. There is a further instance in the TR in 8:1; see n. 133 below.

stands the Spirit material in this letter, therefore, will be affected considerably by one's overall understanding of the letter itself, its purpose and the development of the argument.

But herein lies a major exegetical crux. What is the aim of Romans, and how does the argument accomplish that aim? I have no illusions that I have in fact resolved an issue so complex that it has called forth a major monograph,[3] plus a major collection of studies entitled *The Romans Debate*.[4] But since it is not possible to do exegesis of this letter without some prior assumptions on these matters,[5] I need here to spell out in brief what I understand Romans to be all about and also to note in brief how I perceive the argument to work.

Romans, as I see it, is totally taken up with Paul's passion for the gospel, whose goal is the creation—by redemption—of a single people for God's name out of Jew and Gentile together. It is this latter concern that drives the argument from beginning to end. The dynamics of the letter result from the twin facts (1) that the Roman church is a mixed—perhaps divided—community, who were having difficulty holding Jew and Gentile together as one people of God, and (2) that Paul is attempting to speak to a situation in a community over which he has no jurisdiction but to which he hopes soon to come, in order to find a favorable base for ministry in the West. The issue in Rome apparently stems from the Jewish side, with their concerns about Gentile believers and especially the latter's relationship to Torah.[6]

The practical goal of the letter is to be found in its concluding argument in 14:1–15:13, in which the appeal is for those who do and those who don't, with regard to food laws, to "accept/welcome one another" (15:7; cf. 14:1; 15:1–2). All of which concludes, first, with the benedictory prayer of 15:5–6, that God might grant them as Jews and Gentiles "to live

---

[3] A. J. M. Wedderburn, *The Reasons for Romans* (Edinburgh: T. & T. Clark, 1988).

[4] Edited by Karl Donfried (rev. and expanded ed.; Peabody, Mass.: Hendrickson, 1991), with thirteen additional essays beyond the original ten (Minneapolis: Augsburg, 1977).

[5] All one has to do is to read the commentaries to see that this is so. It is even more true of those who think they come to this letter without such presuppositions. Their unarticulated assumptions determine how they understand almost every text. The clear evidence of this for me is seen when leading a class of students from primarily evangelical backgrounds through the letter, who have been exposed most of their lives to the basic Reformational perspective. In one sense, the goal of my course is to help them to read Romans as if the Reformation had never happened—a major task indeed! It is not that the Reformers' view was wrong, but that it was too narrow and therefore failed to account for so much.

[6] This is evidenced chiefly by the phenomenon of the interlocutor, who emerges throughout and who seems primarily to be raising questions from the Jewish Christian side, usually out of concern for Torah observance. For a view that has some correspondences with this, but sees Gentile rejection of Jews to be the driving force, see Wright, *Climax*, 234–35.

in *harmony with one another,* in accordance with Christ Jesus, so that *together* you may *with one voice* glorify the God and Father of our Lord Jesus Christ" (NRSV). That this is the ultimate aim of the letter seems verified by the appeal that follows (vv. 7–12): they are to welcome one another precisely because Christ's justifying work was for Jew and Gentile alike so that *the* OT promises might be fulfilled, wherein Gentiles glorify the God of Israel, the one and only God. All of this is quite in keeping with the way the letter begins, with a long proemium (salutation and thanksgiving/prayer), in which Paul designates himself as "set apart for the gospel of God" (v. 1) promised by the prophets (v. 2), so as "to bring about the obedience of faith among all the Gentiles" (v. 5).

If that is the aim of the letter, and the evidence throughout points regularly in this direction,[7] then the means to that end is not dissimilar to the argument of Galatians: that the justifying work of Christ is for Jew and Gentile alike, without distinction, as they put their trust in the God who justifies not the righteous (= keepers of Torah) but sinners (= those with and without Torah).[8] Likewise, and again similar to Galatians, the Spirit plays a leading role in this argument, which is not primarily a matter of sanctification following justification, or of the empowering dimension of Pauline paraenesis.[9] Rather, in keeping with Paul's theology elsewhere, the Spirit is seen as the fulfillment of the promised new covenant (7:5–6), wherein Torah is now "fulfilled" in those who walk by the Spirit (8:4).[10] Just as in Galatians, Paul's way of responding to the fear that being done with Torah will lead to unrighteousness is to remind his readers of the central role of the Spirit in Christian life. Indeed, the vast majority of explicit references to the Spirit in this letter are in some way related to this central concern of the letter, that along with Christ's death and resurrection the Spirit has brought an end to Torah observance by empowering its "fulfillment" under the new covenant, thus opening the way for Jew and Gentile together to be God's people, to have

---

[7]Simply note, e.g., that the rhetorical questions in 3:27–31, which seem both to bring the preceding discussion to conclusion and to launch the rest of the argument, have Jew and Gentile relationships as one people of God as their central concern, as that question is related to Gentiles and Torah. Thus, "where is boasting [= boasting before God on the basis of Torah]?" "is God a God of the Jews only, and not also of the Gentiles?" and "do we thereby abolish Torah through faith?"

[8]What is new here is the elaborate argument of 1:18–3:20 that Torah advantages no one, because those without Torah can live righteously just as well as those who have Torah; and those who have Torah have proven to be sinners every bit as much as those who do not have Torah.

[9]After all, one is intrigued in this letter by the paucity of explicit references to the Spirit in 12:1–15:13 in contrast with Gal 5:13–6:10—although, as will be argued here, the Spirit is to be understood as lying behind the whole of this section of Romans as well.

[10]In this regard see on Gal 5:13–15, 16–18.

and do his righteousness, but apart from Torah. Most of the other references to the Spirit occur in passages where Paul is referring to his own Spirit-inspired ministry through which "the sanctification of the Gentiles" (15:16) has been accomplished.

The letter fits the standard formal parts of the Pauline letter. A proemium (salutation and thanksgiving), in this case a rather long one (1:1–15[17]), is followed by the body of the letter, also in this case an exceptionally long one (1:18–15:13), in which Paul argues on the basis of the work of Christ and the gift of the Spirit that there is only one people of God composed of Jew and Gentile alike on the equal grounds of faith in Christ Jesus. This is followed by some personal words related to his own ministry and long-time desire to visit Rome, which he hopes will finally be realized (15:14–33). This is followed in turn by a word of commendation for Phoebe, who bears the letter (16:1–2), and personal greetings to various members of the Roman community who are Paul's personal friends and acquaintances from the past (16:3–16). The letter concludes with the standard fare of closing exhortations, greetings, and benediction(s) (16:17–27). The Spirit plays a leading role in most of this, especially in the argument, as well as in the surrounding personal matter.

The logic of the argument, which ultimately has to do with "the righteousness of God," can be easily traced, even though many of its details are knotty: Paul begins with the failure of Torah to bring about righteousness—both positional and behavioral; thus Torah has not advantaged the Jew (1:18–3:20). The Spirit first emerges in 2:29, as the new covenant answer to Torah and circumcision by creating the true "Jew" (= person of God) by a "circumcision of heart." This is followed by the affirmation of Christ's having effected such righteousness through the cross, to be received by Jew and Gentile alike on the basis of faith (3:21–31). As his way of "upholding the Law," Paul further contends that Abraham serves as primary evidence that God has always intended to create a people for his name on the basis of faith, since Abraham in his trusting obedience became the father of all peoples—Jew and Gentile alike (4:1–25). Thus in the confessional and transitional passage of 5:1–11 Paul both concludes the argument to this juncture and begins the next (5:12–8:39), by pointing out the crucial role of Christ, who effected reconciliation, and of the Spirit, who appropriates to the believer God's love manifested in Christ, whereby one also lives in hope in the midst of present suffering. Most of 6:1–8:30 is taken up with the question of righteousness in terms of conduct; if one lives apart from Torah, one does not thereby live apart from righteousness. Both Christ's death and resurrection and the gift of the Spirit lead to a "walk" in which Torah is "fulfilled." After addressing the matter of God's faithfulness and Jewish disobedience (chs. 9–11)—key to this letter but by the nature of its argumentation lacking references to the Spirit—Paul then takes up the character of the new Torah-less (or "fulfilled Torah") righteousness that the Spirit effects (12:1–15:13). He first describes such righteousness (ch. 12) and illustrates how it works out in some general settings (ch. 13); finally he uses the matter of food laws to illustrate and to appeal for a Torah-less, Spirit-led righteousness (14:1–15:13), in which the Spirit again is seen to play the key role (14:17; the kingdom has to do not with "food and drink" but with "righteousness—not to mention peace and joy—in/by the Holy Spirit"). Thus, even though there is an understandably higher concentration of Spirit language in ch. 8, throughout the argument Paul repeatedly notes the role of the Spirit in God's effecting righteousness for Jew and Gentile alike.

So also with the proemium and concluding matters (from 15:14), which are designed to justify his sending this letter[11] and to pave the way for his coming in person, hopefully soon. Here, too, especially with regard to his own ministry and its relationship to the gospel and Gentile inclusion into the people of God, the Spirit plays the leading role.

The net result is as full-orbed a picture of the person and work of the Spirit in Pauline "theology" as one gets in any of Paul's letters. The Spirit is both the Spirit of Christ and the Spirit of God, whom God has sent into the hearts of believers, thus pouring his love into them, circumcising their hearts, sanctifying them. Not only so, but the eschatological Spirit is both the certain evidence of our belonging to God and the "firstfruits" of our final glory. As such the Spirit empowers us to abound in hope in the present, and intercedes for us in the midst of our present weaknesses. The Spirit thus fulfills the old covenant, so that the life described by the Torah is now lived by the power of the Spirit; accordingly, the Spirit represents a new "law"—that of life, given by Christ Jesus. As such the Spirit is the source of love, joy, and peace in the present, as one awaits the certain future. Finally, the Spirit empowers ministry, not to mention individual and corporate life in all its facets. The Spirit, as always in Paul, is thus portrayed as God's empowering presence, as the way God is present to create and enable his people under the new covenant.

ROMANS 1:1–15

Romans begins with an especially long and, in terms of content, surprising proemium, in which Paul's standard salutation and his

---

[11] This is what best explains the rather long list of persons to be greeted in 16:3–16. The very fact that he already knows so many in the church, and can greet them by name, serves as a kind of backdoor entrée into their midst by means of this letter. That is, he is not altogether presumptuous in writing such a letter to this church that he did not found, since so many among them are already known to him.

thanksgiving/prayer report have both been elaborated in terms of his ministry and of his relationship to the church in Rome.

The salutation (vv. 1–7) is basically a long elaboration of the phrase, "having been set apart for the gospel of God" (v. 1), whose emphasis is threefold: that the gospel has continuity with the old covenant as the fulfilled promise—Christ is of royal David's lineage (vv. 2–3); that the content of the gospel is first of all christological, having to do with Christ's earthly ministry and his present exaltation in power (vv. 3–4); and finally that Paul's own calling and apostleship for which he had been "set apart" was to bring about "the obedience of faith among all the Gentiles" (vv. 5–6). The emphasis in the thanksgiving, which is soon swallowed up by a prayer report (vv. 8–17),[12] lies exclusively with his desire to come to Rome, so that he might be able to say in person what now he will write in a letter.[13] The unusual length and surprising content of this proemium are almost certainly related to its content: since the church in Rome is of some long standing and since it is not one of his own churches, he feels a special compulsion to justify the writing of this letter, which at the same time will pave the way for his own hoped-for soon arrival.

The Spirit material in the proemium, which tends to appear in rather incidental fashion, is also some of the more ambiguous in his letters. But if our exegesis is correct, then the Spirit is first of all the sphere of the Risen Lord's present eschatological existence; the Spirit is also the sphere in which Paul serves the Risen Lord; and finally the Spirit is the source of the gifting with which Paul hopes to come among the Roman believers some future day—and comes now by way of letter.

ROMANS 1:2

. . . which [God] promised beforehand through his prophets in the sacred Scriptures.

The "prophets" mentioned in this passage refer to the Old Testament prophets; the reason for noting the passage here is that the collocation of "prophets" and "sacred Scriptures" reflects something of Paul's view of Scripture as inspired by the Spirit,[14] and thus it also anticipates what is said more clearly in 2 Tim

---

[12]Even though vv. 16–17 seem intended to set forth the themes of the argument that follows, syntactically they belong to the prayer report that begins in v. 9b, which itself is all but lost sight of in favor of an elaboration that has a single concern: his desire to come to Rome and to minister as effectively among them as he has elsewhere. Thus vv. 16–17 bring this expression of personal desire to its proper conclusion and introduce the main concerns of the subsequent argument.

[13]This is said in reverse, in terms of how Paul actually expresses himself in the letter. That is, it is because he cannot now come and "impart some Spirit gift" that he writes instead, undoubtedly hoping the letter to function as the shared "gift of the Spirit" in place of his personal presence. See on v. 11 below.

[14]H. Schlier (next n.) argues that this combination is non-Pauline and therefore an indication that it belongs to the alleged pre-Pauline tradition cited in vv. 3–4. See

3:16. The point does not need belaboring, but the connection seems certain. Whatever else may be true about Paul's understanding of the OT prophets, the connection between the Spirit and prophecy in his own churches and letters demonstrates that the same relationship existed beforehand with the OT prophets. Prophets, whether in ancient Israel or in the contemporary church, speak by the Spirit. Here Paul is at one with the Judaism within which his spiritual life was nurtured. That "the prophets" are mentioned as now existing "in the sacred Scriptures" indicates that Spirit "inspiration" of the Scriptures is a Pauline presupposition, even if it is articulated but once in his extant letters.

ROMANS 1:3–4[15]

[3] . . . concerning his Son, who came from the seed of David according to the flesh, [4]who was declared Son of God with power according to the Spirit of holiness by the resurrection from the dead, Jesus Christ our Lord.

This first mention of the Spirit, which occurs in a clause bristling with exegetical difficulties,[16] is among the more difficult Spirit passages

---

n. 16 below. This, however, takes the question of pre-Pauline tradition beyond the bounds of common sense and leads to exegetical nihilism. Two observations: (1) Paul gives no indication that he is citing something; this is our discovery, not his disclosure. (2) The sentence as it now stands was *dictated* to Tertius as a Pauline sentence, which we may assume he intended the Romans to take at its face value. Thus, whether he used traditional material or not (and I am open on this one), the present sentence is a Pauline construct which has *incorporated* the tradition in such a way that Paul takes ownership of it—all of it. Therefore, it is methodologically proper for us to use it to discover Paul's perspective. Cf. Moo 49: "Methodologically, it is necessary at least to maintain that whatever Paul quotes, he himself affirms."

[15]*Bibliography*: P. **Beasley-Murray**, "Romans 1:3f: An Early Confession of Faith in the Lordship of Jesus," *TynB* 31 (1980) 147–54; M.-E. **Boismard**, "Constitué Fils de Dieu (Rom. I.4)," *RevistB* 60 (1953) 5–17; J. D. G. **Dunn**, "Jesus—Flesh and Spirit: An Exposition of Romans 1:3–4," *JTS* 24 (1973) 40–68; N. Q. **Hamilton**, *The Holy Spirit and Eschatology in Paul* (SJTOP 6; Edinburgh: Oliver and Boyd, 1957) 12–15; R. **Jewett**, "The Redaction and Use of an Early Christian Confession in Romans 1:3–4," in *The Living Text: Essays in Honor of Ernest W. Saunders* (ed. D. E. Groh and R. Jewett; Lanham, Md.: University Press of America, 1985) 99–122; P.-E. **Langevin**, "Une confession prépauliniennes de la 'Seigneurie' du Christ. Exégèse de Romains 1,3–4," in *Le Christ hier, aujourd'hui, et demain* (ed. R. Laflamme and M. Gervais; Quebec: Université Laval, 1976) 298–305; R. P. **Menzies**, *The Development of Early Christian Pneumatology*, 287–95; V. S. **Poythress**, "Is Romans 1[3–4] a Pauline Confession After All?" *ExpT* 87 (1975–76) 180–83; H. **Schlier**, "Eine christologische Credo-Formel der römischen Gemeinde. Zu Röm 1:3f," in *Neues Testament und Geschichte* (Festschrift O. Cullmann; ed. H. Baltensweiler and B. Reicke; Zürich: Theologischer, 1972) 207–18; B. **Schneider**, "Κατὰ Πνεῦμα Ἁγιωσύνης (Romans 1,4)," *Bib* 48 (1967) 359–87; E. **Schweizer**, "Röm 1:3f. und der Gegensatz von Fleisch und Geist vor und bei Paulus," *EvT* 15 (1955) 563–71; J. M. **Scott**, *Adoption*, 223–44.

[16]This is another of those many passages in the Pauline corpus, beginning in 1 Thes 1:9–10 and continuing throughout, which appear to be creedal or semi-creedal. Since there are so many of them, and since no two are alike—or indeed even remotely

in the letter. The clause is one of two in the proemium in which the gospel is given content. The other, vv. 16–17, is strictly soteriological and sets forth the themes of the argument of the letter, which is ultimately a matter of soteriology; this one is as obviously christological, and seems intended from the outset to emphasize for the sake of Paul's Jewish Christian readers that the gospel, which has Christ as its primary subject matter, is the fulfillment of God's promises in the OT (v. 2) and that Christ is the fulfillment of Jewish messianic expectations (v. 3). The promises, of course, include God's blessing on the Gentiles, which is what this letter is ultimately all about.

In the present christological clause, two points are made, set in contrast to each other. First, as to his earthly life, Christ fulfilled Jewish messianic hopes by being of the "seed of David." Second, his earthly life was followed by his present exalted status as "Son of God with power,"[17] predicated on his having been raised from the dead. Thus both clauses are modified by twin prepositional phrases (ἐκ σπέρματος Δαυίδ/ἐξ ἀναστάσεως νεκρῶν [from the seed of David/from the resurrection of the dead]; κατὰ σάρκα/κατὰ πνεῦμα ἁγιωσύνης [according to the flesh/according to the Spirit of holiness]), which seem intended to be in Semitic parallelism, that is, in poetically balanced contrast[18] whose structures can be easily displayed (the whole results in a pair of chiasms):

περὶ τοῦ υἱοῦ αὐτοῦ	A	
τοῦ γενομένου	B	
ἐκ σπέρματος Δαυὶδ		C
κατὰ σάρκα		D
τοῦ ὁρισθέντος υἱοῦ θεοῦ ἐν δυνάμει	B	
κατὰ πνεῦμα ἁγιωσύνης		D
ἐξ ἀναστάσεως νεκρῶν,		C
Ἰησοῦ Χριστοῦ τοῦ κυρίου ἡμῶν	A	

similar in terms of language and structures—one cannot tell whether Paul is here dipping into the common creedal pool of the early church, or whether they reflect his own tendencies to express the basic truth of the gospel in this kind of creedal way. Most scholars assume the former (although Poythress expresses doubts and Scott, *Adoption*, 227–36, offers a considerable refutation). In any case, here as always, *in its present expression* we are dealing with *a Pauline sentence* and must therefore assume Pauline authorship of the arrangement (see n. 14 above). Cf. Gal 4:4–6 (q.v.).

[17] As with most commentaries (e.g., Cranfield, Dunn, Morris, Moo) and translations (NIV, NRSV) I take the phrase ἐν δυνάμει ("with power") to modify "Son of God," not the participle ὁρισθέντος (declared/appointed, as SH). The contrast seems obviously to be between his being Son of God "in weakness" during his incarnation and his having received divine "appointment" as Son of God *with power* on the basis (or from the time) of the resurrection.

[18] Not necessarily intending, of course, by "contrast" that they are thereby "antithetical"—which in this case they surely are not, *pace* Dunn, "Jesus," 49 et passim.

Concerning *his* Son,
> *who* came
>> from the seed of David
>> according to the flesh
> *who* was declared Son of God with power
>> according to the Spirit of holiness
>> from the resurrection from the dead

Jesus Christ *our* Lord

The difficulties with the Spirit phrase are three: first, the meaning of the phrase itself, κατὰ πνεῦμα ἁγιωσύνης ("according to the Spirit [spirit?] of holiness"), which is unique to the Pauline corpus;[19] second, how the phrase is to be understood in relation to the preceding κατὰ σάρκα ("according to the flesh") in v. 3, to which it undoubtedly stands in some form of contrast; and third, its relationship and meaning to the rest of the words within its own clause, and thus its "meaning" in the sentence. It should be noted further that the meaning of the first clause (v. 3) is rather straightforward regarding Jesus' earthly life, and that the questions, therefore, all emerge with the second clause, which seems just as clearly intended to speak of the Son of God in terms of his present, post-incarnational exaltation. The way this second clause has been phrased is what has created our difficulties.

Let us begin by looking at the first two matters together: the meaning of the phrase, but in light of its intended contrast with v. 3. First of all, while there can be little question that Paul intended the two clauses in vv. 3 and 4 to contrast one another, there can likewise be little question that the first clause is intended to speak *affirmatively* of Jesus' earthly life. The gospel, Paul says, is about God's Son, who in terms of his human life (κατὰ σάρκα) came in fulfillment of the prophetic word noted in v. 2— from royal David's own lineage. Thus, even though elsewhere in Paul "flesh" and "Spirit" usually stand in strong antithetical contrast, here that is clearly not the case.[20] "Flesh" is basically theologically neutral

---

[19]Indeed, in almost the whole of Greek literature, occurring only here and in Test. Lev. 18:11 (καὶ πνεῦμα ἁγιωσύνης ἔσται ἐπ' αὐτοῖς, "and the Spirit of holiness shall be on them"), plus on a Jewish amulet (see Erik Peterson, "Das Amulett von Acre," in *Frühkirche, Judentum und Gnosis: Studien und Untersuchungen* (Rome: Herder, 1959) 346–54 (351–52). The phrase is a literal rendering of the Hebrew רוּחַ קָדְשׁ, which occurs in the OT in Ps 50[51]:11 and Isa 63:10, 11 (cf. 1QS 4:21; 8:16; 9:3; 1QH 7:6, 7; 9:32), and which in each case has been translated in the LXX as τὸ πνεῦμα τὸ ἅγιον (Holy Spirit). The distinct, and unusual, Semitic flavoring of this phrase is one of the stronger arguments in favor of the pre-Pauline existence of this passage. But see Poythress, "Romans 1³⁻⁴," 181, who points out the difficulties here as well.

[20]Contra Dunn (see n. 18 above), whose position is only slightly moderated in his commentary (13), followed by Menzies, *Development*, 291–94. If reader response criticism counts for anything, and it must in this case since the Romans for the most part had not heard Paul in person, then it is hard to imagine the circumstances in which they could have understood Paul as Dunn presents him to be arguing. In an

here,[21] and the preposition κατά denotes "relationship to something" (= "with respect to, in relation to").[22] Since the other repeated preposition has basically the same sense in both clauses,[23] there is every good reason to think the same holds true with the κατά phrases.[24] If so, then κατὰ πνεῦμα ἁγιωσύνης means something like "in keeping with, or with respect to, the Spirit of holiness." If the "flesh" phrase thus has to do with "the sphere of his human life," then the "Spirit" phrase probably has to do with "the sphere of Spirit life," which in Paul would be another way of referring to the sphere of our final eschatological existence, which will be Spirit life par excellence. Thus, very much like the first two lines of the Christ-hymn in 1 Tim 3:16 (q.v.), these two phrases describe what is absolutely characteristic of the two expressions of existence, what is

---

otherwise useful overview of the use of σάρξ in Paul, Dunn concludes that the σάρξ/πνεῦμα contrast in vv. 3–4 is primarily to be understood in Paul's more characteristically theological way—so much so that to speak of Christ as "descended from the seed of David κατὰ σάρκα" is ultimately pejorative. He was thus "bound and determined by the weakness and inadequacy of the human condition, *allowed worldly considerations to determine his conduct* [emphasis mine], he was merely Son of David and no more—Messiah indeed, but a disappointing, ineffective, irrelevant Messiah" (57). And this in a Pauline sentence that begins: "The gospel of God which he promised beforehand through his prophets in Sacred Scripture"! How could the Romans, one wonders, have so understood κατὰ σάρκα?

[21]That is, in terms of Paul's frequent usage, where σάρξ represents humanity in its fallenness and hostility toward God. The present usage reflects its OT roots, emphasizing human life in its creatureliness, hence "weakness," but not in terms of fallenness (cf. Käsemann 11).

[22]So BAGD II.6.

[23]Gk. ἐκ (ἐξ), one of whose basic meanings is "to denote origin, cause, motive, reason" (BAGD 3). In this case the first clause means "origin as to family, race, etc." (BAGD 3b); the second denotes "effective cause or reason" (BAGD 3e,f). Thus Jesus "came *from* the lineage of David"; he "was declared Son of God with power *from* (= stemming from; on the basis of) his resurrection from the dead." This is not a universal view; many see it as temporal here (= from the time of the resurrection); see inter alia, Barrett 20, Cranfield 1.62; Käsemann 12; Scott, *Adoption*, 240. But on this one, Morris 47 surely has it right: "There is certainly some reference to time, but this is not primary. Rather, the emphasis is on the fact that the resurrection is that whereby Christ is seen to be the Son of God in power." So most commentaries.

[24]Otherwise, Hendriksen 43, Menzies (*Development*, 288n1), and Scott (*Adoption*, 240), who would make it instrumental here ("by the Spirit"), Hendriksen because he believes the Spirit to be the one who raised Christ, Menzies because he needs such a view for his overall argument, and Scott because of his view that this is "an adoption formula," reflecting 2 Sam 7:14 and corresponding to the role of the Spirit in our "adoption as 'sons' " (see on 8:16). But one wonders whether κατά is ever as baldly instrumental in the sense that Hendriksen and Scott would make it, as a precise equivalent of ἐν. Even in 1 Cor 12:8, the most commonly noted example, it is not an equivalent of the accompanying ἐν and διά phrases, but is rather an extension of its basically relational sense, meaning "in keeping with [the working of] the same Spirit." That Paul believed the Spirit to have raised Christ simply does not hold up exegetically; on this matter see esp. on Rom 8:11 and the discussion in ch. 12.

earthly and what is heavenly, but in this case not in a cosmological but temporal/eschatological sense. The one is κατὰ σάρκα, truly human and belonging to the present age that is passing away; the other is κατὰ πνεῦμα, belonging to the eschatological age inaugurated by the resurrection and the advent of the Spirit.[25] In this one clause Christ's present exaltation as Son of God in power, over against the time of his humiliation in the weakness of our "flesh," our merely human life, is related to the two ultimate eschatological realities—Christ's resurrection and the Spirit.[26]

If that is the intent of the contrasts, and Pauline usage elsewhere leads in that direction,[27] then that leads to some conclusions as to the meaning of the phrase itself. To be sure, some have argued otherwise, that it refers to Christ's (transcendently holy) human spirit,[28] or to his divine nature (vis-à-vis his human nature designated by κατὰ σάρκα),[29] or for a meaning of "spirit" that approximates "attitude" or "disposition."[30] But these views face nearly insurmountable difficulties: First, the former two views derive from a poor understanding of κατὰ σάρκα in v. 3, which does not so much refer to Christ's physical body as to his "human life," thought of in its totality;[31] neither the human "spirit" nor divine "nature" contrast well with this (proper) understanding. Second, apart from the possibility that a similar reference occurs in the hymn in 1 Tim 3:16,[32] there is not the slightest hint that Paul thought of Christ's earthly and exalted existence in terms of his "flesh" and "spirit." Third, it is difficult in any case to determine what the phrase "according to the spirit of holiness" could possibly mean as referring to Christ's human spirit, and especially as a contrast to the flesh of his incarnation. And finally,

---

[25]Dunn, "Jesus," 57, argues that κατὰ πνεῦμα ἁγιωσύνης has also (especially) to do with Jesus' earthly life ("In Paul's view the sonship of the earthly life was constituted by the Holy Spirit"). Although this latter is clearly the view of Luke, and therefore might be assumed to be Paul's perspective, nowhere does Paul make such a point, and it can scarcely be asserted to be true by the circuitous means by which Dunn arrives at it in this article.

[26]Thus some would take the Spirit phrase to refer to the subsequent outpouring of the Spirit by the exalted Son of God as evidence of his present exaltation.

[27]See esp. the discussion of 1 Cor 15:42–46 above, as well as on 1 Tim 3:16 below.

[28]E.g., Meyer 46–47; SH 9.

[29]E.g., Haldane 27, Hodge 20.

[30]This seems to be what the NRSV has in view: "according to the spirit of holiness"; cf. NIV[mg]: "who as to his spirit of holiness."

[31]Cf. the usage of the same phrase in 1 Cor 10:18 (consider Israel κατὰ σάρκα = Israel in terms of its literal, historical life), Rom 4:1 (Abraham, our forefather κατὰ σάρκα = in terms of our human descent), and Eph 6:5 (your κατὰ σάρκα masters = your masters in terms of this earthly life). Dunn's attempt ("Jesus") to make even these passages moral and pejorative fails to impress, since he seems to bend the evidence to make it work.

[32]Which we have concluded to be highly improbable. See the discussion in ch. 11.

the last view seems impossible simply on the grounds of Pauline usage. One is hard pressed to find such a meaning for "spirit" in Paul, and even more so to see it as a proper contrast to Christ's earthly life.

Most likely, therefore, as he usually does with this contrast, Paul intends to refer to the Holy Spirit. But if so, one is still left with the difficulty of ascertaining the sense of and the reason for ἁγιωσύνης ("of holiness"). The two most likely options are (1) that it is a periphrasis for "Holy Spirit." In this case the genitive ἁγιωσύνης is qualitative, or descriptive, so that the phrase means something like "the Spirit, whose character is holiness," or "who is characterized by holiness."[33] But if so, then why such an unusual designation at all, and especially why here? That is, why not simply say "Holy Spirit," if that is what is intended?[34] The alternative is (2) that the genitive is to be taken in its dynamic sense (= the Spirit who gives/supplies holiness)[35] and thus anticipates much of the argument of the rest of the letter,[36] including the description of Gentile believers in 15:16, who are "sanctified by the Holy Spirit" (ἡγιασμένη ἐν πνεύματι ἁγίῳ). All things considered, and especially in light of the OT background to the term, this is the preferred option, although the difficulty as to *why* such a designation here, in a description of the exalted Christ, is not thereby resolved. That, it would seem, must finally be spoken to in relationship to the overall sense of the phrase in its clause.

If this is the correct sense of the phrase and of its contrast with "respect to his earthly descent" in v. 3, how then are we to understand its point? Why this way of expressing Christ's present exalted position? It is altogether possible, of course, that Paul did not "mean" anything by it at all, beyond what has already been suggested. That is, in contrast to his earthly descent, Christ's current heavenly existence as "Son of God with power" is to be understood in terms of the eschatological Spirit, who characterizes all final eschatological existence. At the same time, by designating him as "the Spirit who is holy in character and thus supplies

---

[33]So Swete, *Holy Spirit*, 212.

[34]Some would argue that if the passage represents an adaptation of a pre-Pauline creedal formulation, then this question becomes moot, since Paul may have taken it over from his source and so did not "mean" anything by it at all. It refers to the Holy Spirit, pure and simple. But that might be too easy. For example, how could the phrase have originated in a Hellenistic setting (as many assume because of the Son of God terminology)? But if it originated in an Aramaic setting (as others argue), why did the translator choose this literal rendering rather than that of the LXX where this phrase occurs in the OT (see n. 19 above), especially since in Christian circles the latter became the *name* of the Spirit? Since the "why" question applies at every turn, one may as well begin by applying it to Paul. He did use it, after all; if traditional, he chose *not* to "translate" it into "Holy Spirit." Thus we are thrown back on the original question: Why *this* language *here*?

[35]So also Schneider, "Κατὰ πνεῦμα," 381.

[36]So Jewett, "Redaction," 117, although his elaborate scheme of reconstruction that gets him to this interpretation I do not find convincing.

holiness," he may be marking off the concerns of the letter from the beginning. If Christ is both the content and therefore the source of the gospel, offering "God's righteousness" freely to all who trust him, then the Spirit, in whose sphere the exalted "Son of God with power" now resides, is not simply the *Holy* Spirit, but the Spirit *of holiness itself*—the one who effects the "righteousness of God" in the lives of the believing community, Jew and Gentile together, in terms of their individual and corporate behavior.

We should also note that at the outset of the letter, in terms of Christ, Paul has placed their present existence in the "already" but "not yet" framework that he will spell out in some detail in 5:1–5 and 8:18–30 in light of their own experience of life in the Spirit. As Christ in his exaltation is now κατὰ πνεῦμα ἁγιωσύνης, so too they are presently κατὰ πνεῦμα, destined for glory with Christ and conformed to his likeness.[37]

We need only to note further that, far from supporting a "Spirit Christology," as some maintain,[38] our passage refers to the Spirit in such a way that, although he is closely related to the Son—indeed in 8:9–11 he will be declared to be the "Spirit of Christ"—he is plainly distinct from Christ. The passage does *not* say that Christ has now assumed Spirit existence. Furthermore, neither does our passage imply that the Spirit is the "means" whereby God raised Christ from the dead.[39] In keeping with the Pauline view as expressed everywhere in his letters, God himself raised Christ from the dead, with no reference to his having done so by his Spirit. Rather the Spirit in the passage probably has to do with the heavenly, eschatological sphere of life, into which Christ by resurrection has now entered, and into which all who are his will finally enter.

This, then, is indeed a Spirit passage in this letter, and it sets forth the Spirit as the sphere of present, not to mention future, eschatological existence for Christ; by implication he is also therefore the same for us. If Christ's "declaration" as Son of God with power is in relationship to the Spirit of holiness, how much more will our present eschatological existence in Christ be with respect to "the Spirit who gives holiness"?

ROMANS 1:9

For God is my witness, whom I serve with my S/spirit in the gospel of his Son . . .

Spirit language occurs twice in the thanksgiving/prayer report (here and in v. 11), although this is one of the more complex uses of πνεῦμα in

---

[37]Cf. Leenhardt 37.

[38]See, e.g., Hamilton, *Holy Spirit*, 12–15.

[39]For this view see Hamilton, ibid., Hendriksen 44, Scott, *Adoption*, 240; cf. any number of scholars who assume that Paul has said as much in Rom 8:11, which in fact he neither does nor implies (see the discussion below, and also on 1 Cor 6:14).

the Pauline corpus. There is little question that the chief referent is anthropological and that Paul is referring to his own spirit as the location or means of his divine service. Several factors indicate that it also refers to the Spirit of God at work in his own spirit.[40]

First, nothing else resembles this in the corpus. In the places where Paul's usage is anthropological he speaks of "being refreshed in my/his/ your spirit" (1 Cor 16:18; 2 Cor 7:13), or of his "spirit having no rest" (2 Cor 2:13). These reflect a concern for anxiety/rest in one's inner person, and in one case (2 Cor 2:13) is set in contrast with not finding rest physically (7:5). Otherwise Paul uses πνεῦμα in conjunction with other anthropological terms to refer to the entirety of one's being (1 Thes 5:23; 1 Cor 7:34). Apart from the passages about to be noted, where there is a clear intersection between the human spirit and the divine (cf. Rom 8:16), the closest thing to the present usage occurs in the four grace-benedictions, where he prays for "the grace of our Lord Jesus Christ to be with your spirits" (Gal 6:18; Phlm 25; Phil 4:23; 2 Tim 4:22).

But when Paul elsewhere refers to his πνεῦμα in the context of "spiritual" life[41] (1 Cor 14:14–15; 1 Cor 5:4), he intends something like the present translation. He does indeed serve God with his own spirit; but he does so, as always, because his spirit is yielded to the Spirit of God. Just as the Spirit prays or sings through his own spirit (1 Cor 14:15), so also the Spirit is the source of Paul's serving God through his spirit. Thus, "whom I serve with my S/spirit."

Second, and closely related, is to ask why Paul uses this most unusual way of expressing service to God, if he did not in fact intend at least an indirect reference to the Spirit of God? Again, it is the *uniqueness* of the phrase—not solely in terms of content, but in terms of its use at all—that calls for explanation. The "standard" Pauline expression here would be to say, "whom I serve in the gospel of his Son." Why the qualifier, "with my πνεῦμα"? And if the Holy Spirit is not indirectly in view as well, why single out his spirit? Does he thereby intend to exclude his body?

The best guess is related to his use of the verb λατρεύω, which in biblical usage refers exclusively to "the carrying out of relig[ious] duties, esp[ecially] of a cultic nature, by human beings" (BAGD). Paul uses it four times, twice of himself (here and 2 Tim 1:3, in a clause very much like this one), once of pagans (Rom 1:25), and once of believers vis-à-vis those who falsely "serve God" by submitting to circumcision (Phil 3:3 q.v.). The latter passage is especially instructive, since it occurs with similar language and in a similar overall context. There he describes believers in Christ as those "who serve by the Spirit of God, and put no

---

[40]So also Meyer 58, Godet 87, Leenhardt 43, Ziesler 66, Schweizer, *TDNT* 6.435; otherwise Dunn 29.

[41]The word "spiritual" is now used in its more modern nuance, referring specifically to "religious duties/activities" such as worship, ministry, prayer, etc.

confidence in the flesh." The contrast is not between external and internal, but between that which belongs to the former covenant, in the former age, and that which belongs to the present, through the work of the Spirit. As in 2 Cor 3:3–11, the new covenant of Spirit has done away with the old.

What is noteworthy is the remarkably similar language used here. Paul serves God "with/by my S/spirit." The reason for his pointing that out is best understood in the context of the letter, where life in the Spirit, the new "service to God" (cf. 12:1), contrasts to all former ways of "serving," especially all of those related to the time of the Law. Service to God is now rendered by one's "spirit" by means of the Spirit, as over against that rendered in the flesh, by means of adherence to Torah.

Third, and especially important, when Paul returns to these matters in 15:14–33, the same two concerns recur as in this thanksgiving/prayer report: his own ministry among the Gentiles, related to his desire to come to Rome. In describing his ministry in that passage, especially in 15:16 (q.v.), he does so in thoroughly sacerdotal language. The "grace that has been given him" (v. 15)—a recurring Pauline way of speaking about his own ministry[42]—in this case is expressed in no less than four sacerdotal terms, the final one of which describes the Gentiles as a "sacrificial offering . . . sanctified by the Holy Spirit." Moreover, his whole ministry in that passage is described in terms of Spirit activity (15:18–19).

If all of this sounds a bit subtle for an apparently straightforward expression, one needs only to note again how extremely unusual this qualifier is otherwise, and that such an interpretation fits both Pauline usage elsewhere and the greater context of this letter, which is quite in keeping with several of the unique features of this proemium.

It should be noted in passing, that if this understanding is correct, then we are confronted with yet one more incidental "Trinitarian" text. Just as in Phil 3:3, one "serves" God, by the Spirit, because of the prior activity of Christ (in Phil 3:3 expressed in terms of "boasting in Christ Jesus" vis-à-vis "the flesh"; here in terms of "serving God" in his proclamation of "the gospel of his Son").

ROMANS 1:11

For I long to see you, so that I might share with you some Spiritual gift so that you might be strengthened,

This sentence, with its unique collocation of χάρισμα ("gracious gift") and πνευματικόν ("Spiritual"), occurs in the continuation of the thanksgiving/prayer report, begun in v. 8. As with the salutation, the present material is unique to the corpus and full of surprises. Ordinarily in his prayer reports Paul includes items that concern him about the commu-

---

[42]Cf. 1 Cor 3:10; 15:10; Gal 2:9; Eph 3:2, 7; cf. Col 1:25.

nity. But in this case, although he does mention that he prays for them (v. 9b), he uses the "prayer report" primarily as an opportunity to express his longstanding desire to come to Rome, especially to visit the Christian community there, a matter that has obviously been on his mind for some time. Thus the content of his prayer has to do with "whether I shall somehow succeed at last, in the will of God, to come to you" (v. 10b). The very way this is phrased ("whether I shall somehow succeed at last") begins a movement away from a report of Paul's prayer, toward an expression of his concern to visit them. Our sentence, with its explanatory γάρ, makes this transition complete. Thus all of vv. 11–15 deal with his yet unfulfilled desire to come to see them, the final clause of which (vv. 14–15) serves as a springboard (by way of yet another explanatory γάρ) for him to state the theme of the letter.

All of this suggests that we need to take seriously that this letter is supposed to function very much as 1 Thessalonians and 1 Corinthians, namely, as a second-best substitute for a personal visit. Since he cannot come now (15:25–29), Paul writes this letter to express what he would have said had he been able to be among them. This suggests that we should also take seriously that *the stated reasons for wanting to come to them in the future* are *the express reasons for the present letter.* Thus, despite the disclaimer in v. 12, his reason for wanting to come to them is expressed no less than three times:

v. 11: in order that I might share with you some Spiritual gift,
    so that you might be strengthened;
v. 13b: in order that I might have fruit also among you;
v. 15: so that I might preach the gospel also to you who are in Rome.

The second and third of these are expressed in more general terms, relating to his ministry among the Gentiles everywhere, but focused on his desire to come to Rome. But the first, our present text, suggests in keeping with 15:15 that Paul is writing by way of reminder, and that his concern, now as always, is with the Gentile mission of the gospel.

This set of purpose clauses suggests that he desires to speak to the actual situation of the church in Rome, however much he knows about it; he is not writing merely to "get it off his chest" and thereby to gain their support for his intended Spanish mission. The burden of this letter throughout, just as in Galatians and elsewhere (2 Corinthians 3; Philippians 3), has to do with Gentiles as full and equal recipients in the covenant promises made to Israel—and that without excluding Israel. Since this is the burden of the letter, what he would want to "impart" if he were there in person, surely this is also the best way for us to understand our present clause with its unique juxtaposition of χάρισμα and πνευματικόν.

First, a word about the language (cf. ch. 2). This collocation is the surest Pauline evidence that the word χάρισμα on its own does not refer

to "gifts of the Spirit."[43] As noted in chapter 2, the noun is formed from
χάρις and primarily means "a concrete expression of grace." Thus in this
letter it is used for the gift of eternal life (5:15–16; 6:23), for the various
privileges granted to Israel (11:29, referring to 9:4–5), and for various
ways individual members of the community express the grace of God
given to them for the sake of others (12:6). In this latter case, since the
list begins with "prophecy," the word also moves toward its unique usage
in 1 Corinthians, where in 1:7 and 12:4 and 31 it refers to those special,
extraordinary Spirit giftings that Paul in 1 Cor 12:7 calls "Spirit manifestations." Precisely because that is not the first meaning of χάρισμα, Paul
qualifies the word here with the adjective πνευματικόν, so as to make clear
that in this case the "gracious gift" he wishes to "share with," or "impart
to,"[44] them is a special Spirit gifting.[45]

In light of this evidence, both the meaning of the term and the
context, what then is the "Spirit gifting" that he wishes to share with
them? It is possible, of course, that he had in mind some expression of
Spirit gifting such as those enumerated in 1 Cor 12:8–10 or Rom 12:6–8.[46]
But if so, then we can never know which, if any in particular, he
intended. Far more likely, however, this common interpretation represents a thoroughly noncontextual view of this term. In its present context, and especially in light of the letter as a whole, the "Spirit gift" that
he most likely wishes to share with them is his understanding of the
gospel that in Christ Jesus God has created from among Jews and Gentiles
one people for himself, apart from Torah. This is the way they are to be
"strengthened" by Paul's coming, and this surely is the "fruit" he wants
to have among them when he comes (v. 13).[47] If so, then in effect our
present letter functions as his "Spirit gifting" for them.[48] This is what he
would impart if he were there in person; this is what he now "shares"

---

[43]Contra Käsemann 19, who considers the combination "most unusual," because
he (incorrectly) concludes that "according to 1 Cor 12:3ff. all charismata are πνευματικά [= Spiritual gifts]." But that is an assertion, pure and simple, and it does not
come close to the Pauline data. Cf. also Barrett 25, Morris 60 ("the idea is already
there in the noun"), and Schatzmann, *Theology*, 14–15 (apparently). That is simply
not so, as this usage, and the other uses in Romans, make plain; how, one wonders,
could the Romans have possibly known that the word χάρισμα meant "spiritual gift"
without the qualifier? The fact that Paul so qualifies it for them also shows, therefore,
that he knew that it did not inherently carry notions about gifts of the Spirit.

[44]Gk. μεταδῶ, which means to impart or share something with someone; cf.
1 Thes 2:8; Eph 4:28.

[45]On the meaning of πνευματικόν, as the possessive adjective for Spirit, see ch. 2
above, pp. 28–32.

[46]So SH 21, and others.

[47]Käsemann 19 suggests that it here refers "to the blessing which comes with
preaching."

[48]Cf. Denney 588: "No doubt, in substance, Paul imparts his spiritual gift through
this epistle."

since he cannot presently come to Rome. Just as in 1 Thes 3:9–10, where Paul prays to be present with the Thessalonians "to fill up what is lacking," but since he could not then return, he wrote our 1 Thessalonians instead, so too in this instance.

Since Phoebe is about to go, and since his long-time companions Prisca and Aquila are back in Rome (who with their house church are the obvious first recipients of this letter, 16:3–5), he sends along this "Spirit gift" with Phoebe, trusting that it will be his present means of "having fruit" among them, just as he has had among Gentiles everywhere (v. 13).

If this is the correct understanding of this term here, then along with such passages as 1 Cor 5:3–5, we have in these words strong evidence that Paul, who considered himself to be a prophet (cf. 1 Cor 14:37), also considered his letters to serve as something akin to prophetic words, given by the Spirit; they were certainly so to be understood when read in the gathered community—precisely the place where the Spirit was present in the end-time community of faith.

Romans 2:29[49]

[28]*For not the person who is so outwardly is a Jew, nor is circumcision an outward matter performed in the flesh; [29]but the person who is so inwardly is a Jew, and circumcision is of the heart—by the Spirit, not by letter—whose praise is not from people but from God.*

This mention of the Spirit that seems so off-handed both in its context and in this sentence comes as something of a surprise. In terms of the argument, the Spirit first appears in 5:5, in a passage that seems designed to present the reality of the Spirit early on as the key to Christian life, a usage which will then become foundational for the argumentation of 6:1–7:6 as well as in anticipation of the full discussion in chapter 8. That kind of proleptic (foreshadowing) usage is most likely what lies behind this mention of the Spirit as well. What is said here will receive its reaffirmation and explication in the argument of 7:1–6, especially in vv. 5–6.

Thus, even though the Spirit's role in this argument appears somewhat incidental, his role in Paul's understanding of the old and new covenants, expressed in this pregnant phrase, is crucial—and quite in keeping with the first occurrence of this language in 2 Cor 3:6. Although not articulated here in the same way, the same theology of the new covenant as superseding and thus replacing the old seems to be the presupposition of this phrase.[50] The gospel is *the fulfillment of God's*

---

[49]For bibliography on "Spirit and letter" in Paul, see above on ch. 5, p. 305, n. 71.

[50]One of the weaknesses of Westerholm's otherwise helpful study on "Spirit" and "letter" in Paul (" 'Letter and Spirit' ") is that he starts with this passage, rather than

promises (1:2) in the Son of David (1:3), who by the resurrection and *in accordance with the Spirit* has been designated Son of God with power (1:4); the Spirit now serves as the key to the working out of that covenant in the life of those who believe.

Paul opened the argument by asserting that the gospel is God's power unto salvation for *everyone* who believes, Gentile as well as Jew, and that in the gospel God's righteousness has now been made available to the one who has faith, since "the righteous will live by their faithful trust in God" (1:16–17). To make that point stick, that such a gift of righteousness is for *all* who have faith, he feels compelled first of all to demonstrate that such is so for the Jew as well as the Gentile (1:18–3:20). After all, Paul's point is not foremost that all need God's righteousness—that is assumed and will be stated at several points (3:19–20, 23–26; 5:12–21)—but that the Jew also (especially?) is related to God by faith in Christ and therefore has no prior advantage in having/keeping Torah or in being circumcised. Thus Paul's basic concern in 1:18 through 3:20 is to show that all must live by faith precisely because all—Jews as well as Gentiles—are equally disadvantaged through sin. To put that another way, in order to demonstrate that God's salvation is for *Gentile as well as Jew*, he must first demonstrate that it is *by faith* for *Jew as well as Gentile*. His fellow Jews would surely agree on the former, that salvation is ultimately for Gentile as well as Jew; but they would equally resist the latter, if "faith" meant that Jew and Gentile were equally in need of such faith, or if "faith" meant that Gentiles did not also need to adopt the evidences of the covenant, by accepting circumcision and adhering to Torah.

To get at his point Paul basically has a twofold argument: First, in 1:18–2:11, on the predicate of divine impartiality, he argues that all who are wicked and ungodly—and suppress the truth in their wickedness—are without excuse and therefore are all equally under divine wrath. Since God is absolutely impartial, that means that both Gentile and Jew are without excuse before God, who will judge each alike. Secondly, and building on that predicate, in 2:12–27 he argues further, and this is where our text comes in, that there is absolutely no advantage to Jews in their having Torah, since Jews sin just as do Gentiles—the one with and the other without Torah. The aim of all of this is the conclusion in 3:19–20 that Torah encompasses all under sin and offers no help, since it merely shows up sin. In order to make this point work, that the Jew has no advantage in having Torah, Paul argues logically that just as Jews are also sinners, despite having the Law, so Gentiles can exhibit righteousness, despite not having the Law. Thus by sin Jewish "circumcision turns into uncircumcision," and by keeping what is required in Torah, Gentile

---

with the earlier one in 2 Corinthians 3, which I would urge offers the exegetical and theological keys to this one, rather than the other way around.

"uncircumcision can be reckoned as circumcision." Paul's concern, however, is not with Gentile "righteousness" but with Jewish "sinfulness."

It is at this juncture that our text appears; its immediate function is to offer an explanatory elaboration of vv. 26–27, in which Gentile observance of the righteous requirements of the Law[51] is said to function for them as circumcision, and thus, their keeping Torah despite their uncircumcision will also serve to judge those who, even though they have the "written code" (γράμμα) and circumcision, nonetheless transgress the Law. "For," Paul now goes on to explain, "true circumcision is not a matter of literal, fleshly (ἐν σαρκί) circumcision based on the written code (γράμματι)." Rather, true circumcision, just as God has already said through Moses (Deut 10:16; 30:6), is a matter of the heart, so that with such "heart circumcision" one will readily walk in the ways of God and receive God's "praise," whereas, for Paul, the literal circumcision of Gentiles would serve merely for "human praise."

In making this point, Paul sets up a series of contrasts as to what constitutes a "true Jew" (= one who truly belongs to the people of God). Such a "Jew" is (1) "inward" (ἐν τῷ κρυπτῷ) not "outward" (ἐν τῷ φανερῷ) that is, (2) their circumcision is not in the "flesh" (literally, and for Paul, theologically[52]) but "of the heart," which is then interpreted (3) as ἐν πνεύματι (by the Spirit) and not γράμματι (by "letter" = "written code"), so that the net result is (4) praise from God and not from fellow humans. Our concern is especially with number 3, the interpretation of "inward" and "of the heart" in terms of the Spirit, whereas "outward" and "in the flesh" is of "the letter."

First, it should be noted that Pauline usage in general, the present context, and the OT background to this argument seem to rule out altogether a translation like the NRSV's ("it is spiritual and not literal"), a translation that is especially misleading because it suggests that "Spirit" and "letter" are but one more way of saying "inward" not "outward."[53]

---

[51]Gk. τὰ δικαιώματα τοῦ νόμου; cf. 8:4, where "we who walk by the Spirit" are said to "fulfill τὸ δικαίωμα τοῦ νόμου."

[52]That is, as in Gal 3:3, ἐν σαρκί here refers first of all to the literal flesh that is circumcised; but it also carries all kinds of theological overtones as well, since to live on the basis of Torah is for Paul still to live "in the flesh," whereby one "boasts" in human achievement rather than in God's grace, and worse, to live in the flesh is to continue in all the sinful practices for which Torah has no remedy.

[53]Which perhaps explains why Swete, Holy Spirit, omitted this text altogether; such an understanding is also perpetuated in many of the commentaries (e.g., Haldane, Dodd, Barrett, Black) and recently by Sanders, PLJP, 127; Ervin, Conversion-Initiation, 112–13; it is given as an even possibility by Morris. But if Pauline usage means anything at all, this is an impossible view; there is no use of πνεῦμα in the entire corpus that even remotely connotes "inward" or "spiritual" in the sense suggested here. In any case, Paul's prior usage in 2 Cor 3:1–6 must be seen as determinative here, and in that passage πνεῦμα can refer only to the Holy Spirit.

But that will hardly do, since these are obviously *interpretive* words, as even the NRSV recognizes; and the interpretation is not simply one more way of repeating the same thing.[54] To the contrary, *the interpretation is the theological key to the whole passage* and explains how Paul can get away with what he says here so boldly.

In order to hear Paul, therefore, some words about the OT background are imperative, since that is the key to what Paul is about.[55] The idea of "heart circumcision" is fundamental to the perspective of Deuteronomy. It is found first in 10:16, as a command to those who are about to enter the land, and is seen as the obvious necessity if God's people are truly to walk in his ways and love him with their whole hearts. Its second occurrence is in 30:6, now in the twin contexts of God's making a covenant with his people (29:12), but doing so in anticipation of making a new covenant with those who return from exile, where they have gone because of having broken the first covenant (30:1–5). Here the former command is turned into promise, "God will circumcise your hearts," the net result of which will be love and obedience from the heart; indeed, the Law is "very near to you; it is in your mouth and in your heart, for you to observe" (v. 14).[56] In light of his later use of this text in 10:5–10, it is arguable that Paul had nurtured his Christian life on this passage; it is also clear, from the argument in 2 Corinthians 3, that Paul had read this passage in light of Jeremiah (31:31–34 [LXX 38:31–34]) and Ezekiel (11:19; 36:26–27; 37:1–14), in which the promises of Deuteronomy 30 had already been taken up by the prophets in terms of a new covenant, the Spirit being the key factor to make "the obedience of the heart" a possibility. For Paul all of this has been fulfilled in the "new covenant of the Spirit," available to all—Gentile and Jew alike—who put their trust in Christ (see above on 2 Cor 3:1–18).

Therefore, in light of the contrast between "Spirit" and "letter" which Paul had already used to his theological advantage in 2 Cor 3:6, the little interpretive insertion, "by Spirit not by letter," is to be understood first of all in terms of the Spirit as fulfilling the covenantal promises. The Spirit has performed the "circumcision of the heart," that makes one a true Jew inwardly, in that the "righteousness required by Torah" is fulfilled by those who walk in the Spirit (8:4).

But what of the contrast, "not by letter"? Four matters in the text of Romans provide the clues that Paul is referring primarily to Torah as a written code requiring obedience:[57] first, he already used this language

---

[54]Cf. Murray 88, Cranfield 1.175, although not put quite this way.

[55]It is noteworthy that the language "inward" and "outward" also occurs in the same Deuteronomy text (29:29, where "what is inward" is said to "belong to God").

[56]A passage, it should be noted, that plays a key role in the argument of Rom 10:4–13.

[57]Käsemann 76 suggests that it means "the Torah as instruction."

in v. 27 to refer to the requirements of the Law as they appear in the written word of Torah; second, since this is an insertion intended to *interpret* "inward" and "outward," that would seem also to fix its meaning as referring to circumcision as a form of keeping the written requirements of Torah; third, in its own phrase the contrast is not simply with what is "inward," but with the Spirit, who in Paul's usage elsewhere is the fulfillment of Torah and therefore the one who brings an end to Torah as "regulation requiring obedience"; and finally, when this language is picked up again in 7:5–6, the "letter" there clearly refers to the Law, which has been set aside by the death of Christ and the coming of the Spirit.

All of this suggests, then, that the Spirit is mentioned here as the way God now creates a people for his name, who will walk in his paths in fulfillment of the promised new covenant, and that "the letter" to which the Spirit stands in contrast refers to the written requirements of Torah, which are understood by Jewish Christians as still binding on the people of God, including Gentiles who come to faith in Christ. Not so, says Paul here and elsewhere. In light of Israel's failure God had decided on a new covenant, a covenant of Spirit which "fulfilled" the aim of Torah and thus did away with its regulations requiring "observance." One is no longer a part of the people of God by adhering to the boundary markers of Jewishness; one is part of the people of God on the basis of Christ and the Spirit alone. Thus this little insertion is full of theological grist that will be milled for all it's worth later in this letter.

ROMANS 5:5

. . . and hope will not result in shame[58] *because the love of God has been poured out in our hearts through the Holy Spirit who has been given to us.*

This second mention of the Spirit in the argument of Romans[59] appears as the hinge point[60] in one of the several exalted moments in the letter, where argument turns into confession and worship (in this case, vv. 1–11). The fact that the other three moments occur as "conclusions" to major sections of the argument (8:31–39; 11:33–36; 15:5–13) suggests the same to be true here. But in this case the paragraph also

---

[58]Although the standard editions of the Greek text read the present tense καταισχύνει, that was an arbitrary choice and tends to miss the eschatological thrust both of this passage and of Paul's use of this idea elsewhere. More likely, therefore, it is a future and should be accented καταισχυνεῖ (so Moo 312). On its meaning see n. 67 below.

[59]Cf. 2:29 above; the references to the Spirit in 1:4, [9], and 11 belong to the proemium, whose concerns will be picked up again, with an abundance of Spirit language, in 15:14–33.

[60]So also Godet 189, who calls this verse "the central saying of the entire passage."

launches the next section of the argument, which will "conclude" with a similar confessional affirmation in 8:31–39; the motif of God's love through Christ that dominates this passage dominates there as well.[61]

Here is another of those marvelous passages in the Pauline corpus about which one fears to use too many words, lest its own grandeur and power are trivialized by our verbiage. Nonetheless, since it is such a crucial Spirit passage in this letter as well as in the corpus, some observations about the structure of the whole may help one to hear it better.

Four features about the passage[62] stand out: First, its *confessional nature.* The first person plural pronoun or verb form occurs no less than 18 times. Paul has obviously moved from argument to application that comes close to praise. Second, its *eschatological orientation.* Here is another passage where Paul's "already but not yet" perspective dominates his thinking. The passage oscillates throughout between salvation as a present and certain reality and its future consummation (our hope of attaining God's final glory), which is equally certain, predicated on God's love poured out into our hearts by the eschatological Spirit. Third, and related to the second, its *juxtaposition of present suffering and future glory.* Here is the heart of Paul's understanding of our eschatological existence, held together in this instance by the repeated applicational imperatives, which form the core of vv. 1–5: "let us boast in our hope of the glory of

---

[61]This seems to be the best answer to the long and undecided debate as to the place of 5:1–11 in the argument and whether the major break in the argument occurs here or at 6:1. There can be little question that 5:1–11 concludes what has preceded (the οὖν "therefore," followed by the aorist passive participle, "having been justified by faith," seems to demand as much). Indeed the whole section (vv. 1–11) flows directly out of 4:24–25, where the "reckoning of Abraham's faith" is applied to "us" who have also believed, as did Abraham, in the God who raises the dead—in this case "our Lord Jesus Christ, . . . who was handed over to death for our trespasses and was raised for our justification." This is precisely what 5:1–2 reaffirm and what 5:6–11 spell out, now in terms of God's love for us.

At the same time, given the apparent inclusio that this passage sustains with 8:31–39, with both reflecting on the death and resurrection of Christ as the full expression of God's love and therefore of the believer's absolute security, it is hard to escape the conviction that this passage also serves as the beginning of the argument that will be taken up in earnest in 5:12 and 6:1. This is further supported by several phenomena: (1) the language of "justification" and "faith," which occurs in vv. 1–2, now disappears from the argument until ch. 9; (2) the matter of Christ's death *and* resurrection as evidencing God's love and securing our salvation, both present and future, becomes the major thrust of 6:1–23; (3) the fact that Jew-Gentile concerns, which are always present just below the surface of the argument in 5:12–8:39, are not specifically mentioned again until ch. 9, while the new emphases of this section (the contrasts between sin and righteousness, death and life, Spirit and Torah, Spirit and flesh) are begun here and in 5:12–21, the latter being tied to the former by the διὰ τοῦτο ("for this very reason") of v. 12.

[62]Some of these comments reflect the whole passage, vv. 1–11, although our present concerns are basically limited to the two sentences that make up vv. 1–5.

God" and not only so, but "let us also boast in our sufferings." Fourth, its *Trinitarian structure*. As so often happens in these truly grand soteriological moments, salvation is the work of God the Trinity: based on God the Father's love that is its ultimate predicate; effected historically through the death of Christ, which is here expressly the historical outworking of God's love; and appropriated experientially through the gift of the Spirit, whom God has given to us and through whom we actualize the love of God in Christ.

Even though the Spirit is mentioned but the one time in v. 5, as the realized surety of God's love in Christ, it should be noted that later in the argument (8:14–17, 23, 26–27) the Spirit is the key to items two and three as well.[63] Thus in many ways this mention of the Spirit, casual as it may appear at first, moves us toward the center of Paul's understanding of our new existence in Christ.[64] Therefore, it is also, as in 2:29, a foreshadowing of much that is yet to be said about the Spirit in the letter.[65]

Thus, the first five verses, which hold our current interest, come in the form of two sentences, which are held together by the verb καυχώμεθα ("let us boast"[66]) in vv. 2 and 3—first in our hope of attaining God's final

---

[63]Indeed, much of what is said in vv. 1–5 appears elsewhere in Paul as the effectual working of the Spirit in Christian life, not in the sense of securing such life but of realizing or experiencing it. Thus the "peace with God," here made possible by Christ, meaning the cessation of hostilities (as the theme of reconciliation in vv. 10–11 makes clear), in 14:17 is the activity of the Spirit to effect "reconciliation" between Jew and Gentile over food laws. And the "access" (προσαγωγή) to God (the picture is that of a suppliant who deserves punishment before a king who shows mercy) in v. 2 appears in Eph. 2:18 as the work of the Spirit, who, on the basis of the cessation of hostilities between Jew and Gentile through Christ's death, brings *both* together into the very presence (προσαγωγή) of God.

[64]Cf. Käsemann 135–36.

[65]So Bruce 117, Harrison 58.

[66]This translation is predicated on the conviction that the original text in v. 1 is ἔχωμεν (with ℵ* A B* C D K L 33 81 630 1175 pm lat bo; Marcion—a considerable array of witnesses indeed!) and not the poorly attested ἔχομεν of the later Greek tradition (F G P 104 365 1241 1739 1881 pm). The latter is usually preferred (1) on the (false) basis of the frequency of an omega/omicron interchange in the textual history of the NT (in fact, it occurs infrequently, even in places where one might most expect it, and *seldom in places where either the subjunctive or indicative are distinctly required by the sense of the passage*), and (2) on the (presumptuous) basis that the context demands the indicative, which seems to be a polite way of saying that scholars have difficulty believing that Paul would argue differently from themselves (Lietzmann is so bold in this instance that he would opt for the indicative even if the entire textual tradition read the subjunctive, on the grounds that that is what Paul meant in any case!). (For this argument see esp. Metzger, *Textual Commentary*, 511; cf. Lietzmann, Barrett, Cranfield.) Not only does the weight of external evidence favor the subjunctive, but so does its nearly universal appearance in the early church (how many times, one wonders, would such an interchange need to have happened for the subjunctive to have so totally suppressed the "original" indicative?). The fact that the later Greek tradition is generally unanimous in favoring the indicative suggests only

glory and second in our present sufferings. What leads to the first "let us boast" is the effectiveness of Christ's redemptive work ("having been justified by faith"), which in turn leads to the first exhortation ("let us enjoy peace with God through Christ, through whom we also have obtained access to God"). Thus on the basis of what Christ has done:

> Let us have peace with God
> > and
> Let us boast in our hope of God's glory.

But not only so, Paul adds:

> Let us also boast in our sufferings.

The rest of this second sentence, then, bridges the distance between the two boasts by showing the path from suffering (namely, through endurance and character) to hope. And hope, he concludes, is not mere wishfulness, nor will it result in our experiencing shame.[67] To the contrary, hope is certainty, because it is predicated on the love of God himself, love which is experienced by us ("poured out in our hearts") through the appropriating work of the Spirit and which was demonstrated and effected for us by Christ (vv. 6–8).

Thus the crucial role the Spirit plays in Pauline "theology," that is, in his and his churches' *experience of God's saving grace*. For Paul the "love of God" was no mere abstraction. God's love, the most essential reality about his character and the absolute predicate of our existence, has been demonstrated historically in its most lavish and expansive expression through Christ's death for his enemies (vv. 6–8, thus the basis for "peace with God" and "access" to his gracious presence). But neither is such love merely an objective historical event. God's love, played out to the full in Christ, is an experienced reality in the "heart" of the believer by the presence of the Spirit.[68] *This* is what the Spirit has so richly "shed abroad in our hearts." If one is not thus overtaken by God himself at this one crucial point, then all else is lost, and one is without peace, groveling

---

that later scribes believed as later scholars that one can make better sense of the text as an indicative. Better by far to go with Paul, whose use of the subjunctive here functions as an "imperative" only in a more distant sense. Indeed, most such subjunctives in Paul *assume* the prior indicative and thus embrace it as part of the exhortation (so, correctly, Murray 161n5). Paul's point is application, pure and simple. Given what Christ has done, let us then enjoy its benefits: peace with God now and "boasting" in our inheritance of God's final glory.

[67]In the biblical sense of this word, as it occurs most often in the Psalmist, that one will never be brought to shame or disgrace because of having trusted in God. Thus it does not mean "be ashamed," but refers to not being put to shame at the eschaton, as though one's trust in God were unfounded (cf. Käsemann 115). On this matter see below on Phil 1:19–20.

[68]Cf. Murray 164–65: "[This clause] is a striking example of the combination in few words of the objective grounds and the subjective certainty of the believer's hope."

before God, living with little real hope, and thus experiencing present sufferings as a cause for complaint and despair rather than for "boasting." What rectifies all of this for us is not simply the *fact* of God's love—although in some ways that would surely be enough—but that God's love has been effectively realized in the experience of the believer.[69] God's love for us has been "poured out,"[70] as a lavish and experienced reality, by the presence of the Holy Spirit, whom God has also lavishly poured out into our hearts (see on Titus 3:6).[71]

Crucial to all of this is the central role the Spirit plays not only in our realizing God's love, as that has been demonstrated through Christ (vv. 6–8), but also in our present existence "between the times," as we exult both in our hope and in our sufferings. As Paul will spell out in greater detail in 8:14–27, the Spirit's presence serves as guarantor of our glorious future inheritance as well as our sustainer and helper in the midst of sufferings and weaknesses as we await the final realization of this hope. Just as in the grace-benediction in 2 Cor 13:13[14], God's love is the predicate, Christ's grace is the effective and effectual outworking of that love, and the "participation in the Holy Spirit" is our means of realizing the salvation which that love and grace have effected.

When one finally asks about this section (5:1–11) the crucial exegetical question, "what is its point in the overall argument?" the answer is probably twofold, and the Spirit plays a key role in each instance. First, in light of the argument up to this point, and especially in light of chapter 4,

---

[69]Some (e.g., Leenhardt 135) would tend to downplay the experiential dimension of this text for a more cognitive one (the Spirit reveals God's love); but nothing in the text remotely suggests as much, and everything in the text is against it: the language of love, the verb ἐκκέχυται (the language of Pentecost that implies lavish and abundant experience), the mention of the Spirit, and the location "in our hearts." On this one Dunn (252–54, 265) surely has it right that this reflects the same kind of vivid and experienced entry into life in the Spirit as in Gal 3:2–5, so that Paul can simply appeal to it as a universal phenomenon.

[70]On the vb. ἐκχέω cf. below on Tit 3:6. The OT background for this usage lies in such texts as Joel 2:28 and Mal 3:10, where God will "pour out" his Spirit/blessings on his people.

[71]I suppose of all my memories of the Pentecostal tradition in which I was reared (which differs in many significant respects from that of today), this particular expression of "Pentecostal piety" has left its most indelible imprint on my consciousness. Here were people—often poor, and sometimes suffering, people—whose experience of the Spirit in "Spirit baptism" had assured them of God's love and of their own future glory. The gospel songs on which I was raised were the most constant reinforcement of this reality. If to the outsider, we looked as if we were looking for "pie in the sky" and living as escapists (cf. Robert Mapes Anderson, *Vision of the Disinherited* [reprint Peabody, Mass.: Hendrickson, (1979) 1992]), in fact we were merely expressing what we believed Paul and his churches also to have experienced— that God loves us despite outward appearances to the contrary. And it was our experience of the Holy Spirit, who poured out this love of God into our hearts, that gave us this certainty.

here is the word of grace that transcends all Torah observance, all other identity symbols. Christ's dying for the helpless—sinners *all* (Jew and Gentile alike)—demonstrates God's impartiality toward Jew and Gentile alike. All were enemies; all are alike beloved. The experience of the Spirit is the realization of that love. Second, this is also the great word of assurance, especially to those whose attachment to Torah is emotionally interwoven with their relationship to God. Paul here seems to be saying that Gentiles are not in fact put into jeopardy with God by their not coming under the obligations of Torah observance. Christ's death and the gift of the Spirit are God's guarantees that his love for us is unshakable; this, therefore, gives us certainty about the present and the future.

Finally, it need only be noted that once again the Spirit is spoken of in terms of "gift." Since the verb is aorist, it probably refers to the experience of conversion.[72] But in contrast to previous such passages, where the Holy Spirit is given "in your hearts,"[73] here he is simply God's gift; that the locus of the "gift" is the human heart is evidenced by the fact that the resident Spirit "pours out God's love into our hearts," precisely because he is resident there. Once more Paul's language assumes the Spirit to be the empowering presence of the person of God.

ROMANS 5:15–16

. . . [15]*But not just as the transgression, so also the gracious gift. For if the many died because of the transgression of the one man, how much more shall the grace of God and the gift abound to the many through the grace of the one man, Christ Jesus?* [16]*And not as through the transgression of the one is the gift; for on the one hand, judgment [came] from the one unto condemnation; on the other hand, the gracious gift [comes] on the basis of many transgressions unto justification.*

Without going into the complexities of the argument of this section (vv. 12–21), one needs to note the two occurrences of χάρισμα ("gracious gift") in this passage. Here is certain evidence that the word does not primarily mean "gift of the Spirit," but in fact has to do with "a concrete expression of grace," thus "gracious gift" (see the discussion in ch. 2). The association with "grace" and "gift" in v. 15b is self-evident in the Greek text; that Paul uses χάρισμα at all here probably results from his rhetoric, since its opposite, παράπτωμα, referring to Adam's deed, means "a concrete expression of sin." Thus Christ's deed is here referred to as χάρισμα, which likewise means "a concrete expression of grace." The Spirit is simply not to be found in such usage.

---

[72]Not baptism, as is so often suggested (e.g., Barrett, Black, Käsemann). As Dunn 254 has rightly argued, such a view emanates from a time in the church where the experience of the Spirit was so quiescent that appeal is made to the only "experience" that is known, baptism. But Paul himself neither makes a point of the "experience" of baptism nor directly ties the coming of the Spirit to baptism. His appeal here and elsewhere is to the vividly experienced dimension of the coming of the Spirit, the dynamic nature of whose presence allowed him thus to refer to the Spirit in this way. See esp. on Gal 3:2–5.

[73]See, e.g., 2 Cor 1:22; Gal 4:6; cf. 1 Thes 4:8; 1 Cor 6:19.

Romans 6:1–8:39

Although there is considerable debate over the structure of Romans, especially the role of the two major sections of chapter 5 in the argument as a whole, there is little question that 6:1–8:39 forms a major section in the letter, basically responding to the double questions about sin posed in 6:1 and 15 and to the related double questions about the Law posed in 7:7 and 13. The issue is still that of "righteousness," but now in terms of behavior and directly related to the argument of chapters 1–5, which have for all practical purposes eliminated Torah completely—despite the protests in 3:1–2 and 31. The obvious question from the perspective of Paul's Jewish Christian interlocutor is, What happens to righteousness (= righteous living), if one dispenses with Torah? That is the basic question addressed throughout this section, although at the same time Paul feels compelled to defend Torah, since his own statements could easily lead to the conclusion that Torah was no gift at all (3:1–8), but rather an unfortunate burden placed upon God's ancient people.

Paul's answer to the primary question, what happens to righteousness, or what do we do about sin if Torah is eliminated, is answered in 6:1–7:6 and 8:1–30, first (6:1–7:6) in relation to the work of Christ and second (8:1–30) in relation to the work of the Spirit. As such, of course, in keeping with the basic concern of the entire letter, such righteousness is available to all, Jew and Gentile alike, apart from the Law, through the death and resurrection of Christ and the gift of the Spirit. Thus for Paul the gift of righteousness is not just a matter of right standing with God, but is also a matter of living out the life of this righteous God in the present age. After all, the argument of this section concludes on the note that whom God foreknew he also predestined to be conformed to the image of his Son, whom God designated to be the firstborn among many "brothers and sisters."

The obvious key to such a lived-out righteousness is the gift of the Spirit, which is the point of the extended argument of 8:1–30. What is noteworthy, therefore, is the absence of any mention of the Spirit in the argument of 6:1–23, where the relationship of the believer to sin is taken up in some detail, especially so, since when one finally comes to Spirit language in 7:5–6 and 8:1–30, all kinds of linguistic correspondences suggest that the Spirit has been a presupposition behind much of what is said in 6:1–23. In 6:4, for example, in the first imperative in the letter,[74] Paul urges, "thus let us also *walk* in *newness* of *life*," language which is echoed of the Spirit in 7:6 (in *newness* of *Spirit*), 8:2 (the *Spirit* of *life* = the Spirit who give life), and 8:4 (who *walk* according to the *Spirit*).

---

[74]Assuming that the hortatory subjunctives in 5:1–3 are not intended to be imperatival but words of encouragement.

Similarly, in 6:5–11 the new life of righteousness is related to the believers' identification with Christ in his death and resurrection, ideas that are conjoined in 8:10–11 through the Spirit of Christ, and "for the sake of righteousness." So also in 6:12–14 he speaks about sin reigning in our mortal bodies, language picked up in slightly different form in 8:13: "by the Spirit put to death the deeds of the body."

Since these linguistic phenomena are scarcely accidental, the question persists, why then is there no direct mention of the Spirit in 6:1–23, but only these linguistic anticipations? The answer seems to lie in Paul's thoroughly (economic) Trinitarian view of life in the present age. The key to righteousness for Paul is to be found in the work of both Christ and the Spirit. The role of Christ in bringing such righteousness to God's people apart from the Law lies in their identification with him in his death and resurrection; thus *the whole argument of 6:1–7:6 is predicated on the work of Christ*, whose death and resurrection effected righteousness for God's people, both as right standing with God and as lived-out righteousness; whereas *the whole argument of 8:1–30 is predicated on the role the Spirit plays in working out this righteousness in the life of believers*. What is noteworthy is that the Spirit is brought forward at the conclusion of the first argument (7:6) as the necessary ingredient for bringing it off; while Christ is repeatedly brought forward at the beginning of the second argument as the prior predicate for such life to have been made available at all (8:1, 2, 3).

In light of these structural phenomena, one is tempted in a study like this to go through all of 6:1–7:6 as if it presupposed the life of the Spirit that is finally articulated in 8:1–30. Rather than yield to that temptation, however, I intend here to overview the major sections of the argument, as I perceive them, and to point out the correspondences of concerns and of language that will recur in chapter 8.

The main point of 6:1–7:6 is to argue that trusting in the death of Christ as the way of obtaining God's righteousness (as right-standing) does not in fact lead to *un*righteousness in terms of behavior—as some Jewish Christians apparently argue that it will (v. 1). Quite the contrary, Paul contends, the death of Christ does more than merely "justify the sinner." Because Christ's death and resurrection are integrally bound up in God's righteousizing act (as 5:6–11 makes clear), so the one who is joined to Christ in faith is also joined to Christ's death and resurrection, as evidenced by baptism in which the significance of that joining is actually reenacted. Thus faith in Christ is not merely trust that one has thereby received God's forgiveness; inherent in that faith is faithfulness, a new and faith-ful relationship with God that means walking in "newness of life." Paul works out that point in an argument—interspersed now with imperatives—that comes in three recognizable parts: (1) in 6:1–14, using the experience of baptism as imagery, he develops an argument that death and resurrection lead to the newness of life and thus to release from one's former enslavement to sin; (2) in 6:15–23, picking up themes from vv. 12–14 and now using the imagery of slavery and freedom, Paul elaborates on the fact that those in Christ are enslaved not to sin but to God, and therefore they are free *from* sin and *for* righteousness; and (3) in 7:1–6, using the metaphor of death within marriage, he reintroduces Torah and argues that through the death of Christ we have died to the *whole* of our former "marriage"—sin, the flesh through which sin operates, and Torah which arouses sin in the flesh.

In this final argument in particular the Spirit now appears as the crucial ingredient, to be picked up again in 8:1 after he takes a considerable, but crucial, by-path to explain the connection between Torah and the flesh and sin. Although we tend to want things to be a bit tidier theologically,[75] the absence of mention of the Spirit until 7:5–6 is not surprising, in light of Paul's own emphases. We need only to note that when Paul comes to the section where the work of the Spirit predominates the argument (8:1–30), he does in fact go back and revise some of the crucial language of ch. 6, now with reference to the Spirit. Thus in 8:9–11 all kinds of language and motifs that in 6:5–11 refer to the work of Christ (esp. the death and resurrection imagery) are repeated in terms of the Spirit. Likewise in 8:12–15 there is a similar repetition, again in terms of the Spirit, of the language of slavery, freedom, and "sonship" from 6:15–23, which was expressed in terms of Christ.

All of this suggests, first of all, what we have noted frequently elsewhere: God's saving work in behalf of his people is brought about through Christ and the Spirit—Christ effects it; the Spirit appropriates it to the life of the believer. And second, about the argument in Romans, whereas Paul firmly distinguishes between the work of Christ and that of the Spirit, he just as surely sees the work of each to be about the same thing overall—God's redeeming a people for his name. From both perspectives, that of Christ and that of the Spirit, the same result is effected. Christ's death and resurrection free the believer from sin; the Spirit's indwelling frees the believer from sin. The work of Christ is obviously the central reality, ever and always for Paul; but without the work of the Spirit that of Christ goes for naught. All of this also suggests that one needs to read this letter in a very Trinitarian way, if one is going to make sense of the overall argument.

ROMANS 6:4

. . . We have therefore[76] *been buried with him through baptism into death, in order that just as Christ was raised from the dead through the glory of the Father, so also we ourselves might walk in newness of life.*

---

[75]Which, of course, is another way of saying why couldn't Paul have been just a bit more like our better selves!

[76]The OL versions and Origen attest a text that reads γάρ instead of the οὖν of

Although this sentence is not a Spirit text in itself, there are two reasons for noting it here. First, it has been argued[77] that the phrase "through the glory of the Father" is a veiled reference to the Spirit, hence the Spirit is here to be seen as the agent of Christ's resurrection. While one may grant that the phrase is peculiar, it is difficult to imagine that the Roman recipients of this letter, who at best would know Pauline theology only second-hand, could possibly have so understood this phrase. On what linguistic or theological grounds could they have made such an association, which is never made by Paul or by anyone else known to us?

Second, and more relevant to the purposes of this study, the language "walk in newness of life"[78] anticipates the usage in 7:6, where the contrast between Torah and the Spirit is expressed in terms of "the newness of the Spirit" and "the oldness of the letter." When Paul resumes the argument again in 8:1–4, the "newness of Spirit" is expressed in terms of the Spirit as the source of "life" (8:2) and as the one by whom believers now "walk" so as to fulfill the aim of Torah—righteousness in terms of behavior.[79] Thus, even though the Spirit is not expressly mentioned in this text, there can be little question that lying behind the language is the life of the Spirit that Paul will go on to explicate, once he has dealt fully with the role of Christ's death and resurrection in bringing about this "newness of life."[80]

ROMANS 6:23

. . . For the wages of sin is death, but the gracious gift of God is eternal life in Jesus Christ our Lord.

Here is another occurrence of the word χάρισμα ("gracious gift") which gives further evidence that it denotes not primarily a "Spirit gifting," but a "concrete expression of grace"—in this case again without any reference to the Spirit. Although in 8:10 and 13 Paul will refer to the Spirit as the source of this life, the χάρισμα in this instance is not thought of in terms of its source or effective

---

the rest. This is a secondary reading that attempts to make better sense of the connection between this sentence and v. 3.

[77]See, e.g., Hamilton, *Holy Spirit*, 14, who is especially keen to demonstrate what seems nondemonstrable, that Paul understood Christ to have been raised from the dead through the agency of the Holy Spirit. Thus he asserts (rather than demonstrates): "Glory suggests the state to which Christ attained at His exaltation, and behind that state lies the Spirit. Then we may conclude that that same Spirit is the agent at work behind the glory which raised up Christ." This seems altogether speculative, and doubtful.

[78]Depending on whether one sees the emphasis to rest on "newness" or "life," this genitive construction has been variously perceived either as objective ("the newness that leads to life"; Moo 383) or as qualitative ("newness characterized by life"; MHT 3.213 [although Turner takes it in a different direction from this]) or epexegetic (appositional = "newness which consists in life"; Murray 217). The primary emphasis is most likely on the word "newness," which will be picked up as Spirit-empowered in 7:6; hence it is probably qualitative.

[79]As Dunn 315 observes, this ἵνα (purpose) clause, "in order that we might walk in newness of life," "answers to the false and blasphemous ἵνα of v. 1."

[80]So also Moo 383, an obvious(?) connection that is not made by the majority of commentaries.

mediator, but in terms of its content. Here it stands in contrast to the "earned wages" of sin as the "gracious bestowal" of God on those who trust him.

Romans 7:4–6

[4]*So then, my brothers and sisters, you yourselves have died to the Law*[81] *through the body of Christ, so that you might belong to another, to him who was raised from the dead, in order that we might bear fruit unto God.* [5]*For when we were in the flesh, the passions of sin, which were [aroused]*[82]*through the Law, used to be at work in our members, so as to bear fruit unto death;* [6]*but now, having died,*[83] *we have been released from the Law by which we were bound, so that we might serve in newness of Spirit and not in oldness of letter.*

With these words, and by picking up the "before and after" form of argumentation from vv. 17–22, Paul applies the analogy of vv. 1–3 to the present argument. Even though the application is not especially tight—the wrong "person" dies, as it were[84]—Paul's point is clear enough: as death breaks the bond of husband and wife in marriage, freeing the wife to remarry, so death (of believers, in Christ) breaks the bond of people (now believers) to Torah—not to mention to sin and the flesh. That, and nothing more, is Paul's singular concern, as his application makes plain.[85]

---

[81]As in the parallel in Gal 2:19, τῷ νόμῳ is a dative of reference; thus: "you have died as far as the Law is concerned."

[82]This word is not in the Greek text; it is supplied from vv. 7–12 as making the best sense of Paul's otherwise awkward prepositional phrase.

[83]Several witnesses, primarily Western (D F G it vg[cl] Ambrosiaster Or[mss]), have adjusted the text from ἀπὸ τοῦ νόμου ἀποθανόντες ("from the Law, having died") to ἀπὸ τοῦ νόμου τοῦ θανάτου ("from the Law of death"), in conformity to 8:2. But that misses the immediate context, where Paul is now applying the metaphor set out in vv. 1–3.

[84]This, of course, is what leads to some confusion in our reading the passage. The points of reference seem certain (although see Wright, *Climax*, 196, for a different view):

(1) wife	(2) husband	(2A) husband dies	(1B) wife is free
=	=	=	=
(1) "believer"	(2) Torah	(1A) *"believer"* dies	(1B) believer is free

The breakdown occurs at the point of "death." By the way the points of reference have been set up, the Law itself should "die"; but that makes little sense. Since in the preceding argument, the believer has died with Christ, that is how Paul now "applies" the analogy in vv. 4 and 6. In any case, Paul's intent seems unmistakable: by identification with Christ in his death, believers, as the wife whose husband has died, are no longer bound to the Law, which existed for them only so long as they remained alive (= before Christ).

[85]That is, Paul's point has to do with death severing one's relationship with the Law, *not* with a precise identification of the points of reference. In Denney's language (637): "The inference is drawn rather from the principle than from the example." Missing this has led to the spilling of much more ink over this passage than is warranted, the (unnecessary) refutation of which would only add to the flow.

At the same time, this application concludes the present argument—and anticipates what follows. Indeed, vv. 5–6 serve very much like thesis sentences for the next two sections of the argument (7:7–25 and 8:1–17).[86]

What is significant here is Paul's tying together the Law with sin and the flesh. These sentences affirm two things about this relationship. First, in keeping with the argument of Gal 5:13–24, both the Law and the flesh belong to the past, on the pre-Christ, pre-Spirit side of eschatological realities.[87] The death of Christ and the gift of the Spirit have ended Torah observance; likewise they have dealt the decisive blow to one's entire former way of life, characterized now by the loaded theological term "flesh." Second, unlike the argument in Galatians but in keeping with what has been said regularly in this letter,[88] Torah is explicitly declared to serve as an agent for the passions of sin which "used to be at work"[89] in our flesh. That repeated motif will finally need explanation, as also will the relationship of Torah, sin, and flesh to the Spirit, the former as belonging to the believer's past, the latter as the active agent of the "newness of life" in the present. Thus vv. 7–25 will explain the former relationship (of Torah to sin, flesh, and death), asserted in v. 5, while 8:1–17 will explain the latter relationship (of Spirit to Torah and flesh), expressed in v. 6.

As elsewhere, our interest in these texts lies specifically with what they tell us about Paul's understanding of the Spirit, not with all of their various details.

4 Picking up on the theme of "death" and "resurrection" as that applies to ethical life (6:1–11),[90] Paul now refers to that "death" as having brought an end not only to the reign of sin (6:1–23) but to the reign of Torah as well.[91] As before, death is followed by resurrection, so that

---

[86]Cf. Leenhardt 179.

[87]Cf. Sanders, *PLJP*, 72; contra Cranfield 1.331, who suggests that "the Law" to which believers have died is merely "the law's condemnation." But that is to miss the eschatological and covenantal character of much of this language as well as to read into the text something Paul neither says nor implies.

[88]See 3:20 ("through Torah is knowledge of sin"); 4:15 ("Torah works death; and where there is no Torah there is no transgression"); 5:13–14 ("sin was not reckoned apart from Torah"); 5:20 ("Torah entered to increase the transgression"); and 6:14 ("*Sin* shall not rule over you, for you are *not under Torah*"). Cf. Sanders, *PLJP*, 70–72, for the point that this is unlike Galatians.

[89]Gk. ἐνηργεῖτο. This imperfect is almost always lost sight of in the debate over the present tense in 7:14–25 (see the discussion on 7:14 and 18 that follows).

[90]Note esp. the distinct echoes of the language of Gal 2:19–20 as well.

[91]Some (e.g., Ziesler 174) have questioned how Paul in writing to a predominantly Gentile church can say "*you* yourselves [καὶ ὑμεῖς = "even you"] have died to the Law." The answer lies within the larger presupposed context of his Jewish interlocutor, to whom Paul responds indirectly, that Gentiles do not need to come under Torah in order to have righteousness in either sense of that term. Thus to the Gentiles

"we"[92] who belong to Christ might fulfill God's aim in giving Torah in the first place: by "bearing fruit unto God."[93] Paul is still responding to the blasphemous charge raised in 6:1 and is thereby anticipating 8:4–13's caution that freedom from Torah does not mean freedom from righteousness. At the same time, by this language Paul is discernibly moving toward the life of the Spirit, who in Gal 5:22 is responsible for producing such fruit. The two purpose clauses in this sentence[94] thus bring into focus the two concerns of the argument to this point. First, the death of Christ, which severed their relationship with Torah, has thus brought believers into relationship with him as the Risen One; they "belong" to him through whom they have received righteousness in its first sense in this letter, as a gift from God that puts them into right relationship with himself. Hence: "so that you might belong to another, to him who was raised from the dead." Second, the ultimate aim[95] of that relationship is to effect righteousness in its second sense, as conduct that is in keeping with God's character—his own righteousness, if you will—which is effected in the life of the believer by the Holy Spirit. Hence: "so that we bear fruit unto God."

5 The "for" with which this sentence begins suggests that Paul is about to explain by elaboration the point he has just made in v. 4. Picking up on the verb "to bear fruit," he now sets forth with stark contrasts life *before* Christ. The Law, it turns out, instead of leading to righteousness, "bore fruit" unto sin and death. What is of special import in this sentence is the statement, reminiscent of Gal 5:24 (q.v.), that "life in the flesh" does not belong to our eschatological present, but to our past. It can hardly be plainer: "*When we were* in the flesh." The phrase "in the flesh" refers not to our earthly existence,[96] but to

---

he can say confidently that in Christ *even you* have died to Torah; there is no need for you to come under its rule.

[92]On this shift from *you* (plural) to *we*, so as to include himself in the gracious activity of God, see above on Gal 4:4–6.

[93]This language so vividly echoes 6:21–22 (τὸν καρπὸν ὑμῶν εἰς ἁγιασμόν, "[you have] your fruit in holiness") one wonders how so many (e.g., Meyer, Godet, SH, Barrett, Black) could have fixed on the metaphor of marriage here, as though this were the "offspring" of a "new marriage"—especially since offspring is not so much as hinted at in the analogy itself (vv. 1–3; cf. Moo 442). At the same time, and what the Romans themselves could not have known, this language also echoes Gal 5:22, where the righteousness called for in this passage is called "the fruit of the Spirit."

[94]In this case, vis-à-vis those in Gal 3:14 and 4:5 (q.v.), the second depends on the first, as the content and the change in conjunctions confirm. Thus the εἰς τό (grammatically) expresses the penultimate purpose, the ἵνα the ultimate purpose.

[95]At least in the grammar of this sentence; see also 8:29–30, where "conformity to the image of the Son" has glory (God's glory) as its final goal.

[96]As in 2 Cor 10:2 (q.v.), where Paul makes a play on the language of being "in the flesh" (= our present earthly existence) and living "according to the flesh"

our former way of life that was in opposition to God and therefore full of sin.[97] Only by a most convoluted kind of reasoning can one argue that to be "in the flesh" in the former sense means also to be "in the flesh" in the latter.[98] This passage, as well as the further explanation in 8:1–17, not to mention Gal 5:13–24, makes it certain that for Paul believers are not "in the flesh" in the sense of living in keeping with the values and from the perspective of the former age, which is now passing away.[99] This does not mean, of course, that sin itself is past, or that the desire of the flesh is not still about; but it does mean that one no longer lives within the sphere of the "life of the flesh," any more than one lives under obligation to Torah. The past tense in the opening clause and the contrast "but now" with which v. 6 begins ensure this as Paul's intent.

Although this sentence in some way recapitulates what Paul has said about the Law, it conjoins several things in a new way that calls for explication, especially the sequence: Torah → flesh → sin → death. Even if we did not have the elaboration in vv. 7–25, from this sentence alone we could have figured out the relationship. *Torah* arouses "the passions of *sin*" that are resident in one's *flesh*, which, yielded to, lead to *death*. As Paul will state with utmost confidence in 8:2–4, Christ's death and the Spirit's presence have effectively brought an end to all four of the offending particulars (Law, flesh, sin, death), while at the same time ushering in the life of the future, lived by the power of the Spirit, in which the goal of Torah is fulfilled. But that sentence will only explicate what is affirmed already in v. 6, which here sharply contrasts with the former way of life spelled out in this sentence.

6 With the "but now"[100] Paul moves his readers from their Jewish or pagan past to their life in Christ. But in keeping with the argument of the letter thus far, he zeros in only on Torah. The relationship between Torah and sin will be spelled out in the following section; for now the

---

(= living on the basis of the values and perspective of the former age that is passing away). Cf. Ziesler 176, Moo 442.

[97]And as 8:5–8 will make plain, is still the way of life for those without the Spirit, whose "minds are on the things of the flesh" and thereby do not, and cannot, submit to God's Law and thus please him.

[98]Which is what Dunn has argued in effect in "Jesus," 43–48, perpetuated in his commentary (363), partly because of his (mistaken) view of 8:5–8 as reflecting an internal struggle within believers between life in the Spirit and the life of the flesh, a meaning that seems foreign to both the language and the context of that passage.

[99]On this whole question, and the Pauline perspective, see on 2 Cor 5:14–17 and Gal 5:16–18 above. Cf. Moo 442–43, who also rightly observes that "in the flesh" cannot here equal "the sinful nature" of the NIV. Although it derives from anthropology, the term has become for Paul an eschatological, more than an anthropological, term.

[100]As with 8:1 (q.v.), this νυνὶ δέ is at least (and therefore primarily) temporal (so Cranfield 1.338), stressing the before and after of vv. 5 and 6. It is by that very fact also "logical," but not equally so (contra Barrett 137, Morris 275).

issue remains as it has been from the beginning of the analogy in v. 1.
The ultimate result of (reason for?)[101] release from Torah is that one is
now free to "serve" by the Spirit. Thus Paul begins the sentence by
picking up the point of the analogy once more: death—Christ's death in
which we have participated—means that "we have been released from the
Law by which we were bound," language that now abandons the metaphor
(vv. 1–3) for that of 6:12–23. The consequence of such "release" is that we
"serve" God no longer under Torah but by the Spirit, through whom, he
will go on to explain in 8:4–13, the purpose of Torah is carried out in our lives.

To underscore that, Paul picks up the contrast between "letter" and
the Spirit mentioned in 2:29, but expressed now in the language of 6:4
("newness of life"). The present emphasis is on *both* terms in the two
phrases.[102] "Oldness" and "letter" belong to the past. This is the relationship (to the "letter") severed by Christ's death; this is the "oldness"
brought to an end through the resurrection. "Newness" and "Spirit"
belong to the present. The Spirit is God's effective replacement of Torah
observance; "newness" has to do with life over against the death resulting from the "oldness of letter." Thus, even more explicitly than in 2:29,
the contrast is articulated in terms of "before" and "after," with reference
to the coming of Christ. "Service"[103] toward God *now* (in our present
eschatological existence ushered in by Christ's death and resurrection) is carried forth "in the newness" of the Spirit[104] (in the new
covenant ratified by Christ and characterized by the life of the
Spirit).[105] The new has thus replaced the old,[106] which was ratified by

---

[101] The ὥστε properly introduces a result clause, but lying behind it is the concept
of "reason for."

[102] Cf. Cranfield 1.339, and Dunn 366 ("double antithesis . . . all the more emphatic
for its doubling").

[103] Gk. δουλεύειν; cf. 6:6, regarding "service" to sin, and 12:11 and 14:18 regarding
"service" to Christ. See discussion in Gal 5:13. The verb is a strong one, expressing
one of the paradoxes of Paul. Freedom is what Christ has brought us (8:2), but such
glorious freedom brings obligation to "serve." See further on 8:12 below.

[104] Cranfield 1.339 considers these two genitives as appositives (newness, that is,
the Spirit); more likely they are qualitative (= newness characterized by the Spirit);
cf. on 6:4.

[105] As with 2:29 and 2 Cor 3:6, the contrast between Spirit and "letter" has
nothing to do with the several popularizations of this language: e.g., between "the
spirit and letter" of the law, or between "internal and external," or between "literal
and spiritual"! This is eschatological and covenantal language. "Letter" has to do
with the old covenant that came to an end through Christ and the Spirit. As 2 Cor
3:6 makes clear, the new covenant is a covenant characterized by the effective
presence of the Spirit. Cf. Bruce 139, Käsemann 190, Moo 445–46. It is missing the
eschatological and covenantal aspects of this language that in part has led Cranfield
to a more totally theological view which seems to miss so much in chs. 6–8.

[106] In the expressive language of Käsemann 191, "Christianity is not just a Jewish
sect which believes in Jesus as the Messiah. It is the breaking in of the new world of
God characterized by the lordship of the Spirit."

Moses and Israel on Sinai and characterized by "written regulations requiring obedience."

Just as in 2 Cor 3:3–18, the Spirit serves for Paul as the essential element of the new covenant. With these words Paul now projects into the argument of Romans that dimension of life in the new age ushered in by Christ by which everything is made effectual: the Spirit of God himself.[107] This is what will be explained in the rest of the argument (8:1–30) as well as in the application of the whole to the life of the church in Rome in 12:1–15:13.

But before that, since Paul has been so hard on Torah to this point, and since he is about to leave the issue of Torah observance,[108] he feels compelled to exonerate Torah, despite its failure to secure what so many thought it promised—the righteousness of God, in both senses of that term. Thus the "digression" in vv. 7–25, whose sole concern is to defend Torah as a good thing, despite its failure to secure righteousness and effectively deal with sin.

ROMANS 7:14, 18[109]

[14]For we know that the Law is Spiritual, but I am fleshly, sold under sin. . . .

[18]I know that good does not dwell in me, that is, in my flesh.

---

[107] In light of Paul's usage in 2 Cor 3:3–18, with which this passage has significant parallels, Dunn's suggestion (367, 373) that there is enough ambiguity in the term so that it could also refer here to the human spirit is unconvincing. Paul at least had no ambiguity; he meant the Holy Spirit, pure and simple.

[108] At least as far as the argument proper is concerned. In the paraenesis and application in 12:1–15:13 the obsolete nature of Torah will emerge again (e.g., 13:8–10).

[109] *Bibliography:* P. **Althaus**, "Zur Auslegung von Röm 7:14ff." *TLZ* 77 (1952) 475–80; R. **Bultmann**, "Romans 7 and the Anthropology of Paul," in *Existence and Faith* (London: Hodder & Stoughton, 1960[Ger. original 1932]) 173–85; **Dunn**, "Romans 7:14–25"; R. Y. K. **Fung**, "The Impotence of the Law: Toward a Fresh Understanding of Romans 7:14–25," in *Scripture, Tradition and Interpretation* (Festschrift E. F. Harrison; ed. W. W. Gasque and W. S. LaSor; Grand Rapids: Eerdmans, 1978) 34–48; **Jewett**, *Terms*, 391–401; M. J. **Karlberg**, "Israel's History Personified: Romans 7:7–13 in Relation to Paul's Teaching on the 'Old Man,' " *TrinJ* 7 (1986) 68–69; W. G. **Kümmel**, *Römer 7 und die Bekehrung des Paulus* (Leipzig: Hinrichs, 1929); J. **Lambrecht**, "Man before and without Christ: Romans 7 and Pauline Anthropology," *Louvain Studies* 5 (1974) 18–33; C. L. **Mitton**, "Romans 7 Reconsidered," *ExpT* 65 (1953/54) 78–81, 99–103, 132–35; D. J. **Moo**, "Israel and Paul in Romans 7:7–12," *NTS* 32 (1986) 122–35; J. I. **Packer**, "The 'Wretched Man' of Romans 7," *SE* II (1964) 621–27; E. P. **Sanders**, *PLJP*, 70–86; K. **Snodgrass**, "Spheres of Influence: A Possible Solution for the Problem of Paul and the Law," *JSNT* 32 (1988) 93–113; K. **Stendahl**, *Paul*, 92–94; D. **Wenham**, "Christian Life"; N. T. **Wright**, "The Vindication of the Law: Narrative Analysis and Romans 8:1–11," in *Climax*, 193–219. For further bibliography see Dunn 374–75.

Without question this is one of the more surprising uses of the adjective πνευματικός in the Pauline corpus. In this attempt to exonerate the Torah,[110] one can well understand Paul's having said in v. 12 that the Law is holy, and the commandment holy, righteous, and good. After all, these three words reflect the understanding of Paul and his heritage about the essential character of God; and since the Law comes from God, who is himself holy, righteous, and good, so also with the Law. But in light of the strong contrasts between Law and Spirit in 2:29, 7:6, and especially 2 Cor 3:3–18, one is not quite prepared for this affirmation of Law, that it belongs to the Spirit side of things, not that of flesh.

Not only that, but immediately following these words appear some of the most controversial in the letter, which have bearing on our present concerns: Paul's personification of sin in vv. 8 and 11 is now expressed (in vv. 14–25) in the *first person* singular and in the *present tense* and as taking root in the flesh, but in 7:5 and 8:3 (cf. 8:9) flesh has been put in the *past tense* through the work of Christ and the coming of the eschatological Spirit, and in 8:5–11 those in the flesh are set in contrast to believers, who walk by the Spirit. At issue, therefore, is the tension some feel between the flesh as in the past for Paul, but now expressed with deep emotion as in the present. My concern here is twofold: first, to offer a brief word about "Spiritual" in v. 14; and second, to offer an overview as to how I perceive 7:7–25 to fit into the argument as a whole, and especially as to Paul's use of the past and present regarding "the flesh."

First, then, about the meaning of πνευματικός in v. 14. The word catches us by surprise here, especially in this argument and in light of Paul's letters as a whole. Everywhere else the Law and the Spirit are basically contrasted to each other. To be "led of the Spirit," Paul said in Gal 5:18 means that one is "not under Torah," which pretty well sums up Paul's basic attitude and is precisely the perspective presented in two of the first three references to the Spirit earlier in this letter (2:29 and 7:6). To belong to the one, the Spirit, means to be done with the other, the Law. How, then, can he now say that the Law belongs to the Spirit side of things?

The answer to this lies partly with the basic eschatological framework within which all of Paul's theologizing is expressed, and partly with

---

[110] Apparently sensing the need to do so because of the obvious tensions he himself has set up by the very positive statement in 3:2 ("they have been entrusted with the very words of God") and those noted above in n. 88, to the effect that the Torah has only increased the problem of sin. That this is an attempt to vindicate Torah seems so clearly to be the case, based on the questions Paul sets up (for his imagined interlocutor) in vv. 7 and 13, one wonders how Dunn ("Romans 7:14–25") can address this passage and its place in Pauline "theology" without mentioning the role of the Law in his discussion, but treating the whole as though the issue were primarily anthropological.

the meaning of the adjective itself. The contrast in v. 6 between "the newness of Spirit" and "the oldness of letter" is mainly between life under the new and old covenants, now expressed eschatologically—i.e., between existence in the former age, whose end Christ has inaugurated through his death and resurrection, and existence in the coming age, which was ushered in by that same death and resurrection. One of the ways of expressing life in the former age is "under Torah," whereas life in the new age is characterized above all by the Spirit. Hence the contrasts in v. 6 are not between something good and bad, or even between something good and better, but between two different kinds of existence, one "before" and the other "after" Christ. Since Torah belongs to the "before," Paul is insistent—and is so in a dogged way throughout this letter—that the time of Torah is past. Only when that which served to identify Jews vis-à-vis Gentiles as the people of God has come to end, can God's eschatological salvation be made available to all people, Jews and Gentiles alike, and on equal terms.

But that does not mean that Torah itself is bad, even though it finally brought death to the very people it marked off as belonging to God. Rather, precisely because it also is God's doing—it is the former covenant, after all—Paul can declare that the Law is holy, and its "commandment" is holy and just and good (v. 12). Not only so, he now goes on, the Law is also "Spiritual." As always in Paul, and especially in this context, where it stands in contrast to one's being "fleshly," this can mean only that it "pertains to, or belongs to, the Spirit." How so? Because in Paul's view the Law belongs to the Scriptures, which are God-breathed and therefore come by way of the Spirit. Thus even though for Paul the old covenant failed because it was not accompanied by a giving of the Spirit to the people who received the Law, he nonetheless views the Law as ultimately of the Spirit.[111] The problem lies not in its inherent quality as from God, and therefore as good and of the Spirit. The problem, we come to learn in this passage, has to do with inherent sin and the flesh, which Torah exposed and aroused, but over against which it stood utterly helpless. And that leads, then, to the second issue that concerns us, the role of 7:7–25 in the argument and the place of "fleshly" (v. 14) and "in my flesh" (v. 18).

At issue in the great debate over this passage are (1) the question of context and (2) where one will finally place one's emphasis regarding the two issues that appear to be in conflict: (a) whether the "I," the present tense, and the impassioned manner in which vv. 14–24 are expressed are seen as determinative,[112] or (b) whether Paul's own questions in vv. 7

---

[111] This of course is fully in keeping with the Jewish tradition of which he still considers himself a part.

[112] Even a cursory reading of Dunn ("Romans 7:14–25"), for example, demonstrates how much this is true. In this article, which is written over against Kümmel,

and 13 and the clear statements on either side (7:6 and 8:2–4) that both Torah and the flesh belong to the past are determinative. That at least is the central exegetical issue. At stake also, however, is how one perceives the role of these verses in the overall context, whether they refer to the life of the believer or whether they describe life before and outside of Christ. From my perspective, everything except the present tense of vv. 14–25 favors the second option—the content, the issue being addressed, and the nature of what is said in 6:1–7:6 and 8:1–39.[113]

There are three matters which seem overwhelmingly to favor the view that Paul is here describing life before and outside of Christ,[114] but from the perspective of one who is himself now in Christ. First, the questions as Paul himself puts them forward, and to which he offers a response, have to do with Torah, and therefore life under Torah, *not with life in Christ*, which for Paul is decidedly *not under Torah*.[115] For me this is the decisive issue.[116] The questions put by Paul's imagined interlocutor

---

he identifies the two principal issues as having to do with the surrounding context and how the "I" and present tense fit into that; he mentions the issue of "exonerating Torah" only in passing. Thus he sets the agenda on his own terms, but fails to address what most others would see as the central issue—namely, what is driving Paul's argument is not his personal experience, but the question of whether Torah itself is evil (cf. Wright, *Climax*, 224n25, for whom this became the basic issue that brought about his change of mind). The title for this section in Dunn's commentary is the sure giveaway as to his starting point ("*But* the Law is *still exploited* by Sin and Death, As Experience Demonstrates" [emphases mine]). This seems to move well beyond the questions Paul raises and addresses.

[113] The bibliography on this matter seems endless. For the view expressed here, but not necessarily in the same way or with the same emphases, see, inter alia, the items by Kümmel, Stendahl, Sanders, Wright, and the commentaries by Käsemann and Moo; for the opposing viewpoint, and again not always in the same way or with the same emphases, see inter alia, the items by Dunn and Packer, and the commentaries by Cranfield and Dunn (it is also adopted by Morris, but without the same degree of advocacy). Dunn ("Romans 7:14–25," 51) regards his view as "the minority interpretation"—probably correctly as far as scholarship is concerned. My own experience with the popular literature, in the classroom, and in the church would suggest that it is otherwise within the church at large (so also Moo 471).

[114] Cf. Sanders, *PLJP*, 76: "the obvious and telling arguments against the autobiographical explanation."

[115] And it will do no good, as is so often attempted, to bring in Torah through the back door in some theological way that lies beyond Paul's concerns—as though for Paul Torah is still about, even though we may not be under it. That may work for some theologically, but it is decidedly not an issue raised by Paul either here or anywhere else in Romans. Thus Fung, ("Impotence," 40) suggests that Paul's purpose is "to show that the law is powerless to sanctify the Christian," but his exegesis of vv. 14–25, as well as that of many others, is carried out as if the question in v. 13 had never been asked at all.

[116] Cf. Moo 449–50: " . . . for we must insist again that the central topic of these verses is not human nature or anthropology, but the Mosaic law. Because this is the case, the most important teaching of the section is the same however the 'I' is identified." See also n. 121 below.

are two: (1) In light of all that has been argued, and especially in light
of the assertion in v. 5 that "the passions of sin" are "through the Law,"
is the Law itself therefore to be understood as sinful in some way? To this
Paul's ringing response is μὴ γένοιτο, whose flavor the KJV captures best,
"God forbid." The explanation offered is the well-known one, that the
problem lay with indwelling sin, now personified, which lay dormant
until the Law came and aroused it. In so doing, despite its essential
goodness, the Law became implicated in the death of the person under
Law.[117] That in turn leads to the second question in direct response to
this first answer; (2) by thus arousing sin which "killed me," *was this good
thing, the Law, responsible for my death?* To this too Paul responds, "God
forbid"; sin alone is responsible for death. It is Paul's elaboration of this
last response that has led to our difficulties. The ultimate key to this
elaboration lies with his playing on the language of "law." The (good)
Law attested to the existence of another "law," that of sin and death,
which was already inherent in my fallenness, i.e., in my flesh.[118] Thus
the good Law, whose goodness one can freely assent to, turned out to be
powerless in the face of the more powerful law of sin and death, resident

---

[117] The tension in this argument in fact has little to do with present life, but
rather with Paul's form of argumentation. On the one hand, the clear *aim* of this
excursus is to defend, and thereby exonerate, Torah as such, which he certainly does
in terms of its nature and character. At the same time, on the other hand, and here
is the root of the problem, Paul cannot quite let it go at that, because of Torah's role
in arousing sin—even though the latter alone is responsible for death. Hence, despite
his chief aim, the second matter, Torah's implication in my death, receives the greater
hearing.

[118] Contra several attempts to see νόμος here as still referring to Torah (e.g.,
Denney 642; Dunn 392; Snodgrass, "Spheres," 105–6; Wright, *Climax*, 198). Such a
view seems to stretch the meaning of ἕτερος beyond recognition (so also Moo 491).
One wonders how the Romans could have understood "I see ἕτερον νόμον (*another
law*) *in my members*," which stands over against (indeed, "wars against") *the Law* of
my mind (= the Law of God to which my mind assents) as referring to the same Law.
Without playing all the word games with "law" here, to which Wright rightly objects
("principle," etc.), I nevertheless find the best way through the maze is to see Paul
doing what he often does at such points: making a word play. Wright's objection that
he would be doing so "exactly when it is most likely to be confusing" (199) is not very
helpful, since I find his own solution to be even more "confusing" for the reader. That
there is a word play going on not only resolves the tensions, but seems to be indicated
by two other factors: (1) Paul himself intends to clarify between the two "laws" by
designating the Torah as "the Law of God" in v. 22 (repeated in v. 25, precisely at the
point of making clear distinctions between the two "laws"), a designation not
otherwise found in the corpus (except in 8:7, which picks up the language used here);
(2) he will use the same word play again in 8:2 about the Spirit. In both cases (sin
and Spirit) the designations "the 'law' of sin" and "the 'law' of the Spirit" exist only
here in Paul. This suggests that on his own and in other settings Paul would never
speak of sin and the Spirit in that way and that he does so here because he is making
a word play on νόμος. Since this makes sense both of the usage and of the argument,
such a view seems preferable. See further on 8:2 below.

in my flesh.[119] Thus the Law is exonerated[120] in terms of the basic questions being raised and answered: Is the Law sinful? Did the Law cause my death? No, Paul responds vigorously. Nonetheless, the Law failed at the *more crucial point* of our human life, namely, in its inherent inability to do anything about the sin it aroused. Hence the cry of anguish in v. 24a, by the one who lives under Torah and is caught between two laws, both of which ultimately lead to death: the one, the law of sin, because that is the curse upon sin; the other, Torah, because having aroused sin, it then stands helplessly by while I am held captive to the flesh and thus led to death.[121]

My point is that the *only* questions Paul himself raises in this entire passage have to do with *Torah*—whether it is good or evil—and, once that is answered affirmatively, how this good thing is still implicated in death. The personal dimension thus refers to *life under Torah*. That, and that alone, is under scrutiny.[122] What is abundantly clear in Paul, in this letter and everywhere else, is that the new people of God, whose existence is predicated on the new covenant ratified by Christ and effected by the life-giving Spirit, are *not under Torah*. They have died to Torah, are released from its imprisonment, and serve God in the new way of the Spirit (vv. 4–6). Whatever else, this passage does *not* describe a struggle within the believer between his or her flesh and the Spirit, but rather describes what it is like to be under the Law while in the clutches of sin and the flesh; and according to both 7:1–6 and 8:1–4 for the believer that all belongs to the past.[123] Even in one's fallenness, one can assent to the essential goodness of the thing that God requires; but, and this is what

---

[119] It should perhaps be noted that the ad hoc nature of his letters means that Paul never feels constrained to resolve the inherent tensions created by this answer and that given in Gal 3:19–22, where Torah came into existence "because of the transgressions," which in that case meant to hem people in until Christ should come.

[120] For the view that this is the basic issue in 7:7–25, and not the experience of the "I" of vv. 14–25, see Stendahl, *Paul*, 92–94, and Wright, *Climax*, 196–200, 217–19, who would extend this "vindication of the Law" to 8:1–11.

[121] Paul's response to this second question (vv. 14–25), therefore, is essentially in two parts: vv. 14–20 express the tyranny of sin and one's utter helplessness in the face of it; vv. 21–25 speak to the helplessness of Torah to do anything for the person described in vv. 14–20. These two lead to the cry of despair in v. 24a, to which, in typical fashion, Paul feels an immediate urgency to respond (v. 25a). But the argument of vv. 14–25 has not been wrapped up yet, so he returns to that in summary fashion in v. 25b. If that is not tidy to our way of thinking, it is at least explicable and easy enough to see. Cf. the more detailed analysis in Wright, *Climax*, 217–19.

[122] This is so whether one thinks more personally in terms of Paul as a Christian helping his interlocutor to look at life under Law from his now Christian perspective, as I think, or whether the "I" represents Israel, as Wright, *Climax*, argues.

[123] Note esp. 7:5: "When we *were* in the flesh, the passions of the flesh *used to be at work* [see n. 89 above] aroused as they were through the Law." Only a theological or existential a priori can get around something as transparent as that.

ch. 8 responds to, the (first) Law could not deliver one from that fallenness (the more powerful "second" law).

Second (and this is related to the first), Paul does not so much as
mention the Spirit in this passage—at least not in terms of the believer.[124] The absence of the Spirit in this picture affirms that Paul is not
describing life under the new covenant. The *only* struggle pictured here
is that between the two "laws," a struggle that for Paul belongs to life
before, not after, Christ, because on the "after" side there has come a
third "law"(!), that of the Spirit who gives life (8:2).

Third, that this is the correct view of this passage is finally corroborated by the argument that precedes and follows.[125] Verses 8:1–4 are
intended to resume and elaborate the assertions of 7:5–6, now of course
by way of the intervening content; therefore 7:7–25 seem to function just
as we have described them, as something of a digression—although
crucial to Paul's overall enterprise. Not only so, but in 8:5–8, where Paul
finally sets forth the contrast between the flesh and the Spirit, there is
not a hint of some internal struggle within the Christian breast. Rather,
Paul here simply describes—without struggle—two absolutely incompatible kinds of existence, between "*those* who live according to the flesh"
and therefore *cannot* obey "the Law of God," and "*us* who live according
to the Spirit and thereby fulfill the Law."[126] Again, both the language
and the argument belong to Paul's basic eschatological outlook. He is
neither affirming nor denying that believers are tempted or that they can
be overtaken by sin; that is not at issue here. Rather, Paul is describing
life before and after Christ; the one is characterized by flesh, the other by
the Spirit. Only once in that passage does he allude to the language or
content of 7:7–25, and that is to repeat in 8:7 that the person living in
the flesh cannot submit to God's Torah. But as the contrasting "but as
for you" in v. 9 certifies, that describes *those outside of Christ.*

---

[124] The only mention of the Spirit/flesh contrast appears in v. 14, noted above,
and it does not describe Christian existence. Rather, with consummate irony, Paul
there places the Spirit on the side of Law, as indeed it was before Christ came and
people under Law still lived out of the flesh. Cf. 8:7–8, where people live in the flesh
and thus do not have the Spirit and cannot submit to God's Law. In each case the
Spirit is described not as within the believer, not "the Spirit joining battle *in Paul* with
the flesh" (Dunn, "Romans 7:14–25," 55), but "outside" and on the opposite side of
the one in the flesh—especially in 7:14. In this passage, after all, the Spirit is not
"aiding" the believer. Improbable also, therefore, is the view in Dunn's commentary
(387) that Paul begins his argument by asserting that there are "two dualities," one
within the Law and another within himself, and that these are therefore finally
complementary. See the further refutation in Moo 480.

[125] Moo 475 focuses particularly on the tension created for the "autobiographical"
view by the sharp contrasts between the "objective status" (1) of being "sold under
sin" (7:14) and "set free from sin" (6:18, 22), and (2) of being "imprisoned by the power
of sin" (7:23) and "set free from the law of sin and death" (8:2).

[126] Cf. Sanders, *PLJP*, 74. See below on 8:5–8.

Finally, in an offhanded way, 8:12–13 confirm that 8:5–8 does not describe Paul's personal struggle with the flesh. There he includes himself along with them as being under obligation to live by the Spirit (v. 12), but changes the "we" to "you" when he offers up the warning and affirmation of v. 13. Were this passage a description of Paul's Christian life, and one of such intense struggle and constant defeat, it is hard to account for this casual exclusion of himself here, where his inclusion would have been so appropriate.

Thus, as we noted in our discussion of Gal 5:17, this question has been largely fought in the arena of "the introspective conscience of the West." In so doing it has dealt with a real issue for believers, to be sure, namely, that of besetting sin, but in fact Paul does not speak to that issue either here or in the Galatians passage.[127]

Romans 8:1–30[128]

In this section Paul elaborates what he had previously established in 7:5–6: the Spirit as God's alternative to Torah and antidote to the flesh, since both of these belong to the "before Christ" side of things. The Spirit is therefore the key to our new relationship with God, as children who are heirs with Christ of eternal glory. Not only so, but the Spirit is also the key to our enduring present suffering while we await that final glory. But before examining this extensive Spirit material in some detail, we need a prior sense of how all this fits into the whole.

Because of our tendency, rightly so, to identify personally with this material, it is easy for us to lose the perspective of the larger context, with its three overriding concerns: (1) Jew and Gentile, equally disadvantaged through sin and thus equally advantaged through Christ, form *one*

---

[127] I have deliberately skipped the issue that those on the other side begin with and make their primary point, namely, the "I" and the present tense of the verbs. As noted, these are the two features that may favor the view that Paul is describing his current life in Christ. But since the context and the actual content being addressed seem so clearly against such a view, one must begin there and then try to explain the first person and the present tense. Along with many others, I take it to be representative, but of what? Here the house divides. Since the description of the Law could have come about for Paul only after he had encountered Christ and entered the life of the Spirit, I take it to be a heightened way of bringing his Jewish Christian interlocutor into the argument. This is one Christian speaking to another Christian about life under Torah, once one looks back on that from the life of the Spirit. The point is that neither an unbeliever nor a Jew could possibly have expressed themselves as Paul does here, nor would they care a whit about such. This is a *decidedly Christian perspective* on an issue about which Paul obviously still feels very keenly.

[128] *Bibliography:* E. **Fuchs**, "Der Anteil des Geistes am Glauben des Paulus: Ein Beitrag zum Verständnis von Röm 8," ZTK 72 (1975) 293–302; M. L. **Loane**, *The Hope of Glory: An Exposition of the Eighth Chapter in the Epistle to the Romans* (London: Hodder & Stoughton, 1968); A. S. **Wood**, *Life by the Spirit* (Grand Rapids: Zondervan, 1963).

people of God, which means (2) that not only is there no advantage to
Torah, but that the time of Torah has come to an end with Christ; but
(3) that does not mean that righteousness has come to an end. To the
contrary, *what the Law could not do because Sin was stronger than Law,
Christ and the Spirit have now done.* All three of these concerns, but
especially the first and third, still dominate the argument. Whereas one
can more easily see the third concern being addressed in this section, too
much is lost if the first, which drives the whole argument of the letter
from beginning to end, is not recognized in much of what is said here.
Thus the present material needs to be read consistently within the whole
of the letter: the emphatic declaration in v. 9 means that they [both Jew
and Gentile] are not in the flesh but in the Spirit; led by the Spirit they
[both together] are therefore God's "children" and thus his eternal heirs
(vv. 14–17); for those who [together] were called for his purposes, who
were thus foreknown and predestined to be conformed to Christ's character, and who have been justified and (finally will be) glorified, the Spirit
works all things for good (vv. 28–30); and even though there is present
suffering, no one can bring any charge against those who are his [Jew
and Gentile alike and together], nor can anything in the whole created
order separate them [Jew and Gentile together] from the love of God (which
was poured out into their hearts together by the Holy Spirit; vv. 31–39).

This section, therefore, climaxes the soteriological dimension of the
argument that began in 1:18, and one can scarcely miss the crucial role
played by the Holy Spirit. Even though it is never said in quite this way,
the Spirit is the experiential, life-giving linchpin to everything that has
been argued to this point. The coming of the Spirit means the end of the
time of Law (we serve God in newness of Spirit, not in oldness of mere
"letter"); the Spirit makes both Jew and Gentile God's children and thus
heirs together of God's final glory; at the same time the Spirit makes
possible the righteousness which the Law, weakened through sin and the
flesh, could not; and finally the Spirit is the eschatological down payment, the firstfruits, of the future, including the final resurrection and
glorification of the present mortal body.

Especially noteworthy is how much this material breathes the language
and concerns of 5:1–11; 6:1–7:6; and 7:7–25—now in reverse order.[129]
Thus, vv. 1–8 take up the matters raised in 7:7–25, namely, that God,
through Christ and the Spirit, has done what the Law could not—deal
with sin itself, not simply with occasional sins. In vv. 9–13, which belong
integrally to vv. 1–8, the "Spirit of life" is God's response to the "law of
death" as well as of sin. Here emerge the concerns of 6:1–23; hence this
section is full of linguistic echoes from that argument, but now in terms
of life in the Spirit. Finally, in vv. 14–17, by the Spirit the old slavery to

---

[129] Cf. Moo 501 (a "ring composition").

sin and Law (cf. 6:6, 16–7:4) has been replaced with adoption into God's family as children who are full heirs of God's glory.

This final word, adoption as children who are full heirs, is qualified, however, by current realities—that "we also suffer with Christ." Thus in vv. 18–30 and 31–39 Paul returns to twin themes first struck in 5:3–5, namely, that the indwelling Spirit is guarantor of our hope even in the midst of present suffering and that this is so because he has infused our hearts with God's love. The Spirit guarantees our very existence as God's people, who can neither be charged by others nor separated from his love by anything.

In terms of the argument of 5:1–8:39, even though the Spirit is mentioned at the beginning only in 5:5 (as the one given so as to guarantee our hope and God's love) and is not specifically mentioned at the end (8:31–39, where separation from God's love in Christ is asserted as unthinkable), nonetheless the Spirit is the experiential key to the whole: God in love is creating a people for his name, apart from the Law, composed of Jew and Gentile alike and made possible and effective through the death and resurrection of Christ. All of this is actualized in the church (and the believer as well, of course) by the Spirit whom God has given.

To be sure, the Spirit is not the chief matter; but neither is he the least. In these chapters Paul's Trinitarian presuppositions stand out everywhere. God is the prime mover, the principal actor in all things. God has brought about this salvation, this new people for his name, through the death and resurrection of his own Son (8:3). And God has brought all of it to realization through the gift of his Holy Spirit, who is also the Spirit of his Son.

The present argument has three easily recognizable parts, vv. 1–17, 18–30, 31–39. In vv. 1–17 in particular, where most of the Spirit material is concentrated, all subdivisions into smaller parts have a degree of arbitrariness about them.[130] This is a continuous piece, in which argument and appeal blend and the various "parts" are integral to one another. But for the sake of tracing the flow of thought, and for convenience, I have chosen to look at the material in its smaller units. A word is therefore needed about the relationship of these smaller parts to one another.

(a) Vv. 1–2 function in two ways. On the one hand, they respond directly to 7:7–25, and especially to both parts of v. 25; on the other hand, v. 2 serves as a kind of "lead-in" to what follows. Here is introduced the "third law," that of the Spirit, which sets God's people free from the "second law," that of sin and death. Freedom from sin and death is what will be taken up in vv. 3–8 and 9–11 respectively.

(b) Vv. 3–4 respond directly to v. 2 by arguing that Christ and the Spirit are God's new way over against the "first law," Torah, as well. As

---

[130] There is some discussion, for example, as to whether the first "major" break is at v. 12 or v. 14. But in both cases (vv. 12–13 and 14–17), even though a slightly new direction takes place in the argument, they are integral to what has preceded.

Paul had argued in 7:14–25, Torah was utterly helpless in the face of the "second law," sin and death. But by sending his Son God condemned the sin that exists in the flesh. Not only so, but by the gift of the "third law," the Spirit, God also effectively dealt with the other failure of Torah—to produce true righteousness, here described as "walking according to the Spirit" and thus over against life "according to the flesh."

(c) Vv. 5–8 then elaborate on the two kinds of existence, characterized respectively by "flesh" and "the Spirit." The contrast itself is set forth in vv. 5–6 in two sets of perfectly balanced clauses in an AB, AB pattern. Vv. 7–8 elaborate the A sentences, and explain why the "mind of the flesh is death"—because such people are in enmity to God, neither submitting nor able to submit to God's Torah (cf. 7:14–25), thus being quite incapable of pleasing him. With this sentence Torah fades from the argument until 9:31.

(d) Vv. 9–11, the more complex sub-paragraph in this section, function in at least three ways. First, and most obviously, they designate the Roman believers as the alternative (the B sentences of vv. 5–6) to those who live in the flesh in vv. 7–8. Second, they also speak to the second matter from v. 2, namely, that Christ and the Spirit have also freed God's people from side two of the "second law," namely, the "law of death." Third, in so doing, Paul also brings into focus the final eschatological outcome of salvation in Christ, which will dominate the argument from v. 17 to the end.

(e) Vv. 12–13 directly apply to the believers in Rome what has been argued to this point. Because of what Christ and the Spirit have done, the Romans must live no longer as those who are "according to the flesh." Their "obligation" is not to the flesh, but to the Spirit, by whom they are urged to "put to death" the "deeds of the body." This application is the closest thing to an imperative in the argument. It should also be noted that the word "flesh" now drops from the argument as well, to reappear only once more (13:14).

(f) Vv. 14–17 elaborate the appeal of vv. 12–13 by describing Spirit life in the language of "sonship" over against "slavery," echoing the language and metaphors of Gal 4:4–6. Through the Spirit they have received "adoption as children," evidenced by the Spirit-inspired *Abba*-cry, which means that they are destined to inherit God's glory with Christ himself—provided they also share in his sufferings in the present.

These final words of v. 17 lead to the second part of the argument, vv. 18–30, which make a decided shift toward the role of the Spirit in the present life of suffering, while at the same time serving as guarantee of the future, thus harking back to 5:3–5. This section comes in three distinct parts, the Spirit especially playing the key role in the first two.

(a) Vv. 18–25, picking up the theme of present suffering from v. 17, put that suffering into the broadest possible creational context. All of creation stands on tiptoe awaiting our final redemption, signaled by the "redemption of our bodies." We groan along with the groaning creation, because we have received the firstfruits of such redemption, the Spirit himself. But precisely because the Spirit serves as the "firstfruits," God's own guarantee of the final harvest, we live in hope despite the groaning.

(b) Vv. 26–27 return (after dealing with our certain future) to the theme of our present groaning, and the role of the Spirit in that. It turns out that our "groaning" takes the form of the Spirit's intercession in our behalf.

(c) Vv. 28–30 then conclude this reflection on the present and the future, by placing everything in the context of God's overarching design. The Spirit works in us for good, because God's call—which brought us to life through Christ and the Spirit—reflects his own purposes that belong to eternity past, that we should be "conformed to the image of his Son," and to eternity future, that the justified shall also be glorified, which brings Paul back to where this began in v. 17. This text also concludes the present argument and reminds us that despite the reflection on suffering and glory in vv. 18–25, the concern throughout is with "righteousness," effected by the Spirit, who as the Spirit of the Son recreates children for God who are "joint-heirs" with the Son because they have by the Spirit been conformed into his likeness.

ROMANS 8:1–2[131]

[1]Now[132] *therefore there is no condemnation to those who are in Christ Jesus.*[133] [2]*For the "law" of the Spirit of life has in Christ Jesus set you*[134] *free from the "law" of sin and death.*

---

[131] *Bibliography*: C. E. B. **Cranfield**, "The Freedom of the Christian according to Rom 8:2," in *New Testament Christianity for Africa and the World* (Festschrift H. Sawyerr; ed. M. E. Glaswell and E. W. Fasholé-Luke; London: SPCK, 1974) 91–98; F. S. **Jones**, *"Freiheit" in den Briefen des Apostels Paulus* (Göttingen: Vandenhoeck & Ruprecht, 1987) 122–29; L. E. **Keck**, "The Law of 'The Law of Sin and Death' (Romans 8:1–4): Reflections on the Spirit and Ethics in Paul," in *The Divine Helmsman: Studies on God's Control of Human Events, presented to Lev. H. Silberman* (ed. J. L. Crenshaw and S. Sandmel; New York: KTAV, 1980) 41–57; E. **Lohse**, "ὁ νόμος τοῦ πνεύματος τῆς ζωῆς: Exegetische Anmerkungen zu Röm 8:2," in *Die Vielfalt des Neuen Testaments* (Göttingen: Vandenhoeck & Ruprecht, 1982) 128–36; S. **Lyonnet**, "Christian Freedom and the Law of the Spirit According to St Paul," in *The Christian Lives by the Spirit* (ed. I. de la Potterie and S. Lyonnet; trans. J. Morris; Staten Island: Alba House, 1971) 145–74; H. **Räisänen**, "Das 'Gesetz des Glauben' (Röm 3:27) und das 'Gesetz des Geistes' (Röm 8:2)," *NTS* 26 (1979/80) 101–17; K. **Stalder**, *Werk*, 387–487; N. T. **Wright**, *Climax*, 193–216.

[132] This especially crucial νῦν has been (typically) omitted by the first hand of D (also sy^p).

[133] For understandable reasons, the later manuscript tradition added from v. 4, first the words "who walk not in keeping with the flesh" (A D[1] Ψ 81 365 629 pc vg) and finally the whole phrase, "who walk not in keeping with the flesh, but in keeping with the Spirit" (MajT a sy^h). These are secondary additions, since one can scarcely imagine the situation in which these words would have been omitted, either accidentally or deliberately, had they been originally in the text.

[134] The second singular σε is found in most—and certainly the best—of the early evidence, both Greek and versional (א B F G 1506* 1739* a b sy^p Tertullian Ambro-

At the end of the long litany describing the intense sense of helplessness that one feels who, while living in the flesh and mastered by sin, is
confronted by God's good and holy Law, Paul's "I" cries out, "O wretched
man that I am; who can deliver me from this 'body of death'?" Whatever
else, Paul simply cannot leave his "wretched man" there, and he is thus
compelled to offer the divine solution immediately at the end of that cry:
"Thanks be to God, [deliverance has come] through our Lord Jesus
Christ." At the same time, however, he had not yet "summed up" the
argument of 7:14–23, which despite its intensely personal form is argument nonetheless. So rather than immediately following up on the divine
response of v. 25a with the words of our present text, he first (v. 25b)
offers a summation[135] of what had been said that elicited such a cry. Thus
Paul created what is for us the enigmatic flow of thought in vv. 24–25.[136]
Crucial for our concerns is the repetition in v. 25b of the two "laws" from
vv. 22 and 23: the Law of God, Torah, which brought about this whole
discussion in the first place; and the "law of sin," to which those before
and outside of Christ are held captive because they are yet in the flesh.
Both of these "laws" are what 8:1–13 are responding to.[137]

---

siaster); the first person singular με is read by most of the rest (A D MajT lat sy[h] sa
Clement [Ψ bo Epiphanius read ἡμᾶς]). UBS[4] gives the σε reading a {B}, while its
predecessor gave it a {D} (see the committee's rationale for such reading in Metzger,
Textual Commentary, 516). By all counts the second singular reading is to be preferred
as the original. The possibility of an inadvertent error (the repeating of the preceding
-σεν) is fanciful in this case (it argues for carelessness across two textual traditions
at a very early stage, and of a kind from which the early Egyptian witnesses are
generally quite free). On the other hand, the σε is the obviously more difficult reading
in every way. In light of the argumentation of 7:7–25, one can well imagine a scribe
conforming σε to με, while it is nearly impossible to account for the reverse under
any circumstances, even accidental. So also Cranfield 1.376–77. For a suggested reason
for the σε see n. 158 below.

[135] That this is a summation of vv. 14–24 is evidenced both by the strong
inferential conjunction "therefore" (ἄρα οὖν; cf. 8:12) and the content, which basically
repeats what was said in v. 23. The new element, the verb "serve," picks up the
language of 6:6 ("no longer serve sin") and 7:6 ("serve [God] in newness of Spirit").

[136] As in all such difficult moments of argumentation in Paul, some (e.g.,
Bultmann, "Glössen im Römerbrief," *TLZ* 72 [1949] 197–202; Käsemann 211) would
"resolve" the issue by suggesting interpolations (vv. 25a, b, and v. 1); but as always
this doesn't resolve much. It may make Paul out to be a tidier writer (or "theologian")
than he actually was, but it never explains how *someone else* created such conspicuous
difficulties for himself and others by fashioning such interpolations.

[137] On the question of whether νόμος refers to Torah in both of these clauses, see
n. 118 above. While some have "no basic problem" (Wright's language) with seeing
the word refer to Torah throughout, I find it a most unnatural reading of the text,
especially in light of the two qualifying genitives. The first, "of God," is most likely
possessive or descriptive (i.e., God's Law, or the Law that has to do with God) and is
used expressly to delineate the good and holy Torah from sin (hence the way Paul
"exonerates" Torah). The genitive with the second "law" (and note the strong
adversative δέ) is most likely appositional, although it could also be descriptive (i.e.,

1 "*Now*[138] therefore," Paul begins his response, again employing the "before" and "after" form of argumentation from 6:17–23 and 7:4–6. Despite the present tense of the verbs in v. 25b, the split "I" is pictured as under "servitude"—to the two forms of "law" which describe life before and outside of Christ. What the person described in vv. 14–25 lacks is the freedom that comes from being "in Christ Jesus." Hence the cry of despair, and the reason for Paul's immediate response in 7:25a, "through Jesus Christ our Lord," which is about to be explicated, first by this sentence and then in more detail in v. 3.

But before that, Paul's immediate concern is twofold: first, to describe Christ's work in terms of its net results, "no condemnation,"[139] precisely because of the "[deliverance] through our Lord Jesus Christ" (v. 25a). For those[140] who *once* knew only despair there is *now* no condemnation. The future judgment and condemnation by God which we all so richly deserve have been put into our past, laid upon Christ Jesus (v. 3), so that we might be set free from both of the former "laws" (vv. 2–3) which brought about the condemnation expressed in the cry of 7:24. Second, Paul is setting up his next argument, which picks up on the statements about our former life "in the flesh" and present life "in the Spirit" from 7:5–6. Both of these concerns are united in v. 2, where the Spirit is now brought into the argument in a thoroughgoing way.

2 The "for" with which this sentence begins suggests that Paul is about to explain what he has just asserted in v. 1. Indeed, as suggested above, this sentence serves as the "lead in," a sort of "thesis sentence," to the whole of vv. 2–30.[141] But more is going on here, and the "more"

---

the "law" consisting of sin itself); this "law" is what holds people captive and therefore incapable of responding to God's Law.

[138] Gk. νῦν; cf. the similar usage in 5:9, 11; 6:19, 21; 11:30, 31 (cf. the νυνὶ δέ in 7:6), which in each case is unambiguously temporal, not logical. So here, despite some to the contrary (e.g., Hodge 249, Haldane 311, Hendriksen 245—almost always on the basis that 7:5–25 and 8:1 refer to the same person simultaneously). To make this other than temporal in this argument is go full in the face not only of the context but also of the clear and consistent usage of the adverb throughout this letter. Cf. inter alia Meyer 40, Denney 644, Leenhardt 301, Dunn 415, Morris 300, Ziesler 201.

[139] Gk. κατάκριμα, which can refer either to the process of "judgment" or its result, "condemnation." That Paul intends "condemnation" here is demonstrated by his use of the cognate verb two sentences later (v. 3), where it can only mean "condemned." In either case, it is surely to be understood eschatologically, referring to the end-time judgment (with its condemnation), which in Christ Jesus has been taken out of the believer's future and put into the past.

[140] Note that when Paul moves into present realities, he moves from the first singular (v. 25) to the third plural (here), which in typical fashion becomes first plural in v. 4—which is what makes the second singular "you" in v. 2 so striking.

[141] Cf. Keck, "Law," 46: "This suggests that v. 2 functions as a topic sentence and that vv. 3–30 are its exposition."

is what makes the sentence so complex.[142] The problems (for us) are several: What means "the *law* of the Spirit of life?" What does the prepositional phrase "in Christ Jesus" modify? What, then, is the relationship between these two phrases and the freedom from the other law, that of sin and death? And, finally, in light of 7:25b, to what does the "law of sin and death" refer, to both or only one of the former two "laws"? The way through for us is to note several of the distinctive features of the sentence, with special focus on what is here said about the Spirit.

1. The place to begin is with the phrase that has created so many of our difficulties, "the law of the Spirit of life." This is surely an ad hoc creation,[143] predicated on the word play on "law" that has already been going on in 7:22–23 and 25b. The divine antidote to the two former "laws" (sin *and* Torah), Paul declares, is yet a third "law"! This usage reinforces our understanding that the language "law" in relationship to sin and death (7:22–23, 25) is a word play, pure and simple. Such a rhetorical device is made possible, to be sure, because νόμος ("law") can also mean something close to "principle, rule, or norm." But to translate "the law of sin" with any of those words[144] is to kill it. Since it is a word play that works better in Greek than in English, our best way out is to put quotes around "law" when it refers to something other than Torah, which has brought about the word play in the first place. Hence, "the 'law' of the Spirit of life has in Christ Jesus freed us from the 'law' of sin and death."[145] The point is that νόμος does not mean "law" at all in this sentence, at least in any substantive way.[146] This is rather Paul's way of keeping the argument alive by a striking linguistic move.[147] What he

---

[142] It is the first of several sentences in the argument that follows, in which Paul's intent seems clear enough, but which break down grammatically or get overloaded because he is trying to cover so much ground with so few words. See below on vv. 3, 10, and 15.

[143] There is simply nothing else like this in the corpus. It is hard to imagine the circumstances in which Paul on his own would ever have used language like this to refer to the activity of the Spirit.

[144] As though Paul meant "sin principle" or some such thing. See Louw and Nida, *Greek English Lexicon* §33.333.

[145] Cf. the translation in Moo 502.

[146] Although one might agree with Wood (*Life*, 22) that Paul "did not cast off restraint when he came to Christ; he submitted to a new law," it is doubtful that Paul himself intended something like this. This sentence has to do not with ethics but with deliverance.

[147] Cf. Sanders (*PLJP*, 98) who also calls it a "word play," and Loane (*Hope*, 21): "a phrase of tremendous paradox coined by St. Paul to clinch his point." This, of course, is hardly a universal view! Most, calling the usage "figurative" (or not describing it at all), prefer to give the word some substance here: most often, "power," "inner principle," or "binding authority" (which is true even of Moo 507, despite his observation that the usage in both instances in this verse "has more rhetorical than material significance"). A growing number, following a lead that goes back to Chrysostom, prefer to see here yet another reference to Torah (cf. inter alia Lohse,

intends, of course, is that the Spirit *of life* is God's response to the "living death" of those who are under Torah and captive to sin.[148]

2. By starting his sentence with this arresting word play as its grammatical subject, however, Paul has also set in motion some of the other difficulties we encounter, especially the placement of the phrase, "in Christ Jesus." This phrase could modify "the law of the Spirit of life," which it immediately follows.[149] This would mean that both the grammatical and conceptual subject of the sentence is "law," which Paul then modifies three times: "law" itself is modified by "of the Spirit," which is modified by "of life," which in turn is modified by "in Christ Jesus." If so, then "of life" would probably be a qualitative genitive (= the Spirit who is characterized by life), and "in Christ Jesus" would indicate the source

---

Snodgrass, Wright, Dunn 416–17; for more extensive bibliography see Moo 505n7 and Sanders 15n26). For this view see nn. 118 and 137 above, and the critique in the next note.

[148] Cf. Käsemann 215–16. Many object to this view (see preceding note) on the twofold grounds (1) that Paul often speaks *positively* about the Law in Romans (e.g., 3:1–2, 31; 4:16; 9:3–5; 10:4 [from one point of view]) and therefore that this whole discussion (from 7:7) which tries to vindicate Torah should be seen in a more favorable light than traditional Protestantism tends to do; and (2) that in any case one should expect a consistency in the use of words unless there are self-evident reasons to think otherwise. This is not the place for a larger discussion, but from my perspective the resolution to (1) lies with our accepting the ambivalence Paul himself expresses throughout this letter, rather than to try to line up all νόμος references on one side or the other. For Paul there is both continuity and discontinuity; at times the emphasis will lie with continuity, rightly so—a "new covenant" after all does not mean the former covenant was bad. Indeed it was not "bad" at all. Its content and purpose were right on; what it lacked was the power to deal effectively with sin, on the one hand, and to give life, on the other. But precisely because Christ has done what Torah could not do regarding sin and righteousness (= right standing) and the Spirit has done regarding life and righteousness (= obedience), there is also discontinuity. I see the greater emphasis in Romans on discontinuity; the scholars mentioned in the preceding note see greater emphasis on continuity. As to (2) the fact that Paul so regularly allows the ad hoc moment to dictate his language, so that different nuances of the same word and word plays of this kind abound in his letters, tends to make the appeal to consistency fall on deaf ears. Not only so, but in this case the express use of "*another* 'law' " to describe "sin" and the qualifier "*God's* Law" to describe Torah, plus the clear bifurcation of "laws" in v. 25b, are for me the "self-evident reasons to think otherwise." At the same time, what *is* lacking is some signal that by this language of differentiation (which by normal usage implies two different "laws") Paul intended rather to point to a dual understanding of the one Law—which could have been expressed clearly and unambiguously. Cf. the critique in Räisänen ("Gesetz," 113–16) and Moo 505–6.

[149] As, e.g., the KJV, RSV, NRSV, NASB, Weymouth; cf. Godet 296, Denney 644, Michel 189, Leenhardt 252, Ziesler 202, Wright, *Climax*, 209. The majority (e.g., Meyer, SH, Hendriksen, Cranfield, Dunn, Moo, Loane) adopt the position taken here (Murray, Harrison, and Morris are undecided). Godet's objection that Paul in this case would have used the pronoun ἐν αὐτῷ is more rhetorical than substantive—after all, this could cut both ways!

of the life that characterizes the Spirit.[150] Although possible, this makes for a very cumbersome reading of the text; but of even greater concern, it seems to miss Paul's own point by a considerable margin.

The difficulty has been set up by Paul's starting with this unusual subject, "the law of the Spirit of life." The appropriate verb for the sentence, it should be noted, is the one Paul uses (ἠλευθέρωσεν, "set free").[151] But this combination sets Paul up for something that is less than exact theologically, so he adds the prepositional phrase "in Christ Jesus" (= "by the work of Christ") before the verb. Thus his sentence, strange as it may seem at first to our ears, makes perfectly good sense: The reason there is now no condemnation (in spite of the other two "laws") to those in Christ Jesus, is that God has provided a third "law," the Spirit of life—by setting us free, *through Christ Jesus*, from the second "law," that of sin that leads to death. Thus the logic of the sentence and its parts, not the grammar as such, must superintend our understanding. The *grammar* reads that the "law of the Spirit of life" sets us free; the *logic* has it (1) that Christ Jesus set us free from sin and death (which v. 3 will spell out in more detail), but (2) that God's current, ongoing remedy for sin and death is the indwelling, life-giving Spirit.[152] Our sentence says that in a highly condensed fashion.

3. The word play on "law" in the first instance also sheds light on the second reference to "law." On the one hand, since the present argument resumes what had been left hanging in 7:4–6, and since in earlier passages such as 4:15 ("Torah works wrath; where there is no Torah there is no transgression")[153] Torah has been linked directly to sin and death, it is possible that "the 'law' of sin and death" from which one has been freed *also* includes Torah. That is, one has been freed from Torah, which in its own way has also led to sin and death.[154] But there are two good reasons for thinking otherwise.[155]

First, at least part of the design of 7:7–25 has been to correct any wrong impressions about the relationship of the Law to sin and death that his earlier statements may have (understandably!) created. Hence, the first point of reference for the present phrase must be the usage in 7:23 and 25, where indwelling sin has been referred to as the "law" of

---

[150] Cf. Weymouth's translation: "The Spirit's law—life in Christ Jesus."

[151] For at least two reasons: (1) the "wretched person's" relationship to the "law of sin" in 7:23 is "imprisonment" and in 7:25b is "servitude"; yet (2) the alternative words, "redeemed" (Gal 4:5) or "release" (Rom 7:6), do not respond adequately to the word "condemnation" in v. 1.

[152] Cf. Keck, "Law," 45.

[153] See n. 88 above.

[154] So, inter alia, Haldane 317–18, Hodge 250, Barrett 155, Dunn 418–49, and those mentioned in nn. 118, 147, and 148 above.

[155] As most commentaries (e.g., Meyer, Godet, Liddon, Denney, SH, Hendriksen, Leenhardt, Harrison, Ziesler, Moo; cf. Loane, *Hope*, 18).

sin. That this "law" is also here referred to as "of death" results both from the logic of the preceding argument, that sin alone leads to death, and (especially) from the preceding designation of the Spirit as "of life."

Second, although I would not press this point were the preceding one not convincing on its own, there seems thus to be a kind of chiastic structure to the "law" talk that begins in 7:13:

A 7:13 The (first) Law, Torah, is good, just, holy.

    B 7:14–24, 25b But the first Law was "used" by another "law," Sin, which in turn led to death.

        C 8:2a Enter the third "law," the Spirit of life.

    B′ 8:2b The third "law" sets one free from the second "law," both sin *and* death.

A′ 8:3–4 The third "law" fulfills the intent of the first Law, which was incapable of dealing with sin and thus producing righteousness.

What is crucial to our purposes is that the second "law" is now designated, in contrast to "the Spirit of life," as "the 'law' of sin *and* death." In light of the preceding argument that can only mean "the 'law' of sin that issues in death." The Spirit *of life*, Paul asserts, sets God's people free from *both* of these aspects of the second "law." He will spell this out in the argument that follows: in vv. 3–8 he sets forth the Spirit as God's response to the "law" of sin; in vv. 9–11 the Spirit *of life* is also offered as God's response to the "law" of death that issues from sin. Hence this serves as the "topic sentence" for the argument that follows.

4. That leads us, then, back to the phrase "the Spirit of life," which is perhaps the single most significant designation of the Spirit in the Pauline corpus. He is the Spirit of life first of all precisely because he is the Spirit of God. Whatever else may be true of the OT understanding of God, Yahweh, by his very name, is forever known in Israel as "the living God." This is what marks Yahweh off from all other gods. He is the *living* One, and the source of life in all that lives. Paul reflects this usage in his earliest letter to a Gentile community, which had turned from idols to serve "the living and true God" (1 Thes 1:9–10). Therefore, because he is the Spirit of God, the Spirit is also *the Spirit of life*.[156]

But that terminological background serves simply as the predicate for Paul's current concern, namely, that the Spirit is the source of life for all who come to God through Christ Jesus. He is the Spirit who gives life, over against the death that issues from the "law of sin"; he is the Spirit who gives life and peace over against the death associated with life in the flesh (v. 6); and despite the death of the body, to be indwelt by the

---

[156] This assumes, of course, on the basis of normal usage (Moo 530) that the genitive "of life" modifies "Spirit" not "law" (contra Bruce 160).

Spirit of Christ means life, both now and forever (vv. 10–11). The Spirit of God is thus the Spirit who is the source of life for those who believe.

This understanding, of course, assumes the correctness of our exegesis of the phrase "in Christ Jesus," noted above. As vv. 3 and 10 make clear, Paul's interest in inserting "in Christ Jesus" into this sentence is not that Christ's death provides life for believers—although it does that indeed. Rather, the Spirit himself is the source of that life through the believer's *experience* of freedom in Christ—for both Jew and Gentile alike and together, it must be emphasized, since that is, after all, the main point of everything.

Just as in Gal 5:25 (q.v.), where mention of the crucifixion is followed by the assertion that "we live *by the Spirit*," so here Paul intends "the Spirit of life" to refer to the life that believers now live as the direct result of the Spirit's indwelling. This is also in keeping with 2 Cor 3:6, where in a context of the new covenant's superseding the old, the Spirit is designated as "the life-giving Spirit." As noted on that passage, this usage reflects Ezekiel 37, where the Spirit of God breathes on the dry bones and they "live." Whatever else may be said of the Spirit, primary to Paul's understanding is that he is the Spirit who brings life and who is the source of the life that one consequently leads.

5. A final word. It is possible for us to become so involved in the debate over Paul's use of "law" language in this sentence that we miss its main point: that Paul is now bringing the Spirit into the picture in terms of the deliverance/freedom from the tyranny of sin that has already been expounded in 6:1–23. In contrast to the use of "freedom" language in Galatians, where it referred exclusively to the freedom of God's children vis-à-vis their former "enslavement" to Torah observance (and by extension to "the elemental spirits of the universe"), in this letter "freedom" language refers predominantly to "deliverance" from the tyranny of sin. This has been argued vigorously in 6:1–23 as our inheritance through identification with Christ's death and resurrection. Now the emphasis will rest on the role of the Spirit in this freedom. The key to this lies in the language of "indwelling." In 7:17 and 20 sin, personified as the tyrannical master of those who live outside Christ, is said to "dwell in" such a person. The freedom from this "law" of sin and death comes from "the law" of the life-giving Spirit, who, after Christ has effectively dealt with sin on the cross, now "indwells" the believer in the very place sin once lived.[157]

Deliverance from sin, of course, does not mean sinlessness or freedom from "the desire of the flesh"; but it does mean deliverance from its tyrannical hold on our lives so that we are no longer enslaved to it, sold as slaves to its tyrannical mastery, as the "wretched person" in 7:14–25.

---

[157] Cf. Keck, "Law," 50–51.

Such a person, Paul cries out in 7:24a, is "living in death." God's twofold response to such tyranny is the work of Christ and the Spirit. As he will go on to explain in vv. 3–4, God broke the back of sin's tyranny by presenting Christ as the ultimate sin-offering. But the realization of that freedom comes from the life-giving Spirit, signaled in this text as the one who, because of the work of Christ, has freed us from the enslavement to sin that leads to death. That is the freedom, both now and finally in the resurrection of the body, that Paul will spell out in the argument that follows. But before that he needs to unpack this dense sentence theologically, which is what vv. 3–4 are all about.

What finally is crucial to note, therefore, and will be noted again on vv. 9–11, is that Paul simply cannot bring himself to enter into a long discussion of the role of the Spirit in Christian life without making sure that that role is explicitly and inextricably woven together with the work of Christ, whose Spirit, after all, he is. This interlacing of the Spirit's activity to the work of Christ becomes even more clear in vv. 3–4.[158]

ROMANS 8:3–4[159]

[3]*For what the Law was unable to do in that it was weakened through the flesh, God, having sent his own Son in the likeness of the flesh of sin and for sin [as*

---

[158] Although it is not directly related to our interests in this study, perhaps a word is in order as to how one might understand the unusual second person singular that appears as the object of "set free" in this sentence. It is possible, on the one hand, that Paul "means" nothing by it; i.e., just as in Gal 4:7, he uses the second singular to individualize for his readers what God has done for them in Christ Jesus (cf. MHT 3.39). On the other hand, in light of the preceding argument and the regular appearance of the interlocutor throughout, this may be a word directed toward him. This is an especially attractive option, since the interlocutor may be assumed to underlie the questions in Rom 7:7, 13. Since this person is best understood as one raising questions from the Jewish Christian side, especially in his concern over Torah and Paul's setting it aside through the work of Christ, Paul would here be addressing the interlocutor as a way of pulling him into the preceding argument. In that case, the "I" in what has preceded may well be representative throughout of the unenviable position into which the interlocutor has placed himself by trying to maintain loyalty to Torah. Thus Paul speaks to the interlocutor's situation, but indirectly through his own person, since he had been there once himself. But now, on the other side of things, when he comes to freedom in Christ, he addresses the interlocutor directly, "The law of the Spirit of life has through Christ Jesus set *you* free from the law of sin and death." That, at least, seems to be a viable option and could make sense of both the "I" in ch. 7 and the "you" here.

[159] *Bibliography:* V. P. **Branick**, "The Sinful Flesh of the Son of God (Rom. 8:3): A Key Image of Pauline Theology," *CBQ* 47 (1985) 246–62; F. M. **Gillman**, "Another Look at Romans 8:3: 'In the Likeness of Sinful Flesh,' " *CBQ* 49 (1987) 597–604; R. W. **Thompson**, "How Is the Law Fulfilled in Us? An Interpretation of Rom 8:4," *Louvain Studies* 11 (1986) 31–40; T. C. G. **Thornton**, "The Meaning of καὶ περὶ ἁμαρτίας in Romans viii.3," *JTS* 22 (1971) 515–17; N. T. **Wright**, "The Meaning of περὶ ἁμαρτίας

a sin-offering],[160] *condemned sin in the flesh,* [4]*in order that the righteous requirement of the Law might be fulfilled in us, who walk not in keeping with the flesh but in keeping with the Spirit.*

This grammatically complex[161] but theologically loaded[162] sentence functions to explain by elaboration the "topic sentence" in v. 2; at the same time it brings Torah back into the picture. Thus Paul returns to the concerns of 7:5–6, that the time of Torah has been brought to an end through Christ and has been replaced by the Spirit. But at the same time he is offering the theological—not to mention historical and experiential—grounds for his twofold assertion in v. 2 that freedom from sin and death has been achieved by Christ Jesus and realized for believers through the life-giving Spirit. In doing so, Paul goes back to the forensic language of v. 1 and explains our deliverance in terms of the reversal of "condemnation"—that which was formerly our due has been transferred to sin itself, the sin that resides in our flesh.[163] As noted above, Paul simply will not move on to talk about Spirit activity without grounding it squarely upon the work of Christ.[164] But neither should one, by concentrating solely on what is here said about Christ, lose the *aim* of the argument, which remains the same as it began in v. 2: deliverance from the tyranny of sin, effected through the atoning work of Christ, as an experienced ongoing reality, is the work of the indwelling, life-giving Spirit.[165]

The ungrammatical nature of the sentence is most likely due to two factors: Paul's concern over Torah—as ineffective and therefore now obsolete—which caused him to start with this matter; and his tendency, when referring to the work of Christ, to make it his central focus. These two concerns simply collide grammatically.[166] Nonetheless, despite the

---

in Romans 8:3," in *Climax,* 220–25; J. A. **Ziesler,** "The Just Requirement of the Law (Romans 8:4)," *AusBR* 35 (1987) 77–82.

[160] For this translation see the discussion below; the phrase was omitted in a few witnesses (1912 pc), almost certainly due to homoeoteleuton.

[161] In my translation I have tried to reproduce the complexities so that the following comments will make some sense. This sentence, even more than the preceding (v. 2), seems to be the result of Paul's desire to get in all the necessary particulars.

[162] Cf. Wright, *Climax,* 200, who observes: "vv. 3–4 . . . form . . . the driving force of the whole paragraph [vv. 1–11]."

[163] Imagery that is possible, it should be noted, because of the personification of sin in the preceding argument of 7:7–25.

[164] See Gal 5:24 above and v. 10 below.

[165] On this whole question see esp. Käsemann 218.

[166] The opening clause was probably intended as the object of a sentence that had "God" as its subject, with a predicate that could take this clause as its object (e.g., "did, effected, worked out"). Thus: "What the Law could not do, God did through Christ, etc." What appears to have happened, however, is that after dictating the subject, "God," instead of offering the verb, Paul immediately launched into his ultimate concern—Christ, God's means of accomplishing what the Law could not do.

complexities, Paul's intent is relatively clear and his emphases stand out: (1) Torah's time is past, because (2) of what Christ has done to (3) sin and the flesh, and (4) its purpose is now fulfilled by the Spirit. The net result is another of those profound, creed-like, soteriological moments in Paul,[167] none of which is very much like any of the others—because they are so ad hoc and thus linguistically adapted to their own contexts—but most of which are either explicitly or implicitly Trinitarian. This one is no exception.

Our chief concern is v. 4: the role of the Spirit in "the fulfillment of the righteous requirement of Torah," where Paul returns to the theme begun in v. 2. In order to get there, a few observations are needed about the role of Torah and Christ and the matter of sin and the flesh.

1. That the concern is once more with Torah—as obsolete—is made plain by the way the sentence begins and ends. The opening clause, "what the Law was unable to do in that it was left weak through the flesh," reproduces the point of 7:14–24 with slightly different language. It is placed first because this is what Paul now wants to emphasize, which means that the argument that began in 7:1 is not quite finished. The emphases are precisely those of the preceding argument: the Law, a good thing in itself, was ill-equipped to take on the flesh (cf. 7:14); in fact, the Law was left in a weakened state by the flesh, meaning that in the matter of sin our "flesh" was stronger than Torah;[168] indeed the flesh proved Torah helpless, thus "weakened." What the Law was incapable[169] of doing, of course, in its "weakened condition" was to deal with the problem of indwelling sin,[170] which issues in death.[171] This failure of Torah, which

---

And right there the sentence breaks down, because in describing the work of Christ he reverted to the concerns of the preceding sentence and argument—the flesh and sin. Sin, after all, is the problem, not Torah. Torah was incapable of doing anything about sin, which rendered it obsolete in light of what Christ *did do*. Thus, once having mentioned Christ as the "Son whom God had sent," Paul then describes both what Christ did and how he did it; and in so doing, Paul started the sentence over and left the opening clause to dangle. Not tidy, but explicable. Cf. Moo 506.

[167] See the list in n. 39 (p. 48) in ch. 3.

[168] Thus as in 7:14–25 Paul by this phrase ("weakened through the flesh") both exonerates the Law and also points out its failure. Cf. Cranfield 1.379.

[169] There has been considerable debate as to whether τὸ ἀδύνατον is "active" or "passive" in force, emphasizing respectively either Torah's inability to do anything or its "powerlessness" (Wright). While I tend to join those who think it more active, in light of the next clause, it seems that Paul comes out at pretty much the same place whichever way one understands it. Cf. Moo 509.

[170] At issue throughout is not the problem of forgiveness, i.e., of dealing with "sins," but with the tyrannical nature of indwelling sin.

[171] At least, one would assume so from what is actually said in this sentence (and so most commentaries). Wright (*Climax*, 202) and others, on the basis of 8:2 and 6 (cf. 7:12), which emphasize the Spirit as the source of life, prefer to express the failure of Torah more positively, as the failure to bestow life (cf. Gal 3:21). While this may be Torah's ultimate failure, especially as depicted in the covenantal language of 2 Cor 3:4–6, it is difficult to see that as even latent in this passage—and in any case it does

appears as the first concern, leads to the central focus of the sentence: Christ as God's way of effectively dealing with both sin and the flesh.

Torah emerges once again at the end of the sentence, where our primary interest lies, in language that echoes 7:12, "the righteous requirement[172] of the Law." In rendering Torah obsolete and in effectively dealing with sin, Christ has opened the way for the Spirit to "fulfill" the very purpose for which Torah existed but which it was unable to provide: righteousness.[173] Thus at both ends of the sentence—primarily through the work of Christ, but in the last instance through the ongoing work of the Spirit—God has brought the time of the Law to an end, the very point of 7:1–6. Even though one may recognize Torah for what it is, God's good and holy thing, its ineffectiveness with regard to sin has finally rendered it basically finished; it is now "the *oldness* of the letter," replaced through the effective work of Christ by "the *newness* of the Spirit."[174]

2. The work of Christ is the obvious central concern of the sentence; it is also the matter in this text on which the greatest amount of ink has been spilt. As with Gal 4:5, with which this passage has some similarities, I do not intend here to try to resolve or even to discuss fully the majority of the issues raised, except to note that in a condensed way Paul seems to refer both to Christ's preexistence (and thus to his incarnation) and to his atoning sacrifice.

First, as to Christ's preexistence and incarnation, Paul neither argues for such, nor is such an understanding necessarily essential to his present point.[175] Nonetheless, such realities seem to be the natural *pre-*

---

not seem to be present in the way that Wright asserts and adopts as the basis for much of his argument.

[172] Gk. τὸ δικαίωμα τοῦ νόμου. This noun is found in Paul only in this letter (1:32; 2:26; 5:16, 18; in 1:32 and 2:26 with the modifier "of the Law") and seems to be another example of a concretizing noun formed with the -μα suffix (see 5:15–16 above, on χάρισμα and παράπτωμα). Thus it does not mean "the righteousness found in the Law," as much as "the righteous requirement of the Law." Although these may ultimately come out at the same point, the present usage emphasizes the "concrete expressions of righteous behavior" called for by the Law. In this case it seems also to hark back to the adjective δίκαιος in 7:12, where it actually modifies "commandment."

[173] Here one should not miss the grammar of the sentence, which puts this matter in the form of a purpose clause, as the *reason* for Christ's having done what Torah could not do, namely, to deal effectively with sin. This in turn gives reason to pause regarding Wright's suggestion (*Climax*, 202) that Torah's real failure was its inability to give life (see n. 171 above).

[174] With that, we should note further, Paul is basically done with Torah in the argument. The whole issue will be raised again in 9:31, as Paul discusses God's faithfulness, despite Israel's unfaithfulness (in chs. 9–11). Although see Wright, *Climax*, 201, who argues (1) that in 8:1–11 Paul is still "vindicating" Torah, and (2) therefore that vv. 7–8 serve as a kind of climax to this recapitulation of 7:7–25.

[175] As has often been pointed out (e.g., Käsemann 217, Moo 510–11).

supposition of Paul's language. Despite some occasional demurrers to the contrary,[176] the threefold combination of "having sent," "his *own* Son," and "in the likeness of sinful flesh," which assumes that Christ had not experienced "flesh" before he was sent, bears witness in its own way to this theological perspective.[177] To put all of that in another way, given Paul's belief in Christ's preexistence and incarnation from other passages,[178] that such a presupposition lies behind the language makes far more sense of that language than otherwise.

Second, as to Christ's atoning sacrifice, even though it may not appear to be mentioned directly in this sentence, two matters favor its being understood. As above, there is the *presuppositional* aspect, discussed more fully below, of the language "condemned sin in the flesh" and "as a sin-offering." Furthermore, this sentence occurs a considerable distance into the letter, and anyone who has read thus far does not need to be told explicitly that atonement took place through the death of Christ.

The point to make, of course, is that precisely this understanding is what makes Paul's argument effectual. In 7:7–24 he has grappled with the failure of the Law at the very point of its inability to do something effective with regard to sin. In response to the cry of despair in v. 24 he offered the divine solution, "through Jesus Christ our Lord." Now we have the *how* of that triumphant response to human despair. As elsewhere,[179] Paul uses language from Torah itself to speak about its obsolescence with the coming of Christ. Thus (1) by his having come in the likeness of the very thing that needed to be dealt with, the flesh with its sin, and (2) by his dealing with "sin in the flesh"—indeed *condemning*[180] it—by himself becoming "a sin-offering," (3) Christ became the eternal remedy for sin where Torah offered only a partial remedy through its sin-offerings.

3. Much of the difficulty with the Christ material in this sentence has been raised by Paul's use of flesh and sin language when describing the

---

[176] See esp. Dunn 420–21, who thinks the "Adam-christology" latent in some of this language rules against such a view; cf. his *Christology*, 38–40, 44–45, where this is argued in greater detail. Why one could not have an Adam-christology with a presuppositional understanding of Christ as the Incarnate One remains a singular mystery to me.

[177] So most commentators. Cf. Käsemann 216: "a liturgical statement which describes the incarnation of the preexistent Son of God as the salvation of the world."

[178] Such seems absolutely certain from 2 Cor 8:9; 1 Cor 8:6; and Phil 2:6 (although some object to this latter); cf. the discussion on Gal 4:5. One is struck by how often the argumentation of those who oppose such a view in Paul takes the form of trying to "get around" what seems clearly to be at work in the text.

[179] See esp. in this regard, Gal 3:13–14.

[180] Gk. κατέκρινεν; the word play with v. 1 seems obvious and intentional. We have no "condemnation" because Christ "condemned" the very thing that would have led to our condemnation, sin itself.

work of Christ. As at other such times in Paul, we have manufactured some of the difficulties ourselves by our tendency to read the text as a kind of theologoumenon (theological statement) on its own, apart from the present context that alone offers the *reason* for such language. Thus, if we may not be sure of the finer nuance of the three phrases, "in the likeness of the flesh of sin," "and for sin," and "condemned sin in the flesh," we may be reasonably sure as to why Paul has used this unique language in this particular instance. All of the "sin" and "flesh" language in this passage is directly attributable to Paul's singular concern, the intended contrast between *what Christ did* and *what the Law was incapable of doing*—namely, dealing effectively with sin and the flesh. This observation should at least ease our way into dealing with these phrases. As with the play on "law" language above, the word "flesh" affords Paul the flexibility needed to carry all the points he wants to make.

(a) The first phrase "in the likeness of the flesh of sin" harks back to this combination that began in 7:14 ("I am *fleshly*, sold under *sin*"), picked up again in vv. 18–20. In v. 18 "in me" is defined as "in my flesh," which in v. 20 is expressed in terms of "the *sin* that dwells *in me* [= 'in my flesh']." Paul now says of Christ that he came "in the *likeness*" of such, meaning that he was similar to our "flesh" in some respects but dissimilar in others.[181] The similarity in this case is to be found in the flexibility of the word "flesh," which now has a slightly altered nuance from that in 7:14–20; that is, Christ came "in the flesh," to be sure, and therefore identified with us in our flesh, our humanness, even though ours was riddled with sin. But his was not "flesh" of this latter kind, the flesh now understood as fallen and opposed to God. Thus he came "in the *likeness* of the flesh *of sin*," meaning that he shared "flesh" with us all, but only in the "likeness" of our "flesh" which in our case was laden down with sin.

---

[181] Cf. BAGD (on ὁμοίωμα), "It is safe to assert that [Paul's] use of our word is to bring out both that Jesus in his earthly career was similar to sinful men yet not absolutely like them." That this is Paul's intent, *pace* recent suggestions to the contrary (e.g., Branick, Gillman), seems certain from the use of this word (and this is so whether it means "likeness" or "form"). Had Paul intended a more complete identification with us in our sinfulness, he would surely have said simply "in sinful flesh." All the words of this phrase are necessary (i.e., "likeness," "flesh," "of sin") because of the preceding argument. Christ must effectively deal with sin, thus come in "our flesh" (which in our case is full of sin), but only in the "likeness" of such, because though "in the flesh" he was not in sin (as 2 Cor 5:21 makes clear). Thus, despite our (correct) use of the adjective "sinful" to translate the genitive "of sin," Paul did not in fact use the adjective but a genitive qualifier. Because he is speaking of Christ's incarnation, it is "flesh" characterized in our case by sin, but not in his. But see Cranfield 1.379–82, who argues for the other side of things, that even though he was Son of God and shared our humanness, he nonetheless never ceased to be the eternal Son of God.

(b) To this clause Paul immediately appends, "and for sin," which almost certainly means "and as a sin-offering." That is, God sent his own Son so that "in the likeness of our flesh," riddled with sin as ours was, he might be a sin-offering in our behalf. On its own, of course, this phrase could be understood simply to reflect Christ's death as "for our sins," as in 1 Cor 15:3. But it is not on its own. In the Greek this phrase is the exact language found repeatedly in the LXX as a translation for "sin-offering."[182] Very likely that is what Paul intends here, especially in a context where Christ is seen as accomplishing what Torah could not do and thus bringing "fulfillment" to the aim of Torah.

(c) Finally, by Christ's coming "in the likeness of the flesh of sin" and thus becoming a sin-offering, God effectively "condemned sin in the flesh." Sin has absolutely dominated Paul's concern from 5:12—sin, which Torah not only could do nothing about but actually ended up exacerbating. Through his presenting Christ as a sin-offering, God has judged and condemned the very sin that stood in judgment against us and condemned us. But what does "in the flesh" refer to in this clause, to the flesh of Christ's incarnation/crucifixion just mentioned or to our flesh, which is the reason for his death in the first place? The best answer would seem to be that it refers to both: in his death "in the flesh" he condemned the sin that resides in our "flesh." Thus, in light of the previous phrase "in the likeness of the flesh of sin" *flesh* refers first of all to Christ's own "flesh" in which he bore our sinfulness to the cross, but in light of the argument as a whole it also refers to our flesh, that fallenness in us in which sin had its abode.[183]

Paul's concern, of course, has to do not with a theory of atonement, but with the fact of it. In Christ God has effectively dealt with sin and the flesh, not by eradicating them to be sure, but by "condemning" them— i.e., passing sentence on them in Christ—so that, on the one hand, "sin shall not rule over you" (6:14) and, on the other hand, being "in the

---

[182] Indisputably so in Lev 5:8; 6:25, 30; 7:7; 9:7, 10, 22; 10:17, 19[2x]; 14:13[2x], 19; 16:25; Num 29:11; very likely so in many others (see Wright, *Climax*, 222n12). On this question see now, Wright, "Meaning," who adds to this linguistic data the contextual matter of "sinning inadvertently," which is always the case in the OT "sin-offering" and is paralleled in Paul's description of the "wretched person" in 7:14–25.

[183] It should be noted that this is a decidedly minority opinion. Most scholars, suggest that ἐν τῇ σαρκί modifies the verb "condemned" and not the object τὴν ἁμαρτίαν, and rightly so, given the article τὴν with ἁμαρτίαν, which one would expect to be repeated had he intended "the sin which is in the flesh." My point is that the ambiguity lies not in the present prepositional phrase, but in the preceding identification of Christ's flesh with ours and in the clear location of sin in the flesh in 7:14–25. To say, therefore, that "the sin in our flesh" is also involved is neither redundant nor restrictive (as it has been argued); rather, it simply advances Paul's point in the previous argument.

flesh" and thus following "the passions of sin" can be spoken of as in the past (7:5). This is what the Law could not do, even though it was intended to lead people into righteousness. And this is why its time of usefulness is past, because Christ did what the Law could not do because it was "weakened" by our very flesh that Christ has condemned in the cross. Since this clause is intended to elaborate on v. 2 (as the γάρ makes clear), what Paul has in sight is freedom from sin. Therefore, although the *language* of this passage is primarily judicial, so that the "condemnation" takes the form of God's sentence upon sin, nonetheless its *meaning* is that sin's stranglehold on our human lives has been broken.[184]

4. That brings us finally to the material of our central interest, v. 4, which is expressed in a purpose clause, whose final phrase is further qualified by a participial "clause" ("who walk not according to the flesh but according to the Spirit"). Thus:

> *in order that*
> the righteous requirement   might be fulfilled
>   of the Law   in us
>   who walk
>   not according to the flesh
>   but according to the Spirit

At issue is (1) whether by the language "fulfilled in us" Paul is pointing backward to the work of Christ and is therefore still thinking in more purely forensic terms (what the Law required was perfectly fulfilled in Christ's substitutionary death and becomes effective "in us" as we are "in him"),[185] or (2) whether Paul is already anticipating the participial construction and, in language similar to Gal 5:13–15, is moving toward the more behavioral aspect of righteousness effected by the Spirit as we "walk" in him.[186] That is, at issue is what is "fulfilled" and how it is so "in us."[187]

On the one hand, there is much to be said for the first position. The arguments are both linguistic and theological: (a) that the word δικαίωμα

---

[184] So Murray 282 (emphatically), Cranfield 1.382–83, and most commentaries. Some (e.g., Käsemann 216, Moo 513) downplay, or eliminate, this aspect altogether, in light of the clear juridical nature of the language of vv. 3–4; but that does not take into account the very practical concern of this passage or its role as an explanation of v. 2. A forensic judgment on sin matters little if it does not result in "freedom"—the breaking of the back of the tyranny itself. This, after all, is quite the point of the whole argument that began in 5:12.

[185] A view found, inter alia, in Calvin 160, Haldane 325–26, Hodge 254, Leenhardt 204–5, Morris 304, Moo 515–17, Loane (*Hope*, 27–28), Byrne ('*Sons,*' 93–95).

[186] As in most commentaries, many of which see this sense as so natural as not even to recognize the other option exists.

[187] Although it is arguable that at issue also is whether Paul's concern here is ultimately christological or pneumatological, and thus whether it is more theological per se (if christological) or practical (if pneumatological).

("righteous requirement"; see n. 172) is a forensic term that refers in summary form (note the singular) to "the concrete expressions of behavior that the Law calls for"; (b) that the emphasis on the passive "might be fulfilled" and the preposition "in us" imply not something we do, but something that is done for and in us by God himself, and that what is fulfilled must correspond adequately to "what the Law could not do" at the beginning of the sentence; (c) that an emphasis on our (not perfect!) behavior as the fulfilling the "righteous requirement" of the Law seems to fall short of the kind of "fulfillment" the sentence calls for and puts the emphasis on what we do rather than on what God has done in Christ. The net result, therefore, is seen as a clause that is primarily forensic and points to Jesus, who as our substitute "fulfilled the righteous requirement of the Law" in his atoning sacrifice.

On the other hand, despite the cogency and justifiable concerns of this argumentation, Paul's own concerns seem to point toward "fulfillment" in terms of our "walking in keeping with the Spirit." First, a demurrer. To see the "fulfillment" motif as pointing toward the work of the Spirit does not in fact shift the emphasis from God's activity to our own, as though by our walking in keeping with the Spirit we ourselves fulfilled the righteous requirement of Torah.[188] Paul's theological proclivities would never allow him to put it so carelessly. The emphasis is still and always on the divine initiative and activity. Nonetheless, both this sentence and the larger context indicate that Paul's ultimate concern finally finds expression in this purpose clause with its emphases on *how* the "fulfilled Torah" works out in the lives of those whom the life-giving Spirit has set free from the "law of sin and death."

Three factors lead to this conclusion. First, the believer's freedom from sin and death through the work of the life-giving Spirit is after all the point of the argument. That is, beginning in v. 2, and picking up the statement in 7:6, Paul has begun to shift his emphasis from the work of Christ to that of the Spirit. The Spirit *of life* has freed us from the tyranny of sin and death. But as we observed above, since that is not quite precise theologically Paul apparently felt compelled to point out that the ground

---

[188] A concern expressed especially in Moo 515, who has good cause for concern in light of such statements as that by Hendriksen 248: "The purpose and result of Christ's work of redemption was that his people, by means of the operation of the Holy Spirit in their hearts and lives, should strive, are striving, to fulfill the law's righteous requirement." If that is the only way one could interpret the emphasis on the Spirit which I take to be present in this clause, then one has every right to be concerned. There is no "striving" language here at all, nor is the point that we should struggle, with the Spirit's help, "to fulfill the law's righteous requirements"—as though our relationship with Torah were not really past. As Moo rightly argues, Paul's language is purely descriptive: "Fulfillment" happens "in us who walk in keeping with the Spirit." But the fulfillment lies in those who walk by the Spirit, not in the perfect sacrifice of Christ.

of that freedom lies in the atoning death of Christ. Thus the tyranny of sin, which Torah was helpless to do anything about, has been overcome through Christ's death; but the "righteous requirement"—the *real aim* of Torah, if you will—is now fulfilled in us by God through his Spirit and is evidenced by the fact of our walking in the Spirit and not in the flesh.[189]

Second, this seems to be the clear direction that the purpose clause takes. That is, by the very way he has structured this clause, Paul is moving from the work of Christ to that of the Spirit. Paul knows full well that the real problem of sin was taken care of by Christ, not by the Spirit (hence the prepositional qualifier in v. 2 "by Christ Jesus"); this is the reason for v. 3, which is to explain/elaborate on 7:25a, 8:1, and the prepositional phrase in v. 2. But the clause is constructed in a way that allows Paul to offer his own definition of "fulfillment" in the final participial construction, toward which the whole has been aiming from the beginning.

Third, all of this seems confirmed by Paul's use of "fulfillment" language in similar contexts: in Gal 5:14; 6:2, and later in this letter in 13:8–10. The Spirit himself fulfills Torah by replacing it, and he does so by enabling God's people to "fulfill" the "whole of Torah"—which in other contexts is expressed in the love command,[190] the initial fruit of the Spirit. In bringing the time of Torah to an end, God did not thereby eliminate its purpose, but through the Spirit has brought that purpose to fruition. After all, Paul does not say that Torah is now "obeyed" or "kept" or "done"—the ordinary language for Torah observance—but that what Torah requires is now "fulfilled" *in us*.[191]

As in Gal 5:14, the Spirit is regarded as the "fulfillment" of the goal or aim of Torah, namely, to bring about righteousness. Thus Torah is here described in language reminiscent of 7:12. Torah was not evil; to the contrary it was good, holy, and righteous. But it proved ineffective to bring about the righteousness that it called for. Hence the reason for

---

[189] The relationship with v. 2 seems to me to clinch the matter. There Paul has already put forward the Spirit as "the Spirit of life" over against "the law of sin that issues in death." This new "law" has through Christ Jesus set us free from the former "law." As a kind of inclusio to v. 2, the Spirit now concludes the present sentence as the way God has provided to "fulfill the righteous requirement of Torah," now that sin, flesh, and Torah have been effectively dealt with through the death of Christ. Cf. Cranfield 1.383 and especially Käsemann 218.

[190] Although see Ziesler, "Just Requirement," who argues that for Paul the issue is the tenth commandment, as noted in 7:7.

[191] Gk. ἐν ἡμῖν, which in this case almost certainly is not instrumental, but locative (had Paul intended an instrumental sense, he would surely have followed this passive verb with ὑπό with the genitive). We as his people are the sphere in which God by his Spirit has fulfilled his divine purposes set forth in the Law. Stalder, *Werk*, 406, has argued (correctly) that this reference is both to the individual and (especially) to the believing community—in this case, I would add, composed of Jew and Gentile alike. It is *in us*, in the believing community of Jew and Gentile, that God is fulfilling his purposes.

the coming of the Spirit, to effect, that is to "fulfill," the righteousness that Torah called for but could not produce.[192] But what is being fulfilled is not "Torah observance"; that is what the agitators of Galatians argued for and what Paul (apparently) assumes to lie behind the view of his present Jewish Christian interlocutor. The "righteous requirement" of Torah turns out to have little or nothing to do with "observance." It has everything to do with being conformed unto the likeness of Christ (8:29), of having one's mind renewed (by the Spirit) so as to know and live in ways that are good and pleasing to God (12:1–2). Thus when Paul comes to the particulars in 12:1–15:13, "the righteous requirement of Torah" takes the form of love of neighbor—which "fulfills Torah" (13:8)—or "righteousness, peace, and joy in the Holy Spirit"—which have nothing to do with food laws as such (14:17).

As in Gal 5:16 this "righteous requirement of Torah" is fulfilled "in us" as "we walk in keeping with the Spirit." The difference between walking πνεύματι ("in/by the Spirit") in Galatians and κατὰ πνεῦμα ("according to the Spirit") here is slight. The emphasis in Gal 5:16 is on the Spirit as the source (or sphere) of such walking, on the Spirit as "empowerment" as it were. Here the emphasis, as in Gal 5:25b, is on the character of life that such walking represents. It is *in keeping with the Spirit*, which means that by that very fact it is no longer "in keeping with the flesh"— the former way of life that has been judged and condemned through the death of Christ. That this is Paul's point is evidenced by the elaboration that follows, where the emphasis lies not on the "source" of one's walking, but on that which characterizes the two different ways of life.

Thus, also as in Gal 5:13–25, the present life of the Spirit is sharply contrasted to the former way of life, which characterizes those before and outside of Christ. Neither this text nor Galatians hints of some kind of internal warfare going on in the life of the believer between these two ways of life. Rather, on the basis of the "before" and "after" of the flesh and the Spirit already expressed in 7:5–6 and 8:2–4, they are set out as two absolutely contradictory, incompatible ways of life. Spirit people no longer walk in keeping with the flesh; those in the flesh, by way of contrast, neither "mind" the ways of the Spirit nor can they submit to God's will expressed in Torah. For Paul this is simply a description of two mutually exclusive ways of life, not exhortation.[193]

That does not mean, of course, that the flesh is not still about or that believers do not have to resist its "desires." Indeed, because believers live "between the times"—between "this age" that is passing away and "the age to come" that has already been inaugurated by Christ and the

---

[192] Cf. Hübner, *Law*, 147.
[193] Contra Dunn 425, who asserts the opposite, but without an appeal to what Paul actually says in the text, which points toward description, not exhortation.

Spirit—they must "*reckon* themselves as dead as far as sin is concerned" (6:11). And they do so by "putting to death the deeds of the body *by the Spirit*" (8:13). But this does not represent a struggle for Paul; it represents experienced realities. The accent here falls decidedly on the work of the Spirit to bring it off, not on some constant tug-of-war that believers must endure between their life in the Spirit and the pull of the flesh.

But that belongs to the next paragraph. Before turning to that, we need only call attention as so many times before to the thoroughly Trinitarian nature of this soteriological moment. As always, God is once again the subject of the "saving verb"; Christ is the means whereby at one point in our human history salvation was effected as an objective, historical reality; and the Spirit is the means whereby that salvation is effectively worked out in the life of the believer. It is the Spirit who identifies the people of God over against those who still live according to the present age; it is the Spirit who effects the "righteousness" that Torah aimed at but could not produce.

ROMANS 8:5–8

⁵For those who are according to the flesh set their minds on the things of the flesh; but those according to the Spirit on the things of the Spirit. ⁶For the mind of the flesh is death, but the mind of the Spirit is life and peace—⁷because the mind of the Spirit means enmity against God, for it is not subject to the Law of God, for neither can it be; ⁸and those who are in the flesh are not able to please God.

The "for" with which this set of sentences begins indicates that this is not something new, but rather the elaboration of the final word in v. 4, that God's people "walk not according to the flesh but according to the Spirit"—both because the flesh has been condemned to death through the death of Christ, and because the Spirit has come to make possible the righteous commandment of Torah that Torah itself could not effect. That the present material is integral to vv. 2–4 is further evidenced by the description of life in the flesh as "death," and life in the Spirit as "life and peace." In vv. 7–8 Paul also characterizes life according to the flesh in terms closely resembling those in 7:14–23, where the person in the flesh not only is *not* subject to "God's Torah," but *cannot* be, with the net result that such a person cannot please God.

Nonetheless, this material has its own distinct function in the argument beyond what is said in vv. 3–4. The present interest appears to be twofold. First of all Paul is describing the absolutely incompatible nature of the two ways of life, not because believers constantly struggle between the two, but because they belong to the one and therefore must not live as those who belong to the other, as the application in vv. 12–13 makes clear. But second, his present interest is particularly in the "life of the flesh," so that he can set off the Roman believers as Spirit people over against such a life with the starkest possible contrast. Thus he concludes, "those who are 'in the flesh' cannot please God"; to which he will respond in vv. 9–11, "but as for you, you are *not* 'in the flesh' but 'in the Spirit.' "

The motif that holds all of this together is that struck first in the "thesis sentence" of v. 2: the Spirit who liberates is none other than the Spirit who gives life. By these contrasts Paul shows that only Spirit people have life now (vv. 6, 10) and are destined for life forever (vv. 10–11). Those who "are according to the flesh" cannot have life, because they lack the source of life, the Spirit himself; their minds are on what leads to death; thus they stand in radical opposition to God and "the righteous requirement of Torah" (v. 7).

The present material is in two parts. The first (vv. 5–6) describes what is basic to, and characteristic of, the two ways of life; the second (vv. 7–8), in the form of a causal or inferential clause, gives the reason why life in the flesh results in death: its essential character is enmity against God. The flow of thought can be easily structured:

A   Those who are κατὰ σάρκα have set their minds on the things
           "of the flesh";
       but

B   those who are κατὰ πνεῦμα have set their minds on the things
           "of the Spirit."
       For

A′   the "mind" of the flesh means death,
       but

B′   the "mind" of the Spirit means life and peace;
          because

A^1 the "mind" of the flesh is in enmity against God,
            in that it is not subject to the Law of God,
              for
           neither can it be.
         The result: (δέ)

A^2 those who are in the flesh cannot please God

This is description, not exhortation, whose intent is to elaborate what had been said earlier in 7:5, by drawing the sharpest possible distinctions between life before Christ and the present life of the Spirit; the imperatival application will be given in vv. 12–13. No struggle within the believer is mentioned or hinted at.[194] Rather, in light of vv. 2–4 Paul is reminding

---

[194] Contra what is often asserted; see, e.g., Loane, *Hope,* 31: "St. Paul therefore in this passage describes the *flesh* and the *Spirit* as *two rival forces which both strive for control in man's inmost being*" (emphases mine; cf. Cranfield, Dunn). But this is an assertion that lacks any basis in the text. Paul does not so much as hint that flesh and the Spirit are warring or "striving" for control. For Paul that matter was settled

the Roman believers of that which characterizes "the flesh," which belongs to their past, and of that which characterizes "the Spirit," which
belongs to the present. That the major part of the present paragraph
describes life in the flesh does not mean either that Paul sees the believer
as basically helpless against the flesh—that is not suggested anywhere—
or that the major emphasis in this argument lies here.[195] Paul's point is
exactly the opposite. The concern throughout (from 6:1) has to do with
"what happens to righteousness once one does away with Torah observance." For Paul the Spirit is God's answer. But the Spirit is far more
than the answer to mere "righteousness based on Law." He is the divine
response to that which plagues the human race in all its fallenness: the
flesh with its basic enmity against God, which by its very nature cannot
submit to God. Paul describes, therefore, not the believer's struggle
against the flesh, but that deep-rooted fallenness that life in the Spirit
stands over against. Thus his ultimate concern is to set up vv. 9–11,
which depict the Spirit as the divine provision that makes possible what
is described in 6:1–7:6.[196]

5 With an explanatory "for" Paul proceeds to juxtapose the life of
the Spirit against that of the flesh. That this is "descriptive"[197] and not
argumentative or paraenetic is shown by the persistent use of the third
person plural ("those who"). This also indicates that Paul is not describing the "inner life" of the believer. These depict *two different* groups of
people—"flesh" people and Spirit people, those who belong to Christ and
those who do not.[198] On the Spirit side of things, of course, one is to
understand "those who" to be "*us* who walk by the Spirit" in v. 4. But
Paul is not relating the life of the believer per se, but the two radically
opposed kinds of existence that now exist side by side in the "already but
not yet" of the eschatological realities ushered in by Christ and the Spirit.
Believers, both Jew and Gentile, once belonged to the one, but do so no
longer, as 7:5 and 8:9 show.

In its barest form the two kinds of existence are first described as
"having a mind for"[199] what belongs to the two opposite ways of life.

---

through Christ. Thus what *he* asserts is that "*when* we *were* in the flesh . . . ; but now
. . . we serve in the newness of the Spirit" (7:5–6).

[195] As Wright, *Climax*, 201, would have it, thus seeing these verses as the climax
of yet one more "vindication" of the Law.

[196] There has been some debate, mostly among earlier works, over whether
πνεῦμα here refers to the human spirit (energized by the Spirit, to be sure) or to the
Spirit himself. But in light of the Pauline evidence it would take considerable courage
to defend such a position in this passage.

[197] Cf. Barrett 157: "This verse is a definition."

[198] So most commentaries, contra Dunn 425, who spends most of his energy on
this verse trying to discount what is plainly here.

[199] Gk. φρονέω, a verb which means more than simply "think in a certain way,"

That is, those who are "according to the flesh" are first of all people whose minds are set on, completely given to, the ways of the flesh. In colloquial parlance, such people "think flesh, eat flesh, sleep flesh." This obviously has nothing to do with life "in Christ Jesus"; it rather describes those completely outside Christ.

The opposite is true of believers. They "have set their minds on the ways of the Spirit," which is precisely what makes them so incompatible with life in the flesh. Thus the absolutely basic description of Christian life, as Paul perceives it, begins not with behavior as such, but with that which lies behind all life and behavior—a mind set on God and his ways and that is intent upon what is in keeping with the Spirit. Hence in 12:2 the basic imperative in this letter will take the form of "not being conformed" to *this age*, that is to the life of the flesh, but of "being transformed by the renewing of the mind [by the Spirit, is implied]," so that they may be able to discern God's will.

6 With yet another explanatory "for," Paul pictures the outcome of the two "mindsets" described in v. 5; and he does so by going back to the language of v. 2, where the Spirit *of life* is portrayed as having freed us from the "law of sin *and death*." "The mind set on the flesh,"[200] Paul says, means "death." There is nothing new here; this has been stated in various ways since Paul first picked up this theme in 5:12 and spelled it out in detail in 7:14–25. The "wretched man" of 7:24 is said to be "living in death," precisely because of the presence of sin in the flesh, aroused by the good but helpless Torah. This theme will be reintroduced in a slightly different way in v. 10. Death is the result of sin, which is resident in the "flesh of sin" (v. 3).

Again, the polar opposite prevails for "the mind set on the Spirit." Such a mindset issues in life and peace. Life, of course, is not simply the opposite of death, but the primary character of the Spirit. He is "the Spirit of life," the life-giving Spirit of the living God, as noted above on v. 2. But why add "and peace"? Almost certainly because Paul anticipates the *enmity* that further characterizes life in the flesh spelled out in v. 7. Thus he is echoing the metaphor of sin as hostility to God found in 5:1–11.[201] Because of the reconciling work of Christ, the hostility is overcome and the former enemy has "peace with God."[202] Here we learn what does not

---

but has to do with "setting the mind on, or being intent on, something." It occurs regularly throughout the rest of Romans, esp. in chs. 12–15, and is a predominate verb in Philippians.

[200]Gk. τὸ φρόνημα τῆς σαρκός, a noun phrase that compresses the first clause in v. 5.

[201]Cf. 14:17 and 15:13, where the contexts there rule in favor of "peace" as having to do with wholeness within the believing community.

[202]Cf. also Moo 520. Many interpreters (e.g., Morris 306) take it to refer to the

surprise us, that in Paul's view the source of that peace is the Spirit himself. This incidental reference to the Spirit and "peace" only demonstrates what should be presuppositional in our understanding of Paul, namely, that he does not always need to mention the Spirit for him to think of the Spirit as present in all of the experienced life of believers, in their relationship both to God and to one another.

7–8 These two sentences conclude the description by focusing on "the mind set on the flesh" and by offering the reasons as to why it issues in death. At the same time, of course, it sets up the contrast with life in the Spirit in vv. 9–11, where the indwelling Spirit assures us of life both now and in the Eschaton. Picking up on the theme of "peace" [with God] from the preceding sentence, which characterizes "the mind set on the Spirit," Paul suggests that what lies behind the "mind of the flesh" is an unrelenting hostility toward God, such as he had already described in 1:18–32. This obviously refers neither to Christian life nor to some basic struggle taking place in the believer's heart. Ever and always in Paul this describes those outside Christ.

Not only so, he adds by way of further explanation, and reflecting one final time on the argument of 7:14–25, but such people neither submit nor can they submit to God's Torah. It is this clear collocation of life in the flesh as lived by those outside Christ and hostile to God with the person being described in chapter 7, that finally clinches our contention that 7:14–25 had nothing to do with a struggle that goes on in the life of the believer. In both cases the reason they cannot submit to God's Torah is that they live apart from the Spirit.

Finally, Paul concludes that such people, who are "in the flesh," therefore "cannot please God." This final phrase will not be reflected on immediately, as far as life in the Spirit is concerned, but becomes the primary expression of such life in the "topic sentence" (12:1) when Paul sets out to apply in detail how Spirit life works out in the paraenesis of 12:1–15:13. The person whose "mind" has been renewed by the Spirit seeks above all else to live so as to please God. This can be done by the empowering presence of the Spirit.

ROMANS 8:9–11

⁹*But as for you,*[203] *you are not in the flesh but in the Spirit, since indeed the Spirit of God dwells in you. Now if anyone does not have the Spirit of*

---

subjective well-being or "peace of mind" that comes to those who have received the life of the Spirit. I do not doubt that this, too, is present, but it is so first of all because they are at one with God objectively.

[203]This attempts to capture the emphasis of the ὑμεῖς δέ, which stands in emphatic first position in obvious contrast to those in v. 8 who are in the flesh and therefore cannot please God.

Christ, this person is not of him. [10]*But, if Christ is in you, on the one hand, the body is dead because of sin; on the other hand, the Spirit is life because of righteousness.* [11]*Now if the Spirit of him who raised Jesus from the dead dwells in you, then he who raised Christ Jesus from the dead*[204] *will give life to your mortal bodies as well, because of*[205] *his Spirit who dwells in you.*

With an emphatic "but as for you," and in vivid contrast to those in vv. 7–8 who "mind the things of the flesh," Paul brings the argument that began in vv. 1–2 to its preliminary conclusion. Switching from the

---

[204]A confusing array of alternative readings exists at this point, having to do with both the order of words and the add/omit of Ἰησοῦν. My translation represents the text of Egypt (א* A [C 81] 630 1506 1739 1881 pc), which has both the "addition" of Ἰησοῦν and the unique word order ἐκ νεκρῶν Χριστὸν Ἰησοῦν (found nowhere else in the corpus). This seems to represent the original text on all counts: external evidence (B has clearly abandoned its tradition here) and transcriptional probability—it is the one reading that explains how the others emerged. The editors of NA[26]/UBS[4] opt for Χριστὸν ἐκ νεκρῶν (with B F G and the MajT [which adds τόν before Χριστόν]) as "the least unsatisfactory reading," considering the "addition" of "Jesus" as possibly due to assimilation to the immediately preceding clause (Metzger, *Textual Commentary*, 516). But that scarcely explains the unique word order, or why, if assimilation were at work, there was not a simple substitution of "Jesus" for "Christ." Such an explanation falls far short of carrying conviction.

[205]The logic of the argument (as noted in the discussion below), as well as the weight of both external and internal evidence, favors the reading τὸ ἐνοικοῦν αὐτοῦ πνεῦμα ("will live *because of* his Spirit who dwells in you"; read by B D F G K Ψ 33 181 1241 1739 1881 lat MajT Origen); the alternative, τοῦ ἐνοικοῦντος αὐτοῦ πνεύματος ("*through* the Spirit who dwells in you"), is read by א A C 81 88 104 326 436 2495 pc and NA[26]/UBS[3]. The UBS[3] committee made its choice first of all by negating the witness of B ("in the Pauline corpus the weight of B when associated with D G . . . is quite considerably lessened") and then favoring the genitive "on the basis of the combination of text-types, including the Alexandrian (א A D 81), Palestinian (syr[pal] Cyril-Jerusalem), and Western (it[61]? Hippolytus)" (Metzger, *Textual Commentary*, 517). But that will scarcely do in this case. The same combination of text-types exists even more strongly for the alternative reading (B 1739, which in combination more often represent the "Alexandrian" text than otherwise; the preponderance of Western witnesses, early and widespread; and several "Palestinian" Fathers [Methodius, Origen, Theodoret]). The issue therefore must be decided on the grounds of transcriptional probability, since the variation can only have been deliberate, not accidental. Here the evidence weighs altogether in favor of the accusative, since that is not what one expects when διά modifies a verb for resurrection (cf. 6:4; 1 Cor 6:14)—all the more so when agency would make such perfectly good sense. Cranfield 1.392 to the contrary (who suggests that it might have been changed to the accusative on the basis of the accusatives in v. 10), one cannot in fact imagine the circumstances in which the very natural genitive would have been changed so early and often to the much less common accusative—especially so in light of 6:4, where the διὰ τῆς δόξης τοῦ πάτρος not only reflects Paul's ordinary habits but also, by its very difficulty, begs to be changed to the accusative (which would seem to make so much more sense)—yet no one ever did so. Intrinsic probability—the argument as here presented—only adds to the weight of this conclusion.

more general "those who" in vv. 5–8 to the second person plural, he now concludes regarding the new "law" of the "Spirit *of life*," that the Spirit has not only freed us from the "law of sin" (vv. 3–8), but also from "the law of death." At the same time, as in vv. 3–4, even though the argument is dealing with the life of the Spirit as God's provision for "fulfilling the righteous requirement of Torah," in *both* paragraphs (vv. 3–8, 9–11) Paul *sets forth the work of Christ in conjunction with that of the Spirit*, which will serve as a key to some of the difficulties one encounters in the present paragraph.

Indeed, on the surface, this appears to be a very confused—and confusing—set of sentences, especially in an English translation.[206] Three factors contribute to the confusion: First, Paul's rhetoric frequently dictates how things are said, which on their own would undoubtedly have been expressed more lucidly. This is especially true when, by the use of balanced (parallel) clauses and sometimes with various kinds of shorter and longer chiasms, he sets out items in contrast. His rhetorical style thus helps to explain both the suppositional nature in which all of this is said and some of the difficult expressions in v. 10. Second, because of Paul's concern to tie the work of the Spirit to that of Christ, now in light of what was said in 6:1–14, he oscillates between calling him the Spirit of God and the Spirit of Christ, and in one case substitutes Christ himself for the Spirit of Christ, further adding to the reader's sense of bewilderment. Third, in anticipation of vv. 18–30 Paul now picks up the eschatological dimension of life in the Spirit which has been missing in the argument to this point. The sudden turn everything takes in v. 10 is therefore quite unexpected.

In this case especially, therefore, we need to look at the paragraph as a whole before trying to make sense of the details, and the easiest way to do this is to display structurally the basic argument (with some slight abbreviation):

<pre>
     ⁹But (as for you) you are   not in the flesh
                                    but in the Spirit,
      [A]   since indeed   the Spirit of God   dwells in you.

      [B]   Now if anyone does not have   the Spirit of Christ,
                      this person is not of him [Christ].
      [B′]   ¹⁰But if Christ is in you,
              [C]   that means: μέν the *body* is *dead*   because of sin,
              [D]   δέ the *Spirit* is *life* because of righteousness.

     [A′] ¹¹Now if   the Spirit of him [God] who raised Jesus . . . dwells in you,
              then   he [God]   (who raised Christ Jesus from the dead)
           [(C)/D′]   will also give *life* to your *mortal bodies*,
                                    because of his *Spirit* who dwells in you.
</pre>

---

[206]The sense of confusion obviously lies "below the surface" as well, as a careful reading of the commentaries, especially the earlier ones, reveals.

This structural display affords several helpful observations for unpacking this compact set of sentences.

1. We begin with the *form* of argumentation, which is quite similar to that of 1 Cor 15:12ff. Paul starts, *"you are* (one thing), *if indeed* (this reality holds true at all)" [A]. But rather than immediately spelling out the positive results of this reality, he proceeds to explain the result were this reality *not* so ("if not . . . , then the result would be that you are not . . . ") [B]. This is then followed by its positive opposite, which is where the argument was going in the first place ("since this is so for you, here is what results") [B']. The major difference between the present argument and that of 1 Corinthians 15 is that in the latter case some of the Corinthians actually were denying a future bodily resurrection, hence the emphasis there was on what would be the result if their (untrue) suppositions were in fact true (that is, if what *is not* so, were so). Here the suppositions function quite differently: to set out in an especially emphatic way the results of what in fact *is* so, that is, what is certified for us by the reality of the indwelling Spirit.

2. That means, therefore, that the *point* of the argument lies in the two "D" clauses in vv. 10 and 11, which express the result of the reality of the indwelling Spirit. First (v. 10), since the Spirit is none other than the Spirit of Christ, that means "life" for us as the direct result of the "righteousness" effected by the Christ whose Spirit now indwells the believer—despite the fact that the body is destined for death because of sin (cf. 5:12 and 21). Second (v. 11), since the indwelling Spirit is none other than the Spirit of the God who raised Christ from the dead, then the Spirit therefore is also God's own surety in our lives that, just as Christ was raised, so too our "mortal" bodies are going to live again through resurrection.

3. Thus the *flow* of argumentation can be easily traced. Verse 9 spells out the two basic alternatives, flowing directly out of the preceding argument (vv. 5–8) with their striking contrasts of life in the flesh (= death), and life in the Spirit (= life and peace): one either has the Spirit and thus belongs to Christ, or one does not and is therefore not a believer at all. Verse 10, then, picks up the first result for those who have the Spirit. The emphasis in this first instance is on the work of Christ and the presence of the "Spirit of life" as the direct result of that work; the Spirit is thus called "the Spirit of Christ." This in turn takes the shorthand form of "Christ in you," meaning "if Christ dwells in you by his Spirit." The result of Christ's presence by his Spirit, stemming from his redemptive work of securing righteousness for his people, is that one has "life" (= the gift of eternal life that is already ours; 6:23). Verse 11, in turn, points toward the future. Picking up the two motifs of v. 10—our having life through the Spirit, despite our "dead bodies" as the result of sin—Paul argues further that the presence of the Spirit is the guarantee of our

resurrection. And since, as always in Pauline theology, God himself is responsible for resurrection, both Christ's and ours, the Spirit is now designated once again as "the Spirit of God."

4. That leads, finally, to some summary observations about the *function* of this paragraph in the argument to this point and beyond:

a. The argument as a whole (from 7:6, picked up again at 8:1–2) and the paragraph itself both indicate that Paul's chief interest is in the Spirit's role in "the righteousness of God" that comes "apart from Torah through faith in Christ Jesus" (3:21–22), and in this instance the clear emphasis is on the role/function of the *indwelling* Spirit. In v. 2 Paul had said, "The 'law' of the *Spirit of life* has freed us from the 'law' of death." This paragraph elaborates that point.

b. At the same time the linguistic ties to 6:4–14 are so unmistakable[207] that it is difficult to escape the conclusion that Paul is intentionally tying together what was said there about Christ with what is said here about the Spirit. The singular difference between this passage and that one is that the "death/resurrection" motif in the former had essentially to do with sin and righteousness in terms of behavior, while this one has to do (primarily) with eschatology in terms of a future bodily resurrection.

c. Furthermore, while the paragraph advances the argument in its own right, it also serves as transition for what follows. On the one hand, it gathers up former themes of "life" and "death" and relates them in particular to life in the Spirit; on the other hand, with its future orientation it sets into perspective the true nature of the present tension of living by the Spirit in the "already/not yet." For the person living in the Spirit, the struggle is not between "flesh" and "Spirit," but between present weaknesses and suffering (evidenced by bodies that are destined for "death because of sin") and future glory (evidenced by the resurrection of those same "dead [mortal] bodies"). Thus the present paragraph anticipates the longer discussion of these matters in vv. 18–30.

We should therefore note in this regard that this passage is yet another excellent example of the eschatological tension in Paul between the "already" (the indwelling Spirit of God/Christ means life *now*, predicated on the righteousness Christ has provided) and the "not yet" (even though sin means death for the mortal bodies, the indwelling Spirit means

---

[207] This takes place esp. in the apodoses of vv. 10–11: (1) "The body is dead because of sin" echoes "the body of sin" and "sin reigning in our mortal bodies" in 6:6, 12; (2) "the Spirit is life because of righteousness" echoes 6:13, where we are to present ourselves as "alive" from the dead (because of Christ's death and resurrection in which by faith we participate) and our members as instruments "of righteousness" for God; (3) "he who raised Christ from the dead shall also give life to our mortal bodies" echoes "Christ was raised from the dead through the glory of the Father" in 6:4 and "if we died with Christ . . . we shall live with him" in 6:8.

life both now and forever, through resurrection). Thus it is because of the Spirit's presence now that our *future* resurrection is guaranteed.[208]

Before summarizing the Spirit material from this paragraph, we need to look at several of the details which have been assumed in the presentation to this point, but which need to be demonstrated a bit more thoroughly.

9 Not much more needs to be said about this verse. We have noted above that it functions primarily as the transition between vv. 5–8 and 10–11, and does so by picking up the contrasts from vv. 5–8 and spelling out the alternative possibilities they represent—life in Christ or life apart from Christ. Thus, despite the suppositional nature of the two sentences in this verse, for Paul they are not suppositions at all. Believers, including those in Rome, are in fact *in the Spirit*,[209] because the Spirit of God does in fact *dwell in them*.[210] And those who do not have the Spirit of Christ by that very condition manifest that they are still "in the flesh" and do not belong to Christ at all. Thus this opening thrust seems to verify our interpretation of the preceding paragraph that Paul is not there dealing with a "flesh/Spirit" tension in the life of the believer, but is spelling out in its starkest form the difference between two kinds of existence: life in the Spirit and life in the flesh, the life of the believer and the life of the unbeliever.[211]

We must also note the ease with which Paul moves from "the Spirit of God" to "the Spirit of Christ." This is now the second instance in his

---

[208] Nygren 322 sees the function of the paragraph as reiterating the concerns, as he sees them, of vv. 5–8 and 7:13–15, that the believer is simultaneously under death and under life; hence the outer man (the body) is dead because of sin, but the spirit is alive because of righteousness. This seems to miss Paul's concerns by a wide margin precisely because this commentary is so totally driven by theological interests.

[209] SH 197 note the subtle shift from "if anyone," when speaking negatively in v. 9b, to the assumption that his readers have the Spirit when speaking on the positive side.

[210] This shift from their being "in the Spirit" and the Spirit's "dwelling in them" merely reflects the shift in emphasis between the believer's activity and that of the Spirit. In either case, Paul perceives the believer as "walking by the Spirit" because the Spirit indwells the believer. One of the idiosyncrasies of an earlier era of interpreters was their readiness to interpret ἐν πνεύματι as "in one's own spirit" (with the Spirit's help, of course), as though vv. 4–8 expressed an anthropological contrast rather than an eschatological one. See, e.g., SH 196, who then feel compelled to offer explanations that distinguish the human πνεῦμα from the divine.

[211] Meyer 2.54 sees it differently, as spelling out the difference between two kinds of Christian life: "It is not the *non*Christians, but the *seeming*-Christians . . . who are characterized as those who have not the Spirit." Only theological predispositions could possibly yield such a meaning. Dunn's discussion (428) seems to be guilty of the same. He recognizes the Pauline distinction, but then without warrant either from anything said in the text itself or from the context he includes what appears to be a wholly irrelevant series of comments designed to bring the text into conformity to his view of vv. 5–8 noted above.

letters in which he refers to the Spirit as "of Christ."[212] This in itself is the strongest kind of evidence for Paul's high Christology, that a person steeped in the OT understanding of the Spirit of God as Paul was, should so easily, on the basis of his Christian experience, designate him as the Spirit of Christ as well. We have already noted the *reason* for this transfer of language: the argument is now returning momentarily to an emphasis on the work of Christ and *his* relationship to the Spirit, which will be quite the point of v. 10. And in this sentence in particular, the emphasis is on being a Christian believer, on "belonging to Christ," the evidence of which, therefore, is to "have" the Spirit of Christ.[213]

Paul does not frequently use "have" with reference to the Spirit's presence (here, v. 23, and 1 Cor 6:19). As both this context and the clear language of 1 Cor 6:19 demonstrate, one "has" the Spirit only in the loosest sense of this verb. That is, this is a form of popular speech to reflect the reality of the indwelling Spirit.

10 This tightly packed sentence generates most of our difficulties with this passage. Five items make it so: first, the switch from "having the *Spirit of Christ*" in v. 9 to "*Christ in you*" in this verse; second, the fact that the μέν ("on the one hand") clause, with its content of "the body being dead because of sin," appears *after* Paul has said, "if Christ is in you," implying that this, too, is part of what it means for Christ to be in you; third, the meaning of "the body is dead"; fourth (and fifth), the meaning both of πνεῦμα and of the prepositional phrase "because of righteousness" in the final clause. A few words about each of these:

1. Everything about the argument and the context suggests that "Christ in you" is simply Pauline shorthand for "the Spirit of Christ in you," or perhaps better in this case, "Christ in you by his Spirit."[214] That is, it is doubtful either that Paul has made some kind of "identification" of the Risen Christ with the Spirit so that this language reflects that confusion,[215] or that Paul somehow envisioned both Christ and the Spirit indwelling the believer, "side by side" as it were. Rather, very much as in Eph 2:22, where the church is seen as the "habitation of God by the Spirit," so here the believer is the "habitation" of Christ, also by the Spirit.

---

[212] See on Gal 4:6; he will do so again in Phil 1:19 (q.v.).

[213] The point is not, therefore, on the believing *community* "having the Spirit of Christ" (Black 116), as good as the sentiment is, but on the *individual* believers who make up the community and their own reception of the Spirit.

[214] So also, Calvin 165, Cranfield 1.189; but cf. Barrett 159 who thinks of "union with Christ" as the prior ground, which is now understood in terms of the Spirit.

[215] On this question see my contribution to *Jesus of Nazareth*, 312–31, entitled "Christology and Pneumatology in Rom 8:9–11—and Elsewhere: Some Reflections on Paul as a Trinitarian."

On the language of Christ as "indwelling" the believer see the discussion of Gal 2:20.

The *reason* for this language is not difficult to find. As mentioned above, the fact that in vv. 10–11 Paul picks up so much of the language from 6:4–14 suggests that he is deliberately tying the work of Christ as noted in that passage to the life of the Spirit noted in this one. Since his emphasis is momentarily on what Christ has accomplished—just as in vv. 2 and 3 above—the emphasis of "indwelling" therefore also shifts to the presence of Christ in the believer's life. This, of course, could just as easily have been accomplished by repeating "if the Spirit of Christ is in you." The reason for not doing so probably lies in the μέν/δέ contrast in the apodosis, especially in the δέ clause, where Paul intends to speak of the Spirit as bringing life *because of righteousness*. That is, as we will note below, the final prepositional phrase finds its meaning in the fact that Christ, not the Spirit, is *the subject of the protasis*. By doing so, Paul indicates his intent in the final phrase. Thus, "if *Christ* is in you by his Spirit, then the presence of the Spirit means life for you precisely because of the righteousness *Christ* effected for you."

2. The awkward order of these three clauses is also easily accounted for.[216] As was noted at the outset, Paul's rhetorical style sometimes dictates how things are stated. His obvious concern lies with what the presence of Christ by the Spirit means for the believer both now and for the future. Rather than "clean up" the order of the sentence for the sake of logical niceties, he allows a certain awkwardness for the sake of his rhetoric. Thus, first, the only real apodosis to, "If Christ be in you," is line D: "then the Spirit means life because of righteousness."[217] At the same time, Paul wanted to set life in the Spirit in sharp, but closely connected, contrast with present bodily existence. Hence the use of μέν/δέ in this place with its resulting awkwardness, as though Christ's presence were in some way the cause of "the body being dead because of sin."[218] That is to speak nonsense, and Paul is not intending nonsense. The point is that the μέν/δέ contrast stands on its own, apart from the protasis as such—although the δέ clause is surely to be understood as the "then" part of the sentence. This means that in context the best way to handle the μέν clause is to make it concessive in relation to the clause that follows it: "If Christ is in you, that means that *even though* in your present existence the body is dead because of sin, the presence of the Spirit also means that you have life—both now and forever—because of righteous-

---

[216] Some, of course, reject that there is awkwardness here and interpret "the body is dead" as something brought about by Christ, not by sin. See the discussion on p. 550 below.

[217] Cf. Bruce 164: "the true apodosis to the conditional clause, 'if Christ be in you' is 'the Spirit is life because of righteousness.' "

[218] Although see p. 550 below; some indeed have taken it in this way.

ness."[219] Thus the "body is dead" in the sense of 5:12; because of the entrance of sin through Adam, "death passed to all people, in that all have sinned."[220] With this stark language Paul declares the inevitable: sin has resulted in the death of all, so that even though alive in one sense, the body is dead in the truest sense and is therefore subject to, or destined for, death.

3. Several attempts have been made—but not very successfully[221]— to suggest that Paul did indeed intend to say that the "body is dead because of sin" as a result of Christ's indwelling presence. The best of these argues that, on the basis of baptism in 6:2–4, Paul means that for the one in whom Christ dwells "the body is dead with reference to sin."[222] But this solution founders on the preposition διά: "with reference to" lies quite beyond its range of meanings.[223] Not only that, but such a view misses the logic of Paul's own wording; in v. 11 he uses the synonym θνητά ("subject to death," hence "mortal") to interpret this phrase.[224] Hence he can only mean that the body is dead in the sense that "because of sin the body must be already considered dead," since it is destined for death. Body here does not so much represent the whole person,[225] but is singled out precisely because for Paul that is the locus of resurrection.

4. It is often argued, because of the apparent contrast with "the body" in the μέν clause, that τὸ πνεῦμα in the δέ clause must therefore also refer to a constituent of the human person. Thus the contrast is understood to be that between the body, destined for death because of sin, and the (human) spirit, destined for life because of righteousness (received as the gift of Christ).[226] But this also runs aground on v. 11, where Paul elabo-

---

[219] Cf. RSV, NRSV, NEB, Calvin, Bruce, Cranfield, Dunn, Moo.

[220] Cf. 2 Cor 5:14, where Paul argues that since Christ died for all that means that all have died. As with the present clause, this means that those who live in these "dead bodies" are under the sentence of death.

[221] For a list of such options, see Meyer 2.55–56 (for earlier interpreters) and Käsemann 224 (for more recent ones).

[222] Most recently, Käsemann 224; cf. Barrett 159 ("the human self is dead—to sin"); Ziesler 211 (preferable "because it fits with a leading Pauline theme").

[223] So also Murray 289; Cranfield 1.389; Michel 193n1. Those who take this position regarding the clause uniformly ignore this damaging grammatical problem.

[224] Cf. Murray 289; Moo 524.

[225] As Bultmann suggests (*New Testament Theology*, 192–203), whose influence on this matter has spread widely (see, e.g., Barrett's interpretation in n. 222 above); but see Gundry, *SOMA*, who has convincingly called into question whether σῶμα ever means this in Paul.

[226] For this view see, inter alia, SH 198 ("clearly"); Meyer 2.99. As late as 1959 Murray 289 could call this the "all but uniform exegetical opinion." But the view is (for good reason) currently on the wane and is rejected by almost all commentators since 1960 (e.g., Michel, Cranfield, Harrison, Käsemann, Morris, Dunn, Moo; although, surprisingly, it is held by Wright, *Climax*, 202). It was held by Ziesler in *Righteousness*, 204, but has been moderated in his commentary (212). But the English versions have been slow to catch up (cf. NIV, "your spirit is alive"; so NASB; RSV "your spirits"; but see now NRSV, "the Spirit is life").

rates on the meaning of this text by insisting that the presence of the Spirit of God indwelling the believer is the ground of our confidence that God will give life to "our mortal bodies." That is, what is destined for life is not the human spirit,[227] separated from the body that has died because of sin, but the *mortal body itself*—despite the fact that because of sin it is destined for death. Furthermore, "body" and "spirit" as basic constituents of the human person are found only twice in Paul (1 Thes 5:23; 1 Cor 7:34), and in both cases they occur together as to what is essential to being human; nowhere does Paul ever set "body" and "spirit" in contrast to each other in the way that the alternative interpretation demands in this case.

Thus, we may conclude with considerable confidence that by his μέν/δέ contrast, Paul is speaking not about two constituents of the human person but about Christian existence as "already/not yet." In this case, both the body as destined for death and the Spirit as present with life are "already" for the believer; at the same time, the body and the Spirit are "not yet"—the body in terms of resurrection, the Spirit as the present guarantee of all future realities yet to be realized.

5. That brings us to the more difficult issue: the exact nuance of the prepositional phrase διὰ δικαιοσύνην, which I have consistently translated "because of righteousness." The issue is related to the larger question as to the meaning of this word in Romans. Does the usage here reflect the meaning, for example, in 3:21–22, where "the righteousness of God" refers primarily to the gift of righteousness that Christ's death and resurrection have made available to those who trust him? Or does it reflect the usage in 6:13–20, where righteousness has to do with behavior that is in keeping with the "righteousness of God" that has been given through faith in Christ? That is, does Paul intend "The Spirit means life because of the righteousness Christ has provided" or "The Spirit means life for the sake of righteous behavior"?

The latter is a particularly attractive option in this case,[228] especially in light of the emphasis in vv. 4–8 on "walking in the Spirit" so as to fulfill "the *righteous requirement*" of Torah. That this telic sense of διά is possible in Paul is demonstrated by the striking parallel in 4:25, where Paul argued that Christ's death was "διά (*because of*) our transgressions," and that he was raised "διά (*for the sake of*) our justification." Nonetheless, two matters finally undermine this view. First, despite the larger context, the nearer context, beginning with the unusual shift to "Christ in you" in the protasis, suggests that Christ, not the Spirit, serves as the conceptual subject of the action in this clause. Thus, Christ in you means life in the Spirit precisely *because of the righteousness that he has brought to you.* Second,

---

[227] As is often pointed out (e.g., Barrett 159), if this were intended one would expect Paul to have written, τὸ πνεῦμα ζῇ ("the spirit lives"), not "the spirit is life."

[228] See esp. Käsemann 224. It was adopted by Ziesler in *Righteousness*, 168, a direction in which he leans, but more moderately, in his commentary (212).

the Spirit talk in this paragraph has little or nothing to do with behavior as such, but has rather to do with eschatological existence (evidenced by the Spirit's presence), both now—despite the mortal body—and forever.

Thus, to put all of this together in a paraphrase, Paul is urging that "if Christ by his Spirit is dwelling in you, even though your bodies are destined for death because of sin, the presence of the Spirit (because he is the 'Spirit of life') means that you also have life both now and forever, because of the righteousness that Christ has effected for you."

11 With this sentence Paul arrives at the point of the paragraph, that the presence of the indwelling Spirit guarantees our future resurrection, wherein the mortal body is "given life." Since most of what needs to be said about this sentence was noted in the overview of the paragraph, only a few matters need elaboration here, some by way of reinforcement.

First, the emphatic repetition of "him [God] who raised Christ from the dead," as a way of identifying the indwelling Spirit, is probably intended as a deliberate reiteration of the closeness between Christ's resurrection and ours—his being the ground of ours, as Paul has made abundantly clear in 1 Corinthians 15. The "supposition" in this case tells the story: since the one (his) is true, then the other (ours) is true as well.

Second, as in v. 10, Paul's point lies with the apodosis, by which he not only ties this sentence to that one, but also elaborates, and thereby interprets, v. 10. This is further demonstrated by the otherwise unusual way of referring to our resurrection, as "giving life to our mortal bodies." As he does when referring to Christ, Paul ordinarily speaks about "our being raised from the dead" (1 Cor 6:14; 15:12–58). The language "shall give life to mortal bodies"[229] exists solely because of what was said in v. 10. The body, which is destined for death because of sin, is also destined to be raised to life because of Christ's resurrection.[230]

Third, as noted above (n. 205), the role of the Spirit in all of this is not that of agency, but as the surety for our future resurrection, just as in v. 10.[231] This is the second way he is the "Spirit of life," not only as

---

[229] Paul could hardly have stated it more clearly that he intends the raising of *mortal bodies*. Thus Leenhardt 210 ("the allusion here is to the vivifying energy of the Spirit, who liberates from the tyranny of sin" as in 6:12–23) and Ziesler 212 ("whole persons rather than . . . a strictly physical resurrection") seem miles away from Paul's intent.

[230] Cf. especially in this regard the language of the LXX in Ezek 37:1–14. The "dry bones" of Israel are not raised to life, but are given life through the Spirit that is breathed into them.

[231] Most scholars note the divided nature of the external evidence for this variant, hesitatingly opt for the genitive, but conclude, "intrinsically one reading is not preferable to the other" (SH 199; cf. Käsemann 225). I demur; as noted above (n. 205) the accusative is preferable on all textual grounds and was chosen because it reflects Paul's standard eschatological view of the presence of the indwelling Spirit as God's guarantee of our future (cf. 2 Cor 1:22, etc.).

the one by whom we walk "in newness of life" (cf. 7:6 with 6:4), but also as the one who as the source of present life thus guarantees the giving of life to the "dead body."

Finally, despite much that is asserted or argued to the contrary, Paul neither says nor does the logic of the sentence demand[232] that God raised Christ by means of the Spirit. In fact, despite the prevalence of this idea in Christian circles,[233] Paul nowhere explicitly suggests as much; it is doubtful whether it is implicit in the few texts—including this one—that are often read this way.[234] One can understand how this sentence might easily be misread,[235] but such an idea is quite beside Paul's point. His reason for identifying the Spirit as "the Spirit of him who raised Christ from the dead" is not to say something about the role of the Spirit in Christ's having been raised, but to make the closest possible connection between Christ's resurrection and ours. For Paul the presence in our lives of the Spirit of the God who raises the dead does not imply agency, but rather expresses certainty about our future, predicated on the Risen Christ and by the already present Spirit; that, after all, is quite the point of the repeated "who dwells in you," and especially in its second instance, "*because of* the Spirit who *indwells*[236] in you."

What, then, do we learn about the Spirit from this paragraph? Not much that is new, but much that reinforces in a different way what is found elsewhere in Paul's letters.

1. In v. 9 Paul puts into an emphatic, declarative sentence what we have learned in passages like 1 Cor 2:6–16 and Gal 3:1–4:7: the presence or absence of the Spirit is the one thing that distinguishes those who are Christ's from those who are not.[237] As over against all "boundary markers" predicated on some form of Law, the Spirit alone marks off the genuinely Christian person. Here is the absolutely essential matter for

---

[232] As is sometimes asserted; e.g., Scott, *Adoption* 256; cf. Dunn, "Jesus," 67.

[233] One can find references to such an idea in all kinds of places, scholarly and popular. Unfortunately, it served as a main thrust for Hamilton, *Holy Spirit*, 12–15, and Turner, "Significance of Spirit Endowment," 58–69 (64, 66), who in dealing with our text asserts, "The Spirit *raised* Jesus" (64, emphasis his). Cf. Byrne, '*Sons*,' 96; Menzies, *Development*, 288n1; Scott, *Adoption*, 256; A. W. D. Hui, "The Concept of the Holy Spirit in Ephesians and its Relation to the Pneumatologies of Luke and Paul" (Ph.D. diss., University of Aberdeen, 1992) 153, 161–69 (ch. 9, n. 1).

[234] The others are 1 Cor 6:14 (q.v.); Eph 1:19–21 (q.v.); and Phil 3:21. Hamilton, *Holy Spirit*, 14, would include Rom 6:4, but the exegesis is strained (see n. 77 above).

[235] Since the subject of the sentence is "the Spirit of him who raised Jesus from the dead"; but the predicate for the Spirit is not "raised Jesus from the dead" but "dwells in us." The one who raised Jesus is God himself. Indeed, had Paul intended the Spirit as the one who raised Jesus, the qualifying "Spirit *of him*" is unintelligible.

[236] The verb in this instance is changed from the simple "dwells" (οἰκεῖ) to "indwells" (ἐνοικεῖ).

[237] Cf. Ziesler 210: "The Spirit is thus not a highly desirable extra to Christianity, but the heart of the matter."

Christian life. Thus, as in vv. 5–8 and Gal 5:16–25, "flesh" is not a Christian alternative; to live in the flesh is to live outside Christ altogether.

2. As elsewhere in Paul, the emphasis in this passage is on the "indwelling" nature of the Spirit. The Spirit is not an "it," a kind of aura that influences one from the outside. Rather, the Spirit is none other than the way the eternal God and his Christ have come to us in the present, as personal presence taking up residence within the life of the believer.[238] In the eschatological present ushered in by Christ and the Spirit, the place of God's habitation has been transferred from the temple to his new temples, the life of the believer and the corporate gathering of his people.

3. If vv. 5–8 emphasized the believer's walk "in the Spirit" as evidence of one's present position in Christ, then this passage emphasizes the "indwelling Spirit" as the basis of our eschatological existence. As the "Spirit of life," he is God's surety in our current existence that we have already entered into the life of the coming aeon, to be realized at the End, through either the resurrection or the transformation of our present bodily existence. Thus, along with Christ and his resurrection, the gift of the Spirit is the ground of our hope.

4. As with 2 Cor 13:13[14] and other passages, the very way all of this is said demonstrates the thoroughly Trinitarian presupposition of Paul's way of talking about "salvation in Christ." On the one hand, despite what may appear to be somewhat fluid usage in v. 11, Paul clearly distinguishes between the Three, and does so in terms of the distinctive role of each in salvation. God is the ground of all things and the one who raises the dead; Christ is the one who has brought righteousness; and the Spirit is the presence of both God and Christ in the present, thus giving life now and guaranteeing life for the future. On the other hand, the fact that Paul can so easily interchange the Spirit of God and the Spirit of Christ implies that the two designations refer to the one divine being; this interchange suggests the closest possible links—ontological links, if you will—between the Father and the Son.[239]

At the same time, the passage as a whole, although it demonstrates the closest kind of link between the Risen Christ and the Spirit, also demonstrates by the distinctions it makes that Paul knew nothing of a "Spirit Christology." While it is true that our present experience of the Risen Christ, just as with our present experience of God, is mediated through the presence of the indwelling Spirit, it does not follow that Paul therefore confuses them or somehow identifies them as one and the same reality. There is mystery here, but not confusion—at least not in Paul's mind as that is revealed in what he says.

---

[238] Cf. Morris 308: "The Spirit is not an occasional visitor; he takes up residence in God's people."
[239] Cf. Calvin 164.

ROMANS 8:12–13

¹²*Therefore, brothers and sisters, we are debtors, not to the flesh to live according to the flesh; ¹³for if you live according to the flesh, you are going to die, but if by the Spirit you put to death the deeds of the body,*[240] *you will live.*

The indwelling Spirit, who for us means life now and forever, also opens up for us new possibilities for righteousness unknown before. By his Spirit God fulfills in us his purposes for Torah. But the indwelling presence of God by his Spirit also puts us under obligation; God's new people must *serve* in the new way of the Spirit (7:6, q.v.).

With these words Paul applies the affirmations of vv. 1–11 to the lives of the believers in Rome. Noticeably absent to this point has been anything imperatival—either directly or by implication.[241] But imperative is the certain implication of these sentences.[242] In typical Pauline fashion the whole is expressed by way of contrasts; and the motifs of vv. 4–9 dominate ("flesh/Spirit"; "death/life"). Paul's interest is unmistakable, and he is no longer merely describing: they are to live as people of the Spirit, that is, in keeping with what Christ and the Spirit have done for them, as described in vv. 2–4 and 9–11, and in contrast to those who are "in the flesh" in vv. 5–8. Indeed, they are "indebted" to do so.

All of this seems clear despite some structural and detail items that are less so. In terms of structure, here is one of those few places where Paul (apparently) began a "not/but" contrast that he failed to complete. What one expects, and is probably there by implication in any case, is:[243]

> *Therefore* (brothers and sisters)
> *We* are debtors   *not*   to the flesh
> to live in keeping with the flesh,
>
> *but*
> to the Spirit
> to live in keeping with the Spirit.

---

[240]The Western witnesses (D F G 630 pc latt) understandably changed "body" here to read "flesh."

[241]Although some, to be sure, have so read parts of vv. 5–8 and 9–11. See v. 5 above.

[242]Cf. Murray 293; Käsemann 225.

[243]Although one must be duly cautious about trying to "read the mind" of an ancient author as to what he did not do, this seems to be a legitimate expectation in this case, for three reasons: first, the word order ὀφειλέται ἐσμὲν οὐ ("debtors we are, not to . . . ") seems to demand "not to . . . but to" (cf. Cranfield 394). Had he intended only to single out no "indebtedness" to the flesh, the word order would surely have been, οὐ ὀφειλέται ἐσμέν ("not [= no longer] are we under obligation to . . . "). Second, the running contrasts between "those in the flesh" and "those in the Spirit" in vv. 4–9 seem to set us up to expect an antithetical "but" clause to follow the "not" clause. Third, such an antithetical, neatly balanced, parallel is typical of Paul, as e.g., in Gal 6:8, which is so similar to this one in concern and content, although not in metaphor.

But what we get in fact is a sentence that pauses at midpoint for an explanation of the "not" clause, an explanation which echoes the language of v. 6 and comes off as straight warning. That sentence in turn, which came in the form of a first class (real) condition, is the one that receives its (somewhat balanced) alternative, but no longer as a "not/ but" contrast. Rather it is expressed as a second real condition—that if the opposite condition prevails, so also does the opposite result, and warning turns into reaffirmation. Thus Paul's sentences:

> *Therefore* (brothers and sisters)
> *We* are debtors   not to the flesh
>   to   live in keeping with the flesh;
>   *for*
>   if   *you*   live in keeping with the flesh
>   *you*   are going to die;
>   *but*
>   if   *you*   put to death the deeds of the body,
>   *you*   will live

The play on the themes of life and death (cf. vv. 2, 6, 10) is thorough-going and repeats what has been said up to here. The Spirit of life gives life (eschatological life, both now and in the future) to those who are Christ's; those who do not know Christ are in the flesh and are thus destined for death. Paul's point is plain: *Therefore*, because his readers are not in the flesh but in the Spirit (and therefore destined not for death but for resurrection), they must live accordingly. *How* he expresses this point is what catches our attention. As before, nothing here either suggests or presupposes a constant struggle on the part of the believer. This is as straightforward as vv. 5–8 and 9–11. On the one hand, believers are Spirit people, meaning that they live now and have the promise of life hereafter (vv. 10–11). Therefore, they must live so. Rather than representing spiritual *struggle*, this is a typically Pauline way of pressing the imperative (in terms of behavior) as the only proper response to the indicative (the gift of righteousness, v. 10).

On the other hand, as in Gal 5:16–25 and despite the passive "are led by the Spirit" that follows, neither is there a hint of triumphalism in Paul—as this text makes clear. Spirit people they are to be sure, and that as an act of pure grace; as such they must put to death the deeds of the body (cf. 13:12–14). They are not merely passive recipients or onlookers, nor is anything automatic. They must engage in the life of the Spirit.

12 The applicational nature of this sentence is signaled by both the strong inferential conjunction, "therefore,"[244] and the vocative, "brothers and sisters." The sentence itself is straightforward. Free though we

---

[244]Gk. ἄρα οὖν; cf. 7:25 above.

are through Christ and the Spirit (v. 2), we are nonetheless under "obligation." The intended obligation is undoubtedly to Christ and the Spirit as the direct result of what has just been said in vv. 9–11. But to get there Paul begins with (and never finishes) the "not" contrast, picking up especially the contrasts in vv. 5–8. Precisely because we[245] are Spirit people, in whom the Spirit of Christ dwells and by whom (because of Christ's gift of righteousness) we live (v. 10), we owe the flesh no debt whatsoever; therefore we must not "live according to the flesh."[246]

For us the surprising element in this sentence, besides the fact that the Spirit side is not given, is the concept of "obligation," which occurs rarely in Pauline paraenesis[247]—perhaps because of his sense that "obligation" belongs to Torah observance (cf. 4:4). Nonetheless, in 13:8 he will play on the term as metaphor ("*Owe* no one anything, except of course the 'obligation' to love"). This usage is probably related to its appearance in connection with "the flesh." People who live κατὰ σάρκα are in servitude to the flesh, thus under obligation to it. Paul's point then: Spirit people have no obligations of any kind to the flesh, that cruel task-master whose only "pay" is death (cf. 6:23). Through Christ and by the Spirit they have been set free from this former "obligation" (v. 2).

But the implication on the other side is just as clear. The word "debtors," after all, stands in the emphatic first position. Paul is not hung up on the concept of obligation, as many of his interpreters have been. For him as in this series of sentences, obligation stems from grace—not just the pronouncement of grace but the experience of it. Not that one could ever "pay God back"; freedom and life, the result of the indwelling Spirit of God, do not free one to go back to the very things from which deliverance has come. Rather, one is now under obligation to live by the Spirit who has given one life. The imperative follows the indicative, but not as some kind of heavy-handed requirement. The new "servitude" is the outflow of gratitude for grace received, for liberation from sin and death.

13 But Paul is not quite finished with the flesh. Thus, rather than offer the Spirit alternative to the "not" of v. 12, he instead offers one

---

[245]Note again Paul's inclusion of himself when reflecting on what is true for all believers; cf. v. 4 above.

[246]In light of the demarcation in vv. 5–8 and 9–11, where flesh and Spirit identify the two spheres of eschatological existence of the unbeliever and believer respectively, one is surprised to learn that this text "teaches beyond all question that the believer still has the sinful nature within himself, despite having been crucified with Christ" (Harrison 92). Despite the recent defense of this position by Dunn 448, this text teaches no such thing. That life in the present always has the possibility of choosing to conform to the thinking of the present age is presuppositional in Paul; but that is not the same thing as translating flesh as "sinful nature" and internalizing it in a text like this one. Cf. further the critique of Dunn in Moo 527.

[247]Gk. ὀφειλέται; cf. 13:8; 15:1.

further reminder as to "why not" regarding v. 12. Thus he begins with
an explanatory "for" and, in the form of a real condition, repeats the
basic content of v. 6a. At the same time, he reflects the antitheses of
Deuteronomy (in this case, 30:11–20), by which so much of his own
spiritual life had been formed.[248] Even though indwelt by the Spirit of
God (v. 11) and led by that same Spirit into the ways of the Lord (v. 14),
God's people are under obligation, and choice is ever present. Those who
have chosen flesh, who live "according to the flesh," are destined to die.
But in contrast to vv. 5–8, where Paul is describing those outside of
Christ, here he applies that content to the Romans by way of warning.
The warning is typical; it neither suggests nor implies that some are
indeed living this way. Rather, even though it comes by way of an
explanatory comment on v. 12, it sets up his real concern, the alternative
that follows. By the power of the Spirit, they must "choose life." But
Paul's way of putting that in the final clause calls for comment.

The opposite of the death that results from living in the flesh is the
life that the Spirit brings (as in v. 6b), this time pointing to its eschatological fulfillment:[249] "you *will* live." But how this is expressed is not
quite expected. The reason for the apparent strangeness of language has
to do with how Paul has set up the first clause. Having said that believers
are under no obligation to "live according to the flesh," he elaborates,
"if you *live* thus, you are going to *die*." The "live" in this clause has to
do with one's "way of life" in the present; the "die" belongs to the
eschatological future. But the precise antithesis to that does not work so
well (= "if you *live* according to the Spirit, you will *live*"). Thus Paul does
a better thing. He keeps the precise eschatological antithesis in the
apodosis ("you will *live*"), since the concern lies there. But he offers a
linguistic antithesis in the protasis (the "if" clause), and thus enriches
the metaphor. Rather than simply "live according to the Spirit," therefore, he urges them "by the Spirit" to "put to *death* the deeds of the
body."[250]

This is metaphor, pure and simple. The language "death" carries on
a linguistic play on the term "die" in the preceding clause. And what
they are to "put to death" are "the deeds of the body"—not the flesh,
because believers are no longer "in the flesh." Nor does he intend now
to locate sin in the physical body, any more than he did with the language
"flesh" in Gal 5:16–21. This language in fact comes directly from v. 10.

---

[248] See on 2:29 above.

[249] Which in this case is in keeping with both the preceding clause (such people
are going to die = eschatologically) and the immediately preceding emphasis in v. 11
on the future bodily resurrection of believers.

[250] Thus he does not say "kill," although it comes out at the same point, because
that Greek word is not a linguistic parallel. Cf. Gal 5:24, where he uses the verb
"crucify."

The "body" is destined for death because of sin; now they are urged to put to death the deeds associated with the body thought of in that way (as in v. 10). And in any case, "body" is the only proper object for this verb. Thus, even though the metaphor is strange in terms of language, Paul's intent is clear enough. They are to be done with the various forms of sin associated with "life in the flesh."[251] Since this is still theological argumentation, not paraenesis, he does not here spell out those "deeds."[252] But since the life of the flesh describes those outside of Christ, he most likely intends his readers to recall the list of Gentile "deeds" in 1:28–30, or the list of Jewish "deeds" in 2:21–23, including covetousness from 7:7.

As always in Paul, the empowerment for such comes from the indwelling Spirit. As elsewhere, even though the metaphors differ,[253] Paul calls upon God's people to be done with sin. They are not even to engage it in battle; rather, by the Spirit's help they are to put it to death.[254] All of this must be understood, of course, within the framework of Paul's "already but not yet" eschatological perspective. They are already in the Spirit; but they have not yet arrived. If there is no internal struggle with sin evident in Paul's theologizing, neither is there triumphalism. Temptation exists. The possibility of thinking like those who belong to the present age is ever present (12:2). Old habits die hard.[255] But God's people are Spirit people. They must resist such temptation by relying upon the empowering of the indwelling Spirit.

Therefore, by the Spirit's help they are to "become what they are." And *what they are* and *are to become* is what he will go on to spell out in vv. 14–17. Thus the Spirit not only serves for Paul as the empowering for "walking" in the ways of the Lord and therefore for producing the fruit of godliness (= God-likeness), but he is also understood to be the active agent in counteracting sin.

---

[251] See esp. 13:11–14. This text confirms that the Spirit is to be understood in that passage as presupposition.

[252] Gk. τὰς πράξεις = "practices" (cf. Col 3:9).

[253] As, e.g., the metaphor of "putting off" as a garment the life of sin expressed in 13:11–14 and Col 3:5–11, or of "not sowing" to the flesh in Gal 6:8.

[254] For the more practically minded, of course, such imperatives can cause great frustration. "Fine," they say, "but *what* does that mean in terms of everyday life and *how* does one go about it?" For which, unfortunately, there is no direct Pauline answer. In light of the basic thrust of v. 6 and 12:1–2, it at least means that one must put the "renewed mind" to it; that is, it must be focused and intentional.

[255] Cf. Moo's analogy (527, on the "obligation" of v. 12): "Like freed slaves who might, out of habit, obey their old masters even after being released 'legally' and 'positionally' from them, so Christians can still listen to and heed the voice of that old master of ours, the flesh." Which, of course, is precisely why the emphasis here is on "by the Spirit." Those who are no longer in the flesh, but in the Spirit, must by the Spirit put to death the vestiges of the former way of life. See esp. on 12:1–2.

Romans 8:14–17

[14]*For as many as are being led by the Spirit of God, these are the*[256] *"sons"*[257] *of God;* [15]*for you did not receive the Spirit of bondage again unto fear, but you received the Spirit of adoption as "sons," whereby we cry, "Abba, Father."* [16]*The*[258] *Spirit himself bears witness with our spirits that we are God's children,* [17]*and if children, also heirs, heirs of God and fellow-heirs with Christ, provided we suffer with him, so that we might also*[259] *be glorified with him.*

Paul now brings the argument that began in v. 1 to this somewhat surprising conclusion, surprising since nothing said to this point prepares us for what happens here. What begins in v. 14 as a further explanatory word to v. 13 becomes in vv. 15–17 further explanation of v. 14, and thus a further description of life in the Spirit in its own right. The metaphor is not altogether new, either to us or to the original recipients. For us it serves as a further, less impassioned, elaboration of the Father-son metaphor articulated in Gal 4:4–6;[260] for them it comes as an echo of, but now alternative to, the "slave" metaphor in 6:14–23.

The flow of thought is easily traced. The introductory "for" of v. 14 indicates a further elaboration or explanation of the final clause in v. 13, a point that is easy to miss, since it is expressed in entirely different language. But that very fact seems to be what leads to vv. 15–17. Paul

---

[256] Although there is no definite article in the Greek text, the original word order (whether as in B F G pc or in ℵ C D 81 630 1506 1739 pc) places the predicate noun before the verb, and thus appears as another support for "Colwell's rule"—that when a predicate noun precedes the verb, it is definite even if there is no article expressed.

[257] For this translation of υἱοί see on Gal 4:4–7. That Paul intends "children" is evidenced by the shift to that word (τέκνα) in vv. 16–17. That also shows that the reason for the language "sons" is singularly attributable to the metaphor "adoption as sons" (υἱοθεσία) in v. 15, since in this case, vis-à-vis Galatians, the connection with the "Son of God" does not appear at all.

[258] Codex D has added a ὥστε ("so then") at the beginning of this clause, in an attempt to clarify its relationship to what has preceded. It is extremely doubtful that this is the nuance of relationship Paul intends.

[259] P[46], alone among the Greek witnesses, omits this καί. This is probably a copying accident; in any case, it misses too much. For Paul "knowing Christ" is to know *both* the fellowship of his sufferings *and* the power of his resurrection.

[260] Jewett (*Terms* 198–99), following Michel 199n1 et al., suggests that Paul is here using a piece of "traditional parenetic argument," the same he has used previously in Gal 4:4–7. But one wonders about the methodology behind such an assumption, inasmuch as (1) both passages are found only in Paul; (2) even though they have some similar language and follow a general pattern, they have a considerably different character; and (3) if so, then Paul has adapted either one or both to the respective contexts. How, then, is one to "discover" the original pre-Pauline material? Which form is closer? And how does one explain how Paul so thoroughly eliminated from this one the christological element that holds the Galatians passage together? This looks like a clear case where "if Paul used sources, he wrote them all himself" (an adaptation of a line from Pierson Parker on John's Gospel).

himself is (apparently) aware that he has introduced a new metaphor, "sons of God," which needs some explaining. Thus v. 15 puts the metaphor into perspective. When they received the Spirit what transpired was not a return to "slavery" and "fear" (cf. 6:14, 16) but "adoption as 'sons' " (cf. Gal 4:5, q.v.), evidenced by the Spirit's causing/enabling us to cry out the well-known "*Abba*, Father." In this way, Paul goes on (v. 16), the Spirit himself bears witness with our own spirits that we are, as affirmed in v. 14b, "God's very children." Nor is that all (v. 17), for being a child in terms of the metaphor "adoption as 'sons' " means also to be full heirs, in this case heirs of God and thus fellow-heirs with Christ, his Son. A nice place to stop, for us, but not so for Paul. Glory there will be, to be sure; but in the meantime as we await that glory there will also be "suffering together with Christ." That launches Paul into one of his finer moments (vv. 18–30), in which he explicates with vivid metaphors the present life of the Spirit as one of "already but not yet"—full of hope for the glory that is coming, but living in the midst of suffering and weakness while eagerly awaiting that hope.

It is not difficult, therefore, to see how Paul's thinking progresses. But what is the goal of all of this, and how does it relate to what has preceded, both the affirmations of vv. 1–11 and the implied exhortation of vv. 12–13? The concern about "righteousness" that predominates vv. 1–13 (even though not always expressed in that language but there nonetheless) has faded somewhat into the background here. But when that concern reemerges for the final time in the present argument (until spelled out in particulars in 12:1–15:13), it does so with this metaphor as the primary focus: God's foreordained purpose for us is to be conformed to the likeness of his Son, Firstborn of many brothers and sisters (v. 29). But for now the emphasis seems to have shifted to affirmation and encouragement. The Spirit who has freed us from Torah, sin, and death (v. 2), the Spirit by whom we walk so as to fulfill the righteous requirement of Torah (v. 4) in contrast to those who live in the flesh (vv. 5–8, 12–13), the Spirit who leads us (in the paths of righteousness for his name's sake, v. 14a) is none other than the same Spirit by whom we became believers, and thus God's own children (vv. 14b–17). If the emphasis up to v. 14a, either expressed or implied, is on the Spirit as the one who "fulfills" what Torah could not, namely, the "doing" of true righteousness over against "the flesh," then the emphasis in the rest of this section (vv. 14b–17) is on being and relationship. That is, true righteousness is not so much obedience to behavioral regulations as it is the living out of a new relationship with God—as his "sons," conformed to the likeness of his Son. Therefore, even though not expressed in so many words here, "like Father, like 'S/son(s)' " lies very close to the surface, given the context of the present argument.

Two further observations before looking at the details: First, much of the imagery of vv. 14b–16 modifies the identical imagery from Gal

4:4–7. Thus, much of that discussion will be only cross-referenced here. What interests us are the modifications and thus the special emphases in this presentation, most notable of which is the thoroughly christocent-ric—and Trinitarian—soteriological focus in Galatians. Conversely, in the present passage the focus is altogether on the Spirit, so much so that the "adoption of 'sons' " which *Christ* effected in Gal 4:5 is now referred to as the *Spirit's* thing: he is "the Spirit of 'adoption as sons.' "

Second, a linguistic phenomenon that emerges in v. 16 and carries through to 9:1 needs to be noted, even if it cannot be fully explained: the sudden and repeated occurrence of σύν-compounds (words that are com-pounded with the Greek preposition "together with" so as to form new words). This is true first of all regarding the indwelling Spirit, who "bears witness together with our own spirits" (v. 16), and who "comes together with us in our weaknesses to offer aid" (v. 26). Likewise it is probably the Spirit who works all things together for good (v. 28). In 9:1 this will play in reverse: Paul's own conscience bearing witness together with him by the Spirit. But it is also true of the believer's relationship with Christ, with whom one is "heir together with," provided one also "suffers to-gether with" in order to be "glorified together with" (v. 17), and into whose likeness one is finally to be "formed together with [= conformed]" (v. 29). Even creation gets in on it, "groaning together with" as it "suffers birth pangs together with" (v. 22). Elsewhere in Paul this compound, when not merely an everyday word, tends to emphasize the closest kind of relationship between two people or matters. Is this Paul's own, perhaps unconscious, way to bring this "argument" to its fitting climax?

14 The γάρ ("for") that ties this sentence to the preceding (implied) exhortation of v. 13b indicates that Paul intended the closest kind of relationship between the two sentences, the latter offering further ex-planation, or elaboration, of the former. This means that the language "as many as are being led by the Spirit of God" is best understood as a kind of positive rephrasing of "putting to death the deeds of the body by the Spirit." That is, the somewhat negative-appearing approach to "righteousness" in v. 13, set up because it was expressed vis-à-vis life in the flesh, is properly to be understood by its positive counterpart. Believ-ers are not just those who do not live "according to the flesh," who do not practice "the deeds of the body," but are in fact people who are being led by the Spirit of God.[261] And all those who are so led, Paul says further, "are the 'sons'[262] of God." Thus, life in the Spirit for Paul is not to be

---

[261] So also Cranfield 1.395, Moo 534; cf. Byrne, *'Sons,'* 98, who notes that this clause also "catches up beyond this all the various descriptions of life in the Spirit of the preceding section (vv. 4, 5, 6, 9, 10 & 11)."

[262] On this translation of the word "son" here, rather than "children," see n. 115 on Gal 4:4–7; cf. n. 257 above.

understood as one constant round of putting out fires started by the flesh
(= "putting to death" the flesh with its passions and desires). Rather, it
means being people who are led by the Spirit. Two matters are of significance for our purposes.

1. For the passive verb "are being led" modified with "by the Spirit,"
see above on Gal 5:18. Even more than in that instance this phrase has
no connotation either of "ecstasy" or "Spirit seizure,"[263] on the one hand,
or of "guidance" in the sense of direct help for the details of one's life,[264]
on the other. As always in Paul, the primary place to turn for such usage
is to the OT, where in a whole variety of ways God is said to "lead" the
people of God in the ways of God. Thus, for example, Ps 23:3: "He leads
me in paths of righteousness for his name's sake." That is almost certainly what Paul intends here, that God's people are led by the Spirit *of
God* "into paths of righteousness for the sake of God's name," and such
people thereby show evidence that they are the children *of God.*[265] Such
an understanding best explains both the unexpected appearance of the
designation "Spirit *of God*" and the emphatic nature of the apodosis,
"*these* the 'sons' *of God* are." Such people will obviously not live "according to the flesh," but neither will they simply sit back and "let the Spirit
do it." They are those who *walk* in the ways of the Lord, who by the Spirit
fulfill the "righteous requirement of Torah" (v. 4). Thus the passage has
nothing to do with "guidance" as it is sometimes popularly understood,
but, as the context demands, with righteousness, being led by the Spirit
of God in the ways of God.[266]

2. The close connection between being "led by the Spirit of God" and
"being the 'sons' of God" is also of considerable importance. This is
brought out by both the content and the word order, which in Paul's
sentence runs:

| As many as | by the Spirit of God | are led, |
| These | the 'sons' of God | are. |

---

[263] In an earlier form, see Godet 309: " . . . something like a notion of holy violence;
the Spirit drags the man where the flesh would fain not go." More recently, and
vigorously, Käsemann 226, followed by Dunn 450, translated it "driven by the Spirit"
(despite lacking lexical evidence for such), asserting that Paul has thus appropriated
"the vocabulary of the enthusiasts according to 1 Cor 12:2." But there is no contextual
warrant for such a view (see on Gal 4:6 for the verb "cry out"), and one wonders
how the Romans could possibly have so understood it. Dunn considers this the "most
natural sense," but his supporting texts (e.g., 2 Tim 3:6) will hardly convince.

[264] As in the popular phrase, "the leading of the Spirit," meaning that a certain
decision, conscious or unconscious, was the result of the Spirit's guidance.

[265] Godet 308 makes the altogether unlikely suggestion that this refers to "a more
advanced stage of the Christian life," and thus paraphrases: "Ye have a right to the
title of *sons* as soon as ye let yourselves be led by the Spirit."

[266] So also Harrison 92; Loane, *Hope*, 52.

Paul's point is emphatic. The true evidence of "sonship" is not Torah observance; rather it is to be marked as one who follows in the paths of the Spirit's leading. These (and no others, is implied[267]) are God's children. As in Gal 3:1–5, the Spirit alone identifies the people of God under the new covenant. Thus the sentence simultaneously emphasizes the Spirit's role in righteousness and in identifying God's people. This new identity is now expressed in the imagery of family (= "God's children"). Although this imagery is not common in Paul, except in the regular use of the vocative "brothers and sisters," this is nonetheless a fundamental imagery for the church. It probably derives from the OT, where (infrequently to be sure[268]) God refers to Israel as "his son" and the people as his "sons [and daughters],"[269] language which Paul in 2 Cor 6:18—7:1 sees as an eschatological "promise," fulfilled in the new people of God. As Gal 3:26–4:7 and this passage demonstrate, under the new covenant of the Spirit God's people are now identified as the "children of God."

15 The shift of imagery to "sons" in v. 14b was both sudden and unexpected. Hence Paul apparently feels compelled to explain the relationship between that imagery and the gift of the Spirit, an explanation that will take him down through v. 17, and at the same time will launch him into the next clearly definable section of this "argument." Drawing on imagery of slavery (to sin) from 6:12–18, but in effect reworking his own imagery from Gal 4:1–6, he notes that the *Abba*-cry, which they themselves had experienced as believers, not only comes from the Spirit, but is also therefore evidence that they have received "adoption as sons." Over against their past with its "slavery," "being led by the Spirit of God" does *not* mean slavery of any kind. To the contrary, the Spirit's presence involves an entirely new relationship with God: by the Spirit we have been "adopted as 'sons,' "[270] so that we are God's rightful heirs.[271]

---

[267] Cf. Meyer 2.63: "The emphatic position of the pronoun has an excluding and contrasting force"; cf. Murray 295n15. This view is rejected by Godet, but on the improbable grounds that Paul's point has to do with advanced Christian life, rather than Christian life as such.

[268] This plural occurs only in Deut 14:1; Isa 43:6; Hos 2:1 LXX (cf. Wis 5:5), which in turn is based on God's referring to Israel as "my son" (Exod 4:22; Jer 31:9; Hos 11:1) and to himself as their "father" (Deut 32:6; Jer 3:19).

[269] So also Moo 534. In this regard one should also note that some of the OT references to Israel as God's "son" or "children" are linked to the concept of their "being led" by God (Jer 31:9; Hos 11:1–4).

[270] On the meaning of this term, see Scott, *Adoption*, who argues for a connection with 2 Sam 7:14. In any case, it also refers to the Greco-Roman practice of the "legal" adoption of a son as an heir. See esp. F. Lyall, "Roman Law in the Writings of Paul—Adoption," *JBL* 88 (1969) 458–66.

[271] Ziesler 214 notes that the point of the imagery is not obedience (sons and slaves both obey) or intimacy, but "future destiny" (v. 17). Slaves do not inherit; children do.

Thus, as in Galatians, the Spirit is evidence of "sonship"; but unlike Galatians there is here no close tie between "sonship" and Christ as God's "Son." That is finally expressed circuitously in v. 17—as "children" we are "fellow-heirs" with Christ; but in fact Christ is nowhere referred to as "Son" in the present passage. On the matter of the metaphor "adoption as 'sons' " and of the *Abba*-cry itself, as well as the tension involved in such a passage between the individual believer and the community at worship, see on Gal 4:4–6. Our interests lie with the differences from that passage, which will help us better to understand the role of this material in the present argument. At least four matters are significant:

1. Although the imagery of "sonship" occurs by way of contrast with "slavery" in the Galatians passage, the latter imagery functions differently here. First of all, Paul's way of setting up these contrasts has created considerable misunderstanding. Despite the implication of most translations, the phrase "πνεῦμα of adoption" does not refer to an attitude or disposition;[272] neither, worse yet, is Paul suggesting that there are two kinds of "spirits" about: a "spirit of slavery" and the "Spirit of sonship." Rather, the phrase is an ad hoc creation of Paul's own rhetorical style.[273] Just as in 1 Cor 2:12 (cf. 2 Tim 1:7), his interest lies with what he is about to say about the Spirit, namely, that the reception of the Spirit meant that they had thereby received "adoption as sons." But to get there he sets up a (typical) negative contrast to their former way of life.[274] Formerly they were "slaves" living in "fear." The Spirit has replaced that with the realization of "sonship." Thus, Paul's point can best be construed by paraphrase: "Your reception of the Spirit did not issue in your returning to slavery and fear, rather it issued in your adoption as 'sons.' "[275]

What is less clear in this case is the form of slavery to which Paul is referring, which depends largely on how one perceives Paul's audience.[276] In any case, for him "slavery" equally describes Jews under the

---

[272] As, e.g., SH 202–3.

[273] So also Meyer 2.63, Barrett 163, Murray 296–97, Cranfield 1.396, Moo 576, Loane, *Hope*, 55–56.

[274] This explains the significance of the πάλιν ("again"), which English translations have such a difficult time finding a place for. Paul's Greek goes, δουλείας πάλιν εἰς φόβον ("slavery again unto fear"). The problem is whether to translate "slavery again" (= once again to become slaves [cf. NIV]) or "unto fear again" (= to be led back into fear [cf. NRSV, NASB, NAB, NJB, REB]).

[275] Cf. the GNB, which is the only English translation I know of that adequately captures Paul's sense: "For the Spirit that God has given you does not make you slaves and cause you to be afraid; instead, the Spirit makes you God's children." Missing this stylistic pattern has led to all kinds of convoluted attempts to explain "the spirit of slavery," as though Paul recognized such an entity (see inter alia, Haldane 353–54, Godet 329, SH 202–3).

[276] A point apparently not considered by those who make it refer exclusively to "the bondage of Torah," as in Galatians (e.g., Loane, *Hope*, 56). The problem with

tyranny of sin awakened by Torah and thus fearful of God, or Gentiles under the tyranny of sin without God and therefore without hope and full of fear. His point is a simple one, and picks up the metaphor of "freedom" from v. 2: the Spirit person has moved from servitude and fear into the freedom of children who have attained their majority.

2. In Gal 4:5 our "receiving υἱοθεσία (= adoption as 'sons')" resulted directly from Christ's sacrificial death: God sent his Son "in order to redeem those under the Law, in order that we might receive adoption as 'sons.' " Christ is not so much as mentioned here, where the primary focus is on the Spirit. Hence Paul calls him "the Spirit of adoption [as sons]," as noted above a phrase constructed over against its opposite, "Spirit of slavery." The genitive in both cases functions as a predicate, indicating the *effect* of the Spirit's presence.[277] The Spirit, who does *not* lead to slavery, on the one hand, is in fact the agent of "adoption as 'sons,' " on the other. Here again we can see Paul's basic Trinitarian soteriological perspective at work.[278] Such adoption was secured for us by Christ, as Galatians makes clear; here it has been made effective in the life of the believer through the work of the Spirit.

3. The language for the believer's experience of the Spirit is "you received," a standard formulation that in Paul refers to Christian conversion.[279] In the immediate context, however, as over against Galatians, the focus is not on conversion, but on their ongoing relationship to God as his children. Hence, in the modifying clause that follows, Paul shifts from the past tense, "whom *you received*," to their—and his—present realization of such adoption: "By whom *we cry 'Abba*, Father.' " And this emphasis in turn carries into the next sentence, "The Spirit *bears witness* with our spirits that we *are* God's children." The reason for this shift, of course, is related to the emphasis throughout, which is on the present

---

this, of course, is that the letter specifically assumes largely Gentile congregations, with little or no evidence that some are actually trying to bring them under Torah.

[277] Contra Meyer 2.63, who rejects this on the basis of Gal 4:5–6. But that will hardly do in this case, since Paul clearly is not thinking in terms of that passage. Contra also Barrett 163, who in light of v. 23 sees this as referring to the future. Contra also Scott, *Adoption*, 261n143 (cf. Byrne, *'Sons,'* 100), who has argued for a genitive of quality on the grounds that there is "no grammatical category" for the genitive to be construed as I have it here. But that is only partly true: the genitive "God of hope," in 15:13 is parallel. God himself can hardly be characterized as full of hope; rather, he is the "God of hope" because he guarantees our hope and thus fills his people with hope. For this kind of usage see John Beekman and John Callow, *Translating the Word of God* (Grand Rapids: Zondervan, 1974) 263.

[278] A subtlety that would have been lost on the Romans, of course.

[279] See above on 1 Cor 2:12; Gal 3:2; cf. 2 Cor 11:4. It is much more common in Luke–Acts, and there, too, refers primarily to Christian conversion. Cf. Dunn 451. The view of Ervin, who finally argues that the Spirit is not intended (*Conversion-Initiation*, 87–88), fails to appreciate either the nature of the rhetorical feature or the context.

reality of the Spirit as evidential and effective, for both "sonship" and righteousness. Thus Paul recalls their conversion only momentarily, in the clause "you received the Spirit"; his interest lies in the ongoing life of the Spirit, who assures us in the midst of the "already/not yet" eschatological tension that we are God's children and thereby heirs of his glory.

4. Whereas in Gal 4:6 it is the Spirit himself who cries "*Abba*, Father" from within the believer's heart, here Paul says, "the Spirit . . . by whom[280] *we* cry." This is surely the more precise way of expressing it. For Paul it is always a dictum that "the Spirit of the prophets is subject to the prophets." That is, we speak as the Spirit inspires. For Paul this cry is not so much "Spirit speech" in itself, as it is evidence of the Spirit's indwelling and empowering presence. This is borne out even more in v. 16, which is quite unique to the Pauline corpus. The Spirit is God's abiding presence, but he does not eliminate our humanity; he has redeemed it and now works through it.

16 Without the aid of a nuancing particle or conjunction,[281] Paul further unpacks what he has just affirmed about the Spirit and our "adoption as 'sons.' " "The Spirit himself," he says, "bears witness with our own spirits[282] that we are God's children." That is, as we cry "*Abba*" to God, we do so in full awareness that we are God's children, but we are also aware that we do so *by* the Spirit who has preceded us by giving us birth and is now prompting our cry. In saying this, Paul picks up the language of his heritage ("out of the mouth of two witnesses") and indicates that our *awareness* and *assurance* of this new relationship with God has the twofold witness of God's Spirit together with our own spirits.

But why this emphasis here? Very likely Paul is being neither corrective nor instructive. That is, one simply reads too much into such a sentence to see it as correcting some kind of misguided perspective in Rome. But neither is Paul trying to "teach" them something about the Spirit and their own spirits. Most likely its intent is one of affirmation, pure and simple. How do "we" know that we are God's children? Because by inspiring *us* to cry "*Abba*-Father," the Spirit of God thereby bears

---

[280] Gk. ἐν ᾧ, which elsewhere in Paul tends to mean "in that" or "because" (cf. 8:3); but since there is such a clear antecedent for the pronoun in this case, the instrumental usage seems certain. Cf. Moule, *Idiom Book*, 131, and most commentaries.

[281] See Cranfield 1.398 for a refutation of the punctuation in WH[mg], noted by Denney 648 and Barrett 164, and adopted by Moffatt and RSV (and retained in the NRSV): "When we cry, 'Abba, Father!' it is the Spirit himself bearing witness with our spirit."

[282] Gk. τῷ πνεύματι ἡμῶν, another example of a distributive singular; cf. the discussion in n. 341 on Gal 6:18.

witness with us (= our own spirits) that we belong to God as his children. Thus it stands primarily as a further word of assurance and in response to "slavery that leads to fear."

Even though that seems clear enough, not all think so. Thus three further matters need to be addressed:

1. By the very way Paul speaks of God's Spirit bearing witness with ours, he is saying something about his anthropological perspective—that we "have" a "spirit" (are a "spirit"?), which is distinguishable from the body. This is probably equal to "the inner person" to whom Paul refers in 2 Cor 4:16.[283] This seems so clear, and so matter-of-fact, that all other πνεῦμα texts in Paul that refer to the human spirit need to be heard in light of this one.[284] Which means further that, along with 1 Cor 2:10–12 (q.v.), this verse would seem to invalidate all talk about the divine Spirit as replacing the human spirit or becoming the only form of "spirit" known in Paul's anthropology.[285]

2. What Paul intends by his use of the verb συμμαρτυρέω has created difficulties for some. Disturbed by the supposed theological infelicity of Paul's sentence, that he appears to allow that we know we are God's children *apart from* the Spirit, some argue for a watered down sense to the verb ("assures our spirits") or take the dative as an indirect object ("bears witness *to* our Spirit").[286] But these are unnecessary expedients that abandon Pauline usage for the sake of a prior theological concern that is not involved here. Such objections appear to assume that the text is referring to Christian conversion;[287] but as pointed out above, both the shift to the present tense in v. 15b and the larger context indicate that Paul is rather speaking to the situation of the life of the believers, not to the moment of conversion. This is the "witness" of those whose spirits have already been renewed by the Spirit of God. His point would best be understood as suggesting: "I bear witness, 'I am God's child,' because the

---

[283] Cf. Dunn 454.

[284] Alongside 1 Cor 2:10–12, these two texts together should serve as the *starting point* for the discussion.

[285] On this matter see esp. Jewett, *Terms*, 167–200, and in the present study the discussion on 1 Thes 5:23 and Gal 6:18. Jewett's discussion proceeds on the basis of a tenuous assumption (that the only anthropological "spirit" Paul knows is the "apportioned Spirit" of God), which leads to a view that seems nearly indefensible (that the Spirit is merely bearing witness to himself). But cf. Käsemann 228–29, Ziesler 216 (tentatively), Schweizer, *TDNT* 6.436. A better methodology would call for the two clear texts (this one and 1 Cor 2:10–12) to be the starting point for Pauline anthropology, and for interpreting the others in light of these two.

[286] E.g., Godet 311, Leenhardt 215, Cranfield 1.402–3 (an extensive argument that manifestly begins with this theological agenda in hand), Morris 316 (convinced by Cranfield).

[287] Indeed, Cranfield, appealing to a "logical" reversal of vv. 15 and 16, argues that the witness of the Spirit *to* our spirits (in conversion is implied) leads us to say "*Abba*, Father."

Spirit has already borne witness, 'You are God's child'; and the evidence for this is the cry of '*Abba*,' which I make, but do so by the Spirit's prompting."

This means that those who make much out of the concept of "the inner witness of the Spirit"[288] are probably also missing Paul's point. One need not doubt that such an "inner witness" results, as it were; but Paul is almost certainly not speaking to some deep, interior witness that the Spirit makes within us. Rather, as already suggested, he is simply elaborating on the significance of the *Abba*-cry, that by our crying out to God the Spirit thus bears witness with our spirits that we are God's children.[289]

3. What is more significant for our purposes is the clear sense one receives from this passage, which will be picked up again in v. 26, that the Spirit has not come to "take over," as it were, so that our own human responsibility is diminished. Here Paul says directly what we have noted in passing elsewhere: for him the coming of the Spirit does not overtake or overwhelm. Rather the Spirit has come to do what Torah could not—inscribe obedience on the heart in such a way that God's people will follow in God's ways by his direct help. The Christian life is *by the Spirit*; but *we* cry, or walk, or conform our behavior, or follow, as the case may be. Thus, the Spirit is present, and in this case "bears witness," but he does so as an entity apart from ourselves, to whom we yield and whose lead we follow or by whose inspiration we speak.

We need finally to note how emphatically personal this sentence reveals Paul's understanding of the Spirit to be. By both the intensive pronoun, "the Spirit *himself*" and the verb "bears witness with," Paul asserts the Spirit's discrete personal existence. One does not speak of "the influence itself" as "bearing witness with" another person. Combined with vv. 26–27 that follow, this text opens up for us the personal dimension of the Spirit that will not allow anything less.

17 This final sentence, which has no direct reference to the Spirit, spells out the further, now eschatological, ramifications of the affirmation of v. 16 that the Spirit's presence assures us that we are God's children indeed. Here is the final glorious outcome of our "adoption as 'sons.' " Still following the general sense and order of the prior passage in Gal 4:4–7, Paul now elaborates on the ultimate significance of our being "children" of God—that we are thus his "heirs," which means further that we are "fellow-heirs" with Christ. Heirs of all of God's eternal glory, that is the eschatological denouement of our story. It staggers the imagination.

---

[288] As, e.g., Harrison 93; Wood, *Life*, 94–95.
[289] Cf. Murray 297.

But for the purposes of the present study, the significance of this sentence is that it leads directly to the next section, to vv. 18–30, where Paul wraps up the argument from 5:1 by setting out life in the Spirit within the full context of his "already but not yet" eschatological perspective. Present suffering and future glory both gain their meaning from the presence of the firstfruits of the final eschatological harvest—the Spirit of God himself.

ROMANS 8:18–30

With a considerable turn in the argument, but not in his overall concern, Paul now sets out to respond to the final word of v. 17 ("if indeed we share in his sufferings, we shall also share in his glory"), which in turn takes us back to the twin exhortations of 5:2–3 ("let us boast in our hope of God's glory"/"let us also boast in our sufferings") where the Spirit likewise played a leading role. Thus Paul begins and ends on the note of the "hope of glory" (v. 18, "the glory to be revealed in us"; v. 30, "whom . . . he also glorified"). But everything in between deals with life in the present, for believers a time of "suffering" (v. 18), "weakness" (v. 26), "groaning/sighing" (vv. 23, 25; cf. 22), and "endurance" (v. 25), while "eagerly awaiting" the glory that is to be (vv. 23, 25; cf. 19). Indeed, the whole created order, itself subject to bondage and decay, stands on tiptoe,[290] "eagerly awaiting the revelation of the 'sons' of God."

Despite some unexpected turns along the way, the flow of thought is basically manageable. Verse 18, which responds directly to v. 17, sets the stage for the whole with its contrast between our present suffering and future glory. The one is simply not worthy of being reckoned alongside the other. But having concluded that sentence in terms of "the glory *about to be revealed in*[291] us," Paul pauses to reflect momentarily on the "witness" to that "revelation," namely, the "eagerly expecting creation" (v. 19). That in turn needs explaining, which he does in vv. 20–22. The whole created order,[292] it turns out, has also been subject to bondage

---

[290]This is an attempt to capture the sense of ἀποκαραδοκία in v. 19—a point that Paul obviously feels the need to explain, hence the brief digression in vv. 20–21. It was pointed out to me that Phillips had already so translated it.

[291]Gk. εἰς ἡμᾶς, which, given the context, probably has something of a telic sense; that is, the glory to be revealed has us as its goal and purpose. But in the present sentence that is difficult to convey, since it also has "us" as the locus of that revelation. Hence, with Cranfield 1.410, I think the English "in us" is still the best we can do.

[292]Gk. πᾶσα ἡ κτίσις, which with most commentators I take to refer especially to the whole of the non-human creation (esp. the earth), which suffered "bondage to decay," apparently referring to the curse at the Fall (Gen 3:16). This reflects a view

and decay and thus awaits its "redemption" in ours. Not only so, but it also shares both in our groaning and in our pain.[293] And this is where we come in (vv. 23–25). We, too, having already received the firstfruits of the future glory, the Spirit himself, eagerly await that same "revelation," now expressed as a *future* υἱοθεσία ("adoption as 'sons' "; cf. v. 15), which is interpreted as the "redemption of our bodies," thus reiterating this motif from v. 11. But in the meantime we join the created order in "groaning." All of this is said in v. 23. Verses 24–25 and 26–27, respectively, take up the two themes of our "eagerly awaiting" the future and our present "groaning." Thus Paul first reaffirms our certain future. We have been saved in *hope*, a word which in the NT never connotes mere wishfulness, but full assurance with regard to what is yet to be; it has merely to be "revealed." Meanwhile vv. 26–27 return to the theme of "groaning," which turns out to be a form of praying in the Spirit. And this too is full of hope—both because the Spirit helps us in our weakness when we do not know how to pray as we ought, and also because God knows the mind of his own Spirit, which assures us that such praying is "according to God" and "on behalf of the saints." In vv. 28–30 all of this is brought to its theological conclusion, with the Spirit (probably) working all things for the good of those whom God has called, having predestined us to be conformed to the likeness of the Son.

The net result is one of Paul's finest hours, in terms of his fundamental eschatological framework. Here is both the already and the not yet, with emphasis on the absolute certainty of the "not yet" and concomitant emphasis on present suffering that is full of hope and glory. One can scarcely miss the central role the Spirit plays in all of this. On the one hand, he is the firstfruits of the future harvest, God's guarantee in the present of final redemption. On the other hand, he is the one who makes the present workable at all, helping us in our "groaning" by interceding in our behalf as we await that final revelation, and finally "working all things" for the good of those for whom he intercedes.

It needs to be noted finally that this is the only "tension" one ever finds in Paul regarding our life in the Spirit; and it is clearly an eschatological tension between what we are and what we shall be, not an existential internal tension between our "flesh" and the Spirit, in which

---

similar to that in Isa 55:12, where at the restoration of Israel "the mountains and the hills will burst into song before you and the trees of the fields will clap their hands."

[293] Gk. συστενάζει καὶ συνωδίνει. Cf. Gen 3:16 in the LXX, where the woman's curse includes στεναγμός in childbearing. The "together with" in this case probably refers to all the parts of creation together with each other. The word group στενάζω/στεναγμός, found three times in this passage (vv. 22, 23, 26), occurs elsewhere in Paul only in 2 Cor 5:2, 4, likewise in a context of "groaning" in the present while awaiting the resurrection body. The word has a rich LXX background, especially in Job, the prophets, and the laments. It pictures a people who groan under the weight of circumstances, longing and crying out for deliverance.

the flesh ordinarily wins. To the contrary, here is a tension between our present "adoption" and our future "adoption," between our being God's own people and living in a world in which God's people are given to suffering of the same kind as their Lord's. Indeed, in Pauline theology, life in the "already" means identification with Christ in his sufferings, so that in the "not yet" we shall also identify with him in his present glorification. There is no truly Christian life that does not so identify with Christ. Thus Paul can "boast" in this tension; it is unthinkable that he could ever boast of the other kind, nor does he hint at such. The key to all of this resides in the dynamic, experiential dimension of the Spirit's invasion of their lives and communities. For Paul and the early church— in this case one cannot simply say "and his churches"—the Holy Spirit was no mere item in the creed, nor was he just some ineffective influence that people believed in but scarcely knew. Rather, the reason Paul can boast in his sufferings is that the Spirit was an experienced reality, the experience of the empowering presence of God, who thus guarantees the eternal presence.

As before, despite the special temptation to do otherwise here, we shall limit our closer investigation to the two Spirit passages, which are interrelated, as the linguistic tie between "the Spirit" and "groaning" attests.

ROMANS 8:22–23[294]

[22]*For we know that the whole creation groans together and suffers birth pangs together to this very hour;* [23]*and not only so but even we ourselves, having the firstfruits of the Spirit, we also ourselves groan within ourselves, as we eagerly await adoption as "sons,"*[295] *the redemption of our bodies.*

Both the larger context and the nature of the argument indicate that v. 23 is the main point of everything in vv. 18–27. Its relatively late appearance is the result of Paul's momentary digression on the role of creation in the present eschatological order of things. As it turns out, our present mortal bodies share in being subject to the same decay from which the whole creation awaits its final freedom. Thus the created order not only anxiously awaits our "revelation," but also "groans and suffers birth pangs together." Once that point is made, Paul returns to the twofold concern with which he began in vv. 17c and 18—our present

---

[294] *Bibliography:* P. **Benoit**, " 'We too groan inwardly as we wait for our bodies to be set free': Romans 8:23," in *Jesus and the Gospel* (trans. B. Weatherhead; London: Darton, Longman & Todd, 1974) 2.40–50; **Scott**, *Adoption*, 255–59; J. **Swetnam**, "On Romans 8:23 and the 'Expectation of Sonship,' " *Bib* 48 (1967) 102–8.

[295] The omission of υἱοθεσίαν by P[46(vid)] D G 614 t Ambrst is secondary on all counts (despite Benoit to the contrary). While it is easy to see why in light of 8:15 someone may have omitted it, it is not possible to imagine the circumstances in which someone would have *added* this word at this point.

suffering and future glory. Having described the created order in terms of "groaning" and "eagerly awaiting," he now uses that same language with regard to our own present existence. Although a few details of the sentence are not fully clear, the point itself is. Precisely because we have received the firstfruits of the final harvest, the Spirit himself, even though we also "groan" in the present, we do so as those who are assured of our final "adoption as 'sons' " in the form of the "redemption of our bodies." After a brief word about our hope, he concludes in vv. 26–27 by explicating the nature of the Spirit's role in our present groaning.

"Firstfruits" is the third image of its kind[296] used by Paul to illustrate the role of the Spirit in our present existence as "already" but "not yet." As with "the down payment of the Spirit," this genitive is appositional[297] and means "the firstfruits, the Spirit himself." Paul uses this same imagery in an eschatological setting in 1 Cor 15:20, 23, to refer to the Risen Christ as the "firstfruits" of the final eschatological harvest (of resurrection), which his own resurrection has thus guaranteed. So here, and exactly as with the imagery of "down payment," the presence of the indwelling Spirit functions for us as God's guarantee of that which we "eagerly await." The reason for the use of this imagery, and not "down payment," is that the present setting is thoroughly eschatological, and "firstfruits," which elicits the eschatological imagery of "harvest,"[298] fits that context more precisely than "down payment," whose first emphasis is on the present "installment."

Again, this verifies that for Paul the Spirit was an essentially eschatological reality. For him and the Judaism he represented, the outpouring of the Spirit and the resurrection of the dead were the key elements to their eschatological hopes. For the early church, including Paul, the resurrection of Jesus and the subsequent gift of the eschatological Spirit meant that the future had therefore already arrived in some measure. But the future had only "dawned," it was not yet fully realized. "Raised"

---

[296] The others are ἀρραβών ("down payment, first installment"; see on 2 Cor 1:21–22; 5:5; Eph 1:14) and σφραγίς ("seal"; see on 2 Cor 1:21–22; Eph 1:13).

[297] Some consider this genitive to be partitive, implying that only a portion of the Spirit has been realized in the present, with his fullness to be realized at the End (e.g., Gunkel, *Influence*, 43; Meyer, SH, Murray, Lietzmann, Delling, *TDNT* 1.486). In light of Pauline theology and the clear eschatological parallel with "down payment," this would seem to be a nearly impossible view.

[298] And not sacrifice, as Dunn 473 would have it. Rejection of such a view has nothing to do with a dislike for such imagery, but with the facts that (1) sacrifice is never present with this imagery in the NT, and (2) nothing in the present context even remotely suggests it. Moreover, in Paul the Spirit is never directly associated with sacrificial imagery—for good reason, since it is the physical "body" (carcass) of the animal that is sacrificed, and the "spirit" would simply never hover around this particular imagery. This may explain in part why the Spirit is not expressly mentioned in 12:1–2, where one otherwise might have expected it.

with Christ already (Col 3:1; cf. Rom 6:4), we nonetheless await "the [final] redemption of our bodies." Adopted as "sons" already, evidenced by the Spirit's empowering us to cry *"Abba,* Father," we nonetheless await our final "adoption as 'sons,' "[299] which will take place at the resurrection (the final redemption of our bodies).

Thus Paul pulls together, with the present reality of the Spirit as the key element, several features from the preceding argument and places them within the framework of this eschatological tension: redemption (3:24), the resurrection of the body (8:11; cf. 6:8), and "adoption as 'sons' " (8:15). Despite the fact that our present suffering was the way into this discussion (v. 17), the emphasis to this point has been on the *certainty of the future.* Everything is in eager expectation for what is about to unfold— despite present "bondage" and weaknesses. Thus Paul reuses images that have referred to what is already present (redemption and adoption) and now indicates that in another sense they are also "not yet."[300]

But if the Spirit serves in the "already" as the evidence and the guarantee of our future, then the evidence that the future is "not yet" is to be found both in our present suffering with our sighing for deliverance and in the fact that we still live in bodies that have not yet experienced their final redemption. Hence, as in 2 Cor 5:2 and 4, we "groan" in the present, longing for the final redemption to be realized at the resurrection, when our mortal and decaying bodies are transformed into immortality and incorruptibility. The role of the Spirit in this "groaning" will be spelled out in an unexpected manner in vv. 26–27, and this is probably the solution to the knotty question as to the meaning of ἐν ἑαυτοῖς, which ordinarily in Paul refers to the community (= "among ourselves"),[301] but here seems to mean something more like "within ourselves."[302] It is doubtful, however, whether it thus means "inwardly," as the NRSV, NIV, and others have it, as though the groaning were an inward, and there- fore, *unexpressed* reality. Despite the confidence with which this is often asserted,[303] the phrase does not ordinarily function as a mere synonym

---

[299] Contra Barrett, e.g., who on the basis of this text considers the "adoption" in v. 15 to refer to the same future reality.

[300] Which suggests that the primary sense of the participle "having the Spirit" is not concessive, as though Paul were saying, "Even though we have the firstfruits of the Spirit, we nonetheless groan also" (as e.g., Meyer, Godet). That tends to put too negatively what in vv. 26–27 Paul will see as on the plus side of Spirit life. Rather, the force of the participle is "attendant circumstance" (= "in that we have the firstfruits of the Spirit, we too groan while we await"). The majority, it should be noted, consider it to be causal: (*because* we have the Spirit, the firstfruits of the future, we groan for the final consummation).

[301] See 1 Thes 5:13 ("be at peace ἐν ἑαυτοῖς"); 2 Cor 10:12; cf. Rom 1:27. So Käsemann 237.

[302] As in 2 Cor 1:9.

[303] See Cranfield 1.418, Dunn 74, Morris 324, Moo 324, Loane, *Hope,* 89.

for inaudible, as over against aloud. When used with verbs of speaking it generally means "to oneself," as over against "to others," which may be audible or not. The phrase therefore probably does not refer to whether or not such groaning is expressed, but that it is not expressed in the context of others. Very much like tongues speech in 1 Cor 14:28, this probably does not so much mean "without sounds," but "to ourselves and to God."

ROMANS 8:26–27[304]

[26]*Likewise also the Spirit assists us in our weaknesses;*[305] *for we do not know for*[306] *what we should pray as we ought, but the Spirit makes appeal [in our behalf]*[307] *with inarticulate groanings.* [27]*And he who searches our hearts*

---

[304]*Bibliography:* W. **Bieder**, "Gebetswirklichkeit und Gebetsmöglichkeit bei Paulus: das Beten des Geistes und das Beten im Geist," *TZ* 4 (1948) 22–40; A. **Dietzel**, "Beten im Geist: Eine religionsgeschichtliche Parallele aus den Hodajot zum paulinischen Beten in Geist," *TZ* 13 (1957) 12–32; G. D. **Fee**, "Some Reflections on Pauline Spirituality," in *Alive to God: Studies in Spirituality presented to James Houston* (ed. J. I. Packer and L. Wilkinson; Downers Grove: InterVarsity, 1992) 96–107; E. **Gaugler**, "Der Geist und das Gebet der schwachen Gemeinde," *IKZ* 51 (1961) 67–94; E. **Käsemann**, "The Cry for Liberty in the Worship of the Church," in *Perspectives on Paul* (London: SCM, 1971) 122–37; G. **MacRae**, "A Note on Romans 8:26–27," *HTR* 73 (1980) 227–30; K. **Niederwimmer**, "Das Gebet des Geistes," *TZ* 20 (1964) 252–65; E. A. **Obeng**, "The Spirit Intercession Motif in Paul," *ExpT* 95 (1983/84) 360–64; idem, "The Origin of the Spirit Intercession Motif in Romans 8:26," *NTS* 32 (1986) 621–32; J. **Schniewind**, "Das Seufzen des Geistes, Röm 8.26, 27," in *Nachgelassene Reden und Aufsätze* (Berlin: Töpelmann, 1952) 81–103; K. **Stendahl**, "Paul at Prayer," in *Meanings: The Bible as Document and as a Guide* (Philadelphia: Fortress, 1984) 151–61; A. J. M. **Wedderburn**, "Romans 8:26—Towards a Theology of Glossolalia," *SJT* 28 (1975) 369–77.

[305]Gk. τῇ ἀσθενείᾳ, which I take to be a distributive singular (see discussion below), as did the later MajT tradition, which changed the singular to plural. The Western alterations to τῆς δεήσεως (F G) and its conflation (τῇ ἀσθενείᾳ τῆς δεήσεως; it Ambrosiaster) are secondary attempts to have the sentence speak more directly to the concern about prayer that follows. The versional reading, "with our weakness in prayer," is the earliest of many who have understood "weakness" in this way. See the discussion below.

[306]Gk. τὸ γὰρ τί προσευξώμεθα; the τὸ makes the rest of the clause the object of the verb. The τί might correctly be understood to say "what we should pray." But it can also refer to "for what," not meaning specific things asked for, but the content of the prayer itself. The particle can also mean "how"; in which case it would not refer to "method" but, as in my translation, "how" in the sense of "for what."

[307]The words "in our behalf," which are implied in the compound ὑπερεντυγχάνει, were supplied early on in the earliest of the versions (Latin, Syriac, Coptic), for the same translational reasons I have put them in brackets here. Eventually the words were supplied in the Greek text as well and thus became the Majority text reading (found as early as C Ψ). The reading without ὑπὲρ ἡμῶν is that of all the early Greek evidence (א* A B D F G 6 81 945 1506 1739 1881 [P46 has a lacuna, but it does not appear to be in the MS]), plus it[b].

knows what the mind of the Spirit is, because he [the Spirit] prays according to God on behalf of the saints.

The "likewise also"[308] with which these sentences begin ties them to something said before this. Since this adverb places the second matter on the same terms as the earlier one, and since vv. 24–25 reflect none of the content of this passage and v. 23 says nothing about what the Spirit *does*, Paul is therefore probably intending to draw the argument back into the larger whole by referring back to v. 16.[309] Thus: "The Spirit himself bears witness (συμμαρτυρεῖ) with our own spirits"; "likewise also the Spirit assists us (συναντιλαμβάνεται) in our weakness." The content of these sentences, however, also indicates that they further serve to respond directly to the issue of endurance in v. 25 and to elaborate the Spirit's role in our present groaning in v. 23. Thus these sentences bring to conclusion the entire discussion of the role of the Spirit in Christian life that began in v. 1, but especially from v. 18.[310]

Having articulated the certain, but not yet realized, nature of our hope in vv. 24–25, Paul concludes that word on the repeated note of "awaiting" that hope, but now "through *endurance*," implied throughout as the way we are to live in the "already." Since we live in hope, Paul says, "we *patiently* await" its realization. That leads him back to the role of the Spirit mentioned in v. 23, but now especially his role as we "await our hope with endurance." What we learn is that the Spirit's presence not only guarantees our future hope (v. 23), but he also takes an active and encouraging role as we await its realization by assisting us in prayer and interceding with God on our behalf. By the very nature of things our praying is carried on in the weakness of our present eschatological existence. The Spirit "comes to our aid" in the midst of that weakness as an intercessor on our behalf.

---

[308] Gk. ὡσαύτως δὲ καί, which occurs elsewhere in the Pauline corpus only in the traditional words of the institution of the Lord's Supper (1 Cor 11:25) and in the Pastoral Epistles (for the present usage see esp. 1 Tim 2:9; 3:8 and 11).

[309] As far as I have been able to discover, no one else has taken it this way. The debate is whether it refers *conceptually* to vv. 24–25 (e.g., Moo 559: "In the same way [as hope sustains us] . . . ") or to the *content* of v. 23 (e.g., Cranfield, Dunn, and the majority). It is fair to say that if v. 16 were *closer* to v. 26, everyone would go this way. Even though a link to v. 16 may seem too remote, it is not necessarily so for this adverb (as 1 Tim 3:8 and 11 demonstrate). Such a tie back to v. 16 also helps to explain the role of vv. 18–25 in the argument as well as the internal structure of the present argument—that vv. 19–22 are somewhat digressive and that the key issue is the role of the Spirit (vv. 23 and here) in our present eschatological existence alluded to in v. 17c and elaborated in this passage.

[310] Cf. Käsemann, *Perspectives*, 127, 135. To miss this point is to condemn these verses to something of an addendum (e.g., Harrison 95: "at length Paul arrives at the final ministry of the Spirit"!), or worse yet as something basically dealing with personal, internal piety.

That much seems easy enough. But our distance from Paul's own spirituality and from that of the churches with which he was associated, not to mention from their culture in general, has left us largely in the dark, and therefore with some considerable discussion, as to what precisely he was describing in this passage.

Before entering that discussion—against the majority, I fear[311]—let us first try to describe, with minimal interpretation, what Paul actually says. He begins by stating that "the Spirit assists us in our weakness." That is followed by a second sentence, in the form of a "not/but" contrast, which is intended to explain the first one by elaboration.[312] This is *how* the Spirit assists us in our weakness. The "not" clause is probably best understood as picking up on "our weakness" from the prior sentence: in our present weakness (however we are to understand that), we do not know what to pray for as we ought. Some details remain to be clarified, but that at least seems to be its function. Thus, because we do not know what/how to pray, "the Spirit himself appeals in our behalf," and he does so, now picking up the language of v. 23, with "groanings" that are ἀλαλήτοις (which will remain untranslated at this point since many of the difficulties arise here). At the least, this phrase describes a kind of praying the indwelling Spirit does on our behalf. Apparently anticipating that these might be troubling words for his first readers as well, Paul concludes with a word of assurance regarding these "groanings." The God who searches our hearts also knows the mind of the Spirit; thus the Spirit's "appeal" is simultaneously in keeping with God (i.e., according to God's will) and on our behalf. And from that Paul moves on to what *we know* as the result of such praying in our behalf, that "for those who love God, the Spirit it working all things out for their good" (despite appearances to the contrary). Finally, we should perhaps note how matter-of-fact all of this is. Paul is certainly not arguing *for* something; rather, he seems to be referring to something that is common ground for both himself and

---

[311] One does a lot of soul-searching before concluding that a text refers to something different from what the majority of scholars believe, especially so, when it also means changing one's own position (see Fee, "Pauline Literature," *Dictionary of Pentecostal and Charismatic Movements*, 680). Although it is altogether possible that I am coming to this text with my Pentecostalism well in hand, it seems to me just as likely that others come to the text with their experience of church and prayer in hand as well. Thus, the soul-searching. Moreover, I find myself coming to the conclusions here presented with far less passion than one might expect. For the reasons here given, I think this interpretation moves in the right direction; but it would take more bravado than I could stir up to insist that it must mean this. I should add that I came to this position quite apart from any "hermeneutical tradition" on this text. After writing this section, I looked through a variety of Pentecostal interpretations and found them divided. To take two more recent works as examples, R. W. Graves (*Praying in the Spirit* [Old Tappan, N.J.: Chosen, 1987] 42) assumes such a view, while D. Lim (*Spiritual Gifts: A Fresh Approach* [Springfield, Mo., 1991] 140n3) rejects it.

[312] Note the explanatory γάρ ("for").

his readers. There is no suggestion that this is the only way they prayed, but neither is there the slightest hint that something unusual is going on.

But some things are left unclear. Since the Spirit does the praying in this case, are we involved in it in some way? That is, does the Spirit sort out our prayers for us and make them effective? Does he pray while we keep silent, or is he to be understood as praying through us while we pray? And, of course, what does ἀλαλήτοις mean, since the word by its very nature (= not spoken) is unusual, and therefore ambiguous? Does it mean "inexpressible" (= that for which there are no words), or "silent" (= not vocalized at all), or "inarticulate" (= sounds that are not recognizable as known words)? Since most of the difficulties surround this ambiguous word, let us begin by looking first of all at the surrounding matter, and later try to decide what expression of Christian spirituality Paul is referring to in this phrase.

Our first concern, then, is with the meaning of "assist[313] us in our weakness," especially whether "our weakness(es)"[314] refers to the weakness associated with the present suffering, as in 2 Cor 10:10–12:10, or to our weakness in prayer itself.[315] Most likely, given the context and Paul's use of this term in such contexts elsewhere, he is referring to the "weakness" which is regularly associated with our "suffering" in this present age.[316] It is in this context of *endurance*, living in hope but not at all certain about the present, that we discover ourselves in a regular and ongoing way "not knowing what to pray for as we ought."

This suggests, therefore, that our "not knowing what to pray for as we ought" first of all does not refer to our not knowing *how* to pray, as though method or method and content together were at issue. That seems completely unfounded in light of what Paul says about prayer

---

[313] Gk. συναντιλαμβάνεται, another of the συν-compounds in this passage, found elsewhere in the NT in Luke 10:40 in Martha's complaint to Jesus about Mary that she should "assist" her in the making of the meal. The word means to "come to the aid of" someone.

[314] The singular τῷ ἀσθενείᾳ with the plural pronoun "our" is almost certainly a distributive singular, similar to the τοῦ σώματος ἡμῶν ("our bodies") in v. 23 (cf. on 1 Cor 6:19 and Gal 6:18). Thus it refers not so much to our general corporate weakness as believers, as to the weakness each believer knows in association with the suffering of this present age. In keeping with his overall perspective, Dunn 477 would include our sinfulness as well ("the subvertedness of the flesh"). While one may have no trouble with that theologically, it should be noted that Paul himself never makes that association with this word. Instead, it is used almost exclusively in conjunction with illness or suffering, or with the present bodily existence that is subject to decay.

[315] As Käsemann, *Perspectives*, 128, contends; cf. Denney 651, SH 213, Leenhardt, Hamilton, *Holy Spirit*, 36.

[316] This would include weakness in the former sense, of course, but would not limit it exclusively to our inability to pray knowingly—which seems to miss both the context and Pauline usage by too much. So also Meyer, Godet, Murray, Harrison, Ziesler, Moo, Niederwimmer, "Gebet," 257–59.

elsewhere, and especially of his directives regarding prayer, all of which assume that believers do *not* need instruction on prayer because they already know how to pray.[317] Rather, these words imply that over and again during times of prayer, and in light of the present realities of suffering and endurance, our lack of knowledge has to do with the larger picture, as it were, thus "*what* to pray."[318] In the midst of the "already/not yet" of our salvation, with its present suffering and endurance yet full of hope as it is, we are left with an overwhelming sense of the enormity of our own weaknesses. Our "not knowing" is related to our *present weaknesses* in light of our *future redemption*, our final revelation as God's children, clothed in resurrection bodies which have replaced the current ones which are subject to the same decay as the groaning creation. Since the Spirit is the firstfruits of this glorious future, but is so as God's empowering presence in the context of our present weaknesses, Paul therefore assures us that the Spirit himself[319] "makes appeal for us." Although this verb is often translated (correctly so) as "intercedes for us," the problem with that translation is that it can connote what moderns refer to as "intercessory" prayer, prayer being made on behalf of one by another. That is indeed what the Spirit is here pictured as doing in our behalf; what is not implied is that we do not know how to intercede *for others*, hence the Spirit helps us make intercession on their behalf. To the contrary, the appeal is before God on *our* behalf, the Spirit's appealing to God for us because in our weakness we do not know how to pray in our own behalf.

That leads us then to the troublesome, "with στεναγμοῖς ἀλαλήτοις." The noun "groanings" seems easy enough; minimally at least it picks up the sense of the verb in vv. 22 and 23. This is what we and creation have in common during this time of present "bondage to decay." Despite its anthropomorphic use with creation, however, the concept of "groaning" makes very little sense as something silent.[320] Yet this is in fact the

---

[317] Cf. Käsemann, *Perspectives*, 127, who (correctly) speaks of such an interpretation as a "softening" of τί into πῶς.

[318] This is clearly the implied sense of the indirect question, τί προσευξώμεθα (= "what shall we pray?"). As Käsemann, *Perspectives*, 127, points out, it is also the certain implication of "as we ought" and "according to God."

[319] Gk. αὐτὸ τὸ πνεῦμα; cf. v. 16. This reflexive use of the personal pronoun has caused some consternation among translators. Historically, because πνεῦμα was neuter, and because "spirit" was understood nonpersonally, it was translated "the Spirit itself" (KJV); but that is unsatisfactory in English, since this text especially implies the personal character of the Spirit. The NJB has a nice touch, "the Spirit personally," thus keeping Paul's point but eliminating the inherent difficulty with the masculine pronoun.

[320] On the basis of the use in vv. 22–23, Moo 562 considers the usage throughout as strictly metaphorical; but that does not seem to take 2 Cor 5:2–4 quite seriously enough as the "source" of this language for Paul in the first place. One must begin with v. 23, not v. 22, in this case, since the latter is indeed metaphor; but not so for God's people who await the "redemption of their bodies."

majority view, based in part on an understanding of "within ourselves" in v. 23 as meaning "inwardly," and in part on the accompanying adjective ἀλαλήτοις, which on the surface at least seems to mean "without the use of words," hence "wordless." The majority, however, understand it not to refer to audible groaning, without the use of words; rather, they understand it to mean "inexpressible," that is, groaning of a kind that cannot be put into words at all. Thus, the NRSV and NASB translate "too deep for words"[321] (i.e., of a kind that is so deep and profound there simply are not words available for the Spirit to use). The upshot seems to be that such praying is not really "groaning" at all, but is simply silent praying.[322] Such a view seems supported further by the explanation that God "searches the heart," implying that what he sees in the heart need never be spoken by us. And since such silent praying is what the majority of contemporary Western Christians do when praying privately, it seems perfectly natural that such prayer is what the apostle had in mind.

But there are good reasons for pause, not the least of which is that these words are probably not to be understood as the key to the passage. Rather, they indicate the *manner* in which, when "we do not know what to pray for as we ought, . . . the Spirit intercedes for us according to God's will." Several matters, therefore, join to suggest that Origen probably had it right,[323] in understanding these sentences as a whole and this phrase in particular to refer to a kind of private ("to oneself") praying in tongues that Paul speaks about as part of his resolution of the practice of uninterpreted tongues in the worshiping community in Corinth.[324]

---

[321] Suggested by BAGD; cf. NIV, "that words cannot express"; JB, "that could never be put into words"; NAB, "cannot be expressed in speech."

[322] A point of view that often emerges in the literature (e.g., Leenhardt 229–30, "the culminating point of our inner life"), which Käsemann (*Perspectives*, 129) correctly recognizes as reflecting our own "contemporary devotional practice."

[323] See Origen *De oratione* 2. In recent times it has been taken up by Zahn, Hamilton (*Holy Spirit*, 36), Delling (*TDNT* 1.376), Stendahl ("Paul at Prayer," 155), and esp. Käsemann (*Perspectives*, 122–37; commentary ad loc). Almost all objections to this point of view have been directed against Käsemann's vigorous pursuit of it in his article. The strength of that piece lay in his attempt to place the phenomenon in the larger pattern of Pauline pneumatology (as he understands it) and in the present context. Its weaknesses are damaging: the assumption of indulgent "enthusiasm" of the Corinthian kind in Rome, the assertions that this passage deals with the community at worship and that Paul is therefore "correcting" tongues by asserting it to be an expression of weakness, not of "glory."

[324] Käsemann argues vigorously against "private prayer." Although he recognizes that vv. 18 and 23–25 deal with the individual believer (p. 135), he insists, on the basis of his (questionable) understanding of vv. 15–16, that these verses deal with glossolalia in the assembly (and therefore offer a radically different [theological] "solution" to that matter). What makes this view untenable is that the supporting evidence from 1 Corinthians 14, which I also see as crucial to understanding this text, is all found in those moments where Paul is describing private, as over against public,

1. Much of the discussion about this language has taken place within the context of a Western culture in which the majority of people who, when praying privately, do so silently, without either speaking aloud or "mouthing words." It remains doubtful whether this was often the case in the ancient world. Praying was very much like reading, where even in private one read "aloud"—to oneself, to be sure, but by "mouthing words" nonetheless[325]—just as children still do until they are "taught" otherwise. The casual evidence for this in the NT, of course, is Philip's "hearing" the Ethiopian eunuch as he is "reading" from Isaiah (Acts 8:30). So also with praying. Not only does the narrative in Daniel 6 assume that Daniel prayed "aloud" when praying alone, but so does the parable of Jesus in Luke 18:9–14, as does Luke's narrative about Jesus' praying in 11:1 as well as the Synoptic narrative about his prayer in the Garden. In all of these cases the narrator assumes a culture where people prayed "aloud," that is, articulated for themselves as they prayed.

2. The present sentences, in fact, correspond remarkably with what Paul elsewhere calls "praying with/in the Spirit" (1 Cor 14:14–15; Eph 6:18).[326] These correspondences occur at two crucial points: (a) the Spirit is the subject of the verb "interceding," that is, the Spirit himself is seen as praying from within us and (b) the persons involved do not understand what the Spirit is saying—or not saying, as the case may be.

When we turn to Paul's other notations about prayer, especially private prayer, besides the prayer reports of various kinds (which describe intelligible praying), we have especially the description of his own prayer life in 1 Cor 14:14–15, that it is of two kinds: praying with his mind and praying with his S/spirit. Although this text is too allusive for us to know for sure what "praying with his mind" meant, the context suggests that it does not mean "prayer without words," that is, inaudible, but prayer in which he could *understand the words that he spoke* because they basically *generated from within his own mind*. As we noted in our discussion of that text, "praying in the Spirit" in that context can refer only to the praying in tongues about which he speaks in vv. 2, 19, and 28—private, articulated but "inarticulate" with regard to his mind (that is, the Spirit prays and the mind itself is unfruitful in this case), and "to himself and to God." He further affirms that he does this more than all of them

---

praying in tongues (vv. 2, 13–15, 19, 28). Thus there is no reason to flip suddenly from the believer in v. 25 to the worshipping community in v. 26 as Käsemann does.

[325] On the whole question of the basic orality of classical antiquity, and the fact that private reading was ordinarily done aloud (although he does not note the parallel with prayer), see P. J. Achtemeier, "*Omne verbum sonat*: The New Testament and the Oral Environment of Late Western Antiquity," *JBL* 109 (1990) 3–27 (esp. 16–17).

[326] Cf. Godet 321, who, even though he rejects glossolalia here, has recognized how analogous these two passages are; so also Käsemann, although he misses Paul's discussion by taking "prayer in the Spirit" into the public arena, which Paul roundly rejects (1 Cor 14:19).

(v. 18), and wishes such prayer for all of them (v. 5) precisely because it edifies the one so praying (v. 4)—but not in the assembly, of course (v. 19), because there it does not edify the community as a whole (v. 4).

Even though there is still some mystery here—for all of us—several features about that second form of praying are noteworthy for our present purposes: (a) On the one hand, Paul himself distinguishes between the uninterpreted tongue in private prayer and that which is public and therefore needs interpretation (v. 19). (b) On the other hand, Paul indicates (14:14–15) that private "praying in tongues" requires no interpretation; rather, one's prayer is "by him/herself" and "to God" (vv. 2, 28); thus in such praying "the mind" does not enter into the prayer as such (v. 13). (c) Such prayer is specifically said to be "by the Spirit" (v. 2); and in vv. 14–15 he says "my S/spirit prays," i.e., the Spirit prays in tongues through me. (d) In such prayer by the Spirit one *speaks "mysteries" to God.* (e) That such praying is "vocalized" almost goes without saying; how does one "speak" in a "tongue" and not do so "aloud"? And (f) even though such prayer does not proceed by way of the mind, Paul is nonetheless adamant that he will engage in it (vv. 14–15) and that those so praying are "edified" (v. 4). Finally, since this is the only form of prayer in Paul's letters that is specifically said to be πνεύματι ("by the Spirit"), and since Paul wishes that all would so pray (v. 5), it is arguable, although not certain, that this is also what he meant when he urged the Ephesians to "pray ἐν πνεύματι" (6:18, q.v.).

The significant areas of correspondence are (a) that the Spirit prays within the believer, and (b) does so with "words" that are not understood by the person praying.[327] The other possible correspondence, of course, is between "speaking mysteries by the Spirit" in 1 Cor 14:2 and "the Spirit interceding with inarticulate groanings" in our present passage.[328]

3. This correspondence also helps to explain another troublesome matter. On the one hand, all recognize that the word "groaning" in v. 26 is picked up from v. 23; yet in v. 23 *we* groan, while here *the Spirit* intercedes with groanings. This kind of "mixed" message is not significantly different from what we find in 1 Corinthians 14, where "by the Spirit" in v. 2 becomes "my S/spirit prays" in v. 14; likewise with the *Abba*-cry, which in Gal 4:6 is expressly that of the Spirit ("the Spirit cries *Abba*, Father"), but in v. 15 above it is by the Spirit that *we* cry "*Abba*, Father." Almost surely in all three cases Paul intends that the Spirit indeed does the praying/crying through our own "spirits," using our mouths, but in one instance the emphasis is on the Spirit, while in the other it is on our participation.

---

[327] In rejecting this view, Obeng ("Spirit Intercession," 363) seems to miss the significance of the data in 1 Corinthians 14 by a wide margin.

[328] Byrne, *'Sons,'* 112–13, suggests that the Pauline analogy is to be found in 1 Cor 2:6–16. But his "parallels" are doubtful at best.

4. That leads us then to ἀλάλητος itself, which indeed can mean "unspoken," but can also mean "without words" or "wordless" (BAGD), not necessarily implying without sound or vocalization of some kind, as though it were the equivalent of "silent." In any case, there is no inherent reason to believe that it should here mean either something for which there are no words or something that remains unspoken, thus silent. If Paul intended "inexpressible" why not use the appropriate word which unambiguously means so?[329] And if he had intended "silent," why not simply say so? Given that it modifies "groanings," and given that the context is that of prayer, which in the ancient world was primarily vocalized even in private, there is good reason to think that the word means something close to "inarticulate": not "silent" or "inexpressible," but without the kind of articulation we associate with the use of words— that is, with *words that we understand with our own minds.*[330]

5. That Paul now describes such prayer in the language of "groaning" is a typically Pauline adaptation to context. It seems highly unlikely that he would ever have used this word had it not been for the prior usage in vv. 22 and 23. On the other hand, the very use of this language to refer to prayer by the Spirit seems to necessitate some kind of audibility as a part of the praying. Granted the Spirit is now pictured as making his appeal in our behalf by joining us in our groaning, but for this to be simply a picture of "private, silent prayer" seems to ask too much of the language and the context.

6. That the "praying in the Spirit" here described is other than what Paul in 1 Cor 14:14–15 describes as "praying with the mind" is certain by the final, explanatory sentence, which attempts to reassure the readers that God knows what the Spirit is "saying" even if we do not. Such a sentence is totally unnecessary if what Paul is describing is a form of personal prayer, in which the Spirit is merely "assisting" our own praying and whose content we know perfectly well. That God knows the mind of the Spirit, who is appealing in our behalf, is what gives one confidence, even though he intercedes with "inarticulate (to us) groanings."

7. We should also note that for Paul this is not primarily theological argumentation. Rather, he seems to be speaking about a common, everyday *experience* of prayer for himself and others. At the same time he is also *interpreting* that experience as "intercession by the Spirit" on our behalf. Thus, this sentence grows out of (a) the experience of the Spirit, which (b) Paul is now interpreting.[331]

---

[329] Gk. ἀνεκλάλητος, as in 1 Pet 1:8; cf. Polycarp *Phil.* 1:3. This word is used throughout antiquity to mean what we intend by "inexpressible" in English.

[330] See Wedderburn, "Rom 8.26," who allows that such an understanding may be a valid one.

[331] This leaves some doubts as to the relevance of the two articles by Obeng (see n. 304), who seems to suggest that the origins of this passage lie with Paul's theologizing, not with his own experience.

8. The final problem is the hermeneutical one. First, there is no other known phenomenon, either in Paul or the early church, apart from the prayer in the Spirit described in 1 Corinthians 14, that even remotely resembles what Paul now describes in such a matter-of-fact way.[332] What most interpreters finally come down to in this passage is a form of praying for which there is not only no evidence in the early church, but which they themselves have great difficulty describing in a phenomenological way, since neither is there any widespread contemporary expression of such prayer. The net result is that rather than Paul's describing the common experience of believers, as most urge he is doing, they *fail to describe any known phenomenon* that they or the church engage in that looks like this. What usually happens is a subtle shift from what Paul says ("the Spirit intercedes with groanings, which we do not understand") to what we do, namely, struggle in silent prayer—but we are *almost always very well aware of what we are praying*. Thus it becomes nearly the opposite of what Paul actually describes, and we end up with silent prayer "with my mind," which in Paul's view *stood vis-à-vis praying with the Spirit*. That does not make one kind of prayer better than the other, of course—not in Paul's view certainly—but for him they are prayer of two different kinds. The one, praying with the mind, even though it may not be spoken, nonetheless takes the form of "words," since most of us cannot think apart from the word symbols we use to give meaning to our thoughts. But Paul is here describing *not* "praying with the mind," but *praying with the Spirit*, in which the Spirit prays, "by oneself" as it were, directed toward God, and yet with "inarticulate groanings/sighings."

Since these are the same phenomena that Paul describes in 1 Corinthians 14 as belonging to "praying in tongues," I am prone to think that this is what he also had in mind here. I do not think that it is thereby proven, but it seems to make good sense both of the present text and of the larger context of Pauline spirituality. But there are also two substantial objections[333] to this view that give reason for pause: (a) the difficulty

---

[332] A point also made by Käsemann, *Perspectives*, 127, but which has largely been ignored by scholarship. In fact, one is taken aback a bit by the way scholarship treats this otherwise isolated phenomenon (if in fact it is not related to 1 Cor 14) as a kind of everyday thing, yet reject the one "everyday thing" in Paul that has such obvious phenomenological correspondence.

[333] Almost all other objections are insubstantial in that they assume an understanding of 1 Corinthians 12 and 14 that is highly questionable: that "tongues" was a gift only for a few (see below, and the discussion above of the appropriate passages of 1 Corinthians), that it was limited to praise (speaking "mysteries" to God may be praise indeed, but that is strange language for such), or that the tongue-speaker in 1 Cor 14 *did* know what he or she was saying (which flies full in the face of the evidence). See Cranfield 1.423; cf. Obeng, "Spirit Intercession," 362. Indeed, these objections can be found in some form or another in most commentaries (with the notable exception of Dunn).

with the meaning of ἀλάλατος; and (b) that if Paul had intended tongues why not say so, rather than use this apparently circuitous description.[334] The first problem, of course, remains a difficulty for all interpretations. The second one can be answered contextually. On the one hand, there is no hint even in 1 Corinthians 14 that Paul would use the concept of "speaking/praying in tongues" in this adverbial way. That is, his usage always goes the other way: one "speaks in tongues *by the Spirit*"; he does not say "the Spirit prays *by means of tongues*." And since what is at issue in our present sentence has the Spirit as subject, not modifier, it probably would never have occurred to Paul to create such a solecism as "the Spirit makes his appeal by means of tongues."

What needs to be addressed, finally, is whether "praying in tongues" was as common a phenomenon in the early churches as this interpretation implies,[335] since the assumption is that this is how the Romans would have understood στεναγμοῖς ἀλαλήτοις (after all, the reading of the letter begins at the house church of Aquila and Priscilla; 16:3–5a). This is moot, of course, but silence about it in the other Pauline letters, at least in the language of "speaking in tongues," counts for little; few NT scholars, one needs to be reminded, would believe that the Lord's Table was celebrated in the Pauline churches were it not for the *abuse* of it in Corinth. This text seems to suggest the same was generally true about speaking in tongues, namely, that it was the common, everyday experience of the early churches to pray in this manner, which we learn about chiefly because it was abused in the gatherings of God's people in Corinth. That Paul prayed in this way more than even the Corinthians indicates that this was a regular part of his own personal spirituality; it is difficult to imagine, given the otherwise generally phenomenological approach to the presence of the Spirit described throughout the NT, that he was alone in this in the early church.

Finally, a few further words are needed as to what Paul says about the Spirit in the final clause, "the One who searches our hearts knows what the mind of the Spirit is, that he makes his appeal in keeping with God and for the saints." That such praying by the Spirit is "in behalf of the saints," in their existence "between the times," has been the point right along. What is of significance for our purposes is the relationship Paul expresses regarding the Spirit and God, which is what gives us confidence when we are engaged in such praying.

First, what is said here is the precise counterpart to what Paul has said about the Spirit and God in 1 Cor 2:10–12. There he was trying to illustrate how we come to know the cross as God's wisdom on our behalf:

---

[334] Cf. Dunn 479, "had he wished his readers to think of glossolalia he would probably have written with greater care."

[335] On the improper use of 1 Cor 12:29–30 as speaking against it, see the discussion of this passage, as well as 14:23, in ch. 4 above.

because the Spirit has revealed it to us. That takes him off onto a brief excursion about the relationship of the Spirit to God in terms of how the Spirit can so perfectly know "God's mind." Since by analogy only our own "spirits" know our minds, the same is true with the Spirit. God's own Spirit knows what God is about. But now that plays in reverse: How can we be sure that God hears us when we pray by the Spirit "with inarticulate groanings"? Precisely because God, who is first of all described in biblical terms as the one who knows the hearts of all (meaning us people) also knows the "mind of the Spirit." Thus what we do not understand, we can be sure God does, because even if the "groanings" are "inarticulate" and therefore not understandable to our minds, Paul reassures his readers, they are not so to God. He knows the mind of the Spirit.

That the content of this passage assumes very personal action on the part of "the Spirit himself" and that in a few sentences later much the same thing will be said of Christ in heaven indicate in the strongest possible way that Paul understood the Spirit as "person," not as some kind of influence or force upon our lives. Not only so, but the Spirit has a "mind" that is known to God. Such language also implies distinction, not identity. While one may readily grant that ontology (the question of being and relationships) is of little interest to Paul, such sentences as these are the stuff out of which all future ontological discussions take place. Here is presuppositional Trinitarianism, even if the implications are never addressed by Paul himself.[336]

Second, in knowing the mind of the Spirit, what God knows further is that the Spirit thus makes his appeal "in accordance with God himself." That is, his appeal will never be muddied by our own personal agendas. The Spirit appeals "on behalf of the saints," to be sure; but he does so always as one who, as very God, makes the appeal in keeping with God's will and his ways. Hence the one who leads us in the ways of God, demonstrating that we are indeed children of God (v. 14), is pictured as appealing in our behalf with the language of and in conformity to heaven. Rather than seeing praying in the Spirit ("tongues speech" if you will) as some sort of mindless activity, Paul sees it as a highly significant expression of prayer. In it the believer can take special encouragement even in the midst of present exigencies (weaknesses, suffering, endurance), for the Spirit is praying in keeping with God's will and with "inarticulate groanings" that God himself well understands, since he knows the mind of the Spirit. One may not understand how all of that works out in practice, but Paul, at least, sees it as a powerful encouragement from the "firstfruits" of the Spirit.

---

[336] Cf. Dunn 480: "The fact that Jewish monotheism could encompass such a stretching of its twofold assertion of divine immanence and divine transcendence suggests that it had more room for the Christian experience in a Trinitarian direction than is usually recognized."

ROMANS 8:28–30

[28]*And we know that for those who love God [the Spirit]*[337] *works all things together for good, to those called in keeping with [God's] purpose;* [29]*because whom he knew in advance, he also predestined to be conformed unto the likeness of his Son, so that he might have the status of Firstborn among many brothers and sisters;* [30]*and whom he predestined, these he also called; and whom he called, these he also justified; and whom he justified, these he also glorified.*

With these words Paul concludes the argument that began in 6:1, and more especially that part of the argument first expressed in 7:6 and picked up again in 8:1. There remains only the application, in vv. 31–39. The argument from 8:1 is basically an explication of what it means for God's newly constituted people to "serve in newness of Spirit," now that Torah observance and the passions of the flesh have been rendered obsolete in Christ. The whole is dominated by Paul's essential eschatological framework of "already" but "not yet," in which the Spirit plays the leading role. As children, made so through Christ and evidenced to be so through the Spirit, we are Christ's fellow-heirs, who will be "glorified together with him," if we also "suffer together with him" (v. 17). Thus in vv. 18–27 Paul takes up the role of the Spirit in our present "suffering together with him." As the firstfruits of our final redemption, the Spirit comes to our aid in the present by interceding in our behalf with inarticulate groanings.

Paul now closes this portion by pointing out God's present and future purposes in the lives of those whom he has called and who thereby also love him. God purposes our good, which takes the form of our being "conformed" into the image of his Son—this is what we have been predestined for—which in turn concludes with our finally being glorified with him. Thus what began in v. 17 is herewith brought to conclusion, as Paul steps into the future for a moment and looks back on the whole of our relationship with God, which begins in his divine purposes and foreknowledge and concludes with our being glorified together with Christ. Its place in the argument suggests that our being "conformed into

---

[337] Because the πάντα (P[46] reads the singular πᾶν) can be either nominative or accusative, it is quite impossible to tell whether Paul therefore intended it as the object or subject of the sentence. This matter was clarified in P[46] A B 81 sa by the addition of ὁ θεός ("God"), which is obviously secondary not only because it clarifies the ambiguity but also because one cannot imagine a reason for its being omitted (either accidentally or deliberately) had Paul dictated such a clear subject to his sentence. Cf. Metzger, *Textual Commentary*, 518; and C. D. Osburn, "The Interpretation of Romans 8:28," *WTJ* 44 (1982) 99–109 [109]; contra J. M. Ross, "*Panta sunergei*, Rom. VIII.28," *TZ* 34 (1978) 82–85. For Paul's probable intent see the discussion below.

Christ's likeness" includes not only behavior in keeping with his, but also suffering together with him.

Our interest, however, lies not simply with these clauses as the conclusion to the present argument, which is full of Spirit talk, but especially with the meaning of the first clause in v. 28. On this matter there has been considerable and long-standing debate, as evidenced by the addition among the early Egyptian witnesses of the subject "God." Did Paul intend, "And we know that for those who love God all things work together for good,"[338] or "And we know that for those who love God he works all things together for their good"?[339] And if the latter, which is more likely, did he intend the subject to be "God" or "the Spirit"?[340] Although from this distance there is no way one can demonstrate to the satisfaction of all that Paul intended one or the other of any of these three options, there are good reasons to believe that he intended the subject to be the same as in the preceding sentence ("he [the Spirit] intercedes for them according to God's will"). Since this lies beyond "proof" as such, I simply offer the various reasons for believing this to be Paul's intent.

1. Several factors of usage stand over against the traditional reading found in the KJV and picked up most recently in the NRSV. First, on his own Paul never uses πάντα ("all things") as the subject of an active verb.[341] On the other hand, in the frequent instances where πάντα appears as the object of a personal verb, it almost always precedes the verb,[342] as it does in this case. Not only so, but in the two other occurrences of this verb in Paul[343] the verb has a personal subject. These factors of usage alone would seem to spell the death knell to the traditional reading, "all things work together for good." Although it is arguable that such a reading comes out at very much the same place as the other, in

---

[338] As the Vulgate, KJV, RV, Williams, NRSV; cf. Murray, Hendriksen, Barrett, Cranfield, Käsemann, Morris, Moo.

[339] So RSV, NIV ("in all things God works for the good"), TCNT, Goodspeed, NASB, JB, NJB, NAB; cf. SH, Denney, Dodd, Harrison, Bruce.

[340] So NEB, REB; cf. J. P. Wilson, "Romans viii.28: Text and Interpretation," *ExpT* 60 (1948/49) 110–11; and Matthew Black, "The Interpretation of Rom viii 28," in *Neotestamentica et Patristica; eine Freundesgabe, Herrn Professor Dr. Oscar Cullmann zu seinem 60. Geburtstag überreicht* (NovTSupp 6; Leiden: Brill, 1962) 166–72, followed by Pinnock, "Concept," 184–85. Dunn is hesitant, but open.

[341] The only exceptions are in response to the slogan, "all things are permitted," where Paul keeps the "formula" intact with "but not all things profit/edify" (1 Cor 6:12; 10:23).

[342] 1 Thes 5:21; 1 Cor 2:10; 9:12; 9:23; 9:25; 10:31; 11:2; 13:7[4x]; 14:26; 15:27; 16:14; 2 Cor 6:10; 7:14; Eph 1:22; 6:21. It is of some interest that this matter of usage is not noted by those who consider πάντα as the subject to be the "most natural sense."

[343] 1 Cor 16:16, referring to everyone who "labors together" in the gospel; 2 Cor 6:10, referring to his own ministry.

fact it seems totally foreign to Paul's own theological proclivities that he himself should ever speak so.[344]

2. That leaves, then, the question as to whether "God" or "the Spirit" is the more "natural" antecedent to the "he" that functions as the subject of "works together." In favor of "God" is the fact that God is the most recently mentioned personal noun ("those who love God"), and would function as the natural antecedent in much the same way "the Spirit" does in the preceding sentence. Since God is clearly the subject of the verbs in the clauses that follow, it is reasonable to assume that God has already become the subject with the present clause.[345]

3. All other matters, however, seem to favor "the Spirit" as the most natural subject:

a. The context itself favors this reading. Not only has the Spirit been the conceptual subject of the whole argument from 8:1, but in this case he is also the grammatical subject of the preceding clause. Unless there are strong reasons for thinking otherwise, the more natural way to read the text would be to assume the continuation of the same subject as in the preceding sentence.

b. We noted above[346] that beginning in v. 16, there is a sudden increase in σύν-compounds in the argument, a phenomenon that carries through to 9:1. In several of these the Spirit is the subject of the verb, which probably serves as something of a structural key to the argument. Thus in v. 16 "the Spirit bears witness together with (συμμαρτυρεῖ) our spirits"; *likewise also* "the Spirit assists (συναντιλαμβάνεται) us in our weaknesses" (v. 26); now Paul adds, "and we know that the Spirit works all things together (συνεργεῖ) for good."

c. Language such as this exists in the Testament of Gad 4.7. Referring to the force of love over against hatred the author says that "the Spirit (τὸ πνεῦμα) of love works together (συνεργεῖ) with the Law of God for the salvation of people." Whether Paul knew this text or not, it indicates that the use of πνεῦμα with this verb already existed in Paul's Jewish heritage.

d. Such an understanding also makes the best sense of the way this clause begins, "and we know that" (οἴδαμεν δὲ ὅτι). Even though vv. 29–30 clearly indicate that these several clauses are intended to bring to conclusion the argument that began in v. 17, these introductory words otherwise appear as an interruption, thus making v. 28 as a whole something of an intrusion. But if we take "the Spirit" to be the natural subject of the sentence, then these opening words respond directly to the

---

[344]Especially so in one who changes such theological infelicities when he catches himself in the midst of them, as in 1 Cor 5:7 and Gal 4:9.

[345]So Cranfield, Morris, Moo, and others who acknowledge the contextual strength of reading "the Spirit" as the subject, but cannot overcome what to them is a greater breakdown in grammar with the sudden shift to yet another subject in v. 29.

[346]In the introduction to vv. 14–17 (p. 562).

beginning of v. 26, that "we do not know" for what to pray as we ought (οὐκ οἴδαμεν). The Spirit therefore prays in our behalf, and thus "we do know that" he is working all things together for our good.

In this understanding of the sentence, therefore, Paul brings closure to everything that has preceded since v. 17. As we suffer together with Christ in our present existence, we have the Spirit as the firstfruits of our certain future redemption; therefore we live in great hope. Meanwhile the Spirit assists us in our present weaknesses, interceding in our behalf in keeping with God's will when we do not know what to pray for as we ought. Thus what we *do know*, and this is further cause of great assurance, is that "the Spirit works all things together for the good of those who love God."

We would have the same assurance, of course, if the subject were "God." But by reading the text in this contextually more natural way one keeps the subject matter flowing toward the final conclusion of vv. 29–30, when Paul returns to the eschatological note struck in v. 17. The Spirit not only aids us as we pray in the Spirit, by speaking "inarticulate groanings" in our behalf that are well understood by God, but in so doing encourages us to trust the Spirit thus to work all things together for our ultimate good, as we are being conformed by that same Spirit into the image of the Son of God.

Thus Paul concludes this lengthy discussion of the life in the Spirit. It seems appropriate at this point to list the various affirmations about the Spirit he makes in this chapter:

1. On the basis of the work of Christ, the Spirit, as the Spirit of life, sets us free from the "law" of sin and of death.

2. As we walk in the Spirit, the righteous requirement of Torah is thereby fulfilled in us, thus bringing its time of usefulness to an end.

3. People who live by the Spirit are materially and behaviorally in a different mode of existence from those who live by the flesh. Thus the presence or absence of the Spirit is the one single distinguishing "mark of identity" for God's people in the present age.

4. The Spirit is both "the Spirit of Christ" and "the Spirit of God." Since he indwells the believer in the present age, this is how Christ and the Father are currently present with God's people. The Trinitarian implications of this passage are thoroughgoing.

5. As the indwelling Spirit who now gives life to God's people, the Spirit is the present guarantee of the future, especially in the form of the resurrection of the body.

6. Since God's people are Spirit people, they must not live in keeping with the flesh; and it is by the Spirit that they thus "put to death" the deeds of the flesh, that is, the sin that belongs to their past.

7. On the positive side, God's people are described as "being led by the Spirit," which means that he leads them in the paths of righteousness that fulfill Torah.

8. The Spirit is the certain evidence that God's people are his children, having been "adopted as children" through the work of the Spirit and evidenced by the *Abba*-cry which the Spirit inspires. Indeed, the Spirit himself bears witness with us that we are God's children.

9. The Spirit is the "firstfruits" of the final eschatological harvest. He is the essential element of eschatological life, and his presence now in the lives of believers is both evidence that the future has begun and guarantee of its glorious consummation, wherein the children realize their inheritance.

10. But in the meantime, during our present sufferings and weaknesses, the Spirit assists us in prayer. By praying in the Spirit, believers have the assurance that the Spirit is not only appealing on their behalf before God, but is doing so according to God's own will and ways, and thus working all things together for their good.

11. Our confidence in such praying is directly related to who the Spirit is: the Spirit of God himself, whose mind God knows and thus guarantees that what the Spirit prays through us is heard and understood.

Here is the wonder of grace that leads Paul to the final rhetoric of vv. 31–39—that God should do all of this (vv. 1–30) for us, sinners all, who once walked in the ways of the flesh that led to death, but now by the Spirit know the love of God in Christ from which nothing can separate us. The Pentecostal in me is wont to say, "Hallelujah!"

ROMANS 9:1

I am speaking the truth in Christ,[347] I am not lying; my conscience bears witness with me by the Holy Spirit, that . . .

As he turns from the argument of 5:12–8:39 to the larger question of God's faithfulness with regard to his ancient people, despite their present rejection of Christ, Paul feels bound to assert at the outset the deep personal pain that Jewish rejection brings him—particularly so, since the argument to this point has more or less eliminated the very things that identify Jews as Jews. In light of what has preceded, and what is about to be said, he begins with this oath formula, one of four such in his letters[348] where either the significance of what he is about to say, or else the unexpectedness of it, leads him to call on God as his witness. In this case he is surely anticipating the unexpectedness of what he is about to say (in vv. 2–3), plus underlining its special importance as

---

[347] Given the solemn oath that Paul is here engaging, several Western witnesses (D G a vg^s) heightened its solemnity by adding Ἰησοῦ. See the discussion in 4, below.

[348] See 2 Cor 11:31 ("God . . . knows that I am not lying"); Gal 1:20 ("before God I am not lying"); and 1 Tim 2:7 ("I speak the truth, I am not lying"). Cf. the similar, "God is my witness," in 2 Cor 1:23; Rom 1:9; Phil 1:8 (cf. 1 Thes 2:5).

a preface to this crucial section of the letter. In so doing he also makes a somewhat unexpected reference to the Spirit, which indicates how rich an understanding of the Spirit in the life of the believer Paul really had.

In the two previous oaths, Paul offers one simple disclaimer, "I am not lying," and calls on God as his "witness." Here he claims, first, that the truth he speaks is as one who is "in Christ Jesus,"[349] which emphasizes either his *union* with Christ, meaning falsehood is impossible, or his being in the *presence* of Christ, who will attest to his truthfulness as he speaks.[350] Then, second, to strengthen the oath, he reverses it, asserting that not only is he about to speak sober truth, but neither therefore is he lying. In this case, he calls as his second witness his own conscience, which as in 2:15 he appears to understand as an internal, somewhat independent, arbiter,[351] who bears witness with himself as he speaks that he is not lying. But since there is a ring of subjectivity to such a witness, Paul adds "by the Holy Spirit," meaning that just as Christ attests to his speaking truth, so the Spirit attests to the trustworthiness of his conscience as it bears its independent witness to his veracity. Four matters are of interest to us in this sentence.

1. Although the Spirit phrase is awkwardly expressed,[352] Paul probably intends his readers to hear the echoes of this same language ("bear witness together with") from 8:16. There the Spirit is said to bear witness with our spirits that we are God's children. Although in this instance the phrase "by the Holy Spirit" is a modifier of the verb, Paul probably intends that the Spirit is again to be understood as bearing witness, this time as he attests to the "witness" of Paul's conscience that he is speaking the truth. His intent seems clear: the same Spirit about whom so much has been said in the previous argument is now called upon in a practical way as attesting Paul's truthfulness. If his conscience bears clear witness within himself on this matter, that is so because of the presence of the Holy Spirit, who has already borne such witness within him—and them—as to their relationship with God.

2. Although this might have been missed by the Romans, we should nonetheless note that in previous instances Paul makes his oath *before* God, who "knows I am not lying." Here that same role is played by Christ

---

[349] That ἐν Χριστῷ modifies the verb "I speak" and not "the truth" is the nearly universal opinion of scholarship. For the discussion see Cranfield 2.451.

[350] Most commentaries take the former position, which in light of Paul's usage elsewhere seems the more likely. The latter position is suggested by Käsemann 257. In either case, the phrase can hardly mean here something like "as a Christian," which quite misses the point of calling Christ and the Spirit as witnesses.

[351] On this usage here and in Rom 2:15, see esp. Jewett, *Terms*, 441–46. This somewhat independent nature of conscience is recognized by several commentators.

[352] What Paul literally says is that "his own conscience" bears witness together with himself, and that by the Spirit.

and the Spirit. If the Romans themselves would not have known that elsewhere Paul thus speaks of God as his witness, in light of what has been said about the Spirit in 8:1–30 and of Christ in 8:31–39, they could scarcely have missed that Paul is claiming divine attestation to the truthfulness of what he is about to say. In its own subtle way both this combination and their functioning in a way that God himself ordinarily functions for Paul are full of Trinitarian implications as to Paul's thinking about Christ and the Spirit.

3. Likewise, that the two ἐν-phrases are so distinct ("in Christ" and "by the Holy Spirit") and function in such different ways[353] seems also to play the lie to the suggestion of Deissmann,[354] followed by others,[355] that for all practical purposes these two phrases function as one and the same reality—as though "in Christ" and "in the Spirit" were nearly interchangeable realities for Paul. That is simply not so, and in fact there is no place where Paul uses this phrase regarding the Spirit, where he implies that one is thereby "in Christ." As the distinctions in 8:26–27 and 34 between the Spirit's and Christ's intercession show, the "location" of Christ is in heaven, at the right hand of God, whereas the Spirit dwells on earth within and among the people of God. Such distinctions are maintained in the twin phrases in this sentence.

4. The somewhat unusual[356] use of the full name, "by the *Holy* Spirit," probably has no special meaning or bearing on what is being said, except that it reflects the gravity of the oath.[357] In most cases this emphasis on the Spirit as holy carries with it ethical implications for the people of God, who are indwelt by and live empowered by the Holy Spirit. But that seems less likely to be the case here.

What remains for us to note, therefore, is that in a kind of formula that Paul otherwise expresses in terms of being "before God," Paul now

---

[353] That is, the "in Christ" formula is almost certainly locative; Paul is either himself "in Christ" or he stands "in [the presence of] Christ." On the other hand, ἐν πνεύματι ἁγίῳ can only be instrumental, even if one prefers to translate "in the Holy Spirit." In this case, it is not Paul who is "in the Holy Spirit," but the Holy Spirit who is "in him," and thereby can attest to his truthfulness because the Spirit is responsible for Paul's trustworthy conscience.

[354] See esp. *Die neutestamentliche Formel "in Christo Jesu."* For English readers a succinct overview of his position can be found in *St. Paul: A Study in Social and Religious History*, 123–35.

[355] E.g., Wilhelm Bousset, *Kyrios Christos* (Göttingen: Vandenhoeck & Ruprecht, 1913); trans. by John E. Steely (Nashville: Abingdon Press, 1970) 160: "The two formulas coincide so completely that they can be interchanged at will." Cf. David Hill, *Greek Words and Hebrew Meanings* (SNTSMS; Cambridge University Press, 1967) 276.

[356] For the statistics see ch. 2, pp. 15–24.

[357] That he does not do the same with "in Christ" (see n. 353 above) is probably due to the formula itself, that is, the emphasis lies not on the authority of his full name, "our Lord Jesus Christ," but on his (Paul's) being in Christ, thus verifying his veracity.

expresses the Spirit's activity regarding his own conscience. Not only does that imply the presence of the Spirit within, guiding his conscience and enabling him to say elsewhere that he has nothing on his conscience (1 Cor 4:4), but also this way of speaking about the presence of the Spirit's activity in his life suggests that on any other given occasion, and for whatever reason, he could attribute almost everything he thinks and does as a believer to the presence of the Spirit in his life. It may indicate the folly, therefore, of a book like the present one, if one were to think that simply because one has looked at all the passages where Paul expressly refers to the Spirit, we thereby have grasped the full-orbed nature of Paul's own understanding of life in the Spirit. A text like this one alerts us that Paul's understanding is too large for us to encompass it by merely collecting particular texts and looking at them.

ROMANS 11:8

. . . *Even as it is written, "God gave them a spirit of stupor."*

This is the one appearance of πνεῦμα in Romans that unquestionably neither refers nor alludes to the Holy Spirit. Paul is simply "citing" Deut 29:4, using the language of Isa 29:10. The phrase is a periphrasis referring to the way "stupor" came on the people, by means of a "spirit of stupor." This usage, "spirit of . . . ," which is a thoroughgoing OT idiom, probably lies behind Paul's own occasional use of it. See further on ch. 2.

ROMANS 11:29

. . . *For the gracious gifts and calling of God are irrevocable.*

This is yet another occurrence of the word χαρίσματα ("gracious gifts"), this time in the plural, that gives evidence that the basic sense of the word has nothing to do with "Spirit gifting." The "gracious gifts" referred to are singled out in 9:4–5.[358] These "gifts" are by their very nature "irrevocable." It is especially doubtful that Paul thought of these in terms of the Spirit. On this usage in Romans, see on 1:11, 5:15–16, and 6:23, as well as 12:3–8.

ROMANS 12:1–15:13[359]

We come now to the fourth major section of the argument of this letter, a letter which has primarily to do with Jew and Gentile as one

---

[358] So most of the commentaries who comment on it at all; e.g., Denney 684, Leenhardt 294, Murray 2.101, Michel 283, Cranfield 2.581, Harrison 125, Käsemann 316, Dunn 686, Morris 424.

[359] *Bibliography:* V. P. **Furnish**, *Theology and Ethics in Paul* (Nashville: Abingdon, 1968) 98–106; **Hemphill**, *Gifts*, 129–50; M. **Thompson**, *Clothed with Christ:*

people of God, apart from Torah, predicated on the death and resurrection of Christ Jesus and the ongoing ministry of the Holy Spirit. All of the major concerns have now been addressed: that the righteousness of God has come for Gentile and Jew alike, through Christ, based on faith, and apart from Law (1:18–5:11); that such righteousness includes righteous living, which Torah called for but was unable to accomplish, but has now been realized through Christ and the Spirit (5:12–8:39); that, despite Jewish rejection of Christ and Christ's having brought the time of Torah to an end, God's faithfulness is not thereby called into question, since he will still show mercy on his ancient people as he has on the Gentiles (9:1–11:36). But one concern remains, that of getting all of this to work at the practical level of Jew and Gentile as one people of God in their life together, both as a believing community and in the world. And that is what 12:1–15:13 is all about.

In a sense the whole letter has been aiming toward the practical, but delicate, issue of how the "righteousness of God" argued for in chapters 1–11 is going to work in a setting where Jewish Christians are still Torah-observant while Gentiles are not. Paul's concern, finally, as expressed at the conclusion of the whole argument, is that they might *together with one voice* glorify God, even the Father of our Lord Jesus Christ." The means toward this end is to "accept one another," even as Christ has accepted them for "the glory of God" (15:5–6).[360]

One needs to be careful, therefore, not to read this block of material as just so much paraenesis (exhortation). For even though it is full of imperatives—it is exhortation, after all—most of it (12:9–21 excepted) comes in the form of argumentation. Explanatory γάρ's ("for") and consequential language ("so then," "therefore") abound, and in Paul this is the stuff of argumentation. Indeed, one of the unique features of this material is that for the most part[361] it takes the form of an imperative, followed by argumentation that either explains or supports it.[362] The

---

The Example and Teaching of Jesus in Romans 12.1–15.13 (JSNTS 59; Sheffield: JSOT Press, 1991).

[360] Christ "accepted them" by his having been a "servant of the Jews, . . . so as to confirm God's promises to the patriarchs and so that the Gentiles might glorify God on account of his mercy [to them]" (vv. 7–9). Paul then concludes with a catena of OT passages that have to do with Gentile inclusion among the people of God, who thus "glorify God." When one looks at the letter as a whole it is hard to escape the conclusion that it was all heading toward this objective.

[361] Apart from the genuinely paraenetic material in 12:9–21 and the opening imperative (vv. 1–2), which functions as a kind of "heading" for the whole.

[362] Thus in 12:3–8 an opening imperative (v. 3) is followed by supporting argument and illustration (vv. 4–8); in 13:1–7 an opening imperative (v. 1a) is followed by argumentation (vv. 1b–5), a pattern repeated in vv. 6–7; in 13:8–10 an opening imperative (v. 8a) is followed by argument (vv. 8b–10); in 13:11–14 this plays in reverse

argument's content has to do with their life together as inhabitants of
Rome (12:17–21 [in part] and 13:1–7), but especially with their life together as a believing community composed of Jew and Gentile.

The flow of thought can be easily traced.[363] Paul begins with the
imperative (vv. 1–2) and argument (vv. 3–8), which seem intended as the
"heading" for the whole. Here he offers the basic theological premise for
the imperative (vv. 1–2: the mercies of God call us to service of God,
predicated on a renewed mind that can determine what pleases God),
while the argument (vv. 3–8) offers the basic theological understanding
of the believing community as the arena in which all of this functions.
This is followed by a series of imperatives (12:9–21), which in a variety
of ways illustrates how vv. 1–8 work out both in community life and in
relationship to the world. In 13:1–7 Paul focuses on their relationships to
the world, particularly regarding attitudes toward governing officials as
well as the juicy matter of taxes. This in turn is followed by a paragraph
(13:8–10), which as in Gal 5:13–15 serves as the linchpin to hold together
all that preceded and what will follow: Torah observance is over, since
the love command "fulfills" its aim. After a final "slaying of the dragon"
(life in the flesh; 13:11–14), intended for Gentiles who need to be reminded
that the end of Torah does not mean the end of righteousness, he brings
the whole to its conclusion with a final application to Jew and Gentile as
the one people of God (14:1–15:13). The issues are two, taken directly from
Torah observance itself: food laws and the observance of days. Paul's
obvious goal is for a victory for *neither* side, but only for Christ and his
kingdom.

What is perhaps the single most notable feature in all of this is the
general absence of references to the Holy Spirit. On the one hand, here
is the kind of material where one might expect such references to abound,
but in fact there are only two that are definite:[364] in 14:17, at the crucial
moment in that argument, and in 15:13, in the final prayer that they
might realize all that has been argued for. On the other hand, our
puzzlement over such an absence of direct Spirit talk may reflect only on
our expectations, not on Pauline theology. Three matters call for further
observation.

First, even though it is much briefer, we may take the similar material in Gal 5:13–6:10 as something of a pattern. When arguing theologically for a righteousness apart from Torah which nonetheless fulfills the

---

(argument [11–13], imperative [14]); and finally in 14:1–15:13 imperative and exhortation (14:1, 13, 19; 15:7) are interspersed with argumentation.

[363] After reading the literature, I wondered whether this assertion might not be
too facile. Most of the commentaries see little or no "train of thought" (e.g., Leenhardt
200; cf. Furnish, *Theology*, 100–101; most do not even raise the question). For
somewhat different readings of the "flow" see Käsemann 323–24 and Dunn 705–6.

[364] See below about the doubtful status of 12:11.

design of Torah, the key lies with the ongoing work of the Spirit (Gal 5:16–25); thus Spirit talk dominates. But when all of this is applied in practical ways to their lives (5:26–6:6), the Spirit is rarely mentioned. The reason seems obvious: the whole of the "practical exhortations" *presupposes* the preceding argument with the central role of the Spirit. Paul scarcely needs to insert Spirit language at every turn; he assumes that they will read as though πνεύματι ("by the Spirit") modified every verb, as it were. So with this argument. The theological presentation of Christian life as life in/by the Spirit is what 8:1–30 has been all about. Surely Paul assumes that the Romans will read all of this with that presupposition in hand.

Second, beyond the perspective from which the Romans themselves would have read this material, we have the advantage of the larger corpus and thus know that much of what is said here Paul attributes in other settings to the work of the Spirit. For example, the church as the body of Christ is a Spirit creation (1 Cor 12:13); prophecy is a Spirit manifestation (1 Cor 12:7–10); and love, joy, peace, and endurance are the Spirit's fruit (Gal 5:22–23). Thus we could easily—but will not—work our way through the whole and demonstrate that the Spirit lay behind all of this ethical activity as presuppositional.

But that brings us, third, to those few passages we will note, where the Spirit lies so close to the surface of the language that comment seems necessary. That is especially true of items in the opening imperative and its accompanying argument (vv. 1–2 and 3–8). Apart from that, and except for those passage where πνεῦμα language appears (12:11; 14:17; 15:13), we will briefly note 13:8–10 and 13:11–14, in light of what is specifically said about the role of the Spirit in the "fulfilling" of Torah in 8:4 and the similar passage in Gal 5:14.

ROMANS 12:1–2[365]

[1]I appeal to you therefore, brothers and sisters, by the mercies of God, that you present your bodies as a sacrifice that is living, holy, and acceptable to God, which is your "spiritual" act of worship; [2]and do not be conformed[366] to

---

[365] Bibliography: H. D. **Betz,** "Das Problem der Grundlagen der paulinische Ethik (Röm 12:1–2)," ZTK 85 (1988) 199–218; C. F. **Evans,** "Romans 12:1–2. The 'True Worship,' " in Dimensions de la vie chrétienne (Rom 12–13) (ed. L. De Lorenzi; Rome: Abbaye de S. Paul, 1979) 7–33; E. **Käsemann,** "Worship in Everyday Life: A Note on Romans 12," in New Testament Questions of Today (London: SCM, 1969) 188–95. For a much more extensive bibliography see Dunn 706–7; for the most part these further items reflect interests different from the present one.

[366] The majority of witnesses in the Western and Byzantine traditions read the infinitive συσχηματίζεσθαι (and μεταμορφοῦσθαι) over against the imperative of the Egyptian tradition (P[46] B* L P 104 365 1241 1739 pm). This does not differ significantly,

this age, but be transformed by the renewing of the mind,[367] *so that you may discern the will of God—what is good and acceptable and perfect.*

This well-known exhortation is as surprising for what it does not say, as for what it does. What is surprisingly missing, in light of the argument of chapter 8, is any direct reference to the Holy Spirit. Nonetheless, the Spirit is presupposed everywhere[368] and lies close to the surface in the imperative "be transformed by the renewing of the mind." But something needs also to be said about the word in v. 1 commonly translated "spiritual,"[369] since the Greek word is unrelated to the πνεῦμα word group. But before that, a couple of observations about the whole.

First, besides the "therefore" with which this passage begins, there are other ties to the preceding argument, in particular (a) the "mercies of God" as the theological foundation, which picks up the argument as a whole, but now especially by way of 11:30–32, even though not with the same language, and (b) the language "present your *bodies,*" which, even though chosen here because of the language of sacrifice, is at the same time a direct reflection of 6:11–19.[370]

Second, the sacrificial language in which v. 1 is couched can scarcely be missed, nor would it have fallen on deaf ears—either Jewish or Gentile—in Rome. Metaphors from the sacrificial system are not common in Paul.[371] Its usage here is almost certainly in light of the preceding

---

except that the infinitive ties v. 2 more closely to the infinitive of v. 1 ("I urge you to present your bodies . . . and not to be conformed, but to be transformed"). This is probably secondary; since it makes such perfectly good sense, one wonders why the change if original, unless of course it was purely accidental (since ε and αι were pronounced alike during this period), in which case it could easily go either way.

[367] Never quite content to let the article function as the personal pronoun, the majority of witnesses (א Ψ Maj latt sy) supply the implied ὑμῶν. It is missing in P[46] A B D* F G 6 630 1739 1881 pc; Clement Cyprian.

[368] For example, with the adjective "holy" that modifies "sacrifice." Not only is this a word that has become uniquely Christian because of the presence of the Holy Spirit, but in this case in particular Paul employs similar imagery in 15:16 to refer to Gentiles as an "offering" to God, which has been "sanctified by the Holy Spirit." Käsemann 327 seems to miss Pauline usage here by arguing that "holy" does not have ethical overtones. Granted, the word is called forth by the cultic metaphor ("separated unto God"), but Paul's use of this word and its clear relationship to the Holy Spirit must receive its due weight (see on 1 Thes 4:8); cf. Cranfield 2.601n1.

[369] See ASV, RSV, NASB, NAB, NIV, NRSV.

[370] Cf. most commentaries (e.g., Leenhardt 301, Murray 2.111, Michel 291, Harrison 127, Käsemann 327, Bruce 235, Dunn 708, Morris 434, Ziesler 292; cf. Thompson, *Clothed,* 79). Cranfield 2.598 objects, because the word "presented" carries a nuance from the sacrificial system here that is missing in ch. 6; but the point is that it "echoes" the language, not that it repeats it in precisely the same way.

[371] But they flourish more in Romans than elsewhere. See D. L. Olford, "Paul's Use of Cultic Language in Romans. An Exegetical Study of Major Texts in Romans Which Employ Cultic Language in a Non-literal Way" (Ph.D. diss., University of Sheffield, 1985).

argument. The time of Torah is over; but here is Torah in its new form, radically transformed. Rather than the sacrifice of the dead carcasses ("bodies") of animals, one now gives oneself wholly back to God in the form of a "living sacrifice" (hence "bodies")[372], as those "alive" from the dead (6:11, 13).

Two concerns prevail: (1) God and his purposes absolutely predominate. The appeal is based on God's (prior) mercies. The metaphor of sacrifice suggests the giving of oneself back to God—totally, no strings attached, as holy and pleasing to him—and the renewed mind of v. 2 has to do with approving God's will and thus being pleasing to him.[373]

(2) The nature of such a living sacrifice takes the form of a "renewed mind," which, since it stands over against "this age," presupposes the eschatological life of the Spirit described in ch. 8. The purpose of this "renewed mind" is that one may test and thereby approve (δοκιμάζειν) the will of God, which has to do, of course, with walking in his ways. How the "renewed mind" works out in the believing community is what vv. 3–8 is all about.

That leads to the two matters that are of particular interest for us: the meaning of "spiritual worship," and the phrase, "transformed by the renewing of the mind."

1. Our difficulties with the Greek word λογικήν are three: to get at its precise nuance, the reason for Paul's using it, plus finding a proper English equivalent. The word itself,[374] which has nothing at all to do with the Spirit,[375] does not occur in the LXX, but appears frequently in

---

[372] Thus, much of the discussion aroused by Bultmann (*NT Theology*, 1.192), who saw in this usage justification for understanding "body" as an anthropological term for the whole person, seems in this instance quite misguided. One may grant that "body" is finally equal to "oneself" in this passage, and that any further significance is to be found in 6:11–19 and 12:1: the body, though "dead" because of sin, is nonetheless destined for resurrection and is thus the "location" of our present life in the world. But here the usage is primarily due to the imagery: "bodies" are what are sacrificed, pure and simple. By missing this point, commentators offer a variety of ploys to help Paul out (see, e.g., Leenhardt 302, who suggests that "body" refers to "the reality of existence," by which Paul avoids "pure interiority"). What theological ghosts metaphors let loose in the world. Jewett's history of the discussion is especially helpful (*Terms*, 201–50).

[373] All of this seems deliberately framed so as to respond to 2:18, where the one boasting in Torah thus boasts that he "knows the will [of God]" and properly "discerns" (δοκιμάζεις) the things that matter.

[374] See the more complete discussions in Cranfield 2.602–4; Käsemann 328–29; Dunn 711–12; and G. Kittel, *TNDT* 4.142–43.

[375] Some would argue otherwise; e.g., Leenhardt 303, via a circuitous journey through the use of λογικός in Greek philosophy, sees this phrase as connoting "by a characteristic reversal the cult inspired by the Holy Spirit"; cf. Ziesler 293. I do not doubt that a reversal is ultimately in view, but it is doubtful that this word carries such freight. Käsemann 329 sees a connection by way of 1 Pet 2:2 and 5, but that is also doubtful.

the Greek philosophers, where it often refers to human beings as "rational" vis-à-vis the animals. And because humans had such reasoning faculties not found among the animals, they should offer praise to the gods.[376] Paul probably reflects this usage.[377]

But why *this* word in a context where ethical life is being urged through metaphors from the sacrificial system? Perhaps the best way of getting at that question is to ask what it might stand in contrast to. Most often this is answered either as "rational" vis-à-vis "unthinking, merely ritual observances,"[378] or as "spiritual [= internal]" over against "external rites"[379] as such.[380] Most likely this traditional way of setting up the question leads to emphases that are foreign to Paul's in the present context. Overall two factors seem best to account for the term.

First, the metaphor of a "living sacrifice," itself a kind of metaphorical oxymoron—sacrifice, after all, implies the death of the sacrificed victim—calls for a different kind of "service" to God, predicated on the eschatological realities addressed in v. 2. This new kind of "sacral service,"[381] that of a "living sacrifice," is λογικήν, that which a living human being who belongs to the new eschatological existence ushered in by Christ and the Spirit rightly owes to God.[382] By tying it to the sacrificial metaphor, as the new form of "sacral service," Paul has already released it from its philosophical moorings. The present usage, therefore, is best

---

[376] See, e.g., Epictetus 1.16.20: "If indeed I were a nightingale, I should be singing as a nightingale; if a swan, as a swan. But as it is, I am λογικός, therefore, I must be singing hymns of praise to God."

[377] Although some see here an adaptation of its use in Philo, who employs the word frequently, sometimes in this sense (*Spec. Leg.* 1.277), but more often in keeping with the OT motif of true worship as that of the heart and not of external rites per se, a usage picked up later by the mysticism evidenced in the *Hermetica*. The phrase λογικὴν λατρείαν occurs in this later material in particular to express "true [= spiritual over against material/external] worship." It is the habit of many to read this usage back into Philo and the philosophers, who tended also to disdain sacrifices, but never with these two words in combination, nor by using λογικός vis-à-vis the sacrifices as such.

[378] Cf., e.g., Murray 2.112: "We are not 'Spiritual' in the biblical sense except as the use of our bodies is characterized by conscious, intelligent, consecrated devotion to the service of God. Furthermore, this expression is very likely directed against mechanical externalism."

[379] Cf., e.g., Bruce 226: "in contrast to the externalities of Israel's temple worship."

[380] Those who take this course then have some difficulty with Paul's equating such "worship" with the presentation of one's *body*.

[381] Some object to "service" as a translation of λατρείαν, preferring "worship" instead (see esp. Cranfield 2.601, Ziesler 293). But the word "worship" in English has to do with the adoration of God and tends to refer to what people do together in congregational gatherings; this word, as both the context and Paul's use of the cognate verb elsewhere demonstrate (1:9), has to do with service to God that eventually takes the form of loving concern for others.

[382] Cf. Hemphill, *Gifts*, 135–36, who translates it "appropriate worship."

understood as an anticipation of the "renewed mind" of v. 2. In that sense
it is "Spiritual," but its tie is with the renewed *mind*, not with the renewal
itself that is effected by the Spirit.

Second, and directly related to this first suggestion, are the linguistic
ties with the dreadful picture that began the whole argument in 1:18–
32,[383] and to which this passage offers a positive response. There people
created in God's image, instead of offering to God their λογικὴν λατρείαν,
worshiped and served (ἐλάτρευσαν) the creature rather than the Creator.
In so doing, they evidenced "foolish reasonings" and "senseless hearts"
(1:21). Their behavior was such that God gave them over to a "worth-
less/base mind" (ἀδόκιμον νοῦν, v. 28). But now through his mercies,
offered to them through Christ and the Spirit, God has loved them and made
them his own (5:1–11; 8:31–39). Their response to this is to offer back to God
as their "λογικὴν worship" a "sacrifice" that is "living, holy, and pleasing"
to God, which in this case will take the form of conduct radically the
opposite of the fallenness described in 1:18–32. And they will do so with
a νοῦς (mind) renewed by the Spirit and capable of δοκιμάζειν (discerning
and approving God's will) over against their formerly ἀδόκιμον νοῦν
(disapproved = worthless/base mind).

But how, then, shall we translate it? Almost certainly not as "spiritual,"[384] since that "accordion word"[385] is thoroughly misleading, in the
direction either of the Holy Spirit or of a "spirituality" of a nebulous kind,
usually connoting "interiority." Neither concept is inherent to this word
or reflects Paul's present concerns. Even if the cultic metaphor remains
in view here, to transfer from ritual or cultic observances to the life of
the Spirit does not mean a transfer from "outward" to "inward," but from
the old covenant, with its sacrificial system in which (now) dead animals
were offered, to the offering of living persons, full of the Spirit, whose
renewed minds are reflected in their conduct and relationships. At the
same time, the word "reasonable" of the KJV and others, while keeping
the emphasis on the rational, likewise contains all kinds of pitfalls. Since
λογικήν almost certainly anticipates the "renewed mind" of v. 2, perhaps
it can best be captured by some kind of periphrasis ("the service that a
rational being created in God's image, with a mind renewed by the Spirit,
can offer"[386])—which leads to our second concern and to the fact that

---

[383] I am indebted for this insight to Thompson, *Clothed*, 79–83, who rightly
observes how seldom this has been noted by scholarship. The linguistic ties are
thoroughgoing; and as a response to chapter 1, this otherwise strange word makes
a great deal of sense.

[384] Contra most contemporary translations and commentaries.

[385] That is, a word that is so fluid or so ambiguous, that it means both too much
and too little, depending, accordion-like, on how much air one pumps in or out of it.

[386] My wife Maudine suggested, "worship that makes sense [as befitting those
who belong to Christ]," which may indeed "make the most sense" in the end.

despite no direct reference to him, the Spirit of God lies ultimately behind
this entire passage.

2. Scholars have regularly (and rightly) noted that the key phrase, "be
transformed by the renewing of the mind" denotes for Paul the particular
work of the Spirit.[387] First, we noted on 1 Cor 2:16 and 7:40 that "having
the mind of Christ" and "having the Spirit of God" are nearly interchangeable ideas, suggesting that to have a renewed mind is equal to
having the Spirit. Moreover, the verb ἀνακαινόω (lit. = "make new again")
is specifically attributed to the Spirit in Tit 3:5, an understanding that is
surely presuppositional here, especially in a letter where life in Christ
vis-à-vis Torah observance is described as "in the newness of the Spirit"
(7:6). [388] Not only so, but the verb Paul uses regarding the renewed mind
("transformed") is found once elsewhere in the corpus (2 Cor 3:18) where
the Spirit causes us to be "transformed" into God's own likeness. That
the "renewed mind" represents eschatological existence over against
"this age," plus its place in the argument (picking up from 8:1–30), also
seems to point to the Spirit as presuppositional; over against those who
belong to this age, who live in the flesh and therefore cannot please God
(8:8), the Spirit person can discern and do what is pleasing to God. Thus
in a variety of ways the Spirit hovers close to the surface in this language.

In some respects it is surprising that Paul addresses the ethics of
Spirit life by way of a renewed mind. The language itself responds to the
just mentioned "λογικήν worship." But for the believer—and this is what
makes the translating of that word so difficult—it is scarcely a matter of
human rationality as such, but of the kind of service that is the direct
issue of a mind that has been renewed by the Spirit. The renewed mind
moves in two directions. On the one hand, through the action of the
Spirit in "transforming" believers, they no longer live in "conformity" to
the present age, from which they have been delivered by the death and
resurrection of Christ. The reason for such "trans-formation"[389] is "conformation"[390] into the likeness of Christ himself; believers thus live no
longer in "con-formity"[391] to the present age. Believers are an eschato-

---

[387] E.g., Harrison 128: "In this activity the working of the Holy Spirit should no
doubt be recognized"; cf. inter alia, Cranfield 2.607, 609; Bruce 227; Dunn 714; Morris
435.

[388] So also Cranfield 2.609.

[389] Gk. μετα-μορφοῦσθε; cf. 2 Cor 3:18, where the Spirit is directly responsible for
such "transformation" into God's own likeness as one, by the Spirit, beholds his glory
in the "face" of his Son. Cf. also Gal 4:19, where Paul uses the simple verb (μορφόω)
to image Christ's being "formed" in his people, with Rom 8:29, where the same idea
is reflected with the compound συμμόρφους (being "con-formed" to the image of his
Son) expressing God's ultimate purpose in election.

[390] See previous note.

[391] Gk. συσχηματίζεσθε; it is no longer popular (rightly so) to make much of the
two words μορφή (inward expression) and σχῆμα (external form). But the word σχῆμα

logical people who have experienced the firstfruits of the future, the Spirit; accordingly they stand over against the present age that is passing away. "Behavioral modification" is the aim of all this, to be sure, but it comes as the direct result of a radically renewed mind, of a totally new way of viewing everything, brought about by the Holy Spirit.[392] Thus, with different language, and now in the form of exhortation, Paul calls believers to live in keeping with the indicative of their new existence in Christ and the Spirit expressed in 6:1–7:6 and 8:1–31. The present age, condemned in the cross and now on its way out, is the arena of the flesh. As people of the Spirit whose minds have been renewed by the Spirit, they are now equipped to discern what God's will is, that is, what the good and pleasing thing is that they are to do as those who bear the likeness of Christ.

On the other hand, a mind renewed by the Spirit becomes the key to all the community relationships that will be urged in the imperatives and their supporting argumentation that follow, all of which begins with a considerable word play on "mind" in v. 3. But before that, a couple of further observations in passing.

We should perhaps note what the first readers of this letter could hardly have missed, namely, that these words follow hard on the heels of the doxology of 11:33–36, where the ways of God are described as "past finding out"; after all, "who has known the mind of the Lord?" But what may be true of the larger questions, God's mysterious dealings with Jew and Gentile, Paul now urges is not true of those who by the help of the Spirit have had their minds renewed. They can "test and approve" what God's will is; but they can do so only as those who have the Spirit. Arrogance is out in either direction, because at one level we cannot know God's mind at all, while at another we can, but only by the Spirit's help. As Paul will argue vigorously in v. 3, a renewed mind is not an arrogant mind, but a sensible one.

Finally, in 8:4 Paul urged that those who thus walk in the Spirit "fulfill" the righteous requirement of Torah; in 13:8–10 he will pick that up again in terms of the love command from Torah. What follows is how such "fulfillment" by the Spirit works out. What is significant is how radically different from Torah observance such Spirit-empowered, Spirit-directed "righteousness" really is. It is the result of a renewed mind, which walks in obedience to God by conforming to his character, not by the observance of rules of conduct. Lying close at hand is Christ, the "pattern" for righteousness. And because it is the life of the Spirit, Paul "appeals" to them so to live; he does not give them "commandments" to

---

is used by Paul in precisely this pejorative way in 1 Cor 7:31 to refer to the "form" of this present age that is passing away.

[392] Thus, the eschatological dimension of this passage also argues for the Spirit as presupposition.

observe.[393] How this works out in the context of Torah observance is addressed in the remarkable passage in 14:1–15:13.

ROMANS 12:3–8

[3]*For by the grace given to me I say to everyone among you not to think more highly of oneself than one ought to think, but to think with a view toward a sensible judgment about oneself,[394] to each as God has apportioned a measure of faith. [4]For just as in our one body we have many parts, and all the parts do not have the same function, [5]so the many [of you] are one body in Christ, and individually parts of one another, [6]having gracious endowments that differ, according to the grace given to us, whether prophecy, according to the proportion of one's faith, [7]or service, by serving, or the one who teaches, by teaching, [8]or the one who encourages, by encouraging, the one who gives, with generosity, the one who cares for [others],[395] with ardor, the one who does acts of mercy, with cheerfulness.*

Both the explanatory "for" and the word play on "thinking" in v. 3 (n. 394) indicate that Paul is setting out to explain how the "renewed mind" will behave; here are some samplings of what is good and pleasing to God. At issue is community life; each believer must soberly take stock of his or her own gracious gifting with the benefit of the community in view. In keeping with the form of argumentation noted above, the imperative is given in v. 3, the rest elaborates by illustration and exhortation. In v. 4 Paul states the analogy in its barest form (in our one body we have many parts, each of which has a different function), and in v. 5 he applies it to his readers (the many of them form the one body of Christ, and individually constitute its many parts). Verses 6–8 then illustrate v. 5 with seven different ways of "serving" the church, which Paul calls

---

[393]Leenhardt 307 is right that all of this represents "a categorical imperative"; obedience is not optional. But the goal of the imperative, which transcends mere "commands to be observed," is conformity to Christ—hence, the appeal at the end (15:1–9) to Christ as exemplar of the "servanthood" called for here.

[394]There is a considerable word play taking place that is not quite possible to catch in English. Picking up the word φρονεῖν from 8:5–6, and now directly by way of vv. 1–2, with the "service that makes sense" from a "renewed mind," Paul uses the verb four times (not to be ὑπερ-φρονεῖν, to "think beyond" what is proper φρονεῖν, but φρονεῖν with a view toward σω-φρονεῖν, to think wisely, sensibly). Perhaps something like "not to have a mindset that overestimates one's own importance, but a mindset that has a sensible self-estimation"; nonetheless, that becomes stilted and misses some of the word play.

[395]Gk. προϊστάμενος, which can also mean to "manage" or "lead." But sitting as it does between "giving" and "showing mercy," the emphasis in this context, as in its other uses in Paul, seems to be on the "care for the others" that those in leadership demonstrate. See 1 Thes 5:12, and especially 1 Tim 3:4–5, where the interchange of the synonym ἐπιμελέομαι ("take care of") seems decisive.

χαρίσματα (*charismata*). The first four primarily reflect the community gathered for worship, while the final three single out various "care givers" within the community. The result is an appeal for them to think in terms of the value of their diversity and their individual contributions resulting from "the renewed mind."

As with vv. 1–2, here is another passage noticeable for its lack of specific reference to the Holy Spirit, especially since it reflects clear verbal and conceptual ties with 1 Cor 12:4–14 (q.v.). There can be little question that in Paul's thinking the Spirit lies directly behind the body imagery and these exhortations; but how much the Romans could have known that without the aid of 1 Corinthians is moot.[396] Three matters interest us: the analogy of the body, the use of the word χαρίσματα to describe the activities in vv. 6–8, and the mention of prophecy. Since this material has already been discussed in chapter 4, my concern here is twofold, first, to hear it from the Romans perspective and therefore *without* the aid of 1 Corinthians,[397] but second, to look at it from the Pauline perspective *in light of* 1 Corinthians, especially by way of contrast to what is said there.

1. In a much pared down form, what is said here is very close to the way the body analogy *functions* in 1 Corinthians 12, although there Paul was quite ready to press the matter of "one body" as well.[398] There is none of that here,[399] only a concern that, with a proper and sober self-estimation based on their "renewed minds," they get on

---

[396] In one of his less convincing moments, Käsemann 332–35 has argued that this section (and thus all of ch. 12) is a "polemic against enthusiasm." But this reads into the text a large number of features that are not here at all, in particular a prior understanding of χαρίσματα from 1 Corinthians that will not hold up under scrutiny— especially in light of usage in Romans, toward which Käsemann shows an interesting ambivalence. Not only so, but he ignores the difficulty with v. 11, if in fact "enthusiasm" were an issue that Paul feels the need to address one more time.

[397] A fault which tends to plague the exegesis of this passage. That is, the tendency is to *start* with 1 Cor 12:4 in hand and to *assume*, because of the body imagery and the use of χαρίσματα, that Paul is elaborating on or readdressing that issue—without asking for a moment how the Romans might have been privy to that former argumentation.

[398] Käsemann 335 suggests also the christological emphasis from 1 Corinthians is carried over here; but that is especially moot, since Paul himself in 1 Corinthians, when he actually *applies* the metaphor, makes little of what for him is simply inherent in the metaphor. In any case, one is hard pressed to find that emphasis here.

[399] One of the major weaknesses of Cranfield's discussion of this text, and especially of the key phrases "measure of faith" (v. 3) and "proportion of faith" (v. 6), is his assumption, finally expressed on 2.614, that the issue in this passage is the *unity* of the church ("his apparent purpose in vv. 4ff. [is] to encourage the Christians in Rome to conduct themselves in such a way as to maintain their brotherly unity unimpaired"). This probably explains both his failure to come to terms with the verb μερίζω in v. 3 (see n. 411 below) and his passing over the obvious point of the whole expressed in v. 4: "But all the parts do not have the same function."

with their various "ministries" within the believing community. Whether they would have also heard the Spirit overtones that we hear in this analogy (because we have read 1 Corinthians) is especially doubtful, since there is nothing inherent in the analogy that calls such to mind.

2. The same holds true for Paul's use of χαρίσματα, which he employs to describe the variety of ways each of them has been given a different expression of the grace of God for the sake of others. This is not to say that they would not have recognized the various activities in vv. 6–8 as Spirit-endowed. It would be difficult to think otherwise, given what has preceded in 8:1–30 and 12:1–2, and given that the first item, prophecy, would have been understood by all to be a Spirit-endowment par excellence. Even so, there seems to be no way for the Romans to have understood vv. 6–8 as a listing of "Spiritual gifts." Both the immediate context of v. 6 and all other uses of the word χάρισμα in this letter in fact point in the opposite direction: that they would not think of this (very Pauline[400]) word as having special association with the Spirit at all, but with the gifts of God.[401] In 1:11 it took the adjective πνευματικόν to turn this word into a "*Spirit* gifting," and all other uses have to do with a gift from God (5:15, 16; 6:23; 11:29). Moreover, in this context χαρίσματα is immediately qualified as "in accordance with the χάριν [grace] that has been given to you," which links the word with God's grace, not with the Spirit.

Given this evidence, it is fair to say that, despite the special use of this word in 1 Cor 12:4 to refer to Spirit manifestations, even for Paul χάρισμα does *not* mean something like "Spiritual gift,"[402] as though one could draw up a list of such Spirit endowments and analyze them in some way. Rather, here and always it means precisely as the present qualifier indicates, a "concrete expression of grace," which may or may not be understood as some kind of special Spirit endowment or manifestation. Thus, we probably have overstepped legitimate exegetical boundaries by a fair margin when we use this "list," alongside 1 Corinthians 12–14, to develop a theology of "Spiritual gifts."[403]

---

[400]The word is especially rare in the literature of the ancient world, appearing for the first time in Paul, about which Käsemann 333 says: "This can hardly be said with the same certainty of any other word or formula."

[401]Cf. Cranfield 2.619.

[402]Contra Käsemann 333, whose entire discussion of the paragraph is marred by his reading of this term in light of 1 Cor 12:4, which he (incorrectly) understands basically to be an equivalent of πνευματικά (which he understands to mean "Spiritual gifts"). Not only is that a questionable understanding of 1 Corinthians (see the discussion in ch. 4), but to bring that baggage into this passage obfuscates what is otherwise a much more straightforward passage (and would have been heard so by the Romans) than Käsemann allows.

[403]As e.g., Käsemann 333 and innumerable expressions of popular literature.

On the other hand, this is not to say that what Paul lists here he would not ultimately attribute to the Spirit; we know enough from his extant letters to argue quite the opposite. Even if χάρισμα does not mean "gift of the Spirit," and it does not, the overlap between God's good giftings and the activity of the Spirit is such that Paul would surely have understood all of vv. 6–8 as the working of the Spirit in their community life. As the "gift" of salvation itself generates from God, is "graced" by Christ through his sacrifice, and is effectively worked out in the life of the believer and believing community by the Spirit, so with what Paul calls χαρίσματα. These are concrete expressions of the grace of God at work in the life of individuals for the sake of others; but for him they would not be "Spiritual gifts," but *gifts of God which are effectively brought into the life of the community by the Spirit.*

3. That brings us finally to the mention of "prophecy," which for Paul, as with all the early church, was indeed a clear manifestation of the Spirit in their midst. Two matters need attention.

a. The fact that it strides atop the listing, as it does most often where it is mentioned by the apostle, suggests that for him this was the *primary* way the Spirit evidenced himself in the gathered community. If we were correct in our view of 1 Cor 11:4–5 (q.v.), that "praying" and "prophesying" represent the basic kinds of "speech" that make up Christian worship, God-directed and people-directed, then as there and everywhere else prophecy is the primary form of people-directed speech within the Christian community. On the meaning of the term, see on 1 Cor 12:10 and chapter 15 below.

b. Of special interest in this case, and a matter on which there is considerable debate, is the nature of the qualification of this gift. Prophecy,[404] Paul insists, is to be exercised[405] "according to the ἀναλογίαν τῆς πίστεως." Everything about this phrase bristles with difficulty: its relationship to the "measure of faith" in v. 3, the meaning of the word

---

[404]Gk. προφητεία, which has to do not with a prophetic utterance in this case, but with the act of prophesying, as the qualifier and the rest of the list demonstrate.

[405]At this point we have to face yet another difficulty. It is possible to take all of v. 6 as a further modifier of the "we are" in v. 5 (as in my "translation"). Cf. Dunn 725, who argues for this and sees the whole as "descriptive." But even so, there seems to be an implied imperative in the presentation. For this reason, most scholars presume Paul's sentence to be an anacolouthon (doesn't follow grammatically). Thus he starts with the participle "having," which picks up the verb from the analogy ("we have many parts in our bodies"), a clause that concludes with the adjective διάφορα ("differ"), which in turn launches him directly into his sevenfold illustration of these "different *charismata*." The result is that he never completes his sentence with its main verb. If that is the case, and I have no great urgencies here, we might guess that he intended something like, "Having gifts . . . that differ, let us serve accordingly, whether prophecy . . . " In any case, some kind of verb seems required to make sense of what Paul is saying; one might *have* prophecy, but in community that is *expressed* in some way. The difficulty is to find a verb that adequately gets at the sense Paul intends.

ἀναλογίαν, the use of the article with "faith," the meaning of the word "faith," and the reason for such a qualification in the first place. The word ἀναλογίαν by derivation indicates that one thing "corresponds to" another; thus it means either "in relationship to" or "in proportion to." Does Paul, therefore, intend something like "in keeping with the analogy of faith," that is, in keeping with the gospel, or "in keeping with the proportion of faith" that one has received, or "in correspondence to one's faith [in Christ]"? At the heart of this discussion is the meaning of the word "faith." Does Paul intend something within us (i.e., "our faith") or something *extra nos* (i.e., "*the* faith" = the gospel)? And if he intends the former, what sense does it carry, faith = trust in Christ, or faith = the gift of faith for various ministries (as described in vv. 6–8).[406]

Let us begin with an item that is generally downplayed—or overlooked altogether—in these discussions, namely, that in contrast to the phrase in v. 3, the word "faith" here is accompanied by the definite article. On the one hand, this could be merely anaphoric, referring back to the previously mentioned faith in v. 3. Thus: "according to the proportion of *the* faith that has been apportioned to each person"; in this case it could also be translated by the personal pronoun, "his or her faith." On the other hand, the article's presence could mean "*the* faith," which in Paul is a way of referring not to Christian doctrine, but to the gospel or its content.[407] While the presence of the article cannot alone be decisive, it does open up the possibility that Paul meant to qualify prophecy in particular with a kind of "testing" word and that it should be "in keeping with that which corresponds to the faith, that is, the gospel which we have been expounding in this letter." His concern would then be that prophecy not run amuck; its content must always be in keeping with the gospel if it is to be understood as a genuine working of the Spirit and thereby beneficial for the believing community.[408]

---

[406]The very obtuseness of some of the discussion indicates a measure of the difficulties. One wonders, e.g., what Harrison means when, on the one hand, he follows Cranfield and understands "measure of faith" in v. 3 to mean "that one's faith [= trust in Christ] should provide the basis for a true estimation of himself, since it reveals that he, along with other believers, is dependent on the saving mercy of God in Christ," yet on the other hand concludes by stating, "It should be added that faith, as used in this passage, is hardly saving faith [!], but faith in the sense of grasping the nature of one's spiritual gift and having confidence to exercise it rightly." No wonder readers of commentaries sometimes complain of confusion. Unfortunately, Harrison is not alone on this one.

[407]As e.g., in 1 Cor 16:13 and Gal 1:23. The usage in 14:1 is equally ambiguous, where the one "weak τῇ πίστει" might be "weak regarding the faith that he or she has [= trust in Christ]," or, more likely, "weak regarding the faith of the gospel."

[408]This view is held, inter alia, by Käsemann 341–42; Bultmann, *TDNT* 6.213 ("perhaps"); Schweizer, *TDNT* 6.427n630; Aune, *Prophecy*, 204–5.

The advantage of this view is that it falls in line with Paul's comments elsewhere that prophecy must be "tested," not blindly accepted as the genuine working of the Spirit. Paul's "rule" appears in his earliest letter (1 Thes 5:20–21): "Do not disdain prophetic utterances; but test all things." If that is what is going on here, then we have yet another substantial criterion for such testing:[409] it must be in accord with the gospel. What differs in this case, however, is that Paul would thereby be calling not for a community testing, but for the one speaking forth a prophetic word to ensure that it is in accord with "the faith." And that, plus the fact that in this view the phrase does not correspond with the "measure of faith" in v. 3, gives us reason to pause, since there is nothing really analogous to such a "test" on the part of the speaker in the other letters.

Despite the attractiveness of this option, therefore, it seems more likely that "according to the ἀναλογίαν τῆς πίστεως" corresponds directly to v. 3,[410] and has to do with prophesying according to the faith that has been apportioned to those with the prophetic gift. In v. 3 the phrase "measure of faith" serves as the object of the verb "God has apportioned [or distributed, or 'dealt out']"[411] in a clause that begins with "to each one" in the emphatic first position. Thus the whole clause functions as the grounds on which people with renewed minds may view themselves temperately and sensibly: "to each just as God himself has apportioned a measure of faith." The explanatory γάρ that begins v. 4 indicates that the analogy of the body (vv. 4–5) and its application (vv. 6–8) are intended to elaborate further the concern of this clause, whose point is clearly expressed in v. 4b ("but not all the parts have the same function") and in the emphatic position of the adjective "differ" in v. 6a. All of this suggests, therefore, that the emphasis in v. 3b has to do with what *distinguishes* each person, namely, that each one has a *different* χάρισμα. Thus, the "measure" which God has apportioned must mean something close to "portion," not in a quantitative sense, but in the sense of the "difference," or distinctiveness, of the "faith"[412] that has been given to each person.[413] Consequently, "faith" cannot mean either "saving

---

[409]See on 1 Thes 5:19–22; 1 Cor 12:10; 14:29–30.

[410]It has therefore been noted by several that the Syriac Peshitta renders both words, "measure" and this one, by the same Syriac word, so this understanding goes back at least that far (5th c. CE).

[411] Gk. ἐμέρισεν. For the active, which is the only meaning that counts here, see 1 Cor 7:17 and (especially) 2 Cor 10:13; the latter also has the word "measure," but adds the word "canon" to make it mean "standard." But it is plain that what Paul is referring to is something distinctively "apportioned" to him. Paul's use of this verb particularly spells doom to Cranfield's position (see n. 413 below).

[412]Cf. Hemphill, *Gifts*, 140: "The emphasis is on the individuality of the portion and not on the quantity."

[413]Thus the point seems to be exactly the opposite of that made by Cranfield, in "μέτρον πίστεως in Romans xii.3," *NTS* 8 (1961/62) 345–51, usefully summarized in

faith"[414] or "*the* faith,"[415] but must refer to the gift of faith to serve the believing community in keeping with the distinctive "gracious bestowment" (χάρισμα) that God as apportioned to each one.[416]

Thus, "in proportion to one's faith" in v. 6 probably does not refer to some "degree" of faith required for prophesying, but to the distinct "expression" of faith that has been apportioned to those who prophesy. They do so precisely in keeping with the "faith" to do so that they have received.[417] If this be so, and it makes good sense of both the phrase and its context, then one can thereby explain the (unusual) qualifiers that follow: "the one who serves, *by serving*; the one who teaches, *by teaching*; the one who encourages, *by encouraging*." This is Paul's way of saying about each of these gifts, that they are to be exercised according to the "measure (portion) of faith" distinctively distributed to each—the one who teaches, for example, in keeping with the gift of faith for teaching that he or she has received. So too with prophecy, it should be done by prophesying; this is "in accordance with the prophet's portion of faith."

On the whole this seems to make the best sense of this admittedly difficult phrase. That being the case, it should finally be pointed out that Paul is not hereby setting up either "ministries" or "offices" in the church. He is simply describing how gifted people function within the community of faith, both as a gathered community for worship (prophesying, serving, teaching, encouraging), and in various ways of caring for the needs of others (giving, caring for, showing mercy). For us there is some obvious tension between Paul's emphasis in this text that people

---

his commentary (2.613–16), and followed inter alia by Fitzmyer (*Jerome Bible*), Harrison, Morris, and Ziesler. Cranfield suggests that the aim of the analogy is the *unity* of the body (see n. 399 above) and that "measure" therefore means "standard," while "faith" means what it most often means in the letter, trust in Christ Jesus. It is of more than passing interest that in his commentary Cranfield has four pages of discussion of this phrase, but not a word about the verb μερίζω, which cannot mean simply "give," as he renders it (see n. 411 above).

[414] Contra Dunn 725, e.g., who not only suggests that it refers to "faith = trust in Christ," but has the boldness to argue that such faith has been *quantitatively* apportioned to each person, a view that supports his understanding of chapter 7, but which seems altogether unlikely.

[415] Nor, one might add, to that special gift of faith for the working of miracles (as in 1 Cor 12:10 and 13:2), as is often suggested; and especially not to the variety of other suggestions that all assume some kind of quantitative measurement to be involved: e.g., Ziesler 299, "not go beyond the confidence that it is God who is really speaking through the prophecy."

[416] Cf. Bruce 227 ("the spiritual power given to each Christian for the discharge of his special responsibility"); cf. Käsemann 335: "According to the context Paul could speak equally well of the measure of the Spirit or of grace (Michel). The Spirit and faith are reverse sides of the same thing."

[417] Thus Hemphill, *Gifts*, 141, observes (correctly) that "the measure of faith" in v. 3 refers to the proper "discernment" of one's gifting, whereas "according to the proportion of one's faith" in v. 6 to its "utilization."

have sensible estimations of themselves and that they minister within the community in keeping with God's own gifting, and the otherwise realistic fact that many of these "gifts" can be exercised by any one person (Paul, after all, functioned in most of these ways) and that no one of them is some kind of "exclusive gift for the church" that belongs to a given individual. Paul is concerned with proper self-estimation and the necessary differences that make the body work. Thus he is not concerned with χαρίσματα per se. These that are here listed merely illustrate his twofold concern.

A final observation about prophecy in this passage. That Paul not only lists it first, but also qualifies it in a way that *presupposes* that the Roman community—where Paul lacks firsthand acquaintance—is well acquainted with the phenomenon, indicates how widespread this Spirit manifestation was in the early church.[418] This is almost certainly due to their understanding of the Spirit as a primarily eschatological reality. Set up especially by the prophecy in Joel 2:28–29, they came to understand the Spirit as the evidence not only that the "last days" had dawned, but that the widespread gift of prophecy for old and young, male and female alike, testified to the "turning of the ages."

ROMANS 12:11

not lagging in zeal, being fervent in S/spirit, serving the Lord.

This is one of the more difficult exegetical decisions as to the meaning of πνεῦμα in the Pauline corpus. What does Paul mean by τῷ πνεύματι ζέοντες: "be aglow with the Spirit" (RSV) or "be ardent in [one's own] spirit" (NRSV), as one serves the Lord? That is, is he referring to the fervency the Spirit provides for service, or to the manner in which such service is carried out? A good contextual case can be made on either side, and the commentaries and English translations tend to be split.[419]

First, a note about context, which ultimately offers minimal substantive help in either direction. The overall structure of this set of materials (12:9–21) is not at all easy to ascertain. I take the opening word ("let love be genuine") to be a kind of "title" for the rest, which is then followed (through v. 13) by a series of pairs and triplets which primarily speak to attitudes and virtues necessary for their life together and for the service of Christ. Our phrase falls in the middle of the first set of triplets, the first two of which seem to serve as the basis for the third. It must be admitted

---

[418] Cf. Dunn 726.

[419] A sampling indicates that English translations favor "spirit" (KJV, NIV, NASB, NRSV, JB, NAB, GNB, NEB; otherwise RSV, Goodspeed), while commentaries favor "Spirit" (Calvin, Barrett, Michel, Cranfield, Käsemann, Bruce, Dunn; others prefer the human spirit inspired by the Holy Spirit: Godet, SH, Leenhardt, Morris); otherwise Erdman, Murray, Harrison.

that either view of the meaning of πνεύματι can work just as effectively
in such a setting. That is, it may well be that early on Paul is calling
attention to the need for the Spirit's "fire" if they are effectively to serve
Christ. But, since he has just said negatively, "not lagging in zeal," an
appeal to fervency in one's spirit would make an appropriate positive
parallel.[420] The issue, therefore, must finally be resolved (if indeed it can
be) on other grounds.

In favor of "aglow with the Spirit" are four considerations:[421] the
combination of ζέω with πνεῦμα, the use of πνεῦμα in the dative, the
possible parallelism with the next clause, and the close proximity to
chapter 8 and how the Romans would have thus heard it. First, then, the
verb itself means to "boil" or "seethe." Since "fire" is a common metaphorical association with the Spirit, occurring twice in Paul (1 Thes 5:19
and 2 Tim 1:6, especially the latter, "fan the gift [of the Spirit] into
flame"), the combination of this verb with "by the Spirit" could easily fit
Paul's view of the Spirit. Second, that this dative occurs so often in Paul,
always instrumental and always referring to Spirit activity, seems to
clinch matters. Third, the apparent parallelism of τῷ πνεύματι ζέοντες /
τῷ κυρίῳ δουλούοντες suggests a possible connection between *the* Spirit
and *the* Lord. Fourth, it is hard to imagine in light of chapter 8, and
whatever Paul himself might have "intended," that the Romans themselves would not have heard this as a call to fervency in the Spirit.

But there are also two reasons to think otherwise, which seems
finally to favor "ardent in spirit." First, as pointed out in chapter 2, the
difference between this dative and those unambiguously referring to the
Spirit is that the latter lack the definite article. In fact—excepting this
passage for the moment—Paul is consistent on this matter. When he
refers to the human spirit, he always includes the definite article; when
he refers to the Holy Spirit, he seldom does—never in this formula
and otherwise dependent on emphasis or grammatical case. Thus, what
many see as the strongest point in favor of a reference to the Holy Spirit
turns out to be very little help at all.

Second, as to the use of the verb ζέω in this phrase, it so happens
that Luke uses this exact combination to describe the pre-Christian
Apollos (Acts 18:25), where it can only mean "ardent in spirit," or "full
of burning zeal."[422] While one grants that Lukan usage may not neces-

---

[420]Nor is it of much use to argue in either direction that the Spirit is otherwise
not mentioned until 14:17. It could be argued that he thus reminds them early on of
the role of the Spirit in all of this; as it could be asserted that since Paul does *not*
mention him elsewhere in this entire section, why do so only at this one place?

[421]Käsemann 346 adds a fourth: "the emphatic participle allows only a reference
to the divine Spirit." But one is not quite sure how this is so.

[422]Käsemann 346 suggests, but certainly incorrectly, that this too is a reference
to the divine Spirit.

sarily determine Paul's, it does indicate that a "Paulinist," who himself is unquestionably keen on the ministry of the Spirit, can use this phrase in a way that has no reference to the Spirit.

How, then, shall we conclude? While my own instincts are to go with the former and see this as yet one more Spirit text in the corpus, my better sense tells me that the combination of Pauline grammar and known usage of the phrase should prevail. Even so, as in most cases where the human spirit is probably in view, in Paul the ministry of the Spirit is not far away.[423] And in light of how we might guess the Romans to have "heard" what is said here—would they have been aware of the subtleties regarding Paul's use of the article?—I tend to lean once more toward middle ground. Thus, I have again opted for the inelegant "be fervent in S/spirit."

ROMANS 13:8–10

... [8]*Owe nothing to anyone, except to love one another; for the one who loves another has fulfilled the Law.* [9]*For the commandments, "you shall not commit adultery, you shall not murder, you shall not steal, you shall not covet," and whatever other commandments there are, are summed up in this one, "you shall love your neighbor as yourself."* [10]*Love works no evil toward one's neighbor; therefore love is the fullness of the Law.*

There is no direct reference or allusion to the Spirit in this paragraph. I include it here because it is another of many texts that presuppose the Spirit without mentioning him. The connections are obvious:[424] In 8:4 Paul has argued that those who "walk in the Spirit" thus "fulfill" the "righteous requirement of the Law." Having begun the general paraenesis dealing with relationships with the word that "love must be sincere" (12:9), Paul now tells them that the love-command, which "sums up" all other commands,[425] is precisely how the "righteous requirement of Torah" is "fulfilled." Thus in 14:15 the one who disregards a brother or sister on the issue of food is "not *walking* in *love*." Not only so, but in Gal 5:22 this love that "fulfills" Torah is expressly designated as the "fruit of the Spirit" (cf. Rom 15:30),[426] whose very existence puts one in a sphere where Law no longer pertains. Even though not mentioned in this passage, what is said here about love "fulfilling" the Law is in Pauline understanding a direct outworking of the Holy Spirit in the life of the believer.[427]

---

[423]So Leenhardt 314; Morris 446.

[424]Cf. Harrison 141, who calls attention to these same links.

[425]In this case, of course, thinking only of one's relationship with others, not one's relationship with God.

[426]A link that one might expect to be made more frequently; but see Nygren 435, Harrison 141, Dunn 782–83, Morris 469, and Thompson, *Clothed*, 127.

[427]Thompson, *Clothed*, 122, suggests a further link with the Spirit through the language of "obligation" in v. 8, which echoes our "obligation" to walk in the Spirit in 8:12–13.

The point, of course, is that Paul does not need to mention the Spirit in order for the Spirit to be the theological presupposition of such a passage. The language is that of "fulfillment," which is eschatological language for Paul. In our new eschatological existence inaugurated by Christ and the Spirit, the Spirit, in whose sphere we live and by whom we are empowered, is himself the "fulfillment" of the new covenant (2 Cor 3:6), and by replacing the former covenant of Torah he thus also "fulfills" the purpose of Torah by leading us in those paths of love that reflect God's own character. Against such there is no Torah.

The paragraph may be more intentionally situated to play a more central role in the present "argument" than some allow. Having dealt with conduct in more general terms, both within the believing community and without, Paul is about to address the final issue in the letter, their life together on matters of Torah observance where they openly differ. The way to that material is through this paragraph,[428] which ties together the argument of chapter 8, the introductory paraenesis of 12:1–21, and the final practical concern in 14:1–15:13 (see 14:15).[429] Since this final material in particular will *favor the Gentiles theologically*—although it favors the Jews in actual practice—before moving on to that material Paul takes one final swipe at the former way of life that the Gentiles knew and insists that having had Torah "fulfilled" by Christ and the Spirit does not open the door to a return to that way of life (13:11–14).

ROMANS 13:11–14

. . . [11]*And this, knowing the time, that it is already the hour for you to be aroused from sleep; for now is our salvation nearer than when we believed.* [12]*The night is far gone; day is at hand. Let us therefore lay aside the deeds of darkness, and put on the weapons of light.* [13]*As in the day, let us walk decently, not in carousing and drunkenness, not in sexual promiscuity and licentiousness, not in strife and jealousy,* [14]*but clothe yourselves with the Lord Jesus Christ and give no forethought to the flesh for its desires.*

This is yet another passage in this large section of paraenesis in which the Spirit is not mentioned, but which those hearing the letter read aloud would be expected to associate with what had been said previously in 8:12–13. With a thoroughgoing play on the eschatological imagery of night and day, which he has used before to urge "daytime" behavior of his Gentile converts (1 Thes 5:1–11), Paul spells out specifically the "deeds of the body" that they are to "put to death by the Spirit" (8:13). These are a sampling of life "according to the flesh," which leads to eschatological death (8:12).

While much could be said about the paragraph as a whole, what needs especially to be noted are the pairs of sins that belong to the "flesh." The first two pairs are readily associated with the "flesh" (carousing and drunkenness, and

---

[428]Cf. Thompson, *Clothed*, 121. But see Käsemann 360, who considers it along with vv. 11–14 to function as a summary of 12:1–13:7. That is does, but as 14:15 suggests, it also functions to introduce what follows.

[429]Thus even though Käsemann 361 is right that there is here no polemicizing against the Law, in light of the larger context of the letter and especially of 8:4, the love that the Spirit produces fulfills Torah's just requirement, and the Spirit replaces Torah in the life of the believer.

profligate sexual immorality). These, of course, are mentioned first because of the imagery; whatever else, in Greco-Roman culture (not to mention most other cultures!) these are "night time" vices. So it is all the more striking that in the midst of this imagery, which is maintained from beginning to end,[430] Paul should include "strife and jealousy"—almost deliberately so, it would seem, so as not to leave the impression that he thought of sin purely in its more grotesque forms of debauchery.[431] The point, of course, is that "the flesh" has to do with far more than the flesh. Strife needs to be put aside, put to death if you will, every bit as much as sexual immorality and carousing. The antidote for all of this in 8:14 is to be led by the Spirit into the ways of the Lord.

Romans 14:1–15:13

With this section we come to the climax of the letter. In a sense, everything has been aiming toward this specific end. Given that the time of Torah has come to an end, how, then, do Torah-observant Christian Jews and nonobservant Gentiles get along together as the one people of God? This is the sticky issue here addressed.[432] Although the section is not full of Spirit talk, there are two such texts, one of which (14:17) is central to the argument; the other (15:13) turns out to be the final word of the argument of the letter and thereby indicates the central role of the Spirit in Paul's understanding of Christian faith and experience. But before that, here in particular, both the argument as a whole and its nature need to be noted, in order to furnish a proper context in which to understand these two texts.

---

[430]Unusually so for Paul. Even "walk decently" is a play on being clothed appropriately for going out in the day; so also clothing oneself with "weapons" for war, which begins to move toward different imagery, gets swallowed up in the present imagery—soldiers dress appropriately for duty during the day.

[431]Cf. in this regard the "works of the flesh" in Gal 5:19–21.

[432]This is said more confidently than some will think warranted, since Jews and Gentiles are (carefully?) not mentioned until the end. Paul's own language is "the weak as to the/their faith" (14:1–2) and "the strong" (15:1). Many see connections with 1 Corinthians 8–10 and suggest that the food in question is the "idol meat" of the Corinthians passage (see esp. Ziesler 322–27). This seems unlikely since (1) 1 Cor 8:1–10:22 has to do with attendance at idol temples, and the issue is not food but idolatry; (2) the question of food per se is addressed only in 10:23–11:1, and there Paul vigorously defends his right to eat such food, although acknowledging a willingness to forbear in contexts outside his own lodgings; whereas (3) idolatry is not so much as mentioned here. The issues involved (food and days), namely, that food is a matter of "clean" or "unclean" (14:14, 20), and the final application in 15:5–12, which assumes Jew and Gentile, favor the position taken here. This is the most common view (most recently Cranfield 2.694–95, Dunn 795, Thompson, *Clothed*, 233–34 and passim). In light of the considerable debate, Morris 475 prefers to be noncommittal, but also overlooks the Jewishness of much of the argument (e.g., 14:14, 20).

The argument is crucial, and full of interest. The *goal* is expressed in 15:5–7: that God will give them both the grace to think along the same lines, so that *together*, with *one mouth*, they may glorify the God and Father of our Lord Jesus Christ. Therefore, he urges them, "accept one another." This is why all of this is crucial: the glory of God is at stake, and the gospel must work out in real life, at this intersection of real differences among them, if it is going to count for anything at all.

How Paul gets there is what makes it so full of interest. On the issue itself, he obviously assumes the stance of the Gentiles; he holds fast to what he has asserted elsewhere, "in Christ neither circumcision nor uncircumcision—nor food nor days—counts for a thing." Nonetheless, the argument presumes to speak primarily to the *Gentiles*, to encourage love for the Jews by not forcing Gentile freedom on them. Even so, the nature of the theological dimension of the argument, though addressed to the Gentiles, seems just as clearly intended to get the *Jews* to take a different view of things in light of Christ and the Spirit. Is this, then, his own rhetorical ploy—asking the Gentiles to back off while at the same time exploding the Jewish position? One can see this kind of argumentation at work throughout, but it can be illustrated most easily in the central theological passage holding our interest (14:16–18), which we will note momentarily.

The argument is in four parts:

(a) *14:1–12* begins with a word to Gentiles, but thereafter is an appeal to *both*. The issues are "food" (vv. 2–3, 6b) and "days" (vv. 5–6a). It is clear that God cares nothing at all about observance. But since both the observant and nonobservant are accountable to God alone, any form of judgment (by the observant) or scorn (by the nonobservant) is out. Both will appear before God in judgment, which serves as both warning and assurance—to both. The aim of all of this seems twofold: to remove these matters from the area of genuine righteousness, and to insist that Jews and Gentiles are responsible to God alone on such matters, and therefore they may not be judged or scorned by the other. Thus Paul simultaneously protects his gospel and those who would be abused by others.

(b) *14:13–23* is a word directed primarily to the Gentiles. Whatever they do in private before God, they are under obligation to love the Jews; they are not to offend or cause to stumble. Here in particular, the whole is directed *practically* toward the Gentiles, but *theologically* in fact *takes the side of* the Gentiles, thereby demolishing the position of the Jews.

(c) *15:1–6* is a final appeal to the Gentiles, supported by an appeal to the example of Christ, but which also brings in the Jews, by way of a final prayer.

(d) *15:7–13* serves as the conclusion to the whole argument: first, it becomes an appeal for both to accept one another (just as Christ has accepted *you* [surely both in this case]); second, it acts as a supporting argument to the appeal in v. 7 that the Christ who has accepted them both did so by way of Judaism, but for the sake of Gentiles; and third, the final result of this is that Jew and Gentile are one people, together praising God, thus fulfilling the covenantal promises. All of which concludes with a final prayer.

The repeated imperative, προσλαμβάνεσθε ("accept/receive"), which serves as a kind of inclusio, further confirms this structure. Thus in 14:1 they are to accept the one who is weak as to the faith; in 15:7 they are to accept one another. In both cases the appeal is reinforced by the comparable divine action of "accepting."

ROMANS 14:16–18

[16]*Therefore do not let your*[433] *good be spoken of as evil;* [17]*for the kingdom of God is not a matter of food and drink, but of righteousness and peace and joy in the Holy Spirit.* [18]*For the one who serves Christ in this way*[434] *is pleasing to God and approved by people.*

Here we come to the heart of matters for the present argument. Verse 17 in particular simultaneously offers the theological justification for his word to the Gentiles to back off regarding Jewish observances *and* for the Jews to take a completely different view of the essential character of the kingdom of God. That the "strong" (Gentiles) are primarily being addressed is evidenced by the structure and content of the larger section (vv. 13–23), which takes the form of chiasm,[435] and for which our text serves as the center and therefore the point of emphasis. On either side are the twin imperatives of vv. 15 and 20, which deal with "destroying" others through "food." In both instances, however, the imperatives are set in contexts insisting that such matters in themselves are inconsequential (i.e., on the matters themselves, the Gentiles are right). This seems to be the reason for the appeal to the example of Christ; such matters, either abstention or partaking, *cannot* become matters of Law, but are matters of relationships within the body that call for walking in love—living the life of the Spirit—for the sake of the other.

---

[433]For this ὑμῶν (P[46] ℵ A B C 048 Maj lat sy[h] co) the Western tradition (D F G Ψ 1506 pc lat Clement Ambrosiaster) has substituted ἡμῶν. This secondary reading tilts the argument considerably—from "what you consider to be good" (thus picking up on 12:2) to "our good" (thus suggesting the gospel [our good] will be blasphemed). See n. 436 below.

[434]The later MajT has made this singular into a plural, "in these things" (a reading that goes back as far as Tertullian), probably referring back to the righteousness, peace, and joy in v. 17.

[435]On this matter see esp. Thompson, *Clothed* 201–4, whose analysis is much to be preferred to that of H. V. D. Paranuk, "Transitional Techniques in the Bible," *JBL* 102 (1983) 525–49 (536).

This same ambivalence of argumentation is particularly noteworthy in the present passage. Verse 16 concludes an argument directed toward Gentiles. They simply must not let their own understanding of the good (cf. 12:2!)[436] be reviled[437] by their attitude toward their Jewish brothers and sisters (by "scandalizing" them, v. 13). Verse 17 then gives the reasons for such forbearance, and in light of vv. 15–16, it is still addressed to the Gentiles.[438] The reasons are two: first, because the kingdom of God has nothing at all to do with food and drink; and second, because true righteousness, along with peace and joy, has to do with life in the Holy Spirit. For these reasons they should easily be able to forbear regarding something deemed "good" in itself. Verse 18 further explains that those who *in this way* (just outlined in v. 17)[439] serve Christ are thereby "pleasing to God"[440] and approved by others. Ultimately this is what it means not to be conformed to the present age but to be transformed by the renewing of the mind, so that one can discern the will of God—what is good and pleasing to him.

---

[436]Cf. NIV: "Do not allow what you consider good to be spoken of as evil." One cannot be certain, of course, of this interpretation of ὑμῶν τὸ ἀγαθόν, and indeed there is considerable debate here. Many take it to refer to the gospel (e.g., Cranfield, Hendriksen, Morris, Thompson, *Clothed*, 203; cf. Dunn 821, "all of God's covenanted blessings"), but against this are several strong arguments: (1) Paul nowhere else refers to the gospel with this language; (2) Paul has referred to "doing τὸ ἀγαθόν" throughout this argument (12:2, 9, 21; 13:3, 4; 15:2; 16:19), and one wonders why only here does it take on a different meaning (Käsemann 376 points to 8:28 and 10:15, but in neither case is it τὸ ἀγαθόν); and (3) the emphatic vernacular possessive, ὑμῶν τὸ ἀγαθόν, which is relatively rare in Paul (only here, e.g., in Romans [a point missed by most interpreters]), seems to emphasize not what is "the good" to all believers, but what the "strong" deem to be "the good," hence "*your* good" (so, inter alia, Godet 461, SH 391, Denney 705, Barrett 264, Murray 2.193, Käsemann 396). The "strong" insisting on "their good" when it is hurtful to others will finally bring disrepute on the gospel, to be sure. But the use of ὑμῶν τὸ ἀγαθόν to refer to the gospel seems obtuse at best.

[437]Part of the issue for interpreting this passage has to do with who one understands "the revilers" to be. The interpretation offered above (preceding note) on this passage is greatly enhanced if we take them to be nonChristian Jews who are especially turned off by such Gentile "belief."

[438]A crucial point in the argument, one would think, but seldom noted in the commentaries, who become much more interested in the principle itself than in its application to the argument (but see SH 391–92; Murray 2.193; Cranfield 2.718).

[439]So also Käsemann 374, Dunn 824, Thompson, *Clothed*, 204; otherwise Black 164, Cranfield 2.719, Morris 489 et al., who take it to refer to the righteousness, peace, and joy in the Holy Spirit mentioned in v. 16, thus agreeing with the early interpretation that changed this singular to a plural (see n. 434 above).

[440]The recapitulation of this language from 12:1 also adds weight to the interpretation of vv. 16–17 just offered. The "renewed mind," after all, should be able to discern "what is good and well-pleasing" as to the will of God. Paul's point seems to be that such discernment has not to do with whether something is "clean" or not (v. 14), but whether it promotes the righteousness, joy, and peace that come from the Spirit.

At the same time, as v. 14 shows, this is also a word to Jewish Christians. Since Christ himself spoke to this matter,[441] Paul can remind them that "nothing in itself is unclean."[442] On this matter Paul and his Lord are one: There is no objective "uncleanness" to anything external or material. However, Paul's addition of the "excepting" clause, which admits to "subjective uncleanness" to those who consider it so, while it may indeed be a word to the Gentiles to treat Jewish Christians kindly on this matter, can nonetheless scarcely have been missed by the Jews,[443] however obliquely Paul herewith demolishes their position. So, too, with v. 17. It is surely intended for the Gentiles, as theological justification for toleration with regard to the "weaknesses" of others. But at the same time theologically it cuts the very ground from underneath the weak. The kingdom of God has nothing whatsoever to do with matters of food and drink—even though some do indeed abstain as unto the Lord (v. 6)!

Thus we end up with two responses in this crucial text. On the one hand, practically, the "strong" (Gentiles) have been set up by a series of passages not to judge those who are still Torah-observant—even though the time of Torah is past. In 8:4, in a considerably different context, Paul has argued that even though Torah has had its day, the "righteous requirement of Torah" is still about, now fulfilled by those who walk by the Spirit. In 10:4 he declared Christ to be the "goal" of Torah for those who believe. I take this to mean that Christ has brought it to an end by fulfilling its reason for being in the first place. Then in 13:8–10 Paul has argued that the *way* Torah is fulfilled, or summed up, is by obedience to the love command, since love "does no wrong to one's neighbor." Now, in v. 15, he repeats that one who hurts another in this matter is not "walking according to love." The Spirit, who empowers such "walking in love," and who alone brings about such "righteousness," is also all about "peace"—and "joy."

---

[441] Which is how I take Paul's appeal, "I am persuaded in/by the Lord Jesus," who did in fact speak to this very question—or at least this is what the early church understood him to be about with regard to the question of food laws, as Mark 7:17–23 makes abundantly plain. Most take it to be the equivalent of "as a Christian," but that does not take the Pauline distinctions between "in Christ" and "in Jesus" seriously enough. On this question see esp. Thompson, *Clothed*, 185–99.

[442] Gk. κοινόν = "common," meaning *ritually unclean*. Cf. v. 20; see esp. Matt 15:11, where the cognate verb κοινόω means "to defile"; cf. Acts 10:14. This language is another indication that the issue is Jew/Gentile over ritual eating, not "idol food" (see n. 432 above). Cf. Cranfield 2.695.

[443] Or so one would think; experience in the church suggests that this is far too optimistic. One of the truly amazing bits of hermeneutical reversal that takes place among pietistic groups is that they read this text as though they, the abstainers, were the "strong," while the nonabstainers are considered to be the weak. Thus they promote abstinence for the sake of the others, because in fact they "the strong" are quite offended by someone else's indulgence! Such people simply read around texts like this one.

The theological reason for such an attitude of forbearance is plain. Along with the "canon" that "neither circumcision nor uncircumcision counts for anything" (Gal 6:15), this text also makes clear that the issue is not Torah observance per se. On this matter Paul insists that God cares not a whit. What is at issue, therefore, throughout the argument of this letter—and Galatians—is *making Torah observance count for something*, by insisting that Gentiles become observant. On that issue Paul comes out fighting; but on the issue of whether Jews should continue in the practices that have marked them as Jews for generations, he cares very little at all. And that is precisely because of the first theological dictum, "the kingdom of God has nothing at all to do with such matters." Thus Jews may continue to be observant if they wish; but Gentiles must not, because that would make Torah observance count for something after all.[444]

But there is another side of things that the observant must hear, and hear well. If these theological assertions can be appealed to as reasons for forbearance, they also serve, theologically, to eliminate the possibility that one can ever give significance to being observant.[445] Precisely because God cares nothing at all about such things, neither may they, even as they continue faithfully to be observant. The kingdom of God[446] has nothing at all to do with such; righteousness, he reminds them here, effected by Christ, has to do with life in the Spirit,[447] and is of a radically different kind from observances. Life in the Spirit is like that urged on them in 12:9–21, which has to do with the character of God being reproduced and expressed in the life of his children.

Finally, we must note the three items associated with the Spirit in this passage[448] that are designed first of all for the sake of Gentile believers. Righteousness, of course, is what the whole letter is about—God's gift of righteousness, effected through Christ's death and resurrec-

---

[444]On this question see the "theology of (no) change" that Paul addresses in 1 Corinthians 7:17–24; see Fee, *1 Corinthians*, 307–9.

[445]The only one I know who has made this point is T. W. Manson, as cited (favorably) by Black 169.

[446]This is not a frequent term in Paul, usually referring to the future kingdom. But here as in 1 Cor 4:20 (q.v.) Paul is referring to the kingdom as a present reality.

[447]I take the ἐν here to be primarily locative of sphere. The emphasis is not so much on the Spirit as the empowering agency for righteousness, peace, and joy, but on the Spirit as the sphere of existence wherein these find expression. In such a case, the instrumental sense (favored by Cranfield 1.318n5) is not ruled out altogether. Cf. Dodd 218, Dunn 824 (who argues for both).

[448]Some (Meyer, Michel, Black, Cranfield, Thompson, *Clothed*, 204n1) have argued partly on the basis of 1 Thes 1:6 that "in the Holy Spirit" modifies only "joy." While this is possible, it is highly improbable. Peace and joy are companions again in 15:13, where the Spirit is the assumed source, and appear together as fruit of the Spirit in Gal 5:22. Not only so, but the repeated καί suggests that the three nouns belong together and are together modified by the prepositional phrase (so also most commentaries; Dunn is noncommittal).

tion, apart from Torah, which is then evidenced in the lives of God's people as they walk by the Spirit and thus fulfill the "righteous require-ment" of Torah.[449] Hence it is "righteousness in the Holy Spirit,"[450] that is, the righteousness that finds expression as one lives in the Spirit.

That one seems easy enough; so too is the second. Drawing on what in Gal 5:22 Paul calls a fruit of the Spirit, he insists that the kingdom of God involves "peace." In our discussion of that word in Galatians we suggested that it did not chiefly have to do with one's inner tranquility of spirit; nor does it here have to do with the "peace with God" of 5:1–2,[451] but with *shalom* as characterizing their life together. In this case, that is specifically stated, for the next imperative (v. 19), again directed toward the Gentiles, is: "Let us pursue *the things that have to do with peace and with the building up of others.*" That, too, is the work of the Spirit. But it does not come by sitting by and "letting the Spirit do it." Such *shalom* among the people of God, empowered by the Spirit, results from their "pursuing" it with diligence. It means at times giving up "one's own good" for the sake of others.

Finally, there is joy. It is more difficult to find contextual reasons for this one. One wonders whether in Paul's own understanding, these two—peace and joy—simply go together, as they will again in the prayer in 15:13. Thus, peace among God's people is also reflected in their joy. In any case, Paul understood joy to be one of the major signs of life in the Spirit. See further on 1 Thes 1:6 and Gal 5:22.

ROMANS 15:13

And may the God of hope fill you with all joy and peace in believing/trust-ing,[452] *so that you may abound in hope by the power of the Holy Spirit.*

---

[449]Debate as to whether this refers to one or the other meaning of "righteous-ness" in this letter is probably misguided. Many limit it to the gift of righteousness (Calvin, Hodge, Michel, Cranfield, Käsemann, Dunn); others to ethical righteousness (Meyer, Godet, SH, Barrett, Murray, Harrison). Both views seem too narrow. In context, it must finally refer to ethical righteousness lived out in the community of faith (after all, the contrast is between "eating and drinking" and life in the Spirit), but in this letter ethical righteousness flows out of the gift of righteousness. So also Denney 795, Godet 461–62, Morris 489.

[450]That righteousness essentially involves conduct is further evidenced by this use of the full name, the *Holy* Spirit, which is somewhat rare in Paul (see ch. 2, pp. 15–24), and usually occurs either when there is a special gravity or emphasis on his person in the context (cf. 9:1 above), or as here when the emphasis is on "holy" conduct (see 15:16 below; cf. 1 Thes 4:8; 1 Cor 6:19; Eph 4:30).

[451]As argued by Leenhardt 355, Cranfield 2.719, Dunn 824–25. Again, one could scarcely deny that the peace for which Paul appeals in v. 19 is ultimately predicated on "peace with God," as Dunn points out. But that hardly seems to be the primary referent in this context. So also most commentators; cf. Thompson, *Clothed*, 204.

[452]This is a case where the verb "to believe" (πιστεύω) is very difficult to translate. For Paul it carried with it the double sense of "believing the gospel" as he has outlined

With these words Paul rings off the "argument" of the letter that began in 1:18. More specifically, of course, they conclude the last section of the argument that began in 14:1. This argument has been brought to its concluding moment with a final exhortation that Jews and Gentiles, who together form the one people of God, "accept one another" (15:7). This in turn is supported with a final appeal to the example of Christ, who "accepted you for the *glory* of God," and did so as a "servant from among those who are circumcised" so that (1) he might confirm the promises made to the Fathers, and that (2) "the Gentiles might *glorify* God for his mercy." This is followed by a catena of four OT passages, all of which have to do with Gentiles sharing in the promises and thus "praising God." The last of these is from Isa 11:10 and concludes with the words, "in whom [referring now to Christ] the Gentiles hope." With that the argument comes to an end. But in typical fashion Paul rounds it off with a prayer-wish that they might realize all of this.

The prayer does not, as some prayers do(!), recapitulate everything that has been said; rather, it focuses on four realities: that the "God of *hope*" (picking up the final word of the Isaiah quotation) might: (1) fill them with the Spirit's *joy and peace* as they (2) continue to put their trust in Christ, so that as they do so he (the God of *hope*) might cause them (3) to *overflow with hope*, and as they (4) are empowered by the Holy Spirit, which somewhat incidentally but perhaps symbolically becomes the final word in the argument. Although technically "by the Holy Spirit" modifies only the final clause, Paul's sentence structure and language elsewhere indicate that the Holy Spirit should be understood also as the means whereby God fills them with joy and peace as they trust in Christ: God by his Spirit fills them with joy and peace as they continue to trust in Christ, whose purpose finally is that they might overflow with hope by the same Holy Spirit.[453]

This is not a familiar triad (joy, peace, hope) in Paul—one is more used to "faith, love, and hope"—but it has already been brought together in 5:1-5, the great confessional conclusion to 1:18-4:25.[454] Thus Paul returns, by way of prayer, to the basic eschatological framework of his

---

it in part in this letter, but such "believing the gospel" for him always meant to put one's trust in the Christ, whose "gospel" one is "believing." (The phrase is missing altogether from D F G b m, almost certainly due to homoeoteleuton, which is the same reason the next phrase is missing in B 945 2495 pc.)

[453] Cf. Black 173 and Murray 2.207, who notes that the whole sentence is aimed at the final clause. Otherwise Dunn 853, who makes the unlikely suggestion that the two ἐν-phrases are parallel, thus suggesting that it is by trusting that they are filled with joy and peace. To the contrary, the joy and peace are present by the Spirit *as* they trust; what is coordinate, but not parallel, are the two articular infinitive phrases "as you trust," "so that you might overflow."

[454] "Joy" in that case (Rom 5:2-3) being understood as inherent in the verb "to boast," so that many actually translate it "rejoice" (e.g., RSV, KJV, ASV, TEV).

theology. By their trust in Christ, God's people "already" know joy and peace and thus live in hope, absolute certainty regarding the "not yet." The key to all of this, of course, is the Holy Spirit, who empowers life in the present and guarantees its future consummation—so much so that Paul prays for them to "overflow with hope(!)" by the power of the Spirit.[455] Three matters call for further comment:

1. Paul has already (in 14:17) signalled "joy" and "peace" as the result of life "in the Spirit" (cf. Gal 5:22). Thus he is here returning to that language, as that which should characterize God's people in the present. On these words, see on Gal 5:22 and Rom 14:17. As in those instances, "peace" probably has not here to do with "inner tranquility"[456] but with the very thing that 14:1–15:12 is all about: Jew and Gentile glorifying God together as his one people. For this to happen they must pursue "the matters having to do with peace" (14:19). And such "peace" among them should express itself in "joy," that distinctive mark of Christian piety, brought about by the effective work of the Spirit, who has not only applied to our lives the saving work of Christ, but has also guaranteed our glorious future despite the nature of our present circumstances.

2. That God's people live in hope by the presence of the Spirit also brings us back to an earlier moment in this letter (8:23–27). Such hope is the direct result of the indwelling Spirit, the firstfruits of the guaranteed future. But now Paul prays that by the empowering of the Spirit they may "abound in hope." One is somewhat taken aback by this remarkable language. We are more accustomed to the concept of "abounding" or "overflowing" in such things as "faith," or "earnestness," or "love" (cf. 2 Cor 8:7). But here Paul prays that they may live in the Spirit in such a way that they overflow with the confidence that is theirs as to their certain future. Such "future-oriented" people live in the present in a way different from the rest—not as "too heavenly minded to be of any earthly good," but as so confident of the future that they can pour themselves into the present with utter abandon, full of joy and peace, because nothing in the present can ultimately overwhelm them. Such people make the Christian faith a truly attractive alternative.

3. Finally, at the end of the argument, Paul uses Spirit language of a kind that is almost certainly to be understood as presuppositional throughout. All of the "by the Spirit" phrases that have preceded, modifying a whole variety of verbs (the pouring out of God's love, walking, being led, living, putting to death the deeds of the body, bearing witness), all of these are to be understood presuppositionally as effected *by the*

---

[455] Contra Dunn 851, who argues for a combined locative and instrumental sense; but the use of δυνάμει seems to rule out the locative. The power of the Spirit is the means by which one can abound in hope.

[456] So Käsemann 387, Dunn 851 (who allows both); contra W. Foerster, *TDNT* 2.417 ("undoubtedly"), Cranfield 2.748, Morris 507.

power of the Holy Spirit. For Paul and the early church the Spirit and power belong together; one cannot imagine the one (Spirit) without the other. Hence it is so seldom put in those terms. But it is so here, a reminder that such is always the case.

Paul will pick this language up again momentarily, when reflecting on his own worldwide ministry (15:18–19), as accompanied by, and thus attested by, "the power of signs and wonders," which is then explained as "by the power of the Spirit of God." In light of such a text, and especially with its repeated emphasis on "power," one can easily fall into the trap of thinking of power especially along these lines—of more visible and extraordinary (miraculous, if you will) manifestations of the Spirit's presence. But this text should stand as a corrective to that kind of "one way" thinking. The presence of the Spirit always presupposes power for Paul, but being filled with "joy and peace" and "overflowing with hope" are equally "accompanying and attesting" evidence of the presence of "the Holy Spirit with power."

What an engaging way for the argument of this letter to conclude. Dare one suggest, I wonder, that we might all do well to pray that Paul's prayer for the Romans might be more truly and effectively fulfilled in the life of the church today? One wonders what it would be like, in terms both of our relationships with one another and of our effectiveness as witnesses to the world, if we as individuals and communities were "filled" with joy and peace and "overflowed with hope" by the power of the Spirit.

ROMANS 15:14–33

Although the argument of Romans has ended with the prayer-wish in 15:13, Paul feels compelled to conclude with further remarks that will fill in some of the blanks as to his personal reasons for writing. These reasons are closely related to the passionately missionary context both of his life and his gospel, and therefore are especially pertinent to his soon-to-be-formed relationship with the Romans. This section, therefore, is filled with personal matters—far more of them than one finds at the conclusion of most of Paul's extant letters. What is striking, and therefore probably typical of his everyday life in Christ, is the frequent mention of the Spirit, with regard both to his own ministry and to the Roman believers' life in Christ and relationship to Paul. Before looking at each of these texts in turn, a word is needed about the overall flow of thought; this will allow us to fit them more easily into their respective contexts.

The whole passage needs first of all to be understood as a return to the matters of the proemium (especially 1:9–15) and Paul's twofold concern about the presumption of writing such a (now) long letter to a community which he long desired to, and now hopes soon to, visit. The present materials are consequently both apologetic and informational in nature. The apologetic goes in two directions: (a) that he should write such a long letter to *them*, as though they needed his instruction at all; and (b) for his ministry in the past and (hopefully among and beyond them) in the future. The latter gets by far the most press, since he feels compelled, first, to validate his past and present ministry, and, second, to explain why he cannot now come, but at the same time to hope that when he does they will not only warmly receive him but aid him on his way west. Although the whole is continuous narrative, and any breaking it up into smaller parts is somewhat arbitrary, nonetheless, one can follow the narrative by looking at its various twists and turns.

He begins (v. 14) by apologizing for writing such a letter to a community that scarcely needs it, so in v. 15 he sets out to explain his effrontery: God has "graced" him especially to be Christ's "ministrant" to bring the gospel to the Gentiles (vv. 15–16, a passage filled with allusions to the Jewish cult). That leads him to speak of those things about which he has a "boast" before God (vv. 17–21), namely, his worldwide (from Jerusalem to Illyricum),[457] Spirit-empowered ministry among Gentiles in places where others have not gone—which in turn explains in part his long delay in getting to Rome (v. 22). So in vv. 23–24 he announces his plans to come to Rome, and be sent on his way by them to further "unreached" Gentile territory (Spain). But before that he must go to Jerusalem with his gift from the Gentile churches for the Jewish believers in Jerusalem (vv. 25–27), his own tangible way of expressing Gentile and Jew as one people of God. All of this (vv. 22–27) is recapitulated in vv. 28–29; he concludes (vv. 30–32) with a request for their prayers that the two next items on his agenda (Jerusalem and Rome) might meet with divinely appointed success, and with his own prayer for them (v. 33).

The Spirit appears in a variety of ways throughout, both directly and indirectly: in v. 14, indirectly, as the source of the empowering of the believers in Rome; in v. 16, in another Trinitarian moment, as the one who has sanctified "the offering" composed of Gentile converts; in vv. 18–19 as the empowering source of Paul's ministry; in v. 27, indirectly, as reflecting the nature of the Jewish "mission" to Gentiles; and finally, in v. 30, as the source of the love on which his appeal for their supporting prayer is made.

ROMANS 15:14

. . . And I am persuaded, my brothers and sisters, even I myself concerning you that you yourselves are full of goodness, filled with all knowledge, empowered also to instruct one another.

---

[457] This bit of geography could hardly have been missed by the Romans. The next stop after the Dalmatian coast is Italy; but since the latter has already been evangelized, Spain is the obvious place to go beyond Rome.

Although there is no mention of the Spirit in this opening "apologetic" word, nonetheless, three factors converge to suggest that the Spirit is assumed behind most of the language, two of which flow directly out of the preceding prayer for them. First, the language "filled with," is a direct reflection of the Spirit activity in the preceding prayer. Paul has prayed that they might be filled with joy and peace and thus abound in hope, all by the power of the Holy Spirit. Now he declares his confidence in them that they are already "full of goodness, having been filled with all knowledge." Goodness, it needs to be noted, secondly, is for Paul a fruit of the Spirit (Gal 5:22);[458] and "all knowledge" is directly attributed to the Spirit's activity in 1 Cor 12:8 and 13:2 and 8. Finally, that they are also thereby "empowered" to instruct one another (without the need for his instruction is implied) is the verbal equivalent of the word "power" associated with the Holy Spirit in the preceding prayer.

Whether the Romans would have caught all of this is moot, to be sure, although the linguistic echoes in these two juxtaposed passages would make one think so. In any case, here again, without Paul's mentioning the Spirit by name, we may assume from what we know of Paul elsewhere that the Spirit is behind all of this.

Romans 15:16

So that I might be a priestly servant of Christ Jesus for the Gentiles, serving the gospel of God in priestly fashion, in order that the offering that consists of the Gentiles might be acceptable, sanctified as it is by the Holy Spirit.

This clause expresses the goal of "the grace given to [Paul] by God," mentioned in the preceding main clause (v. 15). The goal is expressed in two purpose clauses, the second dependent on the first. That is, God has "graced" him with the special goal in mind of his "priestly ministry" with regard to the gospel, which has as its ultimate goal the Gentile mission to which his life has been devoted, all of which is expressed with thoroughgoing sacerdotal imagery (which I have tried to capture in translation). The sudden profusion of such imagery is probably best explained, as in 12:1–2, as an indirect way in which Paul himself tries to hold Jew and Gentile together—by using the language of the Jewish cultus while referring to his own ministry among Gentiles.

Our special interest lies not in all the marvelous play on that imagery, but in the final expression of it, wherein Paul's "offering" turns out to be the Gentiles themselves, evidenced to be so because they have been "sanctified by[459] the Holy Spirit." Here, probably, is a final word to the

---

[458] Indeed, it is a rare word in the NT, used only by Paul (here, 2 Thes 1:11, Gal 5:22, Eph 5:9).

[459] As often with this dative, one cannot tell whether Paul intends it be instrumental (the Spirit as empowering agent, as most think) or locative of sphere (as they live in the Spirit, as Lenski argues).

Jewish contingent to "welcome the Gentiles" (15:7); those who were formerly unclean have now been sanctified by the Holy Spirit.[460] This is Paul's version of "do not call unclean what God has cleansed" (Acts 10:15). Their reception of God's Holy Spirit was the ultimate act of creating a "sanctified offering" of Gentiles, which Paul now images as his offering to God. As in 1 Cor 1:2 and 6:11, "sanctified" is best understood as a metaphor for conversion. But it is a rich metaphor, whose overtones should not be missed.

First, the reason for using it here belongs to the metaphor. The offering Paul presents to God in his role as "priestly servant"[461] is, as it must be, a "consecrated" one, in this case "consecrated" by the Holy Spirit. But since Paul's actual ministry, and especially the conversion of Gentiles, has nothing to do with the sacrificial system, one can be sure that Paul intends us to hear his ordinary nuance in this word, "sanctified," meaning now "set apart for God's own holy purposes." And this in turn always for Paul carries with it the connotation of godliness, including godly behavior. After all, in the cultus only pure, unblemished sacrifices could be offered. From Paul's perspective, in any case, flesh and Spirit do not mix. His ministry has thus been that of Christ Jesus who has delivered Gentiles from their former way of life, designated by Paul as "the flesh."[462]

Here is one of the more telling references to the Holy Spirit in the Pauline corpus. The key lies in the word "holy," which for the early Christians was a word brought over from their Jewish past, but now infused with radically new meaning by their experience of the *Holy* Spirit of God (cf. 1:4). Thus, the primary way by which believers are identified in the new age that Christ and the Spirit have ushered in is by the Spirit, himself Holy, who by his presence makes his people also "holy." For Paul this is the ultimate "offering" that he can present to God.

Finally, the latent Trinitarianism of this passage must not be missed.[463] The good news of which Paul is a minister has its origins in God; in taking it to the Gentiles he is a "priestly minister" of Christ Jesus, the content of this good news; the effectual appropriation of the good news in the lives of Gentiles is the working of the Holy Spirit. The pattern remains the same as one finds it everywhere, only the language and imagery have changed.

---

[460]Cf. Bruce 260, Morris 511–12.

[461]Gk. λειτουργός, the noun of the person who performs the λειτουργεῖν ("the service of God") used to describe the "ministry" of Gentiles toward Jewish believers in v. 27—another case of using the language of the cult when referring to Gentile ministry.

[462]See above on 7:5–6; 8:5–8 and 12–13; cf. 13:11–14.

[463]Cf. Barrett 275 ("by accident, as it were"); Morris 512.

ROMANS 15:18–19

[18]*For I shall not dare*[464] *talk about anything*[465] *except that which Christ performed through me for the obedience*[466] *of the Gentiles, by word and deed,* [19]*by the power*[467] *of signs and wonders, by the power of the Spirit of God; so that from Jerusalem all the way around to Illyricum I have brought [the preaching of] the gospel to completion.*

With these words Paul introduces himself, in terms of his ministry, to the church in Rome, whose members, of course, already know something about him/it through the presence of his close friends Priscilla and Aquila. Along with 2 Cor 12:12, and in a very similar, almost off-handed way, we discover things about that ministry that we would know otherwise only from Acts.[468] Three things are said, and each one needs to be heard with Paul's emphases:

First, the subject of the verb, and thus of the entire clause, is Christ, whom Paul understands to be the one carrying out his own "work"[469] in the ministry of his apostle. Thus the christocentric nature of this entire passage (vv. 14–33) can hardly be missed.[470]

---

[464]In an unusual departure from form, Codex B has four singular readings in this sentence. Here the aorist τολμήσω has been changed to the present; it has added λόγων after "through me," which here would mean "matters" ("[except] of those matters which . . . "); it has ἀκοήν ("hearing") for ὑπακοήν ("obedience"); and has omitted the θεοῦ ("of God") that accompanies the Spirit in this case.

[465]For reasons that are not at all clear, this little phrase τι λαλεῖν ("to say anything") has had a tortured textual history: the "anything" has been omitted (P[46]); the two words have been transposed (MajT); and the verb has been made into an aorist, but with two different verbs (εἰπεῖν D F G; λαλῆσαι 1881 2495), a more understandable change. The (probable) original is read by ℵ A B C P 81 365 629 630 1506 1739 pc.

[466]On the reading of Codex B, see n. 464 above.

[467]Apparently in an attempt to make sense of the awkward double ἐν δυνάμει ("by the power of . . . "), some early witnesses (P[46] D* F G m) added an αὐτοῦ ("his"), so that in the first instance it is by the power of Christ and in the second by the power of the Spirit. But in so doing they have created an even more awkward situation with the words σημείων καὶ τεράτων, which the scribe of P[46] alleviated by inserting a τε after "signs," resulting in "by his [Christ's] power, of both signs and wonders, by the power of the Spirit of God."

[468]And which, therefore, for many scholars is highly suspect. Luke would be viewed as a typical first-century teller of stories with great interest in "wonders," which would be suspect because the world view of so many does not include such things.

[469]Gk. κατειργάσατο, a compound of the verb ἐργάζομαι ("work"), having the force of effective working, hence "accomplish, carry out, perform." Note the use of the same verb in the passive in the similar passage in 2 Cor 12:12.

[470]In this regard see vv. 14, 16, 17, 18, 19, 21, 29, and 30.

Second, what Christ is accomplishing through him is "for the obedience of the Gentiles," a phrase that echoes the language of 1:5. This, of course, has been one of the issues that has driven the letter from the beginning (see 1:5–6) and guides much of the argumentation throughout. It is the other predominant note of the present passage.[471]

Third, and the place where our interests lie, the agency of Christ's accomplishing this work through Paul is the Holy Spirit, expressed in this case in the fullest way found in his letters, "by word and deed, by the power of signs and wonders, by the power of the Spirit of God." Paul has spoken of the effective nature of his ministry in language similar to this in 1 Thes 1:4–5; 1 Cor 2:5 (cf. 4:19); and 2 Cor 12:12. In two of these instances (1 Thes 1:4–5; 1 Cor 2:5) I have argued that he is referring primarily to the effectiveness of his ministry in terms of its results, the conversion of the Thessalonians and Corinthians respectively. Whether the "power" terminology also refers to what Paul here calls "signs and wonders" is moot in both cases. On the other hand, the testimony of 2 Cor 12:12 unambiguously refers to the latter. What is unique about this passage is that Paul insists that his ministry involves both dimensions of Spirit empowerment. Christ has been at work in him both through "word" (i.e., by his proclamation of the gospel) and "deed" (i.e., through signs and wonders). Both together are the result and evidence of Spirit empowering.

The phrase is somewhat awkward, but the result is clear enough. Paul begins by indicating the two means by which Christ has been effectively at work through him: by "word" and "deed." "Word" surely refers to his proclamation of the gospel; but "deed" calls for some explanation, so he immediately adds, "by the power of signs and wonders."[472] But this is strangely said, even though Paul's intent seems clear. His interest is to define what he means by "deed," that is, he says, by signs and wonders. But how he says that needs further explanation, which is immediately forthcoming: "What I mean," he says, "is by the power of the Spirit of God." That suggests that the first modifier therefore is a kind of shorthand for "by the power of the Spirit evidenced through signs and wonders." But at the same time the final explanatory modifier is intended to go back and pick up *both* dimensions of his ministry, that is, "word" as well as "deed." The result, now in "longhand," goes something like this: "by proclamation and deed, that is, through signs and wonders, all of which was accomplished by the power of the Spirit of God."[473] We

---

[471] Cf. above on 5:13; here see 15:16, 18, 19, 21, 24, and 26–27.

[472] Otherwise Cranfield 2.759 et al., who take ἔργον to refer to all of Paul's missionary activities, excluding proclamation.

[473] So Meyer 2.348; cf. Murray 2.213. It is doubtful that the two ἐν phrases form a chiasm with word and deed, as though the power of signs and wonders related to "deed" while the power of the Holy Spirit related only to "word," as Denney 713

have noted above on 15:13 that "power" language for Paul is not limited to the miraculous. On the language "signs and wonders" see the discussion on 2 Cor 12:12.

Three additional notes about the Spirit in this passage:

1. As so often in Paul, we note again the latent Trinitarianism in this text as well. In v. 17 he has referred to his "boasting" in Christ Jesus, regarding the things that have to do with God; in our text Christ is the one who accomplishes the work, by the Spirit, who again is designated as the "Spirit of God." Lying behind all of that is the threefold ministry of the Trinity in effecting salvation.[474]

2. In light of our discussion on 8:9–11, we also note the relationship between Christ and the Spirit expressed in this passage. As with 8:10, so here Paul understands the Spirit (of God in this instance) to be the means whereby Christ accomplishes his work in the present age. This makes clear distinctions between Christ and the Spirit that simply disallow a Spirit Christology.

3. Finally, we emphasize again, what we noted in our discussion on 2 Cor 12:12, namely, how matter-of-fact all of this is. Whatever Paul understood by "signs and wonders"—and one would need special bravado to deny that he intended what we call miracles—he speaks of them as though one might add, "well, of course; what else might you expect?" The difficulties moderns feel toward this passage are not exegetical, having to do with Paul's meaning, but hermeneutical in the larger sense of that word, having to do with what we do with a text like this in a day like ours.

On the one hand, what is of interest is how easily a certain segment of evangelical faith can dismiss from today's agenda the miraculous dimension of this text, as though that were as plain as day in the text. But such dismissal in this case is born out of bias, not exegesis. What no one is willing to limit only to the apostolic period is the need for "word" accompanied by the power of the Spirit. But in this sentence one simply cannot easily disentangle "word" from "deed." For Paul they obviously go together. It should be further noted that the frequent ploy to get around what the text explicitly says is to attribute the sentence to an "apology for Paul's apostolic authority," which authority no longer obtains. But how, under any stretch of exegetical imagination, can one argue that this sentence is an attempt to establish his apostleship? To the contrary, after 1:1, Paul has bent over backward not to press

---

(hesitantly), Michel 361, Leenhardt 369, Black 175, Rengstorf, *TDNT* 7.259 (esp. Black, who boldly says, "the 'signs' are wrought by the apostles; it is the Spirit who inspires the Word"!).

[474]Cf. Murray 2.213, who rightly observes, "It is not a case of artificially weaving these persons into his presentation; it is rather that his consciousness is so formed by and to faith in the triune God that he cannot but express himself in these terms."

apostleship per se on this congregation. He is not here undoing that by an under-the-table appeal to his authority; rather, he is in a most matter-of-fact way describing his ministry among the Gentiles, apparently as an appeal for acceptance in this basically Gentile community. There is no hint of any kind that what he describes is limited either to himself or to the apostolic age. This is simply the way Christ has been at work to bring about "the obedience of the Gentiles." Those who argue for such ministry to continue, as long as there are still "Gentiles" who need to come to the obedience of faith, have the better of it hermeneutically.

On the other hand, since this is something Christ does by his Spirit, neither is it some kind of ministry that one can reproduce on one's own. Here, it would seem, one would need to learn anew to walk in the Spirit in ways that are known better today in the emerging world than in the Western world by and large. We are probably guilty of "reasoning" away the works of God of these kinds, whereupon we spend a great deal of hermeneutical energy trying to "justify the ways of God with men" as we have now defined what God can do among us.

ROMANS 15:27

For they were pleased to do so even as they are indebted to them; for if the Gentiles have shared in their [the Jewish believers in Jerusalem] Spiritual things, they [the Gentiles] ought to serve them with their material goods.

In his description of the hoped-for net effects of his taking the offering to Jerusalem, Paul once again uses the language πνευματικός and σαρκικός (cf. 1 Cor 9:11, q.v.) to describe the reciprocal relationship between those ultimately responsible for the ministry of the gospel and those who in turn shared of their material goods. As with the Corinthian passage, there can be no question that σαρκικός here refers to "material goods." There is also no question that the nature of the prior πνευματικός sharing had to do with the sending out of the message of the gospel.[475] But Paul's choice of words is probably dictated in part also because of its overtones with the ministry of the Spirit that is involved. Hence, as before, πνευματικοῖς for Paul are "things having to do with the Spirit."[476]

---

[475] So Michel 371, Cranfield 2.773, but without reference to the Spirit.
[476] See Meyer 2.358, who saw this connection clearly; cf. Denney 715, Barrett 279, and Dunn 876, who, however, is ready to see *both* words as reflecting, in a new way to be sure, the flesh/Spirit contrast that appears so often in Romans.

ROMANS 15:30

Now I beseech you, brothers and sisters,[477] *through*[478] *our Lord Jesus Christ and through the love of the Spirit to strive together with me in your prayers to God for me.*[479]

This final mention of the Spirit in this letter is also one of the more intriguing ones, since "love" followed by a genitive of one of the divine persons most commonly involves God the Father (5:5; 8:39; cf. 2 Thes 3:5; 2 Cor 13:13[14]; Eph 2:4) or Christ (8:35; cf. 2 Cor 5:14; Eph 3:19). Only here in the corpus does Paul speak of the "love of the Spirit," and it is not certain what specifically this implies.

On the basis of 5:5, one is tempted to see an appeal to the "love of God [manifested in Christ's death] that has been poured into our hearts by the Spirit." The "love of the Spirit" thus becomes a kind of shorthand for the former; with this usage one might compare the "love of Christ" with the "love of God which is in Christ Jesus our Lord" of 8:35 and 39. If this is the case, then the appeal is predicated on the work of the triune God on his and their behalf. "Through our Lord Jesus Christ" then becomes an appeal to the "grace" of Christ on their behalf, and the second clause then refers to "the love [of God] known to them because of the Spirit in their hearts."[480]

But as attractive as that understanding might be, and as fitting as it is in this letter, the repeated διά ("through," meaning "efficient cause" [BAGD]) more likely indicates that Paul's appeal has a twofold basis.

---

[477] The vocative is missing in P⁴⁶ and B. On the one hand, this may very well represent the original text, since this combination carries considerable weight and there is no good reason, either by accident or deliberately, for these words to have been omitted had they been original. On the other hand, these two witnesses represent a single variant, whose ancestor may have omitted the word in the process of copying; simply because the idiom is so well known, it would have been unnecessary to consult the *Vorlage,* and thus the vocative was passed over.

[478] A few secondary witnesses (L 1881 pc) add the words ὀνόματός μου before "Lord," probably to balance this phrase with the Spirit phrase that follows. Thus, it becomes "through *the name* of our Lord Jesus Christ and *the love* of the Spirit."

[479] The awkwardness of the Greek (μοι ἐν ταῖς προσευχαῖς ὑπὲρ ἐμοῦ πρὸς τὸν θεόν; lit., "with me in prayers for me to God"), brought about by Paul's overloading the sentence with his desire that they be concerned for him, has been ameliorated in the Western tradition (F G d* m vgᶜˡ) by changing the "for me" to "your," thus creating the much smoother, "with me in your prayers to God." In typical fashion, Codex D has a conflate reading (ὑμῶν ὑπὲρ ἐμοῦ; "your prayers for me"). The "your" in my translation does not reflect this reading; rather it stands for the ταῖς.

[480] So Leenhardt 376 (apparently), and Barrett 279; it is argued for vigorously by Murray 2.221 (on the basis of its being "parallel" with the Christ phrase), who is followed by Harrison 159. But it is decidedly the minority view, not even noted as an option in most commentaries.

First, it is "through our Lord Jesus Christ," meaning "on the basis of what Christ has done for us all as outlined in the argument of this letter"; second, it is "through the love of the Spirit," meaning "on the basis of the love for all the saints, including myself, that the Spirit engenders."[481] Thus, we have another text[482] in which Christian love for one another is first of all predicated on the love of God as it has been demonstrated in Christ Jesus and secondly has been made an effective outworking in our lives through the ministry of the Holy Spirit.

Significantly, this is yet another text in which the work of Christ and the Spirit are brought into close proximity but at the same time are seen as distinct in their own right.[483] It is perhaps fitting that in the final mention of the Spirit in this letter, one is also brought again to see how Trinitarian Paul's basic assumptions about God actually are.[484] Prayer is to be made to God; Paul's appeal for such prayer is predicated on the work of Christ and the Spirit. Besides working havoc with the idea of a Spirit Christology, a text like this indicates how thoroughly Paul thought in terms of the work of Christ and of the Spirit as conjoined in the ongoing life of the believer. Everything is based on the prior work of Christ; but included is the ongoing work of the Spirit who engenders the love that will cause them to take this appeal seriously.

It should perhaps be noted in passing that this concern that they pray for him, predicated on the love that the Spirit effects, brings the letter itself full circle—before he finally signs off with commendations and greetings in ch. 16. The most unusual feature of the proemium, that Paul's prayer report is turned into a prayer that he might visit Rome (see on 1:11), is now repeated in his request that they pray for him. To be sure, the first concern in the prayer is that his trip to Jerusalem be successful in terms of its first purpose: the deliverance of the offering, which has Jew and Gentile as one people of God as its underlying driving force. But beyond that he wants prayer that he himself will be "delivered"—from those who would endanger his life—and finally be brought safely to Rome, for the purposes outlined earlier in the letter (1:10–15; 15:23–29).

---

[481] So Calvin 317, Meyer 2.360, Godet 486, SH 415, Denney 716–17, Erdman 152, Michel 373, Cranfield 2.776, Käsemann 407, Bruce 263, Dunn 878 ("doubtless"), Morris 523.

[482] In this regard see esp. Gal 5:13 and 22, and Col 1:8.

[483] As SH 415 note, the parallelism with Christ indicates that πνεῦμα is personal.

[484] So Barrett 279, who describes this phenomenon as "another 'unintended' Trinitarian formulation"; cf. Morris 523. Otherwise Ziesler 346, whose objection is based on the language Trinitarian that connotes a later development. Granted, but this is precisely the kind of talk that leads to—indeed forces—the later development; and it is thoroughgoing in Paul, and presuppositional, as 2 Cor 13:13[14] makes clear.

CONCLUSIONS

A summary of conclusions at the end of this chapter is scarcely necessary. In fact, the Spirit appears more often in the course of the argument of this letter than anywhere else in the corpus; and there is scarcely an area of Spirit life that is not covered. This calls for two final observations:

First, if Romans is, as most scholars think, a bit more deliberate than most of the other letters in the corpus, then one must take seriously how absolutely central to Pauline experience and theology the Spirit truly is. There is scarcely a dimension of Christian life, from the proclamation that calls people to faith (15:18–19), to their conversion (e.g., 8:14–17), to ethical life (8:12–13), to community relationships (14:17) and worship (12:3–8), that is not covered in this letter, with the Spirit as the crucial reality. Not only so, but there is scarcely a dimension of what is essential to Pauline theology where the Spirit is not mentioned as a central factor (theology proper, Christology, soteriology, eschatology, ecclesiology, continuity/discontinuity [covenant]). Here is the certain evidence that one simply cannot have a truly Pauline theology without giving serious attention to the role of the Spirit in that theology.

Second, the wide range of materials in which the Spirit is mentioned should also lead to a more fully integrated and balanced view of Spirit life than is often the case. On the one hand, the Spirit is obviously the key to Christian life, both conversion and ethics. It is by the Spirit that one also "boasts" in present suffering (5:3–5; 8:23, 26–27), as one "abounds in hope" by the power of the Spirit (15:13). On the other hand, and at the same time, there is evidence of the Spirit's ministry in extraordinary and miraculous ways. The Spirit inspires prophecy within the community of faith, and the proclaimed word is accompanied by signs and wonders, empowered by the Spirit. The tendency in the later church to play these two dimensions of Spirit life over against one another is surely one of the tragedies of the church. The Spirit will not be—indeed cannot be—wedded to our own agendas. It is clear from this letter that the presence of the Spirit means "both/and" not "either/or."

Finally, in keeping with the primary focus of this book, one can scarcely miss that Paul throughout this letter understood the Spirit as God's own empowering presence, both within and in the midst of his people.

8

THE CAPTIVITY EPISTLES: PHILEMON AND COLOSSIANS

We come now to a set of four epistles which have in common that they were written while Paul was in prison. Three of them (Philemon, Colossians, Ephesians) clearly belong together, since they have common references to people and their movements, plus a commonality of ideas and language. Because there is so much Spirit material in Ephesians, it deserves a chapter of its own. Philippians likewise warrants separate treatment, since it betrays little of the concerns or language of the other three; moreover, it reflects an imprisonment of some duration and distress, which Paul seems to think will soon be resolved, hopefully in his favor.

There has been considerable debate in scholarship over the place of this imprisonment—or imprisonments, if Philippians is from another period. The tradition is that all four were written from Rome during the imprisonment referred to in Acts 28. Some who reject the tradition opt for the Caesarean imprisonment narrated in Acts 23–26, while others have argued for Ephesus. Without going into all the reasons pro and con,[1] I am convinced that the tradition has the better of it with regard to all four letters—with the first three coming from the earlier part of the imprisonment, and Philippians considerably later.

PHILEMON

PHILEMON 25

The only appearance of the word πνεῦμα in this letter is in the grace-benediction in v. 25, "the grace of the Lord Jesus be with your[2] spirit [= spirits]." This formula

---

[1]See ch. 10, n. 2.
[2]Gk. ὑμῶν. This use of the "distributive singular" in this personal letter indicates,

has already been discussed in Gal 6:18 (q.v.). Philemon thus turns out to be the only letter in the extant Pauline corpus in which the Holy Spirit is neither mentioned nor alluded to in some way.

COLOSSIANS

Commentaries:[3] T. K. **Abbott** (ICC, 1897); R. G. **Bratcher** and E. A. **Nida** (1977); F. F. **Bruce** (NIC, ²1984); G. B. **Caird** (1976); H. M. **Carson** (TNTC, 1960); H. **Conzelmann** (NTD, 1965); M. **Dibelius** (HNT, 1953); J. **Eadie** (1856; repr. 1957); C. R. **Erdman** (1933); M. J. **Harris** (1991); W. **Hendriksen** (1964); J. B. **Lightfoot** (1890); E. **Lohmeyer** (MeyerK, 1964); E. **Lohse** (Herm, 1971); R. P. **Martin** (NCB, 1972); C. **Masson** (CNT, 1950); H. A. W. **Meyer** (MeyerK, 1875); P. T. **O'Brien** (WBC, 1982); A. S. **Peake** (EGT, 1903); P. **Pokorný** (THNT, 1987); L. B. **Radford** (WC, 1931); A. T. **Robertson** (1928); E. **Schweizer** (1982 [Ger. original 1976]); C. **Vaughan** (EBC, 1978); B. F. **Westcott** (1914); N. T. **Wright** (TNTC, 1986).

Colossians is one of the letters in the Pauline corpus whose authenticity is doubted by many NT scholars;[4] and one of the oft-repeated arguments against Pauline authorship is "the almost complete lack of

---

as if vv. 2 and 3 were not enough, that even "personal letters" within the early Christian communities were intended to be community documents.

[3]The following commentaries are referred to in this chapter only by the author's last name.

[4]For me this is one of the more puzzling "assured results" of NT scholarship. Even though there are some obvious differences between this letter and the so-called acknowledged letters, they are not nearly as great as is often made out and are no greater than any one of the others has with its companions (indeed, on the basis of the criteria used here, one could easily show either Romans or 1 Corinthians to be inauthentic, in light of the other). Normal shifts of emphases and corresponding changes in vocabulary in one's life, and especially differences in the kinds of opposition encountered, make perfectly good sense of these phenomena, while they are almost impossible to explain, as over-subtle to the highest degree, in the case of a forgery.

On the other side, the denial of Pauline authorship faces the nearly insurmountable difficulties posed by the specific relationship of Colossians to Philemon, which all accept as authentic. It is difficult to imagine the historical circumstance in which a pseudepigrapher not only would have had access to such a letter as Philemon, but also would then have used its *merely incidental references to people and their movements* as his one clear tie to the other Pauline letters. It would seem that one must either reject Philemon as well if one rejects Colossians, or else accept them both. Having the one without the other presents historical difficulties all out of proportion to the lesser difficulties of some acknowledged differences in language, thought, and form of argumentation. On this matter see esp. Luke T. Johnson, *The Writings of the New Testament: An Interpretation* (Philadelphia: Fortress, 1986) 357–59.

references to the Spirit,"[5] a lack considered striking since Colossians is a somewhat polemical letter. But this argument fails at two points.

First, it does not take seriously enough the essential difference between the polemic of this letter, which does not intrinsically call for Spirit talk, and that elsewhere, where the Spirit plays a major—and crucial—role. In the earlier letters where the Spirit plays such a predominant role (1 Corinthians, Galatians, Romans), the issues are raised in the first instance by the Corinthians themselves as to what constitutes genuine Spirituality, and in the second instance by Paul's own insistence that the reception of the Spirit is the certain evidence that one neither "gets in" nor "stays in" Christ by means of Jewish boundary markers. Thus the key role of the Spirit in these letters is determined by the issues: in Galatians and Romans, the issue is how one becomes and remains a believer in Christ (the experienced Spirit is the evidence that it is by faith in Christ, and the same Spirit is the key to all subsequent life in Christ), whereas in 1 Corinthians the issue is how the Spirit person lives and worships (marked by the crucified One and intelligibly and orderly in the worshipping community.)

The issue in Colossians, by way of contrast, is almost entirely christological—as to both Christ's nature and his relationship to the believing community. One should no more expect a great deal of Spirit talk in such a polemic than one should in a letter of friendship (and exhortation) thanking his friends for a recent gift (Philippians).[6]

That leads us, secondly, to note that the Spirit language that does appear in this letter, as with 1 Thessalonians and Philippians, is incidental but not unlike what appears elsewhere in Paul. There is indeed only one specific mention of the Spirit (1:8); there Paul expresses thanks to God for their love for him (and one another?) "in/by the Spirit." But there are four other references to the Spirit's activity that are also thoroughly Pauline. Two of these (1:9; 3:16) appear in the adjective form, πνευματικός: as in 1 Corinthians these refer respectively to "Spiritual understanding" (insight into God's will that the Spirit provides; cf. 1 Cor 2:6–16), and "Spiritual songs" (Spirit-inspired response to God's saving activity in Christ in the form of song; cf. 1 Cor 14:26). The other two are "power" texts (1:11; 1:29), both of which, as in 2 Thes 1:11 or 2 Cor 6:7, probably

---

[5]Schweizer 17. This is repeated in the most recent NT introduction to come across my desk (E. D. Freed, *The New Testament: A Critical Introduction* [2d ed.; Belmont, Calif.: Wadsworth Publishing Co., 1986] 305).

[6]Schweizer 38 suggests otherwise, namely, that "many statements which Paul always or very frequently associates with the Spirit are found here without any such reference." This is a particularly thin argument from silence. Not only are Schweizer's illustrations less than convincing, but with the same kind of argument one could condemn all the other letters. For example, on the basis of Gal 5:22, Rom 5:5, and Col 1:8, a lack of reference to the Spirit should condemn all other passages in Paul that speak to the issue of love in the Christian community. Arguments against authenticity, even as only "supporting evidence," must be made of "sterner stuff" than this.

reflect the empowering activity of the Spirit in the believer's life—a theme that will become more thoroughgoing in Ephesians.

COLOSSIANS 1:7–8

[7] *. . . even as[7] you learned [it][8] from our beloved fellow-slave Epaphras, who is a faithful servant of Christ in our[9] behalf, [8]who also informed us of your love in the Spirit.*

This clause concludes the thanksgiving period of the letter. Although most of Paul's thanksgiving periods anticipate the content of the letter proper, in this case that happens more in the prayer report that follows (vv. 9–14). The thanksgiving turns out to be more general, as one might well expect of a letter to a church not founded by Paul directly; and that in fact is the point of this final clause (vv. 7–8)—to authenticate his writing the letter. The earlier, and more general, part of the thanksgiving is expressed in the common triad of faith, love, and hope.[10] In this case there is a clear spelling out of the direction of these three virtues: faith is in/by Christ Jesus; love is for all the saints; and hope is laid up in the heavenly places. What is noteworthy about the final clause in vv. 7–8 is the isolation of love from the other two and the typical way Paul rather off-handedly indicates the source of this love.

The Spirit language in this clause is therefore especially Pauline,[11] in form and content—not to mention in its ambiguity! The dative ἐν πνεύματι ("in/by the Spirit") is in keeping with that formula throughout the Pauline corpus,[12] and the association of the Spirit with love is a

---

[7]The MajT has added καί after καθώς, on the pattern of the two preceding καθὼς καί's in v. 6. But those two are balanced ("even as also in the world"; "even as also among you"), whereas this is the more standard explanatory/causal καθώς found in other thanksgivings (e.g., 1 Cor 1:6; Phil 1:7).

[8]The unexpressed object in this case is "the grace of God" that they have come to know (in v. 6).

[9]Contra the UBS committee (see Metzger, *Textual Commentary*, 619–20), the ἡμῶν of P[46] ℵ* A B D G pc is much to be preferred to ὑμῶν (C K 33 1739 Maj lat cop syr). Rather than ὑμῶν having been changed by attraction to the preceding ἡμῶν, as Metzger suggests, it is far more likely that several scribes independently and early changed the original ἡμῶν to ὑμῶν in the interest of preferred sense, namely, that the direction of the thanksgiving and Epaphras's preaching of the gospel was "for your sakes." But Paul's concern at the conclusion of the thanksgiving is to direct their attention to his authority among them, specifically that Epaphras, Christ's servant though he is, was among them "on Paul's behalf."

[10]Also found in his earliest thanksgiving (1 Thes 1:3).

[11]Contra, e.g., Schweizer.

[12]See on Rom 14:17, χαρὰ ἐν πνεύματι ἁγίῳ ("joy in/by the Holy Spirit"), which is identical in construction and, as yet another of the Spirit's fruit, exhibits the same relationship to the Spirit. Schweizer 38 suggests that because ἐν πνεύματι "is without the article," its "point presumably is only that a spiritual love is to be distinguished

particularly Pauline understanding of the Spirit's activity.[13] Therefore, the ambiguity lies not in whether Paul here refers to the Spirit—he does indeed[14]—but (1) in the *direction* of the love (whether within the community or toward Paul) and (2) the *nuance* of the dative (whether locative, "in the Spirit," or instrumental, "by the Spirit").

The first of these matters can be settled with high probability by the context. Paul has already spoken about "the love which you have for all the saints." That, of course, includes their mutual love for one another, as well as their love for believers beyond their own community. But toward the end the thanksgiving takes a decided turn, in which Paul indicates the source of his knowledge about their faith, love, and hope: Epaphras. This mention of Epaphras picks up two concerns, crucial for Paul's being heard in this letter. First, he reminds them that Epaphras, even though Christ's servant, is in fact Paul's fellow "slave," who ministered among them on Paul's behalf. Paul's own authority to address their "heresy" rests partly on this reality. Second, Epaphras has now also been a "servant" to Paul on their behalf: he has revealed to Paul their love for him. This too is crucial for what he is about to say, in that his confidence of their love for him, even though he is not known to them personally, will give him freedom to speak directly to their present situation. Thus their "love for all the saints," mentioned already in v. 4, is now acknowledged as specifically directed toward Paul as well.[15]

Whether ἐν πνεύματι is locative or instrumental is more difficult to determine.[16] When this formula lacks the preposition, it is invariably instrumental; but it also is so in most cases with the preposition. This is not a crucial matter, since their love for the saints and now especially for Paul results from the Spirit's activity in their midst—and in their hearts. Nonetheless, in keeping with Paul's usage elsewhere, the nuance is most likely instrumental. That is, it is not so much that by their being "in Spirit" love flows out toward him—although one could scarcely argue against that theologically—but that the Spirit is the specific source or cause of such love, the one who has brought it to pass.[17] As in Gal 5:22, this is the "fruit of the Spirit" (cf. Rom 15:30).

---

from one that is purely worldly." That represents a considerable misreading of the Pauline evidence. On this usage in Paul see ch. 2 above, pp. 21–24.

[13] See on Gal 5:22–23; Rom 5:5; 15:30.

[14] As most commentaries (e.g., Eadie, Meyer, Lightfoot, Abbott, Peake, Westcott, Robertson, Erdman, Radford, Carson, Hendriksen, Lohse, Martin, Vaughan, O'Brien, Bruce, Wright, Pokorný, Harris).

[15] So Chrysostom, Abbott 201, Peake 498, Robertson 44, Erdman 39, Martin 50, O'Brien 16; otherwise Westcott 36, Radford 155, Carson 34, Hendriksen 33, Lohse 25, Bruce 44, Wright 56, Pokorný 37. Vaughan and Harris are noncommittal. Meyer 261 thinks it refers to their love for Epaphras, which seems especially unlikely.

[16] Eadie (19) suggests both: "the source and sphere" of love.

[17] So also Meyer 261, Abbott 201, Peake 498, Carson 34, Lohse 23.

Thus in an off-handed way, Paul once again reflects the thorough-going Spirit-orientation of his understanding of Christian life and experience. That believers in his congregations have been filled with love is for him both presupposition and evidence of the Spirit's presence in them and among them.

Colossians 1:9–12

⁹For this reason we also, from the very day we first heard [of your faith in Christ], never cease praying and asking in your behalf that you will be filled with full knowledge of God's will in all Spiritual wisdom and understanding, ¹⁰so that you may walk worthy of the Lord so as to please him in all things, bearing fruit in every good work and increasing in the knowledge of God, ¹¹being empowered with all power, in keeping with his glorious might, for every kind of endurance and longsuffering, with joy ¹²thanking the Father who has qualified you for your part of the inheritance with the saints in light.

As noted above, rather than in the thanksgiving, it is in this prayer report[18] in particular that Paul anticipates some matters he wishes to address in this letter.[19] The concerns are basically two:[20] (1) that they have a better grasp of what God is doing—and wants to do (= have full knowledge of what God's will is), and (2) that they themselves live more fully to God's glory (since this is in fact what God's will is all about). This is the point made in the two purpose clauses, the second of which ("to walk worthy of the Lord") is then spelled out in the four participial phrases that follow. The basic structure of the whole sentence is thus easily displayed:

Paul prays:

(1) that you will be filled
            with the knowledge of God's will
            by means of the Spirit's wisdom, etc.

(2) so that you may walk worthy
            of the Lord
            so as to please him in every way

---

[18]However, in 2 Thessalonians and Philippians it happens in the thanksgiving and the prayer.

[19]This in itself weighs especially heavily in favor of authenticity. It is one thing for a pseudepigrapher to know that Paul often begins his letters with both a thanksgiving period and prayer report (which do not occur in Philemon, the one certain letter he had access to), but it would require insight of the kind prayed for in Paul's sentence for him to be able to enter Paul's less up-front consciousness and anticipate the rest of the letter in this way in the prayer report.

[20]As also in Philippians.

by your:

> (a) bearing fruit in every way
> (b) increasing in the knowledge of God
> (c) being empowered for endurance and patience
> with all power
> in keeping with his might
> (d) giving thanks with joy to the Father

On this view of things the first purpose clause expresses penultimate purpose (knowing God's will by the Spirit's wisdom), so that they may get on with the ultimate purpose found in the second clause (walking worthy of the Lord). This means, therefore, that their *conduct as believers* is the primary concern in the prayer, not their better understanding of the Christian faith. Paul's urgency is with their becoming complete believers, whose faith in Christ is such that it produces the kind of reconciled and changed lives that can be accounted for on the basis of that faith alone.

The compounding of participles that marks this long sentence is typical of Paul in his thanksgivings and prayers, as is the concern itself, which ultimately is for them to live in keeping with God's will—fruitfully, patiently, and thankfully. What is less typical, at least in the earlier letters, is the language, especially "knowledge" and "power" terminology. As in most such cases in Paul, shifts of terminology are usually attributable to the situation being addressed; most likely this reflects language being used by those who are currently deviating from the faith into "empty philosophy."

9 The phrase that concerns us here is "with all Spiritual wisdom and understanding [or insight[21]]," which modifies their "being filled with the knowledge of the will of God." Several pieces of data confirm that Paul intends, "by means of all *the Spirit's* wisdom and understanding/insight":[22]

(1) The use of πνευματικός.[23] Unless there is strong contextual evidence to the contrary, this word should ordinarily be understood as the adjective for "the Spirit," just as κυριακός is the proper adjective for "the Lord." As with κυριακός,[24] it has a kind of "possessive" sense to it: something is πνευματικός in the sense that it properly and essentially belongs to the sphere of the Spirit.[25] This is all the more so when one

---

[21]Gk. σύνεσις; apart from the citation of the LXX in 1 Cor 1:19, this word occurs only in the later Pauline epistles (Colossians, Ephesians, 2 Timothy).

[22]So Eadie 24, Meyer 263, Lightfoot 137, Abbott 202, Peake 499, Robertson 49, Erdman 41, Carson 35, Hendriksen 57, Lohse 26–27, Martin 51, Bruce 46. Otherwise O'Brien 22 and Wright 56, who speak of it as being on "a spiritual level," without elaborating what that might mean. Harris 31 is noncommittal.

[23]See the discussion of this word in ch. 2, pp. 28–32.

[24]On this word see the discussion on 1 Cor 11:20 in Fee, *1 Corinthians*, 539–40.

[25]So also Eadie 24.

asks in any given context, what is the understood *contrast* to πνευματικός? If something is properly described as πνευματικός, what would be its natural opposite? Here the implied contrast is not "material" or "earthly" (= belonging to the earth) or "natural," but "fleshly," that is, wisdom and insight that is merely of this present world, "earthly" in this pejorative, fallen sense.[26] This is precisely what is said in 2:8 and 23 about the "empty philosophy" to which they are currently being subjected.[27] Paul wants for them its opposite, knowing God's ways by means of the wisdom the Spirit gives. As in 1 Cor 2:13–3:3, therefore, πνευματικός refers to what belongs to the Spirit, as over against what is merely ψυχικός ("natural") or σαρκικός ("belonging to the flesh").

(2) Pauline usage. Elsewhere when Paul constructs phrases of compound words, one of which is modified by πᾶς ("all") and the second by another adjective, he intends both adjectives to modify both words.[28] Almost certainly Paul intends the same here, meaning that πᾶς and πνευματικός together modify "wisdom" and "insight."[29] Thus, he is not talking about two things ("all wisdom" and "spiritual understanding"), but a compound reality, "all Spiritual wisdom and understanding." This usage almost certainly reflects the LXX, which not only uses these two words in compound, but does so in connection with the Spirit of God.[30] The further point to make, of course, is that both of these are elsewhere understood by Paul to be Spirit possessions or Spirit endowments (cf. 1 Cor 2:6–16; 7:40; 12:8).

(3) The similarity to Eph 1:17 (q.v.). Exactly the same point is made there, but with slightly different (but still Pauline) language: πνεῦμα σοφίας καὶ ἀποκαλύψεως ("the Spirit of wisdom and revelation").[31] In

---

[26]See esp. 2 Cor 1:12, where behavior opposed to the grace of God is based on σοφίᾳ σαρκικῇ ("on fleshly wisdom").

[27]In 2:8 the "heresy" is described as "empty philosophy" that is based on "merely human tradition," which is "in accordance with the elemental spirits of the universe." In 2:23 the resultant asceticism is described as "making a show of *wisdom*," but as in fact having no true remedy for *the flesh*.

[28]Cf. e.g., 2 Thes 2:17, ἐν παντὶ ἔργῳ καὶ λόγῳ ἀγαθῷ ("with every good work and word").

[29]So also Abbott 202, Peake 499, Erdman 41, Hendriksen 57, Lohse 27, O'Brien 22, Wright 58, Harris 31. The older commentaries tended not only to take them separately, but also tried to find different nuances to the two words (e.g., Eadie 23, Meyer 263, who saw "spiritual insight" as specifying the more general "all wisdom"). The two words occur together regularly in the LXX (Exod 31:3; 35:31, 35; Isa 10:13; 11:2), which best accounts for the usage here.

[30]See esp. Exod 31:3, of Bezalel, who was filled with πνεῦμα θεῖον σοφίας καὶ συνέσεως ("the divine Spirit of wisdom and understanding"; cf. 35:31), and Isa 11:2, of the Messiah, upon whom will rest the Spirit of God (πνεῦμα τοῦ θεοῦ), the Spirit of wisdom and understanding (πνεῦμα σοφίας καὶ συνέσεως).

[31]In the Ephesians passage in particular Paul is adopting the language of Isa 11:2 (LXX), which *specifically* speaks of this πνεῦμα as "the Spirit of God."

both cases the phrase simply means σοφία καὶ σύνεσις τοῦ πνεύματος ("the Spirit's wisdom and insight").

(4) Pauline theology. As noted in the discussion of 1 Cor 2:6–16, it is an especially Pauline view that understanding the ways and mind of God is an endowment of the Spirit for those who have come to faith in Christ Jesus. We have the "mind of Christ" precisely because we have the Spirit; we therefore understand to be the wisdom of God what is foolishness from a merely human point of view. Only the Spirit can reveal the will of God.[32]

All of this together, therefore, suggests that to translate πνευματικός as "spiritual," understood either as dualistic (belonging to the heavenly as opposed to the earthly sphere)[33] or as some merely vague, nonphysical idea, is to miss Paul's usage by a wide margin. To the contrary, Paul prays for them to be filled with the knowledge of God's will (cf. 4:12), which comes by way of the wisdom and understanding that the Spirit endues.[34] As in 1 Thes 4:1–3, God's will means to walk in God's ways, which is precisely how the prayer goes on. Thus Paul is anticipating one of the chief concerns of the letter, that they come to know and live out genuine Christ-likeness; the way forward is through the gift of the Spirit, who in the first place gives understanding as to what God's will is. But the Spirit also empowers such a life, and that is where the "power" language of v. 11 fits in.

11 The third participle modifying "to walk worthy of the Lord" expresses the empowering dimension for their bearing fruit in every way and increasing in the full knowledge of God.[35] Paul's prayer for their obedience to the will of God also therefore contains the means whereby they may do so, "being empowered with all power,[36] in keeping with his glorious might." Although the Spirit is not explicitly mentioned, nor can one be sure that the original recipients would have picked up on it, one can be rather certain nonetheless that as with many such "power" texts the Spirit is very close to the surface in Paul's mind. There are two reasons in particular for thinking so here:

(1) Although "power" appears sometimes in the abstract in Paul, as presuppositional to God's being, in this case the abstract idea is specific-

---

[32]This is not dissimilar to 1 Thes 4:7–8, where the gift of the Spirit brings both insight and empowering for the holiness that is "the will of God for you."

[33]So Schweizer 38.

[34]See also the discussion on Rom 12:1–2, where it was argued that "the renewing of the mind" in order to determine the will of God had the work of the Spirit as its basic presupposition.

[35]These two ideas go together in this letter: to know God fully is to know his character and thus to conform one's life accordingly. See below on 3:10.

[36]This somewhat stilted translation attempts to capture the Semitic redundancy of the original, ἐν πάσῃ δυνάμει δυναμούμενοι.

ally expressed in the next phrase, "in keeping with his glorious might." This latter phrase, therefore, points to "might" or "power" as a quality of the nature of God, which is manifested for the Colossians as they themselves "are empowered by God's power."

(2) That "power" in this context refers to the Spirit's empowering is expressly stated in a parallel passage in the companion letter (Eph 3:16 and 20, q.v.). There, also in a prayer for his readers, Paul desires that they be strengthened "with power" so as to know fully the love of Christ. In the case of 3:16 Paul specifically clarifies "with power" by adding "through his Spirit." This is picked up again in the concluding benediction (v. 20), but once more in terms of "power" only: "To him who empowers . . . according to his power that is at work in you." The context, therefore, requires us to understand "power" in v. 20 as "the power of the Holy Spirit." Since this passage is so similar in language and concern to our present text, by analogy one may rightfully assume the Spirit also to be the source of power here.

As usual in such passages, however, where power language occurs without a specific mention of the Spirit, the emphasis lies on power terminology, not on the presence of the Spirit per se. The Spirit, therefore, must be understood as the presupposition of this language, not as its direct reference point. God is the obvious subject of the empowering; from all kinds of texts in Paul we may assume this means "by the power of God's Holy Spirit."

That this is so is also suggested by two other features of the immediate context: First, the goal of this empowering is "for every kind of endurance and longsuffering." In Gal 5:22 "longsuffering" is listed as one of the fruit of the Spirit. Second, in the participial phrase that immediately follows, the final expression of their walking worthy of the Lord lies in their "giving thanks with joy," yet another of the Spirit's "fruitful" activity in their lives.[37]

Therefore, this is almost certainly another indirect Spirit text, which we should rightly understand to mean, "being empowered with all the Spirit's power, in keeping with his glorious might, for every kind of endurance and longsuffering." It is perhaps worthy of note that this empowering text has nothing to do with "signs and wonders" and everything to do with patience and endurance in the present struggle. The power of the Spirit in Paul thus reflects a full-orbed understanding of Christian life, as both "already" and "not yet," which includes both the miraculous, on the one hand, and patient endurance in the midst of hardship, on the other. And he simply does not see these two kinds of empowering as being in opposition to one another.

---

[37]On this see especially the discussion on 1 Thes 5:16–18; cf. Gal 5:22; Rom 14:17.

COLOSSIANS 1:29

. . . to which purpose also I labor, contending[38] *in keeping with his [God's] working that is at work in me with power.*

These words form the conclusion of the first paragraph of that section of the letter (1:24–2:5) in which Paul (a) "introduces" himself and his ministry to these believers (1:24–29), who otherwise know him only through their mutual friend Epaphras, and (b) expresses his long-term pastoral concern for them (2:1–5). One can hardly escape the christocentric nature of both paragraphs. The problem in Colossae clearly lies here, with their understanding—or lack of full under-standing—of Christ and his work.

This concluding clause (v. 29) is full of Paulinisms: the verb "labor" to describe his ministry; the athletic metaphor "striving/contending" to express something of its difficulty; the fact that he is "energized"[39] for the task by God himself; and that God's "energy" is at work in him "with power."

Our interest here is with this final phrase, yet another "power" text which has the Holy Spirit as its unexpressed presupposition.[40] In light of the foregoing discussion (of 1:11), we will not belabor this point, except to note how often this phrase, ἐν δυνάμει ("with power"), is found in Paul in connection with the Spirit's working in him with regard to his apostolic ministry (1 Thes 1:5; 2 Cor 1:4–5; 6:7; Rom 15:18–19). That is surely so here as well, even if not explicitly stated. Thus: "in keeping with his [God's] working that is at work in me by the power of his Spirit."[41]

Again, as in all of these texts, the apostle expresses his absolute conviction that his ministry, which requires his own "labor" and is full of the struggles of an athlete, is ultimately empowered by God, who is at work in him by the Spirit. Even though this paragraph begins by focusing on his sufferings (v. 24), he nonetheless rejoices in the midst of those sufferings, because for him the greater reality is the presence of God by his Spirit, powerfully at work in him to carry out his divine appointment, as the results throughout the Gentile world offer full evidence.

COLOSSIANS 2:5

For if indeed I am absent in the flesh [= in person], I am nonetheless with you in S/spirit, rejoicing and beholding your good order and the steadfastness of your faith toward Christ.

---

[38]Gk. ἀγωνιζόμενος, an athletic metaphor that occurs frequently in Paul in contexts referring to his apostolic ministry, as here.

[39]As with 1:9 above, this is another Semitic reduplication: κατὰ τὴν ἐνέργειαν αὐτοῦ τὴν ἐνεργουμένην. This combination of "working" and "power" is unique to the Prison letters (Eph 1:19; 3:7; 3:20; Phil 3:21). The use of this verb as a way of expressing God's "energy" at work in Paul for the task of ministry (Gal 2:8) and for Christian life in general (1 Thes 2:13; 1 Cor 12:6, 11; Gal 5:6; Phil 2:13) is uniquely Pauline in the NT.

[40]So also Westcott 86, Hendriksen 94, Wright 93.

[41]This seems to be far more likely than to see the phrase as merely adverbial ("mightily"), as Meyer 335, O'Brien 91, Harris 74.

On this somewhat perplexing usage, see the corresponding passage in 1 Cor 5:3. The significant difference in this case is that Paul uses the term "flesh" rather than "body" as the contrast to his presence with them in S/spirit. But not much can be made of that,[42] since (1) the contrast in neither case is between spirit/body or spirit/flesh, but between Paul's being absent "in person" but present in S/spirit,[43] and (2) the two anthropological terms (body/flesh) are easily interchangeable in Paul when one's human, physical presence is in view.

But what does this enigmatic phrase mean? As with 1 Cor 5:3, the commonly held, but highly unlikely, view is that even though Paul is personally absent, the Colossian believers are nonetheless *in his thoughts*.[44] It is extremely doubtful whether Paul, or any first-century person for that matter, would have used this contrast for such an idea; in any case, Paul uses plain speech when what he intends has to do with his readers' being in his thoughts, as the many prayer reports in his letters demonstrate. It is, after all, quite different for him to say that he thanks God "at every remembrance" of someone, and to say, as he does here and in 1 Cor 5:3, that he considers himself actually to be present with them ἐν τῷ πνεύματι ("in his spirit" or "in the Spirit").[45]

The key to all of this lies with taking Paul's letters much more seriously as consciously written to be read at the gathering of God's people for worship. Most likely, therefore, something very close to the sense of 1 Cor 5:3 is in view, where Paul considers himself as truly present by the Spirit, as they gather in the presence and power of the Spirit for the reading of his letter. It is, after all, "as present in S/spirit" that he both "rejoices" and "sees" what God is doing among them.

COLOSSIANS 3:10

[9] *. . . since you have taken off the old humanity with its practices* [10]*and have clothed yourself with the new, which is ever being made new unto full knowledge after the fashion of him who created the new humanity.*

---

[42]*Pace* Schweizer 119–20.

[43]Hence Harris's objection (87) to a reference to the Spirit seems to miss the point here.

[44]See, e.g., Eadie 120, Meyer 346, Radford 218, Hendriksen 106, Vaughan 196 ("spiritual oneness with them"). Erdman 63 recognizes the difficulty with this view and in its place offers "vividly imagining himself present."

[45]Cf. Westcott 95, Lohse 83, Martin 76, O'Brien 98, Pokorný 91. Schweizer also took this view in *TDNT* 6.436, but rejected it in his later commentary (119–20). He is one of the few NT scholars who seems to have rightly grasped the sense of 1 Cor 5:3; his rejection of that same view here, as his argument makes plain, has not to do with what is actually said, but with his prior commitment to the non-Pauline authorship of the letter. His own view that this expresses the "psychic reaction" of the "apostle" at the news of their steadfastness seems especially far-fetched, although this enigmatic comment may perhaps be another way of stating the commonly held view.

The reason for the inclusion of this passage in the present volume is the appearance of the verb ἀνακαινόω ("being made new"), which elsewhere in Paul has the closest kind of association with the Spirit. Not only so, but one of the linguistic parallels to this passage in Ephesians (3:16) actually speaks of being strengthened "in the inner person" by the power of the Holy Spirit.

Thus in Titus 3:5 Christian conversion is explicitly called a regeneration, a "making new" by the Holy Spirit. Likewise, the Spirit is very close at hand when Paul uses this language in 2 Cor 4:16 and Rom 12:2 (q.v.), even though as here he is not explicitly mentioned. The verb in this passage is another example of the "divine passive" in Paul, where God is to be understood as the unexpressed subject. Therefore, since this language in Paul belongs to the activity of the Spirit, it is altogether likely that lying behind this "renewing" activity is God the Holy Spirit.[46]

Although the language of "putting off" and "putting on" probably reflects baptismal imagery, the concern itself lies at the heart of Paul's gospel and has to do not with baptism but with the work of the Spirit: those who are Christ's must bear his likeness in their behavior. Therefore, just as in Gal 5:13–26, but now with different imagery, the concern is for the Colossians to exhibit in their everyday lives that kind of behavior which is in keeping with the character of the One who created the new person in the first place. Believers are to understand themselves as continually[47] being made new by the Holy Spirit so as to enter into "full knowledge" (of God, is implied), which knowledge is demonstrated when those who bear his likeness live in keeping with his character, which will be spelled out in particular in vv. 12–15.

COLOSSIANS 3:15

And let the peace of Christ rule in your hearts, unto which you were also called in one body.

Here is another passage in this letter in which the Spirit is not mentioned, but where both the parallel in Eph 4:3–4 (q.v.) and Pauline theology elsewhere (esp. 1 Cor 12:13) insist that even though unexpressed, Paul understands the "calling" in one body to have been effected by the Spirit. This becomes even more plausible in light of v. 16 that follows, where the Spirit is the unmistakable presupposition of the whole. But as with the preceding passages, the Spirit is not mentioned in this text because that is merely the presupposition for Paul; his emphasis and concern in this passage lies elsewhere—with the fact that they were all called into the one body, the concluding word which ties together the whole of the preceding paraenesis.

---

[46]Cf. Meyer 432, Westcott 146, Hendriksen 150, Harris 152 (as one possibility).

[47]The present tense of the participle stands in contrast to the aorists that precede and follow. Thus at conversion believers are "clothed with" the new humanity, that is, "created" as new people by God himself; once believers have been clothed with this new humanity, the work of the Spirit is to effect a continual renewal into the image of the creator. Here is a clear case where Paul understands the goal of redemption in Christ to be the restoration of the lost image of God, which was rolled in the dust by the Fall. Cf. 2 Cor 3:18; Rom 8:29.

COLOSSIANS 3:16[48]

Let the word of Christ[49] dwell in your midst richly with all wisdom teaching and admonishing one another with psalms,[50] hymns, songs spiritual with grace/gratitude[51] singing with your hearts to God.[52]

Cf. EPHESIANS 5:18–19[53]

[18]*. . . but be filled with the Spirit,* [19]*speaking to one another with psalms, hymns, and Spirit songs singing and making music with your hearts to the Lord.*

This passage comes toward the conclusion of the paraenesis that began in v. 12, all of which has community life in purview. Verses 12–15, therefore, speak mainly to *relationships* within the community, concluding in v. 15 with the reminder that they have been called to become "one body." Our passage picks up these concerns by focusing on their *corporate worship* as the place where they will both praise God and be reminded of these obligations to one another.

---

[48]The nearly impossible "translation" given here, including the lack of commas, attempts to help the reader see the difficulties of the Greek text, whose word order is followed as closely as possible. For the various exegetical problems involved, see the discussion.

[49]Χριστοῦ is undoubtedly the correct reading, not θεοῦ "God" (A C* 33 451 1241 1984 pc) or κυρίου "Lord" (ℵ* I 2127 Clement pc). Not only is it the reading of the preponderance of witnesses, from all parts and very early, but its uniqueness (the only occurrence of "word of Christ" in the NT) makes it the more difficult reading, which was variously altered to a more common expression.

[50]The MajT has added a καί between the three words in the series in conformity to Eph 5:19.

[51]There are two interrelated difficulties here. Did Paul write ἐν χάριτι (ℵ* A C D[2] Maj) or ἐν τῇ χάριτι (P[46] ℵ[2] B D* F G Ψ 6 1739 pc)? Surely the latter. It is supported by the earliest and best evidence; an omission can be easily accounted for as conforming to Pauline style, whereas one is hard pressed to account for an addition (see 4:6, where no one has added a τῇ). If so, then what does "*the* χάριτι" mean? See the discussion.

[52]On this textual matter I quote Metzger (*Textual Commentary,* 625) in full: "In place of θεῷ, which is strongly supported by early and diversified testimony (P[46vid] ℵ A B C* D* G Ψ[c] 33 81 1739 it[d.g.86] vg syr[p.h] cop[sa.bo] arm Clement Speculum *al*), the Textus Receptus, influenced by the parallel in Eph 5.19 (where there is no variation), substitutes κυρίῳ, with C[2] D[c] K Ψ* 614 *Byz Lect* it[61] goth *al.*"

[53]I do not intend to discuss the Ephesians passage in full at this point; that will be reserved for its proper place in the next chapter. Since the parallel in this case is so close, but is expressed in slightly different ways, reference to this parallel is almost mandatory in order for us to make decisions at some difficult points in the Colossians passage. Therefore, it seemed useful to have the Ephesians text in sight as we think our way through the present text. As before, the "translation" is completely wooden and without punctuation.

Here, then, is a passage full of intriguing information about worship in the Pauline churches; but it also has more than its share of exegetical uncertainties, mostly having to do with how we are to understand the several modifiers, beginning with "with all wisdom." But before that, some preliminary observations about the opening clause ("let the word of Christ dwell in your midst richly") are of considerable importance for this study.

First, everything about the immediate context, and the language of this sentence in particular, indicates that Paul is reflecting on the Christian community. These are not words for the individual believer,[54] but for believers as the people of God in relationship with one another. Beginning with v. 12, where the character of the "new person" in Christ is spelled out in some illustrative detail, all of the paraenesis takes the form of community concerns. Everything is for, or in light of, "one another." Thus in the immediately preceding exhortation (v. 15), which sets the pattern for the present one, they are to let the *shalom* of Christ rule in their hearts, since it is to this that they have been called together as one body. Our passage views these relationships within the context of the gathered people of God at worship, where they are to teach and admonish *one another* as one way that the word of Christ will dwell "in them" richly. This means that the prepositional phrase ἐν ὑμῖν ("in/ among you"), even though it modifies the verb "indwell"[55] and would ordinarily mean "within you," must here mean "in your midst."[56] The indwelling "word of Christ," therefore, in its two forms of "teaching and admonishing one another" and of "singing to God" has to do with the church at worship.

Second, and in the same vein, it is significant to note that the compound participles, "teaching and admonishing," are the same two that Paul used in 1:28 to describe his own ministry. Here, then, is plain evidence that Paul did not consider "ministry" to be the special province of either apostles or office-holders.[57] As in the earliest of his letters

---

[54]*Pace* Peake 541, Robertson 167, Schweizer 209—as though Paul were urging them individually to let the word of Christ dwell richly in them, so that they could help others and sing with thanksgiving to God.

[55]Gk. ἐνοικέτω. This is a Pauline compound in the NT (2 Cor 6:16 [LXX]; Rom 8:11; 2 Tim 1:5, 14); in Rom 8:11 and 2 Tim 1:14 it refers specifically to the indwelling Spirit.

[56]Despite Eadie 250, Peake 541, e.g., to the contrary, who object to rendering ἐν ὑμῖν with ἐνοικέω as "among you." But the context demands something very much like this. If it is "in you," then Meyer 448 correctly notes that it means "in your church." Better, then, to translate it "in your midst." Cf. G. Delling, *TDNT* 8.498n63, Radford 282, Hendriksen 160, Lohse 150, O'Brien 207, Bruce 157 (tentatively). Harris (167, 172) opts for both.

[57]One suspects, although one cannot be sure, that this reality lies behind an earlier tradition of interpretation that saw this text as dealing not with worship but with Christian life in general. Only "office-holders" were to do such things in the assembly! One might add that such "teaching and admonishing" activity would have

(1 Thes 5:14), these kinds of activities in the Christian assembly are the responsibility of all.[58] This is in keeping with the picture that emerges in 1 Cor 14:26 as well (q.v.).

Third, the primary concern of the exhortation is with the "word of Christ," that is, the message of the gospel with its central focus on Christ.[59] This, after all, is what the letter is all about: Christ the embodiment of God, Christ the all-sufficient one, Christ, creator and redeemer. Paul now urges that this "word of Christ," which in part he has already articulated in 1:15–23, "dwell in their midst" in an abundant way. In so doing, part of their activity will be directed toward one another ("teaching and admonishing one another"), and part toward God ("singing to God with your hearts"). Thus the "riches" of the gospel are to be present among them with great "richness." The structure of the sentence as a whole indicates that songs of all kinds are to play a significant role in that richness.

Fourth, as the parallel passage in Ephesians makes explicit, Paul considers all of this activity to be the result of their being filled with the Spirit.[60] Thus, however we are to understand πνευματικός ("spiritual") in relation to the various expressions of song, Spirit songs are but one expression of the Spirit's presence, whose "fullness" will guide and inspire all of the worship in its several expressions.

This much at least seems certain. But how we are to understand the remaining phrases and their relationships to one another is not at all clear, although some are more easily decided than others. The difficulties are six:

1. What does "with all wisdom" mean, and what does it modify?
2. Do the three kinds of songs modify "teaching and admonishing" or "singing"?

---

also included the women. After all, one of the specific persons addressed is Nympha (4:15), in whose house one of the churches met. (On the basis of later prejudices, she was turned into a man by later scribes [D F G MajT], who clearly recognized the implications of a church meeting in her house.)

[58]So also Hendriksen 161, O'Brien 208, Wright 144. Meyer 449 recognizes these implications, so he removes the activity from corporate worship and places it in their life together. See preceding note.

[59]This takes the genitive τοῦ Χριστοῦ ("of Christ") as objective, expressing the content of the "word" (so Lohse 150, Martin 115, O'Brien 206–7, Wright 144), not subjective, as some consider it (see Abbott ["most comm."], Radford 282, Bruce 157n148). This view alone seems to keep the whole letter intact. Most scholars consider 1:15–18, whose focus is altogether on Christ and his work, to be from an early Christian hymn. That is what is taught through singing. And so throughout the letter. Thus the concern here is not on Christ's speaking to them as they gather—although that too could happen through prophetic utterance—or with his teachings, but with their letting the concern of this letter, the message of gospel with its total focus on Christ and his work, dwell richly in their community life.

[60]Cf. Lohse 150–51.

3. What does πνευματικός ("Spiritual") mean, and what does it modify?
   Related to this, are the three kinds of songs distinguishable from one
   another, and if so, how?
4. What does ἐν τῇ χάριτι ("by/with the grace/gratitude") mean?
5. What does "with your hearts" mean, and what does it modify?
6. What is addressed to God, the singing or the thanksgiving?

Although solutions to these several options could be variously ar-
ranged, most of the problems center on item 2, what to do with "psalms,
hymns, and songs," and on 4, since items 5 and 6 depend on how
one understands item 4. The most common arrangements are two, and
are best grasped by structural displays. The traditional view has it as
follows:[61]

Let the word of Christ dwell in your midst richly,

        by teaching[62]
            and
      admonishing one another
         in all wisdom
          with psalms,
            hymns,
              spiritual songs
    by singing to God
        from your hearts
        with gratitude

Most recent English versions and commentaries have it:

Let the word of Christ dwell in your midst richly,

       as you teach
           and
       admonish one another
         in all wisdom;
    and as you sing
         with psalms, hymns, and spiritual songs
         to God
         with gratitude
         in your hearts [so NEB, JB]

    or:

        . . . sing
           with gratitude
           to God
           in your hearts [so NRSV, NIV]

---

[61]This is my translation; the *arrangement* is that of the KJV and NASB.
[62]For this modal sense to the participle, see also Meyer 448 and O'Brien 207.

Let us consider the difficulties one by one:

1. The placement of "with all wisdom" is generally agreed to belong to the participles that follow rather than with "let the word of Christ dwell in your midst."[63] The principal reason for this is that "in your midst" and "richly" already follow the verb, with the latter in what appears to be an emphatic final position. To add one more prepositional phrase to this verb overloads it unnecessarily. Not only so, but this same phrase also modifies these two participles in the parallel in 1:28. Moreover, the meaning of "wisdom" in this letter seems to fit better as a modifier of "teaching and admonishing" than of "indwelling." As in 1:9 the "wisdom" in view is that of the Spirit, and as such it stands over against the futile philosophy of the opposition. It is with this wisdom, the Spirit's wisdom, that they are continually to be teaching and admonishing one another.

2. As to the placement of the three kinds of song, despite the modern consensus there are good reasons for adopting the traditional view:[64] (a) Since the Ephesians passage is both a clear parallel to this one and by the same author, the nonambiguity of that passage seems decisive. Without our hangups over the logic of it,[65] Paul there explicitly says that they are to *speak to* one another with their singing. Rather than rearrange Paul's logic, we should perhaps do better to try to understand how singing can be both "to God" and a means of "teaching one another."[66] (b) By placing these words with "singing," one creates an even greater overload of modifiers for that participle than would be the case to take "with all wisdom" with the opening verb. The net result, therefore, is a structural arrangement that is quite out of balance and considerably awkward, even in Greek:

> with all wisdom,
>   teaching and admonishing one another

---

[63]As Lightfoot 224 prefers; cf. Radford 283. The common view is held by Eadie, Meyer, Abbott, Peake, Westcott, Carson, Hendriksen, Lohse, Martin, Vaughan, Schweizer, O'Brien, Bruce, Wright, Harris.

[64]So also Meyer 448–49, Lightfoot 224, Abbott 290, Peake 541, Westcott 158, Robertson 167, Erdman 90, Radford 283, Carson 90, O'Brien 208–9. For the modern consensus, see inter alia Delling, *TDNT* 8.498, Hendriksen 161, Lohse 151, Vaughan 216, Schweizer 210, Bruce 158, Wright 149, Harris 167. The latter is particularly instructive, since he recognizes the difficulties with this view, yet proceeds to adopt it without convincing argumentation in its favor.

[65]Hendriksen 161n138 cites Ridderbos with approval, "The idea that this mutual teaching and admonishing must be carried out by means of song seems rather unnatural to us." That says baldly what lurks just below the surface in the discussions of several others.

[66]Indeed, as we will note momentarily, the fact that hymns function in this two-dimensional way in both the OT and Paul is yet another argument *for* this view.

> with psalms, hymns, spiritual songs
> with gratitude,
>> singing
>>> in your hearts
>>> to God

This has also created the unlikely translations of the NRSV and NIV, which have the thanksgiving (if indeed it is that) addressed to God, whereas the Greek intends it to be the singing (see number 6 below).[67]

On the other hand, the older view results in a (typically Pauline) nicely balanced set of ideas,[68] each of which expresses the twin dimensions of Christian worship—horizontal and vertical—with the various kinds of songs as the "swing component" that conceptually ties the two parts together. Thus:

> in all wisdom
>> teaching and admonishing one another
>>> with psalms, hymns, and spiritual songs

> in grace
>> singing
>>> with your hearts
>>> to God

3. As we have already argued on 1:9, the adjective πνευματικός ordinarily refers to the Spirit, unless there are especially strong contextual grounds to think otherwise. Here in particular, as most recognize, the ordinary meaning prevails.[69] We are dealing with songs that are inspired by the Spirit. As noted on 1 Cor 14:15–16 and 26, this most likely indicates a kind of "charismatic hymnody" in which Spirit-inspired, and therefore often spontaneous, songs were offered in the context of congregational worship.

Therefore, even though πνευματικός could well modify all three nouns[70]—the psalms and hymns would also be "of the Spirit"—it is more

---

[67]It should be noted further that the NRSV, GNB, JB, and NIV, which take psalms, hymns, and songs as objects of the verb ᾄδω are grammatically quite wrong, since this verb invariably takes the accusative for its direct object (see, e.g., Exod 14:32 [LXX]; Rev 5:9; 14:3; 15:3). This might be contended for as simply a form of "dynamic equivalent," but it comes about by an unnecessary expedient that seems to miss the balanced structure of Paul's sentence.

[68]Indeed, Meyer 448 argues (correctly): "the symmetry of the following participial clauses, each of which begins with ἐν (ἐν πάσῃ σοφίᾳ . . . ἐν τ. χάριτι), ought not to be abandoned without some special reason." In light of Eph 5:19 and of the fact that singing was both praise to God and didactic in the OT and the early church, it is especially difficult in this case to produce "some special reason."

[69]But see Erdman 91, who thinks it means little more than "religious" vis-à-vis "secular"; cf. Hendriksen 162, Schweizer 210, Wright 145. But even if "secular" is part of the intended contrast, for Paul its opposite is not "religious," but the activity of the Spirit.

[70]So Lohse 151; cf. Martin 116, O'Brien 210.

likely that it is intended to modify "songs" only, referring especially to this one kind of Spirit-inspired singing.[71] This word, after all, is the one which the recipients of the letter would least likely associate with worship, since it covers the whole range of "songs" in the Greek world, whereas the other two are usually sung to a deity.

But having said that, it is doubtful whether we are finally able to draw fine lines between the three words. The "psalm," for example, may well include the OT Psalter, now taken over into the worship of the Christian communities; but one would be bold indeed to limit it to such. This, after all, is the word used for the (apparently) more spontaneous singing of 1 Cor 14:26, and its corresponding verb is likewise used in 1 Cor 14:15 to refer to Spirit-inspired "praise to God." Thus, even though NT usage is undoubtedly conditioned by the fact that the hymns of Israel were called "psalms," there is no good reason to understand it as limited to those hymns. What is suggested by this word, of course, is a song that is in praise of God. So also the word "hymn."[72] In the Greek world, this word was used exclusively of songs sung to deities or heroes, and thus would never be used, for example, of the bawdy songs of the bistro. Therefore, "hymns" also refer to singing praise to/about God, or in the case of the NT to/about Christ as well, as the evidence from the Revelation makes especially clear.[73]

4. The decision about the meaning of ἐν τῇ χάριτι is more difficult, having to do in particular with the presence or absence of the article.[74] Despite the nearly universal acceptance of "with gratitude" in the twentieth-century English versions and commentaries, one has good reason to pause. There is no other place in the NT where χάρις means "gratitude" when the article appears with it;[75] however, Paul does at times use the article in otherwise unqualified references to grace (meaning, *the* grace ["of God" being implied]).[76] Thus the KJV reads, "singing with grace in your hearts." So also Chrysostom, who understands it to

---

[71]It is doubtful, as some contemporary charismatics would have it, that it includes singing in tongues as well, since one neither teaches nor admonishes with unintelligible words. But see Martin 115, who despite what is said in 1 Cor 14:26, Eph 5:19, and here, nonetheless allows this as a possibility.

[72]Which occurs only here and in Eph 5:19 in the NT, although its cognate verb occurs four times (Matt 26:30; Mark 14:26; Acts 16:25; Heb 2:12).

[73]Even though the word "hymn" itself does not occur. See esp. in this regard, Rev 4:11, which is addressed to God and introduced with λέγοντες ("saying"), and Rev 5:9, which picks up the identical language but is introduced, "they sing a new song, saying . . . " See also 5:12, 13.

[74]See n. 51 above.

[75]For Paul see especially 1 Cor 10:30.

[76]See esp. the grace-benediction at the conclusion of this letter (4:18; *the* grace [of our Lord Jesus Christ] be with you); cf. Phil 1:7.

refer to the grace of God that comes from the Spirit, and thus as instrumental, "by means of the divine grace."[77]

Despite the use of the article, however, almost all the twentieth-century English versions render it "with gratitude." Part of the reason for this is the parallel in Eph 5:19–20, where thanksgiving to God is stated expressly and unambiguously. Those who note the article consider it anaphoric, that is, as referring to *the* thanksgiving already referred to in v. 15, to be picked up again in v. 17.[78]

Although I have considerable ambivalence on this one, my instincts are to go with the grammar and to understand it, as does Chrysostom, as referring to our standing in grace that makes such singing come from the heart. Thus the focus is not so much on *our* attitude toward God as we sing, but on our awareness of *his* toward us that prompts such singing in the first place.[79]

5. But even if this is the meaning of "in grace," the KJV probably has it wrong as to the meaning of "in your hearts." Following Tyndale, the KJV translators understood this phrase to modify "with grace," thus making it a locative, "with grace in your hearts." This is also carried over to the NRSV and NIV, who translate "with gratitude in your hearts." But the separation of these two phrases in the Greek by the participle "singing" makes that an especially difficult option[80]—all the more so when one thinks of the letter as a document to be read, not studied. The natural way to take this phrase is as a modifier of the participle that immediately precedes it. If so, then in this case it almost certainly is not locative, as though the singing were to take place "in your hearts." Rather, as the parallel in Eph 5:19 makes clear, it expresses accompaniment or manner, "singing with your whole heart."[81]

6. That leads us, finally, to note that the final words in the sentence, "to God," in all probability refer to God as the one to whom *the singing* is directed. The rendering of the NRSV and NIV, "with gratitude in your

---

[77]Cf. Meyer 451–52, Eadie 252, Lightfoot 225–26, Erdman 91, Carson 91, Lohse 152, Delling, *TDNT* 8.498n65. Some of these take it as locative: it is as one stands "in grace" that one sings to God.

[78]So, e.g., Abbott 201; but that will scarcely do, since anaphora by their very nature require a linguistic, not a conceptual, antecedent.

[79]Lightfoot 225, consistent with his view about the placement of "with all wisdom," takes the phrase to go with the preceding participles.

[80]Radford 284 says "the Greek forbids [this] connexion." I am inclined to agree, despite Wright 145, who argues for it.

[81]So also Eadie 252, Lightfoot 226, Erdman 91, Carson 91, Hendriksen 161, Martin 116, O'Brien 210. An older view, expressed inter alia by Meyer, Peake, and Radford, viewed the singing as "the silent praising of God, which belongs to self-edification in the inner man" (Meyer 451). This probably says more about nineteenth-century Western culture than it does about Paul. In a culture where both private reading and praying were "aloud" (see on Rom 8:26–27), one is hard pressed to imagine "silent singing"!

hearts to God," is purely gratuitous.[82] What set up such a view in the first place was a (probably incorrect) overloading of the participle "singing" with adverbial modifiers; hence one solution was to make some of the phrases modify others. Moreover, this view does not take seriously enough the actual word order. Since the dative "to God" not only goes naturally with the participle "singing," but also *stands closer to it in the sentence*, it is altogether unlikely that Paul intended it to modify ἐν τῇ χάριτι (even if he did intend "with gratitude").

That leads, finally, to some summary conclusions about worship in this passage, and the corresponding role of "Spirit-inspired songs."

1. It needs to be noted, first of all, that where the Spirit of God is there is also singing. The early church was characterized by its singing; so also in every generation where there is renewal by the Spirit a new hymnody breaks forth. If most such songs do not have staying power, some of them do, and become the treasure trove of our ongoing teaching and admonishing of one another, as well as of our constantly turning to God the Father and God the Son and offering praise by inspiration of the Holy Spirit.

2. Very likely we have fragments of such psalms, hymns, and Spirit songs embedded in our NT documents. The Revelation, for example, is full of "new songs" sung to God and to the Lamb. That is probably the case with Eph 5:14 and 1 Tim 3:16 as well (q.v.). But more significantly for this letter, the considered opinion of most NT scholars is that 1:15–18 also reflects such a hymn about Christ.[83] If this is so, and there are no good reasons to doubt it, then that would also explain why Paul thinks of these various kinds of hymns and Spirit songs as a means of their "teaching and admonishing one another." Such songs are at the same time creedal, full of theological grist and give evidence of what the early Christians most truly believed about God and his Christ.

3. The background to such two-dimensional worship, hymns that are at once directed toward God and didactic for the participants, resides in the OT Psalter. There we find dozens of examples of hymns addressed to God in the second person, which also have sections in the third person, extolling the greatness or faithfulness of God for the sake of those singing to him.[84] The use of hymns in the NT documents indicates how clearly

---

[82]*Pace* Wright 144–45.

[83]See most recently N. T. Wright, "Poetry and Theology in Colossians 1.15–20," *NTS* 36 (1990) 444–68.

[84]This happens throughout the Psalter. See, e.g., Psalm 30, which offers praise to God in the second person in vv. 1–3, then encourages singing on the part of the "congregation" in vv. 4–5, predicated on the fact that "his favor lasts a lifetime," and returns to second person address in vv. 6–9. Cf. inter alia Psalms 32, 66, 104, 116; so also the many hymns that call on the congregation to praise God in light of his character and wondrous deeds.

they also function in this two-dimensional way for the early church. Most of them are about Christ, and as such are both in worship of him and for the continuing instruction of God's people. The inescapable implication of 1 Cor 14:15–16 and 26 is that "Spirit songs" in the Pauline communities are also to be understood in this way. Singing "with the mind" (= singing intelligible words by the Spirit) is understood as praise to God, but something to which the rest respond with the Amen; and the "psalm" in 14:26 is precisely for the "building up" of the others. Unfortunately, many contemporary Christians do not think of their singing in these terms and consequently miss out on one of the significant dimensions of our reason for singing.

4. Finally, in its own nonreflective way, this too is a "Trinitarian" text. But in contrast to the various soteriological texts, where the Father initiates what the Son effects and the Spirit applies, here the order is reversed. Christ still plays the central role, hence they must let the "word of Christ" dwell lavishly in their midst. But the same Spirit who applied salvation now helps to initiate response through Spirit-inspired songs reflecting the message about Christ, and all to the praise of God.

CONCLUSIONS

Even though there is much less direct Spirit talk in this letter than in the others we have examined thus far (Philemon excepted), what we find is quite in keeping with what has gone before. Missing, to be sure, is any mention of the Spirit's role in Christian conversion. But the Spirit is perceived as present for life in Christ. The Spirit is the source of their love, even for one whom they have not personally met, and the source of their coming to know more fully the will of God. The power of the Spirit is present in their lives for endurance and patience, and in Paul's life for effective ministry. And finally, through songs that are especially of the Spirit they both instruct one another about Christ and offer praise to God. If this is not the full range of Spirit activity, it is a wide range, and fully in accord with what we find throughout the corpus.

9

THE CAPTIVITY EPISTLES: EPHESIANS

Commentaries:[1] T. K. **Abbott** (ICC, 1897); M. **Barth** (AB 34AB, 1974); F. W. **Beare** (IB, 1953); F. F. **Bruce** (NIC, 1984); G. B. **Caird** (NCB, 1976); R. W. **Dale** (1887); J. **Eadie** (1883); G. G. **Findlay** (Expositor's Bible, 1892); J. **Gnilka** (HTK, 1971); W. **Hendriksen** (1967); J. L. **Houlden** (PNTC, 1970); R. C. H. **Lenski** (1937); A. T. **Lincoln** (WBC 42, 1990); J. A. **Mackay** (1952); H. A. W. **Meyer** (MeyerK, 1880); C. L. **Mitton** (NCB, 1973); A. G. **Patzia** (NIBC, 1990); J. A. **Robinson** (²1904); S. D. F. **Salmond** (EGT, 1903); H. **Schlier** (1957); R. **Schnackenburg** (1991; Ger. original 1982); E. F. **Scott** (MNTC, 1930); J. R. W. **Stott** (1979); B. F. **Westcott** (1906); A. S. **Wood** (EBC, 1978).

Other significant works are referred to by the following short titles:

Arnold, *Ephesians* (= Clinton E. Arnold, *Ephesians: Power and Magic. The Concept of Power in Ephesians in Light of Its Historical Setting* [SNTSMS 63; Cambridge: University Press, 1989]); **Chotka**, "Spirit" (= David R. Chotka, "Spirit versus spirit: An Examination of the Nature and Function of the Holy Spirit Against the Backdrop of the False Spirit in Ephesians," unpubl. Th.M. thesis [Regent College, 1992]); **Hui**, "Concept" (A. W. D. Hui, "The Concept of the Holy Spirit in Ephesians and its Relation to the Pneumatologies of Luke and Paul," unpubl. Ph.D. dissertation [University of Aberdeen, 1992]); **Lemmer**, "Pneumatology" (H. R. Lemmer, "Pneumatology and Eschatology in Ephesians. The Role of the Eschatological Spirit in the Church," unpubl. Ph.D. dissertation [University of South Africa (Pretoria), 1988]).

Ephesians is the only letter of its kind in the Pauline corpus. It is neither addressed to a specific Christian community,[2] nor do its recipients

---

[1]The following commentaries are referred to in this chapter only by the author's last name.

[2]English translations to the contrary, there is no church named in the original text (ἐν Ἐφέσῳ is missing in P⁴⁶ ℵ* B* 6 1739 Origen). While it is possible that these

know the apostle personally (1:15; 3:2; 4:21).[3] Moreover, in places it has a turgid style, with impossibly long sentences and a compounding of clauses and phrases unlike anything else in the corpus. These factors, plus its unusual relationship to Colossians,[4] have caused most scholars to opt for inauthenticity. For them the obvious Pauline dimension of the thought and vocabulary are best accounted for as the work of a "Paulinist," a second-generation disciple of the apostle, who was so immersed in Paul's language and thinking that he could write as though he were the apostle himself.

For others, including myself, the Pauline nature of the epistle, particularly the subtleties of vocabulary, language, and theology, are such that it is difficult to imagine someone so thoroughly imbibing the thinking of another as to reproduce him in this way.[5] Just as the (considerable) differences between Galatians and Romans[6] are best explained on the

---

words were suppressed by a scribe who recognized the difficulty of Paul's writing to a church where he ministered for nearly three years as to those who do not know him at all (1:15; 3:2; 4:21), it seems much more likely that a strong "Ephesian" tradition (perhaps the letter ended up in the capital?) caused the designation to be added at a later time. For a more complete discussion, see Lincoln 1–4; and E. Best, "Ephesians i.1," in *Text and Interpretation* (ed. E. Best and R. McL. Wilson; Cambridge: University, 1979) 29–41; idem, "Ephesians i.1 Again," in *Paul and Paulinism: Essays in Honour of C. K. Barrett* (ed. M. D. Hooker and S. G. Wilson; London: SPCK, 1982) 273–79.

[3]Indeed, there are no personal references of any kind about the recipients themselves or about Paul's relationship with them. The closest thing to a personal note comes in 1:15, where Paul mentions that he has heard of their faith in Christ and their love of believers, which indicates that he had certain people in mind as he wrote, but not necessarily a specific Christian community.

[4]For the details of this matter see Lincoln xlvii–lviii. On the question of authenticity as a whole see (con): Lincoln lix–lxxiii; C. L. Mitton, *The Epistle to the Ephesians: Its Authorship, Origin, and Purpose* (Oxford: Clarendon, 1951); D. E. Nineham, "The Case Against the Pauline Authorship," in *Studies in Ephesians* (ed. F. L. Cross; London: Mowbray, 1956) 21–35; and (pro): Barth 1.36–61; Johnson, *Writings*, 367–80; A. Van Roon, *The Authenticity of Ephesians* (NovTSup 39; Leiden: Brill, 1974).

[5]In the final analysis the issue is not provable. One is left with a choice as to probabilities: (a) that a Paulinist who used Colossians so slavishly, yet understood it so poorly (as it is alleged), could have at the same time imbibed the Paul of the other letters so thoroughly that he issues forth in a Pauline manner in the most subtle and unexpected ways; or (b) that Paul, who had just written Colossians, could write a letter of this unique kind, picking up from the themes of Colossians but going beyond them in several ways, so that he himself varies from the Paul of the other letters in several significant ways. At this point a great deal of subjectivity comes into the argument as to what an ancient author "could have" or "could not have" done. I find "Paul varying from himself"—option *b*—an easier historical scenario to imagine than that of a Paulinist of the undoubted brilliance of this author finding it necessary to clothe himself in Paul in order to express his concerns. This is especially so if we take with appropriate seriousness Johnson's view of authorship as a "production by Paul *and his fellow workers*" (*Writings*, 367 [emphasis his]).

[6]Which were probably also written in close temporal proximity. The analogy, I maintain, is a valid one and should give all of us reason to pause with regard to the

basis of the differences in their respective historical contexts, and thus in occasion and purpose, so here. The reasons for doubt are indeed considerable. Nonetheless I think one can make more sense of the document as a circular letter to the churches of Asia,[7] in which the apostle, reflecting on the issues raised by Colossians, addresses yet again the great concern of his apostleship—Jew and Gentile as one people of God, on the basis of Christ and the Spirit—but in this instance he does so against the backdrop of the "powers" before whom the Asian believers stood in fear, or at least in reverential awe.

The thoroughly Pauline nature of the theology of this letter is nowhere more evident than in the Spirit materials,[8] both in their quantity[9] and specific usage. The word πνεῦμα specifically refers to the Holy Spirit twelve times.[10] In one further occurrence (4:23) it probably refers to the human spirit as that is renewed by the Holy Spirit. As in Colossians, the word πνευματικός occurs two times in contexts that decisively favor its

---

relationship of Ephesians to Colossians. The differences between Romans and Galatians are of such kind—nearly insurmountable in some ways!—that one could easily apply to Romans the method used to demonstrate Ephesians as inauthentic and thereby demonstrate the unlikelihood that Paul wrote Romans, if we concede that he actually wrote Galatians.

[7]Part of the difficulty with the letter involves determining how much of it is case specific. Arnold (*Ephesians*) has argued strongly for a case-specific letter (Ephesus). There is much to be said in favor of this, but I would alter the perspective slightly. Since it is difficult to explain how in writing to such a congregation Paul should feel required to use language like that in 1:15 and 3:1–2, I tend to side, on the one hand, with those who see the letter as either having been originally intended for Laodicea (Col 4:16) or, more likely, as something of a circular letter to the churches of Asia. On the other hand, on the basis of 1:15 I am also ready to see the situation as much more case-specific than most who hold this view tend to allow.

[8]On this matter see now the dissertation by Hui, who argues convincingly, on the basis of a careful comparison of the pneumatology of this letter with that of Paul and Luke–Acts, that "in its pneumatology, Ephesians is fundamentally and distinctively Pauline" ("Concept," 412). Cf. Dunn, *Jesus*, 347, who considers its pneumatology one of the strong arguments for authenticity. This is acknowledged specifically by Schnackenburg 118–19, and indirectly by Schweizer, *TDNT* 6.444–45, who says, "the Pauline usage is somewhat watered down in Eph."; but he then goes on to describe nothing that is not fully and consistently Pauline! One is therefore surprised to read in W. Carr (*Angels and Principalities: The Background, Meaning, and Development of the Pauline Phrase* hai archai kai hai exousiai [SNTSMS 42; New York: Cambridge University Press, 1981] 95) that "a dynamic understanding of the Spirit is largely lacking; it is difficult to understand the Spirit in terms of Christian experience." He then proceeds to chide Käsemann (195n9) for not recognizing this. One wonders how learning to love through the power of the Spirit (3:16), being brought into God's presence through the Spirit (2:18), praying in the Spirit (6:18), etc. are less than "dynamic" and removed from Christian experience!

[9]For statistics, see Chotka, "Spirit," 3–4.

[10]1:13, 17; 2:18, 22; 3:5, 16; 4:3, 4, 30; 5:18; 6:17, 18; the full name, "the Holy Spirit," occurs in the first instance (1:13), while in 4:30 there appears the combination, "the Holy Spirit of God," which is unique to the corpus.

being an adjective for the Spirit (1:3; 5:19). Unique to Ephesians, but quite in keeping with its concerns, is the use of πνεῦμα in 2:2 to designate Satan, as well as the companion use of the adjective πνευματικός in 6:12 to refer to satanic spirit powers. In this connection we must also note the frequent occurrence of "power" language, much of which arguably is an indirect reference—almost a circumlocution in some cases—to the Spirit, especially in contexts over against the "powers" and the false "spirit."

Three concerns dominate the letter, and the Spirit plays a central role in each. The *first* is the passion of Paul's life—the Gentile mission, especially in terms of God's reconciling both Jew and Gentile to himself and thereby making of the two a new ἄνθρωπος (humanity) as the ultimate expression of his redeeming work in Christ. This theme first emerges at the end of the opening "blessing of God" (1:11–14); it is developed in a thoroughgoing way in 2:11–22, and is picked up again in 3:1–13, with the Spirit playing a leading role in each case. It is also this "unity of the Spirit" (between Jew and Gentile) that chs. 4–6 are all about by way of exhortation. Thus the whole letter is held together by this theme, admittedly more predominantly so in chs. 1–3 than in 4–6.[11]

The *second* concern, which emerges in a variety of ways throughout the letter, has to do with Christ's victory over the powers for the sake of the church, with the Spirit playing a key role in his readers' participation in that victory. Crucial to the letter is the way that Paul brings these first two concerns together, especially in ch. 3, where the reality of Jew and Gentile together as one people of God is on display before the "powers" so that they become aware of their present—and ultimate—defeat in Christ. This in turn lies behind the *third* concern, which finds expression in the second major part of the letter (chs. 4–6): that they maintain the "unity of the Spirit" (4:1–16) by the way they "walk,"[12] that is, by the way they live out the life of Christ in their corporate relationships, including their worship (4:1–5:20), and in their Christian households (5:21–6:9). All of this is brought into final focus in 6:10–20, where through the weapons and armor provided by Christ and the Spirit they are urged to stand as one people in their ongoing conflict with the powers.

The flow of thought seems to follow these lines, which we briefly trace out below, so as to point out the significant role of the Spirit throughout the letter:

1:3–14 are an opening "blessing" of the God who has blessed them through redemption in Christ and through the gift of the Spirit, who is God's authentication and guarantee of their existence, both now and

---

[11]This is not a universal point of view, especially regarding 1:11–14. On this matter see the discussion below, and esp. n. 37.

[12]This Pauline verb (περιπατέω; see above on 2 Cor 12:18 and Gal 5:16) for Christian conduct in its broadest sense occurs first in 2:2 and 10 (as the "inclusio" of that section) and is thoroughgoing in chs. 4–6 (4:1, 17[2x]; 5:2, 8, 15).

forever. Here the two major notes are struck: first, the Spirit's blessings, provided through Christ, are theirs in the heavenly realm, the place of the habitation of the powers to whom they were formerly in bondage (v. 3); and second, these blessings have come to Jew and Gentile alike through the Spirit, so that both together inherit the final glory of God (vv. 11–14).

1:15–23 are a thanksgiving-prayer report, which functions primarily to set the stage for the affirmations of their present position in Christ, who presently "sits" at God's right hand as head over the powers for the sake of the church. Thus the prayer report (vv. 17–19) evolves into an affirmation of Christ's victory over the powers (vv. 20–23).[13] The Spirit is the key to the prayer report (v. 17), as the one who will reveal to them a fuller understanding of God and what he has done in Christ, and will also reveal the power that has now been made available to them (v. 19).

2:1–10 flow directly out of vv. 20–23, reminding the readers both of their past enslavement to the powers (vv. 1–3) and their present "session" with Christ in the heavenly realm, where he sits enthroned above the powers. This is the only major section of the letter in which the Spirit is not directly mentioned.

2:11–22 return to the theme of Gentile and Jew together as the one people of God, made so first through the death of Christ, who tore down the barriers that divided them and thereby reconciled them to God and to one another, and secondly through the Spirit, by whom they together have access to the Father as one family/household (vv. 18–19) and indwelt by whom they function together as God's temple, the place of God's present habitation on earth (vv. 20–22).

3:1–13 return to the prayer report lost sight of at 1:20, but again it is interrupted, this time for Paul to speak of his own role in the proclamation of God's "mystery": the fact that Gentiles are co-heirs with Jews and thus form with them the one people of God (vv. 2–9), but now especially as a reality set before the powers. Here again the Spirit plays a leading role, as the one through whom this revelation has been made known to him and to other "apostles and prophets."

3:14–21 finally conclude the prayer report, but now in the form of another prayer altogether, which aptly concludes the concerns of chs. 1–3 and anticipates the exhortations that follow in chs. 4–6. The urgency is for his readers to know the "unknowable" love of Christ and thus to be filled with all the fullness of God himself. The prayer concludes with a praise-benediction, which extols the power of God who will bring it off. What makes the prayer achievable is the strengthening of believers

---

[13]In this regard one might note the similarities between chs. 1–3 of this letter and chs. 1–3 of 1 Thessalonians, which in effect become an extended thanksgiving and prayer report, interrupted by Paul's calling to their remembrance the realities about which he is giving thanks.

in their inner person through the power of the Spirit (v. 16), whose power is also the key to the benedictory response in vv. 20–21.

4:1–16 bring Paul to the third major concern: an exhortation that they maintain "the unity of the Spirit," already noted in 2:18–22. He gives an opening exhortation (vv. 1–3), followed by the Trinitarian basis for it (vv. 4–6), the Spirit serving as the key to the one body and the one hope. This in turn is followed by a theological reflection on the gifts Christ has given to the church for its "growing up" into this unity, among whom are "prophets," people who speak by the Spirit (v. 11).

4:17–6:9 then apply all of this to their corporate and household existence as God's people in the world. Most of the sins mentioned are those that destroy harmony in human relationships. To continue in such sins is to give place to the devil (4:27) and thus to grieve the Holy Spirit (4:30). Indeed, the hinge exhortation[14] is "be filled with the Spirit" (5:18).

6:10–20 conclude the letter by urging them, in light of all that has been said thus far, to contend against the powers by means of the armor provided through redemption in Christ (vv. 13–17a) and the weapons of the Spirit (vv. 17b–20)—the word of God and prayer.

Thus Spirit language abounds, in all three areas of concern.[15] Before looking at these texts in detail, as well as in the larger contexts in which they appear, two prefatory notes are in order: First, one must be especially careful in this letter not to read these texts as referring primarily to the individual believer. As elsewhere, though the life of the Spirit is experienced and entered at the individual level, these texts have to do with the people of God as a corporate whole. This is especially so in the opening "blessing" and thanksgiving-prayer report; but it is equally true of the affirmations in ch. 2, as well as the exhortations in chs. 4–6.

Second, as everywhere in Paul, the Spirit, along with the resurrection of Christ, is the key element to the basic theological framework from within which all of Paul's thinking as a Christian takes place: the eschatological nature of present existence as both "already" and "not yet." By the resurrection of Christ and the gift of the Spirit, God has inexorably set the future in motion, heading toward its final consummation. In

---

[14]In that it concludes those in 4:17–5:17 and is the verb for which the following participles (vv. 19–24) serve as modifiers. See the discussion below.

[15]Given the considerable role the Spirit plays in this letter, for both of its major themes, it is remarkable that only recently has any interest been shown in the pneumatology of this letter. In fact, apart from several lengthy discussions of the appropriate passages in Barth (1.101–2, 135–44, 2.547–50) and the helpful section by Bruce 233–35 on "the Parousia and the Spirit," one looks to the commentaries in vain for a discussion of the role of the Spirit in the argument of this letter (the one page by Westcott 130–31 is too abbreviated to be helpful). But see now J. Adai, *Der Heilige Geist als Gegenwart Gottes in den einzelnen Christen, in der Kirche und in der Welt* (Frankfurt: Peter Lang, 1985); and the unpublished theses by Lemmer, Hui, and Chotka (n. 1).

Christ, and thus in their relationships to one another and to the world, believers already live the life of the future: God-likeness as it is patterned in Christ (5:1–2). Because of the nature of the situation Paul addresses, there is more emphasis in this letter on the "already" than in other letters;[16] but it is not totally so, and the Spirit, as everywhere in Paul, plays the key role in our present eschatological existence. The Spirit is both evidence and guarantee of the future inheritance, already begun in Christ, to be realized on the day of redemption (4:30).

All of this, we should note finally, is so thoroughly Pauline that even if the letter were written by a disciple, it was a disciple who had gotten "inside Paul's skin," as it were. Hence, one can look at this material as from the apostle himself, since most probably it does in fact come directly from him.

EPHESIANS 1:3–14[17]

In place of the more standard "thanksgiving," this letter begins with a *berakah*, a Christianized version of the traditional Jewish "blessing" of God[18] which Paul had previously used in 2 Corinthians. The more traditional Pauline thanksgiving with its companion prayer-report begins at v. 15.

The *berakah* itself is another of those remarkable moments in the Pauline corpus,[19] where one fears to say too much, lest its grandeur be replaced by our own pedestrian prose. In keeping with its form, the whole comprises one long "sentence" in the Greek text,[20] held together by a

---

[16]Which is another factor that has led many to deny Pauline authorship. But here also is a clear case of "how one reads the letter as a whole" determining how one understands its parts. The future eschatological dimension is diminished only in the eye of the beholder, not in the epistle itself.

[17]*Bibliography:* B. **Ahern**, "The Indwelling Spirit, Pledge of Our Inheritance— Eph. 1:14," *CBQ* 9 (1947) 179–89; E. **Best**, "Fashions in Exegesis: Ephesians 1:3," in *Scripture: Meaning and Method* (Festschrift A. T. Hanson; ed. B. P. Thompson; Hull: University Press, 1987) 79–91; D. R. **Denton**, "Inheritance in Paul and Ephesians," *EvQ* 54 (1982) 157–62; P. L. **Hammer**, "A Comparison of κληρονομία in Paul and Ephesians," *JBL* 79 (1960) 267–72; H. R. **Lemmer**, "Reciprocity between Eschatology and Pneuma in Ephesians 1:3–14," *Neot* 21 (1987) 159–82; A. T. **Lincoln**, "A Re-Examination of 'The Heavenlies' in Ephesians," *NTS* 19 (1973) 468–83; J. **McNicol**, "The Spiritual Blessings of the Epistle to the Ephesians," *EvQ* 9 (1937) 64–73; P. T. **O'Brien**, "Ephesians I: An Unusual Introduction to a New Testament Letter," *NTS* 25 (1979) 604–16.

[18]Cf. inter alia 1 Kings 8:15–21; Ps 68:19–20 [LXX 67:19–20]; Ps 72:18–19 [LXX 71:18–19]; Luke 1:68–75. Cf. the Qumran hymns as well.

[19]On the questions of form and structure, which lie beyond the concerns of this study, see the helpful overview, plus a discussion of the literature, in Lincoln 10–19; cf. O'Brien, "Ephesians I," 506–9.

[20]This is often pressed as one of the sure signs of non-Pauline authorship; but in fact in this instance sentence length probably counts for very little. The only question is whether Paul would be capable of creating such a "blessing," since its

series of relative pronouns, all referring to Christ and the "blessings" we have received through him. Its length is in part the result of its well-known Trinitarian form. Even though the whole is a "blessing" of God himself, it is so for what God has accomplished for his people through Christ and the Spirit. As such it therefore also serves as an "introduction" to the content of the letter.[21]

Paul is thus blessing God for "salvation in Christ," the "history" of which is the key to its Trinitarian framework: in vv. 3–6 is found the blessing of God, the cause and initiator of our salvation from before history; in vv. 7–12, the work of Christ, who has effected our salvation within history; and in vv. 13–14, the work of the Holy Spirit, who has appropriated this salvation first in the personal histories of Paul and the Jews and now also in those of his Gentile readers, and who thereby also functions as the guarantor of its final consummation beyond history. As always, Christ is the center of everything. He is the one "in whom" God has done, and will do, all things—so that our own salvation, which takes place within history, is now seen in its cosmic dimensions, so that *in him* God will finally reconcile the whole cosmos to himself. The work of Christ, therefore, even more than the Trinitarian structure, absolutely dominates the whole; indeed, its most natural divisions follow the various "in him"/"in whom" phrases which move the "blessing" forward from one theme to the next.

Accordingly, "in him" God in love has chosen "us" (Jew and Gentile together) for "adoption as 'sons,' "[22] all to the praise of God's own glory (vv. 4–6); "in whom" we (both) have realized God's redemption and through whom God will yet "sum up" all things earthly and heavenly (vv. 7–10); "in whom" we Jews were the first to experience God's saving plan (vv. 11–12); "in whom also" you Gentiles have heard the good news of your salvation (v. 13a); "in whom also," having believed in Christ, you were "sealed" by the Holy Spirit for the full realization of redemption, both now and forever (vv. 13b–14).

Our present interest is limited to vv. 3 and 13–14, where the Spirit is actually mentioned. We should simply note in passing that the Spirit underlies much else as well, especially (a) the theme of "adoption as 'sons,' " which in both Gal 4:5–6 and Rom 8:15–16 is realized by us as the Spirit cries out from within our hearts the language of *the* Son, "*Abba,* Father," thus demonstrating our "sonship," and (b) the language "making

---

length is due to the singular factor that the whole is a single *berakah*, which by its nature is held together by compounding relative pronouns.

[21]Although one must also grant with O'Brien, "Ephesians I," 512, that it does not thereby introduce all of the themes of the letter.

[22]Gk. υἱοθεσία; see the discussion of this word above in Gal 4:4–6 and Rom 8:15, including the reasons for this translation.

known to us with all wisdom and insight the mystery of his will," which
in this letter (1:17; 3:5) is attributed directly to the work of the Spirit.

EPHESIANS 1:3

Blessed be the God and Father of our Lord Jesus Christ, who has blessed us
with every Spiritual blessing in the heavenlies in Christ.

These opening words of the *berakah* function as a kind of "sub-title"
for the entire letter as well as the "topic sentence"[23] for the blessing in
particular. The letter itself is all about (1) God, who (2) through Christ
has (3) effected our salvation (described here, in keeping with the *berakah*
formula, as "every kind of blessing"), which (4) is directly related to the
Spirit's activity (thus "*Spiritual* blessing") and (5) has taken place in the
heavenly realm, where Christ is now seated above the "powers" that have
been a life-long cause of fear for those who are the primary recipients.
That, at least, seems to make the best sense of the adjective πνευματικός
in this opening clause, a sense that is in keeping with the use of this
adjective throughout the corpus.

Paul plays on the term "blessing" in the same way that in the *berakah*
of 2 Cor 1:3–7 he plays on the term "comfort." The God whom we "bless"
is none other than the God who has already "blessed" us with every kind
of Spirit "blessing" in Christ. In the same way that our singing in worship
(5:19–20) is in praise of our Lord and in thanksgiving to God for his prior
love and saving activity in our behalf, so here our vocal "blessing" of
God is in response to his prior redemptive blessing of us through Christ,
now experienced in an ongoing way through the Spirit.

Three matters call for special attention: First, on the meaning of
πνευματικός, see the discussion in ch. 2 and especially on Col 1:9. As
elsewhere, πνευματικός is an adjective for the Spirit,[24] that is, "pertaining
to or belonging to the Spirit"; thus "πνευματικός blessings" mean "Spirit
blessings, blessings that pertain to the Spirit." The use of this adjective
rather than the genitive of the word "Spirit" indicates that the emphasis
is on the *nature* of the blessings,[25] rather than their source.[26] But having
said that, that the blessings are those that properly pertain to the life of

---

[23]Cf. Gnilka 60 ("Themasatz").

[24]Some (e.g., Abbott 4, Caird 33) have suggested that it functions here as an
adjective for the human πνεῦμα, describing blessings that have to do with the inner
person. But that runs aground on all known uses of the word, which is primarily a
Pauline word in antiquity in any case.

[25]Cf. Lincoln 19–20: blessings "resulting from the presence and work of the
Spirit."

[26]As most interpreters, who correctly see the relationship with the Spirit; e.g.,
Meyer 34, Eadie 14, Dale 28, Findlay 25, Scott 139, Schlier 446, Barth 1.101–2; cf.
Lemmer, "Pneumatology," 168–69.

the Spirit, one is not very far away from describing their source as well. What is not helpful is the translation "spiritual" to describe the nature of these blessings, since that word is almost always understood over against an antonym of some kind, in a way that "Spirit" is not. Thus it is understood to refer to "heavenly blessings" vis-à-vis "earthly,"[27] or "spiritual" vis-à-vis "material,"[28] or "secular," or "worldly." On the contrary, this is Paul's way of expressing in condensed form what he spells out further in this letter and everywhere else—that the Spirit is the present means whereby God appropriates to the believing community the "blessings" that flow from the redemptive work of Christ.

This understanding is made the more certain, second, when one considers the broadly inclusive nature of these "blessings": with *all* the blessings the Spirit bestows. These are not to be understood in some nebulous way, as so often happens with the word "blessing" in English. On the contrary, "all the Spirit's blessings" with which God has blessed us in Christ are precisely those that Paul will spell out in the rest of the *berakah* (beginning with v. 4):[29] that God in love has chosen us to be blameless before him; that he has "marked us out for himself"[30] for adoption as his own children; that he has lavished his grace on us to this end in Christ Jesus; that this "adoption" was effected for us historically through the death of Christ, who thereby procured our redemption; and that Jew and Gentile have realized this redemption together as one people, having received the Spirit as the down payment on our final inheritance.[31] All of these, and more, are made known to us and realized by us through the gift of the indwelling Spirit.

That leads us, third, to the more difficult question in this opening clause, the meaning and placement of the prepositional phrase, "in the heavenlies,"[32] which is unique to this letter. As in most cases of unique language in a Pauline letter, its appearance is most likely attributable to the historical situation of the recipients—the various churches of the province of Asia, who had formerly been enslaved to magic and the

---

[27]As e.g., Salmond 246, although he does not use this precise language.

[28]This is the most common suggestion, usually in contrast to the "blessings" promised Israel in Deut 28:1–14; so Robinson 20, Westcott 7, Hendriksen 73, Wood 27, Stott 34, Bruce 253, Patzia 150. But it is extremely doubtful whether Paul would have thought of the blessings associated with the Spirit as being over against such "material blessings."

[29]Some earlier interpreters, cited by Eadie 14–15, suggest a correlation with the "Spiritual gifts" of 1 Cor 12:4–11; but this has nothing in its favor either linguistically or contextually.

[30]This is the NJB's helpful translation of the προορίσας of v. 5.

[31]Cf. the notes to the NJB, where six such "blessings" are enumerated from the passage.

[32]Gk. ἐν τοῖς ἐπουρανίοις; cf. 1:20; 2:6; 3:10; 6:12; cf. also ὁ ἀναβὰς ὑπεράνω πάντων τῶν οὐρανῶν ("He who ascended above all the heavens") in 4:10.

spirit powers who are understood to inhabit "the heavenly realm." Thus, in this letter Satan is described as "the prince of the power of the air" (2:2) and the "spirit forces" against whom we are currently engaged in conflict dwell "in the heavenlies" (6:12; cf. 3:10). But in typical Pauline fashion, he enlists the language of the current situation in the service of the gospel, so that Christ himself is now seated "in the heavenlies" as "head over" all the spirit powers for the sake of the church (1:20–23), and God in the richness of his mercy has seated us all (Jew and Gentile together) with Christ "in the heavenlies" (2:6). This, then, is the note struck at the outset, that the blessings of God in Christ made available to us by the Spirit take place for us "in the heavenly realm"—right in the presence, as it were, of the powers themselves.[33] By seating us in the heavenly realm as redeemed, adopted, and forgiven, God by his Spirit has made us the recipients of his lavish grace manifested in Christ as well as the certain victors in our "warfare" against the powers.

Finally, we should perhaps note, as a way of returning to our opening point regarding the function of this clause as the "topic sentence" for the whole *berakah*, how inherently Trinitarian the opening "blessing" is. As everywhere in the corpus, God's love initiates redemption, Christ's death effects it historically, and the Spirit appropriates it to the life of the believer and believing community.

EPHESIANS 1:13–14

[13]*In whom you*[34] *also, having heard the message of truth, the gospel of your*[35] *salvation, in whom also having believed, you were sealed by the Holy Spirit of promise,* [14]*who*[36] *is the down payment of our inheritance, for the redemption of his possession, for the praise of his glory.*

---

[33]Thus it does not affect the meaning much in either direction, whether one considers "in the heavenlies" to modify the participle ("who has blessed us in the heavenlies") or, more likely, to modify our phrase ("with every Spirit blessing in the heavenlies"). Paul's point is that our *experience* of these blessings takes place as we ourselves are "in Christ" in the heavenly realm.

[34]Quite misunderstanding Paul's contextual concern about Jew and Gentile as one people of God (see the discussion below), several manuscripts (א[1] A K L Ψ pm) generalized this text by turning the ὑμεῖς ("you") into ἡμεῖς ("we"). This is a patently secondary reading; the original is read by P[46] א* B D F G Maj latt sy co.

[35]See preceding note. In the interest of consistency, many of the same manuscripts changed "your" to "our" here as well.

[36]As Metzger (*Textual Commentary*, 601–2) points out, it is difficult to decide whether Paul himself here wrote (dictated) the neuter ὅ, in agreement with its antecedent πνεῦμα (as P[46] A B F G L P 6 81 104 365 1175 1739 1881 2495 pm), or the masculine ὅς, by attraction to its predicate noun ἀρραβών (as א D Ψ Maj). The external evidence heavily favors the neuter; transcriptional probability can go either way (i.e., a scribe could have made either change just as easily, and for the same reasons, as Paul would have originally written one or the other). In any case, the point made by

Having "blessed" God in vv. 4–10 for the redemption provided for "us" in Christ (i.e., all of those who believe, both Jew and Gentile) and for God's having made all of this known to us (vv. 8–9, by the Spirit, is implied), Paul concludes by "blessing God" because redemption, which came to the Jew first as an inheritance (vv. 11–12), has come as an inheritance to the Gentile recipients of this letter as well (vv. 13–14)![37] Thus two themes emerge in this final clause, both triggered by the concept of "inheritance": (1) Gentiles and Jews together as one people of God in fulfillment of God's promise to his ancient people, and (2) the eschatological dimension of redemption, that the inheritance has already been realized in part and will be realized in full at the Eschaton.

As elsewhere in Paul, the Spirit plays the key role in both of these merging themes. By having given them "the Holy Spirit of promise," i.e., the Holy Spirit promised to Israel, God thus "sealed" the Gentiles as his own possession. By that same token God also guaranteed the final inheritance for both Jew and Gentile alike, since the Spirit is God's ἀρραβών ("down payment") of *our* inheritance (Jew and Gentile together). Thus with a subtle shift of pronouns Paul moves from "our" (= Jews) having obtained the inheritance, to "your" (= Gentiles) having been sealed by the "promised Holy Spirit," to the Spirit as God's down payment on "our" (= Jew and Gentile together) final inheritance.

The Spirit material itself is full of echoes from earlier letters. The combination of "seal" and "down payment" appears earlier in 2 Cor 1:21–22 (q.v.). The Holy Spirit as the fulfillment of the "promise" that includes Gentiles among the people of God echoes Gal 3:14. These and other items call for further comment.

1. On the imagery of the Spirit as God's *seal*, see on 2 Cor 1:21–22. As in that passage, the metaphor images ownership—and authentication—in this case ownership of a very significant kind. By giving them his Holy Spirit, God stamped the Gentile recipients of this letter as "his own possession," marking them off as his inheritance to be realized at the final redemption. As before, there can be little question that the Spirit himself is the "seal," the mark of ownership.

W. D. Chamberlain in his *Exegetical Grammar of the New Testament* (New York: Macmillan, 1941 [49]) that the relative in the masculine might imply that Paul understood the Spirit in personal terms will hardly hold. This would be true whichever way one went with the textual choice.

[37]This understanding of things has a long history in the interpretation of this letter. It has recently been rejected by several interpreters, usually by those who also reject Pauline authorship (e.g., Gnilka, Schnackenburg, Lincoln), chiefly on the basis that such a contrast is not specifically spelled out in the present text. Indeed, were this the only such reference in the letter, it is doubtful whether very many would go this route. But when one reads this material in light of 2:11–22 and especially 3:6, it is difficult not to see this as a typical Pauline foreshadowing of a motif developed more fully later in the letter.

Also as in the 2 Corinthians passage, there is no allusion to water baptism in this context.[38] Unless one could prove that for Paul the imagery *inherently* carried such an allusion—and such proof is currently unavailable—there is nothing that suggests a baptismal motif. All the more so in this letter, where in the Trinitarian formula of 4:4–6, the *one Spirit* is paired with the *one body* (= the church), while the "one faith" and "one baptism" are paired with the "one Lord." The point to make, of course, is that for Paul, vis-à-vis the later church, the Spirit, not baptism, is the "seal" of ownership, the primary evidence that one belongs to the new people of God.

Although there is little emphasis on it here, this description almost certainly refers to their conversion(s). That is, it does not refer to some subsequent reception of the Spirit,[39] but to that reception that is absolutely essential for people to belong to Christ at all. The emphasis in the passage, after all, is *not* on individual conversions, but on the reality that the reception of the Spirit by these Gentile believers is what brings them into the inheritance of the new covenant and guarantees their final destiny. Therefore, as always in Paul, the Spirit is the sine qua non of Christian existence. The Spirit, and the Spirit alone, marks off the people of God as his own possession in the present eschatological age.

2. The description of the Spirit as "the Holy Spirit of the promise"[40] puts in reverse order the similar description in Gal 3:14, where Paul spoke

---

[38]So also Eadie 66, Abbott 22 ("no reason to suppose such a reference here, which would be too obscure"), Barth 1.145–53, Lincoln 39–40; cf. Dunn, *Baptism*, 160; G. W. H. Lampe, *The Seal of the Spirit: A Study in the Doctrine of Baptism and Confirmation in the New Testament and the Fathers* (2d ed.; London: SPCK, 1967) 3–18, 64–94. Even Schnackenburg, whose book on baptism might lead one to expect such a view, rightly demurs here. Otherwise inter alia Scott 148, Gnilka 85, and Patzia 158–89, whose defense is especially circuitous and unrelated to the present context and usage.

[39]Contra the suggestion that is sometimes offered on the basis of the aorist participle that "believing in Christ" (equated with conversion) precedes the reception of the Spirit (as e.g., in Hunter, *Spirit-Baptism*, 46, and Ervin, *Conversion-Initiation*, 122–24; cf. Meyer 61). But that is to find what Paul did not intend. That the aorist participle intends something antecedent to the main verb need not be doubted (*pace* Dunn, *Baptism*, 158–59, Bruce 265, Lincoln 39); but the two verbs have nothing to do with separate and distinct experiences of faith. Rather, the one ("having believed [in Christ]") logically precedes the other ("you were sealed"); but from Paul's perspective these are two sides of the same coin, thus "attendant circumstance." There is simply nothing in the context, nor anything inherent in this bit of grammar, that would cause one to think that Paul intends to refer here to two distinct experiences. The argument, in fact, has to do with the reality that these Gentiles in becoming believers in Christ also received the promised Holy Spirit, thus indicating that they too are God's own possession. Arguments about individual Christian experience are therefore beside Paul's point.

[40]The unusual wording and order, τῷ πνεύματι τῆς ἐπαγγελίας τῷ ἁγίῳ (= the Spirit of the promise, the Holy), is best explained in light of the *berakah* itself, which begins with the equally solemn "God and Father of our Lord Jesus Christ." At the same time it places emphasis on both the "promise" and the adjective "holy."

of the "promise of the Spirit." In that case the genitive most likely referred to the Spirit as the fulfillment of the promise made to Abraham; similarly, the Spirit is here seen as the fulfillment of what has been promised, but now the "promise" probably refers to the coming of the Spirit in the new covenant of Ezek 36:26–27 and 37:14, understood eschatologically by way of Joel 2:28–30. Thus the genitive is to be understood as adjectival (qualitative) and refers to "the promised Holy Spirit." What is significant in this passage, of course, is that the Holy Spirit, the crucial element of the promised new covenant with Israel, has been received by Gentiles as the seal that they too are God's possession as the new eschatological age unfolds. This motif will be addressed even more directly in 2:11–22 and especially in 3:6.

3. On the metaphor of the Spirit as "down payment" see the discussion on 2 Cor 1:21–22 and 5:5. Whereas the Spirit as present guarantee of the final glory was understood as inherent to the metaphor in the former passages, now that is spelled out explicitly by the addition of the genitive, "of *our* inheritance." We have already noted the significant shift from "you" to "our" in this clause, which is predicated on Paul's use of the word "inherit" as a verb in v. 11, where he speaks of Jews as having come into their inheritance[41] as the "first" to have put their hope in Christ. Thus when Paul joins Gentile and Jew together as recipients of one and the same inheritance, he reverts to "our," the same "our" as in vv. 3–10 (Jew and Gentile together).

The combination of this usage with that in v. 11 also indicates how thoroughly Paul's understanding of the Spirit reflects the basic "already but not yet" structure of his eschatology. On the one hand, God's people have already entered into their inheritance; the Spirit as "down payment" means present possession of what has been promised. On the other hand, as "down payment" the Spirit also guarantees the future consummation of what is now realized only in part. As noted above, the emphasis in Ephesians is more on the "already" side of things than in most of Paul's letters—which has little or nothing to do with Paul's situation but much to do with that which he is addressing. This passage, as well as 4:30, indicates that the Spirit is to be understood throughout as fulfilling his ordinary eschatological role in Pauline thought. Along with the resurrection of Christ, the Spirit is the certain evidence that the future has been set in motion; and the Spirit's indwelling presence serves as God's own guarantee that we are to inherit all that has been promised.

4. It is in this context that we are also to understand the unusual phrase that follows, "for the redemption of his possession." The preposi-

---

[41]At least that is the most common understanding of the verb ἐκληρώθημεν, since it is so strongly supported by v. 13. For a different view, that sees the Jews (or Christians in general) as God's own inheritance, see Robinson 34, Caird 41, Stott 46.

tion εἰς in this case expresses God's goal in his having sealed us by the Spirit. "You were sealed by the promised Holy Spirit," Paul tells his Gentile readers, "for the [final] redemption of what belongs to God as his own possession."[42] "Redemption," as in Rom 8:23 where the companion metaphor "firstfruits" appears, most likely refers to the final consummation of the redemption that we have already realized through Christ (v. 7). Thus this phrase, following "who is the down payment of our inheritance" as it does, also reflects the "already but not yet" eschatological perspective of this sentence.

With this clause, therefore, Paul not only brings the *berakah* to its striking and majestic conclusion, but at the same time brings into focus the third member of the divine triad, the Holy Spirit of God, as well as the guaranteed future realization of the redemption for which most of the *berakah* praises God. All of which is to the praise of God's own glory, which has thus been revealed in Christ and realized by the Spirit.

EPHESIANS 1:15–2:10

The preceding *berakah* focused especially on the redemption that God has effected in Christ, with a twofold emphasis at the end on (a) Gentile participation by the Spirit in the promised inheritance made to Israel and on (b) its eschatological consummation. This in turn is followed by a thanksgiving and prayer report (vv. 15–19), which in typical fashion evolves into theological affirmations (vv. 20–23), focusing on the second major emphasis in the epistle: Christ's victory over the powers on behalf of his people. This in turn[43] calls forth further reflection on the readers' own past and present as participants, first as among the "walking dead" enslaved to the prince of the powers (2:1–3), and second as now raised from the dead and seated with Christ in the heavenlies on display, as it were, both to the powers and to the present fallen world (vv. 4–10).

---

[42]Gk. περιποίησις; cf. 1 Pet 2:9, alluding to Mal 3:17. Otherwise Abbott 24, Salmond 269, Schnackenburg 67, who take "possession" as something belonging to believers; cf. RSV, " . . . our inheritance until we acquire possession of it," but corrected in the NRSV.

[43]Because of our present chapter break, the very close connection between vv. 20–23 and 2:1–10 is often missed. The connection in this case, however, is not only conceptual, as pointed out in the present discussion, but grammatical: this is one of those rare instances in Paul (and in Ephesians as well), where a major shift in the flow of thought is begun with a paratactic καί. Note: parataxis has to do with the joining of major clauses by an "and," rather than by subordination or, in Greek at least, with one of the more common particles (conjunctive signals) that nuance the material in some way.

As with the *berakah*, the thanksgiving-prayer report is one long sentence in Greek,[44] in this case held together by a series of subordinate clauses.[45] Our interest is in the mention of the Spirit in v. 17, which is a key moment for the whole prayer. Moreover, we also meet for the first time in the letter a profusion of "power" terminology (vv. 19–20), some of which seems very likely to refer indirectly to the Spirit. Therefore, a brief overview of the whole will help to place our concerns in their larger context.

Paul begins in v. 15 with what has been reported to him about them, which is followed in v. 16 by a typical thanksgiving, which in Paul is almost always tied to a notation on prayer (i.e., he gives thanks as he prays). Verses 17–19, introduced with a "that" clause, contain the actual prayer report, in which he tells them what he prays in their behalf: for the Spirit to make God known to them and to reveal to them the rich benefits that are theirs in Christ. The final focus is on the greatness of the power that is "unto us who believe," evidenced in particular through the resurrection of Christ (v. 20) and his present session "in the heavenlies" far above all the spiritual powers (v. 21), and all of this for the sake of his people, the church (vv. 22–23).

EPHESIANS 1:17–20

[17]*that the God of our Lord Jesus Christ, the Father of glory, might give you the Spirit of wisdom and revelation in the knowledge of him,* [18]*the eyes of your*[46] *heart having been enlightened, so that you may know what is the hope of his calling, what*[47] *are the riches of his inheritance in the saints,* [19]*and what is the surpassing greatness of his power unto us who believe, according to the*

---

[44]This is true at least through v. 21; vv. 22–23 form a sentence of their own that begins with καί, which makes the second καί in 2:1 all the more telling in terms of structure (see preceding note). The sentence or paragraph break at v. 20 has nothing to do with grammar (in fact it is a subordinate clause that begins with a relative pronoun whose antecedent is ἐνέργειαν ["working"] in v. 19), but is simply a recognition that the prayer report at this point evolves into theological affirmation.

[45]Although some of its language—not to mention grammar and style—is unlike what we meet elsewhere in Paul, the subtle shift from prayer report to theological affirmations that takes place at v. 20 is typical of the apostle. The newness of things in terms of content is due (typically) to the situation to which Paul is speaking.

[46]The ὑμῶν ("your") is missing in the better MSS (P[46] B 6 33 1175 1739 1881 pc); this is probably the original text, since there is no certain evidence for early scribal activity that made grammatical "improvements" toward a more classical style. Thus, as often in Paul, the definite article functions as the possessive, which later scribes clarified by adding the pronoun itself.

[47]In typical fashion the later manuscript tradition added a καί between the first two members of this triplet, which is missing in all the early evidence (except for Jerome and it[a]). See the discussion below.

working of the strength of his might, ²⁰*which he worked*[48] *in Christ when he raised him from the dead and seated him at his right hand in the heavenlies.*

Perhaps the best way to get at the significance of the mention of the Spirit in this prayer report is by way of a structural analysis:

```
 . . . mentioning in my prayer
       17that
   God . . . might grant    you    the Spirit
                                     of wisdom
                                     and
                                     of revelation
       [1]                               in your knowledge of him [God]
                            the eyes of your heart having been [thus] enlightened
                                     18so that you might know:
       [2]                           (a') the hope of his calling
                                     (a") the riches of the glory
                                                of his inheritance
                                                    in the saints
                             19and
                                     (b) the surpassing greatness of his power
                                                unto us who believe
                                                which is in keeping with the working
                                                    of the strength
                                                        of his might
```

Since the Spirit is the object of the verb "grant," it does not take great insight to recognize the Spirit's key role in this prayer. The prayer is for God to grant them *the Spirit,* characterized here in terms of wisdom and revelation: through the Spirit's wisdom and revelation they will thus (1) come to have a more thorough knowledge[49] of God, and through the Spirit's enlightenment of their hearts will understand the certainty of their eschatological future (2a', a") and God's power (through the same Spirit) in their behalf as they await that future (2b). The text, however, is not as straightforward as that, at least in the eyes of many; some further comments are therefore necessary.

1. Given the central role of the Spirit in what seems to be a straightforward expression, one is taken aback somewhat by the majority of English translations[50] and several commentaries[51] who here render πνεῦμα

---

[48]Gk. ἐνήργησεν, the cognate verb of the preceding "working" (ἐνέργειαν), which makes for awkward English but seems necessary at this point in order for the English reader to see the connection.

[49]Gk. ἐπιγνῶσις, a compound of γνῶσις, which carries the sense of "knowing exactly, completely, through and through" (BAGD [on the verb]); cf. 1 Cor 13:12, where it is used of God's knowing us and of our final eschatological knowing of God.

[50]E.g., KJV, ASV, RSV, NRSV, JB, NJB, NASB, NAB, NIV^{mg}, Conybeare. Otherwise NIV, GNB, Williams; cf. REB: "the spiritual gifts of wisdom and vision."

[51]E.g., Abbott 28, Westcott 22, Patzia 164–65 (unfortunately citing Westcott's misinformation); Robinson 38–39 makes much (incorrectly) of the absence of the

as "a spirit." One can perhaps explain the reasons for it: the lack of the definite article; that the expression "spirit of wisdom" is a semitism that can simply mean "a wise spirit"; the sense that the emphasis is on wisdom and revelation, not on πνεῦμα. But the reasons for recognizing a direct reference to the Spirit[52] far outweigh these:

(a) The presence or absence of the definite article has nothing at all to do with whether Paul is here referring to the divine Spirit or the human spirit. On this matter see the discussion in ch. 2. In this case the absence of the article is related to its absence from the two nouns in the genitive as well. Paul would ordinarily write either "*the* Spirit of *the* wisdom and *the* revelation" or "Spirit of wisdom and revelation," both of which mean exactly the same thing. That is, in these kinds of constructions Paul almost always uses the article with both the accusative and its qualifying genitive, or he uses it with neither. Therefore, this accusative is no more to be understood to say "a spirit of wisdom" than in Rom 8:14 the nonarticular πνεύματι θεοῦ means "by a spirit of God/or a god."

(b) That the phrase itself is a semitism need not be doubted, but not of the kind that has been suggested. After all, the language derives directly from Isa 11:2,[53] where the Spirit who is to rest on the Messiah is further described as πνεῦμα σοφίας καὶ συνέσεως (= "the Spirit who grants wisdom and understanding").[54] This is the exact combination Paul used in Col 1:9; the reason for the substitution here of "revelation" for "understanding" is that the emphasis in this prayer is on the Spirit as the revealer, rather than on his granting wisdom. Thus the Spirit who grants wisdom is also (especially) the one who grants the revelation of God and his ways. For the further significance of this language in our letter see the discussion on 3:5.

(c) One may further allow that the emphasis in the present passage is finally on the wisdom and revelation the recipients need, both to know God more fully and thereby also to be assured of their future hope and the power available to them in the present. But that is the *ultimate* concern. The key to all of this lies in the *penultimate*, the object of the verb: the Spirit himself. To skip past the Spirit, the source of both the revelation and the empowering, is to miss Paul's prayer by too much, not to mention the concerns of this letter.

---

article ("without [the article] some special manifestation or bestowal of the Holy Spirit is signified," which for him is therefore less than "the personal Holy Spirit").

[52]So the majority of commentaries: Meyer 69–70, Eadie 82, Dale 128, Salmond 273, Scott 153 (hesitantly), Schlier 78, Hendriksen 96–97, Caird 45, Wood 29, Stott 54, Schnackenburg 74, Bruce 269, Lincoln 56–57; Arnold, *Ephesians*, 76. Gnilka 90 and Barth 1.162 make it apply to both the human spirit and divine Spirit equally.

[53]Cf. also Exod 28:3; 31:3; 35:31, where the first part of the phrase occurs (πνεῦμα σοφίας).

[54]One should also note the anarthrous usage in this passage.

(d) That this is in fact what Paul is up to in this sentence rests finally on the fact that in his understanding of things, wisdom and revelation in the ongoing life of the believing community are expressly associated with the Spirit. In 1 Corinthians in particular wisdom is one of the Spirit's *charismata* (12:8), and the Spirit is the means of revelation whereby believers come to understand the wisdom that lies in the folly of the cross (2:10–13). Not only so, but in Ephesians the Spirit is explicitly noted as the source of the revelation of God's mystery (3:5), which Paul wants his recipients also to understand.

(e) It should be noted finally that the ultimate difficulty with the alternative understanding lies with the word "revelation." Whereas one might be able to understand "a spirit of wisdom" to mean something like "a wise disposition" or "a wise spirit," to speak that way of "revelation" is to speak near nonsense. What, one wonders, can "a spirit of revelation" possibly mean in *any* sense in English?

The upshot of all this, then, is that Paul is herewith praying that God will gift them with the Spirit yet once more,[55] and that the Spirit in turn will supply the wisdom to understand what he also reveals to them about God and his ways. Thus, "I remember you in my prayers and ask God . . . to give you the Spirit, who will make you wise and reveal God to you, so that you will know him" (GNB). It is that same Spirit who will "enlighten the eyes of their minds" so that they may understand what God has done in their behalf as expressed in vv. 18–19. To leave nothing undone, of course, Paul will go on in the first part of this letter to spell out for their "revelation" what God has done, and is doing, on their behalf.

2. Since the renewed "receiving" of the Spirit lies behind their realization of this prayer, a few further words are needed about its content. As I have tried to indicate in the structural analysis, the content of the revelation is twofold: (1) a more complete knowledge of God himself, which (2) will evolve into a better understanding of their own existence in light of what God has done for them. The latter is expressed in the form of three noun clauses ("what is . . . , what is . . . , and what is . . . "), but not all are agreed as to how we are to understand their relationship to each other. It may be, of course, that Paul was the first to use good English style (!) and place his "and" only between the second and third members of a threefold listing.[56] More likely the "and" points to one of

---

[55]On the "popular" level of understanding the renewed gift of the Spirit to those who are already Spirit people, see on 5:18 below, 1 Thes 4:8, and Gal 3:5. That is, the prayer is not for some further Spirit reception, but for the indwelling Spirit whom they have already received to give them further wisdom and revelation. The emphasis, therefore, is not in receiving the Spirit as such, but on receiving (or perhaps realizing?) the resident Spirit's gifts.

[56]The point is that in listings of three or more items, Greek style calls for either a conjunction between all of the items or no conjunction at all. This explains the

two other possibilities. Some see the second two as an explanation of the first.[57] As indicated in the structural analysis, I have opted for the alternative, that the first two form a pair, which together are paired with the third; in this case the first two are in apposition to one another, as two sides of the same eschatological coin, while the third brings them back into the present in terms of the Spirit's work on their behalf.[58] Although one cannot be certain here—because of some inherent difficulties in understanding the middle clause—there can be little question, it would seem, that the first and third clearly point to their eschatological future, on the one hand, and the present realization of divine power, on the other. Both of these need a further word:

(a) The eschatological thrust of the first pair picks up what has just been affirmed in the *berakah*, namely, that their future is certain because it has been guaranteed by the presence of the Spirit. Paul now reflects further on that "hope," praying that the Spirit's revelation of God will cause them to understand how sure their hope is.[59] The emphasis now rests on the divine initiative that leads them to have such hope, which is predicated first of all on God's call. For Paul that generally settles everything.[60] But in a sense that is still to see the future from the perspective of their own experience of God. That is, they have *hope* for a certain, although yet unrealized, future[61] precisely because they have experienced God's call to become his people. The other side of that eschatological coin is to look at that hope from the divine perspective, as it were.[62] Thus he prays that they may also understand how splendid ("wealthy") is the glory that is to be in terms of the final inheritance that God has laid up for them. Or is it, that God himself has an "inheritance," to be realized when "the saints"[63] are finally brought to rest in the place

---

addition of καί by the later textual tradition, which understood them to be a threefold listing (see n. 47 above). See the discussion of 1 Thes 1:5 for a similar phenomenon. On the other hand, this may yet be what Paul was intending, as most modern interpreters take it (e.g., Stott, Schnackenburg, Bruce, Patzia, Lincoln, Arnold).

[57]Cf. Schlier 81–82, Barth 1.150.

[58]Although not put quite this way, this view can be found, e.g., in Westcott 24 and Scott 154.

[59]See esp. 4:1–4 below, where this language combination is found in v. 1 ("walk worthy of the calling unto which you were called") and v. 4 ("one body and one Spirit, even as you were called in one hope of your calling").

[60]See esp. on Rom 8:28–30; 1 Cor 1:2, 26 and throughout the corpus.

[61]Lincoln 59 suggests that hope here is to be understood as both "already" and "not yet." But it is hard to see the realized dimension of this word in this context. Patzia 167, in contrast, makes no mention of the future at all.

[62]Meyer 74, et al., see this rather as a spelling out of the object of the hope.

[63]This reflects a decided understanding of the phrase ἐν τοῖς ἁγίοις (lit. "among/in the holy ones"). Many (e.g., Schlier 84, Gnilka 91, Schnackenburg 74, Lincoln, *Paradise*, 144 [but see now his commentary]) consider this to refer to angels, as it most likely does in the prayer in 1 Thes 3:13 and in the companion text in Col 1:12.

of his glory?[64] In either case, the reference to "inheritance," following "hope," probably emphasizes its future realization. Thus, the same Spirit who in vv. 13–14 serves as God's surety of their final redemption is now the source of their understanding how certain this hope is and how splendid it will be when finally fully realized.

(b) Paul next leads them from contemplation about the future to a new understanding of the present.[65] The same God who has thus guaranteed their lives for eternity has not left them to their own devices as they face the "powers" in the present. Paul therefore also prays that their Spirit-enlightened hearts may understand how "surpassing great is God's present power" unto "us[66] who believe." Further, this power is quite in keeping with that previously manifested in the resurrection and present session of Christ himself. There is nothing else in the corpus quite like this especially high concentration of power terminology,[67] which leads us to our final Spirit concern in this passage.

3. Although Paul does not here equate the Spirit with the word δύναμις ("power"), nor should we, it must nonetheless be noted that Paul sees the closest kind of relationship between the presence of the Spirit and the concomitant presence of God's power. In previous letters that relationship was spelled out in the combination "by the power of the Spirit" (e.g., Rom 15:13). In this letter it will be spelled out specifically in the next prayer report (3:16), where Paul prays that they might be strengthened in the inner person "with power through God's Spirit." There is no reason to doubt that for Paul that same combination is to be understood as lying behind this usage, even though it is not here specifically stated.

But nothing in the present context prepares the readers for such an understanding; and given the usage in 1:1, plus the clear reference to the people of God and their inheritance in vv. 13–14, it is difficult to imagine how the first readers could have heard this as referring to angels. See the more complete discussion in Lincoln 59–60.

[64]This, of course, is not a universal view. The problems are twofold: (a) whether "inheritance," as in the two other occurrences (1:14; 5:5), refers to the future realization of what is already theirs as God's people or to something already present; and (b) whether the combination with the pronoun "his" picks up the OT motif that we as God's people are his inheritance, now and forever or, as in the preceding "his call," it refers to our inheritance that God has provided for us (with the emphasis on his providing it, hence "his inheritance" rather than "our inheritance" as in v. 14).

[65]Meyer 76 and Schnackenburg 75–76 see this affirmation as being primarily future in its orientation as well; but that seems to go against not only what is actually said, but the whole context of the letter as well.

[66]On this shift to the first person plural, while addressing others but reflecting on what is common to him and them, see inter alia on Gal 4:4–7; Rom 8:2–4, 14–17.

[67]Besides the four terms, δύναμις (the regular term for "power" of all kinds), ἐνεργεία (denoting "mighty working"; cf. 3:7; 4:16; Col 1:29; Phil 3:21, of God's working; and 2 Thes 2:9 for Satan's), κράτος (the abstract noun for "might," appearing often in NT doxologies referring to God: 1 Tim 6:16; 1 Pet 4:11; 5:11; Jude 25; Rev 1:6; 5:13), and ἰσχύς (referring to the "strength" that is displayed in specific expressions of God's "might"), Paul begins with the compound "surpassing greatness."

But having said that, one needs especially in this instance to note that the prayer is not for them to experience something triumphalistic, as though through the power of the Spirit God would extricate them from difficulties or enable them "to defeat the enemy" with some sort of visible manifestation. When all of this is spelled out in greater detail in the next prayer report (3:14–19), including its doxology (vv. 20–21), it has to do with being "empowered in the inner person" by the indwelling of Christ, so that they may (a) comprehend the immeasurable greatness of Christ's love for them, and (b) thus be filled with "all the fullness of God."[68]

Paul's concern here is not with any petty victories over the powers, but with his readers' understanding of their position in Christ, who has himself assumed the place of authority over the powers for their sakes. The reality of what God has done for them in Christ is to be realized as they are seated together with him "in the heavenly realm," the realm that Satan and the powers still inhabit. Thus this text is not to be played off against the regular Pauline theme of "power in weakness"; rather, it helps us better to grasp the magnitude of the "power" side of that equation in Paul. But the empowering takes place in the midst of every-day life. To understand the magnitude of such empowering, one needs the revelation of God that the Spirit alone can bring to his people.

EPHESIANS 2:2

among whom you once walked, according to the age of this world, according to the ruler of the authority of the air, of the spirit[69] *who is now at work among the children of disobedience.*

With Christ firmly invested in the heavenly realm, raised from the dead by the power of God (of the same kind presently available to God's people) and seated at God's right hand as "head over the powers for the sake of his body the church," Paul naturally thinks of his readers, for whose sake all of this is being said. In so doing, he reminds them of their former association with the "powers," as those who were among "the walking dead," subject to the prince of the powers,

---

[68]Cf. Bruce 271.

[69]Gk. τοῦ πνεύματος. This genitive is not at all easy to account for, which places considerable stress on our understanding of this sentence. It is most often viewed as in apposition to "ruler" (τὸν ἄρχοντα), with the genitive understood as an attraction to the two immediately preceding genitives. But since for many that makes for careless Greek, and since the two preceding words ("authority," "air") are in the genitive, either of them has been suggested as the appositional antecedent (e.g., "authority," Meyer, Robinson, Abbott, Lincoln; "air," Schlier, Caird). Although not of immediate and easy solution, this is a case where the "ungrammatical" understanding is the one that makes far more sense of the passage than do the other two. That is, it is easy to see how the genitive came about, as Paul piles up terms describing both the arena and the nature of the "prince" of the spirit powers. Since "the spirit" is described in very personal terms (as now working among the disobedient), it seems unlikely that in the midst of describing the chief of demons Paul suddenly elaborates on his activity in more impersonal terms. So most interpreters (cf. Arnold, *Ephesians*, 59–62).

Satan himself. But Paul does not call him the devil here (as in 4:27; 6:11); rather, he describes him with a variety of terms that seem intended to elicit a degree of emotional response from his readers.

Numerous obvious difficulties exist with this passage;[70] our interest is simply to note that this is the single instance in the corpus where Paul actually designates Satan also to be a "spirit." Although one cannot be certain, it is altogether likely that the designation is an intentional parody,[71] similar to that of the "parousia of the man of lawlessness" in 2 Thes 2:8–9 (q.v.). Thus, just as the people of God walk according to the Spirit, so those outside of Christ also walk according to a "spirit," who is also designated as the "prince of the authority of the air." The false "spirit's" realm is also in the heavenlies; but God by his power raised Christ to sit above the powers and to be head over them for the church (1:20–23). From here Paul will go on to emphasize that God has also raised his people to sit "in the heavenlies" with Christ, and therefore they are no longer under the dominion of, or in fear of, the "spirit who is now at work among the disobedient."

This turns out to be the only major section of the letter (2:1–10) in which the Spirit is not specifically mentioned; but we would not be far afield if we were to recognize him in this parody. The "spirit now working among the disobedient" has more than met his match in Christ, whom God by his surpassing great power has raised from the dead, and in the Spirit, the present expression of God's power among and for his people as they live out the life of the future in the present age (vv. 9–10) awaiting the hope of their calling, the realization of their final inheritance.

EPHESIANS 2:3 (2:11)

Among whom also we all once lived in the passions of our flesh, doing the will[72] of the flesh and of our minds, and we were children of wrath as the rest of humankind.

This is obviously not a Spirit text; it is included because of the double mention of "the flesh." My concern is to point out that what is said here is precisely what Paul also says in Rom 7:5. Paul's present concern is to make sure that his Gentile readers understand that from the new perspective in Christ, their own sinfulness described in vv. 1–2 is no greater than that of Paul and his fellow Jews. To do this he uses the language and ideas of Romans 1–7. Two things need to be noted, both of them in keeping with what Paul has said in Rom 7:5. First, by "passions of the flesh," followed immediately by "the will(s) of the flesh," he cannot mean "physical desires."[73] As noted above (n. 72), the perspective is that of Romans 7, where in our pre-Christ existence we lived in keeping with what "the flesh" desired, which is then further described as living by what "the flesh" wills in its over-against-God mindset.[74]

---

[70]See preceding note.

[71]Cf. Chotka, "Spirit," ch. 3.

[72]This is one of the more unusual combinations of singulars and plurals in the corpus (τὰ θελήματα [pl.] τῆς σαρκὸς [s.] καὶ τῶν διανοιῶν [pl.]). Most likely he intended something like: "doing the things that the flesh—and our minds—will(s)." In any case, it reflects the view of Romans 7 that "the flesh," which describes us in our former, pre-Christ condition, has a "will" of its own that is absolutely contrary to the will of God.

[73]As BAGD 61 (under ἀναστρέφω 2bβ, "= be a slave to physical passion").

[74]Cf. Arnold, *Ephesians*, 133.

Second, by the very way this is stated, Paul once again presupposes an attitude toward the "flesh" that understands it not to belong to Christian life, but to characterize the "before and outside of Christ" perspective of our common fallenness. As in Romans 7, it is by means of the flesh, as the place where sin dwells, that Jew and Gentile find common ground in their need of Christ's redemption.

In this regard one should also note the usage of "in the flesh" in v. 11 to describe Gentile and Jews. The "Gentiles in the flesh" means Gentiles, "humanly speaking," that is, with regard to their national origins. The usage almost certainly stems from the next clause which refers to the Jews as "circumcised in the flesh." This usage is thoroughly Pauline (cf. Gal 3:3), in that it has its origins in the actual "flesh" of circumcision, but now has significance as belonging to the present age that is passing away.[75]

While there is no direct Spirit-flesh contrast in this letter,[76] this passage makes it clear that this perspective is absolutely presuppositional here as well.

EPHESIANS 2:11–22

The next instances of Spirit language in this letter occur at the end of this second major section of what began as an interruption of the prayer report in 1:20 and ended up as a reminder of who they are, as members together (with Jews) in the one body of Christ. In the first section (vv. 1–10) Paul reminded his readers, in light of Christ's present position of authority over the powers, that they too share in his resurrection triumph over them; thus Paul's readers are no longer to "walk" (= live) as those who belong to the false "spirit" (vv. 1–3), but are to walk as those who are God's "masterpiece" of reconciliation, in the good works he has ordained for them (vv. 8–10).[77]

In the present section Paul picks up the theme of their "before and after" in terms of what it means for them as Gentiles to become with Jews the one people of God: one "body" (v. 16); fellow "citizens"; members of

---

[75]These are subtleties that are innate to an author, but are extraordinary in the highest degree for someone writing in Paul's name.

[76]Although Robinson 72, followed by Lincoln 152, makes the point that vv. 11–22 are "enclosed" by the twin phrases "in the flesh" and "in the Spirit" in vv. 11 and 22, as describing the Gentiles' two modes of existence before and after.

[77]More than many interpreters, I see the Jew-Gentile focus as also at work in this passage: (a) in the "you" of vv. 1–2 and the "we" of v. 3, in which, as in Rom 1:18–3:20, Paul thus includes Jews along with Gentiles as in need of grace; and (b) esp. in v. 6, where, following v. 5 in which he has included them both as made alive "together *with* Christ," he now speaks of them as "raised together with [one another is implied] and seated together with one another *in Christ*." I would not think so, if this were not what was spelled out specifically in the passage that follows, so that both those who are far off (Gentiles) and those who are near (Jews) are together granted "access to God by the one Spirit." This kind of "pre-echoing" of what will be spelled out later in an argument is typical of Paul.

God's "household" (v. 19); bonded together as God's "temple" (vv. 21–22). Our present interest lies in the specific mention of the Spirit in vv. 18 and 22, and of prophets in v. 20, where these images of the church tumble over each other to find expression. But to get there, we need to see how these texts function in the larger argument.

Paul begins in vv. 11–13 with the "before and after," by noting first their past existence as Gentiles ("without God and therefore without hope" and "aliens with regard to citizenship in Israel, with its covenants and promises") and second their current place in Christ (once "far away" but now "brought near"). Verses 14–18 then spell out both the *how* (through the cross) and the *what* (Jew and Gentile reconciled and formed into one new humanity, in "one body") of their present existence in Christ. The final clause of this section (v. 18) brings in the ministry of the Spirit, as he joins that of Christ by bringing both together as one people into the presence of God. Verses 19–22 conclude by returning to the political imagery of vv. 11–13, but at the same time shifting it slightly to that of household, which in turn evolves into that of temple. Gentiles are no longer "aliens"; on the contrary, they are members together of God's household. Indeed, they are God's temple in whose midst God now dwells. At the end, the images fall all over themselves, but the points are clear and certain. The Spirit in whom they jointly have "access" to God (in the heavenly realm, is implied) is the same Spirit by whom God himself now dwells in their midst (on earth, is implied). That is, in the Spirit we are united as one in God's own presence; and also by the Spirit God's presence is manifest on earth in the community of faith.

EPHESIANS 2:17–18

[17]*And he [Christ] came*[78] *and preached the good news of peace to you who were far off and to those who were near,* [18]*because*[79] *through him we both in one Spirit*[80] *have access to the Father.*

---

[78]Because of the aorist participle, some interpreters (e.g., Meyer 137–38, Salmond 297, Abbott 66) make a point of what is here described as coming after the event of the cross itself, and therefore feel compelled to find a historical moment for this coming (e.g., in the coming of the Spirit). That Paul intended it to follow the event of the cross need not be doubted, but the usage is metaphorical and therefore does not refer to some specific event; rather, it refers to what naturally followed the event of the cross, namely, its proclamation to Jew and Gentile.

[79]Gk. ὅτι; some older interpreters, noted by Meyer 139 and Eadie 186, considered this ὅτι to introduce a noun clause, giving content to "peace." I could find no modern interpreter who holds this view, and for good reason. This clause gives the proof of the former.

[80]Gk. ἐν ἑνὶ πνεύματι. As often is true of this construction in Paul, one cannot tell whether it is to be understood as instrumental or locative (agency or sphere). As noted below, this particular form of the expression is probably to be understood as locative, but an instrumental idea does not trail far behind.

These words appear as a summation at the end of the long sentence (vv. 14–16) in which Paul describes *how* God brought about the reconciliation (with God and with one another) that he asserted in v. 13 ("in Christ Jesus you who were once 'far off' have been brought 'near' through the blood of Christ"). Christ did it "through the cross," by which he destroyed the enmity that existed between Jews and Gentiles, the "dividing wall of hostility" evidenced by the Law with its commandments and regulations. In place of the two he thus created one new humanity, and in so doing established peace. Our sentence summarizes the results by joining the language "far off" and "near" from v. 13 with that of "peace" from vv. 14–16, the result being that both Jew and Gentile together have "access to the Father," which is how Paul will now spell out what it means for them to be "brought near." Indeed, as the "because" indicates, their access to God as one people in the Spirit validates the truth of what is asserted in v. 17.

Four matters are noteworthy regarding v. 18:

1. The subject of the clause, "we both," which may simply mean "we both *alike* have access,"[81] more likely implies in this context that "we both *together* have access." While the latter emphasis is not inherent in the word itself, this is in fact the emphasis in the two occurrences of "both" in the preceding sentence. Christ is our peace by his having made "the both of them one," and he did so by abolishing the Law in order that he might reconcile "the both of them in one body." Thus it is not merely that individual Jews and Gentiles alike now have access to the Father, true and glorious as that is, but that both of them as one new humanity have such access. Jew and Gentile stand together as one people in God's presence with old distinctions no longer having significance.[82]

Given the distinct allusions in v. 17 to Isa 52:7 and 57:19, where in the former the Messiah is the proclaimer of peace and in the latter the peace is for "those who are far and near," it is altogether likely that Paul is here reflecting once again his understanding of the "promised Holy Spirit" as fulfilling the eschatological promise that includes the Gentiles.[83] If so, then "in the one Spirit" replaces the temple as the place of "access" into the presence of God.

2. It is precisely at this juncture that the work of the Spirit comes to the fore. On the one hand, Christ's death made the new humanity, the one body, a possibility; and he accomplished this by abolishing that which divides. But the realization of this "one body" comes through their being one people

---

[81] As the RSV; cf. Bruce 301.

[82] Cf. Findlay 142: "Coming 'in one Spirit to the Father,' the reconciled children join hands again with each other. Social barriers, caste feelings, family feuds, personal quarrels, national antipathies, alike go down before the virtue of the blood of Jesus."

[83] See above on 1:13–14; cf. Gal 3:14 and Rom 15:7–13.

together in the one Spirit of God.[84] In contrast to some English translations,[85] and in contrast to ἐν πνεύματι ("in/by the Spirit") that occurs elsewhere in this letter (2:22; 3:5; 5:18; 6:18), the phrase in this case is most likely a locative. That is, it is as both are "united in the one Spirit" (TCNT) or are "in the fellowship of one Spirit" (Conybeare) that they together have access to the Father. Several matters support this understanding.

a. This best explains the appearance of the modifier "one" in this clause, which occurs elsewhere with the Spirit in 1 Cor 12:8, 13 and Phil 1:27 (q.v.; cf. 4:4 below).[86] The usage here closely resembles 1 Cor 12:13 (q.v.), where all believers (including Jew and Gentile!) are "immersed" in the one Spirit so as to form the one body of Christ. For Paul it is the common experience of the one Spirit, by Jew and Gentile alike, that attests that God has created something new in the body of Christ (cf. v. 15). Thus, the one Spirit who has formed them into the one body, also brings them together as that one body into the presence of the Father. It is as they live together in the common sphere of the Spirit that they have entrée with God. Two matters of the immediate context further support this view.

b. The word order argues for such, where "in the one Spirit" immediately follows the subject "the both [of you]." Thus, the emphasis is not on the activity of the Spirit here, but on the Spirit as the common sphere of their life together.

c. This sentence seems to be intentionally in parallel with v. 16,[87] where Paul has previously emphasized that "through the cross Christ has reconciled *the both in one body* to God," where the parallel "in one body" can only be locative. The intent of the parallel seems to be that they are both in the one body because they are also both in the one Spirit, which is precisely how we are then to understand the words of 4:4, "there is one body and one Spirit." What has made one body possible is the death of Christ; what makes the one body a reality is their common, lavish experience of the Spirit of God. As they live together in the Spirit they now have access to the Father.

3. It must be understood that Paul emphasizes that as one people of God in the one Spirit we have access *into God's very presence;*[88] now the

---

[84]Which is exactly the point Paul will make in 4:1–4; they are to maintain the unity of the Spirit, since there is one body and one Spirit.

[85]E.g., NIV ("access to the Father by the Spirit").

[86]Scott 174 takes the nearly impossible view that this means "in one spirit" (= "the new attitude of worship now available to all"); cf. Barth 1.265–66, who allows for both. This is an altogether modern use of the word πνεῦμα, which Paul himself would scarcely recognize. On this question see the discussion on Phil 1:27.

[87]Thus:

that he might reconcile to God	We have access to God
the both	the both
in one body	in one Spirit
through the cross	through him

[88]This is the distinct force of the preposition πρός, thus the translation "access

locative sense also merges with the instrumental. Not only did the "dividing wall of hostility" alienate Jew and Gentile, but our common fallenness (vv. 1–3) equally served as a dividing wall of hostility between us and God. That wall too has come tumbling down in Christ, which makes it possible for Jew and Gentile together now to have access to God. Equally sinful, both have been equally given life and have been raised together and seated together in the heavenlies in Christ. Thus we have another of the "Spirit's blessings": not only reconciliation with one another through Christ, but reconciliation with God through Christ; and our being together in the one Spirit in God's very presence attests that God has brought it off. Therefore, those who were once dead and subject to wrath are now not only no longer so, but in fact have been "brought near"—as near as one can get(!), into the very presence of God. And there they find what Paul has stressed elsewhere about the Spirit's ministry: the eternal God is none other than our heavenly Father,[89] the one unto whom we cry by the Spirit's empowering, "*Abba*, Father."

The word "access"[90] is that used in Rom 5:2,[91] in a similar context of "peace with God" effected by Christ's death. As in that passage, the imagery is that of a suppliant before a king, who deserves "wrath" (2:3) but receives mercy (v. 4), and not only so, but by the Spirit has ready and free access to the king, who is none other than our Father, through our Lord Jesus Christ. We might note finally that, as it does in that passage, the imagery will shift from our being in God's presence (here and Rom 5:2) to his presence being with us (v. 22 and Rom 5:5), and in both instances this occurs as the result of the presence of the Spirit. The basic difference between the two passages is that in Romans the emphasis falls on the individual believer (Jew and Gentile alike); here it is on the corporate life of the believing community (Jew and Gentile together as one people of God).

4. This is yet one more passage in Paul in which "salvation in Christ" is conveyed in Trinitarian terms. Through the work of Christ and by the present ministry of the Spirit, we have access to the Father. This is a thoroughly Pauline view of things.

EPHESIANS 2:19–22

[19]*Therefore you [Gentiles] are no longer aliens and strangers, but you are fellow-citizens with the saints and members of God's household,* [20]*having been built upon the foundation of the apostles and the prophets, Jesus Christ himself*

---

into the presence of God" is quite legitimate.

[89]Cf. the "Father of our Lord Jesus Christ" (1:3), "the Father of glory" (1:17), the Father from whom all peoples ultimately derive their name (3:14–15).

[90]Gk. τὴν προσαγωγὴν . . . πρὸς τὸν πατέρα.

[91]Cf. also 3:12 in this letter.

the cornerstone, [21]in whom the whole[92] building, having been joined together, grows into a holy temple in the Lord, [22]in whom also you are being built together so as to become God's[93] dwelling place by the Spirit.

These words apply the affirmations of vv. 11–18 directly to the situation of the recipients of the letter. Returning to the political metaphor in v. 12, Paul affirms that their alien status no longer obtains. To the contrary they are "fellow-citizens" with their Jewish brothers and sisters. But in typical fashion that metaphor leads to the closely related metaphor of the Greco-Roman household, so that they are not only "fellow-citizens of the saints" but also "members of God's own household." That in turn calls forth the metaphor of the "house" itself as a building (v. 20); the "household of God" thus becomes the "house of God,"[94] which then yields to yet more building imagery, that of the "temple" (vv. 21–22). Most of this is typical and has antecedents: the rapid-fire shift from metaphor to metaphor (cf. esp. 2 Cor 2:14–17 and 3:1–6); the final shift of metaphors from a "building" to the "temple" (1 Cor 3:9–16); the Spirit as the key to the temple metaphor.[95] Indeed, the most troublesome item (for many) in the passage, the mention of the "apostles and prophets," reflects the companion metaphor of the body in 1 Cor 12:27–28, where Paul affirmed that God has placed in the church "first, apostles; second, prophets." What differs (apparently) is the metaphorical role of the apostles and prophets in the building as the foundation, whereas in 1 Cor 3:10–11 that role was taken by Christ. In the present imagery Christ functions as the cornerstone, a metaphor not found elsewhere in Paul.[96]

---

[92]Gk. πᾶσα οἰκοδομή (so ℵ* B D F G Ψ Maj). A few MSS have tried to assist Paul by inserting the article ἡ between the two words, but this is an unnecessary expedient and misses Paul's intent. Since the "building" is viewed as still in process, the present combination probably refers to "all that has gone into the building as it is being constructed." See the lengthy and helpful discussions in Abbott 73–75 and Robinson 69–71. Some older interpreters (e.g., Meyer 146–47) argued that it should carry its precise sense, "every building," but that misses the point Paul is making in the present context.

[93]Codex B alone has the reading "Christ's" (Χριστοῦ) here. In some ways that might seem to be the more difficult reading, because just above Christ is the "cornerstone" of the temple. But both its uniqueness and the context suggest that this is a pure solecism. God's household has now become "God's temple," made so "in the Lord" by "the Spirit."

[94]Which in Greek closely resembles our usage in English, "the house of Windsor," etc.

[95]Acknowledged by Schnackenburg 125 and Lincoln 152.

[96]For some such a shift is nearly impossible to imagine as having come from Paul, especially since this appears to them to be a move away from charismatic leadership toward "offices." But this again seems to be a matter of the "eye of the beholder"; if they were convinced on other grounds that Paul did not write 1 Corinthians, such scholars would be as equally convinced that 1 Cor 12:28 could not have come from the apostle. But since they believe Paul wrote that letter, they read 1 Cor

Thus we need to look at both v. 20 and v. 22 in some further detail, since the Spirit is expressly mentioned in the latter and is assumed in the former (in the mention of "prophets").

20 This is the first of three instances in this letter (cf. 3:5 and 4:11) where Paul joins together "apostles and prophets"[97] as having a role of some significance in the church.[98] On the meaning of the terms, see on 1 Cor 12:28, where this same combination appears—in equally striking fashion. In 1 Corinthians they are "placed in the church" in the context of the imagery of the body; but in keeping with the concern of that argument, Paul carefully avoids identifying them with any of the actual parts of the body. But there can be little question of their significance for the "building up of the church" in that passage. There we also meet the tension (for us) between the prophet as person and prophesying as a function. There is none of that here, because the imagery and context are so different.

What is striking, of course, is Paul's placing the "prophets" (along with the apostles) as the "foundation" of the building.[99] But they do not thereby replace Christ. Whether architecturally astute from our perspective or not, Paul and his Jewish contemporaries considered the "corner-

---

12:28, which for me is the more difficult text by far, as though it very naturally spoke of "charismatic" leadership—as it probably does, but certainly not very naturally. The only really troublesome matters here are (1) whether one will allow that Paul could so remarkably shift his points of reference in a similar metaphor, to which the answer is "yes, indeed"; and (2) whether seeing them as "foundation," plus the language of "holy apostles" in 3:5, implies a much more significant role than in 1 Cor 12:28, to which the answer would seem to be no—in light of their function in 4:12–16, which is not as "officials" in the church structures, but as those who equip the saints for the ministry of the church.

[97]Gk. τῶν ἀποστόλων καὶ προφητῶν. Because of the single article controlling both nouns, some have argued, following Granville Sharpe's "rule" (most recently, Hui, "Concept," 384–89), that the same people are in mind (= apostles who are prophets). There can be little question that Paul, for example, functioned in both roles (see 1 Cor 14:37). But the evidence of 4:11 and 1 Cor 12:28 seems determinative here that Paul intends two different kinds of establishing ministry, which in his case clearly overlap.

[98]Many interpreters in an earlier day were prone to see here a reference to the OT prophets, but absolutely nothing favors such a view and everything is against it. See the refutations in the older commentaries (e.g., Meyer 143–44, Eadie 193–95).

[99]That, at least, seems to be the plain sense of the text, thus seeing the genitive as "qualitative" or "appositional" (= foundation consisting of the ministry of the apostles and prophets). Earlier interpreters, on the basis of the "analogy of Scripture," could not imagine that the role of Christ has now been replaced by that of the apostle and prophets (which it does not, of course; see the discussion). Thus they argued for a genitive of source (= foundation laid by the apostles and prophets); cf. e.g., Meyer, Eadie, Salmond, NEB. Attractive as that might appear, it founders on the immediate qualifier (Christ himself the cornerstone), which seems deliberately added so that one will not make more of the apostles and prophets by this imagery than is intended.

stone"[100] to be the more significant item in the building. Hence the "apostles and prophets" move into his former role, not as the foundation upon which the church is erected, but as foundational for its existence at all. But much of this is quibble. One must be especially careful not to make metaphors walk on all fours. It is decidedly plain from the larger context of the letter (3:1–7; 4:11–16) that apostles and prophets are not "offices" upon which the organizational structure of the church is built, but are, as in 1 Corinthian 12–14, ministries that are necessary for the founding (therefore, "foundational") of the church,[101] as well as for its subsequent growth into a healthy and mature community of faith. That Paul uses the imagery of "foundation" for the building makes exactly that point. In the further mention of their ministries in 4:11–16, now in the context of the body imagery, apostles and prophets function similarly—to help the body grow into maturity—and again there is no sense of "office," only ministries. To find "ministerial offices" in this passage, therefore, is to read back into this text the realities of a later time,[102] but with the significant transfer from the "offices" of that time to a nonexistent "prophetic office" in the earlier period.

21–22 On the imagery of the church as God's temple, made so by the indwelling presence of the Spirit,[103] see on 1 Cor 3:16–17 and 2 Cor 6:16.[104] Two additional emphases emerge in this sentence: First, the recipients are described as "fitted together" and "being built together" (with the Jews, is still implicit) so as to "grow" into such a temple. Thus, the emphasis in this imagery is almost identical to that of the body in

---

[100]There is a large debate as to whether this refers to the traditional cornerstone of the Semitic building, which was in many respects more significant than the foundation, or whether it refers to the "keystone." Given the close and immediate approximation to the "foundation" and its ties to Isa 28:16, the former seems far more likely (*pace* Lincoln 157).

[101]Cf. Bruce 304. This metaphor therefore means nothing more than what Paul intends when saying to the Corinthians (15:11): "Therefore whether it be I or they (other apostles), so I preach and so you believed."

[102]Which, of course, is what Schnackenburg 122–23 does, since he considers the letter to come from a later time. What is not clear is how one who lives in this later time, when there is no prophetic "office," reads his own "institutional life" back into the time of Paul and chooses "prophets" as one of the "offices," since such an "office" never existed in the church, as the Didache bears sufficient witness.

[103]Some have understood ἐν πνεύματι to mean "spiritual" (= a spiritual temple vis-à-vis the material or literal temple in Jerusalem); e.g., Chrysostom, Robinson 72, Scott 179; cf. Hendriksen 144. But there is nothing in Pauline usage, or in the present context, that remotely allows such a view. If "replacement" is in view, and it very well may be, it is not "spiritual" over against "material," but the *new* temple of the Spirit replacing the old.

[104]Cf. also 1 Cor 6:19–20, where the imagery is reapplied to the individual believer.

4:11–16: their growing together into the people of God and their doing so in unity with one another. That the Spirit lies behind that emphasis is confirmed not only by the previous expression in v. 18, that it is in "the one Spirit" that they have common access to God's presence, but also by the language "unity of the Spirit" in 4:3, which is explicated in the following affirmation in terms of one body (because there is only) one Spirit.

Second, and this is where the Spirit language actually occurs, this imagery especially emphasizes the church as the "new temple," the present place of God's habitation on our planet. Here is the place of God's presence—in the midst of his people, especially as they are gathered to worship him and to instruct one another (as 5:18–20 indicates).[105] This is the same point made in 1 Cor 3:16 ("you are God's temple, in that the Spirit of God dwells in your midst"). They are being built into a habitation of God by the Spirit, which means that God *by his Spirit* abides among them.[106] Here, then, is how one is to understand all the "indwelling" terminology in Paul: by the indwelling of the Spirit, both in the individual and in the community, God (or Christ) indwells his people. Here is the ultimate fulfillment of the imagery of God's presence, begun but lost in the Garden, restored in the tabernacle in Exodus 40 and in the temple in 1 Kings 8. It is God's own presence among us that marks us off as the people of God and, in the language of Moses, is "what distinguishes [us]

---

[105] This stands over against many (e.g., Lincoln 158), who see the present passage as dealing with a nebulous entity called "the church universal." I do not deny that such exists (after all, in such a "circular letter" one could hardly speak otherwise when Paul probably has several congregations in view). But for Paul such a "church" finds expression at the local level, even in this letter, which is what *all* of 4:1–6:10 *presupposes*. Therefore, just as "love" can be expressed in a nebulous, universal way in 3:14–21, Paul's intention that love be taken seriously at the local level is precisely what chs. 4–6 are all about. So with the so-called church universal; it finds local expression as a gathered community "filled with the Spirit" and thus "teaching and admonishing one another" in the various kinds of songs, including those of the Spirit (5:18–19). Thus, God does not indwell the church universal in the heavens, as Lincoln would have it, but on earth, whenever the many churches to whom this letter is addressed gather for worship, "filled with the Spirit."

[106] Thus, both the word order (ἐν πνεύματι follows "for a habitation of God") and Pauline usage elsewhere argue for this meaning of the phrase, "by the Spirit." One may grant that this word order is somewhat ambiguous, that "in/by the Spirit" could modify either its preceding prepositional phrase (as above) or the verb (= are being built together by the Spirit into a habitation for God); so Meyer 149–50. But in response: (a) the latter could have been said without ambiguity syntactically, by placing ἐν πνεύματι immediately following the verb, which is not in fact what Paul does; (b) Paul's emphasis here in not on the *how* but the *what* of their becoming God's temple; that is, this final clause is expounding on what it means for them to "grow into a holy temple in the Lord" (*pace* Arnold, *Ephesians*, 159). One might also remark how thoroughly Pauline—and subtly so, too much so for a pseudepigrapher, it would seem—is the usage ἐν πνεύματι (without the definite article) to describe the work of the Spirit. So also the usage ἐν ἑνὶ πνεύματι in v. 18; cf. 6:18.

from all the other people on the face of the earth" (Exod 33:15). So not only do we have access to the presence of God (v. 18), but God himself by the Spirit has chosen to be present in our world in the gathered church.

We should finally note briefly that this is one more Trinitarian text. Through the Lord Jesus Christ the church comes into existence and is growing into a *holy* temple as it lives in him; as such it thus becomes the habitation of God by his Spirit.

EPHESIANS 3:1–13

Following the long digression that began in 1:20, regarding Christ's present victory over the powers for the sake of the church, and evolved into a long affirmation of the church as Jew and Gentile together as one people of God, in 3:1 Paul writes as though he were going to resume his prayer. What happens instead is another long interruption (vv. 2–13) in which the key issues of the preceding materials (Christ as victor over the powers and Jew and Gentile as one people in Christ) are specifically brought together through Paul's own apostolic ministry. Verses 6 and 10 are therefore the key matters in this section, along with the surrounding words about Paul's own role in all of this. In effect the passage becomes a long introduction of the apostle to churches that do not know him personally; but in it his concerns (Jew and Gentile) and theirs (the powers) merge in his own ministry. That is, God by his Spirit has revealed the formerly hidden mystery, whose content is given in v. 6; Paul in turn has "administered" this mystery among the Gentiles themselves, so that the one people of God are now on display before the powers (v. 10), both as evidence of God's ultimate triumph over them and as security against their threat of subjugation.

Much of what is said here, therefore, picks up motifs that have already surfaced. What is new is the use of "mystery" to describe what has just been set forth in 2:1–22,[107] now in terms of Gentiles as one *body*

---

[107] The term is not new; in fact it is a particularly Pauline term in the NT and is used here in a thoroughly Pauline way (to describe what was once "hidden" in God but is now revealed to believers through the Spirit; see on 1 Cor 2:6–16). Thus, only the content of the mystery is new (Gentile inclusion in the people of God). But such a shift (from the cross as God's wisdom) is hardly unPauline; after all, the usage in 1 Corinthians was thoroughly conditioned by its context. It is of some interest that scholarship tends to see the usage in 1 Corinthians as determinative as to what Paul "could have written" about this word, when that context is so ad hoc that it should always be suspect as to what is determinative in Paul. What we do not know is how Paul might have used it in a completely independent context—perhaps as in Rom

together with Jews *participating* in, and therefore *inheriting*, the *promises* of God that had formerly been made to Israel (v. 6). It is precisely at this point that the Spirit surfaces as well (v. 5), as the one through whom the revelation of the "mystery" has come to Paul (v. 3) and to others of the apostles and prophets as well (v. 5). Although this is the only text in which the Spirit is specifically mentioned, the power language in v. 7 also presupposes the presence of the Spirit.[108]

EPHESIANS 3:3–7

³how that the mystery was made known to me by revelation, even as I have just written in brief, ⁴so that by reading, you will be able to recognize my insight into the mystery of Christ, ⁵which to previous generations had not been made known to the human family[109] as now it has been revealed to his holy apostles[110] and prophets by the Spirit, ⁶that by Christ Jesus through the gospel the Gentiles are heirs together [with Jews], members together of the body, and participants together in the promises [made to Israel],[111] ⁷of which [gospel] I became a servant according to the gift of God given in keeping with the working of his power.

3, 5 In Jewish tradition "mysteries" are revealed to prophets by the Spirit of God; therefore Paul understands God's now disclosed "mystery" (Gentiles as full and equal participants with Israel in the covenant promises) to have been revealed to him by the Spirit. The link between vv. 3 and 5, therefore, is deliberate and significant—and helps to explain further both the prayer in 1:17 and the unusual mention of the apostles and prophets as foundational for the church in the immediately preceding Greek sentence (2:20).

Paul begins in v. 3 by noting his role as recipient of this revelation. But since he introduces himself to them in this section as a "prisoner of

---

16:25–27, which many scholars have also rejected on grounds similar to those invoked here, but a doxology which fits Romans excellently and is the prior use that leads to this one.

[108] So also, one might add, does much of the language of v. 6 ("fellow heirs, fellow members of the body, fellow participants in the promises"), all of which in this letter are elsewhere specifically tied to the ministry of the Spirit (1:13–14; 4:3–4). But the Spirit involvement in these matters lies outside Paul's immediate interests, hence I simply point them out.

[109] This is an attempt to render the Semitic "sons of men" into a dynamic equivalent that is gender neutral, just as the idiom itself is.

[110] This word is omitted in B b Ambrosiaster, probably due to homoeoteleuton.

[111] These words are added to make sense of the σύν-compounds, which by their very nature cannot refer to Gentiles' experiencing these realities together among themselves. The Majority text tradition has added an αὐτοῦ ("his"), which detracts some from Paul's obvious concern over Gentile participation in the promises made to Israel.

Christ Jesus for the sake of you Gentiles," he apparently feels compelled not only to justify the assertion of v. 3, but also to do so in a way that includes himself among the prophets. Thus in vv. 3–5 there are three interlocking assertions: that this "mystery" has been revealed to Paul himself; that they should be able to recognize it by what he has just written (probably 2:1–22); but that what really legitimizes him is that the Spirit, the source of all Christian revelation,[112] has revealed this mystery to "the holy[113] apostles and prophets." One can now understand the reason for the inclusion of "the prophets." As an apostle Paul was responsible for the *founding* of churches, especially among the Gentiles; as a prophet he was given to *understand* what God had done in Christ on behalf of the Gentiles. Hence the "revelation" that came to him did so because the revelation of the mystery was given to Christ's holy apostles and prophets. By this circuitous third person affirmation, he simultaneously affirms that the revelation has come to a much larger circle than just himself, while at the same time he includes himself within that circle.

This in turn helps to explain why the apostles and prophets serve as foundational ministries for the church—because through their ministry, based on the revelation of the Spirit, the church has been established among the Gentiles, "built" in such a way that it includes Jew and Gentile together as one people of God. It is in this same context we may now return to 1:17 with a better sense of understanding, especially as to why "the Spirit of wisdom *and insight*" of Col 1:9 was altered to "the Spirit of wisdom *and revelation* in their knowledge of God." It is through the Spirit's revelation that his readers will be able also to understand their place in the people of God.

That the *revelation* of God's "mystery" comes *by the Spirit* is a note that has already been struck by Paul in 1 Cor 2:6–12; that the content of the "mystery" has changed merely reflects what happens often in Paul

---

[112] Because of the word order, τοῖς ἁγίοις ἀποστόλοις αὐτοῦ καὶ προφήταις ἐν πνεύματι, some have argued that ἐν πνεύματι modifies "prophets" only (Eadie 218–19, who leans this way before rejecting it; Schlier 150–51, Schnackenburg 133–34; cf. Lincoln 180, who gives it credence before [rightly] rejecting it). Not only is that awkward in the highest degree, but it misses the connection with v. 3—which is the point after all—not to mention missing Pauline usage, even in this letter. On this use of ἐν πνεύματι see on 2:18 and 22 above; on its usage in Paul, see ch. 2 above.

[113] The use of this adjective to describe the apostles and prophets, and in the third person, is one of the items that gives reason to pause as to Pauline authorship. On the one hand, this sounds like someone from a later time looking back. On the other hand, it is equally difficult to understand how a pseudepigrapher could have made such a gaffe and then write in v. 8 that Paul is the least of all the saints. One can at least explain Paul's own detachment in v. 5 in light of v. 3; but it is especially difficult to understand why someone writing in Paul's name, who has caught all the subtleties of his thought and language, would not have written, "to *us* apostles and prophets." The usage itself reflects Paul's Jewish background; cf. Luke's use of "his holy prophets" in Luke 1:70 and Acts 3:21, in the "Semitic" materials in these two works.

from letter to letter, as the historical context changes (see n. 107 above). What is less certain is both the nature and the timing of the "revelation." This language occurs in Gal 1:15–16 to refer to Paul's basic revelatory experience on the Damascus road; in Gal 2:2 and 1 Cor 14:6, 26, 30 (cf. 13:2) it refers to those kinds of special ad hoc "revelations" that prophets receive for the sake of the community; while in 2 Cor 12:1 it refers to visionary kinds of experiences. The usage here, however, seems to correspond to none of these, but more to that found in 1 Cor 2:10, where revelation does not refer to a specific visionary or revelatory experience as such, but to the revelation by the Spirit that comes to the believing community, and especially its apostles and prophets, having to do with the overall nature of the gospel. This in turn is quite in keeping with the prayer in 1:17, that this kind of revelation by the Spirit might be theirs as well.

7 At the end of this long sentence (from v. 2) Paul refers to his ministry in nearly identical language to that of Col 1:29, "in keeping with the working of his power." As in that passage (q.v.), this is one of those uses of the term δύναμις ("power") in which, because of Paul's usage in similar contexts elsewhere, one is tempted to hear the word as almost interchangeable with "Spirit." Or at least this reflects the near redundancy that we will meet in the next text (v. 16), where we read that God is at work in him "through the power of the Spirit." In any case, Paul's understanding of his own ministry is encapsulated in this clause: (a) he himself is a servant [of Christ or the gospel, is to be understood], (b) as a direct result of "grace that as been given to him," which (c) is made effective by the empowering of the Holy Spirit.

EPHESIANS 3:14–21

With this well-known prayer and benediction Paul finally concludes the prayer report begun in 1:15, but now as a second prayer report, which, though linked to the first in a number of ways, at the same time anticipates what comes next (4:1–6:20).[114] What is striking is that he begins "for this reason" (cf. v. 1), then scarcely refers to the content of 1:20–3:13. Instead, one hears echoes of the opening blessing (1:3–14) and prayer report (1:16–19) and catches a glimpse of the ethical dimension of life in Christ that will be taken up next. At the same time, it is filled with language that permeates this letter, in this case especially various "empowering" terminology.

Since the ensuing exhortations also follow logically the argument of 2:1–22, however, one may assume that the content of that argument is fully presupposed in this prayer, and in fact is the ultimate reason for

---

[114] Cf. Robinson 82.

it.[115] It does no good for Jew and Gentile together to have access to God and for them in turn to be his family and to be built together into the temple of God's present habitation if they do not have the same kind of love for one another that God had for them both as demonstrated through the death of Christ. Thus "for this reason" Paul prays as he does here, and for the same reason he inserts "with all the saints" in the middle of the prayer.

As with all such moments in this letter, it is a single Greek sentence, full of complexities both in its language and in determining how some of the modifiers function. Our interest is in the mention of the Spirit in v. 16 and its relationship to the indwelling Christ in v. 17. To get at these a brief overview of the whole is needed. The basic parts of the content may be displayed thus:

> [16]*that* [ἵνα]
> [God] might grant you
> > [1a] that you be strengthened   in the inner person
> > > with power
> > > through his Spirit
> > [1b] [17]that Christ dwell   in your hearts
> > > through faith
> > > being rooted and grounded in love,
> > *so that* [ἵνα]
> > [18]you may be able
> > > [2a] to grasp   the breadth, length, height, depth
> > > > with all the saints
> > > [19]and
> > > [2b] to know   the love of Christ that surpasses knowledge
> > > *so that* [ἵνα]
> > > [3] you might be filled
> > > > unto all the fullness of God

Despite the complexities, the sequence of ideas is manageable.[116] The concern is that (1) by the presence of Christ through God's empowering Spirit, (2) they come to know the "unknowable" love of Christ so that (3) they thereby might be filled with all the fullness of God. Their own redemption as the result of the God's love manifested in Christ lay at the heart of the opening *berakah*; that they themselves so live in love toward one another lies at the heart of the succeeding exhortations. This prayer thus serves as the transition between these two expressions of love: God's love for us in Christ, and ours for one another in Christ. This is how we are filled up to "the fullness of God."

---

[115] Cf. Schlier 146, Arnold, *Ephesians*, 86; otherwise Meyer 179, who denies the link between vv. 1 and 14 and sees "the reason" as referring to Paul's affliction in v. 13. But this seems unlikely.

[116] This is true even of other schemes, such as those who see the three ἵνα clauses as parallel, or the second two as parallel and dependent on the first.

The concluding doxology (vv. 20–21) is in praise of the God whose power, for which Paul has just prayed, is able to bring it off, so that his glory will be manifested in the church (composed of Jews and Gentiles who love one another) both now and forever. The connection of v. 20 with v. 16 seems obvious and therefore also needs to be looked at in terms of the Spirit.

EPHESIANS 3:16–17

[16]that in accordance with the riches of his glory he [God] might grant you to be strengthened with power through his Spirit in the inner person, [17]so that Christ may dwell in your hearts through faith, . . .

The mention of the Spirit in this prayer appears in the first step of the sequence, that God strengthen them with power through the Spirit in the inner person. Three matters concern us: the relationship between "with power" and "through the Spirit," the meaning of "the inner person," and the relationship of this clause and these phrases to the next clause that speaks of Christ's indwelling their hearts.

1. The two phrases "with power" and "through his Spirit"[117] sit on either side of the infinitive "to be strengthened."[118] There can be little question that the second functions to elaborate, or give content to, the first. The first emphasis lies on God's empowering; but in this case Paul ensures that his readers understand the source of such empowering—it is by God's own Spirit. Thus we meet again a common collocation of terminology,[119] which derives ultimately from the OT and which Paul has in common especially with Luke in the NT.[120] This "interpretation" of "power" in terms of the Spirit leads one to conclude that the power of the Spirit is also in view in v. 20 as well as in 1:19. As with Rom 15:13 (q.v.), this passage shows that for Paul the "power of the Spirit" is not only for more visible and extraordinary manifestations of God's presence, but also (especially) for the empowering necessary to be his people in the world, so as to be true reflections of his own glory.

2. This strengthening in turn is to take place "in the inner person."[121] This is a uniquely Pauline phrase in the NT, used to refer to the interior

---

[117] Gk. διὰ τοῦ πνεύματος αὐτοῦ; the αὐτοῦ clearly refers to God in this case.

[118] Gk. κραταιωθῆναι; cf. 1 Cor 16:13. Luke uses the combination of this verb with the Spirit to refer to the growth of the John the Baptist in Luke 1:80 (cf. Luke 2:40 of the young Jesus).

[119] On this matter see the discussions of 1 Thes 1:5; 1 Cor 2:4; 2 Cor 6:6–7; Rom 15:13, 19; and 2 Tim 1:7, where this collocation appears, as well as of 2 Thes 1:11; 1 Cor 4:20; 2 Cor 4:7; and Col 1:29, where "power" language most likely refers to the Spirit. Cf. on 1:19 and 3:7 above.

[120] See Luke 1:17, 35; 4:14; Acts 1:8; 10:38; for the OT see pp. 905–7 below.

[121] Gk. εἰς τὸν ἔσω ἄνθρωπον, a phrase that is unique to Paul in the NT (cf. 2 Cor 4:16; Rom 7:22). This is not the same as the "new person" in Col 3:10 (cf. Eph 4:24 below), where the contrast is between "before and after" becoming a believer. In Paul

of our being. This is not only the seat of personal consciousness, but the seat of our moral being.[122] In this regard, therefore, it gives objective expression to concepts which occur elsewhere in terms of "indwelling" or "in the heart," both of which occur in the next clause. Thus, when Paul elsewhere says that God dwells in us by his Spirit, in another context he could say that God dwells in our inner person by his Spirit. Likewise when he refers to the Spirit being given "into our hearts" (2 Cor 1:22), that amounts to the same thing that is said here: that God strengthens us in "our inner person" by the power of the Spirit, the goal of which is to know Christ's love, not just cognitively, but experientially.

This phrase, of course, with its companion in the next clause, "in your hearts," refers to the experience of Christ and the Spirit at the individual level. Even though the emphasis throughout this letter, including the rest of the prayer, is on the people of God as a community of believers in the world, one both enters that community and lives out the life of Christ within it at the individual level. Hence Paul prays that all of them will know this Spirit-empowering in their inner persons. But it is not so that the individual believer will "be blessed," as it were, but so that they might live out the life of Christ *together*, that is, so that the "one body of Christ" composed of Jew and Gentile together might really work.

3. That leads to the more difficult question of the function and relationship of this clause to the next. Despite my structural analysis above, this second clause is probably to be understood as dependent on the first one. But it is not dependent in a consequential way, as though they need to be strengthened by the Spirit so that Christ might be able to dwell in their hearts.[123] Rather, this clause is be understood as an elaboration/explanation of the first one.[124] This is what it means for them to be strengthened by the Spirit in the inner person, namely, that Christ himself thus dwells in their hearts; all of this transpires by faith. This means, therefore, that in keeping with Rom 8:9, the way that Christ dwells within the believer, and by extension within the believing community, is in the same way that in 2:22 Paul expressly says that God dwells among them, namely, by the Spirit.

This is the fifth time in the corpus that Paul speaks of Christ as indwelling the believer.[125] His more usual way of speaking about "indwell-

---

even the unregenerate person in Rom 7:22 has an "inner person" that can recognize the Law to be good.

[122] Cf. Meyer 178: "the essence of man which is conscious of itself as an ethical personality."

[123] As e.g., Eadie 246–47, Salmond 314, and Wood 51 would have it.

[124] So also Barth 1.369–70; cf. Schnackenburg 149, as well as most of those who see the two clauses as parallel and equally dependent on the verb "give" (e.g., Meyer 179–80, Abbott 96, Findlay 188, Westcott 151, Hendriksen 181, Schlier 169, Gnilka 184, Mitton 133, Bruce 326–27, Lincoln 206, Arnold, *Ephesians*, 89).

[125] See above on Gal 2:20 and Rom 8:9–10; cf. 2 Cor 13:5 and Col 1:27.

ing" is by the Spirit. As with the other passages, Paul most likely intends that Christ lives in the heart of the believer by the Spirit. As with Gal 2:20, the reason for speaking this way in this context is that the emphasis rests ultimately on Christ and his love being present in the believers, and finally through them unto the larger context of the people of God.

The result of all of this is that the prayer, in keeping with other such moments in Paul, asks God by his Spirit to produce the fruit of the Spirit in their lives, the same love for one another that Christ has for them. Not only so, but in its own way this reflects the theological concern that Christian ethics is basically having "Christ formed in us," so that we reflect the character of God as that is disclosed to us in his Son. Being filled to all the fullness of God means to have God's character reproduced in the life of the believer by the power of the Spirit. That this is the essence of things is demonstrated by the doxology that follows, where "what we ask" has to do with Christ's love being manifest in the church, "according to the power that is at work *in/among* us." For Paul this is the ultimate empowering of the Spirit, where the indwelling Spirit of God, who is also the Spirit of Christ, reproduces the likeness of God's character in our lives; ultimately this is what the fruit of the Spirit is all about.

EPHESIANS 3:20–21

[20]*Now to the one who has the power*[126] *to do exceedingly beyond what we ask or think, according to the power that is at work in/among us,* [21]*to him be glory in the church and*[127] *in Christ Jesus unto all the generations of the ages of the ages. Amen.*

That this doxology not only follows the preceding prayer, but includes some of the language of that prayer ("according to the power at work in us"), not to mention the language of prayer itself ("what we ask"), indicates that it is not a general doxology but belongs to this prayer in particular.[128] "The power that is at work in us" is precisely what was said above in vv. 16–17: "to be strengthened by his power through the Spirit in the inner person," which takes the form of "Christ [and thereby his love] dwelling in our hearts by faith."[129] It is this

---

[126] Gk. τῷ δυναμένῳ, ordinarily rendered, "who is able." Our translation reflects the clear ties with the "power" terminology in this prayer.

[127] Probably in the interest of theological precision, the later textual tradition omits this καί, so that it reads "in the church, by Christ Jesus."

[128] Contra Wood 52–53, e.g., who sees it as "the climax of the first half of Ephesians," which in a sense is true; but to say that at the expense of seeing it as the doxology of this prayer is to miss too much.

[129] So Findlay 205: "This power is the same as that he invoked in verse 16—the might of the Spirit of God in the inward man"; cf. Salmond 318, Mitton 136, Barth 1.375, Bruce 320, Lincoln 205. Given this seemingly obvious connection, one is

combination, the collocation of "with power through the Spirit" in v. 16 and the present combination, "power at work in us,"[130] that makes one think that the Spirit is in view in 1:19 as well (q.v.).

If the emphasis in vv. 16–19 is on Christ himself, and his love, as the way the empowering of the Spirit works in the church, then the emphasis here is on the empowering of God to bring it to pass. In both cases, therefore, as throughout the corpus, the Spirit is obviously at the heart of things for Paul, in terms of the working out of present life in Christ. But also as throughout the corpus, the Spirit is not front and center in the actual theological spelling out of things. He is there, to be sure, and he is frequently mentioned because he is there, but for Paul the center of things is always to be found in Christ himself, by whom God has effected so great salvation, a salvation worked out at the everyday level through the power of the Spirit.

EPHESIANS 4:1–16

With the opening exhortation of this section, Paul in effect also defines his third major concern in the letter, that they live in keeping with their "calling" that he has set forth in the first three chapters. This section also sets the stage for what follows in 4:17–6:9, which spells out in some detail how the exhortation is to work out in various community and household relationships.

Because of the (apparently) parenthetical material in vv. 7–10, the "logic" of this section is not easily seen. But the passage does in fact cohere. The exhortation, that they live worthy of their calling by maintaining "the unity of the Spirit" (vv. 1, 3), is accompanied by the necessary virtues for such unity (v. 2) and its Trinitarian basis (vv. 4–6). This leads Paul to reflect on the gifts (ministries) necessary for it (vv. 7–11) and on the role of such ministries in light of the opening exhortation: to equip the whole body for "ministry," so that it might "grow up" into a healthy (mature) body, with Christ at the head and all of the body drawing its life-forces from him as it grows into his likeness (vv. 12–16).

Our interests lie in vv. 3 and 4–6, where the Spirit is mentioned directly, and in v. 11, where the Spirit is assumed at least in the mention of prophets.[131]

---

surprised by the number of commentaries that do not mention it (Meyer, Eadie, Abbott, Robinson, Westcott, Scott, Schlier, Hendriksen, Gnilka, Wood, Schnackenburg, Patzia, Arnold).

[130] Gk. κατὰ τὴν δύναμιν τὴν ἐνεργουμένην ἐν ἡμῖν; cf. 1:19 τὸ ὑπερβάλλον μέγεθος τῆς δυνάμεως αὐτοῦ εἰς ἡμᾶς τοὺς πιστεύοντας κατὰ τὴν ἐνέργειαν τοῦ κράτους τῆς ἰσχύος αὐτοῦ.

[131] It should also be noted that several scholars (e.g., Abbott 116; Lincoln, *Paradise*, 156–63 [comm. 243–47]; G. B. Caird, "The Descent of Christ in Ephesians

EPHESIANS 4:1–6[132]

¹*Therefore, I, the prisoner in the Lord, beseech you to walk worthily of the calling by which you were called,* ²*with all humility and gentleness, with forbearance, bearing with one another in love,* ³*making every effort to maintain the unity of the Spirit in the bond of peace.* ⁴*[There is] one body and one Spirit, even as also*[133] *you were called in one hope of your calling,* ⁵*one Lord, one faith, one baptism,* ⁶*one God and Father of all, who is over all and through all and in all.*[134]

This opening exhortation, followed by its Trinitarian basis, is the "topic sentence" for the rest of the letter (to 6:9). That is, all of the subsequent exhortations should be understood as a kind of "spelling out" of what it means to walk worthily of their calling, to do so in love and thus to maintain the unity of the body. At the same time, it reaches back to pick up the essential matters from chs. 1–3 (their calling, the prayer for love, the people of God as one body in the Spirit, and the Trinitarian basis of everything).

The exhortation itself is straightforward (v. 1). It is followed (v. 2) by a series of three modifiers that include four graces (humility, gentleness, forbearance, love) necessary for the final participial clause (v. 3), which gives the aim of the exhortation (to maintain the unity of the Spirit in the bond of peace). This final clause leads Paul to state in a kind of confessional way the Trinitarian basis of the exhortation. The central role of the Spirit in all of this can scarcely be missed. Not only (1) is their unity expressly stated as coming from the Spirit, but (2) four of the five graces listed in vv. 2–3 are among the fruit of the Spirit in Gal 5:22–23; and (3) in the Trinitarian confession that follows, pride of place is given to the Spirit, precisely because the *one body*, which is Paul's present concern, is the result of their common experience of the *one Spirit*, whose

---

4:7–11," *SE* II [ed. F. L. Cross; Berlin, 1964] 535–45) consider the descent of Christ in v. 10 to be a reference to the gift of the Spirit at Pentecost. But this view has very little in its favor contextually: it is based on an association of Ps 68 with Pentecost (how would the recipients have known this, one wonders?) and the mistaken notion that Paul (or the Paulinist) had a "Spirit Christology" (see the refutation of this idea in ch. 13 below). The most telling blow against this view, of course, is Paul's insistence that the one who descended is none other than he who ascended, who can only be Christ. Thus, without a Spirit Christology the view does not work at all, and there is simply no such Christology in Paul.

[132] *Bibliography:* F. **Martin**, "Pauline Trinitarian Formulas and Church Unity," *CBQ* 30 (1968) 199–219; R. R. **Williams**, "Logic *Versus* Experience in the Order of Credal Formulae," *NTS* 1 (1954) 42–44.

[133] Several MSS, including some early ones (B 323 326 pc lat syᵖ sa bo), omit this καί, either by accident or as unnecessary to the sense.

[134] The Western tradition, followed by the later Byzantines (D F G Ψ Maj lat sy), try to "rescue" Paul from what could be understood as something too universalistic and insert a ἡμῖν here (= "in us all").

presence in their lives is also the predicate of their *one hope*. Each of these matters needs closer scrutiny.

2 Although the Spirit is not mentioned in this series of modifiers, one suspects that Paul intended his readers to understand them as the work of the Spirit, since he is the key to the unity that is here being urged. Grammatically, the whole series modifies the main verb; conceptually, they belong with the final participial clause toward which all of this is heading. Thus:

The exhortation	[that you] walk worthily of [your] calling,
The necessary	with all humility[135]
virtues	and
	gentleness
	with forbearance
	bearing with one another
	in love
The goal	making every effort to maintain[136] the unity of the Spirit
	in the bond of peace.

Only as humility, gentleness, and forbearance exist among them—those virtues that stand in such direct opposition to the flesh with its self-centeredness—do they have any hope for maintaining the unity of the Spirit. The mention of forbearance leads directly to the first participial phrase, "*bearing* with one another *in love*," which is paired with the final phrase spelling out the goal of the exhortation of v. 1: that by such forbearing love they maintain the unity of the Spirit that expresses itself in a community characterized by *shalom* (peace, wholeness).

What needs to be noted here is that even though his recipients would not have known it, four of the five virtues in this sentence occur in the ninefold list of the fruit of the Spirit in Gal 5:22–23 (gentleness, forbearance, love, peace).[137] The point to make, of course, is that the unity that is theirs by virtue of their common experience of the Spirit will be maintained only as the Spirit also produces the virtues necessary for it.

The phrase, "the unity[138] of the Spirit,"[139] recalls in a very direct way 2:18, where Paul says that through Christ we both (Jew and Gentile)

---

[135] Gk. ταπεινοφροσύνης, the only virtue in the present sentence that does not appear in the list of Spirit fruit in Gal 5:22–23. But see esp. Col 3:12, where it makes a similar list of "Spirit fruit," and Phil 2:3, where it likewise serves as the virtue necessary for harmony in the community of faith.

[136] Gk. τηρεῖν, which can bear either the nuance "guard" or "maintain" (as most interpreters). The latter seems more likely, since the context suggests something more pro-active, rather than simply defensive.

[137] Noted also by Bruce 334; cf. Hemphill, *Gifts*, 164.

[138] Gk. ἑνότης, found only here and in v. 13 in the NT.

[139] Some earlier scholars (e.g., Calvin 267–68) held the view that this phrase means "unity of spirit," that is, a kind of *esprit de corps* among themselves, while

together in the one Spirit have access to God. That is, even though finally at the practical level this will have to do with personal relationships within the community, in its first instance it refers to the "union" of the two peoples into the one new humanity, the one new people of God. The "unity of the Spirit" does not refer to some sentimental or esoteric unity that believers should work toward. Rather, Paul is speaking of something that exists prior to the exhortation. Whether they like it or not, their lavish experience of the Spirit, which they have in common with all others who belong to Christ, has made them members of the one body of Christ, both on the larger scale and in its more immediate expression in the local community and in their own (believing) households. So they may as well get on with "liking it" and demonstrate as much by the way they live. All of this, then, underscores that for the unity of Jew and Gentile to happen on the larger scale, it must first of all happen among people who regularly rub elbows with one another. They *are* the one body of Christ by their common life in the Spirit; the exhortation is that they bend every effort to maintain this unity of which life together in the Spirit is the predicate.

As elsewhere in Paul,[140] the word that best describes the nature of their "unity of the Spirit" is "peace," here expressed in terms of "the bond[141] of peace."[142] Along with Rom 14:17 and 15:13, this passage is the clear indication that for Paul "peace" as fruit of the Spirit refers not so much to inner tranquility as to the necessary *shalom* that Christ has effected, in bringing an end first of all to the hostility between God and people, and secondly to the similar hostility between people(s). Since Christ *is* our *peace*, who has made of the two one new people of God, they are here being urged to maintain their "oneness," which has bound them together in peace. "The war is over; let us keep the peace" is Paul's point. Again, that will necessarily first express itself in family and community relationships; hence most of the exhortations of 4:17–6:9 are against

---

others understood it as referring to the human spirit (both Robinson 178 and Westcott 57–58 lean this way). Both the context and Pauline (and contemporary) usage make these views all but impossible (see esp. on Phil 1:27 below).

[140] See above on Gal 5:22 (under "peace"); Rom 14:17; 15:13.

[141] Gk. σύνδεσμος, referring to that which holds something together. The genitive τῆς εἰρήνης is almost certainly appositional (= "the bond that consists in peace," BAGD; cf. Meyer 197, Eadie 271, Salmond 321, Abbott 107, Schlier 185, Hendriksen 184).

[142] There is some debate as to whether the ἐν is to be understood as instrumental (e.g., Hendriksen 184–85, Mitton 139, Wood 55, Schnackenburg 164–65, Stott 152, Patzia 230, Lincoln 237) or locative (e.g., Meyer 197–98, Eadie 271–72, Salmond 321, Abbott 107, Hemphill, *Gifts*, 168). In terms both of Pauline usage and the sequence of these participles and their modifiers the latter is preferred. Peace is not the "means" to unity, but its primary evidence. Thus the first three graces are the prior expressions of the Spirit necessary for unity, love is the means, and peace is the end result.

those various kinds of sins that break "the bond of peace" that Christ has established between and among those who are his.

4–6 Without employing a conjunctive signal and without a verb, Paul follows the opening exhortation with a sevenfold list of "ones" that are common to all of Christian life. The sevenfold list, however, is basically threefold, since it turns out to be one of the more certain and specific Trinitarian passages in the corpus.[143] Here especially a structural display will help the reader to see what Paul has done:

[A] 1   *one* body
       and
   2   *one* Spirit,
       even as also you were called
   3   in *one* hope of your calling,
[B] 4   *one* Lord,
   5   *one* faith,
   6   *one* baptism,
[C] 7   *one* God and Father of all,
       who is   over all
          and
         through all
          and
         in all.

At first blush, and for many scholars after much perusal as well,[144] this looks for all the world as though Paul is citing some early Christian creed. But just as with the benediction in 2 Cor 13:13[14] (q.v.), there are several indicators suggesting that whatever "creedal pool" Paul may have dipped into, the listing is in fact an ad hoc creation, spun off at the moment in light of the present context.[145] As such it reflects the Trinitarian basis on which so much that has preceded has been predicated, and will serve as the basis for what follows. The demonstration of its ad hoc character will also serve as the discussion of the text as a whole:

1. The *order* can scarcely be that of an actual creed, which in Paul and all early confessions takes the order of Father, Son, and Spirit. It is noteworthy that the present order is identical to the ascending order of

---

[143] See above on 1 Cor 12:4–6; 2 Cor 13:13[14]; for the broad range of implicit and explicit Trinitarian assumptions in Pauline soteriological statements, see p. 78n146 and p. 79 on 2 Thes 2:13.

[144] So most contemporary scholars; see the discussion in Lincoln 228–29. Findlay 217 suggested a "spiritual song." Otherwise Barth 2.462–64.

[145] The point to be made is that (*pace* Lincoln) not only can one not demonstrate that a preexisting creed (or creeds) lay behind this material, but that even if it were so, asserting as much is irrelevant. One need not doubt that such materials (in some other order, surely) preexisted, but the present formulation can be easily shown to make good sense in the present context and was therefore "created" for such purposes.

1 Cor 12:4–6, which likewise concludes with the mention of the one God, who "works *all things* in *all people*." In both cases, the Spirit is mentioned first for contextual reasons:[146] in 1 Corinthians because Paul is trying to correct an abuse of Spirit manifestations in the assembly, and here because he has just exhorted them to "maintain the unity of the Spirit in the bond of peace." The *basis* of that exhortation comes from 2:16 and 18. Through Christ both have been reconciled "in the one body" (2:16) and have been granted access to the Father "in the one Spirit" (2:18).

2. The immediate context also explains the reason for the order of the first two items: Paul begins with the one body because that is the primary concern in this entire series of exhortations. He follows immediately with the one Spirit, not only because of the immediate context (v. 3), but also because in Pauline theology the "one body" is the direct result of their immersion in the one Spirit (1 Cor 12:13). In the current context these first two items thus declare both who they are in Christ (one body) and how they became that way (one Spirit). At the same time, this also maintains the order of the prepositional phrases in 2:16 and 18.

3. The next clause (referring to their one hope) even more obviously points to an ad hoc creation, since (a) it quite disrupts what otherwise would have been a nicely balanced "sevenfold basis for unity" and (b) it picks up the argument by addressing the readers in the second person plural. Paul began in v. 1 by reminding them of their calling; he now refers again to that calling, but in light of the Spirit's role first mentioned in 1:13–14. The "calling" to which he has referred in v. 1 is undoubtedly the call to Christ, and therefore the call to Christian "vocation" in the theological sense of that word—Christian life as vocation. But having just mentioned the Spirit (v. 3), he now brings the two (calling and Spirit) together in a clause which points to the eschatological conclusion of their calling, for which the Spirit serves as both evidence and guarantee. Thus, the reason for walking worthy of their calling by maintaining the unity of the Spirit in the bond of peace is that they (Jew and Gentile alike) are *one body* (2:16), made so because of their common experience of the *one Spirit* (1:13–14, 2:18), who serves for them as the surety of their *one hope* (1:14), the final eschatological outcome of their calling (1:18).

4. Having begun with a series of "ones," all related to the work of the one Spirit, Paul cannot quite leave it there, since behind all of this is the *one God* who has effected eternal salvation for them and made them his own people through the *one Lord*. So without elaboration, he continues the enumeration. There is also only "one Lord" (for Jew and Gentile alike), he goes on; and now we see further the ad hoc nature of things. Rather than elaborate on the work of Christ, as he has momentarily on

---

[146] As Williams ("Logic") points out, the order is that of *experience*, not of theological logic.

that of the Spirit (one hope), Paul follows "one Lord" by enumerating two "entry" experiences,[147] whereby believers become associated not only with their "one Lord," but also with the "one body." Hence he adds, "one faith,"[148] referring to the faith in Christ that is common to all who are members of the one body, and "one baptism,"[149] referring to the common response to the one faith in the waters of baptism. As with other passages in Paul and throughout the NT, such an enumeration indicates that baptism was the immediate—and universal—consequence of faith in Christ. Having gone that far, Paul can conclude only with the "one God" who is the ground and source of everything.

Two final observations: First, since this seems so clearly the structure and intent of Paul's sentence, it is especially significant to underscore the "connections" that Paul makes between our common experience of the Christian faith and the members of the divine triad. Whereas the later church commonly associated "hope" with Christ and "baptism" with the Spirit, Paul does not do that, at least not here. Although hope often has Christ as its "object" (as in 1 Thes 1:3), Paul probably associates it with the Spirit in this enumeration for contextual[150] reasons related to his understanding of the Spirit as a primarily eschatological reality (cf. 1:13–14). That is, the mention of "one Spirit" in a context of God's "call" (v. 1) elicits an apparently automatic association with the Spirit, as the guarantor of the eschatological *hope* implicit in their calling. But no such contextual reason exists for the mention of baptism; and this enumeration suggests that for Paul a connection between the Spirit and baptism does not naturally come to mind, whereas it does with Christ (as in Rom 6:1–11). This text, therefore, rather than associating baptism with the Spirit, as has sometimes been asserted,[151] in fact does quite the opposite. It indicates that Paul recognizes no direct relationship with the Spirit and water baptism. Such a relationship was foreign to his own experience as

---

[147] Which best explains why Paul does not mention the Lord's Supper, a question frequently asked in the earlier literature.

[148] Some (e.g., Findlay 223, Westcott 58–59) have suggested that "one faith" refers to its objective content (= *what* we believe) rather than to trust in Christ (= in *whom* we believe), as the vast majority of commentators. That seems especially difficult to sustain under any view of this passage, since the two items qualify "one Lord," and since the second one, "one baptism" can refer only to water baptism as response to the "one Lord." To make "one faith" refer to the gospel, therefore, not only breaks the sequence, where the two associated items are related to the "one Lord," but also adds something extraneous to the present concern. This applies as well to those (e.g., Barth 2.468, Wood 56) who suggest that it can refer to both.

[149] Some more adventuresome souls have actually suggested that this refers to "Spirit baptism," but that is well-nigh impossible in light of the argument and the sequence of this enumeration.

[150] The attempt by Stott 159 to associate "hope" with the "one Lord" founders on the grammar, not to mention on the context and order.

[151] E.g., Patzia 233.

narrated in Acts;[152] it may or may not have existed among others who had come to faith in Christ (the evidence of Acts is varied on this matter). But for Paul there is no clear and direct connection between them. Baptism in water, essential as it was understood to be, followed faith in Christ; the actual "moment" of Spirit reception was probably related more closely to their "one faith." But that is something about which we have little or no Pauline evidence to go on. Both Spirit reception and water baptism belonged to the beginning of life in Christ, but there is no evidence in Paul that they happened at the same time.

Second, as with 1 Cor 12:4–6 and 2 Cor 13:13[14], both the very ad hoc way in which all of this is expressed and its clear delineation of the three "persons" of the Godhead indicate how presuppositional such "Trinitarianism" was for Paul. As always this is "economic Trinitarianism," the Trinity in terms of God's saving activity on our behalf. Moreover, the affirmation about the one God is not at all distressed by associating the "one Spirit" and the "one Lord" on nearly equal terms. One must say "nearly equal" because in all such moments in Paul there is an obvious sense of "subordination" on the part of the Son and the Spirit. But Paul merely *asserts* Trinitarian realities—because he *presupposes* them, based on his and the early church's experience of God as Father, Son, and Spirit. The later church was left to grapple with how the one God can be three and how statements that imply equality stand side by side with those that suggest subordination. Our concern is not to work those out for Paul, but simply to point out that a text like this one clearly has such presuppositions, and we do Paul no favor to suggest otherwise.

EPHESIANS 4:11–12

[11]*And he gave some to be apostles, some prophets, some evangelists, some pastors and teachers*[153] [12]*for the equipping of the saints for the work of ministry, for the building up of the body of Christ;*

This well-known passage comes as something of a surprise, related in part to our difficulty with what immediately precedes (vv. 8–10). The surprise has to do with its relationship to v. 7, whose point v. 11 seems intended to pick up; yet Paul accomplishes this in a way quite different from what that sentence might lead one to expect.

The whole began with an exhortation to maintain the unity of the Spirit—because they are one body as the result of their common experi-

---

[152] This is the obvious force of the narrative in Acts 9:17–18, in which receiving the Spirit is associated with the laying on of hands, which is then followed by baptism.

[153] The "some" translates the repeated definite article, which is lacking in the case of "teachers." Grammatically this suggests that the last two items are to be understood as closely associated. For a possible solution see the discussion below.

ence of the Spirit and common faith in the one Lord and common
baptism, all of which stems from the one God and Father of all. In typical
Pauline fashion that emphasis is immediately followed by an equal accent on the (necessary) diversity that makes the one body work at all.
Thus v. 7, very much like Rom 12:3–6, emphasizes the "grace" given *to
each one of us*, in keeping with what Christ has apportioned to each one.
On the basis of our reading of Romans (cf. 12:6–8), we might well have
expected some delineation of these various graces, pointing out both the
unity of the body and the role of the many within that unity. What
happens instead is that the final phrase in v. 7 ("according to the measure
of the gift of Christ") prompts a digression based on Ps 68:18 [LXX 67:19]
vindicating Christ as the dispenser of gifts to the church. But in keeping
with the concerns of this letter, Paul "interprets" the language of "ascent" in that text so as to link Christ's giving of gifts with the cosmic
scope of his victory over the powers.

But when Paul returns in our passage to what he began in v. 7, a
decided shift also takes place. From the "each one" as *recipients* of gifts
in v. 7, and in light of vv. 8–10, Paul now enumerates the *nature* of some
of the "gifts" themselves and their function for the building up of the
body so that it might mature in its unity. Thus, instead of listing ways
that "grace has been given *to each of us*," he lists some of the gifted people
who are themselves gifts to the church. This results in a passage that
began very much like Rom 12:3–8 but ends up looking more like 1 Cor
12:28, where a similar "shift" has taken place. But unlike 1 Corinthians,
where Paul returns to the emphasis on the giftedness of "each one," here
he elaborates on the role of these ministries for the carrying out of the
imperative in vv. 1–3. The return to "each one" takes place in our passage
in v. 12,[154] in the form of "the saints" who have been "equipped" by the
ministries he lists. These ministries empower the whole body to carry out
its ministry[155] of building up the body for maturity, soundness, and
unity, drawing its life-flow from its one head, Christ Jesus.

Our interest lies with the mention of the "ministries" in v. 11, which
have several interesting features. First, we note that Paul lists *people*, who

---

[154] So also Findlay 223, Salmond 331.

[155] This is based on an understanding of the sequencing of prepositions in v. 12,
so that the πρός which immediately follows the enumeration of people expresses
penultimate purpose, while the paired εἰς phrases that follow indicate the ultimate
goal, that of the ministry of the saints in building up the body. Cf. Findlay 238, Salmond
331, Robinson 182, Westcott 63, Mitton 151, Barth 2.478–81 (argued for in detail),
Stott 166, Bruce 349. This seems to be the natural sense of the prepositions (cf.
Robinson, Westcott, Bruce; contra Lincoln 253); for all three to qualify the enumeration of v. 11, one would expect all three to be the same. Otherwise Meyer 219, Eadie
358, Abbott 119, Lincoln 253 (related to his view of authorship), and E. E. Ellis (*Pauline
Theology: Ministry and Society* [Grand Rapids: Eerdmans, 1989] 4n11; related to his
view of ministry).

function in certain ways, not gifts or ministries per se. Noticeably missing is the term χαρίσματα, but neither is there any other term designating who they are (gifts, ministries, leaders, officers, etc.). As in 1 Cor 12:28 and Eph 2:20 (3:5) above, and especially in light of v. 7 and of the function of the ministries in v. 12 to "equip the saints," the enumeration almost certainly has to do with *function*, not with office.[156] Also as with all such enumerations, they are ad hoc and probably representative, not exhaustive or definitive. Whatever else, the people are to be understood as gifted in keeping with "the gift of Christ that has been apportioned" to them (v. 7); they are therefore to function in light of that gifting. Surprisingly absent also is any mention of the Spirit; but his presence can be assumed not only because of the mention of "prophets," but also because of the partial correspondence of this list to that of 1 Cor 12:28.

Second, the nature of the list itself is intriguing. We have already met "apostles and prophets" (2:20, 3:5), and their "foundational" role in establishing the churches. Moreover, "apostles, prophets, and teachers" also appear in 1 Cor 12:28, and in this order—except that in the present instance prophets and teachers are separated by two words that occur in no other such enumeration in the Pauline corpus: evangelists and shepherds. What we are to make of this list, in terms of function within the church, is moot—although some speculations are given with a great deal more certainty than we have data to support. The most probable suggestion[157] is:

(1) In light of 2:20 and 3:5 and the fact that Paul himself functioned as both apostle and prophet, the first three designations refer primarily, though in the case of prophets and evangelists not exclusively, to *itinerant ministries* among the early churches. Itinerant workers founded churches by evangelizing and built them up through prophetic utterances. There can be little question that this is the understanding of the term "apostle" in Paul's letters.[158] Since the itinerant Timothy is called upon to do the work of an "evangelist" (2 Tim 4:5), with no mention of "shepherd," and since Luke designates the itinerant Philip in the same way, this term seems therefore also to refer to an itinerant ministry.[159]

---

[156] Contra almost all of the older commentaries and a few more contemporary ones (some of whom like Lincoln are prone to say "both-and"). So much was "office" engraved on the world view of an earlier time that Abbott 119 rejects the most probable understanding of v. 12 (preceding note) on the grounds that "where offices in the Church are in question, διακονία can only mean official service; and this does not belong to the saints in general." This seems to be a most distorted understanding of διακονία in Paul.

[157] The view suggested here has been taken earlier by Meyer 218, Findlay 240, Salmond 330, Robinson 181, Hendriksen 196–97.

[158] On this matter see esp. 1 Cor 9:1–2; 2 Cor 10:15–18; and Rom 15:17–20.

[159] Although there is no inherent reason to limit such a designation in terms of later ministries in the church.

As with 1 Cor 12:28 and Eph 2:20, the more difficult term is "prophet," since prophecy is more clearly a church-wide phenomenon and not at all limited to leadership or to itinerants who prophesied. The reasons for thinking so here (and perhaps 1 Cor 12:28 as well) include its close relationship with "apostle" in this letter as a "foundational" ministry (2:20; 3:5) and Paul's insistence in 1 Cor 14:37 that he was also a prophet and must be recognized as such. This may be further supported by our suggestion that Paul regarded his own letters to be a form of "prophetic word" to his congregations.[160] If so, then "prophet" in this listing may refer not to the congregational prophesying like that in 1 Thes 5:19–22, 1 Cor 14:1–40, or Rom 12:6, but to people like Paul and his co-workers who also functioned in this way among the churches.

This is not to say, of course, that either prophets or evangelists were not local ministries as well, since such is clearly so in the matter of prophecy. At issue finally, in terms of this ad hoc enumeration, is whether Paul is thinking first in terms of a local congregation or of the church in its broader sense. One cannot be certain here; my sense is that Paul is thinking first of the church in the broader sense of the many churches that make up the church. But by that very fact he would also be thinking of its local expression—which is what makes any fine distinctions lie beyond Paul's own point.

(2) The final two designations, in any case, almost certainly reflect the nature of leadership at the local level, when itinerants are no longer present. This might also account for the fact that they are held together by a single definite article in the Greek text, since Paul is not so much thinking of "offices," but of functions, and the same people would tend to function in both of these capacities. Such a view makes sense of the varied nature of our data; but of course none of it can be proved—except to note that v. 14 seems to indicate that all of these ministries were related to the proclamation and exposition of the gospel.

Finally, then, this is a Spirit text by way of context and usage elsewhere. Whether it belongs also to a discussion of *charismata* is moot, since that connection comes only by the circuitous route of usage elsewhere, but in contexts where it is not at all certain that Paul ever intended to designate *people* as *charismata* (1 Cor 12:28; Rom 12:6–8). On the other hand, if we are correct that the emphasis here is as much on the function as on the people themselves, then those various functions may well be styled *charismata*, in keeping with what is plainly Pauline usage. And in any case, Paul sees their function not in terms of office, but of ministering within the church in such a way as to enable others for the ministry of the church as such.

---

[160] See on 1 Cor 5:3–5; Rom 1:9–15; and Col 2:5.

EPHESIANS 4:17–6:9

This section consists of a series of paragraphs that spell out in some detail how local congregations and households should follow the exhortation of vv. 1–3. Although an overall scheme seems to be at work, attempts to refine the flow of thought too closely have not proven altogether satisfactory. At least four major sections can be isolated, three of them on the basis of the repeated exhortation "walk" (cf. v. 1): (1) 4:17–24 are introductory, taking up the typical "before" and "after" motifs, this time in terms of no longer "walking" as Gentiles (vv. 17–19), but as those who have "learned Christ" (vv. 20–24); (2) 4:25–32 then spell out in seriatim fashion a variety of ways, negatively and positively ("not/but"), in which the "new" must be different from the "old"; (3) 5:1–14 continue the former series of admonitions, but now prefaced with an appeal to "walk in love" and thus to "imitate God," whose love was ultimately demonstrated in Christ's own giving of himself for us; (4) 5:15–6:9 then urge them to "walk wisely," which is spelled out first in terms of their community worship (vv. 18–20) and finally in terms of the three basic relationships within the believing household (husbands/wives, parents/children, masters/slaves).

Several matters call for attention: that the body imagery is continued throughout, although spasmodically (4:25; 5:30); that the basic exhortation is to walk in love (5:2, 25, 28), recalling 3:14–21 (cf. 4:2, 15); that most of the sins mentioned express the self-centeredness that contradicts love and disrupts the unity of the body. In this indirect way, therefore, the Spirit lies behind everything, since the Spirit is responsible for the body and its unity (2:18; 4:3–4), and love itself is empowered by the Spirit (3:16). For our present purposes, however, we will look closely only at those texts where πνεῦμα or πνευματικός occur (4:23, 30; 5:18, 19), plus two other texts (5:9, 14) where some in the ancient church thought they saw the Spirit at work.

We need also to note one further matter: the primary focus throughout is on God, his character and his deeds that reflect his character. Thus, Gentiles are aliens to "the life of God" (4:18), whereas those who have "learned Christ" have put on a "new person," created κατὰ θεόν ("according to God"; NIV, "to be like God," 4:24). Those who forgive and walk in love are "imitators of God" (4:32–5:2). The significance of this emphasis for our purposes concerns 4:30, where in the middle of the first set of prohibitions/exhortations, Paul says, "And do not grieve the Holy Spirit *of God*."

EPHESIANS 4:23–24

[23]*And be renewed in the spirit/Spirit of your mind* [24]*and put on the new person, who has been created according to God in the righteousness and holiness of the truth.*

Although most scholars find this occurrence of πνεῦμα to be a straight-forward reference to the human spirit,[161] I find it the most problematic use of this word in the epistle. On the one hand, the phrase, "the πνεῦμα of your mind(s)" lacks any analogy either in the NT or in the whole of ancient Greek literature. Moreover, Paul distinguishes between praying with "my mind" and praying with "my S/spirit" (1 Cor 14:15), in which he refers to his human spirit as the place where the Holy Spirit prays. Consequently, it is not at all clear that this is a kind of redundancy for the inner person, as most seem to think.[162] Not only so, but neither is it clear what precisely such a phrase might mean when referring to the human mind. One can easily understand one's mind being renewed, or one's spirit; but what exactly would "the spirit of the mind" be referring to?[163]

On the other hand, as is also frequently noted, v. 23 has significant conceptual correspondence with Rom 12:2 ("but be transformed by the *renewing*[164] of the mind"). One wonders, therefore, whether this phrase is not a kind of shorthand for, "be renewed in your minds by the Spirit."[165] The advantages of thinking so are maximal: this probably reflects Paul's intent in the Romans passage (q.v.); in any case, it reflects Paul's own theological position;[166] it eliminates the need for circumlocutions to find ways otherwise to give some meaning to the phrase; it is quite in keeping with the overall perspective in the present letter, with its emphasis on the work of the Spirit; and, finally, it seems to fit the context so well, both the larger context that goes back to v. 3 and the immediate context as that is spelled out in the companion clause of v. 24. To urge them to have a mind renewed by the Spirit and to "put on the new person" are two ways of expressing the same reality, placing emphasis, as in Rom 12:1–2, on the role of the "renewed mind" in Christian

---

[161] I can find no one to defend the position reflected in the NIV: "in the attitude of your minds"—for good reason, since it is a well-nigh impossible reading of Paul.

[162] This is by far the majority view both in earlier and present times. The technical term for this "redundancy" is pleonasm (hence the NEB, "in mind and spirit," even though it is questionable whether the Greek will allow as much); but it is doubtful whether "spirit" and "mind" are so closely linked in Pauline thought that they can be "run together" like this (although see on 1 Cor 2:16). In any case, there is absolutely no analogy for it. Robinson 191 suggests the analogy of "his body of flesh" in Col 1:22; but that is hardly analogous, since the genitive "of flesh" is qualitative and means "body consisting of flesh." No one would argue that the present phrase means "the spirit consisting of mind."

[163] The most common answers are either "the spirit by which your mind is governed" (Meyer 249) or "man's innermost self, the real self within" (Mitton 165). But by any reading of the text, this is a most unusual way of expressing such an idea.

[164] Although it must be noted that a different word appears here. In Romans 12:2 Paul uses ἀνακαίνωσις; here the verb is ἀνανέομαι.

[165] So in antiquity by Oecumenius and Theophylact, and more recently by Schlier 220, Gnilka 230, Houlden 319, Schnackenburg 200.

[166] See, e.g., Rom 7:6, Tit 3:5.

ethics, as well as on the "new person" that results from life in Christ empowered by the Spirit.

But there are two things that speak against this view as well, one a matter of grammar, the other a matter of usage:

(1) This is an admittedly awkward way of expressing such an idea, and especially of making the genitive "of the mind" work. But of course that problem exists on all sides.[167] In any case, as strange as the grammar is, it is perhaps not as serious a problem as most opponents of this view imagine. If Paul is speaking of the Spirit, then the genitive functions very much as it does in a phrase like "a spirit of infirmity" (= a spirit that causes infirmity) or "the Spirit of gentleness" (= the Spirit whose fruit is gentleness). Although the analogy is not precise, in this case Paul is urging them to be renewed "by the Spirit of their minds," meaning by the Spirit as he works within your minds. The chief objection to this view is that Paul does not actually say "in the mind," but "of the mind." An additional complaint includes that "it is improbable that God's Spirit would be described as 'of your mind.' "[168] But that simply does not take 1 Cor 14:14 seriously, where Paul, referring to praying in tongues by the Holy Spirit, uses this same kind of "shorthand"—"my πνεῦμα prays." In light of all of this, I would find it easy to throw my lot in on this side of things, were it not for the next matter.

(2) The problem of usage is for me the crucial one. Fully in keeping with usage throughout the corpus,[169] in this letter Paul uses the definite article with πνεῦμα only in those instances where it is qualified by, or qualifies, an accompanying noun that also has the definite article (1:13; 4:30; 6:17) or when it is accompanied by the possessive pronoun (3:16). In all other cases, and especially when it is instrumental or locative, he writes the standard ἐν πνεύματι without the article.[170] One might argue, of course, that this is a case where it is accompanied by a noun qualifier with the article. But that is precisely where grammar and usage coalesce. As noted above, even if we take the genitive to be a kind of shorthand for "of the mind by the Spirit," the genitive "of the mind" no longer truly qualifies πνεῦμα. Thus, on the basis of grammar and usage together, had Paul intended "renewal of the mind by the Spirit," we might have expected him to state it clearly: ἐν πνεύματι τοῦ νοὸς ὑμῶν.

The net result is that one seems to be left with a highly peculiar way of speaking about the interior life of the human person. But, since the original recipients cannot be expected to have been alert to fine points of usage, it seems most likely to me that they would have heard this

---

[167] While most take it as a form of pleonasm, they scarcely deal with the nature of the genitive as such.

[168] Mitton 165; cf. Lincoln 287, and many before them.

[169] See the full discussion in ch. 2 above.

[170] See 2:22; 3:5; 5:18; 6:18.

phrase in terms of the Spirit, either directly or indirectly, as lying very close to whatever renewing work takes place in their own spirits. Probably, therefore, this is yet another instance where we should recognize the human spirit as the first referent, but be prepared also to recognize the Holy Spirit as hovering nearby, since in Paul's own theology, such renewal is indeed the work of the Spirit.

Ephesians 4:30

And do not[171] grieve the Holy Spirit of God in whom you were sealed for the day of redemption.

This is the second of two such solemn interruptions in the series of paraenetic materials that began in v. 25. The first, "and neither give a place to the devil" (v. 27), follows the first two exhortations on speaking truthfully (v. 25) and not sinning in one's anger (v. 26). These are then followed by two further contrasts between the "old person" and the "new": working with one's own hands to provide for the needy vis-à-vis stealing (v. 28); speech that builds others up and benefits those in need vis-à-vis "unwholesome[172] talk" (v. 29). Our text appears right at this point,[173] to be followed in turn by a series of five vices that are to be done away with ("bitterness, rage, anger, shouting, slander"), along with all other evils (v. 31). On the contrary, they are to be kind and forgiving toward one another in the same way that God has forgiven them through Christ (v. 32). These observations can thus be set out in barest outline:

> Do not lie,
> > but speak truthfully;
> Do not sin in your anger;
> > *Neither give room to the devil.*
> Do not steal,
> > but work, and give to the needy;
> Do not speak garbage,
> > but speak what builds up the needy;
> > *And do not grieve the Holy Spirit of God.*
> Get rid of all evils:
> > bitterness, rage, anger, shouting, slander;
> Be kind and forgiving,
> > *just as God has forgiven you in Christ.*

---

[171] This μή is omitted in P[46], thus turning the prohibition into an indicative: "And you are grieving the Holy Spirit of God." Although this is the "more difficult" reading, it is so suspect contextually that it must be judged a solecism by that scribe.

[172] Gk. σαπρός, which literally means "decayed, rotten" (referring to perishables) or "unsound, crumbling" (referring to nonperishables, including buildings).

[173] The close connection between the Spirit and speech has been noted by Robinson 113, and reemphasized by Lincoln 307–8; see on 4:11 above and esp. on 5:18–19 below.

It does not take much imagination to recognize that all of this is directed specifically toward the concerns in vv. 1–16 that they "maintain the unity of the Spirit" because they are the one body of Christ by the one Spirit. The sins described here destroy relationships within the community of faith; likewise the righteousness here described presupposes life in the believing community. Life in Christ means to live the life of God in the context of "one another" (v. 32).

But one needs also to observe that these exhortations flow directly from vv. 17–24, where the paraenesis began by setting out the two ways of "walking," and concluded with the imagery of putting off the "old person," and of "being renewed in their minds [by the Spirit]" and thereby putting on the "new." These exhortations not only offer specific examples of the two ways of walking, but also indicate their respective sources: the sins that divide and thereby destroy the unity of the body come directly from Satan; to continue in any of them is to grieve the Spirit, who both has "sealed them for the day of redemption" and is the one responsible for the behavior that maintains their unity. And, of course, the pattern for all of this is none other than the living God, whose Holy Spirit is grieved when his people fail to walk in his ways. There are several items about this text as a Spirit text that call for further attention.

1. As elsewhere in Paul,[174] these words not only "echo" the language of an OT passage, in this case Isa 63:10,[175] but at the same time reflect interests similar to that passage (Isa 63:1–19). Thus, after picturing the messianic judgment by him who treads the wine press alone, the prophet applies that oracle to Israel's present situation, but in light of their past. Verse 10 comes at the end of the section describing God's gracious redemption of Israel in the exodus (vv. 7–9), describing Israel's rebellion in terms of "grieving his Holy Spirit." The prophet uses this language because this is his understanding of "the divine presence" in the tabernacle in the wilderness: "It was no messenger or angel but *his presence* that saved them" (v. 9)[176]—a direct recall of Exod 33:12–14. This in turn

---

[174] See esp. the discussion of Phil 1:19; cf. Rom 2:29.

[175] Paul's Greek reads καὶ μὴ λυπεῖτε τὸ πνεῦμα τὸ ἅγιον τοῦ θεοῦ; the LXX of Isa 63:10 reads καὶ παρώξυναν τὸ πνεῦμα τὸ ἅγιον αὐτοῦ. That Paul is "citing" the LXX best explains both the unusual "fullness" to the name and the word order. In the only other place where he says something similar (1 Thes 4:8), the αὐτοῦ comes between "the Spirit" and "the holy." The two linguistic differences are easily explained. Paul substitutes τοῦ θεοῦ for αὐτοῦ because in Paul's sentence the pronoun would have no antecedent (but in making the substitution he keeps the word order of the LXX). Paul substitutes λυπεῖτε for a form of παροξύνω because the latter means "irritate" or "vex," and Paul understands the Hebrew וְעִצְּבוּ to mean "grieve" (correctly so; this is the only instance in the LXX where עצב is rendered with παροξύνω).

[176] This reflects the text of the LXX (cf. NRSV, NAB, JB, NEB), which in turn reflects one way of punctuating and reading the Hebrew text. The difficulty lies with the combination בְּכָל־צָרָתָם לֹא צָר. The LXX translator understood בְּכָל־צָרָתָם to go with the

is followed by a call for Yahweh to return to his people's present distress, in which the prophet once more recalls the glories of the exodus. Again in light of Exod 33:12–14 he equates God's presence with his Holy Spirit.[177]

The rest of our reflections on this text do not mean that Paul, by "citing" Isa 63:10 in this way, is necessarily reflecting on the whole of the Isaiah passage; but it would add considerably to our understanding if such were the case. Here is the one certain place in the OT, whose language Paul is "echoing," where the motif of God's presence is specifically equated with the Spirit of God. Such an equation is certain in Paul by his use of the temple metaphor (= the place of God's presence), now understood in terms of the Spirit's dwelling within and among his people.[178] It is likely, therefore, that we should be prepared to hear this text in light of 2:22, where God's dwelling in his temple, the church, is specifically equated with the presence of the Spirit. In any case, the Spirit as God's personal and empowering presence is the key to our hearing Paul's own concerns in this prohibition.

2. It should be noted that this echoing of Isa 63:10 is the only place in the corpus where Paul uses the full ascription, the *Holy* Spirit *of God*.[179] In context this usage is almost certainly intentional, both as an "echo" of Isa 63:10 and for effect.[180] Elsewhere when Paul wants to underscore the relationship of the Spirit to God, he refers simply to "the Spirit of God," and (sometimes) when he wants to emphasize the aspect of holiness he uses the full name, "the Holy Spirit." Here the full ascription is not just a form of solemn speech, calling special attention to the role of the Spirit in ethical life, but also an emphatic declaration that the *Holy* Spirit is none other than the Spirit *of God*. Thus, the ascription itself draws a bead on the concluding words of the introductory paragraph (vv. 23–24): that they are to be renewed in their minds [by the Spirit] and thereby to put on the new person, *created to be like God* in the

---

preceding line ("became their savior in all their distress") and either had צִיר [= envoy] in his Hebrew text or read צִיר for צַר ("distress"). Paul almost certainly knew the LXX in this case, although his (proper) substitution of λυπεῖτε for παροξύνω indicates that he also knew the Hebrew text as well. In any case, the Greek text more accurately reflects the text of Exodus 33, to which the prophet is clearly alluding, than does the more common English translation of the Hebrew ("the angel of his presence saved them," RSV, cf. NIV, NASB).

[177] This is the clinching evidence that the prophet is reflecting on the theme of God's presence = God's Holy Spirit, since he says in v. 14, "The Spirit of the Lord gave them rest," which directly recalls Exod 33:14, "My presence will go with you and I will give you rest."

[178] See on 1 Cor 3:16–17; 2 Cor 6:16; and Eph 2:22.

[179] Gk. τὸ πνεῦμα τὸ ἅγιον τοῦ θεοῦ, although see 1 Thes 4:8, where the companion ascription occurs: "God . . . who gives *his Holy Spirit* [τὸ πνεῦμα αὐτοῦ τὸ ἅγιον]."

[180] So many interpreters (Meyer, Eadie, Salmond, Bruce); cf. Lincoln 307: "that Spirit who is characterized by holiness and who is God himself at work in believers."

righteousness and holiness that come from the truth (the gospel). Both of these aspects—the Spirit as the presence of God and the Spirit's relationship to ethical life—need closer examination.

3. We noted above in the introduction to this section (4:17–6:9) the special emphasis in this paraenesis on God, both as to his character and his deeds that reflect his character. For Paul the goal of the "new creation" is none other than our being recreated in the "image of God" that was rolled in the dust in the Garden. Thus, the "glory of God" is the ultimate purpose of all that God has done for us people and our salvation. But such glory is not simply that which comes to God as the result of his grace in redemption, which is the first and most obvious point of reference for such language.[181] It is also for the "glory of God" that we are to bear the fruit of righteousness (Phil 1:11). That is quite the point of the prayer in 3:14–21: that as we are empowered by the Spirit, Christ might live in us in such a way that we come to know his love and thus *be filled unto the fullness of God.* Paul's purpose in using this language in part, therefore, is that when God's people do *not* live "like God" they thereby grieve the Holy Spirit *of God.*

Our immediate concern, however, is not merely the ethical one—which we will note in a moment—but the personal one. This text joins many others in making it explicit that Paul understood the Spirit in fully personal terms. Using the terminology of Isa 63:10 and reflecting its conceptual context, Paul appeals to his readers not to *grieve* God's Holy Spirit.[182] One can only grieve a person, and our misdeeds grieve God, who has come to indwell us individually and corporately by his Spirit. One of the misfortunes of the language "spirit," and concomitantly of our impersonal images of the Spirit (wind, fire, water, oil), lies right here. Since "spirit" does not tend to call forth personal images, and since our view of God is often laced with a kind of transcendence that keeps him especially distant from our everyday lives, it is easy for us to pass off our sins in a much too casual way. Here, then, is the text that forever reminds us that such sins bring grief to God. Presuppositional to this exhortation is the prayer in 3:16, that we are indwelt by God's empowering presence in the person of his Holy Spirit. Our misdeeds, therefore, which reflect the character of Satan, bring grief—not just to ourselves and the ones whom we have injured, but to the God who in mercy has chosen to

---

[181] See esp. the repeated refrain in the opening *berakah* (1:3–14), "the praise of his glory," which first of all has to do with redemption per se, but finally with the fact that he has created a new humanity out of Jew and Gentile alike. Such a refrain recurs throughout the corpus (2 Cor 4:4, 6, 15; Rom 15:7; Phil 2:11; 1 Tim 1:11), but so does the refrain that by living in keeping with his character we too reflect or reveal that glory (1 Cor 10:31; 2 Cor 3:17–18; Phil 1:11).

[182] Schlier 227 notes that this language stands in sharp contrast to joy, one of the most distinctive evidences of the Spirit's presence.

indwell us. Hence the weightiness of this solemn word to God's people, who are urged to walk worthy of their calling by maintaining the unity of the Spirit: And do not grieve *the Holy Spirit of God.* Do not, as Israel, reject God's very presence, his Holy Spirit, whose dwelling within and among us is the evidence of "salvation" and his giving us "rest."

4. That leads to further words about the role of the Spirit in ethical life from the Pauline perspective. Passages such as Gal 5:16–6:10 and Rom 8:4, 13–14 show that Paul understood the Spirit to be the *empowering* presence of God, enabling the ethical life which has God's glory as its ultimate goal. That note has already been struck in this letter in 3:16, and is the presupposition behind 4:3–4 (and 23, if it refers to the Spirit). Although the present exhortation is expressed negatively, these words presuppose that the Spirit is grieved precisely because he is present to empower us for better things: truthful and edifying speech, giving to the needy, kindness, and forgiveness. But more is involved. As with the emphasis on the full name, the *Holy* Spirit of God, so also the imagery of the Spirit as God's seal speaks to the ethical dimension of life in the Spirit.

This is now the third occurrence of the imagery "seal" in the corpus.[183] The primary referent in 2 Cor 1:21–22 and in 1:13–14 above is to "ownership." By the *seal of the Spirit* God has placed his divine imprint on our lives indicating that we are his—for now and forever.[184] But inherent in this imagery is also the notion of "authentication," and that seems to be the primary referent here. Granted, the final emphasis is on our eschatological future, but in this context Paul is probably urging that by "sealing" us with his Holy Spirit so as to walk in ways that are "like God," God has authenticated us as those who are truly his own. To put that in another way, it is as we live the life of God empowered by his Holy Spirit that we demonstrate ourselves to be the authentic people of God. As always in Paul, the Spirit is the singular identification mark of believers, an identification that is demonstrated precisely at the point where the Spirit replaces Torah in our lives as the one who fulfills the new covenant by indwelling us and thus causing us to walk in the ways of the Lord.

5. We need also to note the eschatological dimension of this text. As we have seen throughout the corpus, this is the first theological reality for Paul regarding the Spirit: he is "the Holy Spirit of promise" (1:13) and is the fulfillment of Jewish eschatological hopes. By his presence in our lives we are guaranteed our certain future. Thus, he urges that they not

---

[183] For a discussion of the imagery, see on 2 Cor 1:21–22; cf. 1:13–14 in the present letter.

[184] My contemporizing language should not obscure an important Pauline point, hinted at by Robinson 194, that in 1:13 this imagery functioned to certify his Gentile recipients of this letter as sharers in God's promises to Israel. By living like Gentiles (4:17), they grieve the Holy Spirit who has thus sealed them for the day of redemption.

grieve the Holy Spirit of God, "by whom you have been sealed *for the day of redemption.*" This language is reminiscent of Rom 8:23, where the Spirit is imaged as the firstfruits of the final redemption, the consummation of our having been "adopted as his children." One cannot be certain why Paul has added this final touch in this instance. It may simply have been the natural continuation of his having decided to refer them back to 1:13–14 with the imagery of the Spirit as God's seal. But it may also be a way of emphasizing that even though the future is certain, guaranteed by the presence of the Spirit, *that future is be lived out in the present* until "the day of redemption." Thus, the Spirit is both the sign of ownership and authentication and the empowering presence of God for living to the glory of God until we finally arrive at the promised glory which is our own inheritance (Rom 8:17).[185]

6. One final word: it is surely not incidental that this exhortation occurs as a balanced response to the first set of exhortations that conclude, "neither give room to the devil." In this letter in particular, which was written in part to reassure its recipients of Christ's victory over the powers, the Spirit plays a leading role in that motif as well. Thus it is fitting in this first series of paraenesis, which follow hard on the heels of the descriptions of the two ways of walking in vv. 17–24, that Paul should set the Spirit over against "the devil." Satan, the prince of the power of the air (2:2), is the "spirit" who leads people in the ways of "the Gentiles," described here in terms of speaking falsehood, giving way to anger, stealing, using unwholesome speech, slander, and all such evils, while it is the "Holy Spirit of God" who leads people in the ways of God that reflect God's likeness. Thus, lying close at hand in this text is also the contrast of the Spirit of God with the "false spirit," the enemy of God's people.[186]

EPHESIANS 5:9

For the fruit of the light[187] *is in all goodness and righteousness and truth.*

Although this is a Spirit text in the *Textus Receptus,* and therefore in the King James Version, there can be little question as to the original text in this case. Later scribes substituted "Spirit" for "light" on the analogy of Gal 5:22, where Paul speaks of the "fruit of the Spirit," which there includes the first member of

---

[185] Some (e.g., Findlay 316, Barth 2.550) have seen here an underlying threat that those who grieve the Spirit risk forfeiting the future. But that is hard to discern in either the imagery or the language of this sentence, which accents the reality of the future, not its possible forfeiture.

[186] On this question see Chotka, "Spirit," chapter 7.

[187] This is the reading of P[49] ℵ A B D* F G P 6 33 81 629 1739* 1881 2464 pc latt sy[p] co; the MajT, anticipated in this case by P[46], has (understandably) changed φωτός to πνεύματος, influenced by Gal 5:22.

the present triad, "goodness." Thus this text adds nothing to our understanding of the Spirit in this letter.

EPHESIANS 5:14

For the light makes everything visible; therefore he [it] says: "Awake, O sleeper, arise from the dead, and Christ will shine upon you."

Although there is no mention of the Spirit in this text, I include it because some early Fathers, especially Theodoret, considered the citation, which alludes to no obvious biblical passage, to be an example of 1 Cor 14:26, where Paul says, "Each one of you has a hymn."[188] Although this suggestion cannot be proved, it does give us an idea as to how some in the early church understood the language "Spiritual songs" in Col 3:16 and Eph 5:19: as an expression of early Christian hymnody. The likelihood of such a suggestion lies with the introductory formula, which Paul used in 4:8 to cite Ps 68:18. Such introductory language for an early hymn puts it into the same category of Spirit inspiration as that of the Psalter. Whereas all of this seems likely, at this point in time it cannot be demonstrated.

EPHESIANS 5:18-21

[18]*And do not be drunk with wine, in which there is dissipation, but be filled with the Spirit, [19]speaking to one another with psalms, hymns, and Spirit[189] songs, singing and making music with[190] your hearts to the Lord, [20]giving thanks always for all things in the name of our Lord Jesus Christ to our God and Father, [21]submitting yourselves to one another in the fear of Christ.*

These well-known words function by way of transition as Paul moves toward bringing closure to the long section of paraenesis that began in

---

[188] "But some interpreters have asserted that he [Paul?] composed some hymns deemed worthy of a spiritual gift; and this is hinted by the divine apostle in the letter to the Corinthians: 'Each of you has a hymn' " (PG 82.844–45). Barth 2.574n83, with others, suggests that this goes back as far as Origen (in the *Catenae*); but Origen does not actually attribute the words to a hymn. He simply says, "But another will say that the apostle is putting forward something spoken by the Spirit for the urging of repentance."

[189] The word πνευματικαῖς is missing in some important early witnesses (P[46] B b d Ambrosiaster). Since the word seems necessary to distinguish "songs" of all kinds from those inspired by the Spirit (see on Col 3:16, where it is firm), it seems more likely that it was omitted because of homoeoteleuton (it follows ᾠδαῖς, which has the same ending), than that it was added by the whole copying tradition on the basis of the parallel in Colossians.

[190] Most of the later MS tradition add an ἐν here in conformity to Col 3:16; it is missing in P[46] ℵ* B 1739 1881, which most likely represents the original text. But in either case the phrase cannot possibly mean "in the heart" as opposed to public, vocal singing (as e.g., Salmond 364, Mitton 192, Wood 73). It is hard to imagine a less likely understanding either of Paul or of early Christian life in the Spirit. When one's heart sings it does not do so silently! Not only so, but the first participle, "speaking to *one another* with songs of all kinds," presupposes the community at worship, not the private life of the individual believer. See further the discussion on Col 3:16.

4:17. With a summarizing "therefore" (v. 15) he reminds his readers a final time that they must give great care as to "how you walk." In doing so, he picks up the theme of the "renewed mind" from 4:23 and urges them to walk "wisely" (v. 15), as those who understand what the will of God is (v. 17). With the words of our text he brings this series of exhortations to conclusion,[191] by urging them to be filled with the Spirit (v. 18), an imperative which he then develops in two directions: first, they need to be full of the Spirit for their corporate worship (vv. 19–20); second, they need to be full of the Spirit in order to maintain the "unity of the Spirit" in their several relationships in a believing household (v. 21), which are then spelled out in detail in 5:22–6:9.

The imperative in v. 18, therefore, plays the key role both to bring the long series of exhortations from 4:17 to its fitting conclusion (as summation of the whole) and to launch Paul into the final series of exhortations that move from relationships in the community in general to the very specific ones within a Christian household.

What is often missed in our English translations is that all of vv. 19–21 take the form of a series of participles that modify the primary imperative in v. 18. In its basic contours the sentence may be structured thus:

> Do not get drunk   on wine,
> But be filled   by/with the Spirit,
>   speaking *to each other*
>   with psalms, hymns, and Spirit songs,
>   singing and making music *to the Lord*,
>   with your hearts
>   giving thanks *to God*
>   for all things
>   in the name of our Lord Jesus Christ
>   submitting yourselves *to one another*
>   in the fear of Christ,
>   wives to husbands, etc.

Our interest is with v. 18 in particular; plus we will briefly examine vv. 19–20 in conjunction with its companion passage in Col 3:16, where the content of this text has already been discussed at some length.

---

[191] Despite most English translations, the imperative "but be filled with the Spirit" is the last one in the series that began in 4:25. The present sentence actually continues through v. 23. But because of the distinct shift in subject matter at v. 22, most translations start a new sentence with the participle in v. 21. In doing so, they help the reader to see that Paul is in fact beginning something new; but that also means the reader fails to see that v. 21 is not an imperative, but a participle dependent on v. 18—and intentionally so, I would argue (*pace* some commentators to the contrary; the so-called imperatival participle is not nearly as certain as some avow, and in this case there is no need for it at all).

18 Although in some ways this looks like a straightforward imperative, it has just enough striking features to give us reason to pause. First of all, readers are slightly unprepared for the opening prohibition, the key to which lies not in Acts 2:13 but in the preceding materials, beginning with v. 8. This whole section (4:17–5:21), one needs to recall, is determined by the initial set of contrasts put forth in 4:17–24 between the "before" and "after" of living like Gentiles but now as those who have "learned Christ." One of the characteristics mentioned in 4:18 of people outside of Christ is that their understanding is "darkened." This motif is then picked up in 5:8, where Paul plays on it in a variety of ways: darkness/light, hidden [shameful]/revealed, sleep/awake, and finally foolish/wise (in terms of how one uses "the time"). This is a common motif among early Christians; it appears in the earliest letter in the Pauline corpus (1 Thes 5:1–11) and emerges again in the paraenesis of Rom 13:11–14. Common to both of these earlier expressions of this motif, and this is where our present text fits in, is the theme of drunkenness, another "night time" activity, one of the deeds of darkness.

This association best accounts for its appearance here.[192] But unlike the earlier development of this motif, where the more natural contrasts to drunkenness—sobriety and decency—are found, here the contrast is between being drunken with wine and being filled by the Spirit, with the tenses of the two imperatives indicating "never do so" in the former case, and "always be so" in the latter. As always in Paul, the emphasis rests altogether on the "but" clause.[193] Paul is not so much telling them not to get drunk—that is assumed under walking in the light and thus walking wisely—as he is urging them continually to live in/by the Spirit. Whether the contrast in this case is triggered by an outsider's view of someone "filled with the Spirit" as in Acts 2:13 is moot.[194] One can only

---

[192] So also Schnackenburg 236 and Lincoln 345–46. This is not a universal view. Some have suggested an association with 1 Cor 11:21, where it is alleged (though doubtful) that drunkenness at the Lord's Table was at issue; this view dates to the nineteenth century (de Wette, Koppe, Holzhausen [cited by Meyer 284]), and has been variously picked up (Findlay, Robinson, Schlier, Gnilka, Houlden; Dunn, *Jesus*). It is argued that the context of worship supports such a view. But in fact there is nothing *in the text* to support it; and Paul's response ("which is dissipation") is much too casual, one would think, if drunkenness at the Lord's Table were really an issue. Furthermore, how would Paul have learned about such dissipation in churches he did not know personally?

[193] So also Bruce 379, a point too often overlooked by interpreters.

[194] So with the intriguing suggestion put forth by many (e.g., Scott 234) and elaborated by C. Rogers ("The Dionysian Background of Ephesians 5:18," *BSac* 136 [1979] 249–57) that the background is to be found in the cult of Dionysus, the god of wine, where in drinking too much wine the "worshipers" experienced any number of frenetic and frenzied kinds of activity (although it is extremely doubtful that this could have been the result of wine alone, since alcohol is a depressant, not a stimulant; very likely the cult had discovered the use of drugs, perhaps of a psychedelic kind,

allow that it might be possible; but one must insist here that the context in which this imperative appears does not emphasize the "ecstatic" character of the Spirit's presence, but the "fullness" of his presence. And this, so that the preceding imperatives might be lived out in an ongoing way and especially so that their worship and lives together in households might be to the praise of God's glory. This imperative, therefore, is not just another in a long string; rather, it is the key to all the others.

But having said that, in terms of Paul's interests, one can scarcely miss the richness of this metaphor. First of all, it is merely another way, a more powerfully metaphorical way to be sure, of repeating Paul's basic imperative found in Gal 5:16: "Walk in/by the Spirit." All truly Christian behavior is the result of being Spirit people, people filled with the Spirit of God, who live by the Spirit and walk by the Spirit. The richness of the metaphor comes in part from its contrast to being drunken with wine and in part from the verb "be filled." Together they do not picture a person who is "drunk on the Spirit," as it were,[195] as if there were virtue in that, but a person—and in this case, a community!—whose life is so totally given over to the Spirit that the life and deeds of the Spirit are as obvious in their case as the effects of too much wine are obvious in the other.

The actual expression of the imperative is unusual: Paul says not, "be full of the Spirit,"[196] as though one were full of Spirit in the same way that another is full of wine, but "be filled by the Spirit," with the

---

with which they laced the wine and kept its adherents coming back! After all, all the frescoes from the cult picture a kind of gaiety and wild dancing that is not usually associated with drunkenness).

[195] This was the common interpretation of my Pentecostal heritage, where the context was scarcely considered and the individual, personal *experience* of the Spirit tended to be uppermost. A similar view, somewhat modified, appears frequently in the literature as well. Thus Meyer 285: "The *contrast* lies . . . in the two *states*—that of intoxication and that of inspiration," and Findlay 344: "For the drunkards of Ephesus the apostle finds a cure in the joys of the Holy Ghost"; cf. Salmond 363, Scott 234, Mitton 190, Barth 2.582.

[196] Gk. πληροῦσθε ἐν πνεύματι. The NT data on the use of this verb in the passive are varied. As the substance of "filling" in Paul alone it takes an accusative (Col 1:9), a genitive (Rom 15:14), or a dative (Rom 1:29); and despite assertions to the contrary it also appears with the preposition ἐν as an instrumental (Gal 5:14). Part of the problem in this instance is that the contrasting οἴνῳ occurs without the preposition; on the other hand, the dative ἐν πνεύματι fits with the other datives in this letter, most likely reflecting "means." But when one asks, "but with what 'substance'?" it is but a short step to seeing the Spirit as that substance as well. Thus, very much as in 3:19, where being "filled unto the fullness of God" means finally to be filled with God himself, so here, being filled by the Spirit means finally to be "full" of the Spirit's presence. In an earlier generation some found this expression so difficult that they were willing to argue that it meant "be filled in one's own spirit" (so Abbott 161–62, Westcott 81, Lenski 619, Beare 714); but there is nothing in Pauline usage, in the immediate context, or in the context of the letter as a whole that allows even the possibility of such a view.

emphasis on being filled to the full by the Spirit's presence. Very likely Paul is recalling the final purpose clause in the prayer of 3:14–19, that they be empowered by the Spirit so that as Christ thus dwells in them by the Spirit they come to be "filled unto the fullness of God" himself. Here, then, is the ultimate imperative in the Pauline corpus: God's people so filled by/with the Spirit's own presence that they come to know God in all his fullness and reflect such in the way they live in relationship to one another and to God himself.

That leads, then, to note finally that one misses too much if this text is completely individualized, as so often happens. True, as with all such moments, the imperative can be responded to only by individuals; and here, indeed, is a great need in the contemporary church, for God's people individually to take this imperative with all seriousness. But in its immediate context the imperative has to do with community life. Here, perhaps, is an even greater need—that God's people collectively be so "full of God" by his Spirit that our worship and our homes give full evidence of the Spirit's presence: by song, praise, and thanksgiving that simultaneously praise and adore God and teach the community, and by the kind of submission of ourselves to one another in which the concern is not "who's in charge around here," but how to love in the family as Christ loved the church and gave himself for her.

So then, Paul urges the communities to whom the letter is written, be filled with the fullness of God by his Spirit, and let that be evidenced not by Spirit-inebriation, but by behavior and worship that give full evidence of God's empowering presence.

19–20 The speech of those filled with the Spirit differs in every possible way from that of those full of wine! For the content and meaning of this set of participles, see the full discussion on Col 3:16. I merely underscore here what I tried to show in the structural display above, namely, that in this case the participles and their modifiers are unambiguous and thereby clear the way for understanding the ambiguous way this text appears in Colossians. As before, singing of all kinds, including Spirit songs, functions both to instruct the believing community and to praise and adore God. The most significant difference in this text from the former one is that the singing in this case is "to the Lord," which in this letter as throughout the corpus can refer only to Christ.

This is another of those subtle moments in Paul in which a "high" Christology surfaces unintentionally. We know from evidence within and without the NT that from earliest times believers "sang hymns to Christ as to God."[197] That such hymning of Christ is accompanied by thanks-

---

[197] These are the words of the younger Pliny in his letter (10.96.7) to the emperor Hadrian requesting information as to what he should do with the Christians he had investigated.

giving directed to "our God and Father" only increases the christological impact. That is, believers, filled with the Spirit, sing hymns to Christ, while also thanking God in the name of Christ for "all things." As always in Paul, God the Father is the ultimate source and goal of all things; but we sing to Christ while we also thank God, precisely because of who Christ is and for what he has done. And all of this is because we are filled with the Spirit. Therefore, one should note in passing, it is doubtful that the "all things" for which one gives thanks refers to all the circumstances of one's life, good or ill, but to the richness of God's blessings that have been lavished on us in Christ.[198] Thus, this passage toward the end of the letter picks up the themes of the *berakah* with which it all began.

We should note finally the subtle, but dynamic, Trinitarianism that emerges in this passage, as in Col 3:16. It all begins and ends with God. We thank him for "all things" that he has done for us in Christ, which have been carried out in our lives by the Spirit. Now, filled with the Spirit, we play it in reverse: singing hymns to Christ that are full of the message of Christ so that we thereby instruct one another, accompanied by thanksgiving to God the Father for all things.

EPHESIANS 6:10–20

Given the nature of ancient rhetoric, in coming to this final section of the letter we also most likely are coming to Paul's primary concern for his recipients. That is, Paul's placing this material in the emphatic final position suggests that he has been intentionally building the letter toward this climax right along. The "powers" have been a concern from the opening words of the *berakah* in 1:3, where the blessings associated with the Spirit belong to God's people "in the heavenlies," in the habitation of the "powers." The reasons for his recipients' being able to experience such blessings "in the heavenlies" are then spelled out in a variety of ways throughout: Christ is portrayed as over the powers for the sake of the church (1:20–23); Gentile believers once subject to them are now, through participation in Christ's resurrection, seated with him in the heavenlies where he is over the powers (2:2–7); Gentiles and Jews as one people of God, God's now revealed mystery, has been made known to the powers in the heavenlies through the church (3:3–12); Christ's descent and ascent "far above all the heavens" afforded him the right to give gifts of ministry to the church. Among other reasons, these gifts equip the

---

[198] Cf. Meyer 288. I do not intend by this to eliminate thanksgiving while one is in times of suffering; to the contrary, this would be a fully Pauline view. At issue is not the circumstance *within which* one gives thanks, but the rich blessings of Christ *for which* we continually give thanks in any and all circumstances.

saints so that they will not be blown about by every kind of deceit (4:7–16); and in the exhortations they are urged to live no longer as Gentiles, thus making no room for Satan (4:17, 27).[199]

But having assured them of the reality of Christ's victory over the powers, of their being seated together with him in that triumph, and of their inclusion as Gentiles along with the Jews in the new, reconciled people of God as evidence to the powers of Christ's triumph, Paul concludes the letter on this note of realism. As with their redemption in Christ, which, evidenced by the Spirit's presence, is "already" but "not yet," so too with Christ's triumph over the powers. It is "already," so they need no longer live in fear of them; but it is also "not yet," so they themselves must both be aware that the conflict goes on and be equipped by Christ and the Spirit to stand against them.

This final exhortation, therefore, is basically in two parts, the second of which evolves into a third: Verses 10–12 set out the basic imperatives (vv. 10–11, that they be empowered in the Lord, and that they put on God's armor so as to withstand the devil) and the reason for them (v. 12, because of the ongoing war against the powers). Verses 13–17(18) repeat the second imperative and then spell out the nature of the equipment, which consists of the armor of Christ to withstand their attacks and the weapons of the Spirit so as to take them on. But the mention of the "sword of the Spirit" in v. 17 evokes the further concern that they "pray in the Spirit," which is then elaborated in vv. 18–20.[200]

As throughout the letter, the Spirit again plays a significant role, being put at the climax of the enumeration of the armor metaphor (vv. 17–18). But we must also note the use of "spirit" language in v. 12, where Paul describes the powers as "spiritual forces of evil in the heavenlies."

EPHESIANS 6:12

because our[201] *struggle is not against blood and flesh but against the principalities, against the powers, against the world rulers of this darkness, against the spiritual forces of evil in the heavenly places.*

---

[199] On this question, see Arnold, *Ephesians.*

[200] Translation that captures Paul's Greek is not easy, for two reasons: grammatically, v. 17 begins a new sentence, which continues through v. 20; but conceptually, the final mention of armor is in v. 17, which means that as this new sentence began it was a continuation of vv. 14–16. One could argue, as I will, that even though "praying in the Spirit" is not actually included by way of metaphor in the enumeration of armor, Paul intends it as the final, most vital weapon against the powers.

[201] This is the reading of ℵ A D² I 0230 Maj a g* vg syʰ co Clement Tertullian Origen; ὑμῖν ("your") is read by P⁴⁶ B D* F G Ψ 81 1175 pc it syᵖ Lucifer Ambrosiaster. This is an especially difficult textual choice (as is evidenced by the {D} rating in the UBS³ [changed to {B} in UBS⁴]; cf. the discussion in Metzger, *Textual Commentary,* 610). The manuscript evidence clearly favors "your." The transcriptional evidence can go either way: either "your" is original and scribes universalized it, or "our" is

This description of the "powers" collects into one place a variety of terms and language from throughout the epistle that ensures (1) that we have been dealing throughout with malevolent "spirit" beings,[202] (2) that they inhabit what Paul has referred to frequently as "the heavenlies," and (3) that this is a major concern of the letter. Of the four terms used in this passage, two have occurred before (ἀρχάς and ἐξουσίας = "principalities" and "powers"; 1:21; 3:10), while the third (κοσμοκράτορας = "world rulers") occurs for the first time in known literature. Clinton Arnold has made an especially good case for its originating in the "magical/astrological tradition," which Paul has taken over, made into a plural and made equivalent with the "evil spirits" that follow.[203] Our interest lies with the final term, τὰ πνευματικὰ τῆς πονηρίας (= "the spirit forces of evil"), which is probably to be understood not as a fourth category of spirit beings, but as a more comprehensive term that embraces all the former ones,[204] including the others in 1:21—"might" and "dominion," and especially "every name that is named," which probably reflects the magical tradition, where conjurers invoked the names of every imaginable "deity" in their incantations.

What is striking is the use of the word πνευματικός in this way. As we have observed elsewhere, and argued in chapter 2, this word is an adjective that has been formed from the noun πνεῦμα, which in Paul ordinarily means belonging to, or pertaining to, the Spirit. This usage is best explained in light of his prior use of πνεῦμα in 2:2 to refer to Satan. Just as this adjective ordinarily refers to some activity of the Spirit (cf. 1:3 and 5:19 above) for the building up of the people of God, so the "spirit" who stands over against God and who must be resisted by God's people (v. 11) is the "prince of the power of the air" and thus chief among the many "spirit forces of evil," whose purpose is to tear down and destroy or to keep people in bondage. This unique usage is therefore probably related to the larger theme of Spirit activity in this letter, where Christ and the Spirit have triumphed over the "false spirit" and his "evil spirits," even though in the "already but not yet" scheme of things they must be resisted—by the armor provided by Christ and the weapons of the Spirit.

---

original and scribes particularized it. On the one hand, Paul regularly universalizes these kinds of moments; on the other hand, everything on either side of it is second plural, so scribes may have conformed it to the context. On the whole, the text of the UBS[4] is the more likely; probably some early scribes changed in this one instance of the first plural to conform to the surrounding second plurals.

[202]One may grant that in the earlier occurrences there is nothing said that might make one think so, except for the strong implication created by the juxtaposition of the "powers" in 1:21–23 with Satan in 2:1–3. Nonetheless, this passage vividly indicates that they are so. Thus we must do what the first recipients did not need to: go back and read the letter a second time with this passage in mind. They had no need to do so because they knew from the outset that Paul was speaking to their situation. Carr's attempt (*Angels*, 104–10) to eliminate this text as a second-century interpolation, on the (unsupportable) grounds that such beliefs were not current in the first century, seems to be a counsel of despair. This text—not to mention the data in the Gospels and Acts—makes his thesis untenable. See the refutation in C. E. Arnold, "The Exorcism of Ephesians 6:12 in Recent Research," *JSNT* 30 (1987) 71–87.

[203]See Arnold, *Ephesians*, 65–67. By doing so, therefore, Paul is also "disarming" the "world ruler" of having any significance for his readers.

[204]Cf. Arnold, *Ephesians*, 68; Lincoln 444.

Our difficulties with this text lie not so much in understanding it in context, but in trying to come to terms with it in our own day. The tendencies are toward one extreme or the other, to deny the existence of such beings as "the mythology of another day," or to recognize their existence and then to attribute to them a prominence all out of proportion to that which Paul here affords them. As in most such matters, Paul's position lies in the "radical middle": to take them with dead seriousness, but also to recognize that they are a tethered foe, restrained by Christ's victory over them in the cross and resurrection (Col 2:15; Eph 2:6–7). In our present existence as "already but not yet," one would be foolhardy indeed to deny the presence of such "spirit forces of evil" or understand them in some kind of "demythologized" way as mere "forces" and not true spirit beings. But we need also to recognize that the thrust of this passage is not for us to become enamored with them, but to withstand them through the armor provided by Christ in the gospel and through the weapons of the Spirit, to which we now turn.

EPHESIANS 6:17–20

[17]*And take the helmet of salvation and the sword of the Spirit, which is the word of God,* [18]*through every prayer and request praying at all times in the Spirit, and to this end staying alert with perseverance and prayer for all the saints,* [19]*and for me, that the message may be given to me when I open my mouth boldly to make known the mystery of the gospel,* [20] *for which I am an ambassador in chains, in order that in it I might have boldness to speak as I ought.*

Although there is great interest and considerable literature on the imagery of Christian armor that forms the heart of this passage (vv. 14–17),[205] our interest is limited to the final two items in vv. 17–18 which set forth the role of the Spirit in this "spiritual warfare." What is noteworthy is that what precedes the mention of the Spirit are various aspects of the gospel, which are associated with forms of armor, all of which are for defense. This should not surprise us, since the basic imperative is one of leaning on the power provided by Christ so as to "stand against the wiles of the devil" (v. 11) and his minions (v. 12). Thus Paul calls on his readers to make use of "the truth" (as a belt), "righteousness" (as a breastplate), "the gospel of peace" (as shoes), "faith" (as a shield), and "salvation" (as a helmet). How much one should make of the relationship of the various aspects of the gospel singled out and their associated pieces of armor seems moot. Collectively, they call attention to most of the equipment worn in battle by a Roman soldier and associate that armor with the gospel as it is looked at from different vantage points.

---

[205]Part of the interest is with the background, which is probably to be found in Isa 11:4–5; 52:7; and 59:17, especially since Paul's letters are so full of Isaiah material. Paul used this imagery earlier in 1 Thes 5:8. The slight changes here are related in part to the time gap between these two letters and in part to the pregnant nature of the metaphor. Cf. the use of the Isaiah imagery in Wis 5:15–23 and the use of Paul by John Bunyan in *Pilgrim's Progress* and *The Holy War*.

The final piece of equipment is the soldier's weapon, his sword, which in this use of the metaphor is (appropriately) associated with the Spirit and then further identified as "the word of God." That is followed in turn by another participial phrase, urging prayer as well, but in this case "prayer in the Spirit," which suggests the closest kind of relationship between vv. 17 and 18. But what Paul intends by "the sword of the Spirit, which is the word of God," and how these final clauses relate to one another and to the whole imagery are more difficult to determine.

Our difficulties with this passage begin with the first part of v. 17. The imagery to this point (vv. 14–16) appears as a series of four participles, all of which modify the first word in the sentence, the imperative "stand therefore." The participles are all modal, taking the sense of "stand therefore, by doing this, and by doing this, etc." But the final one, "faith," receives special mention, prefaced as it is with "besides all these" and then elaborated by tying it back to v. 11, in the form of quenching the enemy's fiery missiles. Thus, when he comes to the final piece of armor, Paul starts a new sentence,[206] placing the piece of armor before the verb, which is then followed by its second object, "the sword of the Spirit." The result is a series of clauses whose bare outline looks thus:

Stand therefore,
    by girding yourself
           with the truth
    by putting on the breastplate
           of righteousness
    by shoeing your feet
           with the gospel of peace,
   and besides all these,
    by taking the shield
           of faith,
              with which to quench the enemy's fire
   and
the helmet   receive
    of salvation
   and
the sword
    of the Spirit,
       which is the word of God,
  through every prayer
      praying at all times
      in the Spirit.

---

[206]This seems to be the most likely reason for the "break" in structure at this point, vis-à-vis the suggestion that it is "for stylistic reasons" (Gnilka 313, followed by Arnold, *Ephesians*, 106). Robert Wild observes also that this is a point of transition from aspects of the gospel in which the believer is involved in some way to matters that are pure gift to be "received" ("The Warrior and the Prisoner: Some Reflections on Ephesians 6:10–20," *CBQ* 46 [1984] 284–98 [297]).

The difficulty lies with v. 18, prayer in the Spirit, and how—or whether—that relates to the preceding clause about the sword of the Spirit, and thus to the preceding imagery as a whole. But before that we need to look more closely at the Spirit phrase in v. 17.

17 It is not surprising that as the final piece of equipment in the believers' armor Paul urges them to take as their weapon, "the sword[207] of the Spirit." Clad with the gospel of their salvation, they must not only withstand the enemy's fiery missiles, but they must take the offensive as well. And that is precisely the role of the Spirit in the believer's life—to take the things of Christ and not only make them known to the believer, but also appropriate them in such a way that one penetrates the darkness with the light of the gospel (if one may be allowed a Pauline change of metaphors). The genitive, "of the Spirit," in this case is either source (= "given by the Spirit"[208]) or possessive (= "belonging to the Spirit").[209] That much seems obvious enough; the difficulties begin with the further identification, "which is the word of God."[210]

In Paul one expects "the word of God" to refer to the message of the gospel, since that is the way he ordinarily uses this kind of language.[211] But in this case, in place of the ordinary word for "message" (λόγος, *logos*), he uses the word ῥῆμα (*rhēma*). While these words are near synonyms and therefore can often be used interchangeably,[212] ῥῆμα tends to

---

[207] Gk. μάχαιρα, the short double-edged dagger used for close fighting, rather than ῥομφαία, the heavy broad sword in most pictures.

[208] But not so much in the sense of "origin," as though the sword came from the Spirit, but in the sense that the Spirit makes it effective (cf. Schnackenburg 279; Lincoln 451).

[209] Were it not for the following relative clause, which elaborates the "sword" as "the word of God," we would probably understand it to be appositional (= take the Spirit as your sword), just as with the three preceding genitives ("of righteousness," "of faith," "of salvation"). A few interpreters in an earlier time argued for apposition here, but hardly convincingly.

[210] Part of the difficulty rests with the fact that the relative pronoun grammatically has "Spirit" as its antecedent, whereas the sense of the clause demands that it should be "sword." This seems to be a clear case of "attraction," where the relative clause is intended to modify the whole phrase ("sword of the Spirit") together, not just "sword" (cf. Lincoln 451). Thus it is "attracted" to the immediately preceding word, "Spirit."

[211] See, e.g., 1 Thes 1:8; 2:13; 2 Thes 3:1; 1 Cor 14:36; 2 Cor 2:17; 4:2; Col 1:25; cf. "the word of Christ" in Col 3:16. On the other hand, "the word of the Lord" in 1 Thes 4:15 probably refers to some saying of Jesus or to some revelation Paul himself received from the Lord. In contrast to our own habits, Paul never uses this language to refer to Scripture.

[212] See, e.g., Rom 10:17, where Paul uses ῥῆμα τοῦ Χριστοῦ to refer to the message about Christ, although even here ῥῆμα is probably chosen because of the preceding emphasis on "hearing." Thus the emphasis is on the "speaking" of the message of Christ, which is "heard" by those to whom it is spoken. See the preceding note for the use of λόγος where one might have expected ῥῆμα.

put the emphasis on that which is spoken at a given point, whereas λόγος frequently emphasizes the content of the "message." If that distinction holds here, then Paul is almost certainly referring still to the gospel, just as he does in Rom 10:17, but the emphasis is now on the actual "speaking forth" of the message, inspired by the Spirit.[213] To put that in more contemporary terms, in urging them to take the sword of the Spirit and then identifying that sword with the "word of God," Paul is not identifying the "sword" with the book, but with the proclamation of Christ, which in our case is indeed to be found in the book.

In any case, the single weapon that Paul specifically urges them to use is the "word that comes from God,"[214] as that is proclaimed under the empowering of the Spirit of God. He would simply not have understood the fascination with "words" that one finds among some contemporary charismatics, as though what we speak against the devil is what will defeat him. Paul's aim is higher than that. God has something to say, to be sure, but it is not some ad hoc word directed at Satan. Such an understanding surely endows Satan with far more authority in our present world than this text allows. Rather, as vv. 18–20 confirm, the "word of God" that is the Spirit's sword is the faithful speaking forth of the gospel in the arena of darkness, so that men and women might hear and be delivered from Satan's grasp.[215]

18 As noted above, this passage contains inherent difficulties: (1) the relationship of this participial clause to v. 17 and thereby to vv. 14–16, (2) the precise intent of the language "praying in/by the Spirit," and (3) the relationship of this phrase to the rest of the sentence (vv. 19–20).

1. Interpreters and translators commonly start a new imperative with v. 18.[216] The reasons for this are understandable, since the actual imag-

---

[213] So Salmond 388, Barth 2.771, Lincoln 451. Contra Mitton 227, Houlden 339, Patzia 290, who stress the ad hoc nature of the spoken word: "all the words of God that come from his Spirit" (Patzia). Paul is not saying that every word a person speaks by the Spirit is the word of God; rather, he is identifying this weapon with something otherwise known, the speaking forth of the message of the gospel.

[214] Understanding this genitive, therefore, as "source," rather than subjective (= the word that God speaks).

[215] Luther caught the sense of this text in his great hymn, *A Mighty Fortress:*
And though this world, with devils filled, should threaten to undo us;
We will not fear, for God has willed his truth to triumph through us.
The prince of darkness grim, we tremble not for him;
His rage we can endure; for lo! his doom is sure;
One little word shall fell him.
That word above all earthly powers, no thanks to them, abideth;
The Spirit and the gifts are ours, through him who with us sideth.

[216] Cf. NIV, which starts a new imperative with v. 18 and a new paragraph at v. 19, with the NRSV, which starts both a new imperative and new paragraph with v. 18.

ery, both as a whole and of the armor in particular, does not seem to be carried beyond v. 17. Not only so, but the content of vv. 19–20 seems to take off in a new direction, elaborating what is said in v. 18, but without an immediately apparent relationship to the warfare imagery.

On the other hand, there are better reasons for thinking that in v. 18 Paul is continuing the metaphor[217] and that "praying in the Spirit" is to be understood as yet a further weapon in the warfare, even though it is admittedly not associated with armor as such. The most obvious reasons for thinking so are two. First, the grammar of the sentence favors such a view, since the participle in v. 18 modifies the verb "receive" in v. 17.[218] To see it otherwise requires one to appeal to an instance of grammar for which there is less than certain evidence—the participle used as an imperative[219]—and in any case it is imperatival here only because it is dependent on the imperative in v. 17. One cannot complain, therefore, about translating it as an imperative as long as the connection with v. 17 is maintained. Second, the metaphor that follows our phrase is most likely intended to continue the imagery of the Christian soldier: "to this end (i.e., for the purpose of praying in the Spirit at all times) *being on the alert* with all perseverance and prayer." Not only so, but these two motifs naturally go together in Paul.[220] Proclaiming the word of God is speech directed toward people; prayer is speech directed toward God. And since Paul himself deliberately ties the latter to the former by means of the Spirit, there is every good reason to believe that he intended his readers to hear "praying in the Spirit" as the final expression of Christian weaponry in the conflict with the "powers." Thus they are urged also to appeal to the "captain" as they continue in the fight.

2. But what does he intend by "praying in/by the Spirit"? Given the context, and that he has just mentioned the Spirit in association with proclamation, Paul at least intends to associate the empowering of the Spirit with one's praying as well.[221] There is every good reason to think that Paul intends this phrase precisely as he has used it elsewhere—especially in 1 Cor 14:14–15 (cf. Rom 8:26–27)—to refer specifically to that form of prayer in which the Spirit assumes a special role in the

---

[217] So also Schnackenburg 281, Patzia 290. Robinson 117 and Scott 254 make the connection even more closely, suggesting that "the word of God" in v. 17 is best understood as "prayer in the Spirit" in v. 18.

[218] This is clearly so, even though conceptually it is arguable that both this participle and its verb ("receive") are to be understood as ultimately dependent on "stand" in v. 14, as several suggest (Meyer 341, Salmond 389, Abbott 187, Lincoln 451, Arnold [*Ephesians*, 106]).

[219] See n. 191 above on 5:18–21.

[220] See above on 1 Cor 11:4–5.

[221] Some earlier interpreters (Westcott 97; see further list in Meyer 342) understood this to refer to the human spirit (= heartfelt, over against merely with the lips). This is hardly Paul's perspective!

praying, especially, though probably not exclusively, praying in tongues. In that passage Paul distinguishes between two forms of prayer: one he will do "with the mind" and in the public assembly; the other he will do "in/by the Spirit" and in the privacy of his own life of devotion before God. If that catches some of us off guard because it is so little a part of the prayer life of most people in the church, we probably ought not to read our experience of church back into the life of Paul. What Paul says about this kind of praying in 1 Cor 14:1–5 and 14–19 demonstrates that he engaged in it regularly, and that he urged the believers in Corinth to do so as well. The same is most likely true of Rom 8:26–27 (q.v.). If this more specific "praying in the Spirit" is in view, then one must also be prepared to enlarge one's understanding of the nature of such praying; it is not only speaking mysteries to God, or praise and blessing God, or "inarticulate groanings" in times of present weakness, but a way of engaging the enemy in the ongoing conflict.

Whether one takes such a stance or not, what this text does show is that, unlike most contemporary believers, Paul considered prayer to be above all an activity empowered by the Spirit. It also indicates the crucial role the Spirit plays in our continuing "warfare" against Satan. For Paul, the concern was not only that they be clothed with the armor that Christ provides in the gospel, but that they take the enemy on by Spirit-empowered proclamation and by Spirit-inspired praying. The context is that of conflict, warfare against "the prince of darkness grim"; only "praying in the Spirit" will suffice in such conflict.

Perhaps we should note further that the feeble prayers of God's people, spoken in their own strength and often in desperation, while heard on high, are surely not the stuff of "routing the foe." Because we do not know how to pray as we ought, we need to lean more heavily on "praying in/by the Spirit," however one is to understand that phrase. Prayer is not simply our cry of desperation or our "grocery list" of requests that we bring before our heavenly *Abba*; prayer is an activity inspired by God himself, through his Holy Spirit. It is God siding with his people and, by his own empowering presence, the Spirit of God himself bringing forth prayer that is in keeping with God's will and his ways.

3. But what about the rest of the sentence (vv. 18b–20)? Is it related to all of this as well? Probably so. Even though Paul regularly signs off his letters with a request for prayer on his behalf, our present sentence includes that but also moves in quite a different direction. First of all, it begins with a tie to what has preceded: "to this end," that is, to the end that they pray in the Spirit as part of their means of "warfare." And what he wants them to do "to this end" is to "be on the alert" with all perseverance and prayer. These ties with v. 18a suggest that even here the imagery of "spiritual warfare" has not been lost altogether. But the main emphasis of these clauses lies with the two-directional focus that such persevering prayer is to take.

First, he wants them to "pray in the Spirit" on behalf of all the saints, to keep on the alert in their behalf and persevere in doing so. In context this seems to be the place where Paul returns the individual "soldier" to the believing community, not just to the local community but to the larger community of saints everywhere. Not only so, it is the place where they join that community by engaging in prayer in behalf of others so that they will stand empowered in the ongoing conflict with the enemy. This is Paul's recognition that the enemy is real and that fellow-believers need "prayer in the Spirit" in their behalf.

Second, he wants them to "pray in the Spirit" for himself, especially so that, even though presently chained for the sake of the gospel, when he has opportunity to speak he will do so boldly as "an ambassador" of the gospel. Thus, the final word in this letter is a word of evangelism. And prayer in the Spirit is not merely so that God's people will stand against the foe, but so that Paul will be bold to make Christ known.

This final word ties everything together. Just as the Spirit functions as the weaponry against the foe, by empowering the proclamation of the word, so "praying in the Spirit" is not only so that people will be able to withstand the enemy's onslaught, but so that Paul will be enabled to carry the gospel forward. In his final word in this letter he therefore directs them away from their own present conflict to the need for the gospel to continue to be heard in the world, where the prince of darkness still holds sway. To do less than pray in the Spirit in this way, one could argue, is to betray the gospel itself, since the gospel for Paul is the goal of everything.

CONCLUSIONS

The foregoing analysis of the various Spirit texts indicates that one runs the risk of reading Ephesians very poorly if one fails to recognize the central role that the Spirit plays both in this letter and in Paul's understanding of the gospel in general. As with the so-called chief epistles, especially Romans, there is hardly an aspect of Christian life in which the Spirit does not take the leading role, and there is hardly an aspect of the Spirit's role that is not touched on in this letter. Indeed, as Paul suggests in 1:3, all the blessings that God has bestowed on us in Christ in the heavenly places pertain now to the work of the Spirit.

As throughout the corpus, the Spirit is the key to the basic eschatological framework within which Paul's theological assertions and reflections take place. The Spirit is first of all "the Holy Spirit of the promise," whose coming is in fulfillment of the promised new covenant and thereby sets the future into motion. The Spirit thus functions for believers as both the "down payment" on the promised inheritance and the "seal" that we belong to God unto the day of redemption (1:13–14; 4:30). By the Spirit we are marked as belonging to God; at the same time the Spirit is both evidence and guarantee that the future has begun and that its consummation is certain.

The Spirit is the experiential *sine qua non* of our life in Christ, both at its beginning (1:13–14) and in its ongoing expression. He is the empowering presence of God who serves as the key to Christian ethics (3:16, 20; 4:3–4, 30; 5:18) and to our life together in the believing community (2:18, 22; 4:3–4; 5:18–19). In conjunction with the work of Christ himself, the Spirit is responsible for the formation of the church (4:4); his presence in the believing community is how God is now present in our world (2:22); the Spirit is responsible for the unity of believers with one another (4:3–4); as we are continually filled with the Spirit our worship takes the form of song and praise by which we instruct one another and praise God (5:18–20).

Furthermore, the Spirit is crucial for our understanding both of God and of what God is about in our world (1:17–19), in terms not only of our salvation but of our place in God's plan and his victory over the "powers" (1:17–21). Indeed, the Spirit also empowers us in our ongoing conflict with the enemy by enabling the proclamation of the gospel in the midst of the conflict and by praying through us for one another and for the further spread of the gospel (6:17–18).

Finally, the Spirit, as always, is understood as the personal presence of God. It is as we are empowered by the Spirit in the inner person that we will be filled up to the fullness of God (3:16–19), in whose likeness we are being recreated (4:23–24, 30). And when we fail to be like him, we grieve none other than the Holy Spirit of God himself (4:30). In this letter, therefore, we hear the ultimate imperative: keep filled with the Spirit. Here is how God is now present in our world; and as we are filled with the Spirit, both our worship and our behavior reflect his character.

Most of this is said explicitly; some of it appears in presuppositional ways. But all of it together points to the central place the Spirit has in Paul's understanding of life in Christ.

10

THE CAPTIVITY EPISTLES: PHILIPPIANS

Commentaries:[1] K. **Barth** (1962; Eng. trans. from ⁶1947); F. W. **Beare** (HNTC, 1959); F. F. **Bruce** (NIBC, ²1989); J. **Eadie** (1858); J. **Gnilka** (HTK, ⁴1987); G. F. **Hawthorne** (WBC, 1983); W. **Hendriksen** (1962); J. L. **Houlden** (PNTC, 1970); R. **Johnstone** (1875); H. A. A. **Kennedy** (EGT, 1903); H. A. **Kent** (EBC, 1978); J. B. **Lightfoot** (1913; repr. 1953); E. **Lohmeyer** (MeyerK, ⁸1930); R. P. **Martin** (NCBC, 1976); H. A. W. **Meyer** (Eng. trans. 1875); J. H. **Michael** (MNTC, 1928); J. A. **Motyer** (BST, 1984); H. C. G. **Moule** (CGT, 1897); J. J. **Müller** (NIC, 1955); P. T. **O'Brien** (NIGNT, 1991); M. **Silva** (WEC, 1988); M. R. **Vincent** (ICC, 1897).

In stark contrast to Ephesians, Philippians is a very personal letter, written to the first Christian community in Macedonia. Those believers had come to be among Paul's dearest friends in Christ. The letter breathes with the warmth and affection that they mutually shared, and that same congeniality underlies most of the matters spoken to. Their affection for Paul had caused them to send a material gift by way of Epaphroditus, while Paul was imprisoned in Rome.[2] But on the way (apparently)[3]

---

[1]The following commentaries are referred to in this chapter only by the author's last name.

[2]This is debated, of course. Some think Ephesus (although the lack of a praetorian guard there has caused most scholars to abandon this view); others think Caesarea (on the basis of a known imprisonment and the fact that Luke mentions Herod's praetorium there [Acts 23:35]). Rome is the traditional view, based not only on a known imprisonment (Acts 27–28), but also because Rome was the home of the praetorian guard (Phil 1:13), and because of the mention of Caesar's household (Phil 4:22). Since there are no internal grounds to cause one to think otherwise (see the next note for the problem of distance), there is also no good reason to think the tradition to be wrong. For an advocacy of Caesarea, see Hawthorne, xxxvii–xliv; for the tradition, see (most recently) Silva 5–8 and O'Brien 19–26.

[3]One of the alleged difficulties for a Roman provenance (see preceding note) is the distance between Philippi and Rome and the number of trips (by various people) necessary between the two cities on the basis of what is said in the letter (up to five have been suggested—and often considered as too many for such a distance). The

Epaphroditus became sick, so that he was near death (2:30); but God spared him, and now his return to Philippi served as the occasion for Paul's writing to them. Besides thanking them for the gift, he also explained how things were going with him (fine, thank you, inasmuch as the gospel is still being advanced); in typical fashion he also took the opportunity to exhort them (to unity) and to warn them again[4] (against Judaizers).

Understandably, the Spirit is not mentioned frequently—only four times—in such personal correspondence, where the subject matter does not lend itself to many such references.[5] Nonetheless, since, like the legendary King Midas, everything Paul touches turns to gospel, and since gospel for Paul includes the work of the Spirit, it is not surprising that these few incidental references echo several crucial facets of Paul's understanding of the Spirit's activity.

In the first instance (1:19) Paul expects their prayer for him to result in a fresh "supply" of "the Spirit of Jesus Christ," whose effective presence in him will cause Christ to be magnified whether Paul gains his freedom or is put to death. In the next instances (1:27; 2:1), as in 1 Corinthians and Ephesians, life in the Spirit serves as the ground for an appeal to unity within the believing community. And finally (3:3), the Spirit is again put forward as God's own effective alternative to flesh and Torah, in this case in one of the more unusual, but powerful, contrasts in Paul's letters.

---

best solution is that Epaphroditus became ill on the way to Rome and that one of his entourage returned home with that news, while Epaphroditus (and others, probably) went on to Rome with the gift. For a similar reconstruction see C. O. Buchanan, "Epaphroditus' Sickness and the Letter to the Philippians," *EvQ* 36 (1964) 157–66. This cuts the number of trips to three (news of Paul's imprisonment reaches Philippi; Epaphroditus [and others] come to Rome; Epaphroditus returns to Philippi), and even the first item does not necessarily require someone to have gone to Philippi from Rome.

[4]This takes with all seriousness that Paul had previously spoken to them on this issue (3:1).

[5]Although in terms of Pauline theology, the Spirit is surely to be understood, as several commentators have noted, as the agent of the "fruit of righteousness" in 1:11 and of God's being at work in/among them both to will and to do of his pleasure in 2:12–13. Others have perceived the Spirit also to lie close behind the language of 3:15–16 ("God will reveal it to you"; "let us live up to what we have already attained" [cf. Gal 5:25]). But in keeping with the basic parameters of this book none of these texts will be considered in this chapter. There is also a significant "power" text (3:10, "the power of his resurrection"). But that passage, despite its unique language for power in association with Christ's resurrection, is shaped by its present context (esp. vv. 11–16) and is so plainly christocentric that "power" here is almost certainly not a metonym for the Spirit; indeed it is doubtful whether the Spirit lies even distantly behind the language in this case. The same can be said for Max Turner's assertion that "the Spirit appears under the guise of the 'power which enables him to subject all things to himself'" in 3:21 ("Significance," 57). None of this language is used explicitly elsewhere to refer to the Spirit.

Philippians 1:18c–20

[18]*What is more,*[6] *I shall rejoice,* [19]*for*[7] *I know that this shall turn out for me unto "salvation,"*[8] *through your prayers*[9] *and the supply of the Spirit of Jesus Christ,* [20]*in keeping with my own earnest expectation and hope, that in no respect will I experience shame; but to the contrary that with total openness now as always Christ will be magnified in my body, whether it be through life or through death.*

Paul is in the process of sharing his perspective on how things have been—and are—going with him.[10] He has just concluded a reflection on his imprisonment with a word of joy (vv. 12–18b); now he turns toward the future, which will also be a cause for joy. Our passage offers the basis for that further joy. The earlier reflection in fact turned out to be totally given over to explaining how his imprisonment is affecting the gospel; with our passage he shifts to more personal matters: how he is faring, and what is to happen to him. But even here the focus is still on Christ and the gospel.

The explanation itself (vv. 19–20) has several exegetical difficulties,[11] most of which have to do with the initial clause ("this shall turn

---

[6]For this translation of ἀλλά, see Margaret E. Thrall, *Greek Particles in the New Testament: Linguistic and Exegetical Studies* (Grand Rapids: Eerdmans, 1962) 14; cf. BAGD, who note this usage as "ascensive," to be explained elliptically (= and not only this [v. 18ab] but also).

[7]p[46] B 1175 1739 1881 Ambrosiaster read δέ. Although one is reluctant to go against this combination of witnesses, most likely the δέ is secondary here. If it were original, the preceding ἀλλά would seem to lose its genuinely contrastive force, and the clause ἀλλὰ καὶ χαρήσομαι would then belong to v. 18 (as many hold [e.g., Meyer, 41]): "Christ is preached and in this I rejoice, indeed I shall rejoice. But I know . . . " The γάρ, which is by all counts the more difficult, and therefore the original, reading, means that Paul has begun a new clause, giving reasons for his avowal of future joy: " . . . and in this I rejoice. And not only so, but I shall also rejoice, for I know that . . . " (cf. Hawthorne 39, O'Brien 107).

[8]Gk. σωτηρία, a word elsewhere in Paul referring to eschatological salvation; but in this case its meaning is complicated by the fact that this entire clause ("this shall turn out for me unto σωτηρία") is a verbatim "citation" of Job 13:16 (LXX). See the discussion below.

[9]Even though δεήσεως is singular, this is the proper understanding of what is almost certainly a "distributive singular." See the discussion, inter alia, on 1 Cor 6:19 and Gal 6:18.

[10]The key to the structure of the first two chapters seems to lie with the oscillation between the phrases τὰ κατ' ἐμέ (1:12; "my affairs"); τὰ περὶ ὑμῶν (1:27; "your affairs"); and τὰ περὶ ὑμῶν/τὰ περὶ ἐμέ ("your affairs"/"my affairs") in 2:19, 20, 23. The whole thus moves from an explanation about "*my* affairs" (how things have been, and are, with me; 1:12–26), to a concern about "*your* affairs" (that they stand as one person in the continuing struggle for the truth of the gospel; 1:27–2:18), and finally to "*our* affairs" (the present coming of Epaphroditus and later coming of Timothy to catch you and me up on one another in a more personal way; 2:19–30).

[11]Including (1) what "this" refers to in the first clause; (2) the nuance of the key word σωτηρία ("salvation"), whether it means eschatological salvation, deliverance

out for my σωτηρία [= salvation, vindication, deliverance]"), which the Spirit phrase modifies. Is Paul referring to deliverance from prison[12] or to "salvation" in some other sense? Since our understanding of what is said about the Spirit in this clause is conditioned largely by our understanding of the whole sentence, we must first look at the latter.

The interpretive key to this passage lies with a phenomenon literary critics call "intertextuality,"[13] the conscious embedding of fragments of an earlier text into a later one. Since Paul's spiritual life and theology are thoroughly imbued with OT realities,[14] we should not be surprised to find him not only quoting the OT to support an argument, as in most cases, but also, as here, at times borrowing or "echoing" the language and setting of a specific OT passage or motif and refitting it into his own setting. That seems precisely to be what he has done in this sentence, which echoes the situation of the "poor man" in the OT, especially Job and the psalmists, who in their distress look to God for "salvation/ vindication." Thus the first clause, "this shall turn out to me for salvation/vindication,"[15] is actually a verbatim borrowing of the language of Job 13:16 (LXX);[16] and the second clause, with its collocation of "shame" and "magnifying," picks up the language of the "poor man" in Psalms like 34:3–6 or 35:24–28.[17] Thus, even though

---

from prison/death, or something closer to "vindication"; (3) how we are to understand the phrase "through your prayers and the supply of the Spirit of Jesus Christ"; and (4) how we are to understand the final "that" clause, which seems to be the point of everything.

[12]As in the RSV (and NRSV), "this will turn out for my deliverance" (cf. NASB, NIV, NEB, GNB). See Hawthorne 39–44 for the most recent advocacy of this view.

[13]On this question see esp. Richard B. Hays, *Echoes of Scripture in the Letters of Paul* (New Haven: Yale, 1989), who uses this text in his first chapter (pp. 21–24) as an illustration of such intertextuality, where Paul both "echoes" the earlier text, with its literary milieu, and thus seems to have transferred some of that setting to his own situation, and at the same time does so with some obvious contrasts between himself and Job. This view, without the refinement of a later time, was first proposed by Michael 46–48.

[14]The evidence for this is writ large in the corpus. See the discussion on Rom 1:2 and 2 Tim 3:16. Both Paul's theological presuppositions and therefore his thought-world are thoroughly conditioned by the OT.

[15]The word σωτηρία carries in part its ordinary sense of "salvation before God," but in this case, as in the LXX, in the special sense of the final vindication of the passion of Paul's life, the gospel of Christ and therefore of Christ himself.

[16]This has often been overlooked by interpreters, because in this case we have no introductory formula (e.g., "Scripture says"). But the language is so precise, and the "settings" are so similar, that it is nearly impossible that Paul's language here could be mere coincidence.

[17]Noted also by O'Brien 114. This second instance, of course, is an "echo" of a slightly different kind, where in a less case-specific way than with the Job "citation" Paul echoes a repeated OT *motif*.

this is now Paul's own sentence, and must be understood within its present context, the very choice of such language is best understood as intentionally echoing the somewhat similar circumstances of Job[18] and the Psalmists.

This twofold echo of the OT suggests that both parts of Paul's sentence, vv. 19–20a and 20b, are reflecting on the same reality regarding Paul's situation. Thus the key to understanding v. 19 is to be found in the final "that" clause in v. 20, where Paul spells out the content of his "eager expectation and hope."[19] His obvious concern is *not* that he will be "delivered" from his imprisonment, but that no matter how his current circumstances are resolved (we learn only later in vv. 25–26 that he expects a favorable resolution), God will both "save" Paul[20] and vindicate Christ and the gospel. Like the Psalmist, Paul's hope in God is such that he expects his upcoming trial not to be an experience of "shame"[21]—for himself or his gospel—but rather one where Christ will be magnified in his "body,"[22] whether he lives or dies.

Thus the structure of Paul's sentence:

---

[18]Job 13 is one of the more poignant of the speeches where Job abjures the perspective of his "comforters," who insist that his present situation is the result of "hidden sin." Job knows better and pleads his cause with God, who "put my feet in the stocks" (13:27). Job's hope is in God, before whom he will plead his innocence. Indeed the very hope of appearing before God in such a way "will be my salvation" because the godless will not come before him (v. 16). And salvation for Job means "I know that I will be vindicated" (v. 18).

[19]Contra Hawthorne 39–43, who understands this ὅτι as a second object clause with the verb "I know" ("I know that . . . , that . . . "). Besides putting considerable strain on this second ὅτι-clause (the absence of a preceding καί is especially difficult), this seems to miss the point of the sentence as a whole, as argued for here.

[20]In the sense that, as with Job, he expects to receive vindication at the heavenly tribunal.

[21]This phrase especially needs to be understood as an echo of OT values and not in more traditional Western terms of "shame" having primarily to do with "feelings" of dishonor, disgrace, or embarrassment. The OT view of shame, as repeatedly expressed in the Psalter, is most often tied to one's relationship with God. When one of God's righteous ones cries out not to be brought to shame but rather to be vindicated ("saved") by him, God's own honor is at stake. For such a person to be brought to shame reflects unfavorably on God; hence the cry is always filled with trust and hope that God will therefore vindicate the one who has trusted in him. Classic illustrations of such an understanding may be found, e.g., in Ps 25:1–3 and 34:4–6. On this matter see H. C. Kee, "The Linguistic Background of Shame in the New Testament," *On Language, Culture and Religion: In Honor of Eugene A. Nida* (Paris: Mouton, 1974) 133–47, esp. 137f.

[22]Paul uses σῶμα here as the only anthropological term that makes sense in the present context. Had he been reflecting only on "living," he would probably have used ψυχή μου (in the sense of "my life"). But the inclusion of "death" rendered that term inadequate; hence the use of "body" as the one term appropriate for the situation of both life and death.

What is more, I *will* rejoice,
>   *for*
> I know *that*
>> this will turn out to be salvation/vindication
>>>>> for me
>>> through your prayers
>>> and
>>> the supply of the Spirit
>>>>> of Jesus Christ
>> in keeping with my   earnest expectation
>>>> and
>>>> hope
>>>> *that*
>>> in no way
>>>> shall I be brought to shame,
>>>>> *but*
>>> with all openness
>>>> Christ will be magnified
>>>>>> in my body
>>>>> as always,
>>>>> so now,

>>>>>> whether through life
>>>>> or   through death

The reflective soliloquy that follows further confirms that Paul's concern is not with "getting out of prison," but exactly as in vv. 12–18: that whether Paul is released or not, Christ will be glorified; and for Paul that could happen through his death as well as by his life. Besides, he will go on, "as for myself personally, if I could choose, *death* would be preferable because that would mean finally to have 'gained Christ,' but in reality I have no choice, and *life* will be better for you, because that will mean growth and joy for you."

Thus Paul needs their prayer and the consequent supply of the Spirit not for "deliverance"—as though the Spirit would help him get released from prison—but for the kind of "openness" or "boldness"[23] that will cause Christ to be glorified when Paul finally has his hearing, however that might turn out. Thus both parts of this personal reflection on his

---

[23]Gk. παρρησία, one of the more difficult words in the Pauline letters. Its basic meaning is "outspokenness" or "plainness of speech" that "conceals nothing and passes over nothing" (BAGD); but it soon crossed over to mean "openness to the public," hence "publicly." Eventually it acquired the nuance of "bold speech," hence "confidence/boldness" of the kind that only the privileged would have before those in authority. Here it probably has to do with "openness," that is, that in a very open and public way Christ will magnified through Paul's coming trial, no matter what its outcome.

"present affairs" (vv. 12–18b; 18c–26) have their singular focus on the effect of his imprisonment on Christ and the gospel.

What, then, of the modifying phrase, "through your prayers and the supply of the Spirit of Jesus Christ"? Several matters require our attention:

1. First, this is a single prepositional phrase, with the two nouns ("prayers" and "supply") serving as compound objects of one preposition with one definite article. Grammatically this suggests that Paul envisions the closest kind of relationship between their prayer and the supply of the Spirit. Paul is referring not to two realities ("your prayers" and "the Spirit's help," as the NIV), but to twin sides of a single reality. Through their prayers, and with that, God's special provision of the Spirit, his most eager expectation and hope about Christ's being magnified through him will be realized.

2. The greater issue has to do with the meaning of the word ἐπι-χορηγία ("supply,"[24] frequently translated "help"[25]) and the issue of whether "Spirit" is an objective or subjective genitive (= supply or supplier). In some ways these are related issues, because the meaning "help," despite Bauer's *Lexicon* and many recent commentators to the contrary, seems to be an invented meaning for which no known lexical evidence can be mustered in support; rather, it evolved precisely because scholarship was generally convinced that the Spirit was the subject of "supply," not its object.[26]

The noun is not a common one, occurring elsewhere in the NT only in Eph 4:16 (RSV, "with which it is supplied"), where Markus Barth has shown convincingly that the normal meaning is both lexically and contextually to be preferred.[27] It derives from the cognate verb, ἐπιχορηγέω, which always and only means "to supply, furnish, or provide for." Its noncompounded form originated as a term for supplying choristers and

---

[24]Debate exists in the literature as to whether the compound ἐπιχορηγία implies generous supply. Lightfoot, Michael, Beare, and Motyer are so inclined; Vincent thinks not. Most do not mention the possibility. This is a more difficult one, since both the noun and its cognate verb appear infrequently in the extant literature. In any case, if it does not imply "generous," all known uses do suggest "full" or "adequate" supply.

[25]See, e.g., NIV, RSV, GNB, JB, NAB, Phillips, Hawthorne.

[26]One can almost trace the evolution of this meaning through BAGD and the commentators (see esp. Müller 58n2 and Hendriksen 74n50; both of whom move from "supply" to "help" without offering lexical evidence). Convinced that the Spirit is the subject of the verbal idea in this noun, and having difficulty offering an object to the translation, "through the Spirit's supply," the evolution was an easy one. Since the verb is used in the papyri in marriage contracts, where husbands promise to "provide for" their wives, the English word "support" in this financial sense came to be used (indeed, this is the only meaning offered in BAGD). The next step, from "support" to "help" or "aid," seemed only natural—but only in English (or German), one might add! There is simply no evidence for such a meaning in the Greek materials.

[27]See his commentary on Ephesians 2.448.

dancers for festive occasions. But even as it moved beyond that original specific sense, it always kept the nuance of supplying or providing someone with something. Thus the verb, and the verbal idea of this noun, is clearly transitive, requiring or expecting an object in terms of what is supplied. It need only be pointed out that the English word "help," which almost never carries such a nuance, has to do with coming to someone's aid. One would not deny that when the rich provide for the poor or a husband contracts to provide for his wife[28] in that sense the recipients are being helped. But the nuance of this word is not with the idea of helping, but with the "provision" or "supply" itself.

If the lexical evidence were not sufficient proof that Paul here intends the Spirit as the "supply," the almost identical usage of the cognate verb in Gal 3:5 (q.v.) virtually guarantees it; there it can only mean "God supplies you with the Spirit." In Galatians he appeals to believers who had already "received" the Spirit (v. 2) that God's continuing "supply" of the Spirit, including miracles, is further evidence that "works of Law" do not count. Likewise here he is not thinking of the Spirit's "help" but of the gift of the Spirit himself, whom God continually provides.[29]

3. That means, therefore, that the oft-debated question as to whether the genitive is to be understood as "objective" or "subjective" is nearly irrelevant. Since the noun does not mean "help," but "supply," and an object is implied by the very word itself, the genitive in this case must be objective.[30] The Spirit of Jesus Christ is the "object" to be supplied so as to magnify Christ, not the one who as "subject" will help Paul as he faces trial.

We must not let personal theological proclivities invent meanings for Paul that would have been foreign to him. As we have noted elsewhere,[31] Paul has none of our hang-ups over whether a Spirit person can "receive the Spirit."[32] If that language does not work well for us, it did for Paul.

---

[28]These are two of the specific uses in the literature. See 1 Clem 38:2; cf. the papyri cited by MM 251.

[29]Moffatt's translation has thus captured the sense: "and as I am provided with the Spirit of Jesus Christ."

[30]This may seem a bit strong in light of the decided majority of commentators who argue for a subjective genitive. But the evidence in this case seems overwhelming, especially since the word is such a rare one; yet Paul himself uses it in precisely this way in the only other instance where "supply" and "Spirit" occur together. Those who argue for a subjective genitive tend to dismiss this one piece of solid Pauline evidence much too casually (e.g., Eadie). An objective (or, similarly but less likely, appositional) genitive is also adopted, inter alia, by Moule 23, Michael 49, Lohmeyer 52, Bruce 53, Silva 79 (cf. G. P. Wiles, *Prayers*, 280). Lightfoot argued for both meanings (gift and giver).

[31]See, e.g., on 1 Thes 4:8; Gal 3:5; Eph 5:18.

[32]Cf. the objection voiced by Meyer 43, which seems to lie unexpressed behind that of others: "as genitive of object . . . the expression would be inappropriate, since Paul already *has* the Spirit" (emphasis his). Some have also argued for an analogy

He could not imagine the Spirit in static terms. Hence he can speak of believers' being "given" the Spirit (1 Thes 4:8), or being "supplied" with the Spirit (Gal 3:5; here), or of fanning the Spirit into flame (2 Tim 1:6). For Paul the resident Spirit is ever being given or "supplied" anew in the individual believer's or community's life. So here. Paul knows his own need of the Spirit in a fresh way if Christ is to be magnified in him personally in the soon-to-be-unfolding events of his present imprisonment.

4. All of this is supported by the final matter, namely, that Paul identifies the Spirit in this instance as "the Spirit of Jesus Christ."[33] This unusual designation argues most strongly both for the meaning of the whole sentence presented here and for the meaning of "supply," which the lexical evidence requires.

This qualifier is yet another genitive construction, which again could be construed as subjective (i.e., the Spirit sent by Christ[34]). But the close tie of this phrase to the prayer of the Philippians indicates a considerably different sense. As most often in Paul prayer is directed toward God the Father, in this case that Paul might be supplied with the Spirit of God's Son.[35] This is how Christ lives in him (Gal 2:20), by his Spirit. The genitive, therefore, is best understood as designating relationship or identification. The Spirit, who for Paul is primarily thought of as the Spirit of God, is here identified as the Spirit of Jesus Christ. Finally, when Paul reflects on the Spirit as helper he invariably speaks in terms of the Spirit *of God*.

Why, then, does he here use this more unusual qualifier? The answer lies in the context: Paul's concern throughout this "explanation" has been on Christ and the gospel. Now, in anticipation of the final clause that expresses the content of his "salvation/vindication," he knows that Christ will be glorified in his life or death only as Paul is filled with the Spirit of Christ himself.[36] That is, it is Christ resident in him by the Spirit[37] who alone will cause both that Paul—and therefore the gospel—would not be brought to shame and that Christ would be magnified through him.[38]

---

with the Johannine Paraclete, as the one who comes alongside to aid the believer. But here is a patent example where John can be of very little help in understanding Paul.

[33]In fact, this exact phrase occurs only here in Paul. On two other occasions he refers to the Spirit as "of Christ" (Gal 4:6; Rom 8:9), but in neither instance with the full name.

[34]So Eadie 45, Michael 49, Kent 117, O'Brien 111.

[35]Very much as in Gal 4:6, where God is said to have sent forth "the Spirit of his Son."

[36]Cf. Meyer 43. This seems a better option than the more theological explanation offered, e.g., by Eadie, that the genitive is of origin or source; thus the Spirit is bestowed by the exalted Lord; cf. Michael 49.

[37]Cf. Barth 34, "the *Spirit* . . . is the Lord in Person."

[38]Hamilton (*Holy Spirit*, 12, 35) offers the totally improbable suggestion, without argument or lexical support, that Paul sees the Spirit as God's "equipment . . . against losing his relationship with Christ in the face of death" (12). Hui ("Concept," 70–71)

Thus this phrase is not incidental. Here is the key to Christ's being glorified in every way: by Paul's being "supplied" the Spirit of Jesus Christ, who will live powerfully through Paul as he stands trial. At the same time, from such a phrase and its close relationship with the prayer of the believing community, one learns a great deal about Paul's own spiritual life and his understanding of the role of the Spirit in that life. He rejects thinking of Christian life as lived in isolation from others. He may be the one in prison and headed for trial; but the Philippians—and others—are inextricably bound together with him through the Spirit. Therefore, he assumes that their praying, and God's gracious supply of the Spirit of his Son, will be the means God uses yet once more to bring glory to himself through Paul and Paul's defense of the gospel.

That such an understanding of spiritual life is front and center in Paul corresponds with the final imperatives in the letter probably penned not too many months earlier, noted at the end of the preceding chapter. As the "Ephesians" *pray in the Spirit at all times* (6:18) they will be able both to be strong in the Lord themselves (6:10) and to aid Paul "to make known with boldness the mystery of the gospel, for which I am an ambassador in chains" (6:19–20). If the later church has not always taken seriously this crucial—and dynamic—relationship of prayer and Spirit, there can be little question that for Paul this lies at the heart of Christian life.

PHILIPPIANS 1:27

Only live out your citizenship worthy of the gospel of Christ, so that whether I come and see you, or whether absent from you I hear about your situation,[39] *that you stand firm in one Spirit, contending as one person in the faith of the gospel;*[40]

With this imperative Paul moves from "my affairs" (v. 12) to "your affairs,"[41] which in a specific way will be the concern from here through

---

offers the intriguing suggestion that Paul is reflecting on Jesus' promise of the Spirit in face of trial (Matt 10:20 and parallels), which finally founders lexically (against all known evidence he translates ἐπιχορηγία "assistance").

[39]This somewhat stilted translation reflects an attempt to make sure that the neuter plural article (τά) is included. The vast majority of English translations have simply "about you," which is not quite precise and causes readers to miss the fact that this little phrase offers the structural signal which relates 1:27–2:18 with both 1:12–26 and 2:19–30. See n. 10 above.

[40]This phrase is especially difficult to translate, thus I have followed the Greek very literally. Does it mean "in your commitment to the gospel"? (less likely) or "in the faith, that is in the gospel"? (more likely, despite the alleged "unPauline" use of "faith" in this case). Cf. "the truth of the gospel" in Gal 2:5, 14; Col 1:5.

[41]See n. 10 above. That this is so is further confirmed in vv. 12–26, where the first person singular pronoun predominates, whereas from this sentence through 2:18 it is all second person plural.

2:18. Paul has learned (apparently from Epaphroditus) that some disharmony exists in the community, evidenced in particular by the failure of
two leaders, Euodia and Syntyche, to see eye-to-eye on some matters.
The problem falls short of "strife" or "division" within the community;[42]
but some posturing is taking place, including some "murmuring and
arguing" (2:14) that smells of pride and selfish ambition (2:3). And Paul
feels constrained to nip it in the bud, not only because such posturing is
so unlike Christ (2:5–11), but also because these are dear friends.[43]

Two of the Spirit texts in this letter thus emerge near the beginning
of this section (1:27–2:18), which assumes the form of an appeal that they
live out their "citizenship" in Philippi as "citizens" of their heavenly
homeland.[44] The first of these is actually not so obviously a Spirit text,
especially in the English translations. At issue is whether Paul is encouraging them to stand firm "in one spirit"—understood either as "one
person" or with a common mind—or to stand together in[45] the "one
Spirit" of God.[46] Most translations and commentaries understand Paul
to mean the former, primarily because in the Greek text this phrase is
followed immediately by the μιᾷ ψυχῇ ("one soul/person") of the next
clause, which is seen as parallel to, or explanatory of, the first,[47] and
because the modifier "one" seems to put the emphasis on their own unity
"of spirit."

Despite this widely held point of view, several matters related to
Pauline usage give reason to pause: First, while this kind of terminology
("in one spirit") may seem to make perfectly good sense to us, finding

---

[42]As found, e.g., in Corinth. This is verified both by the kinds of appeals that Paul
makes and by the lack of the language of "quarreling" and "division." For this view
of the situation, cf. Kennedy 430: "We have no reason to suppose that there had been
serious divisions in the Philippian Church, but the case of Euodia and Syntyche (iv.2)
discloses perilous tendencies."

[43]Hence the "over-loading" (as it might appear to us) of terms of endearment,
when Paul returns to this matter in 4:1 ("my beloved, longed-for brothers and sisters,
my joy and my crown").

[44]The imperative, πολιτεύεσθε, with its cognate noun πολίτευμα in 3:20, is a word
play, related to the fact that the Philippians had Roman citizenship. His concern is
not, as some have suggested, that they live as good citizens of Rome, but how they
live out their true "citizenship," their heavenly one, as they continue to live in Philippi
until the coming of Christ. For a helpful recent discussion of this question see O'Brien
146–47.

[45]If the Holy Spirit is in view here, as I will argue, it is possible that the ἐν ἑνὶ
πνεύματι is instrumental, "by one Spirit"; but Pauline usage elsewhere with the verb
στήκετε suggests that the usage is locative. See esp. 4:1, "stand firm ἐν κυρίῳ" (cf.
1 Thes 3:8; 1 Cor 16:13).

[46]Several commentators (e.g., Vincent, Michael, Barth, Müller, Houlden, Kent)
suggest both, but with the emphasis primarily on the Philippians' own "spirit
of unity."

[47]So, e.g., Eadie 72, Meyer 61, Kent 118, Bruce 57, and esp. Hawthorne 56–57,
followed by Silva 94 and O'Brien 150.

any analogy for it in Greek literature is difficult, especially in Paul and the NT. In fact it is not easy to determine exactly what this translation might mean.[48] Ordinarily, it suggests something attitudinal,[49] that is, a "community spirit"[50] or (worse yet, in terms of Pauline usage) "a common mind."[51] But Paul never elsewhere uses πνεῦμα as an anthropological term for the human mind,[52] and when he does use πνεῦμα in the sense of an "attitude," he always qualifies it with a genitive modifier which specifies the kind of "spirit" he intends (e.g., "gentleness"; 1 Cor 4:21). What is missing in Paul is any hint that "spirit" might be an anthropological *metaphor* for a *community disposition*. Although the French have a word for it (*esprit de corps* = "spirit of the body"), the Greeks apparently did not; and it is highly questionable whether Paul is here creating such a usage.

Second, although the two phrases ἐν ἑνὶ πνεύματι/μιᾷ ψυχῇ stand in juxtaposition in Paul's sentence, it is gratuitous to argue that the clauses are therefore synonymous parallels or that the second "explains" the first.[53] This juxtaposition is undoubtedly for rhetorical effect, but that says very little about their meaning. To put that another way, no reason exists as to why the meaning of the first of these phrases should be dictated by the meaning of the second, while on the other hand there are several good reasons why it should not. Indeed, it is doubtful whether many would have thought "in one πνεῦνα" refers to something other than the Holy Spirit had there been no juxtaposed "one soul."

Third, the two phrases seem to have different relationships to their respective verb forms, predicated on the use of the preposition ἐν ("in") in the first instance which is missing in the second. Elsewhere when Paul qualifies the verb στήκω ("stand firm") with ἐν, it is invariably locative, indicating the sphere in which they are to stand firm.[54] If it were here

---

[48]Thus Eadie (72), "pervaded with one genuine spiritual emotion"; Meyer (61), "the perfect *accord* of their minds in conviction, volition, and feeling"; Michael (65), "the disposition of the community"; Lohmeyer (75) "die innere Geschlossenheit" (= "the inner resolution of purpose"; cf. O'Brien [150], "with one common purpose").

[49]Cf. Vincent 33, who suggests "disposition" as the proper sense of πνεύματι here.

[50]This is the language of Hawthorne 56.

[51]Cf. Kent 118.

[52]In this letter he uses the verb φρονεῖν when he wants to make this point (2:2; 4:2) and in 1 Cor 1:10 he uses the actual words for "mind" and "opinion." Moreover, in 1 Cor 2:10–16 the πνεῦμα is said to know the mind of God or people.

[53]Some older commentators (e.g., Lightfoot) not only saw the two terms as anthropological, but also were willing to distinguish the two, with "spirit" designating "the principle of the higher life," vis-à-vis the "soul, the seat of the affections, passions, etc." (106).

[54]Thus in 4:1, when he renews this charge, he urges them to "stand firm in the Lord." So also in 1 Thes 3:8, while in 1 Cor 16:13 it is "stand firm in the faith." By analogy, this appeal is for them to stand fast "in the one Spirit" by whom they have all been incorporated into Christ. Cf. Motyer 95, who also notes this usage.

to mean "in one spirit" then the phrase functions not as a locative but as manner, which, though possible, is unlikely in light of the combination στήκετε ἐν. The phrase "one soul," on the other hand, which does not have the preposition, is almost certainly dative of manner, indicating the way in which they are to join in the struggle together, "as one person."

Fourth, and related to the preceding two points, in the resumption of the appeal that follows in 2:1–4 these two words are picked up again by Paul and used exactly as we are suggesting he uses them here. Thus in v. 1, he appeals to their "participation in *the Spirit*" and in v. 2 argues that they be "soul brothers and sisters" in this matter. Why the first of these words should carry a different meaning, not only from all other Pauline usage but also from its meaning in a resumptive passage, is not easy to discern.

Fifth, and most significantly, Paul has used this identical language (ἐν ἑνὶ πνεύματι, "in one Spirit") in a recent letter (Eph 2:18; cf. 4:4) as well as in 1 Cor 12:13 to describe the Holy Spirit, *precisely in passages where the emphasis is on believers' common experience of the one Spirit as the basis for unity.* No one would imagine in these cases that "in one Spirit" refers to the *esprit de corps* of the community. Paul's obvious concern is that their being one in Christ is the direct result of the Spirit's presence in their individual and community life. So too in this case.

That leads, finally, to the contextual observation that understanding the phrase in this way not only makes good sense in terms of Pauline usage, but also in terms of the present appeal and of his theology as reflected elsewhere. The present appeal is for their unity in the face of opposition. That Paul should *twice* urge them to hold firm and contend with unity of purpose makes for a much weaker appeal than that he should urge them first to stand firm in the "one Spirit," and by the Spirit thereby to contend "as one person" against their opposition. This is such a thoroughly Pauline viewpoint that one wonders why it should even be imagined that ἐν ἑνὶ πνεύματι might mean something like *esprit de corps*.

But even more so, it is an especially Pauline view that the Spirit is the key to unity in the church. This is expressly stated in such passages as 1 Cor 12:13 or Eph 4:4, and is implied in many other texts. Moreover, in the next paragraph (2:1) he further appeals to their common fellowship in the Spirit as one of the bases for his renewed appeal to unity. That he should qualify the Spirit as "the *one* Spirit" underscores the *source* of their unity. By standing firm in the one Spirit they can then hope to contend as "one person" against their opposition. We should therefore not be surprised that this is the first thing said in the long appeal for unity (1:27–2:18) that begins with this sentence.

PHILIPPIANS 2:1

¹Therefore, if there is any encouragement in Christ, if there is any comfort of love, if there is any fellowship of Spirit, if there is any compassion or pity, ²fulfill my joy, so that you have the same mind, having the same love, . . .

Both the "therefore" and the content of this sentence (vv. 1–4) signal that the preceding paragraph had primarily to do with a concern for unity/harmony in the Philippian congregation—although in the first instance as a concern in the face of opposition. The appeal thus began in 1:27, but the mention of opposition in v. 28 led to momentary theological reflection on the role of suffering. With the present text Paul now returns to the appeal, beginning with a fourfold basis for it, each item of which has to do with their common life in Christ.

But the meaning of these various clauses is not easy to pin down. To get at the problem, and for the convenience of referral, an analysis and structural display of the basic elements in Paul's sentence may prove helpful. In form the sentence is "conditional," with a fourfold protasis (the "if" clauses) and elaborated apodosis (the "then" clause). The result is a sentence in four parts: a compound protasis (v. 1), the apodosis (2a), a result (or noun) clause explaining how the apodosis will be "fulfilled" (2b), which is then elaborated with a series of modifying participles and nouns (2c–4) that offer the means to fulfillment contrasted with their opposite, which undoubtedly gives content to the problem in Philippi ("selfish ambition" and "empty conceit"). But despite the form, the "conditional" disappears as the sentence evolves. The "if" clauses turn out not to express supposition, but presupposition.[55] These therefore are better translated something closer to "since there is . . . "; and the apodosis, therefore, instead of expressing the "then" side of a supposition, takes the form of an imperative based on the presuppositions. Thus (very literally following Paul's own wording):

	Therefore	
(*protasis*)	[1] If any	encouragement in Christ
	[2] If any	solace of love
	[3] If any	fellowship of Spirit
	[4] If any	compassions and mercies

---

[55]Cf. in this regard, J. L. Boyer, "First Class Conditions: What Do They Mean?" *GTJ* 2 (1981) 106; and BDF §371 (and most commentators), over against W. Barclay, "Great Themes of the New Testament" *ExpT* 70 (1958–59) 40, who considers the clause to be suppositional.

(*apodosis*)	Fulfill my joy,
	so that
(*explanation*)	you think the same thing
(*elaboration*)	by having the same love,
	being soul brothers/sisters[56]
	thinking the one thing
	nothing according to selfish ambition
	nothing according to empty conceit
	but
	with humility
	considering one another
	more important than oneself

The interpretive difficulties have to do with the modifiers (in Christ, of love, of Spirit) in lines 1–3, which in turn affect how one understands the entire passage. There can be little question that Paul is appealing to their common experience of the Christian faith; what is less clear is the nature of the *relationships* intended, or even whether the same relationships are assumed in all three lines.[57] Using line 2 to illustrate,[58] basically three options exist. Did Paul intend (1) solace that comes from Christ's love for them; or (2) solace from the Philippians' mutual love for each other; or (3) solace from their mutual love with Paul? Or in the case of line 3 which concerns us, did he intend (1) fellowship with the Spirit himself,[59] or (2) fellowship with one another created by the Spirit,[60] or (3) their common fellowship (theirs and Paul's together) that comes from their common experience of the Spirit.[61]

---

[56]Gk. σύμψυχοι, lit. "united souls" (Alford).

[57]On this larger question and for a helpful and more detailed discussion of the three lines, see now O'Brien 167–75.

[58]The meaning of line 1 is more complicated, since the word παράκλησις has a considerable range of meanings ("appeal, exhortation, encouragement, comfort"), and since its modifier is not a genitive but the locative ἐν Χριστῷ ("in Christ"). Thus it has been variously understood to mean (1) "if there is any consolation in Christ" = recall your status as a community loved by Christ; (2) "if there is any appeal in Christ" = if our common life in Christ allows any grounds for appeal; (3) "if there is any encouragement in Christ" = an obligation to unity arises directly out of their (the Philippians') common life in Christ; or (4) "if there is any encouragement that comes from *our* common bond in Christ."

[59]In the sense of participation in the Spirit and therefore in the life of the Spirit. Cf. Vincent 54. On this matter see the discussion on 2 Cor 13:13[14]. As there, and under the influence of Seesemann, this is the view of Martin 87 (cf. his commentary on 2 Corinthians and his contribution to the Beasley-Murray Festschrift).

[60]So, inter alia, Moule 34; Kennedy 432; Barclay, "Great Themes," 40; Hawthorne 66; Motyer 103.

[61]Beare 71 wants all three senses here. Many early commentators argued that the Spirit is not in view at all, but that the phrase denotes only community of feeling among themselves; but both the parallel in 2 Cor 13:13[14] and Pauline usage and theology in general have sounded the death knell to such a view.

This is not at all easy to determine, since the answer in the case of our clause is related in part to Pauline usage elsewhere (2 Cor 13:13[14]),[62] in part to how one understands all four of the "if" clauses and their purpose, and in part to how one understands the larger context. Indeed, so difficult is this decision, that a convincing case can be made for each of the options. In the final analysis, the option that seems to make the best sense of the overall argument is preferred. The ultimate question, therefore, is whether the context emphasizes (1) Christ and the Spirit's prior work of grace in their midst,[63] (2) the Philippians' common life in Christ that they have experienced heretofore,[64] or (3) the relationship that they and Paul have together in the bonds of Christ and their common participation in the Spirit.[65]

Despite my theological proclivities toward the first option and the plain concern in context for the second, the imperative in the apodosis seems to point to the third. It is true that their sharing in the Spirit would serve as a powerful theological basis for unity; it is likewise true that if our understanding of the Spirit phrase in 1:27 is correct, then Paul has already urged them to stand firm in the one Spirit who is the common denominator of their life in Christ and therefore of their unity. Nonetheless, the immediate context seems to favor an appeal to their mutual (his and theirs together) life in Christ, their mutual love for one another, and their mutual sharing in the life of the Spirit. Thus, although the work of Christ and the Spirit are the ultimate ground of the appeal, the expression of it in these clauses most likely has to do with their relationship with Paul.

Three items argue decisively in this direction. First, their mutual relationship with Paul is quite the point of the immediately preceding "digression" about suffering in 1:29–30. Not only is their present struggle and suffering a gift of God's grace[66] (v. 29), but he and they are in this together, inasmuch as the Philippians are involved in *the same* "struggle" they have previously seen Paul go through and have more recently heard that he is now enduring (v. 30).

Second, that commonality is precisely why our sentence, which renews the appeal that began in 1:27, is connected to vv. 29–30 with a

---

[62]We have already noted the difficulty with the phrase "fellowship of the Holy Spirit" in this grace-benediction; but even if we are right in that instance, namely, that it has to do with participating in the Spirit himself—that is, mutual sharing in the life of God through his Spirit—there can be no guarantee that that meaning will hold here as well.

[63]So Beare, O'Brien.

[64]So Lightfoot, Moule, Silva.

[65]So Eadie, Michael, Barth.

[66]The choice of the verb χαρίζομαι ("give graciously as a favor") is scarcely accidental. They have been "graced" by God, not only to trust in Christ, but also to suffer "for him" (ὑπὲρ αὐτοῦ).

"therefore."[67] "Therefore," Paul is saying, "since we are in this thing together as to suffering, if there is any encouragement that comes from our being in Christ, if there is any comfort to be found in our mutual love, if our common sharing in the Spirit means anything at all, if anyone has any compassion or pity, fulfill my joy. . . ."

Third, and most important, their common lot is especially the point of the imperative in the apodosis. Paul wants them to "fulfill *his own joy*," joy which is his in Christ and which they are to him because of their common relationship to Christ (cf. 4:1). That is, the *appeal* is for the Philippians to "work out their common salvation" (2:12) by being united in Christ, but the *ground* of the appeal is their common relationship with Paul in Christ and the Spirit.

That means, therefore, that "fellowship of the Spirit," as is most likely also the case in 2 Cor 13:13[14], refers to the sharing "in the Spirit" that believers have first with God through the Spirit and then with one another because they live and breathe by the same Spirit. They not only live and breathe by means of the Spirit whom God has given them, but they are also thereby united to Christ and to one another in Christ. The Spirit is the empowering agent of all that God is currently doing among them, "both to will and to do of his good pleasure" (v. 13).

Thus even the order of these clauses is full of Pauline theology. Everything has to do with their being "in Christ." The first result of such life in Christ is mutual love; hence in v. 2 the first participial elaboration as to how they can "fulfill Paul's joy" is by their having this same love for another that they have mutually had with Paul over many years. The experienced reality that has brought them together into Christ and has given them this mutual love in Christ is their common participation in the life of the Spirit.[68]

PHILIPPIANS 3:3

For we are the real circumcision, who offer service[69] by the Spirit of God[70] and put our boast in Christ Jesus and have no confidence in the flesh.

---

[67]Otherwise Eadie 81, who sees it as going back to v. 27; cf. Kennedy 432, Vincent 53 ("clearly"!).

[68]Lohmeyer 82, followed by Motyer 103, sees the three lines as reflecting on the divine triad, very much as in 2 Cor 13:13[14]. Thus: the "grace" of Christ, now expressed as "encouragement"; love's solace is that from God the Father; and the communion of the Spirit. While this is perhaps possible, one wonders whether the Philippians could have caught this sense.

[69]For the difficulties in translating λατρεύοντες here, see the discussion that follows.

[70]The original text reads either οἱ πνεύματι θεοῦ λατρεύοντες ("who serve by the Spirit of God"; ℵ* A B C D² F G 1739 Maj) or οἱ πνεύματι θεῷ λατρεύοντες ("who serve God in spirit" [Moffatt]; ℵ² D* P Ψ 365 1175 pc lat sy) or οἱ πνεύματι λατρεύοντες ("who

This final mention of the Spirit in this letter comes in one of its more difficult sections. If the structure of the flow of thought in chs. 1–2 can be traced with relative ease (see n. 10 above), the same cannot be said about ch. 3, in terms either of its inner coherence[71] or of its relationship to what precedes and follows.[72] For reasons not immediately apparent to us, Paul feels constrained in this letter to warn them yet one more time of the dangers of incursions from Jewish Christian missionaries,[73] who probably insist on Gentile circumcision as necessary for reaching the eschatological goal. Just as in the two previous letters where such argumentation takes place (Galatians and Romans), the Spirit is brought into the foreground as evidence against such "boasting in the flesh."

Especially significant in this regard is the argument in Gal 3:2–3, where Paul uses "flesh" in the same way as here, as referring first to the actual "flesh" cut away in circumcision, but at the same time as the primary descriptive word of life before and outside of Christ. Thus, as in that passage, "Spirit" and "flesh" stand juxtaposed as eschatological realities that describe existence in the overlap of the ages.[74] One lives either "according to the Spirit" or "according to the flesh." These are mutually incompatible kinds of existence; to be in the one and then to revert to the former is spiritual suicide from Paul's perspective.

What is striking in this case is the nature of the rhetoric by which all of this is said. The Philippians are to "beware the dogs," who in

serve by the Spirit"; P[46]). Both the supporting witnesses and transcriptional probability favor the first option (the phrase seems so unnatural and the concept of "serving God" so normal [cf. Rom 1:9], it is difficult to imagine scribes deliberately changing from either of the latter to the former). Cf. Metzger, *Textual Commentary*, 614. Otherwise Kennedy 449, who prefers the dative on the mistaken notion that it provides a better parallel with σαρκί.

[71]One of the difficulties has to do with how the "opponents" in vv. 17–19 are related to those warned against by the rhetoric of v. 2, whether they are the same, or whether Paul is fighting on more than one front.

[72]As suggested above in n. 4, I take the τὰ αὐτά ("the same things") in v. 1 with all seriousness as an indication that Paul has formerly warned them of such "mutilators of the flesh." Solutions to the twin problems of the abruptness of this warning and of the repeated "finally, rejoice in the Lord" that take the form of multiple letters and interpolations finally solve nothing. The text as we have it comes with the difficulties intact. Solutions of interpolation merely presuppose that Paul is a tidier writer than the alleged interpolator, tidier than we might have any a priori grounds to believe him to be. Since such solutions are propounded to overcome similar difficulties in several of his letters, perhaps that should clue us in to Paul as a writer; he is not nearly as tidy as we think he should be (perhaps we prefer him to reflect what we think of our better selves?).

[73]Not all are agreed even on this. Hawthorne, e.g., argues strongly for Jews as such, but his position is a minority one. For the position assumed here, see O'Brien 26–35.

[74]For this emphasis on "flesh" and "Spirit" as primarily eschatological realities, see Silva 170–71.

the third instance are described with a striking word play on circumcision. By insisting on Gentile circumcision (περιτομή = to cut *around*), the opponents are themselves the κατατομή (= cut *to pieces*, hence "the mutilation"). "For" he now goes on in our sentence by way of contrast, "we ourselves *are* the circumcision, who offer service by the Spirit of God." All of this echoes what Paul had said earlier to the Romans (2:28–29, q.v.). But in this case the contrast takes a slightly different turn.

The crucial term here is the verb λατρεύω, which most English translations render as "worship," a rendering which in this case can be misleading. In Jewish and Christian literature this verb was used only for the offering of service to God, particularly "the carrying out of relig[ious] duties, esp[ecially] of a cultic nature" (BAGD).[75] Paul uses the same word in Rom 1:9 to describe his ministry as a whole and in Rom 12:1 (in its noun form, and also in a context of religious imagery) to describe Christian life as "service that makes sense." The verb, therefore, is not the one for "worship" in the sense of what the congregation does together as a gathered people, but for service rendered to God as a form of devotion to him. The choice of words here is dictated almost entirely by the play on the theme of circumcision.[76] Rather than offer service to God in the form of "cutting away the flesh," so as to be identified with the people of God under the former covenant, Paul asserts rhetorically that he and the Philippians[77] are *the* circumcision, who have exchanged a form of "ritual service" for that which takes place in the realm of the Spirit. Thus, Paul has in view not external rite over against internal, "spiritual"[78] service, but two ways of existing—in the "flesh," which, as in Galatians and Romans, he understands as life centered in the creature as over against God, or as the eschatological people of God, evidenced as such by the Spirit of God, through whom all life in the present is now service and devotion to God.

---

[75]There is great insight in Barth's translation (94): "we who through the Spirit are religious."

[76]Cf. Lightfoot 145, who notes that this choice is very likely a deliberate borrowing from the LXX, where it "had got to be used in a very special sense to denote the service rendered to Jehovah by the Israelite race, as His peculiar people."

[77]There has been some debate on the sense of the ἡμεῖς here. H. Koester's view that this refers to Paul's Spirit-endowed apostleship as over against that of his opponents is of interest, but related to his unique view of the passage as a whole ("The Purpose of the Polemic of a Pauline Fragment (Philippians iii)," *NTS* 8 [1961–62] 317–32). Nor does it refer to Paul and Timothy. On this question see esp. D. E. Garland, "The Composition and Unity of Philippians. Some Neglected Literary Factors," *NovT* 27 (1985) 170n100.

[78]As, e.g., the NEB, "we whose worship is spiritual"; cf. Lightfoot 145, Beare 105, Hawthorne 126–27. Although this view is often tied to John 4:24, that misses the genuinely radical nature of life in the Spirit as Paul elsewhere articulates it.

What is less certain is the precise nuance of the dative. Some make it locative:[79] the Spirit is the sphere in which those who "boast in Christ Jesus" offer all service to God, that is, we render proper service to God as we live in the Spirit. While one could scarcely argue against that theologically, Pauline usage seems determinative here. In most other instances in Paul this dative is instrumental, and is arguably so in all cases; we offer such service to God by means of the Spirit,[80] which in this case probably has little to do with "doing" anything, but rather with simply living and walking in the Spirit as over against putting confidence "in the flesh."

Finally, Paul qualifies Spirit by the genitive "of God." This designation occurs often enough in Paul that one should perhaps not make too much of it here—this is who the Spirit is, after all. Nonetheless, since Paul does not often use this qualifier in this construction,[81] there might be more emphasis than at first meets the eye. This may in fact be a pointed contrast to those who think of themselves as rendering service to the one God not only by being circumcised themselves but also by urging (insisting?) that Gentiles offer themselves to God in the same way. True service *to God* is that which has been engendered by the Spirit *of God*, where in living by the Spirit the believer thus "boasts in Christ," who has brought an end to the time of "the flesh."

PHILIPPIANS 4:23

On the use of πνεῦμα in this grace-benediction ("the grace of the Lord Jesus Christ be with your spirit [= spirits]," see the discussion of the nearly identical formula in Gal 6:18.

CONCLUSION

Even though there are but four direct references to the Spirit in this brief letter, they continue to reflect the central role of the Spirit in Paul's understanding of Christian life and experience. Believers in Christ are the people of God in the Coming Age that has already dawned, because they have received and live in the Spirit—in contrast to those who continue to live in the past ("in the flesh") by insisting on circumcision. Moreover,

---

[79]E.g., NRSV, "who worship in the Spirit of God." Cf. NASB, NAB.

[80]So also Meyer 199, Vincent 93. Pinnock, "Concept," 125–26, suggests that the "natural" sense of the dative πνεύματι is as the object of the participle λατρεύοντες, "we who serve God's Spirit." But the subsequent discussion and Paul's usage elsewhere indicate a meaning more closely aligned to an instrumental dative.

[81]That is with the dative πνεύματι; Rom 8:9 is the one exception.

life in Christ is so thoroughly life in the Spirit that the Spirit is the key to their unity, both in their united front against opposition and in their own life together as a believing community. Finally, their relationship with Paul is such that as they pray he expects God to supply him yet again with the Spirit of his Son so that Christ will be magnified in Paul, however his trial turns out. Although such references in one sense are incidental, in another sense it is their very incidental nature that indicates how thoroughly such an understanding of Christian life had pervaded Paul's experience, and therefore his thinking.

11

THE PASTORAL EPISTLES

Commentaries:[1] H. **Alford** (1865); C. K. **Barrett** (NClarB, 1963); J. H. **Bernard** (1899); N. **Brox** (1969); J. **Calvin** (1548); **D-C** = M. **Dibelius** and H. **Conzelmann** (Herm, 1972); R. **Earle** (EBC, 1978 [1–2 Tim only]); B. S. **Easton** (1948); C. R. **Erdman** (1923); R. **Falconer** (1937), G. D. **Fee** (NIBC, [2]1988); G. D. **Gealy** (IB, 1955); D. **Guthrie** (TNTC, 1957); A. T. **Hanson** (NCB, 1982); W. **Hendriksen** (NTC, 1965); J. L. **Houlden** (PNTC, 1976); R. J. **Karris** (NTM, 1979); J. N. D. **Kelly** (BNTC, 1963); H. A. **Kent** (1958); A. R. C. **Leaney** (TBC, 1960); W. **Lock** (ICC, 1924); H. A. **Moellering** (1970); R. St J. **Parry** (1920); J. D. **Quinn** (AB, 1990 [Titus only]); W. M. **Ramsay** (in *The Expositor*, 1909–10); E. F. **Scott** (MNTC, 1936); E. K. **Simpson** (1954); C. **Spicq** ([4]1969); N. J. D. **White** (EGT, 1910).

Other significant works are referred to by the following short titles:

Elliott, *Text* (= J. K. Elliott, *The Greek Text of the Epistles to Timothy and Titus* [SD 36; Salt Lake City: University of Utah Press, 1968]); **Fowl**, *Story* (= Stephen D. Fowl, *The Story of Christ in the Ethics of Paul: An Analysis of the Function of the Hymnic Material in the Pauline Corpus* [JSNTSS 36; Sheffield: JSOT Press, 1990]; **Hanson**, *Pastoral Epistles* (= A. T. Hanson, *Studies in the Pastoral Epistles* [London: SPCK, 1968]); **Knight**, *Sayings* (= George W. Knight III, *The Faithful Sayings in the Pastoral Letters* [Grand Rapids: Baker, 1979]); **Quinn**, "Spirit" (= Jerome D. Quinn, "The Holy Spirit in the Pastoral Epistles," in *Sin, Salvation, and the Spirit* [ed. D. Durken; Collegeville, Minn.: Liturgical Press, 1979] 345–68); **Towner**, *Goal* (= Philip H. Towner, *The Goal of Our Instruction: The Structure of Theology and Ethics in the Pastoral Epistles* [JSNTSup 34; Sheffield: JSOT Press, 1989]); **Wilson**, *Luke* (= Stephen G. Wilson, *Luke and the Pastoral Epistles* [London: SPCK, 1979]).

---

[1]The following commentaries are referred to in this chapter only by the author's last name.

Without doubt the most controversial aspect of this book is the inclusion of the Pastoral Epistles in a study of the Holy Spirit in Paul. On the other hand, nothing else in NT studies quite so clearly demonstrates how presuppositions affect conclusions as how one views the Pauline elements in these letters.[2] And in this regard, nothing does so any more than how one handles the Spirit texts. If the letters are read as late first/early second century forgeries, then the Spirit texts could have been written by Ignatius of Antioch;[3] if they are read as basically from Paul, then these same texts can be shown to be fully in keeping with the rest of the Pauline corpus. In any case, the theology of these letters is "much nearer to that of the earlier Paul than [is] often allowed,"[4] as Towner has recently demonstrated—fairly and convincingly, to my mind.

First, it should be noted that there are not many Spirit texts,[5] the most frequent of which refer to Timothy's personal experience of the Spirit, especially in the context of his "call" to ministry (1 Tim 1:18; 4:14; 2 Tim 1:6–7; cf. 1:14). Although these texts have some well-known exegetical difficulties, they nonetheless exemplify the fully Pauline perspective that ministry is charismatic, i.e., that it is Spirit-endowed and Spirit-empowered. In two other passages (1 Tim 3:16; Titus 3:5–6), as he does frequently, Paul dips into the creedal/hymnic traditions of the church to bolster his argument. In one instance, referring to Jesus, the question of "spirit" or "Spirit" is especially acute; in the other, as often in Paul, the Spirit plays the central role in the appropriation of God's eschatological salvation. Finally, in 1 Tim 4:1 Timothy is to recognize in the present situation in Ephesus exactly what the Spirit prophesied about the "latter times."

---

[2]It is the conviction that these letters are far more Pauline than otherwise, so that one might still speak of them as ultimately having come from him and not from a later pseudepigrapher, that caused me to subtitle this study "The Holy Spirit in the Letters of Paul" rather than "The Spirit in Paul."

[3]For an extreme example see Hanson (26–42, and the commentary throughout), whose assertions far more often betray Hanson's presuppositions than they reflect what is actually in the texts themselves. In this regard, Dunn (*Jesus*, 346–50) does not fare much better. On these matters Barrett 71 is more circumspect: "The Pastorals are not inconsistent with Paul's teaching, though they mark a later stage of development." Cf. Quinn, "Spirit," 345.

[4]Towner, *Goal*, 256. On the whole this is a persuasive study, which should help to redress some of the grievances of what Towner calls "the modern interpretation of the letters." It does not follow, of course, that Paul is their author; but what Towner has demonstrated is that, "when . . . the modern interpretation . . . is brought face to face with the actual theological and ethical outlook of their author, . . . the Pastorals are less easily dissociated from Pauline thought" (256).

[5]This in itself has often been a reason for condemning them as not from Paul (most recently Freed, *Introduction*, 401). But this is an argument from silence of the poorest kind, which takes into little or no consideration the occasion and purpose of these letters. On the same grounds one may as well condemn Philemon, which contains no references to the Spirit, or Philippians, which has proportionately about the same as the Pastorals.

Besides texts that speak of the Spirit or prophecy, there are two "power" texts in 2 Timothy (1:8; 3:5), which most likely are indirect references to the Spirit, as is the language of inspiration in 2 Tim 3:16, that scripture is "God-breathed."

What emerges in these final Pauline letters, therefore, is exactly what emerges elsewhere in Paul: The Spirit plays the crucial role in Christian conversion and ongoing Christian life; the Spirit is the key to Christian ministry; the Spirit is perceived in terms of power; and the Spirit is present in the church partly through gifts experienced by individuals within a community context.[6]

1 Timothy

The Spirit texts in this letter are especially bound up with its occasion and purpose. My view on these questions is spelled out in the Introduction to my commentary (pp. 5–10); here I outline the essential matters.

In contrast to an older view, which treated 1 Timothy as a kind of "church manual,"[7] the key to understanding the letter lies in taking seriously that Paul's *stated* reason in 1:3 for leaving Timothy in Ephesus is the *real* one; namely, that he had been left there to combat some false teachers, whose asceticism and speculations based on the Law are full of empty words, engendering strife and causing many to go astray.

Several pieces of converging evidence suggest that the false teachers, who in this case are insiders, not outsiders as elsewhere, are actually elders, just as Acts 20:17–35 presents Paul as prophesying some years earlier.[8] Some new ideas that had been circulating just a few years earlier in Colossae and Laodicea apparently had made their way to Ephesus, but now as the "official" line. These straying elders must be stopped, and Timothy was left in Ephesus to do it.

---

[6]If there is not more Spirit talk, that probably says more about the nature of the specific life setting of each of the letters than about Paul and his gospel. Since in real life neither Timothy nor Titus would need abundant rehearsals of the *content* of Paul's gospel, arguments from silence are in this case especially thin.

[7]This is especially prevalent among those who opt for pseudepigraphy, where the Pastoral Epistles are understood to reflect "early Catholicism," and Timothy is taken as the "model pastor." But this view breaks down at almost every point in terms of what the text actually says. Timothy and Titus are still itinerants; Timothy is not "setting the church in order"—although Titus is—since elders are already in place; it is not "pastoring" that is in view, but stopping false teaching. Timothy and Titus in fact are apostolic representatives within their respective communities, whose positions are no more permanent than the apostle's. If "church order" had been the forger's purpose, he was neither clear in that purpose nor did he help himself by creating so many "blips" with regard to that purpose.

[8]As noted in my commentary (29n16), this is a significant datum whether the content of that speech was written before or after the fact.

The *purpose* of 1 Timothy arises out of this complexity. The letter betrays indications everywhere that it was intended ultimately for the church itself, not just for Timothy. But because of *defections in the leadership*, Paul does not, as before, write directly to the church, but to the church through Timothy. The reason for going this route would have been twofold: (1) to *encourage Timothy* to carry out this most difficult task of stopping the erring elders, who were creating strife as well as promoting errors, and who obviously carried a good deal of clout;[9] and (2) to *authorize Timothy before the church* to carry out his task. At the same time, of course, the church will be having the false teachers/teachings exposed before them, plus Paul's instructions to Timothy about what he was to do.

The Spirit texts fit squarely into this dual concern over the false teaching (3:16; 4:1) and Timothy's task of stopping the false teachers (1:18; 4:14).

1 TIMOTHY 1:18

This charge I entrust to you, child Timothy, in keeping with the prophetic utterances once spoken over/about you,[10] so that by means of them you may keep on waging[11] the good warfare.

These words renew the charge to Timothy begun in v. 3, and seem primarily intended to bolster Timothy's courage for the task of stopping the straying elders.[12] To do so, he reminds Timothy of his "call" to ministry, which was both ordained and (according to 4:14) effected by the Spirit. "This charge," he says, "is quite in keeping with the prophetic utterances spoken about you many years ago."

Paul's intent and concern seem clear. He is urging Timothy to stay with the "battle" and at the same time reminding the church of Timothy's "authority" to be among them in this way. Thus this reminder that the charge comes ultimately from the Spirit, not from Paul. Moreover, Paul urges him to do battle by the power of the Spirit (here, "by means of the prophecies"), which he will urge even more explicitly in 2 Tim 1:6–8 and 14.

---

[9] The fact that the "excommunicated" Hymenaeus (1 Tim 1:20) is still at work in the church over a year later (2 Tim 2:17) indicates that he did not give up easily.

[10] Gk. ἐπὶ σέ. The preposition ordinarily means "over" (hence the JB: "the words once spoken over you by the prophets"); but the nature of such utterances would therefore be "about" Timothy (thus, GNB NIV NRSV NASB and most commentaries).

[11] The present tense (א² A D² F G H Maj) is to be preferred to the aorist (א* D* Y 1175 pc), on grounds both transcriptional (scribal tendencies are away from the present and toward the aorist as the more common tense with the subjunctive) and intrinsic (the concern is continuation, not getting started). Cf. Elliott, *Text*, 21, who offers different reasons. Although this way of translating the Greek present is somewhat pedantic, it seems proper in this instance in order to bring out the force of the renewed charge (from v. 3).

[12] This becomes more clear in light of the immediately following mention of the ringleaders of the movement, Hymenaeus and Alexander, who had been excommunicated, but one of whom, according to 2 Tim 2:17, remains active in the church.

So significant is this concern (that Timothy rely on the Spirit) that Paul reminds him on three separate occasions in the two letters (see 4:14; 2 Tim 1:6–7)[13] of the Spirit origin of his life in Christ and of his calling and ministry. Each of these, however, is tailored to its immediate context, and there are just enough differences among them so as to create difficulties for us in trying to define the precise nature of the experience(s) to which Paul refers. Even so, the *reason* for all of these reminders is plain enough: Timothy's need to depend on the Spirit for the task at hand. Indeed 2 Tim 1:6–7 indicates that the concern is not simply for Timothy to remember his beginnings—although for his encouragement that is important as well—but that he "fan into flame" the gift of the Spirit, whose indwelling also brought enabling power.

Paul here describes the experience as κατὰ τὰς προαγούσας ἐπὶ σὲ προφητείας (lit. "in keeping with the formerly spoken over you prophecies"[14]). From the other two passages we learn that the experience involved more than Timothy's simply being singled out for ministry by prophetic utterances; through the Spirit he also received a gift that Paul describes as *in him*. But here his presence in Ephesus to combat error is *in keeping with* some earlier prophecies; what the Spirit had said about him many years before, Timothy is now to understand as pertaining to his involvement in the current conflict. The present emphasis therefore is twofold: (1) that the experience goes back to his *origins* in this ministry; and (2) that it was *the Spirit himself* who expressly *singled Timothy out* for this ministry in which he had long been involved, and which is now being tested in Ephesus.

It is possible, however, to understand the phrase "formerly spoken over you" in a slightly different way. The ambiguity[15] of the Greek participle has caused some to argue that the prophecies "lead the way" to Timothy, i.e., they "pointed out Timothy to Paul."[16] But there is solid contemporary evidence for the temporal use of this participle;[17] and since

---

[13] Although most scholars think that these three texts probably refer to the same event in Timothy's life, there are good reasons to think otherwise about 2 Tim 1:6–7 (q.v.). Nonetheless, all of them are concerned to remind Timothy of his Spirit origins—both as a believer and as an itinerant servant of Christ. The two passages in this letter most likely refer to the same event as that recorded in Acts 16:1–5, where Timothy joined the Pauline circle in Lystra. Some (Bernard 72, Lock 54) suggest a more recent event in Ephesus; but that is the result of an ecclesiastical reading of 4:14. Second Timothy suggests that Paul is especially concerned to recall Timothy's origins (see 2 Tim 1:5, 6–7; 3:10–11, 14–16). See Fee 175–77.

[14] Cf. the KJV, "according to the prophecies which went before on thee."

[15] προάγω, which can mean either to "lead the way, precede" in a spatial sense (cf. 5:24, "the sins of some *go on before* them into judgment") or to "go before" and thus to have *happened* previously in a temporal sense.

[16] Thus NEB, "which first pointed you out to me"; RSV, "which pointed to you" (but changed in the NRSV to the position argued for here, "made earlier about you"). So also Chrysostom, White, Kent, Guthrie, and several others as an equal option (Lock, Scott, Barrett, Kelly, Earle). Otherwise Bernard, Erdman, Hendriksen.

[17] E.g., Heb 7:18 ("the former regulation" NIV); cf. the papyri examples in MM.

Paul's concern is not, as some would have it, with recognizing Timothy as Paul's authentic "successor,"[18] but rather with encouraging Timothy to continue the battle, the view of the majority is much to be preferred.

Because of the ad hoc nature of such statements,[19] the questions of when, by whom, and what (= the content of the prophecies) are less than certain. As to when, both the tenor of the two letters to Timothy and the content of the three crucial texts point to the time when Timothy began his association with Paul.[20] This is the obvious perspective of 2 Tim 3:10–11. To suggest that this is an event in which the Ephesian elders "ordained" Timothy to ministry is not only the perspective of a later time, but is impossible if we are correct that the false teachers are elders.

By whom? In light of the singular noun "prophecy" in 4:14,[21] the plural here is suggestive. Perhaps it points to more than one occasion;[22] more likely it suggests a variety of prophetic activity on the one occasion referred to. Perhaps the plurality of the utterances was itself a form of "discerning" the prophecies, in which the word to Timothy came from several people in the community, each in its own way affirming the word of the others. In any case, Calvin seems to have had it right in suggesting that the plural firmly places the experience in the broader context of the church, not in the narrower context of Paul and Timothy together.[23]

The content, of course, can only be surmised; but in view of the concern in this context and in light of 4:14, the most obvious surmise is that they were spontaneous utterances of the Spirit through those so gifted in the community, which would commission—or confirm—Timothy as one whom God had singled out for itinerant ministry with Paul. Thus it is a Pauline illustration of what he himself experienced in the church in Antioch, narrated in Acts 13:1–2.[24]

Finally, Timothy is also urged "by means of these prophecies" (lit. "in them") to engage in the noble warfare. While this prepositional phrase is somewhat ambiguous, it probably means something like

---

[18]E.g., Scott 16.

[19]Because Paul and Timothy are fully aware of the particulars, there is no need to elaborate. Timothy is simply being reminded of the event. Pseudepigraphers, on the other hand, tended to fill in such details—for the sake of their own audiences.

[20]See n. 13 above.

[21]See below on 4:14, where προφητεία almost certainly refers not to a singular "prophetic utterance" but to the phenomenon itself, collectively understood. Contra BAGD, 3b.

[22]As Lock 18 asserts; Kelly 57 is uncertain.

[23]Contra Guthrie 67, e.g., who suggests "predictions in some way granted to Paul concerning Timothy before his call to ministry." This does not take 4:14 seriously enough, not to mention the Pauline understanding of prophecy as a corporate reality.

[24]Some among those "ministering" in that church are specifically designated as "prophets and teachers." This is one of the correspondences between Acts and the Pastoral Epistles that led Wilson (Luke, 58) to see the hand of Luke in these letters.

either "standing in the strength of such prophecies"[25] or "by means of the encouragement drawn from such prophecies."[26] In either case, the appeal is for Timothy both to remember the origins of his present ministry many years earlier as the singular work of the Spirit and by that remembrance to keep at the task in Ephesus, despite the obvious difficulties that entailed (the warfare imagery is not for naught). Indeed, this appeal to former prophecies, plus the urging not to neglect his gift (4:14) but to fan it into flame (2 Tim 1:6–7), is to be understood precisely in a context of what in contemporary terms would be called "spiritual warfare." This is further clarified in 4:1–2, where the false teaching is demonic and the false teachers are under the influence of "deceiving spirits." Thus "by them" (the Spirit's prophetic utterances) Timothy is to keep on waging the war against the enemy of people's souls.

Such emphasis, it need only be pointed out in passing, is thoroughly Pauline. Timothy will be successful in Ephesus to the degree to which he remains dependent on the work of the Spirit.

1 TIMOTHY 3:16[27]

By common consent[28] great indeed is the mystery of the godliness [we affirm]:[29]

---

[25]Cf. White 101, *"in them,* as in defensive armour"; so also Erdman.

[26]Cf. RSV, "inspired by them"; Calvin 201, "Timothy, relying on this approval God has given him."

[27] *Bibliography:* Reinhard **Deichgräber,** *Gotteshymnus und Christushymnus in der frühen Christenheit: Untersuchungen zu Form, Sprache und Stil der frühchristlichen Hymnen* (Göttingen: Vandenhoeck & Ruprecht, 1967) 133–37; **Fowl,** *Story,* 155–94; Robert H. **Gundry,** "The Form, Meaning and Background of the Hymn Quoted in I Timothy 3:16," in *Apostolic History and the Gospel: Biblical and Historical Essays presented to F. F. Bruce on his 60th Birthday* (ed. W. W. Gasque and R. P. Martin; Grand Rapids: Eerdmans, 1970) 203–22; W. **Metzger,** *Der Christushymnus 1 Tim. 3,16* (Stuttgart: Calwer, 1979); E. **Schweizer,** "Two New Testament Creeds Compared," in *Current Issues in New Testament Interpretation: Essays in honor of Otto A. Piper* (ed. W. Klassen and G. Snyder; New York: Harper, 1962) 166–77; D. M. **Stanley,** *Christ's Resurrection in Pauline Soteriology* (AnBib 13; Rome: Pontifical Biblical Institute, 1961) 236–39; W. **Stenger,** *Der Christushymnus 1 Tim. 3.16: Eine structuranalysche Untersuchung* (Frankfurt: Peter Lang, 1977); **Towner,** *Goal,* 87–93.

[28]Although ὁμολογουμένως usually means "confessedly, admittedly," the context suggests that the more pregnant idea inherent in the word group ("confession" or "agreeing") is foremost in Paul's mind, especially in light of the adversative δέ that begins 4:1, which contrasts the demonic teaching that *disagrees* with this. Cf. Fowl, *Story,* 183–84, who notes the usage in Jos. *Ant.* 1.180; 2.229, where it means something close to "by common assent." This is much to be preferred to Hanson's view that the author is here dependent on 4 Maccabees for "an academic" phrase with philosophical overtones (see *Pastoral Epistles,* 21–28).

[29]For this translation see the discussion below.

> *He who*[30] *was manifested in the flesh,*
> *was vindicated in the Spirit,*
> *appeared to angels,*
> *was preached among the nations,*
> *was believed on in the world,*
> *was taken up in glory.*

The consensus of NT scholarship is that Paul (or the non-Pauline author) is here quoting from an early Christian hymn, focusing on Christ. The reasons for this belief are basically three: (1) The rhythmic nature of the whole (all begin with an aorist passive; and all but line 3 are modified by a dative with ἐν); (2) the apparent parallelism of the lines; and (3) the terse form of the six lines, which speak to different aspects of Christ's "life" with some ambiguity and without elaboration. If this is not a hymn to be sung, there can be little question of its creedal nature. Here Paul is dipping into the church's common confession of Christ to make a point in his argument.

But after that, there is considerable difference of opinion—on three crucial matters: (1) the structure and meaning of the hymn as a whole; (2) the meaning of the first two lines, especially line 2, our present interest: ἐδικαιώθη ἐν πνεύματι ("was vindicated in the spirit/Spirit"); and (3) how all of this fits into the context of the present argument. In this case these three matters are rather thoroughly interwoven; so let us begin with the latter and see how that might affect our understanding of the first two.

The question of context usually either is neglected[31] or at best receives mere lip service,[32] mostly because the passage seems to sit like a

---

[30]That ὅς (ℵ* A* C* G 33 365 442 2127 syr cop arm goth eth Origen Epiphanius Jerome), and not its corruption ὅ (D latt), nor θεός (MajT), is the original text is assured by all the canons of textual criticism. It is the reading of all the early evidence, confirmed in this case by the fact that not a single one of the ancient versions is translated from a text that read "God." In fact the corruption can have happened only in Greek, and on the basis of the abbreviation of the *nomen sacrum* (ΘΣ); this was easily corrupted from ΟΣ, on the basis of the apparently ungrammatical nature of the latter; indeed a change in the other direction is nearly impossible to account for under any circumstances. See further Fee, "The Majority Text and the Original Text of the New Testament," 116–18.

[31]As e.g., in Bernard and Earle. The majority think it simply illustrates the "mystery of godliness," and therefore the truth of which the church is guarantor; so e.g., Lock, Scott, Guthrie, Hendriksen. D-C style it "transitional," intended "to present the concept of tradition"; Kelly 93 specifically calls it a "brief digression extolling the Christian mystery." All of these have in common that they do not see it as advancing the argument itself in any specific way.

[32]Calvin 232 and Barrett 57, e.g., relate it directly to ch. 3, as giving "the reasons why men should behave suitably (for example, in the conduct of their ministry) in the Church of God" (Barrett). At best this is weak; at worst it misses the genuine break at v. 14 and the adversative nature of the δέ in 4:1, and never fully faces up to

rock in the middle of the argument.[33] But there are reasons to think otherwise.[34] The clues lie in three areas. First, v. 14 functions transitionally, concluding the whole argument thus far and setting up what is to follow. Thus the concern over conduct in God's household refers not so much to chapter 3, but to the larger behavioral concerns brought about by the false teachers; Paul is writing not so that Timothy or church leaders will know how to behave in church, but so that all of God's people will know how to behave in God's household, the community of faith.[35] Second, the δέ ("but") in 4:1 is best understood as a true adversative to 3:16, suggesting that what Paul is about to say stands in contrast to what is expressed in the hymn. Third, what holds this argument together (from 3:14) is the concern over εὐσέβεια ("godliness");[36] the hymn is intended to give content to εὐσέβεια; the pursuit of it is about to be urged on Timothy (4:6–10) in direct antithesis to the false teachers and their errors (4:1–5). This suggests, therefore, that the content of the hymn may best be understood over against the content of the false teachings as they are delineated in 4:3–5.

Thus the argument: Since Paul cannot return to Ephesus immediately, he writes to Timothy so that people will know how to live as God's household. This concern over proper behavior serves as the catalyst to move him directly toward the exposure of the false teaching that is

---

the problem of why *this* particular content should have been quoted, since it seems irrelevant to the reason offered. White's suggestion is even less convincing: "The connexion of thought lies in a feeling that the lofty terms in which the Church has been just spoken of may demand a justification" (118); cf. Hanson 86.

[33]Nothing in the immediately preceding context prepares us for this content; furthermore, the argument seems to begin anew in 4:1 and, from this distance, with no immediately apparent conceptual connection to 3:16. Scott 40 states it baldly, "[The words] . . . are thrown in, as one might cite a verse of poetry, to conclude and dignify a passage of argument."

[34]In what follows I am indebted to insights from both Towner, *Goal*, 87–93, and esp. Fowl, *Story*, 174–94. In my commentary I had advanced a twofold suggestion as to context: that it was probably in contrast to the Christology of the false teachers, and that it prepared the way for the denouncement of the false teaching in 4:1–5. The studies of Fowl and Towner have advanced these suggestions considerably, and I herewith acknowledge my debt to them in the exegesis that follows—although I continue to differ from them in some details.

[35]On this see Fee 91, 95; cf. Fowl, *Story*, 180–81.

[36]Cf. Fowl, *Story*, 183–84; Towner, *Goal*, 88–89. There can be little question of the importance of this word in the Pastoral Epistles. Since it is unique to these letters in the Pauline corpus, this is seen as a sign of pseudepigraphy. On the contrary, I have suggested that its usage is more typically Pauline; as in 1 Cor 1:18–3:23, he takes a word that is important to his opponents and turns it over against them and fills it with his own content (Fee 63). In this case, Towner (*Goal*, 147–54) has argued convincingly that the word refers to "the manner of life that issues from a [proper] knowledge of God" (149), and thus includes both right thinking and right living. That is surely the primary clue to the question of context in this passage.

leading to all kinds of "ungodliness" in this community. The church, therefore, is to be understood as the guarantor of the truth; "indeed," he goes on, "by common confessional consent great is the mystery of the εὐσέβεια that we affirm in our hymn/creed."

After citing (in our text) some matters essential to a proper understanding of "godliness," he immediately plunges into the contrast, the present scene in Ephesus, which is something that the Spirit has expressly warned about. Indeed the false teaching is ultimately demonic, from "deceiving spirits," and its content is decidedly over against the Christian understanding of creation. As Fowl has argued, the false teaching spelled out in v. 3 and argued against in vv. 3–5 separates God from the created order. And it is exactly such a notion that, by pointing to Christ, the hymn resists.[37]

If this properly views the flow of the argument, and it seems to make eminently good sense of things, that in turn should inform our understanding not only of the *reason* for the hymn at this point, but also of the meaning of the crucial opening lines. All concur that these two lines give the focus and are the clue to understanding the whole. It is likewise agreed that the two are to be held together, in some antithesis to be sure, by the contrasting pair, ἐν σαρκί and ἐν πνεύματι ("flesh" and "spirit"). The disagreement comes in determining their points of reference.

Line 1 almost certainly refers to our Lord's incarnation. But in what way, and with what emphasis? Despite the use of "manifested,"[38] the emphasis does not seem to be on divine self-disclosure as one finds in John's Gospel. Moreover, although the language seems to presuppose preexistence,[39] neither is that a concern here. Rather, in light of the language of "vindication" in line 2, most likely this line emphasizes, at least in this context, the *reality* of Christ's having been present "in the flesh." What is less certain is the precise referent of "flesh," which in turn affects how one understands πνεῦμα in line 2. Does it refer to Jesus' "body" per se,[40] or to his humanity in a more general sense?[41]

---

[37]This also helps to explain the most striking feature about the hymn as a piece of early Christian creedal formulation, namely, the lack of reference to Christ's death. Some (e.g., Stanley, *Resurrection*, 237) have argued, but with little success in terms of persuading others, that line 1 "ought to be understood as an allusion to Christ's death in its redemptive character." That is to find what one is looking for, not what seems to be inherent in the language itself.

[38]Gk. ἐφανερώθη; cf. Titus 1:3; 2 Tim 1:10. The verb is common in Paul.

[39]So Bernard 63, Lock 45, and many others, contra Dunn, *Christology* 237, whose determination to read preexistence out of Paul makes him read several texts in what appears to be a very unnatural way.

[40]This is contended for by Gundry, "Form"; cf. the NIV, "He appeared in a body."

[41]Because of prior commitments to their views of the hymn as a whole, some limit the reference to Jesus' birth (Alford) or the crucifixion (Stanley, *Resurrection*); but these seem altogether unlikely. See the critiques in Gundry, "Form," 204, 209–10.

If "flesh" equals "body," then πνεῦμα in the next line seems logically to refer to Jesus' human spirit.[42] But there are several reasons for rejecting this view of "flesh"[43] and its corresponding view of "spirit," not the least of which is that this contrast never occurs in Paul anywhere.[44] More likely the phrase "in the flesh" means something like that in the similar passages in Rom 1:3–4 and 1 Pet 3:18, namely, "in the sphere of humanity," i.e., in truly human existence. Although the term is not intended to be pejorative regarding our human life, it does indeed speak to its limitations and weaknesses. Thus in quoting this hymn Paul is not suggesting that Christ's appearing in "flesh" was an unfortunate expression of his existence. To the contrary, "he was *manifested* in the flesh": the "mystery" of "godliness" has been revealed through Christ's sharing our human life, despite its weaknesses.

On this interpretation of "flesh," line 2 is then best understood as denoting God's vindication[45] of Christ's earthly life. But exactly how this vindication is to be understood is moot. Several English translations[46] take ἐν πνεύματι as instrumental and as referring to God's vindication of his Son through the power of the Spirit, either during his earthly ministry[47] or in the resurrection, suggesting the Spirit to be the agent of his resurrection. But attractive as that view might be, it fails on three counts: (1) it is not the most natural contrast with "in the flesh" in line 1; (2) it seems to strain the verb "vindicated" to suggest that this refers to his earthly ministry;[48] and (3) it is not elsewhere explicitly stated in the NT that God raised Christ by the power of his Spirit.

---

[42]Some (Kent 146, Simpson 61, Earle 370) take the nearly impossible view that it refers to his divine nature. Gundry argues for a reference to Jesus' human spirit (cf. Bernard 63, White 119, Erdman 47). The NIV, however, understands line 1 in this way, taking ἐν πνεύματι as instrumental ("He appeared in a body, was vindicated by the Spirit"; cf. Hendriksen 140, Barrett 65). About this view see the discussion below.

[43]Particularly so in the form that it appears in Gundry, "Form." See esp. the critique in Fowl, *Story*, 160–62.

[44]The one passage that might seem to do so, 1 Cor 5:5, almost certainly does not (see above on this passage). Otherwise Paul uses σῶμα and πνεῦμα ("body/spirit") to express the two basic parts of our humanity (see 1 Cor 7:34).

[45]For this understanding of the verb δικαιόω in Paul, see 1 Cor 4:4 and esp. his citation of Ps 50:6 (LXX) in Rom 3:3, regarding the "vindication of God." Quinn, therefore, is not quite correct in asserting that this usage is "by no means Pauline" ("Spirit," 355; cf. D-C 62).

[46]E.g., NIV, GNB, JB, all of which have some form of "by the Spirit." The RSV, NASB, NAB are more ambiguous with their "in the Spirit."

[47]E.g., Calvin 233–34, Alford 334, Lock 45–46 (as one option); cf. Metzger, *Christushymnus*, 83–90, although he also includes the resurrection as the final act of this vindication.

[48]That is, the NT does not elsewhere suggest that the Holy Spirit's presence in Christ was for him some kind of "vindication"; rather, the Spirit evidenced God's presence and the source of his empowerment (cf. Luke 4:14, 18–21; 5:17; Acts 1:2; and esp. 10:38).

The best understanding of "in the spirit," therefore, seems to be as the natural antonym of "in the sphere of humanity." What is being set out, as has often been suggested,[49] are two spheres of existence, the natural and supernatural,[50] that is, "two orders of being, the flesh representing human nature in its weakness, its proclivity to evil . . . , the spirit representing the consequence of God's incursion into human affairs, the presence and activity among men of the Spirit of God."[51] Thus, "in the spirit" most likely refers to the new "spiritual," supernatural realm of existence, entered by Christ through his resurrection. However, this choice of words is scarcely accidental. Whatever else, this new "sphere" is precisely that of the Spirit.[52] Just as Christ when "in the flesh" ministered in the power of the Spirit, so now Christ, by virtue of his resurrection, has entered the spiritual/supernatural realm, the realm of the Spirit, which is the final goal of those for whom the present gift of the Spirit is the ἀρραβών ("down-payment").

If that be the case, then two further remarks are necessary about the understanding of the Spirit in this passage. First, this is another instance of the Spirit as the key element to the new eschatological order that God began through the death and resurrection of Christ and instituted in history through his gift of the Spirit, an understanding that is also implicit in 4:1 that follows. Second, in this passage Christ's "vindication" by having entered this new sphere, following his short period in the sphere of our humanity, is not to be understood as "over against" his flesh, but as the full vindication of his having been manifested in the flesh. That is, life in the flesh is not to be scorned; it is not to be separated from God, as the false teachers were plainly doing. The Spirit, therefore, in Pauline theology is not over against the physical world, as with so many of Paul's opponents. Rather, the Spirit, as God, affirms the created order.[53]

That leads, finally, to a few words about the hymn as a whole,[54] although this will little affect the understanding of the first two lines just

---

[49]See esp. W. J. Dalton (*Christ's Proclamation to the Spirits: A Study of 1 Peter 3:18–4:6* [Rome: Pontifical Biblical Institute, 1965] 127–32) on the similar contrast in 1 Pet 3:18. Cf. D-C 62; Towner, *Goal*, 90–92; Fowl, *Story*, 159–64; Schweizer, "Creeds," 169; Quinn, "Spirit," 355. Otherwise Kelly 90–91, who interestingly takes "in the flesh" in this way, but thinks "in the spirit" must refer to his "spiritual nature."

[50]Cf. in this regard Paul's contrast between the "natural" and "supernatural" (πνευματικόν) body in 1 Cor 15:44.

[51]Dalton, *Proclamation*, 127.

[52]Cf. Towner, *Goal*, 91, who speaks of the Spirit as the "operative Agent" of this spiritual/supernatural sphere of existence.

[53]Cf. esp. in this regard the argument in 1 Cor 6:13–14 and 15:35–58.

[54]For both a helpful overview of the history of interpretation and a discussion of the various structural options, see Gundry, "Form," 203–9 (although he apparently has found no takers for his own view, which sees line 2 as referring to the vindication

argued for. The issue, it should be noted, is raised by line 6, where language that elsewhere in the NT is reserved for Christ's ascension appears here *after* he has been proclaimed among the nations and believed on in the world. Were it not for this line, everyone would see the whole as chronological.[55]

Currently there are two basic views, with some variations within each. The majority view finds 3 strophes, with alternating sets of antitheses, set to an AB/BA/AB pattern, contrasting the earthly and heavenly realms of Jesus' existence (lines 1/2, earth/heaven), proclamation (lines 3/4, heaven/earth), and reception (lines 5/6, earth/heaven). In this scheme the beginning of each of the final two strophes also corresponds directly to the last line in the preceding strophe. Although there is much to be said for this view, it tends to disregard the natural parallelism of lines 4/5 and in turn creates some especially unnatural "antitheses."[56]

The alternative view finds 2 strophes of three lines each, the first two lines forming a parallel, the third a kind of "refrain." The hymn is thus seen as an expression of *Heilsgeschichte*, one strophe celebrating Christ's earthly life and its vindication (lines 1/2, with line 3 celebrating his present exaltation), the other celebrating his ongoing "vindication" in the world (lines 4/5, with 6 again celebrating his present exaltation).[57]

---

of Christ's human spirit "before the resurrection" and line 3 as referring to his appearing to "the spirits in prison" of 1 Pet 3:19, interpreted as hostile powers; see the critique in Fowl, *Story*, 165–67).

[55]For a fascinating presentation of this view, see Lock 42, who put the whole into contemporary verse:

In flesh unveiled to mortals' sight,
Kept righteous by the Spirit's might,
    While angels watched him from the sky:
His heralds sped from shore to shore,
And men believed, the wide world o'er,
    When he in glory passed on high.

An earlier form of this view held by Alford has been critiqued by Gundry, "Form," 203–4. A more recent—and considerably different—expression of it was advocated by Barrett 65, who took line 6 to refer to Christ's final victory at his Parousia. As far as I can tell, he has found no followers. Cf. the critique in Gundry (204).

[56]For further critique, see Fee 93–96. It is extremely doubtful that anyone would have ever considered lines 3/4 and 5/6 to be antithetical parallels if they had not been set up by lines 1/2. But whereas lines 1/2 form a known and natural set, the contrast between "angels" and "nations" is both forced and unnatural—there is nothing like it in all of Christian literature. So also the "antithesis" between "world" and "glory" in line 6—all the more so if "in glory" is considered to be locative, as most do who hold this view. But "in glory" does not function well as a locative; its nuance is "manner" or "attendant circumstance" and describes the nature of Christ's ascension: it was "in/with glory." The natural antithesis to world, after all, is the true locative, "into heaven."

[57]For a more thorough presentation of this option, and the reasons for it, see Fee 93–96. Lock 45 argues for this structure, but sees the whole quite differently.

What is finally significant for our purposes is to note that whatever view one takes on this question, lines 2 to 6 all seem to vindicate the one who "was manifested in the flesh."[58] The vindication is both by God (lines 2 and 6) and before angels (line 3) and humans (lines 4 and 5). Thus Christ himself stands as God's response to the demonic errors of the false teachers, who would separate creation from God. And it is about this that the Spirit has something to say, which is what 4:1–2 is all about.

1 TIMOTHY 4:1–2

[1]*But the Spirit expressly says that in latter times some people will fall away from the faith, by giving heed to deceiving spirits and the teachings of demons,* [2]*by the hypocrisy*[59] *of speakers of falsehoods,*[60] *whose consciences have been branded.*[61]

Following hard on the heels of 3:16 as it does, and set in contrast to it by the δέ with which it begins, this passage brings us to the heart of the matter in 1 Timothy. That Spirit in whose sphere Jesus now exists as the "vindicated" and "exalted" one is the same Spirit who has told us about the present "latter" days. What the Spirit says is that the latter days will see an apostasy brought about by "spirits" from the other side, Satan's own demonic forces, whose deceits and falsehoods are currently being propagated by the false teachers. Thus, along with 6:3–5, this is the strongest denunciation of the false teachers in the letter. They are not merely those who "teach different doctrines," who "promote speculations" and love "controversies"; they are dupes of Satan, and their teaching is inspired by "deceiving spirits."

---

[58]This point is made especially strongly by Schweizer, "Creeds," 169–70.

[59]It is not absolutely certain how this prepositional phrase ἐν ὑποκρίσει ψευδο-λόγων functions in the clause. It possibly modifies the verb ("people will fall away . . . by giving heed to . . . , through the hypocrisy of speakers of falsehoods"); more likely it modifies the verbal idea in διδασκαλία ("teachings of demons that come by way of").

[60]Although the substantive ψευδολόγων is most often translated "liars" (NIV, NASB, GNB, RSV, NRSV, JB), that could be misleading in English. "Liars" has to do with telling deliberate untruths in order to deceive. This word has to do with speaking falsehood as over against the truth of the gospel. Thus Weymouth has it right: "through the hypocrisy of men who teach falsely" (cf. NEB, "through the specious falsehoods of men whose . . . ").

[61]This participle can mean either "seared as with a hot iron" or "bearing the brand of someone." In context the latter seems to be preferred. The problem is not that the false teachers have had their consciences seared so as not to be able to distinguish truth from error (although that may well be true), but that they bear Satan's own brand mark as those whose teaching is from "deceiving spirits." By teaching in the guise of truth what is actually false, they show that they have been branded by Satan as belonging to him and doing his will. Cf. Barrett 67, Fee 98–99.

The meaning of "the Spirit expressly says" is moot. On the one hand, such a formula is never used by Paul to refer to the OT.[62] Because of the present tense of λέγει ("the Spirit *says*" = "the Spirit *is saying*"), it is sometimes suggested that the Spirit is now speaking through Paul.[63] A more likely alternative is that this refers to the prophetic Spirit speaking in the Pauline churches.[64] But if so, then what the Spirit says now is nothing more than what he has already said before,[65] especially through the teaching of Jesus. Along with 2 Tim 3:1–5, here we have another reflection of a common apocalyptic motif that the time of the End would be accompanied by a time of intense evil,[66] which would include a "falling away" of some of the people of God.[67] Thus "the Spirit" in this case probably refers not to some specific prophetic utterance in the churches—although that may very well be included—but to what he has been saying in a whole variety of ways from the time of Jesus.[68] In any case, according to Acts 20:29–30, Paul had prescience about this matter some years earlier and spoke it directly to the elders of this church, many of whom can therefore be expected to be hearing it yet another time.

Here, then, is another instance of understanding the presence of the Spirit as an essentially eschatological phenomenon. Living in "the latter times" does not stress "imminence," but rather reflects the radically altered understanding of existence brought about by the presence of the Spirit. The time of the End has already begun; believers are already the people of the future in the present age, even though the consummation of what has begun still lies before them. Thus Christian existence always belongs to "the latter times," already begun through the gift of the eschatological Spirit. And one of the things "the Spirit expressly says" about "our times" is that some people will also give way to the deceptions of Satan.[69]

---

[62]Kent 149 refers to Dan 7:25; 8:23, and concludes that Paul perhaps intends the "continual stream of the Spirit's prophesying, beginning in the Old Testament and continuing to the time of the apostles." But in light of Pauline usage elsewhere, and especially in light of the present content ("giving heed to deceiving spirits"), this seems highly unlikely. It is not simply apostasy that the Spirit here speaks to, but an apostasy in which the false teachers are themselves given over to "deceiving spirits and the teachings of demons." Bernard 64–65 suggests, but rejects, the possibility that Paul is referring to some "forgotten" prophecy in an apocryphal work.

[63]E.g., Calvin 235–36, White 120, Hendriksen 146. Scott 44 suggests that the alleged pseudepigrapher specifically had Acts 20:29–30 in mind.

[64]So Bernard 65; cf. Lock 47.

[65]Cf. Erdman 50, "such had been predicted already and with great definiteness by men who were divinely inspired."

[66]See, e.g., 2 Thes 2:8–12; Mark 13:5–8, 14–23.

[67]See, e.g., Matt 24:12; Jude 17–18; 2 Pet 3:3–7.

[68]The ῥητῶς, therefore, does not refer to "some known available source," but rather means "explicitly," in the sense of "unmistakably" (cf. Jos. *Ant.* 1.24, "there he was making his meaning ῥητῶς [absolutely plain]").

[69]It is hard not to see, as most commentators do, an intentional contrast between

Hence the warfare imagery in 1 Tim 1:18 and Eph 6:10–17 to connote the nature of the conflict in which God's Spirit people are currently engaged.

In light of Paul's language in 1 Cor 12:10 ("the discernment of πνεύματα") and 14:29–32, where the "spirits" of the prophets are subject to the prophets and their utterances must be "discerned," it is an attractive suggestion[70] that "the deceiving spirits" refer to charismatic activity in the church, some of which should be tested and exposed. The grammar and structure of the sentence, however, suggest that "deceiving spirits" refers directly to demons.[71] This, then, is the only place in the Pauline corpus where demons are specifically called πνεύματα—although some would see such a reference in "the discernment of spirits" in 1 Cor 12:10 (q.v.); and Satan is called "the spirit that is now at work among the disobedient" in Eph 2:2. But such a designation does not lie very far below the surface in such passages as 1 Cor 10:20–21 (where demons are recognized as the true reality inherent in idols), or in the "principalities and powers" of Ephesians and Colossians. Precisely because this is so, that is, because the false teachers and their teachings are ultimately demonic, Timothy was urged in 1:18 to carry on the good warfare (= engage in spiritual warfare) by means of the prophecies that came from the Spirit of the living God—and will be urged in 2 Tim 1:6–7 to "fan into flame the gift" of the Spirit.

Thus this first explicit mention of the Spirit in these letters is full of theological presuppositions thoroughly consonant with what we have met regularly in Paul's earlier letters. The prophetic Spirit is still actively speaking to the situation of God's eschatological community; and what he says distinctly places that community in "the latter times" in which they are involved in spiritual warfare against the "principalities and powers" of the present age.

1 TIMOTHY 4:12

Let no one disparage your youthfulness, but rather become an example of believers[72] in speech, in conduct, in love,[73] in faithfulness, in purity.

---

the Spirit of God, who speaks truth, and the demonic "spirits," who, because they are from Satan, speak not truth but only falsehood and deceit.

[70]So, e.g., Calvin 237.

[71]The two objects of "giving heed to" are most likely complementary, the second specifying the first, in other words, "deceiving spirits, that is, the teachings of demons." That means the false teachers themselves are not in view until the ἐν ὑποκρίσει ψευδολόγων of v. 2. This is the means whereby the teachings of the demons are propagated, through the "hypocrisy of those who speak falsehoods."

[72]That is, of what believers are, rather than an "example for other believers to follow"—although that is not very far behind.

[73]The MajT, against all early evidence from every known source, includes ἐν πνεύματι following "in love." Metzger (*Textual Commentary*, 642) suggests that the

The addition of ἐν πνεύματι ("in spirit" KJV) following ἐν ἀγάπῃ in this list of virtues that Timothy is to model is one of the more perplexing textual variations in the Pauline corpus. On the one hand, the history of the transmission of the NT text simply disallows it any claim to originality.[74] Had Paul written it, it is nearly impossible to account for its having been omitted so thoroughly across the board, so that it fails to show up in a single piece of our extant early textual evidence.[75] It is not found in a single one of the ancient versions, which means that they were all translated in a period—and in many different geographical settings—in which the variant was unknown. The earliest Greek evidence for the reading is in the ninth-century uncials K L P, which means for all practical purposes it is a reading that is unique to the Greek Orthodox Church.[76]

On the other hand, it is equally difficult to imagine what might have prompted someone in the early Byzantine church to insert "in spirit" right at this point in Paul's text. Not only does it not seem to "fit," but it is equally difficult to imagine what ἐν πνεύματι might have meant to the interpolator. In any case the interpolation would have happened so late that we would need to seek for its meaning within the early history of the Greek church (600–800 CE). Calvin suggests "fervent zeal for God," but allows that it might be more general than that. Particularly doubtful is that the interpolator would have had the Holy Spirit in mind.

1 TIMOTHY 4:14

Do not neglect the gift that is in you, which was given to you through prophecy[77] accompanied by the laying on of the hands of the presbytery.[78]

---

addition happened "perhaps under the influence of Col 1.8." Bernard 64 offers 1 Cor 4:21 as another possible source, while White 126 suggests 2 Cor 6:6. The hesitant nature and the unlikelihood of these suggestions (the usage in both cases is considerably different from what is said here) indicate the difficulty of this variation in terms of transcriptional probability. See the discussion.

[74]The fact that it is not even included in the apparatus of the UBS⁴ indicates how thoroughly it has been dismissed as an option by NT textual critics. That Elliott, *Text*, 70, on the other hand, adopts the reading says something about the bankruptcy of so-called rigorous eclecticism, which pays no attention to the history of transmission or textual relationships.

[75]Elliott, *Text*, 70, suggests that it dropped out through the common beginning ENαγαπηΕΝπνευματιΕΝπιστει, which might partly make sense had it happened once; but in this case one must ask, (1) why only this word in the list, and (2) why this word so often and in so many different geographical areas that it failed to appear at all in the first nine centuries?

[76]Since it is unknown to Chrysostom, *Hom. 13 on 1 Tim.*, it is unlikely to have arisen even in the Byzantine church until after the fifth century at the earliest.

[77]Although this might mean "a prophetic utterance" (cf. BAGD, NIV, NEB), in light of the plural in 1:18 this more likely refers to the event of prophecy as such, rather than to the content of a specific utterance.

[78]Both the first hand of ℵ and 69 have πρεσβυτέρου ("of an elder"); these reflect independent—and corrected—mistakes in copying.

For the second time Paul reminds Timothy of his Spirit-initiated, Spirit-directed experience of "call" to ministry. As before (1:18), it is set in the context of his need to combat, by example and by direct confrontation, the "profane myths" (v. 7) of the false teachers, which in vv. 1–2 are described as originating from "deceiving spirits." Also as before, the present text signals that 1 Timothy is a three-party document. Although the imperative is directed to Timothy, and is therefore surely for his own sake—both to bolster his courage and to encourage him to action—the two imperatives in vv. 11 and 12 verify that it is also intended to authenticate Timothy before the community. This twofold audience probably accounts for most of the peculiarities in the sentence. The χάρισμα ("gift") is affirmed to be ἐν σοί ("in you")[79]—for Timothy's encouragement. The emphases on its Spirit-given nature (διὰ προφητείας "through prophecy") and on its recognition/affirmation by the elders (μετὰ ἐπιθέσεως τῶν χειρῶν τοῦ πρεσβυτερίου "accompanied by the laying on of the hands of the presbytery") are surely intended as much for the sake of the Ephesian church as for Timothy's own exhortation/encouragement.

Thus the *reason* for this imperative in its present context is easier to decide than is the precise meaning of its various components: what is the χάρισμα; how is it "in him" by means of "prophecy"; how are the two activities of prophecy and the laying on of hands related; what/who is the "presbytery"; and how is this text to be reconciled with—or otherwise understood to be in relationship to—1:18 and 2 Tim 1:6–7.[80]

One may dismiss as both prejudicial and unwarranted Bauer's definition of χάρισμα as here referring to "the gift of an office."[81] Not only does nothing in these letters speak in favor of such a view,[82] but the clear statements of the text itself, and of its companion text in 2 Tim 1:6–7, speak strongly against it. First, Timothy is here urged "not to neglect" or "disregard" his χάρισμα. In itself, and without the ἐν σοί ("in you"),

---

[79]The "enclosed" word order τοῦ ἐν σοὶ χαρίσματος ("the in you gift"), which occurs often in the Pastoral Epistles (e.g., 1 Tim 3:16; 2 Tim 2:14; cf. 1 Cor 6:19 above), must be understood as emphatic.

[80]On the question of *when*, see above on 1:18.

[81]See under χάρισμα, § 2. This is repeated by H. Conzelmann ("Χάρισμα," *TDNT* 9.406) and is standard fare in those studies that see 1 Timothy as a forgery (e.g., D-C 70; Scott 51; cf. Dunn, *Jesus*, 348). To the contrary, see R. Y. K. Fung, "Ministry, Community and Spiritual Gifts," *EvQ* 56 (1984) 5.

[82]Only the most biased reading of this letter sees Timothy as "holding an office" in Ephesus. On the contrary, he is there as Paul's delegate to put a stop to the straying elders and their false teachings. Nothing in the letter points to an "office" for him; as always with Paul and his co-workers, Timothy is an itinerant, who in 2 Timothy is being called once more to Paul's side and is being replaced by Tychicus (2 Tim 4:9, 12). Cf. the similar, clearly itinerant, nature of Titus' ministry on Crete (Titus 3:12). Interpreters should not hope to have their cake and eat it too. If these are forgeries intended to set up Timothy and Titus as model "office-holders," then the forger cannot also have them move on so casually.

that might be seen as referring to an office, which he is being called upon to take more seriously. But that goes against the plain sense of 2 Tim 1:6–7. There he is called upon to "fan into flame" the χάρισμα τοῦ θεοῦ ("gift of God"). Only with the most severely strained stretching of terms and ideas can this be understood to refer to something so external as an "office." One does not "fan into flame" an "office";[83] that is to speak nonsense.

Second, the χάρισμα in both passages is specifically, and emphatically, affirmed to be "in you." Such language does not fit well any normal understanding of the concept of "office." An office is a position that one is called to *fill*; thus it is external to the office holder. This is a χάρισμα that indwells Timothy, which he can be commanded "not to neglect" and encouraged "to fan into flame." Even if the author's reference is unclear (whether Paul or not), it makes little sense to see it as an "office" in the church.[84]

But to what then does it refer? On this, one might well expect divided opinion, because nothing is said specifically as to its nature. In light of the internal evidence, Paul is probably referring to his specific giftedness for ministry that is present through the gift of the Spirit.[85] Thus it includes, but is not limited to, the "public reading, proclamation/exhortation, and teaching" that Timothy is urged to "devote himself to" in the preceding imperative. In the larger context of the letter it concerns the whole range of his ministry in Ephesus. Through the gift of the Spirit, Timothy has been especially gifted for a ministry similar to Paul's. Hence Paul can later urge him to "guard the sacred trust by means of the Spirit who dwells *in us*" (2 Tim 1:14).

In the present passage the tie between Spirit and gift is made through the prepositional phrase διὰ προφητείας ("through prophecy"). The problem concerns finding the relationship between διά, the Spirit, and the prophetic utterances. How does the gift come to be "in Timothy" yet "*through* prophecy"?[86] The best answer stems from the ad hoc nature of the epistle. It is typical of Paul in highly ad hoc moments[87] to express

---

[83]Not even the "apostolic office," even if one were to allow such foreign language for Paul's understanding of his own calling.

[84]Dunn's assertion that "Spirit and charisma have become in effect subordinate to office, to ritual, to tradition" (*Jesus*, 349) is just that, an assertion, based on several preceding assertions, none of which seem to accord with the texts themselves.

[85]Cf. Kelly 106: "The reference . . . is to the grace of the Holy Spirit which Timothy had received. . . . [C]harisma . . . denotes a special endowment of the Spirit enabling the recipient *to carry out some function* in the community" (emphasis mine).

[86]It should be noted that διὰ προφητείας could be either genitive singular or accusative plural ("because of prophecies"). Bernard 72 notes that "some have taken it" as the latter—although I have found none in recent times. Not only is it difficult to find an adequate meaning for the accusative plural, but the companion text in 1:18 seems to make "through prophecy" certain.

[87]See on 1:18 above (esp. n. 19). The more ad hoc a letter is, i.e., the more case-specific it is, the more an author assumes between himself and the recipient(s). Timothy does not need explanations of something that was such a vital part of his

himself in something of a "shorthand" way, where much is assumed between him and his readers, but in a way that appears to us as somewhat
odd. According to Pauline theology, the giftedness exists "in Timothy" as
the direct result of the *Spirit's* indwelling him (hence 2 Tim 1:6–7, q.v.); the
prophecies therefore are those words from the Spirit through the lips of
others[88] so gifted in the community, spoken in spontaneous, ad hoc ways,
that confirm—or commission—such giftedness both for the sake of its
recipient (Timothy in this case) and for that of the rest of the believing
community.[89] This fully conforms with the picture that has already emerged
in 1:18. But because the concern here is with the "gift that is *in you*," as well
as with his *divine* appointment to this ministry, the gift itself is said to come
to him "through prophecy." The fully Pauline—in the sense of fully "charismatic"—nature of this passage can scarcely be gainsaid.[90]

But in this context Paul is concerned not only with the divine origins
of Timothy's Spirit-given ministry, but also *with its full recognition by the
believing community*—especially in the form of its leadership.[91] This surely
is how we are to understand the next prepositional phrase, "with the
laying on of the hands of the presbytery."[92] This phrase is commonly
regarded as a quasi–instrumental,[93] i.e., that the gift came to Timothy
through the twofold instrumentality of a prophetic utterance and the
laying on of hands, as though the latter "conferred" on Timothy his gift.[94]

---

own personal spiritual history. Paul is merely recalling the event, without details.
The items he mentions, however, probably point beyond Timothy to the church that
will have this letter read in its hearing.

[88]Thus taking the διά in its normal usage as expressing a secondary agent.

[89]This is how we are to understand the narrative in Acts 13:1–3, where in the
context of "prophets" in the church, the Holy Spirit "speaks" by calling out Saul and
Barnabas for an appointed task. This is a kind of special "equipping" for their next,
divinely appointed, task of ministry.

[90]Despite the assertions of some (Dunn, *Jesus*, e.g.), such "charismatic endowment" is not the view of a later time; this is squarely in keeping with what one finds
elsewhere in Paul.

[91]Scott 16 (on 1:18) has it backwards when he says, "no important step was taken
in the Early Church until the sanction of the Spirit had been obtained through the
utterance of prophets." That sounds altogether like Delphi and almost nothing like
the early church, where the Spirit primarily initiated and directed, rather than was
"consulted" through its prophets.

[92]This is so despite the more "instrumental" language in 2 Tim 1:6 regarding
Paul's relationship to Timothy and his gift.

[93]See, e.g., the GNB, NIV, JB, RSV, NEB (blatantly!); cf. Simpson 71 and M. J. Harris
(*NIDNTT* 3.1182), who tries to find justification for it. Grundmann (*TDNT* 7.772n36)
rightly includes this passage with others in the NT where in combination with σύν,
μετά "means 'together with.' "

[94]This prepositional phrase in particular has influenced the view that the χάρισμα
refers to an "office." Here one has the "clear evidence" of the conferring of office by
those who already hold office. But not only is that an unwarranted assumption, it
does not measure well with what the text actually says.

On the contrary, the preposition μετά has no known instance in the *Koinē* of an instrumental sense. Rather, this is a case of "other accompanying phenomena," as Bauer rightly suggests.[95] The laying on of hands does not confer anything; just as in Acts 13:3, it is the community's own recognition and commissioning of the recipient in light of the prior activity of the Holy Spirit.[96] The reason for its inclusion here, and not elsewhere, has to do with the "authenticating" nature of the present argument (4:6–16). Timothy may well be encouraged by this reminder, but the church in Ephesus is also being reminded that Timothy's presence there—and his ministry among them of stopping error and teaching "healthy doctrine"—not only came by the Spirit's giftedness, but was recognized to be so by elders in that earlier setting.

One should make very little, therefore, of the singular (for Paul) use of πρεσβυτέριον in this passage. For the reasons already spoken to, it is altogether unlikely that this genitive is telic—for the purpose of Timothy's *becoming* a presbyter.[97] Not only does this twist the preposition μετά, but also it rather misses the point of the passage. As in its other occurrences in the NT[98] and beyond[99] the word πρεσβυτέριον refers to the group of elders as a whole. And it is a matter of undue skepticism to suggest that such did not exist from the earliest times in the Pauline churches.

Thus, totally in keeping with the larger Pauline corpus, this text affirms (1) that the Spirit is seen as the key to ministry; (2) that the Spirit came to Timothy for this ministry in a very charismatic way and in the context of the believing community; and (3) that the Spirit was both an experienced and evidenced reality in the Pauline churches.

It must be noted finally that it is unwarranted to argue as some do that because Paul speaks thus to Timothy, the "author" betrays himself as belonging to a time when "charismatic gifts" are the special province

---

[95]BAGD A.III.2. So also most commentaries, contra most English translations.

[96]Very likely the background for this phenomenon is to be found in Judaism, which had been influenced by the account of Moses' laying hands on Joshua as his true successor (Num 27:18–23 and Deut 34:9). These two texts share a phenomenon not unlike that of our present text and 2 Tim 1:6, inasmuch as in Numbers, Moses is to lay hands on Joshua precisely because God has already given him of his Spirit, while in Deuteronomy the "spirit of wisdom" is said to come to Joshua through the laying on of Moses' hands. These reflect a similar change of perspective and emphasis with regard to the same reality. What is *not* similar in the present passages is the suggestion that they refer to some kind of "succession" that Paul is conferring on Timothy. These passages clearly refer to an event at a much earlier time in Timothy's life, to which the apostle can appeal as a means of encouragement and authentication.

[97]See Calvin 247, who waffles, but seems finally to favor this view. It has been revived more recently—apart from Calvin—by D. Daube (*The New Testament and Rabbinic Judaism* [London: University Press, 1956] 224–46), and adopted by Barrett 72 and Kelly 107–8.

[98]See Luke 22:66; Acts 22:5.

[99]See the many passages in Ignatius listed in BAGD.

of official office-holders.[100] That in itself betrays a prior commitment to authorial purpose that does not hold up well under scrutiny, as well as presenting an argument from silence of the worst kind.[101] After all, the "prophecies" both in this passage and in 1:18 come from the charismatic community, with not a hint that they are the special preserve of office-holders.

TITUS

This letter fits much better the designation "church manual" than do either of the letters to Timothy, in that Titus has obviously been left in Crete to set matters in order (1:5). Rather than a church with a considerable history, as in Ephesus, here is a situation where Titus is to take care of some unfinished business. What needs to be put in order is the appointment of elders, who will themselves stand up against the (apparently) Jewish Christian errors that are prevalent on the island.

The letter has a much less urgent appearance than 1 Timothy and was therefore probably written some time later as a kind of prophylactic against similar false teaching. But because the situation there lacked the urgency of that in Ephesus, the prominent motif in Titus urges believers toward exemplary behavior for the sake of outsiders.[102] This concern had surfaced already in 1 Timothy (3:7; 6:1); it becomes thoroughgoing in this letter. Paul's concern is both *prophylactic* (against false teaching) and *evangelistic* (encouraging behavior that will be attractive to the world).

Because of its smaller size and singular purpose, very little actual content of the gospel per se is given, except for two marvelous passages (2:11–14 and 3:4–7), in which Paul once more dips into the church's creedal traditions and reformulates them to serve as the theological basis for his appeal to "good works." The second of these, containing the only mention of the Spirit in the letter, is a more complete formulation, with a twofold emphasis: first, *God's mercy*—not "good works"—is the basis of their common salvation; and second, *the regenerating work of the Spirit* is the effective agent of their salvation. Thus, even though the passage bristles with exegetical difficulties, the result is yet one more creedal formulation in Paul where salvation is the activity of the triune God, and the Spirit plays the crucial role in "bringing it off" in the life of believers. But before that, one other text calls for our attention, where Paul uses the word "prophet" to refer to a pagan epigramist.

---

[100]This is a particularly common assertion in the literature. For a stark expression of it, see Dunn, *Jesus*, 348–49.

[101] See n. 5 above.

[102] Note the frequent emphasis on doing good ("good works," 1:8, 16; 2:7, 14; 3:1, 8, 14), or on exemplary behavior with outsiders in view (2:5, 7, 8, 10, 11; 3:1, 8).

Titus 1:12

A certain one of them, from among their own prophets, said: "Cretans are always liars, vicious brutes, lazy gluttons."

Paul gives his argument against the Cretan false teachers a remarkable turn by noting that their conduct is very much in accord with the known reputation of Crete, expressed in an epigram from Epimenides (ca. 600 BCE). What seems even more remarkable is his willingness to consider Epimenides a prophet. This in fact is the only occurrence of this word in the Pauline corpus that does not refer either to the OT prophets or to Christian prophets, both of whom speak by the Spirit of God.

Several possibilities exist: (1) that Paul here intended something similar to John 11:49–51, where Caiaphas is considered to have spoken "prophetically" without having done so by design;[103] (2) that the false teachers styled themselves as prophets, and with this word Paul turns the tables on them;[104] or, more likely, (3) the present usage simply reflects the common reputation of Epimenides, whom Plato called a "divine man" and of whom Aristotle said, "He used to divine, not the future, but only things that were past but obscure."[105] For Paul the fact that what he said about the Cretans has proved true in the case of the false teachers makes the title a permissible one.

This usage, therefore, says very little about Paul's understanding of charismatic phenomena outside the Christian faith. Even the fact that Epimenides spoke truly says nothing about whether Paul would actually have considered him a "prophet," that is, as one who was in fact inspired of the Spirit. After all, the very strongly worded, "from among themselves, a certain one of their own prophets," emphasizes that Epimenides was being appealed to as one whom the Cretans themselves ought to believe. All that can be said for sure is that this is the reputation Epimenides already had, and that Paul is willing to speak of him by that common designation, probably because what he said in this case was indeed true in a very specific sense. The result is powerful irony.[106] A nonChristian "prophet" speaks truly about some would-be Christian leaders, who because of their false teaching and behavior are true "Cretans," liars all.

Titus 3:5–6[107]

[5] *. . . but in keeping with his mercy he saved us, through washing of regeneration and renewal of*[108] *the Holy Spirit,* [6]*whom he poured out on us richly through Jesus Christ our Savior.*

---

[103] So Barrett 131; cf. Spicq 609.

[104] See White 189.

[105] Plato, *Laws* 1.642D; Aristotle, *The Art of Rhetoric* 3.17 (LCL).

[106] So also Quinn 108–9; cf. Simpson 100, "with a twinkle in his eye."

[107] *Bibliography:* **Beasley-Murray,** *Baptism,* 209–16; **Dunn,** *Baptism,* 165–70; **Ervin,** *Conversion-Initiation,* 128–30; **Hunter,** *Spirit-Baptism,* 51–52; **Knight,** *Sayings,* 80–111; **Towner,** *Goal,* 112–18.

[108] Several Western witnesses (D* F G b Lucifer) try to resolve the difficulties created by the compounding of genitives in this clause by inserting a διά (= "renewal

As noted above this remarkable clause falls in the middle of one of the two great creedal moments in this letter, the last of such passages in the Pauline corpus in which the Spirit plays a central role.[109] On the one hand, as with most such moments, which have so much new vocabulary and which seem to be dipping into, and reformulating, the tradition(s) of the church, there is always a question about its pre-history and whether or not it therefore truly reflects Pauline theology. On the other hand, as Morna Hooker has rightly argued about Phil 2:5–11, "even if the material is non-Pauline, we may expect Paul himself to have interpreted it and used it in a Pauline manner."[110] As with other such passages (e.g., 2 Thes 2:13; 1 Cor 6:11; 2 Cor 1:21–22; Gal 4:4–6), here again one cannot miss the absolutely central role the Spirit plays in Pauline formulations of the gospel whose central concern is Christian conversion.[111]

In order to catch the place of the Spirit clause in this formulation, a display of the whole, with a description of the function of its parts, may be useful:

```
                   But
WHEN          when   the goodness
                            and                  appeared,
                     the lovingkindness
                            of God our Savior
WHAT          He saved us
                     not on the basis of works of righteousness,
                                                  which we have done
BASIS                but in keeping with his mercy,
MEANS                through washing
                            of  regeneration
                                 and
                                 renewal
```

---

through the Holy Spirit"). This probably reflects a very early understanding of the phrase as having two parts, one referring to baptism, the other to the Spirit ("through washing of regeneration, and renewal through the Holy Spirit").

[109] There are three further such traditional pieces in 2 Timothy (1:9–10; 2:8, 11–13), but because the interest in these does not lie in the saving event as conversion, there is no mention of the Spirit.

[110] Morna D. Hooker, "Philippians 2:6–11," in *Jesus und Paulus: Festschrift für Werner Georg Kümmel zum 70 Geburtstag* (ed. E. E. Ellis and E. Grässer; Göttingen: Vandenhoeck & Ruprecht, 1975) 152.

[111] That this is so can be seen especially by the subtle shift in time from v. 4 ("when the goodness and lovingkindness of God our savior appeared," which points to the historic event of Christ), to vv. 5–6, which by means of the prepositional phrase "through washing by the Holy Spirit" focuses the whole sentence on the experienced reality of salvation in the life of the believer.

AGENT   by the Holy Spirit
                                whom
                         He poured out richly
                                  upon us
MEANS   through Jesus Christ our Savior
                           so that
                      having justified us
AGENT   by the grace of Christ
GOAL   we might become heirs
                                     in keeping with the hope
                                            of eternal life

Here is yet another Trinitarian formulation, which as in most such creedal moments in Paul emphasizes salvation as ultimately grounded in God and his mercy, effected historically by Christ through his act of grace, and effected experientially by the active work of the Holy Spirit. What is striking in this case[112] is the central role of the Spirit; so much so that even though the Spirit himself is poured out through Jesus our Savior, the work of the Spirit is spoken of prior to the work of Christ. This does not make it more important, of course; all Pauline soteriological formulations have their central focus on the work of Christ.[113] But it does suggest that the *emphasis* lies here, first, on God's mercy—not the "good works" appealed to so often in this letter—as the basis of salvation, and second, on the regenerating/renewing work of the Spirit as the absolutely crucial event that effects both the washing away of the sins in which we all once walked (v. 3) and the regeneration necessary for the good works now urged upon God's new people (vv. 1–2, 8).

This overview, however, tends to obscure—and in this case to make assumptions about —the ambiguities of the genitives in the Spirit-phrase and therefore of the relationship of the Spirit to the words that precede it. The problems here are considerable and are related in part to the use of λούτρον ("washing") to describe the renewing event, and in part to the compounding of genitives and the role of the καί ("and") between the words "regeneration" and "renewal."[114] These issues in fact are interrelated. First, as to λούτρον, the question is whether this is a metonym for baptism[115] or a metaphor for the washing away of sins; or whether it is

---

[112] But cf. 2 Thes 2:13; 2 Cor 1:21–22.

[113] Note that even here, where the experience of salvation through the Spirit precedes the grace of Christ that effected it, the Spirit himself is "poured out through Jesus Christ our Savior."

[114] Not to mention that here is a passage to which most scholars bring considerable vested interests. Since I am not immune at this point, the best I can hope for is a reasonable explanation as to why I go the way I do.

[115] It takes a liturgical churchman of another generation like Bernard 178 to say, "that the 'washing of regeneration' is the Water of Baptism is undoubted."

something in between (i.e., a metaphor, which has baptism lurking very close to the surface). Second, does the "and" suggest two ways that salvation is effected ("through the washing of regeneration *and* through the renewal of the Holy Spirit"), or does it join a set of synonyms ("regeneration" and "renewal"), both of which describe the nature of the "washing" and all of which are effected by the Holy Spirit?[116]

First, as to the meaning of λουτρον. This, of course, is an especially difficult and vexing issue. The problem has to do in part with how soon in the early church the "washing" in the rite of baptism was understood as going beyond the metaphor inherent in the act to some kind of reality itself; i.e., how soon a connection was made between the water used in the rite and the actual "washing away of sins" and "the interior cleansing of the life." In light of Paul's infrequent mention of baptism—especially so in conversion texts—and in light of his expressed attitude toward and clear separation of baptism from the work of the gospel in 1 Cor 1:13–17, one is especially hard pressed to see a connection either between baptism and the work of the Spirit or between baptism and conversion per se in the apostle Paul.[117] The evidence of the preceding several hundred pages makes it abundantly clear that for Paul the crucial matter for Christian conversion is the work of the Spirit, and, as we have shown, it is extremely doubtful whether the three texts most often brought into the conversation here (1 Cor 6:11; 12:13; 2 Cor 1:21)[118] are referring directly to baptism at all. Therefore, in light of the Pauline evidence (including the use of λουτρον in Eph 5:26), it is likely that Paul did not intend "washing" to stand for "baptism" here. After all, he could have easily said that, had he so intended.[119]

That suggests, then, that the usage is metaphorical and should be translated "washing."[120] That is, Paul is not saying that God saved us through baptism, but "through the spiritual washing effected by the Holy

---

[116] See the especially helpful overview of the grammatical issues, in schematic fashion, in Quinn 218–19.

[117] Contra Beasley-Murray, *Baptism*; but the very limited number of texts he has to discuss—and the fact that several of them are almost certainly *not* baptismal texts—is evidence enough. See the discussion in ch. 14 below (pp. 860–63).

[118] Other texts are also sometimes brought forward (Eph 1:13; 4:5, 30), but as we have noted, the connection between Spirit and baptism in these texts is even more remote. That connection can only be found when read in the light of later evidence, not on the basis of the evidence in Paul himself. On this whole question, see Dunn, *Baptism*. Contra Kelly 252; for all the strengths of his commentary, Kelly's own enviable acquaintance with the second-century data is probably also the commentary's greatest fault, in that he regularly reads Paul in light of the second century, rather than the other way about.

[119] The point must be stressed that Paul has the word "baptism" available to him. The use of "washing" here is first of all a metaphor, even if he does intend to refer to baptism—a point that is too often missed in the discussion.

[120] Cf. the discussion by J. A. Robinson, *Ephesians*, 205–6.

Spirit."[121] On the other hand, the richness of the imagery makes it difficult to imagine that Christian baptism is not lying very close to the surface in such a metaphor. What is doubtful is that Paul considered baptism itself as the place where regeneration took place.[122] This for him, always and ever, is the work of the Spirit. It is even more doubtful, especially in light of the grammar of this passage and what he says elsewhere, that Paul considers baptism to be the place where the Holy Spirit is received. The disavowal in 1 Cor 1:14–16 in light of 2:4–5, even if Paul is not playing down baptism as such, makes such a view nearly impossible to sustain. It takes the later church, where the dynamic quality of life in the Spirit had tended to subside and, correspondingly, where rites tended to become more prominent, to make that connection.

That leads, secondly, to the grammatical question, which basically boils down to whether Paul has one or two events/experiences in view, even though they might be seen as closely related. Despite the historical tendency[123] to read the text as referring to two events, baptism and the coming of the Spirit,[124] there are several reasons to think otherwise.

(1) The whole phrase is controlled by a single διά. That means that from the author's perspective this is a single "event." That of course does not completely rule out a single event with two parts to it;[125] but if that were the case, one still might have expected two prepositions.

(2) The two nouns, παλιγγενεσία and ἀνακαίνωσις ("regeneration" and "renewal") are obvious synonyms, both having to do with "being made new."[126] If Paul intended "the washing of regeneration" and "the re-

---

[121] Cf. Hippolytus, *Dan.* 59: "those who come . . . through the spiritual washing [πνευματικοῦ λουτροῦ] of regeneration"; also Dunn, *Baptism*, 168; Towner, *Goal*, 116.

[122] That is precisely the step that no previous Pauline texts allow. Those asserting that "washing" equals baptism read too much later Christianity into that expression, since it is not the "washing" but the Spirit that effects regeneration and renewal.

[123] One can see a decided shift in perspective before and after World War II. Almost all recent studies (Beasley-Murray, Dunn, Knight, Hunter, Towner, Quinn) take the position argued for here.

[124] How these two events are perceived depends on one's ecclesiastical context. As early as the fifth century Theodoret suggested baptism and confirmation. More often it has been conversion and sanctification. Most second-blessing theologies perceive it as conversion and "baptism in the Spirit," a view still argued for by Ervin, *Conversion-Initiation*, 128–30.

[125] As Bernard 178, e.g., perceives it.

[126] Cf. Beasley-Murray, *Baptism*, "it is fairly certain that [they] represent the same reality" (210); Dunn, *Baptism*, "they are virtually synonymous" (166). So also Knight, Towner, and others. For a useful discussion of the two words see, Knight, *Sayings*, 97–102. The former occurs only here and in Matt 19:28 in the NT; it is an eschatological word, referring in Matthew to the "regeneration" of all things at the end. But the thought is not foreign to Paul, as 2 Cor 5:17 shows. With the coming of Christ and the Spirit, "a new creation," the new order, is in effect. For the second word, "renewal," and its relationship to the Spirit in Paul, see earlier on 2 Cor 4:16 and Rom 12:2.

newal of the Holy Spirit," then two things happen to the phrase: First, the
two nouns become separated from one another and no longer function as
synonyms at all; the parallels are now "washing of regeneration" and
"renewal of the Holy Spirit," with the words in parallel now being "washing
and renewal" and "regeneration and Holy Spirit." Thus, second, the compound object of the preposition now becomes "washing" and "renewal," and
the two genitives "regeneration" and "Holy Spirit" function in quite different
ways: in the first instance as objective (= washing that effects "regeneration") or adjectival (= washing characterized by regeneration), in the
second as subjective (= renewal effected by the Holy Spirit). These obviously do not balance, nor is there the "chiasmus" that some think they find.

It is unlikely, therefore, that two separate events are in view, since
for all practical purposes the words mean exactly the same thing. The
καί should thus be understood either as a hendiadys (= "the washing of
regeneration, that is, the renewal of the Holy Spirit"),[127] or, more likely,
as two metaphors for the same reality, controlled by the metaphor "washing." In that case the two genitives function in the same way, not
"washing" effecting regeneration and renewal, but "washing" characterized by regeneration and renewal.

(3) This is further confirmed if, as seems most likely, lying behind the
language of this text is that of Ezek 36:25–27 (LXX), where Yahweh
promises to "wash" his people with "pure water," which is immediately
identified as cleansing from all uncleanness and idolatry and followed by
the promised gift of a "new Spirit," God's own Spirit. It is hardly possible
that Ezekiel had two events or experiences in view; rather, as here, the
Spirit is the means of effecting this "washing" from sin.

(4) As v. 6 shows, the focus of the whole of vv. 5–6 is on the work of
the Holy Spirit. The emphasis in Paul's sentence distinctly rests on the
Spirit who is "lavishly poured out on us,"[128] not on the metaphor of
washing. Thus, the Spirit not only renews, but in Pauline theology effects
the washing away of sins and the making new of the believer's life.[129]
Not only so, but the Trinitarian nature of the entire sentence noted above
argues for such a focus here.

(5) Finally, those who see two separate events and consider the
second to be confirmation, sanctification, or Spirit baptism, build their
whole case on internal aspects of the phrase.[130] But that will not do. The

---

[127] So Beasley-Murray, *Baptism*, 211.

[128] Calvin 383 is mistaken to see this οὗ as referring to λουτρόν. The attraction of
the relative in this case is to the word which immediately precedes it, and which is
therefore its antecedent.

[129] See esp. 1 Cor 6:11.

[130] In this regard, see esp. Ervin, *Conversion-Initiation*, 128–29, who treats the
phrase as if it really were a creed, in which the pieces could be looked at in isolation
from the rest.

entire phrase is soteriological, pure and simple, modifying the main verb in the sentence, the aorist ἔσωσεν ("he *saved* us"). This διά phrase can thus refer only to the *means of salvation*. To force it to refer to something more is to read into the text what is not there.

What that suggests, then, is that what Paul is emphasizing by a series of metaphors is the effective work of the Holy Spirit,[131] both to cleanse away former sins, such as those in v. 3 to which this whole passage serves as response, and to recreate God's new people in such a way that the lavish ("richly") outpouring of the Spirit into the life of believers will equip them for the good deeds to be urged on them in v. 8.[132] Thus the GNB seems to have it right: "he saved us, through the Holy Spirit, who gives us new birth and new life by washing us."

Several features now need to be brought into focus concerning what we learn of Paul's pneumatology in this passage:

1. We have already noted its decidedly Trinitarian implications. As always in Paul, God is the subject of the saving verb; he has provided eternal salvation through the work of Christ (here, "justified by the grace of that one" v. 7) and brought it off in the lives of believers by the Spirit.

2. We have also noted the crucial and central role the Spirit plays in the entire passage. Consonant with previous passages, this emphasis emerges whenever Paul's concern is with the effective working out of the saving event in the lives of believers.

3. In keeping with the preceding point, the context suggests that the emphasis on the Spirit here is related to Paul's concern that believers' abandon former sins and live a truly Christian life in the world—in this case so that outsiders will be affected by such lives. Thus the concern is not simply on conversion as such, but on the behavior of those who are so converted.

4. The subject of the verb "poured out" in v. 6 again is God. As in most places in Paul, the Spirit is understood to have been given by God, not by Christ (whatever else, *filioque* is not a Pauline point of view). But in this case, God has given the Spirit διὰ Ἰησοῦ Χριστοῦ τοῦ σωτῆρος ἡμῶν ("through Jesus Christ our savior"). This is indeed a new wrinkle and might be argued as a non-Pauline element. But it is also plainly the common understanding of the early church. Thus Luke in Acts 2:33 speaks of the exalted Lord as "having received from the Father the promise of the Holy Spirit, he has poured out this that you both see and

---

[131] It comes as something of a surprise, therefore, to open commentaries (such as Bernard, Lock, or Kelly) and find them discussing the effects of baptism, as though the Spirit were a mere addendum. Indeed, the comments by Lock on this passage do not so much as mention the Spirit!

[132] Lock 155 suggests that v. 6 refers to the historic event of Pentecost; but that misses too much, including the thrust of the ἐφ' ἡμᾶς ("on us"), by which Paul intends to include himself with his readers in their own actualization of God's mercy.

hear"; and the Johannine Jesus speaks of the Paraclete, "whom I will send to you from the Father" (John 14:26). All of this coincides with Jewish messianic expectations that the Messiah would be both the unique bearer of the Spirit and the one who pours out the Spirit, in keeping with the prophecy of Joel 2:28.

5. Finally, one cannot escape the bold Pauline emphasis on the lavish nature of the outpouring of the Spirit. Picking up the verb "pour out" from Joel 2:28–30, he adds the adverb πλουσίως ("richly"). Just as in the twin metaphors of 1 Cor 12:13 ("baptism" and "drink to the fill"), and in line with Paul's understanding of the close relationship between Spirit and power, so here the Spirit is poured out in an abundant way upon us. The God who saves on the basis of his mercy does not scrimp! As elsewhere in Paul such language tends to undercut all arguments for maintaining a status quo of spiritual anemia. The very lavish supply of Spirit is what makes the imperatives in v. 8 not only possible, but within reach of all who trust in God for their salvation.

2 TIMOTHY[133]

In contrast to the earlier two letters, Paul is no longer free to evangelize and to strengthen his churches in person. Again arrested, he is in an imprisonment that, in contrast to that of Philippians, is burdensome for him. The motif of suffering dominates the letter from beginning to end; he is "chained like a common criminal" (2:9); Onesiphorus had to search for him until he found him (1:17); there are defections in Asia (1:15) and desertions in Rome (4:10); and from this imprisonment Paul obviously does not expect to be delivered (4:6–8, 16–18).

It is out of this context, and with considerable anxiety about the situation Timothy leaves behind in Ephesus, that Paul writes the letter,

---

[133] This letter in particular creates difficulties for theories of pseudepigraphy. For even though it touches on some of the issues of 1 Timothy, it fails to accord with any of the proposed reasons for 1 Timothy and Titus as pseudepigraphs. Why, one wonders, would a pseudepigrapher go to the trouble to write three letters and make the occasion and historical setting of this one so radically different? And why, one wonders further, if the goal is to present Timothy as a model of one who carries on the Pauline gospel, does he present him as one who is urged to leave Ephesus, so that his functioning in the role of model pastor in this community is thereby completely overthrown? But even more difficult are the many very personal touches, of a kind for which the word "pseudepigraphy" is too polite; if not from Paul himself in some way, this is blatant forgery, and one is especially hard pressed to find an adequate motive for it. Indeed, I would hazard the guess that if we did not also possess 1 Timothy and Titus, which NT scholarship has such difficulties with, the majority of NT scholars would find a way of attributing this letter to Paul.

the final one in the Pauline corpus. Its immediate purpose is to call Timothy to his side; but its greater purpose, especially in light of the defections, desertions, and false teachers, is to appeal to Timothy's abiding loyalty—first of all to his own personal ministry (and thus to Christ and the gospel) and then to Paul, Christ's loyal servant of the gospel. The whole letter, therefore, is one long appeal (1:6–2:13; 3:10–4:15), set against the immediate backdrop of the desertions in Asia (1:15) and the continuing successes of the false teachers (2:14–3:9).

Although the Spirit is mentioned only twice (1:6–7 [+8] and 14), these occur at the beginning and ending of the opening appeal that sets the stage for the whole, and thus serve as the framework within which Timothy is to read the entire letter. Therefore, the urgency of the letter is that Timothy be renewed in the Spirit, and that by the power of the Spirit he take his share in the suffering and guard what has been deposited to his care.

2 Timothy 1:6–7

⁶For which reason [vv. 3–5] I remind you to fan into flame the gift of God, which is in you through the laying on of my hands; ⁷for God did not give us the Spirit of cowardice, but of power, love, and sound-mindedness.

These words, which flow directly out of the thanksgiving (vv. 3–5), form the opening appeal of the letter and become the ground for all subsequent appeals.[134] The thanksgiving is full of "memory" words; Paul in prayer gives thanks as he continually *remembers* Timothy (v. 3), especially when he *remembers* his sincere faith (= genuine faithfulness; v. 5) or is *reminded* of Timothy's tears at their parting (v. 4). Because Paul has such fond memories of Timothy and of his loyalty, he now turns and appeals to him by way of *reminder* to stir up in his own heart the work of the Spirit, since it by this and this alone that all the remaining appeals will work.

Thus the argument begins with an *appeal* ("fan into flame the gift of God"), which is followed by the *ground* of the appeal (for God gave him the Spirit for power, not cowardice), which in turn is followed by a *second appeal* that rests on obedience to the first one ("therefore [since the Spirit empowers] do not be ashamed of either Christ or me, his prisoner; rather take your part in the present suffering—by the power of God [i.e., through the Spirit]").

---

[134] This seems so obvious both from Paul's syntax and from the larger structure of the argument that one is puzzled by the translations that present their paragraphs as 3–7 and 8–14 (NIV, RSV, GNB; cf. White, Hendriksen). The arrangement argued for here is that of NA²⁶ (cf. JB, NEB; so also, Bernard, Erdman, Lock, Scott, Kelly, Barrett, Spicq).

This is the third time in the two letters to Timothy that Paul reminds him of this event, or a related one, that lies near the beginning of their association in the gospel (cf. 1 Tim 1:18; 4:14). But this is also the passage that creates tensions in relationship with the other two. Indeed, one wonders how this text would have been understood in the church, had 2 Timothy been the only one of these letters to have survived. The difficulties stem from the combination of striking similarities in language to 1 Tim 4:14, and some equally striking differences. Thus, on the one hand, both passages speak of a "χάρισμα that is in you," associated with the "laying of hands"; and the appeal to "fan it into flame" seems to correspond to "do not neglect" in 1 Tim 4:14. On the other hand, in 1 Tim 4:14 the laying on of hands is an accompanying act by the body of presbyters, while the gift comes through the agency of prophecy. Here, the gift comes through the agency of Paul's laying on of hands, with no mention of the group of elders or of prophecy. Furthermore, what was described in 1 Tim 4:14 as the "in you χάρισμα" is here qualified as the "χάρισμα of God that is in you through the laying on of my hands."

These tensions are most commonly resolved in terms of the specific focus of the two letters. The concern in 1 Tim 4:14 was for both Timothy's and the church's sake; here it is narrowed to their own personal relationship. Hence there is here no mention of prophecy, and no thought of the group of elders. The focus is now on Paul alone, who was undoubtedly part of the group of elders who laid hands on him. And in contrast to 1 Tim 4:14, the laying on of hands is now expressed in the language of secondary agency ("through the laying on of my hands"), which functions to telescope two moments into one (prophecy and the laying of hands), which are seen as closely related but separate moments in the former text.

But despite the nearly universal assumption (or assertion) of this point of view,[135] the fuller description in 1 Tim 4:14 and the actual language of this passage give good reason to pause. Given the very real differences between them, it is at least possible that this laying on of hands is not identical to that in 1 Tim 4:14, especially so in light of the evidence from Acts that the laying on of hands in the early church was not used strictly for ordaining/commissioning, but also for the reception of the Spirit.[136]

At issue in particular is the meaning of χάρισμα in this passage, which is regularly assumed to be identical to the usage in 1 Tim 4:14,

---

[135] White 155 is an exception: "We have no right to assume that hands were laid on Timothy once only. Thus Acts ix.17 and xiii.3 are two such occasions in St. Paul's spiritual life."

[136] For commissioning, see Acts 6:6; 13:3 (both with the identical formula, προσευξάμενοι ἐπέθηκαν αὐτοῖς τὰς χεῖρας); for the reception of the Spirit, 8:17, 18, 19; 9:12, 17; 19:6; for healing, 28:8 (perhaps also 9:17).

and therefore to be referring to Timothy's gift of ministry—either in the broadest and best sense of that term or in the narrower sense of "pastoral office"[137] (a view which has nothing to commend it here). On the other hand, it seems more likely that, even though *ultimately* Paul may have Timothy's "ministry" in view, the χάρισμα in this case refers more directly to the source of his ministry, the Spirit himself. There are several reasons for thinking so: (1) In contrast to 1 Tim 4:14, the χάρισμα in this case is specifically referred to as the "gift *of God*" that is in him. Although that language occurs in Rom 6:23 to refer to eternal life, elsewhere in Paul the Holy Spirit is expressly spoken of as *given* by God to be *in* believers (1 Thes 4:8; 1 Cor 6:19; 2 Cor 1:22). (2) In the same vein, when Paul gives the ground of the appeal in v. 7, he specifically says that "God *gave* us the *Spirit*." That is, the Spirit is designated as what is given by God, not the gift of ministry. It is the Spirit, therefore, who is the main focus in this passage. (3) This is further confirmed by the imagery of rekindling a fire that begins the sentence. Along with 1 Thes 5:19 this is an instance where Paul uses the common imagery of fire with reference to the Holy Spirit. It is certainly arguable that if the fire of the Spirit can be quenched (1 Thes 5:19), so also it may be "fanned into flame."[138] (4) Finally, vv. 6–14 hold together as a single unit of appeal. At the end of this appeal, in v. 14, Paul returns to the focus at the beginning (our passage) and urges Timothy to guard the good deposit "through the *Holy Spirit who dwells in us*." This does not refer to his ministerial gift, but to the Spirit.[139] Thus, even though the concern is with Timothy's loyalty to the gospel, the focus is on the empowering of the Spirit to accomplish it.

All of this suggests, therefore, that even though this passage is probably related in some way to 1 Tim 4:14, what Paul is referring to here is not Timothy's giftedness for ministry; rather, Paul's concern here is focused more directly on the gift of the Spirit himself, a gift that originally came to Timothy when Paul laid hands on him. And it is this association, Timothy's reception of the Spirit through Paul, that is being recalled. Timothy is about to be spurred to a loyalty to the gospel that will require his taking part in suffering for Christ. It is not his "gift of

---

[137] A view that goes back at least as far as Chrysostom; cf. Calvin. One can find it throughout the literature. But see Bernard 109, who, if this view is correct, more properly speaks of the χάρισμα as "the special grace received by Timothy to fit him for his ministerial functions." We are thus dealing with function, not office.

[138] In 1 Thes 5:19 the Spirit is quenched by stifling the prophetic gift; here he is "fanned into flame" as Timothy girds himself by the help of the Spirit for ministry in the face of increasing hostility and suffering.

[139] Furthermore, in v. 6, just as in 1 Tim 4:14, Paul refers to the "gift" as being "in Timothy"; but in v. 7 he broadens the scope to speak of the Spirit as being given to *us*. In v. 14 Paul brings these two items together and specifically refers to the "*Spirit who lives in us*." The Spirit is the obvious point of focus.

ministry" that needs to be aroused, but his utter reliance on the Holy
Spirit, and that is what v. 7 is all about.

Given all of this, it is all the more surprising that so many consider
πνεῦμα in v. 7 to refer to a disposition, "a spirit of," rather than to the
Holy Spirit.[140] On the surface this is understandable, especially in light
of the negative side of the "not/but" contrast. Indeed, were this the only
thing said, it would be universally granted that Paul is speaking of "a
spirit of timidity," that is, a disposition toward cowardice.[141] But it is not
the only thing said, nor does this common view take seriously enough
the nearly identical usage in 1 Cor 2:12 and Rom 8:15[142] (q.v.), where the
Holy Spirit is also plainly in view. The key lies with Pauline usage: in the
vast majority of his οὐ/ἀλλά contrasts the negative is not the point,
although it is crucial to the point; Paul's concern is always expressed in
the ἀλλά ("but") phrase or clause. Thus one may usually take out the
"not [something], but" and thereby get directly to Paul's point. So here:
"For God gave us the Spirit of power, love, and sound-mindedness,"
meaning that in giving us his Spirit, God thereby gave us power, love,
and a sound head. This is corroborated by the context, as we have noted
above, and by the fact that "power" and "love" in Paul are specifically
related to the activity of the Spirit in the believer's life. If Paul does not
elsewhere use "sound-mindedness,"[143] he does list "self-control" in Gal
5:23 as one of the fruit of the Spirit.[144]

But to get there Paul begins by setting up a contrast vital to the
present argument, but expressed in such a way as to make his meaning
almost impossible to render in English without some jockeying with the

---

[140]E.g., White 55, Lock 85–86 (who as in Titus 3:5–6 does not so much as mention
the Holy Spirit in his comment on v. 7; cf. Simpson 123–24), Kelly 150, and others.
The English translations are especially faulty; however, their faultiness is excusable
in this case, since Paul's Greek is not easily rendered into English without a dynamic
equivalent.

[141]Gk. δειλεία, which means more than simply timidity. It is frequently used in
contexts of struggle or warfare of those who pull back from the struggle as cowards.
See 1 Macc 4:32; 2 Macc 3:24; Jos. Life 172; Ag. Ap. 2.148.

[142]Hanson 29 has argued that the pseudepigrapher has used and rewritten Rom
8:12–17 as the basis for 1 Tim 1:6–9 ("this is certainly based on the Romans passage"),
and here in particular has "deliberately [made] a play on Paul's words." It is hard to
imagine a comment at once more prejudicial and more distant from the actual data.

[143]Gk. σωφρονισμοῦ. This is another of the words/word groups nearly unique to
these letters in the Pauline corpus (but see the use of σωφρονέω in Rom 12:3 and 2 Cor
5:13; the latter passage in particular shows that the present usage is thoroughly
Pauline).

[144]In this regard note Rom 12:3, where as the first matter of paraenesis Paul
insists that the Roman believers not think more highly of themselves than is proper,
but that they "think with sober judgment" (NRSV; Gk. εἰς τὸ σωφρονεῖν), and especially
so in light of v. 2, that they be "transformed by the renewing of the mind." How Paul
could write those words but not these is indeed a mystery.

words and their word order. To put it another way, here is a case where
so-called literal translation must give way to a dynamic equivalent in
order to say in English what Paul's Greek intends. What God has given
is the Spirit; what that means for Timothy is that "cowardice" is out, and
"power, love, and a sound head" are in. The GNB has captured Paul's
intent: "For the Spirit that God has given us does not make us timid;
instead, his Spirit fills us with power, love, and self-control." Precisely.

That means, finally, that when Paul shifts from "in you" in v. 6 to
"to us" in v. 7, he is not intending, as is often suggested,[145] to refer to
their individual "ordinations," thereby limiting the whole to Timothy's
and Paul's respective gifts of ministry. On the contrary, this is typical of
Paul's argumentation everywhere; in offering the theological basis for an
appeal or exhortation, he almost always includes himself (and by implication, others) as well.[146] That is not to suggest that Paul is thinking of
Pentecost; he is not. Rather he is thinking of Timothy's own, and thereby
his, and by implication all others', individual reception of the Spirit. The
inclusion of himself, of course, is especially noteworthy in this context,
since he will next remind Timothy of his (Paul's) own suffering for the
gospel, which thereby exemplifies the point of v. 7 and thus serves as a
personal model for it.

What all of this means, therefore, is that this passage picks up the
concern for Timothy's *ministry* as such only secondarily at best. Rather,
Paul focuses on the *source* of that ministry, in order to urge Timothy to
abiding loyalty to the gospel. As such, these verses take their place with
others in the Pauline corpus which emphasize the Spirit as God's gift, the
Spirit as indwelling the believer, the Spirit as power, and love as the fruit
of the Spirit.

2 TIMOTHY 1:8

*Therefore, do not be ashamed of the testimony of our Lord or of me his prisoner,
but take your part in suffering for the gospel according to the power of God.*

---

[145] Kelly 159 is typical of this point of view, "The aorist **gave** . . . recalls the
ordination service which he has mentioned, while by **us** he means Timothy and
himself." This runs aground not only on Pauline usage as argued here, but also on
v. 14 (q.v.).

[146] This phenomenon is found at the outset (1 Thes 1:9–10, "how *you* turned to
God from idols, to await his Son Jesus, who delivers *us* from the coming wrath"; cf.
4:13–14; 5:5–10), and continues throughout. See, inter alia, 1 Cor 5:7–8 ("Cleanse out
the old leaven that you might be a new loaf, for Christ *our* Passover was sacrificed;
let *us* therefore celebrate the feast"); 15:1–3 ("the gospel *you* believed, in which *you*
stand; how that Christ died for *our* sins"); 2 Cor 5:17–18 ("if anyone is in Christ, behold
the new creation; . . . now all things are from God who reconciled *us* to himself");
Gal 4:6 ("because *you* are sons, God sent the Spirit of his Son into *our* hearts"!). When
exhortation or theology turns to the *experience* of the gospel, Paul habitually includes
himself.

With the two imperatives comprising this sentence we come to the central burden of the letter. The appeal is to loyalty—to the gospel and to Paul. The problem is with defections, especially in the face of suffering related to Paul's (probably political) imprisonment. Thus, he began in v. 6 by reminding Timothy of his experience of the Spirit, as the ground for the present appeal. The Spirit, he reminds him, has nothing to do with cowardice, but is God's empowering for times like this. "Therefore," he now implores, "do not be ashamed of either the gospel, the witness about our Lord, or me, the Lord's prisoner because of the gospel; on the contrary take your own share of suffering for the gospel." And with that Paul takes him back to vv. 6–7, that Timothy take his share of suffering *by the power of God,* meaning by the Spirit whom God has given so that he may be empowered to share in such suffering.

While it is true that in Paul δύναμις does not always refer directly—or even indirectly—to the Holy Spirit, the full context in this case, as in Eph 3:20, demands such an interpretation,[147] especially in light of v. 7 with its combination of Spirit and power over against cowardice. Thus, Timothy's need to "fan into flame" the gift of the Spirit, who resides in him, because it is by the power of the Spirit that he will need to "take his own part in suffering for the gospel." This is one further piece of evidence of the very close tie in Paul between the presence of the Spirit and the presence of God's power in the life of the believer.

2 TIMOTHY 1:14

Guard the good deposit entrusted to your care through the Holy Spirit who dwells in us.

With these words Paul concludes the appeal that began in v. 6. As noted above, his concern for Timothy is threefold: that he be loyal to Christ, to Paul, and thus to his own ministry, which is for Christ and under Paul's tutelage. The appeal is that he fan into flame the gift that is in him; the ground of the appeal is the Holy Spirit whom God has given him and in so doing has therewith empowered him. Having described the "deposit," the gospel itself, in vv. 9–10, and having reminded Timothy once more of his (Paul's) own loyalty to this gospel and of God's own commitment to guard what has been committed to him until the final day (vv. 11–12), Paul in v. 13 turns once more to Timothy (last addressed in v. 8) and urges him to keep to the sound teaching of the gospel, and to do so by the power of the indwelling Spirit.

---

[147] Some (e.g., Alford, Kent) understand the κατά (*according to* the power of God) to refer to that power displayed in "our salvation" that is spelled out in vv. 9–10. While this is possible grammatically, it seems unlikely in context. Rather, the κατά means "in keeping with the power of God we have just mentioned."

Here is the last explicit mention of the Holy Spirit in the Pauline corpus. Some find this sentence altogether too static to be authentic Paul, whose view of the Spirit is much more dynamic, we are told.[148] But that view seems to be based on a prior commitment that disallows that Paul would ever write such a letter in the first place. Given the historical circumstances as they emerge in this letter—an especially onerous imprisonment, defections of people from whom he expected more, and the almost inevitable prospect of death—how else might one expect the apostle to speak to his closest and dearest companion in ministry?[149]

In any case, the metaphor of "guarding the deposit" is not intended to be "static"—not in these letters in any case. On the contrary, the metaphor appeals to Timothy's abiding loyalty to the gospel, to which he had indeed been committed for so many years.[150] In this context it is an understandable and powerful metaphor, drawn from one of the truly sacred trusts of the ancient world.[151] The "deposit" is obviously the gospel, which has been briefly summarized in vv. 9–10 in terms appropriate to the context, to which Paul has been loyal to the point of his present suffering (vv. 11–12). It is this same gospel to which Timothy must be loyal as well, especially in light of the defections in v. 15 and the false teachers in 2:14–3:9. "Guarding" therefore does not mean to "sit on it," but to stay loyal to it, even to the extent of taking his share in the suffering.[152]

Thus the role of the Spirit is precisely that of vv. 6–7 and 8. Timothy's continued loyalty, which as the rest of the letter proves is hardly a static concept, is being urged in the face of considerable hardship. Under such

---

[148] In this regard see esp. Dunn, *Jesus*, 349. "The Spirit has become the power to guard the heritage of tradition handed on from the past," he says of this verse. But not only is such a view too narrow as to what Paul is "allowed" to say, by our standards, but it also betrays a lack of sensitivity to the real concern in this whole appeal.

[149] And what kind of prejudice is it, one wonders, which disallows beforehand that this combination of circumstances is possible for the apostle?

[150] Apart from the actual metaphor itself, therefore, this differs little from the concern expressed very early in Paul, which recurs in a variety of ways throughout the corpus, that his friends "hold fast the traditions which they were taught through word or letter" (2 Thes 2:15).

[151] The metaphor (Gk. παραθήκη) first appears in 1 Tim 6:20–21, although it is hinted at in the use of the verb παρατίθημι in 1 Tim 1:18. It reflects one of the highest forms of obligation in ancient society, in which a person going on a journey entrusted what was of value (family or goods) to a friend for safe-keeping. The person so entrusted was under sacred duty to keep "the deposit safe" (see, e.g., Lev 6:2, 4, where παραθήκη is used in the LXX; cf. Tob 10:13; and esp. 2 Macc 3:15). Cf. the helpful discussions in W. Barclay, "Paul's Certainties, VII. Our Security in God—2 Timothy i.12," *ExpT* 69 (1958) 324–27; and in Lock 90–92.

[152] After all, it is by means of the prophetic Spirit that Timothy was earlier urged to engage in the ongoing spiritual warfare (1 Tim 1:18).

circumstances he will need the help of the Spirit to hold to the pattern of sound teaching.

Also as in v. 6, and elsewhere in Paul, the emphasis is on the Spirit as *indwelling* Timothy for such a task; moreover, as in v. 7 the mention of the indwelling Spirit causes Paul to broaden the perspective to include himself, "who dwells *in us.*" The frequent suggestion that "in us" refers only to Paul and Timothy and to their gift of ministry thus misses the argument by a wide margin.[153] It is not ministry that is in view, but *persons*, two men who are in ministry to be sure, but who with all other believers are indwelt by the Spirit, in whose strength alone they can continue their loyalty to Christ and the gospel in the face of their present hardships.[154] To make 2 Timothy refer primarily to ministry simply misses too much in this letter.

2 TIMOTHY 3:5

. . . holding to the outward form of godliness, but denying its power.

With these words Paul concludes a long vice list describing the last days, by focusing directly on the false teachers. He thereby includes the false teachers in Ephesus as part of the increase of evil that is the harbinger of the final eschatological day. As noted above on 1 Tim 3:16, the great concern in the two letters to Timothy is εὐσέβεια ("godliness"), which has to do with both right thinking about God and right living for him. This indictment of the false teachers suggests that they are in favor of εὐσέβεια all right, as 1 Tim 6:5 also makes plain. But for them "godliness" involves ascetic practices and other "outward forms"[155] that make a show but have none of the real substance of Christian faith or life.[156]

In this case the substance that is denied is "the power" found in true εὐσέβεια. This, of course, might mean nothing more than denying "its effective power,"[157] and as such it would stand over against the "outward form" by emphasizing the

---

[153] So e.g., Lock 89, Kelly 167, Hanson 125 (with some antipathy toward the author, who would "attribute to the members of the ordained ministry" what "Paul predicates of all Christians"!). Proponents of this view commonly see the whole of this passage as dealing with Timothy's "ministry" as such, and in particular contend that vv. 6–7 refer to his "ordination." Barrett 98, on the other hand, who also sees vv. 6–7 as referring to "ordination" nonetheless wisely counsels of this passage, "There is no reason for confining *within us* to the ministry; the Holy Spirit dwells within all Christians, and thus lends special aid to ministers in their special responsibilities."

[154] To suggest otherwise is similar to arguing (absurdly, to be sure) that the appeal to the Spirit as indwelling the "bodies" of the Corinthians in 1 Cor 6:19 limits the meaning of the indwelling Spirit in that passage only to the sanctification of the body.

[155] Gk. μόρφωσις, which refers to the outward form that something takes. Philo (*Plant.* 70) similarly refers to some "who were a semblance of piety [τῶν ἐπιμορφα-ζόντων εὐσέβειαν]").

[156] Very much like the false teaching in Colossians 2; see esp. 2:20–23.

[157] So Guthrie 158.

inherent power of the gospel to regenerate and to *transform* so that ascetic practices are quite unnecessary and irrelevant. But the contrast closely resembles Paul elsewhere, as in 1 Cor 2:5 or 4:20,[158] where the "power" of our εὐσέβεια is none other than that of the Spirit. Thus, even though the Spirit is not mentioned here (the contrast does not easily lend itself to doing so), this is probably another "power" text in which the Spirit lies close below the surface.

If that be so, then this is but one more text in Paul in which the Spirit is seen in terms of power, and power is understood as the Spirit's effecting in believers' lives what "outward form" of any kind simply cannot do. Indeed, every *substitution* of "form" for the genuine experience, be it fundamentalist legalism or high church ritualism or Pentecostal enthusiasm, is an effective denial of the power of the Spirit to work out the Christian faith—genuine faith—in our lives.

2 TIMOTHY **3:16**

All scripture is God-breathed[159] *and is profitable for teaching, for reproof, for correction, and for training in righteousness.*

In this passage, which is one of the two in the NT on which the doctrine of the divine inspiration of scripture is primarily predicated,[160] Paul is giving the theological ground for his confidence in scripture to make Timothy "wise unto salvation" (v. 15): it is totally "God-breathed," that is, it is completely of divine origin. The word describing its divine character and origin, θεόπνευστος, brings the passage into our present discussion.[161] Although this does not articulate a doctrine of inspiration, both the language (πνευστος) and Paul's attitude toward scripture elsewhere[162] indicate that he shares with his Jewish heritage the conviction that the sacred scriptures were given by divine in-"spiration," that is, by the "breath" of God, the Holy Spirit.[163]

---

[158] So White 171.

[159] The grammar of this sentence is not certain. Did Paul say, "All scripture is God-breathed" or "Every God-breathed scripture is . . ."? For the former see the discussion in Hendriksen, Kelly, or Hanson; for the latter, Bernard, Spicq, or Barrett. In favor of the translation as given is the similar construction in 1 Tim 4:4 ("every creation of God is good, and . . .") and the context (the scripture that is able to make Timothy wise unto salvation can do this because it is God-breathed in its totality). The other reading is traceable to an early period, effected in some of the Old Latin versions by omitting the καί that follows "God-breathed."

[160] The other is 2 Pet 2:21.

[161] Not all see the Spirit behind the language "God-breathed." See, e.g., Schweizer, *TDNT* 6.653–55. But his disdain for a "mechanical" view of inspiration causes Schweizer to understate the case here. For the perspective argued here, see Quinn, "Spirit," 361–62 (cf. Hendriksen 301–3).

[162] Several things are instructive. It is clear, for example, that in scripture God speaks (note the formula "God says"); so much so, that in Gal 3:8 and 3:22 "scripture" functions as the subject of sentences where one would normally expect "God."

[163] It is therefore totally beside the point for Schweizer to assert that Paul is "far . . . from an authenticating theory of inspiration" (*TDNT* 6.454n7). *Theories of*

Behind this view in Judaism is that reflected in 2 Pet 2:21, which understands the OT as the writings of the "prophets" (including Moses)[164] and thus links those writings with the Spirit, the acknowledged source of prophetic inspiration. Even though Paul makes no point of this particular doctrine elsewhere, there can be little question that he shared the common view that the Spirit inspired the writers of the OT. Thus in Rom 1:2 he speaks of "what God promised beforehand through his prophets in the sacred scriptures." Precisely that combination, God speaking through prophets and thus creating "holy scripture," is what lies behind the use of the word "God-breathed" in this present passage.

2 TIMOTHY 4:22

On the use of πνεῦμα in this grace-benediction ("the Lord be with your spirit; grace be with you"[165]), see the discussion of the nearly identical formula in Gal 6:18.[166]

CONCLUSIONS

With these letters the Pauline corpus comes to a close. As we have noted throughout, their special circumstances (written to long-time companions and trusted colleagues, but as third-party documents) tend to limit the number of references to the Holy Spirit. But what does emerge in these letters fully accords with the dynamic of life in the Spirit recorded throughout the corpus.

At the heart of a typical soteriological formulation in Titus 3:5–6, the Spirit plays the key role in God's people's experience of salvation. God saves them through the work of the Spirit (here seen, as in 1 Cor 6:11, in terms of the metaphor "washing"), who has been lavishly poured out upon them through Christ.

---

inspiration are unnecessary for those who hold the Spirit's inspiration of the OT as common ground.

[164] For this attitude cf. Acts 2:30 (of David in the Psalms); 3:24–25; 13:20.

[165] The "your" in the first clause is singular; in this second clause it is plural. For the final plural, see the note on Phlm 25. This separation of the grace into two parts, one for Timothy and one for the rest, is surely a final touch of affection in this letter, and with it another strike for authenticity.

[166] Although see Quinn, "Spirit," 363, who sees this usage as continuing "the link of Timothy with the Spirit . . . to the very last words of PE." The final prayer of the apostle for Timothy is thus to be understood as a request that the Lord "stay with and protect that spirit in Timothy that has been the gift of the Holy Spirit." But this tends to see the grace-benediction strictly in terms of the Pastoral Epistles, without adequate appreciation for Pauline usage elsewhere, which as we have shown scarcely reflects the activity of the Holy Spirit.

The Spirit, however, is not only "poured out" upon believers, he is the personal presence of God ("the χάρισμα of God") who has come to dwell within believers. As such he empowers them for life in the present—in Timothy's case to equip him for loyalty to the gospel in the midst of hardship and suffering. Thus the Spirit is the source of power and fruit (love), as throughout the Pauline corpus. Indeed, it is the denial of such power in favor of "outward show" that marks the false teachers as belonging to the final apostasy.

Furthermore, the Spirit is also present, as always, in the community of faith through the prophetic word. The Spirit who breathed authority and usefulness into sacred scripture, continues to speak through prophetic words. As such he is the eschatological Spirit who "expressly says" that the present days of demonic activity through the false teachers are evidently "the latter days."

It was also in the community of faith that the prophetic word and the gift of the Spirit joined to "gift" Timothy for his ministry, which is especially being tried in the difficult situation in Ephesus. By remembering that gifting of many years earlier, he will be encouraged not only "not to neglect his gift," but also to engage in the present warfare against Satan and his dupes, the straying elders.

If this is not the full-orbed view of the Spirit one finds in some of the earlier letters, it is nonetheless part and parcel with the full understanding of the Spirit that emerges in the letters as a whole. Therefore, it is altogether proper that this evidence be included in the theological synthesis that follows.

PART 2

SYNTHESIS

Preface to Part II:
Finding a Place to Begin

Having examined all the Pauline texts that speak directly about the Spirit, and many that seem to do so indirectly, we now face the problem of finding a place to begin. How does one bring coherence to the mass of material that lies before us? That in itself is a daunting task. But of still greater moment is the existential one. How do we reflect on this material so that it has something to say to us? That, after all, is the reason for this book in the first place. And our problems are even more complex because none of us approaches these questions *tabula rasa*. Our own experiences of Christ, the Spirit, and the church, both individually and corporately, not only prepare us to read the texts in a certain way, but also tend to dictate how we go about the task of thinking through them with some kind of coherence.

Most of the readers of this book, including its author, live in a time when neutrality about the work of the Spirit is scarcely an option. The basic reason for that, for good or ill, stems from the Pentecostal and charismatic movements. There is hardly anyone who does not have an opinion—or a positive or negative experience—regarding the renewal of Spirit phenomena in the contemporary church. Part of the problem here is one of polarization; far more people tend to take sides for such phenomena or against them than try to embrace Spirit phenomena within the confines of historic Christianity. Historically, Spirit movements have a poor track record within the boundaries of more traditional ecclesiastical structures. From my perspective the fault lies on both sides: reformers tend to burn structures and try to start over (and when they do they only create a new set of structures for the next Spirit movement to burn down); those with vested interests in the structures consequently tend to push Spirit movements to the fringe—or outside altogether. Thus there is a hardening of "orthodoxy," on the one hand, that tends to keep the Spirit safely domesticated within creeds and office; on the other hand, when Spirit movements are forced (or choose) to exist outside the proven tradition(s) of the historic church, there is a frequent tendency to throw theological caution to the wind. The result all too often is a great deal of finger-pointing and name-calling, without an adequate attempt to embrace both the movement of the Spirit and existing tradition(s) simultaneously.

This historical phenomenon, which provides us with our own starting point in coming to these texts, may also happily serve us in finding a starting point in Paul—since in their own way our difficulties reflect the kinds of tensions that Paul faced, most of which have to do with the basic eschatological framework within which he lived presuppositionally. The tension results from living simultaneously within the "already" and the "not yet" of God's eschatological salvation that has come present in Christ and the Spirit. For Paul this tension surfaced particularly in a community like Corinth, where a large dose of the "already" appears to have motivated their spirituality, so that they had little time or concern for the "not yet." How *does* one square the appearance of the "powers of the age to come," manifested in specific forms of Spirit gifting, with the mundane matters of everyday life? How *does* one hold "signs and wonders" together with suffering and weakness? And here is where we come in, because most of us find it difficult to do as Paul, to hold them together simultaneously as accepted realities.

Our experience of the church or the Spirit, on either side, causes us to lean toward an "either-or" approach to the life of the Spirit. For some the emphasis will lie with power manifested in various expressions of "enthusiasm" or in signs and wonders; for others it will be with power manifested in the fruit of the Spirit or in the normal activities of everyday life. Thus it is enthusiasm vis-à-vis ethics, or signs and wonders vis-à-vis weakness and suffering. Anyone who has taken the time to work through the preceding texts, whether in agreement with all the details of my discussions or not, can scarcely miss the fact that these are false dichotomies as far as Pauline pneumatology is concerned.

But even when we acknowledge that for Paul it was "both-and" not "either-or," the more intensely existential question persists. How do any of us, on either side of these emphases in terms of tradition or experience, not just acknowledge the Pauline perspective, but learn to realize it again in a time when so much water has gone under the bridge? Those of us in the Western church at least can scarcely come to this question with the "innocence" of the primitive church. Both the long-time "safe" approach of the historic church and the Enlightenment have had their innings, and try as we might, it is difficult to make the water go back under that bridge. Westerners are instinctively nervous about spirit activity, be it the Spirit of God or other spirits; it tends not to compute rationally and is therefore suspect. Hence our difficulties with regard to any genuine "restoration" of the experience and life of the early church.

Nonetheless, this question must finally be addressed and thus will be touched on briefly at the end. But first, we must try to come to terms with Paul's own experience and theology, in as comprehensive a way as possible.

To do so we will try to enter into the Pauline world at the one crucial place where his presuppositions tend to be *radically different* from those of the later church, but are the absolutely basic "theological" or experiential framework for everything he experienced or thought. For Paul, through the resurrection of Christ and the subsequent gift of the Spirit, God himself had set the future inexorably in motion, so that everything in the "present" is determined by the appearance of the "future." It is necessary for us to start here, not with "theology" proper (the doctrine of God as such), because this is *the experiential starting point for Paul* and the early church. In contrast, the "doctrine" of God was presuppositional, but was tested in significant ways through their new experience of God through Christ and the Spirit. That, too, must be addressed.

As noted in chapter 1, the elusive "center" in Paul's theology is probably best distilled in a phrase like "salvation in Christ," which must be expressed in such a way as to include (1) the eschatological framework of Paul's existence and thinking, (2) his understanding of Christ, (3) his understanding of salvation itself, and (4) his understanding of the people of God, the sphere of God's eschatological salvation in Christ.[1] The following chapters proceed along these lines, in each case focusing on how Paul perceived the role of the Spirit in these matters (although ch. 13, by the very nature of things, will deal with the larger question of the doctrine of God, rather than focus on Christology). The result should force us not only to come to terms with the crucial role played by the Spirit in Paul's scheme of things, but also to ask the larger questions about our own existence in Christ and the role of the Spirit in our individual and corporate lives.

A final word to the reader: Because of the approach in this study (see ch. 1, pp. 9–11), a certain amount of repetition is inevitable. At times one will note that I chose not to try to invent new ways of saying the same thing. On the other hand, most of what follows synthesizes in such a way as to offer conclusions only; thus I make assertions of a kind for which the reader will need to turn to Part I to find their exegetical basis. I have thus tried to cross-reference to the exegesis rather thoroughly, especially in the footnotes that read, "see the discussion on [a given passage]." I am assuming the reader will take the time to look at the discussion of those texts before, or in conjunction with, what is here said in more summary fashion.

---

[1]Cf. Pinnock, "Concept," 3, who uses precisely these four themes to illustrate how broad and significant the concept of the Spirit is in Pauline theology, and Hui, "Concept," who in comparing Pauline and Lukan pneumatologies with that of Ephesians divides his study into these four categories.

12

THE SPIRIT AS ESCHATOLOGICAL FULFILLMENT

Probably the one feature that distances the New Testament church the most from its contemporary counterpart is its thoroughly eschatological perspective of all of life. In contrast to most of us, eschatology—a unique understanding of the time of the End—conditioned the early believers' existence in every way. The first clue to this outlook came from Jesus' own proclamation of the kingdom—as a present reality in his ministry, although still a future event. But it was the resurrection of Christ and the gift of the promised (eschatological) Spirit that completely altered the primitive church's perspective, both about Jesus and about themselves. In place of the totally future eschatology of their Jewish roots, with its hope of a coming Messiah and the resurrection of the dead, the early church recognized that the future had *already* been set in motion. The resurrection of Christ marked the beginning of the End, the turning of the ages. However, the End had only *begun*; they still awaited the final event, the (now second) coming of their Messiah Jesus, at which time they too would experience the resurrection/transformation of the body. They lived "between the times"; *already* the future had begun, *not yet* had it been consummated. From the New Testament perspective the whole of Christian existence—and theology—has this eschatological "tension" as its basic framework.

THE PAULINE FRAMEWORK[1]

This changed eschatological perspective absolutely determines Paul's theological outlook, how he talks about Christ, salvation, the church,

---

[1]On this question, the classic is G. Vos, *The Pauline Eschatology* (Princeton: University Press, 1930 [repr. Baker, 1979]), esp. pp. 1–61, a book that was some years ahead of its time.

ethics, the present, and the future. This is reflected both in his language and in many of the presuppositions that determine how he expresses himself. "We are those," he reminds the Corinthians, "upon whom the ends of the ages *have come*" (1 Cor 10:11). Christ's death and resurrection, he tells them on another occasion, have already passed sentence on the present age (2 Cor 5:14–15), which is thus "passing away" (1 Cor 7:31). With the coming of Christ the new order has begun; all things have become new (2 Cor 5:17).

For Paul, therefore, salvation in Christ is a thoroughly eschatological reality, meaning first of all that God's final (eschatological) saving of his people has already been effected by Christ. The future condemnation which we all richly deserve has been transferred from the future into the past, having been borne by Christ (Rom 8:1–3). Thus we "have been saved" (Eph 2:8). But since our final salvation has not yet been fully realized, he can likewise speak of salvation as something presently in process ("we are being saved," 1 Cor 1:18) and as yet to be consummated ("we shall be saved," Rom 5:9). "Redemption" is both "already" (Eph 1:7) and "not yet" (Eph 4:30), as is our "adoption" (Rom 8:15 and 23) and "justification" (= the gift of righteousness; Rom 5:1 and Gal 5:5). It is this understanding of salvation, as both "already" and "not yet," that keeps Paul from being a triumphalist. Because we are "already," we presently experience the power of Christ's resurrection; but because we are "not yet," we also presently participate[2] in his sufferings (Phil 3:10).

This essential framework likewise conditions Paul's understanding that the church is an eschatological community, whose members live in the present as those stamped with eternity. We live as expatriates on earth; our true citizenship is in heaven (Phil 3:20). Ethical life, therefore, does not consist of rules to live by. Rather, empowered by the Spirit, we now live the life of the future in the present age, the life that characterizes God himself. That is why, for example, Paul appeals to present and future eschatological realities as the reason believers may not adjudicate present grievances before pagan courts (1 Cor 6:1–4). Their eschatological existence trivializes such grievances—and puts believers in the awkward position of asking for a ruling by the very people that they themselves will eventually judge.[3] Believers have tasted of the life to come; and the full and final realization of the future is so certain that God's new people are completely radicalized as they live "already" but "not yet."

Since such a framework is both so thoroughgoing and so completely conditions Paul's outlook on everything, our first task in this "synthesis" is to look at the crucial role the Spirit plays in God's eschatological

---

[2]For this understanding of κοινωνία, see on 2 Cor 13:13[14] and Phil 2:1.

[3]For a full discussion of this text and the eschatological framework which conditions Paul's response, see Fee, *1 Corinthians*, 228–48.

"salvation in Christ." We will then point out how this understanding of the Spirit affects several interrelated, key areas of Pauline theology, especially those related to the central passion of Paul's life, the Law-free mission to the Gentiles. Thus we will note in turn how the Spirit as the realization of the eschatological promise determines Paul's changed attitude toward the Law, his understanding of "the flesh," and his ability to embrace present existence simultaneously as one of empowering and weakness.

THE ROLE OF THE SPIRIT[4]

For Paul this "changed eschatological perspective" derives from two experienced realities, both of which took place at the very beginning of his life in Christ: his encounter with the risen Christ on the Damascus Road ("I have seen the Lord," he avows to the Corinthians) and the subsequent gift of the eschatological Spirit. In Paul's own prior understanding of things, the resurrection of the dead and the gift of the Spirit were the two primary events that marked the end of the ages. Both of these have now been set in motion.

First, the resurrection of the dead is for Paul the final event on God's eschatological calendar, the unmistakable evidence that the End has fully arrived.[5] For Paul *the* resurrection has already taken place when Christ was raised from the dead, thus setting in motion the final doom of death and thereby guaranteeing our resurrection. Christ's resurrection makes ours both inevitable and necessary—inevitable, because his is the first-fruits which sets the whole process in motion; necessary, because death is God's enemy as well as ours, and our resurrection spells the end to the final enemy of the living God who gives life to all who live (1 Cor 15:20–28). Believers therefore live "between the times" with regard to the two resurrections. We have *already* been "raised with Christ," which guarantees our *future* bodily resurrection (Rom 6:4–5; 8:10–11).

Second, and now to our present concern, I have above regularly referred to the Spirit as the "eschatological Spirit." That is because apart from the eschatological dimension of "promise and fulfillment" and "already but not yet," neither Paul's own experience of the Spirit nor his

---

[4]For the discussion of the texts on which this section is based, see on 1 Thes 4:8; 2 Thes 1:11; 2:2; 1 Cor 1:4–7; 13:8–13; 2 Cor 3:1–6, 16–18; 4:10–12, 16; 5:5, 16–17; 6:16–7:1; 12:12; Gal 3:3, 14; 5:5–6, 16–18, 21; 6:7–10; Rom 5:1–5; 8:11, 17–30; 15:13; Eph 1:13–14, 17–20; 4:4, 30; 1 Tim 4:1. See also Hamilton, *Holy Spirit*, 17–40; Pinnock, "Concept," 279–301; Hui, "Concept," 151–76.

[5]That Paul never lost this perspective on things is witnessed most vividly in 1 Cor 15:20–28. When Christ raises the believing dead, that spells the death of death itself; thus Christ turns over all things to the Father, who is all and in all. See Fee, *1 Corinthians*, 746–60.

perception of that experience are intelligible.[6] From his Jewish heritage he well understood that the Spirit was part of the promise for the future. The promises of the new covenant had been put into an eschatological frame by Jeremiah and Ezekiel and had become thoroughgoing in later Jewish expectations on the basis of Joel 2:28–30. This is why the Spirit is so crucial to Paul's understanding of Christian existence. The gift of the out-poured Spirit meant that the messianic age had already arrived. The Spirit is thus the central element in this altered perspective,[7] the key to which is Paul's firm conviction that the Spirit was both the *certain evidence* that the future had dawned, and the *absolute guarantee* of its final consummation.

THE PAULINE METAPHORS

This twofold role of the Spirit (as both evidence and guarantee of the future) in Paul's "already but not yet" understanding of existence emerges in a variety of ways throughout the corpus, but nowhere more prominently than in three metaphors for the Spirit that are unique to him: down payment, firstfruits, and seal. All three images are aptly chosen; in turn each may emphasize the Spirit either as the present evidence of future realities or as the assurance of the final glory, or both of these simultaneously.

1. The metaphor of "down payment," which occurs three times (2 Cor 1:21–22; 5:5; Eph 1:14), occurs exclusively in Paul in the New Testament; and he uses it exclusively to refer to the Spirit. The word itself is amply attested in the Greek commercial papyri as a technical term for the first installment (hence "down payment") of a total amount due.[8] As such, it both establishes the contractual obligation and guarantees its fulfillment. For Paul it thus serves in all three instances to emphasize *both* the "already" *and* the "not yet" of our present existence.[9] This is expressly stated in Eph 1:14, where the "promised" Holy Spirit is actually desig-

---

[6]Failure to recognize this reality, plus a penchant to see more influence from the hellenistic side (see Appendix, n. 3), rather totally negates the value of the chapter on Paul in E. F. Scott (*Spirit*). This failure also mars Horton's, *What the Bible Says about the Holy Spirit*, but for different reasons; his book is devoted almost totally to the Spirit in the life of the individual believer.

[7]F. F. Bruce (*Commentary on Galatians*, 232) rightly calls this "the most distinctive feature in Paul's doctrine of the Spirit." Cf. Hamilton, *Holy Spirit*, who, despite the inadequate exegesis of so many passages, has correctly perceived this central dimension of Pauline thought.

[8]See MM, 79; cf. the discussion on 1 Cor 1:21–22.

[9]So much is this so, that the NIV translates ἀρραβών in both 2 Corinthians passages as "a deposit, guaranteeing what is to come." That is a true "dynamic equivalent," although the phrase "guaranteeing what is to come" is only inherent in the metaphor itself; it does not occur in Paul's own sentence as such.

nated as the "down payment on our inheritance."[10] The "already/not yet" presuppositions of this language can scarcely be missed. On the one hand, the "Holy Spirit of the promise" and "our inheritance" come directly out of the eschatological expectations of Paul's Jewish heritage: the Spirit whom we have received is *the fulfillment of the promise.* On the other hand, this "fulfilled promise" is likewise *the guarantee of our future inheritance.* The Spirit, therefore, serves as God's down payment in our present lives, the certain evidence that the future has come into the present, the sure guarantee that the future will be realized in full measure.

2. As with "down payment," the metaphor "firstfruits," used of the Spirit in Rom 8:23, is especially serviceable to image the Spirit's role in Paul's "changed eschatological perspective." This metaphor, used previously of Christ's resurrection as the guarantee of ours (1 Cor 15:20, 23), reflects in a special way the tension of present existence as already/not yet *and* the guarantee of our certain future. The larger context of Rom 8:14–30 is especially noteworthy. With the Spirit playing the leading role, Paul in vv. 15–17 has struck the dual themes of our present position as children (who are thus joint-heirs with Christ of the Father's glory) and of our present existence as one of weakness and suffering as we await that glory. These are the two themes taken up in vv. 18–27. By the Spirit we have already received our "adoption" as God's children, but what is "already" is also "not yet." Therefore, by the same Spirit who functions for us as *firstfruits,* we await our final adoption, in the form of the redemption of our bodies. The first sheaf is God's pledge to us of the final harvest. Thus, in one of the clearest passages in the corpus in which Paul delineates his basic eschatological framework, the Spirit plays the essential role in our present existence, as both evidence and guarantee that the future is now and yet to be.

3. The third metaphor, "seal," also occurs three times with direct reference to the Spirit (2 Cor 1:21–22; Eph 1:13; 4:30). When used literally, a "seal" usually referred to a stamped impression in wax, denoting ownership and authenticity, and carrying with it the protection of the owner. In contrast to "down payment," there is nothing inherently eschatological in this image; nonetheless, when Paul uses it as a metaphor for the Spirit it carries a decidedly eschatological overtone. As Eph 1:13 and 4:30 make certain, the "seal" is the Spirit, by whom God has marked believers and claimed them for his own. Intrinsically this metaphor can emphasize either the present or the future. Thus in 2 Cor 1:21–22, the gift of the eschatological Spirit in the lives of the Corinthians serves as the "seal" which both marks them off as God's possession and

---

[10]Which suggests further that the genitive "of the Spirit" in 2 Cor 1:22 and 5:5 is appositional to down payment. Thus "the down payment of the Spirit" = "the down payment, that is, the Spirit." See on 2 Cor 1:21–22.

authenticates Paul's apostleship among them. Likewise, in Eph 1:13 by "sealing" them with the Holy Spirit, God stamped the Gentile recipients of that letter as his own possession. At the same time, the eschatological guarantee in the metaphor is expressly stated in Eph 4:30 ("with whom you were sealed *for the day of redemption*").

Although this perspective occurs in a variety of other ways, these metaphors serve as starting points for us to penetrate Paul's understanding. The Spirit is the evidence that the *eschatological promises of Paul's Jewish heritage have been fulfilled.* At the same time, the Spirit as God's empowering presence enables the people of God not simply to endure the present as they await the final consummation, but to do so with verve (with "spirit" if you will). And that is because the future is as sure as the presence of the Spirit as an experienced reality, hence the significance of the dynamic and experiential nature of the Spirit's coming into the life of the believer.[11]

THE SPIRIT AND RESURRECTION

The most prominent feature of what is "not yet" in Pauline eschatology is the bodily resurrection of believers. But explanations of the precise role of the Spirit in this reality appear in some unfortunately confused ways in the literature, where it is often suggested, based on the prior assumption that the Spirit was the agent of Christ's resurrection, that the Spirit is the agent of ours as well. Although there are no inherent theological difficulties with this position, there are considerable exegetical ones. In fact, Paul's position on this issue is consistent throughout. Resurrection, both Christ's and ours, is invariably expressed in terms of God's activity, attributed at times to God's power;[12] the Spirit is not the *agent* of our resurrection, but its *guarantor.* Moreover, since the final resurrection takes place in the sphere characterized above all by the Spirit's final eschatological presence, Paul sees the closest kind of connection between the Spirit and the nature of the resurrection body. A few words about each of these matters:

1. The mistaken notion that the Spirit is the agent of resurrection is based primarily on the questionable exegesis of a few texts, of which Rom 8:11 is chief: first, it is asserted that *the Spirit is the agent of Christ's resurrection,* and therefore also of ours; second, in one textual tradition of Rom 8:11, assumed to be original despite its patently secondary character,[13] Paul is made to say that *"God will also raise us through the Spirit who indwells us."* But such an understanding of Rom 8:11 is highly suspect.

---

[11] See the further discussion of this matter in ch. 14 below.

[12] See 1 Thes 1:10; 1 Cor 6:14; 15:15; 2 Cor 4:14; 13:4; Gal 1:1; Rom 4:24; 6:4; 8:11; 10:9; Col 2:12; Eph 1:20; plus the texts where Christ's resurrection is expressed in the "divine passive" (1 Thes 4:14; 1 Cor 15:12, 20; 2 Cor 5:15; Rom 4:25; 6:9; 7:4; 8:34).

[13] On this question see esp. nn. 205 and 231 on Rom 8:10–11.

a. Despite the frequency with which it is asserted,[14] no text in Paul in fact attributes the resurrection of Christ to the work of the Spirit, especially not Rom 8:11. Paul did not say, "If the Spirit who raised Christ dwells in you." Rather he said, "If the Spirit *of him [God] who raised Christ* dwells in you. Paul's point is that if the *Spirit dwells in us*, that is, the Spirit *of the very God who raised Christ*, then that says something significant about our own future—that the presence in our lives of the Spirit of the God who raised Christ guarantees the "future life" of our mortal bodies as well, destined for death though they still be (v. 10). Thus this text in particular not only does *not* attribute Christ's resurrection to the agency of the Spirit, but on the contrary attributes it, as always in Paul, to God alone. All other texts that are enlisted to support this mistaken reading of Rom 8:11 are equally suspect.[15] The one that might have the most in its favor is 1 Cor 6:14, where Paul says that both Christ's resurrection and ours are "through God's power." If there were any place where Paul expressly stated either that the Spirit raised Christ or that he will raise us, then "power" in this text might easily be seen as referring to the Spirit; but since Paul nowhere says such a thing, "power" in this case refers to God's power in the abstract, as the "might" inherent to his being by which he raises the dead (cf. Eph 1:20).

b. The only text, therefore, which attributes resurrection, in this case *our* resurrection, to the Spirit is the aforementioned textual variant of Rom 8:11. But this variant is clearly a corruption of the text of Paul, supported as it is by the inferior textual tradition and representing as it does the *lectio facilior*, the easier reading created by the scribes for the very reasons some would argue for its originality. What Paul himself wrote fully accords both with his whole theological perspective and especially with the point of v. 10: that we can be certain that our bodies, though destined for death, will be given life, precisely *because* of the Spirit who indwells us. Thus, in this passage, as in all others that speak to the question, the Spirit is the guarantor of our future, including our bodily resurrection. That is the clear sense of the metaphor "down payment" in 2 Cor 5:5 and the metaphor "firstfruits" in Rom 8:23. In each case the metaphors signal the Spirit's presence in our lives as the sure guarantee that we shall realize our final "adoption, the redemption of our bodies."[16] Thus, even though one could hardly object to the Spirit's agency of this final realization of the future, Paul's point is a consistently different one, namely, that the Spirit is both the evidence and guarantee of the future, including its final expression.

---

[14]For bibliography see n. 233 on Rom 8:11.
[15]See the discussion on 1 Cor 6:14; Rom 1:3–4; 6:4; 8:23.
[16]So also Pinnock, "Concept," 288–89.

2. That leads, then, to a word about the nature of our redeemed bodies, since in 1 Cor 15:44–48, Paul insists on calling them "spiritual bodies." As we noted in the exegesis of these texts, this does not refer to their "substance," as though Paul intended to compare them with our present bodies composed of material substance. Rather, he is contrasting our present existence with our heavenly one; the future body is super-naturally fitted for the final life of the Spirit, totally unhindered by any of its present weaknesses. Left to his own, and apart from the language dictated by his opponents in Corinth, Paul later speaks of the two modes of our bodily existence as "the body of our [present] humiliation" which God will transform into the likeness of "the body of Christ's [present] glory" (Phil 3:21). The "body of glory" is his "Spiritual body," the body supernaturally transformed for existence in the final realm of the Spirit. Thus, the "redemption of the body" has to do with the present body's becoming a "Spiritual body," in that it will be so totally transformed that it will be fully adapted for the life that is to be, of which the Spirit's presence now is the guarantee.

We note finally in this regard that Paul's eschatology lacks alto-gether any Greek influence in which the body is relegated to a secondary status, despised and subdued in the present and finally to be sloughed off as believers attain true spirituality. Apparently this was the Corinthians' position, and Paul attacks it twice in his letters to them. For them the Spirit meant present ecstasy, life above and beyond mere bodily weak-nesses, and thus evidence of being released finally from bodily existence altogether. For Paul the Spirit meant empowering for life in the midst of present bodily weaknesses in a body obviously in the process of decay. Thus in 2 Cor 5:5 he reaffirms his position from 1 Cor 15:35–58 that the presence of the Spirit means that these "decaying bodies" have also been stamped with eternity; they are destined for resurrection and thus trans-formation into the likeness of Christ's now glorified body. God, Paul argues, "has fashioned us for this," and the Spirit, whom the Corinthians have come to understand in a triumphalistic way, is rather the guaran-tee, the down payment from God that these bodies are also destined for a "Spiritual" (= glorified) future.

In light of all this evidence, therefore, it is fair to conclude that the Spirit is the key to the future orientation of Paul and the early church. By the Spirit's presence believers tasted of the life to come and became oriented toward its consummation. But despite what is often implied to the contrary, Paul's primary emphasis is not on the certain and eagerly awaited future that the Spirit guarantees. That is always there, to be sure, but by the very nature of things[17] Paul's emphases lie with the

---

[17] Specifically, that Paul's letters are ad hoc and far more often corrective than merely instructional.

Spirit as the demonstration that the future has already been set in motion. This is especially true at the very heart of matters for him: a Law-free, but not lawless, mission to the Gentiles, to which matter we now turn.

THE SPIRIT AS THE FULFILLED PROMISE

The Gentile mission was the passion of Paul's life. But for him this mission was not simply to "make believers out of Gentiles." Rather, his passion was the inclusion of Gentiles into the people of God, Law-free and on equal terms with Jews, so that there were not two peoples of God but one, composed of Jew and Gentile alike, who "together with one voice might glorify the God and Father of our Lord Jesus Christ" (Rom 15:6). On the basis of the argument in Galatians 3, we know that Paul saw the inclusion of the Gentiles as the fulfillment of the Abrahamic covenant (Gen 12:3). The catena of Old Testament citations in Rom 15:9–12, which concludes the argument of this letter, further indicates that Paul understood Gentile inclusion in terms of eschatological fulfillment. One is not surprised, therefore, that in the two places where Paul equates the Spirit with the language of "promise," he does so in the context of the inclusion of the Gentiles into the eschatological people of God (Gal 3:14 [cf. vv. 21–22]; Eph 1:13–14). The two places where the Spirit is tied directly to the word "hope" occur in similar contexts (Rom 15:13; Eph 4:4).

THE SPIRIT AND THE INCLUSION OF THE GENTILES

The key passage in this regard is Gal 3:14, since the promise of the Spirit is equated with the blessing of Abraham, even though in the Old Testament passage there is no mention of the Spirit. Since the "blessing of Abraham" came in the form of a "promise," the latter word is the one Paul uses throughout this argument to refer to the blessing. Crucial to this argument is Paul's assertion that the fulfillment of this promised blessing for the Gentiles is to be found in their having experienced the Spirit as a living and dynamic reality. The blessing of Abraham, therefore, is not simply "justification by faith." Rather, it refers to the eschatological life now available to Jew and Gentile alike, effected through the death of Christ, but realized through the dynamic ministry of the Spirit—and all of this by faith.

Likewise in Eph 1:13–14, addressing his Gentile readers directly, Paul assures them that they, too, have been sealed by God as his own possession, by giving them "the Holy Spirit of the promise" (= the Holy Spirit promised to Israel). By that same token God also guaranteed the final inheritance for Jew and Gentile alike, since the Spirit is God's "down payment" of *our* inheritance (Jew and Gentile together). Thus, with a subtle shift of pronouns Paul moves from "our" (= Jews) having obtained the inheritance, to "your" (= Gentiles) having been sealed by the "promised Holy Spirit," to the Spirit as God's down payment on "our" (= Jew and Gentile together) final inheritance. This is eschatological language. The Spirit as the "fulfilled promise" confirms that God's eschatological salvation has now come. Jew and Gentile together have obtained the inheritance, which they also patiently await. "A person is not a Jew 'outwardly,' " Paul says in another place (Rom 2:29), nor is true circumcision a matter of cutting off the foreskin but is rather "by the Spirit, not by the letter." This, too, for Paul has to do with eschatological fulfillment, this time of Deut 30:1–6, with its promise of a renewed people whose hearts God has circumcised.

So also with the language of hope. In Eph 4:1–3, Paul's concern is that his readers "maintain the unity [of Jew and Gentile as one people of God] effected by the Spirit." The one body, he goes on in v. 4, formed by the one Spirit, also lives in one hope of their calling, precisely because through the Spirit Gentiles have become fellow-heirs with Jews of the final inheritance (1:13–14). And in Rom 15:13, having noted that Christ is the fulfillment of Isa 11:10—he is the one in whom the Gentiles now hope—Paul concludes by praying that his predominantly Gentile readers will "abound in [this] hope by the power of the Spirit." Thus the Spirit for Paul is the key to the present fulfillment of the eschatological inclusion of the Gentiles in the people of God.

THE SPIRIT AND THE NEW COVENANT

This same theme is picked up in a slightly different way in those passages where Paul contrasts the past and present in terms of the old and new covenants.[18] The emphasis now, however, is not so much on Gentile inclusion per se, but on *their inclusion totally apart from Torah*, which served as the "identity marker" of the former covenant. The Spirit, and the Spirit alone, Paul argues in Galatians, identifies the people of God under the new covenant. The failure of the former covenant, the covenant of Law, was that even though Paul considered the Torah to be "Spiritual" in the sense that it came by way of Spirit-inspiration (Rom 7:14), and even though it came with glory (2 Cor 3:7), it was *not* accompanied by the empowering Spirit. Indeed, it was written on stone tablets,

---

[18]See the discussion of 2 Cor 3:1–18; 3:6; Gal 4:23–29; Rom 2:29; 7:6. Although covenantal language occurs in connection with the Spirit in a direct way only in 2 Corinthians 3, it is closely connected in Gal 4:29 by way of v. 24. The very language of Rom 7:6, "newness of Spirit/oldness of letter," implies the old and new covenants, as does the echo of Deut 30:6 in Rom 2:29.

which for Paul imaged its "deadness," its basic inability to set people free. It had become a covenant of "letter" (= a merely written code of laws requiring obedience) leading to death (Rom 2:29; 7:6; 2 Cor 3:5–6); and a veil like that which covered Moses' face to hide the fading glory now covers the hearts of all who hear it read (2 Cor 3:14).

In contrast, the new covenant, by means of the life-giving Spirit, is written on "tablets of human hearts" (2 Cor 3:3); its rite of "circumcision" is that "of the heart" (Rom 2:29). The gospel and its ministry are accompanied by a much greater and more enduring glory, the ministry of the Spirit himself (2 Cor 3:8). The new covenant is life-giving, because its content, Christ, is administered by the Spirit, through whom also we behold—and are being transformed into—the glory of the Lord (2 Cor 3:4–18). The promised new covenant has replaced the old, and the gift of the Spirit proves it.

Essential to this view of things, of course, is that Paul understood the gift of the Spirit in terms of the new covenant promise of Jer 31:31–34, as that had come to be read in light of Ezek 36:36–37:14. The reason for a new covenant was the failure of the old to effect a truly meaningful righteousness, a righteousness coming from an obedient heart, rather than finding expression primarily in observances—as though God's people could be identified by circumcision, the observance of days, and food laws. The Old Testament itself is abundantly clear that God's intent with Torah was for his character to be revealed in the way his people worshiped and lived,[19] hence the crucial role played by the Spirit. The Spirit, promised as part of the new covenant, would effect the righteousness the former called for but failed to produce. The eschatological Spirit has now been experienced by Jew and Gentile alike, and that quite apart from Torah. Thus, the Spirit, as the eschatological fulfillment of the promised new covenant, plays a central role in Paul's argumentation whenever Gentile inclusion, Torah-free, is the issue.[20]

THE SPIRIT AND TORAH

The gift of the eschatological Spirit as the new covenant *replacement* of Torah and the new covenant *fulfillment* of its "righteous requirement" is also the key to another of the persistently nagging questions in Pauline studies: how are we to understand Paul's view of the Law?[21] Our primary

---

[19]See, e.g., among scores of such texts, the powerful appeal of Isaiah 58.

[20]See on 2 Cor 3:1–4:6 [cf. 11:4]; Gal 3:1–4:7; 4:29; 5:1–6, 13–24; Rom 7:4–6; 8:1–30; Phil 3:2–3.

[21]For helpful introductions to the issues and the debate on "Paul and the Law," see esp. S. Westerholm, *Israel's Law and the Church's Faith: Paul and his Recent Interpreters*, and F. Thielman, *From Plight to Solution: A Jewish Framework for Understanding*

difficulty here, and one of the places where the opposition lines up, stems
from the tension we feel over the many statements in Paul that seem to
speak of the Law in a highly pejorative way, as having had its day, which
stand side by side, sometimes in the same contexts, with other statements
that affirm Torah as good and as being "established by faith." Here as
much as at any other place one faces the complications of continuity and
discontinuity in Paul.

Thus, on the one hand, Paul can speak of the Law as bringing
knowledge of sin (Rom 3:20; 7:7–12) or as "arousing sin" (7:5); indeed, it
was "added so that the trespass might increase" (5:20). To be under the
Law is to be in prison, to be under slavery (Gal 3:23; 4:1); it means to be
a descendant of Hagar rather than of Sarah (Gal 4:21–31). Having increased the transgression, it led to condemnation (2 Cor 3:9); and it was
helpless to do anything about it (Rom 7:14–25; 8:3). For this reason the
Law ultimately deals in death, not life (2 Cor 3:6; Gal 2:19; Rom 7:5, 9).
Those who promote Torah observance therefore belong to "the mutilation" (Phil 3:2); they are enemies of Christ, whom Paul wishes would go
the whole way and castrate themselves (Gal 5:12). With the coming of
Christ and the Spirit, therefore, the time of Torah has come to an end
(Rom 10:4; Gal 5:18, 23). In all of these passages the emphasis is clearly
on discontinuity.[22]

On the other hand, Paul sees the Law as "holy" and "Spiritual" and
its requirements as "holy, righteous, and good" (Rom 7:12, 14). The
singular advantage of the Jews is that they have "been entrusted with
the very words of God" (Rom 3:2; cf. 9:4); and to these words Paul appeals
again and again as having authority still for God's people. Thus "faith
does not nullify the Law"; rather it "establishes, or upholds, it" (Rom
3:31). If circumcision is out, the same cannot be said of "the commandments of God" (1 Cor 7:19).

How, then, shall we reconcile such diversity?[23] Traditionally, the
way through was seen to be theological: the Law as a means of achieving
right standing with God has had its day, to be replaced by faith in Christ.
There is a considerable measure of truth in this traditional view; nonetheless, as many have shown, it tends to read the Old Testament rather
poorly, as though "keeping the Law" *were* a means of gaining God's favor
in the Old Testament.[24] In response to this, others have understood the

---

Paul's View of the Law in Galatians and Romans (NovTSup 61; Leiden: Brill, 1989), esp.
chs. 1 and 2.

[22]Indeed, much of the literature on Paul and the Law stems from the need to
explain how a Jew like Paul could bear such unJewish sentiments toward Torah.

[23]Putting the question this way, of course, assumes that these matters can be
reconciled, contra H. Räisänen, *Paul and the Law* (Philadelphia: Fortress, 1986).

[24]E. P. Sanders has argued that the same holds true for contemporary Judaism,
that is, that the Christian church, reading it through the eyes of Jesus' and Paul's

Law in Paul in terms of "covenantal nomism,"[25] in which the Law was seen by many contemporary Jews to be ethnic as well as religious, as a way of identifying the people of God vis-à-vis the Gentiles. In this view, the Law as a "boundary marker" has been brought to an end, but the Old Testament continues to have authority for Paul. Again, as useful as this is to help us understand in part the significance of the Law for contemporary Judaism, it is doubtful whether it is adequate to deal with the intensely religious nature of the Law that is presupposed—and frequently expressed—in Paul.

The solution to all of this, I propose, is to take more seriously the role of the Spirit in Paul's understanding. The experience of the promised eschatological Spirit, after all, not "righteousness by faith," forms the core of Paul's argumentation in the one letter (Galatians) devoted primarily to this issue. To be sure, regarding the above debate, the problem with Torah observance in this letter leans much more heavily toward the Law as "identity marker" (especially in the form of circumcision, food laws, and observance of days); but it is surely not limited to that. "Those who are led by the Spirit," Paul says, "are not under Torah" (Gal 5:18), period. For Paul the Spirit marks the effective end of Torah, both because the coming of the Spirit fulfills the eschatological promise that signals the beginning of the new covenant, thus bringing the old to an end, and because the Spirit is sufficient to do what Torah was not able to do in terms of righteousness, namely, to "fulfill in us who walk by the Spirit the righteous commandment of Torah" (Rom 8:4). What has come to an end, therefore, is *any form of Torah observance*, be it "boundary markers," the "observance of sabbaths," or any other "work of Law" understood religiously, all of which for Paul are predicated on "the doing" of the Law and not on faith in Christ Jesus. What has come to pass with the Spirit is God's promised new covenant, in which "I will put my Spirit in you and cause you to follow my decrees" (Ezek 36:27).

Discontinuity, therefore, lies in the area of Torah observance, the use of Torah either to identify the people of God or to identify one's relation-

---

anti-Pharisaic polemic, have missed the main thrust of contemporary Judaism. But the jury is still out on this one. There can be little question that Sanders and others, before and after him, have brought about a much-needed corrective to a rather one-sided and sometimes distorted view of Judaism. But, as others have pointed out, the polemic of Jesus and Paul did not take place in a vacuum, and an understanding of Law-keeping as gaining favor with, or securing one's relationship to, God can in fact be found among some of the rabbis.

[25]This language stems from E. P. Sanders and refers to an understanding of the Law as a gift, given in connection with the covenant, in which people did not try thereby to earn God's favor, but tried to walk in his ways because they had experienced his favor. The present description, however, is from Dunn, who has taken Sanders's view in this direction. See the collection of essays in *Jesus, Paul and the Law*, esp. chs. 6, 7, and 9.

ship with God. Continuity lies in the Spirit's "fulfilling" Torah by leading
God's people in the paths of God to live in such a way so as to express
the intent of Torah in the first place—to create a people for God's name,
who bear God's likeness in their character, as that is seen in their
behavior. Thus the key to Paul's view of the Law lies with the gift of the
eschatological Spirit.[26] The fruit of the Spirit is none other than the
Spirit's bearing in our lives the "righteousness of God" (= the righteousness that characterizes God). When this is happening Torah is fulfilled
in such a way that for all practical purposes it has become obsolete;
however, Torah as part of the Old Testament story, of which ours is the
continuation, is never obsolete. In this sense it will endure as long as this
"between-the-times" existence endures—not as a means of righteousness, nor as a means of identity, but as a means of pointing us to the
"righteousness of God," which the Spirit brings to pass in our lives in the
present expression of the eschatological future.[27]

Paul, of course, is also a realist. The coming of the Spirit to replace
Torah by effecting its intended righteousness is itself both already and
not yet. That is, the coming of the Spirit means not that divine perfection
has set in, but "divine infection." Our lives are now led by the one
responsible for inspiring the Law in the first place. But that does not
mean that God's people cannot still be "overtaken in a fault" (Gal 6:1).
The resolution of such "between-the-times" trespassing of God's "righteous requirement" is for the rest of God's Spirit people to restore such a
one through the Spirit's gentleness. It means forgiveness and grace; but
it does not mean constantly living in sin, as though the Spirit were not
really sufficient for life in the present. And that leads us to a discussion
of the Spirit and "the flesh."

THE SPIRIT AGAINST THE FLESH[28]

The gift of the eschatological Spirit, especially as empowering
changed attitudes and behavior in the already, also serves as the key to
understanding Paul's well-known contrast between living κατὰ σάρκα
(kata sarka, "according to the flesh") and κατὰ πνεῦμα (kata pneuma,
"according to the Spirit"). Although this language does not occur as

---

[26]Cf. Hamilton, *Holy Spirit*, 30; Pinnock, "Concept," 196.

[27]For the exegesis that leads to these various conclusions, see on 2 Cor 3:1–18;
3:4–6, 7–11; Gal 3:1–5, 14; 4:4–7, 29; 5:5–6, 13–15, 18, 19–23; Rom 2:29; 7:5–6, 14, 18;
8:1–2, 3–4; 12:1–2; Phil 3:3.

[28]See the discussions on 2 Cor 5:14–17; 10:2–3; 12:7; Gal 3:3; 4:29; 5:13–6:10; Rom
7:4–6, 14, 18; 8:3–4, 5–8, 12–13; 13:11–14; Phil 3:3.

often as we are sometimes led to believe by the rhetoric of New Testament scholarship,[29] nonetheless, these phrases do capture much that is at the heart of Paul's understanding of our present eschatological existence. Indeed, even though the term "flesh" originated as an anthropological term, in Paul these two phrases have become primarily and essentially eschatological. They describe two kinds of existence: one that belongs to and is conditioned by the present age that is passing away; the other describing our new eschatological existence set in motion by Christ and the Spirit.

Basic to Paul's view of things is that, as with Torah observance, the time of the flesh is over. Living according to the flesh belongs to our existence *before* and *outside of* Christ; it is totally incompatible with life "according to the Spirit." Paul, therefore, contrary to popular—and much scholarly—opinion, does not view life in the Spirit as a constant struggle between the flesh and the Spirit, in which the flesh generally has the upper hand. That may indeed be the experience of many of God's good people, but they can find no comfort in that existence on the basis of Pauline theology. Nor again does Paul's view represent triumphalism, as though people who lived by the Spirit were never tempted by the old life in the flesh or that they never succumbed to such. They have, and they do; and there is forgiveness for such, and gracious restoration. My point is a simple one: *Nowhere does Paul describe life in the Spirit as one of constant struggle with the flesh.*[30] He simply does not speak to that question. Where it might appear as though he did, his point rather is *the sufficiency of the Spirit* as we live in our present "already but not yet" existence. Thus for Paul the language "according to the flesh" describes both the perspective and the behavior of the former age that is passing away; those who so live will not inherit the kingdom of God (Gal 5:21). We, on the other hand, have entered the new aeon, where the Spirit is sufficient and stands over against the flesh in every way.

The exegesis of the key texts (Gal 5:17 and Rom 7:14–25), demonstrates that this is the Pauline perspective and will not be repeated here. Rather, after a brief outline of Paul's usage of the word "flesh,"[31] I gather the several lines of evidence from the exegesis that reflect Paul's perspective on this matter.[32]

---

[29]It is found basically in Gal 5:13–6:10 (cf. the analogy in 4:29); Rom 8:3–17; and Phil 3:3.

[30]See the discussion of Gal 5:13–15, 16–17, 19–23, 24–26; 6:7–10; Rom 7:4–6; 8:4, 5–8; 13:11–14; Phil 3:3.

[31]In this case especially in light of the analysis by Dunn in his "Jesus–Flesh and Spirit," affirmed most recently by Menzies, *Development.*

[32]As noted in the exegesis of these passages, the strongest advocate of the opposite position in recent years has been Dunn. Much of what is said here, therefore, appears in the form of a response to Dunn's work.

THE MEANING OF σάρξ IN PAUL[33]

The ultimate questions here are two and inter-related: (1) whether or not in Pauline usage σάρξ is primarily anthropological or eschatological, or perhaps some combination of both, and (2) whether it usually carries *morally* pejorative overtones in Paul, as Dunn suggests.[34]

The place to begin such an inquiry is with the Old Testament, since Pauline usage originates there. The Hebrew בָּשָׂר (*baśar*) primarily refers to the flesh of bodies, and by derivation, therefore, sometimes to the bodies themselves; on a few occasions the term is extended to describe human frailty and creatureliness, usually in contrast to God the creator. Thus a common expression for all living beings, especially humans, is "all flesh," meaning "every creature." When the Psalmist asks in light of his trust in God, "What can flesh do to me?" (Ps 56:4), he means that with God as his protector what can a mere human do to him (cf. Jer 17:5). In his anguish Job asks God, "Do you have eyes of flesh? Do you see as humans see?" While "flesh" is not a "neutral" term when used in this way, neither does it carry moral overtones. It is not pejorative; rather, it expresses human weakness and frailty as a creature. It would be unthinkable to the Hebrew that sin lay in the flesh, since sin's origins lie in the human "heart."

Although Paul rarely uses σάρξ in its basic sense, as referring to the physical body, he regularly uses it in the extended sense as referring to our humanity in some way or another. Thus he can speak of "Israel κατὰ σάρκα" (1 Cor 10:18), or Abraham as our forefather κατὰ σάρκα (Rom 4:1), or of Jesus as descended from David κατὰ σάρκα (Rom 1:3), neither of which is either pejorative or depreciatory, but rather means "humanly speaking."[35] In the same mode Paul recognizes present human life as still "in the flesh" (e.g., Gal 2:20; 2 Cor 10:3), not at all intending a morally pejorative sense to the word.[36]

---

[33]On this question see E. Schweizer, et al., *TDNT* 7.98–151; A. C. Thiselton, *NIDNTT* 1.671–82 (for further bibliography see Thiselton, 682).

[34]Dunn actually allows that σάρξ is basically "neutral" in 1 Cor 10:18 ("Jesus," 47). But in effect his article pushes toward a view that "flesh" is always pejorative in Paul.

[35]This is the opinion of almost all who have ever written on the subject, and they are surely correct. Dunn's attempt to make these also carry morally pejorative overtones ("Jesus–Flesh and Spirit," 44–47) is made by fiat rather than by careful demonstration from the data. See above on Rom 1:3. Unfortunately, Dunn's confusion of "frailty, weakness" with "morally pejorative," so that even Jesus in his earthly life is understood to be so, is imported into Paul in such a way that Dunn understands human "weakness" and "suffering" as ultimately on the "flesh" = "sinful" side of life. In part this accounts for his failure to handle either Rom 7:14 and 18 or Gal 5:17 within their Pauline contexts.

[36]Again contra Dunn, "Jesus," 49, who asserts the opposite to be true, but without evidence from the Pauline contexts themselves.

The uniquely Pauline sense, in which life κατὰ σάρκα is seen as over against life κατὰ πνεῦμα, "according to the Spirit," derives ultimately from the Second Temple period where there is a tendency to use this extended meaning of the word in a more heightened way, so that "flesh" forms part of both a cosmological and anthropological dualism.[37] But Paul puts his own stamp on this idea, a stamp that is predicated on his understanding of our present life as primarily eschatological. Through the work of Christ and the Spirit, God has ushered in the coming, messianic age. Since for Paul the main evidence of that reality is the gift of the eschatological Spirit, it was easy for him to describe present eschatological existence as "in keeping with/according to the Spirit." The natural contrast to this way of describing present existence was to refer to life in the old age as "in keeping with the flesh." But "flesh" now denotes not simply humanity in its *creatureliness* vis-à-vis God, but humanity in its *fallen* creatureliness as utterly hostile to God in every imaginable way. Thus, what began as a purely anthropological term in the physical sense, evolved into an anthropological term in a more theological sense ("creatureliness," thus human frailty), and finally into Paul's unique usage in a thoroughly eschatological sense. For this reason also, the translation "sinful nature"[38] fails to convey Paul's meaning, since that tends to make it an anthropological term without adequately recognizing that for Paul it functions principally in an eschatological way.

The clearest instance in which Paul plays on the two basic senses of this word is in his conflict with the Corinthians in 2 Cor 10:2–4. Accused of being "according to the flesh" in the morally pejorative sense, Paul allows, for the sake of his argument, that he does indeed live "*in* the flesh," by which he means "in the weaknesses and limitations of present mortality." But, he goes on, I do not engage in warfare "*according to* the flesh." This argument, it needs to be pointed out, does not work at all if "flesh" is morally pejorative in both instances.

Our interest lies strictly with this latter sense, which has completely lost its relationship to the physical[39] and has become strictly eschatological—and pejorative—describing existence from the perspective of those who do not know Christ, who thus live as God's enemies. Our point here is that in Paul's understanding such a life describes those *outside* of Christ, and thus describes believers *before* they came to be in Christ and live by the Spirit. To the demonstration of this assertion we now turn.

---

[37] On this matter see Meyer and Schweizer, *TDNT* 7.110–24.

[38] As it is frequently, but inconsistently, rendered in the NIV when used in its morally pejorative sense (e.g., see 1 Cor 5:5; Gal 5:13, 16, 17[2x], 19, 24; 6:8; Rom 7:5–8:13; Col 2:11, 13; Eph 2:3; but "worldly point of view" in 2 Cor 5:16 [cf. 1:12, 17; 10:2] and "flesh" in Phil 3:3–4!).

[39] See esp. the discussions of Gal 5:13–15, 16–18, 19–21; note as well that of the fifteen "works of the flesh," very few of them can be located in the physical body.

THE SPIRIT-FLESH CONTRAST IN PAUL

That Paul viewed the flesh as belonging to one's past in the same way as he viewed Torah observance can be determined by several lines of evidence.

1. The earliest appearance of the morally pejorative use of σάρξ language in Paul occurs in 1 Cor 3:1. Here the usage refers to two forms of eschatological existence. Paul's problem with the Corinthians is not that they struggle between living in the flesh and in the Spirit, but that they believe themselves to be fully Spirit people—despite their attitude toward Paul and the message of the cross. The irony of Paul's sentence lies in the fact that these πνευματικοί (Spirit people) are thinking just as they did before they met Christ, just like those leaders of this passing age, who crucified Christ in the first place (2:6–8). His urgency is singular: to get people who have entered the new aeon, the age of the Spirit, to stop conforming their thinking to the old age that is passing away. This is obviously *eschatological* terminology, not *anthropological*; moreover, it does not reflect some *internal struggle in the believer* between these two kinds of existence. On the contrary, it describes the essential characteristics of the two ages, which exist side by side in unrelieved opposition in our present "already but not yet" existence. The one, "flesh," has been condemned and is on its way out; the other, Spirit, is the sure evidence and guarantee of the future.

2. The same holds true for the pejorative uses in 2 Corinthians (1:12, 17; 5:16; 10:2–3; 11:18). To think, or make plans, or "boast" κατὰ σάρκα means to live in keeping with the values of the old aeon that has been judged by Christ and stripped of its grip on God's people; therefore, it is totally inconsistent with present realities for God's people to revert to thinking that conforms to values they had before they met Christ. This comes out most vividly in the argument of 5:14–17. To be sure, the old age continues, and those who are not in Christ still think and live "according to the flesh," but this way of thinking and living is no longer an option for those who in Christ have experienced death and resurrection. "From now on," Paul says in v. 16, meaning from the time of the death and resurrection noted in v. 14, we "can no longer regard anyone, least of all Christ, from the perspective of the flesh." That is because we now live "from the perspective of the Spirit."

Furthermore, this statement in v. 16 is followed in v. 17 with the language of the "new" and the "old," in this instance the new and old orders. The old order has gone, he declares, the new "creation" has come in its place—not just in the life of the individual, but in the total sense of what God is doing in the world through Christ and the Spirit. This, of course, is the language used earlier in 2 Corinthians 3 to describe the two covenants, which reflect God's specific activities toward his people in these two orders. The old covenant is now obsolete because the new covenant, the covenant of Spirit, has come.

The death and resurrection of Christ and the gift of the Spirit have changed everything. The former order of things is described in terms of "flesh," that basically self-centered, creature-oriented point of view, which has caused the Corinthians to regard Paul as he had formerly regarded Christ, as "weak" and therefore not of God. The "flesh" perceives things from the old age point of view, where value and significance lie in power, influence, wealth, and wisdom (cf. 1 Cor 1:26–31). But in Christ, all of that has passed away; behold, the new has come, the time of the Spirit, in which there has been a total, radical restructuring of value and significance. The paradigm is the cross: the power lies not in externals, but in the Spirit, who indwells believers and by grace is renewing the "inner person" (4:16), transforming us into God's own likeness (ultimately portrayed in Christ through the cross). To be sure, the Spirit stands over against life κατὰ σάρκα, but in Paul's argumentation there is no hint of an internal struggle within the believer's heart.

3. Similarly, in the later contrast in Phil 3:3, warning the Philippians against those who would insist on circumcision, Paul describes believers as those who serve "by the Spirit of God" and who put no confidence in "the flesh." Here again, even though "flesh" refers to self-confidence based on an advantaged covenantal relationship with God evidenced by circumcision, these are basically eschatological realities. To revert to circumcision, that is, to put "confidence in the flesh," is to go back to the way that has come to an end with the death and resurrection of Christ and the gift of the Spirit.

4. Finally, in the controverted passages, Gal 5:17 and Rom 7:14–23, the contrast between flesh and Spirit is also *chiefly* eschatological in nature. The contrast, it must be noted, comes at the heart of two different passages dealing with the same urgent question: since Torah observance is now a thing of the past because of the coming of Christ and the Spirit, what is to ensure righteousness? That is, Paul is arguing against (perhaps anticipating) Jewish-Christian opposition that would see his bypassing Torah observance as a sure invitation to license and ungodliness. Indeed, as Rom 3:7–8 makes clear and Rom 6:1 implies, Paul has been charged with this very thing. My first point, then, is that the flesh-Spirit contrast in Paul never appears in a context in which the issue has to do with "how to live the Christian life"; rather, it appears in this case in an argument with those who have entered into the new eschatological life of the Spirit, but who are being seduced to return to the old aeon, to live on the basis of Torah observance, which for Paul is finally but another form of life "according to the flesh."[40] In both passages, Paul is arguing for the

---

[40]See esp. on Gal 3:3; cf. 5:17–18 and Phil 3:3–6.

sufficiency of the Spirit for life in the new eschatological existence where
Torah is no longer operative.

All of this to say, then, that the phrases "according to the flesh" and
"according to the Spirit" refer not to "physical" and "spiritual" existence
or to the "sinful nature" that drags one down over against the Spirit who
lifts one up, but to living by the power of the indwelling Spirit in a world
characterized by "the flesh," where the old values and behavior still
predominate. As far as the believer is concerned, Christ's death and
resurrection have pronounced a death sentence on the "flesh." As with
the "old age" to which it belongs, the "flesh" is on its way out; it has
been rendered ineffective through death, which is the meaning of Rom
7:4–6. Through the death of Christ and the gift of the Spirit, "the flesh"
has been decisively crippled—"killed," in Paul's language. It is not possible, therefore, that from Paul's perspective such a Spirit person would
be living in such a way that she or he is "sold as a slave to sin," who is
unable to do the good she or he wants to do because of being "held
prisoner to the law of sin." Whatever is done with the "I" and the present
tense in Rom 7:14–25, they can scarcely describe life in the Spirit. In fact,
Paul specifically says that he is describing *life under Law*, lived "according
to the flesh," *before* the death of those two enemies took place in Christ.

Thus believers live "between the times." The already crippled flesh
will be finally brought to ruin at the coming of Christ. The Spirit, already
a present possession, will be fully realized at the same coming. To the
degree that the old aeon has not yet passed away, we still must learn "to
walk by the Spirit," to behave "in keeping with the Spirit," and to "sow to
the Spirit." But we do so precisely because the Spirit is sufficient, not because
we live simultaneously "according to the flesh" and "according to the
Spirit." In Paul's view, we live "in the flesh," meaning in the body and
subject to the realities of the present age; but we do not walk "according
to the flesh." Such a way of life belongs to the past, and those who so live
"shall not inherit the [final, eschatological] kingdom of God" (Gal 5:21).[41]

THE SPIRIT, POWER, AND WEAKNESS[42]

Present eschatological existence as already/not yet is also the key to
a final set of contrasts in Paul, in which the presence of the eschatological

---

[41]Students often express their frustration with this perspective on things, partly
because of their years of being taught otherwise in the church and partly because of
their own personal concerns. They even become angry that Paul may not have
addressed the issue of their personal struggle with sin as a believer—as though he
had some duty to do so. But this is an issue we bring *to* the text, not derive *from*
the text.

[42]See on 1 Thes 1:5–6; 1 Cor 2:4–5; 4:18; 2 Cor 3:1–18; 4:7; 5:5, 13; 6:6–7; 12:1–10,
12; 13:3–4; Rom 8:18–30, 26–27; 15:18–19; Col 1:29; Phil 1:19–20; 2 Tim 1:6–7, 8, 14.

Spirit again plays a major role, sometimes resulting in tension for later believers. At issue is the relationship between the Spirit as God's empowering presence and the theme of weakness in Paul. Here in particular it is easy to miss the "radical middle" in which Paul himself walked and to err with unPauline emphases on one side or the other.

On the one hand stands a view that by default is easily that of the majority.[43] This view has a subtlety to it that makes it look more Pauline than it actually is; in fact it leans toward a defeatism that is especially difficult to square with Paul. At issue here is a tendency on the part of some to confuse the term "weakness," i.e., life *in* the flesh, with life *"according to* the flesh." Thus when Paul says, for example, that "the Spirit assists us in our weakness" (Rom 8:26), "weakness" is taken to encompass all of our present existence, including our sinfulness. Paul's "glorying in his weaknesses" then is seen to embrace the alleged Spirit-flesh struggle as well as the various bodily weaknesses and sufferings that Paul actually refers to.[44] But Paul never makes that equation, as any careful study of the term "weakness" in Paul demonstrates.[45] This term does indeed apply to life "in the flesh," that is, our present life in the Spirit that is still lived in the context of suffering and debilitation. But as noted above, life *in* the flesh is not the same as life *according* to the flesh.

The best evidence that Paul does not include the Spirit-flesh antithesis within his understanding of being empowered in weakness is that he can speak so positively of living in weakness, so much so that it is for him a cause for "boasting/glorying" and thus for eschatological joy. It is unimaginable that he should rejoice over life "according to the flesh"—nor in fact does he do so. The result is an "under-realized" eschatological perspective. Even though there is much talk about the Spirit in this view, there is a strong tendency to leave God's people to "slug it out in the trenches" more or less on their own, with some lip service paid to the Spirit but with little of the Pauline experience of the Spirit as the empowering presence of God.

On the other side lie some equally strong tendencies toward triumphalism, especially in a culture like late-twentieth-century America, where pain of any kind is rejected as a form of evil and where suffering is to be avoided at all costs. Here the difficulty is not between an internal struggle and a human penchant to sinfulness, but between the promised—and experienced—power of the Holy Spirit and our culture's view

---

[43]The default stems from a general failure to take the Spirit seriously as God's empowering presence.

[44]The chief proponent of this view is Dunn, *Jesus*, 326–42, which for all of its powerful moments and keen insights nonetheless makes a confusion at this point that is simply foreign to Paul.

[45]In this regard see D. A. Black, *Paul, Apostle of Weakness:* Astheneia *and Its Cognates in the Pauline Literature* (American Univ. Studies; New York: Peter Lang, 1984).

of suffering and pain as something inherently evil. That suffering and pain stem from evil is not to be doubted; that they are the direct result of our own evil—or lack of faith, as some would have it—is not only to be doubted but to be vigorously rejected as completely foreign to Paul. The result on this side is something of an "over-realized" eschatological perspective, with an unPauline view of the Spirit as present in power which negates weakness in the present as something dishonoring to God.

The problem here lies with the tendency to separate some realities that in Paul gladly coexist.[46] Paul knows nothing of a gospel that is not at the same time God's power, power manifested through the resurrection of Christ and now evidenced through the presence of the Spirit. That includes "miracles" in the assembly (Gal 3:5), to which Paul can appeal in a matter-of-fact way as proof that salvation in Christ is based on faith and not on Torah observance. It also includes the effective proclamation of Christ accompanied by the Spirit's manifest power in bringing about conversions (1 Thes 1:5–6; 1 Cor 2:4–5), despite the obvious weakness of the messenger himself (1 Cor 2:1–3; 2 Cor 12:7–10). For many, especially the Corinthians (and their legion of present-day followers), the latter is incongruous. How can there be miracles, but no miracle in one's own behalf? How can one glory in the power of the resurrection and the life of the Spirit and not appropriate it for oneself regarding physical weaknesses and suffering? "Physician, heal thyself" was not just a word spoken to Christ; it is always the bottom line of those for whom God's power can be manifest only in visible and extraordinary ways, who never consider that God's greater glory rests on the manifestation of his grace and power through the weakness of the human vessel, precisely so that there will never be any confusion as to the source!

Let us begin, then, with another look at the word "power," since part of the problem for us is again semantic. We cannot always be sure what "power" might have meant for Paul. Frequently it refers to visible manifestations that evidence the Spirit's presence (e.g., 1 Cor 2:4–5; Gal 3:5; Rom 15:19). The evidence from 1 Thes 5:19–22; 1 Corinthians 12–14; Gal 3:2–5; and Rom 12:6 makes it certain that the Pauline churches were "charismatic" in the sense that a dynamic presence of the Spirit was manifested in their gatherings.[47] And even where power means that believers apprehend and live out the love of Christ in a greater way (Eph 3:16–20), Paul recognizes here a miraculous work of the Spirit that will

---

[46]I say "gladly" not because Paul "enjoyed suffering," but because he saw suffering so distinctly in terms of discipleship. That is, he saw suffering as following in the ways of Christ, who suffered before entering into his glory, and who through that suffering redeemed the people of God. Hence Paul's willingness not only to suffer for Christ's, and thus the church's, sake, but to rejoice in suffering, inasmuch as it confirmed for him the reality of his discipleship.

[47]On this matter, see the conclusions to ch. 15; cf. Dunn, *Jesus*, 260–65.

be *evidenced* by the way renewed people behave toward one another. It is this dynamic, evidential dimension of life in the Spirit that probably more than anything else separates believers in later church history from those in the Pauline churches. Whatever else, the Spirit was *experienced* in the Pauline churches; he was not merely a matter of creedal assent.

On the other hand, Paul also assumes the closest correlation between the Spirit's power and present weaknesses. Without explicitly saying so, passages such as Rom 8:17–27 and 2 Cor 12:9 indicate that the Spirit is seen as the source of empowering in the midst of affliction or weakness. In Paul's view, "knowing Christ" means to know *both* the power of his resurrection *and* the fellowship of his sufferings (Phil 3:9–10).[48] Suffering means to be as the Lord, following his example and thus "filling up what was lacking in his sufferings" (Col 1:24). Nonetheless, Paul also expects God's more visible demonstration of power, through the Spirit, to be manifested even in the midst of weakness, as God's "proof" that his power resides in the message of a crucified Messiah. In 1 Cor 2:3–5, therefore, Paul can appeal simultaneously to the reality of his own weaknesses and the Spirit's manifest power in his preaching and the Corinthians' conversion; and in 1 Thes 1:5–6, he reminds these new believers that they became so by the power of the Spirit, but in the midst of suffering that was also accompanied by the joy of the Holy Spirit.

All of this reflects Paul's basic eschatological understanding of Christian existence as "already/not yet," a tension that Paul was able to keep together in ways that many later Christians can not. For him it was not simply tension in which the present was all weakness and the (near) future all glory. The future had truly broken into the present, as verified by the gift of the Spirit; and since the Spirit meant the presence of God's power, that dimension of the future had already arrived in some measure. Thus present suffering is a mark of discipleship, whose paradigm is our crucified Lord. But the same power that raised the crucified One from the dead is also already at work in our mortal bodies.

This paradox in Paul's understanding is what creates so many difficulties for moderns. We have tended to emphasize either to the neglect of the other. Paul, and the rest of the New Testament writers, hold these expressions of Spirit and power in happy tension. After all, for Paul, the preaching of the crucified One is the fulcrum of God's power at work in the world (1 Cor 1:18–25), and Paul's own preaching in a context of weakness and fear and trembling certified that the power that brought

---

[48]This is almost certainly how one is to understand the καί . . . καί that follows τοῦ γνῶναι αὐτόν. There are not three things that Paul longs to know, but one: to know Christ. But in context that means to know him simultaneously in two ways, both the power of his resurrection and the fellowship of his sufferings, the latter very likely being a corrective against some form of triumphalism that Paul is going to elaborate on in vv. 12–21.

about the Corinthians' conversion lay in the work of the Spirit, not in the wisdom or eloquence of the preacher. Paul thus steers a path through the "radical middle" that is often missed by both Evangelicals and Pentecostals, who traditionally misplace their emphasis on one side or the other.

Whether or not a (sometime) companion of Paul, the author of the epistle to the Hebrews seems to capture this paradox in a slightly different way, through the several examples of "faith" (= faithfulness, perseverance) in 11:32–38. Some lived "in faith" and saw great miracles performed; others also lived "in faith" and were tortured and put to death. But all were commended for their faith, the author concludes. So with the Spirit and power in Paul. The Spirit means the presence of great power, power to overflow with hope (Rom 15:13), power sometimes attested by signs and wonders and at other times by joy in great affliction. But precisely because the Spirit has not brought the final End, but only its beginning, power does not mean final perfection in the present age, but rather leads to maturity in Christ.

Thus the whole of Paul's understanding of our present life in the Spirit, paradoxical as it may seem at times, is put into proper perspective if we begin by realizing that the Spirit is both the fulfillment of the eschatological promises of God and the down payment on our certain future. We are both already and not yet. The Spirit is the evidence of the one, the guarantee of the other.

13

THE SPIRIT AS GOD'S PERSONAL PRESENCE

By the very nature of things, the Pauline letters serve chiefly not as theological, but as pragmatic, documents; nonetheless, they are full of theological presuppositions, assertions, and reflections of a kind that allow us to describe them theologically. At the heart of these descriptions lies the mystery of the Trinity, but it does so in a presuppositional, experiential way, not by reflective theologizing. By that I mean that Paul expresses his experience of God in a fundamentally Trinitarian way, but never grapples with the theological issues that this experience raises. It is common among scholars, therefore, to deny that Paul was a Trinitarian at all and to contend that such an understanding belongs to a later time, when the influences of Hellenistic philosophy began to predominate among those who were doing the theologizing.

Part of the demurrers here are semantic. Trinity itself is the language of a later time, which landed on this word to express the church's faith in the One God, whom they knew to be in a unity of three divine Persons.[1] But part of the objection also stems, I have come to believe, from the early reaction on the part of biblical theology as it struggled to free itself from what it perceived as the heavy-handedness of dogmatics. One way to do that was to assert, on a regular basis, that if the New Testament reflected Trinitarianism, it did so in an incipient, nonreflective way, so that, whatever else, "it was not the Trinitarianism of a later day such as Chalcedon." But that seems so self-evident that one wonders why it needed to be repeated so often. Consequently one wonders further, whether our

---

[1] And even our language "Person" causes all kinds of difficulties, partly because it stems from a Latin word that does not carry all the baggage that our word does. For example, our word "person" implies self-consciousness, so that "three Persons" should mean three separate and distinct expressions of "self-consciousness," but neither the Greek *hypostasis* (ὑπόστασις) nor the Latin *persona* carries such a nuance.

difficulties do not also stem from our own experience of the church and the Spirit, where the Spirit is understood in such nonpersonal ways—as divine "influence" or "power"—that it is a very short step from our experience of the Spirit as a "gray, oblong blur" (see p. 6 above) to our becoming practical binitarians:[2] I believe in God the Father; I believe in Jesus Christ, God's Son; but I wonder about the Holy *Ghost.* The Spirit has become God's specter, if you will, an unseen, less than dynamic, vibrant influence, hardly God very God.

The problem with such hesitations is that their frequent repetition finally comes home to roost, and within scholarship, at least, scholars are skittish of using language of this kind to describe the New Testament witness. But despite the frequency of the demurrers, and for want of a better term, Pauline theology can hardly be examined without wrestling with the fundamental issues of Trinitarian theology, because Paul himself, an avowed monotheist, nonetheless spoke of Christ as the preexistent Son of God (see on Gal 4:6–7) and attributed every imaginable activity to him which Paul's Judaism reserved for God alone. Granted that Paul never lets us in on how he could do so, but the scholar denies that he did so at great peril of misunderstanding the apostle. Thus, the two basic issues of Trinitarianism are traceable to Paul (and the rest of the early church as well, of course): that God is one; that God is now known and experienced as Father, Son and Holy Spirit, each distinct from the other, yet as only one God.

Despite all our resistance to the contrary, therefore, and even if the language "Trinity" or "Trinitarianism" were limited to the time in which the church wrestled with the ontological issues of *how,* we cannot escape the fact that Paul himself is partly responsible for such a need in the later church. So we cannot avoid the ontological questions, even if Paul does not speak directly to them.

But in fact, that is only one side of *Trinitarianism,* since historically the issue of God's nature was forced upon us first of all because of the primitive church's faith in Christ as Savior and Lord. "Lord," after all, was the OT equivalent for God. There can be little question, therefore, that the early church would have finally expressed itself in a *binitarian* way, had it never done so in a *Trinitarian* way. So the further question about the Pauline understanding of God is not only what he believed about Christ, but also what he believed about the Spirit, since the Trinity not only expresses Christian conviction about God as one being in three *persons,* but as one God in *three* persons, including God the Holy Spirit. Thus the questions raised in this chapter have to do with Paul's under-

---

[2]Cf. Pinnock ("Concept," 2): "Modern Christians are largely content to be trinitarian in belief, but binitarian in practice"; he notes that much the same had been said by A. M. Hunter (*Interpreting Paul's Gospel* [London: SCM, 1954] 112) and F. C. Synge ("The Holy Spirit and the Sacraments," *SJT* 6 [1953] 65).

standing of God, and especially with his understanding of the Spirit as God. Did Paul in fact have a Trinitarian faith, even if he did not use the language of a later time to describe God? All the evidence from the preceding analysis of the texts points to a singularly affirmative answer to that question.[3]

But since not all NT scholars think so, part of my concern in this chapter is not simply to catalogue the data, but to argue that the data do point in the direction just affirmed.[4] The first question before us, therefore, is basically twofold: Did Paul consider the Holy Spirit as *Person*, and as *one with, but distinct from*, God the Father and Christ the Son? And, secondly, if so (and the data all point in that direction), then how are we to understand Paul's perspective, or can we?

THE HOLY SPIRIT AS PERSON

Paul's main interest in the Spirit is experiential, so that his Spirit talk is limited basically to the Spirit's *activity*; but that situation also cracks open the door for our understanding. Thus, even though Paul does not speak directly to the question of the Spirit's *person*, nonetheless, several converging pieces of evidence assure us that he understood the Spirit in personal terms, intimately associated with both the Father and the Son, yet distinct from them.

First, it must be acknowledged that the Spirit is most frequently spoken of in terms of *agency*—that is, the Spirit is the agent of *God's* activity—and that such language does not presume personhood. Nonetheless, a casual glance in chapter 2 at the uses of πνεῦμα in the genitive and dative cases shows how often agency finds personal expression. For instance, the Thessalonians' conversion is by the sanctifying work of the Spirit (2 Thes 2:13; cf. 1 Cor 6:11; Rom 15:16), as is their accompanying joy (1 Thes 1:6; cf. Rom 15:13). Revelation comes through the Spirit (1 Cor 2:10; Eph 3:5); and Paul's preaching is accompanied by the power of the Spirit (1 Thes 1:5). Prophetic speech and speaking in tongues directly result from speaking by the Spirit (1 Cor 12:3; 14:2, 16). By the Spirit the

---

[3]This conclusion stands in rather sharp contrast to Lodahl's attempt (*Shekinah Spirit: Divine Presence in Jewish and Christian Religion* [New York: Paulist, 1992]) to ameliorate between Christianity and Judaism by rethinking the Christian doctrine of the Spirit. While I sympathize with Lodahl, I doubt whether his reading of the NT data is adequate. It has all the appearance of yet another theologically driven look at the texts and resembles the very historical orthodoxy that he argues against. In the process the concerns of the Pauline texts themselves seem to lose out.

[4]So also Pinnock, "Concept," 116–18, who likewise notes that the later *expression* of Trinitarian faith grows out of a Trinitarian encounter with the one God in his saving work.

Romans are urged to put to death any sinful practices (Rom 8:13). Paul desires the Ephesians to be strengthened by means of God's Spirit (Eph 3:16). Believers serve by the Spirit (Phil 3:3), love by the Spirit (Col 1:8), are sealed by the Spirit (Eph 1:13), and walk and live by the Spirit (Gal 5:16, 25). Finally, and especially, in Titus 3:5, believers are "saved through washing by the Spirit, whom God 'poured out' upon them."

On the one hand, a passage like the last one might suggest "agency" in quite impersonal terms. The concept of "pouring out" does not invoke the idea of personhood, nor does the imagery of "washing" by the Spirit. On the other hand, a careful look at most of these passages and others indicates that personhood is either implied or presupposed, and that the language of "pouring out" is imagery, pure and simple. This is especially true in a passage like 1 Cor 6:11, where God "washes, justifies, and sanctifies" by the double agency of "the name [authority] of the Lord Jesus Christ" and "by the Spirit of our God." The point to make, of course, is that what Paul says of the Spirit in terms of agency parallels what he says in scores of places about Christ, whose "agency" can only be personal. By implication, not to mention by direct statements elsewhere, to suggest that the Spirit's agency is any less personal than that of Christ is difficult to say the least. Not only so, but one is struck by the scarcity of impersonal images in Paul. In contrast to Luke, he never speaks of being "filled with the Spirit";[5] his primary language has to do with God's "giving his Spirit into you,"[6] or of our "receiving" or "having" the Spirit.[7] None of these imply personhood, but neither do they imply what is impersonal, as so many other Spirit images do (wind, fire, oil, water).

In any case, personhood is confirmed, secondly, by the fact that the Spirit is the subject of a large number of verbs that demand a personal agent: The Spirit *searches* all things (1 Cor 2:10), *knows* the mind of God (1 Cor 2:11), *teaches* the content of the gospel to believers (1 Cor 2:13), *dwells* among or within believers (1 Cor 3:16; Rom 8:11; 2 Tim 1:14), *accomplishes* all things (1 Cor 12:11), *gives life* to those who believe (2 Cor 3:6), *cries out* from within our hearts (Gal 4:6), *leads* us in the ways of God (Gal 5:18; Rom 8:14), *bears witness* with our own spirits (Rom 8:16), *has desires* that are in opposition to the flesh (Gal 5:17), *helps* us in our weakness (Rom 8:26), *intercedes* in our behalf (Rom 8:26–27), *works* all things *together* for our ultimate good (Rom 8:28), *strengthens* believers (Eph 3:16), and is *grieved* by our sinfulness (Eph 4:30). Furthermore, the fruit of the Spirit's indwelling are the personal attributes of God (Gal 5:22–23).

---

[5]Despite our common translation of Eph 5:18 (q.v.) and the fact that the Spirit is ultimately the "element" of filling, as well as the agent.

[6]See on 1 Thes 4:8; cf. 2 Cor 1:22; 5:5; Rom 5:5; Eph 1:17; 2 Tim 1:7; cf. "the supply of the Spirit" in Gal 3:5 and Phil 1:19.

[7]For "receive" see 1 Cor 2:12; 2 Cor 11:4; Gal 3:2, 14; Rom 8:15; for "have" see 1 Cor 2:16; 7:40; Rom 8:9.

Some of these texts seem determinative, as for example Rom 8:16, in which the Spirit who gives us "adoption as 'sons,'" attested by his prompting within us the "*Abba*-cry," in turn, and for this very reason, becomes the *second (necessary) witness* along with our own spirits to the reality of our being God's children. Likewise in Rom 8:26–27, not only does the Spirit intercede in our behalf, thus "knowing us" being implied, but we can be assured of the effectiveness of his intercession because "God knows *the mind* of the Spirit," who in turn thus prays "according to God['s will]." Whatever else, this is the language of personhood, presuppositionally so, and not that of an impersonal influence or power. The language πνεῦμα may have the imagery of "wind" inherent in it, but Paul never uses it in this manner.

Finally, the Spirit is sometimes the subject of a verb or implied activity that elsewhere is attributed either to the Father or to the Son. Thus in 1 Cor 12:6 and 11, in successive passages Paul says of God (the Father is implied) that he "produces" (ἐνεργεῖ) all of these activities in all people (πάντα ἐν πᾶσιν, v. 6), while in a similar sentence in v. 11 the Spirit is the subject of the identical verb with a similar object (πάντα ταῦτα, "all these things," now referring to the many Spirit manifestations enumerated in vv. 8–10). Likewise, in Rom 8:11 the Father "gives life," while in 2 Cor 3:6 it is the Spirit; and in Rom 8:34 Christ "intercedes" for us, while a few verses earlier (8:26) this was said of the Spirit. In a related way, but now with the Spirit as the "object" of the verb, in Gal 4:5–6, in consecutive sentences Paul asserts that "God sent forth his Son" and that "God sent forth the Spirit of his Son" (cf. 1 Cor 6:11). Both the parallel and the fact that the activities of the Son and of the Spirit (redemption and crying out from within the heart of the believer) are personal activities presuppose the Spirit as person.

This evidence alone, it is arguable, indicates that for Paul the Spirit is never thought of as "it," but as "person." But what of the issue of "one with, but distinct from"? On this issue the data again point in the direction of historical orthodoxy, but in this case there is a considerable body of scholarly opinion that thinks otherwise. Hence these data will be examined in light of what has been suggested to the contrary.[8]

THE SPIRIT AND THE GODHEAD

One of the idiosyncrasies of NT scholarship with regard to the Pauline view of the Spirit is to speak of the relationship between the risen Christ

---

[8]Some of the following material appears in part in my forthcoming contribution to the I. Howard Marshall Festschrift (entitled "Christology and Pneumatology in Romans 8:9–11—and Elsewhere: Some Reflections on Paul as a Trinitarian").

and the Spirit so as to blur the distinctions between them. This perspective goes as far back as Gunkel's seminal work on the Spirit in Paul[9]
and was carried forward with special vigor in the influential work of
Adolf Deissmann[10] and Wilhelm Bousset.[11] This perspective became so
dominant that by 1923 E. F. Scott could say that "in many presentations
of Paulinism it has become customary to assume, almost as self-evident,
that in Paul the Spirit and Christ are one and the same."[12] The post–
World War II impetus to this theological perspective came especially
from Neill Q. Hamilton,[13] Ingo Hermann,[14] and, more recently, J. D. G.
Dunn.[15]

The common thread in all of these studies, from Gunkel to Dunn—
and in many whom they have influenced[16]—is to start by noting the

---

[9]By which he "felled the giant" of nineteenth-century liberalism, wherein
the Spirit had been identified with consciousness. See *Die Wirkungen des heiligen
Geistes nach der populären Anschauung der apostolischen Zeit und der Lehre des Apostels
Paulus* (Göttingen: Vandenhoeck & Ruprecht, 1888); trans. by Roy A. Harrisville and
Philip A. Quanbeck II, *The Influence of the Holy Spirit: The Popular View of the Apostolic
Age and the Teaching of the Apostle Paul* (Philadelphia: Fortress Press, 1979). The
giant-killing analogy is from Harrisville's introduction, p. x. Gunkel's discussion can
be found on pp. 112–15; his supporting texts, in his order, are 1 Cor 15:45; 6:17; and
2 Cor 3:17.

[10]See esp. *Die neutestamentliche Formel "in Christo Jesu."* For English readers a
succinct overview of his position can be found in *St. Paul: A Study in Social and Religious
History*, 123–35.

[11]In *Kyrios Christos*, 154–55 and 160–64.

[12]*The Spirit in the New Testament*, 178. In keeping with the nature of the book this
is stated without documentation.

[13]In his published Basel dissertation (under Oscar Cullmann), *The Holy Spirit and
Eschatology in Paul*. In his first chapter (pp. 3–16), Hamilton offers a (much too brief
to be convincing) analysis of the key texts (2 Cor 3:17; 1 Cor 12:3; Rom 8:9; Gal 4:6;
Phil 1:19; Rom 1:3–4; 1 Cor 15:45) so as to demonstrate that "Christology [is] the key
to pneumatology." One can trace the influence of this study in almost all the
subsequent literature.

[14]*Kyrios und Pneuma: Studien zur Christologie der paulinischen Hauptbriefe.* This
study has also had considerable influence, but only among those who really do think
that 2 Cor 3:17 is saying something christological, since in effect Hermann's whole
case is based on a demonstrable misunderstanding of this passage.

[15]In articles on two of the key texts ("Jesus," 40–68 and "I Corinthians 15.45,"
127–41); later in summary form in *Jesus*, 318–26, and *Christology*, 141–49. On the
other hand, Dunn also wrote specifically against finding support for this view in 2 Cor
3:17 ("2 Corinthians III.17"). For those who write on this issue, and have been
influenced by these various scholars, one can trace a parting of the ways between
those who follow Hermann and those who follow Dunn as the result of this latter
article.

[16]See, among others, Hendrikus Berkhof, *The Doctrine of the Holy Spirit* (London:
Epworth Press, 1964) 21–28; David Hill, *Greek Words and Hebrew Meanings*, 275–83
(although Hill, to be sure, does so with considerable qualification); W. C. Wright, *Use*,
206–59.

Pauline texts, usually beginning with 2 Cor 3:17,[17] and then to use such language as "identification,"[18] "equation" (Gunkel, Dunn), or "merge" (Bousset) to speak about this relationship.[19] To be sure, in most cases all of this is said with the proper qualifications that Paul does indeed also recognize distinctions,[20] that the identity is "dynamic" rather than "ontological,"[21] or that the identity is not so complete that the one is wholly dissolved in the other.[22] But there can be little question that "identification" is the stronger motif, especially at the level of Christian experience of the risen Christ and the Spirit, which is asserted for all practical purposes to be one and the same thing.[23]

That the emphasis clearly lies with "identification" rather than "distinction" is confirmed by another thread that runs through these studies

---

[17]Although Dunn is an obvious exception here. He starts with 1 Cor 15:45 (q.v.).

[18]Obviously this is the operative word; see, e.g., Gunkel, Scott (hesitantly), Hamilton, Hermann, Berkhof, Hill ("virtual identification"); cf. Walter Kasper: "That is why Paul can actually identify the two (2 Cor 3.17)" (in *Jesus the Christ*, 256).

[19]Another thread common to many of these studies is the assertion that Paul's "in Christ" and "in the Spirit" formulae amount to one and the same thing, a view which in particular may be traced back to Deissmann (*Formel*), whose thesis in part depends on this interchange; cf. Bousset (160): "The two formulas coincide so completely that they can be interchanged at will." Cf. Hill, *Greek Words*, 276. But this seems to be a considerable overstatement, since in fact there are some significant differences: Paul always uses the preposition "in" (ἐν) with "Christ," whereas he alternates between πνεύματι/ἐν πνεύματι with "Spirit." This reflects that the predominant usage of πνεύματι/ἐν πνεύματι is instrumental, whereas the predominant usage of "in Christ" is locative. The differences are demonstrated in Rom 9:1, the one sentence where both formulae appear together. In his asseverations as to his own truthfulness, Paul "speaks the truth [as one who, with them, is] in Christ Jesus"; moreover, his own conscience, "by the [inner witness of] the Holy Spirit," bears witness to the same. Thus the two formulae are scarcely interchangeable, except for those places where the soteriological activity of Christ and the Spirit overlap, such as "sanctified in/by Christ Jesus" in 1 Cor 1:2, where the emphasis lies on Christ's redemptive activity; and "sanctified by the Holy Spirit" in Rom 15:16, where the emphasis is on the appropriation by the Spirit of the prior work of Christ. Cf. the more detailed critique of Deissmann in F. Büchsel, " 'In Christus' bei Paulus," *ZNW* 42 (1949) 141–58; F. Neugebauer, "Das paulinische 'in Christ,' " *NTS* 4 (1957/58) 124–38; and M. Bouttier, *En Christ: Etude d'exégèse et de théologie pauliniennes* (Paris: Presses Universitaires, 1962).

[20]Scott 183 in fact stands apart from the others mentioned above in that he thinks the "identification" was not deliberate on Paul's part, but that it was "forced upon him in spite of himself."

[21]Hamilton, *Holy Spirit*, 6, 10.

[22]This is the objection to Hermann (*Kyrios und Pneuma*, 123) of Herman Ridderbos, *Paul: An Outline of His Theology*, 88, who takes a position similar to the one argued for here, except that he is willing to allow that some of these texts point toward "a certain relationship of identity with each other" (87).

[23]Cf. Dunn, "*If Christ is now experienced as Spirit, Spirit is now experienced as Christ* [emphasis his]" (*Jesus*, 323).

as well, namely, the rather strong denial that Paul's experience and understanding of God can be properly termed "Trinitarian." This is pressed vigorously by Hermann, who goes so far as to argue that the identification of Christ with the Spirit is so complete that one can no longer press for a personal identity of the Spirit, separate and distinct from Christ, hence distinct in traditional Trinitarian terms.[24] Despite demurrers, Hamilton and (especially) Dunn do not seem far from this, so much so that in effect to speak of Trinitarianism in Paul is probably to use inappropriate language altogether.[25]

I have called this view "idiosyncratic," because it seems to be based on an inadequate reading of the Pauline data. Three matters give reason to pause: (1) the data from the Pauline Spirit texts taken as a whole move in a different direction; (2) this point of view is predicated on a reading of certain "obscure" texts, none of which can be demonstrated to mean what is affirmed about them in this regard; which in turn (3) points to a considerable methodological failure, in terms of how one should pursue such a matter. To each of these we turn in brief.

THE SPIRIT AS THE SPIRIT OF GOD

While it is fair to say that the coming of Christ forever marked Paul's understanding of the Spirit,[26] what does *not* seem to cohere with the data is the oft-repeated suggestion that "we have to think of the Spirit in

---

[24]*Kyrios und Pneuma*, 132–36.

[25]Thus Hamilton (*Holy Spirit*, 3): "An attempt to deal with the Spirit in the traditional way as an aspect of the doctrine of the Trinity would be inappropriate to Paul. This is not to deny that the Spirit is for Paul a distinct entity over against the Father and the Son. The problem of the Trinity, which is the occasion of the doctrine of the Trinity, was for Paul no problem." Thus "to deal with the Spirit in the tradition of the New Testament is to avoid all speculation about the nature of the being of the Spirit." (One of course could say the same about Paul's assertions about Christ, which means therefore that one in effect should cease christological discussion altogether!) Dunn ("1 Corinthians 15.45," 139): "*Immanent christology is for Paul pneumatology* [emphasis mine]; in the believer's experience there is *no* [Dunn's emphasis] distinction between Christ and the Spirit. This does not mean of course that Paul makes no distinction between Christ and Spirit. But it does mean that later Trinitarian dogma cannot readily look to Paul for support at this point." If by "immanent christology" Dunn denotes the traditional sense of "Christ as he is in himself," then this statement seems far removed from Pauline realities.

[26]One must put it that way, of course, because even though the *experience* of the Spirit for the earliest believers followed their experience with Christ, incarnate and risen, their *understanding* of the Spirit begins with the OT, and it is that understanding that is being transformed by Christ, just as was their understanding of what it meant for the Messiah to be Jesus, not to mention their understanding of God.

strictly christocentric terms."[27] That is considerably overstated. Here I call attention to the statistics noted at the beginning of chapter 2: of over 140 occurrences of πνεῦμα, the full name, Holy Spirit, occurs in 17 instances, "the Spirit of God"/"His Spirit" occurs 16 times, "the Spirit of Christ," or its equivalent, but 3 times. Some observations about these statistics:

1. Paul refers to the Holy Spirit as a full name in the same way as, and at about the same ratio that, he refers to Christ by the full name, our Lord Jesus Christ. This use of the full name in itself suggests "distinction from," not "identity with," as the *Pauline presupposition*.

2. Despite suggestions to the contrary, Paul thinks of the Spirit *primarily* in terms of the Spirit's relationship to God (the Father, although he never uses this imagery of this relationship). Not only does he more often speak of the "Spirit of God" than of the "Spirit of Christ," but God is invariably the subject of the verb when Paul speaks of human reception of the Spirit.[28] Thus God "sent forth the Spirit of his Son into our hearts" (Gal 4:6), or "gives" us his Spirit (1 Thes 4:8; 2 Cor 1:22; 5:5; Gal 3:5; Rom 5:5; Eph 1:17), an understanding that in Paul's case is surely determined by his OT roots, where God "fills with" (Exod 31:3) or "pours out" his Spirit (Joel 2:28), and the "Spirit of God" comes on people for all sorts of extraordinary ("charismatic") activities (e.g., Num 24:2; Judges 3:10).

Two passages in particular give insight into Paul's understanding of this primary, presuppositional relationship. In 1 Cor 2:10–12 he uses the analogy of human interior consciousness (only one's "spirit" knows one's mind) to insist that the Spirit alone knows the mind of God. Paul's concern in this analogy is with the Spirit as the source of *our* understanding of the cross as God's wisdom; nonetheless, the analogy itself draws the closest kind of relationship between God and the Spirit. The Spirit alone "searches all things," even "the depths of God"; and because of this unique relationship with God, the Spirit alone knows and reveals God's otherwise hidden wisdom (1 Cor 2:7).

In Rom 8:26–27 this same idea is expressed obversely. Among other matters, Paul is here concerned to show how the Spirit, in the presence of our weaknesses and inability to speak for ourselves, is able to intercede adequately on our behalf. The effectiveness of the Spirit's intercession lies

---

[27]This is the language of Berkhof, *Doctrine*, 24 (emphasis mine). Cf. Marie E. Isaacs, *The Concept of Spirit: A Study of Pneuma in Hellenistic Judaism and its Bearing on the New Testament* (Heythrop Monographs 1; London: Heythrop College, 1976) 124: "For all N.T. writers the power and presence of God, signified by πνεῦμα, is grounded exclusively in Jesus, the Christ."

[28]That is, there is no firm evidence that Paul considered the Spirit also to be sent by the Son. The only texts that might be read thus are two of the three "Spirit of Christ" texts (Rom 8:9 and Phil 1:19); so Hui, "Concept," 64–67, 69–72. But as noted in the exegesis of these texts, this is almost certainly an incorrect understanding of the genitives. *Filioque* is simply not a Pauline idea, and a couple of debatable genitives are hardly the kind of data to make it so.

precisely in the fact that God, who searches our hearts, likewise "knows the mind of the Spirit," who is interceding for us.

Some mystery is involved here, because finally we are dealing with divine mysteries. There can be little question that Paul sees the Spirit as distinct from God; yet at the same time the Spirit is both the interior expression of the unseen God's personality and the visible manifestation of God's activity in the world. The Spirit is truly God in action; yet he is neither simply an outworking of God's personality nor all there is to say about God.

3. Given these data, the cause for wonder is that Paul should *also* refer to the Spirit as "the Spirit of Christ." That he does so at all says something far more significant about his Christology than about his pneumatology—although the latter is significant as well. Here is evidence for Paul's "high Christology": that Paul, steeped in the OT understanding of the Spirit of God, should so easily, on the basis of his Christian experience, speak of him as the Spirit of Christ as well.[29]

4. A careful analysis of all the texts in which Paul identifies the Spirit either as "the Spirit of God" or "the Spirit of Christ" suggests that he customarily chose to use the genitive qualifier when he wanted to emphasize the activity of either God or Christ that is being conveyed to the believer by the Spirit. Thus the church is God's temple because God's Spirit dwells in their midst (1 Cor 3:16), or God gives his Holy Spirit to those he calls to be holy (1 Thes 4:8), and so on. So also in the three texts in which the Spirit is called the Spirit of Christ, the emphasis lies on the work of Christ in some way. In Gal 4:6 the emphasis is on the believers' "sonship," evidenced by their having received "the Spirit of God's Son," through whom they use the Son's language to address God. In Rom 8:9 Paul seems to be deliberately tying together the work of Christ in Romans 6 with that of the Spirit in chapter 8, hence the evidence that they are truly God's people is that they are indwelt by the Spirit *of Christ*. And in Phil 1:19 Paul desires a fresh supply of the Spirit of Christ Jesus so that when he is on trial, Christ will be magnified, whether by life or by death.

All of this suggests, as argued above on Phil 1:19, that these genitives primarily designate relationship or identification. That is, the Spirit to whom Paul is referring is the Spirit who is to be understood in terms of his relationship either with God or with Christ. "God" and "Christ" in each case give "identity" to the Spirit, in terms of what relationship Paul is referring to.

5. Finally, in Rom 8:9–11 Paul clearly and absolutely identifies "the Spirit of God" with "the Spirit of Christ"; on the other hand, nowhere does he equate the risen Christ with the Spirit, including those handful of texts that might appear to suggest otherwise.

---

[29]It is of some interest that this point is so seldom made in the literature.

THE SPIRIT AS THE SPIRIT OF CHRIST

In Christian theology in general and Pauline theology in particular, the coming of Christ has forever marked our understanding of God. The transcendent God of the universe is henceforth known as "the father of our Lord Jesus Christ" (2 Cor 1:3; Eph 1:3; 1 Pet 1:3), who "sent his Son" into the world to redeem (Gal 4:4–5). Likewise the coming of Christ has forever marked our understanding of the Spirit. The Spirit of God is also the Spirit of Christ (Gal 4:6; Rom 8:9; Phil 1:19), who carries on the work of Christ following his resurrection and subsequent assumption of the place of authority at God's right hand. To have received the Spirit of God (1 Cor 2:12) is to have the mind of Christ (v. 16). For Paul, therefore, Christ gives definition to the Spirit: Spirit people are God's children, fellow heirs with God's Son (Rom 8:14–17); they simultaneously know the power of Christ's resurrection and the fellowship of his sufferings (Phil 3:10); at the same time Christ is the absolute criterion for what is truly Spirit activity (e.g., 1 Cor 12:3). Thus it is fair to say with some that Paul's doctrine of the Spirit is christocentric, but only in the sense that Christ and his work give definition to the Spirit and his work in the Christian life.

But such an understanding of the relationship between Christ and the Spirit is a far cry from the "Spirit Christology" that is spoken of so confidently by many. That view is based chiefly on three texts (1 Cor 6:17; 15:45; 2 Cor 3:17–18[30]) in which Paul is understood to speak of the risen Lord in such a way as to identify him with the Spirit. But such an identification is negated by a contextual understanding of these texts. The main text, 2 Cor 3:17–18, where Paul's language seems to imply an identification, in fact does no such thing. As noted in the exegesis of this passage, Paul's clause "the Lord is the Spirit" is strictly anaphoric, i.e., "the Lord" just mentioned in v. 16 (alluding to Exod 34:34), to whom people *now* turn, is the Spirit—the Spirit of the new covenant, who brings freedom and transforms God's people into "the glory of the Lord." In the case of both 1 Cor 6:17 and 15:45 the language has been dictated by their contexts, where contrasts set up by the argument call forth the usage. Neither of these passages offers a theology of the Spirit or an identification of the Spirit with the risen Lord.

On the other hand, that the risen Christ and the Spirit are clearly *distinct from one another* in Paul's thinking is demonstrated from all kinds of evidence. Besides the Trinitarian passages noted below, other kinds of (nonsoteriological) texts indicate that the activities of the risen Christ

---

[30]Some also appeal to Rom 1:3–4 and 8:9–10 (see, e.g., Hamilton, *Holy Spirit*, 10–15); however, not only do these not suggest any identification, but they actually demonstrate the opposite. See the discussions in ch. 7.

and the Spirit are kept separate in his understanding. This is true of passages as diverse as Rom 9:1, where the formula "in Christ" and "by the Spirit" function quite differently—but characteristically—in one sentence (see n. 19 above), and Rom 15:30 ("through our Lord Jesus Christ and through the love of the Spirit"), where the repeated διά indicates the twofold basis of Paul's appeal. First, it is "through our Lord Jesus Christ," meaning "on the basis of what Christ has done for us all as outlined in the argument of this letter"; second, it is "through the love of the Spirit," meaning "on the basis of the love for all the saints, including myself, that the Spirit engenders."

Perhaps the most significant text in this regard, thinking only of passages where Christ and the Spirit appear in close approximation, is the combination of Rom 8:26–27 (the Spirit intercedes for us) and 8:34 (Christ intercedes for us). On the surface one could argue for "identification" in function; but what one gets rather is the clearest expression not only of "distinction" but of the fact that the risen Christ is not now understood by Paul to be identified with the Spirit. The role of the Spirit is on earth, indwelling believers in order to help them in the weakness of their present "already/not yet" existence and thereby to intercede in their behalf. The risen Christ is "located" in heaven, "at the right hand of God, making intercession for us."[31] The latter text in particular, where Paul is not arguing for something but asserting it on the basis of presuppositional reality, negates altogether the idea that the Spirit in Paul's mind could possibly be identified with the risen Christ, either ontologically or functionally—which means, of course, that there is no warrant of any kind that Paul had a "Spirit Christology."

Nonetheless, although Paul does not make this identification, he does assume the same kind of close relationship between the Spirit and Christ as with the Spirit and God. Thus, at times he moves easily from the mention of the one to the other, especially when using the language of "indwelling" (e.g., Rom 8:9–10, from "have the Spirit of Christ" to "Christ is in you"; cf. Eph 3:16–17). Thus when Paul in Gal 2:20 (q.v.) speaks of Christ as living in him, he almost certainly means "Christ lives in me *by His Spirit*," referring to the ongoing work of Christ in his life that is being carried out by the indwelling Spirit.

This fluid use of language most likely results from the fact that Paul's concern with both Christ and the Spirit is not ontological (= the nature of their *being* God), but soteriological (= their role in salvation)—and experiential. It is precisely at this juncture that we meet the Trinity in Paul; and to this matter we now turn.

---

[31]Cf. Arthur W. Wainwright, *The Trinity in the New Testament* (London: SPCK, 1962) 260.

THE SPIRIT AND THE TRINITY

The real problem with those who support a "Spirit Christology" in Paul is methodological. The common denominator of this position is that its proponents *begin* with this handful of (mostly obscure) texts full of notorious exegetical difficulties, which can be demonstrated not to carry any of the weight they wish to give them. Furthermore, these texts serve not simply as the *primary* basis but as the *only* basis for Paul's alleged Spirit Christology, as though it were clear to all who would read Paul. In turn, the plain and certain Trinitarian texts are then either negated by disclaimers or in some cases not considered at all. Thus scholars begin with what they *assume* Paul to be saying in a few obscure texts and either avoid or treat with diffidence what he unambiguously says elsewhere and in all kinds of unmistakable ways.[32]

Paul, on the other hand, began at a different point. Here is a thoroughgoing monotheist, whose encounter with Christ on the Damascus Road, and subsequent encounter with the Holy Spirit, forever radically altered his understanding of God and of his (now Christian) existence. At the heart of Pauline theology is his gospel, and his gospel is essentially *soteriology*—God's saving a people for his name through the redemptive work of Christ and the appropriating work of the Spirit. It is his encounter with God soteriologically, as Father, Son, and Holy Spirit, that accounts for the transformation of Paul's theological language and of his understanding of God—although this is never worked out at the level of immanent, or doxological, Trinitarianism. In light of this reality and the preponderance of texts that support it—and with Trinitarian language—it might be assumed that these texts should serve as the methodological starting point, and that the more obscure ones should be interpreted in light of these, not the other way around.

That Paul's understanding of God was functionally Trinitarian and that the distinctions between Father, Son, and Spirit were presuppositional for him[33] can be demonstrated from two sets of materials: several explicitly Trinitarian texts (2 Cor 13:13[14]; 1 Cor 12:4–6; Eph 4:4–6) and the many soteriological texts that are expressed in Trinitarian terms.

1. As noted in our exegesis of 2 Cor 13:13[14], this remarkable grace-benediction offers us all kinds of theological keys to understanding both Paul's soteriology and his theology proper (i.e., his understanding of

---

[32]Dunn, therefore, seems to work at cross purposes with a methodology he has himself spoken against (*Baptism*, 103–4). Cf. his similar critique of Hermann in "2 Corinthians III.17," 309; yet he turns about and does this very thing on the basis of his own exegesis of 1 Cor 15:45 and Rom 1:3–4.

[33]On this whole question, and especially on Paul as a Trinitarian, see the section entitled "What About the Trinity?" by David Ford, in Frances Young and David Ford, *Meaning*, 255–60.

God). The fact that the benediction is ad hoc only increases its importance in hearing Paul. Thus what he says here in prayer appears in a *thoroughly presuppositional* way—not as something Paul argues for, but as the assumed, experienced reality of Christian life.

First, it serves to encapsulate what lies at the very heart of Paul's singular passion: the gospel, with its focus on salvation in Christ, equally available by faith to Gentile and Jew alike. That the *love of God* is the foundation of Paul's soteriology is expressly stated with passion and clarity, in passages such as Rom 5:1–11, 8:31–39, and Eph 1:3–14. The *grace of our Lord Jesus Christ* is what gave concrete expression to that love; through Christ's suffering and death in behalf of his loved ones, God effected salvation for them at one moment in human history. The *participation in the Holy Spirit* expresses the ongoing realization of that love and grace in the life of the believer and the believing community. The κοινωνία τοῦ ἁγίου πνεύματος (note the full name!) is how the living God not only brings people into an intimate and abiding relationship with himself, as the God of all grace, but also causes them to participate in all the benefits of that grace and salvation, indwelling them in the present by his own presence, guaranteeing their final eschatological glory.

Secondly, this text also serves as our entrée into Paul's theology proper, that is, into his understanding of God himself, which had been so radically affected for him by the twin realities of the death and resurrection of Christ and the gift of the eschatological Spirit. Granted, Paul did not wrestle with the ontological questions which such statements beg to have addressed. Nor does he here *assert* the deity of Christ and the Spirit. But what he does is to *equate the activity of the three divine Persons* (to use the language of a later time) *in concert and in one prayer*, with the clause about God the Father standing in second place. This suggests that Paul was truly Trinitarian in any meaningful sense of that term—that the one God is Father, Son, and Spirit, and that when dealing with Christ and the Spirit one is dealing with God every bit as much as when one is dealing with the Father.

Thus this benediction, with its affirmation of the distinctions of God, Christ, and Spirit, also expresses in shorthand form what is found everywhere elsewhere in Paul, namely, that "salvation in Christ" is the cooperative work of God, Christ, and the Spirit. Affirmations like this shut down all possibilities that Paul could ever identify the risen Christ with the Spirit so that in Paul "immanent Christology is pneumatology."

The same fully Trinitarian implications also appear in 1 Cor 12:4–6 and Eph 4:4–6. In the former passage Paul is urging the Corinthians to broaden their perspective and to recognize the rich diversity of the Spirit's manifestations in their midst (over against their apparently singular interest in glossolalia). He begins in vv. 4–6 by noting that diversity reflects the nature of God and is therefore the true evidence of the work of the one God in their midst. Thus the Trinity is presuppositional to the entire argument.

In Eph 4:4–6 one finds this same combination as in 2 Cor 13:13[14]—a creedal formulation expressed in terms of the distinguishable activities of the triune God. The basis for Christian unity is one God. The one body is the work of the one Spirit (cf. 1 Cor 12:13), by whom also we live our present eschatological existence in one hope, since the Spirit is the "downpayment on our inheritance" (Eph 1:13–14). All of this has been made possible for us by our one Lord, in whom all have "one faith" and to which faith all have given witness through their "one baptism." The source of all these realities is the one God himself, "who is over all and through all and in all."

If the last phrase in this passage reemphasizes the unity of the one God, who is ultimately responsible for all things—past, present, and future—and subsumes the work of the Spirit and the Son under that of God, the entire passage at the same time puts into creedal form the affirmation that God is *experienced* as a triune reality. Precisely on the basis of such experience and language the later church maintained its biblical integrity by expressing all of this in explicitly Trinitarian language. And Paul's formulations, which include the work of the Spirit, form a part of that basis.

2. That this "soteriological Trinitarianism" is foundational to Paul's understanding of the gospel is further corroborated by the large number of soteriological texts in which salvation is formulated in similar Trinitarian terms. This is especially true of the larger, explicit passages such as Rom 5:1–8; 2 Cor 3:1–4:6; Gal 4:4–6; or Eph 1:3–14 (cf. Titus 3:4–7). But it is also true of many other texts, primarily soteriological, in which salvation is either explicitly or implicitly predicated on the threefold work of the triune God, as encapsulated in 2 Cor 13:13[14]. Thus:[34]

1 Thes 1:4–5, where the love of God has brought about the realization of election through the Gospel (the message about Christ) empowered by the Holy Spirit.

2 Thes 2:13, where God's people are "beloved by the Lord (through his death)," because God elected them for salvation through the sanctifying work of the Spirit.

1 Cor 1:4–7, where God's grace has been given in Christ Jesus, who in turn has enriched the church with every kind of Spirit gifting.

1 Cor 2:4–5, where Paul's preaching of Christ crucified (v. 2) is accompanied by the Spirit's power so that their faith might rest in God.

1 Cor 2:12, where "we have received the Spirit that comes from God," so that we might know the things given to us (in the cross is implied in context) by God.

---

[34]For the complete listing of relevant texts that are addressed exegetically in this book, see n. 39 on 1 Thes 1:4–6.

1 Cor 6:11, where God is the conceptual subject of the "divine passives" (you were washed, justified, sanctified), effected in the name of Christ and by the Spirit.

1 Cor 6:19–20, where the believer has been purchased (by Christ; cf. 7:22–23) so as to become a temple for God's presence by the Spirit.

2 Cor 1:21–22, where God is the one who has "confirmed" believers in a salvation effected by Christ, God's "Yes" (vv. 19–20), evidenced by his giving the Spirit as "down payment."

Gal 3:1–5, where Christ crucified (v. 1, picking up on 2:16–21) is conveyed to believers by the Spirit, whom God yet "supplies" among them (v. 5).

Rom 8:3–4, where God sent his Son to do what the Law could not in terms of securing salvation, and the Spirit does what the Law could not in terms of effecting righteousness in behavior ("walking" = living in the ways of God).

Rom 8:15–17, where the God-given Spirit serves as evidence of "adoption" as children, and thus "joint-heirs" with Christ, who made it all possible.

Col 3:16, where in worship it is all played in reverse: as the message of Christ "dwells richly among them," they worship the God from whom salvation has come, by means of a Spirit-inspired hymnody.

Eph 1:17, where the God of our Lord Jesus Christ gives the Spirit of wisdom and revelation so that they may understand the full measure of the work of Christ in their behalf.

Eph 2:18, where "through [the death of] Christ" (vv. 14–16) Jew and Gentile together have access to God by the one Spirit, whom both alike have received.

Eph 2:20–22, where Christ is the "cornerstone" for the new Temple, the place of God's dwelling by his Spirit.

Phil 3:3, where believers serve (God is implied) by the Spirit of God and thus boast in the effective work of Christ Jesus.

The result of these data, therefore, is that Paul would not so much as recognize the language or the theological assertions of those who consider him to have had a Spirit Christology. His presuppositions lay elsewhere, with the one God, now bringing salvation through the cooperative work of the three divine Persons: Father, Son, and Spirit. At points where the work of any or all overlaps, so could Paul's language tend to be flexible—precisely because salvation for him was the activity of the one God. If his Trinitarian presuppositions and formulations, which form the basis of the later formulations, never move toward calling the Spirit God and never wrestle with the ontological implications of those presuppositions and formulations, there is no evidence that he lacked clarity as to the distinctions between, and the specific roles of, the three divine Persons who effected so great salvation for us all.

THE SPIRIT AS GOD'S PRESENCE[35]

If Paul's soteriological *experience* of God is the starting point for understanding his inherent Trinitarianism, so also his experience of the Spirit in particular serves as the starting point for penetrating his understanding of the Spirit in personal categories. The clues here are a combination of three related Old Testament realities that Paul sees "fulfilled" by the coming of the Spirit: (1) his association of the Spirit with the new covenant; (2) the language of "indwelling"; and (3) his collocation of the Spirit with the imagery of the temple. The result is an understanding of the Spirit that not only is personal, but sees the Spirit as the way God has "fulfilled" both the new covenant and the renewed temple motifs, and therefore as the way God himself is now present on planet Earth. The temple is the place of God's "dwelling"; the Spirit is the way God now "dwells" in his "holy temple," both in the individual believer and in the gathered community.

1. We have already noted in the preceding chapter the role of the Spirit as the eschatological fulfillment of the new covenant. My concern here is to point out in particular how Paul perceives *the role* of the Spirit in the new covenant. Almost certainly as the result of his own—and others'—experience of the Spirit, Paul understood this role especially in terms of Ezek 36:26–27 and 37:14. Paul combines motifs from these two passages in such a way that in the coming of the Spirit into the life of the believer and the believing community God fulfilled three dimensions of the promise: (a) that God would give his people a "new heart"—Jeremiah's "heart of flesh" to replace that of stone (Jer 31:31–33)—made possible because he would also give them "a new spirit" (Ezek 36:26). In Paul this motif finds expression in 2 Cor 3:1–6, where the Corinthians are understood to be the recipients of the new covenant in that they were "inscribed" by "the Spirit of the living God" on "tablets of human hearts" (v. 3). Paul himself is the minister of this new covenant which has no longer to do with "letter" but with the Spirit who "gives life" (vv. 5–6). (b) This "new spirit" in turn is none other than God's Spirit, who will enable his people to follow his decrees (Ezek 36:27). As noted in our discussions of Rom 8:3–4 and Gal 5:16–25, the Spirit's fulfillment of this motif is Paul's answer to the question of "what happens to righteousness" if one does away with Torah observance. (c) God's Spirit in turn means the presence of God himself, in that by putting "my Spirit in you . . . you will live" (Ezek 37:14). Again, Paul picks up this motif in 2 Cor 3:5–6. As

---

[35]On the theme of the divine presence as the key to biblical theology, see Samuel Terrien, *The Elusive Presence: Toward a New Biblical Theology* (San Francisco: Harper, 1978).

the Spirit *of the living God*, the Spirit provides for God's people the one essential reality about God. "The Spirit," Paul says in the context of the new covenant, "*gives life.*"

Similarly, the language of 1 Thes 4:8 is expressly that of Ezek 36–37. Any rejection of holiness on the part of the Thessalonians is a rejection of the God who "gives his Holy Spirit into you." It is the presence of the holy God himself, by his Holy Spirit, whom they reject if they reject his call to holy living. Thus, for Paul, Christ has effected the new covenant for the people of God through his death and resurrection; but the Spirit is the key to the new covenant as a fulfilled reality in the lives of God's people.

2. Intimately related to this theme and these OT passages are the many texts in Paul that speak of the Spirit as "dwelling" in or among the people of God. This is found first of all in the various texts that locate the Spirit "in the heart" of the believer, or simply "in them." The Spirit is spoken of as being "in you/us" in 1 Thes 4:8; 1 Cor 6:19; 14:24–25; and Eph 5:18 (in the imagery of "filling"). The location of "in you/us" is the "heart" in 2 Cor 1:22; 3:3; Gal 4:6; Rom 2:29; 5:5. This in turn becomes the language of "dwelling in" in 1 Cor 3:16; 2 Cor 6:16; Rom 8:9–11; and Eph 2:22.

Two of these passages (1 Cor 14:24–25 and 2 Cor 6:16) are especially instructive in that Paul cites OT texts that speak of *God's dwelling* in the midst of his people, which Paul now attributes to the *presence of the Spirit*. Thus, when pagans turn to the living God because their hearts have been exposed through the prophetic Spirit, Paul speaks of this in the language of Isa 45:14: "Surely *God is among you.*" Similarly, in the temple imagery of 2 Cor 6:16, which presupposes the presence of the Spirit in the life of the community from 1 Cor 3:16, Paul understands God to be present among his people. In making that point, Paul draws upon the language of the new covenant promise of Ezek 37:27: "I will dwell among them and they shall be my people." This latter passage in turn points toward the ultimate expression of the language of "indwelling" in the imagery of the temple.

3. As we observed in chapter 1, for Paul the Spirit is the key to fulfillment of the motif of God's presence among his people, especially as that was understood in Israel in terms of the temple. This imagery occurs four times in Paul, three times in keeping with its OT antecedents (1 Cor 3:16; 2 Cor 6:16; Eph 2:22), where God dwells *in the midst of the people* by means of the tabernacle and the temple. What is significant for our purposes is that Paul specifically uses this imagery and the OT motif of God's presence in the context of *the Spirit's presence in the midst of the people of God* as they are constituted on the basis of the new covenant, effected by Christ and actualized by the Spirit. Here is how the living God is now present with his people, expressed most clearly in Eph 2:22: the

church is being raised up to become a holy temple in the Lord, built up together as "a dwelling for God by his Spirit."

It is of more than passing interest, therefore, that in urging his readers in Eph 4:30 "not to grieve the Holy Spirit of God" Paul does so by "citing" the language of Isa 63:10, the one certain place in the Old Testament where the concept of the divine presence with Israel in the tabernacle and temple is specifically equated with "the Holy Spirit of Yahweh." This equation is the presupposition behind Paul's own prohibition. The divine presence in the form of God's own Spirit, not an angel or envoy, journeyed with God's people in the desert. By the Holy Spirit God's presence has now returned to his people, to indwell them corporately and individually so that they might walk in his ways (hence the significance in Paul of "being led by the Spirit").

Here, then, also lies the significance of 1 Cor 6:19–20, where Paul expresses this motif in terms of his soteriological understanding of the Spirit's presence in the life of the individual believer. The result is that God not only "dwells" in the midst of his people by the Spirit, but that has likewise taken up residence in the lives of his people individually, as they are indwelt by the life-giving Spirit. The Spirit for Paul is therefore none other than the way God's presence has returned to his people, not only corporately as they gather for worship, but individually as well.

Thus for Paul, the Spirit is not some merely impersonal "force" or "influence" or "power." The Spirit is none other than the fulfillment of the promise that God himself would once again be present with his people. The implications of this are considerable, not only in terms of Paul's understanding of God and the Spirit, the concern of this chapter, but in terms of what it means for us individually and corporately to be the people of God, which is the concern of the next two chapters. The Spirit is God's own personal presence in our lives and in our midst, who leads us into paths of righteousness for his own name's sake, who "is working all things in all people," and who is grieved when his people do not reflect his character and thus reveal his glory.

It is for God's people of a later time like ours once more to appropriate these realities in an experienced way, if we are truly to capture the Pauline understanding. Perhaps a beginning point for us would be to downplay the impersonal images, as rich as they are in terms of aspects of the Spirit's ministry, and to retool our thinking in Pauline terms, where we understand and experience the Spirit as the personal presence of the eternal God.

14

THE SOTERIOLOGICAL SPIRIT

In the preceding two chapters, in conjunction with our chief concerns, we also noted the central role of the Spirit in Paul's scheme of "salvation in Christ." First, salvation is an essentially eschatological reality in which God brings to pass the promised eschatological salvation, which included Jew and Gentile on the same basis of faith in Christ and of their common experience of the Spirit (cf. 1 Cor 12:13). Second, salvation finds its meaning in the character of the triune God, whose redemptive love initiated (the Father), effected (the Son), and made effectual (the Spirit) our salvation. Salvation is *in Christ*, wrought by him through his death and resurrection; it is realized in the life of the believer by *the Holy Spirit*, the empowering presence of God. Thus the presence of the Spirit is both the evidence that salvation has come and the guarantee of our inheritance, of our sharing in the final glory of God through Christ.

The result of this understanding of salvation, which stems both from the work of Christ himself and from Paul's experience of the eschatological Spirit, is that again there is both continuity and discontinuity with Paul's Jewish heritage. The continuity is to be found in the fact that God is still "saving a people for his name" (cf. e.g., Num 6:27; Deut 28:10; 2 Sam 7:23), a people who fulfill the promise made to Abraham (Gen 12:2–3). The discontinuity is to be found in the individualizing factor, that the people of God are no longer constituted on the basis of "nation," but on the basis of individual entry through faith in Christ Jesus and the gift of the Spirit.

Paul can hardly help himself: his focus and concern are ever and always on the people as a whole. Though entered at the individual level, salvation is *never thought of simply as a one-on-one relationship with God*. While such a relationship is included, to be sure, to be saved means especially to be joined to the people of God. In this sense, Cyprian had it right: there is no salvation outside the church—since God is saving *a people* for his name, *not a disparate group of individuals*. Nonetheless, since both "getting in" and "staying in" happen at the individual level, our look at the role of the Spirit in salvation, at least in terms of "getting in," must begin at this level.[1]

We should note also that for Paul "salvation in Christ" includes *both* "getting in" *and* "staying in"; that is, Paul's view of "getting saved" had to do with faith in Christ that also includes "faithfulness"[2] in terms of a life being continually transformed into the likeness of God. Paul knows nothing of salvation that does not include both the indicative (salvation by grace through faith) and the imperative (faith lived out in one's relationships and behavior). This presents us with considerable difficulty, therefore, as to where properly to discuss ethics in Pauline theology. Do they belong in this chapter, on "salvation in Christ," so as to emphasize that the ethical life is part of what it means to be saved? Or do we discuss them, as I have chosen to do, in the next chapter, so as to emphasize that ethics, though carried out individually, have to do with being the people of God together?

In any case, in order to understand Paul correctly, we must think of what is said here as it points toward the next chapter. Nonetheless, neither may we minimize that salvation, the focus of the present chapter, begins in the heart of the individual believer. After all, this emphasis on the individual is not the product of the Renaissance and Reformation— although at times these have resulted in an unfortunate and unbiblical focus on the individual to the point of an enculturated narcissism. The new place for the individual originates in part in Paul himself and arises from his altered eschatological perspective that includes Jew and Gentile alike on the same grounds. So it is fitting in this chapter to focus on this aspect of "salvation in Christ," but we must always remind ourselves that, despite our cultural and theological biases, this is not the whole story in Paul.

THE SPIRIT AND THE HEARING OF THE GOSPEL

We must note at the outset that Paul's statements about the role of the Spirit in salvation are primarily experiential and altogether ad hoc;

---

[1]Cf. Ewert, *Holy Spirit*, 168, who also shows concern that by starting with the individual one may skew the data, but that if one does not take the individual into account, one will also skew Paul's overall theology. The failure to come to grips with this is one of the weaknesses of Horton's book (*What the Bible Says about the Holy Spirit*). It is typical of the pietistic tradition of all strands to read Scripture as if it were primarily written to individual believers.

[2]The one word, πίστις, expresses for Paul *both* of these ideas: trust, and trusting faithfulness. Thus πίστις is listed among the fruit of the Spirit (Gal 5:22), as well as serving to denote our proper response to God's saving grace.

thus they do not easily yield to a precise scheme as to the *ordo salutis* ("order of salvation"). What one does find are several components that make up the complex of Christian conversion (hearing the gospel, faith, various metaphors for conversion, the gift of the Spirit, baptism in water); and there is indeed a certain logic as to how they are mentioned. But everything beyond that is more speculative. What is crucial to realize is that the Spirit plays the central role in most of the process—except for baptism, which is understandable, since Paul (apparently) understood baptism as the human response to the prior divine activity.

For Paul Christian life begins with the hearing of the gospel, which both precedes faith (Rom 10:14) and is accompanied by faith (1 Thes 2:13; 2 Thes 2:13–14; Eph 1:13). "How," he asks, "can they believe in the one of whom they have not heard? And how can they hear without someone preaching to them? And how can they preach unless they are sent?" (Rom 10:14–15 NIV). This view of "hearing the gospel" accounts in part for Paul's own missionary urgencies. Nor is it surprising, therefore, that according to Paul the Holy Spirit, who plays the central role in the conversion process itself, should play the central role here as well. Two things are involved here: the gospel as God's very word (1 Thes 2:13) and therefore the truth that must be believed (2 Thes 2:13; 1 Tim 2:4), revealed as such by the Spirit; and the dual act of preaching and responding, which are also the work of the Spirit. We begin with the latter.

THE SPIRIT AND PROCLAMATION[3]

In 2 Cor 3:8, contrasting his own ministry with that of Moses—and indirectly with that of the "peddlers of another Jesus"—Paul refers to his as "the ministry of the Spirit," meaning the ministry of the new covenant, which is empowered by the Spirit and results in others' receiving the Spirit. Such ministry, he insists, despite the earthenware vessel through which it comes, is accompanied by far greater glory than that which accompanied the ministry of Moses. The "far greater glory," it turns out in this context, is the work of the Spirit, who not only brings us into the presence of the living God, but does so by removing the veil that otherwise keeps people from beholding God's glory in the face of Christ Jesus and from consequently being transformed into his likeness.

Paul thus frequently refers to his own effective ministry as a direct result of the work of the Spirit. This work included not only conviction concerning the truth of the gospel, but also signs and wonders, all of which resulted in changed lives. Indeed, and appropriately, the first reference to the Spirit in the Pauline corpus (1 Thes 1:5–6) strikes this

---

[3]On this question see the discussions on 1 Thes 2:4–6; 1 Cor 2:4–5; 2 Cor 6:6–7; 12:12; Rom 15:18–19; Eph 3:3–7.

note. Paul begins his encouragement of this new—and persecuted— Christian community by reminding them of two Spirit-experienced realities: his ministry among them, and the nature of their conversion. They became converts (v. 5) not on the basis of Paul's proclamation alone, although "word" was involved as well, but because that proclamation was accompanied by the power of the Spirit, including a deep conviction (probably both in Paul as he preached and in them as they heard). Whether the "power of the Spirit" in this first instance also included accompanying "signs and wonders" is moot (I think it did); but in any case Rom 15:18–19 indicates that such was regularly the case. The Thessalonians' reception of the gospel was itself accompanied by much affliction and with the joy of the Holy Spirit (v. 6), that untrammeled joy the Spirit brings to those who have come to know the living and true God (v. 9).

So also with 1 Cor 2:1–5. In defending his ministry in Corinth against his detractors (cf. 4:1–21; 9:1–27), Paul in this paragraph takes up the matter of his preaching when first in the city. Both the content (1:18–25) *and* the form of his preaching lacked persuasive wisdom and rhetoric; indeed, his preaching was far more effective than that, Paul argues. It was accompanied by a demonstration of the *Spirit's* power, evidenced by the conversion of the Corinthians themselves (cf. 2 Cor 3:3). And it was so, Paul adds, in order that their faith might rest in "the power of God," not in merely human wisdom. These passages, and the next, make it abundantly clear that Paul understood Christian conversion to begin with Spirit-empowered proclamation, which by the same Spirit found its lodging in the heart of the hearer so as to bring conviction—of sin (as 1 Cor 14:24–25 makes clear), as well as of the truth of the gospel.

But the Spirit's role in Paul's preaching was not limited to an "anointing" of Paul's own words, thus carrying conviction as to the truth of the gospel itself. In Rom 15:18–19 he insists that his preaching all the way from to Jerusalem to Illyricum was an effective combination of "word *and* deed," both of which were the work of "the power of the Spirit." By "word" he undoubtedly refers to the proclamation of the gospel; he explains "deed" as referring to "signs and wonders through the power of the Spirit."

For Paul this double display of power (empowered words and powerful deeds) appears as presuppositional to his understanding of the role of the eschatological Spirit. That is, he never argues *for* such empowering, nor does he allow anyone to authenticate either his ministry or their faith on that basis (2 Cor 5:13). But neither would he understand the presence of the eschatological Spirit without such a double expression of power. We are dealing with the Spirit of God, after all, the present eschatological fulfillment of God's empowering presence. It would never occur to him that the miraculous would *not* accompany the proclamation of the gospel, or that in another time some would think of these two empowerings as "either-or." For Paul, it is simply a matter of, "of course." Thus, speaking of his ministry as a whole, he can confidently say to the Colossians, "to which purpose also I labor, contending in keeping with God's working, which is at work in me with power" (1:29), which in Paul means "by the power of the Spirit."

Although the evidence is more scanty, what was true of Paul's ministry is probably how he understood the effective preaching of the gospel in general. "And take the sword of the Spirit," he urges the recipients of Ephesians, which he then interprets as "the word of God" (6:17). In that context this almost certainly refers to speaking forth the truth about Christ in a world where the powers are still at work. Thus he is urging them to be involved in a Spirit-empowered proclamation of Christ.

Similarly, this understanding of the relationship of the Spirit to ministry lies behind three passages addressed to Timothy (1 Tim 1:18; 4:14; 2 Tim 1:6–7; cf. v. 14), in which Paul recalls Timothy's experience of "call" to ministry. Because of context, each emphasizes a different aspect of that experience. Several things may be deduced from the passages together: (1) Timothy's gift (χάρισμα) refers first to the Spirit (2 Tim 1:6–7), but is also broadened to refer to the gift of ministry that came by the Spirit (1 Tim 4:14). The experience therefore is first of all something that happened to (within) Timothy. He experienced a Spirit-directed, Spirit-given "call," singling him out for the ministry of the gospel. (2) The experience, however, took place in a community setting of some kind, since it also came by way of prophetic utterances spoken about and to him (1 Tim 1:18; 4:14). (3) The community of elders responded to the prior work of the Spirit by the laying on of hands (4:14; 2 Tim 1:6; cf. the similar sequence in Acts 13:1–3). The gift itself did not come through their laying on of hands; rather, their act was one of recognition and affirmation of the prior work of the Spirit that had come through prophetic utterances. The Spirit as an *experienced* reality is the obvious key to these appeals.

THE ROLE OF REVELATION[4]

Part of Paul's conviction that his message would be, and was, accompanied by the Spirit's power was his corresponding conviction that

---

[4]On this question, both as to its Jewish background and its Pauline usage, see especially, Bockmuehl, *Revelation*. My interest at this point is in "revelation" as it refers to Paul's—and his churches'—hearing and understanding the gospel. But quite in keeping with his view of salvation as all-inclusive, having to do with both "getting in" and "staying in," "revelation" becomes a part of Christian life, as God's people, by the Spirit, come to discern God's will for their ethical life. See the further discussion in ch. 15 below.

the essential content of the gospel came to him by revelation, again as the work of the Spirit. Both 1 Cor 2:10–16 and Eph 3:5–7 affirm that his own insight into the gospel came by the Spirit's revelation.

This revelation involved a twofold unveiling of God's mystery. First, in 1 Cor 2:6–16 the Spirit is understood to have revealed what was formerly hidden—and is still hidden to those without the Spirit. Only by the Spirit (v. 10) could he and his converts possibly understand what the human mind could not so much as conceive (v. 9), namely, that God in his own wisdom had chosen to redeem our fallen race through the crucifixion of Christ. Thus Paul's preaching of the cross came with "words taught by the Spirit" (v. 13), which included "explaining spiritual things by spiritual means" (= the things *taught* by the Spirit with *language appropriate* to the Spirit). To have the Spirit in this way means not to be subject to merely human judgments; rather, it means to have the mind of Christ (vv. 15–16; cf. 1 Cor 7:25, 40).

Crucial to Paul's argument is that this revelation should be the common experience of all who have received the Spirit.[5] Paul's problem with the Corinthians was that they considered themselves to be people of the Spirit, yet were abandoning the cross for human wisdom and rhetoric. Hence the crucial role of the Spirit, who has revealed to those who love God what was formerly hidden (2:9–10), namely, what God in Christ has freely given us (v. 12).[6] It is not esoteric wisdom that has been revealed by the Spirit, but the content of the gospel, God's "mystery." The need for revelation by the Spirit at this point is considerable, since it requires an understanding that merely human wisdom could not penetrate in ten thousand years. The gospel, after all, at its most crucial and therefore at its deepest point stands in utter contradiction to human wisdom: that God has redeemed our fallen race by means of the ultimate

---

[5]Otherwise Bockmuehl, *Revelation*, 164–65, who sees the "us" as more narrowly referring to "the apostles." I do not doubt that part of the purpose of this passage is apologetic; but in this case, at issue is the *Corinthians'* failure to understand what God was about in Christ, which they should have known precisely because they did have the Spirit—hence the powerful irony within the passage as a whole. See the discussion in ch. 4 above.

[6]It is this contextual factor which makes the alleged linguistic parallels between this passage and Wis 9:9–17 nearly irrelevant (see, e.g., most recently, Menzies, *Development*, 303–15, and the literature cited on 315nn3, 4; cf. the discussion below in the Appendix, pp. 911–13). First, because Paul's use of "wisdom" language in this passage comes from the Corinthians, not from his own argumentation, and the tie of "wisdom" to "revelation" and "the Spirit" is so circuitous in this passage and otherwise so rare in Paul, one would expect a bit more caution from its more vigorous advocates. Second, the linguistic correspondences between this passage and Wisdom 9, which make the alleged parallels work at all, are themselves so remote in terms of meaning and content that this has all the earmarks of a fishing expedition rather than a case of Paul's "knowing and being influenced by." If Paul was *influenced* by Wisdom, such a demonstration will need to be made of firmer stuff than this passage.

oxymoron, a crucified Messiah. Without the Spirit, who alone knows the mind of God, human beings do not stand a chance to penetrate this "hidden mystery." This is what "eye has not seen nor has it entered into the heart of human beings"; and this is what the Corinthians should have come to recognize, precisely because they, too, had received the Spirit that they might be taught by means of the Spirit the things of the Spirit.

Second, in Eph 3:2–13 this mystery, God's hidden wisdom now revealed by the Spirit, includes the fact that "Gentiles are heirs together with Israel, members together of one body, and sharers together in the promise in Christ Jesus" (v. 6). Since these words reflect the primary focus of the argument of Galatians and Romans as well, it is not surprising that Paul here speaks of these matters in terms of "revelation" which came "by the Spirit." Therefore for Paul both the revelation of it and the actual inclusion of Jews and Gentiles together in Christ (1:13–14; 2:18, 22) are the work of the Spirit. This, too, obviously needs the revelation that only the eschatological Spirit can bestow. What required revelation was not that Gentiles were to be included in the eschatological blessings of God—that was common stock for all—but that they would be included Torah-free and on equal grounds with Jews, so that God in Christ had formed one new humanity of the two peoples. Such an understanding could have come only through the Spirit's revelation, both through Jews' and Gentiles' common experience of the Spirit (1 Cor 12:13) and the cognitive understanding of what Christ and the Spirit had done (Eph 3:5).

A further aspect of revelation connected with the hearing of the gospel occurs in 1 Cor 14:24–25. Here the revelation comes by means of prophetic utterances within the believing community when unbelievers are present. What is revealed in this case are the secrets of the unbelievers' hearts, leading them to repentance and conversion. We should pause here to note that in the present overview of Pauline theology, focusing as we are on the role of the Spirit in that theology, there is no mention of the human predicament that made salvation a necessity. That is because Paul sees not the Holy Spirit, but the evil spirit, Satan himself, as at work in those whose minds he "has blinded so that they cannot behold the light of the gospel in face of God's glory, Christ himself" (2 Cor 4:4). Believers can see the glory because the Spirit has removed the veil, in this case the "blindfold." The present passage indicates in part at least how the Spirit removes the veil—by means of a prophetic utterance that penetrates into the unbeliever's heart and lays it bare before all. The "revelation" in this case has probably to do with the unbeliever's own sinfulness, which in turn leads him or her to hear the greater "revelation" that has taken place in Christ. Such "revelation" by the prophetic Spirit, we should note further, serves for believers as the sure sign of God's favor and presence among them (1 Cor 14:22). All of this is the work of the Spirit.

THE SPIRIT AND FAITH[7]

The relationship of the Spirit to faith is one of the more complex issues in the corpus; indeed, its very complexity bears mute witness against our attempt to fit all of Paul's words about the Spirit into our own prior categories. On the one hand, in Gal 3:2–5 Paul is adamant that the gift of the Spirit is the result of "faith in Christ Jesus." According to any "systematic" presentation that should demand that faith itself precedes the reception of the Spirit. On the other hand, in 1 Cor 12:8 and 13:2 "faith" is considered one of the manifestations of the Spirit. If those passages can be dismissed as referring (correctly so) to that unusual gift of faith that accompanies the miraculous, the same can scarcely be said of the "faith" that is the fruit of the Spirit (Gal 5:22), which refers to "saving faith" in its continuing expression, or of 2 Cor 4:13, where Paul refers to "having the same Spirit who effects faith as the Psalmist had," who leads us "to believe."

This prompts us to suggest, therefore, that faith itself, as a work of the Spirit, leads to the experienced reception of the Spirit that also comes through that same faith. Although it does not fit our logical schemes well, the Spirit is thus both the cause and the effect of faith. This same close relationship of the Spirit to faith is also presupposed in Gal 5:5, where Paul urges that *we*, in contrast to *them* (the Jewish Christian agitators), "by the Spirit, on the basis of faith, await the final righteousness for which we hope." The object of faith, as always, is Christ; the Spirit is the means whereby such faith is sustained.

What all of this means, then, is that for Paul both the *understanding* of the gospel and the *event of preaching*, including *the hearing that leads to faith*, are the work of the Spirit. In this sense one may legitimately argue that faith itself is also a prior work of the Spirit in the life of the one who becomes a believer, since "we have the same Spirit who inspires faith" so that "we believe" (2 Cor 4:13).

THE SPIRIT AND CONVERSION

The Spirit who empowers and accompanies the preaching and hearing of the gospel also plays the crucial role in the actual conversion of the believer. Our concern here is, first, to demonstrate this assertion and, second, by means of the Pauline metaphors to examine the role played by the Spirit.

---

[7]See the discussion on 1 Cor 12:8; 13:2; 2 Cor 4:13; Gal 3:1–5.

The Crucial Role of the Spirit[8]

Although he would not have used such language, for Paul, Christian conversion has both an objective and subjective dimension to it. On the one hand, Christ's death and resurrection have secured eternal salvation for those who believe. This objective *historical* reality is conveyed with a variety of metaphors, each of which emphasizes a significant aspect of the believer's new relationship with God (redemption, reconciliation, washing, propitiation, justification, adoption, birth). At the point of conversion, this objective historical reality becomes for the believer an objective *positional* reality as well, in terms of the individual's relationship to God through Christ. But for Paul this reality also involves a clearly subjective, *experiential appropriation* that results in some radical changes in the believer; and the Spirit is the absolutely crucial element for this dimension of conversion.[9] This can be illustrated in several ways:

1. Quite in passing Paul frequently refers back to his readers' conversion(s), and he does so regularly in terms of the Spirit. Thus, God gave them his Spirit (Rom 5:5), anointed them with the Spirit (2 Cor 1:21), poured out his Spirit generously on them (Tit 3:6), and sealed them with the Spirit (Eph 1:13; 4:30). Obversely, believers have received the Spirit (1 Cor 2:12; 2 Cor 11:4), have been saved through the sanctifying work of the Spirit (2 Thes 2:13; Rom 15:16), have been circumcised in their hearts by the Spirit (Rom 2:29), and have been joined to Christ so as to become one S/spirit with him (1 Cor 6:17). As well as "by the name of Christ," believers have been "washed, sanctified, and justified" by "the Spirit of our God" (1 Cor 6:11). In the analogy of Ishmael and Isaac in Gal 4:29, the former is "born of the flesh," while the latter (= the Galatian believers) was born of the Spirit.

2. In several "conversion" texts, the Spirit plays the leading role in *describing what has happened to the believer* (Gal 3:2–5; 1 Cor 6:11; 12:13; Eph 1:13–14; Tit 3:5–7). Most significant of these is Gal 3:2–5, made so by the nature of Paul's appeal. To counteract the influence of the Jewish Christian agitators who are promoting the circumcision of Gentiles in order for them to belong fully to the people of God, Paul begins by appealing to the Galatians' own conversion(s), precisely because they were experienced and visible. So he asks not, "Were you saved, or justified, etc.," but "Did you *receive the Spirit* by Torah observance, or by

---

[8]The texts here are many and varied; see, e.g., the discussions on 1 Thes 1:4–6; 2 Thes 2:13; 1 Cor 2:6–3:1; 6:11, 19–20; 2 Cor 1:21–22; 3:1–18; 11:4; 13:13[14]; Gal 3:1–5; 4:6; 5:5–6; 5:13–6:10; Rom 5:5; 7:4–6; 8:1–30; 14:16–18; 15:13, 16; Eph 1:13–14; 4:1–6, 30; Phil 3:3; Titus 3:4–7.

[9]In the perceptive words of Swete (*Holy Spirit*, 206): "Without the mission of the Spirit the mission of the Son would have been fruitless; without the mission of the Son the Spirit could not have been sent."

believing what you heard? Are you so foolish? Having *begun by the Spirit*, are you now trying to come to completion through the 'flesh'?" For Paul the Spirit is the crucial element to *all* of Christian life; therefore his argument stands or falls on their recalling their own experience of conversion at the beginning in terms of the Spirit. "Have you experienced so many things [referring to the working of the Spirit] in vain?" he goes on. Later, in 4:5–6 (cf. Rom 8:15) he again refers to this experience, this time with the metaphor of adoption as children; and again the Spirit, who has made them children as evidenced by the Spirit's crying out to God as *Abba*, is clearly the crucial element in terms of their actual experience of conversion.

Titus 3:4–7 is significant in yet another way, since Paul here describes conversion in language that has a clearly creedal ring to it. What is remarkable is the crucial role the Spirit plays in this formulation, even preceding mention of the work of Christ in this case, since the emphasis is on what has happened to the believer. God has saved them, the creed goes, through the washing and renewing work of the Spirit, whom God lavishly poured out on them through Christ the Savior.

For Paul, therefore, whatever else happens at Christian conversion, it is the experience of the Spirit that is crucial; and therefore it is the Spirit alone who identifies God's people in the present eschatological age.

3. In three texts Paul distinguishes believers from nonbelievers in terms of the former having the Spirit, while the latter do not (1 Cor 2:6–16; 12:3; Rom 8:9). Most significant of these is 1 Cor 2:6–16, where he sets out the basic contrasts between the "natural" and "spiritual" person. The "natural person" is one who does not have the Spirit and is therefore incapable of understanding what God has done through the cross; whereas the opposite prevails for the believer. Likewise no one can make the basic Christian confession of Jesus as Lord, except by the Holy Spirit (1 Cor 12:3); and, finally, he says it plainly, "If anyone does not have the Spirit, that person does not belong to Christ at all" (Rom 8:9). In a former time Paul had divided the world between "us" and "them" in terms of "Jews" and "Gentiles." The new division is between those who belong to Christ and those who do not; and what characterizes the former is that they have the Spirit, while the others do not. Whatever else, the newly constituted eschatological people of God are Spirit people. They have come to life by the life-giving Spirit (Gal 5:25; 2 Cor 3:3, 6); they walk by the Spirit, and they are led by the Spirit. For Paul therefore to "get saved" means first of all to "receive the Spirit."

THE PAULINE SOTERIOLOGICAL METAPHORS

How Paul perceived this converting work of the Spirit is best seen by looking at his various soteriological metaphors. On the one hand, the more common metaphors are seldom used in conjunction with the Spirit.

Justification is connected with the Spirit in 1 Cor 6:11;[10] redemption, propitiation, and reconciliation are not at all. The reason for this is close at hand; these metaphors emphasize the positional or relational aspect of salvation and therefore are used exclusively to refer to Christ's saving work in our behalf. On the other hand, metaphors that emphasize the believer's *experience* of salvation are frequently expressed in Spirit language.

1. *Adoption.* This metaphor appears first in Gal 4:4–6, where Paul contrasts living under Law with the life of faith, life in the Spirit. Living under Law is like being a son before he has attained his majority; he may technically own the whole estate, but he is still no better off than a slave. So with believers, who are no longer under slavery (which for the sake of Paul's Gentile readers is seen as slavery to the "powers," the so-called elements of the world); rather they are "sons" with full rights, the evidence of which is their experience of the Spirit, especially the Spirit's cry in them of "*Abba*, Father." Thus, the primary evidence that we are God's "sons" is that the Spirit within us cries out in the very language of Jesus, the Son. This emphasis is heightened in the Romans parallel, where our ongoing recognition of our "sonship" is the result of "the Spirit himself bearing witness with our spirits that we are the children of God." To which Paul appends, "and if children, then heirs; heirs of God, and fellow-heirs with Christ."

The difficulties in the Galatians text come with v. 6, where Paul, in making his new point (after vv. 4–5), starts the sentence by saying that *because* they are "sons," God has sent the Spirit of his Son into their hearts. That sounds as if the one thing (objective sonship) preceded the other (the gift of the Spirit). But this "awkwardness" is the result of reading the text as though Paul were offering a chronology of individual salvation. But v. 5 does not refer to the individual believer's salvation history at all. Rather, Paul here presents the work of Christ as an objective, once-for-all, historical reality, by which Christ procured "adoption" for all who would ever trust him. The experience of the individual believer is historically subsequent to and predicated on this prior work of Christ. Thus, the cause and effect relationship is that between "sonship" provided for us by Christ's death on the cross, and "sonship" as actualized experientially by the Spirit in the life of the believer. That Paul has little concern for the "ordering" of things can be seen both from 3:2–5, where the Spirit alone is the key to their conversion, and from the parallel in Rom 8:15–17, where the Spirit is understood as responsible for adoption. Hence Paul's intent in both texts is to remind believers that their reception of the Spirit is what *makes* them children, as is *evidenced* by the cry "*Abba*."

---

[10]Most likely in terms of the believer's appropriation. Cf. Rom 14:17, although only indirectly (see ch. 7, pp. 620–21, n. 449).

Nor should we pass too quickly over the significance of this cry, pointed out in our discussion of Gal 4:6. Here is the certain evidence of our entrance into God's family; we speak to God in the language of family. This is not simply the language of infancy; in Semitic homes it was the language of children of all ages, expressing both intimacy and special relatedness. What may begin as "baby-talk" is not thereby to be outgrown; on the contrary it is to be grown into. That we are the beloved children of the eternal God is knowledge "shed abroad in our hearts by the Spirit" (Rom 5:5) and by that same Spirit is manifest in our lifelong cry to God as our heavenly *Abba*, the one on whom we depend for everything. The experience of the Spirit should lead the believer not only to a position of justification before God but also to an ongoing awareness of the privileges of childhood—personal relationship and companionship with God himself. Being "in the presence of God" through Christ and by the Spirit (2 Cor 2:17; Eph 2:18) was for Paul not a cause for fear, but for confidence in his Spirit-anointed ministry.

2. *Washing/Rebirth/Life-giving.* These three terms need to be examined together, partly because in some cases they occur in the same texts and partly because some issues raised by them belong in discussion together.

a. The metaphor "washing" as a work of the Spirit first occurs in 1 Cor 6:11. Many see here reference to baptism, especially in this case because it is followed by the phrase "in the name of the Lord Jesus Christ," which is argued to be a baptismal formula. But as pointed out in the exegesis, that runs aground both on Paul's usage elsewhere and on the structure of the sentence, where both prepositions modify all three verbs.[11] That it might allude to baptism need not be doubted, but in context the emphasis falls on the metaphor of "washing away of sin," especially those sins just mentioned in vv. 9–10. Our point is that the Spirit is specifically singled out as the means of such "cleansing."

This metaphor occurs again, along with the metaphors of "rebirth" and "renewal," in the very difficult phrase in Tit 3:5. As the central feature of salvation Paul says (literally), "God saved us . . . through washing of rebirth and renewal of the Holy Spirit." Although there are some inherent difficulties with this phrase, the evidence points most strongly to an interpretation that sees this not as referring to two experiences (the washing of rebirth and the renewal of the Spirit = baptism and confirmation, or conversion and Spirit baptism), but to one (a washing that involves rebirth and renewal, all of which are effected by the Spirit).

But opinion is also divided among those who take this position. Does "washing" refer to water baptism or more simply to the "washing away

---

[11] That is, "in the name of our Lord Jesus" and "by the Spirit of our God" together modify the three verbs "washed, sanctified, justified."

of sin," and what relationship does the Spirit have to this "washing"? Again, that it probably alludes to "baptism" one need not doubt; but that Paul uses a metaphor and *not* the word "baptism" itself implies that his own emphasis is on the metaphor as such, not on the event of baptism. In any case, the final genitive, "of the Spirit," is the key to the whole. Salvation is not appropriated through baptism—that is foreign to Paul (see below)—but through the work of the Spirit, which in this case is imaged as a "new birth" (cf. John 3:3) or a "renewal" in the new believer's life.

b. The two words "new birth" and "renewal" are as close as one comes to the concept of "regeneration" by the Spirit in the Pauline corpus. But if this metaphor is itself infrequent, the idea behind it is thoroughly Pauline, namely, that at the beginning of one's life in Christ one has been given life by the Spirit himself. Such "new life" is otherwise pictured as a "renewal" (cf. Rom 12:2; Col 3:10). Absolutely basic to Paul's understanding of becoming a believer in Christ, therefore, is not simply that one is given a new "objective standing" with God—redeemed, forgiven, cleansed, "justified." In Paul's view, the "washing" is that "of the Spirit," which includes rebirth and renewal. By the Spirit God not only cleanses people from past sins, but also transforms them into his people, "reborn" and "renewed" so as to reflect God's likeness in their lives.

Paul understands a radical change to have taken place at conversion; it means a thoroughgoing reorientation of one's entire life. This "radicalization" of life is directly tied to the work of the Spirit. Theologically one may refer to this as a "rebirth," even though that metaphor is not front and center in Paul's view of things. For him, because his primary focus is always on the work of Christ, what happens to the believer is "death" and "resurrection" (2 Cor 5:14; Gal 5:24; Rom 6:1-6; Col 2:20–3:4). And this is where conversion as the experience of the "life-giving Spirit" comes in.

c. Whatever else may be said about God in the Old Testament, the main reality about him, which is revealed even in his name, is that Yahweh is the living and life-giving God. That God lives and gives life to all that lives is absolutely foundational to biblical faith. What is crucial to Pauline understanding of Christian conversion is that the Spirit whom believers receive is none other than the "Spirit of life" (Rom 8:2, 6), who "gives life" to those who turn to Christ (2 Cor 3:6). For Paul the old (flesh, sin, Torah observance) has been crucified (Gal 5:24); we have been raised with Christ to live in "the newness of the Spirit" (Rom 7:6). If anyone is in Christ, *a new creation*; the old (life κατὰ σάρκα) is gone; the new (life κατὰ πνεῦμα) has come. This is why Christian conversion from Paul's perspective also includes walking in "newness of life." Thus he implores, following his assertion that the flesh was crucified with Christ, that "if we live (following our crucifixion with Christ) by the Spirit, then let us also behave in keeping with the self-same Spirit" (Gal 5:25). For Paul there is no such thing as a believer who is not thereby brought to life—life now and forever—by the coming of the life-giving Spirit. But such life must manifest itself in the radically new life of God given by the Spirit.

Paul's understanding of Christian conversion as essentially the work of the Spirit, therefore, has no place in it for the "white-washed sinner," the person who is still sinful, but "justified before God" anyway. The only coming to Christ known to Paul is one in which the life of the believer has been invaded by the life-giving Spirit, who not only applied the redemptive work of the cross but also transformed one from within, by the "renewing of the mind" (Rom 12:2). All of Paul's metaphors of "before" and "after," therefore, speak in the same way of the radical transformation of life that the Spirit brings (death/life; old ἄνθρωπος [person]/new person; darkness/light; etc.), which is also brought into focus by the next metaphor as well.

3. *Sanctification.* Paul's primary use of the term "sanctification" is also as a metaphor for conversion, not a reference to a work of grace *following* conversion. This can be seen most clearly in 2 Thes 2:13, where Paul refers to the Thessalonians' experience of salvation as being effected "by sanctification of the Spirit and belief in the truth." The metaphor is drawn from Jewish religious practices, where the sacred rites and utensils have become so by their having been "sanctified" unto God, i.e., set apart solely for God's holy purposes. This same use of the metaphor, referring now especially to Gentile conversions under Paul's ministry, is found in Rom 15:16. The Jewish Christians in Rome may not call "common or unclean" (because of failure to be circumcised) those whom God has "sanctified" by the Spirit. The Gentiles' reception of the Spirit was God's ultimate act of creating for himself a "sanctified offering" composed of both Gentile and Jew. On the other hand, the usage of the same imagery to refer to the Corinthians' conversion (1 Cor 6:11) is intended to emphasize that conversion includes the sanctifying work of the Spirit that disallows the kind of behavior in which they formerly engaged. "Such were some of you," he asserts, "but you have been . . . sanctified . . . by the Spirit of our God."

4. When one adds to these the metaphors "anointing," "seal," "down payment," and "firstfruits" (see ch. 12 above), firm conclusions can be drawn: (a) The wide variety of metaphors in itself indicates that no single one will do. The work of Christ, appropriated by the Spirit in Christian conversion, is simply too multifaceted to be captured by a single metaphor. In almost every case the choice of metaphors is related to the perspective on the human condition that is addressed in the context. Thus, *propitiation* responds to our being under God's *wrath*; *redemption* to our being *enslaved* to sin; *justification* to our guilt before the *Law*; *reconciliation* to our being God's *enemies*; *sanctification* to our being *unholy*;

washing to our being *unclean*; etc. (b) The metaphors tend to be used in keeping with the emphasis of the moment, thus the point in context is what is at issue, not the precise timing or relationships in conversion. (c) There is no such thing as Christian conversion that does not have the coming of the Spirit into the believer's life as the crucial ingredient. However variously expressed, the presence of the Spirit is the one constant. (d) It is highly doubtful whether Paul saw the Spirit as connected directly to water baptism or whether his language implies yet a second experience of the Spirit after conversion. To these latter two issues we must turn in further detail.

THE SPIRIT AND WATER BAPTISM

In the early church water baptism was the believer's immediate response to God's saving action by the Spirit. Since some of the texts discussed above may seem to suggest a close connection between the two, some (esp. within the liturgical Christian traditions) have argued that the Spirit actually comes to the believer through the event of baptism itself—much like the dove descended on Jesus in the waters of baptism, which is viewed as a paradigm for later Christians.[12] The key texts here are 1 Cor 6:11; 12:13; and Tit 3:5, although some would add Gal 3:28–4:6, the imagery of the "seal" in 2 Cor 1:21–22, and Eph 1:13–14; 4:30.[13]

The problem here is partly methodological (how does one proceed to discover the Pauline perspective?) and partly ecclesiological (one tends to argue on the basis of one's own experience of the church, not on the basis of the biblical data[14]). There are basically three avenues of approach, none of which is totally free from the factor of bias: (1) to look at the texts themselves, which we have done in the preceding exegetical chapters; (2) to look at texts where Paul speaks about water baptism in an unambiguous way, and see whether they might also be seen as connected to the Spirit in some way; and (3) to look at the texts where conversion is unambiguously expressed in terms of the Spirit and see whether baptism might also be presupposed.

---

[12]A paradigm, interestingly, which Pentecostals have seen as expressing Spirit baptism as subsequent to his birth by the Spirit.

[13]What follows assumes the exegesis of these texts from Part I.

[14]One is interested to read in Hoyle (*Holy Spirit*, 32), for example, that "in the early church . . . the reception of the Spirit *generally followed* upon baptism, though in exceptional cases it might precede it" (emphases mine), with the "exceptions" in Acts noted in a footnote. Since the "exceptions" are significantly more numerous than the "rule," one might think the exception was the rule!

1. In the preceding exegetical chapters, we examined in some detail texts where "baptism" and "the Spirit" appear in collocation and concluded that in Paul no direct tie exists between water baptism and the reception of the Spirit. Some further observations about these texts might be useful. First, the actual language of "baptism" and "the Spirit" occurs in collocation only once in Paul, in 1 Cor 12:13. Metaphorical language appears in the other texts, which may or may not refer to baptism; but even if it does, as seems likely in some cases, Paul makes no direct tie between baptism itself and the reception of the Spirit. Second, we have noted that it is altogether unlikely, given that there are no contemporary linguistic grounds for it at all, that Paul understood the metaphor "seal" to refer to baptism—especially so, since in one of these passages at least the seal is nearly equated with the Spirit (2 Cor 1:21–22, "God sealed you by[15] giving you the Holy Spirit"). Third, the only "connection" between baptism and the Spirit in these passages is conceptual, i.e., the metaphors for baptism and the mention of the Spirit happen to occur in the same sentence. What is missing is a direct link between the metaphor and the coming of the Spirit. In fact, in no place does Paul express the kind of relationship between the two that those assume who assert that baptism is the place where one *receives* the Spirit. Indeed, apart from 1 Cor 12:13, Paul always puts the relationship in instrumental terms, where the Spirit is responsible for the "washing" or "sealing." To argue for the other relationship at least one piece of direct, explicit evidence would seem to be required.

That leads to a few further words about the one text where the two words actually occur together: First, one should note again that Paul's actual language has to do not with the reception of the Spirit at water baptism, but with the believer being "baptized *in* the Spirit." In light of Pauline usage one is hard pressed to suggest that this is a "metaphor" for water baptism.

Second, as to the text in its context, Paul's concern in saying that they were "all baptized ("immersed") ἐν ("in") one Spirit εἰς ("into") one body, . . . and all were made to drink to the fill of the one Spirit," is *not* to explain how people become believers, but how believers from such diverse sociological contexts (Jew, Greek, slave, free) all form the one body of Christ. To make this point, Paul, with a fine piece of Semitic parallelism, uses two metaphors (immersion into and drinking one's fill of) to express their common, lavish experience of the Spirit, almost certainly at their conversion(s). Moreover, Paul's usage elsewhere strongly suggests that the prepositions ἐν and εἰς should be translated respectively as locative (the Spirit is the "element" into which they were

---

[15]This to take the καί that joins these participles as a hendiadys, suggesting that the two for all practical purposes are saying one and the same thing.

submerged) and telic (= so as to form one body). The point is that Paul is not referring to water baptism at all—although again an allusion to it might be recognized. That falls outside his frame of reference in this context. *It is not baptism that makes them one body; it is the Spirit*—as the Corinthians themselves would agree, which is why Paul uses such a metaphor in the first place. In the context his ultimate interest is to argue for the need for *diversity* in the one body. To achieve his purpose he must appeal to the fact that they are indeed one body, and as they should well appreciate, the Spirit alone makes them one.

The result, therefore, is that in no text does Paul associate the gift of the Spirit with water baptism, either as cause and effect or as occurring experientially at the same time.

2. Paul's explicit and unambiguous references to water baptism support this claim regarding the relationship between the two: 1 Cor 1:13–17 (cf. 10:2; 15:29); Gal 3:27; Rom 6:3–4; Col 2:12; Eph 4:5. Two features about these passages stand out. First, in every instance the association between the believer and baptism is invariably with reference to Christ, not to the Spirit. Two instances are especially instructive. In Gal 3:27 Paul refers to "putting on Christ." This is precisely the kind of language that is missing throughout the corpus with regard to the Spirit. That is, in baptism one is pictured as being clothed with Christ, but never so with the Spirit. Moreover, in Eph 4:4–6 Paul deliberately, in a highly creedal way, associates various facets of Christian life with the Spirit and with Christ. The one body and one hope are associated with the Spirit; faith and baptism are associated with Christ.

Second, despite all disclaimers, in 1 Cor 1:13–17 Paul deliberately subordinates baptism to the proclamation of the gospel. This does not mean that he minimizes baptism; what he will not allow is that it holds the same level of significance as the preaching of Christ. My point: *in this same argument he specifically associates the reception of the Spirit with his proclamation of the gospel, not with baptism.* In Paul's mind baptism stands on a different level, apparently as response to grace received through the Spirit's coming in connection with the hearing of faith at the time of proclamation. It is nearly unthinkable that Paul could speak so casually of baptism and of his having baptized only two of them (plus one household that he had to be reminded of!), if in fact he understood the Spirit to come at their baptism. But in 2:1–5, he insists that the Spirit came on *them* precisely at the point of *his* ministry, through proclamation, which would hardly be true if it came during baptism, since he baptized so few of them, one of whom he had actually forgotten about (1:14).

3. This last text seems conclusive that Paul understood the reception of the Spirit to take place at conversion, in the hearing of the gospel by faith, not later at baptism. One can scarcely imagine Paul to have argued the way he does in 1 Cor 1:13–2:5, if in fact the Spirit came on believers at baptism. This is supported further by most of the texts we have already

noted in this chapter. Thus, for example, in Gal 3:2–5 the reception of the Spirit, Paul says, which came by faith and was dramatic and evidential, is the certain evidence that the Galatians belong to the newly constituted people of God. Nothing in this text even remotely suggests that Paul presupposes this reception to have taken place at baptism; indeed, his argument loses its point if the reception of the Spirit were simply being transferred from one rite (circumcision) to another (baptism). This could perhaps look like an inconclusive argument from silence were it not for the several texts in which Paul ties his converts' reception of the Spirit directly to his own proclamation of the gospel. For Paul the Spirit came in the context of his preaching and of their hearing the gospel (1 Thes 1:5; Rom 15:16, 18–19). By his own admission he rarely engaged in the actual baptizing of converts. Thus, it seems scarcely possible that Paul himself understood the reception of the Spirit to be in response to their baptism in water. For him it would have been exactly the opposite.

This is not to say, of course, that at times what is pictured by Luke in a passage like Acts 19:1–7 did not happen in the Pauline context. But what all of this evidence together does suggest is that the close tie of water baptism to the Spirit does not come from a close reading of Paul, but stems from reading back into Paul the later experience of the church.

CONVERSION AND SPIRIT BAPTISM

The urgent question on the nonliturgical side, especially for the various Spirit movements that have left their mark on the church throughout its history, is whether Paul also envisaged a work of grace beyond conversion to which the language "the baptism of the Spirit" might correctly apply. To be sure, some of the Pauline texts have been interpreted in this way (e.g., 1 Cor 12:13; Gal 4:4–6),[16] but the full contextual data make this doubtful. On the other hand, whether Paul *knew* of such an experience is a moot point, argued against primarily on the basis of silence. Two further points need to be made.

First, as was pointed out in chapter 2 and throughout, Paul makes a clear connection between the Spirit and the experience of power. What becomes evident from the preceding discussion is that the Spirit was not

---

[16]See, e.g., Horton, *What the Bible Says about the Holy Spirit*, 215–17, cf. 173. The most ambitious attempt in this regard is by Ervin, *Conversion-Initiation*, which for the most part does not succeed in convincing, precisely because he came to the texts with a non-Pauline agenda in hand and simply "exegeted" them accordingly; H. Hunter, *Spirit-Baptism*, whose exegesis fares only a little better, is more cautious, and tries to open the door to the possibility that several texts in Paul make room for such.

only *experienced* in conversion, but was experienced in a *dynamic*, undoubtedly *visible*, way. This is precisely why Paul appeals to the Spirit, the lavish experience of Spirit, to make his points in both Gal 3:2–4 and 1 Cor 12:13. This is made the more certain by Gal 3:5, where as further evidence that the Galatians have no relationship to Law, Paul specifically appeals to their ongoing experience of the Spirit as dynamically present among them with miraculous deeds—one can scarcely interpret the two present tenses otherwise ("God gives the Spirit and works miracles among you"). By reemphasizing this dimension of Christian life in their experience of "baptism," Spirit movements tend (correctly, I would argue) to see themselves as having recaptured what is at the heart of Paul's understanding of the Spirit and Christian life, even if they have (less convincingly) also made a virtue out of their timing of this dimension as well.[17]

Second, as is pointed out in the next chapter, Paul does not see life in the Spirit as the result of a single experience of the Spirit at conversion. The Spirit is the key to all of Christian life, and frequently Paul implies there are further, ongoing appropriations of the Spirit's empowering. This is certainly intended in Gal 3:5; it is the further implication of such present tense verbs as in 1 Thes 4:8 and Eph 5:18, and the consequence of prayer in Phil 1:19. In 1 Thes 4:8 Paul's first referent is surely to their conversion; but the argument in context and the verb's present tense ("God *gives* you his Holy Spirit") imply that what happened at conversion needs renewed appropriation in light of their pagan past. All of this suggests that perhaps too much is made on both sides of single experiences. For Paul life in the Spirit begins at conversion; at the same time that experience is both dynamic and renewable.

Life in the Spirit

Although I have argued to the contrary, the reading of this chapter might lead one to believe that "salvation in Christ" for Paul had to do with conversion, pure and simple. Nothing could be further from the Pauline perspective. To "get saved" from his perspective means to be joined to the people of God by the Spirit; and to "be saved" means "to live the life of the saved person." Conversion by the Spirit involved a commitment to a life of walking in the Spirit, being led by the Spirit, sowing to the Spirit. The Spirit who engenders the faith by which one

---

[17]On this question, see G. D. Fee, "Baptism in the Holy Spirit: The Issue of Separability and Subsequence," in *Gospel and Spirit* (Peabody, Mass.: Hendrickson, 1991) 105–19.

believes (2 Cor 4:13) is the same Spirit whose fruit in the believer's life includes "faith," meaning now "faithful walking in his ways." The primary way this tends to surface in Paul is in the area of ethical life. But for him it meant far more than that. The whole of one's new eschatological life is now lived in and by the Spirit. We will take up ethical life in the next chapter; my concern here is to emphasize the place of the Spirit in the whole of the ongoing life of the individual believer.

Part of the present concern is to point out that the dichotomy that so often occurs in the church between the people of God and the individual is a false one as far as Pauline experience and theology are concerned. Moreover, this dichotomy sometimes takes the form of resistance to personal piety, including "spirituality," in the name of corporate church life, that is, of "belonging to the church," or assenting to its common faith. All pietistic movements come into being in response to a tendency for the individual's relationship with God to get lost or swallowed up in some form of "churchiness." Paul's understanding of the role of the Spirit in the church as the people of God is addressed in the next chapter. Here I want to enter a plea, a Pauline plea if you will, for personal piety and spirituality as a part of life in the Spirit.

OTHER SPIRIT ACTIVITY

As noted above, not all of ongoing Christian life comes under the rubric of ethics. All sorts of other activities are also seen to be the work of the Spirit. Most of these belong to the life of the individual believer. What they demonstrate is how wide-ranging is Paul's view of "salvation in Christ" as life empowered by the Spirit.

For example, our experience of hope—for the certain future noted in chapter 13—is empowered by the Spirit (Gal 5:5; Rom 15:13). Colossians 1:9 indicates that the Spirit also renews, or illumines, the mind so that believers may understand what God's will is (cf. Rom 12:1–2). Similarly, in Rom 9:1 Paul implies that his clear conscience about what he will say as to his own yearning for his fellow-countryfolk is the work of the Spirit in his life. If Rom 12:11 refers to the Spirit at work in the believer's spirit, then the Spirit is also the source of zeal for service. And in Phil 1:19, Paul expects the combination of their praying and the "supply of the Spirit" to make it possible for him to experience either deliverance or death without shaming the gospel, and to the glory of Christ. Furthermore, and even though he makes little of it with regard to apostleship, the Spirit is the key to Paul's "many visions and revelations" (2 Cor 12:1). Again, for him it is not a matter of "either-or," but of "both-and." Life in the Spirit is full and wide-ranging. Indeed, if our understanding of Rom 8:28 is correct, the Spirit, who intercedes in our behalf according to God's will, is also at work in our lives in all things in order to bring about God's ultimate good.

All of these texts together demonstrate further what has already been said—that Paul's view of life in Christ is so thoroughly dominated by the Spirit that the Spirit is the one absolutely essential ingredient for that life. Moreover, both the community imperative in Eph 5:18 ("be filled with the Spirit") and the individual imperative to Timothy in 2 Tim 1:6–7 ("fan the gift into flame") imply the need for ongoing appropriation. The Spirit's presence is the crucial matter, but that presence does not automatically ensure a quickened, fervent spiritual life. Both individuals and the church as a whole are exhorted to keep the gift aflame. One way of doing that, of course, is by mutual encouragement and growth in the context of corporate life, especially in worship. But at the individual level the way to such life is through prayer and by having an awareness that by the Spirit one now lives in the presence of God. On these matters Paul himself serves as exhibit A.

THE SPIRIT AND PRAYER[18]

One of the more remarkable incongruities in Pauline studies is that thousands of books exist that search every aspect of Paul's "thinking," while only a very few seek to come to terms with his life of prayer. Indeed, most people's understanding of Paul is limited either to "Paul the missionary" or to "Paul the theologian." But what is clear from Paul's letters is that he was a *pray-er* before he was a "missioner" or a thinker. His life was devoted to prayer; and his relationship with his converts was primarily sustained by way of thanksgiving and prayer. To eliminate prayer from Paul's personal piety would be to investigate the workings of a gas-combustible engine without recognizing the significance of oil. Paul did not simply believe in prayer, or talk about prayer. He prayed, regularly and continuously, and urged the same on his churches (1 Thes 5:16–18). This is undoubtedly a carry-over from his life before Christ. What needs to be noted here is that for Paul prayer in particular has been radically transformed by the coming of the Spirit.

Whether set prayers were ever said in the Pauline churches cannot be known; in any case, spontaneous prayer by the Spirit is the norm.[19] The beginning of Christian life is marked by the indwelling Spirit's crying

---

[18]On this question see my contribution to the James Houston Festschrift ("Some Reflections on Pauline Spirituality," in *Alive to God: Studies in Spirituality*, 96–107). See also K. Stendahl, "Paul at Prayer" (ch. 7, n. 304); and more recently, D. A. Carson, *A Call to Spiritual Reformation: Priorities from Paul and His Prayers* (Grand Rapids: Baker, 1992).

[19]It has sometimes been noted, as a word either against the personality of the Spirit or against Paul's Trinitarianism, that the Spirit is never invoked in prayer, as are the Father and the Son. Precisely, but the inference being drawn is incorrect. The role of the Spirit in prayer is a different one; he is our divine "pray-er," the one *through* whom we pray, not the one *to* whom prayer is directed.

out "*Abba*" to God (Gal 4:6; Rom 8:15). "On all occasions," Paul urges elsewhere, "pray in/by the Spirit," which is to include every form of prayer (Eph 6:18), including prayer for the enabling of evangelism. With prayer in particular the Spirit helps us in our "already/not yet" existence. Because in our present weakness we do not know for what to pray, the Spirit himself makes intercession for us with "inarticulate groanings" (Rom 8:26–27), which most likely refers to glossolalia.

Prayer (and praise), therefore, seems the best way to view Paul's understanding of glossolalia. At no point in 1 Corinthians 14 does Paul suggest that tongues is speech directed toward people;[20] three times he indicates that it is speech directed toward God (14:2, 14–16, 28). In vv. 14–16 he specifically refers to tongues as "praying with my S/spirit"; and in v. 2 such prayer is described as "speaking mysteries to God," which is why the *mind* of the speaker is left unfruitful, and also why such prayer without interpretation is not to be part of the corporate setting. Paul himself engaged in such prayer so frequently that he can say boldly to a congregation that treasured this gift that he prayed in tongues more than any of them (1 Cor 14:18). Prayer of this kind for Paul was not ecstasy; it meant the Spirit's praying through his spirit without the burden of his mind and in conversation with God. We can trust the Spirit in such prayer, he argues in Rom 8:26–27, precisely because such prayer is a form of the Spirit's assisting us in our weaknesses and God knows the mind of the Spirit, that he prays in keeping with God's will.

Praying "in the Spirit" (however that is to be understood) is also God's provision for his people in another area of weakness—in the ongoing struggle "against the principalities and powers." Besides the defensive armor provided by the gospel, Paul urges the believers to use their two "Spirit weapons" as they engage the enemy: the message of the gospel (penetrating the enemy's territory and rescuing people who are captive to him) and "praying in the Spirit" (Eph 6:18–20). Here in partic- ular the Spirit is our true friend and aid. Precisely because we do not know how to pray as we ought we need to lean more heavily on "praying in/by the Spirit" so as to carry on such "spiritual warfare" more effec- tively. Prayer, therefore, is not simply our cry of desperation or our "grocery list" of requests that we bring before our heavenly *Abba;* prayer is an activity inspired by God himself, through his Holy Spirit. It is God siding with his people and, by his own empowering presence, the Spirit of God himself, bringing forth prayer that is in keeping with his will and his ways.

It is probably impossible to understand Paul as a theologian, if one does not take this dimension of his "Spirit-uality" with full seriousness.

---

[20]As pointed out on 1 Cor 14:5, the interpretation of a tongue does not thereby turn it into human directed speech, but interprets the mystery spoken to God referred to in v. 2.

A prayerless life is one of practical atheism. As one who himself lived in and by the Spirit, Paul understood prayer in particular to be the special prompting of the Spirit, leading him to thanksgiving for others and petition "in the Spirit," even when he did not know for what specifically to pray. Whatever else "life in the Spirit" meant for Paul, it meant a life devoted to prayer, accompanied by joy and thanksgiving.

In this context we should perhaps also include one of the more imponderable dimensions of Pauline Spirituality, the place of visions and revelations. We know about these only because Paul is stepping over onto the Corinthians' turf momentarily in order to dissuade them of the relevance of such experiences as authenticating his—or anyone else's—apostleship (2 Cor 12:1–10; cf. the discussion of 5:13). What needs to be noted is (1) that Paul clearly affirms that he has had such experiences and apparently has had them often; but (2) he disallows that they have any value at all in authenticating ministry. Very much as with glossolalia, therefore, we learn about such matters in his life in the Spirit only because the Corinthians made too much of them. Obviously for Paul both of these kinds of Spirit experiences belonged to his private relationship with God; thus he simply never speaks about them on his own. "Ecstasy" for him was a matter between himself and God; before others he will only be "sober-minded" (2 Cor 5:13).

How different from so much of church history! A parade of private Spirit experiences has all too often been the first "credential" brought forward to authenticate ministry or spirituality. For Paul there was plenty of Spirit activity that had to do with God's dealings with others for him to point to, and usually from within a context of personal weakness (see ch. 12 above.); thus such moments as those described in such self-effacing terms as in 2 Cor 12:1–6 were undoubtedly moments highlighting the richness of his life in the Spirit, life for him in the personal presence of God. But these were too private to be either promoted or paraded.

SPIRIT LIFE AND THE PRESENCE OF GOD

As was pointed out in chapter 13, whatever else the Spirit meant in Paul's understanding, it meant at least that the desire for God's presence had been fulfilled by the coming of the Spirit. While this imagery, as in the Old Testament, refers primarily to the church as God's temple, the place of God's habitation, there are two texts in particular that indicate that Paul also understood this imagery in terms of the individual believer. And herein, I would argue, lies the secret to Paul's personal piety and to his understanding of the Spirit in his own personal life. In both cases, the texts finally point outward; that is, the goal of this dimension of Spirit life is not simply contemplation, but the ethical life that the Spirit produces. Nonetheless, the personal dimension cannot be set aside.

The first text is 1 Cor 6:19–20, where Paul reapplies to the individual believer's body the temple imagery that elsewhere refers to the church corporately. Here is the certain evidence that Paul understood the presence motif of the Old Testament, which Isa 63:9–14 had already equated with the Holy Spirit, to be fulfilled in the life of the individual believer as well as in the gathered community of believers. Indeed, the first locus of God's presence in the new covenant is within his people, sanctifying their present existence and stamping it with his own eternity.

But as is often true of imagery in Paul, by its very fluidity in another context it takes a quite different turn. Part of our way into a proper understanding of 2 Cor 2:14–4:6 is through the combined imagery of "tabernacle/temple" and "presence." It begins in 2:17 with Paul's arguing as to the validity of his ministry—in contrast to the peddlers of another gospel—that he makes his claim as one who "lives in the presence of God."[21] This motif is then picked up in 3:7 and carried through to the end by the contrast of his ministry with that of Moses. Eventually this evolves into a kind of midrash on Moses' being veiled when he came *from* the presence of God, whereas he was "unveiled" when he entered the tabernacle of the Presence. Believers are those who now turn to the Lord, identified as the Spirit of the Lord, the key to God's presence in the present age. By the Spirit we are now unveiled so as to behold the glory of the Lord. It is the play on veil and Spirit that makes the argument so telling; the Spirit of the Presence has now removed the veil—most likely now also alluding to the veil keeping people away from God's presence within the temple. The result is that by the Spirit's coming, the veil is removed, both from our faces and from the presence, so that we can behold the glory of the Lord himself in the face of God's Son, our Lord Jesus Christ.

As we pointed out in the exegesis on this passage, here Paul enters the holy place. By the Spirit's presence one is now behind the veil in the very presence of God, not only beholding God's glory in Christ, but also being transformed into God's likeness from one degree of glory to another. Here is the place where the *Abba*-cry evolves into praise and adoration, and where his children are transformed from the likeness of their former "father," the god of this world who still blinds the hearts of those who do not believe, into the likeness of God himself, so as to bear his image in our present "already but not yet" existence. This is not the only thing Paul believes the Spirit to be doing in our present world, but it is one very significant thing, and we miss Paul by a wide margin if we do not pay close attention to it.

Thus "salvation in Christ" not only begins by the Spirit, it is the ongoing work of the Spirit in every area and avenue of Christian life. We miss both Paul's own life in Christ and his understanding of salvation if we do not see the central role the Spirit plays at every juncture.[22]

---

[21]For this point I am indebted esp. to D. A. Renwick, *Paul*.

[22]On this point see the citations from Pinnock and Neill in ch. 1 (n. 1) above.

15

THE SPIRIT AND THE PEOPLE OF GOD

If "salvation in Christ" is the essence of Pauline theology, then any discussion of that theology requires a careful look at his understanding of the people of God, since for Paul this is the arena in which salvation is being worked out. As noted in the preceding chapter, even though in Paul's new eschatological framework a person becomes a member of the people of God individually, the goal of salvation has remained the same as in the old covenant: "a people for God's name." On this matter, therefore, there is both continuity and discontinuity between Paul and the Old Testament. The continuity lies with the reality that God is saving a people; the discontinuity concerns how God's people are now constituted. It is still by election and grace, to be sure; but election has now taken place in Christ, and people are elect by virtue of their association with Christ through the Spirit.

That Paul is at one with his heritage on the matter of "a people for God's name" is confirmed first of all by his use of Old Testament "people" language to refer to the newly constituted people of God. Thus they are God's λαός ("people"),[1] God's "saints" (οἱ ἅγιοι),[2] because they are God's "elect."[3] Indeed, those who live by the canon of "neither circumcision

---

[1] See 2 Cor 6:16–18; Tit 2:14. Although not particularly popular with Greek writers, λαός was the word chosen by the LXX translators to render the Hebrew עַם, the most frequently used word in the OT (over 2000 times) to express the special relationship Israel had with Yahweh. Their choice of λαός was probably because the more common word ἔθνος was used by Greek writers to refer to themselves as a people in the same way the Hebrews used עַם. Thus for the Jews ἔθνος had come to mean "Gentile," and was so used by the LXX translators. This meant they needed a different word to distinguish themselves.

[2] Although not frequent in the OT, the designation of Israel as God's "holy people" occurs in the crucial covenantal passage in Exod 19:5–6, an expression that in later Judaism referred to the elect who were to share in the blessings of the messianic kingdom (Dan 7:18–27; Ps Sol 17; Qumran); this is Paul's primary term for God's newly formed, eschatological people.

[3] Gk. ἐκλεκτός and cognates; see 1 Thes 1:4; 2 Thes 2:13; Col 3:12; Eph 1:4, 11. As in the OT the term refers not to individual election but to a people who have been

nor uncircumcision" are the "Israel of God" (Gal 6:16), a phrase unique to Paul in all of biblical literature. But the most common designation is "the church" (ἐκκλησία), which for Paul derives not primarily from the Greek *polis*, but from the LXX, where ἐκκλησία is regularly used to translate the Hebrew *qāhāl*, referring most often to the "congregation of Israel." This abundant use of Old Testament "people" language makes it clear that Paul saw the church not only as in continuity with the old covenant people of God, but as in the true succession of that people.

One of the essential features of this continuity is the corporate nature of God's people. God chose, and made a covenant with, not individual Israelites but a people, who would bear God's name and be for God's purposes. Although individual Israelites could forfeit their position in Israel, this never affected God's design or purposes with the people as his people. This is true even when the majority failed, and the "people" were reduced to a "remnant." That remnant was still Israel—loved, chosen, and redeemed by God.

This is the thoroughgoing perspective of Paul as well, but at the same time, as noted in chapter 14, Christ's coming and the gift of the eschatological Spirit also marked the new way by which God's people are constituted. The community is now entered individually through faith in Christ and through the reception of the Spirit, signalled by baptism. Nonetheless, the church itself is the object of God's saving activity in Christ. God is choosing and saving a people for his name.

Perhaps nothing illustrates this as vividly as two passages in 1 Corinthians (5:1–13; 6:1–11), where Paul speaks to the rather flagrant sins of particular individuals. In both cases Paul aims his heaviest artillery not at the individual sinners, but at the church for its failure to deal with these matters. In 5:1–13 the man is not so much as spoken to—he is simply to be put out—and his partner is not mentioned at all. Everything is directed at the church—for its arrogance, on the one hand, and its failure to act, on the other. So also in 6:1–11. In this case he does finally speak to the plaintiff (vv. 7–8a) and the defendant (vv. 8b–11), but only after he has scored the church for allowing such a thing to happen at all among God's eschatological community and for failing to act. What is obviously at stake in these cases is the church itself, and its role as God's redeemed and redemptive alternative to Corinth.

This concern for God's saving a people for his name, vis-à-vis simply saving individual believers, is further evidenced by the frequency of one of the prevailing, but frequently overlooked, words in Pauline paraenesis: ἀλλήλων ("one another/each other"). *Everything* is done ἀλλήλων. They are members of *one another* (Rom 12:5; Eph 4:25), who are to build up *one*

---

chosen by God for his purposes; as one has been incorporated into, and thus belongs to, the chosen people of God, one is in that sense also elect.

another (1 Thes 5:11; Rom 14:19), to care for *one another* (1 Cor 12:25), to love *one another* (1 Thes 3:12; 4:9; 2 Thes 1:3; Rom 13:8), to pursue *one another's* good (1 Thes 5:15), to bear with *one another* in love (Eph 4:2); to bear *one another's* burdens (Gal 6:2); to be kind and compassionate to *one another*, forgiving *one another* (Eph 4:32; cf. Col 3:13), to submit to *one another* (Eph 5:21), to consider *one another* better than ourselves (Phil 2:3; cf. Rom 12:10), to be devoted to *one another* in love (Rom 12:10), to live in harmony with *one another* (Rom 12:16).

Thus, God is not just saving individuals and preparing them for heaven; rather, he is creating *a people* for his name, among whom God can dwell and who in their life together will reproduce God's life and character. This view of salvation is thoroughgoing in Paul. It is evidenced nowhere more clearly than in his references to the Spirit, who plays the obviously crucial role not only in constituting the people of God, but also in their life together and in their worship.

THE SPIRIT AND THE BELIEVING COMMUNITY

THE FORMATION OF THE COMMUNITY

What was noted in the preceding chapter about the individual Christian life, that one's origins lie with the transforming, renewing work of the Spirit, is equally true of the believing community. The people of God as a community of believers owe their existence to their common, lavish experience of the Spirit. Thus, the question Paul answers in 1 Cor 12:13 is not, how do people become believers—although in a sense that is being answered as well—but how do the many of them, composed of Jew and Gentile, slave and free, make up the one body of Christ. Paul's answer: *All* alike were immersed in the same reality, Spirit, and *all* alike were caused to drink to the fill of the same reality, Spirit, so as to form one body in Christ. Likewise, the reason Paul needed no letters of commendation when he came to Corinth is that the Corinthians themselves, inscribed by the Spirit, became an epistle of Christ (2 Cor 3:1–3).

Created and formed *by* the Spirit, the early communities thus became a fellowship *of* the Spirit. The concept of κοινωνία ("fellowship") is a broad one in Paul. It begins as fellowship with God through Christ (1 Cor 1:9), which in turn brings believers into fellowship with one another. In the Trinitarian benediction of 2 Cor 13:13[14], Paul selects κοινωνία to characterize the ministry of the Spirit. Although this refers chiefly to "a participation in the Spirit himself," such participation is common to them all and thus also includes the "fellowship" created and sustained by the Spirit. So also in Phil 2:1–4, part of the basis of his appeal to unity and harmony in v. 1 is their common participation (both Paul's and theirs together) in the Spirit (cf. 1:27, "stand firm in one Spirit"). And common love brought about by the Spirit serves as the basis of an appeal to the Roman believers to support him with their prayers (Rom 15:30; cf. Col 1:8).

As noted in chapter 12, for Paul the inclusion of Jews and Gentiles in God's family is the most remarkable aspect of this newly formed fellowship; God had triumphed over the former prejudices on both sides (Eph 2:14–18). Paul's sense of wonder at this shines throughout Ephesians. Thus 1:13–14 is not first of all about individual conversions; rather, Paul is rejoicing because Gentiles ("you also") have been included in Christ along with Jews as God's inheritance, certified by the singular reality that they were given the promised Holy Spirit as "seal" and "down payment" of that inheritance. This is also the point of 2:18. Just as Christ's death made the "one body" a possibility by abolishing what divided Jew and Gentile, so now through Christ both "have access to the Father *in one Spirit.*" Jews and Gentiles have been formed by the Spirit as one body (4:4), and as they dwell together in the one Spirit they have common access as one people into the presence of God (the temple imagery now played in reverse).

THE PAULINE IMAGES

The centrality of the Spirit to Paul's view of the believing community emerges especially in his three major images for the church (family, temple, body); the first two of these also reflect continuity with the Old Testament.

(a) *The church, God's family.* This image, which occurs explicitly only twice (Eph 2:19; 1 Tim 3:15; cf. 2 Cor 6:18), flows naturally out of Paul's reference to God as Father, believers as brothers and sisters, and the apostle as a household manager. The imagery itself receives no elaboration. What is significant is the role of the Spirit, as both responsible for and evidence of believers' becoming members of God's family. This is expressed most vividly in the parallel passages of Gal 4:6 and Rom 8:14–17. In the Romans passage in particular, the Spirit is actually identified as "the Spirit of adoption," which can only mean, "the Spirit, responsible for their adoption as God's children." The evidence of their being God's children is found in the Spirit's prompting them to cry "*Abba,* Father." The *Abba* cry not only denotes intimacy with God, but especially signifies that this is the language of God's only Son. Now this language is given to those who are his "fellow-heirs." The thoroughgoing use of ἀδελφοί ("brothers and sisters") in Paul and the rest of the New Testament to refer to "the saints," is best explained on the basis of this Spirit-inspired cry to God in the language of Jesus.

(b) *The church, God's temple.* On this image, which four times refers to the church,[4] see the discussion at the end of chapter 13. It is particu-

---

[4]See 1 Cor 3:16–17; 2 Cor 6:16; Eph 2:19–22; 1 Tim 3:15–16.

larly well-suited to the Spirit, since it derives from the sanctuary (ναός) in Jerusalem, the earthly "dwelling" of the living God. The Spirit among God's newly constituted people means that God has taken up his dwelling in the gathered community.

The usage in 1 Corinthians 3 is especially instructive, both as to the role of the Spirit and as an image referring to the church as "a gathered people" of God. Paul's use of the imagery actually begins in v. 9 ("you [the church in Corinth] are God's building"). Their foundation (Christ crucified) had been laid by the apostle, but at the time of Paul's letter the superstructure was being erected with materials incompatible to that foundation (wood and straw, referring to their current fascination with wisdom and rhetoric). They must build with enduring materials (gold, silver, costly stones = the gospel of the crucified One), imagery taken from the building of Solomon's temple (1 Chron 29:2; 2 Chron 3:6). Then in v. 16 Paul asks rhetorically, "Do you not know what kind of building you are? God's temple in Corinth!" As a gathered community, they formed the one temple of the *living* God, God's alternative to Corinth; and what made them his alternative was the presence of the Spirit in their midst.

But the Corinthians were in the process of dismantling God's temple, because their strife and fascination with wisdom meant the banishing of the Spirit from their midst. Hence this strongest of warnings: the people responsible for the destruction would themselves be destroyed by God. This emphasis on the church as God's temple, and therefore God's alternative to Corinth, also lies behind the identical imagery in 2 Cor 6:16–7:1. They must come out from the idolatry of Corinth and purify themselves from every defilement, because they are God's temple, the place of the eternal God's dwelling, in Corinth. This, of course, is the ultimate form in which Paul's understanding of the Presence motif finds expression.

(c) *The church, Christ's body.* With this imagery, which occurs several times in the corpus,[5] Paul essentially makes two points: the need for unity *and* for diversity in the believing community, both of which are the work of "the one and the same Spirit" (1 Cor 12:11).

First, the imagery presupposes and contends for the unity of the people of God. That is the clear point of Ephesians 4. The church, composed of both Jew and Gentile, forms one body (Eph 2:16). The

---

[5]See 1 Cor 10:16–17; 11:29; 12:12–27; Rom 12:4–5; Col 1:18; 3:15; Eph 1:23; 2:16; 4:3–16; 5:23. For the most recent discussion of the imagery in Paul, see G. L. O. R. Yorke, *The Church as the Body of Christ in the Pauline Corpus*, whose primary conclusion is undoubtedly correct (despite some exegetical weaknesses in getting there [cf. Fee, *JBL* 112 (1993) 357–58]): that Paul knows nothing of a "mystical body of Christ" to which believers are joined; rather, Paul's use of the imagery is metaphorical in every case and has the human body as its metaphorical point of reference.

urgency of the appeal that begins with 4:1 and carries through to the end is that they "keep the unity that the Spirit has given them" (4:3). The basis for the appeal is the triune God, as expressed in vv. 4–6, which begins by placing the one body in the closest kind of association with the one Spirit. Furthermore, all of the sins listed in vv. 25–31 are sins of discord. By giving in to sin, they grieve the Holy Spirit (v. 30), who has formed them into a body and whose continuing presence is intended to bring the body to full maturity. Hence the need to "keep filled with the Spirit" (5:18), so as to ensure proper worship (vv. 19–20) and proper relationships (5:21–6:9).

The same holds true in 1 Cor 12:12–26. The earlier use of the imagery in 10:16–17 and 11:29, with reference to the bread of the Lord's Table, had focused on their need for unity. When the imagery recurs in 12:12, unity and diversity are equally stressed. The role of the much-debated v. 13 fits in right at this point. With two sentences (vv. 13 and 14) that begin with the identical applicational signal ("for indeed"), Paul argues first that the many of them (Jew, Gentile, slave, free) are one body because of their common lavish experience of Spirit (v. 13). After v. 14 and its application (vv. 15–20), both of which stress diversity, Paul urges in the second application (vv. 21–26) that there be no "division" among them. This especially recalls the various divisions mentioned throughout the letter. The Spirit has made them *one* body; true Spirituality will maintain that unity, whatever else. Likewise in Philippi, where some bickering and posturing were going on that could lead to disunity, Paul urges his readers, especially in light of their struggle against their pagan opponents, to "stand firm in the one Spirit" (1:27). This appeal is made on the basis of their common (his and theirs) participation in the Spirit (2:1).

Second, the Spirit is also responsible for maintaining a necessary and healthy diversity in the church. This is the basic concern of the argument in 1 Corinthians 12. The Corinthians' singular and imbalanced emphasis on tongues as the evidence of a fully developed spirituality requires some *theological* correctives (chs. 12 and 13) before the specific abuse is corrected (ch. 14). Thus every paragraph in chapter 12 (except for vv. 21–26) has this theme—the need for diversity in order for the community to be built up. God himself as three Persons illustrates—and serves as the basis for—this diversity-in-unity (vv. 4–6); and the Spirit in particular is responsible for its being evidenced among them, especially in the many manifestations of his presence "given to each one for the common good" (vv. 7–11). A body cannot be only one part (v. 14); that is a monstrosity (vv. 15–20). The Spirit who is responsible for their being *one body* is also the basis for the *many parts* necessary for the body to function at all.

Significantly, the body imagery in Ephesians, with its concern for unity, focused primarily on *relationships* within the church. In 1 Corinthians 12, however, the focus is mainly on the church as a *community gathered for worship*; this is true also of the temple imagery in 3:16–17.

This is due to the respective errors that were taking place within the gathered community. The early believers did not have buildings called "churches"; they did not "go to church." They *were* the church, and at appointed times they assembled *as* the church (1 Cor 11:18). As God's temple, inhabited by his Spirit, they formed a powerful fellowship, evidenced by manifestations of the Spirit (1 Cor 12:7), including miracles (Gal 3:5) and prophetic utterances (1 Thes 5:19–20; 1 Cor 14:24–25; outsiders exclaim, "surely God is *among you*"). This emphasis on the gathered community serves as the essential background to Paul's understanding of *charismata*, especially in 1 Corinthians 12–14. But before that, we need to take a closer look at the ethical dimension of life in the Spirit noted in chapter 12 above.

THE SPIRIT AND CHRISTIAN LIFE

For Paul Christian life not only begins by means of the Spirit; the whole of Christian life is a matter of Spirit. In the kingdom of God not only righteousness (including right standing with God and right living), but also peace and joy are effected by the Spirit (Rom 14:17). In Gal 3:3, Paul asked rhetorically (about their conversion), "having made a *beginning* by means of the Spirit, are you now hoping to *be made complete* in the flesh?" The expected reply is "Of course not!" One must finish in the same way as one began, through the empowering and appropriating work of the Spirit. Thus the Spirit is as central to Paul's understanding of all of ongoing Christian life, including ethical life, as it is to conversion itself.

Here again Paul's accent falls heavily on the community. His concern is with the local church as the people of God in their city. Hence most of his indicatives and imperatives are in the second person plural, with the whole church in purview; nonetheless, these indicatives and imperatives are expressed in such a way that they are experienced and obeyed at the individual level. For example, on the one hand, the command to remain filled with the Spirit in Eph 5:18 is not addressed to individuals with regard to Christian life in general; rather, Paul is addressing a community setting in which believers *teach one another* with various kinds of songs. On the other hand, such a text by its nature applies first to individual believers, who must respond to the exhortation if the community is to be filled with the Spirit. So with the majority of texts here under discussion. As noted in chapter 14, these materials could rightly have been included there; I have chosen to include them here, even though they must be responded to at the individual level, because for Paul the focal concern is with the life of the believing community, how the people of God live in a world that has been judged by Christ and is in process of passing away.

THE SPIRIT AND ETHICAL LIFE[6]

The problem of ethics in Paul has several dimensions. First, there is the longstanding issue of the role of ethics in relation to his attitude toward Torah. How can the Paul who insists that one's relationship with God is not predicated on "works of Law" turn about and insist on absolutes with regard to Christian behavior? Second, there is the problem of absolutes at all in an ethics of the Spirit, in which the Spirit leads the believing community into proper relationships and conduct. Consequently, on the one hand, one finds a readiness in Paul to express paraenesis in absolutes, based on the Spirit's presence and without appeal to Torah; on the other hand, one finds almost total flexibility with regard to what Paul deems to be nonessentials. The key to such ethics lies with Paul's understanding of the role of the Spirit in the believer's—and believing community's—life.

We have already argued in chapter 12 that the Spirit is the key to what may appear to be Paul's ambiguous attitude toward Torah, which at the same time is also the answer to the first dimension of the "problem" of Pauline ethics. Discontinuity, we suggested, lies in the area of Torah observance, the use of Torah in any form whatsoever to identify the people of God. On this matter Paul is resolute: "Neither circumcision nor uncircumcision counts for anything; what counts is keeping the commandments of God" (1 Cor 7:19). This means, therefore, that since circumcision counts for nothing, one may not impose it on Gentiles, precisely because that would give it religious significance. On the other hand, Jewish parents may continue to circumcise their sons if they wish, but they must understand that it has no bearing on their being counted among the people of God.

But if circumcision counts for nothing, the same is not true of "keeping the commandments of God." That does count. Is this, then, a new form of "works righteousness"? Hardly. This is simply Paul's way of saying that "righteousness," thought of now in terms of God's character evidenced in his people's attitudes and behavior, is not optional. The reason for this lies with the gift of the eschatological Spirit, who has rendered Torah observance obsolete, but who has at the same time made possible the "fulfillment of the righteous requirement of Torah." That is, the goal of Torah, God's own righteousness, reflected in his people, is precisely what the Spirit can do, which Torah could not. But it is only

---

[6]On the question of Pauline ethics, see esp. V. P. Furnish, *Theology and Ethics in Paul;* for the role of the Spirit in Paul's ethics, see esp. the couple of perceptive paragraphs in Käsemann, *Romans,* 324–25. See also in Part I, the discussion on 1 Thes 4:8; 2 Thes 2:13; 1 Cor 6:19–20; Gal 5:5–6, 13–15, 16–18, 19–23, 24–26; 6:1–3; Rom 6:1–8:39; 7:5–6, 14, 18; 8:1–2, 3–4, 5–8, 12–13; 12:1–2; 13:11–14; 14:16–18; Eph 4:3–4, 30.

those matters which Paul perceives as *having to do with God and his character* that render some moral actions as absolutes; all others are *adiaphora*, nonessentials. Paul's attitude toward all these matters, therefore, can best be found in Rom 14:17, the theological insertion that lies at the heart of Paul's response to some very practical ethical questions. How *do* the observant and nonobservant live together as one people of God, so that "together with one voice" they might "glorify the God and Father of our Lord Jesus Christ" (Rom 15:6)? At the practical level the observant must not condemn the nonobservant, and the nonobservant must not scorn the observant (14:1–6). The reason? "For the kingdom of God has nothing at all to do with food and drink (mere *adiaphora*), but with the righteousness, joy, and peace that the Holy Spirit empowers." Food and drink count for nothing; righteousness, joy, and peace count for everything.

Thus, the crucial role of the Spirit in Pauline ethics: First, *because for Paul there is no such thing as "salvation in Christ" that does not also include righteousness on the part of God's people.* They are not saved by "doing righteousness"—indeed that is unthinkable in Paul, since righteousness in the form of behavior is the product of the Spirit's empowering, and thus can only be the working out of salvation by the same Spirit who has appropriated to their lives Christ's saving work in the first place. But for that very reason ethical life is also required, because both "getting in" and "staying in" are the work of the Spirit, and Paul sees no bifurcation between the two. Second, the Spirit is essential to Paul's ethics *because truly Christian ethics can only be by the Spirit's empowering.* That is why Torah observance does not work; it may make one "religious," but it fails to make one truly "righteous," in the Pauline sense of reproducing the righteousness of God in the lives of believers.

This is also why the ethics of eschatological salvation in Christ starts with a renewed mind (Rom 12:1–2; cf. Col 1:9; Eph 1:17), because only in this way may one determine what God's will is and thus be pleasing to him. Not only does the mind renewed by the Spirit lead one to understand that love must rule over all, but only by such a renewed mind may one determine how best to love. There is a time for speaking, and time for silence, a time for taking another's load on oneself and a time to refrain for the sake of that one's own growth. Only dependence on the Spirit can enable one to know what is pleasing to God.

The passages in Colossians and Ephesians are especially significant in this regard. Although the specific nature and form of the Colossian "heresy" may be shrouded in mystery for us, there can be little question that it included as two of its elements (1) an appeal to something heady (wisdom, so-called philosophy, etc.), probably based on "visions," and (2) an insistence on "religious righteousness" approaching an ascetic ideal ("don't touch, don't taste, don't handle"). Paul's response to this early on in the letter (1:9–11) is to pray for the Colossian believers that they might "be filled with the knowledge of God's will by means of *the Spirit's wisdom and insight,*" and this precisely so that they might walk worthy of the Lord in ways that are pleasing to him (cf. Rom 12:1–2). Thus, rather than give them Christian "rules" he gives them the Spirit. Through the Spirit's wisdom and insight they are to be done with "rules" and advance to living the life of those who by the Spirit are being "renewed into the likeness of the Creator" (3:10), whose character is then spelled out (v. 12) in language reminiscent of the fruit of the Spirit in Gal 5:22–23. This is the new form of "revelation." It is not in "visions," nor what has only "an appearance of wisdom," namely, "rules to live one's Christian life by" (2:23). Rather, it is in the Spirit, who reveals God's will in such a way that ethical life is a reflection of God's character.

Ethics for Paul, therefore, is ultimately a *theological* issue pure and simple. Everything has to do with God, and what God is about in Christ and the Spirit. Thus: (1) the *purpose* (or basis) of Christian ethics is the glory of God (1 Cor 10:31); (2) the *pattern* for such ethics is Christ (1 Cor 4:16–17; 11:1; Eph 4:20); (3) the *principle* is love, precisely because love alone reflects God's character;[7] (4) and the *power* is the Spirit. Hence the crucial role of the Spirit. Since the Spirit of God is the Spirit *of Christ,* and since the first mentioned fruit of the Spirit is *love,* the Spirit, therefore, not only empowers the believer for ethical behavior, but by indwelling the believer the Spirit also reproduces the pattern and the principle of that behavior. Several further observations are needed about these matters.

(a) Walking in/by the Spirit.[8] The central role of the Spirit is most clearly spelled out in Gal 5:13–6:10, where with a series of verbs modified by the phrase πνεύματι ("in/by the Spirit"), Paul urges the Galatians to "make a completion" (3:3) by means of the same Spirit by whom they had been converted. They are commanded to "walk in the Spirit," and promised that those who so walk "will not fulfill the desire of the flesh" (v. 16); such people are "led by the Spirit," attested by "the fruit of the Spirit" (vv. 22–23), and are not under Torah (vv. 18, 23). Since they "live by the Spirit" (= have been brought to life by the life-giving Spirit), they must also "behave in accordance with the Spirit" (v. 25). Finally, only those who "sow to the Spirit" in this way "will reap the *eternal* life" that is also from the Spirit (6:8).

Two things are clear from this passage: that the Spirit is the key to ethical life, and that Paul expected Spirit people to exhibit changed behavior. The first imperative, "walk by the Spirit," is the basic imperative in Pauline ethics. This verb was common in Judaism to refer to a

---

[7]The passages here are numerous: Gal 5:13–14; 1 Cor 8:2–3; 13:4–7; Rom 13:8–10; Col 3:14; Eph 5:2, 25.

[8]See the discussion on Gal 5:13–6:10; 2 Cor 12:18; Col 1:9–11; Eph 4:1–3.

person's whole way of life. Paul adopted it as his most common metaphor for ethical conduct (17 occurrences in all). All other imperatives proceed from this one. The primary form that such walking takes is "in love" (Eph 5:2; cf. Gal 5:6), hence love is the first-mentioned "fruit of the Spirit" (Gal 5:22; cf. 5:14; Rom 13:8–10).

But ethics for Paul is not simply some ideal, to be actualized only by those who are truly "spiritual," as over against some who are still "carnal." Precisely because the Spirit empowers this new life, Paul has little patience for the point of view that allows for people to be "justified sinners" without appropriate changes in attitudes and conduct (cf. 1 Cor, Gal 5–6, Rom 6 and 12, Col 3, and Phil 2–4). Nor would Paul understand an appeal to helplessness on the part of those who live in and walk by the Spirit. If he knows nothing of ethical "perfectionism," neither does he know anything about an internal struggle within the human breast, in which the "flesh" continually proves to be the greater power. The whole point of the argument of Gal 5:13–6:10 has to do with the suffi- ciency of the Spirit, as we continue to live as Spirit people in a world where the perspective of the flesh is still the dominant force. The point of the imperative in Gal 5:16 is *promise*: "Walk by the Spirit, and *you will not fulfill the desire of the flesh.*"

But neither is this triumphalism. As noted in the exegesis of Gal 5:16, the key for Paul lay with the Spirit as a *dynamically experienced reality* in the life of both believers (3:2, 4) and community (3:5). Paul's expectation level was high on this matter because for him and his churches the Spirit was not simply believed in but was experienced in very tangible, visible ways. If our experience of the Spirit lies at a lower level, we must resist the temptation to remake Paul into our image and thereby find comfort in a Paul that did not exist. Paul's answer was, "walk in/by the Spirit," and he assumed that such a walk was available to those who "had experienced so many things" of the Spirit already. If he does not tell us *how* to do that, that is because such a dynamic life in the Spirit was presuppositional to him.

(b) *The Spirit as holy.*[9] Although Paul usually uses the term "sancti- fication" to refer to Christian conversion (see ch. 14 above), the metaphor tends to appear where his concern is with his converts' improper (sinful) behavior.[10] For example, in 1 Thes 4:3–8 he takes up the issue of sexual immorality with a group of former pagans for whom sexual irregularity

---

[9]See the discussion on such diverse texts as 1 Thes 4:8; 2 Thes 1:11; 2:13; 1 Cor 6:11; Rom 15:16; Eph 4:30.

[10]Except for instances where he is making a play on the new and old covenants, such as in Rom 15:16. There his point has to do with formerly "unclean" Gentiles now "sanctified" by the Spirit, so that they may not be judged by Jewish Christians for their lack of ritual "purity," especially their rejection of circumcision and food laws.

was *not* considered a moral issue. The argument begins, "this is God's will for you, even your sanctification" (v. 3), and concludes that the person who rejects his instruction on this matter does not reject what a mere man has to say, "but rejects the very God who *gives* [present tense] you his *Holy* Spirit." This further explains the use of this metaphor in reminding them of their conversion in 2 Thes 2:13, as well as the repeated emphasis on this metaphor in 1 Corinthians (see 1:2, 30; 6:11).

Here one sees at least in part the significance of the early church's referring to the Spirit as the *Holy* Spirit, a name that rarely occurs in the Old Testament.[11] The early believers understood themselves to be dedicated to God, but not in a ritual way, as in the Old Testament use of the term "sanctified." Rather, they were set apart for God, to be his "holy" *people* in the world.[12] Hence the emphasis in 1 Thes 4:3–8.

For Paul "holiness," i.e., walking by means of the *Holy* Spirit, was two-dimensional. On the one hand, it meant abstaining from certain sins—absolutely. Since in Christ they had died to both sin (the flesh) and the law, believers are to serve God "in the newness of the Spirit" (Rom 7:6). They must put to death the former way of life (Rom 6:1–18; 8:12–13; Col 3:5–11), portrayed in Gal 5:19–21 as "the works of the flesh." As we noted in our discussion of the Spirit/flesh contrast in chapter 12, the "flesh" is not primarily an anthropological term, but an eschatological one, referring to life *before and outside* of Christ. Such a life is no longer an option for the new people of God, who are so by the indwelling of the Spirit of God. Paul, therefore, understands such "putting to death" of the works of the flesh as the empowering work of the Spirit (Rom 8:12–13).

On the other hand, "holiness" also (especially) means the *Holy* Spirit living *in* believers, reproducing the life of Christ within/among them, especially in their communal relationships. To do otherwise is to "grieve the Holy Spirit of God" (Eph 4:30), who by his presence has given them both unity and mutual growth. For this reason, Paul's most common language for the people of God is οἱ ἅγιοι ("the saints" = God's *holy* people). They live differently in their relationships with one another, and are empowered to do so, because they are Spirit people, whatever else.

THE FRUIT OF THE SPIRIT

In Gal 5:22–23 Christian ethical life is specified as the *fruit* of the Spirit, in contrast to the *works* of the "flesh." But this is not to be understood as passivity on the part of the believer. Indeed, the imperatival nature of Pauline ethics found elsewhere leaves exactly the opposite

---

[11]The only two texts where it does occur, interestingly enough, are in David's lament over his sin (Ps 51:11) and Isaiah's recall of Israel's rebellion (Isa 63:10).

[12]Cf. Wainwright, *Trinity*, 22–23.

impression. Believers are called to active obedience. What one must not disregard is the element of the miraculous. Just as in conversion, where there is a "hearing of faith" and a receiving of the Spirit, so in Pauline ethics there is a *walking* in the Spirit, that is *led by* the Spirit. The Spirit produces the fruit as believers continually walk with the Spirit's help.

The essential nature of the "fruit" is the reproduction of the life of Christ in the believer. This is confirmed by several pieces of evidence: (1) the Spirit is in fact the Spirit *of Christ*, a point made especially strongly in Rom 8:9–11, in the middle of an argument that places the ethical life of believers within the framework of life in Christ; (2) many of the words used to describe that fruit are used elsewhere of Christ; and (3) Paul elsewhere understands ethical conduct in terms of "learning Christ" (Eph 4:20).

On the nature and significance of the items listed, see the discussion in Part I. Four observations need to be repeated here about the "fruit" enumerated in Gal 5:22–23. First, this list is not intended to be exhaustive, but representative, just as with the preceding list of vices in vv. 19–21. Paul concludes both lists by referring to "such things" (τὰ τοιαῦτα), meaning all other vices and virtues similar to these. All such enumerations, including the descriptions of love in 1 Cor 13:4–7 and of χαρίσματα in 1 Cor 12:8–10, are quite ad hoc, and thus tailored to their contexts. This means that a full discussion of the fruit of the Spirit would need to spread a wide net so as to include, for example, the further items mentioned in Col 3:12–13 (compassion, humility, forgiveness) as well as the specific applications like those in Rom 12:9–21. Not only so, but it also means in terms of specifics in Gal 5:19–23 that even though Paul always throws the net widely enough to help his readers view their specific sins in light of a broad range of iniquity, nonetheless the majority of vices and "fruit" in this case are specifically tailored to a situation in which they are "biting and devouring each other" (5:15). This is the "work of the flesh" that by walking in the Spirit they will not "fulfill"; the fruit of the Spirit provide attitudes and behavior that are quite the opposite.

Second, these "fruit" cover a broad range, including all manner of attitudes, virtues, and behavior. Christian life across the broadest possible spectrum is the work of the Spirit. "Fruit" include the experiences of joy, and peace within the believing community, attitudes such as gentleness, forbearance, and self-control, and behavior such as love, kindness, goodness, and all other kinds of behavior consonant with these experiences and attitudes.

Third, what this list of Spiritual fruit does not include is any attempt to "regulate" Christian behavior by rules of religious conduct. Because truly Christian ethics are the product of walking and living in the Spirit, there can be no Law (Gal 5:23). Truly Christian conduct cannot be "regulated" by reference to rules of behavior. But by that same token, neither is any other form of Torah permitted, especially of the kind that regulates food, the observance of days, and religious practices, or in our cultures, seeks to govern matters such as clothing, entertainment, recreation, etc. These may have an appearance of wisdom, but finally they are of no value at all, since they are but "human commandments" (Col 2:20–23). "Rules and regulations" of this kind directly oppose life in the Spirit. Hence Paul always renounces such strictures whenever anyone would judge another about these things, intending by their judging to make others conform to "the rules"—as though God really did care about such things—and not to Spirit ethics. Rules, after all, are easily regulated and easily performed, without the need of the Spirit's empowering. On the other hand, because such "regulations" have absolutely no value in terms of one's relationship with God, people may practice them if they wish—as long as their "religious practices" are not looked upon as the "fruit of the Spirit," and seen as "requirements" for everyone. For Paul, that is anathema.

Fourth, to bring this discussion full circle, it is especially to be noted that both the fruit of the Spirit and the various imperatives that give specifics to Pauline ethics belong primarily to the believing community, not to the individual believer. Thus, the foremost imperative, "walk by the Spirit," is directed not so much toward the individual in terms of his or her own personal life with Christ, but toward the Christian community, in which some are "biting and devouring" one another and using their freedom in Christ as an occasion for the flesh. The flesh/Spirit contrast in this passage, therefore, has nothing at all to do with one's introspective conscience, but has everything to do with "love, joy, peace, forbearance, kindness, goodness, and gentleness" within the believing community, as believers learn to live as God's people together in a fallen world. While these various attitudes and behaviors must be worked on at the individual level—no one is exempt from walking by the Spirit—they are primarily the ethics not of the individual, but of the community of faith.

According to Col 3:16 and Eph 5:19 one of the forms of teaching and admonishing one another regarding the "message of Christ" was through psalms, hymns, and Spirit songs. This suggests a much closer relationship to ethics and worship than is sometimes noted. In any case, just as with ethics, so with worship: the Spirit was understood by Paul to play a leading role.

THE SPIRIT AND WORSHIP

Because of the ad hoc nature of Paul's letters, they contain nothing close to a systematic presentation of the worship of the early church. What we learn is only in response to problems and is therefore fragmentary. Nonetheless, for Paul the gathered church was first of all a worshiping community; and the key to their worship was the presence of the Holy Spirit. Thus, in Phil 3:3, in his strong attack against the "mutilators of the flesh" (through circumcision), Paul begins by asserting that "*we are the circumcision, who serve/worship by the Spirit of God.*" *Their* worship is a matter of a religious rite performed in the flesh; *ours* is a matter of Spirit.

Not only is the Spirit seen as responsible for worship (see esp. 1 Cor 14:6, 24, 26), but when believers are assembled in this way Paul understood himself to be present in S/spirit (probably in the reading of the letter as his prophetic voice among them), along with the "power of the Lord Jesus" (1 Cor 5:3–5; Col 2:5). Thus, even though he makes no direct allusion to the presence of the Spirit at the Lord's Table (1 Cor 10:16–17; 11:17–34), we may assume his understanding of the bread as representing Christ's body the church (10:16–17; 11:29), made so by the Spirit, to be leading in that direction. In fact, one would not be far wrong to see the Spirit's presence at the Table as Paul's way of understanding "the real presence." The analogy of Israel's having had "Spiritual food" and "Spiritual drink" in 1 Cor 10:3–4 at least allows as much. In any case, the Spirit is specifically noted as responsible for all other expressions of Christian worship.

THE NATURE OF WORSHIP

Several of the *charismata* discussed in the next section belong to the context of corporate worship. This is especially true of those that involve speech directed toward the community, as Paul's correctives in 1 Corinthians 14 make clear. These include prophecy, teaching, knowledge, and revelation (v. 6), however we are finally to define some of these in relationship to each other.

What is most noteworthy in all the *available* evidence[13] is the free, spontaneous nature of worship in the Pauline churches, apparently orchestrated by the Spirit himself. Worship is expressed in a variety of ways and with the (potential) participation of everyone (1 Cor 14:26). There is no hint of a worship leader, although that must not be ruled out on the basis of silence. But neither is chaos permitted. The God whom they worship is a God of peace (v. 33), whose character is to be reflected in both the manner and content of their worship. Therefore, disorder is out. Although *all* may participate (vv. 23, 24, 26, 31), there are some guidelines. Speakers of inspired utterances must be limited to two or

---

[13]And I stress the factor of "available evidence," because what comes to us does so for the most part in the form of correction. We simply do not know enough to make far-reaching, all-inclusive statements about the nature of worship in the Pauline churches.

three at a time, and they must be followed by interpretation and discernment. And they must have respect for one another. Speakers must make way for others, since the "S/spirit of the prophet is subject to the prophet" (v. 32). Thus, spontaneity does not mean lack of order; it means "peace" and "decency and orderliness"—also the work of the Spirit.

If our interpretation of 1 Cor 11:4–5 is correct, the "praying and prophesying" in that passage are not delimiting terms, but representative, in this case of the two basic kinds of activities that happened in Christian worship. Together they designate the two primary foci of gathered worship: God and the believing community. Thus prayer (and song and tongues, according to 1 Cor 14:2 and 15) is directed Godward; and prophesying represents the many forms of speech—especially Spirit-inspired speech—that are directed toward the people of God for their edification (1 Cor 14:3, 16) or toward outsiders for their conversion (14:24–25).

In terms of participation, it should be noted that both men and women apparently shared equally in the praying and prophesying (1 Cor 11:4–5). In the Christian assembly the cry of Moses has been fulfilled: "I wish that all the Lord's people were prophets and that the Lord would put his Spirit on them!" (Num 11:29, NIV). This is quite in keeping with 1 Cor 14:23, where again somewhat in passing Paul says that "all may prophesy." The problem in 1 Cor 11:5–6, therefore, is not with the *fact* that women prayed and prophesied in the assembly, but that they were doing so in appearance similar to men, which Paul considers to be an expression of shame. That women were full participants in the worship of the Pauline churches, including the more preferred expression of Spirit-inspired speech, prophecy, moves considerably beyond the norm of Paul's Jewish background and seems to be quite in keeping with the rest of the New Testament evidence, as little as there is. In terms of ministry within the worshiping community, the Holy Spirit was apparently indiscriminate, inspiring women and men alike, since in Christ Jesus such distinctions no longer have religious value in God's new eschatological kingdom (Gal 3:28).

Since "prayer" has been noted in chapter 14 and "prophecy" will be looked at in more detail below, this is also the occasion to note the place of singing in the Pauline churches. As with prayer, song had become the special province of the Spirit (1 Cor 14:14–15, 26; Col 3:16; Eph 5:19). The evidence from Colossians and Ephesians suggests that some of the singing was corporate; the language of these passages further indicates that besides being addressed as praise to God, hymns served as vehicles of instruction in the gathered assembly. Furthermore, both passages, as well as 1 Cor 14:15, indicate that some of the singing might best be called "a kind of charismatic hymnody,"[14] in which spontaneous hymns of

---

[14]This is the language of Dunn, *Jesus*, 238.

praise were offered to God in the congregation, although some may have been known or inspired beforehand. Both 1 Cor 14:15 and 26 suggest that some of this singing at least was "solo."

THE χαρίσματα AND THE SPIRIT[15]

As already noted, community worship included several extraordinary phenomena Paul variously calls χαρίσματα, πνευματικά, or "manifestations of the Spirit." Such phenomena are especially the activity of the Spirit in the community. This is an area, however, where there is also great diversity in understanding, both among scholars and within ecclesiastical contexts. The primary reason for this is the basic assumption by most that Paul is intending to give instruction in the various places where he mentions χαρίσματα. What we have in fact is ad hoc correction, which is neither systematic nor exhaustive. Part of the difficulty lies with Paul's use of language; for this matter the reader is referred to chapter 2. Here our concern is to describe the phenomena as best we can in light of the available evidence.

THEIR NUMBER AND VARIETY

Several things need to be said about the various lists in 1 Corinthians 12–14. First, none of them is intended to be exhaustive, as though Paul were setting forth everything that might legitimately be called a "gift of the Spirit." This is evidenced in part by the very fact that no two lists are identical—not even the rhetorical repetition in 12:30 of vv. 28–29. It goes beyond the evidence—and Paul's own concerns—to speak of "the nine spiritual gifts."

Second, the items in 12:8–10 are called "manifestations of the Spirit," which in context almost certainly means, "diverse ways the Spirit manifests himself when the community is gathered together." Paul's point here is their need for diversity. The list is especially tailored to the situation in Corinth. Paul's structural signals (the omission of the connective particle δέ along with a different word for "another" for the third and eighth items) suggest a listing in three parts. The first two pick up words that held high court in Corinth ("wisdom" and "knowledge") and seem to be an attempt by Paul to recapture these realities for the Spirit

---

[15]See the discussion in ch. 2 on χάρισμα(τα); and on 1 Cor 1:4–7; 12:1–14:40; 2 Cor 8:7; 11:6; Rom 12:3–8; Eph 4:7–16; 1 Tim 4:14; 2 Tim 1:6–7; plus the notations on all the other uses of this word in the corpus (1 Cor 7:7; 2 Cor 1:11; Rom 1:11; 5:15–16; 6:23; 11:29).

and the gospel. The next five have in common that they are, like glossolalia, extraordinary phenomena. It would scarcely do for Paul to try to
broaden their perspective with regard to tongues by listing less visible
phenomena. Finally, after diversity is well heard, he includes the problem
child, glossolalia, along with its necessary companion—at least in the
community—the interpretation of glossolalia.

Third, attempts to categorize the items in the different lists are ten-
tative at best. When those in Rom 12:6–8 and Eph 4:11 are included as
well, one gets a wide variety of nomenclature (e.g., "motivational,"
"ministerial," etc.) that the apostle would scarcely recognize and that at
best are exegetically suspect. The broad spectrum of phenomena are best
grouped under the three natural headings hinted at in 1 Cor 12:4–6:
service, miracles, and inspired utterance. It should be noted further, that
Paul himself does not refer to visionary experiences such as one finds in
2 Cor 12:1–6 as χαρίσματα—although they belong legitimately to a discussion of Spirit phenomena. Nor are people (e.g., apostles, pastors)
actually called χαρίσματα; to be sure, they are "gifts" to the church, as
Eph 4:11 shows, but only their ministries, not the people themselves are
legitimately termed χαρίσματα, in terms of Pauline usage.

(a) *Forms of service.* Items listed here include "serving," "giving," and
"caring for" (in the sense of leadership) from Rom 12:7–8 and "helpful
deeds" and "acts of guidance" from 1 Cor 12:28. These are the least visibly
"charismatic" of the "gifts" and the least obvious as expressions of corporate worship. They belong to Paul's ever-present interest in relationships within the church. Thus, they are Spirit activity, not so much in
the sense of "Spirit manifestations" within the assembly as in the sense
of the broad range of Spirit activity noted in chapter 14. To include them
in a discussion of χαρίσματα would legitimize discussing any and all Spirit
endowments as χαρίσματα, which means that the category would become
less than useful.

(b) *The miraculous.* Included here are three items from 1 Cor 12:9–10,
"faith" (= the supernatural gift of faith that can "move mountains"; cf.
13:2), "gifts (χαρίσματα) of healings" (of the physical body; also vv. 28,
30), and "workings of miracles" (= all other such phenomena not included in healing). The use of the plurals, "gifts" and "workings," for the
latter two probably means that these "gifts" are not permanent, but each
occurrence is a "gift" in its own right. That such phenomena were a
regular part of the apostle's own ministry is evidenced by 2 Cor 12:12 and
Rom 15:18–19. That they were also the regular expectation of the Pauline
churches is evidenced by Gal 3:5. He would simply not have understood
the presence of the Spirit that did not also include such manifestations
of the Spirit that he termed "powers," which we translate "miracles."

Whether one believes such things happened or not, of course, depends almost altogether on one's world view. The so-called Enlightenment has had its innings, and moderns, helped along by the phenomenal

advances of modern scientific discovery, are prone to unbridled arrogance, leaving Paul and his churches to their own world view—in which they believed in such things—but rather casually dismissing them in terms of reality. Bultmann, for example, speaking for many, caricatured the "three-storeyed universe" of Paul and his contemporaries. So prevalent is this world view that many evangelicals, conservative in their theology and therefore incensed at Bultmann's "rationalism" which so casually dismissed the Pauline affirmations, adopted their own brand of rationalism, as a way of explaining the absence of such phenomena in their own circles: by limiting such Spirit activity to the apostolic age.

But in defense of Paul, two matters about his affirmations must be noted. First, all such statements in Paul are sober, matter-of-fact, and usually offhanded—events that for him would have been open to investigation had anyone felt the need to do so. The reason for this is very simple—and theological. He was born and raised within a tradition that believed in God and could not even have imagined God as not being all-powerful. With their thoroughly non-deistic view of God as one who took an active interest in his universe and in the affairs of his people, it would never have occurred to them that the one who chose to be present with them in the Incarnation and now by his Spirit would do otherwise than graciously intervene in their lives. Those who believe in God as Creator and Sustainer, but who balk at the miraculous both past and present, have created positions for themselves which are difficult to sustain theologically and quite removed from the biblical perspective.

Second, Paul's affirmations about miracles are not the statements of one who is trying to prove anything. That is, not only does he not point to miracles as grounds for accepting either his gospel or his ministry, but on the contrary he rejected such criteria as authenticating ministry of any kind. The cross, with the subsequent resurrection, and the present gift of the Spirit was all the authentication he ever appealed to. Those who need an occasional miracle to keep their belief in God alive and those who feed on such "faith" by promoting the miraculous as authenticating their "gospel" also lie outside the Pauline perspective. His view expected and accepted, but did not demand, and on this matter refused to put God to the test.

(c) Inspired utterance. Included here are "the message of wisdom," "the message of knowledge," "prophecy," "the discernments of S/spirits," "tongues," and "the interpretation of tongues" from 1 Cor 12:8, 10; "teaching" and "revelation" from 14:6; and (perhaps) "exhortation" from Rom 12:8. It might also include "singing" from Eph 5:19 (cf. 1 Cor 14:26). Attempts to distinguish some of these items from one another are generally futile, as is any distinction between their "charismatic" or non-charismatic expression (e.g., teaching or singing).

The "message of wisdom" and "knowledge" is language created by the situation in Corinth. For Paul the "message of wisdom" refers first of all to the preaching of the cross (see 1 Cor 1:18–2:16; the terminology occurs nowhere else); whether it means some spontaneous expression of Spirit wisdom for the sake of the community is possible, but can never to be known. "Knowledge," on the other hand, is closely related to "mysteries" in 1 Cor 13:2, and elsewhere it stands close to the concept of "revelation" (13:8–9, 12; 14:6). Similarly, prophecy is closely connected to "revelation" in 14:6 and especially in 14:25, 26, and 30. Are these to be understood as distinctively different gifts? Or, as seems more likely, do they suggest different emphases for the expression of the prophetic gift, since that, too, seems to fluctuate between "revealing mysteries" and more straightforward words of edification, comfort, and exhortation (or encouragement)? In any case, the use of uninterpreted tongues in the assembly is what brought forth the whole argument, and Paul uses prophecy as representative of all other intelligible inspired utterances that are to be preferred to tongues in that setting.

Both because Paul himself uses glossolalia and prophecy in a running contrast between (edifying) intelligibility and (nonedifying) unintelligibility in 1 Corinthians 14, and because of our inherent interest in these two phenomena, some further suggestions are offered about these two χαρίσματα.

GLOSSOLALIA[16]

Paul's actual term is "different kinds of tongues." Enough is said in 1 Cor 12–14 to give us a fairly good idea as to how Paul himself understood this phenomenon. (1) Whatever else, it is Spirit-inspired utterance; that is made plain by 1 Cor 12:7 and 11 and 14:2. This in itself should cause some to speak more cautiously when trying to "put tongues in their place" (usually meaning eliminate them altogether) in the contemporary church. Paul does not damn tongues with faint praise, as some have argued, nor does he stand in awe of the gift, as apparently the Corinthians had done—and some contemporary proponents of tongues do. As with all Spirit-empowered activity, Paul held it in high regard *in its proper place.* (2) The regulations for its community use in 14:27–28 make it clear that the speaker is not in "ecstasy" or "out of control." Quite the opposite; the speakers must speak in turn, and they must remain silent if there is no one to interpret. Therefore the mind is not detached; but it is at rest, and thus unfruitful. (3) It is speech essentially unintelligible both to the speaker (14:14) and to other hearers (14:16), which is why it must be interpreted in the assembly. (4) It is speech directed basically toward God (14:2, 14–15, 28); one may assume, therefore, that what is interpreted is not speech directed toward others, but the "mysteries" spoken to God.

---

[16]For bibliography, see ch. 4, n. 336 on 1 Cor 12:8–10.

(5) As a gift for private prayer, Paul held it in the highest regard (14:4, 5, 15, 17–18; cf. Rom 8:26–27; Eph 6:18).

Whether Paul also understood it to be an actual earthly language is a moot point, but the overall evidence suggests not. He certainly does not envisage the likelihood of someone's being present who might understand without interpretation; and the analogy of earthly language in 14:10–12 implies that it is not an earthly language (a thing is not usually identical with that to which it is analogous). Our most likely entrée into Paul's understanding is to be found in his description of the phenomenon in 1 Cor 13:1 as "the tongues of angels." The context virtually demands that this phrase refers to glossolalia. The more difficult matter is its close conjunction with "the tongues of people." Most likely this refers to two kinds of glossolalia: human speech, inspired of the Spirit but unknown to the speaker or hearers, and angelic speech, inspired of the Spirit to speak in the heavenly dialect. The historical context in general suggests that the latter is what the Corinthians understood glossolalia to be, and that therefore they considered it one of the evidences of their having already achieved something of their future heavenly status.

Paul shows considerable ambivalence toward this gift. On the one hand, with regard to its use in the public assembly, although he does not condemn it, he obviously is not keen on it. And in any case, tongues should not occur at all if there is not an interpretation. On the other hand, as a gift of private prayer and utterance, tongues are spoken of very favorably, obviously dealing with something that for Paul is very personal and very private. The breakdown for him has occurred when what is personal and private comes into the public assembly, since it has no facility for strengthening the others. Here, again, the central focus on corporate life comes to the fore.[17]

PROPHECY

Of all the χαρίσματα, this is the one mentioned most often in the Pauline letters. It is specifically mentioned in 1 Thes 5:20; 1 Cor 11:4–5; 12:10–14:40; Rom 12:6; Eph 2:20; 3:5; 4:11; 1 Tim 1:18; 4:14; and probably lies behind "through the Spirit" in 2 Thes 2:2 and "in keeping with a revelation" in Gal 2:2. This implies the widest range of occurrence in the Pauline churches. Although it was also a widespread phenomenon in

---

[17]The question as to whether the "speaking in tongues" in contemporary Pentecostal and charismatic communities is the *same* in kind as that in the Pauline churches is moot—and probably somewhat irrelevant. There is simply no way to know. As an *experienced* phenomenon, it is *analogous* to theirs, meaning that it is understood to be a supernatural activity of the Spirit which functions in many of the same ways, and for many of its practitioners has value similar to that described by Paul.

the Greek world, Paul's understanding is thoroughly conditioned by his own history in Judaism. The prophet spoke to God's people under the inspiration of the Spirit. In Paul such "speech" consisted of spontaneous, intelligible messages, orally delivered in the gathered assembly, intended for the edification or encouragement of the people. That they were spontaneous is certain from the evidence in 1 Cor 14:29–32, since a "revelation" comes to another while one person is still "prophesying." Those who prophesied were clearly understood to be "in control" (see 14:29–33). Although some people are called "prophets," the implication of 1 Cor 14:24–25 and 30–31 is that the gift is available—at least potentially—to all.

But it is also clear that it does not have independent authority. The combined evidence of 1 Thes 5:21–22 and 1 Cor 12:10 and 14:29 indicates that all prophesying must be "discerned" by the Spirit-filled community. That is almost certainly the first intent of the gift of the "discernments of S/spirits" in 1 Cor 12:10, since the cognate verb of the noun "discernments" appears in 14:29 as the needed response to prophetic utterances, just as interpretation is needed with tongues.

The actual function of prophecy in the Pauline churches is more difficult to pin down. If our view of Gal 2:2, 1 Tim 1:18 (cf. 4:14), and 1 Tim 4:14 is correct, then, on the one hand, the Spirit directs the lives of his servants in specific ways; sometimes they are singled out for the ministry the Spirit empowers (1 Tim 1:18; 4:14) and sometimes they are directed to undertake a difficult mission to Jerusalem (Gal 2:2). On the other hand, the Spirit also reminds the church, probably repeatedly, that the words of Jesus concerning the increase of evil in the end (1 Tim 4:1) are being confirmed. It was probably a misguided but heeded prophetic utterance that the Day of the Lord had already come (2 Thes 2:2) that led to the distress in Thessalonica. In 1 Corinthians 14 yet another picture emerges of how the community regularly experiences the prophetic Spirit: In the case of believers the Spirit speaks encouragement and edification, and in the case of unbelievers he lays bare their hearts in such a way as to lead to repentance. All of this suggests that "prophecy" was a widely expressed and widely experienced phenomenon, which had as its goal the building up of the people of God so as to come to maturity in Christ (Eph 4:11–16).[18]

Some recent literature on this question has been interested in the question of "backgrounds" and "authority." This problem is related to the inspiration and canonical authority of the Old Testament prophets

---

[18]On the probability that Paul understood himself to be a prophet as well as an apostle, see on 1 Cor 14:37 and Eph 3:5. According to 1 Cor 5:3–4 and Col 2:5 he also understood himself to be present by the Spirit in the gathered assembly, presumably at the reading of his letter. Very likely, therefore, he understood his letters to function in a prophetic way within the churches as they were being read.

and their concern whether the New Testament variety might be understood in the same way.[19] Sometimes related to this discussion is the fact that women prophesied in the Pauline churches; some prior commitments as to the extent of women's "authority" in the church has caused these scholars to find a way around the question of prophecy and authority, which allows women to prophesy but not to have authority.

When such issues precede one's coming to the text, it is not surprising that one finds what one is looking for. The usual "way around" this matter is to suggest either (a) that the kind of prophesying that Paul is referring to is not of the same kind as that in the "classical prophets," but of the more ecstatic kind found, for example, in 1 Sam 10:5–13 or Num 11:24–25; or (b) that the apostles and teachers stand in the line of "authority" with the Old Testament prophets, while New Testament prophecy is simply of a different kind altogether.

But this discussion seems controlled by factors that do not interest Paul at all. He never raises the question of "authority" with regard to prophecy. That he saw the phenomenon as evidence for the outpouring of the eschatological promise of Joel 2:28–30 need hardly be doubted, since whatever else, prophecy existed for the church as an eschatological community that lived between the times (1 Cor 13:8–13). This suggests that questions such as those raised by people with "canonical consciousness" lie totally outside his frame of reference. That also means that he undoubtedly saw the "New Testament prophets" as in the succession of the "legitimate" prophets of the Old Testament, which explains in part why all such prophecy must be "discerned," just as with those in the Old Testament. But the *nature* of the prophecy was also understood to be of a different kind, precisely because of their present eschatological existence. A prophet who speaks encouragement to the church in its "between the times" existence speaks a different kind of word from the predominant word of judgment on ancient Israel. In any case, the only "prophets" Paul ever refers to who are not part of the present Spirit-inspiration are the prophets whose oracles became part of his Bible (Rom 1:2; 3:21). This is slender evidence to go on, but it is all we have that is not based on some prior speculations having to do with "authority." The key to Paul's understanding lies with his eschatological framework and presuppositions; he has no interest at all in the questions raised by our existence in the church some 1900 years later.

---

[19]Typical is Wayne A. Grudem's *The Gift of Prophecy in the New Testament and Today*, whose major concerns have to do with the "authority" of the prophecy and the concomitant (for him) issue of the "authority" of women in the church. For all of the good material in this book, this way of setting up the questions tends to result in speaking to a lot of concerns that are quite different from Paul's.

THE χαρίσματα AND ESCHATOLOGY

Related to the previous discussion is that of the cessation of the χαρίσματα. This question, of course, is related not to questions that concerned Paul, but to those raised by our own history of the church. But in a manner unrelated to the way the question has been raised in our time, Paul does speak to it. It is not surprising that his answer is once again related to his eschatological framework and presuppositions. His resolution in this case seems directed against a misguided understanding of χαρίσματα, especially glossolalia, on the part of the Corinthians. Paul speaks to this question in 1 Cor 13:8–10, in this case arguing against the Corinthians' "overspiritualized" eschatology. Apparently they have emphasized the "already" in such a way as to negate rather thoroughly the "not yet." Already they are rich, full, and have begun to reign (4:8). Glossolalia apparently serves for them as the "sign" (cf. 14:20–22) of their "arrival." Speaking the language of angels (13:1) means they are already partakers of the ultimate state of spiritual existence, leading them to deny a future bodily resurrection (15:12).

As part of his argument against this wrong emphasis on tongues, Paul insists that the gifts do *not* belong to the future, but *only* to the present. On this matter they are deluded. The irony is that the gifts, to them the evidence of future existence, will pass away when the true future existence is attained(13:8a): the χαρίσματα are "partial" (v. 9); they are like childhood in comparison with adulthood (v. 11); they are like looking into a mirror in comparison with seeing someone face to face (v. 12). But this is not a devaluation of the gifts; rather, it is to put them into proper (= "already but not yet") eschatological perspective. We are still in the present, so in 1 Cor 14 Paul not only corrects abuse, but urges proper use. In the present we should pursue love (14:1), because that alone is both for now and forever (13:13); but that also means that in the already we should eagerly desire manifestations of the Spirit so as to build up the community. The final glory (what is complete) awaits.

What does not seem possible to extract from this answer is that Paul expected the χαρίσματα to cease within his lifetime, or shortly thereafter. This particular "answer" to the issue is raised not on the basis of reading the biblical text, but from the greater concern as to their "legitimacy" today. But this is a hermeneutical question, pure and simple, and one that Paul could not have understood. His answer is plain: "Of course they will continue as long as we await the final consummation." Any answer that does not follow in the footsteps of the apostle at this point may hardly appeal to him for support.[20]

---

[20]The most exegetically astute of these various attempts is that by R. Gaffin, *Perspectives on Pentecost*. This book basically raises and answers questions, using

THEIR EXTENT IN THE PAULINE CHURCHES

The very fact that Paul can list all these items in such a matter-of-fact way, especially in 1 Cor 12:7–11, indicates that the worship of the early church was far more "charismatic" than has been true for most of its subsequent history. Some indeed have tried to make a virtue of this lack, arguing that the more extraordinary phenomena were relatively limited in the early church—they belong to more "immature" believers like the Corinthians—but are not needed in more mature congregations. One may as well argue that the other Pauline churches did not celebrate the Lord's Supper, since it is mentioned only in 1 Corinthians.

In fact the evidence is considerable that a visible, "charismatic" dimension of life in the Spirit was the normal experience of the Pauline churches. That Paul should speak to it in a direct way so few times (esp. 1 Thes 5:19–22; 1 Cor 12–14) is the "accident" of history: only here were there problems of abuse. The nature of the problem in Thessalonica, to be sure, is moot; either some of them are "playing down" the prophetic Spirit in their gatherings, or Paul is anticipating some problems and tries to bring it under the rubric of "test all things." More likely it is the latter. If so, then it is similar to that in Corinth. In any case, Paul's response is never to eliminate such phenomena—they are the manifestations of the Spirit, after all—but to correct by urging proper use.

Even more telling are the offhanded, matter-of-fact ways these phenomena are mentioned elsewhere. For example, in 2 Thes 2:2 Paul knows that someone has falsely informed them as to "the Day of the Lord." What he does not know is the source of this false information; one possibility is "through the Spirit" (most likely a "nondiscerned" prophetic utterance). Likewise in 1 Cor 11:2–16 in the matter of head-coverings, Paul refers to worship as "praying *and prophesying*," the two primary ways of addressing God and people in the assembly. In Gal 3:4 he can appeal to their "having experienced so many such things," referring specifically to the experienced dimension of their coming to faith in Christ; and in v. 5 a major point of his argument rests on their ongoing experience of "miracles." Finally, in the case of Timothy's ministry (1 Tim 1:18; 4:14), his own gifting is related to prophetic utterances in the community. In none of these instances is Paul arguing *for* something; rather, the visible, "charismatic" expression of their common life in the Spirit is the presupposition *from* which he argues for something else.

We may conclude, therefore, that all the evidence points in one direction: for Paul and his churches the Spirit is not only the absolute key to their understanding of Christian life—from beginning to end—but

---

Paul in support, to which Paul does not speak at all. Cf. my critique in *Gospel and Spirit*, 75–77.

above all else the Spirit was experienced, and experienced in ways that were essentially powerful and visible. Although in some cases this led to triumphalism—of a dualistic type (Spirit against earthly existence)—for Paul these were part of the package. Paul did not "ethicize" the Spirit, as Gunkel argued;[21] for Paul ethical life by the Spirit was part and parcel of his understanding of the Spirit as the fulfilled eschatological promise of God. That is, the ethical life of the Spirit belonged to the promise and was experienced as such before Paul came to it. His concern was with correction, to ensure that his churches followed in the paths he had taught them from the beginning.[22]

But triumphalism was not the necessary corollary of life in the Spirit, experienced in dynamic and powerfully visible ways, as his own life attests. Here is one who could keep the two together; the empowering Spirit, visibly manifest among them often and regularly in giftings and empowerings of an extraordinary kind; while at the same time Paul was filled with the joy of the Spirit in the midst of suffering and weaknesses of all kinds. Paul's word to the Philippians is worth our hearing and heeding today: "Join with others in following my example, brothers and sisters, and take note of those who live according to the pattern we gave you" (3:17). In the context of Philippians that included both "the power of Christ's resurrection and the fellowship of his sufferings." As noted in chapter 14, his example of a Spirit-empowered, Spirit-directed life was particularly wide-ranging and included personal Spirituality as well as the community phenomena noted in this chapter. So our final word is like the first one: the Spirit for Paul was an experienced eschatological reality who served both as evidence that the future is already at hand and as the guarantee of its final consummation. We are "already" but "not yet," and the only way we can so live is by the power of the Spirit.

---

[21]Nor did he, as Hoyle suggests (*Holy Spirit*, 34), "base all the religious and ethical life of Christians on the quieter, constant, inward working of the Spirit." Paul would not recognize such dichotomies.

[22]How else does one explain the warning in 1 Cor 10:1–6, one wonders, where Paul argues that "*all our Fathers* were baptized into Moses."

16

WHERE TO FROM HERE? THE RELEVANCE OF PAULINE PNEUMATOLOGY

If the preceding pages of exegesis and theology are even moderately accurate, then it must be candidly acknowledged not only that the experience and life of the Spirit were for the most part more radically in the center of things for Paul and his churches than for most of us, but that the Spirit was a more genuinely experienced reality as well. It is that acknowledgment that has led to the title of this final chapter. But proper humility will also acknowledge that "I don't know" is the most appropriate answer to the question. Rather than give "answers," therefore, I propose to conclude (1) by isolating the central features of Pauline pneumatology, (2) by pointing out the frequent distance between Paul and ourselves on these matters, and (3) by offering some minimal suggestions about bridging that distance. What is said here, it should be noted, assumes the essential validity of the Reformation principle that the church must always and simultaneously be "reformed but always being reformed," and that the essential ingredient of true "reformation" and "renewal" is for it to become more self-consciously biblical in its life and outlook.

THE PAULINE PERSPECTIVE: A SUMMARY

The following are what I perceive to be at the heart of Paul's view of things regarding the Spirit:

1. The most obvious point has been repeated in a number of ways throughout, namely, *the absolutely crucial role the Spirit plays* in Paul's Christian experience and therefore in his understanding of the gospel. In the final analysis, there is no aspect of his theology—at least what is fundamental to his theology—in which the Spirit does not play a leading role. To be sure, the Spirit is not *the* center for Paul—Christ is, ever and always—but the Spirit stands very close to the center, as the crucial

ingredient of all genuinely Christian life and experience. For this reason, the Spirit arguably must play a much more vital role in our rethinking Paul's theology than tends now to be the case.

2. Crucial to the Spirit's central role is the thoroughly *eschatological* framework within which Paul both experienced and understood the Spirit. The Spirit had played a leading role in his—and others'—eschatological expectations; along with the resurrection of Christ, therefore, the out-poured Spirit was the primary cause of Paul's radically altered eschato-logical perspective. On the one hand, the coming of the Spirit fulfilled the OT eschatological promises, and was the sure *evidence* that the future had *already* been set in motion; on the other hand, since the final expression of the Eschaton had *not yet* taken place, the Spirit also served as the sure *guarantee* of the final glory. It is impossible to understand Paul's emphasis on the experienced life of the Spirit apart from this thoroughgoing eschato-logical perspective that dominated his thinking.

3. Equally crucial to the Pauline perspective is the *dynamically expe-rienced nature* of the coming of the Spirit in the life of the individual and in the ongoing life of the believing community. This view is fully pre-suppositional for Paul; it also finds frequent expression, not as something Paul argues for, but from. The Spirit as an experienced reality lies behind both the Corinthian abuse and the Pauline corrective of Spirit life in that community (1 Cor 12–14); it is basic to his reminding the Thessalonians about the reality of their conversion (1 Thes 1:4–6); it serves as primary evidence that life in Christ is predicated on faith and apart from Torah (Gal 3:1–5; 4:6–7); it is the presupposition lying behind the (apparently corrective) imperatives in 1 Thes 5:19–22 (cf. 2 Thes 2:2); it serves as corroborating evidence of Paul's own apostolic ministry (1 Cor 2:4–5; 2 Cor 12:12; Rom 15:18–19); it is the predicate on which Paul can argue for the sufficiency of life in the Spirit (Gal 5:13–6:10); and it is essential to his reminder to Timothy to fan Spirit life into flame for the necessary power and courage for ministry in Ephesus (1 Tim 1:18; 4:14; 2 Tim 1:6–7). Both Paul's explicit words and his allusions to the work of the Spirit everywhere presuppose the Spirit as an empowering, experienced reality in the life of the church and the believer.

4. Related to the crucial eschatological framework are several con-verging items which demonstrate that for Paul the experience of the eschatological Spirit meant the return of *God's own personal presence* to dwell in and among his people. The Spirit marks off God's people corpo-rately and individually as God's temple, the place of his personal dwelling on earth. Brought together here in terms of fulfillment are: (a) the Presence motif itself, inherent to the OT tabernacle and temple; (b) the Presence understood in terms of the Spirit of the Lord (Isa 63:9–14; Ps 106:33); and (c) the promised new covenant of the Spirit from Jeremiah and Ezekiel, wherein the Spirit would indwell God's people and cause them to live and to follow in his ways. Paul not only sees these themes

as fulfilled by the gift of the Spirit, but also understands the Spirit as God's personal presence. This best accounts for Paul's general reluctance to refer to the Spirit with impersonal images; to the contrary, he regularly refers to the Spirit's activity with verbs of personal action, used elsewhere of God and Christ. The Spirit is thus "the Holy Spirit of God" and "the Spirit of Jesus Christ"—the way God is currently present with and among his people.

5. In this vein it is also important to note how absolutely fundamental to Pauline theology are his *Trinitarian presuppositions*—although that is neither his language nor his major focus. What makes this presuppositional for him, without his ever discussing it as such, are the fourfold—and thoroughgoing—realities (a) that God is one and personal, (b) that the Spirit is the Spirit of God and therefore personal, (c) that the Spirit and Christ are fully divine, and (d) that the Spirit is as distinct from Christ and the Father as they are from each other. This "modification" of Paul's understanding of the one God lies behind much that makes his soteriology dynamic and effective.

6. Paul's Trinitarian understanding of God, including the role of the Spirit, is thus foundational to the heart of his theological enterprise—*salvation in Christ*. Salvation is God's activity, from beginning to end: God the Father initiated it, in that it belongs to God's eternal purposes (1 Cor 2:6–9), has its origins in God and has God as its ultimate goal (1 Cor 8:6), and was set in motion by his having sent both the Son and the Spirit (Gal 4:4–7). Christ the Son effected eschatological salvation for the people of God through his death and resurrection, the central feature of all Pauline theology. The effectual realization and appropriation of the love of God as offered by the Son is singularly the work of the Spirit. So much is this so that when Paul reminds believers of their conversion experience or of their present status in Christ, he almost always does so in terms of the Spirit's activity and/or presence. There is no salvation in Christ which is not fully Trinitarian in this sense, and therefore there is no salvation in Christ which is not made effective in the life of the believer by the experienced coming of the Spirit, whom God "poured out on us generously through Jesus Christ our Savior" (Tit 3:6 NIV).

7. But despite his key role in the realization of salvation in Christ, the Spirit's major role in Paul's view of things lies with his being *the absolutely essential constituent of the whole of Christian life*, from beginning to end. The Spirit thus empowers ethical life in all of its dimensions—personal, corporate, and in the world. Believers in Christ, who for Paul are "Spirit people" first and foremost, are variously described as living by the Spirit, walking in the Spirit, being led by the Spirit, bearing the fruit of the Spirit, and sowing to the Spirit. Ethics for Paul is likewise Trinitarian at its roots: the Spirit of God conforms the believer into the likeness of Christ to the glory of God. The Spirit is therefore the empowering presence of God for living the life of God in the present. For Paul,

therefore, there is no Christian life that is not at the same time a *holy* life, made so by the Holy Spirit whom God gives to his people (1 Thes 4:8). At the same time, life in the Spirit also includes every other imaginable dimension of the believer's present eschatological existence, including being empowered by the Spirit to abound in hope, to live in joy, to pray without ceasing, to exercise self-control, to experience a robust conscience, to have insight into God's will and purposes, and for endurance in every kind of present hardship and suffering. To be a believer means nothing less than being "filled with" and thus to "live in/by the Spirit."

8. Finally, the Spirit is the key to all truly Christian *Spirituality*. At the individual level the life of the Spirit includes "praying in the Spirit" as well as with the mind. In so doing, the Spirit not only helps believers by interceding for them in their weaknesses, but also gives them great confidence in such times of prayer since God knows the mind of the Spirit, and since the Spirit prays through the believer in keeping with God's own purposes. At the same time, the Spirit's presence, including his *charismata*, helps to build up the believing community as its members gather together to worship God. In the Pauline churches, therefore, worship is "charismatic" simply because the Spirit is the key player in all that transpires. The Spirit, who forms the body and creates the temple, is present with unity and diversity, so that all may participate and all may be built up.

THE PRESENT PERSPECTIVE: A CONTRAST

With no intent to be judgmental, I observe that in much of its subsequent history the church has lived somewhat below the picture of the life of the Spirit just outlined. Indeed, the general marginalizing of the Spirit by the academy and the frequent domestication of the Spirit by the church were noted in chapter 1 as part of the reason for this book in the first place. For a variety of reasons items 1 to 3 waned in terms of the church's actual experience of the Christian life, with the consequence that items 4, 7, and 8 also tended to diminish. The net result was that the key items, 5 and 6, were retained but frequently more theologically than experientially.

For example, the passage of time and the (necessary, but not always helpful) institutionalizing of the church, plus the influence of Greek thought forms on its theologizing, led the church away from its fundamentally eschatological outlook (item 2), in which the experience of the Spirit played the key role to its self-understanding as living between the times—between the time of the beginning of the end and its consummation at the return of Christ—in which it lived "in the world," always calling it into question, but not "of the world," not conditioned by its values and lifestyle.

At the same time, the dynamic and experienced nature of life in the Spirit was generally lost (item 3). At least part of the reason for this was the result of a matter the NT never addresses: How do children of believers become believers themselves? At some point in time the majority of Christians became so as the result of being born into Christian homes rather than through adult conversion. Indeed, much of the tension later believers feel between their own experience of church and that about which they read in the NT can be attributed to this significant factor. All the Pauline epistles, it must be emphasized, were written to first generation believers, all of whom—at least those *addressed* in Paul's letters—were adult converts, whose conversions had included an experienced coming of the Holy Spirit into their lives. That, at least, is the picture that emerges in the letters. But what happens to this experienced conversion, attended by the Spirit, for children born and raised in the homes of such converts? As much as anything, this probably accounts for the subsequent loss of the experienced nature of life in the Spirit and for the general marginalizing of the Spirit in the later church. Again, this is not intended to be a judgmental picture, nor do I suggest that it is true at all times and in all places. But it is of some interest that the subsequent study of "church history" by the church itself has far more often been a history of the institution than of the life of the Spirit in the community of faith as it lived out the life of Christ in the world.

What was not lost in all of this, of course, was the *doctrine* of the Spirit, with its properly biblical understanding of the Spirit in personal terms (item 4), which led to the more formal creedal expressions of the Trinitarian implications of the Spirit's place in the Godhead (item 5) and therefore of his essential role in one's becoming a child of God (item 6). Related to this development is both the joining of the reception of the Spirit to water baptism and the (probably) eventual practice of baptizing infant children born into Christian homes. Inevitably, the Spirit was now no longer perceived as dynamically experienced, although he was still the central factor in the *theology* of salvation.

The general loss of the dynamic and experienced life of the Spirit *at the beginning of Christian life* also accounts for the frequent malaise and unfortunately all too frequent anemia of the individual believer throughout much of the church's later history (item 7). This is obviously not true of everyone, of course. But it does in part account for the rise both of the monastic movement and of various Spirit movements throughout its history. "Holy" and its plural noun, "the saints," which in Pauline Spirituality describes everyday Christian life, came to describe the "special," rather than the normal. And so, too, with Spirituality (item 8). Spontaneity by the many gave way to performance by a few; prayer in the Spirit became fixed in the (often excellent) liturgy of the church; tongues did indeed generally cease and the prophetic word was relegated to the prepared sermon.

To be sure, the church has also had its history of "Spirit movements" of various and sundry kinds. Some of these were co-opted by the church; others were pushed outside the church and usually became heretical and divisive; and still others became reform movements within. The common denominator of most of these movements has been their attempt to recapture the life of the Spirit in some form or another. To the degree that they succeeded they have been a source of renewal and blessing. But Spirit movements tend to make institutions nervous—for good reason, one might add, both positively and negatively. The net result has been that the Pauline perspective of life in the Spirit, as a dynamically experienced reality creating an eschatological people who live for God's glory, has not generally fared well in the overall life of the church.

A WAY FORWARD

If what has preceded paints too bleak a picture or sounds like a denigration of the subsequent work of the Spirit in the church, let it be said again that this is not my intent; nor do I think that if we could turn the clock back, all would be better. To the contrary, I for one not only recognize that the clock cannot be turned back, but also find cause for much rejoicing in the church's history. The creeds, the liturgies, the theologizing, the institutional life are not only with us, but for many, myself included, are seen to be the work of the Spirit in the subsequent life of the church. The plea of this study, therefore, is not that of a restorationist, as if we really could restore "the primitive church," whatever that means and whatever that would look like. Rather, it is a plea for the recapturing of the Pauline perspective of Christian life as essentially the life of the Spirit, dynamically experienced and eschatologically oriented—but *fully integrated into the life of the church.*

From my limited perspective, such a "recapturing" has two dimensions to it. First, rather than "tearing down these barns and building different ones," which all too often has been the history of Spirit movements, especially of the "restorationist" type, let us have the Spirit bring life into our present institutions, theologies, and liturgies. The Spirit not only inspires a new hymnody in every renewal within the church, but makes the best of former hymnodies come to life with new vigor. "Can these 'dry bones' live?" the Lord asked the prophet. "You know," he replied, and then watched as the Spirit brought life to what was already there. Too much water has passed under the bridge for us to believe that somehow we will be miraculously made into one in terms of visible structures, liturgies, and theologies. But time and again, when the human factor is not getting in the way, the Spirit has given God's people a greater sense that they are one across confessional lines. The church is with us—indeed, we are it—in its present shape(s) and structures. May the Spirit of the living God be poured out upon it afresh for its life in the present world until Christ comes again.

Second, a genuine recapturing of the Pauline perspective will not isolate the Spirit in such a way that "Spiritual gifts" and "Spirit phenomena" take pride of place in the church, resulting in churches which are either "charismatic" or otherwise. Rather, a genuine recapturing of the Pauline perspective will cause the church to be more vitally Trinitarian, not only in its theology, but in its life and Spirituality as well. This will mean not the exaltation of the Spirit, but the exaltation of God; and it will mean not focus on the Spirit as such, but on the Son, crucified and risen, Savior and Lord of all. Ethical life will be neither narrowly, individualistically conceived nor legalistically expressed, but will be joyously communal and decidedly over against the world's present trinity of relativism, secularism, and materialism, with their thoroughly dehumanizing affects. And the proper Trinitarian aim of such ethics will be the Pauline one—to the glory of God, through being conformed to the image of the Son, by the empowering of the Spirit.

In recapturing the dynamic life of the Spirit there will also be the renewal of the *charismata*, not for the sake of being charismatic, but for the building up of the people of God for their life together and in the world. What must not happen in such a renewal is what has so often happened in the past: holding the extraordinary *charismata* is such awe that they are allowed to exist untested and undiscerned. Every form of extremism, which is so often the expressed or hidden fear over a renewed life of the Spirit in the church, is ultimately the result of failure to heed the primary Pauline injunction (1 Thes 5:19–22): "Do not quench the Spirit by despising prophesying. But *test all things*; and in so doing, hold fast to what is good and be done with every evil form." The failure to "test the spirits" has led to lack of responsibility and accountability, which in turn has often led to failure on the part of some who were in prominence, as well as to pain and hurt by those who were the recipients of "prophetic words" that were either false or unrealizable.

In sum, I for one think the Pauline perspective has the better of it; and I also believe that that perspective can become our own—dare I say, "must" become our own, if we are going to make any difference at all in the so-called post-Christian, post-modern era. But this means that our theologizing must stop paying mere lip service to the Spirit and recognize his crucial role in Pauline theology; and it means that the church must risk freeing the Spirit from being boxed into the creed and getting him back into the experienced life of the believer and the believing community.

Perhaps the proper way to conclude this study is with prayer, in this case with the aid of earlier Spirit-inspired prayers. The first is from the Psalter, expressing the longing of those who already know God to know him more—and better; it assumes the posture of the first and third beatitudes ("blessed are the poor in spirit"; "blessed are those who hunger and thirst for righteousness"), but is expressed in the passionate language of the soul that knows it has a God-shaped space within, which desperately needs God to fill it with himself:

> O God, you are my God,
>   earnestly I seek you;
> my soul thirsts for you,
>   my body longs for you,
> in a dry and weary land
>   where there is no water (63:1; NIV).

The second is the prayer of Moses, noted throughout this study as lying close to the surface of Paul's understanding of the Spirit as God's empowering presence. Here is that cry of desperation which should mark church and believer alike, who live as God's redeemed and redemptive people in the post-modern era that marks the turning of the centuries—and millennia:

> If your Presence does not go with us, do not send us up from here. How will anyone know that you are pleased with . . . your people unless you go with us? What else will distinguish . . . your people from all the other people on the face of the earth (Exod 33:15–16; NIV)?

And finally from Andrew Reed's hymn, which expresses at the individual level what should perhaps most characterize the nature of our prayer for life in the Spirit:

> Holy Spirit, all divine,
>   Dwell within this heart of mine;
> Cast down every idol throne,
>   Reign supreme, and reign alone.

Amen and amen.

APPENDIX: THE PAULINE ANTECEDENTS[1]

In contrast to many such studies, where the questions of "sources" and "influences" appear early on, I have chosen to relegate this matter to an appendix—not because I think it unimportant, but because I think one can only pursue this question legitimately *after* a careful look at Paul himself. But since it would be anti-climactic for me to make it the final chapter, as though the book were heading in that direction,[2] I have chosen to include it as an appendix.

There can be little question that Paul considered his understanding of the Spirit to flow directly out of the Old Testament. This is writ large throughout the corpus. The Old Testament contains the "covenant" which Christ and the Spirit have replaced; here are found the "promises" which Paul understands to have been "fulfilled" by the gift of the Spirit. In his earliest letter he echoes the language of the LXX of Ezek 37:6 and 14 to speak of God's "giving his Holy Spirit into you" (1 Thes 4:8); the same passage from Ezekiel is joined to a midrash on Exodus 33–34 in 2 Corinthians 3 to try to persuade the Corinthians that the more glorious covenant (of the Spirit) has come, over against the purveyors of Torah observance for God's newly constituted people; in Gal 3:14 Paul sees the gift of the Spirit among the Gentiles as evidence that the promised blessing of Abraham has now been fulfilled; in Rom 2:29 Paul considers the circumcision of the heart by the Spirit to be in "fulfillment" of Deut 30:1–6; and the list could go on.

Nonetheless, as with ourselves (referring now especially to Christians), who read the Old Testament in light of the events of the New, so

---

[1]*Bibliography:* Michael E. **Lodahl**, *Shekinah Spirit: Divine Presence in Jewish and Christian Religion* (New York: Paulist, 1992); R. P. **Menzies**, *Development*, 52–112; **Pinnock**, "Concept," 13–88; W. C. **Wright**, "Use," 6–169.

[2]Which is precisely what Hoyle does (*Holy Spirit*, 1927). His obvious interest is to place Paul on the map, as it were. I care very little for that, except in terms of his continuity and discontinuity with the Old Testament (and Judaism).

Paul was also a man of his own times, who likewise read the Old Testament within the framework of his own historical context and experience. Our task in this chapter, therefore, is twofold: (1) to outline the Old Testament understanding of the Spirit, especially as that impacts our understanding of Paul; and (2) to look briefly at some "developments" within intertestamental Judaism.[3] Our concern is to place Paul within this spectrum, so that we can understand not only the Old Testament view itself, but also how the Spirit was viewed within the continuation of Judaism after the Old Testament, and whether or not that had any measurable influence on Paul.

A very important methodological point needs to be made at the outset. As with all who interpret their existence and the past in light of their own experiences, there are both conscious and unconscious influences. There can be no question of Paul's conscious influences: the canonical Old Testament and his own experience of the Risen Lord and the eschatological Spirit. And he clearly interprets the former in light of the latter, although he considers this way of looking at things in terms of "promise" (the Old Testament) and "fulfillment" (Christ and the Spirit). Our difficulties lie with trying to discover the unconscious influences, since Paul makes no explicit mention of them and does not use their language. Nonetheless, two "influences" seem certain. (1) By his own admission he was "as to the Law a Pharisee" (Phil 3:5); that he moved easily within this tradition is evidenced by his knowledge of pharisaic traditions in 1 Cor 10:4 and by his form of argumentation in Gal 4:21–31. (2) The other certain influence is Jewish "apocalyptic," which in Paul's case refers more to an eschatological perspective held in common with those who produced this literature than to the literature itself, since his letters reveal no explicit literary dependence on these works. Our concern here is a simple one: Is there any evidence from what is actually expressed in these sources that they influenced his *understanding* of his experience of the eschatological Spirit?

THE SPIRIT IN THE OLD TESTAMENT

Of the some 377 appearances of the word רוּחַ (*rûaḥ* = "breath, wind, spirit") in the Masoretic text,[4] our interest lies with the approximately 94 that refer to the Spirit of God. The issue of its meaning in the Old

---

[3]*Pace* E. F. Scott, *Spirit*, 130 ("this Hellenistic bias in Paul's thinking must be taken into account when we seek to understand his doctrine of the Spirit"), the firm judgment of all recent writers (Pinnock, Wright, *TDNT*, *NIDNTT*, Menzies) is that Paul's understanding of his experience of the Spirit, as the Spirit of God, rests entirely within his Jewish frame of reference.

[4]Only 264 of these are translated by πνεῦμα in the LXX.

Testament is a large and complex one, related in part to how one understands developmental schemes in the Old Testament literature.[5] But this latter issue interests us very little, since whatever influence the Old Testament had on Paul, it had in its canonical form, with all the variety and complexity already securely in place. Our interest, therefore, is not in linear development, but in the diverse ways an understanding of the Spirit occurs.

All of the various developments of רוּחַ in the Old Testament can be attributed to two factors: its basic meaning as "air in motion," and the mysterious, intangible, but powerfully effective nature of such רוּחַ. That it should finally be attributed to the mysterious and powerful workings of God, in a whole variety of manifestations, should therefore not surprise one. But at the same time, when רוּחַ is associated closely with God, it was also inevitable that it should be related both to his power and to his moral character. Most of the presuppositions of Pauline usage, therefore, are already at work in the Old Testament. We note a few of these:

THE SPIRIT AS DIVINE POWER

The single most notable characteristic of the Spirit of God is his power. Such an attribution seems inevitable, since God himself is the all-powerful one and the Hebrew interest in רוּחַ lay primarily in its inexplicable power, that is, in its powerful effects, even though רוּחַ itself was invisible. Thus, the Spirit of God is recognized as the invisible power creating or effecting a whole variety of realities. Although the notion of the Spirit as creator is not a fully developed OT concept, the Spirit is seen as responsible for creation (Ps 104:30; cf. 33:6; Gen 1:2), as well as for the eschatological renewal of the earth (Isa 32:15). The רוּחַ of God endows mere humans with extraordinary powers, sometimes with physical strength (Judg 14:6, "The Spirit of the Lord came upon Samson with power"; cf. 14:19; 15:14), sometimes with skill for working

---

[5] *Bibliography* (selected): C. **Armerding**, "The Holy Spirit in the Old Testament," *BSac* 92 (1935) 277–91, 433–41; F. **Baumgärtel**, W. **Bieder**, E. **Sjöberg**, *TDNT* 6.359–89; C. **Briggs**, "The Use of רוּחַ in the Old Testament," *JBL* 19 (1900) 132–45; R. S. **Cripps**, "The Holy Spirit in the Old Testament," *Th* 24 (1932) 272–80; G. H. **Davies**, "Holy Spirit in the Old Testament," *RevExp* 63 (1966) 129–34; J. **Hehn**, "Zum Problem des Geistes im alten Orient und im Alten Testament," *ZAW* 43 (1925) 13–67; P. **van Imschoot**, "L'Esprit de Jahvé, principé de vie morale dans l'A.T.," *ETL* 16 (1939) 457–67; E. **Kamlah**, *NIDNTT* 3.690–93; R. **Koch**, *Geist und Messias* (Vienna: Herder, 1950); S. **Mowinckel**, "The Spirit and the Word in the Pre-Exilic Reforming Prophets," *JBL* 53 (1934) 199–227; W. R. **Schoemaker**, "The Use of *Ruach* in the Old Testament and πνεῦμα in the New Testament," *JBL* 23 (1904) 13–67; N. **Snaith**, *Distinctive Ideas of the Old Testament* (London: Epworth, 1944) ch. 7; P. **Volz**, *Der Geist Gottes und die verwandten Erscheinungen im Alten Testament und im anschliessenden Judentum* (Tübingen: Mohr, 1910); B. B. **Warfield**, "The Spirit of God in the Old Testament," in *Biblical and Theological Studies* (Philadelphia: Presbyterian and Reformed, 1952) 127–56.

(Exod 31:3–4; 35:31, "I have filled Bezalel with the Spirit of God, with skill . . . to make artistic designs"), sometimes with insight and wisdom (Dan 5:14), and sometimes for ecstasy (1 Sam 10:10, "and the Spirit of God came upon him in power, and he joined in their prophesying"; cf. v. 6; Num 11:25, 29; 1 Sam 19:20, 23–24). Likewise, the Spirit causes the cherubim to move (Ezek 1:12, 20), sets Ezekiel on his feet (2:2), lifts him up (3:12; 8:3), or snatches him away (3:14; cf. 1 Kgs 18:12; 2 Kgs 2:16).

The Spirit of God, therefore, meant the effective working of the power of God. It is probably fair to say that even though the two words (spirit and power) are not coterminous, the presence of the one (spirit) always implies the presence of the other (power). As noted throughout the exegesis of texts, this fundamental understanding of the Spirit is presuppositional with Paul.

THE SPIRIT AND LEADERSHIP

One of the major strands of empowering in the Old Testament is for leadership in Israel. This appears first with regard to Moses (Num 11:17) and Joshua (Num 27:18). It becomes thoroughgoing in the Judges, various of whom are specifically noted as having received the Spirit of the Lord as the source of their equipping for leadership. Thus, "the Spirit of the Lord came upon [Othniel], so that he became Israel's judge and went to war" (3:10, NIV); cf. Gideon, ("then the Spirit of the Lord came upon Gideon, and he blew a trumpet, summoning the Abiezrites to follow him" 6:34 [NIV]); Jephthah (11:29); and Samson (14:6, 19; 15:14). The first king of Israel is empowered for an almost identical kind of leadership (1 Sam 11:6, "when Saul heard their words, the Spirit of God came upon him in power"), and the same is said of David at his anointing (1 Sam 16:13).

It is not surprising, therefore, that God's messianic king is characterized first of all as the one on whom the Spirit of the Lord would rest (Isa 11:2), a motif developed more fully with the Servant of the Lord (Isa 42:1–2; 59:21; 61:1).

Given this considerable motif in the Old Testament, it is of some interest that Paul himself does not develop it, in terms either of Christ or of his own apostleship. That he does not so refer to Christ is less surprising, since his references to Christ are predominantly to the Risen Lord, not to the earthly Messiah. But in terms of his own ministry, Paul never directly attributes apostleship, either his or others', to the Spirit. Some, of course, see such an attribution in 1 Cor 12:27, since it occurs in the context of χαρίσματα. But in fact Paul does not refer to apostleship as a χάρισμα; and of apostles he says, "God has placed in the church." This phenomenon is one of the imponderables in Paul.

THE SPIRIT AND PROPHECY

In keeping with the Spirit as the source of divine empowering, the Spirit of God is especially understood to lie behind prophetic activity, especially the prophetic word, as well as behind inspired speech in general. Thus, David says, "The Spirit of the Lord spoke through me" (2 Sam 23:2); cf. 1 Chron 12:18 (of Amasai); 2 Chron 15:1 (Azariah); 20:14 (Jahaziel).[6] But prophetic speech in particular is recognized as the product of Spirit-empowering. This was true of pre-writing prophetism (Num 11:25 [the seventy elders]; 11:26 [Eldad and Medad]; 24:2 [Balaam]; 1 Sam 10:10 [Saul]). According to Zechariah (7:12), it was also true of the pre-exilic prophets ("the words that the Lord Almighty had sent by his Spirit through the earlier prophets"), although they themselves do not often attribute their words directly to the Spirit. Micah 3:8 is the one clear exception: "But as for me, I am filled with power, with the Spirit of the Lord, . . . to declare to Jacob his transgression, to Israel his sin" (NIV). The Spirit as the source of his inspiration is the thoroughgoing perspective of the exilic prophet Ezekiel (11:5 et passim).

Of considerable interest for our purposes is the response of Moses in Num 11:29 to Joshua's jealousy: "I wish that all the Lord's people were prophets and that the Lord would put his Spirit on them." This prayer is taken up eschatologically by Joel as the first expression of God's messianic rule: "I will pour out my Spirit on all people; your sons and daughters will prophesy; . . . even on my servants, both men and women, I will pour out my Spirit in those days" (2:28–29).

Although Paul does not mention the latter prophecy as such, his understanding of prophecy, that "all may prophesy, one by one" (1 Cor 14:31), surely reflects this promise. In any case, prophecy is clearly attributed to the Spirit in 1 Thes 5:19–20 and 1 Cor 12:7–11. In Paul's view, to despise prophetic utterances is to quench the Spirit.

THE SPIRIT AND REVELATION[7]

Closely related to the motif of the Spirit of God as the source of prophetic inspiration is the later development of the Spirit as the source of revelation. During the Second Temple period this motif goes in two directions, both rooted in the Old Testament. First, when God puts his Spirit upon the Messiah in Isa 11:2, the result will be that he will receive the "Spirit of wisdom and understanding." This motif is picked up in the non-canonical wisdom literature, especially Sirach and the Wisdom of Solomon.

---

[6]Cf. the Elihu speeches in Job (32:8, 18; 33:1–4); but one is not sure whether the author intends these ironically or wants them to be taken seriously. In any case, they reflect an understanding that inspired speech comes from the "spirit of God."

[7]On this question, see esp. Bockmuehl, *Revelation*, passim.

It obviously influences Paul's usage in Col 1:9 and Eph 1:17, in Paul's case directly from the Old Testament, not by way of the wisdom literature.

Second, in Daniel (4:8, 9, 18; 5:11, 14) the Babylonians attribute Daniel's ability to interpret dreams and the writing on the wall to his having "the spirit of the holy gods," whereby he has "insight, intelligence, and outstanding wisdom" (5:14). Here the apocalyptic and wisdom traditions clearly coalesce. This motif of the revelation of mysteries by the Spirit is picked up especially in the apocalyptic literature and Qumran. Paul also obviously fits within this tradition by the way he argues in 1 Cor 2:9–12; but it is scarcely a dominant motif in the apostle, and what he does with it is to take all the "mystery" out. The "hidden mystery" of God that is revealed to those who have received the Spirit of God is the "wisdom" in God's folly, salvation through a crucified Messiah.

THE SPIRIT AS GOD'S PRESENCE

The direct connection between God's presence and his Spirit is articulated especially in the Psalter. In his penitential prayer in Psalm 51, David asks: "Do not cast me from your presence, or take your Holy Spirit from me." Indeed, the Psalmist asks in another place, "Where can I go from your Spirit? Where can I flee from your presence?" (139:7). But it is in Isa 63:10–14 in particular, a passage cited by Paul (Eph 4:30), that the divine presence motif is specifically attributed to the presence of the Spirit. This concept is picked up eschatologically by the prophets, who see the restoration in terms of God's Spirit, both in bringing the nation back to life (Ezek 37:14; cf. Isa 34:16) and in fulfilling the new covenant of Jeremiah by dwelling in the hearts of the people (Ezek 36:27). In this light, the post-exilic Haggai, looking back to the Exodus, sees the present restoration in terms of the Spirit: "This is what I covenanted with you when you came out of Egypt; and my Spirit remains among you" (2:5). Likewise, Zechariah encourages Zerubbabel that God will effect his purposes among them "by my Spirit, says the Lord Almighty" (4:6).

Although one may grant that such language is scarcely that of distinct personhood, it is the beginning of the process that develops in the intertestamental period, where terms like word, wisdom, and spirit are personified, that is, accorded individual and personal characteristics in such a way as to appear with God, yet distinct from him. The Spirit as a distinct agency of God was already recognized in the Old Testament, especially in such language as "I will put my Spirit upon him." It is this rich tradition to which the apostle falls heir.

THE SPIRIT AND ESCHATOLOGY

The most traceable influence on Paul's understanding of the Spirit also ties together much of what has been said above: the Spirit as the key to Israel's eschatological future. This emerges in several significant ways in the Old Testament. In Isaiah, the Spirit rests upon the Messiah, the bringer of eschatological salvation (11:2; cf. 42:1; 59:21; 61:1). Among the Isaianic oracles are the further promises (a) that the Spirit will gather the exiles (34:16); (b) that the Spirit will be "poured out upon us from on high," so that the desert becomes a fertile field and the fertile field a forest (the creation motif), in which justice and righteousness will dwell (32:15–16); and (c) that I [God] will "pour out my Spirit on your offspring, and my blessings on your descendants" (44:3).

Eschatological salvation, both for the people of God as a whole and for the individuals who make up this people, is a major motif in Ezekiel as well (11:19; 18:31; 36:26–27; 37:1–14). The Spirit is key both to salvation and to the promise of God's renewed presence among them. Finally, Joel 2:28–30 sees the renewal of prophecy, bestowed by God on all his people, as part of the eschatological restoration of God's people.

The New Testament perspective as a whole, and Paul's especially, is dominated by this Old Testament theme, a theme which continues to have influence in the intertestamental period as well, to which we now turn.

THE INTERTESTAMENTAL DEVELOPMENTS

The single most noticeable "development" of the concept of the רוח of God during the Second Temple period is that there is scarcely any development at all, mostly because there is comparatively sparse mention of the Spirit in the literature. Most of these, not surprisingly, basically reflect continuations of Old Testament motifs, and the most prevalent is the relationship of the Spirit to prophetic inspiration.[8] Apart from three passages in the Wisdom of Solomon, noted below, and a reference to Isa 11:2 in Sir 39:6, the Spirit of God is not so much as alluded to in the Apocrypha. Although the Spirit is mentioned by Paul's slightly earlier Alexandrian contemporary, Philo, his references are basically limited to the Spirit as the source of prophetic inspiration or of esoteric wisdom; Philo has no influence on Paul. A much higher occurrence of Spirit language emerges in the apocalyptic literature and especially in Qumran. It is more difficult to assess the rabbinic materials, since in written form they come much later than Paul, although some of their references to the Spirit undoubtedly go back as far as Paul.

---

[8]On this matter see Menzies, *Development*, 52–111, although this is a bit of an overstatement, with an obvious bias toward the author's conclusions.

Our concerns in this section, therefore, are two: (1) to critique the oft-repeated suggestion that Paul's pneumatology was influenced by the Wisdom of Solomon; (2) to trace the eschatological Spirit motif through the various literatures.

PAUL AND THE WISDOM OF SOLOMON

One of the less salutary legacies of the "comparative religions school" on New Testament studies was its tendency to turn every linguistic correspondence between a hellenistic document and Paul into a conceptual parallel and every alleged "parallel" into an "influence" or "borrowing." Nowhere can this tendency be seen more clearly than in the alleged "influence" of the Wisdom of Solomon on the apostle Paul, especially on his pneumatology, which has a considerable history in New Testament studies.[9] The "parallels" with Paul's pneumatology are alleged to exist between Wis 9:7–18 and 1 Cor 2:6–16 and Gal 4:4–6.

First, it should be noted that even though the word πνεῦμα occurs more often in Wisdom (20 times) than in most of this literature, only a few of these refer to the Spirit of God,[10] and even in these there is scarcely what one might call a developed pneumatology. In fact, the author betrays influences from Alexandria and Stoicism, which he seems to fail to merge satisfactorily with his own clearly Jewish heritage. Thus, although πνεῦμα is understood as the source of life (15:11), it is not the Spirit of God who has so breathed life into living beings, but the "human spirit" which makes them living beings, and which will depart at death (16:14). The same is true of personified Wisdom, who has a "spirit" within her (7:22–23). In the final analysis, the Spirit of God is mentioned only three times: in 1:7, "the spirit of the Lord has filled the world"; in 12:1, which expresses the same thought in a nearly pantheistic way, "Your immortal spirit is in all things"; and in the alleged parallel, 9:17, where the author

---

[9]This is especially true of Hoyle, *Holy Spirit*, 213–19, who acknowledges the earlier work of J. Weiss, P. Wendland, P. Feine, Sanday and Headlam, and A. Plummer. He could have included others (e.g., O. Pfleiderer, *Das Urchristentum* [Berlin: Georg Reimer, 1887] 158–68; H. J. Thackeray, *The Relation of Paul to Contemporary Jewish Thought* [London: Macmillan, 1900] 78). Since Hoyle, it has been taken up in various forms by inter alia G. Kuhn, "Beiträge zur Erklärung des Buches der Weisheit," *ZNW* 28 (1929) 334–41; J. Fichtner, "Die Stellung der Sapientia Salomonis in der Literatur und Geistgeschichte ihrer Zeit," *ZNW* 36 (1937) 113–32; H. Conzelmann, "Paulus und die Weisheit," *NTS* 12 (1965/66) 231–44; E. Schweizer, "Zum religionsgeschichtlichen Hintergrund der 'Sendungsformel' Gal 4:4f. Rm 8:3f. Joh 3:16f. I Joh 4:9," 199–210; R. Scroggs, "Paul: ΣΟΦΟΣ and ΠΝΕΥΜΑΤΙΚΟΣ," 33–55; K. Romaniuk, "Le Livre de la Sagesse dans le Nouveau Testament," *NTS* 14 (1967/68) 498–514; G. W. E. Nickelsburg, *Jewish Literature between the Bible and the Mishnah* (Philadelphia: Fortress, 1981) 184–85; Menzies, *Development*, 303–15.

[10]See 1:7; 7:7[?]; 9:17; 12:1.

traces his understanding of wisdom to God's "having sent his holy spirit from on high." Even to speak of a "pneumatology" in Wisdom, therefore, requires a degree of temerity.[11]

The alleged parallels are found at two points. E. Schweizer in particular found a "double sending formula" in the request for wisdom (9:10) and the gift of πνεῦμα (9:17) "paralleled" in Paul's words about the Father having sent his Son and the Spirit of his Son in Gal 4:5–6. The linguistic tie is asserted to be in v. 10, where "Solomon" prays for wisdom to be "sent," using the verb ἐξαποστέλλω, the verb Paul uses twice in a *heils-geschichtliche* way, speaking first of God's having "sent forth" his Son (at the propitious historical moment), and later of God's having "sent forth" the Spirit of his Son. But what of Schweizer's "sending formula," for which this text in Wisdom is crucial? First, the author does not in fact speak of a double sending. In the first instance, where the use of the verb is the only "parallel"—and indeed the only clue at all—it comes in the form of a prayer, namely, Solomon's prayer to receive Wisdom so that he might rule wisely and justly. But in v. 17 the sending of the "spirit" is expressed in the past tense, with a different verb, and is obviously not a second "sending," but refers to the Spirit of God who provides wisdom. In between is a considerable exposition of the need for wisdom, which mortals could not have at all had God not sent his Spirit. To find here a "double sending *formula*," even in Schweizer's watered-down version of "thought pattern in the tradition," as though the author had historical moments of sending in mind upon which Paul himself is *dependent*, is suspect in the highest degree. "Borrowing" and "influence" must be made of firmer stuff!

The same holds true with the admittedly closer "parallel" between Wis 9:17–18 and 1 Cor 2:6–16. But again the "parallels" are basically (remote) linguistic correspondences that function far below what one might expect from literary and conceptual *dependency*. What is common to both texts is that the Spirit of God is the source of wisdom. Because the verb for "salvation" also appears in Wis 9:18, it is suggested that here, too, is the source of Paul's understanding of the Spirit as a soteriological reality. But the problems with this view are several; I simply list them:

1. The *linguistic* ties between Wisdom and 1 Cor 2:6–16 are so remote as to be nearly nonexistent. Despite assertions by some to the contrary, Paul does not attribute the gaining of wisdom to the Spirit. He speaks rather of what has been once hidden as now revealed. Two matters are crucial: First, wisdom is not a Pauline word. His use of it in this passage is dictated by the Corinthians' fascination with it, not by his own reading of Jewish speculative wisdom. Second, Paul asserts the content of "wis-

---

[11] In Winston's commentary (AB 43; New York: Doubleday, 1979), e.g., no such category is noted, nor does the Spirit appear in the subject index; cf. his entry in *ABD* 6.120–27.

dom" to be the proclamation of a crucified Messiah, which is foolishness to those who do not have the Spirit. This is a far cry indeed from the wisdom praised by the author of Wisdom!

2. On the other hand, there are some discernible linguistic ties with Jewish literature, but it is with Jewish apocalyptic, not Jewish speculative wisdom. As pointed out in our exegesis of this passage, the "background" to Paul's use of language—and concepts—comes from passages like Dan 2:20–23. If the Spirit is missing from the Daniel text, much of the rest of the language is parallel.

3. One should note further that the concerns expressed in 1 Cor 2:6–16 scarcely lie at the heart of Pauline pneumatology. Rather than reflecting the heart of things, it reflects what Paul can do when his opposition sets him up for something. The confirmation for this is that even though Paul does see the Spirit as crucial to "revelation," when he refers to such reality he uses the language of Isa 11:2, not that of Wisdom 9 (see esp. Col 1:9; Eph 1:17). Otherwise there is no connection between the Greek word "wisdom" and the Spirit.

4. But most significantly, the overall pneumatological schemes of Paul and Wisdom are so radically different that one wonders how any could have persuaded themselves to the contrary. Paul's view of the Spirit stems from his *experience* of the Spirit, as that is understood within his basic eschatological framework. The "fulfillment" Paul speaks to stems directly from the Old Testament; this view can scarcely have been mediated through Wisdom, since it lacks totally the Pauline eschatological perspective and makes no allusion of any kind to the promised eschatological Spirit,[12] which is central to Paul's view of things.

If Paul shares some elements in common with the basic anthropology of Wisdom, that is incidental to his pneumatology, and in any case belongs to the milieu of which they both form a part. One may safely judge this view of "influence" on Paul to be both mistaken and misguided. Paul's influence comes from his experience of the Spirit as the eschatological fulfillment of the promises of God (in the OT); the real question is whether this perspective is in a direct line from the Old Testament, or whether it is also a reality shared in common with others of his own time on which he is dependent.

THE SPIRIT AS AN ESCHATOLOGICAL REALITY

Since eschatological salvation is so clearly at the heart of Pauline pneumatology, the real question of "influences" on Paul's thinking need

---

[12]In Wisdom the Spirit has already been given, not as an *eschatological* reality, but as the agency behind Solomon's having received wisdom. The conceptual parallel to this is the attribution of the Spirit's insight to the writers of the apocalyptic literature, since the actual writers do not (cannot?) speak in their own name.

to be sought in this area. And here we can make some prior judgments, namely, that there is no known *literary* parallel between Paul and any of this literature, especially in the area of Pauline pneumatology. What is "parallel" are some common motifs and concerns; this indicates, understandably, that Paul and these writers emerge within the same general milieu of Jewish eschatological expectations, and in both cases they are ultimately dependent on the Old Testament, though they interpret it in independent ways.

First, they commonly recognize that the Spirit is responsible for the "inspiration" of the ancient worthies who spoke for the Lord.[13] Noticeably missing in the intertestamental literature, by way of comparison, is the sense that the Spirit speaks through any contemporary "prophet." This is almost certainly the result of the growth of a tradition called "the quenched Spirit," which begins in the later books of the Old Testament and is found variously during the Second Temple period, to the effect that the time of prophecy had ceased with the last of the writing prophets and would reappear again only in the final eschatological age. Such a view seems to lie behind Zech 13:2–3 and perhaps Ps 74:9 and the anonymity of Malachi. It finds explicit expression in such various places as Josephus,[14] the Apocalypse of Baruch,[15] the rabbis,[16] and perhaps 1 Maccabees (4:46; 9:27; 14:41), although the latter is disputed.[17] This view is clearly presupposed by the early church (with the coming of John the Baptist and the Day of Pentecost; see Luke 1:15, 76; Acts 2:17).

The most noticeable exception to this motif is the Qumran community, where entrance into the community was understood to be accompanied "by the Spirit which thou has put in me to accomplish thy favours towards thy servant forever by cleansing me by thy Holy Spirit" (1QH 16.11–12 [Dupont-Sommer]), by whom also the worshiper has received the knowledge of God (1QH 12.11–12). But what is noteworthy about these expressions regarding the Spirit here is the community's understanding of itself as an eschatological people who awaited the day of the Lord.[18]

---

[13]Cf. *1 Enoch* 91:2; *2 Esdr* 5:22; 14:22; *Mart. Isa.* 1:7; 5:14; *T. Abr*(A) 4:7; *Apoc. Bar.* 6:3.

[14]See *Ag. Ap.* 1.41 ("From Artaxerxes to our own time the complete history has been written, but has not been deemed worthy of equal credit with the earlier records, because of the failure of the exact succession of the prophets"; LCL, 179).

[15]*Apoc. Bar.* 85:3 (" . . . and the prophets have fallen asleep").

[16]See esp. *t. Soṭa* 13.2 ("When the latter prophets died, that is, Haggai, Zechariah, and Malachi, then the Holy Spirit came to an end in Israel"; Neusner's translation). For a convincing argument that this reflects a very old, probably first century CE, tradition, see Menzies, *Development*, 92–96.

[17]See esp. R. Meyer, *TDNT* 6.816 (on "prophecy").

[18]There has been a considerable literature on the concept of רוּחַ in Qumran; see now A. E. Sekki, *The Meaning of* rûaḥ *at Qumran* (SBLDS 110; Atlanta: Scholars, 1989), for an overview and analysis.

Noticeably scarce in these various writings is an explicit expression of anticipation of the outpouring of the Spirit in the "latter days." Although this motif can be found throughout the rabbinic literature, the problem of dating these materials becomes especially acute with regard to this motif. The one significant exception appears in *Jub.* 1:22–25, where the writer has God speak to Moses with a kind of collage of texts from Deut 30 and Jer 31. Among the promises for future Israel is a circumcision of the heart that is accompanied by God's giving them his Holy Spirit. It is precisely this kind of expectation that one finds in Paul as a "fulfilled promise."

In the final analysis, however, one is hard pressed to argue that with regard to his understanding of the Spirit Paul was greatly influenced by the literature of the Second Temple period. The reason for this is not hard to find. It results altogether from his and the early church's dynamic and visible *experience* of the Spirit as a realized phenomenon. Their experience of the outpoured Spirit caused them to turn not to contemporary writings, but to the books God had inspired by the Holy Spirit (2 Tim 3:16). There Paul discovered that he and the newly constituted people of God had been written about beforehand; there was the promise of the eschatological Spirit, who would reveal, reinstate prophecy, bring in a new covenant, and cause God's people to walk in his ways. If Paul does not expressly associate the soteriological dimension of the Spirit with Old Testament texts, that is because such an understanding is assumed in the new covenant, which is evidenced by the *life-giving Spirit*. Thus for Paul the line is not from the Old Testament to the New, but from his experience of the Spirit as the empowering presence of God back to the Old. What he holds in common with his contemporaries was an apocalyptic world view in which the Spirit had been quenched until the time of the End. The lavish outpouring of the Spirit on him and his churches was the evidence for Paul that the End had begun. Thus Paul's understanding is not influenced by the literature of the period; it is primarily influenced by the experience itself. For him the natural place to look for "antecedents" was in the scripture God had given them. In a whole variety of ways Paul assumes and implies what is said explicitly in Peter's Pentecost sermon: "This is that which was spoken by the prophet" (Acts 2:16).

Select Bibliography

[Commentary bibliographies may be found on the first page of each chapter, where they are listed by author and date.]

Achtemeier, P. J. "*Omne verbum sonat*: The New Testament and the Oral Environment of Late Western Antiquity." *JBL* 109 (1990) 3–27.

Adai, J. *Der Heilige Geist als Gegenwart: Gottes in den einzelnen Christen, in der Kirche und in der Welt.* Frankfurt: Peter Lang, 1985.

Agnew, F. H. "The Origin of the NT Apostle-Concept: A Review of Research." *JBL* 105 (1986) 75–96.

Ahern, B. "The Indwelling Spirit, Pledge of Our Inheritance—Eph 1.14." *CBQ* 9 (1947) 179–89.

Althaus, P. "Zur Auslegung von Röm 7:14ff." *TLZ* 77 (1952) 475–80.

_____. " 'Das ihr nicht tut, was ihr wollt.' Zur Auslegung von Gal. 5,17." *TLZ* 76 (1951) 15–18.

Armerding, C. "The Holy Spirit in the Old Testament." *BSac* 92 (1935) 277–91, 433–41.

Arnold, Clinton E. *Ephesians: Power and Magic; The Concept of Power in Ephesians in Light of its Historical Setting.* SNTSMS 63. Cambridge: Cambridge University Press, 1989.

_____. "The Exorcism of Ephesians 6:12 in Recent Research." *JSNT* 30 (1987) 71–87.

Aune, David E. *Prophecy in Early Christianity and the Ancient Mediterranean World.* Grand Rapids: Eerdmans, 1983.

Badcock, F. J. " 'The Spirit' and Spirit in the New Testament." *ExpT* 45 (1933–34) 218–22.

Baird, W. "Letters of Recommendation: A Study of II Cor. 3:1–3." *JBL* 80 (1961) 166–72.

Baker, D. L. "The Interpretation of 1 Corinthians 12–14." *EvQ* 46 (1974) 224–34.

Banks, R. *Paul's Idea of Community.* Grand Rapids: Eerdmans, 1980.

Banks, R., and G. Moon. "Speaking in Tongues: A Survey of the New Testament Evidence." *Churchman* 80 (1966) 278–94.

Barclay, John M. G. *Obeying the Truth: A Study of Paul's Ethics in Galatians.* Edinburgh: T. & T. Clark, 1988.

Barclay, William. *Flesh and Spirit: An Examination of Galatians 5.19–23.* Nashville: Abingdon, 1962.

Barr, J. " 'Abba, Father' and the Familiarity of Jesus' Speech." *Theology* 91 (1988) 173–79.

_____. " 'Abba' isn't 'Daddy.' " *JTS* 39 (1988) 28–47.

Barrett, C. K. *Freedom and Obligation: A Study of the Epistle to the Galatians.* London: SPCK, 1985.

Barth, M. "A Chapter on the Church—The Body of Christ: Interpretation of I Corinthians 12." *Int* 12 (1958) 131–56.

Bartling, W. J. "The Congregation of Christ—A Charismatic Body: An Exegetical Study of 1 Corinthians 12." *CTM* 40 (1969) 67–80.

Bassler, J. M. "1 Cor 12:3—Curse and Confession in Context." *JBL* 101 (1982) 415–18.

Beale, G. K. "The Old Testament Background of Reconciliation in 2 Corinthians 5–7 and its Bearing on the Literary Problem of 2 Corinthians 6.14–7.1." *NTS* 35 (1989) 550–81.

Beare, F. W. "Speaking with Tongues." *JBL* 83 (1964) 229–46.

Beasley-Murray, G. R. *Baptism in the New Testament.* Grand Rapids: Eerdmans, 1962.

Beasley-Murray, P. "Romans 1:3f: An Early Confession of Faith in the Lordship of Jesus." *TynB* 31 (1980) 147–54.

Beekman, John, and John Callow. *Translating the Word of God.* Grand Rapids: Zondervan, 1974.

Beker, J. Christiaan. *Paul the Apostle: The Triumph of God in Life and Thought.* Philadelphia: Fortress, 1980.

Belleville, Linda. *Reflections of Glory: Paul's Polemical Use of Moses-Doxa Tradition in 2 Corinthians 3.1–18.* JSNTSup 52. Sheffield: JSOT Press, 1991.

Benoit, P. " 'We too groan inwardly as we wait for our bodies to be set free': Romans 8:23." In *Jesus and the Gospel.* Translated by B. Weatherhead. London: Darton, Longman & Todd, 1974. 2.40–50.

Berkhof, Hendrikus. *The Doctrine of the Holy Spirit.* London: Epworth Press, 1964.

Best, E. "Fashions in Exegesis: Ephesians 1:3." In *Scripture, Meaning and Method.* Festschrift A. T. Hanson. Edited by B. P. Thompson. Pages 79–91. Hull: Hull University Press, 1987.

_____. "The Interpretation of Tongues." *SJT* 28 (1975) 45–62.

Betz, H. D. *Der Apostel Paulus und die sokratische Tradition: Eine exegetische Untersuchung zu seiner Apologia (2 Kor. 10–13).* BHT 45. Tübingen: J. C. B. Mohr [Paul Siebeck], 1972.

_____. "Eine Christus-Aretologie bei Paulus (2 Cor 12, 7–10)." *ZTK* 66 (1969) 288–305.

_____. "In Defense of the Spirit: Paul's Letter to the Galatians as a Document of Early Christian Apologetics." In *Aspects of Religious Propaganda in Judaism and Early Christianity.* Edited by E. Schüssler Fiorenza. Pages 99–114. Notre Dame: Notre Dame University Press, 1976.

_____. "2 Cor. 6:14–7:1: An Anti-Pauline Fragment?" *JBL* 92 (1973) 88–108.

Bieder, W. "Gebetswirklichkeit und Gebetsmöglichkeit bei Paulus: das Beten des Geistes und das Beten im Geist." *TZ* 4 (1948) 22–40.

Binder, H. "Die angebliche Krankheit des Paulus." *TZ* 17 (1961) 319–33.

Bittlinger, A. *Gifts and Graces: A Commentary on 1 Corinthians 12–14.* ET. Grand Rapids: Eerdmans, 1967.

Black, D. A. *Paul, Apostle of Weakness: Astheneia and its Cognates in the Pauline Literature*. New York: Peter Lang, 1984.

Black, Matthew. "The Interpretation of Rom viii 28." In *Neotestamentica et Patristica: eine Freundesgabe, Herrn Professor Dr. Oscar Cullmann zu seinem 60. Geburtstag überreicht*. Edited by W. C. van Unnik. NovTSup 6. Pages 166–72. Leiden: Brill, 1962.

Blomberg, C. "The Structure of 2 Corinthians 1–7." *Criswell Theological Review* 4 (1989) 3–20.

Bockmuehl, M. *Revelation and Mystery in Ancient Judaism and Pauline Christianity*. WUNT 2/36. Tübingen: J. C. B. Mohr [Paul Siebeck], 1990.

Boismard, M.-E. "Constitué Fils de Dieu (Rom. I.4)." *RevistB* 60 (1953) 5–17.

Bousset, Wilhelm. *Kyrios Christos*. (Ger. original 1913). Translated by John E. Steely. Nashville: Abingdon, 1970.

Bouttier, M. *En Christ: Etude d'exégèse et de théologie pauliniennes*. Paris: Presses Universitaires, 1962.

Bowker, J. W. " 'Merkabah' Visions and the Visions of Paul." *JJS* 16 (1976) 157–73.

Branick, V. P. "The Sinful Flesh of the Son of God (Rom. 8:3): A Key Image of Pauline Theology." *CBQ* 47 (1985) 246–62.

Braswell, J. P. " 'The Blessing of Abraham' versus 'the Curse of the Law': Another Look at Gal 3:10–13." *WTJ* 53 (1991) 73–91.

Briggs, C. "The Use of רוח in the Old Testament." *JBL* 19 (1900) 132–45.

Bruce, F. F. "The Curse of the Law." In *Paul and Paulinism*. Edited by M. D. Hooker and S. G. Wilson. Pages 27–36. London: SPCK, 1982.

_____. "The Spirit in the Letter to the Galatians." In *Essays on Apostolic Themes: Studies in honor of Howard M. Ervin*. Edited by P. Elbert. Pages 36–48. Peabody, Mass.: Hendrickson, 1985.

Buchanan, C. O. "Epaphroditus' Sickness and the Letter to the Philippians." *EvQ* 36 (1964) 157–66.

Büchsel, F. *Der Geist Gottes im Neuen Testament*. Gütersloh: Bertelsmann, 1926.

_____. " 'In Christus' bei Paulus." *ZNW* 42 (1949) 141–58.

Bultmann, R. *Faith and Understanding*. ET. New York: Harper, 1969.

_____. "Romans 7 and the Anthropology of Paul." In *Existence and Faith* (Ger. original 1932). ET. Pages 173–85. London: Hodder & Stoughton, 1960.

Burgess, S. M., G. B. McGee, and P. Alexander, eds. *Dictionary of Pentecostal and Charismatic Movements*. Grand Rapids: Zondervan, 1988.

Byrne, B. *'Sons of God'—'Sons of Abraham.'* AnBib 83. Rome: Pontifical Biblical Institute, 1979.

Callan, T. "Prophecy and Ecstasy in Greco-Roman Religion and 1 Corinthians." *NovT* 27 (1985) 125–40.

Cambier, J. "Le critère paulinien de l'apostolat en 2 Cor 12, 6s." *Bib* 43 (1962) 481–518.

Carson, D. A. *A Call to Spiritual Reformation: Priorities from Paul and His Prayers*. Grand Rapids: Baker, 1992.

_____. *Showing the Spirit: An Exposition of 1 Corinthians 12–14*. Grand Rapids: Baker, 1987.

_____. " 'Silent in the Churches': On the Role of Women in 1 Corinthians 14:33b–36." In *Recovering Biblical Manhood and Womanhood: A Response to Evangelical Feminism*. Edited by John Piper and W. E. Grudem. Pages 140–53. Wheaton: Crossway, 1991.

Chevallier, M.-A. *Esprit de Dieu, Paroles d'Hommes*. Neuchâtel: Delachaux and Niestlé, 1966.

Chotka, David R. "Spirit versus spirit: An Examination of the Nature and Function of the Holy Spirit Against the Backdrop of the False Spirit in Ephesians." Th.M. thesis, Regent College, 1992.

Clemens, C. "The 'Speaking with Tongues' of the Early Christians." *ExpT* 10 (1898–99) 344–52.

Collins, R. F. *Studies on the First Letter to the Thessalonians*. BETL 66. Leuven: Leuven University Press, 1984.

Cosgrove, Charles H. *The Cross and the Spirit: A Study in the Argument and Theology of Galatians*. Macon, Ga.: Mercer University Press, 1988.

Cottle, R. E. "All Were Baptized." *JETS* 17 (1974) 75–80.

Cranfield, C. E. B. "The Freedom of the Christian according to Rom 8:2." In *New Testament Christianity for Africa and the World*. Festschrift H. Sawyerr. Edited by M. E. Glaswell and E. W. Fasholé-Luke. Pages 91–98. London: SPCK, 1974.

_____. "μέτρον πίστεως in Romans xii.3." *NTS* 8 (1961–62) 345–51.

Cranford, L. "A New Look at 2 Corinthians 5:1–10." *SWJT* 19 (1971) 95–100.

Cripps, R. S. "The Holy Spirit in the Old Testament." *Th* 24 (1932) 272–80.

Cullmann, O. *Baptism in the New Testament*. ET. London: SCM, 1950.

_____. *The Christology of the New Testament*. ET. London: SCM, 1959.

Cuming, G. J. "ἐποτίσθησαν (I Corinthians 12. 13)." *NTS* 27 (1981) 283–85.

Currie, S. D. " 'Speaking in Tongues': Early Evidence Outside the New Testament Bearing on 'Glossais Lalein.' " *Int* 19 (1965) 174–94.

Cutten, G. B. *Speaking with Tongues*. New Haven: Yale University Press, 1927.

Dahl, N. A. "A Fragment in its Context: 2 Corinthians 6:14–7:1." In *Studies in Paul*. Pages 62–69. Minneapolis: Augsburg, 1972.

Daines, B. "Paul's Use of the Analogy of the Body of Christ—With Special Reference to 1 Corinthians 12." *EvQ* 50 (1978) 71–78.

Dautzenberg, G. *Urchristliche Prophetie*. Stuttgart: Calwer, 1975.

_____. "Zum religionsgeschichtlichen Hintergrund der διακρίσεις πνευμάτων (I Kor. 12.10)." *BZ* 15 (1971) 93–104.

Davidson, R. M. *Typology in Scripture: A Study of hermeneutical τύπος structures*. AUSSDS 2. Berrien Springs, Mich.: Andrews University Press, 1981.

Davies, G. H. "Holy Spirit in the Old Testament." *RevExp* 63 (1966) 129–34.

Deissmann, A. *Die neutestamentliche Formel "in Christo Jesu."* Marburg: N. G. Elwert, 1892.

_____. *St. Paul: A Study in Social and Religious History*. (Ger. original 1911). ET. London: Hodder & Stoughton, 1912.

Denton, D. R. "Inheritance in Paul and Ephesians." *EvQ* 54 (1982) 157–62.

Derrett, J. D. M. "Cursing Jesus (I Cor. xii. 3): The Jews as Religious 'Persecutors.' " *NTS* 21 (1974–75).

Dietzel, A. "Beten im Geist: Eine religionsgeschichtliche Parallele aus den Hodajot zum paulinischen Beten in Geist." *TZ* 13 (1957) 12–32.

Dinkler, E. "Die Tauferterminologie in 2 Kor. i,21f." In *Neotestamentica et Patristica: eine Freundesgabe, Herrn Professor Dr. Oscar Cullmann zu seinem 60. Geburtstag überreicht*. Edited by W. C. van Unnik. NovTSup 6. Pages 173–91. Leiden: Brill, 1962.

Dodd, C. H. "῎Εννομος Χριστοῦ." In *Studia Paulina in Honorem Johannis de Zwaan Septuagenarii*. Edited by J. N. Sevenster and W. C. van Unnik. Pages 96–110. Haarlem: De Ervem F. Bohn N.V., 1953.

Donaldson, T. L. "The 'Curse of the Law' and the Inclusion of the Gentiles: Galatians 3.13–14." *NTS* 32 (1986) 94–112.

Donfried, K. P., ed. *The Romans Debate*. Rev. and Exp. Peabody, Mass.: Hendrickson, 1991.

Dunn, J. D. G. *Baptism in the Holy Spirit*. SBT 2/15. London: SCM, 1970.

_____. *Christology in the Making*. Philadelphia: Westminster, 1980.

_____. "I Corinthians 15:45—last Adam, life-giving Spirit." In *Christ and Spirit in the New Testament: Studies in Honour of Charles Francis Digby Moule*. Edited by B. Lindars and S. Smalley. Pages 127–42. Cambridge: Cambridge University Press, 1973.

_____. *Jesus and the Spirit*. Philadelphia: Westminster, 1975.

_____. "Jesus—Flesh and Spirit: An Exposition of Romans i:3–4." *JTS* 24 (1973) 40–68.

_____. "Romans 7:14–25 in the Theology of Paul." In *Essays on Apostolic Themes: Studies in honor of Howard M. Ervin*. Edited by P. Elbert. Pages 49–70. Peabody, Mass.: Hendrickson, 1985. [= *ThZ* 31 (1975) 257–73].

_____. "2 Corinthians iii.17 — 'The Lord is the Spirit.' " *JTS* 21 (1970) 309–20.

_____. "The Theology of Galatians: The Issue of Covenantal Nomism." In *Jesus, Paul and the Law*. Pages 242–64. Philadelphia: Westminster, 1990.

_____. "Works of the Law and the Curse of the Law (Gal. 3.10–14)." *NTS* 31 (1985) 523–42; repr. In *Jesus, Paul and the Law*. Pages 215–41. Philadelphia: Westminster, 1990.

Duprez, Antoine. "Note sur le rôle de l'Esprit-Saint dans la filiation du chrétien, à propos de *Gal*. 4:6." *RSR* 52 (1964) 421–31.

Easley, K. H. "The Pauline Use of *Pneumati* as a Reference to the Spirit of God." *JETS* 27 (1984) 299–313.

Ellis, E. E. *Paul's Use of the Old Testament*. Edinburgh: Oliver & Boyd, 1957.

_____. *Pauline Theology: Ministry and Society*. Grand Rapids: Eerdmans, 1989.

_____. *Prophecy and Hermeneutic in Early Christianity: New Testament Essays*. Grand Rapids: Eerdmans, 1978.

_____. "II Corinthians v.1–10 in Pauline Eschatology." *NTS* 6 (1959–60) 211–24.

Engelsen, N. I. J. "Glossolalia and Other Forms of Inspired Speech According to 1 Corinthians 12–14." Ph.D. diss., Yale University, 1970.

Ervin, H. M. *Conversion-Initiation and the Baptism in the Holy Spirit*. Peabody, Mass.: Hendrickson, 1984.

Evans, C. F. "Romans 12:1–2: The 'True Worship.' " In *Dimensions de la vie chrétienne (Rom 12–13)*. Edited by L. De Lorenzi. Pages 7–33. Rome: Abbaye de S. Paul, 1979.

Ewert, D. *The Holy Spirit in the New Testament*. Harrisburg: Herald, 1983.

Fee, G. D. *Gospel and Spirit: Issues in New Testament Hermeneutics*. Peabody, Mass.: Hendrickson, 1991.

_____. "II Corinthians vi.14–vii.1 and Food Offered to Idols." *NTS* 23 (1976–77) 140–61.

_____. "Some Reflections on Pauline Spirituality." In *Alive to God: Studies in Spirituality presented to James Houston*. Edited by J. I. Packer and L. Wilkinson. Pages 96–107. Downers Grove: InterVarsity, 1992.

_____. "Tongues—Least of the Gifts? Some Exegetical Observations on 1 Corinthians 12–14." *Pneuma* 2 (1980) 3–14.

_____. "ΧΑΡΙΣ in II Corinthians i.15: Apostolic Parousia and Paul-Corinth Chronology." *NTS* 24 (1977–78) 533–38.

Fichtner, J. "Die Stellung der Sapientia Salomonis in der Literatur und Geistgeschichte ihrer Zeit." *ZNW* 36 (1937) 113–32.

Fitzgerald, John T. *Cracks in an Earthen Vessel: An Examination of the Catalogues of Hardships in the Corinthian Correspondence.* SBLDS 99. Atlanta: Scholars, 1988.

Fitzmyer, J. A. "Abba and Jesus' Relation to God." In *'A cause de l'Evangile: Mélanges offerts à Dom Jacques Dupont.* Edited by R. Gantoy. Pages 16–38. Paris: Cerf, 1985.

_____. "Glory Reflected on the Face of Christ (2 Cor. 3:7–4:6) and a Palestinian Jewish Motif." *TS* 42 (1981) 630–44.

_____. "Qumran and the Interpolated Paragraph in 2 Cor 6:14–7:1." In *Essays on the Semitic Background of the New Testament.* Pages 205–17. London: Chapman, 1971.

Ford, J. M. "Toward a Theology of 'Speaking in Tongues.' " *TS* 32 (1971) 3–29.

Fowl, Stephen D. *The Story of Christ in the Ethics of Paul: An Analysis of the Function of the Hymnic Material in the Pauline Corpus.* JSNTSup 36. Sheffield: JSOT Press, 1990.

Francis, D. P. "The Holy Spirit: A Statistical Inquiry." *ExpT* 96 (1985) 136–37.

Francis, J. " 'As Babes in Christ'—Some Proposals regarding 1 Corinthians 3.1–3." *JSNT* 7 (1980) 41–60.

Fuchs, E. "Der Anteil des Geistes am Glauben des Paulus: Ein Beitrag zum Verständnis von Römer 8." *ZTK* 72 (1975) 293–302.

Fuller, R. H. "Tongues in the New Testament." *ACQ* 3 (1963) 162–68.

Fung, R. Y. K. "The Impotence of the Law: Toward a Fresh Understanding of Romans 7:14–25." In *Scripture, Tradition and Interpretation.* Festschrift E. F. Harrison. Edited by W. W. Gasque and W. S. LaSor. Pages 34–48. Grand Rapids: Eerdmans, 1978.

_____. "Ministry, Community and Spiritual Gifts." *EvQ* 56 (1984) 5.

Funk, R. W. "Word and Word in 1 Corinthians 2:6–16." In *Language, Hermeneutic, and Word of God.* Pages 275–305. New York: Harper, 1966.

Furnish, V. P. *Theology and Ethics in Paul.* Nashville: Abingdon, 1968.

Gaffin, R. *Perspectives on Pentecost.* Philadelphia: Presbyterian and Reformed, 1979.

Garland, D. E. "The Composition and Unity of Philippians: Some Neglected Literary Factors." *NovT* 27 (1985) 141–73.

_____. "The Sufficiency of Paul, Minister of the New Covenant." *Criswell Theological Review* 4 (1989) 21–37.

Garnier, G. G. "The Temple of Asklepius at Corinth and Paul's Theology." *Buried History* 18 (1982) 52–58.

Gärtner, B. E. "The Pauline and Johannine Idea of 'To Know God' Against the Hellenistic Background." *NTS* 14 (1967–68) 215–21.

_____. *The Temple and the Community in Qumran and the New Testament.* SNTSMS 1. Cambridge: Cambridge University Press, 1965.

Gaugler, E. "Der Geist und das Gebet der schwachen Gemeinde." *IKZ* 51 (1961) 67–94.

Gee, Donald. *Concerning Spiritual Gifts*. Springfield, Mo.: Gospel Publishing House, n.d.

Gillman, F. M. "Another Look at Romans 8:3: 'In the Likeness of Sinful Flesh.' " *CBQ* 49 (1987) 597–604.

Gillman, J. "A Thematic Comparison: 1 Cor 15:50–57 and 2 Cor 5:1–5." *JBL* 107 (1988) 439–54.

Gnilka, J. "2 Cor 6:14–7:1 in Light of the Qumran Texts and the Testaments of the Twelve Patriarchs." In *Paul and Qumran*. Edited by J. Murphy-O'Connor. Pages 48–68. London: Chapman, 1968.

Goldingay, J. *The Church and the Gifts of the Spirit*. Bramcote, 1972.

Gordon, T. D. "The Problem at Galatia." *Int* 41 (1987) 32–43.

Grant, R. M. "Like Children." *HTR* 39 (1946) 71–73.

Graves, R. W. *Praying in the Spirit*. Old Tappan, N.J.: Chosen, 1987.

Grech, P. "2 Corinthians 3,17 and the Pauline Doctrine of Conversion to the Holy Spirit." *CBQ* 17 (1955) 420–37.

Green, M. *I Believe in the Holy Spirit*. 2d ed. Grand Rapids: Eerdmans, 1985.

Greenwood, D. "The Lord is the Spirit: Some Considerations of 2 Cor 3:17." *CBQ* 34 (1972) 467–72.

Grudem, W. A. "1 Corinthians 14.20–25: Prophecy and Tongues as Signs of God's Attitudes." *WTJ* 41 (1979) 381–96.

_____. *The Gift of Prophecy in 1 Corinthians*. Washington: University Press of America, 1982.

Gundry, R. H. " 'Ecstatic Utterance' (N.E.B.)?" *JTS* 17 (1966) 299–307.

_____. "The Form, Meaning and Background of the Hymn Quoted in I Timothy 3:16." In *Apostolic History and the Gospel: Biblical and Historical Essays presented to F. F. Bruce on his 60th Birthday*. Edited by W. W. Gasque and R. P. Martin. Pages 203–22. Grand Rapids: Eerdmans, 1970.

_____. "The Moral Frustration of Paul before His Conversion: Sexual Lust in Romans 7.7–25." In *Pauline Studies*. Edited by D. A. Hagner and M. J. Harris. Pages 228–45. Grand Rapids: Eerdmans, 1980.

_____. *SOMA in Biblical Theology with emphasis on Pauline Anthropology*. SNTSMS 29. Cambridge: Cambridge University Press, 1976.

Gunkel, H. *The Influence of the Holy Spirit*. (Ger. original 1888). ET. Philadelphia: Fortress, 1979.

Gunther, J. *St. Paul's Opponents and Their Background*. NovTSup 35. Leiden: Brill, 1973.

Hafemann, S. J. "The Comfort and Power of the Gospel: The Argument of 2 Corinthians 1–3." *RevExp* 86 (1989) 325–44.

_____. *Suffering and the Ministry in the Spirit: Paul's Defense of his Ministry in 2 Corinthians 2:14–3:3*. Grand Rapids: Eerdmans, 1990.

Hamilton, N. Q. *The Holy Spirit and Eschatology in Paul*. SJTOP 6. Edinburgh: Oliver & Boyd, 1957.

Hanimann, J. " 'Nous avons été abreuvés d'un seul Esprit.' Note sur 1 Co 12, 13b." *NouvRT* 94 (1972) 400–405.

Hanson, A. T. "The Midrash of II Corinthians 3: A Reconsideration." *JSNT* 9 (1980) 2–28.

Harpur, T. W. "The Gift of Tongues and Interpretation." *CJT* 12 (1966) 164–71.

Harris, M. J. "2 Corinthians 5:1–10: Watershed in Paul's Eschatology?" *TynB* 22 (1971) 33–57.

Harrisville, R. A. "Speaking in Tongues—Proof of Transcendence?" *Dialog* 13 (1974) 11–18.

_____. "Speaking in Tongues: A Lexicographical Study." *CBQ* 38 (1976) 35–48.

Hartmann, L. "Some Remarks on 1 Cor. 2:1–5." *SEÅ* 34 (1974) 109–20.

Hays, Richard B. "Christology and Ethics in Galatians: The Law of Christ." *CBQ* 49 (1987) 268–90.

_____. *Echoes of Scripture in the Letters of Paul.* New Haven: Yale University Press, 1989.

_____. *The Faith of Jesus Christ: An Investigation of the Narrative Substructure of Galatians 3:1–4:11.* SBLDS 56. Chico, Calif.: Scholars, 1983.

Hehn, J. "Zum Problem des Geistes in alten Orient und im Alten Testament." *ZAW* 43 (1925) 13–67.

Hemphill, K. S. *Spiritual Gifts: Empowering the New Testament Church.* Nashville: Broadman, 1988.

Hermann, I. *Kyrios und Pneuma: Studien zur Christologie der paulinischen Hauptbriefe.* Munich: Kösel-Verlag, 1961.

Hettlinger, R. F. "2 Corinthians 5:1–10." *SJT* 10 (1957) 174–94.

Hickling, C. J. A. "The Sequence of Thought in II Corinthians, Chapter Three." *NTS* 21 (1975) 380–95.

Hill, David. *Greek Words and Hebrew Meanings.* SNTSMS. Cambridge: Cambridge University Press, 1967.

_____. *New Testament Prophecy.* Atlanta: John Knox, 1979.

_____. "Salvation Proclaimed: IV. Galatians 3:10–14." *ExpT* 93 (1982) 196–200.

Hooker, Morna D. "ΠΙΣΤΙΣ ΧΡΙΣΤΟΥ." *NTS* 35 (1989) 321–42.

Horton, S. *What the Bible Says about the Holy Spirit.* Springfield, Mo.: Gospel Publishing House, 1976.

House, H. W. "Tongues and the Mystery Religions of Corinth." *BSac* 140 (1983) 135–50.

Hoyle, R. B. *The Holy Spirit in St. Paul.* London: Hodder and Stoughton, 1928.

Hübner, H. *Law in Paul's Thought.* (Ger. original 1978). Translated by J. C. G. Gerig. Edinburgh: T. & T. Clark, 1984.

Hugedé, N. *La métaphore du miroir dans les Epitres de Saint Paul aux Corinthiens.* Neuchâtel: Delachaux and Niestlé, 1957.

Hughes, F. W. *Early Christian Rhetoric and 2 Thessalonians.* JSNTSup 30. Sheffield: Academic Press, 1989.

Hui, A. W. D. "The Concept of the Holy Spirit in Ephesians and its Relation to the Pneumatologies of Luke and Paul." Ph.D. diss., University of Aberdeen, 1992.

Hunter, A. M. *Interpreting Paul's Gospel.* London: SCM, 1954.

_____. *Paul and his Predecessors.* 2d ed. London: SCM, 1961.

Hunter, H. *Spirit-Baptism: A Pentecostal Alternative.* Lanham, Md.: University Press of America, 1983.

Hurd, J. C. *The Origin of 1 Corinthians.* 2d ed. Macon, Ga.: Mercer University Press, 1983.

Hurley, J. B. *Men and Women in Biblical Perspective.* Grand Rapids: Zondervan, 1981.

Iber, G. "Zum Verständnis von I Cor. 12:31." *ZNW* 54 (1963) 43–52.

Isaacs, Marie E. *The Concept of Spirit: A Study of Pneuma in Hellenistic Judaism and its Bearing on the New Testament.* Heythrop Monographs 1. London: Heythrop College, 1976.

Jeremias, Joachim. *The Prayers of Jesus.* SBT 2/6. London: SCM, 1967.

Jervell, Jacob. "The Signs of an Apostle: Paul's Miracles." In *The Unknown Paul: Essays on Luke–Acts and Early Christian History.* Pages 77–95. Minneapolis: Augsburg, 1984.

Jewett, R. "The Agitators and the Galatian Congregation." *NTS* 17 (1970–71) 198–212.

————. *Paul's Anthropological Terms: A Study of their Use in Conflict Settings.* AGJU 10. Leiden: Brill, 1971.

————. "The Redaction and Use of an Early Christian Confession in Romans 1:3–4." In *The Living Text: Essays in Honor of Ernest W. Saunders.* Edited by D. E. Groh and R. Jewett. Pages 99–122. Lanham, Md.: University Press of America, 1985.

————. *The Thessalonian Correspondence: Pauline Rhetoric and Millenarian Piety.* Philadelphia: Fortress, 1986.

Johanson, B. C. "Tongues, a Sign for Unbelievers? A Structural and Exegetical Study of I Corinthians xiv. 20–25." *NTS* 25 (1979) 180–203.

Johnson, L. T. *The Writings of the New Testament: An Interpretation.* Pages 367–80. Philadelphia: Fortress, 1986.

Jones, F. S. *"Freiheit" in den Briefen des Apostels Paulus.* Göttingen: Vandenhoeck & Ruprecht, 1987.

Jones, W. R. "The Nine Gifts of the Holy Spirit." In *Pentecostal Doctrine.* Edited by P. S. Brewster. Pages 47–61. Greenhurst, 1976.

Kaiser, W. C. "A Neglected Text in Bibliology Discussions: I Corinthians 2:6–16." *WTJ* 43 (1981) 301–19.

Kamlah, E. "Buchstabe und Geist: Die Bedeutung dieser Antithese für die alttestamentliche Exegese des Apostels Paulus." *EvT* 14 (1954) 276–82.

Käsemann, E. "The Cry for Liberty in the Worship of the Church." In *Perspectives on Paul.* Pages 122–37. London: SCM, 1971.

————. "Die Legitimität des Apostels: Eine Untersuchung zu 2 Korinther 10–13." *ZNW* 51 (1942) 33–71.

————. "The Spirit and the Letter." In *Perspectives on Paul.* Pages 138–66. London: SCM, 1971.

————. "The Theological Problem Presented by the Motif of the Body of Christ." In *Perspectives on Paul.* Pages 102–21. London: SCM, 1971.

————. "Worship in Everyday Life: A Note on Romans 12." In *New Testament Questions of Today.* Pages 188–95. London: SCM, 1969.

Kasper, Walter. *Jesus the Christ.* New York: Paulist, 1976.

Keck, L. E. "The Law of 'The Law of Sin and Death' (Romans 8:1–4): Reflections on the Spirit and Ethics in Paul." In *The Divine Helmsman: Studies on God's Control of Human Events, presented to Lev. H. Silberman.* Edited by J. L. Crenshaw and S. Sandmel. Pages 41–57. New York: KTAV, 1980.

Kemmler, D. W. *Faith and Human Reason: A Study of Paul's Method of Preaching as Illustrated by 1–2 Thessalonians and Acts 17, 2–4.* NovTSup 40. Leiden: Brill, 1975.

Kendall, E. L. "Speaking with Tongues." *CQR* 168 (1967) 11–19.

Kerr, A. J. "ʼAPPABΩN." *JTS* 39 (1988) 92–97.

Kirk, J. A. "Apostleship since Rengstorf: Towards a Synthesis." *NTS* 21 (1974–75) 249–64.

Knight, George W., III. *The Faithful Sayings in the Pastoral Letters.* Grand Rapids: Baker, 1979.

Koch, R. *Geist und Messias.* Wien: Herder, 1950.

Koenig, J. *Charismata: God's Gifts for God's People.* Philadelphia: Westminster, 1978.

Kramer, W. *Christ, Lord, Son of God.* ET. SBT 50. London: SCM, 1966.

Kümmel, W. G. *Römer 7 und die Bekehrung des Paulus.* Leipzig: Hinrichs, 1929.

Ladd, George E. "The Holy Spirit in Galatians." In *Current Issues in Biblical and Patristic Interpretation.* Festschrift M. C. Tenney. Edited by G. F. Hawthorne. Pages 211–16. Grand Rapids: Eerdmans, 1975.

Lambrecht, J. "The fragment 2 Cor. vi.16–vii.1: A Plea for its authenticity." In *Miscellanea Neotestamentica* II. Edited by T. Baarda, A. F. J. Klijn, and W. C. van Unnik. Leiden: Brill, 1978.

_____. "Man before and without Christ: Romans 7 and Pauline Anthropology." *Louvain Studies* 5 (1974) 18–33.

_____. "Transformation in 2 Cor. 3,18." *Bib* 64 (1983) 243–54.

Langevin, P.-E. "Une confession prépauliniennes de la 'Seigneurie' du Christ: Exégèse de Romains 1,3–4." In *Le Christ hier, aujourd'hui, et demain.* Edited by R. Laflamme and M. Gervais. Pages 298–305. Quebec: Université Laval, 1976.

Lemmer, H. R. "Pneumatology and Eschatology in Ephesians: The Role of the Eschatological Spirit in the Church." Ph.D. diss., University of South Africa [Pretoria], 1988.

Lenski, R. C. H. *The Interpretation of St. Paul's Epistles to the Galatians, to the Ephesians, and to the Philippians.* Columbus, Ohio: Lutheran Book Concern, 1937.

_____. "Reciprocity between Eschatology and Pneuma in Ephesians 1:3–14." *Neot* 21 (1987) 159–82.

Lincoln, A. T. *Paradise Now and Not Yet: Studies in the Role of the Heavenly Dimension in Paul's Thought with Special Reference to his Eschatology.* SNTSMS 43. Cambridge: Cambridge University Press, 1981.

_____. " 'Paul the Visionary': The Setting and Significance of the Rapture to Paradise in II Corinthians xii. 1–10." *NTS* 25 (1979) 204–20.

_____. "A Re-Examination of 'The Heavenlies' in Ephesians." *NTS* 19 (1973) 468–83.

Loane, M. L. *The Hope of Glory: An Exposition of The Eighth Chapter in The Epistle to The Romans.* London: Hodder & Stoughton, 1968.

Lodahl, Michael E. *Shekinah Spirit: Divine Presence in Jewish and Christian Religion.* New York: Paulist, 1992.

Lohse, E. "ὁ νόμος τοῦ πνεύματος τῆς ζωῆς: Exegetische Anmerkungen zu Röm 8:2." In *Die Vielfalt des Neuen Testaments.* Pages 128–36. Göttingen: Vandenhoeck & Ruprecht, 1982.

Lull, David John. *The Spirit in Galatia: Paul's Interpretation of* Pneuma *as Divine Power.* SBLDS 49. Chico, Calif.: Scholars, 1980.

Lutjens, R. " 'You Do not Do What You Want': What Does Galatians 5:17 Really Mean?" *Presbyterion* 16 (1990) 103–17.

Lyall, F. "Roman Law in the Writings of Paul—Adoption." *JBL* 88 (1969) 458–66.

Lyonnet, S. "Christian Freedom and the Law of the Spirit According to St. Paul." In *The Christian Lives by the Spirit.* Edited by I. de la Potterie and S. Lyonnet. Translated by J. Morris. Pages 145–74. Staten Island: Alba House, 1971.

MacDonald, W. G. "Glossolalia in the New Testament." *BETS* 7 (1964) 59–68.

MacGorman, J. W. *The Gifts of the Spirit: An Exposition of I Corinthians 12–14.* Nashville: Broadman, 1974.

Maly, M. K. "1 Kor 12,1–3, eine Regel zur Unterscheidung der Geister?" *BZ* 10 (1966) 82–95.

Martin, D. W. " 'Spirit' in the Second Chapter of First Corinthians." *CBQ* 5 (1943) 181–95.

Martin, F. "Pauline Trinitarian Formulas and Church Unity." *CBQ* 30 (1968) 199–219.

Martin, I. J. "I Corinthians 13 Interpreted by its Context." *JBR* 18 (1950) 101–5.

_____. "Glossolalia in the Apostolic Church." *JBL* 63 (1944) 123–30.

Martin, Ralph P. *The Spirit and the Congregation: Studies in 1 Corinthians 12–15.* Grand Rapids: Eerdmans, 1984.

_____. "The Spirit in 2 Corinthians in Light of the 'Fellowship of the Holy Spirit' in 2 Corinthians 13:14." In *Eschatology and the New Testament: Essays in Honor of George Raymond Beasley-Murray.* Edited by W. H. Gloer. Pages 113–28. Peabody, Mass.: Hendrickson, 1988.

_____. *Worship in the New Testament.* 2d ed. Grand Rapids: Eerdmans, 1974.

Martyn, J. Louis. "A Law-Observant Mission to Gentiles: The Background of Galatians." *SJT* 38 (1985) 307–24.

_____. "Apocalyptic Antinomies in Paul's Letter to the Galatians." *NTS* 31 (1985) 410–24.

_____. "Epistemology at the Turn of the Ages: 2 Corinthians 5:16." In *Christian History and Interpretation.* Festschrift John Knox. Edited by W. R. Farmer, C. F. D. Moule, and R. R. Niebuhr. Pages 269–87. Cambridge: Cambridge University Press, 1967.

Matera, Frank. "The Culmination of Paul's Argument to the Galatians: Gal. 5:1–6:17." *JSNT* 32 (1988) 79–91.

Mawhinney, A. "God As Father: Two Popular Theories Reconsidered." *JETS* 31 (1988) 181–89.

McNicol, J. "The Spiritual Blessings of the Epistle to the Ephesians." *EvQ* 9 (1937) 64–73.

McRay, J. R. "*To Teleion* in I Corinthians 13:10." *ResQ* 14 (1971) 168–83.

Menzies, R. P. *The Development of Early Christian Pneumatology with Special Reference to Luke–Acts.* JSNTSup 54. Sheffield: JSOT Press, 1991.

Metzger, B. M. *A Textual Commentary on the Greek New Testament.* London: United Bible Societies, 1971.

Metzger, W. *Der Christushymnus 1 Tim. 3,16.* Stuttgart: Calwer, 1979.

Miguens, M. "1 Cor. 3:8–13 Reconsidered." *CBQ* 37 (1975) 76–97.

Mills, W. E. *Glossolalia: A Bibliography.* New York: Edwin Mellen, 1985.

_____. *The Holy Spirit: A Bibliography.* Peabody, Mass.: Hendrickson, 1988.

Mitton, C. L. "Romans 7 Reconsidered." *ExpT* 65 (1953–54) 78–81, 99–103, 132–35.

Moo, D. J. "Israel and Paul in Romans 7.7–12." *NTS* 32 (1986) 122–35.

Moule, C. F. D. "2 Cor. 3:18b, καθάπερ ἀπὸ κυρίου πνεύματος." In *Neues Testament und Geschichte.* Festschrift O. Cullmann. Edited by H. Baltensweiler and B. Reicke. Pages 233–37. Tübingen: J. C. B. Mohr [Paul Siebeck], 1972.

Mowinckel, S. "The Spirit and the Word in the Pre-Exilic Reforming Prophets." *JBL* 53 (1934) 199–227.

Mullins, T. Y. "Paul's Thorn in the Flesh." *JBL* 76 (1957) 299–303.

Murphy-O'Connor, J. "1 Corinthians, V,3–5." *RB* 84 (1977) 239–45.

_____. "PNEUMATIKOI and Judaizers in 2 Cor. 2:14–4:6." *AusBR* 34 (1986) 42–58.

Neugebauer, F. "Das paulinische 'in Christ.' " *NTS* 4 (1957–58) 124–38.

Niederwimmer, K. "Das Gebet des Geistes." *TZ* 20 (1964) 252–65.

Nisbet, P. "The Thorn in the Flesh." *ExpT* 80 (1969–70) 126.

Noth, Martin. "For All Who Rely on Works of the Law are under a Curse." In *The Laws in the Pentateuch and Other Studies*. Pages 118–31. Edinburgh/London: Oliver & Boyd, 1966.

O'Brien, P. T. "Ephesians I: An Unusual Introduction to a New Testament Letter." *NTS* 25 (1979) 604–16.

_____. *Introductory Thanksgivings in the Letters of Paul*. NovTSup 49. Leiden: Brill, 1977.

O'Collins, G. G. "Power Made Perfect in Weakness: 2 Cor 12:9–10." *CBQ* 33 (1971) 528–37.

Obeng, E. A. "Abba, Father: The Prayer of the Sons of God." *ExpT* 99 (1988) 363–66.

_____. "The Origin of the Spirit Intercession Motif in Romans 8.26." *NTS* 32 (1986) 621–32.

_____. "The Spirit Intercession Motif in Paul." *ExpT* 95 (1983–84) 360–64.

Oesterreicher, J. M. " 'Abba, Father!' On the Humanity of Jesus." In *The Lord's Prayer and Jewish Liturgy*. Edited by J. J. Petuchowski and M. Brocke. Pages 119–36. New York: Seabury, 1978.

Olford, D. L. "Paul's Use of Cultic Language in Romans: An Exegetical Study of Major Texts in Romans Which Employ Cultic Language in a Non-literal Way." Ph.D. diss., University of Sheffield, 1985.

Osburn, C. D. "The Interpretation of Romans 8:28." *WTJ* 44 (1982) 99–109.

Packer, J. I. "The 'Wretched Man' of Romans 7." *SE* II (1964) 621–27.

Park, D. M. "Paul's ΣΚΟΛΟΨ ΤΗ ΣΑΡΚΙ: Thorn or Stake?" *NovT* 22 (1980) 179–83.

Parratt, J. K. "Romans i.11 and Galatians iii.5—Pauline evidence for the Laying on of Hands?" *ExpT* 79 (1967–68) 151–52.

_____. "The Witness of the Holy Spirit: Calvin, the Puritans and St. Paul." *EvQ* 41 (1969) 165.

Pinnock, C. "The Concept of Spirit in the Epistles of Paul." Ph.D. diss., Manchester, 1963.

Plevnik, J. "The Center of Pauline Theology." *CBQ* 61 (1989) 461–78.

Poythress, V. S. "Is Romans 1^{3-4} a *Pauline* Confession After All?" *ExpT* 87 (1975–76) 180–83.

_____. "The Nature of Corinthian Glossolalia: Possible Options." *WTJ* 40 (1977) 130–35.

Price, R. M. "Punished in Paradise: An Exegetical Theory on 2 Corinthians 12:1–10." *JSNT* 7 (1980) 33–40.

Provence, T. E. " 'Who is Sufficient for These Things?' An Exegesis of 2 Corinthians ii 15–iii 18." *NovT* 24 (1982) 54–81.

Quinn, Jerome D. "The Holy Spirit in the Pastoral Epistles." In *Sin, Salvation, and the Spirit*. Edited by D. Durken. Pages 345–68. Collegeville, Minn.: Liturgical, 1979.

Räisänen, H. "Das 'Gesetz des Glauben' (Röm 3:27) und das 'Gesetz des Geistes' (Röm 8:2)." *NTS* 26 (1979–80) 101–17.

Rengsberger, D. "2 Corinthians 6:14–7:1—A Fresh Examination." *StBibT* 8 (1978) 25–49.

Renwick, David A. *Paul, The Temple, and the Presence of God.* BJS 224. Atlanta: Scholars, 1991.

Richard, E. "Polemics, Old Testament and Theology — A Study of II Cor. III,1–IV,6." *RB* 88 (1981) 340–67.

Richardson, P. "Letter and Spirit: A Foundation for Hermeneutics." *EvQ* 45 (1973) 208–18.

Richardson, W. "Liturgical Order and Glossolalia in 1 Corinthians 14.26c–33a." *NTS* 32 (1986) 144–53.

Ridderbos, Herman. *Paul: An Outline of His Theology.* Grand Rapids: Eerdmans, 1975.

Riggs, R. *The Spirit Himself.* Springfield, Mo.: Gospel Publishing House, 1949.

Roberts, P. "A Sign—Christian or Pagan?" *ExpT* 90 (1979) 199–203.

Robertson, O. P. "Tongues: Sign of Covenantal Curse and Blessing." *WTJ* 38 (1975) 45–53.

Robinson, D. W. B. "Charismata versus Pneumatika: Paul's Method of Discussion." *RThR* 31 (1972) 49–55.

Robinson, W. C., Jr. "Word and Power." In *Soli Deo Gloria: Essays for W. C. Robinson.* Edited by J. M. Richards. Pages 68–82. Richmond: John Knox, 1968.

Rogers, C. "The Dionysian Background of Ephesians 5:18." *BSac* 136 (1979) 249–57.

Rogers, E. R. "Ἐποτίσθησαν Again." *NTS* 29 (1983) 139–42.

Romaniuk, C. "Le Livre de la Sagesse dans le Nouveau Testament." *NTS* 14 (1967–68) 498–514.

Ross, J. M. "*Panta sunergei*, Rom. VIII.28." *TZ* 34 (1978) 82–85.

Russell, R. "The Idle in 2 Thess 3.6–12: An Eschatological or a Social Problem?" *NTS* 34 (1988) 105–19.

Saake, H. "Paulus als Ekstatiker: Pneumatologische Beobachtungen zu 2 Kor. xii 1–10." *NovT* 15 (1973) 153–60.

Sanders, E. P. *Paul, the Law, and the Jewish People.* Philadelphia: Fortress, 1983.

Schatzmann, S. *A Pauline Theology of Charismata.* Peabody, Mass.: Hendrickson, 1987.

Schlier, H. "Eine christologische Credo-Formel der römischen Gemeinde: Zu Röm 1:3f." In *Neues Testament und Geschichte.* Festschrift O. Cullmann. Edited by H. Baltensweiler and B. Reicke. Pages 207–18. Zürich: Theologischer, 1972.

Schnackenburg, R. "Apostles Before and After Paul's Time." In *Apostolic History and the Gospel.* Edited by W. W. Gasque and R. P. Martin. Pages 287–303. Grand Rapids: Eerdmans, 1970.

_____. *Baptism in the Thought of St. Paul.* ET. Oxford: Blackwell, 1964.

Schneider, B. "Κατὰ Πνεῦμα Ἁγιωσύνης (Romans 1.4)." *Bib* 48 (1967) 359–87.

Schneider, G. "The Meaning of St. Paul's Antithesis 'The Letter and the Spirit.' " *CBQ* 15 (1953) 163–207.

Schniewind, J. "Das Seufzen des Geistes: Röm 8.26, 27." In *Nachgelassene Reden und Aufsätze.* Pages 81–103. Berlin: Töpelmann, 1952.

Schoemaker, W. R. "The Use of *Ruach* in the Old Testament and πνεῦμα in the New Testament." *JBL* 23 (1904) 13–67.

Schweitzer, A. *The Mysticism of Paul the Apostle.* London: Black, 1931.

Schweizer, E. "Röm 1:3f. und der Gegensatz von Fleisch und Geist vor und bei Paulus." *EvT* 15 (1955) 563–71.

_____. "Two New Testament Creeds Compared." In *Current Issues in New Testament Interpretation: Essays in honor of Otto A. Piper*. Edited by W. Klassen and G. Snyder. Pages 166–77. New York: Harper, 1962.

_____. "Zum religionsgeschichtlichen Hintergrund der 'Sendungsformel' Gal 4,4f., Rm 8,3f., Joh 3,16f., 1 Joh 4,9." *ZNW* 57 (1966) 199–210.

Scott, C. A. A. *Christianity according to St. Paul*. Cambridge: Cambridge University Press, 1927.

Scott, E. F. *The Spirit in the New Testament*. London: Hodder and Stoughton, 1923.

Scott, James M. *Adoption as Sons of God*. WUNT 2/48. Tübingen: J. C. B. Mohr [Paul Siebeck], 1992.

Scroggs, R. "Paul: ΣΟΦΟΣ and ΠΝΕΥΜΑΤΙΚΟΣ." *NTS* 14 (1967–68) 33–55.

Seesemann, H. *Der Begriff κοινωνία im Neuen Testament*. BZNW 14. Giessen: Töpelmann, 1933.

Sekki, A. E. *The Meaning of Ruah at Qumran*. SBLDS 110. Atlanta: Scholars, 1989.

Shelton, James B. *Mighty in Word and Deed: The Role of the Holy Spirit in Luke–Acts*. Peabody, Mass.: Hendrickson, 1991.

Smith, B. L. "Tongues in the New Testament." *Churchman* 87 (1973) 183–88.

Smith, D. M. "Glossolalia and Other Spiritual Gifts in a New Testament Perspective." *Int* 28 (1974) 307–20.

Smith, N. G. "The Thorn that Stayed: An Exposition of 2 Cor 12:7–9." *Int* 13 (1959) 409–16.

Snaith, N. *Distinctive Ideas of the Old Testament*. London: Epworth, 1944.

Snodgrass, K. "Spheres of Influence: A Possible Solution for the Problem of Paul and the Law." *JSNT* 32 (1988) 93–113.

Spicq, C. *Agapè dans le Nouveau Testament*. EB. 3 vols. Paris: Gabalda, 1959.

Spittler, R. P. "The Limits of Ecstasy: An Exegesis of 2 Corinthians 12:1–10." In *Current Issues in Biblical and Patristic Interpretation*. Festschrift M. E. Tenney. Edited by G. F. Hawthorne. Pages 259–66. Grand Rapids: Eerdmans, 1975.

Stalder, K. *Das Werk des Geistes in der Heiligung bei Paulus*. Zürich: Evz-Verlag, 1962.

Stanley, Christopher D. " 'Under a Curse': a Fresh Reading of Galatians 3.10–14." *NTS* 36 (1990) 481–511.

Stendahl, K. "The Apostle Paul and the Introspective Conscience of West." In *Paul Among Jews and Gentiles and Other Essays*. Pages 78–96. Philadelphia: Fortress, 1976.

_____. "Paul at Prayer." In *Meanings: The Bible as Document and as a Guide*. Pages 151–61. Philadelphia: Fortress, 1984.

Stenger, W. *Der Christushymnus 1 Tim. 3.16: Eine structuranalysche Untersuchung*. Frankfurt: Peter Lang, 1977.

Stockhausen, Carol Kern. *Moses' Veil and the Glory of the New Covenant*. AnBib 116. Rome: Pontifical Biblical Institute, 1989.

Sumney, J. L. *Identifying Paul's Opponents: The Question of Method in 2 Corinthians*. JSNTSup 40. Sheffield: JSOT Press, 1990.

Sweet, J. M. P. "A Sign for Unbelievers: Paul's Attitude to Glossolalia." *NTS* 13 (1967) 240–57.

Swete, H. B. *The Holy Spirit in the New Testament*. London: Macmillan, 1910; repr. ed. Grand Rapids: Baker, 1964.

Swetnam, J. "On Romans 8:23 and the 'Expectation of Sonship.' " *Bib* 48 (1967) 102–8.

Synge, F. C. "The Holy Spirit and the Sacraments." *SJT* 6 (1953) 65–76.

Tabor, J. D. *Things Unutterable: Paul's Ascent to Paradise in its Greco-Roman, Judaic, and Early Christian Contexts.* Lanham, Md.: University Press of America, 1986.

Talbert, C. H. "Paul's Understanding of the Holy Spirit: The Evidence of 1 Corinthians 12–14." In *Perspectives on the New Testament: Essays in Honor of Frank Stagg.* Edited by C. H. Talbert. Pages 95–108. Macon, Ga.: Mercer University Press, 1985.

Thackeray, H. J. *The Relation of Paul to Contemporary Jewish Thought.* London: Macmillan, 1900.

Thiselton, A. C. "The Interpretation of Tongues: A New Suggestion in Light of Greek Usage in Philo and Josephus." *JTS* 30 (1979) 15–36.

Thomas, R. L. " 'Tongues . . . Will Cease.' " *JETS* 17 (1974) 81–89.

Thompson, M. *Clothed with Christ: The Example and Teaching of Jesus in Romans 12.1–15.13.* JSNTSup 59. Sheffield: JSOT Press, 1991.

Thompson, R. W. "How Is the Law Fulfilled in Us? An Interpretation of Rom 8:4." *Louvain Studies* 11 (1986) 31–40.

Thornton, T. C. G. "The Meaning of καὶ περὶ ἁμαρτίας in Romans viii.3." *JTS* 22 (1971) 515–17.

Thrall, M. E. "The Problem of II Cor. vi.14–vii.1 in some Recent Discussions." *NTS* 24 (1977–78) 132–48.

Toussaint, S. D. "First Corinthians Thirteen and the Tongues Question." *BSac* 120 (1963) 311–16.

Towner, Phillip H. *The Goal of Our Instruction: The Structure of Theology and Ethics in the Pastoral Epistles.* JSNTSup 34. Sheffield: JSOT Press, 1989.

Tugwell, S. "The Gift of Tongues in the New Testament." *ExpT* 84 (1973) 137–40.

Turner, M. M. B. "The Significance of Spirit Endowment for Paul." *VoxEv* 9 (1975) 58–69.

Turner, N. *Grammatical Insights into the New Testament.* Edinburgh: T. & T. Clark, 1965.

van Imschoot, P. "L'Esprit de Jahvé, principé de vie morale dans l'A.T." *ETL* 16 (1939) 457–67.

van Stempvoort, P. A. "Eine stylische Lösung einer alten Schwierigkeit in I. Thessalonicher v. 23." *NTS* 7 (1961) 262–65.

van Unnik, W. C. " 'Den Geist löschet nicht aus' (1 Thessalonicher v 19)." *NovT* 10 (1968) 255–69.

_____. "Jesus: Anathema or Kyrios (I Cor. 12:3)." In *Christ and Spirit in the New Testament.* Edited by B. Lindars and S. Smalley. Cambridge: Cambridge University Press, 1973.

_____. " 'With Unveiled Face': An Exegesis of 2 Corinthians iii 12–18." *NovT* 6 (1963) 153–69.

Volf, Judith M. Gundry. *Paul and Perseverance: Staying in and Falling Away.* WUNT 2/37. Tübingen: J. C. B. Mohr [Paul Siebeck], 1990.

Volz, P. *Der Geist Gottes und die verwandten Erscheinungen im Alten Testament und im anschliessenden Judentum.* Tübingen: J. C. B. Mohr [Paul Siebeck], 1910.

Wagner, G. "The Tabernacle and Life 'in Christ': Exegesis of 2 Corinthians 5:1–10." *IBS* 3 (1981) 145–65.

Wainwright, Arthur W. *The Trinity in the New Testament.* London: SPCK, 1962.

Walker, D. *The Gift of Tongues.* Edinburgh, 1908.

Walker, W. O. "Why Paul Went to Jerusalem: The Interpretation of Galatians 2:1–5." *CBQ* 54 (1992) 503–10.

Warfield, B. B. "The Spirit of God in the Old Testament." In *Biblical and Theological Studies*. Pages 127–56. Philadelphia: Presbyterian and Reformed, 1952.

Wedderburn, A. J. M. *The Reasons for Romans*. Edinburgh: T. & T. Clark, 1988.

———. "Romans 8:26—Towards a Theology of Glossolalia." *SJT* 28 (1975) 369–77.

Wenham, David. "The Christian Life: A Life of Tension? A Consideration of the Nature of Christian Experience in Paul." In *Pauline Studies*. Edited by D. H. Hagner and M. J. Harris. Pages 80–94. Grand Rapids: Eerdmans, 1980.

Westerholm, S. *Israel's Law and the Church's Faith: Paul and his Recent Interpreters*. Grand Rapids: Eerdmans, 1988.

———. " 'Letter' and 'Spirit': the Foundation of Pauline *Ethics*." *NTS* 30 (1984) 229–48.

———. "On Fulfilling the Whole Law (Gal 5.14)." *SEÅ* 51–2 (1986–87) 229–37.

Widmann, M. "1 Kor 2:6–16: Ein Einspruch gegen Paulus." *ZNW* 70 (1979) 44–53.

Wilckens, U. *Weisheit und Torheit*. Tübingen: J. C. B. Mohr [Paul Siebeck], 1959.

Wild, Robert. "The Warrior and the Prisoner: Some Reflections on Ephesians 6:10–20." *CBQ* 46 (1984) 284–98.

Wiles, G. P. *Paul's Intercessory Prayers*. SNTSMS 24. Cambridge: Cambridge University Press, 1974.

Wilkinson, T. L. "Tongues and Prophecy in Acts and 1st Corinthians." *VoxR* 31 (1978) 1–20.

Williams, R. R. "Logic *Versus* Experience in the Order of Credal Formulae." *NTS* 1 (1954) 42–44.

Williams, Sam K. "Justification and the Spirit in Galatians." *JSNT* 29 (1987) 91–100.

———. "*Promise* in Galatians: A Reading of Paul's Reading of Scripture." *JBL* 107 (1988) 709–20.

Wilson, J. P. "Romans viii.28: Text and Interpretation." *ExpT* 60 (1948–49) 110–11.

Winward, Stephen F. *Fruit of the Spirit*. Grand Rapids: Eerdmans, 1981.

Wood, A. S. *Life by the Spirit*. Grand Rapids: Zondervan, 1963.

Wright, N. T. *The Climax of the Covenant*. Minneapolis: Fortress, 1991.

———. "Reflected Glory: 2 Corinthians 3:18." In *The Glory of Christ in the New Testament: Studies in Christology in Memory of George Bradford Caird*. Edited by L. D. Hurst and N. T. Wright. Pages 139–50. Oxford: Clarendon, 1987.

Wright, W. C., Jr. "The Use of Pneuma in the Pauline Corpus with Special Attention to the Relationship between Pneuma and the Risen Christ." Ph.D. diss., Fuller Theological Seminary, 1977.

Yorke, G. L. O. R. *The Church as the Body of Christ in the Pauline Corpus: A Re-examination*. Lanham, Md.: University Press of America, 1991.

Young, F., and D. F. Ford. *Meaning and Truth in 2 Corinthians*. Grand Rapids: Eerdmans, 1987.

Ziesler, John A. "The Just Requirement of the Law (Romans 8:4)." *AusBR* 35 (1987) 77–82.

———. *Pauline Christianity*. Oxford: Oxford University Press, 1983.

Zmijewski, J. "Kontextbezug und Deutung von 2 Kor 12, 7a: Stilistische und Strukturale Erwägungen zur Lösung eines alten Problems." *BZ* 21 (1977) 265–77.

INDEX OF SUBJECTS

INDEX OF MODERN AUTHORS

INDEX OF ANCIENT SOURCES